Trade
and the
Environment

Trade and the Environment

Law and Policy

Second Edition

Chris Wold
ASSOCIATE PROFESSOR,
LEWIS & CLARK LAW SCHOOL

Sanford Gaines
VISITING PROFESSOR, SCHOOL OF BUSINESS AND SOCIAL SCIENCES,
AARHUS UNIVERSITY (DENMARK)

Greg Block
VICE PRESIDENT, CONSERVATION FINANCE AND EXTERNAL AFFAIRS,
WILD SALMON CENTER

CAROLINA ACADEMIC PRESS
Durham, North Carolina

ISBN: 978-1-59460-816-2
LCCN: 2010933731

Carolina Academic Press
700 Kent Street
Durham, North Carolina 27701
Telephone (919) 489-7486
Fax (919) 493-5668
www.cap-press.com

Printed in the United States of America

To Sue, Zach, and Mats
C.W.

I dedicated the first edition to my wife Cassandra. We jointly dedicate this second edition to the next generations—our children Ingrid and Seth, their spouses Jeremiah and Amy, and our granddaughter Sadie Margaret—with the fervent hope that, as we face urgent challenges today, we will build for them economically sound and environmentally sustainable societies, at home and around the world.
S.G.

To Rosemary Vila, Andrea, and Anton
G.B.

Contents

Preface

General Introduction

In 1991, the *Tuna/Dolphin* dispute brought international trade law to the attention of environmental advocates in many countries. In 1998, with protesters lining the streets of Seattle in turtle costumes in reference to the *Shrimp/Turtle* dispute, the relevance of the World Trade Organization to environmental policy was brought to the attention of citizens worldwide. As the first edition of this book went to press, the United States and Europe were about to become engaged in another trade dispute, this one over trade in genetically modified foods. In late 2010, as this second edition goes to press, the United States is contemplating a possible trade complaint against China for rules and subsidies giving an advantage to Chinese manufacturers of solar panels and wind turbines. Mexico has initiated a dispute over U.S. "dolphin-safe" labels for tuna.

Despite these and other high profile cases, or perhaps because of them, the intersection of trade law and environmental policy remains poorly understood. It is still often portrayed as a struggle between good and evil. In this simplified view, trade experts think liberalized trade is good because it promotes economic efficiency and raises standards of living, and they fear environmental trade measures because they threaten to undo hard-won gains for open market access. For environmental advocates, the simplified view is that trade's promotion of growth increases pollution and depletion of natural resources, open market competition drives standards down, and trade rules limit policy options for pursuing environmental objectives in an environmentally challenged world. By immersing our readers in the detail of the law we hope to challenge these simplified constructions of the relationship between international trade law and the law of environmental protection.

The ambition of this textbook, then, is to present students and other readers with the complexity and ambiguity of the real world where trade and environment meet. Trade law leaves space for environmental trade measures, but trade measures have commercial consequences, so there are pre-conditions for such measures to be allowed. Are those pre-conditions overly stringent? On the other side, open international trade can help with diffusion of green technology and with the environmental battle against agricultural and natural resources subsidies, but governments have proven reluctant to live up to their free trade principles on these matters. The text deals repeatedly with these difficult issues.

The complexity and ambiguity runs deep. Environmental effects of production of traded goods vary from product to product, and are mostly mediated through national regulations that vary from country to country. Equally, the specific effects of trade law on environmental protection efforts depend on the details of regulatory implementation. Sensitive issues also arise in the relationship between international cooperation and independent national action, between harmonization of policy in global markets and national prerogatives to set national goals and requirements. For all these reasons, sweeping generalizations about trade and environment are often misleading. Only a detailed examination of the law and the factual circumstances in each situation will yield meaningful understanding and insight. Extensive excerpts from WTO dispute settlement reports are designed to give readers that detail. In the process, we hope that each community will not only understand the other but with that understanding can earn the confidence and respect of the other.

Trade and the environment is not a subject for specialists only. It is an element of a larger (and endless) discussion about the organization and objectives of our social, economic, and political systems and their situation in the world of natural ecological systems. When and to what extent should the pursuit of nontrade values such as labor rights, human rights, or environmental protection be freed from, or be subject to, the stringent market-opening disciplines of international trade law? In the quest for sustainable development, how are trade and nontrade values balanced and blended? To what institutions — national or international, can we turn for rules and guidance? Such issues are already topics of national discussion and international negotiation. We hope this book encourages teachers and students alike to become participants in that discussion.

Teaching Trade and the Environment

The field of "Trade and Environment" law and policy demands a lot from students — and from professors — because it requires some basic mastery of principles, concepts, and legal doctrines in both the trade realm and the environmental realm. The primary objective of this textbook is to provide the material for students to gain such basic mastery. Each realm has a broad sweep and myriad details; the combination can be daunting, but is at the same time fascinating and, more importantly, an element of the ongoing struggle by international policy makers to forge rules and institutions for a sustainable world.

Study of trade and environment is not made easier — though perhaps teaching is made more interesting — by the clash of cultures and by the endless, occasionally fruitless, debate about how these two realms should best co-exist, if not achieve the ideal state of becoming "mutually supportive." Our textbook presents much of that debate and the cultural differences that underlie it, but tries at the same time to ask critical questions about the arguments presented by all participants in the debate. We hope in that way to provide a reliable and yet provocative introduction to the field and a foundation for further study by both students and professors.

Although all three authors are from the United States and the text material is presented in the style customary for law textbooks at U.S. law schools, we have tried to give the book an international cast so that it can be easily used by teachers around the world who are teaching classes in English. Some of the major WTO cases involve the United States, but others center on environmental issues and trade practices in other parts of the world, providing material to engage the interest of students in all regions of the world. Apart from the WTO cases, the reading selections encompass economics and political science as well as law, and reflect a variety of national and regional perspectives. At appropriate places there are materials specific to U.S. law, EU law, and Canadian law that can be used to give a particular local orientation to the course or as a basis for comparative law analysis of national trade law and policy.

Overall Approach

The numerous linkages between trade and environmental policy made this a rather large book. Chapter 1 begins by exploring the underlying principles of free trade and sustainable development. It sets out the trade and environment debate by highlighting the criticisms and defenses of free trade through a "debate" between Herman Daly, a prominent ecological economist who views trade liberalization as "uneconomical," and Jagdish Bhagwati, a well-known trade economist who believes that trade liberalization is the world's most powerful force for social good. It also explores the goal of sustainable development and asks whether trade liberalization can help achieve that goal.

Chapter 2 takes a close look at the institutions and decisionmaking process of the World Trade Organization (WTO). Because so much of the trade and environment debate is framed by the decisions of trade panels, it also explores in detail the structure and composition of the WTO's Dispute Settlement Body and the legal standards used to decide trade disputes.

Chapters 3 through 8 examine the substantive law of the General Agreement on Tariffs and Trade (GATT) and other WTO agreements. Chapters 3 and 4 introduce the core components of trade law that are central to the trade and environment debate. This material is organized to be taught consecutively, though not all sections of each chapter need to be covered. Chapter 3 explores the GATT rules on tariffs, quotas, and other import and export restrictions and the environmental implications of such measures. It focuses on timber policy—quotas, bans, and taxes—to highlight the environmental implications of these GATT rules.

Chapter 4 examines the GATT's core nondiscrimination obligations: the most favored nation and national treatment obligations. These two obligations are at the heart of the trade and environment debate because they require WTO Members to tax and regulate foreign and domestic "like products" with equal favor. Because environmental advocates want to tax and regulate "green" products more favorably than similar products they deem environmentally harmful, the GATT consistency of such measures hinges on whether those products are considered "like." This chapter assesses whether countries may and should tax or regulate products differently depending on the processes and production methods (PPMs) used to make them.

Chapter 5 looks at the evolving nature of the exceptions to GATT's core obligations for measures necessary to protect human, animal, and plant life or health and measures relating to the conservation of exhaustible natural resources. Early interpretations of the exceptions by trade panels, such as in *Tuna/Dolphin*, made it very difficult for countries to justify their trade-related environmental policies under the GATT. The *Shrimp/Turtle* decisions, however, appear to have opened the door to many of the trade-related environmental policies sought by environmental advocates—provided certain steps are followed.

Chapters 6, 7, and 8 look at specialized agreements within the WTO from which students and professors may wish to select: the Agreement on Technical Barriers to Trade (TBT Agreement), the Agreement on the Application of Sanitary and Phytosanitary Measures (SPS Agreement), and the Agreement on Subsidies and Countervailing Measures (SCM Agreement). Each agreement focuses on unique environmental issues that require an understanding of Chapters 3 to 5, but the Chapters in this set stand independently of each other. Chapter 6 examines the TBT Agreement and its effect on ecolabeling efforts. Chapter 7 asks whether the SPS Agreement adequately balances the public interest in a safe food supply with trade interests in health and safety regulations that do not protect domestic producers. Chapter 8 tackles subsidies and agricultural subsidies by assessing the environmental soundness of subsidies and their economic rationale.

Chapter 9 explores the complicated relationship between international trade agreements and multilateral environmental agreements. This important trade and environment issue receives close scrutiny, because policymakers at the highest levels have been debating whether environmental treaties should be allowed to use trade restrictions in light of the WTO's antipathy to trade restrictions. Because this chapter describes the trade measures used in environmental agreements, it also offers a means to review earlier chapters, particularly Chapters 3, 4, and 5. It also briefly introduces two additional WTO agreements that have unique linkages to specific environmental agreements: the Agreement on Trade-Related Aspects of Intellectual Property Rights and its relation to genetic resources under the Convention on Biological Diversity; and the General Agreement on Trade in Services and its relation to implementation of the Kyoto Protocol to the United Nations Framework Convention on Climate Change. Because these trade and environment concerns are more speculative than other trade-MEA linkages, they are not given full treatment.

Chapters 10 and 11 turn to substantive and environmental provisions of regional agreements and entities, particularly the North American Free Trade Agreement (NAFTA) and the European Union. Chapter 10 focuses on the investment provisions of the NAFTA, which grant rights to private, foreign investors to challenge governmental measures that they believe discriminate against them or their investments or that "expropriate" their investment. Environmental advocates have found investment provisions of free trade agreements particularly pernicious, and we explore whether those concerns have merit. Chapter 11 reviews the specific ways the NAFTA and the European Union incorporate environmental decisionmaking into a trade framework or into trade decisionmaking, something the WTO has so far refused to do.

Chapter 12 closes with an examination of the role of public participation. Environmental advocates have long fought against the culture of confidentiality that dominates trade decisionmaking. Looking at the United States and the European Union, this chapter tracks the strategies that environmental advocates have used to pry open the door to the trade world, sometimes with success and other times with failure. It also reviews the use of environmental impact assessment as a means to evaluate the potential effects of trade agreements.

Because of the complexity and ambiguity of the trade-environment linkage and because of the depth of trade-environment linkages, we have opted not to provide a synthesis or conclusion at the end of this book. Instead, each chapter offers some ideas on how a particular component of trade law can be reshaped to better achieve environmental goals while also achieving trade goals. These sections are entitled, for example, "Rethinking Article XX(g)" or "The Way Forward." We hope that this strategy helps make learning trade law *and* imagining how trade law and environmental law can be made mutually reinforcing more manageable.

The breadth of the subject matter made limiting the scope of this book challenging. In the end, we omitted important influences on trade and environmental issues, such as the role of the International Monetary Fund, the World Bank, and the regional development banks. Although these institutions have played important roles in promoting liberalized trade, the development of environmental law, and the financing of projects that have significant impacts on the environment, we chose to adhere more closely to environmental issues more directly affected by trade rules rather than globalization issues.

In addition, we have not covered in any detailed or systematic way the skewed distribution effects of liberalized trade policies that have failed to alleviate poverty in the least developed countries. Poverty alleviation can have significant impacts on the environment, both positive and negative. This particular issue, while enormously important and closely associated with the defense of globalization, liberalized trade policies, and the achievement of sustainable development, encompasses a broader range of issues and policies than the law related to the trade and environment debate. Nevertheless, we incorporate issues of equity, differential and special treatment, and poverty throughout the book. We also highlight the distinctive perspectives that developed and developing countries bring to bear on trade and environment issues, such as ecolabeling and regulatory distinctions based on processes and production methods, among others. These perspectives of course are often tightly linked to a country's development status or unique economic interests.

A third issue that this book does not explicitly cover is the use of economic power in the development of trade rules and in resolving trade disputes. Until recently, developing countries have found it difficult to use their advantage in numbers to overcome their economic disadvantage. This may be changing, however. Developing countries have stalled negotiations of the Free Trade Area of the Americas and derailed negotiations on multilateral trade issues until the developed countries agree to concessions concerning their agricultural subsidies and other measures restraining market access.

We close with a note of heartfelt thanks to the large number of people who have made important contributions to this book. We would like to thank Ashlee Albies, Candice Rutter, Debby Scott, Josh Smith, Erica Thorson, and Mario Williams, all students at Lewis & Clark Law School, for their valuable research and editing talents. A special thanks to Jessica Yeh and Eleanor Garretson for their fantastic work on this second edition. The staff of the Boley Law Library at Lewis & Clark Law School have provided tremendous assistance; thank you Tami Gierloff, Kim Jurney, Rob Truman, and Lynn Williams. We also thank Andy Marion and Lisa Frenz for assisting with word processing. We would also like to thank our colleagues who took the time to carefully review draft chapters: David Downes, David Gantz, Geoffrey Garver, Patti Goldman, Eban Goodstein, David Markell, John Knox, Richard Tarasofsky, Martin Wagner, Jake Werskman, David Wirth, and Durwood Zaelke. Finally, we would like to particularly note the valuable contributions of Stephen Powell and Errol Meidinger, whose detailed comments on the first edition have improved this second edition. Finally, we are most grateful to our wives—Sue, Cassandra, and Rose—who have patiently endured a seemingly endless writing process.

We welcome comments on the strengths of this book as well as where it can be improved. Comments can be sent to Chris Wold (wold@lclark.edu).

Chris Wold
Sanford Gaines
Greg Block

Portland, OR
November 2010

A General Note on Information and Research Sources

The textbook has a selected bibliography, starting at page 893. We offer here some general notes and commentary on a few of the items in that bibliography, and general guidance on sources for further research.

General Texts

In spite of an active academic and advocacy literature on trade and environment, there are only a few general texts on the subject. Our book remains, as far as we know, the only published text for teachers and students that attempts to cover the whole subject from a legal perspective. The other single comprehensive book on trade and environment policy is the dated but still enormously valuable analysis of the issues by Daniel Esty, now a professor at Yale: Greening the GATT: Trade, Environment, and the Future (1994). In addition, attorneys with the Center for International Environmental Law have recently published a book which provides short summaries and commentaries on, together with large excerpts from, trade-environment reports and other reports with jurisprudential significance. Bernasconi-Osterwalder et al., Environment and Trade: A Guide to WTO Jurisprudence (2006). Another book covers much of the same material as included in this textbook, but from a human rights perspective: Berta Esperanza Hernández-Truyol & Stephen Powell, Just Trade: A new covenant Linking Trade and Human Rights (2009).

A number of books, some from the early years and some more recent, are less comprehensive but nevertheless address the broad interface between trade and environment. Among the more recent is a compendium of views from various experts under the title Trade and Environment: Recent Controversies (2003), edited by Singer, Hatti & Tandon, available from the Indian publishing house Vedams. For a more idiosyncratic theoretical analysis, see Oren Perez, Ecological Sensitivity and Global Legal Pluralism: Rethinking the Trade and Environment Conflict (2004). An earlier edited volume presenting various perspectives is Trade and Environment: Conflict or Compatibility, Duncan Brack, ed. (1998), available from Earthscan. For Francophones, a rare text in French is Sandrine Maljean-Dubois, Droit de L'Organisation Mondiale du Commerce et Protection de L'environnement (2003).

Some very useful volumes focus on trade and environment in a regional context. In particular, there are a number of books examining the North American Free Trade Agreement and its associated environmental agreement. We draw your attention to two of them.

On a general level, for a very useful and up-to-date assessment of NAFTA's environmental consequences by an economist, *see* KEVIN GALLAGHER, FREE TRADE AND THE ENVIRONMENT: MEXICO, NAFTA, AND BEYOND (2004). The best available examination of the operation of the environmental side agreement is JOHN KNOX & DAVID MARKELL, EDS., GREENING NAFTA: THE NORTH AMERICAN COMMISSION FOR ENVIRONMENTAL COOPERATION (2003). In addition, two journal have recent volumes dedicated to trade and environment in a regional context: 45 WAKE FOREST L. REV. (2010) and 28 ST. LOUIS UNIV. PUBLIC L. REV. (2008).

There are a few general texts on trade law that have significant coverage of trade and environment. In our opinion, the best and most current of these is: MITSUO MATSUSHITA, THOMAS J. SCHOENBAUM & PETROS MAVROIDIS, THE WORLD TRADE ORGANIZATION: LAW, PRACTICE, AND POLICY (2d ed. 2006). Another valuable general text is: RAJ BHALA & KEVIN KENNEDY, WORLD TRADE LAW (1998).

In the environmental literature, the best that exists are relatively short chapters on trade and environment in some environmental law teaching texts, including DAVID HUNTER, JAMES SALZMAN & DURWOOD ZAELKE, INTERNATIONAL ENVIRONMENTAL LAW AND POLICY (3d ed. 2006) and PERCIVAL ET AL., ENVIRONMENTAL REGULATION: LAW, SCIENCE, AND POLICY (5th ed. 2006). For serious study of trade and environment issues, the obvious limitation of these environmental textbooks is that they do not, and do not claim to, treat trade-environment issues in a comprehensive way.

At the general level, there are also some reports and a number of advocacy statements. A significant general report that was inadvertently omitted in the Selected Bibliography was prepared by two economists on the WTO secretariat staff: Nordstrom & Vaughan, Trade and the Environment (1999), available through the WTO website.

General Sources

There are many different sources of information and analysis available through the Internet. Here is a sampling of major sites that have substantial materials:

Official

www.wto.org A very complete site with full text of all WTO agreements, dispute settlement reports, minutes of meetings of the Committee on Trade and Environment, and many other documents, reports, data sources, and news items.

www.oecd.org The Organisation for Economic Cooperation and Development has prepared a number of papers and reports on different issues in the trade and environment subject area.

www.unep.org The United Nations Environment Programme has participated on occasion in the international policy deliberations and negotiations on trade and environment issues.

www.cec.org The North American Commission for Environmental Cooperation has been a pioneer in the rigorous analysis of the environmental effects of trade liberalization in North America.

www.nafta-sec-alena.org This is the official website of the NAFTA Secretariat, with full text of NAFTA and NAFTA dispute settlement rulings.

www.worldbank.org/icsid The official site of the International Center for the Settlement of Investment Disputes, which handles many investor-state arbitrations under trade agreements.

Many national trade agencies, maintain sections of their websites devoted to trade and environment. A few environmental agencies do the same. Some examples:

U.S.:   www.ustr.gov (U.S. Trade Representative)

           www.epa.gov (U.S. Environmental Protection Agency)

Canada: www.international.gc.ca/international/index.aspx (Foreign Affairs and International Trade Canada)

EU: europa.eu/pol/comm/index_en.htm
This is the English language portal to all EU activities and bodies dealing with "external trade."

Australia: www.dfat.gov.au/trade/

Academic/Research

www.gets.org (Yale Global Environment and Trade Studies)

www.ictsd.org (International Centre for Trade and Sustainable Development)

www.trade-environment.org A component of the ICTSD website with an interesting collection of studies, news, and other useful information.

ase.tufts.edu/gdae (The Global Development and Environment Institute at Tufts University)

www.iisd.org (International Institute for Sustainable Development)

www.ciel.org (Center for International Environmental Law)

www.american.edu/TED/ted.htm (A website from American University, Washington, DC, devoted to trade, environment, and development)

www.wti.org (The World Trade Institute is an educational and research organization devoted to the law and economics of world trade, based in Switzerland)

Advocacy

Depending on the organization or the particular study, these may include references to reports or other substantive analysis.

www.sierraclub.org

www.publiccitizen.org

www.oxfam.org

www.wwf.org

www.wwfus.org

www.cato.org

Table of Cases

Reports of WTO Panels and the WTO Appellate Body

Note: In the text of the book, we have referred to the date of adoption of the report by the Dispute Settlement Body, not the date of publication by the panel or the Appellate Body. Both dates are included below.

Arbitral, Administrative, Judicial Decisions

List of Acronyms

AIT   Canadian Agreement on International Trade
APA   U.S. Administrative Procedure Act

BECA   U.S.-Mexico Border Environment Cooperation Agreement
BECC   Border Environmental Cooperation Commission
BISD   Basic Instruments and Selected Documents
BITs   Bilateral Investment Treaties

CAFE   Corporate Average Fuel Economy
CFCs   Chlorofluorocarbons
CITES   Convention on International Trade in Endangered Species of Wild
                      Fauna and Flora
CEC   Commission for Environmental Cooperation (of North America)
CTE   Committee on Trade and Environment

DR-CAFTA   U.S.-Dominican Republic-Central American Free Trade Agreement
DSB   Dispute Settlement Body
DSU   Dispute Settlement Understanding

EA   Environmental Assessment
EC   European Communities
EIA/EIS   Environmental Impact Assessment/Statement
EPA   U.S. Environmental Protection Agency
ESI   Environmental Sustainability Index
EU   European Union

FAO   U.N. Food and Agriculture Organization
FACA   Federal Advisory Committee Act
FDI   Foreign Direct Investment
FOIA   Freedom of Information Act
FTAA   Free Trade Area of the Americas

GATS   General Agreement on Trade in Services
GATT   General Agreement on Tariffs and Trade
GDP   Gross Domestic Product
GMF/GMO   Genetically Modified Food/Organism
GSP   Generalized System of Preferences

HTS   Harmonized Tariff System

ICJ	International Court of Justice
ICSID	International Centre for Settlement of Investment Disputes
ISO	International Organization of Standardization
ITO	International Trade Organization
JPAC	Joint Public Advisory Committee
MMPA	U.S. Marine Mammal Protection Act
MEAs	Multilateral Environmental Agreements
MFN	Most Favored Nation
NAAEC	North American Agreement for Environmental Cooperation
NAFTA	North American Free Trade Agreement
NGOs	Nongovernmental Organizations
NEPA	U.S. National Environmental Policy Act
OECD	Organization for Economic Cooperation and Development
PCBs	Polychlorinated Biphenyls
PPMs	Processes and Production Methods
PPP	Polluter Pays Principle
SCM Agreement	Agreement on Subsidies and Countervailing Measures
SPS Agreement	Agreement on the Application of Sanitary and Phytosanitary Measures
TBT Agreement	Agreement on Technical Barriers to Trade
TEDs	Turtle Excluder Devices
TNCs	Transnational Corporations
TPA	U.S. Bipartisan Trade Promotion Authority Act
TRIPs	Agreement on Trade-related Intellectual Property Rights
UNCITRAL	United Nations Commission on International Trade Law
UNCTAD	U.N. Conference on Trade and Development
UNDP	U.N. Development Program
UNEP	U.N. Environment Program
USTR	U.S. Trade Representative
WHO	World Health Organization
WTO	World Trade Organization

Trade
and the
Environment

Chapter 1

The Tension between Trade and Environment

I. Trade and Environment: Congruence or Conflict?

There is no doubt that international trade has grown hugely in importance over the last 50 years and even in the last decade, the global decline of late 2008 and 2009 notwithstanding. In 2008, the last full year for which robust data are available, global merchandise trade (trade in goods) approached US$15.8 trillion, a 250 percent increase from the US$6.3 trillion in trade in 2002, a figure itself that was almost double the value of trade in 1990. World trade in services rose to US$3.7 trillion, more than doubling since 2002. These recent trends are consistent with the entire 1950–2007 period during which world trade has grown on average by about 6 percent per year, far higher than the growth in world output. In short, the proportion of the world's goods and services that crosses a border is now much higher than it was even 10 years ago, much less 60 years ago. WORLD TRADE ORGANIZATION, WORLD TRADE REPORT 2009 4 (2009); WORLD TRADE ORGANIZATION, INTERNATIONAL TRADE STATISTICS 2003 (2003).

For some countries, trade has fundamental economic importance. Exports of goods and services account for 35 to 40 percent of Canada's gross domestic product (GDP). Total trade (exports and imports) is well over 100 percent of GDP for many countries. Even for the United States, with its huge internal market, total trade represents about 25 percent of GDP. World Bank, Indicators, *at* http://data.worldbank.org/indicator. The flow of investments across national borders is similarly vast, though more volatile. Worldwide, foreign direct investments—that is, investments in physical and commercial assets—were more than US$1.7 trillion in 2008, down from nearly $2.0 trillion in 2007 and expected to decline to about $1.0 trillion in 2009. UNCTAD, WORLD INVESTMENT REPORT 2009 1, 4 (2009).

The production of the huge quantities of merchandise that enter the flow of international trade has important environmental effects, from the ecological disturbance of extracting and consuming natural resources (fish, timber, coal, etc.) to the pollution from processing raw materials and manufacturing goods. Beyond this, manufacturing requires vast amounts of energy, and the transportation systems that move these goods from place to place cause additional environmental harm. But as we shall see, the direct environmental effects of trade are the least of the issues that consume the time of policymakers, business people, environmental groups, and scholars who work at the interface of trade policy and environmental policy. No one has captured the central issues in the trade and environment debate more succinctly than Professor John Jackson did almost 20 years ago:

Proposition 1: Protection of the environment has become exceedingly important, and promises to be more important for the benefit of future generations. Protecting the environment involves rules of international cooperation, sanction, or both, so that some government actions to enhance environmental protection will not be undermined by the actions of other governments. Sometimes such rules involve trade restricting measures.

Proposition 2: Trade liberalization is important for enhancing world economic welfare and for providing a greater opportunity for billions of individuals to lead satisfying lives. Measures that restrict trade often will decrease the achievement of this goal.

John H. Jackson, *World Trade Rules and Environmental Policies: Congruence or Conflict?*, 49 Wash. & Lee L. Rev. 1227, 1227–28 (1992).

Professor Jackson also put useful labels on the major viewpoints one can take about the relationship between the two propositions: some see liberalized trade and environmental protection as congruent, others believe they are in conflict.

The 1991 report of a trade tribunal in the *Tuna/Dolphin I* case, which launched the modern "trade and environment" debate, catalyzed the conflict viewpoint. In that case, Mexico sought review by a panel of trade experts under the General Agreement on Tariffs and Trade (GATT) of a U.S. embargo on imports of yellowfin tuna from Mexico. The United States imposed the embargo because Mexican fishermen were not using the dolphin-protective fishing practices that U.S. tuna boats were required to use and that the U.S. Marine Mammal Protection Act required as a condition for importing yellowfin tuna caught in the eastern tropical Pacific. The panel of trade experts determined that this embargo was contrary to the GATT. In the panel's view, the embargo closed the U.S. market to Mexican-caught tuna even though the tuna are just "like" U.S.-caught tuna. Trade rules, they opined, obliged the United States to work toward an international agreement to protect dolphins rather than using a trade embargo to pressure the Mexican government to change its fisheries policy. In succeeding years, decisions by other panels of the GATT and its successor, the World Trade Organization (WTO), have found other environmentally-based trade restrictions impermissible. (The complex facts of these cases and the legal analyses by the GATT and WTO tribunals are taken up in detail in Chapters 3, 4 and 5.)

For many other observers, however, there is more congruence than conflict in the goals of trade liberalization and environmental protection. A year after *Tuna/Dolphin I*, and about the time that Jackson wrote his article, world leaders signed the Rio Declaration on Environment and Development, the key text of the 1992 United Nations Conference on Environment and Development. Principle 12 of the Rio Declaration states:

States should cooperate to promote a supportive and open international economic system that would lead to economic growth and sustainable development in all countries, to better address the problems of environmental degradation. Unilateral actions to deal with environmental challenges outside the jurisdiction of the importing country should be avoided. Environmental measures addressing transboundary or global environmental problems should, as far as possible, be based on an international consensus.

Rio Declaration on Environment and Development, June 14, 1992, U.N. Doc. A/CONF.151/5/Rev. 1, *reprinted in* 31 I.L.M. 874 (1992). Note that Principle 12 expressly disapproves of the kind of unilateral trade restriction at issue in *Tuna/Dolphin I*. Two years later, the world's trade ministers more directly embraced the congruence viewpoint, asserting that "there should not be, nor need be any policy contradiction between … an open … trading system on the one hand, and acting for the protection of the environment and the promotion of sustainable development on the other." Preamble to the Decision of Ministers on Trade and Environment, Marrakesh, April 15, 1994.

More than 15 years after these early statements, the debate on trade and environment can still be strident. Many environmental and social activists continue to take a starkly conflict-based view of trade's implications for the environment. Consider the following from a publication of the U.S. nongovernmental group Public Citizen, which begins a chapter on *Tuna/Dolphin I* and its aftermath with the provocative title, "The WTO's Environmental Impact: First, Gattzilla Ate Flipper":

> In this chapter, we document a systematic pattern of WTO attacks on member nations' vital environmental concerns and policy priorities, and the biases built into WTO rules that promote unsustainable uses of natural resources. Over its almost nine years of operation, the WTO's anti-environmental rhetoric has been replaced by more politic pronouncements even as it has systematically ruled against every domestic environmental policy that has been challenged and eviscerated exceptions that might have been used to safeguard such laws. Instead of seeking to resolve conflicts between commercial and environmental goals, the WTO's largely ineffectual Committee on Trade and the Environment has become a venue mainly for identifying green policies that violate WTO rules.

LORI WALLACH & PATRICK WOODALL, WHOSE TRADE ORGANIZATION? THE COMPREHENSIVE GUIDE TO THE WTO (2004).

Ardent proponents of free-market economics can be just as dogmatic in their defense of unfettered international trade. Consider this excerpt from an analysis by the libertarian Cato Institute:

> There is no inherent conflict between high labor and environmental standards in the domestic economy and success in the global economy. In fact, the evidence points strongly to a positive correlation between high standards, high national incomes, and economic openness. Nations that have opened themselves to the global economy tend to grow faster, achieve higher per capita incomes, and maintain higher labor and environmental standards. The belief that higher standards can be promoted only through tough language in trade agreements is built on a myth.

Daniel T. Griswold, *Trade, Labor, and the Environment: How Blue and Green Sanctions Threaten Higher Standards,* Cato Institute Trade Policy Analysis No. 15, Aug. 2, 2001, at 10.

Over the years since those excerpts were written, much of the debate about the interaction of trade and environment has become more nuanced and complex than these polemical advocacy statements indicate. Nevertheless, even scholarly analyses and government position papers continue to reflect persistently divergent views about the nature, location, and intensity of the policy conflict between open trade and environmental protection and what combination of legal and institutional reforms would enhance policy congruence.

The goal of this textbook is to help you explore many of the legal and policy texts and arguments and look at some of the reform proposals. Although as authors we have our own views on these matters, and don't always agree among ourselves, we try to offer you, our readers, a balanced presentation of the issues. If we succeed in our mission, each of you will gain a basic capacity to formulate your own informed and well-reasoned judgments about desirable national and international law and policy on trade and the environment.

This chapter introduces some of the theory and analysis underlying the policy discourse that lead to the persistently divergent views about whether trade and environment rules and objectives are congruent or in conflict. We conclude this introductory section with three analytical frames for understanding the potential policy conflicts and the opportunities for congruence.

A sophisticated environmental critique of trade policy can rest on the following general propositions enumerated by Professor Daniel Esty:

- Trade in goods has *scale and composition effects* on the environment. "Without environmental safeguards, trade may cause environmental harm by promoting economic growth that results in the unsustainable consumption of natural resources and waste production."

- Trade rules and policies can exert a *regulatory effect*. As it is, trade regulations or market access agreements "can be used to override environmental regulations unless appropriate environmental provisions are built into the structure of the trade system." Prospectively, in the view of environmentalists, trade restrictions should be available as a regulatory policy tool "as leverage to promote worldwide environmental protection, particularly to address global or transboundary environmental problems and to reinforce environmental agreements."

- Many environmental commentators also express concerns over a supposed *competitiveness effect*. "Even if the pollution they cause does not spill over onto other nations, countries with lax environmental standards may have a competitive advantage in the global marketplace and put pressure on countries with high environmental standards to reduce the rigor of their environmental requirements."

Drawn from and quoting from DANIEL C. ESTY, GREENING THE GATT: TRADE, ENVIRONMENT, AND THE FUTURE 42 (1992).

In equally broad terms, economists and other trade advocates offer responses to these three environmental critiques. The following paraphrases arguments of the eminent economist Jagdish Bhagwati:

- In terms of the *scale and composition effects*, even though freer trade may lead to economic growth, growth can improve environmental conditions by altering social preferences for environmental protection and increasing economic resources available to spend on environmental enhancement measures.

- Market access agreements have a positive *regulatory effect* by helping eliminate environmentally harmful subsidies and by removing trade barriers to the transfer of pollution control technology. Nations retain their right to impose national environmental standards (and taxes) of their own choosing.

- In response to the claimed positive *regulatory effect* of trade leverage, trade restrictions, especially unilateral ones, are a second-best approach to international environmental problems and often impose unfair economic burdens for environmental protection on developing countries.

- The *competitiveness effect* is not a legitimate argument in theory or practice. Differences in national environmental standards are justified because each nation has its own set of environmental conditions and its own priorities and preferences. Regardless, in practical terms empirical studies show no measurable trade or business location advantage for countries with lax environmental standards.

Trade and Environment: The False Conflict?, in TRADE AND THE ENVIRONMENT: LAW ECONOMICS, AND POLICY 159 (Durwood Zaelke et al., eds. 1993).

Here is a fuller explanation of these three abiding concerns about the effects of an open system of international trade on the nation's and the world's environmental condition.

Scale and composition effects concern the growing scale of international trade and the composition of that trade; that is the particular mix of goods being traded. Economists often discuss scale and composition as two separate factors, but together they raise the question of sustainability. The overall scale of world economic activity raises significant challenges for all elements of environmental protection, from resource conservation to pollution control, and a growing fraction of that activity involves international trade. By the same token, the composition of trade significantly determines its environmental consequences. For example, trade in fish and in agricultural products has a bearing on fishing effort and land-use practices around the world. Trade in lumber and pulp and paper influences forest conservation and forest management in many countries. As two prominent economists once remarked, "Although many positive things can be said about liberalizing and thus increasing trade, the structure of trade, as we know it at present, is a curse from the perspective of sustainable development." Trygve Haavelmo & Stein Hansen, *On the Strategy of Trying to Reduce Economic Inequality by Expanding the Scale of Human Activity*, in ENVIRONMENTALLY SUSTAINABLE ECONOMIC DEVELOPMENT: BUILDING ON BRUNDTLAND 41, 46 (Robert Goodland et al. eds., 1991).

Regulatory effects concern the way international trade law may limit government policy choices and perhaps restrain the regulatory authority of governments to protect national health and the environment and to secure effective protection of the global environment. In principle, international trade rules may act to limit national or even international regulatory options for protection of the national environment. There have been a small number of high profile trade cases over national environmental or health regulations, and these might exert some chilling effect on new regulatory initiatives, but overall there have been very few international trade challenges to domestic environmental or health regulation. More obviously and more controversially, trade law has been invoked to challenge unilaterally-imposed trade restrictions intended to protect foreign or global resources, such as the U.S. trade embargo in *Tuna/Dolphin I*. For lawyers especially, much of the trade and environment debate turns on the way different analysts evaluate real or perceived effects of trade law on environmental regulatory choices, subjective predilections about whether one country should be able to express or impose its environmental policy preferences on other countries, and questions about how to manage or reduce regulatory effects.

Competitiveness effects concern whether or to what extent differences across countries in their national environmental standards impair the ability of firms in "high-standards" countries to compete with firms in countries with less stringent standards. Although politicians speak frequently about the competitiveness effect, its existence or its magnitude in economic terms is much debated, making competitiveness another issue on which various analysts and activists have widely divergent views. Moreover, economists in particular note that there would be a flip side to any competitiveness-based trade restriction—there could be adverse environmental effects from limiting the access of developing countries to developed country markets for a variety of reasons. *See, e.g.*, Brian R. Copeland & M. Scott Taylor, *Trade, Growth, and the Environment*, 42 J. ECON. LIT. 7, 67 (2004).

As a first illustration of the three effects just described, carefully consider the following real-world situations. Are these examples of conflict? Of congruence? Are the environmental or the trade "facts" clear? Are they knowable? What are the (apparent) motivations of the various participants? Should their motivations matter or only the results? Do these cases demonstrate the predicted effect of trade policy on environmental protection or tend to disprove it?

- *Scale and Composition Effect.* Environmental groups in the Netherlands proposed a law that all wood products sold in the Netherlands carry a label indicating whether the wood was sustainably produced. The Netherlands has scant forests of its own; the measure is clearly addressed to forestry practices in other countries, with special concern for the protection of tropical forests. Is the proposed measure a reasonable consumer-information measure or a disguised restriction on trade? Could it be both? Does your answer depend on whether you come from a "northern" consumer country or a "southern" producer country? Is it relevant that for ten years or more the government of the Netherlands has advocated international agreements on sustainable forest management, but many other governments, including those of tropical forest countries, have argued against any such binding legal regime?

- *Regulatory Effect.* A U.S. company makes a gasoline additive that boosts octane and enhances fuel efficiency. For some years, the U.S. Environmental Protection Agency (EPA) banned this additive on the ground that it interfered with catalytic converter pollution controls on automobiles. After the company showed that the additive does not interfere with catalytic converters, EPA considered banning it under another section of the law for health reasons. Finally, however, EPA decided they lacked sufficient scientific data to support a ban under U.S. law, and the additive became legal in the U.S. Officials in Environment Canada reached the same conclusion about the health effects data under Canadian environmental law. The Canadian environment minister, however, expressing concern about public health in speeches, convinced Parliament to ban the shipment of this additive from one province to another. This internal trade ban within Canada effectively prevented the additive from being marketed to gasoline refiners in Canada. The U.S. company then protested Canada's inter-provincial trade ban under a provision of the North American Free Trade Agreement allowing foreign investors to seek compensation for improper governmental interference with their investments. From an environmental perspective, did the public health concerns of the environment minister justify the internal trade restriction? Should Canada be required to compensate the U.S. company for its lost investment in the Canadian market? Consider these additional facts: In both Canada and the United States there has been a long-running conflict between the automobile manufacturers (who oppose this gasoline additive) and the petroleum refiners (who favor it). The Canadian environment minister's riding (district) is in Ontario, an auto production center. Does this raise suspicions about the bona fides of the minister's actions? Another fact: At the request of an oil-producing province (Alberta), a Canadian domestic trade tribunal determined that Parliament's inter-provincial trade ban on this additive violated Canada's internal trade statute. The Canadian tribunal agreed that trade within Canada could be restricted for public health reasons under Canadian law, but it found no "urgency" to the health concerns over this additive, so it concluded that the federal government must use less trade restrictive means to accomplish its objective. Do these additional facts change your opinion about the minister's action? About Canada's obligation to compensate the U.S. company for its lost investment?

- *Competitiveness Effect.* Air quality management officials for the Los Angeles area adopted very stringent air pollution control standards for volatile organic compounds (VOCs) in the late 1980s as part of the effort to clear Los Angeles's notorious smog. Furniture makers use solvents, paints, and varnishes that release VOCs. Soon after the new regulations were adopted, a few dozen furniture makers (among thousands in the Los Angeles area) relocated to nearby Mexico, where air pollution control requirements are less stringent. Is this an example of companies relocating to a "pollution haven" to take advantage of less stringent environmental standards? About 40 furniture makers moved their operations to Mexico; in the same years a much larger number of Los Angeles furniture makers relocated to Arizona, North Carolina, Michigan, and other places in the United States. Air pollution requirements for VOCs in these other locations are also less stringent than in Los Angeles. Does that change your view of the "pollution haven" hypothesis? Why are the standards in Arizona, for example, less stringent than those in Los Angeles? What other factors may have caused furniture makers to relocate their operations?

The rest of this chapter introduces key trade and environmental concepts that underlie policy and analysis at the intersection of trade and the environment. To put the issues into the broader context of international economic and political relations, Section II below touches on some key themes in the burgeoning literature on globalization. Section III then presents the key economic and environmental concepts that permeate trade and environment policy debates. Section IV then puts a sharper focus on the scale and composition and competitiveness issues through a stylized "debate" between environmental and trade proponents

---

II. Globalization

The trade-environment debate has evolved against a social and political background increasingly aware of "globalization." Canadian commentator Pierre Marc Johnson notes that globalization is not "a new phenomenon," but nevertheless a powerful force:

> The early 16th and late 19th century were, most notably, two "golden eras" of commerce, characterized by open markets, and extensive international trade. The current globalization process, however, is fundamentally different in its scope, depth, and institutional characteristics. The process of economic integration today is truly global, as well as multidimensional. It is market-based, driven by powerful economic forces, and accelerated by a technological revolution. It is also supported and shaped by an extensive web of international organizations and rules, both formal and informal, public and private.

Pierre Marc Johnson, *Beyond Trade: The Case for a Broadened International Governance Agenda*, POLICY MATTERS, June 2000, at 5.

Johnson identifies two other facets of globalization that have important ramifications for international law and policy. One facet is a North-South divide, which arises from the uneven capacity of developing countries to deal with the social pressures of globalization and capture its economic benefits. The other facet is the empowerment of environmental organizations and other elements of civil society on an international scale, with substantial consequences for the way international policy is developed, both formally and informally.

A. Economic Integration

The world has grown ever more interdependent economically, as described in the opening paragraphs of this chapter. Global gross domestic product (GDP) multiplied more than six times in real terms between 1950 and 2000 and has continued to grow at an average rate of about four percent since then. Per capita GDP expanded almost three times, meaning a higher standard of living for millions around the world. International trade increased 14-fold.

In 2006, total trade accounted for more than 50 percent of the GDP of the members of the Organization for Economic Cooperation and Development (OECD), the world's industrial free-market economies. WORLD TRADE ORGANIZATION, INTERNATIONAL TRADE STATISTICS 2008 3 (2008); ORGANISATION FOR ECONOMIC CO-OPERATION AND DEVELOPMENT, INDEX OF STATISTICAL VARIABLES: TRADE AS % OF GDP, *available at* http://www.oecd.org/dataoecd/26/40/38785295.htm#T. But a substantial share of this trade occurs among "preferred" trading partners within regional trading blocs. In the European Union (EU), 68 percent of total trade transactions come from intra-regional trade among the EU's 27 members. Among the three countries of the North American Free Trade Agreement, intra-regional trade accounts for 51 percent of total trade. On the other hand, China's share of world exports more than tripled between 1990 and 2007. China is expected to be the number one merchandise exporter in 2008. WORLD TRADE ORGANIZATION, WORLD TRADE REPORT 2008: TRADE IN A GLOBALIZING WORLD 17 (2008), www.wto.org/english/res_e/booksp_e/anrep_e/world_trade_report08_e.pdf.

Another sub-phenomenon of global economic integration is the high proportion of cross-border trade that takes place between units of single corporate enterprises, such as the shipment of raw materials, components, partly assembled goods, or even final goods from one company location to another or one subsidiary to another. The U.N. Conference on Trade and Development (UNCTAD) estimates that there are 82,000 transnational (multinational) corporations (TNCs) with 810,000 foreign affiliated companies. These TNCs accounted for 11 percent of global GDP in 2007, with sales amounting to US$31 trillion. UNCTAD, WORLD INVESTMENT REPORT 2009: TRANSNATIONAL CORPORATIONS, AGRICULTURAL PRODUCTION AND DEVELOPMENT xxi (2009), http://www.unctad.org/en/docs/wir2009_en.pdf. Although world data on intra-firm trade is not collected, UNCTAD estimates that about one-third of international trade is between related parties.

Johnson identifies rapid financial flows as a "second economic driver of globalization." An astounding US$3 trillion or more in currency changes hands daily; since the management of exchange rates across currencies is a key instrument of national fiscal policy and has a major effect on trade flows, the nearly perpetual exchange of currency puts strong market pressures on government economic policy. The more lasting international financial flows are foreign direct investment (FDI)—private investments in foreign countries. Total world FDI was US$2 trillion in 2007, slipping to $1.7 trillion in 2008, but still way up compared to US$644 billion in 1998. In terms of sustainable development, it is notable that the share of the FDI inflows going to developing and transition economies has increased steadily in recent years, accounting for $621 billion in 2008, or more than one-third of global FDI. Investment is not evenly distributed, however. China alone accounts for US$108 billion of FDI, and Brazil and India together had another $87 billion of inflows. Meanwhile, only US$33 billion went to all 49 of the world's least developed countries. UNCTAD, WORLD INVESTMENT REPORT 2009, at xix and Annex Table B.1. These patterns pose both opportunities and challenges. "FDI has considerable impact on economic growth in the countries where it is massively channeled; indeed FDI has become much more important than Official Development Assistance (ODA) [eds. note: i.e., government-contributed aid] in major developing countries, with obvious structural effects on their economies. At the same time, capital and money markets have demonstrated through their volatility that they can be disruptive and increase the vulnerability of host countries." Pierre Marc Johnson, *Beyond Trade,* at 7.

While trade has grown, so has the world's "throughput"—the flow of raw materials into the human economy and its flow out as waste. World consumption of fossil fuels (coal, oil, and natural gas) reached some 11.43 trillion tons of oil equivalent in 2005, up from 8.76 trillion tons in 1990. Marine fish production from both live catch and aquaculture (which relies on live catch for feed) jumped from 88.3 to 118.6 million metric tons over the same decade. The consumption of paper per person on a world basis increased nearly 20 percent in the 1990s, from 45.15 kg/person in 1989 to 54.48 kg/person in 2005. On a more hopeful note, per capita global production of wood for both industrial and fuel uses ("roundwood") has dropped steadily for more than four decades, from 0.74 cubic meters per person in 1960 to 0.54 cubic meters in 2005. WORLD RESOURCE INSTITUTE, EARTHTRENDS SEARCHABLE DATABASE, http://earthtrends.wri.org/; Gary Gardner, *Roundwood Production Up,* WORLDWATCH INSTITUTE VITAL SIGNS 2007–2008 62 (2007).

Questions and Discussion

1. Some observers are more skeptical than Johnson about the significance of globalization. Robert Gilpin sees the current pattern of globalization as "largely confined to North America, Western Europe, and Pacific Asia." Trade still accounts for a "relatively small portion of most economies," and the "largest portions of foreign direct investment flows are invested in the United States, Western Europe, and China" with only a "very small portion" going to developing countries in sectors other than raw materials. He agrees that the technological revolution in computers and telecommunications has "contributed to the process of globalization," but in other fields, such as biological sciences, the changes in technology, which he says are a "profound development," have "nothing whatsoever to do with globalization as it is commonly conceived." Citing air, water, and soil pollution; deforestation in Brazil, the United States, and Southeast Asia; and the decline of small-scale agriculture as examples, Gilpin concludes: "It would be easy to expand the list of problems generally attributed to globalization that have really been caused by technological changes, by national government policies, or by other wholly domestic factors." GLOBAL POLITICAL ECONOMY: UNDERSTANDING THE INTERNATIONAL ECONOMIC ORDER 364–69 (2001).

2. If the WTO is a symbol of economic globalization, it is pertinent to ask: How has the WTO influenced patterns of international trade? The WTO itself cites the data at the beginning of this chapter as demonstration of its positive influence on world trade and world economic welfare. Environmental critics of trade also assume that market access agreements and WTO trade liberalization rules will result in higher levels of international trade. But in a 2004 paper, economist Andrew Rose contradicts this common as-

sumption: "It turns out that membership in the GATT/WTO is *not* associated with enhanced trade.... To be more precise, countries acceding or belonging to the GATT/WTO do not have significantly different trade patterns than nonmembers." Andrew K. Rose, *Do We Really Know that the WTO Increases Trade?*, 94 Amer. Econ. Rev. 98 (2004) (emphasis in original). Rose suggests as one explanation for this unexpected result that WTO membership in itself has little influence on each member's trade policy; many WTO members, especially developing countries, maintain substantial barriers to trade. *Id.* at 111–12.

B. The North-South Divide

Economic integration is just one part of globalization, and trade just one part of economic integration. For example, sub-Saharan countries export 30 percent of their combined GDP, but remain among the world's poorest countries, because debt-servicing costs absorb all their hard currency revenues. The world's population has grown from 1.6 to nearly 6.9 billion in the last 100 years with more than 75 million people added each year. Most of these people live in the developing world and remain desperately poor.

- 1 billion people live at the margins of survival on less than US$1 a day; 2.6 billion — 40 percent of the world's population — live on less than US$2 a day.

- 28 percent of all children in developing countries are estimated to be underweight or stunted.

- The vast majority of the approximately 10 million children who die each year before the age of 5 die from poverty and malnutrition; they live primarily in the developing world.

- The 40 percent of the world's population living on less than US$2 a day account for 5 percent of global income. The richest 20 percent account for three-quarters of world income. All of sub-Saharan Africa will account for almost one-third of world poverty by 2015, up from one-fifth in 1990.

- Since 1971, the number of Least Developed Countries (LDCs) those countries considered to be extremely poor based on income, economic vulnerability, and other factors (nutrition, health, education, and adult literacy) — has risen from 25 to 50 (35 in sub-Saharan Africa).

- LDCs, representing more than 11 percent of world population (more than 740 million people), accounted for just 0.6 percent of world GDP in 2004.

United Nations Development Programme, Human Development Report 2007/2008 at 25 (2007); United Nations, The Criteria for Identification of the LDCs, *available at*: http://www.un.org/special-rep/ohrlls/ldc/ldc%20criteria.htm.

Pierre Marc Johnson points out that general globalization trends "hide an increasingly divided world where a North-South gulf has taken the place of the traditional East-West divide." He goes on to comment that "the persisting inequalities are a testimony to the considerable challenge of translating growth into human development" which "point to the need for global governance institutions to identify and implement innovative ways of disseminating knowledge and technology." Pierre Marc Johnson, *Beyond Trade*, at 9–10.

The inequities that underlie the North-South divide have numerous implications for trade policy. Deepak Nayyar has observed, "Economic interdependence is asymmetrical.

There is a high degree of interdependence among countries in the industrialized world. There is considerable dependence of the developing countries on the industrialized countries." Nayyar comments that in a condition of interdependence, "the benefits of linking and the costs of delinking are about the same for both partners." The unequal distribution of costs and benefits "implies a situation of dependence." Deepak Nayyar, *Towards Global Governance*, in GOVERNING GLOBALIZATION: ISSUES AND INSTITUTIONS 6–9 (Deepak Nayyar, ed. 2002). Nayyar argues more broadly that globalization "has been associated with an exclusion of countries and people from its world of economic opportunities." The excluded people and countries are those that lack sufficient income to participate in the market. People without assets that yield an income can sell their labor if they have some capabilities, but those capabilities depend on education, training, or experience. People without capabilities are excluded. "In the changed international context, however, the increased openness, interdependence, and integration attributable to globalization have made it more difficult for governments to intervene, particularly through economic policies, to combat such exclusion."

Another Indian, Nobel laureate economist, Amartya Sen, puts the issue more bluntly: "[T]he real issue is the distribution of globalization's benefits." He adds:

> Indeed, this is why many of the antiglobalization protesters, who seek a better deal for the underdogs of the world economy, are not—contrary to their own rhetoric and to the views attributed to them by others—really "antiglobalization." It is also why there is no real contradiction in the fact that the so-called antiglobalization protests have become among the most globalized events in the contemporary world.

Amartya Sen, *How to Judge Globalism*, THE AMERICAN PROSPECT, Jan. 1, 2002, *available at* http://www.prospect.org/cs/articles?article=how_to_judge_globalism.

C. The Rise of the Non-State Actor and the Vertical Loss of Sovereignty

A third facet of globalization that Pierre Marc Johnson identifies is its influence on the processes for making public policy decisions, especially at the international level:

> Nation-states have suffered a vertical loss of power in the globalization process, mainly as a result of the combination of the fiscal crisis of the state and the internationalisation of governance. The fiscal crisis has produced devolution of power to local authorities while states have also delegated aspects of their sovereignty to international regimes. This process has weakened the state and given prominence to new actors.

Pierre Marc Johnson, *Beyond Trade*, at 10. Two of the "new actors"—not really new in themselves, but with new influence on policy—are transnational corporations (TNCs) and nongovernmental organizations of civil society (NGOs). We have already noted the high proportion of international trade that takes place between different affiliates of TNCs and their corresponding interest in maintaining and extending a world-wide system of liberal trade and investment. NGOs have also become influential. By Johnson's count, there were some 30,000 international NGOs in the mid-1990s. Thanks to electronic communications, NGOs have fostered a diverse but highly organized web of organizations, creating a truly global civil society.

Not all commentators, however, agree with Johnson that globalization results in a weakening of nation-state autonomy. Amit Bhaduri challenges the notion that the nation-state is in decline in the face of globalization. He sees instead new tensions and a "reorientation" for the state that strains democratic accountability:

> [T]wo opposing tendencies are being fused together. The nation state is apparently being constrained and weakened on the one hand in exercising its economic and political authority. On the other, however, the nation state is being strengthened in certain respects in so far as it suits global corporate interests in trade, investment, and finance. In this sense, it is not the demise, but a systematic reorientation of the nation state that we may be witnessing as one of the striking features of the current process of globalization. Nevertheless, it tends to create a growing hiatus between the democratic governments of the nation states that have to be accountable for their performance within the electoral timeframes, and the multinationals as central actors in globalizing markets who are not accountable to the wider body of ordinary citizens in any nation.

Amit Bhaduri, *Nationalism and Economic Policy in the Era of Globalization*, in GOVERNING GLOBALIZATION, at 39–40, 42.

Questions and Discussion

1. The role of transnational corporations and nongovernmental organizations, particularly "northern" environmental groups, remains a nettlesome issue in the trade-environment debate. Northern environmental advocates, often believing that governments have become the handmaidens of corporations, propose direct regulation of the international actions of the corporations (*e.g.*, national control of foreign investments and national standards for imported products). Governments of the developing countries typically resist these environmental initiatives even though they are meant to help those countries manage corporate actions. Do the readings help explain these attitudes?

2. Dani Rodrik sees the tensions Bhaduri describes leading to a governance trilemma:

> We want economic integration to help boost living standards. We want democratic politics so that public policy decisions are made by those that are directly affected by them (or their representatives). And we want self-determination, which comes with the nation-state. This paper argues that we cannot have all three things simultaneously. The political trilemma of the global economy is that the nation-state system, democratic politics, and full economic integration are mutually incompatible. We can have at most two out of the three. It follows that the direction in which we seem to be headed—global markets without global governance—is unsustainable.

Dani Rodrik, "Feasible Globalizations," NBER Working Paper 9129 (Sept. 2002), at 1.

Do you see Rodrik's trilemma? That is, why do any two of the things go together, but not all three? Do you agree with Rodrik's prediction that governments tend to sacrifice democratic accountability in their economic policies under these circumstances? What is the likely result of making trade policy more democratically accountable? If promoting integration of environmental and trade policy is a move toward deeper integration, does

Rodrik's trilemma mean environmentalists will need to compromise either on democratic accountability or on national autonomy? Is this why some environmentalists oppose economic integration instead? The next section offers additional food for thought.

D. Globalization and Trade-Environment Issues

What are the implications of the globalization of environmental concerns in conjunction with the economic and social globalization discussed here? A 1999 WTO report on trade and environment stated that the "ongoing dismantling of economic borders reinforces the need to cooperate on environmental matters, especially on transboundary and global environmental problems that are beyond the control of any individual nation." Many would subscribe to Pierre Marc Johnson's view that globalization means that "the WTO cannot escape this new trade and environment/development nexus." Pierre Marc Johnson, *Beyond Trade*, at 12.

S.P. Shukla, for one, offers a contrary view. In his terms, the deeper integration now on the WTO agenda, represented by trade-environment issues, "seeks to achieve the standardization of domestic policies in a wide range of issues." He sees transnational corporations and their home governments as the "propelling force" behind deeper integration in the quest for open markets. The standard economist's efficiency argument for the welfare-enhancing benefits of open markets, he argues, "overlooks the reality of the existence of vast multitudes of people with little or no ability to participate in market processes." From this perspective:

> The newer [trade] regimes being designed for labour and environment standards are also likely to limit weaker members' access to markets. Deeper integration carries the process of exclusion much further, with the ultimate outcome that people are barred from the law-making processes of their countries. In effect, the legislative power of a country is transferred to the invisible control of the transnational corporations who have vested interests in creating "internationally contestable markets." In this sense, the process of deeper integration is anti-democratic.

S.P. Shukla, *From the GATT to the WTO and Beyond*, in Governing Globalization at 254, 273–75.

Amartya Sen puts the policy challenge in overtly ethical terms:

> Globalization has much to offer, but even as we defend it, we must also, without any contradiction, see the legitimacy of many questions that the antiglobalization protesters ask.... [T]he ethical and human concerns that yield these questions call for serious reassessments of the adequacy of the national and global institutional arrangements that characterize the contemporary world and shape globalized economic and social relations.

Amartya Sen, *How to Judge Globalism*, The American Prospect, Jan. 1, 2002.

Questions and Discussion

1. Pierre Marc Johnson and others plausibly describe the current state of world affairs as a combination of deep economic integration and nation-state autonomy. What policy

tensions arise in trying to promote the national interest in an integrated economy? Consider again Rodrik's trilemma.

2. As we have seen, analysts like Robert Gilpin dispute the idea that we have deep economic integration in the world today. The rules of the GATT, in this view, represent only shallow integration and still allow substantial "protection" of national markets. Domestic economic policies (budgetary and fiscal) are still the overwhelming influence on the national economy. If this is an accurate assessment, does that suggest that there is in fact more democratic accountability now than there would be under a more deeply integrated system? What indications do you see of democratic accountability in current economic and trade policies of your own country?

3. What are the implications of an emphasis on democratic accountability in trade policy? In 2001, the World Trade Organization committed itself to a "development round" of trade liberalization to benefit the developing countries, including better access for those countries to the markets of the developed countries, especially for agricultural products. This is known as the Doha Development Agenda or the Doha Mandate. Yet the EU and the United States, responsive to domestic political pressures, have so far (as of late 2010) continued to maintain, if not increase, their barriers to market access for agricultural and other goods from developing countries. Consequently, hundreds of millions of the world's poorest people have seen their living standards decline rather than advance in recent years. According to the U.N. Development Program, the number of people living in "extreme poverty" declined only slightly in the 1990s, leaving nearly one quarter of the world's people in that condition. U.N. DEVELOPMENT PROGRAM, HUMAN DEVELOPMENT REPORT 2003, at 5.

4. For a diverse collection of articles relating to the globalization issues raised in this section, *see* THE GLOBALIZATION READER (Frank J. Lechner & John Boli eds., 2d ed. 2004).

III. Key Concepts in Trade and Environment

The question of whether trade policy and environmental policy work at cross-purposes or can work together for common goals—whether trade and the environment are in conflict or congruent—runs through this whole textbook. So far, we have merely given you a quick glimpse of the ongoing debate over these questions and then tried to situate that debate in the larger framework that affects policymaking at the international level, in particular concerns about globalization and the political tensions arising from the disparity in wealth and political power between the economically developed North and the still developing South. But another difference between the realms of "trade"—the lawyers and economists and government officials who devote their time to trade law and policy—and the realms of the "environment"—which also include scientists and many people in civil society—is that the people who inhabit these two realms usually have different ways of looking at the world born from differences in their training and, it must be admitted, from differences in their paradigms and the values that animate their work. Before we go any further, then, it is time to get acquainted with the key concepts and the intellectual traditions that give each realm, trade and environment, a legitimate claim to a seat at the table of public policymaking.

A. Concepts of International Economics

1. Comparative Advantage

John Jackson, The World Trading System
14–18 (2nd ed. 1997)

Early [trade] theorists developed a "mercantilist" viewpoint. Under this theory, the goal of nations in their economic relations was to amass gold or other treasure, so as to maximize national power (which was not well distinguished from the wealth and power of sovereigns). The goal therefore was to "sell more to strangers yearly than we consume of theirs in value." This theory was soon attacked as flawed by [David] Hume and [Adam] Smith, among others. For one thing, mere accumulation of money did not necessarily promise better living standards or even the instruments of power (warships, etc.). For another thing, accumulating monetary assets could cause inflation, undermining a nation's world-competitive position.

Eighteenth-century classicists focused on the welfare of citizens rather than sovereigns, and noted the advantages of international trade, Adam Smith saying: "What is prudence in the conduct of every private family can scarce be folly in that of a great kingdom. If a foreign country can supply us with a commodity cheaper than we ourselves can make it, better buy it off them with some part of the produce of our own industry...."

It was [David] Ricardo, in 1817, who went a step further and developed the theory of comparative advantage, which, despite refutations from skeptical politicians, has provided a powerful intellectual underpinning, still respected by all major economists, for policies that generally stress the value of "liberal trade"— that is, of minimizing governmental interference with trade flows. We must therefore examine this theory in more detail.

The theory was originally based on a simple model of international trade, involving two countries, two traded products, and one type of input for both products. Often the model uses the United Kingdom and Portugal as the countries, cloth and wine as the products, and labor as the input. Assume that in the United Kingdom a yard of cloth takes 5 hours of labor to produce, and a gallon of wine 10 hours of labor to produce. Assume that in Portugal it takes 10 hours to produce the yard of cloth and 6 hours to produce the gallon of wine. It is obvious that the United Kingdom has an absolute advantage in cloth production and Portugal an absolute advantage in wine production. The total goods produced by an available 90 hours of labor in each country, absent trade (i.e. with autarky), can be summarized as follows:

United Kingdom: 18 yards of cloth or 9 gallons of wine, or some combination of these, such as 10 yards of cloth and 4 gallons of wine.

Portugal: 9 yards of cloth or 15 gallons of wine, or some combination of these, such as 6 yards of cloth and 5 gallons of wine.

Given that citizens in both countries want both products, then without trade both countries will produce some mix of the two products, such as the following:

	United Kingdom	Portugal	Total
Cloth	10 yards	3 yards	13 yards
Wine	4 gallons	10 gallons	14 gallons

If trade between the two countries is opened and each specializes entirely, trading for the product of the other, then the products available or produced in each can be summarized as follows:

	United Kingdom	Portugal	Total
Cloth	18 yards	0 yards	18 yards
Wine	0 gallons	15 gallons	15 gallons

The totals for both products are larger than in the autarky case, and thus more is available for consumption in both countries under trading conditions.

The model above shows a case where each of two countries has an absolute advantage in one of the two products, and trade will help both. The question that immediately occurs, then, is, if one country has an absolute advantage in *both* goods, should these countries trade? Such a case would demonstrate the power of the theory of comparative advantage. The following table summarizes this situation, both before and after trade opens.

	United Kingdom	Portugal	Total
Labor Available	90 hours	90 Hours	
Labor Used Hours per yard Hours per gallon	5 hours 10 hours	10 hours 10 hours	
Autarky Cloth Wine	10 yards 4 gallons	5 yards 4 gallons	15 yards 8 gallons
Trade Cloth Wine	18 yards 0 gallons	0 yards 9 gallons	18 yards 9 gallons

Thus, it is not the difference of *absolute* advantages but of *comparative* advantage that gives rise to the gains from trade. Even when the United Kingdom can produce all goods in the model with no more labor than Portugal, there is an advantage for the two countries to trade if the *ratio* of production costs of the two products differs. In this second case, wine in the United Kingdom costs 2 yards of cloth, whereas in Portugal it costs only 1 yard of cloth; thus it is worthwhile for the United Kingdom to produce cloth and to trade its excess for wine. In fact (going beyond Ricardo), with specialization one may create economics of scale so that the gains from trade would be even more than those represented in this hypothetical case.

The discussion above presents the basic model of the theory of comparative advantage, but it is appropriate to ask whether the model has been confirmed by empirical evidence. The simple model above does not lend itself easily to empirical investigation, partly because it is so simple. Derivative and additive theories complementing the model, however, have been tested with some success. The apparent importance of trade to national and world economic growth and well-being is sometimes seen in statistics showing that trade over several decades has generally grown at a faster rate than the economy as a whole. Strictly speaking, however, this fact does not necessarily confirm the theory of comparative advantage, given that there are many other factors (including the significant decline of transportation costs and other "natural" barriers to trade) that could explain in part the fact.

Elaborations of the simple model, however, all seem to point in the same direction. A large number of studies, based on various plausible theories or analyses of the effects of restraints on trade, exist that show a loss in welfare for the world as a whole and often also for the countries imposing the restrictions. These restraints cause costs to be borne by the economies, usually costs that are imposed on the consumers or other users of the imported product.

The theory of comparative advantage does have strong intuitive appeal. As consumers, individual citizens can easily see the advantage of international trade: it gives them greater choice of products at better prices. Travelers return home raving about their purchases. Buyers in the marketplace observe better available values in some imported goods. Of course the question remains whether Adam Smith was right when he claimed that what is good for families is also good for nations. Most assuredly one does not follow from the other. The advantages that buyers discover in individual cases may result in an overall disadvantage for a nation as a whole.

One thing does seem clear, however. Import trade provides an additional source of competition to domestic producers. Considered intuitively, and on the basis of a large number of studies, competition is almost always deemed beneficial to world or national-aggregate economic welfare. This can be seen intuitively from individual experiences in recent years with electronic consumer goods: calculators costing over $100 during the mid-1970s can now be purchased in better versions for under $8 (although surely some of this discrepancy is a result of technological innovation). The remarkable and seemingly perpetual drop in price of computers is another example.

Yet there are also groups in a national economy that experience loss from shifts to freer trade, such as the employees who lose their jobs in a domestic industry because of competition from imports. Of course, there are numerous other reasons, including other domestic competition, why firms or whole industry sectors decline, causing job loss as well as capital investment loss. Changes of taste, changes in government procurement programs, new technology, and improved efficiency of production processes can all be mentioned. The question is, why should influences from beyond a nation's borders, ones requiring "structural adjustment changes," be treated differently from such influences from within a nation's borders?

Questions and Discussion

1. Economist Paul Samuelson has called Ricardo's theory of comparative advantage "the most beautiful idea in economics." Yet the theory, as Ricardo propounded it, is incomplete in two respects. First, Ricardo used the productivity of labor as the single variable in comparative advantage and assumed that both capital and labor were immobile—that is, could not be exported or imported. In the 21st century, these assumptions are clearly false. Capital in particular is extremely mobile. Some, including Herman Daly, argue from this that the theory of comparative advantage no longer holds. But if the cost of labor were the key factor in comparative advantage, others have pointed out, countries like Bangladesh would be the world's major exporters. Obviously, other factors are important, including economies of scale, access to raw materials, access to markets, need for skilled labor, reliability of the national legal and economic system, and so forth. We explore some of these factors in the notes that follow.

2. The second limitation of Ricardo's original theory is that it described a static situation. What happens if there are changes in the comparative advantage of one country or another, perhaps as a result of the trade itself? Two Swedish economists pondered that question and devised what is known as the Heckscher-Ohlin Theorem. Their idea is elegant, as well as common-sensical. They begin by theorizing that the reason for differences in comparative advantage from one country to another is their different factor endowments. Each product calls for a mix of factors of production—labor, capital, land, etc. Land-rich countries like Canada or the Ukraine have a comparative advantage in wheat, labor-rich countries like India and China have a comparative advantage in sewing garments, and so on. Some factor endowments are subject to change over time, with resulting shifts in comparative advantage. For example, as the United Kingdom's great stores of coal became depleted, the costs of mining it increased until the entire sector collapsed. Some factor endowments can be changed through government intervention; transportation systems and the educational level of the workforce are common examples. Finally, what economist Paul Krugman calls the "new trade theory" looks beyond factor endowments for other sources of comparative advantage and finds that economies of scale and even imperfect (monopoly) competition also play a role. That is, once a country begins specializing in certain products, it may capture economies of scale that enhance its comparative advantage. Paul R. Krugman, Rethinking International Trade (1990).

3. A 2004 study extends the Heckscher-Ohlin analysis to seek a better understanding of "the effect of factor proportions on the commodity structure of production and trade." It comes to two important conclusions. First, "Countries capture larger shares of world production and trade in commodities that more intensively use their abundant factor." This is consistent with the Heckscher-Ohlin theorem. Second, "Countries that accumulate a factor faster than the rest of the world will see their production and export structure move towards commodities that more intensively use that factor." John Romalis, *Factor Proportions and the Structure of Commodity Trade*, 94 Amer. Econ. Rev. 67 (2004). Thus, as Romalis shows, imports into the United States from Bangladesh concentrate in commodities requiring little skilled labor, while imports from Germany capture "large shares of U.S. imports of skill-intensive commodities, and much smaller shares for commodities that sparingly use skilled labor." *Id.* Such data support his first conclusion. The second conclusion is illustrated by the changing pattern of exports from the "miracle" economies of East Asia—Singapore, Hong Kong, Tai-

wan, and Korea. "Their rapid accumulation of human and physical capital has not simply led to more skill-intensive and capital-intensive production of the same goods, with a consequent reduction in marginal prices. Instead, ability to trade has allowed them to shift production to more skill- and capital-intensive industries." *Id.* at 68. One interesting explanation for these changes is that educational quality correlates significantly with shifts of production and exports towards more skill-intensive industries. *Id.* at 88–89.

4. Herman Daly, for one, notes that Ricardo constructed his theory of comparative advantage by looking only at exchanges of goods, assuming that neither labor nor capital were mobile. The modern world is much different, with massive movements of capital from one country to another and moderate amounts of labor migration as well. From this, Daly disputes the continuing validity of the claim that both partners will increase their welfare after trade based on comparative advantage. Virtually all other economists, though, contend that the law of comparative advantage holds as well when capital and labor are mobile. Using the Heckscher-Ohlin focus on factor endowments, they conclude that both capital and labor will also seek out opportunities for higher productivity, the same calculus that drives exchanges of goods or services. In Ricardo's classic example, Portugal will always have a comparative advantage over England in the production of wine due to its climate and soil conditions, and England will have a comparative advantage in cloth because it has greater supplies of water power (and later coal for steam power) for driving the mills. These endowments will not change even if Portuguese workers can seek employment in English cotton mills or British investors can buy up Portuguese vineyards. Ultimately, of course, England lost most of its comparative advantage in producing cloth to the United States, which is now losing it to China. There are at least two reasons for those shifts in comparative advantage: 1) with industrialization, England, and later the United States, moved on to even higher-productivity goods such as machines and automobiles, and 2) changes in technology changed the mix of factor endowments that bestow advantage for making cloth.

5. As noted earlier in this chapter, some of the trade-environment debate is conducted in terms of competitive advantage. What is the difference between *comparative* advantage and *competitive* advantage? It's best to begin with another distinction, that between *absolute* advantage and *comparative* advantage, as illustrated by the following situation: Even though a litigation attorney is a much better legal researcher than any available law clerk, she hires a law clerk to do research so that she can focus on her litigation. The attorney has an *absolute* advantage over the clerk in both research and trial work, because she can do both jobs better than the law clerk. The clerk, however, has a *comparative* advantage as a researcher because he does not give up any more valuable work to do the research, whereas the attorney would need to reallocate her resources away from the more valuable work of litigating cases in order to do research. In international trade terms, it therefore makes sense for the attorney to "import" research services so that she can "export" more of her litigation skills. The law clerk also benefits, of course, because he is paid more for research than, for example, filing. So both the law clerk and the litigation attorney are better off after this trade. It bears emphasis that the "gains from trade" are realized by reallocating jobs from lower-productivity to higher-productivity sectors of the economy. The litigating attorney has reallocated her effort away from research (lower productivity) and toward litigation (higher productivity). Similarly, the law clerk has reallocated his effort from some lower-productivity option (*e.g.*, file clerk) to a higher-productivity job as a research assistant.

6. *Competitive* advantage, in contrast to comparative advantage, refers to characteristics that permit a company to compete effectively with other firms offering the same product or

service due to lower cost or superior quality. Competitive advantage depends on some degree of absolute advantage by one firm over its competitors. When competitive advantage is used to describe characteristics of a country, then, it harks back to a pre-Ricardian mercantilist philosophy in which internal commerce primarily serves to increase a country's financial wealth and exports are viewed as desirable and imports as undesirable unless they lead to even greater exports. *See* John W. Sweetland, Professor of International Economics and Public Policy, University of Michigan, http://www-personal.umich.edu/~alandear/glossary/. Paul Krugman argues strenuously that the typical political discourse about trade, and even much of what passes for sophisticated economic commentary, misconstrues competitive advantage. Paul Krugman, Pop Internationalism (1996). Krugman argues that *firms* compete, but *countries* do not. International trade should always and only be considered as a matter of comparative advantage. The basis for any country's comparative advantage depends on its national circumstances. Countries with little capital, a relative lack of skills, and low worker productivity will find their comparative advantage in low wages. Countries with high capital or skill levels tend to have comparative advantage in producing goods or services with high inputs of those elements. Countries can influence their national comparative advantage in the world market through, for example, fiscal policies (particularly management of currency valuations) and national choices about investments in education and infrastructure.

7. The mutual benefits to both partners in a trade based on comparative advantage does *not* mean that the trade will equalize their incomes, although there may be convergence over time (see the next discussion point below). In our example of the attorney and the law clerk, the attorney will continue to have a higher income than the law clerk (even after using some of her earnings to pay the law clerk's salary). The difference in incomes reflects the absolute higher productivity of the attorney as compared with the law clerk—the attorney has a higher and less common skill level than the researcher, and the market reflects the higher value of her work in the hourly rate that she can charge. Many factors, of course, account for wage and income differentials. On wages, one key factor is the number of available workers. Wage rates in Japan and the United States have been comparable over the last 25 years, but wage rates in China are only 1/20th as high.

8. Trade based on the theory of comparative advantage offers a politically attractive argument emphasizing increased economic efficiency. Senator Bob Dole stated that with the legislation to implement the WTO agreements, the United States "said loud and clear, America will continue to lead the world to a more prosperous place after the Cold War." An executive at a large retailer said that the WTO "will create economic growth and good-paying jobs for Americans, and for us [at Pier 1], that means they will have more discretionary income to spend at Pier 1 stores." Does this make the theory of comparative advantage sound like a global version of "trickle down" economics?

Consider that the United States is essentially a giant free trade area. Businesses and workers may freely move anywhere in the country. Similarly, investors may freely move their money anywhere they want. What has happened to incomes and income inequality over the last 130 years or so? Incomes vary from state to state, but not nearly as much as in the past. In 2002, Connecticut had the highest per capita income at about $42,000 with New Mexico the lowest at $24,000. These "differences are small ... compared with the huge differences that used to exist." Virginia Postrel, *Economic Scene: A Case in Free Trade: American Incomes Converge, But Not at the Bottom*, N.Y. Times, Feb. 26, 2004, at C2. Some states, such as New York, California, New Jersey, Connecticut, and Massachusetts, have maintained higher incomes for at least 100 years, but incomes have grown more slowly than poorer states. Similarly, North Carolina's productivity was only about 24 percent of California's or New York's in 1880, roughly the same as between the United States and Thailand or Morocco in 2004. Virginia Postrel writes that the "North Carolina is still poorer than California or New York, but the difference is much smaller." She concludes that "[t]he free movement of goods, investment capital and labor has in fact helped to equalize regions within the United States—and, at the same time, to make the whole economy more prosperous by spurring productivity." *Id.*

Recall Amartya Sen's statement that "the real issue is the distribution of globalization's benefits." If you are a resident of Connecticut, does the increasing wealth of the whole U.S. economy make up for the decrease in Connecticut's relative wealth? Would you feel the same way if you lived in New Mexico? Is income inequality between Connecticut and New Mexico less important than income inequality between, let us say, the United States and Costa Rica? Why or why not? The strategy of the European Union, as it has expanded to include less wealthy countries, has been to redistribute some wealth by spending enormous sums of money to promote economic development in the newly-admitted countries. Is this a sound strategy economically? Politically?

9. If some politicians tout the economic benefits of trade and comparative advantage, other political forces can limit or distort those benefits. Some of the discussion of globalization above has already alluded to the constraints that liberal trade places on economic sovereignty and democracy. One response to these constraints is the "conservative social welfare function," as phrased by the economist Max Corden in his book *Trade Policy and Economic Welfare*. Corden argues that politicians will seek to avoid "any significant absolute reductions in real incomes of any significant section of the community.... In terms of welfare weights, increases in income are given relatively low weights and decreases very high weights." He explains his argument as follows:

> Firstly, it is 'unfair' to allow anyone's real income to be reduced significantly— and especially if this is the result of deliberate policy decisions—unless there are very good reasons for this and it is more or less unavoidable.

> Secondly, insofar as people are risk averters, everyone's real income is increased when it is known that a government will generally intervene to prevent sudden or large and unexpected income losses. The conservative social welfare function is part of a social insurance system.

> Thirdly, social peace requires that no significant group's income shall fall if that of others is rising. Social peace might be regarded as a social good in itself or as a basis for political stability and hence perhaps economic development. And even if social peace does not depend on the maintenance of the incomes of the major classes in the community, the survival of a government may.

> Finally, if a policy is aimed at a certain target, such as protecting an industry or improving the balance of payments, most governments want to minimize the adverse by-product effects on sectional incomes so as not to be involved in political battles incidental to their main purpose.

W. M. Corden, Trade Policy and Economic Welfare 107–08 (2d ed., 1997). Do you agree with Corden's perceptions of the political economy of trade? Why have nations nevertheless entered into numerous agreements to liberalize trade?

10. There are a number of arguments regularly advanced as to why nations may want to deviate from comparative advantage and liberal trade policies. A principal national prerogative, recognized in the GATT itself, is the possible restriction of trade to ensure

national security. Even Adam Smith recognized that "Defence is more than opulence." Closely related to national security is the argument that a nation should use tariffs or other restrictions to safeguard industries of military significance, such as aerospace or shipbuilding, even if another nation can supply better or cheaper airplanes and ships.

Policies that do not maximize wealth, such as the preservation of a domestic film industry or traditional wine and cheese production methods, or a national symphony or opera, may be desired because citizens have a strong cultural, aesthetic, or other attachment to these industries or products. Do other "nonmaterial" preferences, such as a preference for locally grown food or a desire to protect whales and dolphins, also justify departures from liberal trade principles? What about preservation of the landscape through stewardship by small-scale "family" farms? What about maintaining rural communities dependent on logging activities? There is nothing wrong with such preferences, of course. The question for trade policy is whether trade restrictions should be used as a means, or the means, to secure these objectives. Economists are almost universally skeptical about such deviations from open international competition, seeing them as more costly and less effective than alternatives such as direct support payments to the industries or workers involved. The number of countries using trade restrictions to protect selected industries has dwindled in recent years. Agriculture remains the last major bastion of closed markets and domestic subsidies; we take up that topic in Chapter 8. Jackson, Davey, and Sykes state this general conclusion: "There is little in international trade theory that can refute the validity of such choices on the part of nations, with perhaps one exception. It can be argued that when a nation makes an "uneconomic" choice, it should be prepared to pay the whole cost, and not pursue policies that have the effect of unloading some of the burdens of that choice onto other nations. In an interdependent world, paying the whole cost is not often easy to accomplish." JOHN H. JACKSON, WILLIAM J. DAVEY, AND ALAN O. SYKES, JR., LEGAL PROBLEMS OF INTERNATIONAL ECONOMIC RELATIONS 23 (4th ed. 2002).

---

2. Cost Internalization: The Polluter Pays Principle and Trade Policy

The fundamental concept of cost internalization has a long and honorable history in the field of environmental economics. As early as the 1920s, British economist Arthur Pigou recognized that market prices for goods failed to account for the harm from the pollution generated during their manufacture because the firm did not have to pay for the right to pollute or, in most cases, compensate those who might be injured by its pollution. Pigou's proposed solution was to "tax" the pollution so that it became a cost item for the firm that would be reflected in the price of its product; hence the term "Pigouvian taxes."

But Pigouvian taxes or fees, despite their theoretical appeal, have never been politically popular as a way to control pollution or other environmental damage. Direct regulation has been the norm. When the industrialized countries adopted national environmental clean-up programs in the late 1960s and early 1970s, trade policy experts had a fear—voiced by many environmentalists—that firms might try to eke out a "comparative" advantage by avoiding direct payments for pollution control, and that national governments might abet that process by subsidizing the pollution control costs of their industries. To avert such distortions to the free market of international trade, the industrialized countries, acting in concert through the Organization for Economic Cooperation and Development (OECD), agreed to an economist's solution, the Polluter Pays Principle.

a. The Polluter Pays Principle

Organisation for Economic Cooperation and Development, Recommendation of the Council on Guiding Principles Concerning International Economic Aspects of Environmental Policies

C(72)128, Annex (May 26, 1972)

Introduction

1. The guiding principles described below concern mainly the inter-national aspects of environmental policies with particular reference to their economic and trade implications....

A. Guiding Principles

a) Cost Allocation: The Polluter-Pays Principle

2. Environmental resources are in general limited and their use may lead to their deterioration. When the cost of this deterioration is not adequately taken into account in the price system, the market fails to reflect the scarcity of such resources both at the national and international levels. Public measures are thus necessary to reduce pollution and to reach a better allocation of resources by ensuring that prices of goods depending on the quality and/or quantity of environmental resources reflect more closely their relative scarcity and that economic agents concerned react accordingly.

3. In many circumstances, in order to ensure that the environment is in an acceptable state, the reduction of pollution beyond a certain level will not be practical or even necessary in view of the costs involved.

4. The principle to be used for allocating costs of pollution prevention and control measures to encourage rational use of scarce environmental resources and to avoid distortions in international trade and investment is the so-called "Polluter-Pays Principle." The Principle means that the polluter should bear the expenses of carrying out the above-mentioned measures decided by public authorities to ensure that the environment is in an acceptable state. In other words, the cost of these measures should be reflected in the cost of goods and services which cause pollution in production and/or consumption. Such measures should not be accompanied by subsidies that would create significant distortions in international trade and investment. * * *

b) Environmental Standards

6. Differing national environmental policies, for example with regard to the tolerable amount of pollution and to quality and emission standards, are justified by a variety of factors including among other things different pollution assimilative capacities of the environment in its present state, different social objectives and priorities attached to environmental protection and different degrees of industrialisation and population density.

7. In view of this, a very high degree of harmonisation of environmental policies which would be otherwise desirable may be difficult to achieve in practice; however it is desirable to strive towards more stringent standards in order to

strengthen environmental protection, particularly in cases where less stringent standards would not be fully justified by the above-mentioned factors.

8. Where valid reasons for differences do not exist, Governments should seek harmonisation of environmental policies, for instance with respect to timing and the general scope of regulation for particular industries to avoid the unjustified disruption of international trade patterns and of the international allocation of resources which may arise from diversity of national environmental standards.

9. Measures taken to protect the environment should be framed as far as possible in such a manner as to avoid the creation of non-tariff barriers to trade.

Questions and Discussion

1. The Polluter Pays Principle has been adopted as policy, or at least referred to, by many governments and in a number of international agreements. For example, the Polluter Pays Principle is a binding principle in the European Union. In some contexts, it has also taken on a broader meaning than its original formulation. For a useful review, see the report of the OECD's joint working party on trade and environment, *The Polluter-Pays Principle as It Relates to International Trade*, COM/ENV/TD(2001)44/FINAL .

2. Daniel Esty concludes that environmental policymaking suffers from an economic and political failure to internalize environmental costs. He argues that if environmental costs were fully internalized, then the tensions between trade and environment would be much reduced. ESTY, GREENING THE GATT, at 4. The first question to ask about the Polluter Pays Principle is whether it is a cost-internalization principle. In an associated *Note on the Implementation of the Polluter-Pays Principle*, the drafters state: "In fact, the Polluter-Pays Principle is no more than an efficiency principle for allocating costs and does not involve bringing pollution down to an optimum level of any type, although it does not exclude the possibility of doing so."

3. The more difficult question that Esty's argument raises is: Which "costs" should be internalized? The Polluter Pays Principle requires polluters to bear the expense of meeting what public authorities determine is an "acceptable" environmental state. As explained by the OECD in the note on implementation, "acceptable state" implies a level of pollution where public authorities have presumably concluded that the marginal benefits of more abatement would be less than the marginal costs. Is this a satisfactory definition of what is "acceptable"? Is it the same as an economist's idea of internalizing pollution costs?

4. The Rio Declaration, in Principle 16, seems to conflate cost internalization and the Polluter Pays Principle: "National authorities should endeavour to promote the internalization of costs and the use of economic instruments, taking account of the approach that the polluter should, in principle, bear the cost of pollution, with due regard to the public interest and without distorting international trade." Agenda 21, often called the blueprint for sustainable development, urges businesses and industries to use "free market mechanisms in which the prices of goods and services should increasingly reflect the environmental costs of their input, production, use, recycling and disposal subject to country-specific conditions." U.N. Conference on Environment and Development, Agenda 21, ¶ 30.3, U.N. Doc. A/CONF.151/26 (1992).

5. Observe that the OECD's guidance on the PPP, quoted in point 2 above, explicitly states that the PPP does not require "bringing pollution down to an optimum level

of any type." This means that Country A can have very strict pollution control standards and Country B can have very lenient ones, and as long as both require the firms in their jurisdiction to pay for their own pollution control costs, both will be in compliance with the PPP. How does the PPP recommend addressing that situation? Do you think that recommendation would be effective? We address this question further in the next section.

----

b. Trade Effects of Differences in National Environmental Standards

For trade and environment, the question remains whether a nation's willingness to pollute the environment constitutes a part of its comparative advantage and, if so, whether its trading partners should be permitted to try to offset that advantage. In principle, a difference in the environmental regulations confronting firms in two different countries will give the firm in the country with the "lower" standards a cost advantage, assuming of course that it costs some money to meet environmental requirements and that it costs more money to meet higher standards than it does to meet lower ones. Trade experts acknowledge the theoretical legitimacy of the cost advantage argument. Numerous efforts by economists to detect the expected effect on trade and investment patterns, however, have revealed little or no effect. A World Bank report summarizing the evidence noted that pollution havens have "not happened on a significant scale." The report also reiterates the most widely accepted explanation: "The main reason is that the costs imposed by environmental regulation are small relative to other considerations.... [T]here are large cost differences between locations due to factors such as transport, infrastructure and economic policy. By contrast, the cost of making a plant less polluting is usually remarkably cheap." WORLD BANK, GLOBALIZATION, GROWTH, AND POVERTY: BUILDING AN INCLUSIVE WORLD ECONOMY 132 (2002).

The World Bank report remarks that the "new globalizers" — the developing countries that have engaged intensively in trade — have increased their share of industrial production and their share of pollution intensive industries. It concludes, however, that this increasing production and pollution "was not related to exporting; it largely met domestic demand." *Id.* According to this analysis, then, the severe problems of industrial pollution in developing countries are domestically determined and are not the result of the pollution haven effect. Indeed, foreign-owned firms in these countries tend to be less polluting than domestic firms in the same industry. Other studies looking at industrial location, at trade flows, and at foreign direct investment flows tend, with rare exceptions, to support the view that inter-country differences in environmental standards have little or no effect on patterns of international trade and investment. An economics literature review in 2004 concludes: "While there is evidence of a pollution haven *effect*, it is only one of many factors that determine trade patterns, and there is no evidence that it is the dominant factor." Copeland & Taylor, *Trade, Growth, and the Environment*, at 67 (emphasis in original).

Although the general absence of observed trade effects from differences in environmental standards is telling, it does not altogether negate the argument in favor of national flexibility to use trade measures to offset the environmental advantage of foreign producers. Accordingly, trade advocates carry their argument further, questioning the very policy premises behind the environmentalists' position. Trade economist Jagdish Bhagwati puts the argument this way:

[I]f India pollutes a lake that is wholly within its borders, that is an intrinsically domestic question. If, however, she pollutes a river that flows into Bangladesh, that is an intrinsically international question. So are the well-known problems of acid rain, ozone layer depletion, and global warming. These latter, intrinsically international problems of the environment raise questions that inter-face with the trade questions in a more complex way than the former, intrinsically domestic problems....

A country's solution to intrinsically domestic environmental problems should reflect her own resources, her technical know-how, and her tradeoffs between income and pollution of several varieties. Her solutions should thus be within her own traditional jurisdiction. As long as the environmental question is intrinsically domestic, one may wonder why anyone should object to the conduct of free trade with a country on the grounds that her preferred environmental solution makes free trade with her unacceptable. Yet the fact is that they do. And the objections are directed not merely at free trade, but also at the institutional safeguards and practices, as at GATT [eds. note: now the WTO], which are designed to ensure the proper functioning of an open, multilateral trading system that embodies the principles of free trade. * * *

For instance, polluting now, growing faster, and cleaning up later may be more economical for a country. Or for specific environmental choices, a country may prefer to spend on clean-up or prevention in one industry rather than another, reflecting her own evaluation of environmental impacts in these different industries.

In short, the notion that "international standards" should be set for all, or that the United States should have the power to countervail any "social dumping" it deems to be occurring abroad, ignores the fact that there are legitimate reasons for diversity in environmental regulation across countries.

Jagdish Bhagwati, *Trade and Environment: The False Conflict?, in* TRADE AND THE ENVIRONMENT: LAW, ECONOMICS, AND POLICY, at 164–65, 167.

Bhagwati also argues that a country that imposes sanctions against another country for having different environmental standards is really imposing its ethical preferences on the other country. For example, the U.S. Marine Mammal Protection Act prohibits any person from killing, injuring, or harassing whales, dolphins, and other marine mammals, regardless of a species' conservation status. It protects them all, principally because Americans believe that whales and dolphins are highly intelligent, social animals that should be protected. In other countries, such as Japan, some people prefer to eat dolphins. Mexicans do not value dolphins as highly as Americans, so they do not protect dolphins from fishing nets as the United States does. Did the U.S. embargo on Mexican tuna in the *Tuna/Dolphin I* case, then, rest on a nonenvironmental value (moral) preference?

Reversing the tables, the United States is a large consumer of beef. In many western states, overgrazing of cattle has left much of the range in unsatisfactory condition. Meanwhile, Hindus in India refuse to kill cows because they consider them sacred. Should India be able to impose trade sanctions against the United States because it deems U.S. grazing laws to be environmentally inadequate? Or because it believes that all cows are sacred?

Even where countries share environmental objectives, such as protection from hazardous chemicals, countries may choose to regulate different chemicals. A dense concentration of paper mills in one country may lead it to regulate dioxin levels in wastewater discharges strictly or even to prohibit the use of chlorine for bleaching altogether. A larger country with a more dispersed paper industry, however, may not see the need to regulate dioxin as strictly because dioxin levels in water will be very low.

From these kinds of arguments, Bhagwati concludes:

> The unilateral, governmental imposition of trade sanctions against other nations simply with a view to coercing them into accepting one's idiosyncratic "value" preferences seems therefore unwise on three principal grounds:
>
> • It is essentially intransitive, with each nation able to say its specific values are better than another's; it thus creates the potential for chaotic spread of trade restrictions based on self-righteousness, compounded by likely encouragement of the process of protectionism;
>
> • It is inherently asymmetric toward poor nations with less economic clout, implying that the economically strong nations are also morally superior and their governments must not be constrained by multilateral rules from coercing others into conversion; and
>
> • There are alternative, private options that can be used to create multilateral consensus of shared values, based not on the sword but on precept, example, and even private retribution via boycotts.

Id. at 173–74.

Nonetheless, most agree that truly international concerns may require different approaches to trade issues. Bhagwati, for example, would defend a country's use of unilateral trade restrictions to address cross-border or transboundary physical spillovers, such as when water pollution or acid rain enters a country's territory from another country. *Id.* at 177, 183–84. For truly global issues, such as global warming or ozone depletion, he favors a multilateral approach but recognizes that an effective multilateral approach may be difficult to negotiate.

In this context, though, a new concern arises. Trade restrictions may be applied, not on the grounds of a putative competitive advantage, but to exert economic pressure on governments to change their national environmental policies. This would shift the trade restriction from one based on compensation to one based on sanction. Bhagwati then asks what should happen when a country has scientific or other objections to a multilateral policy favored by many other countries (the refusal of the United States, for example, to ratify the Kyoto Protocol and reduce emissions of greenhouse gases). He argues, "The use of trade restrictions to chastise those who do not go along, condemning them as "rejectionists" or "free riders," would then be unjust.... If such trade restrictions are to be accepted, then it is necessary that they be justified before an impartial adjudicating body such as perhaps a [WTO] dispute settlement panel, as required in order to secure an efficient and equitable solution to a global environmental problem rather than as an instrument to impose an inefficient and inequitable solution an another trading nation." *Id.* at 186–87.

———————

Questions and Discussion

1. The editors of *The Economist* argue that "it is not at all unfair for countries to choose different levels of environmental protection—it is an important part of their competitive advantage." *Why Greens Should Love Trade*, THE ECONOMIST, Oct. 9, 1999, at 17. That is,

to insist on a "level playing field" amounts to an "unfair trade" practice. Do you agree? Is it fair to require Bangladesh, whose per capita GDP in 2006 was only US$1,155, to have businesses meet the same pollution control requirements as those imposed in the United States, whose per capita GDP in 2006 was US$43,968? United Nations Development Program, Statistics of the Human Development Report, *at*: http://hdr.undp.org/en/statistics. Is it reasonable to assume that such disparities in wealth may lead to differences of opinion as to the appropriate level of environmental protection?

2. Recall Bhagwati's comment that "if India pollutes a lake that is wholly within its borders, that is an intrinsically domestic question." Is his position supported by the Polluter Pays Principle? How does the Polluter Pays Principle address differences in pollution control efforts between two trading partners?

3. Is the pollution of a lake in India really an intrinsically domestic question? Might it be an international question? Consider the case of Brazil's Tietê River, which flows wholly within Brazil. The Tietê River is one of the most polluted rivers in the world, flowing with the chemical and human waste of São Paulo and elsewhere. The government of Brazil has borrowed hundreds of millions of dollars from international financial institutions such as the Inter-American Development Bank to clean the river. Does this international investment make the river's condition an international question? Or suppose that the lake in India is an important habitat for migratory birds? Would this make its condition an international question? In either case, if a seemingly "domestic" environmental matter becomes an international question, would that justify a trade rule that requires imports from India to be produced in a way that would meet the importing nation's own environmental standards?

4. An important part of the argument by developing countries against environmentally-based trade restrictions is that poor nations cannot afford environmental protection now or that poor nations simply have different, immediate priorities. When two-fifths of the world's population live on fewer than US$2 per day, how fair is it to ask them to be concerned about—and pay for—global warming reductions or strict requirements for water pollution? Economic development must come first. Only with higher incomes will people have the luxury to "worry" about the environment. Is this argument compelling? If you do not think the argument is compelling, are you willing to tell poor farmers in rural Brazil that they cannot cut trees in the Amazon Rainforest to clear land for crops or cattle because we need the Amazon to mitigate the effects of global warming or to save an endangered bird?

5. Bhagwati repeats the argument that it may be more economical to pollute now and clean up later. But empirical evidence suggests that companies do not choose to locate their businesses based on lax environmental regulation. EBAN GOODSTEIN, THE TRADE-OFF MYTH 55–67 (1999). Doesn't that undercut the idea that countries must grow economically first and protect the environment later?

---

3. The Free Movement of Goods and Core International Trade Principles

The liberal economic regime that now prevails throughout the world has its roots in the economic theories of Adam Smith and his followers. Recall that Smith argued against mercantilist notions of trying to accumulate wealth by hoarding capital and by seeking to have the nation export more than it imported. He urged instead a focus on production and allowing the "invisible hand" of the market to guide independent market participants to choose what products to make, free of intervention by the state.

One of the first national experiments in implementing Smith's principles was the United States Constitution. Among its objectives was to replace the chaotic and inefficient regime under the previous Articles of Confederation, in which each of the states maintained tariffs against the goods of the other states. The Constitution instead envisioned a national market in which the federal Congress alone had the authority to regulate interstate as well as foreign commerce. Early decisions of the United States Supreme Court struck down local and state measures it judged to have direct effects on interstate commerce. Over time, the doctrine of the Dormant Commerce Clause took shape. This doctrine holds that states are not only prohibited from taking action affecting interstate commerce that is contrary to policies established by the Congress, but they are also prohibited from taking any action that would affect commerce in ways not regulated by the Congress unless they are exercising their inherent state powers and the indirect effect on interstate commerce is not "undue" in light of the importance of the state policy being advanced. Direct discrimination by one state against goods from other states is presumptively unconstitutional regardless of the state's policy objective.

The constitutional architecture of the European Union is cut from the same cloth as the U.S. economic law system, though it uses some different terminology to express the concepts. In the language of the Treaty on the Functioning of the European Union, the core market principle is phrased as the "free movement of goods." (It also embraces the free movement of labor and services.) The Member States of the European Union retain substantial independent regulatory authority under the "subsidiarity principle," which provides that issues should be addressed at the most local level at which they can be addressed effectively. Nevertheless, the Member States are expressly enjoined from interfering with the free movement of goods except to advance certain national objectives, among which is protection of the environment. Even in exercising this exceptional authority, however, the national measures may not result in a "disproportionate" effect on the free movement of goods. This is known as the "proportionality principle." When significant effects on trade are likely to arise, the European Union as a whole regularly exercises its authority to set Europe-wide standards or Europe-wide policy objectives to be implemented by each of the Member States.

With those important "national" systems in mind, we see that the multilateral trading system, as it developed in the 20th century, was inspired by the same core principles and developed a strikingly similar set of "constitutional" legal rules. The critical text is the General Agreement on Tariffs and Trade (GATT), conceived and negotiated among the Allied Powers at the end of World War II, which came into effect in 1947. The current version of the GATT, called GATT 1994, is textually virtually the same as the GATT 1947 as that was amended over the succeeding decades. Because every member of the World Trade Organization is a party to the GATT, the discussion that follows will refer to the obligations owed between and among "Members."

The GATT system was designed to ensure the efficient allocation of world economic resources and to prevent a recurrence of the beggar-thy-neighbor escalation of tariffs in the early 1930s, which many believed precipitated or aggravated the Great Depression and fomented the aggressive nationalism that brought on World War II. The basic trade liberalization commitment, embodied in Article II of the GATT, requires each country to bind itself to maximum tariff rates determined after negotiation among all the members. The vision in 1947, successfully realized in the decades that followed, was that countries could be persuaded, by mutual agreement, to reduce those tariff levels. To a considerable extent, the remaining provisions of the GATT can be understood as rules to ensure the fair and impartial application of the agreed tariffs and to prevent members from circumventing those tariff commitments by restricting trade through nontariff barriers.

The cardinal legal principle of the GATT is nondiscrimination. Nondiscrimination has two aspects in international trade. One possible form of discrimination is that a particular country will favor one foreign trading partner over another. To prevent this, Article I of the GATT enunciates the most favored nation (MFN) principle. As expressed in the text of Article I, MFN means that each member must provide unconditionally any advantage or privilege granted to a product from one member to a "like product" imported from, or exported to, any other member. That is, a WTO member cannot offer a lower tax or regulatory standard, or a less advantageous legal or administrative requirement, to a product from one WTO member than it offers the same product from any other WTO member. In short, a WTO member may not discriminate among products on the basis of their national origin. For example, Brazil cannot import automobiles from Europe, but bar automobiles from Japan. Similarly, Brazil cannot require automobiles imported from Europe to have different specifications from automobiles imported from Japan. (Free trade agreements and customs unions are authorized exceptions to the MFN obligation, allowing preferential treatment for trade among the members of the agreement or union.) The MFN obligation is discussed further in Section II.A. of Chapter 4.

The second potential form of discrimination in trade is for a country to have a set of rules for imported products that is in some way more burdensome than the rules for the same product made domestically. To prevent this, GATT Article III sets forth the legal obligation to provide "national treatment": to give an imported product tax or regulatory treatment no less favorable than the treatment of the "like" domestic product. For example, if the United States taxes a class of chemicals, it may assess a tax on the same chemicals imported from abroad, but it may not tax the imported chemicals at a higher rate (although it could tax them at a lower rate). Similarly, the United States may require importers of chemicals to provide, for example, environmental testing documentation, but only if and to the extent that the same documentation is required from domestic producers of the same chemicals. Most of Chapter 4 is devoted to the national treatment obligation and its equivalent in some national systems.

In addition to the nondiscrimination obligations of MFN and national treatment, the GATT contains one other core obligation to ensure that trade is not restricted by any measure other than a tariff. GATT Article XI prohibits members from applying any restrictions other than tariffs to imported products. This provision is commonly paraphrased as a prohibition on quantitative restrictions, such as quotas. Agricultural products aside (where special rules apply), members are not allowed to set a limit on the amount or the value of a particular product that can be imported from all countries or from any particular country. A complete ban or embargo on the import of a product is also construed as a quantitative restriction (a zero quota) in violation of Article XI. That is not to say that a member cannot ban a product altogether from its market. Thus, the U.S. ban on the import of polychlorinated biphenyls (PCBs) is acceptable under the GATT because the U.S. law has a corresponding prohibition on the domestic manufacture and sale of PCBs. On the other hand, the U.S. embargo on Mexican tuna in the *Tuna/Dolphin I* case was deemed a violation of Article XI because tuna was still a legal product and U.S.-caught tuna was still being sold in the U.S. market. Part III of Chapter 4 further explores WTO law on quantitative restrictions.

The final GATT provision of fundamental importance for trade and environment law is Article XX, titled "General Exceptions." Essentially, Article XX recognizes that a country may have compelling reasons of national interest to breach its trade obligations under the other GATT articles. Article XX enumerates those compelling reasons, including 1) imposition of measures "necessary" for the protection of "human, animal or plant life or health," and 2) the imposition of measures "relating to" the "conservation of exhaustible natural resources." (Article XXI also allows members to breach their trade obligations for purposes of national security.) Moreover, in order for a member to establish that its trade restrictions fall within the exceptions provided by Article XX, those measures must be applied in a way that avoids "arbitrary or unjustifiable discrimination" in trade and they must not constitute a "disguised restriction" on trade. Because Article XX is central to the WTO resolution of trade-environment tensions, it gets full treatment in Chapter 5.

On their face, the core obligations of the GATT seem simple to apply, but an extensive and growing body of decisions by arbitral panels convened to settle trade disputes demonstrates otherwise. For example, panels have struggled to define "like product," an essential term for determining whether a member might be in violation of its MFN and national treatment obligations. Likewise, several panels have struggled with the precise meaning of the words used in Article XX. These and other questions are taken up in the succeeding chapters. Finally, we will see that there are many other trade agreements besides the GATT that are important in the trade and environment context. These other agreements often reiterate the core nondiscrimination obligations, but they set their own legal standards on other questions and present their own interpretive challenges. Chapter 11 looks at the world's two largest regional agreements, in Europe and in North America.

B. Environmental Concepts and Principles

As mentioned earlier, Daniel Esty wrote years ago about the clash of cultures and paradigms between the environmental and trade communities. One difference he observed is that environmentalists are accustomed to dealing in objective scientific understanding rather than behavioral prediction. At the same time there are inherent scientific uncertainties about many environmental problems that make it difficult to present them as urgent or amenable to precise management, especially problems such as climate change or biodiversity conservation that involve large scales and long time frames. Another difference is that environmentalists are suspicious of the efficiency orientation and behavioral flexibility that are the hallmarks of economics, usually preferring a law-based approach of uniform rules and strict enforcement, reinforced by a strong conviction that environmental values are a "higher-order concern than trade." ESTY, GREENING THE GATT, at 36–41. This section examines key environmental concerns, concepts, and principles of particular relevance to the trade-environment relationship.

1. The State of the World

A good deal of the difference in viewpoints between trade advocates and environmentalists stems from nothing more than differing perceptions of the scope and urgency of the world's environmental problems. From the environmental perspective, global environmental problems have accelerated with increasing population and increasing consumption of the earth's resources. The human population doubled between 1950 and 1986 and approached 6.9 billion in 2010. Both fossil fuel consumption and gross world production quadrupled between 1950 and 1986. The impacts of such growth are felt throughout the economy and throughout the world. This text is not the place for a detailed assessment of the changes, which can be found in many publications, but we present a few indicators relevant to trade:

- **Agriculture.** About 15 million acres of arable land are converted into desert annually and 40 percent of the earth's land is threatened by desertification. Current rates of desertification threaten to displace 50 million people over the next decade. Nonetheless, 35 percent of global grains are fed to livestock, with another 17 percent used to produce biofuels. International Fund for Agricultural Development, *Desertification*, Nov. 2008, at 2; Brian Halweil, *Grain Harvest Sets Record, But Supplies Still Tight*, WORLDWATCH INSTITUTE, VITAL SIGNS, Dec. 12, 2007, http://www.worldwatch.org/node/5539.

- **Fisheries.** The United Nations Food and Agriculture Organization estimates that 52 percent of marine fish stocks are fully exploited. In addition, 19 percent are overexploited and 9 percent are depleted or recovering from depletion. Catches from these stocks will decrease if remedial action is not taken to abate or eliminate overfishing. U.N. FOOD AND AGRICULTURE ORGANIZATION, THE STATE OF WORLD FISHERIES AND AQUACULTURE 2008 7 (2009), ftp://ftp.fao.org/docrep/fao/011/i0250e/i0250e.pdf.

- **Species Extinction.** Scientists estimate that the present extinction rate, mostly due to human activities, is "hundreds of times greater" than the natural extinction rate of approximately 1–10 species per year and "higher than any other on record." Many scientists thus believe we are living during the sixth great extinction on earth. ALFONSO ALONSO ET AL., BIODIVERSITY: CONNECTING WITH THE TAPESTRY OF LIFE 14 (2001). The latest edition of the IUCN Red List, a comprehensive survey of over 47,000 species worldwide, reports that 809 species are already extinct and another 66 are found only in captivity or cultivation. An additional 17,291 species are threatened with extinction or vulnerable. The data are summarized in IUCN, *Extinction Crisis Continues Apace*, Nov. 3, 2009, *available at* http://www.iucn.org/?4143/Extinction-crisis-continues-apace.

- **Chemicals and Waste.** There are about 100,000 chemicals in commercial production. The world generates an estimated 300 million tons of hazardous waste per year. THEO COLBORN ET AL, OUR STOLEN FUTURE 106 (1996).

- **Consumption Patterns.** The richest 20 percent of the world accounts for more than 75 percent of all private consumption, while the poorest fifth consumes about 1.5 percent. High income countries consume 93.5 kilograms of meat per person compared to just 8.8 kg per person in low income countries, use 49 percent of all energy, consume 63 percent of all paper and paperboard, and own 90 percent of all vehicles. WORLD BANK, WORLD DEVELOPMENT INDICATORS 2008 at 4 (2008); WORLD RESOURCE INSTITUTE, EARTHTRENDS SEARCHABLE DATABASE, *available at* http://earthtrends.wri.org/.

- **Poverty.** As noted earlier, 1 billion people live at the margins of survival on less than US$1 a day; 2.6 billion—nearly 40 percent of the world's population—survive on less than US$2 a day. UNITED NATIONS DEVELOPMENT PROGRAMME, HUMAN DEVELOPMENT REPORT 2007/2008 at 25 (2007).

- **Net Primary Product.** Ecological economists warn that growth cannot be the focus of the economy because humans already appropriate about 40 percent of the land-based primary product of photosynthesis—net primary product (NPP).

NPP is the amount of energy left after subtracting the respiration of primary producers (mostly plants) from the total amount of energy (mostly solar that is fixed biologically). NPP provides the basis for maintenance, growth, and reproduction of all heterotrophs (consumers and decomposers); it is the total food resource on Earth. We are interested in human use of this resource both for what it implies for other species, which must use the leftovers, and for what it could imply about limits to the number of people the earth can support.

Peter Vitousek, Paul Ehrlich, and Anne Ehrlich, *Human Appropriation of the Products of Photosynthesis*, 36 BioScience 368, 368 (1986).

Based on the amount of NPP people and their domestic animals use directly as food, fuel, fiber, or timber, the authors estimate that humans appropriate about 3 percent of Earth's annual NPP, but when cropland and other areas used by humans are included, they estimate that humans appropriate "nearly 40 percent ... of potential terrestrial productivity, or 25 percent ... of the potential global terrestrial and aquatic NPP." *Id.*

————

2. The Challenge of Sustainability

To get at the concept of sustainability in the context of international trade, we turn to the work of a relatively new school of economic analysis known as ecological economics. Ecological economics starts with the fundamental truth that the earth is a thermodynamically closed and nonmaterially growing system. The only input into the global ecosystem from the outside is solar radiation, which is balanced by a continual loss to space of reflected light and infrared radiation—heat. Energy and matter cannot be created or destroyed, but they can be reduced to less available, less useful forms through the process of entropy based on the second law of thermodynamics. For an example of entropy, consider human use of fossil fuels. Coal, oil, and gas have low entropy; they are readily usable, easy to manage, and relatively compact forms of energy. When fossil fuels are burned, heat is generated. Heat is also a useful form of energy, especially if it is contained, as in an automobile cylinder or a power plant boiler. But heat has higher entropy, making it difficult to store, manage, and distribute. Notably, entropy cannot be reversed; heat cannot be repackaged into fossil fuels. (Or, to be more precise, it took vastly more energy over the course of past eons to produce the fossil fuels in the first place than they now yield.) In short, natural systems and natural laws impose limits on the human ability to produce more usable energy and material goods, which are the classic measures of economic growth.

Because the earth imposes limits on the economy, ecological economists stress the importance of recognizing the human economy as a subsystem of the global ecosystem, not the other way around. This brings them to examine scale and distributional considerations through a multidimensional, transdisciplinary approach. One of the key developers of ecological economics, Robert Costanza, explains.

Robert Costanza et al.,
An Introduction to Ecological Economics
78–83 (1997)

The transdisciplinary view provides an overarching coherence that can tie disciplinary knowledge together and address the increasingly important problems that cannot be addressed within the disciplinary structure. In this sense ecological economics is not an alternative to any of the existing disciplines. Rather it is a new way of looking at the problem that can add value to the existing approaches and address some of the deficiencies of the disciplinary approach. It is not a question of "conventional economics" versus "ecological economics"; it is rather conventional economics as one input (among many) to a broader transdisciplinary synthesis.

We believe that this transdisciplinary way of looking at the world is essential if we are to achieve the three interdependent goals of ecological economics discussed below: sustainable scale, fair distribution, and efficient allocation. This requires the integration of three elements: (1) a practical, shared vision of both the way the world works and of the sustainable society we wish to achieve; (2) methods of analysis and modeling that are relevant to the new questions and problems this vision embodies; and (3) new institutions and instruments that can effectively use the analyses to adequately implement the vision.

The importance of the integration of these three components cannot be overstated. Too often when discussing practical applications we focus only on the implementation element, forgetting that an adequate vision of the world and our goals is often the most practical device to achieving the vision, and that without appropriate methods of analysis even the best vision can be blinded. The importance of communication and education concerning all three elements can also not be overstated. * * *

Sustainable Scale, Fair Distribution, and Efficient Allocation. A complementary way of characterizing ecological economics is to list the basic problems and questions it addresses. We see three basic problems: allocation, distribution, and scale. Neoclassical economics deals extensively with allocation, secondarily with distribution, and not at all with scale. Ecological economics deals with all these, and accepts much of neoclassical theory regarding allocation. Our emphasis on the scale question is made necessary by its neglect in standard economics. Inclusion of scale is the biggest difference between ecological economics and neoclassical economics.

Allocation refers to the relative division of the resource flow among alternative product uses—how much goes to production of cars, to shoes, to plows, to teapots, and so on. A good allocation is one that is efficient, that is, that allocates resources among product end-uses in conformity with individual preferences as weighted by the ability of the individual to pay. The policy instrument that brings about an efficient allocation is relative prices determined by supply and demand in competitive markets.

Distribution refers to the relative division of the resource flow, as embodied in final goods and services, among alternative people. How much goes to you, to me, to others, to future generations. A good distribution is one that is just or fair, or at least one in which the degree of inequality is limited within some acceptable range. The policy instrument for bringing about a more just distribution is transfers, such as taxes and welfare payments.

Scale refers to the physical volume of the throughput, the flow of matter energy from the environment as low entropy raw materials and back to the environment as high entropy wastes. It may be thought of as the product of population times per capita resource use. It is measured in absolute physical units, but its significance is relative to the natural capacities of the ecosystem to regenerate the inputs and absorb the waste outputs on a sustainable basis.... For some purposes the scale of throughput might better be measured in terms of embodied energy. * * *

Priority of Problems. The problems of efficient allocation, fair distribution, and sustainable scale are highly interrelated but distinct; they are most effectively solved in a particular priority order, and they are best solved with independent policy instruments. There are an infinite number of efficient allocations, but only one for each distribution and scale. Allocative efficiency does not guarantee sustainability. It is clear that scale should not be determined by prices, but by a social decision reflecting ecological limits. Distribution should not be determined by prices, but by a social decision reflecting a just distribution of assets. Subject to these social decisions, individualistic trading in the market is then able to allocate the scarce rights efficiently.

Distribution and scale involve relationships with the poor, future generations, and other species that are fundamentally social in nature rather than individual. *Homo economicus* as the self-contained atom of methodological individualism, or as the pure social being of collectivist theory, is a severe abstraction. Our concrete experience is that of "persons in community." We are individual persons, but our very individual identity is defined by the quality of our social relations. Our relations are not just external, they are also internal—that is, the nature of the related entities (ourselves in this case) changes when relations among them changes. We are related not only by a nexus of individual willingness-to-pay for different things, but also by relations of trusteeship for the poor, future generations, and other species. The attempt to abstract from these concrete relations of trusteeship and reduce everything to a question of individual willingness-to-pay is a distortion of our concrete experience as persons in community—an example of what A.N. Whitehead called "the fallacy of misplaced concreteness."

The prices that measure the opportunity costs of reallocation are unrelated to measures of the opportunity costs of redistribution or of a change in scale. Any tradeoff among the three goals (e.g., an improvement in distribution in exchange for a worsening in scale or allocation, or more unequal distribution in exchange for sharper incentives seen as instrumental to more efficient allocation), involves an ethical judgment about the quality of our social relations rather than a willingness-to-pay calculation. The contrary view, that this choice among basic social goals and the quality of social relations that help to define us as persons should be made on the basis of individual willingness-to-pay, just as the trade-off between chewing gum and shoelaces is made, seems to be dominant in economics today, and is part of the retrograde modern reduction of all ethical choice to the level of personal tastes weighted by income. * * *

It seems clear, then, that we need to address the problems in the following order: first, establish the ecological limits of sustainable scale and establish policies that assure that the throughput of the economy stays within these limits. Second, establish a fair and just distribution of resources using systems of property rights and transfers. These property rights systems can cover the full spectrum from individual to government ownership, but intermediate systems of common ownership and systems for dividing the ownership of resources into ownership of particular services need much more attention. Third, once the scale and distribution problems are solved, market-based mechanisms can be used to allocate resources efficiently. This involves extending the existing market to internalize the many environmental goods and services that are currently outside the market.

———————

Ecological economics and the concept of environmental sustainability raise several points that are crucial to understanding how comparative advantage and open trade may, or may not, promote sustainable development. These points include the ecological footprint of the human economy; the spatial and temporal distribution of costs and benefits; and questions about Gross Domestic Product as an appropriate measure of human welfare.

a. Ecological Footprints and Effective Consumption Populations

The concept of "ecological footprints" captures the idea of the scale of economic activity convincingly. An ecological footprint calculates the amount of land needed to provide the resources to meet a population's consumption needs. For example, to meet the energy, food, and forestry needs of the people of the Netherlands, the Netherlands needs an area more than 17 times its size. *See* James Salzman, *Sustainable Consumption and the Law*, 27 ENVTL. L. 101 (1998). The concept of an ecological footprint is intimately tied to consumption, even more so now that the analysis incorporates the goods and services purchased by a population. For an excellent discussion of consumption and the unsustainability of western consumption patterns, *see* Paul Ekins, *The Sustainable Consumer Society: A Contradiction in Terms?* 3 INT'L ENVTL. AFFAIRS 242 (1991); ALAN DURNING, HOW MUCH IS ENOUGH? (1992).

A country's "effective consumption population" also illustrates the disproportionate impact that some nations have. For example, as compared with Brazilians, Americans consume 7 times more energy, 7.5 times more paper, 1.5 times more cement, and 1.5 times more meat per capita. Americans thus consume 4.38 times more, based on unweighted averages, than Brazilians for these four products. The real U.S. population of 300 million Americans consumes at a level equivalent to 1.31 billion Brazilians.

If one compares the amount Americans consume to Bangladeshis, the U.S. "effective consumption population" is even more staggering. As compared with Bangladeshis, Americans consume 46 times more energy, 142 times more paper, 10.4 times more cement, and 40.3 times more meat per capita. Again, based on an unweighted average, Americans consume 60 times more of these products than Bangladeshis, meaning that the U.S. population consumes at a level equal to 18 billion Bangladeshis—a number far exceeding the nearly 6.9 billion people currently inhabiting the planet. Consumption data from: WORLD RESOURCES INSTITUTE, EARTH TRENDS, *available at* http://earthtrends.wri.org; W. DAVID MENZIE, ET AL., SOME IMPLICATIONS OF CHANGING PATTERNS OF MINERAL CONSUMPTION (USGS, Oct. 2003), *available at* http://pubs.usgs.gov/of/2003/of03-382/of03-382.html.

Herman Daly raises another consideration about scale, consumption, and ecological footprints. He argues that international trade spatially separates the costs and benefits of environmental exploitation. That is, if the Dutch are buying products from Tanzania and Tanzanians are buying products from Malaysia, consumers never see the environmental or social impacts of buying those products. In the larger context, a country is less likely to know if its economy is operating at an optimal scale, because the impacts of its decisions are felt abroad, not at home. The United States has run a trade deficit for the last

35 years; that is, it imports more than it exports. In Daly's terms, this means that much of the environmental impact of consumption in the United States is felt in other countries, leaving the U.S. environment in better condition than its patterns of consumption would otherwise indicate.

---

b. National Accounting Practices

Despite the negative ecological consequences of mass consumption, the standard measure of economic well-being—Gross Domestic Product (GDP)—values such consumption positively. GDP is merely the sum of all economically productive activity. Policymakers, economists, and the general public generally take a growing GDP as a reliable indicator that we are becoming more prosperous and a declining GDP as a sign that the economy is doing poorly.

But more perceptive economists have shown that GDP is not a true indicator of an economy's stability or health. GDP blindly adds up all economic activity regardless of its relationship to human or environmental welfare. The *Exxon Valdez* spilled approximately 11 million gallons of oil into Prince William Sound. Exxon Valdez Oil Spill Trustee Council, Questions and Answers, http://www.evostc.state.ak.us/facts/qanda.cfm. The spill oiled more than 1,300 miles of Alaskan coastline and, according to best estimates, killed approximately 250,000 seabirds, 2,800 sea otters, 300 harbor seals, 250 bald eagles, up to 22 killer whales, and billions of salmon and herring eggs. *Id.* At least 8 species are not recovering. At its peak, the cleanup effort included 10,000 workers, about 1,000 boats, and roughly 100 airplanes and helicopters; Exxon spent perhaps US$2.1 billion cleaning up the spill. Exxon, fishermen, the federal government, and the Alaskan government have spent hundreds of millions more litigating the spill, with Exxon paying more than a billion dollars in civil and criminal penalties to Alaska and millions more in compensation to fishermen. Exxon Valdez Oil Spill Trustee Council, Settlement, http://www.evostc.state.ak.us/facts/settlement.cfm. All the billions spent on clean up, environmental restoration, and lawyers in the wake of this natural disaster, *added* to U.S. GDP. Similarly, mitigation of soil erosion due to bad farming or silviculture practices also *improve* a nation's GDP. CLIFFORD COBB ET AL., WHY BIGGER ISN'T BETTER, THE GENUINE PROGRESS INDICATOR (Redefining Progress, Nov. 1999).

From an environmental perspective, another key factor missing from GDP is that it does not account for the depreciation or depletion of the nation's capital stock. The value of a ton of coal is added to GDP when it is taken from the ground and sold, but GDP does not show that the nation now has one ton less of remaining coal resources. A policy designed to maximize GDP thus tends to become a policy equivalent to maximizing resource depletion and pollution. REPETTO ET AL., WASTING ASSETS: NATURAL RESOURCES IN THE NATIONAL INCOME ACCOUNTS (1989).

Various models have been proposed to redefine how we measure the economy. The Genuine Progress Indicator (GPI), developed by Redefining Progress, adjusts GDP by subtracting for certain factors, such as crime, resource depletion, pollution, long-term environmental damage, loss of leisure time, and auto accidents. It adds to GDP for other factors, such as parenting, volunteer and household work, and higher education. According to Redefining Progress, whereas the per capita GDP of Australia nearly tripled between 1950 and 2000, rising from $10,208 to $29,928, its GPI grew more slowly, from $8,074 in 1950 to $14,013 in 2000. Significantly, the gap between GDP and GPI has grown tremendously, from just $2,134 in 1950 to $15,916 in 2000. The apparent trend is that "a decreasing proportion of economic benefits registered by the GDP count towards improved welfare as time goes on because such benefits are increasingly offset by the costs associated with growing inequality and deteriorating social and environmental conditions." Dr. John Talberth, et al., The Genuine Progress Indicator 2006: A Tool for Sustainable Development 3 (Redefining Progress, 2006).

––––––––––

Questions and Discussion

1. Although recognition that GDP is a poor indicator of overall welfare has gained currency in policymaking circles, national governments continue to use it. Why? Despite the attraction of the GPI or other alternative measures, do you see any problems with adopting those strategies?

2. Some have proposed a more radical departure from GDP by focusing on human survival needs as well as more existential needs identified by Manfred Max-Neef. The survival needs that must be satisfied to achieve well-being include subsistence, protection, affection, understanding, participation, leisure, creation, identity, and freedom. The existential needs include having (consuming), being (existing without having), doing (participating in the work process), and relating (interacting in social and organizational structures). See Costanza et al, An Introduction to Ecological Economics, at 132–38. How would we measure these factors?

3. In a similar vein, human development is the focus of one important effort to measure national performance. The United Nations Development Program has developed a "human development index" that assesses countries on four development indicators. Per capita GDP is one of the four; the others are life expectancy at birth; rate of adult literacy; and the gross enrollment in primary, secondary, and university education. On this index, the country with the highest per capita GDP, Luxembourg, ranks only 18th in the world in human development, while Australia, the third highest-ranked country on the human development index, ranks only 16th in per capita GDP. Nevertheless, there is a strong correlation between income and human development; every one of the 37 lowest-ranked countries for human development has a per capita GDP of less than US$2,600 per year. U.N. Development Programme, Human Development Report 2007/2008, at 221–32.

4. Environmental sustainability is the focus of another national performance assessment exercise. A team at Yale and Columbia universities, with funding from the World Economic Forum, compiled an "environmental sustainability index," later changing the name to Environmental Performance Index (EPI). The original index evaluated countries on twenty indicators centered on five themes: the state of their environmental systems; efforts to reduce environmental stresses; efforts to reduce human vulnerability to environmental stress; social and institutional capacity to address environmental problems; and stewardship of shared and global resources. But the index confronted problems in data and subjective evaluation. The latest version, from 2008, focuses on more quantifiable "performance" factors measuring progress toward two objectives—"reducing environmental stresses to human health [and] promoting ecosystem vitality and sound natural resource management." The indicators include measures related to policy areas such as environmental health, pollution, biodiversity and habitat protection, management of productive resources (e.g., agriculture), and efforts to address climate change. By these measures, Switzerland, Sweden, Norway, Finland, and Costa Rica garner the top rankings, while sub-Saharan African countries (Mali, Mauritania, Sierra Leone, Angola, and Niger) are at the bottom. One interesting conclu-

sion that the reporters draw is: "Wealth correlates highly with EPI scores and particularly with environmental health results. But at every level of development, some countries achieve results that exceed their income-group peers while others fail to keep up. Statistical analysis suggests that in many cases good governance contributes to better environmental outcomes." YALE CENTER FOR ENVIRONMENTAL LAW & POLICY AND CENTER FOR INTERNATIONAL EARTH SCIENCE INFORMATION NETWORK, 2008 ENVIRONMENTAL PERFORMANCE INDEX 9 (2008), http://sedac.ciesin.columbia.edu/es/epi/papers/2008EPI_mainreport_july08.pdf. More specifically, one governance factor that emerges from the data is that "increased public awareness and public involvement in government have positive effects on all national environmental objectives." *Id.* at 37. Finally, the report concludes that there is a direct correlation between competitiveness and environmental health, but "no discernible correlation" between competitiveness and ecosystem vitality. *Id.* at 38–39.

---

3. Sustainable Development

The concept of sustainable development is built on the recognition in ecological economics of the limits of environmental capacity to support economic activities over time. In addition, sustainable development sees poverty as a major contributing factor to unacceptable environmental conditions for billions of the world's people and as a contributor to social and political instability. Sustainable development, therefore, seeks to integrate economic with social and environmental concerns.

Sustainable development merits our attention because it has been embraced as one of the goals of the multilateral trading system. The very first paragraph of the Preamble of the Agreement Establishing the World Trade Organization explicitly references sustainable development as a goal for the WTO:

> *Recognizing* that their relations in the field of trade and economic endeavour should be conducted with a view to raising standards of living, ensuring full employment and a large and steadily growing volume of real income and effective demand, and expanding the production of and trade in goods and service, while allowing for the optimal use of the world's resources in accordance with the objective of sustainable development, seeking both to protect and preserve the environment and to enhance the means for doing so in a manner consistent with their respective needs and concerns at different levels of economic development, ...

The WTO "strongly reaffirm[ed]" its commitment to sustainable development at its 2001 ministerial meeting in Doha, Qatar, saying that trade liberalization "can and must be mutually supportive" of environmental protection and the promotion of sustainable development. Preamble to the Doha Ministerial Declaration, 14 November 2001, WT/MIN(01)/DEC/1, at para. 6.

Sustainable development, as we will see, is both all-encompassing and amorphous. This section first lays out the basic concept and then explores some of its ramifications for trade. On the one hand, how can trade's promise of greater economic efficiency contribute to sustainable development as a whole? On the other hand, to what extent are the social and environmental considerations of sustainable development in tension with the economic considerations that are central to the trading system?

The conceptualization of sustainable development was the result of years of study and international discussion. Growing awareness of environmental problems and huge disparities in economic and environmental conditions between rich and poor nations formed the backdrop for the environmental and development communities to work together for several years in advance of the 1992 United Nations Conference on Environment and Development, frequently called the "Earth Summit," in Rio de Janeiro. As part of that effort, the United Nations chartered a World Commission on Environment and Development, often known as the Brundtland Commission after its chairwoman, Gro Haarlem Brundtland, then the prime minister of Norway. The prominent international citizens serving on the commission seized on and popularized the concept of sustainable development as the key to achieving environmentally sound economic development. As you read the Brundtland Commission's definition and description of sustainable development, ask how sustainable development should be implemented. Does the attainment of sustainable development require a command and control style regulatory regime? Is it compatible with comparative advantage and free trade rules? Should free trade and environmental protection proceed together? If so, how?

World Commission on Environment and Development, Our Common Future ["The Brundtland Report"]

43–46 (1987) By permission of Oxford University Press

Sustainable development is development that meets the needs of the present without compromising the ability of future generations to meet their own needs. It contains within it two key concepts:

- The concept of "needs," in particular the essential needs of the world's poor, to which overriding priority should be given; and
- The idea of limitations imposed by the state of technology and social organization on the environment's ability to meet present and future needs.

Thus the goals of economic and social development must be defined in terms of sustainability in all countries—developed or developing.

Development involves a progressive transformation of economy and society. But physical sustainability cannot be secured unless development policies pay attention to such considerations as changes in access to resources and in the distribution of costs and benefits. Even the narrow notion of physical sustainability implies a concern for social equity between generations, a concern that must logically be extended to equity within each generation.

The satisfaction of human needs and aspirations is the major objective of development. The essential needs of vast numbers of people in developing countries—for food, clothing, shelter, jobs—are not being met, and beyond their basic needs these people have legitimate aspirations for an improved quality of life. A world in which poverty and inequity are endemic will always be prone to ecological and other crises. Sustainable development requires meeting the basic needs of all and extending to all the opportunity to satisfy their aspirations for a better life.

Settled agriculture, the diversion of watercourses, the extraction of minerals, the emission of heat and noxious gases into the atmosphere, commercial forests, and genetic manipulation are all examples of human intervention in natural systems during the course of development. Until recently, such interventions were small in scale and their impact limited. Today's interventions are more drastic in scale and impact, and more threatening to life-support systems both locally and globally. This need not happen. At a minimum, sustainable development must not endanger the natural systems that support life on Earth: the atmosphere, the waters, the soils, and the living beings.

Growth has set no limits in terms of population or resource use beyond which lies ecological disaster. Different limits hold for the use of energy, materials, water, and land. Many of these will manifest themselves in the form of rising costs and diminishing returns, rather than in the form of any sudden loss of a resource base. But ultimate limits there are, and sustainability requires that long before these are reached, the world must ensure equitable access to the constrained resources and reorient technological efforts to relieve the pressure.

Economic growth and development obviously involve changes in the physical ecosystem. Every ecosystem everywhere cannot be preserved intact. A forest may be depleted in one part of a watershed and extended elsewhere, which is not a bad thing if the exploitation has been planned and the effects on soil erosion rates, water regimes, and genetic losses have been taken into account. In general, renewable resources like forests and fish stocks need not be depleted, provided the rate of use is within the limits of regeneration and natural growth. But most renewable resources are part of a complex and interlinked ecosystem, and maximum sustainable yield must be defined after taking into account system-wide effects of exploitation.

As for non-renewable resources, like fossil fuels and minerals, their use reduces the stock available for future generations. But this does not mean that such resources should not be used. In general the rate of depletion should take into account the criticality of that resource, the availability of technologies for minimizing depletion, and the likelihood of substitutes being available. Thus land should not be degraded beyond reasonable recovery. Sustainable development requires that the rate of depletion of non-renewable resources should foreclose as few future options as possible.

Development tends to simplify ecosystems and to reduce their diversity of species. And species, once extinct, are not renewable. The loss of plant and animal species can greatly limit the options of future generations; so sustainable development requires the conservation of plant and animal species.

So-called free goods like air and water are also resources. The raw materials and energy of production processes are only partly converted to useful products. The rest comes out as wastes. Sustainable development requires that the adverse impacts on the quality of air, water, and other natural elements be minimized so as to sustain the ecosystem's overall integrity.

In essence, sustainable development is a process of change in which the exploitation of resources, the direction of investments, the orientation of technological development, and institutional change are all in harmony and enhance both current and future potential to meet human needs and aspirations.

Our Common Future succeeded in popularizing sustainable development in part because it advocates policies built on both environmental protection and economic growth: "Meeting essential needs depends in part on achieving full growth potential, and sustainable development clearly requires economic growth in places where such needs are not being met. Elsewhere, it can be consistent with economic growth, provided the content of growth reflects the broad principles of sustainability and non-exploitation of others." Our Common Future at 44.

The emphasis of the Brundtland Commission on poverty alleviation and a more equitable opportunity for all people "to satisfy their aspirations for a better life" reflects sustainable development's concern with what is known as "intragenerational equity." Principles of equity show up in related policy statements such as Rio Declaration Principle 7, which speaks of the "common but differentiated responsibility" of countries to contribute to sustainable development. More famously, the Brundtland Commission's one-sentence definition of sustainable development articulated the separate notion of intergenerational equity—that the present generation needs to account for the interests of future generations in its use of the world's resources.

Intragenerational equity and intergenerational equity also have a bearing on the important but often concealed distinction between "development" and "growth." To begin with, there is a strong tendency in the literature to equate "development" with "economic development." This is not correct. As John Dernbach has pointed out, within the international community the term "development" has a much broader sweep, taking in all aspects of personal, social, and even political development, everything from liberty and education to social order and cultural expression. John C. Dernbach, *Sustainable Development: Now More Than Ever*, 32 ENVTL. L. REP. 10003, 10004–05 (2002). Even when focusing on economic policy, though, there is a distinction between development and growth. The thought that humans already appropriate nearly 40 percent of the Earth's net primary production says much about whether we should "grow" the economy or "develop" the economy. The Brundtland Commission estimated that the global economy would need to grow five to ten times bigger to eliminate poverty. Even Herman Daly admits that the economy must grow, but he and the Brundtland Commission also agree that the growth must be carefully planned and targeted. According to Daly:

> The important question is the one that the Brundtland Commission leads up to, but does not really face: How far can we alleviate poverty by development without growth? I suspect that the answer will be a significant amount, but less than half. One reason for this belief is that if the five- to tenfold expansion is really going to be for the sake of the poor, then it will have to consist of things needed by the poor—food, clothing, shelter—not information services. Basic goods have an irreducible physical dimension and their expansion will require growth rather than development, although development via improved efficiency will help.... Sustainable development must be development without growth—but with population control and wealth redistribution—if it is to be a serious attack on poverty.

Herman Daly, *Sustainable Growth: An Impossibility Theorem, in* VALUING THE EARTH: ECONOMICS, ECOLOGY, ETHICS, 267, 269–70 (Herman E. Daly & Kenneth N. Townsend eds., 1993).

Daly and others urge the adoption of four policy guidelines to achieve sustainable development.

- Throughput, the flow of materials into the human economy and out again, must be held constant at present levels by taxing resource extraction heavily;

- Harvesting rates should not exceed regeneration rates;

- Waste emissions should not exceed the renewable assimilative capacity of the local environment; and

- Nonrenewable resources should be depleted at a rate equal to the rate of creation of renewable substitutes.

Id. at 271–72; Robert Goodland & Herman Daly, *Environmental Sustainability: Universal and Non-Negotiable*, 6 ECOLOGICAL APPLICATIONS 1002, 1008 (1996).

Each of these four guidelines points to the most difficult question about sustainability: How much capital, or wealth, should the present generation leave for future generations? In general, three types of capital exist. *Natural capital* is our natural environment, flora and fauna as well as the atmosphere. *Manufactured capital* includes the things humans make, including factories, products, roads, and computer chips. *Human capital* includes people and their knowledge, institutions, education, and information, among other things. The challenge of determining how much of each type of capital to leave future generations ensures that societies will argue over how to implement sustainable development. Take the case of nonrenewable resources. Assume that we know we have a 50-year supply of petroleum remaining at current consumption levels, but we lack an adequate supply of substitutes for petroleum to maintain these rates of energy consumption 51 years from now. How do we calculate whether we are making sufficient investments in human capital in the form of knowledge and ingenuity today to develop adequate substitutes within 50 years?

To identify the correct "formula" for calculating capital, Robert Goodland and Herman Daly devised a model based on different levels of sustainability. "Weak sustainability" would maintain total capital without regard to levels of natural, manufactured, or human capital. Based on an assumption that all forms of capital are substitutable, all natural capital could be depleted and converted to human capital. At the other end of the spectrum, "absurdly strong sustainability" would not permit the depletion of anything—nonrenewable resources could not be used and renewable resources could be used only to the extent that "overmature" stock exists. Between these two extremes, however, Goodland and Daly identify two degrees of sustainability—"intermediate" and "strong sustainability"—that highlight the trade-offs between different forms of capital.

> *Intermediate sustainability*: This would require that in addition to maintaining the total level of capital intact, attention should be given to the composition of that capital from among natural, manufactured, and human. Thus, oil may be depleted as long as the receipts are invested in other capital elsewhere (e.g., in human capital development, or in renewable energy resources), but, in addition, efforts should be made to define critical levels of each type of capital, beyond which concerns about sustainability could arise and these should be monitored to ensure that the patterns of development do not promote decimation of one kind of capital no matter what is being accumulated in the other forms of capital. This assumes that while manufactured and natural capital are substitutable over a sometimes significant but limited margin, they are complementary beyond that limited margin. The full functioning of the system requires at least a mix of the different kinds of capital. Since we do not know exactly where the boundaries of these critical limits for each type of capital lie, it behooves the sensible person to err on the side of caution in depleting resources (especially natural capital) at too fast a rate. Intermediate sustainability is a big improvement over weak sustainability and seems "sensible." Its great weakness is that it is difficult if not impossible to define critical levels of each type of capital, or rather each type of natural capital that is the limiting factor....
>
> *Strong sustainability*. This requires maintaining different kinds of capital intact separately. Thus, for natural capital, receipts from depleting oil should be invested in ensuring that energy will be available for future generations at least as plentifully as enjoyed by the beneficiaries of today's oil consumption. This assumes

that natural and human-made capital are not really substitutes but complements in most production functions. A sawmill (human-made capital) is worthless without the complementary natural capital of a forest. The same logic would argue that if there are to be reductions in one kind of education investments they should be offset by other kinds of education, not by investments in roads.

Robert Goodland & Herman Daly, *Environmental Sustainability: Universal and Non-Negotiable*, at 1006.

The four degrees of sustainability offered by Goodland and Daly address only environmental sustainability. As described in *Our Common Future*, the broader concept of sustainable development integrates economic and social dimensions of sustainability with environmental goals. In fact, while definitions of sustainable development vary widely — one group of authors found at least 25 different definitions — they all integrate economic, social, and environmental goals in some way. By including social well-being, sustainable development casts a wider net that assesses an individual's well-being in far more than simple economic terms. For example, sustainable development asks not only if a person is better off financially, but also whether the person has improved health and better education. Sustainable development also shows increased concern for the distributional aspects of economic development through its focus on intergenerational and intragenerational equity. DAVID PEARCE, ET AL., BLUEPRINT FOR A GREEN ECONOMY 1–2 (1989).

The challenges of choosing a level of environmental sustainability and defining how to achieve it should be readily apparent; informational, institutional, and other barriers pose substantial obstacles to even identifying basic thresholds, such as critical levels of a given resource. When the economic and social dimensions of sustainable development are added to a decisionmaking process, it is easy to see why sustainable development has been so difficult to implement.

At the same time, it has been widely embraced. Almost 20 years after *Our Common Future*, sustainable development remains the international community's central goal for environmental and economic planning. Perhaps one reason for its wide acceptance is its ambiguity. The ambiguity of sustainable development lies in the absence of a prescribed method for integrating and balancing economic, social, and environmental goals. Under what circumstances might sustainable development permit economic priorities to outweigh social or environmental priorities? Might environmental priorities outweigh social priorities in another context? If the answer to these questions is yes, sustainable development becomes easy to support because a country can pursue it by the means it deems most consistent with its condition and its philosophy. As David Pearce and his co-authors wrote: "It is difficult to be against 'sustainable development.' It sounds like something we should all approve of, like 'motherhood and apple pie.'" *Id*. at 1. As a result, the trade community and the environmental community can both champion sustainable development, but in far different ways.

———————

Questions and Discussion

1. The Brundtland Commission report uses much of the same terminology and logic as the ecological economists. Does ecological economics support sustainable development? To the extent it does not, what are the differences? Do the issues of allocation, distribution, and scale, as expressed by ecological economists, relate to sustainable development's effort to integrate economic, ecological, and social factors?

2. While sustainable development and ecological economics have appeal, what problems arise when we try to implement them? When do we know we have achieved sustainable development? Should the ecological, social, and economic factors of sustainable development and ecological economics always carry equal weight? Or can a country initially focus on economic development and after reaching a particular standard of living then address social and ecological concerns? In either case, can liberal trade be a basis for achieving sustainable development?

3. Is "intermediate sustainability," as proposed by Goodland and Daly, a sensible approach to the previous question? How might you define critical levels of each type of capital? Can you think of an approach that avoids the problems of actually calculating sustainability and renewability rates?

4. Daniel Esty has concluded that the term "sustainable development" is so vague and subject to so many variant interpretations and applications that it has become useless as a statement of objectives or as a guide for policymakers. Daniel C. Esty, *A Term's Limits*, FOREIGN POLICY, No. 126, Sept.–Oct. 2001, at 74. On the other hand, a vice-president of the International Court of Justice remarked in a concurring opinion that, "The principle of sustainable development is … a part of modern international law by reason not only of its inescapable logical necessity, but also by reason of its wide and general acceptance by the global community." Gabcikovo-Nagymoros Project (Hung. v. Slovk.), 1997 I.C.J. 3 (Sept 25, 1997) (separate opinion of Vice-President Weeramantry). Who do you think has the better of the argument?

---

4. *The Legal Challenge of Sustainable Development*

To meet the challenge of sustainability and sustainable development, a comprehensive body of international environmental law has developed. More than 200 multilateral environmental agreements (MEAs) address a diverse number of global environmental challenges. The Montreal Protocol on Substances that Deplete the Ozone Layer requires that its parties reduce the consumption and production of ozone depleting substances, such as chlorofluorocarbons. The Convention on International Trade in Endangered Species of Wild Fauna and Flora regulates trade in species of conservation concern to prevent overexploitation. Several MEAs control trade in hazardous waste or chemicals that pose risks to human health and the environment. About 30 MEAs use trade measures to achieve their objectives. The relationship between the trade measures of MEAs and the trade disciplines of WTO agreements is explored in Chapter 9.

A number of principles also guide international environmental law and policy, some of which support trade principles. For example, an underlying principle of international environmental law is that countries have "the sovereign right to exploit their own resources pursuant to their own environmental and developmental policies." *See, e.g.,* Rio Declaration, Principle 2. This right dovetails easily with multilateral trade's principle of comparative advantage and with the broad notion that trade measures of importing countries should not pressure an exporting country to change its laws and policies. However, the right of a country to pursue its own regulatory policies comes encumbered with "the responsibility to ensure that activities within their jurisdiction or control do not cause damage to the environment of other States or of areas beyond the limits of national jurisdiction." *Id.* Thus, many trade proponents acknowledge that transboundary pollution may be a legitimate basis for the affected party to impose unilateral trade measures to prevent further environmental harm.

Some other principles of international environmental law designed to promote sustainability pose more serious challenges for trade law. For example, countries have a general duty to prevent or minimize environmental harm in accordance with the principle of pollution prevention. They are also called upon to assess the transboundary environmental impact of activities under their jurisdiction. These principles reflect general international law principles of consultation with other governments and the avoidance of harm. They also reflect the environmental adage that an ounce of prevention is worth a pound of cure; pollution prevention is almost always less expensive than remediating environmental harm. If a government fails to implement these responsibilities, though, does another country have the right to "enforce" these duties through trade sanctions?

Perhaps most critical to the trade and environment debate is the precautionary principle, which provides, in its most common formulation, that "[w]here there are threats of serious or irreversible damage, lack of full scientific certainty shall not be used as a reason for postponing cost-effective measures to prevent environmental degradation." Rio Declaration, Principle 15. The precautionary principle provides policymakers with a framework to anticipate and prevent the potential harmful effects of products and activities when scientific evidence cannot adequately describe those effects. The precautionary principle is among the most controversial of international environmental principles, however. Most international texts, including the Rio Declaration, call it an "approach," not a principle. *See also, e.g.,* The Stockholm Convention on Persistent Organic Pollutants, art. 1, May 22, 2001, 40 I.L.M. 532 (2001). If a WTO member believes that trade in certain products, such as pesticides, genetically modified organisms, or beef treated with growth hormones, may pose a threat to human health or the environment, may it ban trade in those products on the grounds of "precaution"? This issue is discussed throughout the book. For more complete discussion of the principles of international environmental law, *see* HUNTER, SALZMAN, & ZAELKE, INTERNATIONAL ENVIRONMENTAL LAW AND POLICY, at 463–537; PATRICIA BIRNIE, ALAN BOYLE, & CATHERINE REDGWELL, INTERNATIONAL LAW AND THE ENVIRONMENT (3d ed. 2009); PHILIPPE SANDS, PRINCIPLES OF INTERNATIONAL ENVIRONMENTAL LAW (2d ed. 2003).

At the domestic level, countries implement a variety of environmental policies. For example, command-and-control regulations aim at limiting pollution through emission or process standards. Countries also use tradable permits, subsidies, taxes, and liability schemes, among other strategies, to encourage environmental protection. *See* HUNTER, SALZMAN, & ZAELKE, INTERNATIONAL ENVIRONMENTAL LAW AND POLICY, at 131–41.

Different regulatory approaches may have different effects on the competitive circumstances of individual firms. Some regulatory approaches—subsidies are the prime example—are disfavored by trade policy. Thus, the regulatory and competitiveness effects of international trade exert an influence on domestic environmental policy.

IV. A "Debate" on Two Key Issues: Scale and Competitiveness

In the preceding sections, we have introduced some of the key concepts, intellectual history, and modes of discourse that underpin trade policy on the one side and the enterprise of environmental protection and sustainable development on the other. With that background, and to prompt you to engage actively with the issues that run throughout this textbook, we present here a stylized debate on trade and the environment. In trade and environment policy disputes, the environmental point of view is commonly presented by environmental lawyers and scientists and liberalized international trade is most often defended by economists. The two protagonists in our "debate," however, are both economists. Herman Daly is a proponent, indeed a founder, of the steady-state or ecological economics school presented earlier in section III.B.2. of this chapter. Professor Jagdish Bhagwati is perhaps the best-known publicist among traditional economists who have devoted their careers to the study of international trade. In reading the excerpts below, consider not only the substantive merits of their arguments, but also their style of discourse and the evidence or logic that each advances in support of his point of view.

A. General Premises

Herman E. Daly, *Problems with Free Trade: Neoclassical and Steady-State Perspectives*

Trade and the Environment 147, 151–52
(Durwood Zaelke et al., eds.)

No policy prescription commands greater consensus among economists than that of "free trade based on international specialization according to comparative advantage." Free trade has long been the "default position," presumed good unless proved otherwise in specific cases. This presumption should be reversed. The default position should favor domestic production for domestic markets, with balanced (not deregulated) international trade, as a fall back alternative when domestic production is too inconvenient. * * *

The correct name for "free trade" (who can oppose freedom?) is "deregulated international commerce," which should serve to remind us that deregulation is not always good policy.... [T]he point is not to deny that there are gains from international trade. Rather it is to agree with Keynes that there are gains from national self-sufficiency accompanied by balanced trade in items that are inconvenient to produce nationally:

> I sympathize, therefore, with those who would minimize, rather than those who would maximize, economic entanglement between nations.... [L]et goods be homespun whenever it is reasonably and conveniently possible and, above all, let finance be primarily national.[1]

Jagdish Bhagwati, *The Case for Free Trade*

269 Scientific American 42, 42–43 (Nov. 1993)

Economists are reconciled to the conflict of absolutes: that is why they invented the concept of tradeoffs. It should not surprise them, therefore, that the objective of environmental protection should at times run afoul of the goal of seeking maximum gains from trade. In fact, economists would be suspicious of any

---

1. J.M. Keynes, "National Self-Sufficiency," *The Collected Writings of John Maynard Keynes*, vol. 21, ed. Donald Moggeridge (London, 1933).

claims, such as those made by soothsaying politicians, that both causes would be only mutually beneficial. They are rightly disconcerted, however, by the passion and the ferocity, and hence often the lack of logic or facts, with which environmental groups have recently assailed both free trade and the [WTO], the institution that oversees the world trading system.

The environmentalists' antipathy to trade is perhaps inevitable. Trade has been central to economic thinking since Adam Smith discovered the virtues of specialization and of the markets that naturally sustain it. Because markets do not normally exist for the pursuit of environmental protection, they must be specially created. Trade therefore suggests abstention from governmental intervention, whereas environmentalism suggests its necessity. Then again, trade is exploited and its virtues extolled by corporate and multinational interests, whereas environmental objectives are embraced typically by nonprofit organizations, which are generally wary of these interests. Trade is an ancient occupation, and its nurture is the objective of institutions crafted over many years of experience and reflection. Protection of the environment, on the other hand, is a recent preoccupation of national and international institutions that are nascent and still evolving. * * *

It is surely tragic that the proponents of two of the great causes of the 1990s, trade and the environment, should be locked in combat. The conflict is largely gratuitous. There are at times philosophical differences between the two that cannot be reconciled, as when some environmentalists assert nature's autonomy, whereas most economists see nature as a handmaiden to humankind. For the most part, however, the differences derive from misconceptions. It is necessary to dissect and dismiss the more egregious of these fallacies before addressing the genuine problems.

Questions and Discussion

1. What are the virtues of domestic production for domestic markets, as advocated by Daly? Is there an economic argument for self-sufficiency? What does Daly mean when he says that trade can be useful when domestic production is "too inconvenient"? Is higher cost of production a measure of "inconvenience"?

2. Bhagwati identifies several differences between economists' and environmentalists' ways of thinking. In much the same vein, Professor Daniel Esty attributes some of the hostility between "environmentalists" and "free traders" to three clashes—a clash of cultures, a clash of paradigms, and a clash of judgments. DANIEL C. ESTY, GREENING THE GATT, at 36–41. Do you think policymakers can, or should at least try, to overcome these clashes? Or do they represent irreconcilable differences in values and objectives?

B. Economic Growth and the Problem of Scale

Jagdish Bhagwati, *The Case for Free Trade*

269 SCIENTIFIC AMERICAN, at 43

The fear is widespread among environmentalists that free trade increases economic growth and that growth harms the environment. That fear is misplaced.

Growth enables governments to tax and to raise resources for a variety of objectives, including the abatement of pollution and the general protection of the environment. Without such revenues, little can be achieved, no matter how pure one's motives may be.

How do societies actually spend these additional revenues? It depends on how getting rich affects the desire for a better environment. Rich countries today have more groups worrying about environmental causes than do poor countries. Efficient policies, such as freer trade, should generally help environmentalism, not harm it.

If one wants to predict what growth will do to the environment, however, one must also consider how it will affect the production of pollution. Growth affects not only the demand for a good environment but also the supply of pollution associated with growth. The net effect on the environment will therefore depend on the kind of economic growth. Gene M. Grossman and Alan Krueger of Princeton University found that in cities around the world sulfur dioxide pollution fell as per capita income rose. The only exception was in countries whose per capita incomes fell below $5,000. In short, environmentalists are in error when they fear that trade, through growth, will necessarily increase pollution.

Economic effects besides those attributable to rising incomes also help to protect the environment. For example, freer trade enables pollution-fighting technologies available elsewhere to be imported. Thus, trade in low-sulfur-content coal will enable the users of ... high-sulfur-content coal to shift from the latter to the former.

Herman E. Daly, *Problems with Free Trade*
TRADE AND THE ENVIRONMENT, at 147, 150–51, 155–56

Sustainable scale means that the scale (population times resource use per capita, or total resource throughput) of the economy relative to the containing ecosystem must be biophysically sustainable. In other words, the input of raw materials and energy must be within the regenerative capacity, and the output of waste materials must be within the absorptive capacity, of the ecosystem. * * *

[S]ustainable scale of total resource use, forces us to ask what will happen if the entire population of the earth consumes resources at the rate associated with current real wages in high-wage countries. This question is central to the steady-state paradigm, but remains unasked in the neoclassical view, or is given the facile response that there are no environmental limits.

Steady-state economics suggests the following answer: the regenerative and assimilative capacities of the biosphere cannot sustainably support even the current levels of resource consumption, much less the many-fold increase required by "upward harmonization" of consumption standards worldwide. Still less can the ecosystem afford the upward harmonization of standards for an ever-growing population striving to consume ever more per capita. This heretofore unrecognized limit to development puts a brake on the ability of growth to wash away the problems of allocation and distribution raised by free trade with free capital mobility. In fact, free trade becomes a recipe for standards-lowering competition leading to the downward harmonization of efficient allocation, equal distribution, and ecological sustainability. * * *

The usual pre-analytic vision, the one that supports most neoclassical economic analysis today, is that the economy is the total system and nature is the subsystem. The economy's growth is unconstrained by any enveloping natural system. Nature may be finite, but it is just a sector — the extractive sector — of the economy, for which other sectors can substitute, without limiting growth in any important way. If the economy is seen as an isolated system, then there is no environment to constrain its continual growth.... Sustainable development is development without growth, in other words, a physically steady-state economy that may continue to develop greater capacity to satisfy human wants by increasing the efficiency of resource use, by improving social institutions, by clarifying ethical priorities, but not by increasing the resource throughput.

In the light of the growth versus development distinction, let us return to the issue of trade and consider two questions: What is the likely effect of free trade on growth? What is the likely effect of free trade on development?

Free trade is likely to stimulate throughput growth. Trade offers the possibility of importing environmental carrying capacity in the form of raw materials and waste absorption capacities in exchange for production. It allows a country to exceed its domestic regenerative and absorptive limits by importing these functions from other countries. That tends to increase throughput, other things being equal. But it could be argued that the country exporting carrying capacity might have had to increase throughput even more had it produced those products domestically rather than importing them. Nevertheless, trade does postpone the day when countries must face up to the discipline of living within natural regenerative and absorptive capacities.

Questions and Discussion

1. Does Bhagwati's optimism about growth miss Daly's main point? Are Daly and Bhagwati using "growth" in the same way?

2. A note on environmental Kuznets curves. Bhagwati cites a famous study showing that sulfur dioxide emissions decline as income increases above US$5,000 per year per capita GDP. Gene Grossman and Alan Krueger, Environmental Impacts of a North American Free Trade Agreement (1991). The curve showing the income effect on pollution control is known as the "environmental Kuznets curve." But Kuznets curves do not hold true for all pollutants. For example, carbon dioxide emissions and urban wastes continue to increase with wealth. In *World Resources 1996–97: A Guide to the Global Environment*, The World Resources Institute reviewed the literature with respect to Kuznets curves and drew the following conclusions:

Most environmental conditions that do improve with economic growth are those that have local impact and abatement costs that are relatively inexpensive in terms of money and changes in lifestyle. Environmental problems that improve only at higher income levels (or that continue to worsen as incomes rise) generally create impacts that affect only a few people (e.g., solid waste) or that occur either outside the local area or in the future (e.g., the contributions of carbon dioxide emissions to climate change). * * *

Some studies have also focused primarily on pollution problems and say little about the degradation or depletion of the natural resources on which many of the poorest segments of populations in developing countries depend in a direct way for their livelihood and day-to-day sustenance. Thus, correlations between economic growth and environmental improvement or degradation must be used cautiously; any general claim that economic growth leads to environmental improvement must be heavily qualified.

A number of these studies note that turning points in the relationship between economic growth and environmental quality do not just happen, but result largely from explicit policy actions. They do not imply that societies can automatically grow their way out of environmental problems nor that economic liberalization and other policies that promote economic growth can substitute for environmental policies. * * *

A more recent survey of the literature finds that "there is now a great deal of evidence supporting the view that rising incomes affect the environment in a positive way.... [W]e cannot simply associate increased economic activity with increased environmental damage." Copeland & Taylor, *Trade, Growth, and the Environment*, at 66. Even so, the authors call for further studies "giving a larger role to natural resources, capital abundance and other more conventional factors" besides income. *Id.*

In a similar vein, another analysis finds that any relationship between income and pollution is pollutant specific and that "economic growth by itself may be insufficient to generate a downturn in the pollution-income trajectory, especially for pollutants with a high private abatement cost." Florenz Plassmann & Neha Khanna, *Household Income and Pollution: Implications for the Debate about the Environmental Kuznets Curve Hypothesis*, 15 J. ENVT. & DEV'T 3, 38 (2006). The authors conclude that other factors, such as population density, percentage of registered voters, costs of private abatement, and consumer preferences at the local level, may play significant roles in determining whether pollution levels decline over time. The authors found an income-only relationship with coarse particulate matter (PM10), but that pollution levels peaked at about US$20,000.

C. Competitive Advantage and Downward Pressure on Domestic Regulations

Herman E. Daly, *Problems with Free Trade*
TRADE AND THE ENVIRONMENT, at 148–49, 156

A clear conflict exists if a nation follows a domestic policy of internalization of external costs into prices, and, simultaneously, an international policy of free trade with countries that do not internalize their external costs in their prices. The cost-internalizing country should be allowed to employ a tariff to compensate for the higher cost—not to protect inefficient industry, but to protect an efficient national policy against standards-lowering competition. This does not imply the imposition of one country's environmental preferences or moral judgments on another country. Each country sets the rules of cost internalization in its own market. Whoever sells in another nation's market must play by that nation's rules of cost internalization, or pay a tariff sufficient to remove the competitive advantage of lower standards as a price of admission to that market. * * *

Competition can reduce prices in two ways: by increasing efficiency, or by lowering standards. The lower standards refer to the failure to internalize social and environmental costs. Costs to the firm are reduced by low pollution control standards.... Attaining cheapness by ignoring or externalizing real costs is a sin against efficiency. * * *

If firms are allowed to produce under the most permissive standards and sell their product without penalty in countries with higher standards, they succeed in externalizing costs and bringing pressure to bear on the high-standards country to lower its standards—in effect "imposing their lower standards." * * *

Cost externalization is socially inefficient. A country trying to internalize external costs cannot accomplish that efficient policy if it enters into free trade with countries that do not internalize their external costs. Reduced efficiency results in a higher throughput for any given level of welfare, other things being equal.

Jagdish Bhagwati, *The Case for Free Trade*
269 SCIENTIFIC AMERICAN, at 44

Why do intrinsically domestic environmental questions create international concern? The main reason is the belief that diversity in environmental standards may affect competitiveness. Businesses and labor unions worry that their rivals in other countries may gain an edge if their governments impose lower standards of environmental protection. They decry such differences as unfair. To level the playing field, these lobbies insist that foreign countries raise their standards up to domestic ones. In turn, environmental groups worry that if such "harmonization up" is not undertaken before freeing trade, pressures from uncompetitive businesses at home will force down domestic standards, reversing their hard-won victories. Finally, there is the fear, dramatized by H. Ross Perot in his criticisms of NAFTA, that factories will relocate to the countries whose environmental standards are lowest. * * *

Worry over competitiveness has ... led to the illegitimate demand that environmental standards abroad be treated as "social dumping." Offending countries are regarded as unfairly subsidizing their exporters through lax environmental requirements. Such implicit subsidies, the reasoning continues, ought to be offset by import duties.

Yet international differences in environmental standards are perfectly natural. Even if two countries share the same environmental objectives, the specific pollutions they would attack, and hence the industries they would hinder, will generally not be identical. Mexico has a greater social incentive than does the United States to spend an extra dollar preventing dysentery rather than reducing lead in gasoline.

Equally, a certain environmental good might be valued more highly by a poor country than by a rich one. Contrast, for instance, the value assigned to a lake with the cost of cleaning up effluents discharged into it by a pharmaceutical company. In India such a lake's water might be drunk by a malnourished population whose mortality would increase sharply with the rise in pollution. In the United States the water might be consumed by few people, all of whom have the means to protect themselves with privately purchased water filters. In this example, India would be the more likely to prefer clean water to the pharmaceutical company's profits.

The consequences of differing standards are clear: each country will have less of the industry whose pollution it fears relatively more than other countries do. Indeed, even if there were no international trade, we would be shrinking industries whose pollution we deter. This result follows from the policy of forcing polluters of all stripes to pay for the harm they cause. To object, then, to the effects our negative valuation of pollution have on a given industry is to be in contradiction: we would be refusing to face the consequences of our environmental preferences.

* * *

Jagdish Bhagwati, *Trade Liberalisation and "Fair Trade" Demands: Addressing the Environmental and Labour Standards Issues*

18 THE WORLD ECONOMY 745, 748–49 (Nov. 1995)
Reprinted with permission of the original publishers: Blackwell Publishing Ltd.

But one more worry needs to be laid at rest if the demands for upward harmonisation of standards or ecodumping duties in lieu thereof are to be effectively dismissed. This is the worry that I noted at the outset: that free trade with countries with lower standards will force down one's higher standards. The most potent of these worries arises from the fear that "capital and jobs" will move to countries with lower standards, triggering a race to the bottom (or more accurately a race towards the bottom), where countries lower their standards in an interjurisdictional contest, below what some or all would like, to attract capital and jobs. So, the solution would lie then in coordinating the standards-setting among the nations engaged in freer trade and investment. In turn, this may (but is most unlikely to) require harmonisation among countries to the higher standards (though, even then, not necessarily at those in place) or perhaps there might be improvement in welfare from simply setting minimum floors to the standards.

This is undoubtedly a theoretically valid argument. The key question for policy, however, is whether the empirical evidence shows, as required by the argument, that: (1) capital is in fact responsive to the differences in environmental standards and (2) different countries/jurisdictions actually play the game then of competitively lowering standards to attract capital. Without both these phenomena holding in a significant fashion in reality, the "race to the bottom" would be a theoretical curiosity.

As it happens, systematic evidence is available for the former proposition alone, but the finding is that the proposition is not supported by the studies to date: there is very weak evidence, at best, in favour of interjurisdictional mobility in response to … differences in environmental standards. There are in fact many ways to explain this lack of responsiveness: (1) the differences in standards may not be significant and are outweighed by other factors that affect locational decisions; (2) exploiting differences in standards may not be a good strategy relative to not exploiting them; and (3) lower standards may paradoxically even repel, instead of attracting, direct foreign investment.

As it happens, countries, and even state governments in federal countries (for example, President Bill Clinton, when governor of Arkansas), typically play the game of attracting capital to their jurisdictions: but this game is almost universally played, not by inviting firms to pollute freely but instead through tax breaks and holidays, land grants at throwaway prices, and so forth, resulting most likely in a "race to the bottom" on business tax rates which wind up below their optimal levels! It is therefore not surprising that there is little systematic evidence of governments' lowering environmental standards to attract scarce capital. Contrary to the fears of the environmental groups, the race to the bottom on environmental standards therefore seems to be an unlikely phenomenon in the real world.

I would conclude that both the "unfair trade" and the "race to the bottom" arguments for harmonising ... standards or else legalising ecodumping duties at the WTO are therefore lacking in rationale: the former is theoretically illogical, and the latter is empirically unsupported.

Questions and Discussion

1. The competitiveness argument covers several specific arguments with colorful names — the "pollution haven" hypothesis; the "race to the bottom"; and H. Ross Perot's famous "giant sucking sound," his prediction that the lower environmental (and labor) standards in Mexico would allow Mexico to drain jobs from the United States under the North American Free Trade Agreement. The competitiveness argument also connects to the regulatory effects concern based on the supposition that competitiveness concerns have a "chilling effect" on domestic environmental regulations.

2. How does one determine whether a particular (low) standard is allowing a firm to externalize a cost to society that rightfully should be borne by the firm itself? To the extent that most environmental standards allow some pollution to occur (and thus do not perfectly "internalize" all environmental costs), what is a reasonable approach for trade between two countries with different degrees of cost internalization? Recall the discussion of the Polluter Pays Principle in Section III.A.2. of this chapter.

3. What other factors besides differences in environmental standards are likely to affect price competition between firms in two different countries? One substantial factor, often overlooked, is the exchange rate between the currencies of the two countries. A "weak" currency favors exporters because it makes their goods relatively cheaper in terms of the importer's currency; conversely, a "strong" currency favors manufacturers who rely on imported parts and materials by lowering their costs in terms of their own currency for goods bought abroad. Exchange rate shifts can be dramatic; the value of the U.S. dollar relative to the European Euro has declined by some 40 percent between 2002 and 2009.

4. As some have commented, if competitiveness in international trade had to do only with direct costs to producers, Bangladesh would be an economic powerhouse. Yet, as the U.N. Development Program (UNDP) points out, "While globalization has created unprecedented opportunities for some, others have been left behind. In some countries — India is an example — rapid economic growth has produced modest progress in poverty reduction and in nutrition. In others — including most of sub-Saharan Africa — economic growth is too slow and uneven to sustain rapid progress in poverty reduction. Despite high growth across much of Asia, on current trends most countries are off track for

achieving ... targets for reducing extreme poverty and deprivation in other areas by 2015." HUMAN DEVELOPMENT REPORT 2007/2008, at 25. The UNDP identifies weaknesses in governance, structural problems (such as the geographic isolation of the countries of the Sahel), population growth, the burden of diseases, climate change, and other environmental conditions as factors contributing to the extreme and enduring poverty of the least developed countries.

D. Afterword on the "Debate"

The debate above took shape in the early 1990s. Although there have been many legal and policy developments since then, little has changed at the poles of the debate in either tone or major themes. What has changed is the landscape of the middle ground. More than two decades into the debate, there are many more empirical studies and theoretical analyses in the literature. From this richer context of understanding and with a better appreciation of the complexities of the issues, governments, private interests, and NGOs have less support for some of their initial fears and a stronger evidentiary basis for constructive dialogue in quest of workable solutions.

It is important to be clear that the "debate" presented above, which pits "environmentalists" against "free traders" without any common ground, is oversimplified even for the 1990s. We present it to help encapsulate and dramatize the trade and environment debate. But we emphasize that it does not reflect the many nuances of the relationship between trade and the environment. The mission of this textbook is to uncover and examine many of those nuances. We conclude this introductory chapter with some ideas about the ingredients of a "congruent" approach to trade and environment.

V. Trade and Sustainable Development: A Path to Congruence of Trade and Environment?

The WTO officially espouses the view that trade liberalization "can and must be mutually supportive" of environmental protection and the promotion of sustainable development. Preamble to the Doha Ministerial Declaration, 14 November 2001, WT/MIN(01)/DEC/1, at para. 6. Working with some of the central themes of the conflict-oriented "debate" between trade and environmental advocates, let's explore whether there are ways to reach the more affirmative congruence that the WTO envisions.

A. Trade's Benefits for Sustainable Development *Redux*

To begin with, we have seen that economists and other trade proponents claim that greater market access and world trade rules that prohibit economic discrimination will bring economic benefits that help achieve sustainable development. Here is a simple example. The United States, accepting claims that Argentine farmers were selling the honey they produced at less than its fair value, imposed tariffs on Argentine honey of 66 percent (based on the value of the honey). 66 Fed. Reg. 63672 (Dec. 10, 2001); Larry Rohter, *U.S. and Argentina Fight over Honey*, N.Y. Times, Mar. 5, 2002, at W1, col. 2. With access to the U.S. market thus restricted, the price of Argentine honey dropped from US$1,150 a ton to US$950 a ton, which lowered the incomes of Argentine farmers. In the meantime, prices for honey in the United States increased because honey users were unable to find substitutes for Argentine supplies. While U.S. honey producers gained, Argentine producers and U.S. consumers lost, arguably a poor equation for sustainable development. Stricter adherence to liberalized trade would have allowed Argentine farmers to reap the benefits of international trade and U.S. consumers to purchase higher quality honey at prices lower than domestically produced honey.

A liberal trade regime also contributes to global sustainable development through technology diffusion. The OECD believes that the elimination of import and export controls and improved intellectual property rights regimes should help provide indirect environmental benefits by distributing environmentally sound products and production processes globally. Moreover, "trade-related growth can provide the resources to companies to invest in cleaner technologies and government revenues for financing environmental infrastructure, such as sewage treatment and water supply." Organization for Economic Cooperation and Development, The Environmental Effects of Trade 15 (1994).

The OECD report also takes the view that open trade will have salutary effects on national environmental policies. It should raise overall levels of environmental protection "as more attention and resources are devoted to strengthening environmental laws and enforcement." *Id.* at 17. The OECD maintains, however, that the main environmental benefits will be achieved at the structural level by removing trade-distorting policies:

> Trade liberalisation should reduce or eliminate many policy interventions which now exacerbate environmental problems through their distortive effects on the location and intensity of production and consumption. Freer trade through the removal of subsidies and tariff and non-tariff barriers should likely redistribute world production with some countries increasing output and others reducing output of different goods. It should allow countries to specialise to a greater extent in sectors in which they enjoy competitive advantage, including advantages based on environmental endowments.
>
> For example, trade liberalisation in the agricultural sector should benefit the environment to the extent that distortive policy interventions—such as production supports, export subsidies and quantitative restrictions—have resulted in over-specialisation, intensive farming operations and poor land use patterns. In the forestry and fisheries sectors, reform of trade-related measures which may have contributed to deforestation or overfishing, such as subsidies or tariff differentials on processed and unprocessed products, should prove positive for the environment.
>
> The possibility of negative structural effects from trade liberalisation stems from the expansion of trade in the presence of market and intervention failures which may, in some cases, worsen the distribution and intensity of economic activities from the environmental standpoint. Increased output of particular goods and services following trade liberalisation could, in the absence of environmental policy interventions or in the presence of market externalities, lead to greater environmental degradation. It is the continuing existence of market and inter-

vention failures, and the difficulties in rectifying these failures, that may precipitate the negative structural effects of trade liberalisation.

Id. at 16.

On the social side of sustainable development, trade liberalization has been urged as a way to promote freedom and democracy. Former U.S. President Clinton, for example, supported the WTO membership of the People's Republic of China on the belief that the Chinese government would not be able to contain the free flow of ideas, including democracy, once markets opened to imported goods and foreign investments.

Questions and Discussion

1. Does the preamble to the WTO Agreement, quoted on page 41, commit the WTO to the kind of policy integration envisioned in the Brundtland Commission report? What would an ecological economist say about the WTO's goals of "steadily growing ... effective demand" and "expanding the production of ... goods"? What about the way the WTO seems to link sustainable development with "optimal use of the world's resources"? If you are a government official of a developing country, how would you seek to construe that linkage?

2. Do you agree that democracy and freedom follow freer trade and open markets, as President Clinton hoped? Singapore, with strict controls on personal liberty, has one of the highest standards of living in the world. The Philippines, whose government has been democratically elected since 1986, continues to struggle economically. In 2007, Brazil, with its vibrant democracy, saw its gross domestic product (GDP) grow by 6 percent while China, with its highly authoritarian regime, saw its GDP grow by 13 percent. What other factors may account for the political and economic conditions in these countries? WORLD BANK, KEY DEVELOPMENT DATA & STATISTICS (2009).

B. The Environmental Critique of Trade *Redux*

Principle 8 of the Rio Declaration calls for reducing or eliminating "unsustainable patterns of production and consumption." The promotion of socially established preferences, such as environmental value preferences, is thus a key to the promotion of sustainable development. Many economists call such preferences "uneconomic"; promoters of sustainable development would call them reasonable social and environmental preferences to allocate resources appropriately. Regardless of how they are viewed, no one questions each nation's right to express those preferences in its national law. The harder trade-environment question is whether that expression of national values can also take the form of explicit or implicit restrictions or burdens on trade in goods that do not conform to national preferences.

Many trade proponents see virtually all environmentally-based trade restrictions as subterfuges for economic protectionism. This is an argument both difficult to refute and difficult to prove. Most environmental laws seek in good faith to address serious environmental issues, but they also have significant economic consequences and affect different businesses differently. For example, the United States imposed a tax on those automobile manufacturers that failed to meet prescribed fuel efficiency standards for the cars they produced, including importers of foreign-produced autos. Congress adopted that approach rather than gasoline taxes (which economists would prefer) because gasoline taxes are politically unpopular and because Congress worried, among other things, about the impact of increased gasoline taxes on the domestic automobile industry. Smart environmental protection or surreptitious economic protectionism?

The excerpt that follows looks at a similar controversy. Concerned about a shortage of landfill space, Germany adopted a national packaging law that makes the suppliers of all packaging in Germany responsible for the reuse or recycling of their packaging waste. Yet, the *Economist* calls the German law to reduce packaging waste and a similar law requiring the recycling of cars "nonsense." How can we determine whether an environmental measure is for protectionist purposes and not for environmental protection? Under what circumstances would a domestic environmental measure be legitimate, even if it discriminates against foreign products or companies?

Free Trade's Green Hurdles

THE ECONOMIST (June 15, 1991)

The packaging industry is irate. EC commissioners are unnerved. Both are alarmed by Germany's new law on packaging which crosses, in industry's eyes, the indistinct line between national environmental protection and protection of a more reprehensible sort. The European Commission's response—a packaging directive of its own[.] * * *

... The commission has been bounced into this nonsense by Germany, which took advantage of a ruling by the European Court in 1988 that Denmark could insist that drinks were sold in refillable bottles. Since then, European countries have been busily drawing up their own rules on recycling and on eco-labeling, while the EC has struggled to resolve the clash between the interests of trade and the environment. * * *

Increasingly, countries specify green characteristics for products: cars must have catalytic converters, say, or a kind of plastic must not be used. As long as such standards, whether set by law or by eco-labeling, apply to all producers equally, they do not infringe GATT rules. * * *

Arguably, environmental product standards are no different from others designed to codify local-market requirements. But sometimes their effect is discriminatory.... With Germany's packaging law, importers complain to the EC that it includes a provision, inserted at the last minute, to insist that only 28% of all beer and soft-drinks containers can be "one-trip" (i.e., disposable). Packagers suspect that this clause was inserted for the benefit of small brewers in politically sensitive Bavaria, who will find it easier to collect and refill the empties. Packagers also dislike the new law's insistence that companies collect their used packaging for recycling. The fact that this will be easier for local manufacturers may prejudice retailers in favor of domestically produced goods.

––––––––––

While *The Economist* railed against Germany's packaging law as protecting or providing advantages to German companies, environmentalists cheered the law for being a huge success, because the law has helped reduced waste and create an entirely new business sector in packaging recovery and recycling. According to the German government, used packaging levels dropped 1.4 million metric tons annually between 1991 and 1996. Industry collected and recycled more than 20 million tons of used packaging between 1993 and 1996. Germany reuses 52 percent of its waste packaging and the paper industry has boosted its recycled paper content in its paper production to 60 percent by 1996, four years ahead of its voluntary commitment. Moreover, Germany has 180 certified waste management companies, employing more than 240,000 people with annual revenues of about US$45 billion. All this success has not come without a price, however: owners of incineration and public dump facilities have complained that falling waste levels have meant that numerous waste landfills and incinerators are operating under capacity. *Federal, State Environment Officials Discussing Ways to Amend Packaging Law*, 20 INT'L. ENVT. REP. 1009 (Oct. 29, 1997); Bogdan Turek, *Preparation of Packaging Recycling Law under Way to Meet EU Norms, Official Says*, 22 INT'L. ENVT. REP. 721 (Sept. 1, 1999).

Moreover, while *The Economist* sees the European Union's directive on packaging waste as coerced by Germany's unilateral action, environmentalists see it as a way to apply the successes of Germany's positive waste reduction program throughout the European Union. Similarly, the United States, Japan, and the European Union banned the sale of ivory before the international community did through the Convention on International Trade in Endangered Species of Wild Fauna and Flora. The unilateral action was thought necessary to spur the international community into action. When should countries be permitted to impose trade measures for environmental purposes unilaterally? That question is answered, to some extent, by distinguishing domestic from international problems.

The Economist, like Professor Bhagwati, also viewed efforts to require trading partners to meet an importing country's environmental standards as a "blatant" trade problem, because such efforts force foreign manufacturers to adopt the importing country's ethical preferences. Environmentalists, on the other hand, see such measures as a shield against practices the importing country does not support.

Another criticism of trade from the environmental perspective draws into question trade's preoccupation with efficiency and productivity. Comparative advantage is built on notions of increasing welfare by capturing the economic efficiency gains of increased specialization of production. Herman Daly argues for a broader conception of welfare and espouses the virtues of diversity in production. He agrees that economic diversity "entails some loss of efficiency, but it is necessary for community and nationhood." Robert Costanza et al. make a similar argument in their discussion of distribution and scale, on page 37 above, where they assert that "reduc[ing] everything to a question of individual willingness-to-pay is a distortion of our concrete experience as persons in community."

Questions and Discussion

1. If one takes the communitarian environmentalist perspective seriously, the determinative question may be just how we define the "community" to which we belong. In other words, which of our social relationships is critical when dealing with public goods such as environmental quality and international sustainable development? At its narrowest, our community of concern is our family, our near neighbors and others with whom we have almost daily interaction, our local community. More broadly, for purposes of public policy many people identify themselves as citizens of a particular country. If the country is the relevant community, then its laws and regulations should vindicate the important values collectively shared by the country's citizens. The next step beyond the nation as "community" is a broader regional identity. In some parts of the world, no-

tably Europe, social and political leaders of nations have made concerted efforts to replace national identity, seen as too narrow and often founded on prejudice, with a broader sense of identification as "Europeans," citizens of a regional community that now embraces 27 separate nation-States. Most broadly of all, some people think of themselves simply as world citizens, encompassing within their "community" of concern people of all nations in their varied circumstances. Both the concept of sustainable development and the maintenance of the multilateral trading system through the WTO partake, in significant part, of this last and broadest notion of community. But such a global perspective goes too far for many individuals and engenders deep skepticism about the political legitimacy of such supranational entities.

2. Metaphorically, the Kentucky poet, author, and farmer Wendell Berry writes of the Great Economy, which is filled with mystery and "cannot be fully comprehended." For him, the Great Economy is limited by scale and ecological limits. He asserts that attention to these limits can bring economic benefits:

> Harry Besuden, the great farmer and shepherd of Clark County, Kentucky, compares the small sheep flock to the two spoons of sugar that can be added to a brimful cup of coffee, which then becomes "more palatable [but] doesn't run over. You can stock your farm to the limit with other livestock and still add a small flock of sheep." He says this, characteristically, after rejecting efforts of sheep specialists to get beyond "the natural limits of the ewe" by breeding out of season in order to get three lamb crops in two years or by striving for "litters" of lambs rather than nature's optimum of twins. Rather than chafe at "natural physical limits," he would turn to nature's elegant way of enriching herself *within* her physical limits by diversification, by complication of pattern. Rather than strain the productive capacity of the ewe, he would, without strain, enlarge the productive capacity of the farm — a healthier, safer, and cheaper procedure. Like many of the better traditional farmers, Henry Besuden is suspicious of "the measure of land in length and width," for he would be mindful as well of "the depth and quality."

> A small flock of ewes, fitted properly into a farm's pattern, virtually disappears into the farm and does it good, just as it virtually disappears into the time and energy economy of a farm family and does it good. And, properly fitted into a farm's pattern, the small flock virtually disappears from the debit side of the farm's accounts but shows up plainly on the credit side. This "disappearance" is possible, not to the extent that the farm is a human artifact, a belonging of the human economy, but to the extent it remains, by its obedience to natural principle, a belonging of the Great Economy.

WENDELL BERRY, *Two Economies, in* HOME ECONOMICS 63–64 (1987). Berry probably would not use a phrase like sustainable development, but rather "stewardship." Is stewardship a better way to describe the appropriate scale? Do you think it is more politically acceptable than sustainable development and the four policy guidelines espoused by ecological economists on page 44?

C. Towards Mutually Reinforcing Paradigms

We close this introductory chapter with an excerpt written more than 15 years ago by Stewart Hudson, then with the National Wildlife Federation. Hudson uses sustainable development as his environmental paradigm to try to resolve the trade-environment tension. Consider whether Hudson's effort to find a middle ground has a sound theoretical or experiential basis, or whether he was just being politically pragmatic—looking for alliances. Have changes in the world in recent years made Hudson's view more realistic or less?

Stewart Hudson, *Trade, Environment and the Pursuit of Sustainable Development*

INTERNATIONAL TRADE AND THE ENVIRONMENT
55, 57, 64 (Patrick Low ed., 1992)

If understood in the context of sustainable development, environmental concerns and trade activities are not necessarily at odds, and should be dealt with in an integrated fashion. It is clear that trade policy which does not consider environmental impacts can undermine the natural resource base on which continued, or future, development depends. At the same time, it is obvious that environmental policy, framed without regard to development needs, can be equally shortsighted.

Within the context of sustainable development, trade and environmental policy become means by which to achieve a higher goal. The implications of this approach are captured in an excerpt from the OECD's [Organization for Economic Cooperation and Development] recent Joint Report on Trade and Environment which concludes that:

> It is, therefore, important that trade policies are sensitive to environmental concerns and that environmental policies take account of effects of trade.... Unlike sustainable development, free trade is not an end in itself....

One of the most important keys to understanding the environmental perspective on trade issues is to recognize its basis in the concept of sustainable development. Therefore, it is necessary to correct two misconceptions this perspective seems to have generated. First, the environmental perspective on trade should *not* be construed as antitrade, since trade can be an important instrument by which to achieve development that is economically and environmentally sustainable. Second, this approach is *not* an attempt to extort from trade practices the means to cure all of the world's environmental ills. What is critical is the intersection of trade and environmental concerns.

The dynamic relationship between economic activity and the health of the environment, and the implications of this relationship for sustainable development, are now widely accepted, as is the recognition that change is needed in the patterns of global economic activity in order to better address environmental concerns. * * *

Unfortunately, while free trade agreements can lead to greater economic growth and a greater pool of funds targeted for environmental protection, there is no guarantee that this will *necessarily* occur. Further, while acknowledging that environmental protection *cannot* occur in the absence of some level of economic growth, promoting free trade as a panacea for resolving environmental ills ignores some of the very real costs that it entails. * * *

In the long run, environmental protection will not be successful if it ignores the development needs of the world's population. Conversely, the benefits of a more liberalized trading system cannot be sustained over the long term if environmental and natural resource considerations are not taken into account. To be sure, conflicts between some of the core values of liberalized trade and environmental protection do exist. Nevertheless, an awareness of mutual benefits of an approach to trade and environmental concerns, based on sustainable development, can help overcome the anxiety that this new type of thinking seems to have generated in both the trade and environmental communities.

Hudson advises the trade community to take into account environmental and natural resource considerations, and the environmental community to take into account the benefits of trade, but he does not describe how to bring about this accommodation. The challenge for future trade lawyers and environmental lawyers is to help ensure the goals of sustainability and sustainable development are met through mutually reinforcing policies. The remainder of this book explores the congruence and conflict between trade and environmental objectives and, we hope, provides some ideas about how to resolve conflicts and make trade and environmental objectives mutually reinforcing.

Chapter 2

The World Trade Organization, Dispute Settlement, and the Domestic Legal Effect of Trade Agreements

I. Introduction

The World Trade Organization (WTO) has become the symbolic representation of international trade. That is fitting; as of the beginning of 2010, the WTO has a membership of 153 that account for 90 percent of the world's international trade. More countries, including Iran and Iraq, are actively negotiating toward membership. Among major economies, only the Russian Federation remains, for the time being, outside the WTO.

Many environmental and public interest nongovernmental organizations (NGOs) continue to have a jaundiced view of the WTO. In 1992, advertisements by environmental groups portrayed the WTO's predecessor organization, the GATT, as "GATTzilla." The French version, reproduced on the next page, reads, "Discover the monstrous reality of GATT." Because the WTO has a more coherent structure, broader membership, and presides over a wider array of trade agreements than the old GATT, the WTO is viewed with equal or greater suspicion. One NGO characterizes it as "one of the main mechanisms of corporate globalization." Public Citizen, *Global Trade Watch*, *at* http://www.citizen.org/trade/wto. Another calls it "the most powerful legislative and judicial body in the world" that has "systematically undermined democracy around the world." Global Exchange, *at* http://www.globalexchange.org/campaigns/wto. A third ranks it as "among the most powerful, and one of the most secretive international bodies on earth." International Forum on Globalization, *at* www.ifg.org/wto.html. All of these statements remain unchanged since 2004.

Not surprisingly, the WTO itself offers a more benign view of its role in the world, also unchanged in the last six years. It identifies ten benefits from its work: 1) the system helps promote peace; 2) disputes are handled constructively; 3) rules make life easier for us all; 4) freer trade cuts the cost of living; 5) it provides more choice of products and qualities; 6) trade raises incomes; 7) trade stimulates economic growth; 8) the basic principles make life more efficient; 9) governments are shielded from lobbying; and 10) the system encourages good government. World Trade Organization, *10 Benefits of the WTO Trading System*, *at* http://www.wto.org/english/thewto_e/ whatis_e/10ben_e/10b00_e.htm.

A particular aspect of the WTO that leads to the perception that it holds overbearing power is the binding, enforceable WTO dispute settlement process established by the

"Discover the Monstrous Reality of GATT." GATTzilla: Public Citizen's Global Trade Watch, Washington, D.C., www.tradewatch.org.

WTO's Understanding on Rules and Procedures Governing the Settlement of Disputes, commonly referred to as the Dispute Settlement Understanding (DSU). One environmental text describes it as "one of the most potent dispute settlement systems at the international level." DAVID HUNTER, JAMES SALZMAN, & DURWOOD ZAELKE, INTERNATIONAL ENVIRONMENTAL LAW AND POLICY 1261 (3d ed. 2007). Similarly, a trade text calls it "arguably the most important international tribunal." MITSUO MATSUSHITA, THOMAS J. SCHOENBAUM & PETROS MAVROIDIS, THE WORLD TRADE ORGANIZATION: LAW, PRACTICE, AND POLICY 104 (2d ed. 2006). The WTO has resolved a number of trade disputes relating to environmental regulation. The dispute settlement process is described in detail in Section IV of this chapter.

Although the WTO is the world's only global trade organization, it is important to take note of complementary regional trade arrangements (RTAs) that govern much of international trade. These regional arrangements take two basic forms: free trade agreements and customs unions. In free trade agreements, the participating countries eliminate or significantly reduce tariffs on substantially all trade between them but each country maintains its individual tariff system vis-à-vis the rest of the world. In customs unions, the participating countries eliminate all duties among members and adopt a common external tariff that they all apply to goods from countries outside the union. For the United States, the most important and well-known regional agreement is the North American Free Trade Agreement (NAFTA) covering trade among Mexico, the United States, and Canada. The 27 countries of the European Union (EU) constitute the world's largest customs union[1] with free movement of goods and people within the EU and a single set of tariffs and other trade policies with respect to the rest of the world.

In recent years, RTAs have proliferated. As of early 2010, in addition to NAFTA the United States has free trade agreements in force with 15 other countries, from Australia and Bahrain to Peru and Singapore, including the countries of Central America and the Dominican Republic in an agreement known as DR-CAFTA. Other countries have also paired up to create dozens of bilateral free trade agreements, such as the Canada-Chile Free Trade Agreement and the Mexico-Japan Free Trade Agreement. On a broader scale, nine African countries joined together in 2000 to form the Common Market for Eastern and Southern Africa (COMESA). Various African nations have negotiated eight other major free trade agreements and customs unions. Four countries in South America (Argentina, Brazil, Paraguay, and Uruguay) established their own common market, Mercosur (or Mercosul in Portuguese), and Venezuela was approved to join early in 2010. Chile, Bolivia, Peru, Ecuador, and Colombia are associate members with reciprocal trade benefits. *See* Rafael A. Porrata-Doria, Jr., *Mercosur: The Common Market of the Twenty-First Century?*, 32 GA. J. INT'L & COMP. L. 1 (2004). In 2009, the ten countries in the Association of Southeast Asian Nations (ASEAN) implemented the ASEAN Free Trade Area. The pace of negotiations for such regional preferential trading arrangements shows no sign of slowing. In late 2009, the U.S. Trade Representative notified Congress that it was opening free trade negotiations with the Trans-Pacific Partnership, a trade agreement among

---

1. Until Europe's Lisbon Treaty came into effect on December 1, 2009, the legal representative of the European Union (EU) in the WTO was the "European Communities." Many WTO documents, including dispute settlement report titles, reflect that nomenclature. Note also that each of the EU member states is, in its own right, a WTO member. As a matter of European constitutional law, however, the Commission of the EU is the exclusive representative of the 27 members on most matters under WTO jurisdiction. See Section V.B. of this chapter for further explanation of the European approach to the WTO.

several countries in the greater Pacific region. The handling of environmental issues in RTAs is covered in Chapter 11. For further reading and references on RTAs, see the symposium in volume 28 of the *St. Louis Univ. Public Law Review* (2008).

In spite of the many regional agreements, this book emphasizes the multilateral trading system presided over by the WTO. Whatever opinions are expressed about the virtues or vices of the WTO, it is unquestionably the only international organization establishing global rules for trade between nations. As such, it is the major organizational arbiter of trade and environment policy.

This chapter introduces the WTO as an organization in general and its dispute settlement system in particular. Section II begins by putting the establishment of the WTO in 1995 in the historical context of the evolution of the modern international trading system following World War II. Section III explains the basic structure of the organization and its governance mechanisms. Section IV details the dispute settlement process and explores some criticisms of it from the environmental perspective. Finally, Section V looks at the question of how the rules and decisions of the WTO and other international trade agreements are given effect as a matter of national law, both in the negotiation of trade agreements and in their application once they have been adopted.

II. Creating a Multilateral Trading System

The 21st century constellation of multilateral, regional, and bilateral trade agreements gives liberalized international commerce a sense of inevitability. The multilateral trading system has not always rested on such a firm foundation, however. This section briefly sketches the evolution of the modern world trade institutions from early antecedents to provisional agreement in 1947, through difficult tariff negotiations and fledgling efforts to deal with nontariff barriers to trade in the 1960s, 70s, and 80s, and finally to the formation of the WTO as a full-fledged international organization in 1995.

The following two readings give a brief history of the emergence of a system of trade rules prior to World War II, and the post-war development of the General Agreement on Tariffs and Trade (GATT) as both a legal text and as an organization overseeing implementation and negotiation of multilateral trade rules.

John Jackson, *The World Trading System*
35–36 (2d ed. 1997)

The history of international cooperation to discipline national actions affecting international trade can be traced back to the beginnings of recorded history. During the Middle Ages the development of the city-states and the Hanseatic League were manifestations of this long history, and the "law merchant," later to be incorporated into the Common Law of England by Lord Mansfield in the late 1700s, was another example of the search for predictability and stability in international trading relations. The Treaty of Utrecht of 1713 has been described as a forerunner of GATT.

The development of the bilateral friendship, Commerce, navigation (FCN) treaties during the seventeenth and eighteenth centuries was an important step in regulating economic relations among the emerging nation-states. These treaties also covered matters other than trade in goods, but involved clauses dealing with "most-favored-nation" status and "national treatment" that later became pillars of the GATT structure.

Modern multilateral developments to regulate trade began mainly during the late nineteenth century. In 1890 a treaty was signed Concerning the Creation of an International Union for the Publication of Customs Tariffs. International meetings or congresses were held in 1900, 1908, and 1913 to address problems of customs cooperation. Conferences on this matter were also organized in 1920, 1922, 1923, 1927, 1930, and 1933. The 1923 International Conference on Customs Formalities, sponsored by the League of Nations, completed an International Convention Relating to the Simplification of Customs Formalities that covered many of the matters now treated in GATT. The League of Nations produced a series of studies on trade problems from 1926 to 1936 that later influenced international initiatives concerning trade.

The major initiatives leading to the establishment of the GATT were taken by the United States during World War II, in cooperation with its allies, particularly the United Kingdom. Two distinct strands of thought influenced these countries during the war. One strand concerned the program of trade agreements begun by the United States after the enactment of the 1934 Reciprocal Trade Agreements Act. Between 1934 and 1945 the United States entered into thirty-two bilateral reciprocal trade agreements, many of which had clauses that foreshadowed those currently in GATT.

The second strand of thinking during the war period stemmed from the view that the mistakes made concerning economic policy during the interwar period (1920 to 1940) were a major cause of the disasters that led to World War II. The Great Depression has been partly blamed for this war, as has the harsh reparations policy toward Germany. In the interwar period, particularly after the damaging 1930 U.S. tariff act was signed, many other nations began enacting protectionist measures, including quota-type restrictions, which choked off international trade. Political leaders in the United States and elsewhere made statements about the importance of establishing postwar economic institutions that would prevent these mistakes from happening again.

Thus it was that the Bretton Woods conference was held in 1944. This conference was devoted to addressing monetary and banking issues. It established the charters of the International Monetary Fund and the World Bank (International Bank for Reconstruction and Development), but it did not take up the problems of trade as such. This was undoubtedly because the conference was sponsored by and under the jurisdiction of ministries of finance, whereas trade was under the jurisdiction of different ministries. (It is interesting to speculate, in light of the history of the trade conferences, how history might have been different if the Bretton Woods conference had indeed taken up the entire subject matter of economic relations, including trade.) Nevertheless, the 1944 conference is on record as having recognized the need for a comparable institution for trade, to complement the IMF monetary institutions.

———

Mitsuo Matsushita, Thomas J. Schoenbaum, & Petros Mavroidis, *The World Trade Organization: Law, Practice, and Policy*

1–7 (2d ed. 2006) By permission of Oxford University Press

1. Bretton Woods and the failure of the International Trade Organization

The idea of founding an international organization to develop and coordinate international trade was put forward in 1944 at a conference on economic matters held in Bretton Woods, New Hampshire, but the details were left for later. After the founding of the United Nations in 1945, multilateral trade negotiations were conducted within the framework of the UN Economic and Social Council, which in 1946 adopted a resolution in favour of forming an International Trade Organization (ITO).

Negotiations over the ITO and the post-war international trading system were held in several stages: at Lake Success, New York in 1947; in Geneva in 1947; and in Havana in 1948. The Geneva meetings, which were pivotal, had three objectives: (1) draft an ITO charter, (2) prepare schedules of tariff reductions and (3) prepare a multilateral treaty containing general principles of trade, namely, the General Agreement on Tariffs and Trade (GATT). By the end of 1947, work had been completed on the tariff reductions and the GATT. The final work to complete a charter for the ITO was put off until 1948.

The governments of the countries engaged in the negotiations were left with a problem: how to bring the tariff cuts and the GATT into force right away without waiting on the final round of negotiations to form the ITO. The solution was to adopt a Protocol of Provisional Application to apply the GATT "provisionally on and after January 1, 1948." In this way, the GATT and its tariff schedules could immediately enter into force, later the GATT could be revised to be consistent with the charter, and the GATT and the charter could finally be adopted.

The countries participating in the Havana Conference of 1948 completed work on the ITO charter, but the ITO charter never entered into force. Because the support of the United States was critical, other countries that were ready to adopt the ITO charter waited to see its fate in the United States. President Truman submitted the ITO charter to Congress, but the Republicans won control of Congress in the 1948 election. In 1950, the Truman administration announced that it would no longer seek congressional approval for the ITO. The ITO was dead.

2. The GATT becomes an international organization

The failure to adopt the ITO meant the absence of the "third pillar" on which the Bretton Woods economic structure was to be built. [eds. note: The other two pillars are the World Bank and the International Monetary Fund.] The GATT, which was not intended to be an international organization, gradually filled this void. The contracting parties of the GATT—the GATT could have no members— held meetings every year, and new contracting parties were gradually added. The Interim Commission for the ITO became the GATT Secretariat. The GATT evolved into an international organization based in Geneva, taking as its "charter" the GATT, practice under the GATT and additional understandings and agreements.

Nevertheless, the GATT always suffered from what Professor Jackson has termed "birth defects," inherent weaknesses that handicapped its operation. These birth defects included:

1. The lack of a charter granting the GATT legal personality and establishing its procedures and organizational structure;

2. The fact that the GATT had only "provisional" application;

3. The fact that the Protocol of Provisional Application contained provisions enabling GATT contracting parties to maintain legislation that was in force on accession to the GATT and was inconsistent with the GATT (so-called grandfather rights); and

4. Ambiguity and confusion about the GATT's authority, decision-making ability and legal status. * * *

4. The GATT tariff negotiating rounds

Despite its birth defects, the GATT served as the basis for eight "rounds" of multilateral trade negotiations. These rounds were held periodically to reduce tariffs and other barriers to international trade and were increasingly complex and ambitious. All were successful.

The principal accomplishment of the GATT was its success in reducing tariffs and other trade barriers on a worldwide basis.

The various negotiating rounds were named after the place in which the negotiations began or the person associated with initiating the round. The names and dates of the rounds are as follows:

- Geneva   1947
- Annecy   1949
- Torquay   1950
- Geneva   1956
- Dillon   1960–61
- Kennedy   1962–67
- Tokyo   1973–79
- Uruguay   1986–94
- [• Doha   2001– (suspended in 2008)]

The objectives of the early GATT negotiating rounds were primarily to reduce tariffs. Non-tariff barriers later emerged as a vital concern as well. The objectives of the Tokyo and Uruguay rounds were primarily to reduce non-tariff barriers. The Uruguay Round culminated in the creation of an immense new body of international law related to trade: the basic texts of the WTO agreements exceeded 400 pages, and the Final Act signed in Marrakesh, Morocco on April 1994 was over 26,000 pages.

The Final Act of the Uruguay Round transformed the GATT into a new, fully fledged international organization called the World Trade Organization (WTO).

5. The Creation of the WTO

The idea of creating a World Trade Organization emerged slowly from various needs and suggestions. Even at the beginning of the Uruguay Round, negotiators and observers realized that significant new agreements would require better institutional mechanisms and a better system for resolving disputes. One of the 15 negotiations undertaken at the beginning of the Round was on the "functioning of the GATT system," dubbed with the acronym "FOGS." Negotiators were particularly concerned with how new agreements would come into force and whether they would be binding on all GATT contracting parties. Many countries wanted to avoid the problems of the Tokyo Round, which had resulted in significant new "side agreements" that were binding only on those GATT contracting parties that accepted them (GATT à la carte).

Thus, Uruguay Round negotiators were receptive to the suggestion, first made by Professor Jackson, to use the Uruguay Round as an occasion to found a new "World Trade Organization." Jackson argued that it was time to cure the "birth defects" of the GATT by creating an organization that would be a United Nations specialized agency with an organizational structure and a dispute settlement mechanism. The creation of such an organization could solve the problems of "GATT à la carte." It would be necessary to accept all the Uruguay Round agreements to be a Member of the new World Trade Organization.

The idea of a new world trade organization was taken up in the FOGS negotiation. When the Draft Final Act of the Uruguay Round was issued in 1991, it contained a proposal for a new "Multilateral Trade Organization." Working groups and negotiators did further work, and the name was changed to the World Trade Organization. The Draft Final Act included agreements on transitional arrangements and the termination of the GATT 1947 and the Tokyo Round agreements on subjects covered by new WTO agreements. Finally, the negotiators decided that the WTO would come into being on 1 January 1995. The package of agreements that brought the WTO into being was opened for signature at Marrakesh on 15 April 1994. The package consisted of multilateral trade agreements annexed to a single document, namely, the Marrakesh Agreement Establishing the World Trade Organization (WTO Agreement). Through this ingenious device, all agreements annexed to the WTO Agreement become binding on all Members as a single body of law.

III. The Structure of the WTO

A. Overview

The Agreement Establishing the World Trade Organization, which we will call simply the WTO Agreement, was adopted on April 15, 1994 at the Marrakesh Ministerial, a meeting of world trade ministers, as the main item of "The Final Act Embodying the Results of the Uruguay Round of Multilateral Trade Negotiations." As Professor Jackson writes, the Final Act creates:

> a full-fledged legally constituted international organization, the WTO. Its charter begins by establishing the international organization and then proceeds through the priority elements for creating it, including statements on functions and structure; provision for the highest authority in a ministerial conference to meet at least biannually; and provision for a secretariat, a director-general, and a series of subbodies, including four councils that will be described later in this chapter....

> Nevertheless, no one should expect a very "tidy" text in the Uruguay Round. A number of subtexts have been pasted together, and the relationships among them is often very unclear. Negotiating compromises required the introduction, or at least toleration, of ambiguous phrases in a number of places. The sheer com-

plexity of the agreement assures that a variety of interpretive problems will arise. Trade policy experts generally agree, however, that the Uruguay Round is a remarkable and substantial step forward for the world trade system.

JOHN JACKSON, THE WORLD TRADING SYSTEM, at 48–49.

As Jackson indicates, the WTO Agreement accomplishes several tasks. First, it formally "establishes" the WTO as an international organization and describes the essential details of the scope of its authority. Second, it provides the basic framework for WTO governance and organizational structure. Third, it "integrates" and makes binding on all WTO members the GATT and other multilateral trade agreements annexed to the Agreement. Finally, it indicates the procedures for amendment of the Agreement, for the accession of new members, and for withdrawal of members, as well as the formalities of its entry into force. The WTO Agreement entered into force for its charter members on January 1, 1995 and has added more than 30 members since then.

An immediate explanation is in order of the relationship between the new WTO and the old GATT. The WTO is explicitly built on the foundation of the GATT as both the trade agreement itself, GATT 1947, and the organization that evolved to administer it. Thus, although the WTO has a formal status as an international organization that the old GATT never had, the staff of the GATT and many of the internal arrangements of the GATT carried forward much as before. As a textual matter, the GATT 1994 is the operative basic trade agreement for the WTO. The GATT 1994 replaces the GATT 1947, and with the expiration of the GATT 1947, certain grandfathering provisions and other negotiated arrangements with certain countries ceased to have legal effect. Nevertheless, the GATT 1994 incorporates by reference the complete text of the GATT 1947, including all the amendments and other legal instruments that the GATT contracting parties had agreed to over the years to elaborate the original agreement. The only specific wording change that the GATT 1994 makes to the GATT 1947 is to replace the terms "Contracting Party" or "Contracting Parties" with the terms "Member" or "Members." The change from the GATT 1947 to the GATT 1994 is more than a formality; by having the GATT 1947 expire, all the former contracting parties to the GATT were compelled to adhere to the WTO Agreement, including all its subsidiary agreements, in order to maintain their legal rights vis-à-vis the other GATT parties.

As a result of the ambitious agenda adopted at the outset of the Uruguay Round, the scope of the WTO system is vastly broader than the GATT regime that it replaced. The List of Annexes, reproduced on page 75, gives a sense of the breadth of the new world trade system. As you see, the WTO Agreement has four annexes containing a number of different trade agreements. Most notably, the multilateral system no longer applies solely to goods; new agreements cover trade in services, the trade-related protection of intellectual property rights, and trade-related aspects of the national regulation of foreign investments. The WTO also replaces the rather *ad hoc* and increasingly controversial GATT regime for the resolution of trade disputes with a substantially more formal quasi-judicial process, including specific steps for enforcement of legal determinations and a remedy of authorized trade sanctions in cases of recalcitrance. Dispute settlement is addressed in more detail in Section IV of this chapter beginning on page 82.

Although the texts annexed to the WTO Agreement are called "agreements," they are not all free-standing agreements. Several require reference to the GATT or other documents. Annex 1 contains the mandatory "multilateral agreements" on trade, including various ministerial decisions and declarations and interpretive notes. Annex 1A includes the many agreements on trade in goods, spanning the gamut from the broad principles and obligations of the GATT to agreements on specific practical issues such as preshipment inspection. Annex 1B is the General Agreement on Trade in Services (GATS), and Annex 1C is the Agreement on Trade-Related Aspects of Intellectual Property Rights (TRIPs). Annexes 2 and 3 comprise administrative measures, the Dispute Settlement Understanding (DSU) and the Trade Policy Review Mechanism (TPRM), respectively. Acceptance of these provisions is also mandatory for all WTO members. Annex 4 contains four optional "plurilateral agreements," two of which (those on dairy and bovine meat) were terminated in 1997.

One consequential change from the earlier GATT regime is that the WTO agreements bring more precision and wider coverage to those rules on trade in goods with the greatest potential to affect the environment and environmental regulation. The WTO's Agreement on the Application of Sanitary and Phytosanitary Measures (SPS Agreement), for example, applies detailed and rather complex requirements to national regulations designed to prevent the introduction of plant and animal pests and diseases or to control the contamination of food products. Already, WTO dispute settlement rulings have found certain SPS regulations in Europe, Australia, and Japan to be inconsistent with the SPS Agreement. These cases are discussed in Chapter 7. The Agreement on Technical Barriers to Trade (TBT Agreement) applies to a wide variety of government product regulations and even private standard-setting entities. One contentious environmental issue under the TBT Agreement is whether or to what extent it allows or controls the development and promulgation of ecolabels providing consumers with information about the environmental effects of the way a product was produced. These issues are discussed in Chapter 6.

B. The Administration of the WTO

The brief principal text of the WTO Agreement establishes the WTO as an international organization and defines the WTO's scope, functions, institutional structure, and decisionmaking process. Structurally, the WTO has a hierarchical organization with the following major components: the Ministerial Conference, the General Council, the Dispute Settlement Body, Councils and Committees, and the Secretariat.

1. Ministerial Conference

The ultimate governing authority of the WTO is the Ministerial Conference. Paragraph 1 of Article IV calls for the Ministerial Conference of all members to convene at least once every two years and endows that conference with plenary authority to "carry out the functions of the WTO and take actions necessary to this effect." At the request of any member, the Ministerial Conference is also empowered to "take decisions on all matters under any of the Multilateral Trade Agreements." In other words, the trade ministers of the member countries, meeting together, must make all major policy decisions, initiate new negotiations, and otherwise determine the strategic direction of the WTO. Through October 2010, there have been seven Ministerial Conferences, commonly known by the cities in which they convened: the Singapore Ministerial in 1996, the Geneva Ministerial in 1998, the Seattle Ministerial in 1999, the Doha Ministerial in 2001, the Cancún Ministerial in 2003, the Hong Kong Ministerial in 2005, and after a four year hiatus a low-key Geneva Ministerial in 2009.

Table of Contents of Instruments Creating the WTO

The members and the WTO Secretariat staff put enormous effort into the preparation for these Ministerial Conferences. They operate much like any other multilateral conference. The participating countries agree (or attempt to agree) in advance on the agenda of issues to be addressed and the desired outcome on each issue. Invariably, agreement on some important issues remains elusive until the ministers themselves and their teams of assistants actually convene for the conference and debate the issues face-to-face. Outside groups, including environmental NGOs, attempt to influence the course of the negotiations before and during the conference. Efforts are made, however, to keep the government delegates separated from demonstrations and other ancillary activities by civil society. The Singapore and Doha ministerials were substantially successful, with ministerial declarations memorializing the major decisions. The Seattle and Cancún ministerials, in contrast, adjourned without agreement by the ministers on the major policy proposals and trade negotiation initiatives on the agenda. The failure of these two ministerials to maintain forward momentum on trade policy and further trade liberalization led in each case to a period of reassessment about what the WTO can or should try to accomplish. They also led to proposals, both from within and from without, for major reform of the way the WTO operates. Yet no major reforms have been made, and despite repeated commitments to pursue negotiations, the Doha Development Round remains unfinished after more than eight years.

---

2. General Council

Paragraph 2 of Article IV establishes a General Council, composed of representatives of all the members, to meet periodically to carry out the functions of the WTO between meetings of the Ministerial Conference. The General Council ordinarily meets monthly at WTO headquarters in Geneva. For most members, the General Council representatives are the senior trade officials who head their country's permanent Geneva delegation to the WTO. The General Council is the forum for formal deliberation and decision among WTO members on the broad range of specific trade topics within WTO jurisdiction, especially the month-by-month implementation of the strategic policies determined by the Ministerial Conference. Meetings of the General Council are also the occasion for decisions to give instructions or guidance to subordinate bodies of the WTO, including the Secretariat, the four topical councils and standing committees, and the special committees pursuing negotiation of new agreements.

With respect to decisionmaking, Article IX of the WTO Agreement provides that the members will continue the GATT practice of making decisions by consensus. Where consensus cannot be reached, "Decisions" will be approved by a simple majority vote, with each member getting one vote. "Interpretations" of a multilateral trade agreement included in Annex 1, however, must be approved by a three-fourths majority. With these provisions, the WTO Agreement establishes an institutional structure not unlike those under other international agreements, such as the Convention on International Trade in Endangered Species of Wild Fauna and Flora and the Montreal Protocol on Substances that Deplete the Ozone Layer.

---

3. Dispute Settlement Body

The same representatives that constitute the General Council also function as the Dispute Settlement Body (DSB), the governing entity under the Dispute Settlement Understanding. The DSB is, however, legally distinct from the General Council, with a different chair person and different rules of procedure. The DSB's major responsibilities are to receive requests from WTO members to establish a panel to resolve a particular trade dispute, to act as the final decision maker in each dispute by accepting or rejecting the "report" of the dispute settlement panel or the Appellate Body, and to authorize compensatory remedies if a party to a dispute fails to correct a violation. The DSB also supervises the work of the WTO organs of dispute settlement: the Appellate Body, the dispute settlement panels, and the Secretariat staff that support their work.

---

4. Councils and Committees

Underneath the General Council, the WTO Agreement establishes three Councils and several Committees to oversee the key elements of the system of agreements. All member countries are also members of these councils and committees. There is a council for each aspect of the multilateral trade agreements: a Council for Trade in Goods, another Council for Trade in Services, and a third Council for Trade-Related Aspects of Intellectual Property Rights. The councils can create committees to assist in their work. The membership as a whole established several standing committees addressing specific recurring topics, such as the Committee on Trade and Development. Finally, when formal negotiations toward a new agreement are under way, a Trade Negotiations Committee oversees and coordinates the negotiations.

One of the Ministerial Decisions adopted at Marrakesh in April 1994 established, on a provisional basis, a new Committee on Trade and Environment (CTE). The CTE's original terms of reference, set out in the following box, have subsequently been renewed at each Ministerial Conference, so the CTE has become, in effect, a standing committee of the WTO. The CTE meets about four times per year and prepares reports on its activities for the Ministerial Conferences. Documents prepared by the CTE and minutes of its meetings are available on the WTO website at http://www.wto.org/english/tratop_e/envir_e/wrk_committee_e.htm.

---

5. The Secretariat

The final important component of WTO governance is the Secretariat. The Secretariat is a staff of approximately 625 international civil servants headed by a Director-General who is appointed by the Ministerial Conference for a term of up to four years with the possibility of reappointment for another term not to exceed four years. General Council, *Procedures for the Appointment of Directors-General*, WT/L/509, para. 21 (Jan. 20, 2003). Below the Director-General are four Deputy Directors-General, appointed by the General Council. Each of the four is responsible for particular substantive issue areas and particular administrative functions within the Secretariat.

The Secretariat serves multiple functions for the membership. At a general level, it carries out those administrative responsibilities given to it by the Ministerial Conference. Different divisions of the Secretariat, roughly paralleling the council and committee structure, provide research and administrative support to the councils and committees. One branch of the Secretariat legal staff, for example, provides research and drafting support to dispute settlement panels and to the Appellate Body. The Secretariat can also undertake certain initiatives on its own to assist the WTO members in exploring new strategies

The Committee on Trade and Environment

As part of the Uruguay Round documents, the Ministers drafted terms of reference for a Committee on Trade and Environment (CTE). The two fundamental premises for creating the CTE were that 1) "there should not be, nor need be, any policy contradiction" between the multilateral trading system on the one hand and the protection of the environment and promotion of sustainable development on the other; and 2) coordination of trade and environmental policies within the WTO should be "limited to trade policies and those trade-related aspects of environmental policies which may result in significant trade effects for its members."

With those guides, the Ministers directed the CTE, "with the aim of making international trade and environmental policies mutually supportive," to address the following matters:

- the relationship between the provisions of the multilateral trading system and trade measures for environmental purposes, including those pursuant to multilateral environmental agreements;

- the relationship between environmental policies relevant to trade and environmental measures with significant trade effects and the provisions of the multilateral trading system;

- the relationship between the provisions of the multilateral trading system and (a) charges and taxes for environmental purposes; and (b) environmental product requirements for packaging, labelling, and recycling;

- the provisions of the multilateral trading system with respect to the transparency of trade measures used for environmental purposes and environmental measures and requirements which have significant trade effects;

- the relationship between the dispute settlement mechanisms in the multilateral trading system and those found in multilateral environmental agreements;

- the effect of environmental measures on market access, especially in relation to developing countries, in particular to the least developed among them, and environmental benefits of removing trade restrictions and distortions;

- the issue of exports of domestically prohibited goods;

CTE Terms of Reference from the Marrakesh Ministerial Decision on Trade and Environment, April 14, 1994.

or considering new policy proposals. For example, the Secretariat has helped to develop and propose cooperative work programs between the WTO, the World Bank, and the International Monetary Fund.

The Director-General himself (they have all been men so far) has sufficient stature to be somewhat independent of the membership. This allows him to act, as the occasion may arise, as a publicist for the WTO, as a visionary who puts out provocative proposals, as a champion of the under-represented smaller and least-developed countries, or as the mediator between contending factions within the membership on important negotiations. He is also, of course, the chief executive of the Secretariat.

C. The WTO, the Members, and Environmental Organizations

One of the persistent themes in trade and environment discussions is a double-barreled complaint by environmental organizations about the WTO. Substantively, environmental advocates believe that the WTO, which is by its nature focused on trade liberalization and the enforcement of trade rules, gives insufficient consideration to the environmental consequences of trade and the impact of trade rules on national and international environmental regulation. In a corresponding criticism of decisionmaking procedures at the WTO, environmental advocates complain of the high degree of confidentiality in WTO deliberations, the resulting lack of transparency, and the very tight restrictions on the ability of civil society to participate directly in the policy formulation and dispute settlement processes.

In a study of the CTE, Professor Gregory Shaffer takes a provocatively skeptical view of these environmentalist complaints. Shaffer proposes that the creation of the CTE in the first place, as well as the course of the deliberations in the CTE, can be analyzed according to one of three alternative models:

> (i) An intergovernmental perspective, which holds that the creation of the CTE represents an attempt by states to take control of the trade and environment debate by bringing it to a state-dominated organization. A two-level intergovernmental model incorporates portions of the next two perspectives by maintaining that national positions are shaped by national political processes as well as competition among governmental actors attempting to respond to and shape constituent demands.

> (ii) A supranational technocratic perspective, which appraises the WTO's handling of trade and environment matters as a co-optation of policy-making by a technocratic network of trade policymakers with a neoliberal policy orientation. The network is composed of national trade officials working with the WTO Secretariat within the structure of the WTO trade regime. National trade officials, in turn, receive support from large, well-organized private businesses.

> (iii) A stakeholder/civil society perspective, which views the creation of the CTE as a response to ongoing systematic pressure from non-governmental advocacy groups before international and domestic fora to change the norms of the world trading system.

Gregory C. Shaffer, *The World Trade Organization under Challenge: Democracy and the Law and Politics of the WTO's Treatment of Trade and Environment Matters*, 25 HARV. ENVTL. L. REV. 1, 7–8 (2001). After detailed review of the negotiations leading to the agreement to create the CTE and the course of the first five years of discussions in the CTE, Shaffer concludes that the two-level intergovernmental version of the intergovernmental perspective offers the best explanation of how the CTE has worked. In the course of his analysis, Shaffer examines the efforts of environmental NGOs to pursue the stakeholder/civil society model of WTO decisionmaking and draws a decidedly unflattering picture.

Gregory C. Shaffer,
The World Trade Organization under Challenge
61–68

Different interests have attempted to advance their goals through the institutionalization of trade and environment issues within the WTO, as suggested by neoliberal and stakeholder perspectives. The CTE's failure to recommend any changes in WTO rules has frustrated northern environmental groups, especially regarding the issue most important to them: Item 1, concerning the use of trade measures to enforce international environmental agreements and advance environmental goals through unilateral state action. Because of the stalemate within the CTE, they advocate a stakeholder model under which they would play a greater role in CTE deliberations. They have already used the CTE process to pressure the WTO to make its decision-making more transparent so that NGOs may better coordinate pressure on governments, in particular through the media, domestically and internationally.

Not all NGOs, however, have advocated adopting a stakeholder model of WTO governance. The model has been primarily advocated by environmental groups in the United States and Europe, because southern NGOs, although sometimes large in number, are short on resources and typically localist in orientation. They thus recognize the northern NGOs' advantage in international fora. Just as all states are not equal, all NGOs are not equal. Northern NGOs have more funding, are located closer to WTO offices in Geneva, are more likely to finance international networks, and have greater indirect access to information from their state representatives. Southern NGOs have less access, in part because southern governments themselves have difficulty monitoring all developments in the WTO. One London-based environmental NGO, the Foundation for International Environmental Law and Development ("FIELD"), even negotiated a deal with a developing country, Sierra Leone, to represent it before the CTE. Sierra Leone, beset by violent civil conflict, did not have the resources or the priority to represent its "stakeholder" interests before the CTE. A northern NGO, though with serious conflicts of interest, offered to do so in its stead. FIELD supported the cost of attending and reporting in meetings in exchange for direct access to CTE meetings.

In short, northern NGOs are much better positioned than southern NGOs and southern trading interests to have their views heard at the international level. Given scarce resources, southern states even question the appropriateness of the WTO sending NGO delegates to Geneva for symposia when those resources could be spent on water purification, nutrition, education, and disease control projects in developing countries. While some northern commentators may condescendingly counter that the alternative use of funds will not go to social services, but to line the pockets of southern elite, the fact remains that international NGO conferences remain more of a prerogative of northern governments and constituencies.

Information comes at a price. Northern environmental NGOs such as Greenpeace and WWF, have multi-million-dollar budgets that they use to address environmental matters. Some of their budgets exceed that of the WTO itself….

In these information campaigns, northern environmental NGOs do not represent the environmental perspective. Rather, the term "environment" has vastly different meanings to a northern public than to stakeholders in developing countries. In developing countries, it is much more difficult to separate the notion of the "environment" from that of "development" because people's livelihoods are more intimately connected on a day-to-day basis with the environment. Developing country stakeholders are thus much less likely to adhere to a preservationist perspective of environmental protection when their lives and livelihoods are directly at stake.

While northern environmental NGOs may be internationalist in orientation and more likely than the WTO Secretariat to represent the "trees," they do not represent a "global civil society." They have a specifically northern perspective, and often, even more specifically, an Anglo-Saxon one. Their representatives were raised and educated in the North. Almost all of their funding comes from contributors from the North. They obtain their financing by focusing on issues that strike the northern public's imagination, in particular animal rights and species preservation issues. This was the motivating force for their demand for changes in WTO rules under Item 1 following the two Tuna-Dolphin decisions.

Southern states and southern NGOs thus distrust demands for greater WTO transparency when "transparency" means greater access for private groups to WTO decision-making. Southern interests are wary that this form of transparency will merely permit northern NGOs to better exploit the media to pressure state delegates, the WTO Secretariat, and WTO dispute settlement panelists to take their views into account and thereby advance northern ends. Southern delegates fear precisely these "constructivist" aspects of the stakeholder model. As a developing country consultant to WWF (India) states, "there is an urgent need to contest the anti-environment image of the WTO so assiduously disseminated by northern academics and environment groups" pursuant to their "dual strategy" of pressuring WTO dispute settlement bodies through critiques and amicus curiae briefs, on the one hand, and pressuring northern governments to include trade-environment issues in the next round of WTO negotiations, on the other.

NGOs from the United States and Europe are already relatively powerful in affecting WTO agendas and outcomes precisely because they can work with and through the WTO's most powerful members. They simply lobby and otherwise pressure their national representatives. Developing countries question whether a stakeholder model would, in fact, exacerbate this disequilibrium. While communitarian and civic republican models may work relatively better at the local level, they are much more problematic at the international level where numbers, complexity, and inequality of access to information and decision-makers increase.

_____

Questions and Discussion

1. Is Shaffer being anti-environmental in his approach? Does he give too much credence to the view of environmental organizations as self-interested rent seekers rather than good-faith and issue-driven advocates for "the trees"? Do you think he has overstated the influence of environmental organizations?

2. Recall the introduction to North-South perspectives and the concept of sustainable development in Chapter 1. Have northern environmental groups, as Shaffer suggests, lost

sight of the needs of developing countries? To what extent might southern development considerations be viewed by northern environmental advocates, in good faith, as contrary to sound environmental policy? To what extent should NGOs represent global society? Do you think governments do? Shaffer's critique leads to an important question: whose WTO is it?

3. Shaffer acknowledges that Sierra Leone did not have the resources to represent itself before the CTE. Yet, he criticizes FIELD for representing Sierra Leone. Is that criticism fair? What alternatives does Sierra Leone have? Is it not possible for a "northern" NGO to provide legal assistance to a "southern" government? Does your view change when you learn that FIELD held extensive consultations with the government of Sierra Leone and that the FIELD attorney, Beatrice Chaytor, who became a member of the Sierra Leone delegation, is a native of Sierra Leone and now works for the Sierra Leone government? For Chaytor's view of the relationship between FIELD and the government of Sierra Leone, see Beatrice Chaytor, *Cooperation Between Governments and NGOs: The Case of Sierra Leone in the CTE, in* TRADE, ENVIRONMENT AND SUSTAINABLE DEVELOPMENT: VIEWS FROM SUB-SAHARAN AFRICA AND LATIN AMERICA: A READER 89 (Peider Könz ed., 2000).

4. If Shaffer is correct about the two-level game aspect of trade policy, this has substantial implications for how environmental interests should advance the trade and environment agenda. The focus of effort will have to be to influence individual national governments to shift their positions, not the WTO Secretariat or dispute settlement tribunals, because only the governments, in this view, control the process of reform, and they respond to domestic constituent pressures.

5. With respect to transparency, trade officials of most countries draw a sharp distinction between a discussion forum like the CTE and true negotiations toward a new or amended legal text. For example, the CTE has for years allowed the secretariat staffs of multilateral environmental agreements (MEAs) to attend, and to speak at, CTE meetings as officially sanctioned "observers." But the Doha Ministerial Declaration charged the CTE with negotiating a specific statement on the relationship between the WTO agreements and the MEAs. For this negotiation, which as of early 2010 continues in desultory fashion, the CTE meets in "special sessions" with sharp restrictions on the participation of the MEA secretariats. For further details, see Chapter 9.

6. In a similar way, the WTO membership generally remains opposed to increased transparency and participation in WTO dispute settlement. *See* Section IV.C below.

IV. The WTO's Dispute Settlement System

Perhaps none of the organizational units of the WTO is more important to trade and environment issues than the Dispute Settlement Body (DSB). When popular press accounts discuss "the WTO," they are often referring to the decisions of the DSB. The DSB represents the most widely reported and politically controversial face of the WTO: the WTO as an organization empowered to render legally enforceable decisions directly affecting national laws and policies. More precisely, the public focus is on the written decisions, called reports, of the particular decisionmakers in a WTO dispute, either the three-person panel of independent experts that heard the case in the first instance or, when there is an appeal, the three-member division of the permanent Appellate Body of leading trade law experts.

Article 1.1 of the DSU declares that its provisions "shall apply" to the resolution of disputes among members under any of the "covered agreements," which include all the agreements in Annex 1 to the WTO Agreement. Thus, the DSB has exclusive jurisdiction over any dispute involving the application and interpretation of most of the WTO agreements. To the discomfort of some environmental advocates, nothing in the DSU precludes the DSB from resolving trade disputes where the implementation of environmental laws or requirements implicates trade rules. In reality, however, no alternative dispute resolution process of comparable effectiveness exists under environmental auspices for the adjudication of trade-related environmental disputes; the international community has largely avoided the International Court of Justice as a viable forum. On the one hand, then, environmental advocates see the WTO trade dispute resolution process as "insular, rigid, and narrow," with impenetrable procedures. DANIEL C. ESTY, GREENING THE GATT: TRADE, ENVIRONMENT, AND THE FUTURE 77 (1994). On the other hand, environmental advocates envy the exclusive authority of the WTO and the international recognition of the DSB as a reliable and authoritative international adjudicatory body that regularly resolves disputes with serious economic and political consequences. Consequently, various proposals have emerged from environmental commentators to establish a global or world environmental organization comparable to the WTO in order to establish an authoritative forum for interpretation of environmental agreements and development of environmental policy. Even so, most of these proposals do not specifically recommend an environmental counterpart to the DSB. *See, e.g.,* C. Ford Runge, *A Global Environment Organization (GEO) and the World Trading System: Prospects and Problems,* 35 J. WORLD TRADE 399 (2001); DANIEL C. ESTY & MARIA H. IVANOVA, GLOBAL ENVIRONMENTAL GOVERNANCE: OPTIONS AND OPPORTUNITIES (2002).

The overall responsibility of the DSB is to make recommendations and rulings "aimed at achieving a satisfactory settlement" of each dispute "in accordance with the rights and obligations" under the agreements. DSU, art. 3.4. The DSB has two main roles in the dispute resolution process. First, under Article 2 of the DSU, the DSB supervises the functioning of the procedures and the organizational elements that constitute the WTO's dispute settlement machinery—informal consultations, the establishment of a dispute settlement panel, and the possible appeal of legal questions to the Appellate Body. As part of this function, the DSB oversees, for example, the formal rules of procedure of the Appellate Body. Second, the DSB acts as the final decision maker in every dispute. As a formal matter, in fact, the panels and the Appellate Body are merely adjuncts to the DSB: "The function of [dispute settlement] panels is to assist the DSB in discharging its responsibilities under this Understanding and the covered agreements." DSU, art. 11. Nevertheless, the DSU is framed with the expectation that the DSB will adopt the panel report or, in the case of an appeal, the Appellate Body report: the DSB can decide *not* to give legal effect to any particular report only by consensus. DSU, art. 16.4 (adoption of panel reports); art. 17.14 (adoption of Appellate Body reports).

In practice, the handling of specific disputes has become routine. According to an analysis of disputes initiated by early 2008, there were 369 disputes (though this count includes some cases of multiple complaints by different countries about a single measure that are resolved in a single proceeding). Of the 369, only 36% were litigated. Another 14% were officially notified as settled under DSU article 3.6; no panel was formed for 34% (presumably because consultations between the parties resulted in a mutually satisfactory outcome); 8% were inactive, and 9% were still in process. Mary Kopczynski, "The

Haves Coming Out Behind: Galanter's Theory Tested in the WTO Dispute Settlement System," (2008) *at* http://works.bepress.com/mary_kopczynski/1. For the disputes for which the panel process is set in motion, the DSB plays virtually no further role. After 15 years, the DSB has not even once rejected the final report of a dispute settlement panel or the Appellate Body. The DSB is more than a rubber stamp, however. It exercises political control, albeit indirectly, through two other functions. First, all panel and Appellate Body reports are reviewed and discussed in the DSB, and the statements by governments in the DSB about dispute settlement procedures or about the legal reasoning of specific decisions constitute an influential source of political feedback to the Appellate Body and its supporting secretariat staff. Second, the DSB appoints the members of the Appellate Body, who serve for four-year terms renewable once, and decides on the renewal of the term of any Appellate Body member. The appointment power gives the DSB some capacity to shape the style and substance of WTO jurisprudence. The full text of the DSU provisions is available in many places, including on the WTO website at http://www.wto.org/english/docs_e/legal_e/legal_e.htm.

A. The Legal Character of Disputes in the WTO

According to Article 3.2 of the DSU, "[t]he dispute settlement system of the WTO is a central element in providing security and predictability to the multilateral trading system.... [I]t serves to preserve the rights and obligations of Members under the covered agreements." Article 3.3 underscores that the "prompt settlement" of disputes is "essential to the effective functioning of the WTO and the maintenance of a proper balance between the rights and obligations of Members."

The DSU applies to disputes under the "covered agreements," which are the Agreement Establishing the WTO and all the annexed agreements except for one on the trade policy review mechanism. Since the GATT remains the core text, most disputes arise in whole or in part under the GATT. Moreover, Article 3.1 of the DSU affirms the "adherence" of the WTO members to the "principles" for dispute management "heretofore applied under GATT Articles XXII and XXIII." We begin, then, with a look at those GATT articles.

Mitsuo Matsushita, Thomas J. Schoenbaum, & Petros Mavroidis, *The World Trade Organization: Law, Practice, and Policy*
(2d ed. 2006)
105–08 By permission of Oxford University Press

2. Dispute settlement in the GATT

The WTO dispute settlement system is the result of over 40 years of experience and the evolution of dispute settlement under the GATT 1947. The WTO system can be appreciated only against the background of the GATT regime.

The GATT avoids mention of the term "dispute." The drafters of the GATT did, however, foresee that problems would arise due to future actions or non-actions of one or more GATT contracting parties concerning the matters covered in the GATT. The principal mechanism for dealing with these problems is diplomatic consultation. There are 19 provisions for consultation in the GATT 1947. One of these, Article XXII, is a general provision calling for "sympathetic consideration" and consultation "with respect to any matter affecting the operation of this Agreement."

Article XXIII of the GATT creates a specific mechanism to correct "nullification or impairment" of the GATT. Nullification or impairment can occur for any one of three reasons: (1) failure of a party to carry out obligations under the GATT; (2) the application of a measure by a party regardless of whether the measure conflicts with the GATT; or (3) the existence of any other "situation" that is troublesome. Thus, dispute settlement addresses more than just breaches of the GATT.

Article XXIII specifies a series of steps for dealing with a possible nullification or impairment. Each step is an escalation to be taken if previous attempts to settle the matter are ineffective:

1. ["Written representations or proposals" which must be given "sympathetic consideration."]

2. [Referral to the Contracting Parties collectively, who shall investigate and make recommendations.]

3. [An authorization to suspend the application of concessions or obligations under the GATT as a countermeasure if "the circumstances are serious enough."]

Article XXIII and dispute settlement under the GATT 1947 were shaped by state practice. At first, diplomatic negotiations were the sole means of dealing with controversies. Then "working parties" began to be established to investigate and formulate recommendations.... In 1955, the GATT Contracting Parties began referring disputes to "panels," *ad hoc* groups of experts who acted as neutrals, not government representatives. Panel decisions had no official or binding effect but were referred to the GATT Council, which could make the "appropriate recommendations."

The GATT panel decision process of dispute resolution was successful. Because it was frequently utilized, it became necessary to formalize the panel procedures. This led to a series of agreements and understandings on dispute settlement to supplement the skeleton approach of Article XXIII. [A 1966 "Decision on Procedures," a 1979 "Understanding," and further "Decisions" on procedures in 1982, 1984, and 1989.] Over the years, panels began to take a more rule-oriented, judicial approach to settling disputes. Parties invoked Article XXIII to vindicate their legal rights under the GATT. The panels' recommendations rested on legal, rather than merely diplomatic, grounds. To a remarkable degree, the decisions of the GATT panels adopted by the GATT Council were implemented and observed by states. This was not due to the threat of suspension of concessions, but rather was an accomplishment of the dynamics of the process. A losing party could not ignore a decision based on legal principles. To do so would threaten the entire legal order on which the GATT system was based and which the losing party would need (and might be on the winning side of) in other cases.

Despite the success of the GATT panel dispute resolution process, serious shortcomings inhibited its effectiveness. Such shortcomings included delays in the formation of panels and the panel process, blocking of the adoption of panel reports in the GATT Council and delays in the implementation of Council recommendations. The Tokyo Round of multilateral trade negotiations added dispute resolution procedures to the various Codes approved in 1979. The result was dispute resolution procedures that were confusing in number and were largely uncoordinated.

These difficulties were addressed in the new system of dispute settlement adopted by the WTO.

3. WTO dispute settlement

In the negotiations leading to the establishment of the WTO dispute settlement mechanism, the debate focused on whether a negotiation approach would be superior to a more legalistic, rule-oriented approach. Fears were expressed that reforms to give primacy to legal rules would impair the WTO's credibility because powerful states would inevitably ignore the rules when they go against their national interests.

For better or worse, the judicialized, rule-oriented approach to dispute resolution has prevailed at the WTO.

Questions and Discussion

1. As the above excerpt describes, the DSU brings clarity to several unresolved questions arising under the prior rudimentary GATT process for dispute resolution. Most importantly, the DSU provides a solid legal foundation for the DSB, something the former GATT panel process never had due to its flawed origins. Further, it provides a judicial formality of process that the GATT system lacked. As part of that formalization, it provides that the determinations of WTO panels (or the Appellate Body) are presumptively binding on the parties to the dispute unless there is a consensus among the WTO members, acting through the DSB, to reject the outcome. Another important innovation of the DSU was to create an institutional structure to appeal legal questions to a second panel of legal experts. The DSU establishes a permanent Appellate Body of seven leading trade law experts from around the world who serve for four-year terms renewable once. A division of three members of this Appellate Body sits to hear the appeal from a panel report on questions of law indicated in the statement of appeal.

1. *"Nullification or Impairment"*

As the excerpt above points out, the GATT text does not use the terms "dispute" or "violation." The sole basis an aggrieved WTO member has for invoking the DSU in a complaint brought under the terms of the GATT is to claim that a "benefit accruing" to it under the GATT is being "nullified or impaired" by another member's actions. GATT Article XXIII:1 defines three circumstances in which such nullification or impairment can occur:

(a) the failure of another Member to carry out its obligations under this Agreement;

(b) the application by another Member of any measure, whether or not it conflicts with the provisions of this Agreement; or

(c) the existence of any other situation.

As Professor Jackson has pointed out, nullification or impairment is an "unfortunately ambiguous term." JOHN JACKSON, THE WORLD TRADING SYSTEM, at 115. Why? Article XXIII:1(a) establishes claims for "violations" of the GATT whereas Article XXIII:1(b) creates a claim even where an obligation has not been breached. But how can there be a violation if no obligation has been breached? As to the "any other situation" catch-all of Article XXIII:1(c), no such claims have ever been brought forward, and the DSU, Article 26.2, sets up a special procedure for such claims that will discourage any country that might contemplate such a claim in the future — it makes any recommended decision on Article XXIII:1(c) cases subject to the old GATT rules, meaning that it would have to be adopted by a consensus of the members before it would become binding and trade remedies would not automatically be available.

a. "Violation" Cases

Cases finding a breach of obligations under subparagraph XXIII:1(a) have come to be known as "violation" cases. In general terms, the "benefits accruing" under the GATT were understood to be expectations of fair access to the markets of other members, subject to the restriction of the tariff rates that had been negotiated among the members. Rulings by GATT panels clarified some of the meaning of nullification or impairment. By the time of the 1979 Understanding, it had become established GATT practice that "where there is an infringement of the obligations assumed under the General Agreement, the action is considered prima facie to constitute a case of nullification or impairment." Understanding on the Rules and Procedures Governing the Settlement of Disputes, Annex 2, art. III, §8, B.I.S.D. 26th Supp. at 216 (1994). In *Superfund*, the Panel held that the prima facie presumption that a violation nullifies or impairs benefits could not be rebutted by a claim that trade flows would not be affected, concluding that GATT provisions (in that case, Article III:2) protect "expectations on the competitive relationship between imported and domestic products. A change in the competitive relationship contrary to that provision must consequently be regarded ipso facto as a nullification or impairment of benefits accruing under the General Agreement." United States-Taxes on Petroleum and Certain Imported Substances, GATT Panel Report, L/6175, B.I.S.D. 34th Supp. at 136 (1988) (adopted June 17, 1987).

Compare the Panel's conclusion in *Superfund* with Article 3.8 of the DSU: "In cases where there is an infringement of obligations assumed under a covered agreement, the action is considered *prima facie* to constitute a case of nullification or impairment. This means that there is normally a presumption that a breach of the rules has an adverse impact on other Members ... and ... it shall be up to the Member against whom the complaint has been brought to rebut the charge." Is the DSU language a step back from *Superfund*? Did the *Superfund* Panel go too far? Given repeated statements by WTO panels and the Appellate Body that the benefits of the trade rules relate to conditions of competition and not to volumes of trade, how would a defending country rebut the presumption that violations of trade rules nullify or impair benefits?

---

b. "Nonviolation Nullification or Impairment" Cases

"Nonviolation nullification and impairment" cases arise when a member claims that any benefit accruing to it directly or indirectly under a covered agreement is being nullified or impaired or that the attainment of any objective of a covered agreement is being impeded by another member, regardless of whether that member's action violates the agreement. There have been several holdings of "nonviolation nullification or impairment" under Article XXIII:1(b). Interestingly, each has involved a claim that the defending government's actions have nullified or impaired the expected benefits of prior tariff negotiations between the parties. Perhaps the best known "nonviolation" case is *EEC-Oilseeds*. GATT Panel Report, B.I.S.D. 37th Supp. at 86 (adopted Jan. 25, 1990). The Panel upheld a complaint by the United States that certain agricultural subsidies adopted by the European Economic Community after a round of tariff negotiations had "nullified or impaired" the benefits that the United States had reasonably expected to obtain through reduced tariffs for oilseeds. The tariffs had been negotiated in 1962; the European subsidies were adopted in the 1980s. Was it reasonable for the United States to expect that Europe would not adopt subsidies or other similar measures? Under Article 26 of the WTO DSU, the DSB reports on such disputes are not binding, although a panel may recommend that the losing party make a "mutually satisfactory adjustment," including the payment of compensation.

EEC-Oilseeds is, in fact, the last successful nonviolation claim under the GATT. The United States lost on a nonviolation claim in *Japan-Measures Affecting Consumer Photographic Paper*, WT/DS44/R, adopted by the DSB April 22, 1998. In that case, the United States failed to convince the Panel on two points: 1) that it had reasonable expectations that it had gained some "benefits" in the Japanese market for photographic paper during the prior tariff negotiations; and 2) that the Japanese measures in question had actually caused any nullification or impairment of the supposed benefit. The *Photographic Paper* Panel observed that there have been only eight disputes involving nonviolation claims in the last 50 years and that both Japan and the United States agreed that the nonviolation remedy "should be approached with caution and treated as an exceptional concept." *Id.* at para. 10.36.

In an interesting twist on nonviolation nullification or impairment, a panel under the U.S.-Canada Free Trade Agreement, construing identical language, found a "violation" when the United States acted in a way that "could not reasonably have been anticipated" by Canada. The Panel ruled that the United States had nullified or impaired Canada's rights by breaking off negotiations concerning the safety of ultra-high temperature (UHT) milk even though the United States had not violated any substantive trade rule. In the Matter of Puerto Rico's Regulations on the Import, Distribution and Sale of U.H.T. Milk from Quebec, 1993 FTAPD LEXIS 18 (June 3, 1993).

---

2. *"Actionable Harm"*

In either violation or nonviolation cases, dispute settlement panels need to determine how much and what kind of trade injury (more precisely, loss of benefit) is necessary before a case is "actionable." For example, does Article III prohibit *all* discrimination or is a little discrimination acceptable? If the laws of a member adversely affect a product from one foreign producer but provide an advantage to the same product from another producer from the same country, does the advantage to the one offset the impairment of the trade opportunity to the other? How is the market effect of the trade discrimination measured?

In the early 1980s, many GATT delegates claimed that a complaining party was required to show actual cause-and-effect trade damage. Because of the more pragmatic, less legalistic approach to the GATT that prevailed at the time, this "trade damage" approach had "solid historical grounding." ROBERT HUDEC, ENFORCING INTERNATIONAL TRADE LAW 268 (1993). Nonetheless, a series of cases concerning the GATT's nondiscrimination obligations helped solidify a rule based on the maintenance of competitive opportunities, some of which are summarized in the text and footnotes of this excerpt from a WTO dispute settlement panel report.

United States-Sections 301–310 of the Trade Act of 1974
WT/DS/152/R (adopted Jan. 27, 2000)

7.71 What are the objects and purposes of the DSU, and the WTO more generally, that are relevant to a construction of Article 23? The most relevant in our view are those which relate to the creation of market conditions conducive to individual economic activity in national and global markets and to the provision of a secure and predictable multilateral trading system....

7.73 ... Many of the benefits to Members which are meant to flow as a result of the acceptance of various disciplines under the GATT/WTO depend on the activity of individual economic operators in the national and global market places. The purpose of many of these disciplines, indeed one of the primary objects of the GATT/WTO as a whole, is to produce certain market conditions which would allow this individual activity to flourish....

7.74 The very first Preamble to the WTO Agreement states that Members recognise

> "that their relations in the field of trade and economic endeavour should be conducted with a view to raising standards of living, ensuring full employment and a large and steadily growing volume of real income and effective demand, and expanding the production of and trade in goods and services".

7.75 Providing security and predictability to the multilateral trading system is another central object and purpose of the system which could be instrumental to achieving the broad objectives of the Preamble. Of all WTO disciplines, the DSU is one of the most important instruments to protect the security and predictability of the multilateral trading system and through it that of the marketplace and its different operators. DSU provisions must, thus, be interpreted in the light of this object and purpose and in a manner which would most effectively enhance it. In this respect we are referring not only to preambular language but also to positive law provisions in the DSU itself. Article 3.2 of the DSU provides:

> "The dispute settlement system of the WTO is a central element in providing security and predictability to the multilateral trading system. The Members recognize that it serves to preserve the rights and obligations of Members under the covered agreements ...".

7.76 The security and predictability in question are of "the multilateral trading system". The multilateral trading system is, per force, composed not only of States but also, indeed mostly, of individual economic operators. The lack of security and predictability affects mostly these individual operators. * * *

7.79 ... [T]here is nothing novel or radical in our analysis. We have already seen that it is rooted in the language of the WTO itself. It also represents a GATT/WTO orthodoxy confirmed in a variety of ways over the years including panel and Appellate Body reports as well as the practice of Members. * * *

7.82 Thus, Article III:2 of GATT 1947, for example, would not, on its face, seem to prohibit legislation independently from its application to specific products. However, in light of the object and purpose of the GATT, it was read in GATT jurisprudence as a promise by contracting parties not only that they would abstain from actually imposing discriminatory taxes, but also that they would not enact legislation with that effect.

7.83 It is commonplace that domestic law in force imposing discriminatory taxation on imported products would, in and of itself, violate Article III irrespective of proof of actual discrimination in a specific case.[665] Furthermore, a domestic law which exposed imported products to future discrimination was recognized by some GATT panels to constitute, by itself, a violation of Article III, even before the law came into force.[666] Finally, and most tellingly, even where there was no certainty but only a risk under the domestic law that the tax would be discriminatory, certain GATT panels found that the law violated the obligation in Article III.[667] A similar approach was followed in respect of Article II of GATT 1994 by the WTO panel on *Argentina–Textiles and Apparel (US)* when it found that the very change in system from *ad valorem* to specific duties was a breach of Argentina's *ad valorem* tariff binding even though such change only brought about the potential of the tariff binding being exceeded depending on the price of the imported product.

7.84 The rationale in all types of cases has always been the negative effect on economic operators created by such domestic laws. An individual would simply shift his or her trading patterns—buy domestic products, for example, instead of imports—so as to avoid the would-be taxes announced in the legislation or even the mere risk of discriminatory taxation. Such risk or threat, when real, was found to affect the relative competitive opportunities between imported and domestic products because it could, in and of itself, bring about a shift in consumption from imported to domestic products: This shift would be caused by, for example, an increase in the cost of imported products and a negative impact on economic planning and investment to the detriment of those products. This rationale was paraphrased in the *Superfund* case as follows:

> [5.2.2] "to protect expectations of the contracting parties as to the competitive relationship between their products and those of the other contracting parties. Both articles [GATT Articles III and XI] are not only to protect current trade but also to create the predictability needed to plan future trade".

---

665. A change in the relative competitive opportunities caused by a measure of general application as such, to the detriment of imported products and in favour of domestically produced products, is the decisive criterion.

666. In the Panel Report on *US– Superfund* (op. cit., paras. 5.2.1 and 5.2.2) tax legislation as such was found to violate GATT obligations even though the legislation had not yet entered into effect. See also the Panel Report on *US–Malt Beverages* (op. cit., paras. 5.39, 5.57, 5.60 and 5.69) where the legislation imposing the tax discrimination was, for example, not being enforced by the authorities.

667. See Panel Report on *US–Tobacco*, op. cit., para. 96:

"The Panel noted that an internal regulation which merely exposed imported products to a risk of discrimination had previously been recognized by a GATT panel to constitute, by itself, a form of discrimination, and therefore less favourable treatment within the meaning of Article III. The Panel agreed with this analysis of risk of discrimination as enunciated by this earlier panel."

A footnote to this paragraph refers to the Panel Report on *EEC–Payments and Subsidies Paid to Processors and Producers of Oilseeds and Related Animal Feed Protein*, adopted 25 January 1990, BISD 37S/86, para. 141, which reads as follows:

"Having made this finding the Panel examined whether a purchase regulation which does not necessarily discriminate against imported products but is capable of doing so is consistent with Article III:4. The Panel noted that the exposure of a particular imported product to a *risk* of discrimination constitutes, by itself, a form of discrimination. The Panel therefore concluded that purchase regulations creating such a risk must be considered to be according less favourable treatment within the meaning of Article III:4. The Panel found for these reasons that the payments to processors of Community oilseeds are inconsistent with Article III:4."

Doing so, the panel in *Superfund* referred to the reasoning in the *Japanese Measures on Imports of Leather* case. There the panel found that an import quota constituted a violation of Article XI of GATT even though the quota had not been filled. It did so on the following grounds:

> "the existence of a quantitative restriction should be presumed to cause nullification or impairment not only because of any effect it had had on the volume of trade but also for other reasons e.g. it would lead to increased transaction costs and would create uncertainties which could affect investment plans".

7.85 In this sense, Article III:2 is not only a promise not to discriminate in a specific case, but is also designed to give certain guarantees to the market place and the operators within it that discriminatory taxes will not be imposed. For the reasons given above, any ambivalence in GATT panel jurisprudence as to whether a risk of discrimination can constitute a violation should, in our view, be resolved in favour of our reading.

Questions and Discussion

1. According to this standard interpretation, the GATT and the other WTO agreements are intended to create an opportunity to compete in the marketplace; any deviation from the rules that might have an adverse effect on the competitive position of even a single foreign producer or product is held to be a nullification or impairment of the benefits of the trade agreements. Actual effects on trade flows are considered irrelevant. Robert Hudec noted the importance of eliminating an inquiry into trade damage:

> The trade damage line of cases has been critical to the development of an effective GATT adjudicatory procedure, because … there is no way to prove that a particular trade measure had any cause-and-effect impact on trade. One can identify the trade measure and gather the trade data, but there is no way to link the two in a logically valid manner. If GATT panels are to adjudicate rule violations or [nonviolation nullification and impairment] claims, they must be able to stop at showing that the measure causes a disadvantageous change in competitive opportunity.

ROBERT HUDEC, ENFORCING INTERNATIONAL TRADE LAW 269 (1993). Do the decisions of the panels make sense from a legal perspective? A trade perspective? An environmental perspective? Why might changes in trade flows not be a reliable indicator of the effect of a national measure on competition in the marketplace?

B. The DSU Process

A dispute begins with the initial logging of a complaint and a request for consultations. There is no time limit on the consultation process, but 60 days after the request, the complaining party may ask the DSB to establish a panel. From the establishment of a panel (which can take several months) to the adoption of a final report, the entire DSU process should conclude in 9 months, or in 12 months in cases of appeal. DSU, art. 20.

In early years, the WTO established an enviable record of coming very close to this self-imposed deadline. More recently, complicated facts in many cases involving, for example, anti-dumping measures or fiscal measures have led panels to request additional time, often an extra year or more. In cases where a member has been found in violation of its WTO obligations, still further time may pass before remedial steps are completed or recourse to compensation is authorized.

1. Consultations

A WTO member initiates the dispute settlement process by requesting consultations with another member under Article 4 of the DSU. (A member may also request "good offices, conciliation or mediation" under Article 5, although this is rarely done). Members undertake "to accord sympathetic consideration to and afford adequate opportunity for consultation." As a matter of GATT practice incorporated into the DSU system, consultations are deemed a prerequisite to a request for a panel, as reflected in the Article 4.7 requirement that a complaining party wait at least 60 days from its request for consultations before asking for a panel to be established. Those who have studied the results of such consultations find that they sometimes lead to settlement of disputes and sometimes help the parties to clarify the issues on which they differ. For example, the United States and Europe avoided a nasty dispute over the Helms-Burton law, a U.S. law that among other things bars trade with U.S. and foreign companies trading with Cuba, when the United States, after consultations, agreed to a presidential waiver of the offending provisions. While consultations are often *pro forma* exercises, the data of Kopczynski's study, cited above in the opening paragraphs of Section IV, show that one-third to one-half of all disputes are resolved at this stage.

2. Establishment of a Panel

If the members cannot resolve their dispute through confidential consultations, or if a member receiving a request for consultation fails to respond to the request or fails to consult in good faith, then the member requesting consultations may immediately make a written request to the DSB for the establishment of a panel, identifying the measure or measures at issue and summarizing the legal basis of the complaint. DSU, art. 6. The panel is established, if still requested, at the next DSB meeting, usually a month later. The panel has three members (in exceptional cases five), agreed to by the parties based on persons nominated by the Secretariat. If the parties cannot agree, the Director-General of the WTO, in consultation with others, names the panelists. DSU, art. 8.

The panel determines its terms of reference in consultation with the parties to the dispute, but Article 7.1 of the DSU provides standard terms of reference that are used in most cases. A panel may address only those issues that were part of the consultations and are identified in the terms of reference.

If a member brings more than one complaint about a particular measure, the multiple complaints may be combined into a single panel proceeding. DSU, art. 9. Any member having a substantial interest in the dispute may notify the DSB of its interest. Such third parties may make written submissions to the panel and are afforded an opportunity to be heard at panel proceedings. DSU, art. 10.

3. The Panel Process

The expectation and the common practice under the DSU is that the panel will submit its report within six months after it is established. The panel and the parties establish the schedule of submissions and hearings to meet that deadline. After the parties submit their first written submissions (the complaining party submits first), the panel convenes and hears oral arguments. After the hearing, the parties simultaneously submit their second written submissions, which are in essence rebuttals to the first written submissions and to the arguments made at the hearing. The panel then convenes a second hearing. DSU, art. 12. Some time after the second hearing, the panel issues an interim report on its description of the facts and the legal arguments presented, on which the disputing parties may comment. The panel then prepares a full interim report including its own findings and conclusions. The parties may request a review of certain aspects of the full interim report, which may include a meeting of the disputing parties. If the parties do not request a review, then the interim report becomes final. If a review is requested, the final report will take account of that review. DSU, art. 15.

The panel may request information from the parties or from other individuals, and it may consult with experts if it wishes. DSU, art. 13. Rules are provided for the establishment of an expert advisory group in technically complex cases. This was done, for example, in the *Shrimp/Turtle* and *EC–Hormones* disputes, and the panels referred frequently to the reports prepared by the expert groups.

4. Adopting the Decision

The DSU makes an important change from GATT's procedures that has greatly affected the results of dispute resolution. Panel reports "shall be adopted" by the DSB within 60 days of circulating the report to the members, unless a party to the dispute decides to appeal or the DSB decides *by consensus* not to adopt the report. DSU, art. 16.4. Under this structure the winning member must agree not to adopt the report. In contrast, GATT reports were adopted only if all contracting parties agreed by consensus to adopt it. Thus, the losing party could always block adoption of the report.

5. Appeals

Perhaps the most significant innovation in WTO jurisprudence made by the DSU has been the creation of the Appellate Body. The Appellate Body is a permanent group of seven trade experts, each appointed for a four-year term, renewable once. For any specific case, a division of three members sits. Only parties to the dispute, not third parties, may appeal a panel report, or aspects of it, to the Appellate Body. Article 17.6 of the DSU limits the Appellate Body's authority to issues of law covered by the panel report and legal interpretations developed by the panel. The appeals process is expedited—60 to 90 days, including submission of briefs, oral argument, and writing of the decision. The Appellate Body may affirm, reverse, or modify the report of the panel.

The Appellate Body has been actively used; about two-thirds of panel reports are appealed. As of mid-2009, the Appellate Body had issued reports in 77 separate cases, and an additional 21 reports in the so-called "recourse" proceedings under DSU art. 21.5 (*see* below under "6. Implementation"). In its 77 reports, the Appellate Body has reversed or significantly modified the legal conclusions of many panel decisions. *See, e.g., Asbestos,*

Shrimp/Turtle. As a result, the Appellate Body has become an important means for correcting analytical or reasoning errors in panel decisions that under the GATT could not be reversed because the GATT had no appeal mechanism. Equally significant, the permanent nature of the Appellate Body has allowed it to begin to formulate a coherent and consistent jurisprudence over a series of separate cases, something the *ad hoc* GATT panels were not in a position to do. Appellate Body reports are also automatically adopted ("shall be adopted by the DSB and unconditionally accepted by the parties to the dispute") within 30 days, unless the DSB decides otherwise by consensus. DSU, art. 17.14.

6. *Implementation*

If the DSB accepts a panel or Appellate Body legal conclusion that a WTO member is maintaining a measure inconsistent with its obligations under the WTO agreements, that member is expected to comply with the recommendations of the report calling for the removal of the measure or the relevant parts of the measure. As Article 21.1 of the DSU declares, "Prompt compliance with recommendations or rulings of the DSB is essential in order to ensure effective resolution of disputes to the benefit of all Members." Indeed, most international law scholars view correction of the identified violation as a general obligation under international law. Because compliance with such recommendations may involve rewriting statutes or regulations, the DSU makes allowance for a negotiated "reasonable period of time" for implementation. DSU, art. 21.3.

If the member called upon to comply with recommendations or rulings has not done so within the agreed period, or if the complaining party considers the change made by the member insufficient to remedy the violation, then the complaining party may, under Article 21.5, have "recourse" to dispute settlement—to the original panel, if possible— to get a ruling on the offending member's compliance or noncompliance with the original ruling. In *Shrimp/Turtle*, for example, the United States made some changes to its procedures and practices after the WTO decision but no change to the statute or the basic regulations. One of the complainants exercised its right to recourse, but both the Panel and the Appellate Body in the recourse proceeding found the changes made by the United States sufficient to bring the shrimp embargo provisions into compliance with the original rulings.

7. *Remedies*

For situations in which the legal problems are not corrected by the "losing" member, Article 22 of the DSU establishes clear guidance on compensation and sanctions. As a matter of principle, voluntary compensation and trade retaliation ("suspension of concessions") are permitted only as "temporary measures." DSU, art. 22.1. If the member fails to brings its laws into conformity and the parties to the dispute cannot agree on payment of satisfactory compensation, then the prevailing member may seek authorization from the DSB to "suspend concessions or other obligations," i.e., impose trade sanctions such as higher tariffs, against the losing member equal to the amount of trade lost due to the losing member's inconsistent law. DSU, art. 22.2. The DSB must grant such authorization within 30 days of the expiration of the agreed time-frame for implementation. Disagreements over the proposed level of suspension may be referred to arbitration, which in complex cases can take years. Concessions should normally be suspended in the same sector as that in issue in the case. For services and for intellectual property rights, "sector" is narrowly defined. For disputes involving trade in goods, however, "sector" is broadly defined to include "all goods." For example, despite a WTO dispute ruling that the European Union's ban on the importation of U.S. and Canadian meat that includes bovine growth hormones violates the SPS Agreement, the European Union (EU) refused to repeal the ban. The United States and Canada requested authorization from the DSB for the suspension of concessions to the EU in the amount of US$202 million and Can$75 million, respectively. After the EU asked for arbitration, the arbitrators determined the level of damages suffered to be US$116.8 million for the United States and Can$11.3 million for Canada. As a result, the United States imposed 100 percent *ad valorem* duties on several different goods from the EU, including pork, truffles, and Roquefort cheese. The same procedure has been applied in reverse by the EU against the United States in a dispute over tax benefits for exporters under U.S. law.

The availability of explicitly authorized trade sanction remedies has had a clear impact on the WTO's dispute resolution process. While the contracting parties to the GATT could vote to suspend concessions against another party found to be in violation of a GATT rule, the contracting parties did this only once. On the other hand, the trade sanction remedy can take years to implement, especially if the amount involved is subject to arbitration, and in any case will have little effect if the complaining party is a small country with low volumes of international trade. As a last resort, countries may seek other ways to achieve their objectives. One of the longest-running disputes, spanning 15 years and 14 separate dispute settlement cases, of which 6 remain unresolved, concerned the EU's complex scheme controlling the import and internal distribution of bananas. Colombia finally invoked the "good offices" of the Director-General of the WTO, as provided in DSU Article 3.12 for cases brought by a developing country against a developed country. With the personal involvement of the Director-General himself and his staff, a settlement was negotiated between Colombia and the EU, which at the time of this writing is still awaiting formal approval by the EU.

---

8. Repeal of Trade Suspensions

Although the DSU expressly contemplates the imposition of sanctions, what action on the part of the losing party requires the prevailing party to repeal those sanctions? The DSU is not clear on this subject. Article 22.8 of the DSU provides that sanctions "shall be temporary" and shall only be applied until one of the following three conditions is met:

> the measure found to be inconsistent with a covered agreement has been removed, or the Member that must implement recommendations or rulings provides a solution to the nullification or impairment of benefits, or a mutually satisfactory solution is reached.

Left unanswered is when a measure may be considered "removed," who determines when a measure is "removed," and the process for making that determination.

The Appellate Body in *Hormones II* recently had the opportunity to explore these issues. United States–Continued Suspension of Obligations in the EC–Hormones Dispute, WT/DS320/R (adopted Nov. 21, 2008); Canada–Continued Suspension of Obligations in the EC–Hormones Dispute WT/DS321/AB/R (adopted Nov. 21, 2008). In *Hormones I*, the Appellate Body concluded that the EU's prohibition against the importation of meat containing growth hormones was inconsistent with the risk assessment provisions of the

Agreement on the Application of Sanitary and Phytosanitary Measures (SPS Agreement). Starting in 1999, the United States and Canada imposed additional duties on certain EU goods when the EU failed to comply with the Appellate Body's findings. In 2003, the EU replaced Directive 96/22/EC, which the Appellate Body found inconsistent with the SPS Agreement, with Directive 2003/74/EC. The new Directive maintained the permanent import ban on meat containing the hormone oestradiol–17β and imposed a "provisional" import ban on meat containing five other hormones (testosterone, progesterone, trenbolone acetate, zeranal, and MGA).

Although the new Directive was functionally equivalent to the Directive found inconsistent with the SPS Agreement, the EU claimed it had "removed" the offending measure, that the new ban on hormone-treated beef was supported by valid risk assessments, and that the United States and Canada were impermissibly continuing trade suspensions against the EU. Has the EU removed its measure or implemented the Appellate Body's rulings in *Hormones I*? Must the United States and Canada lift their trade sanctions?

The Appellate Body began by concluding that DSU Article 22.8 "require[s] nothing less than substantive removal of the inconsistent measure." WT/DS321/AB/R, at para. 305. Replacing an offending measure with a similar one is insufficient; otherwise, a WTO member's benefits would continue to be nullified or impaired. *Id.* at paras. 304–05. The Appellate Body found support for this conclusion in the second sentence of Article 22.8, which requires surveillance by the DSB of concessions that have been suspended when the recommendations to bring a measure into conformity have not been implemented. From this, the Appellate Body concluded that authorization to suspend concessions does not lapse until substantive compliance is achieved. The Appellate Body also concluded that the effectiveness of the WTO dispute settlement mechanism would be significantly weakened if suspended concessions must be terminated before substantive compliance is achieved. *Id.* at paras. 309–10. Moreover, ascertaining whether substantive compliance has occurred necessitates a review of the conformity of the new measure with a member's WTO obligations — in this case, the SPS Agreement. *Id.* at paras. 327–32.

The Appellate Body also concluded that any of the disputing parties may initiate a claim to determine whether a measure has been "removed." The original complaining parties may initiate a recourse claim under Article 21.5 that the new measure is inconsistent with the recommendations and rulings of the DSB, or the original responding party may initiate a claim alleging that the continued suspensions are unlawful pursuant to Article 22.8. *Id.* at paras. 347, 352.

Questions and Discussion

1. *The Appellate Body's Reach.* While the creation of the Appellate Body must be seen as a very positive step in trade disputes and in international law generally, it suffers from some constitutional defects. One issue currently without a perfect answer relates to mixed questions of law and fact. Recall that panels are constituted only for the purpose of hearing a specific dispute. Once a panel issues its report, the panel is dissolved. The panel can be reconstituted only for recourse proceedings under Article 21.5; the Appellate Body cannot "remand" to the panel for further proceedings. Thus, if the Appellate Body reverses a legal decision of the panel, what happens when the new legal approach requires determination of facts not found in the panel's report? Does the Appellate Body have "ancillary jurisdiction" to make its own findings of fact? Two provisions of the DSU are

relevant. First, the Appellate Body's powers under Article 17.6 of the DSU are limited to "issues of law" and "legal interpretations." Suppose that the panel, having made certain legal conclusions, fails to examine a separate legal issue? By its terms, the DSU seems to limit the Appellate Body to issues of law "covered in the panel report" and legal interpretations "developed by the panel." A second issue arises in considering whether the panel had complied with Article 11 of the DSU, which requires the panel to make "an objective assessment of the facts of the case and the applicability of and conformity with the relevant covered agreements." What should the Appellate Body do if the appeal raises a question about how the panel assessed the "facts of the case"?

The Appellate Body addressed the first of these issues squarely in the *Shrimp/Turtle* dispute, in which several Southeast Asian countries challenged U.S. restrictions on imports of shrimp due to failures to adopt sea turtle conservation laws (sea turtles often die in shrimpers' nets). In this case, the United States sought to justify the restrictions under Article XX(g) for measures relating to the conservation of exhaustible natural resources. The Panel, however, concluded that the U.S. import restrictions did not meet the discrimination requirements of the Article XX exceptions and thus never determined whether they were consistent with Article XX(g). The Appellate Body reversed, noting that panels must first determine whether a trade restriction is justifiable under one of the ten specific exceptions under Article XX such as XX(g) and then determine whether the restriction meets the discrimination requirements of Article XX.

> 123. Having reversed the Panel's legal conclusion that the United States measure at issue "is not within the scope of measures permitted under the chapeau of Article XX," we believe that it is our duty and our responsibility to complete the legal analysis in this case in order to determine whether Section 609 qualifies for justification under Article XX. In doing this, we are fully aware of our jurisdiction and mandate under Article 17 of the DSU. We have found ourselves in similar situations on a number of occasions. Most recently, in *European Communities-Measures Affecting the Importation of Certain Poultry Products,* we stated:
>
> > In certain appeals, ... the reversal of a panel's finding on a legal issue may require us to make a finding on a legal issue which was not addressed by the panel.
>
> In that case, having reversed the panel's finding on Article 5.1(b) of the *Agreement on Agriculture,* we completed the legal analysis by making a finding on the consistency of the measure at issue with Article 5.5 of the *Agreement on Agriculture.* Similarly, in *Canada-Certain Measures Concerning Periodicals,* having reversed the panel's findings on the issue of "like products" under the first sentence of Article III:2 of the GATT 1994, we examined the consistency of the measure with the second sentence of Article III:2. And, in *United States-Gasoline,* having reversed the panel's findings on the first part of Article XX(g) of the GATT 1994, we completed the analysis of the terms of Article XX(g), and then examined the application of the measure at issue in that case under the chapeau of Article XX.
>
> 124. As in those previous cases, we believe it is our responsibility here to examine the claim by the United States for justification of Section 609 under Article XX in order properly to resolve this dispute between the parties. We do this, in part, recognizing that Article 3.7 of the DSU emphasizes that: "The aim of the dispute settlement mechanism is to secure a positive solution to a dispute." For-

tunately, in the present case, as in the mentioned previous cases, we believe that the facts on the record of the panel proceedings permit us to undertake the completion of the analysis required to resolve this dispute.

United States-Import Prohibition of Certain Shrimp and Shrimp Products, Appellate Body Report, WT/DS58/AB/R (adopted Nov. 6, 1998), *reprinted in* 38 I.L.M. 121 (1999).

Do you agree with the Appellate Body that it may address legal issues not addressed by the panel in order to "complete the analysis," because "[t]he aim of the dispute settlement mechanism is to secure a positive solution to a dispute"? Or do you think that the Appellate Body is just making the best out of a situation for which the DSU fails to provide an adequate solution? If the latter, what should be done to fix this problem?

Former Appellate Body member Mitsuo Matsushita points out a due process weakness of the DSU Article 17.6 dilemma. In *Canada-Periodicals*, mentioned in the *Shrimp/Turtle* excerpt above, the Appellate Body decided to apply GATT Article III:2(2) only after the oral argument. Because DSU procedures make no provision for an additional oral hearing, the parties had no opportunity to brief this new issue. Mitsuo Matsushita, *Some Thoughts on the Appellate Body*, in 1 THE WORLD TRADE ORGANIZATION: LEGAL, ECONOMIC AND POLITICAL ANALYSIS 1389 (Patrick F.J. Macrory et al. eds., 2006).

On the Article 11 problem of mixed questions of fact and law, Matsushita cites the *EC-Hormones I* report, EC-Measures Concerning Meat and Meat Products, Appellate Body Report, WT/DS26/AB/R, WT/DS48/AB/R (adopted Feb. 13, 1998). One of the claims by the EU on appeal was that the panel had ignored some evidence and distorted other evidence about carcinogenicity of hormones in violation of Article 11. This required the Appellate Body itself to review all the evidence (the facts) in order to determine (as a matter of law) whether the panel had been "fair and objective" in its approach to the facts. Notably, similar problems with the panel's review of the evidence came up in *Hormones II*, but because of the complexity of the scientific issues involved, the Appellate Body decided *not* to substitute its own reading of the facts. Because the DSU lacks a remand procedure, the effect is that *Hormones II* ends without a clear outcome, leaving *Hormones I* as the governing determination between the parties.

2. *Third Party Rights.* Article 17.4 of the DSU specifically states that "[o]nly parties, not third parties, may appeal" a panel report but that third parties may make written submissions if a disputing party does appeal. However, the DSU does not make clear if third parties may make submissions only with respect to those issues appealed by the parties or whether they may appeal issues of law not appealed by the parties. Rule 24.1 of the *Working Procedures for Appellate Review* states that a third party may include in its submission "the grounds and legal arguments in support of its position." WTO, Appellate Body, WT/AB/WP/5 (Jan. 4, 2005). By not limiting the arguments of third parties to those appealed by the principal disputing parties, Rule 24 suggests that third parties may appeal any issue contained in the panel report. Is the Appellate Body obligated to address issues raised independently by third parties?

3. Do you think binding dispute settlement is somehow more appropriate than "negotiation and diplomacy" for resolving trade disputes? Recall that the GATT began with no formal procedure for dispute settlement, relying heavily on negotiation and on investigations by "working parties" of other contracting parties. Professor John Jackson, an advocate for the more rules-based approach of the DSU, has argued that the negotiation and diplomacy approach is a "power orientation" that favors larger and more developed countries compared with the more objective and even-handed "rule orientation" of the DSU. Matthew Dunne questions whether such a dichotomy exists; the "Bananas War" to

which he refers below was a case successfully brought by some Latin American countries against a byzantine import and distribution scheme for bananas in Europe that favors bananas from former European colonies in the Caribbean and Africa.

> The Bananas War demonstrates that power orientation and rule orientation are not mutually exclusive. On the one hand, the repeated rulings in favor of low-power states demonstrate the rule-oriented nature of the GATT/WTO dispute settlement system. On the other hand, the EC's successful effort to delay and frustrate the implementation of the panel and AB rulings was a naked exercise of aggregate structural power that vividly illustrates the power-oriented nature of the GATT/WTO dispute settlement system. These aspects of the Bananas War indicate that power orientation and rule orientation can coexist within the same system.

Matthew S. Dunne, III, *Redefining Power Orientation: A Reassessment of Jackson's Paradigm in Light of Asymmetries of Power, Negotiation, and Compliance in the GATT/WTO Dispute Settlement System*, 34 Law & Pol'y Int'l Bus. 277, 325 (2002).

4. Is it possible that the rule orientation of Jackson and others is overly centered on the American experience? Joost Pauwelyn, who has served in the WTO Legal Affairs Division, has written that there are "dark sides" to the "Americanization" of the WTO dispute settlement. For one, it brings "too much law" to the litigation stage (the panel and Appellate Body process) and "not enough law" to pre-dispute consultations and to post-dispute compliance. Pauwelyn would prefer a process in which consultation played a more significant role in the amicable and less formal resolution of disputes. He argues that the legalization of the panel process may hamper resolution of the dispute. Joost Pauwelyn, *The Limits of Litigation: "Americanization" and Negotiation in the Settlement of WTO Disputes*, 19 Ohio St. J. on Disp. Resol. 121 (2003). Do Pauwelyn's arguments sound familiar? In trade and environment disputes, which system do you think would be more likely to lead to environmentally favorable results? Pauwelyn proposes strengthening the consultation procedures both before establishing a panel and before pursuing a recourse proceeding. Do you think that would either reduce the number of litigated disputes through settlement or lead to greater compliance in trade and environment cases? If either the refusal to negotiate or the refusal to comply is due in part to domestic politics, will procedural reforms at the WTO have any effect? Does allowing domestic politics to exert a strong influence help in bringing the environmental perspective forward?

5. Joost Pauwelyn claims that, "[N]egotiated settlements are sometimes the only way out of state-to-state disputes, even those that did go all of the way through litigation." Dunne agrees:

> A growing body of literature argues that strict rule orientation is "counterproductive" and that better results can be obtained through a greater use of soft law measures. Instead of "formally binding obligations," soft law relies on "agreed-upon principles and objectives, and 'a considerable degree of discretion in interpretation and on how and when to conform to the requirements is left to the participants.'" Problems of noncompliance are resolved through the use of transparency (e.g., public exposure of noncompliant behavior), authoritative interpretation of agreements by neutral bodies, capacity building, persuasion, negotiation, and shaming. In sum, the "managerial" approach is "discursive, nonconfrontational, forward-looking, and broadly cooperative."

Matthew S. Dunne, III, *Redefining Power Orientation*, at 336. As noted above in section IV.B.7., Colombia eventually used the "good offices" mechanism to negotiate a settlement of its bananas dispute. In a report on this process to the DSB, the Director-General promotes the flexibility of negotiated settlement, expressly asserting that it is not a "purely legal process." Report of the Director-General, WT/DS361/2, para. 1. With respect to environmental policy, do you agree with Pauwelyn and Dunne?

6. *Dispute Resolution in Multilateral Environmental Treaties.* In creating a binding, rules-based dispute resolution mechanism, the WTO differs from traditional dispute resolution processes of multilateral environmental agreements (MEAs). While most MEAs include provisions for binding dispute resolution, those provisions require the consent of both parties to the dispute. For example, Article XVIII of the Convention on International Trade in Endangered Species of Wild Fauna and Flora (CITES) requires negotiation between two parties to a dispute, but if negotiation fails, the parties "may, by mutual consent, submit the dispute" to binding arbitration. Other MEAs, such as the Montreal Protocol on Substances that Deplete the Ozone Layer and the Convention on Biological Diversity, allow a country the discretion to choose arbitration or submission of the dispute to the International Court of Justice (ICJ). In any event, the jurisdiction of the ICJ is consensual, not mandatory. In contrast to the extremely active DSB, no MEA dispute has been referred to binding arbitration or the ICJ. We return to the relationship between MEAs and the WTO in Chapter 9.

7. Some environmental advocates clearly see the WTO's DSB as a model for enforcing international environmental rules and treaties, an idea that has yet to take hold. *See* Daniel C. Esty, Greening the GATT: Trade, Environment, and the Future 78–82, 85–86 (1993). If countries will not agree to binding dispute settlement within MEAs, why would they agree to it within the WTO? Nonetheless, parties to MEAs appear to be moving away from a reliance on diplomacy and negotiation in dealing with noncompliance. CITES has institutionalized a process for recommending sanctions against a party that has failed to properly implement its obligations. CITES, Resolution Conf. 14.3, *Compliance Procedures* (2004). The Montreal Protocol has created an Implementation Committee that has recommended the withdrawal of a party's "Article 5" status, a status that gives a Party grace periods for implementing the Protocol's obligations and gives them access to funds from the Protocol's Multilateral Fund. *See* David G. Victor, *The Operation and Effectiveness of the Montreal Protocol's Non-Compliance Procedure, in* The Implementation and Effectiveness of International Environmental Commitments 137–76 (David G. Victor et al. eds., 1998). What are the advantages of a binding rules-based approach to dispute resolution for both trade and environmental disputes? What are the disadvantages?

8. *DSB Activity.* With more than 405 disputes initiated in the WTO as of May 2010, the DSB has been extremely active. The disputes have covered several different agreements: the Agreement on Technical Barriers to Trade, the SPS Agreement, the GATT, and the Agreement on Trade-related Aspects of Intellectual Property Rights, among others. In addition, while the majority of disputes still involve the United States, the EU, and Japan either as a complainant or "defendant," a growing number of disputes are between developing countries. *See, e.g.,* Mexico-Antidumping Duties on Steel Pipes and Tubes from Guatemala, WT/DS331 (adopted July 24, 2007) (agreeing with Guatemala that Mexico violated the Anti-Dumping Agreement); Thailand-Customs and Fiscal Measures on Cigarettes from the Philippines, WT/DS371 (initiated by the Philippines; panel report due in mid-2010). For more information on the status of cases and access to all reports, visit the WTO's website at http://www.wto.org/english/tratop_e/dispu_e/ dispu_e.htm#disputes.

C. Transparency, Democracy, and the DSB

Prior to the creation of the WTO and the DSB, environmental and labor advocates strongly criticized GATT panels for their undemocratic and secretive proceedings. Mickey Kantor, the former U.S. Trade Representative, called GATT panels "star chambers." Under GATT rules, GATT contracting parties did not need to notify their own citizens when laws were challenged. Citizens had no right to participate or even attend hearings relating to disputes in which their own countries were participating—the proceedings were conducted in complete secrecy. Not even contracting parties who were not part of the dispute could attend the hearings. Citizens could not submit information to a panel. Citizens could not obtain pleadings in a dispute. The United States finally began to release its submissions when nongovernmental organizations successfully sued the Office of the United States Trade Representative, the U.S. agency responsible for trade policy and negotiations, under the Freedom of Information Act. Public Citizen v. United States Trade Rep., 804 F.Supp. 385 (D.D.C. 1992). Only if the GATT contracting parties unanimously approved the decision of a GATT panel were decisions made public.

Considering the controversy surrounding the secretive nature of the GATT panel proceedings, most environmental advocates heavily criticized the new DSB as business as usual. Robert F. Housman, for example, argued that the WTO Agreement "carries over GATT's undemocratic ways in the troubling area of dispute settlement" and predicting that "it is unlikely the public will gain access to the decisions in GATT disputes." *Democratizing International Trade Decision-Making*, 27 Cornell Int'l L.J. 699, 713 (1994). Housman's pessimistic prediction proved incorrect: every final report of dispute settlement panels and the Appellate Body is made public and a full text is immediately posted on the WTO website. His prediction about availability of government briefs or summaries of government legal arguments was also unduly pessimistic, at least with respect to submissions involving the United States. The United States continues to follow a practice of making nearly full texts of its submissions publicly available, with redactions only to protect confidential business information or confidential statements by other governments. *See* USTR, Dispute Settlement Proceedings, *at* http://www.ustr.gov/trade-topics/enforcement/dispute-settlement-proceedings. The U.S. government has also actively coordinated with environmental NGOs on the drafting of the official U.S. submission and has on occasion appended *amicus* briefs prepared by NGOs to its own briefs so that the briefs are available to the panel. Finally, the style of the written panel and Appellate Body reports has been to provide an exhaustive account of every party's legal arguments, frequently taken *verbatim* from the party's own briefs. In this way, substantial portions of all government briefs become a matter of public record.

Transparency is far from perfect, however. One remaining concern is the lack of public access to dispute settlement proceedings. James Bacchus, who served on the Appellate Body for eight years, called for reforms to lift the veil of secrecy that covers many decisionmaking processes at the international trade body: "There is no reason for WTO proceedings to remain secret, and there is every reason for them to be open to the light of public scrutiny. It is only because the doors are closed that the critics of the WTO can claim any credibility at all in referring to the WTO as a 'star chamber' or as a 'kangaroo court.'" James Bacchus, *Open Up the WTO*, Wash. Post, Feb. 20, 2004, at A25.

1. Public Access to Dispute Settlement Proceedings

In response to such observations and continuing public pressure, some panels and the Appellate Body have made modest steps forward at the request of the parties to some disputes. The first breakthrough came in the panel proceedings in the disputes initiated by the European Communities against the United States and Canada regarding their continuing suspension of trade obligations toward the European Communities as a result of the WTO ruling in the original *EC-Hormones* case. The principal parties agreed that the oral hearings before the panel should be open to public observation. Many third parties in the case disagreed. In its reports, excerpted below, the panel gives the legal analysis behind its decision to open the oral arguments and the meeting with the outside experts to public viewing.

United States-Continued Suspension of Obligations in the EC-Hormones Dispute
Panel Report, WT/DS320R (adopted Nov. 14, 2008)

7.40 On 1 August 2005, the Panel decided to accept the parties' joint request to open the Panel hearings for public observation. The Panel also decided that the meetings at which the parties are invited to appear, as referred to in paragraph 2 of Appendix 3 to the DSU, would be open for observation by the public through a closed-circuit broadcast, keeping in mind the Panel's obligation to ensure that its Working Procedures are objective, impartial and non-discriminatory, and after careful consideration of the existing provisions of the DSU and its Appendix 3. In addition, since not all third parties had agreed that their session with the Panel be open for observation by the public, the Panel decided that that session would remain closed. * * *

7.42 After the Panel decided to consult scientific experts, the opinion of the parties was sought on whether they wished that any meeting with the parties and the scientific experts also be open for public observation. The parties replied affirmatively.

7.43 Since this was the first time in GATT/WTO history that a panel has held hearings open for public observation, the Panel deems it appropriate to elaborate further on the reasons why it agreed to open its substantive meetings for public observation.

7.44 The Panel first wishes to recall that it acted at the joint request of the parties. Some third parties, however, objected to the holding of a hearing that would be observable by the public. As a result, the hearing with third parties was not opened to public observation.

7.45 The Panel considers that the DSU does not expressly contemplate the possibility for meetings of panels to be open for public observation. On the contrary, Paragraph 2 of Appendix 3 to the DSU provides that "the panel shall meet in closed session" and that "The parties to the dispute, and interested parties, shall be present at the meeting only when invited by the panel to appear before it." The Panel understands this to mean that it shall always meet in camera, whether or not the parties and/or interested parties have been invited to appear before it. No reference is made in that provision to other Members or to the general public.

7.46 However, Article 12.1 of the DSU provides that "[p]anels shall follow the Working Procedures in Appendix 3 unless the panel decides otherwise after consulting the parties to the dispute." In other words, the Panel has the possibility to depart from any provision of Appendix 3, its only obligation being to consult the parties to the dispute first.

7.47 This discretion, however, applies only to the provisions of the Working Procedures in Appendix 3, not to any other provision of the DSU. The Panel thus is of the view that Article 12.1 entitles it to proceed with any adaptation of the working procedures contained in Appendix 3, as long as such an adaptation is not expressly prohibited by any provision of the DSU. Therefore, we need to examine whether there is any DSU provision that would explicitly prohibit the opening of panel meetings to public observation.

7.48 The Panel notes in this respect the confidentiality requirements contained in Articles 14.1, 18.2 and Appendix 3, paragraph 3 to the DSU. It also recalls the obligations of its members pursuant to the Rules of Conduct for the Understanding on Rules and Procedures Governing the Settlement of Disputes.

7.49 Regarding the requirement in Article 14.1 of the DSU that "[p]anel deliberations shall be confidential", the Panel first notes that one of the ordinary meanings of the word "deliberations" is "careful consideration, weighing up with a view to decision". The term "deliberations" also applies to "[c]onsideration and discussion of a question by a legislative assembly, a committee, etc.; debate". However, the Panel is not of the view that a panel hearing is similar to a consideration by a legislative body or a committee. Even though exchanges of points of view take place in both instances, the nature of the exchange of arguments by parties to a dispute before an adjudicating body remains different from that of an assembly or a committee. This suggests that the term "deliberation" was not intended to cover the exchange of arguments between the parties, but rather the internal discussion of the Panel with a view to reach its conclusions. We note that our interpretation of the term "deliberation" conforms to the use of that term in the statutes of other international judicial bodies. It is also confirmed by the context of Article 14.1. Article 14 deals with confidentiality in the work of panels *stricto sensu* (deliberations, drafting of the panel report, opinions of panelists), whereas the provisions dealing with the conduct of the proceedings with the parties are contained in Article 12. The Panel therefore concludes that Article 14.1 of the DSU does not apply to panel hearings and that opening the Panel's substantive meetings with the parties to public observation does not breach that provision.

7.50 Regarding the requirement contained in Article 18.2 of the DSU that "[w]ritten submissions to the panel ... shall be treated as confidential", we note that, by opening its hearings to public observation, the Panel did not disclose to the public the content of the parties' written submissions. By making statements to which the public could listen, the parties themselves exercised their right under Article 18.2 to "disclos[e] statements of [their] own positions to the public".... The Panel notes also that Article 18.2 provides that "Members shall treat as confidential information submitted by another Member to the Panel or the Appellate Body which that Member has designated as confidential." We consider that this sentence clarifies the scope of the confidentiality requirement which applies to the Panel and to Members, and that panels have to keep confidential only the information that has been designated as confidential or which has otherwise not been disclosed to the public. Any other interpretation would imply a double standard, whereby panels would have to treat as confidential information which a WTO Member does not have to treat as confidential. The Panel also notes that, by requesting that the Panel hold hearings open to public observation, the parties to this dispute have implicitly accepted that their arguments be public, with the exception of those they would identify as confidential.

7.51 Finally, the Panel notes that Article VII of the Rules of Conduct for the Understanding on the Rules and Procedures Governing the Settlement of Disputes provides that "[e]ach covered person shall at all times maintain the confidentiality of dispute settlement deliberations and proceedings together with any information identified by a party as confidential." ... In this case, the parties waived their right to confidentiality and requested open hearings.... [T]he Rules of Conduct should not be construed in a manner that would restrict the rights of Members under the DSU. The Panel concludes that Article VII does not prevent the Panel from holding hearings open to observation by the public.

7.52 The Panel is mindful that the issue of transparency of panel and Appellate Body proceedings is currently under review as part of the negotiations on improvements and clarifications of the DSU. However, the Panel recalls that the dispute settlement system of the WTO serves to preserve the rights and obligations of Members under the covered agreements, which include the DSU, and to clarify the existing provisions of those agreements in accordance with customary rules of interpretation of public international law. The Panel considers that its role is not to address transparency in general terms, but to determine whether the DSU as it currently stands permits that, under the circumstances of this particular case, the Panel hearing be open to public observation. When called upon to decide on whether to open hearings to public observation, the Panel concluded that this was the case. However, this finding is limited to this particular case and is without prejudice to any approach to the issue of transparency that the Members may negotiate.

7.53 For the reasons set out in the previous paragraphs, the Panel considers that it is entitled, under the particular circumstances of this case and pursuant to Article 12.1 of the DSU, to open its hearings for public observation. This is why the Panel decided to accept the parties' request to open its meetings with the parties for public observation. The third-party session was, however, not open to public observation, due to the absence of consensus among the third parties on this matter.

7.54 The first substantive hearing with the parties was held on 12, 13 and 15 September 2005. The hearing with third parties took place on 14 September 2005. The hearing with the scientific experts was held on 27–28 September 2006. The second substantive meeting with the parties was held on 2 and 3 October 2006.

On appeal in the same dispute, the Appellate Body also decided for the first time to allow closed-circuit broadcast of the oral hearing before the Appellate Body. The following excerpts from the Appellate Body's procedural ruling shed light on some additional issues at stake.

WTO Appellate Body, Procedural Ruling Concerning the Opening of the Oral Hearing to Public Observation in United States-Continued Suspension and Canada-Continued Suspension
WT/DS320/AB/R, Annex IV (2008)

1. ... [W]e invited the third participants to comment in writing on the requests of Canada, the European Communities, and the United States. In particular, we

asked third parties to provide their views on the permissibility of opening the hearing under the DSU and the Working Procedures, and, if they so wished, on the specific logistical arrangements proposed in the requests.... According to [some of the] third participants, the oral hearing forms part of the proceedings of the Appellate Body and, therefore, is subject to the requirement of Article 17.10 of the DSU that "[t]he proceedings of the Appellate Body shall be confidential." * * *

4. The third participants that object to the request to allow public observation argue that the confidentiality requirement in Article 17.10 is absolute and permits of no derogation. We disagree with this interpretation because Article 17.10 must be read in context, particularly in relation to Article 18.2 of the DSU. The second sentence of Article 18.2 expressly provides that "[n]othing in this Understanding shall preclude a party to a dispute from disclosing statements of its own positions to the public". Thus, under Article 18.2, the parties may decide to forego confidentiality protection in respect of their statements of position. With the exception of India, the participants and third participants agreed that the term "statements of its own positions" in Article 18.2 extends beyond the written submissions referred to in the first sentence of Article 18.2, and includes oral statements and responses to questions posed by the Appellate Body at the oral hearing.... Thus, Article 18.2 provides contextual support for the view that the confidentiality rule in Article 17.10 is not absolute. Otherwise, no disclosure of written submissions or other statements would be permitted during any stage of the proceedings.

5. In practice, the confidentiality requirement in Article 17.10 has its limits. Notices of Appeal and Appellate Body reports are disclosed to the public. Appellate Body reports contain summaries of the participants' and third participants' written and oral submissions and frequently quote directly from them. Public disclosure of Appellate Body reports is an inherent and necessary feature of our rules-based system of adjudication. Consequently, under the DSU, confidentiality is relative and time-bound. * * *

7. We note that the DSU does not specifically provide for an oral hearing at the appellate stage. The oral hearing was instituted by the Appellate Body in its Working Procedures, which were drawn up pursuant to Article 17.9 of the DSU. The conduct and organization of the oral hearing falls within the authority of the Appellate Body (compétence de la compétence) pursuant to Rule 27 of the Working Procedures. Thus, the Appellate Body has the power to exercise control over the conduct of the oral hearing, including authorizing the lifting of confidentiality at the joint request of the participants as long as this does not adversely affect the rights and interests of the third participants or the integrity of the appellate process.

* * *

9. The Appellate Body has fostered the active participation of third parties in the appellate process in drawing up the Working Procedures and in appeal practice. Article 17.4 provides that third participants "may make written submissions to, and be given an opportunity to be heard by, the Appellate Body." In its Working Procedures, the Appellate Body has given full effect to this right by providing for participation of third participants during the entirety of the oral hearing, while third parties meet with panels only in a separate session at the first substantive meet-

ing. Third participants, however, are not the main parties to a dispute.... In order to sustain their objections to public observation of the oral hearing, third participants would have to identify a specific interest in their relationship with the Appellate Body that would be adversely affected if we were to authorize the participants' request—in this case, we can discern no such interests.

10. The request for public observation of the oral hearing has been made jointly by the three participants, Canada, the European Communities, and the United States. As we explained earlier, the Appellate Body has the power to authorize a joint request by the participants to lift confidentiality, provided that this does not affect the confidentiality of the relationship between the third participants and the Appellate Body, or impair the integrity of the appellate process. The participants have suggested alternative modalities that allow for public observation of the oral hearing, while safeguarding the confidentiality protection enjoyed by the third participants. The modalities include simultaneous or delayed closed-circuit television broadcasting in a room separate from the room used for the oral hearing. Finally, we do not see the public observation of the oral hearing, using the means described above, as having an adverse impact on the integrity of the adjudicative functions performed by the Appellate Body.

11. For these reasons, the Division authorizes the public observation of the oral hearing in these proceedings on the terms set out below. Accordingly, pursuant to Rule 16(1) of the Working Procedures, we adopt the following additional procedures for the purposes of these appeals:

a. The oral hearing will be open to public observation by means of simultaneous closed-circuit television. The closed-circuit television signal will be shown in a separate room to which duly-registered delegates of WTO Members and members of the general public will have access.

b. Oral statements and responses to questions by third participants wishing to maintain the confidentiality of their submissions will not be subject to public observation.

c. Any third participant that has not already done so may request authorization to disclose its oral statements and responses to questions on the basis of paragraph (a), set out above. Such requests must be received by the Appellate Body Secretariat no later than 5:30 p.m. on 18 July 2008.

d. An appropriate number of seats will be reserved for delegates of WTO Members in the room where the closed-circuit broadcast will be shown.

e. Notice of the oral hearing will be provided to the general public through the WTO website. WTO delegates and members of the general public wishing to observe the oral hearing will be required to register in advance with the WTO Secretariat.

f. Should practical considerations not allow simultaneous broadcast of the oral hearing, deferred showing of the video recording will be used in the alternative.

––––––––––

Panels and the Appellate Body have since made similar rulings in other cases. The United States tallied 8 panel hearings allowing public observation by mid-2008. Trade Policy Review: Report by the United States, WT/TPR/G/200 (2008). The USTR website shows two others in 2009 for which public viewing was allowed.

There is even less transparency in the arbitration tribunals that hear disputes between investors and governments under trade and investment agreements, though there, too, there are recent initiatives to make the proceedings more accessible. *See* the discussion in Chapter 10.

---

2. *Amicus Curiae* Briefs

The secretive nature of the WTO's dispute settlement and meetings of the Ministerial Conference was one of the galvanizing issues that brought tens of thousands of protesters to WTO's Seattle Ministerial meeting in November 1999. One of the easiest ways to enhance participation in dispute settlement, one would think, would be to allow submissions to panels and the Appellate Body of briefs from *amicus curiae* ("friend of the court"), whether environmental NGOs or other groups with something at stake. At odds with the "lesson" of Seattle, though, the WTO members have objected to efforts by the Appellate Body to move in this direction.

In *Shrimp/Turtle*, the Appellate Body ruled that panels were not prohibited from accepting and reviewing *amicus curiae* briefs. *Shrimp/Turtle*, Appellate Body Report, para. 110. The Appellate Body ruled that:

> authority to *seek* information [pursuant to articles 11–13 of the DSU] is not properly equated with a *prohibition* on accepting information which has been submitted without having been requested by a panel. A panel has the discretionary authority either to accept and consider or to reject information and advice submitted to it, *whether requested by a panel or not*. The fact that a panel may *motu proprio* have initiated the request for information does not, by itself, bind the panel to accept and consider the information which is actually submitted.

Id. at para. 108 (emphasis in original). Do you agree both on the right to accept the briefs and on the right to ignore them? Subsequent decisions in environmental and other disputes have affirmed the right of NGOs and businesses to submit *amicus curiae* briefs to the Appellate Body. Consider the following analysis, from the key case in this trend toward openness.

United States-Imposition of Countervailing Duties on Certain Hot-Rolled Lead and Bismuth Carbon Steel Products Originating in the United Kingdom

Appellate Body Report, WT/DS138/AB/R (adopted June 7, 2000)

36. On 7 February 2000, we received two documents, described in their respective covering letters as "*amicus curiae* briefs," from the American Iron and Steel Institute and the Specialty Steel Industry of North America. On 15 February 2000, the European Communities filed a letter arguing that these *amicus curiae* briefs are "inadmissible" in appellate review proceedings, and stating that it did not intend to respond to the content of the briefs. According to the European Communities, the basis for allowing *amicus curiae* briefs in *panel* proceedings is Article 13 of the DSU, as explained in *United States-Shrimp*. The European Communities notes that Article 13 of the DSU does not apply to the Appellate Body and that, in any case, that provision is limited to *factual information and*

technical advice, and would not include *legal arguments or legal interpretations* received from non-Members. Furthermore, the European Communities contends, neither the DSU nor the *Working Procedures* allow *amicus curiae* briefs to be admitted in Appellate Body proceedings, given that Article 17.4 of the DSU and Rules 21, 22 and 28.1 of the *Working Procedures* confine participation in an appeal to participants and third participants, and that Article 17.10 of the DSU provides for the confidentiality of Appellate Body proceedings.

37.... Brazil, in its third participant's submission, and Mexico, in a letter submitted to us on 23 February 2000, agree with the European Communities that the Appellate Body does not have the authority to accept *amicus curiae* briefs.... Mexico underlines that the DSU and the *Working Procedures* limit participation in appellate proceedings and require those proceedings to be confidential....

38. In a letter submitted on 23 February 2000, the United States argues that the Appellate Body has the authority to accept *amicus curiae* briefs, and urges us to accept the briefs submitted by the steel industry associations. The United States notes that, in *United States-Shrimp*, the Appellate Body explained that the authority to accept unsolicited submissions is found in the DSU's grant to a panel of "*ample and extensive authority to undertake and to control the process* by which it informs itself both of the relevant facts of the dispute and of the legal norms and principles applicable to such facts." To the United States, it is clear that the Appellate Body also has such authority, given that Article 17.9 of the DSU authorizes the Appellate Body to draw up its own working procedures, and Rule 16(1) of the *Working Procedures* authorizes a division to create an appropriate procedure when a question arises that is not covered by the *Working Procedures*. The United States does not agree that acceptance of an unsolicited *amicus curiae* brief would compromise the confidentiality of the Appellate Body proceedings, or give greater rights to a non-WTO Member than to WTO Members that are not participants or third participants in an appeal.

39. In considering this matter, we first note that nothing in the DSU or the *Working Procedures* specifically provides that the Appellate Body may accept and consider submissions or briefs from sources other than the participants and third participants in an appeal. On the other hand, neither the DSU nor the *Working Procedures* explicitly prohibit acceptance or consideration of such briefs. However, Article 17.9 of the DSU provides:

> Working procedures shall be drawn up by the Appellate Body in consultation with the Chairman of the DSB and the Director-General, and communicated to the Members for their information.

This provision makes clear that the Appellate Body has broad authority to adopt procedural rules which do not conflict with any rules and procedures in the DSU or the covered agreements. Therefore, we are of the opinion that as long as we act consistently with the provisions of the DSU and the covered agreements, we have the legal authority to decide whether or not to accept and consider any information that we believe is pertinent and useful in an appeal.

40. We wish to emphasize that in the dispute settlement system of the WTO, the DSU envisages *participation* in panel or Appellate Body proceedings, as a matter of legal right, *only* by parties and third parties to a dispute. And, under the DSU, *only* Members of the WTO have a legal right to participate as parties or third parties in a particular dispute....

41. Individuals and organizations, which are not Members of the WTO, have no legal *right* to make submissions to or to be heard by the Appellate Body. The Appellate Body has no legal *duty* to accept or consider unsolicited *amicus curiae* briefs submitted by individuals or organizations, not Members of the WTO. The Appellate Body has a legal *duty* to accept and consider *only* submissions from WTO Members which are parties or third parties in a particular dispute.

42. We are of the opinion that we have the legal authority under the DSU to accept and consider *amicus curiae* briefs in an appeal in which we find it pertinent and useful to do so. In this appeal, we have not found it necessary to take the two *amicus curiae* briefs filed into account in rendering our decision.

———————

Note that the Appellate Body asserts the right to receive and consider *amicus* briefs but declines to take the two briefs in the case into consideration. This is characteristic of the Appellate Body's practice—keeping open its option to use information and arguments offered to it, but exercising that right sparingly. Does this support Matthew Dunne's view that the DSB can accommodate both a "power orientation" and a "rule orientation"?

Despite the apparent breakthrough for the filing of *amicus* briefs, panels and the Appellate Body are reluctant to consider them. In fact, even when the Appellate Body solicited *amicus* briefs in *EU-Measures Affecting Asbestos*, it refused to consider all of the 11 briefs that met the procedural guidelines it had established, though the *Asbestos* Panel took into account two of the five *amicus* briefs submitted to it. The Appellate Body did not explain its reasoning, but it is widely accepted that the Appellate Body rejected the briefs after receiving a stinging rebuke from many WTO members during an "extraordinary Council meeting" called to discuss the Appellate Body's invitation. *See* Petros C. Mavroidis, *Amicus Curiae Briefs Before the WTO: Much Ado About Nothing* (Jean Monnet Working Paper, February 2001).

Despite the minimal degree of consideration of *amicus* briefs, many WTO members have argued against the Appellate Body's procedures in the DSB. In particular, some argue that the ability of NGOs to submit *amicus* briefs may give NGOs greater rights than WTO members. These members have argued that WTO members that are not party to the dispute cannot participate because they must reserve third-party rights within 10 days of a panel's establishment or lose their rights. The Appellate Body disposed of that argument, however, in the *Sardines* dispute. In that case, Morocco had not reserved its third-party rights, but submitted a brief to the Appellate Body as *amicus curiae*. The complaining member, Peru, objected, arguing that acceptance of Morocco's brief "would be to allow a WTO Member impermissibly to circumvent the DSU."

European Communities-Trade Description of Sardines

Appellate Body Report, WT/DS231/AB/R (adopted Oct. 23, 2002)

162. We do not agree. As we said earlier, we found in *US-Lead and Bismuth II* that "nothing in the DSU or the *Working Procedures* specifically provides that we may accept and consider submissions or briefs from sources other than the participants and third participants in an appeal." We also stated in that appeal that "neither the DSU nor the *Working Procedures* explicitly prohibit acceptance or consideration of such briefs." In so ruling, we did *not* distinguish between, on the one hand, submissions from WTO Members that are not participants or third participants in a particular appeal, and, on the other hand, submissions from *non*-WTO Members.

163. It is true that, unlike private individuals or organizations, WTO Members are given an explicit right, under Articles 10.2 and 17.4 of the DSU, to participate in dispute settlement proceedings as third parties. Thus, the question arises whether the existence of this explicit right, which is not accorded to non-Members, justifies treating WTO Members differently from non-WTO Members in the exercise of our authority to receive *amicus curiae* briefs. We do not believe that it does.

164. We have been urged by the parties to this dispute not to treat Members less favourably than non-Members with regard to participation as *amicus curiae*. We agree. We have not. And we will not. As we have already determined that we have the authority to receive an *amicus curiae* brief from a private individual or an organization, *a fortiori* we are entitled to accept such a brief from a WTO Member, provided there is no prohibition on doing so in the DSU. We find no such prohibition.

165. None of the participants in this appeal has pointed to any provision of the DSU that can be understood as prohibiting WTO Members from participating in panel or appellate proceedings as an *amicus curiae*. Nor has any participant in this appeal demonstrated how such participation would contravene the DSU. Peru states only that the DSU provides that participation as a third party is governed by Articles 10.2 and 17.4, and appears to draw from this a negative inference such that Members may participate pursuant to those rules, or not at all. We have examined Articles 10.2 and 17.4, and we do not share Peru's view. Just because those provisions stipulate when a Member may participate in a dispute settlement proceeding as a third party or third participant, does not, in our view, lead inevitably to the conclusion that participation by a Member as an *amicus curiae* is prohibited.

166. As we explained in *US-Lead and Bismuth II*, the DSU gives WTO Members that are participants and third participants a legal *right* to participate in appellate proceedings. In particular, WTO Members that are third participants in an appeal have the *right* to make written and oral submissions. The corollary is that we have a *duty*, by virtue of the DSU, to accept and consider these submissions from WTO Members. By contrast, participation as *amici* in WTO appellate proceedings is not a legal *right*, and we have no duty to accept any *amicus curiae* brief. We may do so, however, based on our legal authority to regulate our own procedures as stipulated in Article 17.9 of the DSU. The fact that Morocco, as a sovereign State, has chosen not to exercise its *right* to participate in this dispute by availing itself of its third-party rights at the panel stage does not, in our opinion, undermine our *legal authority* under the DSU and our Working Procedures to accept and consider the *amicus curiae* brief submitted by Morocco.

167. Therefore, we find that we are entitled to accept the *amicus curiae* brief submitted by Morocco, and to consider it.

———————

The calls for reduced NGO participation generally, but not exclusively, come from developing countries. Why would developing countries in particular want to eliminate the participation of NGOs in the WTO as well as in multilateral environmental agreements? Review Articles 13 and 17 of the DSU. For a skeptical view from a French scholar of the Appellate Body's openness to *amicus* briefs, see Brigitte Stern, *The Intervention of Private Entities and States as "Friends of the Court" in WTO Dispute Settlement Proceedings*, in 1

THE WORLD TRADE ORGANIZATION: A LEGAL, ECONOMIC AND POLITICAL ANALYSIS 1427 (Patrick F.J. Macrory, Arthur E. Appleton & Michael G. Plummer eds., 2006).

D. Selected Issues in WTO Jurisprudence

We have seen earlier that the GATT said virtually nothing about how disputes were to be settled. In particular, given its early emphasis on consultation and diplomacy, it said nothing about what rules of law apply in resolving disputes. Similarly, the DSU provides little guidance for panels and the Appellate Body in terms of which legal rules to apply in disputes. The only clear reference to sources of law is in Article 3.2, which provides that the WTO agreements must be clarified "in accordance with customary rules of interpretation of public international law."

As a result of this scant direction, GATT panels and now WTO panels and the Appellate Body have crafted their own body of procedural and substantive law to guide their decisionmaking. GATT and WTO panels have also considered a wide range of issues relating to the jurisdiction of the panels, including mootness and whether the panel has competence to hear a particular issue (the equivalent of asking if there is a "case or controversy" under U.S. law). Much of the jurisprudence emerges from GATT panel reports. However, because the DSU added little guidance and few procedural rules, WTO panels have only slowly developed their own distinctive jurisprudence.

1. A General Note on Stare Decisis

Common law lawyers, the British even more than the Americans, are schooled in a legal system in which the holdings of a court on a question of law are taken to have, to a substantial degree, binding effect in later cases involving the same legal question. The Latin phrase *stare decisis* is often invoked as a label for this common law tendency. As an equally broad generality, it can be said that the code-based civil law systems originating in continental Europe follow a different principle—that the legal determinations of a court control the case at hand, but that a subsequent court examining the same legal question has free rein, based on a fresh legal analysis, to come to a different conclusion. Finally, it is widely, though somewhat inaccurately, stated that international law follows the civil law approach and does not give binding or near-binding effect to case law precedent on the same legal question.

What is the law on this point in the WTO? The DSU does not address this issue specifically, but two provisions in the DSU and another in the WTO Agreement strongly indicate that panel or Appellate Body conclusions of law have binding effect only in the particular dispute being decided. Article 3.2 of the DSU is very precise that, in settling disputes, the DSB "cannot add to or diminish the rights and obligations in the covered agreements." That is, the text of the agreements and any authoritative interpretation of them adopted by the members themselves constitute the controlling law. Moreover, Article IX:2 of the WTO Agreement itself specifically reserves the authority for binding interpretive decisions to just two bodies, the General Council and the Ministerial Conference.

The lack of a formal legal rule of *stare decisis* in the WTO dispute settlement system means that panels and the Appellate Body are not obligated to follow previous decisions, as a court ordinarily would be called on to do in a common law legal system. For example, the very same issues arose in two disputes involving EU apple restrictions, one in

1980 and one in 1989. The 1989 panel expressly stated that it was not bound by the earlier decision, adopted by the GATT Council, holding that the EU measures complied with the GATT. The 1989 Panel said: "While taking careful note of the earlier panel reports, the panel did not consider they relieved it of the responsibility, under its terms of reference, to carry out its own thorough examination on this important point." European Communities-Restrictions on Imports of Apples, GATT Panel Report, L/6513, B.I.S.D. 36th Supp. at 93, 127 (1990) (adopted June 22, 1989).

Do the panels and the Appellate Body nevertheless follow a *stare decisis* approach? In an exhaustive examination of this subject, Professor Bhala makes a convincing case that the *stare decisis* rule does not apply *de jure* in the WTO, but that a fair reading of panel and Appellate Body reports of recent years indicates that dispute settlement in the WTO follows *stare decisis* in practice, giving substantial and often controlling weight to the resolution of legal questions by prior panels or in prior Appellate Body reports. Raj Bhala, *The Myth about Stare Decisis and International Trade Law (Part One of a Trilogy)*, 14 Am. U. Int'l L. Rev. 845 (1999); *The Precedent Setters: De Facto Stare Decisis in WTO Adjudication (Part Two of a Trilogy)* 9 J. Transnat'l L. & Pol'y 1 (1999); *The Power of the Past: Towards De Jure Stare Decisis in WTO Adjudication (Part Three of a Trilogy)*, 33 Geo. Wash. L. Rev. 873 (2001). Subsequent dispute settlement results confirm his analysis. WTO panels almost invariably decide similar cases similarly and rulings are now replete with citations to previous decisions. In several cases, the Appellate Body has chastised panels for failing to apply or to understand earlier rulings of the Appellate Body, implicitly invoking the *stare decisis* principle that lower courts are bound by the decisions of higher courts.

2. The Legal Effect of Dispute Settlement Findings

Finally, the lack of formal *stare decisis* raises questions about the legal status of panel and Appellate Body reports. In *Japan-Taxes on Alcoholic Beverages,* the Appellate Body reviewed the historical attitude towards GATT panel decisions as binding only between the parties to the dispute and as distinct from official action to interpret the GATT. It then referred to Article IX:2 of the WTO Agreement, which states that the "Ministerial Conference and the General Council shall have the exclusive authority to adopt interpretations of this Agreement and of the Multilateral Trade Agreements." In addition, the Appellate Body noted, Article 3.9 of the DSU states that the provisions of the DSU "are without prejudice to the rights of Members to seek authoritative interpretation of provisions of a covered agreement." From these several points, the Appellate Body concluded that adopted panel reports under the WTO agreements have the same status as they did under the GATT: "Adopted panel reports are an important part of the GATT *acquis*. They are often considered by subsequent panels. They create legitimate expectations among WTO Members, and, therefore, should be taken into account where they are relevant to any dispute. However, they are not binding, except with respect to resolving disputes between parties to that dispute." Japan-Taxes on Alcoholic Beverages, Appellate Body Report, WT/DS8/AB/R, WT/DS10/AB/R, WT/DS11/AB/R, 13 (adopted Nov. 1, 1996). Regarding unadopted panel reports from the GATT era, the Appellate Body was clear that they "'have no legal status in the GATT or WTO system since they have not been endorsed through decisions by the CONTRACTING PARTIES to GATT or WTO Members,'" though "'a panel could nevertheless find useful guidance in the reasoning of an unadopted panel report that it considered to be relevant.'" *Id.* at 14–15, quoting from the panel report with approval. In fact, WTO panels and the Appellate Body rarely refer to unadopted decisions while liberally citing to adopted decisions.

If WTO panel reports have no precedential value *strictu sensu*, what is their legal effect? The only bodies authorized to render definitive legal interpretations of the WTO agreements are the Ministerial Conference and the General Council. This approach makes sense if we remember to think about the panels and Appellate Body as something other than independent judicial organs. As Bruce Wilson has observed:

> The problem [with thinking about WTO dispute settlement in terms of an independent judiciary] is that governments, including the U.S. government, have clearly not yet accepted that proposition, nor are they likely to do so. Fundamentally, the WTO agreements are a series of contractual arrangements between and among sovereign states. They do not, nor were they intended to, establish a comprehensive legal system with an independent judiciary. Consequently, the current DSU was designed to improve on the old GATT system of dispute settlement by implementing time limits, more automaticity in various aspects of the process, a new set of presumptions, and an appellate body. At best, the current dispute settlement system was intentionally designed to be a quasi-adjudicative system with restricted powers, subject ultimately to the control of the WTO members. It was not designed to be an independent judicial system, nor, in my view, do WTO members really want one.

S. Bruce Wilson, *Can the WTO Dispute Settlement Body Be a Judicial Tribunal Rather than a Diplomatic Club?*, 31 Law & Pol'y Int'l Bus. 779, 780 (2000).

As a result, it is not clear whether a WTO member whose law or regulation has been found to be inconsistent with a WTO obligation has the choice to compensate or to comply with the ruling by making its law or regulation consistent with the panel findings. Article 21.1 of the DSU simply states: "prompt compliance with recommendations or rulings of the DSB is essential in order to ensure effective resolution of disputes to the benefit of all Members." Even if the DSU does not *require* compliance in so many words, certain analyses find the requirement in the text nevertheless. One strong argument that the DSU imposes an obligation to comply in "violation" cases looks at DSU Article 26.1(b), which specifically states that in cases of *nonviolation* nullification or impairment, "there is no obligation to withdraw the measure." The fact that the negotiators specifically stated that no obligation exists with respect to nonviolation measures implies that an obligation to comply does exist with respect to violations. *Accord* John H. Jackson, The World Trade Organization: Constitution and Jurisprudence 88 (1998). Moreover, the overwhelming weight of international law authority holds that a nation is under a legal obligation to bring its conduct into conformity with international law, and the DSU specifically refers to "international law" as one of the interpretive guides for determining WTO obligations. Finally, the DSU shows a clear preference that members conform to dispute settlement decisions. *See* DSU, arts 3.7, 19.1, 21.6, 22.1, 22.8. In that light, the provision in Article 22 of the DSU for compensation or a suspension of concessions in the event that a member does not comply with a decision could be viewed as simply a practical remedy for the problem of persistent noncompliance, a key enforcement component of the DSU.

It seems appropriate to end this discussion on a practical note. How are the WTO's dispute settlement organs in fact handling precedent? Richard Steinberg makes the following comment:

> [I]n general, previous decisions and doctrine are so highly persuasive in WTO jurisprudence, and their use is so central to the discourse of dispute settlement, that it may be said that the WTO observes de facto *stare decisis*. This practice is

reinforced by the Appellate Body's procedure of meeting en banc to discuss each case and ensure consistency across decisions, notwithstanding that every decision rests with a three-member division of the Appellate Body. Hence, instances of judicial lawmaking in the WTO do not apply just to the matter at hand but build a body of law that bears on the behavior of all members.

Richard H. Steinberg, *Judicial Lawmaking at the WTO: Discursive, Constitutional, and Political Constraints*, 98 Am. J. Int'l L. 247, 254 (2004).

Questions and Discussion

1. Does the Appellate Body's explanation give you a better sense of the legal status of adopted decisions? Does Steinberg's comment on practice change your view?

2. Article 3 of the DSU declares that WTO dispute resolution is "a central element in providing security and predictability to the multilateral trading system." Does that argue for greater reliance on *stare decisis* principles?

3. *Stare decisis* enhances legal predictability from one forum (court) to another and enhances the disciplinary control of higher courts over lower courts. Are those advantages meaningful in the WTO context where there is no opportunity for forum shopping and there is an automatic right of appeal to a single body, the Appellate Body, which has the final say? Each panel, however, is appointed *ad hoc*, which decreases uniformity; is the Appellate Body enough of a control? Veteran WTO observers seem to think that it is. In recent remarks, Sir Francis Jacobs noted that the Appellate Body disclaims precedent but then uses it, and that it is important to the rule of law. At the same conference, Professor Jackson commented that the Appellate Body's reliance on precedent provides elements of predictability and assurance that are of great value to economic players. British Institute of International and Comparative Law, Tenth Annual WTO Conference, London, May 2010.

4. On a large range of issues, the WTO members have been unable to come to agreement on how to proceed. This includes issues left outstanding from the 1994 Uruguay Round negotiations such as the extent to which the Agreement on Technical Barriers to Trade covers ecolabels (*see* Chapter 6) as well as most of the issues included within the Doha Development Agenda. As a consequence, "more and more of the work of trade relations has shifted away from negotiations and towards litigation and arbitration." Alan Beattie, *From a Trickle to a Flood: How Lawsuits Are Coming to Dictate the Terms of Trade*, Financial Times, Mar. 20, 2007, at 11. Does this trend represent the "rule of reason constraining power politics" or "runaway jurists subverting democracy"? *Id*. On the other hand, the flood may be ebbing. Relatively few disputes were initiated in 2009, and many of the recent disputes are continuations of earlier disputes not yet fully resolved.

---

3. Deference to National Authorities

In a trade dispute, the complaining party is questioning the legality of a national law, regulation, or administrative practice that affects trade. Thus, the WTO faces the delicate question in every case as to the degree of deference to accord the challenged decision of the defending government. Professor Joel Trachtman has called this the question of laissez-regler—to what extent and in what circumstances should the WTO acknowledge the autonomous authority of national governments to regulate as they deem fit? Joel P. Trachtman, *Trade and ... Problems, Cost-Benefit Analysis and Subsidiarity*, 9 Eur. J. Int'l L. 32, 37 (1998). Now that the WTO agreements cover many policy areas, not just trade in goods, the question of deference to national authorities has become more acute. Environmental advocates, of course, are particularly sensitive about "second-guessing" by non-expert outsiders of often complex and controversial national regulatory determinations in the environmental policy arena.

For a first perspective on deference, consider a couple of cases from the GATT era. In the first case, New Zealand argued that, even though a GATT panel may determine whether New Zealand made a finding required by the GATT before imposing antidumping duties, a panel could not review whether New Zealand had adequate grounds for making that finding. In the second case, Canada agreed that the GATT requires a national government to take "such reasonable measures as may be available to it" to make local governments within its jurisdiction conform to the GATT, but argued that a panel could not review the national government's judgment as to what measures are "reasonably available to it." In both cases, the panels rejected these arguments for deference to national judgment and decisionmaking. They ruled that in order to give the GATT's obligations meaning, panels must have the power to determine whether a government's judgment or decision complied with the relevant GATT obligations. *See* Robert Hudec, Enforcing International Trade Law 259 (1993). On the issue in the Canadian case, subsequent GATT panel rulings make clear that panels will rigorously review whether the national government has in fact taken all reasonable efforts within its constitutional power to ensure that provincial or state governments comply with the GATT. *See, e.g.,* Canada-Import, Distribution and Sale of Certain Alcoholic Drinks by Provincial Marketing Agencies, GATT Panel Report, DS17/R, B.I.S.D. 39th Supp. at 27 (adopted Feb. 18 1992).

The refusal to defer to national authorities continues in the WTO. In a complex case relating to the safety of meat and meat products from cattle treated with growth hormones, the EU argued that the Panel should defer to its evaluation of the health risk from the beef. The Appellate Body specifically rejected that argument, citing the obligation of panels under DSU Article 11 to make an "objective assessment of the facts." After carefully scrutinizing the scientific evidence provided by the EU in support of their ban on such meat, both the Panel and the Appellate Body determined that the evidence did not meet the requisite legal standards. The Panel even assembled a group of experts to assess the scientific validity of the EU's scientific papers, an approach expressly allowed by the DSU and affirmed in that case by the Appellate Body. European Communities-Measures Concerning Meat and Meat Products, Appellate Body Report, WT/DS26/AB/R, WT/DS48/AB/R (adopted Feb. 13, 1998), *reprinted in* 37 I.L.M. 749 (1998) [hereinafter Hormones]. In another case, Australia claimed that a Panel had failed to accord "due deference" to matters of fact that Australia presented. The Appellate Body, however, declared that panels "are not required to accord to factual evidence of the parties the same meaning and weight as do the parties." Australia-Measures Affecting Importation of Salmon, Appellate Body Report, WT/DS18/AB/R, para. 267 (adopted Nov. 6, 1998), *reprinted in* 37 I.L.M. 1507 (1998). Both of these cases, as well as the issue of deference, are discussed in more detail in Chapter 7.

The country defending a measure usually has one important advantage: the complaining party must establish a prima facie case that the challenged measure does not comply with one of the relevant trade agreements. Moreover, the key agreements of interest from the environmental point of view explicitly grant each government the unrestricted right to determine the level of health or environmental protection it wishes to achieve. The issue of deference, thus, is generally restricted to the factual basis for the particular regulatory measure or the evaluation of alternative means of reaching the country's declared objective or satisfying its trade obligations.

Questions and Discussion

1. Scholars have also made the argument that WTO panels should defer to national decisionmaking especially with regard to scientific questions. Professor David Wirth, for example, argues that panels should defer to agency decisions because regulators often "work at the frontiers of science." David Wirth, *The Role of Science in the Uruguay Round and NAFTA Trade Disciplines*, 27 CORNELL INT'L L.J. 817 (1995). Do you agree? The expertise rationale that Wirth invokes is a familiar reason for deference by courts to domestic administrative agencies; is the same reasoning pertinent in the WTO context with respect to national authorities? *See also* Steve Charnovitz, *Environment and Health under WTO Dispute Settlement*, 32 INT'L LAW. 901 (1998).

2. By the same token, though, U.S. courts regularly overturn agency decisions that lack a proper scientific foundation or appear to run counter to the available science. In doing so, they apply the "arbitrary and capricious" standard of the U.S. Administrative Procedure Act, 5 U.S.C. §706 (1946), in determining whether an agency has considered all relevant factors and whether it has developed a rational connection between the evidence in the record and the agency's decision. Should the WTO panels have the same authority to scrutinize the government's evidence? When, if ever, should a trade panel or other international court defer to national decisions that are claimed to violate international treaties? If panels defer to national decisionmaking, what standard of review— what level of deference—should it accord those decisions? These questions arise frequently under the SPS Agreement, which we take up in Chapter 7.

---

4. "Case or Controversy": Ripeness and Mootness

We earlier addressed the issue of what kind of "actionable harm" gives grounds for a remedy. Somewhat related but nevertheless distinct questions of "ripeness" and "mootness" arise from time to time in disputes where a particular trade measure has not yet come into effect or, although on the books, has not yet been applied. Both the GATT and now the DSU are silent on this issue.

As is clear from the discussion of "actionable harm" on pages 88–91, however, trade panels have judged their own role expansively. In *Superfund*, the Panel found tax legislation to violate GATT obligations even though the legislation had not yet entered into effect. In *Japan-Measures on Imports of Leather*, a GATT panel concluded that a quota could be challenged as violating the GATT even though the quota was not enforced, because even an unenforced quota, if mandatory, could discourage investment, planning, or other market activities relating to exports. GATT Panel Report, l/5623, B.I.S.D. 31st Supp. at 94 (1985) (adopted May 15–16, 1984). WTO panels have continued this expansive view, as in Argentina-Measures Affecting Imports of Footwear, Textiles, Apparel, and Other Items, WT/DS56/R (adopted Apr. 22, 1997). In that case, the United States challenged Argentina's new mandatory methods for assessing tariffs. Even though the United States had not shown that Argentina had already imposed a duty in excess of bound rates, the Panel concluded that "the competitive relationship of the parties was changed unilaterally by Argentina because its mandatory measure clearly has the potential to violate its bindings, thus undermining the security and the predictability of the WTO system." *Id.* at para. 6.46. Affirmed by the Appellate Body, WT/DS56/AB/R, paras. 53–55 (adopted Apr. 22, 1998).

The flip side of ripeness is whether a dispute has been mooted when the challenged measure has been withdrawn or has expired. As Professor Raj Bhala explains, here too the panels and Appellate Body have interpreted their role expansively.

Raj Bhala, *International Trade Law: Interdisciplinary Theory and Practice*
160 (3rd ed. 2008)

May a panel issue a ruling in a case where the measure in dispute has been withdrawn, or has expired? Again, the *DSU* is silent. Ostensibly, as regards the disputing parties, the ruling would seem to be a waste of time. However, as is observed in the 1998 case of *European Communities–Measures Affecting Importation of Certain Poultry Products*, a terminated measure may have lingering trade repercussions on the export performance of the complaining Member. Thus, the panel in that case rejected the EC's argument that it could not rule on a measure challenged by Brazil. Moreover, consider the interests of non-disputants. If one of them were to consider adoption of a similar measure, then a ruling might be very instructive. In other words, if the dispute is capable of being repeated, why not go forward with the case?

Several pre-Uruguay Round GATT panels took this approach. They tended to issue rulings even after the disputed measure had terminated, but only if the disputed measure was in effect when the terms of reference for the panel were agreed upon, or if there was no objection from either party. The WTO panels and Appellate Body continue this nuanced approach in *Argentina–Footwear* and the 1996 case of *United States–Standards for Reformulated and Conventional Gasoline.* . . . If the measure terminated before the terms of reference were set [for establishing the panel by the DSB], then the issue is considered moot, and the panel will not rule on it. If the measure was still in effect when the terms were established, then it is "fair game."

––––––––––

Questions and Discussion

1. The "case or controversy" doctrine is familiar to American lawyers, but it has its roots in interpretations of the U.S. Constitution and is thus somewhat alien to other legal systems. Other national legal systems allow advisory opinions, for example, and some even provide for an adjudication of the constitutionality of a law before the legislature votes on it.

2. Notwithstanding the previous point, U.S. students may wish to compare the rulings on ripeness and mootness with U.S. law. With respect to "ripeness," the *Superfund* Panel ruled:

[GATT Articles III and XI] are not only to protect current trade but also to create the predictability needed to plan future trade. That objective could not be attained if contracting parties could not challenge existing legislation mandating actions at variance with the General Agreement until administrative acts implementing it had actually been applied to their trade.

Superfund, para. 5.2.2. Under U.S. law, a regulation is ordinarily not ripe for judicial review until there is:

> some concrete action applying the regulation to the claimant's situation in a fashion that harms or threatens to harm him. (The major exception, of course, is a substantive rule which as a practical matter requires the plaintiff to adjust his conduct immediately. Such agency review is "ripe" for review at once, whether or not explicit statutory review apart from the [Administrative Procedure Act] is provided.)

Lujan v. National Wildlife Federation, 497 U.S. 871, 891, 110 S.Ct. 3177, 3190,111 L. Ed. 2d 695, 718 (1990). Is GATT jurisprudence really that different from U.S. law?

3. *Exhaustion of Domestic Remedies.* A related issue is whether a private party or complaining member must use available remedies in the country alleged to have violated its trade responsibilities before resorting to the WTO's dispute settlement process. While the Appellate Body has not yet ruled on this issue, the Panel in *Argentina–Footwear*, cited above, has. In that dispute, Argentina claimed that a U.S. importer should have sought a remedy under Argentina's law to resolve a dispute over a tariff binding before the United States initiated a WTO dispute. The Panel disagreed, noting that Article II of the GATT relating to tariffs imposed unconditional obligations on a WTO member for which recourse to the WTO's dispute settlement process was possible.

---

5. *Approaches to Interpretation and the Relevance of International Law*

For trade and environment disputes, a significant question for the DSB is the degree to which international environmental law should be used as an external guide for interpreting WTO obligations in cases where the trade measure involved has an environmental protection aspect. In this brief introduction to the trade and environment jurisprudence of the WTO, we will see that it has dealt with two different aspects of international environmental law. On one hand, there are in some cases international agreements or actions relating to a specific environmental objective, which present the question of the relevance of that international environmental law to the resolution of the WTO dispute. On the other hand, members challenging or defending certain trade measures have sometimes invoked general international environmental law principles such as the Polluter Pays Principle and the precautionary principle (*see* Chapter 1). The international law status of these principles is not altogether clear, so their application in trade disputes has been problematic.

As a general matter, Article 3.2 of the DSU directs panels and the Appellate Body to clarify WTO rules "in accordance with customary rules of interpretation of public international law." This mandate has given panels and the Appellate Body useful tools for interpreting the meaning of key terms in trade agreements and has brought some discipline and uniformity to decisions. On the other hand, the same article provides that dispute settlement outcomes "cannot add to or diminish the rights and obligations provided in the covered agreements." The tension between these instructions highlights the fundamental challenge faced by the dispute settlement organs of the WTO and national courts alike: to clarify the meaning of ambiguous texts without crossing the nebulous boundary between the judicial and legislative functions; that is, to not "make" law. The challenge is made more difficult because even the "customary rules of public international law offer alternative approaches to interpreting the WTO agreements." Richard H. Steinberg, *Judicial Lawmaking at the WTO*, at 258.

Pursuant to Article 3.2 of the DSU, WTO dispute settlement reports have made frequent references to the Vienna Convention on the Law of Treaties (Vienna Convention) as the authoritative international guide to the interpretation of the GATT and the other WTO agreements. In particular, Article 31 of the Vienna Convention deals with treaty interpretation by adjudicative bodies. Claus-Dieter Ehlermann, a former member of the Appellate Body, reviews its use of the first paragraph of Article 31.

Claus-Dieter Ehlermann, *Six Years on the Bench of the "World Trade Court": Some Personal Experiences as Member of the Appellate Body of the World Trade Organization*
36 J. WORLD TRADE 605, 615–17 (2002)

According to Article 31.1 of the Vienna Convention, "a Treaty shall be interpreted in good faith in accordance with the ordinary meaning to be given to the terms of the treaty in their context and in the light of its object and purpose." Among these three criteria, the Appellate Body has certainly attached the greatest weight to the first, i.e. "the ordinary meaning of the terms of the treaty." ... The second criterion, i.e., "context" has less weight than the first, but is certainly more often used and relied upon than the third, i.e., "object and purpose." * * *

[T]he immediate reference to Articles 31 and 32 of the Vienna Convention, and the acceptance of the prime importance of "the ordinary meaning to be given to the terms of the treaty," have given precious guidance to the Appellate Body Members working in different divisions and interpreting different covered agreements. In other words: the very early consensus on interpretive principles has facilitated decision-making and contributed considerably to the consistency and coherence of Appellate Body reports.

Even greater are the benefits of the open and transparent choice of the Appellate Body's interpretive methods on the outside world. This choice has given clear guidance to Members of the WTO and to panels. It has thus contributed to "providing security and predictability to the multilateral trading system." * * *

The heavy reliance on the "ordinary meaning to be given to the terms of the treaty" has protected the Appellate Body from criticism that its reports have added to or diminished the rights and obligations provided in the covered agreements. On a more general level, the interpretative method, established and clearly announced by the Appellate Body, has had a legitimizing effect, and this from the very beginning of the its activity.

———————

The very first WTO dispute offers an excellent example of the application of the Vienna Convention relevant to trade and environment. As briefly described in Chapter 1, and as will be more fully discussed in Chapter 5, Article XX of the GATT allows countries to adopt measures that otherwise violate the GATT for environmental and other purposes. Depending on the purpose of the exception, the different paragraphs of Article XX authorize the use of a GATT-inconsistent measure in different terms. A country may adopt GATT-inconsistent measures that are, *inter alia,* "necessary" to protect human, animal, or plant life or health or "relating to" the conservation of exhaustible natural resources. GATT panels and the first WTO Panel interpreted the phrase "relating to" the conservation of the resources as meaning "primarily aimed at" their conservation, which they further determined meant something akin to "necessary for" their conservation. In *Reformulated Gasoline,* the Appellate Body used Vienna Convention Article 31(1) to specifically reject that interpretation. Applying the "ordinary meaning" doctrine, the Appellate Body reasoned that different words such as "necessary," and "relating to," must be given their different and ordinary meanings, because "[i]t does not seem reasonable to suppose that the WTO members intended to require, in respect of each and every category, the same kind or degree of connection or relationship between the measure under appraisal and the state interest or policy sought to be promoted or realized." United States-Standards for Reformulated and Conventional Gasoline, WT/DS2/AB/R, 18 (adopted May 20, 1996), *reprinted in* 35 I.L.M. 603 (1996). Professor John Knox explains the significance of this and similar rulings:

> Looking to the ordinary meaning of the language of the text to be interpreted hardly seems a radical innovation. But the GATT Panels in the *Tuna-Dolphin* cases had had relatively little concern for the exact language of the text. With respect to GATT Article XX(g), for example, they had read "relating to" to mean "primarily aimed at" (or even "necessary for"); read "are made effective in conjunction with" to mean "primarily aimed at making effective"; and added "within the jurisdiction of the importing country" after "exhaustible natural resources." As Robert Howse has said, the "tendency of panels to assume they understood the general purpose of a provision, and to give sense to it in light of that purpose, without regard to the individual words and phrases, almost always resulted in rulings tilted towards one particular value among the competing values at stake, namely that of liberal trade," and as a result their decisions ignored the balance the trade agreement actually strikes between trade and non-trade values.

> The Appellate Body therefore took an important step toward placing its decisions on a more secure basis politically as well as legally when it decided that its starting point would always be the ordinary meaning of the text, and relegated the teleological approach favored by the *Tuna-Dolphin* panels to a secondary, or even tertiary, position.

John H. Knox, *The Judicial Resolution of Conflicts Between Trade and the Environment,* 28 Harv. Envtl. L. Rev. 1, 51 (2004).

References to Article 31(1) of the Vienna Convention as a guide to interpretation are well accepted. The DSB has a responsibility to interpret WTO law, and the Vienna Convention offers authoritative guidelines on how to interpret international treaty texts. The matter is not entirely free of doubt, however. Some 60 members of the WTO are not parties to the Vienna Convention, raising the potential for conflicts over its "binding" application in WTO disputes.

On other points, the Appellate Body has applied more controversial aspects of what is, at best, customary international law. Knox identifies what he calls a "two-step interpretive process the Appellate Body has followed in the trade/environment cases: 1) to follow the ordinary meaning of the text before it as far as possible; and 2) when the ordinary meaning is unclear, to look beyond the text for substantive principles with widespread political support, upon which an interpretation can be based." *Id.* at 50. Knox explores some of the implications of the second step.

John H. Knox, *The Judicial Resolution of Conflicts between Trade and the Environment*

28 HARV. ENVTL. L. REV. 1, 52–55 (2004)

The textual focus explains much of the trade/environment jurisprudence, but not all of it. Some provisions, such as the Article XX chapeau itself, do not necessarily have a plain meaning around which political agreement may be assumed. As a result, the Appellate Body has looked beyond the text of the trade agreements. * * *

In *Hormones*, the rejected panel interpretation was not completely implausible.... In explaining why the panel's interpretation failed, the Appellate Body did not stop at the ordinary language of the provisions. It looked also to the object and purpose of Article 3 [of the SPS Agreement], which it said is to harmonize SPS measures in the future, rather than in the "here and now." And it emphasized that the right of each WTO Member to determine its own level of protection of health and safety is an important "autonomous" right ... and that WTO Members had not clearly agreed to impose upon themselves the onerous obligation to conform to international standards. In support, it cited the "interpretative principle of *in dubio mitius*," which it described as stating that "[i]f the meaning of the term is ambiguous, that meaning is to be preferred which is less onerous to the party assuming an obligation." * * *

Another issue that led the Appellate Body to look beyond the language of the text is whether the term "exhaustible natural resources" in Article XX(g) includes living resources, such as endangered species of sea turtles. One can argue, as the U.S. government did in *Shrimp-Turtle I*, that endangered sea turtles fit within the plain meaning of the text: they are indisputably natural resources and, at least when on the brink of extinction, they are obviously exhaustible. On the other hand, the complaining parties argued that a reasonable interpretation would be that the provision refers only to finite resources, such as minerals. They pointed out that reading "exhaustible natural resources" to include living resources appears to make "exhaustible" redundant.

Looking first to the words of the provision, the Appellate Body agreed with the United States that they are not limited to non-living natural resources and that living resources are susceptible to exhaustion or extinction. But, again, it then went beyond the language in search of agreed principles outside of the text. It found them in two treaties—the 1982 UN Convention on the Law of the Sea and the 1992 Convention on Biological Diversity—and two non-binding documents—Agenda 21, adopted by the UN Conference on Environment and Development in 1992, and a resolution adopted in conjunction with the signature of the Convention on the Conservation of Migratory Species of Wild Animals in 1979. All of these documents had been signed or adopted by a very wide range of governments, and each refers to natural resources as including living resources.

How did the Appellate Body tie these indicia of agreement to the text of the provision being interpreted? It said that the WTO Agreement recognizes the goal of sustainable development in its preamble, and, based on that "perspective," it stated that "the generic term 'natural resources'... is not 'static' in its content or reference but is rather 'by definition, evolutionary.'" It then cited the environmental instruments as evidence of what the term had evolved to mean. It also referred to the principle of effectiveness in treaty interpretation in concluding that measures to conserve living, as well as non-living, exhaustible natural resources may fall within Article XX(g). Although it has cited the principle of effectiveness in other cases for the uncontroversial proposition that interpretations should be avoided that reduce "whole clauses or paragraphs of a treaty ... to redundancy or inutility," that proposition could not support the Appellate Body's decision here, since the interpretation of "exhaustible natural resources" urged by the complaining parties could not reduce Article XX(g) to redundancy or inutility. Instead, the Appellate Body seemed to be referring to the principle in a broader, teleological sense, as a method of reading the text to make effective the goal of sustainable development.

Some aspects of what Knox describes about how the Appellate Body "looks beyond" the text are especially controversial. For example, international scholars are divided on the question of the principle of effectiveness and whether treaty terms can have an "evolutionary" meaning. On one side, Myres McDougal has called the principle of effectiveness, through which a treaty is interpreted to make it effective rather than ineffective even if the plain meaning does not necessarily support such an interpretation, "the most widely accepted interpretive standard in the traditional repertoire." MYRES S. McDOUGAL, THE INTERPRETATION OF INTERNATIONAL AGREEMENTS 156–57 (1994). Other eminent scholars, however, argue that treaty terms must be interpreted as they were intended at the time the treaty was concluded, or in accordance with the ordinary meaning to be given to their terms. They argue that the principle of effectiveness suffers from organic defects. *See, e.g.,* IAN BROWNLIE, PRINCIPLES OF INTERNATIONAL LAW 636–37 (5th ed. 1998).

Even more interesting, the Appellate Body in *Shrimp/Turtle* relied on general principles of international law, not merely general principles of treaty interpretation. The Appellate Body referred to aspects of Article XX as being an expression of the principle of good faith, "at once a general principle of law and a general principle of international law" that controls the exercise of rights by states. *Shrimp/Turtle*, at para. 158. While this statement is without controversy, the Appellate Body also stated that one application of the general principle, the doctrine of *abus de droit* (abuse of rights), prohibits the abusive exercise of a State's right. However, the Permanent Court of International Justice, the predecessor of the International Court of Justice, articulated the abuse of rights doctrine only in dicta. *See* Certain German Interests in Polish Upper Silesia, 1926 P.C.I.J., (ser. A) No. 7, at 30 (stating that "such abuse cannot be presumed, and it rests with the party who states that there has been such misuse to prove its statement"); Free Zones Case, 1930 P.C.I.J. (ser. A) No. 24, at 12. Consequently, while most international law scholars agree that the doctrine is a general principle of law, they also appear to agree that it "must be wielded with studied restraint." HERSCH LAUTERPACHT, THE DEVELOPMENT OF INTERNATIONAL LAW BY THE INTERNATIONAL COURT 164 (1958); *see also* IAN BROWNLIE, PRINCIPLES OF INTERNATIONAL LAW, at 447–48; B. CHENG, GENERAL PRINCIPLES OF LAW AS APPLIED BY INTERNATIONAL COURTS AND TRIBUNALS 125 (1953).

General principles of environmental law, such as the Polluter Pays Principle and the precautionary principle, have become core concepts on which national governments and international agreements build more specific rules and regulations. *See* pages 24–27 for a discussion of the Polluter Pays Principle and pages 492–495 for a discussion of the precautionary principle. For example, the Convention on International Trade in Endangered Species of Wild Fauna and Flora (CITES) has structured its rules for regulating trade in species based on the precautionary principle. *See* CITES, Resolution Conf. 9.24 (1994), *at* http://www.cites.org/eng/res/index.shtml. Domestic courts in India, Brazil, Pakistan, and elsewhere have interpreted the precautionary principle and the Polluter Pays Principle as representing customary international law and creating norms from which no country can derogate. *See, e.g.,* Vellore Citizens Welfare Forum v. Union of India & Others, WP 914/1991 Scale (PIL) 1981–97, 703 (India 1996); Zia v. WAPDA, P.L.D. 1994 Supreme Court 693 (Pakistan 1994). On the other hand, for an indication that the precautionary principle (some would say "approach") is not yet accepted without equivocation, see the history of the hard-fought negotiations over the precautionary "approach" in the Biosafety Protocol, recounted in Sean Murphy, *Biotechnology and International Law*, 42 Harv. Int'l L.J. 47, 78 (2001).

In *Hormones*, the EU argued that provisions of the SPS Agreement, which require such measures to be based on scientific information, should be interpreted in light of the precautionary principle. According to the EU, the precautionary principle would permit import restrictions on hormone-treated beef to prevent any potential risk to human health, even if the scientific evidence in the risk assessment did not show any causal link between eating those beef products and human health effects from hormone exposure. The Appellate Body discussed the precautionary principle at some length but noted its uncertain status in international law. It then noted that the SPS Agreement itself contained a provision much like the precautionary principle, specifically granting countries a limited and conditional right to impose SPS measures where the science is uncertain. (The EU had explicitly refused to rely on this provision because of its limits and conditions.) In light of the textual provision, the Appellate Body held that more general international law principles could not be invoked to "override" the agreed provisions of the SPS Agreement. *EC-Hormones*, Appellate Body Report, at paras. 120–25.

As acceptance of these environmental norms as principles of international law grows, however, WTO panels will have greater difficulty avoiding or evading application of them to GATT and WTO rules. The precautionary principle, with its emphasis on taking action before the scientific information is conclusive, could prove invaluable for interpreting whether measures are justifiable as exceptions to the GATT rules for measures "necessary" to protect of human, animal, or plant life or health. It could also prove useful for interpreting the scientific standards of the SPS Agreement. We will return to this issue in Chapter 7.

Questions and Discussion

1. Many of the commentators on the modes of interpretation employed by the Appellate Body, including Professors Richard Steinberg and John Knox, quoted above, emphasize the political nature of WTO interpretation and the care that the Appellate Body seems to take to select interpretive rules that will allow it to reach conclusions that will be accepted by a wide range of WTO members, especially the more powerful members. Steinberg, for example, concludes, "Hence, judicial lawmaking at the WTO will continue to face a hard political constraint.... [J]udicial lawmaking will not fundamentally and adversely shift the balance of WTO rights and responsibilities against the interest of powerful states, or the Appellate Body will be subjected to political correction." Richard H. Steinberg, *Judicial Lawmaking at the WTO*, at 275. Note also the observations above of Claus-Dieter Ehlermann, a former Appellate Body member. On environmental issues specifically, Knox is cautiously optimistic: "Since governments have been unable to reach

a detailed political resolution of trade/environment conflicts, the judicial effort to devise a politically acceptable resolution of such conflicts may have seemed doubtful, or even quixotic. But in fact, as measured by the statements of government representatives at meetings of [the DSB], governments have accepted most elements of the judicial resolution." John H. Knox, *Judicial Resolution of Trade/Environment Conflicts*, at 70.

2. Analysts generally agree that the Appellate Body has, to a degree, used legal rules to accomplish policy change. Is this a wise approach? What would be the result if the Appellate Body were to follow a more conservative, strictly legal approach? If, as with the issue of *amicus curiae* briefs, controversial issues remain deadlocked in the WTO because the members cannot reach a political compromise to a legal dispute, which members would be likely to benefit from a strictly legal approach? More generally, because the political/negotiating aspect of the WTO has become deadlocked in recent years, some see a danger that the DSU could lose legitimacy if members try to use dispute settlement to address issues that would better be resolved politically.

3. Given the emphasis on political acceptance of, or political control of, the jurisprudence of the Appellate Body, would it be more helpful to analogize WTO dispute settlement to a system of agency-managed administrative adjudication rather than to a system of national courts?

V. National Negotiation and Implementation of Trade Agreements

International trade policy poses special problems in the allocation of political authority within national governments because these international agreements have pervasive and detailed effects on national economic policy. Thus, many countries have special constitutional arrangements for trade negotiations and approval of trade agreements to ensure effective political control of trade policy through some sharing of the political responsibility for foreign policy and economic policy. This section summarizes the procedures for policy control and trade agreement approval in several different systems.

A. The United States

1. The "Fast Track" Process

The United States exhibits an extreme, but nevertheless representative, form of power sharing. Article II of the U.S. Constitution grants the President the authority to conduct foreign affairs, including the authority to negotiate international agreements on behalf of the United States. Because this authority is not limited to particular policy areas, the President is thus empowered to negotiate trade agreements. However, Article I, section 8 of the U.S. Constitution assigns to the Congress the authority to "regulate commerce with foreign Nations" and to "lay and collect Taxes, Duties, Imposts, and Excises." Tariff bindings, quota restrictions, and other integral rules of trade agreements obviously affect taxes and duties—matters clearly within the exclusive constitutional powers of the Congress. Nevertheless, the international nature of a trade agreement obviously brings it within the President's exclusive authority to conduct the foreign relations of the United States.

An element of U.S. law that exacerbates this tension is the distinction, accepted in U.S. constitutional law, between a "treaty" and an "agreement." In international law, "treaty," "agreement," and "convention" have the same legal meaning and effect. Under the U.S. Constitution, however, the President must submit a "treaty" to the Senate (the upper chamber of the Congress) for its advice and consent. Only if the Senate consents to ratification by a two-thirds majority can the President "ratify" the treaty and make it binding on the United States. Since the presidency of George Washington, though, presidents have sidestepped the Senate by characterizing some agreements with foreign governments as "executive agreements."

The President and the Congress established, more than 30 years ago, an uneasy truce over such constitutional questions to ensure a strong and effective U.S. trade policy in which both the President and the Congress have a voice. The mechanism is widely known as "fast track," though the most recent legislation on the subject styled it Trade Promotion Authority. *See* Bipartisan Trade Promotion Authority Act of 2002 (TPA), 19 U.S.C. §§ 3801 et seq. (2004). In the case of the TPA, the negotiating authority was originally scheduled to end on June 1, 2005 but was extended through June 1, 2007, at which time it expired. As of early 2010, therefore, the President and the U.S. Trade Representative are operating without explicit delegation of authority from Congress to negotiate comprehensive trade agreements. Even so, the fast-track process of the TPA described here would apply to several agreements already concluded that still require congressional approval.

Legislative Authority to Negotiate. Congress, through trade legislation, grants the President for a fixed period of time the authority to negotiate comprehensive trade agreements (agreements like the Dominican Republic-Central American Free Trade Agreement or the WTO agreements that affect tariffs and other terms of "foreign commerce"). The TPA legislation generally set forth, in lesser or greater detail, nine overall objectives and detailed instructions on 17 separate issues. *Id.* § 3802.

Consultations with Congress. When the President decides to negotiate a trade agreement, he must notify Congress of his intent to do so at least 90 days before initiating negotiations. Before and after submission of this notice, the President must consult the Senate Committee on Finance and the House of Representatives Committee on Ways and Means, as well as the Congressional Oversight group, a new body designed to spearhead consultations with the administration and formulate consultation guidelines. He may also consult with other House and Senate committees that "the President deems appropriate." On agreements relating to specific topics, such as agricultural or fisheries trade, he must consult with specialized committees of the House and Senate. For example, the President must consult with the House Committee on Resources, the Senate Committee on Finance, and the Senate Committee on Commerce, Science, and Transportation on agreements relating to fish or shellfish trade.

Congressional Review. Assuming that negotiations lead to an agreement, the President must notify Congress at least 90 days before he "enters into" the agreement through signature of the agreement, and he must publish a notice to that effect in the *Federal Register.* With Congress and the public thus made aware of the proposed terms of the agreement, the 90-day period gives Congress time to hold committee hearings on the draft agreement and otherwise to solicit and receive input from interested persons. If significant objections to the agreement were to emerge during this period of review, the President would have the opportunity to renegotiate the troublesome provisions. Assuming that no significant problems arise during the 90-day review, the President or his subordinate is authorized to sign the agreement, which signifies that the United States wishes in good faith for this agreement to become binding.

Implementing Legislation. Before the agreement can become binding under U.S. law, however, Congress must enact legislation to make its terms and conditions part of U.S. law. Within 60 days after entering into the agreement, the President must provide Congress with a description of the changes to existing laws that the President considers necessary to bring the United States into compliance with the agreement. Any time after those 60 days, on a date of the President's choosing when Congress is in session, the President must then submit to Congress the final text of the agreement along with several other items: 1) draft implementing legislation with the requisite changes to statutory provisions; 2) a "statement of administrative action" describing any changes to United States regulations or practices that do not require new legislation; and 3) an explanation of how the agreement meets the negotiating objectives set forth in the TPA.

Once the draft implementing legislation is introduced, the process for congressional approval (or disapproval) of the agreement is governed by a law first enacted in 1974. This is where the term "fast track" applies. The relevant congressional committees have up to 45 legislative days (typically about three calendar months) to review the legislative package. The committees can take testimony and deliberate over the implementing legislation bill submitted by the President, but they may not "mark up" the bill with amendments. On or before the end of the 45-day period, the bill is automatically reported by the committees to the full Senate and House of Representatives. Each chamber allots a maximum of 20 hours for floor debate on the legislation and the underlying agreement. Within 60 legislative days of its submission to Congress by the President, the House and Senate vote, by simple majority in each chamber, either to approve or reject the implementing legislation without any amendments. Only after Congress enacts the implementing legislation does the trade agreement enter into force for the United States.

---

2. Trade Promotion Authority and Environmental Issues

The periodic renewal of legislation granting the President negotiating authority has become a flash point for the trade and environment debate. Recognizing that the legislation purports to give direction to the President in negotiating trade agreements, the Clinton Administration, with support from environmental and labor advocates, sought congressional authorization for the President to negotiate environmental and labor standards in any future trade agreement. Business groups and others argued in opposition to keep "nontrade related" issues out of the legislation and had sufficient votes to prevent enactment of legislation. The resulting stalemate between President Clinton and the Congress resulted in a hiatus of several years during which the President lacked "fast-track" authority to negotiate comprehensive trade agreements. Even so, President Clinton negotiated, and Congress enacted implementing legislation for, a free trade agreement with Jordan that contained some environmental provisions. Congress did not attempt to introduce any "poison pill" amendments or delay consideration of the agreement. Hal Shapiro & Lael Brainard, *Trade Promotion Authority Formerly Known as Fast Track: Building Common Ground on Trade Demands More than a Name Change*, 35 Geo. Wash. Int'l L. Rev. 1, 46 (2003).

With a Republican President and Republican Congress in 2001, the political stalemate was broken and Congress granted President George W. Bush new trade negotiating authority through the TPA. The TPA included among its objectives for trade agreements the need to "ensure that trade and environmental policies are mutually supportive." It elaborated its "principal negotiating objectives" with respect to the environment (and labor) as follows:

(A) to ensure that a party to a trade agreement with the United States does not fail to effectively enforce its environmental or labor laws, through a sustained or recurring course of action or inaction, in a manner affecting trade between the United States and that party after entry into force of a trade agreement between those countries;

(B) to recognize that parties to a trade agreement retain the right to exercise discretion with respect to investigatory, prosecutorial, regulatory, and compliance matters and to make decisions regarding the allocation of resources to enforcement with respect to other labor or environmental matters determined to have higher priorities, and to recognize that a country is effectively enforcing its laws if a course of action or inaction reflects a reasonable exercise of such discretion, or results from a bona fide decision regarding the allocation of resources, and no retaliation may be authorized based on the exercise of these rights or the right to establish domestic labor standards and levels of environmental protection; …

(D) to strengthen the capacity of United States trading partners to protect the environment through the promotion of sustainable development;

(E) to reduce or eliminate government practices or policies that unduly threaten sustainable development;

(F) to seek market access, through the elimination of tariffs and nontariff barriers, for United States environmental technologies, goods, and services; and

(G) to ensure that labor, environmental, health, or safety policies and practices of the parties to trade agreements with the United States do not arbitrarily or unjustifiably discriminate against United States exports or serve as disguised barriers to trade.

19 U.S.C. §§ 3802(b)(11).

————————

Questions and Discussion

1. Due to the speed with which the U.S. Congress must conduct its final debate on a trade agreement and Congress's self-imposed inability to amend any of an agreement's provisions, some people have questioned this process as undemocratic. They are particularly concerned that implementing legislation may alter the legal effect of many federal and even state laws without opportunity for specific debate on those issues. For example, Congress approved the NAFTA's implementing legislation less than three weeks after the President submitted it. On the other hand, there was more than a year of often vigorous public debate and intense lobbying of Congress about the NAFTA between the time the negotiations concluded in August 1992 and the passage of the implementing legislation in November 1993, not to mention a presidential election forcing George H.W. Bush out of office and bringing in the Administration of Bill Clinton. JOHN J. AUDLEY, GREEN POLITICS AND GLOBAL TRADE: NAFTA AND THE FUTURE OF ENVIRONMENTAL POLITICS 69 (Barry Rabe & John Tierney eds., 1997).

2. Patti Goldman comes to the following conclusion concerning fast-track procedures:

Since fast-track procedures stand in the way of effective congressional oversight and public participation, they should be eliminated. Every time an agreement has been negotiated and submitted under fast-track rules, Congress has expressed its dissatisfaction with the system and tinkered with the fast-track rules to give

Congress more oversight. Thus, Congress has required more consultations and provided for additional opportunities for Congress to vote on whether fast-track rules will apply. These refinements of the fast-track rules, however, have neither provided an adequate check on presidential power nor compensated for the loss of congressional control occasioned by the no-amendment rule.

The Democratization of the Development of United States Trade Policy, 27 CORNELL INT'L L.J. 631, 666 (1994), Do you agree? How would you change the legislation, if at all? For an argument that fast track is compatible with democracy, see Harold Hongju Koh, *The Fast Track and United States Trade Policy*, 18 BROOK. J. INT'L L. 143 (1992).

3. Due to the U.S. Constitution's silence on the meaning of the word "treaty," scholars have debated whether U.S. fast-track authority and congressional-executive agreements violate the U.S. Constitutional provision requiring the "advice and consent" of the Senate. Some argue that the "executive agreement" has become an accepted practice under the U.S. Constitution. *See* Bruce Ackerman & David Golove, *Is NAFTA Constitutional?*, 108 HARV. L. REV. 799, 804 (1995). Laurence Tribe takes issue with the Ackerman & Golove line of argument but not with the result. Laurence H. Tribe, *Taking Text Seriously: Reflections on Free-Form Method in Constitutional Interpretation*, 108 HARV. L. REV. 1221 (1995). A court of appeals declined to rule on whether the NAFTA constituted a treaty requiring the advice and consent of the Senate. Given the frequent interaction of the President and Congress during major trade negotiations, the court held that the question of what constitutes a "treaty" requiring Senate ratification is a nonjusticiable political question. Therefore, the court lacked jurisdiction under Article III of the Constitution. Made in the U.S.A. Foundation v. United States of America, 242 F.3d 1300 (11th Cir. 2001).

4. Do you think the TPA language on environmental objectives is specific enough to guarantee specific outcomes of trade negotiations? Should Congress have demanded specific conclusions to trade negotiations, such as the exemption of certain environmental laws from scrutiny under trade rules?

5. As of October 2010, three bilateral free trade agreements negotiated under George W. Bush remain signed but unimplemented by Congress: Colombia, Panama, and Korea. President Obama does not need new TPA to seek implementation of these agreements by Congress, because they have already been negotiated and signed. Moreover, he does not need TPA to negotiate any changes to those agreements or to participate in the reengagement of the Doha Development Agenda within the WTO; the procedural rules of the TPA would not apply, but Congress would get a chance to amend any implementing legislation President Obama submitted to it. Nevertheless, the lack of explicit negotiating authority weakens the U.S. hand with negotiators from other countries.

B. The European Union

The European Union (EU) has a revamped governing structure and a new constitutional framework as a result of approval in 2007 by all 27 Member States of the Treaty of Lisbon. The arrangements in the EU for agreeing to negotiate trade agreements, managing the negotiations, and then approving and implementing trade agreements are every bit as complex and constitutionally fragile as the U.S. process described in the previous section. To understand what follows, a brief introduction to the EU governing institutions is in order.

Like the United States, the EU essentially has a legislature, an executive, and a judiciary, but power among them is allocated differently. The legislature is the European Parliament, which meets in Strasbourg, France. On many issues, as we will see, the Parliament must be consulted but lacks direct legislative control of law and policy. The executive has most of the lawmaking power. The political lead for the executive comes through the Council. The "Council" is a council of government ministers of the Member States; it has varying membership depending on the issue to be decided. The key ministers overseeing the common commercial policy, which includes international trade, are the foreign ministers, not the trade ministers. For trade issues, the agriculture ministers also have a role. But most of the executive work is carried out by the European Commission. Based in Brussels, Belgium, and staffed with career civil servants, the Commission has the authority to initiate legislation and regulation on a wide range of issues. As we will see, it also serves as the trade negotiator and trade representative for the EU. In Chapter 4, Section VI.B., you will be introduced to the European Court of Justice, the judicial arm of the EU.

The European Union has been a work in progress for the last 60 years. Its evolution reached its latest culmination when the mammoth Treaty of Lisbon came into force on Dec. 1, 2009, after the Czech Republic gave it formal approval, the last of the 27 Member States to do so. With the Treaty of Lisbon, there are now two separate legal texts that govern the EU: 1) the Treaty on the European Union (TEU), which is a relatively short text setting forth broad rights and principles and the new governance architecture, and 2) the much more elaborate Treaty on the Functioning of the European Union (TFEU), which blends elements of the predecessor European treaties and provides substantial detail about the jurisdiction and policies of the EU vis-à-vis the member states on many issues and the allocation of authority among the different elements of the EU government. As noted at the beginning of this chapter, the terms European Community and European Communities, which you will see in many WTO documents, have passed into oblivion. The European Union, in all its aspects, is now known simply as the European Union, or EU. A consolidated English text of EU treaties incorporating the Lisbon changes, to be cited as O.J. C115, 9.5.2008 is available at http://eur-lex.europa.eu/JOHtml.do?uri=OJ:C:2008:115:SOM:EN:HTML. In the following excerpts, the editors have inserted in brackets the new numbers for the treaty articles.

Europe first adopted a common commercial (trade) policy in the 1957 Treaty of Rome, but the modern role of the EU in trade policy took shape only after a 1971 decision by the European Court of Justice affirming that the treaties had transferred the rights and obligations of the Member States under the GATT to the European level. The "common commercial policy" springs from Article 206 of the TFEU: "By establishing a customs union in accordance with Articles 28 to 32, the Union shall contribute, in the common interest, to the harmonious development of world trade, the progressive abolition of restrictions on international trade and on foreign direct investment, and the lowering of customs and other barriers."

Article 207 of the TFEU sets the procedures for developing and implementing elements of the common commercial policy. Article 207(1) declares the core elements of the policy, with specific reference to "trade in … services, the commercial aspects of intellectual property [and] foreign direct investment" in addition to its traditional coverage of trade in goods and "measures to protect trade such as those to be taken in the event of dumping or subsidies."

Although the European Parliament and the Council are to work together to define the framework for implementing the common commercial policy (Art. 207(2)), it is up to the

Council, upon recommendations from the Commission, to authorize the Commission to negotiate and to oversee any negotiations necessary to achieve the objectives of the policy (Art. 207(3)). Article 207(3) also provides that the Council shall appoint a special committee for the Commission to consult with during the course of negotiations, and that the Commission shall report "regularly" to that committee and to the European Parliament. This special committee has been a feature of European trade policy governance for many years.

Article 207(4) provides that in authorizing negotiations and in accepting the results of negotiations, the Council will ordinarily act on the basis of qualified majority voting (QMV). Without going into the details of QMV (because the rules will be changing in coming years), the QMV process allows the EU to act on many matters without unanimous consent from the Member States. For matters regarding trade in services, trade-related aspects of intellectual property, and foreign direct investment, however, Article 207 expressly requires unanimous approval in most cases because unanimity is required by other parts of the TFEU for internal measures related to those topics. The following excerpt helps to situate EU trade diplomacy in the WTO context.

Jens Ladefoged Mortensen, *The World Trade Organization and the European Union*

THE EUROPEAN UNION AND INTERNATIONAL ORGANIZATIONS
80, 81–83 (Knud Erik Jørgensen ed., 2009)

Who are the EU trade diplomats?

It is helpful to start off by asking a seemingly simple question: Who are the EU trade diplomats? I suggest that these can be understood in terms of overlapping concentric circles, as depicted in Figure 5.1.

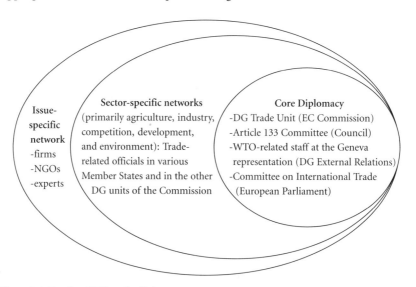

Figure 5.1 Levels of EU trade diplomacy

The legal basis for the Common Commercial Policy is [Art. 207] of the [Treaty on the Functioning of the European Union] that provides for the delegation of powers from the national to the supranational level on all matters concerning international trade. Consequently, the Commission negotiates in Geneva in consultation with the Article [207] Committee (which meets on a weekly basis). All agreements must be ratified by the Council of Ministers by a qualified majority. At the centre is the DG External Trade unit in the Commission. According to latest budget figures, the DG Trade consists of roughly 550 people, currently headed by Commissioner Peter Mandelson [update: as of Dec. 1, 2009, the trade commissioner is Benita Ferrero-Waldner]. It is telling that the former Trade Commissioner, Pascal Lamy, is the current General Director (DG) of the WTO. The first General Director of the WTO, Peter Sutherland, was a former Commissioner for Competition 1985–1989. The 'EU representation to International Organizations in Geneva' is also part of the core trade diplomacy even if it also manages relations with other Geneva-based IOs [international organizations]. It consists of roughly 18 people, being one of the largest in Geneva. To this, one must add each national representation of the member states in Geneva. The relevant European Parliament Committees (like those on International Trade or Development, respectively) are also considered part of the permanent machinery of the EU trade diplomacy. The current status of the EP [European Parliament] is limited to that of an advisor.

One of the peculiar features of the EU–WTO relationship is that the European Community [now EU] is a member of the WTO itself alongside the EU member states. It is common practice to let the EU delegate speak on behalf of all member states in the WTO—even if individual member states are present. A few comments on the voting issue are in order as it is in stark contrast to those relating to EU business in the IMF and World Bank. Since both the European Union and its member states are formally represented in the WTO process, critics have—particularly in the United States—argued that EU interests have double weight in the WTO. Yet, Article IX of the WTO Agreement determines that the number of votes cannot exceed the number of the individual [EU] member states. In any event, the WTO Councils and bodies operate on a consensus voting norm. WTO issues are almost never put to a formal vote. Consensus is determined in the corridors and not by counting votes at meetings. Nonetheless, the special status of the European Union in the WTO is indicative of how prominently the European Union is positioned throughout the WTO process.

The next circle of the EU diplomacy is slightly more fluid, open ended and policy sector specific in its composition. Yet, EU trade diplomacy cannot be understood without references to the different segments of the Commission. Also, as the WTO involves the member states directly, these interests are represented either directly via the Council in the core diplomacy or through sector-specific networks involving the relevant parts of the national governments. The outer layer of the EU trade diplomacy is an extremely fluid trade policy network that includes sections of the civil society, the trade policy expert community and other private actors. This layer is the issue-specific aspect of the EU–WTO process. These networks are increasingly integrated into the policy process, however, as reflected by WTO dispute settlement, anti-dumping proceedings or the trade barriers regulation.

Putnam's two-level game model stresses the fact that trade diplomats play different games simultaneous[ly] in the various capitals, in Brussels, in Geneva and in Washington. An explanation of what the European Union does in the WTO must take the dynamics at different levels into consideration. Putnam-inspired analysis explains trade diplomacy as outcomes of 'synergistic policy linkage' and 're-

verberation' between the external and internal negotiations. The relationship resembles a principal-agent relationship. Member states may well have accepted the
political benefits of having the Commission to speak on behalf of the European
Union in the WTO, but they remain 'at pains to ensure that such de facto authority ... does not lead to an increase in the acquired powers of the Commission'.
When negotiating, DG External Trade meets frequently with the Article [207]
committee (comprised of senior national officials). Member states have also limited the scope of the exclusive competence by excluding audio-visual services,
health services and education (Article [207], para. 5–6). Although the transfer of
powers following Article [207] is uniquely strong, the room of manoeuvre for an
independent-minded Commission in the WTO confronts several control mechanisms. Yet, the power of the EU trade bureaucracy in day-to-day WTO matters
is considerable. Issue-specific WTO governance requires extensive legal and diplomatic expertise. This puts the Commission in the driving seat in most day-to-
day activities in the WTO.

C. Other Countries

Hal Shapiro & Lael Brainard, *Trade Promotion Authority Formerly Known as Fast Track: Building Common Ground on Trade Demands More than a Name Change*

35 Geo. Wash. Int'l L. Rev. 1, 33–34 (2003)

[F]or many foreign countries approval of trade agreements is fairly automatic;
this is most likely in parliamentary systems where the prime minister is by definition the leader of the majority bloc in the legislature, and there is only partial, if any, separation between the legislature and the executive. In Japan and
India, for instance, the legislature plays a limited role in treaty approval—voting only on certain treaties, approving most with little rancor, and lacking the
ability to offer amendments as a practical if not a legal matter.

In other parliamentary countries such as Australia and the United Kingdom,
there is a dualist system in which treaties must be implemented through separate
legislation in order to have the effect of domestic law. The need for domestic implementing legislation creates opportunities for parliaments to offer interpretations or take positions that may not be consistent with the letter or spirit of an
agreement. In some federal systems such as Canada and Germany, the federal
government is limited in its ability to bind states or provinces. Switzerland presents an extreme example of this, where certain types of trade agreements have
traditionally required approval not only by the legislature, but also through a
referendum requiring a majority of the electorate and the Swiss provinces.

Questions and Discussion

1. Compare the European process with that of the United States in terms of degree of
political control over the negotiations and degree of assurance that the political bodies will

agree to the results brought to them by the negotiators. In an earlier analysis, Mortensen observed that the EU process has dangers of fragmentation and inertia, leading many to call for a European "fast track." One substitute was devised near the end of the Uruguay Round negotiations—a "Jumbo Council" of Europe's foreign ministers, trade ministers, and agricultural ministers at which important last-minute compromises within the EU were negotiated. Jens L. Mortensen, *Institutional Challenges and Paradoxes of EU Governance in External Trade, in* THE UNION AND THE WORLD 211, 220 (A. Cafruny & P. Peters eds., 1998).

2. Another feature of the European situation that favors rapid agreement is a so-called "EU policy style" for resolving conflicts through cross-cutting policy networks. *Id.* at 221–22. The Mortensen excerpt above describes those networks. In what ways do these networks differ from the U.S. process?

3. Consider the problem of "mixed agreements" in the EU, agreements for which the European Commission and the Member governments share authority. The most challenging of the mixed agreements are the WTO agreements on services (GATS) and trade-related intellectual property rights (TRIPS). During the Uruguay Round negotiations, the Commission claimed exclusive competence to negotiate these agreements. Several EU Member States contested the power of the Commission to conclude the GATS and TRIPS agreements. The Commission asked the European Court of Justice (ECJ) for an advisory opinion. In its Opinion 1/94, Competence of the Community to Conclude International Agreements Concerning Services and the Protection of Intellectual Property, 1994 E.C.R. I-5267, P 5, [1995] 1 C.M.L.R. 205, the ECJ surprised many observers by splitting the baby. It upheld the Commission's broad power over trade in goods, including agriculture, but held that with respect to services and intellectual property the Commission and the Member States had "joint competences." The ECJ called upon the parties to recognize a "duty to cooperate" while recognizing "the need for unitary representation." The Treaty of Lisbon modifies this outcome by affirming Commission authority to negotiate on services and trade-related intellectual property issues, but with the proviso that such negotiation require unanimous consent of the Member States, thus recognizing their own prerogatives in these matters. On the trade in goods aspect of the ECJ opinion, Jacques H.J. Bourgeois makes the following comment: "It is worth mentioning that Opinion 1/94 put an end to a number of uncertainties that led to recurrent discussions: the [EU] has the power under Article [207] to enter into international agreements including … international agreements on trade in agricultural products, international agreements such as the WTO Agreement on Sanitary and Phytosanitary Measures and the WTO Agreement on Technical Barriers to Trade." Jacques H.J. Bourgeois, *External Relations Powers of the European Community*, 22 FORDHAM INT'L L.J. 149, 161 (1999).

4. Notwithstanding the negotiating authority of the European Commission, it operates under the political shadow of the Member States. Shapiro and Brainard describe the consequences:

> The European Union (EU) requires the European Commission (Commission) to muster a consensus, or at least a weighted majority, among sovereign member nations through the Council of Ministers. Accordingly, the Commission goes to great lengths to build advance support for its negotiating positions among member-states, primarily through the so-called [207] Committee, which consists of national trade officials. Unlike fast track, however, this process does not always involve a formal vote. This has been evident in several instances where one member state (e.g., France) has sharply pulled back the Commission in the endgame of multilateral agricultural negotiations. Following approval of a trade

agreement at the EU level, some member states require additional domestic implementing legislation to ensure national laws are in compliance.

Hal Shapiro & Lael Brainard, *Trade Promotion Authority Formerly Known as Fast Track*, at 34.

5. How does the democratization argument apply in the EU context? Is there better democratic control of the Commission through the Council, where member governments have control, or in the directly-elected European Parliament, which is not connected to any national government?

Chapter 3

Border Issues — Tariffs, Quotas, and Export Restrictions

I. Introduction

Countries regulate goods, services, and investments in their national markets in myriad ways. A number of the WTO agreements focus on the routine ways governments regulate internal markets and respond to international economic forces. The agreements are designed to strike a balance in each case between the right of each country to manage its own economy and the opportunity for foreign providers of goods, services, and investments to compete in every national market on equal terms. The most common mode of government regulation is to establish a rule that applies to a particular good or service within the country: emission standards for automobiles; child-proof caps for medications or other potentially harmful products; and maximum levels of bacteria or other contaminants in food. The WTO agreements that address these kinds of internal measures afford a degree of regulatory flexibility to governments, subject in most cases to the basic requirement that the internal regulation should not discriminate against foreign goods, services, and investments in favor of domestic ones. Chapter 4 begins the discussion of issues relating to internal regulations.

This chapter focuses on the trade law that applies to those measures that more directly affect international trade by controlling, at the national border, the ability of goods, services, and investments to enter or leave the national market. The GATT, in particular, contains important provisions that severely limit the right of governments to exclude foreign products from their market or to prevent their domestic products from being exported. Because the severe limitations against these kinds of border measures contrast with the more lenient approach toward internal regulations, a critical legal issue arises in deciding whether a particular national requirement is a border measure or an internal measure. In GATT terminology, this is the distinction between a border measure applied to the "importation" or "exportation" of a good on the one hand and an internal measure applied to "imported" goods on the other.

By far the most common border measure is the tariff. Tariffs, also known as duties, are taxes imposed on imported products based on the value of the product, the quantity of items imported, or the weight or measure of the product. Because tariffs increase the cost of imports, they improve the competitive position of domestic products — in trade language, they afford protection to domestic production. Although tariffs themselves have not played a significant role in the trade and environment context, they are the foundation or reference point for most of the WTO agreements. Section II of this chapter describes how tariffs operate and how they are controlled by the GATT and other agreements. It also explores the possible environmental impacts of different tariff rates.

The General Agreement on Tariffs and Trade, as its name suggests, allows countries to use tariffs as a tool to hinder imports and thereby protect domestic production and sales. It then tries to assure that *only* tariffs are used for economic protection. Article XI, commonly characterized as the prohibition against quantitative restrictions, is the key GATT provision against nontariff border restrictions. Because tariffs themselves, as well as import or export quotas and other quantitative trade restrictions, are enforced by national customs authorities at the point of import or export, these aspects of international trade law focus on borders to determine the validity of measures used to facilitate or hinder trade. The validity of such measures, however, is not defined by geographic or physical borders *per se* but rather by "doctrinal, conceptual, and ideological" borders. Jeffrey L. Dunoff, *Border Patrol at the World Trade Organization*, 9 Y.B. Int'l Envtl. L. 21, 21 (1998).

Countries may want to impose import and export restrictions on products for any number of reasons. They may want to ban exports or impose export taxes to conserve natural resources or provide cheaper natural resources for domestic industries. They may feel a responsibility to impose export restraints to protect foreign countries and their citizens from harmful substances, such as toxic waste or hazardous chemicals. Import bans serve protectionist purposes by shielding industries from less expensive foreign products, but they may also serve environmental purposes by curtailing harmful environmental practices or protecting citizens from harmful products or waste. Whether the GATT allows such import and export restrictions depends on how key "border" phrases, such as "affecting the internal sale," "on the importation," and "sale for export" are defined. Section III of this chapter begins the discussion of these border issues.

II. Tariffs

A. GATT's Permissible Means of Protectionism

Article II of the GATT provides the authorization to impose tariffs and the basic ground rules for national tariff systems. Within the framework of Article II, countries negotiate with each other and reach binding agreements on the maximum tariffs that each country will impose on particular products. These agreements are called tariff bindings, and the maximum tariff that can be imposed is called a bound tariff. Article II:1(a) of the GATT imposes the most favored nation obligation on tariff setting by requiring WTO members to accord tariff treatment "no less favourable" than that provided in their tariff bindings to all imported products in the same tariff category regardless of their origin. Article I of the GATT, the basic most favored nation provision, covers another tariff situation. A member may offer tariffs lower than its bound tariffs, but unless the lower tariff is applied pursuant to an exception, as discussed below, the most favored nation obligation requires that the WTO member grant the lower tariff to all imported products within that tariff category from all WTO members.

Table 3-1. Tariff Reductions under the GATT

Round	Dates	Number of Countries	Value of Trade Covered	Average Tariff Cut	Average Tariff Afterward
Geneva	1947	23	$10 billion	35%	"not available"
Annecy	1949	33	Unavailable	35%	"not available"
Torquay	1950	34	Unavailable	35%	"not available"
Geneva	1956	22	$2.5 billion	35%	"not available"
Dillon	1960–61	45	$4.9 billion	35%	"not available"
Kennedy	1962–67	48	$40 billion	35%	8.7%
Tokyo	1973–79	99	$155 billion	34%	6.3%
Uruguay	1986–94	120+	$3.7 billion	38%	3.9%

John Jackson, The World Trading System 74 (2d ed. 1998).

In terms of international economic policy, the GATT and WTO have made significant progress in standardizing and reducing tariffs. As Table 3–1 shows, the GATT Contracting Parties negotiated reductions in tariffs of roughly 35 percent at each negotiating round, bringing the average tariff on manufactured goods of industrial countries down from an estimated 40 percent in 1947 to 3.9 percent today.

Because countries have traditionally maintained tariffs to protect domestic producers from competition with foreign products, the tariff reductions over the last 60 years clearly represent a great achievement for the GATT and WTO. Still, the average tariff after the Uruguay Round is in fact an *average*, with countries using tariffs to protect certain domestic goods and industries. For example, the United States imposes tariffs of 20 percent or more on some products, including a 27.9 percent tariff on certain men's clothing and other textiles to shield American businesses from imports from countries such as Pakistan and Honduras. Harmonized Tariff Schedule of the United States (2010) (Rev. 1), HTS 6203.43.40; 6203.49.20, *available at* http://www.usitc.gov/tata/hts/bychapter/index.htm. Of course, developing countries protect their industries too. Although India nearly halved its tariffs during the Uruguay Round, its average bound tariff on nonagricultural goods is still 34.7 percent. Indonesia's average bound tariff on nonagricultural goods is 35.6 percent. WTO et al., World Tariff Profiles 16 (2009).

Countries maintain these protectionist tariffs through negotiations. First, members may simply refuse to negotiate binding tariffs, despite the requirement of GATT Article XXVIII *bis* for negotiations to be reciprocal and mutually advantageous. If a product is not included in the negotiated tariff schedule, then a WTO member may impose any tariff it wants. Developing countries have historically refused to establish binding tariffs due to their development, financial, and trade needs. Developed countries have bound 99 percent of their tariffs, while developing countries on average have bound only 73 percent of their tariffs. WTO, *Goods Schedules: Members' Commitments, available at* http://www.wto.org/english/tratop_e/schedules_e/goods_schedules_e.htm. Many African countries have bound fewer than ten percent of their tariffs for nonagricultural goods; Cameroon, for example, has bound just 0.1 percent of its tariffs on nonagricultural products. Nonetheless, developing countries with stronger economies, including Brazil, Chile, and China, have bound tariffs for all nonagricultural goods; Thailand, the Philippines, and Singapore, among others, have bound a majority of their tariffs for nonagricultural goods. WORLD TARIFF PROFILES, at 14, 16, 18.

Second, the process of negotiating tariffs has always been cumbersome and has become more so as the number of participating countries has risen. Traditionally, each country would negotiate sets of tariffs for thousands of products with several of its major trading partners, but the tariff levels agreed to would apply to all countries under Article II's most favored nation clause. That is, a country was negotiating bilaterally with one country, while at the same time negotiating tariffs with all countries. This made the "rounds" of negotiations amazingly complex, because Country A might agree to reduce its tariff on one product with Country B, but only if Country C reduced its tariff on a different product.

As more countries joined the GATT, this product-by-product negotiating strategy became increasingly problematic. As a result, the parties initiated a process by which a party would offer tariff reductions of, say, 50 percent for all products within a particular sector. If other parties did not accept that offer, then the parties would seek a more limited reduction until agreement was reached. Further nuances to negotiating exist, as well as rules for modification, suspension, and withdrawal of tariff bindings. See ANWARUL HODA, TARIFF NEGOTIATIONS AND RENEGOTIATIONS UNDER THE GATT AND THE WTO: PROCEDURES AND PRACTICES (2001); JOHN JACKSON, THE WORLD TRADING SYSTEM, at 143, 175–211.

Third, other provisions of the GATT and other WTO agreements allow countries temporarily to impose tariffs on selected products at rates much higher than the bound tariffs. Under Article XIX of the GATT, known as the "escape clause," and the related WTO Agreement on Safeguards, a country may impose temporary protective tariffs, called "safeguard measures," to fend off imports of certain products if it can show that there has been a sudden and unexpected increase in imports and that the increase is causing or threatening to cause serious injury to its domestic industry. Under Article VI and its related WTO agreement on anti-dumping, and under the WTO Agreement on Subsidies and Countervailing Measures, countries may also impose extra tariffs to counteract the effects of "dumping" by foreign producers (selling at below cost or at a price lower than in their own domestic market) or the benefits of subsidies that foreign producers receive. These tariffs are allowed only on a showing that the unfair trade practice is causing "substantial injury" to domestic producers. These kinds of defensive tariff measures have been controversial as a matter of trade theory and because of their abuse by many countries, but they remain politically popular.

The most recent negotiations have included efforts to use the tariff schedules as a means to reduce barriers to trade in environmental goods. Paragraph 31(iii) of the Doha Ministerial Declaration calls for negotiations "on the reduction or, as appropriate, elimination of tariff and non-tariff barriers to environmental goods...." Although the governments have not yet agreed on how to define this category, it could reasonably include pollution control equipment and might also include consumer or industrial products with especially good environmental performance characteristics, such as zero-emission vehicles, organic foods, and sustainably-produced timber. In 2007, the United States and the European Union jointly proposed an Environmental Goods and Services Agreement, including removal of all tariffs on a World Bank list of environmental technologies.

B. Exceptions to MFN for Tariffs: Free Trade Areas, Customs Unions, and GSP

Although each WTO member has a standard schedule of tariffs that it negotiated with the other WTO members and that applies to all other WTO members, many members, including the United States and the European Union, have tariff schedules with several tiers of tariffs depending on the origin of the goods in question. The GATT itself permits tiered tariff regimes through two important exceptions to the requirement to implement tariffs consistent with the most favored nation obligation.

The first exception allows preferential tariff rates among members of free trade agreements (such as the North American Free Trade Agreement) or customs unions (such as the European Union), provided that those free trade agreements or customs unions encompass almost all trade among the participating countries. Thus, most goods pass from the United States to Mexico, or from Jordan to the United States, at lower (including zero) tariffs pursuant to free trade agreements than tariffs negotiated through the WTO. Likewise, goods pass tariff-free from Portugal to Poland or Greece to Ireland because these countries are all members of the European Union, which is a customs union.

As noted in Chapter 2, there are many free trade agreements in different parts of the world, and several customs unions as well. Consequently, a substantial fraction of world trade is not subject to tariffs negotiated under the auspices of the WTO, but benefit instead from lower or zero tariffs among the various participating countries to free trade agreements and customs unions. Whether or not these preferential trading arrangements divert trade and undermine the multilateral WTO system is an issue of perennial debate and analysis.

Members may also deviate from their WTO-negotiated tariffs under the Generalized System of Preferences (GSP), which was adopted by the GATT parties in 1971 to bring more of the benefits of liberalized trade to the least developed countries. Without going into detail, the GSP allows each country or customs union to establish its own system, with its own criteria, for granting lower tariff rates to goods from qualifying developing countries than those normally applied on a most favored nation basis. *See* GATT Contracting Parties, *Decision of November 28, 1979 on Differential and More Favourable Treatment, Reciprocity and Fuller Participation of Developing Countries*, para. 2, L/4903 (Nov. 28, 1979), GATT B.I.S.D. (26th Supp.) at 203 (1980). Thus, some wildlife, such as birds from developing countries, may enter the United States under GSP tariffs. HTS 0106.31.00.

The excerpt from the U.S. Harmonized Tariff System on page 142 gives some idea of the complexity of the tariff schedules and the tariff distinctions made pursuant to the GSP and various regional free trade agreements and customs unions. It thus highlights the importance for many trade transactions of "rules of origin," an important practical dimension of trade law which gets only occasional mention in this book.

C. The Special Case of Tariffs on Agricultural Products

Through subsidies, price supports, and tariffs, agricultural products remain some of the most heavily protected of all products in international trade. While the GATT technically applies to trade in all goods, widespread noncompliance with the GATT with respect to trade in agricultural goods has essentially placed these goods beyond GATT discipline. Many lay the blame at the feet of the U.S. Congress, which adopted legislation in 1955 mandating import restrictions on certain agricultural goods. The United States achieved "consistency" with the GATT only when the GATT parties granted the United States a waiver from GATT requirements. Although other countries did not obtain a waiver, they acted as if they did. JOHN JACKSON, THE WORLD TRADING SYSTEM, at 57–58, 314–15.

During the Uruguay Round of trade negotiations, countries made progress on eliminating nontariff barriers on agricultural goods by converting quotas, voluntary export restraints, and other barriers to tariffs that tend to achieve the same level of trade protection. Due to this process of "tariffication," virtually 100 percent of agricultural products now have bound tariff rates. GATT Secretariat, *The Results of the Uruguay Round of Multilateral Trade Negotiations* (Nov. 1994). Because tariffs constitute a quantifiable barrier, many view them as easier to reduce through negotiations than nontariff barriers. Under the separate WTO Agreement on Agriculture, WTO members committed to gradually reduce agricultural tariffs: an average of 36 percent over a six-year period ending in 2000 for developed countries and an average of 24 percent over a 10-year period ending in 2004 for developing countries. Despite these concessions, agricultural tariffs remain high and the Agreement on Agriculture exempts certain primary agricultural products from tariffication. Subsequent Doha round negotiations in 2004 achieved a breakthrough, with members agreeing to a set of principles to achieve "[s]ubstantial overall tariff reductions" on agricultural products. WTO, General Council, Decision on 1 August 2004, WT/L/579, para. 29 (Aug. 2, 2004). Nonetheless, the failure of the members to reach a final agreement has put the Doha round in limbo. The treatment of agricultural tariffs, subsidies, and other domestic support in the Agreement on Agriculture is covered in more detail in Chapter 8.

————————

D. Classification and Valuation of Products

Two other important tariff issues have caused persistent problems: classification and valuation of tariffs. When a foreign good arrives at a port of entry, customs officials must determine what tariff (if any) must be paid before the good can clear customs and enter the market of the importing country. The tariff to be paid depends on three elements: 1) the classification of the good, 2) the value of the good, and 3) the country from which it originated.

With respect to classification, millions of trade transactions occur each year with each product classified into one of about 8,000 different product classifications. Through international negotiation, and now through WTO agreement, countries assign all products to one or another classification based on the Harmonized Tariff System (HTS). The HTS assigns 6-digit codes for general categories; countries that use the HTS are allowed to define commodities at a level more detailed than 6 digits, but all definitions must be within that 6-digit framework. The United States defines products using 10-digit HTS codes. Import codes are administered by the U.S. International Trade Commission (USITC). Exports codes (which the United States calls Schedule B) are administered by the U.S. Census Bureau. *See* http://www.ita.doc.gov/TTFrameset.html. As the excerpt from the U.S. HTS shows in Table 3–2, every item is assigned a unique 10-digit identification code and every 10-digit item is part of a series of progressively broader product categories. It also shows the different treatment accorded to different trading partners. The general rate of duty applies to "normal trade relations." The "special" duty category includes tariff rates pursuant to non-WTO free trade agreements or other programs allowing special tariff treatment, including: the Generalized System of Preferences (A, A* or A+); the North American Free Trade Agreement with Canada (CA) and Mexico (MX); the African Growth and Opportunity Act (D); the Caribbean Basin Economic Recovery Act (E or E*); the Andean Trade Preference Act or Andean Trade Promotion and Drug Eradication Act (J, J* or J+); and free trade agreements or similar arrangements with, among others, Australia (AU); Chile (CL); Israel (IL); Jordan (JO), Singapore (SG) the Dominican Republic and Central America (P or P+); and Peru (PE). The "other" rate of duty, known technically as "column 2," applies only to goods from Cuba and North Korea, with whom the United States does not have "normal trade relations."

Customs officials have the responsibility to classify a product into one of hundreds of possible categories. This important decision could mean the difference between no tariff and a significant tariff. For example, if an energy efficient light-emitting diode (LED) light bulb is classified as an LED, then it may enter the United States duty free under HTS 8541.40.20. If it is classified as some form of lamp, as has been the case in a number of rulings, then it will be subject to a 2.4 percent *ad valorem* tariff under HTS 8539.49. *See* "The Tariff Classification of an LED Lamp from Germany," NY M83236 (May 18, 2006) (placing an LED light bulb in HTS 8539.49.0080 as "other" electrical filament or discharge lamps). To ensure consistency in classifying products, many countries use the Harmonized Commodity Description and Coding System, which creates a single set of product categories. It also provides rules for classification of goods that may reasonably fall into two or more different categories.

Different methods for valuation of products have also led to a harmonized scheme to achieve greater consistency among nations. While some tariffs are based on the weight, number, or other physical measure of the imported product, such as the tuna products found in Table 3-2, most are *ad valorem*, e.g., 5 percent of the value of the product. Determining the value of the product, however, became a concern among GATT parties because countries were using different valuation methods. The GATT contracting parties negotiated the "Valuation Code" to bring some uniformity and perhaps greater simplicity to the valuation process; only minor changes were made to the new WTO agreement on valuation—the Agreement on Implementation of Article VII of the General Agreement on Tariffs and Trade 1994. The basic principle, expressed in Article 1 of the WTO's agreement on valuation, defines "customs value of imported goods" as "the price actually paid or payable for the goods when sold for export to the country of importation." It also includes additional rules and procedures for determining the value when the "price paid" is not available or not reliable, such as when the transaction is between related parties, and for making other adjustments. For more on valuation of goods, *see* WTO, *Customs Valuation: Technical Information, available at* http://www.wto.org/english/tratop_e/cusval_e/ cusval_info_e.htm#1; Raj Bhala & Kevin Kennedy, World Trade Law 316–41 (1998).

Questions and Discussion

1. The classification of goods can sometimes lead to litigation, as in the case of LED lights mentioned above. In another case, the Bureau of Customs and Border Protection classified Certs® Powerful Mints as sugar confectionery subject to a 5.6 percent tariff under HTS 2106.90.00. Warner-Lambert, the producer of Certs®, successfully argued before the Federal Circuit court that the mints were sugar-free and thus duty free "prepa-

Table 3-2. Harmonized Tariff System of the United States (2010)

Heading/ Subheading	Stat. Suffix	Article Description	Unit of Quantity	General Rate of Duty	Special Rate of Duty	Other Rate of Duty
1604		Prepared or preserved fish; caviar and caviar substitutes prepared from fish eggs * * *				
		Fish, whole or in pieces, but not minced:				
1604.14		Tunas, skipjack and bonito (Sarda spp.):				
		Tunas and skipjack				
		In airtight containers				
1604.14.10		in oil...............................	....	35%	Free (A+, AU, BH, CA, D, IL, JO, MA, MX, OM, P, R) 10.5% (CL, SG) 28% (PE)	45%
	10	In foil or other flexible containers weighing with their contents not more than 6.8 kg each..............	kg			
		* * *				
		not in oil:				
1604.14.22		In containers weighing with their contents not over 7 kg each, and not the product of any insular possession of the United States, for an aggregate quantity enter3ed in any calendar year not to exceed 4.8 percent of apparent United States consumption of tuna in airtight containers during the immediately preceding year, as reported by the National Marine Fisheries Service..	....	6%	Free (A+, AU, BH, CA, D, IL, JO, MA, MX, OM, SG) 0.4% (R) 0.8% (P) 1.8% (CL) 4.8% (PE)	25%
		* * *				
		Tunas and skipjack				
1604.14.40	00	Not in airtight containers: (in bulk or in immediate containers weighing with their contents over 6.8 kg each, not in oil)....................	....	1.1¢/kg	Free (A+,AU, BH, CA, CL, D, E, IL, J, JO, MA, MX, OM, P, PE, SG)	2.8¢/kg
		Bonita (Sarda spp.)				
1604.14.70	00	In oil......................................	kg	4.9%	Free (A+,AU, BH, CA, CL, D, E, IL, J, JO, MA, MX, OM, P, PE, SG)	30%
1604.14.80	00	Not in oil..............................	kg	6%	Free (A+,AU, BH, CA, CL, D, E, IL, J, JO, MA, MX, OM, P, PE, SG)	25%

rations for oral or dental hygiene" under HTS 3306.90.00. Warner-Lambert Co. v. United States, 407 F.3d 1207 (Fed. Cir. 2005).

2. The Appellate Body has held that a WTO member's GSP scheme does not need to provide identical tariff preferences to all developing countries. According to the Appellate Body, a member's GSP scheme may be "nondiscriminatory" even if it does not provide identical tariff treatment to all GSP beneficiaries. However, the preference-granting members must ensure that "identical treatment is available to all similarly-situated GSP beneficiaries, that is, to all GSP beneficiaries that have the 'development, financial, and trade needs' to which the treatment in question is intended to respond." Nevertheless, the GSP scheme must provide clear criteria for determining eligibility for GSP preferences. European Communities-Conditions for the Granting of Tariff Preferences to Developing Countries, Appellate Body Report, WT/DSB246/AB/R, para. 173 (Apr. 20, 2004). As a result of this ruling, members may provide GSP benefits based on a developing country's respect for international labor norms, sustainable forestry practices, drug eradication efforts, or other factors.

E. Environmental Impacts of Tariffs

Until the late 1990s, environmental advocates tended to ignore the issue of tariffs and the effects that tariffs might have on the environment. They began to pay greater attention to tariffs when the Asia-Pacific Economic Cooperation (APEC), a negotiating forum for 21 Pacific Rim economies, began discussing a proposal to eliminate tariffs on timber, fish, chemicals, toys, gems and jewelry, medical equipment, environmental goods and services, and energy products. The APEC Ministers also agreed in 1999 to initiate a similar process in the WTO, which became known as the Accelerated Tariff Liberalization, to conclude an agreement to eliminate tariffs in these sectors.

APEC's proposal to eliminate tariffs on timber products galvanized the environmental community, which quickly dubbed the proposal the "Global Free Logging Agreement." Many countries, particularly developing countries, impose significant tariffs on imported timber products as a means to protect their mills from foreign competition. Perhaps unintentionally, high tariffs on timber products may reduce logging rates by increasing the costs of timber products. Higher production costs translate into higher consumer costs, which in turn reduce demand. The U.S. Trade Representative, however, stated that eliminating tariffs for all forest products would "promote sustainable management of forestry to the benefit of both developed and developing economies." Press Release, Executive Office of the President: The United States Trade Representative, Barshefsky Welcomes APEC Sectoral Agreement—Plans to Move Initiative to WTO (Nov. 15, 1998). Environmentalists vehemently disagreed, stating that tariff elimination would increase deforestation. They found support from an unlikely source, a study commissioned by the American Forest and Paper Association, an industry trade group. That report estimated that the elimination of tariffs on timber products would increase consumption of forest products by 3 to 4 percent.

As an initial matter, global demand for forest products continues to grow. Between 1970 and 1996, consumption of roundwood—wood in its natural state—increased by 40 percent to 3,354 million cubic meters (m3). Consumption has leveled off since then, reaching 3,535 m3 in 2006. While per capita consumption is far larger in the United States, Japan, and Europe than in developing countries, consumption is growing most rapidly in poorer countries, particularly China, where rising incomes have increased domestic consumption and rapid development has increased production of wood products.

International trade is an important element of the forest products industry. While only about 4 percent of roundwood is exported, the quantity currently traded has increased by more than 80 percent since 1993, just prior to the completion of the Uruguay Round. In addition, about 31 percent of paper and paperboard is exported with quantities traded increasing by more than 79 percent from 1993, and 35 percent of sawnwood is exported with quantities traded increasing by more than 55 percent from 1993. While most countries engage in some trade in timber products, only a few countries dominate global trade. In 2006, for example, 5 countries accounted for 58 percent of all exports of roundwood and 10 countries for more than 72 percent.

So how might the elimination of tariffs on forest products change production and trade? As with much of the trade and environment debate, this issue is more complicated than described above. First of all, the Uruguay Round negotiations reduced average tariffs on most wood products below 1 percent and a trade-weighted average of about 5 percent; many countries have zeroed their tariffs. Thus, tariffs are already low. Any impact would be felt most in those countries with relatively high tariffs. Second, tariffs alone cannot explain trade flows and environmental impacts. Governments impose a range of subsidies and other nontariff barriers that affect price and availability of timber products, and thus demand. Third, a variety of factors influence how tariffs will affect markets and which countries will experience positive or negative environmental and social impacts from trade liberalization. Consider these points as you read the following excerpt.

Nigel Sizer, David Downes, & David Kaimowitz, *Tree Trade: Liberalization of International Commerce in Forest Products: Risks and Opportunities*

FOREST NOTES (World Res. Inst., Wash. D.C.), Nov. 1999, at 3–6, 8–9

Trade liberalization can be beneficial for forest conservation and sustainable management if domestic forest conservation policies are well developed and implemented, because, all else being equal, it enhances the competitiveness of producers that are more efficient, better managed, less wasteful, and better informed. Thus, a company with mills that convert logs into plywood with less loss of raw material in Malaysia might gain market share from a company in Cameroon that has older and poorly managed equipment, thereby sending more plywood to the market with lower raw log inputs.

The problem is that all else is *not* equal. In many countries, governments subsidize production by offering tax breaks, paying for road construction in logging operations, and helping with marketing, forest inventories, and so on. Weak environmental laws, or poor enforcement of laws, also reduce logging costs. And even illegal logging is tolerated in many places, with zero costs to the producer in taxes and forest management, let alone proper care of employees and local communities. These factors create undesirable comparative advantages for producers, increasing their competitiveness, and positioning them to benefit from greater access to foreign markets at the expense of more responsible producers elsewhere.

International trade, in itself, is not directly a threat to forests and can even provide incentives for responsible forest management. But where improved forest management and environmental and social safeguards do *not* accompany expanding trade, trade-related deforestation and forest degradation can occur. Trade policy also poses risks to implementation of those safeguards themselves. * * *

Tariffs vary greatly by country and product. Tariffs are now quite low … for most products entering the major importing countries. Therefore, for the bulk of trade, further tariff elimination would have relatively small effects at the global level, although even elimination of small tariffs might have a larger than expected impact for highly competitive markets with low profit margins, as is the case for basic commodity products. For wood panels (especially plywood), builders' woodwork materials, and furniture, rates are higher—in the 10 to 15 percent range. Rates are far higher in some non-OECD countries, with tariffs commonly reaching 20 to 40 percent.

Tariff escalation, where import levies are higher for more heavily processed products, is a common feature in many importing countries. Rates increase from logs (generally no tariffs), through sawnwood, panels, joinery, and laminates, to furniture. Such measures have been introduced to protect domestic processing industries from foreign competition. The Uruguay Round of Multilateral Trade Negotiations (signed in 1994) made a substantial dent in tariff escalation for forest products. Escalation for wood-based panels was cut by 30 percent from average pre-Uruguay Round levels; for semi-manufactured wood products, it dropped by 50 percent; and for wood articles, by 67 percent.

Countries whose timber industries would benefit most from tariff reduction include those that currently dominate world wood export markets—namely, Canada, the United States, and Indonesia. These countries are also considered the most competitive in most product classes. Reducing tariffs on plywood, for example, would greatly favor Indonesia's exports. Malaysia might also be a major beneficiary for the same reason. Brazilian exports could be a mid-term beneficiary as investment grows in value-added production. These are also countries where, therefore, increased pressure on forests from logging might be seen following further liberalization. Other forest-rich regions where wood exports are significant, such as the Congo Basin, Papua New Guinea, the Guianas, and Bolivia, could respond to tariff reductions by developing processing industries because they currently ship mostly logs and sawnwood. The net social and environmental impacts on those countries could, however, be negative if trade expands without adequate forest protection frameworks in place. These countries are also home to some of the world's most threatened and important forests, from the perspective of biodiversity, cultural and linguistic heritage, carbon values, and local dependence on natural forests. There could also be environmental benefits from shifts in trade if production were to decline in countries that are forest-rich but less competitive. * * *

Under a global free trade regime, so the theory goes, those who produce the best products at the lowest relative cost will benefit from expanding markets. There are many factors that serve to differentiate costs from place to place, including how well companies are run, the cost of borrowing money, infrastructure quality, local wages, and how quickly trees grow. In some countries, however, costs of production are lower because companies do not have to comply with the strict forest protection regulations, or regulations are simply not enforced. Policies designed to expand trade can therefore stimulate production in parts of the world with the weakest social standards and safeguards for environmental protection, or even where substantial illegal logging takes place, as in Brazil and Indonesia. This could have a number of serious economic, environmental, and social consequences. While different countries may choose different levels of protection and indeed have the right to do so, trade and trade rules are problematic if they exacerbate weaknesses in national policies, undercut national laws protecting forests, or stimulate activity inconsistent with international norms.

Tariff elimination and other changes that reduce the cost of trade will increase consumption of forest products. The increase in consumption will, however, probably be small at the global level. This is because tariffs are already generally low ... and demand for forest products is mostly local and driven primarily by income, population growth, new technology, and interest rates (the latter particularly affecting home building and the construction industry).

The impact of price tends to be higher on total supply than on demand, especially for softwood, but it is still not large. This means that, even if exporters are able to charge more for their products following liberalization, only moderate growth in timber supply will be seen worldwide. There could, however, be significant impacts in specific countries or regions. Areas with a greater response to increased prices (i.e., a higher price elasticity) would expect to see their market share increase. As discussed above, tariff reductions would likely enhance incentives for timber production in certain countries, such as Indonesia, Malaysia, and Canada.

Trade liberalization tends to stimulate increased efficiency of production in response to higher demand and rising prices for producers. Ultimately, this works its way back into the forest and the price of standing timber rises, serving as an incentive to reduce waste, increase recycling, and shift to plantation production. It can also make previously noncommercial species and smaller trees that were of lower value more commercially attractive. Areas of forest that were not previously logged might come into production. There is now rapid global expansion of industrial plants that convert smaller trees and previously less economically attractive species into wood panels, including oriented strand board (OSB), laminated veneer lumber (LVL), medium-density fiberboard (MDF), and particle board. More species and more forested regions are becoming attractive for logging, a trend that increased trade will likely accelerate. Overall, the efficiency improvements that result from trade liberalization may have either negative or positive consequences for the environment depending on specific circumstances.

In Sweden and Finland, it costs about twice as much to produce wood pulp as in Canada and the United States, and almost three times as much as in Indonesia. Sweden and Indonesia both have large state-of-the-art pulp mills. Those in Sweden are consuming logs from managed secondary forests and plantations that have been tightly regulated and now are third-party-certified according to the demanding criteria of the Forest Stewardship Council. In Indonesia, old-growth tropical forests are being cleared and converted directly into pulp (often illegally), with subsidies and no long-term sustainability. It is not surprising that production costs are much lower in the latter. Open competition between the Scandinavians and the Indonesians would be beneficial to the Indonesian economy in the short-term, but would lead to further liquidation of that country's forest resources. In an ideal world, Indonesia would embark on a process of rapid policy reform, crack down on illegal activities, and win substantial foreign aid to improve forest management practices. Sadly, the real world is far from ideal and tariff barriers may, in such an extreme case, be one of the few tools available to prevent expansion of unregulated logging. In the longer term, trade liberalization might lead to expansion of plantation forestry in Indonesia and less harvesting of secondary forests in Scandinavia (which would gradually revert to old growth).

A country where tariff reduction could have unusually large impacts on supply and demand is China, which has import tariffs of more than 20 percent for most categories. Furthermore, last year the government of China banned logging in many of its natural forests and has substantially increased imports, particularly from Indonesia, Laos, Cambodia, Vietnam, Russia and other countries, some of which have very poor records of forest management. With a fast-growing economy and an increasingly literate population, this country could soon become one of the largest importers of forest products.

Questions and Discussion

1. More recent studies have affirmed the key findings of Sizer et al.:

The net effect on social and environmental sustainability impact of possible trade liberalisation under [the] Doha agenda is ambiguous (positive in some areas and negative in others). In most contexts—both in developed countries and in developing countries—trade liberalisation alone is unlikely to cause significant direct negative sustainability impacts. However, it can accentuate negative trends in countries such as Brazil, Indonesia, and Papua New Guinea where forest governance systems are still relatively weak. It is likely that the most serious negative environmental impacts are likely to be experienced in countries, which contain regionally and globally unique biodiversity resources, but which suffer currently from sustainability and governance problems.

Marko Katila & Markku Simula, Sustainability Impact Assessment of Proposed WTO Negotiations: Final Report for the Forest Sector Study, at vii (June 19, 2005). Yet, even improved forest governance may simply shift the problem to other countries. For example, Indonesia and Malaysia have recently cracked down on illegal logging. Because illegal logging in these countries represented a significant source of logs for export, traders will be forced to find substitutes in other countries. Another example is China, which reduced its domestic harvest of trees to prevent flooding. The resulting loss of domestic wood supplies along with China's booming production of wood products for domestic and export markets have made China the biggest importer of raw forest products. What role should trade policy have in addressing these issues?

2. While researchers have focused on forest governance as the primary driver of environmental impacts, trade policy certainly may have profound impacts on trade flows, employment, and the environment. For example, when Tanzania significantly reduced import tariffs on wood products, including paper, a major pulp and paper mill closed because it was unable to compete with higher quality products offered at a lower price. Katila & Simula, Annex 5, at 19. From the perspective of comparative advantage, this is exactly what is supposed to happen. As a matter of sustainable development, what should happen? In addition, China has become a WTO member and slashed its tariffs on timber products, including zero tariffs on logs and pulp, although it maintains tariffs on value added wood products and paper products. China is now the world's largest log importer. Its imports of tropical logs almost tripled from the mid-1990s to 2005. From 1997 to 2005, the value of its raw wood materials and imports of

wood products rose from US$6.4 billion to US$16.4 billion. During the same period, its exports of forest products soared from US$4 billion to US$17 billion. Chinese exports increased by nearly 1,000 percent to the United States and 800 percent to the European Union. Chinese imports of Russian logs have increased 21 times since 1997, from 0.95 million to 20 million m3. UNITED NATIONS ECONOMIC COMMISSION FOR EUROPE/FOOD AND AGRICULTURE ORGANIZATION, FOREST PRODUCTS ANNUAL MARKET REVIEW 2005–2006 at 17, 19 (2006). However, Russia has increased its *export* tariffs on logs from 6.5 percent to 20 percent in 2007 and then to 25 percent in April 2008. It has delayed, for now, an increase to 80 percent, which was scheduled to take effect in January 2009. Russia's export tariffs may be affecting exports, which jumped from about 16 million m3 to a staggering 51 million m3. One report notes that Russian exports of logs through one Chinese port fell 32 percent due to Russia's tariff increases, and some believe that Russian exports to all of China will soon approach zero. China, however, will need to get its logs from elsewhere to feed its growing appetite for wood products. It already is increasing its imports of Russian sawnlogs, which jumped by more than 58 percent after Russia eliminated export tariffs on sawnwood. But it will need to get material for pulp and paper from elsewhere. For more on China and trade in forest products, see Fordaq, *China: Log Imports through Manzhouli Port Fall 32%* (July 10, 2008), *at* http://www.fordaq.com/fordaq/news/log_lumber_imports_ 17340.html; STEVEN NORTHWAY ET AL., RECENT DEVELOPMENTS IN FOREST PRODUCTS TRADE BETWEEN RUSSIA AND CHINA: POTENTIAL PRODUCTION, PROCESSING, CONSUMPTION AND TRADE SCENARIOS (2009); AMERICAN FOREST & PAPER ASSOCIATION, CHINA'S SUBSIDIZATION OF ITS FOREST PRODUCTS INDUSTRY (June 2004).

3. *Tariff Escalation.* Many countries impose higher tariffs on higher value products. For timber products, many countries encourage imports of raw materials by imposing the lowest tariffs on unprocessed products and raising tariffs as the amount of processing increases. This is known as "tariff escalation." When done by industrialized countries, prices for raw logs are kept artificially low relative to value-added products and may make it more difficult for developing countries to establish their own value-added industries. However, tariff escalation by industrialized countries may harm those countries with better technology, skilled people, and cheaper labor as opposed to timber-producing countries.

> [A]lthough developing countries as a group have comparative advantage in simply worked wood and wood manufactures, and possibly veneer and plywood, it is not certain that the timber-producing developing countries within this group would necessarily have the comparative advantage in producing all these products. For example, newly industrialized countries (NICs) that have no or negligible production forests, such as Taiwan, South Korea, and Singapore currently have a greater comparative advantage in more advanced processed products, such as plywood and veneer. Thus, current import barriers may be discriminating more against NICs rather than the timber-producing countries. There may be a knock-on effect of discrimination against the NICs onto the timber-producing countries, but the magnitude of this impact is difficult to determine. The ultimate impacts on forest management and its environmental impacts of both the first-order and second-order effects of timber trade import barriers are therefore hard to discern. The situation is further complicated by the extensive use of non-tariff barriers to processed timber imports from timber developing countries. Bourke found substantial evidence that such barriers are restricting trade from the log producing countries. However, the effects of non-tariff barriers on

trade flows [are] difficult enough to analyze, let alone the impacts on forest degradation.

Ed Barbier, *The Environmental Effects of Trade in the Forestry Sector, in* OECD, THE ENVIRONMENTAL EFFECTS OF TRADE 55, 80–81 (1994). Tariff escalation is highest among developing and newly industrialized countries. India, for example, imposes a 5 percent tariff on unprocessed wood but tariffs of 25 percent and 35 percent for semi-processed and processed wood. As a consequence, if tariff escalation is eliminated or reduced, "it would likely have more impact on South-to-South trade, because of larger reductions in tariffs and because many developing countries already enjoy low preferential tariffs or no tariffs at all for their exports to developed countries." KATILA & SIMULA, at 18.

4. As the materials in this section illustrate, tariffs can powerfully influence markets and the sustainable or unsustainable use of natural resources. Identifying the specific environmental impacts in specific countries, however, remains difficult, and no single tariff regime will ensure the sustainability of forests. To encourage the sustainable use of forest and other products, Hilary French calls for "mutual tariffs." Under this scheme, countries exporting primary commodities (raw materials, such as timber, minerals, oil, as well as agricultural products) would impose an environmental export tariff on their goods and funnel the proceeds toward sustaining that resource. To ensure that primary commodities enter the market on a level playing field, importers would impose a tariff on exporters, if the exporting country does not have a similar tax. According to French, such environmental tariffs would acknowledge that chronically low prices for commodities often cause overexploitation and externalize costs. HILARY F. FRENCH, COSTLY TRADEOFFS: RECONCILING TRADE AND THE ENVIRONMENT 23 (1993). Should countries, especially developed countries, reverse how they levy tariffs? That is, should they levy higher tariffs for raw materials and lower tariffs for manufactured goods? Should countries funnel tariff proceeds from raw materials directly into environmentally related funds rather than to the general treasury?

5. While the American Forest and Paper Association thought that the elimination of tariffs on timber products would increase consumption of forest products by 3 to 4 percent, more recent studies found that the elimination of import tariffs would increase consumption by only 0.4 or 0.5 percent. Shushuai Zhu et al., *Global Effects of Accelerated Tariff Liberalization in the Forest Products Sector to 2010* (U.S. Dep't of Agriculture, Forest Service Res. Pap. PNW-RP-534, Mar. 2002); KATILA & SIMULA, at v. However, tariff elimination would alter the composition of goods in trade and the geographic pattern of production and trade. It is from these projected changes that environmental impacts can be anticipated. For example, tariff elimination would increase wood production in many developing countries, particularly in Indonesia, Malaysia, China, and countries in South America. Because these countries are "all suffering from governance problems ... [i]t can thus be expected that further trade liberalization in these countries will add pressure on the remaining natural forests and may exacerbate existing sustainability problems." KATILA & SIMULA, at 36. Similar trends are projected in the Congo Basin, Papua New Guinea, Thailand, the Philippines, and Myanmar. *Id.* In the absence of data that show exactly where tariff elimination leads to increased harvesting, however, it is almost impossible to predict the exact scope of environmental problems resulting from tariff elimination.

III. The Prohibition against Quantitative Restrictions

While the GATT allows protection through the use of tariffs, its remaining core obligations—most favored nation, national treatment, and the prohibition against quantitative restrictions—are designed to prevent protection of domestic goods and industries through discriminatory practices or through nontariff barriers to trade. These obligations all implicate, in one way or another, the fundamental distinction between border measures applied at the time of importation or exportation on the one hand and internal measures applied to imported products on the other. This section focuses on Article XI's prohibition against importation and exportation restrictions before beginning an inquiry into the difference between Article XI and Article III measures.

Article XI:1 states:

> No prohibitions or restrictions other than duties, taxes or other charges, whether made effective through quotas, import or export licenses or other measures, shall be instituted or maintained by any Member on the importation of any product of the territory of any other Member or on the exportation or sale for export of any product destined for the territory of any other Member.

Because Article XI of the GATT is entitled "General Elimination of Quantitative Restrictions," it is often referred to as the rule against *quantitative* restrictions, such as quotas. The reference to "other measures" in Article XI, however, evinces a broader purpose: the elimination of *all* nontariff restrictions that may affect the *importation and exportation* of products. Dispute settlement panels have acknowledged this broad purpose to conclude that "any form of *limitation* imposed on, or in relation to importation constitutes a restriction on importation within the meaning of Article XI:1." India-Measures Affecting the Automotive Sector, Panel Report, WT/DS146/R, WT/DS175/R and Corr.1, para. 7.265 (adopted April 5, 2002) (emphasis in original). Moreover, "measures" encompass a broader range of restrictions than binding regulations and laws. India-Quantitative Restrictions on Imports of Agricultural, Textile and Industrial Products, Panel Report, WT/DS90/R, para. 5.128 (Sept. 22, 1999).

Against this background, panels have ruled that the existence of an unenforced, yet mandatory, quota could discourage investment, planning, and other market activities. Japan-Measures on Imports of Leather, GATT Panel Report, L/5623, GATT B.I.S.D. (31st Supp.) at 94 (adopted May 15–16, 1984) (1985). Even measures that are not formal legally binding obligations may be prohibited by Article XI provided that "sufficient incentives or disincentives exist[] for non-mandatory measures to take effect." Japan-Trade in Semi-Conductors, GATT Panel Report, L/6309, GATT B.I.S.D. (35th Supp.) at 116, 153–55, para. 109 (adopted May 4, 1988) (1988). "There can be no doubt … that the disciplines of Article XI:1 extend to restrictions of a *de facto* nature." Argentina-Measures Affecting the Export of Bovine Hides and the Import of Finished Leather, Panel Report, WT/DS155/R, para. 11.17 (adopted Feb. 16, 2001). Another panel held that a fine for violating an import ban was inconsistent with Article XI, because the fine of 400 Brazilian Reis per tire, "which significantly exceeds the average prices of domestically produced retreaded tyres for passenger cars (R$100–280)—is significant enough to have a restrictive effect on importation." Brazil-Measures Affecting Imports of Retreaded Tyres, Panel Report, WT/DS332/R, para. 7.372 (adopted Dec. 17, 2007).

As we will see below, the scope and breadth of Article XI affects the choice of trade measures that members may adopt for environmental purposes. However, these cases also underscore how environmental and human health measures can easily mask protectionist purposes.

A. Border Measures and Internal Measures

At the outset, a distinction must be made between Article III measures, often called "internal measures," and Article XI measures, often called "border measures." This distinction is critical, because categorizing a provision of law as an Article III measure or an Article XI measure is often the difference between a GATT-consistent or -inconsistent measure. Article XI establishes a bright line rule: Article XI measures are prohibited. On the other hand, members may implement Article III measures, provided they do so in a nondiscriminatory way. That is, they may tax and regulate foreign products if they do so no less favorably than "like products" of domestic origin.

Article XI governs "prohibitions or restrictions ... instituted or maintained ... *on the importation* of any product." This language suggests that Article XI measures affect an imported product before or at the time of importation. In contrast, Article III applies to taxes and measures "*affecting the internal sale,* offering for sale, purchase, transportation, distribution or use of products." As such, Article III governs taxes, charges, laws, and regulations applied to imported products after those products have cleared customs and border procedures and entered the importing country's internal market.

Normally, identifying whether a measure is an Article III measure or an Article XI is not difficult. Consider the following real-world measures:

- A ban on the importation of DDT, a pesticide known to cause serious environmental problems.
- A ban on the importation of chlorofluorocarbons (CFCs), because they deplete the ozone layer.
- A limit of 500 leopard skins that may be imported from Zimbabwe, a measure designed to protect the species from overutilization due to trade.

All of these measures are Article XI measures. The ivory and CFC import bans prevent these products from entering the importing country's market altogether. The leopard quota, by limiting the number of skins that may be imported from a specific country, is exactly the kind of quota scheme contemplated by Article XI.

Now consider these measures:

- A tax imposed on imported petroleum products that is equivalent to a tax imposed on domestic petroleum products.
- A prohibition on the sale of imported or domestic automobiles unless they include a catalytic converter, a device used to reduce toxic emissions from the combustion of fossil fuel.
- A tax imposed based on the fuel efficiency of the car.

These measures fall within Article III. In the case of the taxes, the products may be imported into the country without restriction but the tax is imposed as a condition of sale. Likewise, a law that requires automobiles to be sold with catalytic converters would be an

Article III measure because it affects the sale of automobiles without actually preventing the importation of automobiles.

Customs practices, however, may complicate the classification of a measure as an Article III or Article XI measure. To simplify the collection of taxes and the enforcement of laws and regulations, most countries have made the point of importation—customs—the point at which they collect taxes and enforce other laws that apply to imported products. In this way, the taxes are collected and laws enforced *before* a product enters the market. An interpretative note to Article III clarifies that these Article III measures, such as the tax on petroleum products mentioned above, are not suddenly transformed into prohibited quantitative restrictions simply because the taxes are collected or regulations are enforced before the product is allowed to enter the internal market of the importing country. The interpretative note reads:

> Any internal tax or other internal charge, or any law, regulation or requirement of the kind referred to in [Article III:1] which applies to an imported product and the like domestic product and is collected or enforced in the case of the imported product at the time or point of importation, is nevertheless to be regarded as an internal tax or other internal charge, or a law, regulation or requirement of the kind referred to in [Article III:1], and is accordingly subject to the provisions of Article III.

This interpretative note clarifies the status of certain taxes as Article III measures. Nonetheless, a small number of laws or regulations may be difficult to characterize as "on the importation" of a product and falling within Article XI or as "affecting the internal sale" of a product and falling within Article III. Consider whether the following examples are Article III measures affecting the sale of goods or Article XI measures "on the importation" of goods.

- The United States requires lobsters to reach a certain minimum size before they may be sold in or imported into the United States. Provided that the lobsters meet this size restriction, there are no other limits on the sale of lobsters. 16 U.S.C. § 1857(1)(J); 50 C.F.R. § 697.20(9).

- In the United States, washers, refrigerators, dishwashers, and other appliances may not be sold unless they meet certain energy standards. Energy Policy and Conservation Act, 42 U.S.C. § 6302(5). Many countries have similar laws, although their standards may differ from those imposed by the United States. Like lobsters, any number of appliances may enter the country provided they meet these standards. If they do not, they are banned from importation. 42 U.S.C. § 6301.

A panel established under the U.S.-Canada Free Trade Agreement was asked to untangle this thorny distinction between Article III and Article XI measures when Canada challenged the U.S. size restrictions on lobsters (*Homarus americanus*). In the Matter of Lobsters from Canada, U.S.-Canada Free Trade Agreement Panel Report, No. USA 89-1807-01, 1990 FTAPD LEXIS 11 (May 25, 1990) [hereinafter *Lobsters*]. Because Articles 407 and 501 of the U.S.-Canada Free Trade Agreement incorporate by reference GATT Articles XI and III, respectively, the Panel made its findings in light of the relevant GATT articles.

The majority concluded that the lobster size restrictions fell within Article III of the GATT, because the measure was imposed at the time of, and as a condition to, the entry of the goods into the importing country. *Id.* at para. 7.12.4. The majority reasoned that the lobster size requirements did not prevent the importation of Canadian lobsters, but rather they were a condition to entry of goods. *See id.* at paras. 7.13.1–.8.

According to the minority, Article XI prohibits a measure that prevents or is intended to prevent a product from entering the market of the importing country or if a measure's "effect is felt before the foreign product enters the commerce of the importing country." *Id.* at para. 8.2.6. In contrast, an Article III measure must "affect" the internal sale, use, or transportation of a product that has already entered into the market of the importing country. As such, the minority concluded that the word "affecting" in Article III presumes the real or potential existence of internal "sale, use, or transportation" of "imported" products in competition with domestic products. Thus, Article III necessarily excludes from its scope the complete prohibition of the sale, transportation, or use of an imported product and applies only to laws, regulations, or requirements influencing or modifying the conditions of internal sale, use, or transportation of an imported product. *Id.* at paras. 8.2.10–8.2.11.

The minority ultimately adopted a simple test to determine whether a measure constitutes an Article III or Article XI measure: "Is the measure one that prevents a product from entering the domestic commerce of the importing country or is it one imposing conditions to be met by the foreign product before it can be marketed in the country?" *Id.* at para. 8.5.1. With respect to the lobster size restrictions, the minority rejected the notion that the size restrictions imposed "a condition on the sale of the Canadian lobster, that it be left in the water long enough to reach American minimum size; this ... is not a condition or term affecting the sale in the United States of a particular lobster, it is an absolute bar to that sale. It cannot be an answer to Article XI to say that the importing party can bar entry this year to the lobster as long as entry will be regained next year or the year after." *Id.* at para. 8.5.5.

Questions and Discussion

1. The *Lobsters* dispute boils down to whether one believes that size requirements are a condition of sale. The point is not an esoteric one. Size requirements are an essential feature of natural resource management, because many species reach sexual maturity at a predictable size. As a result, managers can prohibit the sale of undersized individuals because they have yet to reproduce and/or larger individuals because they represent the breeding population. This biology aside, the majority concludes that the lobster size requirements are conditions affecting sale. Canada can sell a limitless number of lobsters to the United States provided that those lobsters meet U.S. size requirements. The minority, however, believes the size requirements are an absolute bar that "prevents" lobsters of a certain size from entering the market. Who has the better argument? Is this different from a ban on the sale of appliances that fail to meet energy efficiency requirements or the sale of cars without emission controls or catalytic converters?

2. In Canada-Administration of the Foreign Investment Review Act, GATT Panel Report, L/5504, GATT B.I.S.D. (30th Supp.) at 140 (1984) (adopted Feb. 7, 1984), Canada required foreign investors to enter into purchasing undertakings. Some of these undertakings required foreign investors to purchase goods from Canadian suppliers or purchase goods of Canadian origin in specified amounts or in preference to imported goods. The United States claimed that these undertakings violated Article XI by limiting imports and reserving a portion of the internal market for Canadian products. Without detailed analysis, the Panel concluded that these undertakings affected the internal sale of products, not the importation of products. *Id.* at para. 5.14. Do you agree? Are these undertakings similar to lobster size restrictions? In *FIRA*, U.S. exporters could export their

entire stock, but they did not have unfettered access to all potential buyers. In *Lobsters*, all lobsters of Canadian origin could enter the United States, provided that they were of a certain size.

3. Canada's claim in *Lobsters* actually derived from a unique comparative advantage with respect to some lobsters, because the size of lobsters at sexual maturity varies depending on water temperature. In the warm Canadian waters of the Gulf of St. Lawrence, the average size of a lobster at sexual maturity is 3 inches, 3-5/8 inches in the cool oceanic Nova Scotia waters, and 4 inches in the cold Gulf of Maine waters. In theory, Canada maintained a comparative advantage because its Gulf of St. Lawrence lobsters reached sexual maturity at a smaller size than other lobsters and smaller than the 3-5/8 inch size requirement imposed by U.S. law. Against this biological background, do you think the U.S. size restrictions are consistent with Article III? This "discrimination" by the United States appears motivated not by efforts to protect its lobster harvest from Canadian competition but rather from enforcement concerns. Prior to adoption of the outright prohibition of under-sized lobsters, the United States allowed the importation of Canadian lobsters that did not meet U.S. size restrictions. However, U.S. and other fishermen were "laundering" U.S. lobsters as Canadian lobsters and selling them in the U.S. market. Because of this enforcement problem, the United States justified its prohibition against the sale of any lobster failing to meet the U.S. size restrictions.

On these issues, it is worth noting that, despite its conclusion that the size requirements were conditions of sale, the *Lobsters* majority seemed more convinced that the U.S. restrictions were Article III measures because they applied equally to domestic and Canadian lobsters "and would therefore be nonprotectionist measures of the kind covered by Article III." *Lobsters,*. at para. 7.7.5. Do you agree that the U.S. measure applies equally to U.S. and Canadian lobsters? In any event, is the nondiscrimination/nonprotectionism principle of Article III relevant for determining whether a measure falls within the scope of Article III? Don't we first need to address whether the measure is "on the importation" of a product (Article XI) or affects the internal sale of a product (Article III)?

4. In the future, these types of measures may be reviewed as "technical regulations" under the Agreement on Technical Barriers to Trade (TBT Agreement). The TBT Agreement defines a technical regulation as a "[d]ocument which lays down product characteristics or their related processes and production methods, including the applicable administrative provisions, with which compliance is mandatory." Size restrictions would certainly constitute a product characteristic and any dispute concerning size restrictions on lobsters or other fish would likely arise under the TBT Agreement. The TBT Agreement is discussed in Chapter 6. However, the WTO's Appellate Body has said that measures falling within the TBT Agreement must also be consistent with the GATT.

B. Export Restrictions

Many countries have imposed export bans as a means to achieve certain environmental or developmental goals. Brazil, Canada, Indonesia, Malaysia, Papua New Guinea, Thailand, and the United States, among others, have or have had bans or other restrictions on the export of unprocessed timber. Raw log export bans are intended to help conserve forests by eliminating the international market for a country's logs. They may also add value to the lumber in the domestic market by creating processing jobs and industries associated with the use of processed lumber, such as furniture manufacturing. Countries may also adopt export bans or other export restrictions to protect the human health of foreign citizens or the environment of other countries or the global commons. The U.S. Marine Mammal Protection Act and the Australian Environment Protection and Biodiversity Conservation Act prohibit exports of cetaceans and their parts and products, except in very limited circumstances.

Article XI of the GATT provides that "[n]o prohibitions or restrictions other than duties, taxes or other charges ... shall be instituted or maintained ... on the exportation or sale for export of any product destined for the territory of any other Member." As the *Salmon and Herring* dispute below makes clear, Article XI limits a country's options for using export restrictions to achieve its policy goals.

---

1. *The* Salmon and Herring *Case*

Canada first enacted export restrictions on fresh and newly salted herring and sockeye salmon from British Columbia in 1908. The restrictions varied over time but by 1970 Canada prohibited the export of any herring and sockeye or pink salmon unless it was first canned, salted, smoked, dried, pickled, or frozen and was inspected. The United States eventually challenged these regulations. In a case known as *Herring and Salmon*, a GATT Panel found Canada's export ban on unprocessed herring and unprocessed sockeye and pink salmon to violate Article XI:1 of the GATT, and that it was not justified by the exception for measures relating to the conservation of exhaustible natural resource measures under Article XX(g). Canada-Measures Affecting Exports of Unprocessed Herring and Salmon, GATT Panel Report, L/6268, GATT B.I.S.D. (35th Supp.) at 98, paras. 4.1, 4.4–4.7 (1988) (adopted Mar. 22, 1988).

In response, Canada lifted its export bans but introduced new requirements to land in Canada all roe herring and all salmon (sockeye and pink, as well as coho, chum, and chinook) caught commercially in Canadian waters, ostensibly to collect data to assess the status of salmon and herring populations. Under these regulations, Canada required salmon and roe herring to be landed at a licensed "fish landing station" in British Columbia or onto a vessel or vehicle ultimately destined for such a landing station. It also required vessels to submit catch reports, landing station operators to report landings, and landing station operators to allow examination and biological sampling by Canadian fisheries officials.

The United States challenged these new restrictions in a case known as *Salmon and Herring* under the U.S.–Canada Free Trade Agreement. Because that agreement incorporated Article XI of the GATT, the dispute centered on whether or not Canada's landing requirement affected the exportation or sale for export of salmon and herring.

In the Matter of Canada's Landing Requirement for Pacific Coast Salmon and Herring

U.S.-Canada Free Trade Agreement Panel Report, No. CDA-89-1807-01, 1989 FTAPD LEXIS 6 (Oct. 16, 1989)

6.02 The United States argued that Article XI:1 should be given its simple and straightforward meaning—it enjoins "prohibitions or restrictions" on "exportation or sale for export." In accordance with existing GATT decisions, the United States argued, a measure need not refer directly to exports; in order to fall within Article XI:1, it need only have the effect of restricting exports. The United States claimed that the Canadian landing requirement has the effect of placing costs on export sales of unprocessed herring and salmon that are not borne by most domestic buyers, thereby placing many United States buyers at a competitive disadvantage. Such a competitive disadvantage, in the view of the United States, constitutes a "restriction" within the meaning of Article XI:1. According to the United States, while the landing requirement could also be viewed as a restriction on "exportation" it is certainly a restriction on the "sale for export" of such products.

6.03 Canada argued that Article XI:1 forbids restrictions on "exportation"—in Canada's words the "act of exporting." However, the landing requirement does not regulate the act of exporting; it requires that all fish be landed without distinction between fish destined for domestic buyers or fish destined for export buyers. In Canada's view, the GATT decisions relied on by the United States are irrelevant because they deal either with imports or with measures closely related to an export licensing scheme. Canada further argued that a landing requirement is not the type of measure covered by Article XI:1. A reading of that article in accordance with the normal canons of interpretation, according to Canada, requires "other measures" covered by the article to be limited only to those of the same genus as "quotas" or "licences" which are specifically mentioned in Article XI:1. Furthermore, as United States buyers are able to procure unprocessed herring and salmon on the same terms and conditions as Canadian buyers, then there is no restriction on "sale for export" contrary to Article XI:1. Finally, Canada argued that the landing requirement did not constitute a de facto restriction on trade because the United States had failed to discharge the burden of proving that there was any trade impact.

6.04 In the course of the proceedings, the Panel asked the Parties whether the distinction between border measures and internal measures, which applied in the case of imports under Article XI.1, had any relevance to exports under that article. After considering the arguments of the Parties on this issue, the Panel concluded that the "border measures-internal measures" distinction did not apply to export restrictions under Article XI:1. First, although there is an obvious parallel between the word "importation" and the word "exportation," Article XI:1 does not use the word "exportation" alone. It refers to "prohibitions or restrictions ... on the exportation or sale for export of any product." Thus, even if "exportation" was to refer to the act of exporting at the border alone, the concept of "sale for export" extends the coverage of Article XI:1 to restrictions imposed at an earlier stage of the process, before the act of exportation itself.

6.05 Second, there is a good reason for the broader coverage in Article XI:1 in respect of exports, which does not apply in the case of imports. Internal or non-border restrictions placed on imports are regulated elsewhere in the GATT under Article III. That article does not apply, nor could it readily be made to apply, to exports. While an import retains its distinct character as an import throughout its commercial life, and is identifiable as such, an export does not exist as an export until it is committed to the export process. In the Panel's view, the reference to restrictions on "sale for export" in Article XI:1 was designed to deal with this earlier phase of the process and to cover restrictions imposed on goods destined for export even though the restriction does not take effect at the border.

6.06 The Panel concluded, therefore, that there was no justification for applying the "border measures-internal measures" distinction to export restrictions under Article XI:1. The issue before the Panel was whether the landing requirement constituted a restriction on "sale for export" regardless of whether it was an internal or a border measure. If the landing requirement was found to be a restriction on "sale for export," then there would be no need to decide whether it constituted a restriction on "exportation."

6.07 On the question of the scope of the term "restriction" under Article XI:1, the Panel was not convinced that the reference to "other measures" in the definition was limited to a genus confined by the words "quotas, import or export licences." The common genus of these measures might well be that they constitute a restriction on trade. Further, the ordinary meaning of an amplifying phrase introduced by the word "whether" is to affirm the inclusive rather than the limited nature of the term. In this regard, the Panel noted that the definition of "restriction" in Article 410 of the FTA, which is applicable to all of Chapter Four and thus relevant to the interpretation of Article XI:1, elaborates the meaning of restriction to include "permits" and "minimum price requirements" as well as quotas and licences. Moreover, GATT interpretations of Article XI:1 support a liberal approach stressing that the Article should be interpreted broadly enough to accomplish its basic purpose.

6.08 Canada argued that the only measures that can be regarded as "restrictions ... on the ... sale for export" under Article XI:1 are those that actually provide for different treatment of domestic sales and export sales. The Panel noted that such an approach would create a significant limitation on the scope of GATT obligations regarding exports. It would allow governments to impose measures that in fact place heavier commercial burdens on exports than on domestic products, provided only that the form of the measure itself was neutral. The Panel noted that no such limitation is made in the parallel GATT obligation regarding imports in Article III:2 and III:4.

6.09 In considering the Canadian argument, the Panel noted that the landing requirement was not merely a general measure that happened to have an adverse impact on exports. An important reason for the specific rule requiring that all salmon and herring be landed in Canada (as distinct from the rules requiring inspection and reporting) was to make exports more amenable to data collection and this, in fact, is its principal effect. The Panel concluded that where the primary effect of a measure is in fact the regulation of export transactions, the measure may be considered a restriction within the meaning of Article XI:1 if it has the effect of imposing a materially greater commercial burden on exports than on domestic sales. In the view of the Panel it was not necessary to demonstrate the actual trade effects of such a measure. As a practical matter there cannot be data to show what would have happened without the measure and GATT decisions have not required such proof.[14] What has to be shown is

---

14. Japan-Customs Duties, Taxes and Labelling Practices on Imported Wines and Alcoholic Beverages, GATT Panel Report, L/6216, GATT B.I.S.D. (34th Supp.) at 83, paras. 5.10–5.11 (1987); see

that the measure has altered the competitive relationship between foreign and domestic buyers.

6.10 The basic United States argument with regard to the competitive disadvantage of the landing requirement was that a substantial proportion of potential exports to the United States would be required to take steps that would not be required in the case of sales to Canadian buyers. Canadian buyers would be able to land at their chosen processing plant or at a location most convenient to that processing plant. The United States did not deny that some export buyers might find it economically advantageous to land in Canada and ship by truck from there; the problem was that exports had to be landed in Canada whether economically advantageous or not. The United States argued that many export buyers would find it economically advantageous to ship directly from the fishing grounds to United States landing sites by water; for these buyers, the landing requirement would impose the extra expense of landing, unloading and reloading at a Canadian landing station.

6.11 The Panel agreed that while the landing requirement affects both Canadian and United States buyers, the burden on export buyers of having to make an unwanted landing would be additional to the burden of inspection and reporting which is imposed on all buyers. Moreover, while there was no actual data on the proportion of export buyers for whom direct transport by water would be most advantageous, the Panel was persuaded that the proportion would be significant. Water transport is the only means available to export buyers from Alaska. Export buyers from the State of Washington do have the alternative of truck transport, but even in this case the proportion of export purchases shipped directly by water is likely to be significant. The evidence of Canadian landing practice submitted to the Panel showed that a substantial majority of Canadian buyers land their catch directly at their processing plants. There is no reason to assume that a similar proportion of United States buyers would not do the same.

6.12 Both Parties devoted a considerable part of their written submissions and oral argument to demonstrate, on the part of the United States, the nature and extent of the additional costs on United States buyers, and on the part of Canada, that the costs were insignificant. Neither side was able to demonstrate what the actual costs to United States buyers would be. Based simply on the steps that export buyers would be required to take—landing in Canada, unloading and loading for reshipment to the United States—the Panel was satisfied that the cost of complying with the landing requirement would be more than an insignificant expense for those buyers who would have otherwise shipped directly from the fishing ground to a landing site in the United States.

6.13 In sum, although the evidence presented made it difficult to assess the impact of the landing requirement with any precision, and although it was clear that the landing requirement would not be a commercial burden for some ex-

also United States-Taxes on Petroleum and Certain Imported Substances, GATT Panel Report, L/6175, GATT B.I.S.D. (34th Supp.) at 136, para. 5.1.9 (1987).

port buyers, the Panel was satisfied that a considerable number of potential export buyers would find direct shipment by water more economical, and that for most of these buyers the extra expense of making an unwanted landing in Canada would be significant. Accordingly, the Panel concluded that, as presently constituted, the Canadian landing requirement is a restriction on "sale for export" within the meaning of GATT Article XI:1.

Questions and Discussion

1. The *Salmon and Herring* Panel makes two key distinctions to define "exportation" broadly. First, it takes an expansive view of "restriction" in Article XI. Second, the Panel rejects an interpretation of Article XI that would equate Article XI's export scope as essentially the opposite of "importation." Do you think that the Panel's interpretations are supported by the ordinary meaning of the terms in Article XI?

2. The *Salmon and Herring* Panel ultimately concludes that a measure is a restriction on "sale for export" if it "has the effect of imposing a materially greater commercial burden on exports than on domestic sales." At the same time, the challenging party does not need to show any actual trade impacts. How should a party demonstrate that a measure imposes a materially greater commercial burden on exports than on domestic sales? Does the Panel's decision make sense given the underlying principles of free trade? Are you satisfied that the landing requirement actually imposes a greater commercial burden on exports? As we will see in Chapter 4, pages 175–77, dispute panels regularly refuse to investigate whether a measure causes actual trade impacts and instead focus on whether the measure alters the conditions of competition between importers and exporters.

3. The *Salmon and Herring* case highlights a particular problem for panel members—judging real environmental measures from protectionist measures in the guise of environmental measures. Recall that this dispute began when Canada banned the export of unprocessed salmon and herring. Only after a GATT panel found that export ban to violate Article XI did Canada require all salmon and herring to be landed in Canada. In addition, at the time of this dispute the sockeye and pink salmon and herring fisheries gave employment to almost five-sixths of the workers in the British Columbia fish processing industry. Nonetheless, Canada offered an environmental argument for its landing requirement: a 100 percent landing requirement was necessary to ensure that Canada obtained adequate population data on salmon and herring populations. How should a panel judge whether this is a conservation or protectionist measure?

---

2. Environmental Consequences of Export Restrictions

The decisions in *Herring and Salmon* and *Salmon and Herring* affect a country's policy choices to achieve sustainable development. Countries may want to reduce deforestation or ensure that natural resources, including fish and timber, are not exported without processing, because the value of natural resources escalates dramatically from raw material to value-added product. Fine furniture, for example, has considerably more value than a raw log. In fact, export restrictions may help achieve a country's economic objectives to produce more value-added products. When Russia significantly increased export tariffs on raw logs, for example, it saw exports of higher value sawn timber surge. Presumably, these exports of higher value products were accompanied by additional sawmill jobs as well. Russia's export tariffs are protected against an Article XI challenge, because Article XI expressly excludes duties, taxes, or other charges from its scope, although an excessively high export tax could potentially violate Article XI as a *de facto* ban, as the *Retreaded Tyres* Panel concluded (*see* page 150). As seen from the two herring and salmon cases, other types of export restrictions, particularly export bans, run afoul of Article XI.

Whatever the economic impacts might be, strong environmental counter-arguments exist to export bans on natural resources, such as logs and whole fish. For example, rather than conserving forests, log export bans may have just the opposite effect and actually increase deforestation. Log export bans can fuel deforestation by ensuring that timber is supplied at low cost to inefficient mills. Sawmills in the developed world typically are highly computerized and more timber product can be produced from one log at these sawmills than at the less efficient sawmills found in many developing countries. Sawmills in Ghana, Ivory Coast, and Indonesia have historically converted logs into sawn lumber and plywood at a rate about two-thirds of industry standards. But because an export ban prevents sales at higher cost to more efficient mills abroad, domestic sawmills have no incentive to improve their practices.

This is what happened in Indonesia. There, the switch from exports of raw logs to value-added processed timber products slowed the rate of timber extraction in the short-term, but the switch is thought to have increased the rate of deforestation over the medium- and long-term, because the ban reduced domestic wood prices and stimulated inefficient domestic production. Katila & Simula, Annex 5, at 14–15; Barbier, *Environmental Effects of Trade in the Forestry Sector*, at 83.

In other cases, export or even logging bans may simply transfer the problem to another country. A U.S. raw log export ban sent Japanese sawmills to other countries to replace more than US$868 million in logs imported from the United States. A Chinese logging ban forced Chinese sawmills and producers of wood products to search for timber in Russia and elsewhere.

Moreover, the development benefits of export bans and other export restrictions are questionable, at least in relation to their cost. However, both the environmental and developmental shortcomings of timber policy are difficult to pin on any one policy. As the economist Robert Repetto illustrates, competing policies in exporting and importing countries may affect the environmental and developmental outcome.

Robert Repetto, *The Forest for the Trees? Government Policies and the Misuse of Forest Resources*
25–26 (World Res. Inst. 1988)

The Indonesia case illustrates the fiscal costs and risks to the forests that ambitious forest-based industrialization entails. To encourage local processing, the government raised the log export tax rate to 20 percent, exempting sawn timber and all plywood. Mills were also exempted from income taxes for five or six years. Since these tax holidays were combined with unlimited loss-carryover provisions, concessionaires were frequently able to extend the holiday by declaring (unaudited) losses during the five-year holiday provision, or by simply arguing before sympathetic tax officials that the holidays were intended to apply for five years after the start of profitable operations.

With these incentives and the impending ban on log exports, the number of operating or planned sawmills and plymills jumped from 16 in 1977 to 182 in 1983. By 1988, plymills will be on stream with a total installed capacity for processing 20 million cubic meters of logs per year. Sawmill capacity is expected to account for another 18 million cubic meters of logs, of which only 1 million cubic meters will be met from teak plantations on Java. As much as 37 million could come from the natural forests, an annual harvest level 50 percent greater than the maximum levels reached in the 1970s, when log exports peaked. But, according to Government of Indonesia long-term forestry plans, log harvests to feed the mills are expected to continue rising throughout the 1990s as well.

Because of low conversion efficiencies and distortions in relative log and plywood prices in world markets, the jobs this harvest will create are bought at a heavy cost. For example, although a cubic meter of plywood could be exported for US$250 in 1983, the export value in terms of the logs used as raw materials (the roundwood equivalent) was only US$109. However, the logs themselves could be exported for US$100 per cubic meter. In other words, plymills added only $9 in export earnings for every cubic meter of logs used. But, because of the export tax exemption for plywood, the government sacrificed US$20 in foregone tax revenues on every cubic meter of logs diverted to plymills. * * *

The losses involved in producing sawn timber for export were more obvious. Because the average price of sawn timber exported in 1983 was only US$155, a cubic meter of logs that could be exported for US$100 brought only US$89 if processed in local sawmills. The government actually sacrificed US$20 in export taxes in order to lose US$11 in export earnings on every cubic meter of logs sawn domestically. Economic losses, as well as the waste of the natural resources and the sacrifice of public revenues, can result when overly generous incentives permit or encourage inefficient processing operations.

Questions and Discussion

1. While the export bans and taxes did not, in and of themselves, cause environmental harm and minimal development gains, they played a significant role. Is the answer trade liberalization? Consider the following two examples.

China. Trade and logging patterns have been greatly affected by China's participation in APEC and WTO accession in 2001. It has reduced import tariffs and revoked import quotas and licenses. It has reduced or zeroed tariffs for logs, sawnwood, and pulp, although it maintains tariffs on processed goods such as wooden furniture, resulting in tariff escalation. During this period of trade liberalization, China was also experiencing rapid economic growth and a rapid increase in demand for forest products. It also banned logging on about 60 million hectares of natural forest. As a result of these measures and economic growth, China is now the world's largest importer of industrial roundwood and tropical sawnwood and the second largest importer of forest products. Two studies have made the following conclusions about the economic and environmental impact on the forest sector as a consequence of China's WTO accession:

Economic Effects	• Increase in domestic and foreign investment in forest industry (especially in pulp and paper, wooden furniture, and other secondary processed wood products) • Significant increase in imports of forest products (logs, pulpwood, semi-processed products) • Manifold increase in production and export of wooden furniture • More efficient and productive forest industry due to economies of scale and upgrading of technology
Social Effects	• Increased employment especially in export-oriented forest industry • Negative social impacts (e.g., impoverishment of forest dependent communities) in countries which log illegally to export wood to China • Reduction in employment in obsolete straw-based pulp and paper mills which are shut down for competitiveness and environmental reasons
Environmental Effects	• Increased imports have reduced the pressure on China's own natural forests (the pressure has been "transported" to other countries) • The forests "saved" in China due to increased forest products imports have helped to maintain water resources and soil conservation services (indirect impact, pressure transferred to other countries) • Despite more efficient and environmentally friendly forest industries, total increase in production has possibly increased emissions and effluents but a more significant reduction in emissions is likely due to gradual shut-downs of polluting straw-based pulp mills • Increased risk of alien species invasion because of increased imports of roundwood and sawnwood • Forest degradation and deforestation with associated losses in biodiversity in some countries exporting wood to China
Governance Effects	• There appear to be no negative governance impacts in China but increased wood imports have stimulated unsustainable forestry practices and illegal trade in forest products, e.g., in Myanmar, Papua New Guinea, Indonesia, Malaysia, Africa and the Russian Far East • The problems with illegal trade and unsustainable forestry apply only to countries which already have problems with forest governance; increased trade with China is not necessarily creating new problems but aggravating existing ones

INTERNATIONAL INSTITUTE FOR SUSTAINABLE DEVELOPMENT, AN ENVIRONMENTAL IMPACT ASSESSMENT OF CHINA'S WTO ACCESSION: AN ANALYSIS OF SIX SECTORS (2004); KATILA & SIMULA, SUSTAINABILITY IMPACT ASSESSMENT OF PROPOSED WTO NEGOTIATIONS, at 25.

Mexico. Because Mexico has gone through trade liberalization due to the North American Free Trade Agreement, it offers a compelling case study for identifying what might happen with further trade liberalization throughout Central America.

Katila & Simula, *Sustainability Impact Assessment of Proposed WTO Negotiations*
Annex 5, 22–23

4.3 Environmental Impacts

• There is speculation that increased competition from imports is putting pressure on domestic forest industry enterprises, which may avoid improving environmental standards to maintain their competitiveness, but no data is available to confirm the existence of this trend.

• The evidence on impacts on wood production and the size of the forest area are mixed. Trade liberalisation has increased wood production in some areas (especially softwoods) and may have thus contributed to deforestation and forest degradation but such impacts are probably very limited. Prestemon (2000) used a simulation model to predict that increased prices of forest products would increase the area of private forest land and decrease the area of public forest land as a result of the acceleration of natural forest degradation. However, Brooks et al. (1999) predict that full trade liberalisation would reduce the overall harvest level in Mexico in relation to the base scenario.

• The contribution of trade liberalisation in forest products has had a limited impact on the overall deforestation in Mexico. Most of the deforestation and forest degradation is taking place in the tropical forest areas, where agricultural and livestock expansion put pressure on the remaining forests. However, these incremental pressures are partly linked to trade liberalisation under NAFTA, and consequently can be regarded at least partially as cross-sectoral impacts.

• In the northern and central parts of Mexico unsustainable logging is clearly an issue and, to some extent, the problem may have been aggravated by trade liberalisation. However, illegal logging and poor forest management were serious problems already before trade liberalisation. Trade liberalisation has certainly not improved the situation but the domestic market demand is a much more important underlying cause behind negative sustainability trends.

• There is no information available for making conclusions on possible incremental pollution effect caused by increased production of pulp and paper aimed at export markets. Some mills have been rehabilitated which usually also leads to better pollution control.

• Uncontrolled (both sanctioned and illegal) logging is resulting in soil erosion and sedimentation e.g. in Chihuahua and Guerrero, but it is practically impossible to "allocate" these negative environmental trends by source of demand (e.g. domestic consumption vs. increased exports).

As Guerrero *et al.* (2001) stated: it is exceedingly difficult to quantify the degree to which NAFTA has influenced the forest sector and how changes in harvesting and production patterns have affected the forest and other natural resources.

4.4 Social and Governance Impacts

• Trade liberalisation has affected social conditions and forest governance, but the overall evidence is mixed. There are both negative and positive impacts, but quite often it is difficult to attribute a change specifically to trade liberalisation. In some industries employment has increased because of improved international market access but some plants have also been closed because of influx of cheap imports especially from the United States.

• Trade liberalisation appears to have weakened local institutional controls, especially related to community forestry, where natural and social capital levels were already low, whereas it has stimulated improved governance in better-resourced community forest enterprises.

• Trade liberalisation appears to have magnified social conflict and governance problems created by inappropriate sectoral policies and the SAP [Structural Adjustment Program], especially in the community forestry sector. However, forest governance problems appear to be more common and acute for lower-value domestic market production than for export-oriented industries.

• There is evidence of corruption in the forest sector and increased trade may have in some cases created new opportunities for illegal activities. In many areas, forest and environmental laws are not enforced efficiently. However, high level corruption was higher in Mexico before trade liberalisation due to complex import and export procedures involving a high level of discretionary powers.

• Trade liberalisation has made minor contributions to a number of positive institutional developments, including civil society participation, certification, and the location of more law-abiding foreign companies in Mexico. However, other factors have affected these developments more than trade liberalisation.

———————

Given this information, do you think on average that trade liberalization in the forest products sector should be pursued? More generally, how should one determine whether or not to pursue trade liberalization in a given sector? For country-specific case studies and more detailed information on export restrictions and other forest and timber policies, see Katila & Simula, Sustainability Impact Assessment of Proposed WTO Negotiations, at Annex 5; Robert C. Repetto et al., Public Policies and the Misuse of Forest Resources (Robert Repetto & Malcom Gillis eds., 1998).

2. Are there more effective ways to conserve natural resources than through export bans or other regulatory restrictions on exports? For example, how are forests conserved if an export ban on raw logs is not accompanied by restrictions on domestic sales or if an export ban on *raw* logs is not accompanied by export restrictions on *processed* lumber? In the absence of harvest restrictions, do you think export bans help conserve forests?

———————

3. *Domestically Prohibited Goods*

In the early 1980s, Nigeria and Sri Lanka expressed concern that some countries permitted the export of goods whose sale or use was banned or severely restricted on human health and environmental grounds. Developing countries are often unable to make an informed decision about whether or not to import these goods because they lack information about whether and why goods are banned or restricted for sale or use in the exporting countries. In fact, while some countries ban the export of domestically prohibited goods, others permit it. For example, the United States permits the export of pesticides not registered for domestic use if export notification requirements are met, the foreign purchasers sign a statement acknowledging the pesticide's U.S. registration status, and the exports meet domestic labeling requirements. U.S. Federal Insecticide, Fungicide, and Rodenticide Act, 7 U.S.C. § 136o (2006). When a country identifies a product as harmful to human health or the environment and takes action to ban its use or sale, *should* that country also ban the export of such products or take other action to protect the citizens and environment of other countries?

The GATT parties agreed in 1982 to notify the GATT Secretariat of any goods produced and exported by them but whose sale, for health reasons, they had banned in their domestic markets. GATT B.I.S.D., (29th Supp.) at 19 (1983). That notification system failed to achieve its desired effect, however, because governments tended to provide notification of domestically prohibited goods whose export had also been prohibited rather than the ones they continued to export. It also failed because the parties could not agree on which products should be subject to the notification (e.g., products that are "banned or severely restricted in the domestic market" because they pose "serious and direct danger to human, animal or plant life or health or the environment"). Although the 1982 Decision remains in force, no notifications have been received since 1990.

In 1994, the Ministerial Decision on Trade and Environment incorporated domestically prohibited goods into the terms of reference of the new WTO Committee on Trade and Environment (CTE). The CTE has encouraged WTO members to provide technical assistance to other members, especially developing and least-developed countries, to assist these countries in strengthening their technical capacity to monitor and, where necessary, control the import of the domestically prohibited products. Overall, however, the issue has become moribund. While some members have called for a revival of the notification system, no such decision has been made. Secretariat Note, *A Review of the Information Available in the WTO on the Export of Domestically Prohibited Goods*, WT/CTE/W/43 (Apr. 22, 1997).

Questions and Discussion

1. Are export bans to protect foreign citizens and environments paternalistic or do governments have an ethical responsibility to ban exports of products they identify as harmful to human health or the environment? Consider DDT. DDT is known to cause the eggs of birds to thin, thus causing the eggs to break prematurely. DDT is largely responsible for the endangerment of bald eagles, peregrine falcons, and other birds of prey in the United States. The United States now prohibits its use as an insecticide. However, DDT remains an inexpensive and effective means to combat malaria, a life threatening illness in many parts of the world. Should the United States prohibit its export or should other countries decide for themselves whether the importation of DDT is appropriate for their circumstances? Should treatment of domestically prohibited goods depend on whether the prohibition has a health basis or an environmental basis? Should treatment differ between products that will stay in the foreign country, such as hazardous waste, and those that may return to the exporting country, such as pesticides on foods? How should trade law handle these issues—through a notification system or some other approach?

2. WTO members have shown little or no interest in domestically prohibited goods since 2000, perhaps because the United Nations has developed the Consolidated List of Products Whose Consumption and/or Sale Have Been Banned, Withdrawn, Severely Restricted or Not Approved by Governments. The Consolidated List designates products that have been deemed to be harmful to human health or the environment, and which have been banned, severely restricted, or not approved by governments. The list currently includes actions taken by 105 governments on more than 900 pharmaceuticals, agricultural and industrial chemicals, and consumer products. The Consolidated List is designed to provide all countries with information on these products so they may take appropriate regulatory action based on their domestic circumstances and their own assessments of the costs and benefits of control. The Consolidated List, while containing a range of regulatory actions taken by governments to protect themselves against harmful products, does not provide information on whether governments impose any export restrictions for these products. *See* Secretariat Note, *Domestically Prohibited Goods*, WT/CTE/W/161 (Oct. 2, 2000).

3. Within international environmental fora, governments have opted largely for notice and consent provisions rather than export bans of hazardous and other substances. The Basel Convention on the Control of Transboundary Movement and Management of Hazardous Wastes and their Disposal includes a system of prior informed consent through which the importing country must expressly consent to the import of hazardous waste

after being notified of the contents of the shipment. Basel Convention, Mar. 22, 1989, 31 I.L.M. 657 (1989) (entered into force May 5, 1992). African nations, wanting a mandatory ban on exports to their countries, bristled at these notice and consent provisions, even though they grant importing countries the unilateral right to reject shipments of hazardous waste. As a result, they negotiated the Bamako Convention on the Ban of Import Into Africa and the Control of Transboundary Movement and Management of Hazardous Waste Within Africa. Bamako Convention, Jan. 30, 1991, 30 I.L.M. 775 (1991) (entered into force Apr. 22, 1998). The Bamako Convention bans the importation of hazardous waste generated by noncontracting parties. Since the Convention is open only to members of the Africa Union (formerly the Organization of African Unity), it effectively bans the importation of hazardous wastes from all non-African countries. The parties to the Basel Convention approved an amendment to that Convention that prohibits trade in hazardous waste from developed countries to developing countries, but it has not come into effect, in part because many developing countries wish to import certain hazardous waste for recycling as a source of raw materials (e.g., zinc, lead, and scrap metal).

The Rotterdam Convention on the Prior Informed Consent Procedure for Certain Hazardous Chemicals and Pesticides in International Trade also adopts a prior informed consent procedure rather than an export/import ban regime. Rotterdam Convention, Sept. 10, 1998, U.N. Doc. UNEP/FAO/PIC/CONF/2, 38 I.L.M. 1 (1999) (entered into force Feb. 24, 2004). The Rotterdam Convention covers pesticides and industrial chemicals that have been banned or severely restricted for health or environmental reasons by its parties and which have been notified by parties for inclusion in the Convention's prior informed consent procedure. Severely hazardous pesticide formulations that present a hazard under conditions of use in developing countries or countries with economies in transition may also be nominated for inclusion in the procedure. The Convention currently covers 25 pesticides, 4 severely hazardous pesticide formulations, and 11 industrial chemicals. *See* Rotterdam Convention, http://www.pic.int.

The Stockholm Convention on Persistent Organic Pollutants strictly regulates the production, use, import, and export of listed pesticides and industrial chemicals, and unintended by-products. Persistent Organic Pollutants, or "POPs," are chemicals that are highly toxic and persistent, and that bioaccumulate and move long distances in the environment. The Stockholm Convention now covers 21 POPs, including nine pesticides and industrial chemicals slated for elimination. These include aldrin, chlordane, and dieldrin, as well as polychlorinated biphenyls (PCBs). Uses of other POPs must be severely restricted. For example, the pesticide DDT may be used for disease vector control (malaria) until safe, affordable, and effective alternatives are found. The Stockholm Convention restricts the import and export of POPs to cases where, for example, the purpose is environmentally sound disposal. It also requires that POPs not be transported across international boundaries without taking into account relevant international rules, standards, and guidelines. Stockholm Convention, May 22, 2001, U.N. Doc. UNEP/POPS/CONF/2,40 I.L.M. 532 (2001) (entered into force May 17, 2004). *See* the Convention's website *at* http://www.pops.int.

Do these multilateral environmental agreements suggest an answer as to whether developing countries want developed countries to ban exports of dangerous or domestically prohibited substances to their countries?

4. Under the Decision on Notification Procedures for Quantitative Restrictions (Dec. 1995), WTO members are required to notify the WTO Secretariat of any quantitative restrictions that they maintain and to notify changes to these quantitative restrictions when they occur. Members must provide notification of Import and Export Prohibitions, Pro-

hibitions Except under Defined Conditions, and Export Restrictions. Notifications of such quantitative restrictions can, in certain instances, provide information on the export of domestically prohibited goods. Nonetheless, this notification system is not intended to provide information about when exports are allowed.

———

C. Import Quotas and Other Nontariff Barriers

Quotas—specific limits on imports or exports—and other nontariff barriers distort markets in several ways. Perhaps most importantly, they allow countries to protect domestic industries by imposing barriers to imports, usually cheaper imports. The effect or intent, of course, is to increase sales of domestic products. In addition, quotas allow domestic producers to charge higher prices due to a lack of competition. Thus, domestic producers can capture greater profits. At the same time, however, an import quota may generate greater profits for foreign producers. This may occur if demand remains static and the availability of the product is reduced due to the quota. MITSUO MATSUSHITA, THOMAS J. SCHOENBAUM, & PETROS C. MAVROIDIS, THE WORLD TRADE ORGANIZATION: LAW, PRACTICE, AND POLICY 270 (2d ed. 2006).

Quotas, bans, and other restrictions are also used to meet important environmental objectives. Certain multilateral environmental agreements (MEAs), such as the Convention on International Trade in Endangered Species of Wild Fauna and Flora (CITES), use quotas to protect species of conservation concern in part due to trade. Under CITES, the use of quotas offers a highly regulated way to protect species while permitting some trade to occur from healthier populations. Ironically, CITES quotas may actually liberalize trade for species for which the parties would not otherwise permit commercial trade. This is likely true for leopards, where international trade for fur caused significant declines in leopard populations. Other MEAs, such as the Montreal Protocol on Substances that Deplete the Ozone Layer, use trade bans to encourage broad participation in the treaty to address a global problem.

———

Questions and Discussion

1. Daniel Esty claims that "thousands" of environmental and human health and safety laws impose import restrictions with very little, if any, controversy. He claims that import bans only become an issue when used as a "sword" to change the behavior of business in foreign countries. He contrasts bans on the importation of tuna caught by encircling dolphins on the high seas, which he considers to be a "sword," with an import ban on cars that fail to meet emission control standards, which he considers to be a "shield." DANIEL C. ESTY, GREENING THE GATT: TRADE, ENVIRONMENT, AND THE FUTURE 250 (1994). How do these bans differ? Why might governments be more willing to challenge laws such as the tuna ban? Don't both laws ask producers to alter their production to meet requirements imposed by the importing country?

2. The GATT includes exceptions to the prohibition against quantitative restrictions for quotas imposed on certain agricultural products under Article XI, quotas imposed to correct balance-of-payments shortfalls under Article XII, and quotas imposed as a remedy under an Article XIX safeguard action. These exceptions are unlikely to have envi-

ronmental implications, although the agricultural exception under Article XI(2)(a) permits export quotas "to relieve critical shortages of foodstuffs or other products essential to the exporting contracting party." For a more detailed discussion of these exceptions, see RAJ BHALA & KEVIN KENNEDY, WORLD TRADE LAW 106–14 (1998).

3. Some attempts to ban the importation of products deemed environmentally unsound have been resolved more to the satisfaction of environmental advocates. For example, the Appellate Body in *Asbestos* analyzed France's ban on the importation of carcinogenic asbestos products under Article III. European Communities-Measures Affecting Asbestos and Asbestos-Containing Products, Appellate Body Report, WT/DS135/AB/R (adopted Apr. 5, 2001). That decision strongly suggests that import bans, at least when related to product characteristics and accompanied by similar restrictions on domestic production and sales, will be interpreted under Article III. Due to the procedural circumstances of the case, however, the decision should not necessarily be read as suggesting that all such bans will be assessed under Article III. Because the Panel in *Asbestos* found that France violated Article III's national treatment obligation by failing to regulate carcinogenic asbestos fibers the same as noncarcinogenic fibers used for similar purposes, it never reached the issue of whether the ban constituted an Article XI quantitative restriction. On appeal, the Appellate Body found that carcinogenic asbestos fibers and noncarcinogenic fibers were not "like products" and thus could be regulated differently. Like the Panel, it did not determine whether the measure violated Article XI. *See* Chapter 4 at page 191 for a more complete discussion of the *Asbestos* decision.

4. The EU has established the Forest Law Enforcement, Governance and Trade licensing scheme (FLEGT). Council Regulation EC 2173/2005, 2005 O.J. (L 347/1) (EC). Under this scheme, the EU may conclude Voluntary Partnership Agreements with countries and regional organizations in order to impose a legally binding obligation on that partner country or regional organization to implement a licensing scheme for timber products. Under the licensing scheme, certain timber products exported from a partner country and entering the EU should be covered by a license issued by the partner country stating that the timber products have been produced from domestic timber that was legally harvested or from timber that was legally imported into a partner country in accordance with national laws as set out in the respective Partnership Agreement. Compliance with those rules should be subject to third-party monitoring. Timber exported from partner countries into the EU shall be prohibited unless the shipment is covered by a FLEGT license. The EU has concluded agreements with Cameroon and the Republic of Congo with negotiations and other FLEGT activities occurring in several other countries. Might this approach produce better environmental results than the use of tariffs or nontariff barriers? What are the approach's disadvantages?

Chapter 4

Trade and the Regulation of Goods: GATT Article III, "Like Products," and Processes and Production Methods (PPMs)

I. Introduction

In Chapter 3, we tried to ascertain *which* GATT rules apply to traded goods in different circumstances. Our focus there was on the nature and the effect of the government action restricting trade. Was it a measure that placed conditions or limitations on the opportunity for the imported good of that type or origin to enter the market place (suggesting that Article XI applies), or was it a measure more realistically characterized as merely setting forth conditions for sale of such product in the national market (suggesting that Article III applies)?

In this chapter, we explore basic but elusive questions about the goods themselves. Under the GATT, which characteristics of goods or which circumstances surrounding their production provide an appropriate basis for a government to tax or regulate them differently from other competing goods in the market? The focus here will be on the premises underlying the government action in question: has the government identified meaningful differences between competing products that relate to a legitimate regulatory interest of the government? For example, do the GATT's nondiscrimination rules allow a country to tax or regulate paper with a high percentage of recycled content more favorably than paper produced from virgin forests as a means to promote recycling or to reduce impacts on virgin forests? Most importantly, may a government tax or regulate physically identical or similar products differently because of the environmental conditions under which they were manufactured or harvested? For example, do the GATT's nondiscrimination rules allow a country to tax or regulate domestic-caught tuna caught using dolphin-friendly harvesting practices differently from imported tuna caught with harvesting practices not considered dolphin-friendly?

The trade issues in this chapter have central importance for trade-environment policy. Environmental law and regulation strive to reduce the effect of human activities on the environment. One key strategy is to regulate products directly. Governments sometimes set environmental performance standards for products (such as automobile emission standards) or seek better management of resources by specifying product characteristics (such as requirements for returnable beverage containers). Product regulation can be for health and safety reasons as well as protection of the natural environment; food and drug regu-

169

lations are the most common example. For some classes of products, particularly chemical products, governments restrict or even prohibit their production, use, or disposal on health or environmental protection grounds. When any such product-based regulation has the effect of giving some domestically-produced goods a market advantage over imported goods, Article III of the GATT and the "like products" question can come into play.

Broadly speaking, trade law fits easily with product regulation. Trade in products — or more generically, "goods" — is the very stuff of international commerce. As exemplified by the GATT, trade law focuses on the regulation of the trade in goods by setting rules on collection of tariffs and prohibiting most nontariff barriers to trade (Article XI). At the same time the GATT recognizes that all nations have elaborate systems for the taxation and regulation of various goods. Thus, the most favored nation (MFN) obligation of Article I strives to ensure that an importing country taxes and regulates imported products from all countries the same; the national treatment obligation of Article III strives to ensure that national tax and regulatory systems are applied so as not to discriminate between domestic and imported goods of the same type.

A core feature of both the Article I and Article III nondiscrimination obligations is that the nondiscrimination relates to treatment of "like products." This stipulation is both obvious and necessary. With it, governments retain their traditional sovereign autonomy to have different tariff rates, taxes, or regulations for different products, such as automobiles and asbestos. As a corollary, tax or regulatory distinctions between automobiles and asbestos do not become illegitimate under GATT simply because automobiles are domestic products and asbestos is imported. But at some point, products become similar enough that they should be taxed and regulated the same so as to ensure fair competition in the global marketplace. The "like product" problem is to identify just where that point may be with respect to any two products. Is a gasoline-powered automobile "like" an electric car? Is asbestos "like" fiberglass when both are used as insulation? For a challenging analysis of the "like product" issue emphasizing competition in the marketplace as the decisive criterion, see WON-MOG CHOI, LIKE PRODUCTS IN INTERNATIONAL TRADE LAW: TOWARDS A CONSISTENT GATT/WTO JURISPRUDENCE (2003). Section III of this chapter covers the development of WTO law on "like product."

Another key strategy in national environmental regulation is to control the environmental damage that can occur during natural resource harvesting and extraction and the pollution from the processes of energy generation and industrial manufacturing. Laws and regulations for surface mining reclamation and for water pollution control from factories are just a couple of examples of this familiar approach to environmental protection practiced extensively by countries around the world. Trade lawyers distinguish these environmental measures from those that regulate products directly because they regulate processes and production methods (PPMs) rather than final products.

As part of its respect for national regulatory autonomy, trade law generally eschews any intervention into the national regulation of how goods are made; individual countries are free to make their own rules about PPM-based environmental regulation of the producers of goods. More problematically, trade law also generally adheres to the corollary principle that one government should not seek to dictate environmental policy to another. Thus, trade law is hostile to the notion that one WTO member should be allowed to restrict trade in certain goods on the basis of the PPMs by which that good was produced in another country.

The reluctance of the WTO to tolerate trade discrimination between products based on their PPMs has its roots in the "like product" concept. Is sustainably harvested timber "like" unsustainably harvested timber? Is paper from a paper mill with zero discharge of wastewater "like" paper from a mill that pollutes a river? The classic trade position is that the environmentally friendly timber and paper are "like" their environmentally damaging counterparts, because they are physically indistinguishable as products. Environmental advocates and a number of academic observers, though, see virtue in allowing countries to assert their environmental preferences in nondiscriminatory ways through a looser definition of "like product" than trade panels have so far adopted. Section IV delves into the PPMs debate.

Section V explores the issues surrounding "border tax adjustments," a mechanism through which governments may ensure they do not discriminate *against* their own products. Under GATT rules, a country may impose on imported products a tax equivalent to a like internal tax imposed on "like" domestic products. A country may also rebate internal taxes on the exported goods. By allowing such border tax adjustments, products theoretically enter trade "untaxed" and are taxed only in the country of sale. Border tax adjustments may have significant implications for energy conservation policies, such as taxes imposed on energy products or energy efficiency.

Lastly, Section VI takes a relatively brief look at how three "national" systems have dealt with analogous issues of discrimination against "foreign" products. In the United States, there is a considerable body of case law under the Dormant Commerce Clause of the Constitution that tries to determine whether state regulation of a product presents an "undue" burden on interstate commerce. Despite the long line of Dormant Commerce Clause cases, ambiguity persists about just what tests to apply or under what circumstances to apply them. In the European Union (EU), the European Court of Justice faces similarly difficult questions in trying to define the limits on national regulatory authority of member States arising out of the principle of the free movement of goods within the EU. Canada, a federal system with strong provincial power, has tackled the same issues through its Agreement on Internal Trade.

II. The GATT's Nondiscrimination Obligations

A. Article I: The Most Favored Nation Obligation

The most favored nation (MFN) obligation is imposed by the very first paragraph of Article I of the GATT:

> 1. With respect to customs duties and charges of any kind imposed on or in connection with importation or exportation or imposed on the international transfer of money payments for imports or exports, and with respect to the method of levying such duties and charges, and with respect to all rules and formalities in connection with importation and exportation, and with respect to all matters referred to in paragraphs 2 and 4 of Article III, any advantage, favour, privilege or immunity granted by any Member to any product originating in or destined for any other country shall be accorded immediately and unconditionally to the *like product* originating in or destined for the territories of all other Members. (emphasis added).

Note the broad phrasing of the MFN obligation. First, it covers every conceivable aspect of the governmental regulation of trade, both border measures, such as tariffs and quotas, and internal taxes and regulations covered by Article III. Second, Article I uses the very general terms "advantage, favour, privilege or immunity" to cover all different forms of possible preferential or discriminatory treatment. These general terms encompass informal government practices as well as specific formal laws and requirements.

Although MFN issues arise only rarely in trade and environment disputes, the MFN obligation can have both positive and negative environmental effects. On the positive side, it favors nearby sources of imports, thus reducing the environmental burdens of transportation. For example, if both Jamaica and Australia produce aluminum at two dollars per pound, the cost of Jamaican aluminum for a U.S. consumer will be cheaper because transportation costs will be lower. The MFN obligation protects Jamaica from any attempts by the United States to favor the competing Australian product. On the other hand, MFN may hinder sustainable development because it makes it difficult for developing countries to foster "infant industries." If the Jamaican aluminum producer is a new firm with smaller capacity and a less experienced work force than the Australian one, its cost of production may be higher. Under strict application of MFN, it might lose the competitive battle with the Australian firm. Trade officials long ago recognized this problem and agreed to some exceptions to MFN to take into account the special needs and circumstances of developing countries in the global market. One exception allows countries like the United States to give generally reduced tariffs to products from developing countries. GATT Contracting Parties, Decision of November 28, 1979 on Differential and More Favorable Treatment, Reciprocity and Fuller Participation of Developing Countries, L/4903, B.I.S.D. 26th Supp. 203 (1980). For a detailed argument in favor of a much wider tolerance in the WTO for national economic policies like "infant industry" to foster economic development in developing countries, see YONG-SHIK LEE, RECLAIMING DEVELOPMENT IN THE WORLD TRADING SYSTEM (2d ed. 2010).

Questions and Discussion

1. Despite the obligatory nature of MFN and its inclusion in most WTO agreements, the GATT includes a number of important exceptions, including the tariff preferences just mentioned, that permit about 25 percent of global trade to depart from the MFN obligation. The most important exception to MFN permits a country to give more favorable treatment to products originating from partner countries in a customs union or free trade agreement. As described more fully on page 139, because Brazil and Uruguay are members of MERCOSUR, Brazil can treat, for example, meat products from Uruguay more favorably than meat products from the United States. Likewise, the United States may treat meat products from Mexico more favorably than meat products from Brazil, because Canada, Mexico, and the United States are members of the North American Free Trade Agreement.

B. Article III: The National Treatment Obligation

1. The Structure of Article III

The national treatment obligation is a linchpin of the GATT regime. Article III of the GATT states a general principle about national treatment and then addresses itself specifically to the two contexts in which the obligation applies—taxation and regulation. Internal taxation is addressed in paragraph 2; internal regulation is covered by paragraph 4. The "notes" are negotiated parts of the original GATT 1947 text and, thus, have binding effect:

Article III [See note] — National Treatment on Internal Taxation and Regulation

1. The Members recognize that internal taxes and other charges, and laws, regulations and requirements affecting the internal sale, offering for sale, purchase, transportation, distribution or use of products, and internal quantitative regulations requiring the mixture, processing or use of products in specified amounts or proportions, should not be applied to imported or domestic products so as to afford protection to domestic production.

2. The products of the territory of any Member imported into the territory of any other Member shall not be subject, directly or indirectly, to internal taxes or other internal charges of any kind in excess of those applied, directly or indirectly, to like domestic products. Moreover, no Member shall otherwise apply internal taxes or other internal charges to imported or domestic products in a manner contrary to the principles set forth in paragraph 1. [See note] * * *

4. The products of the territory of any Member imported into the territory of any other Member shall be accorded treatment no less favourable than that accorded to like products of national origin in respect of all laws, regulations and requirements affecting their internal sale, offering for sale, purchase, transportation, distribution, or use. * * *

Notes and Supplementary Provisions: Ad Article III

[The first note reproduced here applies to Article III in general; the second note applies to paragraph 2.]

Any internal tax or other internal charge, or any law, regulation or requirement of the kind referred to in paragraph 1 [of Article III] which applies to an imported product and the like domestic product and is collected or enforced in the cases of the imported product at the time or point of importation, is nevertheless to be regarded as an internal tax or other internal charge, or a law, regulation or requirement of the kind referred to in paragraph 1, and is accordingly subject to the provision of Article III.

Paragraph 2: A tax conforming to the requirements of the first sentence of paragraph 2 would be considered to be inconsistent with the provisions of the second sentence only in cases where competition was involved between, on the one hand, the taxed product and, on the other hand, a directly competitive or substitutable product which was not similarly taxed.

———————

Three features of the structure of Article III present difficult interpretational problems. The way GATT and WTO panels have resolved those problems has shaped the understanding of the overall scope and purpose of Article III in general, and the definition of "like products" as used in paragraphs 2 and 4 in particular.

First, the panels have noted the structural separation of policy and obligation. Article III:1 is a mere policy statement. It encompasses a broad range of practices in the administration of internal taxes or regulations, but it merely recites that the WTO members "recognize" that these practices "should not be applied ... so as to afford protection to domestic production." On its face, the Article III:1 language is hortatory, not mandatory. The operative legal obligations appear in Article III:2 and Article III:4. This structural separation leaves interpreters with two big questions: 1) What policy does Article III:1 declare—that is, what does it mean to say that measures ought not to be applied "so as to" protect domestic producers?; and 2) What legal effect or interpretive value should be given to the policy pronounced in the first paragraph when determining the scope of the legal obligations in paragraphs 2 and 4?

The second troublesome structural feature of Article III also relates to the distinction between policy and obligation. Although Article III:1 sets forth the objectives of the national treatment obligation, neither the first sentence of Article III:2 nor Article III:4 make explicit reference to Article III:1. This might not be significant in itself, but Article III:2's second sentence expressly forbids only those practices "contrary to the principles set forth in paragraph 1." As a result, treaty interpreters must establish a meaningful distinction between the explicit reference to Article III:1's policy in Article III:2, second sentence, and its implicit relationship to the other provisions of Article III. As we will see, the Appellate Body uses this structural distinction to shape its reading of "like products" as that term is used in Article III:2, first sentence, and Article III:4.

The third structural feature that presents interpretive problems is that Article III:2, as "clarified" by the Note associated with it, contains two distinct obligations; one or the other will apply according to the circumstances of each case. Article III:4, by contrast, states only a single obligation. Moreover, the distinct nature of the two obligations in Article III:2 hinges on the difference between "like product" (first sentence) and "directly competitive or substitutable products" (Note Ad III:2). As we will see, the Appellate Body has drawn important conclusions about the definition of "like product" based on the dual nature of Article III:2 and the unitary nature of Article III:4.Before proceeding to the analysis of the GATT and WTO panels, let's review the legal questions raised by these structural features. It should now be clear that the "national treatment obligation" is expressed in three different ways, and each of these ways is framed differently by the text of Article III:

- *Internal taxation of "like products" (Article III:2, first sentence).* Internal taxation of the foreign product shall not be "in excess of" the domestic like product. This obligation is stated without express reference to Article III:1. Is this obligation nevertheless conditional on whether the difference in taxes reaches a certain level such that it "affords protection to domestic production"? What is the difference between "like products" (first sentence) and "directly competitive or substitutable products" (second sentence)? Are competitive relationships not relevant in determining "likeness" under the first sentence?

- *Internal taxes or charges on "directly competitive or substitutable products" (Article III:2, second sentence, and Note).* By definition, the fiscal measures being evaluated under the second sentence do not violate the first sentence. Presumably that means that the second sentence only comes into play when the two products being taxed (one foreign, one domestic) are not "like products." Recall also that, in principle, a country should be free to tax different products differently. With those points in mind, by what criteria will it be determined that products that are not "like" are nevertheless protected from differences in taxation under the second sentence? When can it be said that such differences in taxation "afford protection" under the test in Article III:1 which is made expressly applicable? How is that test different from the "in excess of" test under the first sentence? Furthermore, what does the phrase "so as to" mean—that is, under what conditions can it be said that a measure has been applied "so as to afford protection"?

- *Internal regulation of "like products" (Article III:4).* Should "like product" be defined here the same as under Article III:2, first sentence? On the other hand, should "like products" under Article III:4 be defined the same as "directly competitive or substitutable products" under Article III:2, second sentence? How does Article III:1 apply, if at all? That is, are differences in regulation of foreign and domestic "like products" permissible if they do not "afford protection" to domestic producers?

With these perplexing questions in mind, the next subsection, II.B.2, describes the evolution of trade law on general questions of the scope and purpose of Article III. Section III then takes up the central question of the definition of "like products" in the context of environmental taxation and regulation. The principal case there is *EC-Asbestos*, but the legal analysis of the panel and of the Appellate Body in that case cannot be fully grasped without examining *Japan-Alcoholic Beverages II* to understand how the Appellate Body addresses some of the questions just posed.

---

2. The Scope and Purpose of Article III

The agreement of the WTO members to the broad nondiscrimination purposes of the national treatment obligation are set out in the "principles" of Article III:1, namely that national taxes and regulations should not be applied "so as to afford protection to domestic production." That general principle becomes, in binding language, one that requires national treatment through the equivalent application of internal taxes and no less favorable treatment for imported products than for the like domestic products "in respect of all laws, regulations, and requirements affecting" their sale, transport, distribution and use. Through more than 50 years of jurisprudence in disputes under the GATT and now the WTO, dispute settlement panels and the WTO Appellate Body have gradually developed a relatively firm and consistent law about the kinds of national decisions that fall within the scope and the overall purposes of Article III that guide its application in various situations.

By scope, we refer especially to the terms of Articles III:2 and III:4. Article III:2 is, as a matter of scope, simple to interpret and apply. It covers any internal taxes and charges applied to products, which is to say any domestic fiscal measures other than tariffs and customs charges associated with the importation of the product. Article III:4, like the MFN obligation of Article I of the GATT, uses multiple terms in describing its coverage of internal regulations but leaves open for interpretation just what consequence the regulations should have to be covered by Article III.

By purpose, we refer to the difficult interpretive question of how to connect Article III:1 with the obligations of III:2 and III:4. As noted above, it has long been accepted that Article III:1 does not establish any specific obligation but only expresses the general objectives of Article III. Article III:2 and Article III:4 state the substantive requirements, but only Article III:2, second sentence, refers specifically to paragraph 1. Does that mean that paragraph 1 should not be invoked in interpreting the other provisions? If that is not the proper inference, just how should the whole of Article III be interpreted?

In an early GATT case, *Italian Agricultural Machinery,* the GATT parties had occasion to decide what meaning to give to the national treatment obligation. In the years after

World War II, Italy adopted various programs to re-establish agricultural production; one such program offered certain credit services to farmers purchasing agricultural machinery. In an effort to re-establish industrial production as well, Italy decided to give farmers a special, concessional rate of interest on loans to purchase agricultural machinery made in Italy. The United Kingdom complained that this program violated Article III. Italy defended, asserting that nothing in this program impeded the importation or sale of British-made agricultural machinery or set any conditions on their sale. The dispute settlement panel, however, took a broader view:

> [T]he text of paragraph 4 referred both in English and French to laws and regulations and requirements *affecting* internal sale, purchase, etc., and not to laws, regulations and requirements governing the conditions of sale or purchase. The selection of the word "affecting" would imply, in the opinion of the Panel, that the drafters of the Article intended to cover in paragraph 4 not only the laws and regulations which directly governed the conditions of sale or purchase but also any laws or regulations which might adversely modify the conditions of competition between the domestic and imported products on the internal market.

Italian Discrimination Against Imported Agricultural Machinery, GATT Panel Report, L/833, B.I.S.D., 7th Supp. 60, para. 12 (1959) (adopted Oct. 23, 1958) (emphasis in original).

Italian Agricultural Machinery was a watershed decision on both the scope and the purpose of Article III. On scope, its focus on the word "affecting" made clear that any regulation that had the effect, even indirectly, of altering the terms of competition in the marketplace in favor of domestic goods over similar imported goods comes within the scrutiny of Article III. On purpose, its conclusion that Article III is meant to ensure an equality of competitive opportunity between national and imported products has become a staple feature of trade law in cases involving taxation as well as regulation.

Some years after *Italian Agricultural Machinery*, the *Section 337* Panel further broadened the scope of Article III. It held that even procedural rules—in that case, differences between civil procedure in U.S. federal court litigation for protection of intellectual property rights (applicable to domestic products) and the procedural rules for administrative hearings (applicable to foreign products)—were among the "laws, regulations and requirements" that fall within the scope of Article III:4.

As to the purpose of Article III, the *Section 337* Panel (and other GATT panels) further emphasized that Article III was intended to protect not only competition in the marketplace, but also "expectations on the competitive relationship." Accordingly, it was sufficient for the complaining party to demonstrate the "potential impact, rather than … the actual consequences for specific imported products." United States-Section 337 of the Tariff Act of 1930, GATT Panel Report, L/6439, B.I.S.D., 36th Supp. 345, para. 5.13 (1990) (adopted Nov. 7, 1989), quoting in part from United States-Taxes on Petroleum and Certain Imported Substances, GATT Panel Report, L/6175, B.I.S.D., 34th Supp. 136 (1988) (adopted June 17, 1987). The Panel also rejected a U.S. argument that the treatment of imported products under Section 337 was not "less favorable" because, for many importers, the administrative hearing procedure under Section 337 would be less burdensome than litigation in U.S. courts or could result in a more favorable outcome:

> The Panel further found that the "no less favourable" treatment requirement of Article III:4 has to be understood as applicable to each individual case of imported products. The Panel rejected any notion of balancing more favourable treatment of some imported products against less favourable treatment of other

imported products. If this notion were accepted, it would entitle a contracting party to derogate from the no less favourable treatment obligation in one case, or indeed in respect of one contracting party, on the ground that it accords more favourable treatment in some other case, or to another contracting party. Such an interpretation would lead to great uncertainty about the conditions of competition between imported and domestic products and thus defeat the purposes of Article III.

Section 337 Panel Report, at para. 5.14. Nevertheless, the "no less favourable" treatment condition remains a distinct test. That is, a complaining nation must establish not only that the challenged regulation treats foreign and domestic like products differently; it must also show that the differential treatment is "less favourable" to imported products. "[A] formal difference in treatment between imported and like domestic products is thus neither necessary,[1] nor sufficient, to show a violation of Article III:4." Korea-Various Measures on Beef, Appellate Body Report, WT/DS161/AB/R and WT/DS169/AB/R, para. 137 (adopted Jan. 10, 2001).

Another GATT panel addressed the same issues in an environment-related case arising under Article III:2, first sentence. In 1980, the United States enacted the Comprehensive Environmental Response, Compensation and Liability Act, often called Superfund. The Superfund, a fund to clean up hazardous waste sites, was financed by a tax on both domestic production and imports of petroleum and petrochemicals on the theory that petrochemical wastes constituted the predominant share of the hazardous waste to be cleaned up. For reasons that are not altogether clear, the U.S. Congress imposed one tax rate on domestic petroleum and petrochemicals and a slightly higher rate on imported petroleum and petrochemicals. The EU, Venezuela, and Mexico, among others, complained that the higher tax rate for imported products was inconsistent with Article III:2. The United States conceded the difference in the tax rates but argued that the differential was so small that it had no effect in the marketplace and thus did not "nullify or impair" trade benefits within the meaning of GATT Article XXIII. The GATT Panel dismissed that argument:

> An acceptance of the argument that measures which have only an insignificant effect on the volume of exports do not nullify or impair benefits accruing under Article III:2, first sentence, implies that the basic rationale of this provision—the benefit it generates for contracting parties—is to protect expectations of export volumes. That, however, is not the case. Article III:2, first sentence, obliges contracting parties to establish certain competitive conditions for imported products in relation to domestic products. Unlike some other provisions in the General Agreement, it does not refer to trade effects.... For these reasons, Article III:2, first sentence, cannot be interpreted to protect expectations on export volumes; it protects expectations on the competitive relationship between imported and domestic products. A change in the competitive relationship contrary to that provision must consequently be regarded ipso facto as a nullification or impairment of benefits accruing under the General Agreement.

United States-Taxes on Petroleum and Certain Imported Substances, GATT Panel Report, L/6175, B.I.S.D. 34th Supp. 136, para. 5.1.9 (1988) (adopted June 17, 1987).

---

1. Editors' note: In saying that a "formal" difference in treatment is not necessary to show a violation of Article III:4, the Appellate Body is affirming that "informal" differences, or de facto differences, are sufficient even if the regulation appears to be origin-neutral in a "formal" way.

The WTO Appellate Body has reconfirmed these understandings of the scope and purpose of Article III. In doing so, however, it has taken a more formal, text-based interpretive approach. In particular, it has resolved the question of how the policy statement in Article III:1 relates to the substantive obligations of Article III:2:

Japan-Taxes on Alcoholic Beverages

Appellate Body Report, WT/DS8/AB/R, WT/DS10/AB/R, WT/DS11/AB/R, 37–40, 51–54 (adopted Nov. 1, 1996) (*Japan-Alcoholic Beverages II*)

G. Article III:1

The terms of Article III must be given their ordinary meaning—in their context and in the light of the overall object and purpose of the WTO Agreement. Thus, the words actually used in the Article provide the basis for an interpretation that must give meaning and effect to all its terms. The proper interpretation of the Article is, first of all, a textual interpretation. Consequently, the Panel is correct in seeing a distinction between Article III:1, which "contains general principles", and Article III:2, which "provides for specific obligations regarding internal taxes and internal charges." Article III:1 articulates a general principle that internal measures should not be applied so as to afford protection to domestic production. This general principle informs the rest of Article III. The purpose of Article III:1 is to establish this general principle as a guide to understanding and interpreting the specific obligations contained in Article III:2 and in the other paragraphs of Article III, while respecting, and not diminishing in any way, the meaning of the words actually used in the texts of those other paragraphs. In short, Article III:1 constitutes part of the context of Article III:2, in the same way that it constitutes part of the context of each of the other paragraphs in Article III. Any other reading of Article III would have the effect of rendering the words of Article III:1 meaningless, thereby violating the fundamental principle of effectiveness in treaty interpretation. Consistent with this principle of effectiveness, and with the textual differences in the two sentences, we believe that Article III:1 informs the first sentence and the second sentence of Article III:2 in different ways.

H. Article III:2

1. First Sentence

Article III:1 informs Article III:2, first sentence, by establishing that if imported products are taxed in excess of like domestic products, then that tax measure is inconsistent with Article III. Article III:2, first sentence does not refer specifically to Article III:1. There is no specific invocation in this first sentence of the general principle in Article III:1 that admonishes Members of the WTO not to apply measures "so as to afford protection." This omission must have some meaning. We believe the meaning is simply that the presence of a protective application need not be established separately from the specific requirements that are included in the first sentence in order to show that a tax measure is inconsistent with the general principle set out in the first sentence. However, this does not mean that the general principle of Article III:1 does not apply to this sentence. To the contrary, we believe the first sentence of Article III:2 is, in effect, an application of this general principle. The ordinary meaning of the words of Article III:2, first sentence leads inevitably to this conclusion. Read in their context and in the light of the overall object and purpose of the WTO Agreement, the words of the first sentence require an examination of the conformity of an internal tax measure with Article III by determining, first, whether the taxed imported and domestic products are "like" and, second, whether the taxes applied to the imported products are "in excess of" those applied to the like domestic products. If the imported and domestic products are "like products", and if the taxes applied to the imported products are "in excess of" those applied to the like domestic products, then the measure is inconsistent with Article III:2, first sentence. * * *

2. Second Sentence

Article III:1 informs Article III:2, second sentence, through specific reference. Article III:2, second sentence, contains a general prohibition against "internal taxes or other internal charges" applied to "imported or domestic products in a manner contrary to the principles set forth in paragraph 1." As mentioned before, Article III:1 states that internal taxes and other internal charges "should not be applied to imported or domestic products so as to afford protection to domestic production." * * *

Article III:2, second sentence, and the accompanying Ad Article have equivalent legal status in that both are treaty language which was negotiated and agreed at the same time. The Ad Article does not replace or modify the language contained in Article III:2, second sentence, but, in fact, clarifies its meaning. Accordingly, the language of the second sentence and the Ad Article must be read together in order to give them their proper meaning.

Unlike that of Article III:2, first sentence, the language of Article III:2, second sentence, specifically invokes Article III:1. The significance of this distinction lies in the fact that whereas Article III:1 acts implicitly in addressing the two issues that must be considered in applying the first sentence, it acts explicitly as an entirely separate issue that must be addressed along with two other issues that are raised in applying the second sentence. Giving full meaning to the text and to its context, three separate issues must be addressed to determine whether an internal tax measure is inconsistent with Article III:2, second sentence. These three issues are whether:

(1) the imported products and the domestic products are "directly competitive or substitutable products" which are in competition with each other;

(2) the directly competitive or substitutable imported and domestic products are "not similarly taxed"; and

(3) the dissimilar taxation of the directly competitive or substitutable imported domestic products is "applied ... so as to afford protection to domestic production."

Again, these are three separate issues. Each must be established separately by the complainant for a panel to find that a tax measure imposed by a Member of the WTO is inconsistent with Article III:2, second sentence.

Questions and Discussion

1. Why do the GATT and WTO decisions discount actual trade effects of government actions and emphasize the mere "opportunity" to compete as the condition to be pro-

tected by the national treatment obligation? Is that approach consistent with the stated policy of Article III, namely to guard against measures "applied so as to afford protection to domestic production"? If flows of imports are not impeded, how can domestic production be said to have been protected? But even if changes in trade flows would be a more practical measure of "protection," how does a company or a country demonstrate that trade flows have or have not been affected by the challenged measure?

2. The GATT panel reports reach legal conclusions about the competitive relationships to be protected by Article III with scarcely any reference to Article III:1. In the *Japan Alcoholic Beverages II* report, the Appellate Body comes to the same conclusions, but only after parsing the language of Article III:1 and Article III:2 and the connections between the two. Which approach do you find more persuasive? What drawbacks might there be to the formalistic, textual approach of the Appellate Body?

3. The analysis of Article III:1 in *Japan Alcoholic Beverages II* plays a central role, as we shall see next, in the Appellate Body's interpretation of "like product" in Articles III:2 and III:4.

III. "Like Products"

As already noted, the meaning of "like products" underpins the GATT's MFN and national treatment obligations. Broadly speaking, WTO members must tax and regulate "like products" the same. If the products are not "like," then WTO members may, without restraint by trade law, exercise their national prerogative to tax and regulate non-"like" products differently.

Despite the importance of the term "like products," the GATT and other WTO agreements do not define it. Over the years, dispute settlement panels and other trade bodies have taken a case-by-case approach to the criteria for determining when products are "like." In 1970, the Report of the Working Party on Border Tax Adjustments, adopted by the Contracting Parties in 1970, expressly advocated the case-by-case approach for interpreting "like or similar products" generally in the various provisions of the GATT 1947:

> [T]he interpretation of the term should be examined on a case-by-case basis. This would allow a fair assessment in each case of the different elements that constitute a "similar" product. Some criteria were suggested for determining, on a case-by-case basis, whether a product is "similar": the product's end-uses in a given market; consumers' tastes and habits, which change from country to country; the product's properties, nature and quality.

Report of the Working Party on Border Tax Adjustments, Nov. 20, 1970, L/3464, B.I.S.D. 18th Supp. 97, para. 18 (1972). Subsequently, GATT panels added tariff classification of the products as an additional criterion for assessing product similarity. *See, e.g.,* EEC-Measures on Animal Feed Proteins, GATT Panel Report, L/4599, B.I.S.D. 25th Supp. 49 (1979) (adopted Mar. 14, 1978); Spain-Tariff Treatment of Unroasted Coffee, GATT Panel Report, L/5135, B.I.S.D. 28th Supp. 102 (1982) (adopted June 11, 1981).

Despite the presence of this four-part test since the 1970s, the jurisprudence on "like product" has evolved as GATT and WTO panels and the Appellate Body have refined their thinking about how to apply these four factors. The formative cases arose in disputes involving taxes on foreign and domestic products under Article III:2. We take up those cases next. But as described in Section II.B.1 above, Article III:2 and Article III:4 have different structures and define different obligations. It was not until the landmark case *EC-Asbestos* that the Appellate Body decided how to apply the analytical framework of the III:2 cases to the product regulation context under Article III:4. We take up *EC-Asbestos* in Section III.B below.

A. "Like Products" under Article III:2

1. The "Aim and Effect" Test

The first GATT case to undertake a precise interpretation of "like product" in Article III:2 was *Japan-Alcoholic Beverages I*. Several countries complained that Japan's system of taxation of alcoholic beverages discriminated in favor of Japanese-produced beverages and against imported beverages. Because many discrete alcoholic beverages were involved — shochu (a distilled beverage made from rice), vodka, gin, various whiskies, brandy, etc. — the GATT panel undertook an exhaustive determination of likeness of products. It reconfirmed the importance of the Report of the Working Party on Border Tax Adjustments (Working Party) approach as an interpretive guide. The GATT Panel worked through each of the three Working Party factors — physical characteristics, consumer tastes and preferences, and the product's end use — along with tariff classification. It explicitly concluded that no single factor should be applied to make a finding of "like product"; rather, it required a consideration of all the factors together in the context of the specific facts of the case at hand. It reached three determinations with respect to likeness. First, it concluded that, within each beverage category (e.g., vodka, whiskey, brandy, or wine), the Japanese and imported products were "like products." Second, with an emphasis on physical characteristics and end uses, the Panel concluded that the clear distilled beverages shochu and vodka were "like products." Finally, with a heavy emphasis on the end use factor, it held that all these alcoholic beverages together were "directly competitive or substitutable products." The Panel discounted the consumer preferences factor on the grounds that consumer preferences could be "crystallized" by the very differences in taxation that were in dispute. Japan-Customs Duties, Taxes and Labelling Practices on Imported Wines and Alcoholic Beverages, GATT Panel Report, L/6216, B.I.S.D. 34th Supp. 83 (1988) (adopted Nov. 10, 1987) (*Japan-Alcoholic Beverages I*).

The *Auto Taxes* Panel took a different approach. United States-Taxes on Automobiles, GATT Panel Report, DS31/R (Oct. 11, 1994) (unadopted), *reprinted in* 33 I.L.M. 1397 (1994). This case arose when the EU challenged key elements of U.S. policy on automobile fuel consumption that were adopted during the Arab oil embargo in the mid-1970s as measures to conserve petroleum. The measures also had the environmental benefit of reducing air pollution and reducing pressure from the domestic petroleum industry for exploration and production in environmentally sensitive areas like the North Slope of Alaska or coastal waters. The luxury tax was a retail excise tax on certain passenger vehicles (an exemption applied for passenger vehicles for trade, business, and certain other purposes) amounting to 10 percent of the excess of the retail price over $30,000 (later increased to $32,000). The gas guzzler tax of the Energy Tax Act of 1978, 26 U.S.C. §§ 4064 et seq., imposes a tax on the sale by the manufacturer (including the importer) of each automobile within a "model type" whose fuel economy fails to meet certain fuel economy requirements. The legislation exempts "non-passenger" automobiles, such as light trucks, mini-vans, recreational vehicles, and emergency vehicles (as well as the subsequently-developed sport-utility vehicle). The Energy Tax Act required the Environmental Protection Agency (EPA) to separate cars for gas guzzler tax purposes according to the fuel economy of a "model type" for a model year on the basis of characteristics likely to significantly affect fuel economy. Gas guzzler liability calculations are performed before vehicles enter into commerce so that the tax can be displayed on the fuel economy label at the beginning of the model year, thus allowing the consumer to be aware of the fuel economy value and the extra cost at the time of sale.

The central question in the portions of the *Auto Taxes* panel report dealing with the luxury tax and the gas guzzler tax was whether all cars were "like products" that must be taxed the same, as the Europeans argued, or whether it was legitimate for the United States to distinguish one car from another on the basis of certain characteristics. In its analysis, the Panel linked the principle of preserving the competitive relationship with the interpretation of "like product":

> 5.6 ... Thus the practical interpretative issue under paragraphs 2 and 4 of Article III was: which differences between products may form the basis of regulatory distinctions by governments that accord less favourable treatment to imported products? Or, conversely, which similarities between products prevent regulatory distinctions by governments that accord less favourable treatment to imported product?

> 5.7 ... The Panel reasoned therefore that Article III serves only to prohibit regulatory distinctions between products applied so as to afford protection to domestic production. Its purpose is not to prohibit fiscal and regulatory distinctions applied so as to achieve other policy goals. * * *

> 5.9 ... [T]he first step of determining the relevant features common to the domestic and imported products (likeness) would in the view of the Panel, in all but the most straightforward cases, have to include an examination of the aim and effect of the particular tax measure. Therefore the second step of determining whether the tax measure was discriminatory or protective was simply a continuation of the inquiry under the first step. The Panel concluded that its interpretation was consistent with previous ones, but made explicit that issues of likeness under Article III should be analyzed primarily in terms of whether less favourable treatment was based on a regulatory distinction taken so as to afford protection to domestic production.

> 5.10 The Panel then proceeded to examine more closely the meaning of the phrase "so as to afford protection." The Panel noted that the term "so as to" suggested both aim and effect.[129] Thus the phrase "so as to afford protection" called for an analysis of elements including the aim of the measure and the resulting effects. A measure could be said to have the aim of affording protection if an analysis of the circumstances in which it was adopted, in particular an analysis of the instruments available to the contracting party to achieve the declared domestic policy goal, demonstrated that a change in competitive opportunities in favour of domestic products was a desired outcome and not merely an incidental consequence of the pursuit of a legitimate policy goal. A measure could be said

---

129. This term "shows the logical result or purpose of an action done in a specific manner" (Webster's Third New International Dictionary of the English Language (Unabridged)). This meaning is also reflected in the French authentic text of Article III:1 which uses the expression "de manière à."

to have the effect of affording protection to domestic production if it accorded greater competitive opportunities to domestic products than to imported products.

United States-Taxes on Automobiles, GATT Panel Report, DS31/R (Oct. 11, 1994) (unadopted).

Using this interpretive approach, the Panel then found that the aim and effect of the luxury tax was not to afford protection to domestic production. The fact that a large proportion of imports of EU origin (but not necessarily a large proportion of imports from other countries) was affected by the measure did not demonstrate that the legislation was aimed at affording protection to domestic automobiles selling for less than US$30,000. No evidence had been advanced that EC or other foreign automobile manufacturers did not in general have the design, production, and marketing capabilities to sell automobiles below the US$30,000 threshold, or that they did not in general produce such models for other markets. Similarly, with respect to the gas guzzler tax, the Panel found no change in the conditions of competition that favored U.S. auto manufacturers. "In terms of Article III:2, and for the purposes of the gas guzzler tax, foreign automobiles below the 22.5 mpg threshold were not 'like' domestic automobiles above the threshold, and different and less favourable treatment under the gas guzzler measure could therefore be accorded to them." *Id.* at para. 5.26.

Questions and Discussion

1. *Auto Taxes* was seen in the environmental community as a welcome sign that a reasonable interpretation of trade law could create space for regulation affecting trade based on national policy choices for environmental protection and energy conservation. In particular, the "aim and effect" test, analogous to many U.S. court decisions in Commerce Clause cases, seemed to American environmentalists at least to give legal footing to the idea that a *bona fide* environmental protection measure should not be struck down in the WTO just because it had some incidental effect on the terms of competition that was unfavorable to some foreign producers.

2. Even so, the reasoning in *Auto Taxes* raises difficult questions of its own. In the luxury tax section of its report, the Panel never properly determined whether or not the automobiles of various prices were in some sense "like products." Rather, in its eagerness to give broad discretion to national tax policy designers, it conflated the decision on "like products" with the "aim and effect" test, allowing the policy behind the tax to govern the determination of likeness without regard to any of the traditional criteria. Shouldn't a determination of "likeness" come before assessing the measure's aim and effect?

3. *Auto Taxes* was the last ruling under the GATT system of dispute settlement. Like the *Tuna/Dolphin* reports, it was never adopted by the GATT Council. As we will now see, the WTO Appellate Body has not followed its reasoning.

2. Reframing the Issues: Japan-Alcoholic Beverages II

In its first detailed examination of "like products," *Japan-Alcoholic Beverages II*, the WTO Appellate Body takes a more formalistic textual analysis approach to the provisions of Article III. Observe in particular how the Appellate Body handles the "aim and effect" test articulated in *Auto Taxes*. Close examination of the *Japan-Alcoholic Beverages II* analytical approach is relevant to our understanding of the landmark environmental case interpreting Article III:4, *EC-Asbestos*.

The dispute concerned Japan's Liquor Tax Law (Shuzeiho), Law No.6 of 1953, which establishes tax rates for domestically produced and imported alcoholic beverages that are intended for consumption in Japan. The Liquor Tax Law classified the various types of alcoholic beverages into ten categories and additional sub-categories: sake, sake compound, shochu (group A, group B), mirin, beer, wine (wine, sweet wine), whisky/brandy, spirits, liqueurs, miscellaneous (various sub-categories). The tax rate was assessed based on the type of beverage and the alcohol content of the beverage. As a consequence of this scheme, shochu, a distilled "white" liquor native to Japan, was taxed substantially less than vodka, gin, and other "white" liquors, as well as "brown" liquors like whisky. The questions for the Panel and the Appellate Body were whether shochu and other "white" alcoholic beverages are "like products" and whether shochu whisky and other "brown liquors" are "directly competitive and substitutable products."

Japan-Taxes on Alcoholic Beverages

Appellate Body Report, WT/DS8/AB/R, WT/DS10/AB/R, WT/DS11/AB/R, 42–70 (adopted Nov. 1, 1996) (*Japan-Alcoholic Beverages II*)

H. Article III:2 * * *

1. First Sentence * * *

(a) "Like Products"

Because the second sentence of Article III:2 provides for a separate and distinctive consideration of the protective aspect of a measure in examining its application to a broader category of products that are not "like products" as contemplated by the first sentence, we agree with the Panel that the first sentence of Article III:2 must be construed narrowly so as not to condemn measures that its strict terms are not meant to condemn. Consequently, we agree with the Panel also that the definition of "like products" in Article III:2, first sentence, should be construed narrowly.

How narrowly is a matter that should be determined separately for each tax measure in each case. We agree with the practice under the GATT 1947 of determining whether imported and domestic products are "like" on a case-by-case basis. The Report of the Working Party on Border Tax Adjustments, adopted by the CONTRACTING PARTIES in 1970, set out the basic approach for interpreting "like or similar products" generally in the various provisions of the GATT 1947 [quoting Working Party report].

This approach was followed in almost all adopted panel reports after Border Tax Adjustments. This approach should be helpful in identifying on a case-by-case basis the range of "like products" that fall within the narrow limits of Article III:2, first sentence in the GATT 1994. Yet this approach will be most helpful if decision makers keep ever in mind how narrow the range of "like products" in Article III:2, first sentence is meant to be as opposed to the range of "like" products contemplated in some other provisions of the GATT 1994 and other Multilateral Trade Agreements of the WTO Agreement. In applying the criteria cited in Border Tax Adjustments to the facts of any particular case, and in considering other criteria that may also be relevant in certain cases, panels can only apply their best judgement in determining whether in fact products are "like." This will always involve an unavoidable element of individual, discretionary judgement. We do not agree with the Panel's observation in paragraph 6.22 of the Panel Report that distinguishing between "like products" and "directly competitive or substitutable products" under Article III:2 is "an arbitrary decision." Rather, we think it is a discretionary decision that must be made in considering the various characteristics of products in individual cases.

No one approach to exercising judgement will be appropriate for all cases. The criteria in Border Tax Adjustments should be examined, but there can be no one precise and absolute definition of what is "like." The concept of "likeness" is a relative one that evokes the image of an accordion. The accordion of "likeness" stretches and squeezes in different places as different provisions of the WTO Agreement are applied. The width of the accordion in any one of those places must be determined by the particular provision in which the term "like" is encountered as well as by the context and the circumstances that prevail in any given case to which that provision may apply. We believe that, in Article III:2, first sentence of the GATT 1994, the accordion of "likeness" is meant to be narrowly squeezed.

The Panel determined in this case that shochu and vodka are "like products" for the purposes of Article III:2, first sentence. We note that the determination of whether vodka is a "like product" to shochu under Article III:2, first sentence, or a "directly competitive or substitutable product" to shochu under Article III:2, second sentence, does not materially affect the outcome of this case.

A uniform tariff classification of products can be relevant in determining what are "like products." If sufficiently detailed, tariff classification can be a helpful sign of product similarity. * * *

It is true that there are numerous tariff bindings which are in fact extremely precise with regard to product description and which, therefore, can provide significant guidance as to the identification of "like products." Clearly enough, these determinations need to be made on a case-by-case basis. However, tariff bindings that include a wide range of products are not a reliable criterion for determining or confirming product "likeness" under Article III:2. * * *

  (b) "In Excess Of"

The only remaining issue under Article III:2, first sentence, is whether the taxes on imported products are "in excess of" those on like domestic products. If so, then the Member that has imposed the tax is not in compliance with Article III. Even the smallest amount of "excess" is too much. "The prohibition of discriminatory taxes in Article III:2, first sentence, is not conditional on a 'trade effects test' nor is it qualified by a de minimis standard." We agree with the Panel's legal reasoning and with its conclusions on this aspect of the interpretation and application of Article III:2, first sentence.

  2. Second Sentence * * *

  (a) "Directly Competitive or Substitutable Products"

If imported and domestic products are not "like products" for the narrow purposes of Article III:2, first sentence, then they are not subject to the strictures of that sentence and there is no inconsistency with the requirements of that sentence. However, depending on their nature, and depending on the competitive conditions in the relevant market, those same products may well be among the broader category of "directly competitive or substitutable products" that fall within the domain of Article III:2, second sentence. How much broader that category of "directly competitive or substitutable products" may be in any given case is a matter for the panel to determine based on all the relevant facts in that case. As with "like products" under the first sentence, the determination of the appropriate range of "directly competitive or substitutable products" under the second sentence must be made on a case-by-case basis.

In this case, the Panel emphasized the need to look not only at such matters as physical characteristics, common end-uses, and tariff classifications, but also at the "market place." This seems appropriate. The GATT 1994 is a commercial agreement, and the WTO is concerned, after all, with markets. It does not seem inappropriate to look at competition in the relevant markets as one among a number of means of identifying the broader category of products that might be described as "directly competitive or substitutable."

Nor does it seem inappropriate to examine elasticity of substitution as one means of examining those relevant markets. The Panel did not say that cross-price elasticity of demand is "the decisive criterion" for determining whether products are "directly competitive or substitutable." The Panel stated the following:

> In the Panel's view, the decisive criterion in order to determine whether two products are directly competitive or substitutable is whether they have common end-uses, inter alia, as shown by elasticity of substitution.

We agree. And, we find the Panel's legal analysis of whether the products are "directly competitive or substitutable products" in paragraphs 6.28–6.32 of the Panel Report to be correct. * * *

(b) "Not Similarly Taxed"

To give due meaning to the distinctions in the wording of Article III:2, first sentence, and Article III:2, second sentence, the phrase "not similarly taxed" in the Ad Article to the second sentence must not be construed so as to mean the same thing as the phrase "in excess of" in the first sentence. On its face, the phrase "in excess of" in the first sentence means any amount of tax on imported products "in excess of" the tax on domestic "like products." The phrase "not similarly taxed" in the Ad Article to the second sentence must therefore mean something else. It requires a different standard, just as "directly competitive or substitutable products" requires a different standard as compared to "like products" for these same interpretive purposes.

Reinforcing this conclusion is the need to give due meaning to the distinction between "like products" in the first sentence and "directly competitive or substitutable products" in the Ad Article to the second sentence. If "in excess of" in the first sentence and "not similarly taxed" in the Ad Article to the second sentence were construed to mean one and the same thing, then "like products" in the first sentence and "directly competitive or substitutable products" in the Ad Article to the second sentence would also mean one and the same thing. This would eviscerate the distinctive meaning that must be respected in the words of the text.

To interpret "in excess of" and "not similarly taxed" identically would deny any distinction between the first and second sentences of Article III:2. Thus, in any given case, there may be some amount of taxation on imported products that may well be "in excess of" the tax on domestic "like products" but may not be so much as to compel a conclusion that "directly competitive or substitutable" imported and domestic products are "not similarly taxed" for the purposes of the Ad Article to Article III:2, second sentence. In other words, there may be an amount of excess taxation that may well be more of a burden on imported products than on domestic "directly competitive or substitutable products" but may nevertheless not be enough to justify a conclusion that such products are "not similarly taxed" for the purposes of Article III:2, second sentence. We agree with the Panel that this amount of differential taxation must be more than de minimis to be deemed "not similarly taxed" in any given case. And, like the Panel, we believe that whether any particular differential amount of taxation is de minimis or is not de minimis must, here too, be determined on a case-by-case basis. Thus, to be "not similarly taxed", the tax burden on imported products must be heavier than on "directly competitive or substitutable" domestic products, and that burden must be more than de minimis in any given case.

In this case, the Panel applied the correct legal reasoning in determining whether "directly competitive or substitutable" imported and domestic products were "not similarly taxed." However, the Panel erred in blurring the distinction between that issue and the entirely separate issue of whether the tax measure in question was applied "so as to afford protection." Again, these are separate issues that must be addressed individually. If "directly competitive or substitutable products" are not "not similarly taxed", then there is neither need nor justification under Article III:2, second sentence, for inquiring further as to whether the tax has been applied "so as to afford protection." But if such products are "not similarly taxed", a further inquiry must necessarily be made.

(c) "So As To Afford Protection"

This third inquiry under Article III:2, second sentence, must determine whether "directly competitive or substitutable products" are "not similarly taxed" in a way that affords protection. This is not an issue of intent. It is not necessary for a panel to sort through the many reasons legislators and regulators often have for what they do and weigh the relative significance of those reasons to establish legislative or regulatory intent. If the measure is applied to imported or domestic products so as to afford protection to domestic production, then it does not matter that there may not have been any desire to engage in protectionism in the minds of the legislators or the regulators who imposed the measure. It is irrelevant that protectionism was not an intended objective if the particular tax measure in question is nevertheless, to echo Article III:1, "applied to imported or domestic products so as to afford protection to domestic production." This is an issue of how the measure in question is applied.

In the 1987 Japan-Alcohol case, the panel subsumed its discussion of the issue of "not similarly taxed" within its examination of the separate issue of "so as to afford protection." * * *

As in that case, we believe that an examination in any case of whether dissimilar taxation has been applied so as to afford protection requires a comprehensive and objective analysis of the structure and application of the measure in question on domestic as compared to imported products. We believe it is possible to examine objectively the underlying criteria used in a particular tax measure, its structure, and its overall application to ascertain whether it is applied in a way that affords protection to domestic products.

Although it is true that the aim of a measure may not be easily ascertained, nevertheless its protective application can most often be discerned from the design, the architecture, and the revealing structure of a measure. The very magnitude of the dissimilar taxation in a particular case may be evidence of such a protective application, as the Panel rightly concluded in this case. Most often, there will be other factors to be considered as well. In conducting this inquiry, panels should give full consideration to all the relevant facts and all the relevant circumstances in any given case. * * *

[H]aving stated the correct legal approach to apply with respect to Article III:2, second sentence, the Panel then equated dissimilar taxation above a *de minimis* level with the separate and distinct requirement of demonstrating that the tax measure "affords protection to domestic production." As previously stated, a finding that "directly competitive or substitutable products" are "not similarly taxed" is necessary to find a violation of Article III:2, second sentence. Yet this is not enough. The dissimilar taxation must be more than *de minimis*. It may be so much more that it will be clear from that very differential that the dissimilar taxation was applied "so as to afford protection." In some cases, that may be enough to show a violation. In this case, the Panel concluded that it was enough. Yet in other cases, there may be other factors that will be just as relevant or more relevant to demonstrating that the dissimilar taxation at issue was applied "so as to afford protection." In any case, the three issues that must be addressed in determining whether there is such a violation must be addressed clearly and separately in each case and on a case-by-case basis. And, in every case, a careful, objective analysis, must be done of each and all relevant facts and all the relevant circumstances in order to determine "the existence of protective taxation." Although the Panel blurred its legal reasoning in this respect, nevertheless we conclude that it reasoned correctly that in this case, the Liquor Tax Law is not in compliance with Article III:2. As the Panel did, we note that:

> ... the combination of customs duties and internal taxation in Japan has the following impact: on the one hand, it makes it difficult for foreign-produced shochu to penetrate the Japanese market and, on the other, it does not guarantee equality of competitive conditions between shochu and the rest of "white" and "brown" spirits. Thus, through a combination of high import duties and differentiated internal taxes, Japan manages to "isolate" domestically produced shochu from foreign competition, be it foreign produced shochu or any other of the mentioned white and brown spirits.

Our interpretation of Article III is faithful to the "customary rules of interpretation of public international law." WTO rules are reliable, comprehensible and enforceable. WTO rules are not so rigid or so inflexible as not to leave room for reasoned judgements in confronting the endless and ever-changing ebb and flow of real facts in real cases in the real world. They will serve the multilateral trading system best if they are interpreted with that in mind. In that way, we will achieve the "security and predictability" sought for the multilateral trading system by the Members of the WTO through the establishment of the dispute settlement system.

[The Appellate Body then concluded that shochu and vodka are like products and that shochu and other distilled spirits and liqueurs, except for vodka, are "directly competitive or substitutable products."]

Questions and Discussion

1. The very strict rule declared in *Japan-Alcoholic Beverages II* on taxation of like products under Article III:2, first sentence, has been cited with approval in subsequent cases. Korea-Taxes on Alcoholic Beverages, WT/DS75/AB/R, WT/DS84/AB/R (adopted Feb. 17, 1999); Chile-Taxes on Alcoholic Beverages, WT/DS87/AB/R, WT/DS109/AB/R, and WT/DS110/AB/R (adopted Jan. 12, 2000). Note the reciprocal nature of the "accordion" of like products and the strictness of the reading of "in excess of." The strict rule requires a very narrow reading of "like product." Compare that with the more relaxed rule under Article III:2, second sentence, and the correspondingly broad interpretation of "directly competitive and substitutable."

2. Why should the WTO not allow *de minimis* differences in tax rates for "like" products? What are the arguments for and against any differentials in taxation? If one argues for a *de minimis* rule, what would be the measure of whether the difference was or was not *de minimis*? As the Appellate Body says, the GATT is a commercial agreement, so why should trade effects not be considered? Why does the Appellate Body then explicitly permit *de minimis* differences under the "not similarly taxed" language of Article III:2, second sentence?

3. Consider whether *Auto Taxes* would be decided differently under the analytical approach of *Japan Alcoholic Beverages II*. In *Auto Taxes*, were foreign products taxed differently from domestic products? Does Article III:2, first sentence, apply? Could the *Auto Taxes* handling of "like product" be read as a tight squeezing of the accordion of likeness? If Article III:2, first sentence, does not apply, what *was* the basis of the EU's Article III claim? Was it a claim under Article III:2, second sentence? What would the EU have needed to show in the auto taxes context to meet the Appellate Body's tests under Article III:2, second sentence? How different is that from the approach of the *Auto Taxes* panel?

4. The Appellate Body, with its "accordion" simile, definitively concludes that the term "like product" should have different meanings in different contexts. Are you convinced? Does the emphasis on assessing "like-products" on a case-by-case basis coupled with this "accordion of likeness" give panels and the Appellate Body too little guidance and too much discretion? What does "accordion of likeness" suggest about the interpretation of "like product" in the Article III:4 context?

5. *Some Final Observations on the "Aim and Effect" Test.* In *Japan-Alcoholic Beverages II*, both the complaining governments and Japan argued their positions with reference to the "aim and effect" test. Notwithstanding the general acceptance of the test among WTO members, the Appellate Body surprised all observers with its new interpretive approach to the Article III:1 policy against protectionist measures. Essentially, the Appellate Body attempted to formulate a more objective way of considering a measure's aim: "Although it is true that the aim of a measure may not be easily ascertained, nevertheless its protective application can most often be discerned from the design, the architecture, and the revealing structure of a measure."

In the view of the late Robert Hudec, a highly respected trade law scholar, the "aim and effect" test (or "aim and effects," as he called it) served a useful purpose. By setting it aside, he argued, the Appellate Body left trade law without reliable, practical guidance. Consider Hudec's following arguments and prognostications:

> If it is true that the "aim and effects" approach makes the most intuitive sense when trying to discern the difference between bona fide domestic regulatory measures

and disguised trade restrictions, one would expect that the Appellate Body decision in the Japan-Alcoholic Beverages case would have left most participants in the WTO dispute settlement process dissatisfied with the rather wooden kinds of legal tools that they had been left to work with. One would expect, therefore, to see evidence of efforts to circumvent such a doctrinal straight-jacket. It is perhaps relevant, therefore, to note that in the first twelve months after the decision in Japan—Alcoholic Beverages, no less than four major dispute settlement proceedings witnessed a serious effort to introduce versions of the "aim and effects" approach into the legal analysis of violation. First, as just noted, in the panel phase of Bananas III, the panel itself tried to introduce analysis of protective purpose into article III:4. Second, in the appellate phase of Bananas III, the European Community (the dedicated opponent of the "aim and effects" approach) argued that the one-dimensional, head-count approach to identifying de facto discrimination under the GATS agreement had to be blended with considerations of protective purpose. Third, at both levels of the Canadian Periodicals case, Canada (which had supported the EC's assault on the "aim and effects" approach) found itself arguing that the "like product" test of article III:2 had to be accompanied by consideration of whether the legislation had a "discriminatory" purpose. Finally, the panel decision in the Hormones case added an extensive analysis of regulatory purpose, in part based on GATT article III:1, in applying article 5.5 of the SPS Code. The author would suggest, of course, that these four instances are merely the tip of an iceberg.

Robert E. Hudec, *GATT/WTO Constraints on National Regulation: Requiem for an "Aim and Effects" Test*, 32 INT'L LAW. 619, 635–36 (1999).

6. Is Professor Hudec's report on the death of the "aim and effect" test premature? Is the Appellate Body really saying that the intent of a measure is irrelevant? What might have motivated the Appellate Body to avoid a direct or explicit inquiry into a government's intent? Do you think their "design and architecture" approach to discerning intent is workable? Does it amount to the same thing as "aim and effect"? In any event, Professor Hudec wrote his requiem before the Appellate Body's next significant interpretation of Article III, the *EC-Asbestos* report, to which we now turn.

B. "Like Products" and Regulations under Article III:4

A good opportunity for further development of the "like product" issue presented itself in a case brought by Canada against the EU, then known as the European Communities, challenging a French regulation forbidding the sale of chrysotile asbestos and most products containing such asbestos. Asbestos fibers have been used in a variety of products, such as cement pipe, to give the material extra strength. There are about 150 other fibers, including fiberglass and cellulose fibers, that may be reasonable substitutes for asbestos in these products. The French regulation banned chrysotile because it is a recognized carcinogen if inhaled but allowed the continued sale of other noncarcinogenic substitute fibers and products containing them although they, too, present some health risks. Canada, which continues to mine and export chrysotile asbestos and allows asbestos products in its market, argued that all these fiber products were "like products," even if the length and diameter ratio of the different fibers have an effect on their pathogenicity. The EU, on behalf of France, argued that the nature, composition, physical properties, and proven effects on human health of chrysotile asbestos make it a "radically different" product from noncarcinogenic cellulose and other substitute fibers.

The WTO Panel, paying particular attention to the fact that the various fiber products had the same end uses and competed with each other in the marketplace, ruled that the various fibers were "like products." Thus, France had violated Article III in its asbestos regulation by giving asbestos less favorable treatment than the noncarcinogenic products with similar end uses. European Communities-Measures Affecting Asbestos and Asbestos Containing Products, Panel Report , WT/DS135/R (Sept. 18, 2000), *reprinted in* 40 I.L.M. 258 (2001). The Panel purported to apply the traditional four-part test for determining "likeness." It acknowledged that asbestos had unique physical and chemical characteristics and that no substitute has the same properties of asbestos. The Panel found, however, that asbestos has the same uses as many other products. It noted that "[i]f the chemical and physical characteristics were to be recognized as decisive in this case, we would have to disregard all the other criteria and this does not appear to us to be consistent with the flexibility given to panels by the Appellate Body when examining the principle of likeness." *Asbestos Panel* at para. 8.123. Moreover, the Panel asserted that when two products can be used for the same end use, their "properties are then equivalent, if not identical.... [T]he end-use of the products should affect the way in which we examine the properties of the fibres compared.... We therefore conclude that, taking into account the properties criterion, chrysotile fibres are like PVA [polyvinyl alcohol], cellulose and glass fibres." *Id.* at paras. 8.125–8.126. Finally, the Panel ruled that the risk to human health posed by a product could not be considered as part of the "likeness" inquiry under Article III; it could only be analyzed under the Article XX(b) exception for measures inconsistent with the GATT but "necessary for the protection of human, animal or plant life or health." *Id.* at para. 8.130. (The Article XX aspect of *EC-Asbestos* is covered in Chapter 5 at pages 287–293.)

The EU appealed the Panel's conclusions. The Appellate Body's report in *EC-Asbestos* is the first, and thus far the definitive application of the "like product" analysis developed in *Japan Alcoholic Beverages II* as applied to the comparison of products on environmental grounds.

European Communities-Measures Affecting Asbestos and Asbestos-Containing Products

Appellate Body Report, WT/DS135/AB/R (adopted April 5, 2001),
reprinted in 40 I.L.M. 497 (2001)

93. ... In previous Reports, we have held that the scope of "like" products in [Article III:2, first sentence] is to be construed "narrowly." This reading of "like" in Article III:2 might be taken to suggest a similarly narrow reading of "like" in Article III:4, since both provisions form part of the same Article. However, both of these paragraphs of Article III constitute specific expressions of the overarching, "general principle", set forth in Article III:1 of the GATT 1994. As we have previously said, the "general principle" set forth in Article III:1 "informs" the rest of Article III and acts "as a guide to understanding and interpreting the specific obligations contained" in the other paragraphs of Article III, including paragraph 4. Thus, in our view, Article III:1 has particular contextual significance in interpreting Article III:4, as it sets forth the "general principle" pursued by that provision. Accordingly, in interpreting the term "like products" in Article III:4, we must turn, first, to the "general principle" in Article III:1, rather than to the term "like products" in Article III:2.

94. In addition, we observe that, although the obligations in Articles III:2 and III:4 both apply to "like products," the text of Article III:2 differs in one important respect from the text of Article III:4. Article III:2 contains *two separate* sentences, each imposing *distinct* obligations: the first lays down obligations in respect of "like products"' while the second lays down obligations in respect of "directly competitive or substitutable" products. By contrast, Article III:4 applies only to "like products" and does not include a provision equivalent to the second sentence of Article III:2....

95. For us, this textual difference between paragraphs 2 and 4 of Article III has considerable implications for the meaning of "like products" in these two provisions. In *Japan-Alcoholic Beverages*, we concluded, in construing Article III:2, that the two separate obligations in the two sentences of Article III:2 must be interpreted in a harmonious manner that gives meaning to *both* sentences in that provision. We observed there that the interpretation of one of the sentences necessarily affects the interpretation of the other....

96. In construing Article III:4, the same interpretive considerations do not arise, because the "general principle" articulated in Article III:1 is expressed in Article III:4, not through two distinct obligations, as in the two sentences in Article III:2, but instead through a single obligation that applies solely to "like products." Therefore, the harmony that we have attributed to the two sentences of Article III:2 need not and, indeed, cannot be replicated in interpreting Article III:4. Thus, we conclude that, given the textual difference between Articles III:2 and III:4, the "accordion" of "likeness" stretches in a different way in Article III:4.
* * *

98. As we have said, although this "general principle" [in Article III:1] is not explicitly invoked in Article III:4, nevertheless, it "informs that provision." Therefore, the term "like product" in Article III:4 must be interpreted to give proper scope and meaning to this principle. In short, there must be consonance between the objective pursued by Article III, as enunciated in the "general principle" articulated in Article III:1, and the interpretation of the specific expression of this principle in the text of Article III:4. This interpretation, must, therefore, reflect that, in endeavouring to ensure "equality of competitive conditions," the "general principle" in Article III seeks to prevent Members from applying internal taxes and regulations in a manner which affects the competitive relationship, in the marketplace, *between the domestic and imported products involved*, "so as to afford protection to domestic production and consumption."

99. As products that are in a competitive relationship in the marketplace could be affected through treatment of *imports* "less favourable" than the treatment accorded to *domestic* products, it follows that the word "like" in Article III:4 is to be interpreted to apply to products that are in such a competitive relationship. Thus, a determination of "likeness" under Article III:4 is, fundamentally, a determination about the nature and extent of a competitive relationship between and among products. In saying this, we are mindful that there is a spectrum of degrees of "competitiveness" or "substitutability" of products in the marketplace, and that it is difficult, if not impossible, in the abstract, to indicate precisely where on this spectrum the word "like" in Article III:4 of the GATT 1994 falls. We are not saying that *all* products which are in *some* competitive relationship are "like products" under Article III:4. In ruling on the measure at issue, we also do not attempt to define the precise scope of the word "like" in Article III:4. Nor do we wish to decide if the scope of "like products" in Article III:4 is co-exten-

sive with the combined scope of "like" and "directly competitive or substitutable" products in Article III:2. However, we recognize that the relationship between these two provisions is important, because there is no sharp distinction between fiscal regulation, covered by Article III:2, and non-fiscal regulation, covered by Article III:4. Both forms of regulation can often be used to achieve the same ends. It would be incongruous if, due to a significant difference in the product scope of these two provisions, Members were prevented from using one form of regulation—for instance, fiscal—to protect domestic production of certain products, but were able to use another form of regulation—for instance, non-fiscal—to achieve those ends. This would frustrate a consistent application of the "general principle" in Article III:1. For these reasons, we conclude that the scope of "like" in Article III:4 is broader than the scope of "like" in Article III:2, first sentence. Nonetheless, we note, once more, that Article III:2 extends not only to "like products", but also to products which are "directly competitive or substitutable", and that Article III:4 extends only to "like products." In view of this different language, and although we need not rule, and do not rule, on the precise product scope of Article III:4, we do conclude that the product scope of Article III:4, although broader than the *first* sentence of Article III:2, is certainly *not* broader than the *combined* product scope of the *two* sentences of Article III:2 of the GATT 1994.

100. We recognize that, by interpreting the term "like products" in Article III:4 in this way, we give that provision a relatively broad product scope—although no broader than the product scope of Article III:2. In so doing, we observe that there is a second element that must be established before a measure can be held to be inconsistent with Article III:4. Thus, even if two products are "like", that does not mean that a measure is inconsistent with Article III:4. A complaining Member must still establish that the measure accords to the group of "like" *imported* products "less favourable treatment" than it accords to the group of "like" *domestic* products. The term "less favourable treatment" expresses the general principle, in Article III:1, that internal regulations "should not be applied ... so as to afford protection to domestic production." If there is "less favourable treatment" of the group of "like" imported products, there is, conversely, "protection" of the group of "like" domestic products. However, a Member may draw distinctions between products which have been found to be "like", without, for this reason alone, according to the group of "like" *imported* products "less favourable treatment" than that accorded to the group of "like" *domestic* products. In this case, we do not examine further the interpretation of the term "treatment no less favourable" in Article III:4, as the Panel's findings on this issue have not been appealed or, indeed, argued before us.

101. We turn to consideration of how a treaty interpreter should proceed in determining whether products are "like" under Article III:4. As in Article III:2, in this determination, "[n]o one approach ... will be appropriate for all cases." Rather, an assessment utilizing "an unavoidable element of individual, discretionary judgement" has to be made on a case-by-case basis. The Report of the Working Party on *Border Tax Adjustments* outlined an approach for analyzing "likeness" that has been followed and developed since by several panels and the Appellate Body. * * *

102. These general criteria, or groupings of potentially shared characteristics, provide a framework for analyzing the "likeness" of particular products on a case-by-case basis. These criteria are, it is well to bear in mind, simply tools to assist in the task of sorting and examining the relevant evidence. They are nei-

ther a treaty-mandated nor a closed list of criteria that will determine the legal characterization of products. More important, the adoption of a particular framework to aid in the examination of evidence does not dissolve the duty or the need to examine, in each case, *all* of the pertinent evidence. In addition, although each criterion addresses, in principle, a different aspect of the products involved, which should be examined separately, the different criteria are interrelated. For instance, the physical properties of a product shape and limit the end-uses to which the products can be devoted. Consumer perceptions may similarly influence—modify or even render obsolete—traditional uses of the products. Tariff classification clearly reflects the physical properties of a product.

103. The kind of evidence to be examined in assessing the "likeness" of products will, necessarily, depend upon the particular products and the legal provision at issue. When all the relevant evidence has been examined, panels must determine whether that evidence, as a whole, indicates that the products in question are "like" in terms of the legal provision at issue. We have noted that, under Article III:4 of the GATT 1994, the term "like products" is concerned with competitive relationships between and among products. Accordingly, whether the *Border Tax Adjustments* framework is adopted or not, it is important under Article III:4 to take account of evidence which indicates whether, and to what extent, the products involved are—or could be—in a competitive relationship in the marketplace.

[The Appellate Body then reversed the key conclusions of the Panel. It found that the Panel's decision to conclude that asbestos and non-asbestos products were "like product" based on one of the four criteria—end use—was inappropriate. Para. 109. It then turned to the question of the relevance of the health effects of asbestos.]

114. Panels must examine fully the physical properties of products. In particular, panels must examine those physical properties of products that are likely to influence the competitive relationship between products in the marketplace. In the case of chrysotile asbestos fibres, their molecular structure, chemical composition, and fibrillation capacity are important because the microscopic particles and filaments of chrysotile asbestos fibres are carcinogenic in humans, following inhalation. In this respect, we observe that, at paragraph 8.188 of its Report, the Panel made the following statements regarding chrysotile asbestos fibres:

> ... we note that the carcinogenicity of chrysotile fibres has been acknowledged for some time by international bodies. This carcinogenicity was confirmed by the experts consulted by the Panel, with respect to both lung cancers and mesotheliomas, even though the experts appear to acknowledge that chrysotile is less likely to cause mesotheliomas than amphiboles. We also note that the experts confirmed that the types of cancer concerned had a mortality rate of close to 100 per cent. We therefore consider that we have sufficient evidence that there is in fact a serious carcinogenic risk associated with the inhalation of chrysotile fibres. Moreover, in the light of the comments made by one of the experts, the doubts expressed by Canada with respect to the direct effects of chrysotile on mesotheliomas and lung cancers are not sufficient to conclude that an official responsible for public health policy would find that there was not enough evidence of the existence of a public health risk.

This carcinogenicity, or toxicity, constitutes, as we see it, a defining aspect of the physical properties of chrysotile asbestos fibres. The evidence indicates that PCG fibres, in contrast, do not share these properties, at least to the same extent. We do not see how this highly significant physical difference *cannot* be a consideration in examining the physical properties of a product as part of a determination of "likeness" under Article III:4 of the GATT 1994.

115. We do not agree with the Panel that considering evidence relating to the health risks associated with a product, under Article III:4, nullifies the effect of Article XX(b) of the GATT 1994. Article XX(b) allows a Member to "adopt and enforce" a measure, *inter alia*, necessary to protect human life or health, even though that measure is inconsistent with another provision of the GATT 1994. Article III:4 and Article XX(b) are distinct and independent provisions of the GATT 1994 each to be interpreted on its own. The scope and meaning of Article III:4 should not be broadened or restricted beyond what is required by the normal customary international law rules of treaty interpretation, simply because Article XX(b) exists and may be available to justify measures inconsistent with Article III:4. The fact that an interpretation of Article III:4, under those rules, implies a less frequent recourse to Article XX(b) does not deprive the exception in Article XX(b) of *effet utile*. Article XX(b) would only be deprived of *effet utile* if that provision could *not* serve to allow a Member to "adopt and enforce" measures "necessary to protect human ... life or health." Evaluating evidence relating to the health risks arising from the physical properties of a product does not prevent a measure which is inconsistent with Article III:4 from being justified under Article XX(b). We note, in this regard, that, different inquiries occur under these two very different Articles. Under Article III:4, evidence relating to health risks may be relevant in assessing the *competitive relationship in the marketplace* between allegedly "like" products. The same, or similar, evidence serves a different purpose under Article XX(b), namely, that of assessing whether a *Member* has a sufficient basis for "adopting or enforcing" a WTO-inconsistent measure on the grounds of human health.

116. We, therefore, find that the Panel erred, in paragraph 8.132 of the Panel Report, in excluding the health risks associated with chrysotile asbestos fibres from its examination of the physical properties of that product.

117. Before examining the Panel's findings under the second and third criteria, we note that these two criteria involve certain of the key elements relating to the competitive relationship between products: first, the extent to which products are capable of performing the same, or similar, functions (end-uses), and, second, the extent to which consumers are willing to use the products to perform these functions (consumers' tastes and habits). Evidence of this type is of particular importance under Article III of the GATT 1994, precisely because that provision is concerned with competitive relationships in the marketplace. If there is—or could be—*no* competitive relationship between products, a Member cannot intervene, through internal taxation or regulation, to protect domestic production. Thus, evidence about the extent to which products can serve the same end-uses, and the extent to which consumers are—or would be—willing to choose one product instead of another to perform those end-uses, is highly relevant evidence in assessing the "likeness" of those products under Article III:4 of the GATT 1994.

118. We consider this to be especially so in cases where the evidence relating to properties establishes that the products at issue are physically quite different. In such cases, in order to overcome this indication that products are *not* "like", a higher burden is placed on complaining Members to establish that, despite the pro-

nounced physical differences, there is a competitive relationship between the products such that *all* of the evidence, taken together, demonstrates that the products are "like" under Article III:4 of the GATT 1994. In this case, where it is clear that the fibres have very different properties, in particular, because chrysotile is a known carcinogen, a very heavy burden is placed on Canada to show, under the second and third criteria, that the chrysotile asbestos and PCG fibres are in such a competitive relationship.

119. With this in mind, we turn to the Panel's evaluation of the second criterion, end-uses. The Panel's evaluation of this criterion is far from comprehensive. First, as we have said, the Panel entwined its analysis of "end-uses" with its analysis of "physical properties" and, in purporting to examine "end-uses" as a distinct criterion, essentially referred to its analysis of "properties." This makes it difficult to assess precisely how the Panel evaluated the end-uses criterion.... It is only by forming a complete picture of the various end-uses of a product that a panel can assess the significance of the fact that products share a limited number of end-uses.... In these circumstances, we believe that the Panel did not adequately examine the evidence relating to end-uses.

120. The Panel declined to examine or make any findings relating to the third criterion, consumers' tastes and habits, "[b]ecause this criterion would not provide clear results." ... A panel cannot decline to inquire into relevant evidence simply because it suspects that evidence may not be "clear" or, for that matter, because the parties agree that certain evidence is not relevant. In any event, we have difficulty seeing how the Panel could conclude that an examination of consumers' tastes and habits "would not provide clear results", given that the Panel did not examine *any* evidence relating to this criterion.

121. Furthermore, in a case such as this, where the fibres are physically very different, a panel *cannot* conclude that they are "like products" if it *does not examine* evidence relating to consumers' tastes and habits. In such a situation, if there is *no* inquiry into this aspect of the nature and extent of the competitive relationship between the products, there is no basis for overcoming the inference, drawn from the different physical properties of the products, that the products are not "like."

122. In this case especially, we are also persuaded that evidence relating to consumers' tastes and habits would establish that the health risks associated with chrysotile asbestos fibres influence consumers' behaviour with respect to the different fibres at issue. We observe that, as regards *chrysotile asbestos and PCG fibres*, the consumer of the fibres is a *manufacturer* who incorporates the fibres into another product, such as cement-based products or brake linings. We do not wish to speculate on what the evidence regarding these consumers would have indicated; rather, we wish to highlight that consumers' tastes and habits regarding *fibres*, even in the case of commercial parties, such as manufacturers, are very likely to be shaped by the health risks associated with a product which is known to be highly carcinogenic. A manufacturer cannot, for instance, ignore the preferences of the ultimate consumer of its products. If the risks posed by a particular product are sufficiently great, the ultimate consumer may simply cease to buy that product. This would, undoubtedly, affect a manufacturer's decisions in the marketplace. Moreover, in the case of products posing risks to human health, we think it likely that manufacturers' decisions will be influenced by other factors, such as the potential civil liability that might flow from marketing products posing a health risk to the ultimate consumer, or the additional costs asso-

ciated with safety procedures required to use such products in the manufacturing process.

123. Finally, we note that, although we consider consumers' tastes and habits significant in determining "likeness" in this dispute, at the oral hearing, Canada indicated that it considers this criterion to be *irrelevant*, in this dispute, because the existence of the measure has disturbed normal conditions of competition between the products. In our Report in *Korea-Alcoholic Beverages*, we observed that, "[p]articularly in a market where there are regulatory barriers to trade or to competition, there may well be latent demand" for a product. We noted that, in such situations, "it may be highly relevant to examine latent demand" that is suppressed by regulatory barriers. In addition, we said that "evidence from other markets may be pertinent to the examination of the market at issue, particularly when demand on that market has been influenced by regulatory barriers to trade or to competition." We, therefore, do not accept Canada's contention that, in markets where normal conditions of competition have been disturbed by regulatory or fiscal barriers, consumers' tastes and habits cease to be relevant. In such situations, a Member may submit evidence of latent, or suppressed, consumer demand in that market, or it may submit evidence of substitutability from some relevant third market. In making this point, we do not wish to be taken to suggest that there *is* latent demand for chrysotile asbestos fibres. Our point is simply that the existence of the measure does not render consumers' tastes and habits irrelevant, as Canada contends.

124. We observe also that the Panel did not regard as decisive the different tariff classifications of the chrysotile asbestos, PVA, cellulose and glass fibres, each of which is classified under a different tariff heading. In the absence of a full analysis, by the Panel, of the other three criteria addressed, we cannot determine what importance should be attached to the different tariff classifications of the fibres. * * *

140. Finally, we note that chrysotile asbestos fibres and the various PCG fibres all have different tariff classifications. While this element is not, on its own, decisive, it does tend to indicate that chrysotile and PCG fibres are not "like products" under Article III:4 of the GATT 1994. * * *

147. Thus, we find that, in particular, in the absence of any evidence concerning consumers' tastes and habits, Canada has not satisfied its burden of proving that cement-based products containing chrysotile asbestos fibres are "like" cement-based products containing PCG fibres, under Article III:4 of the GATT 1994.

148. As Canada has not demonstrated either that chrysotile asbestos fibres are "like" PCG fibres, or that cement-based products containing chrysotile asbestos fibres are "like" cement-based products containing PCG fibres, we conclude that Canada has not succeeded in establishing that the measure at issue is inconsistent with Article III:4 of the GATT 1994.

149. One Member of the Division hearing this appeal wishes to make a concurring statement. * * *

151. In paragraph 113 of the Report, we state that "[w]e are very much of the view that evidence relating to the health risks associated with a product may be pertinent in an examination of 'likeness' under Article III:4 of the GATT 1994." We also point out, in paragraph 114, that "[p]anels must examine fully the physical properties of products. In particular, ... those physical properties of products that are likely to influence the competitive relationship between products in

the market place. In the cases of chrysotile asbestos fibres, their molecular structure, chemical composition, and fibrillation capacity are important because the microscopic particles and filaments of chrysotile asbestos fibres are carcinogenic in humans, following inhalation." This carcinogenicity we describe as "a defining aspect of the physical properties of chrysotile asbestos fibres", which property is not shared by the PCG fibres, "at least to the same extent." We express our inability to "see how this highly significant physical difference *cannot* be a consideration in examining the physical properties of a product as part of a determination of 'likeness' under Article III:4 of the GATT 1994." (emphasis in the original) We observe also that the Panel, after noting that the carcinogenicity of chrysotile asbestos fibres has been acknowledged by international bodies and confirmed by the experts the Panel consulted, ruled that it "[has] sufficient evidence that *there is in fact a serious carcinogenic risk associated with the inhalation of chrysotile fibres*." (emphasis added) In fact, the scientific evidence of record for this finding of carcinogenicity of chrysotile asbestos fibres is so clear, voluminous, and is confirmed, a number of times, by a variety of international organizations, as to be practically overwhelming.

152. In the present appeal, considering the nature and quantum of the scientific evidence showing that the physical properties and qualities of chrysotile asbestos fibres include or result in carcinogenicity, my submission is that there is ample basis for a definitive characterization, on completion of the legal analysis, of such fibres as *not* "like" PCG fibres. PCG fibres, it may be recalled, have not been shown by Canada to have the same lethal properties as chrysotile asbestos fibres. That definitive characterization, it is further submitted, may and should be made even in the absence of evidence concerning the other two *Border Tax Adjustments* criteria (categories of "potentially shared characteristics") of end-uses and consumers' tastes and habits. It is difficult for me to imagine what evidence relating to economic competitive relationships as reflected in end-uses and consumers' tastes and habits could outweigh and set at naught the undisputed deadly nature of chrysotile asbestos fibres, compared with PCG fibres, when inhaled by humans, and thereby compel a characterization of "likeness" of chrysotile asbestos and PCG fibres.

153. The suggestion I make is not that *any* kind or degree of health risk, associated with a particular product, would *a priori* negate a finding of the "likeness" of that product with another product, under Article III:4 of the GATT 1994. The suggestion is a very narrow one, limited only to the circumstances of this case, and confined to chrysotile asbestos fibres as compared with PCG fibres. To hold that these fibres are not "like" one another in view of the undisputed carcinogenic nature of chrysotile asbestos fibres appears to me to be but a small and modest step forward from mere reversal of the Panel's ruling that chrysotile asbestos and PCG fibres are "like", especially since our holding in completing the analysis is that Canada failed to satisfy a complainant's burden of proving that PCG fibres are "like" chrysotile asbestos fibres under Article III:4. That small step, however, the other Members of the Division feel unable to take because of their conception of the "fundamental", perhaps decisive, role of economic competitive relationships in the determination of the "likeness" of products under Article III:4.

154. My second point is that the necessity or appropriateness of adopting a "fundamentally" economic interpretation of the "likeness" of products under Article III:4 of the GATT 1994 does not appear to me to be free from substantial doubt. Moreover, in future concrete contexts, the line between a "fundamentally" and

"exclusively" economic view of "like products" under Article III:4 may well prove very difficult, as a practical matter, to identify. It seems to me the better part of valour to reserve one's opinion on such an important, indeed, philosophical matter, which may have unforeseeable implications, and to leave that matter for another appeal and another day, or perhaps other appeals and other days. I so reserve my opinion on this matter.

Questions and Discussion

1. Does the *Asbestos* decision have any impact beyond allowing WTO members to differentiate between carcinogenic and toxic substances on the one hand and their noncarcinogenic and nontoxic substitutes on the other? Does it suggest that paper with a high percentage of recycled content can be regulated differently from paper derived from virgin forests? Heirloom tomatoes, conventional tomatoes, and genetically modified tomatoes? What lessons from *Asbestos* apply to environment-related cases not involving health risks?

2. The *Asbestos* Panel had concluded that asbestos was "like" PCG and other non-asbestos fibers because the different fiber products have the same or similar end uses and thus compete with each other in the marketplace. The Appellate Body finds fault with the Panel's failure to seriously consider the other Working Party factors. From this report, can we tell where the Appellate Body would draw the line between "like products" in other cases?

3. The "concurring statement" by one member of the Appellate Body (paras. 149–154) is highly unusual in WTO practice. In what way does his analysis differ from that of his colleagues? Why did he think that difference was important enough to merit an expression of his own view? Given that this "concurring statement" is the view of just one member of the Appellate Body, how much weight should it be given in terms of how broadly or narrowly to read the *Asbestos* analysis of "like product" in subsequent health-related cases under Article III:4?

IV. Processes and Production Methods (PPMs)

The *EC-Asbestos* report shows that the dispute settlement organs of the WTO are not totally deaf to environmental and health concerns; they are prepared to grant member governments considerable freedom to keep out imported products in order to protect public health or the environment. But that regulatory freedom still has discernible limits. In particular, the product-process distinction identified in the *Tuna/Dolphin* disputes still prevails. The key result of *EC-Asbestos*—that a country may restrict trade in a product when that product itself is reasonably understood to threaten national health or welfare— is part of the traditional argument of trade experts to minimize conflict between trade law and environmental regulation. But whether countries should be able to tax or regulate imported products differently from similar domestic products based on processes and production methods (PPMs) is another question altogether and remains a lively issue in the trade and environment policy debate:

> Clarifying the PPM issue is one of the most important and difficult challenges in the trade and environment debate. Environmentalists argue that the existing

rules fail to provide policy-makers with sufficient clarity about the kinds of measures governments may take to address environmental impacts. Preventing or limiting countries from distinguishing between goods according to the environmental impact of their production gives foreign countries a competitive edge and places downward pressure on domestic environmental standards. It also forces importing countries to import and consume unsustainably produced goods. Trade theorists respond that differing countries may set their own environmental standards and that different preferences for environmental quality are a valid source of "comparative advantage."

DAVID HUNTER, JAMES SALZMAN, & DURWOOD ZAELKE, INTERNATIONAL ENVIRONMENTAL LAW AND POLICY 1274 (3d ed. 2007).

An abiding concern of trade advocates is that domestic industries have had repeated success in lobbying for economic protection to avoid foreign competition. They consider the national treatment obligation a bulwark against such protectionist erosion of open markets and fair competition. Given the routine use of PPM-based standards in national environmental programs, trade advocates fear that a special exemption for PPM-based environmental measures, however narrowly drawn, would undermine this basic control against discriminatory measures. Some are already concerned that a more relaxed interpretation of GATT Article XX has opened the door too wide to protectionist measures in the guise of environmental protection.

Environmental advocates do not dispute that PPM-based measures are a core environmental protection tool that will be widely used. More often than not, it is not the goods themselves but how they are made that creates serious environmental problems, from climate change and deforestation to pollution of oceans and the poisoning of the air we breathe. The opportunity to produce goods for export to other countries should not, in their view, become an incentive for continued use of environmentally-damaging production systems. Likewise, democratic governments of importing countries should have the right to establish some basic PPM standards for imported products to reflect important and widely-held environmental protection preferences within the country.

The *Tuna/Dolphin I* and *II* decisions launched the trade and environment debate with a narrow reading of the permissible scope of product regulation under Article III that drew a sharp distinction between product and nonproduct characteristics such as PPMs. *Auto Taxes* and *Reformulated Gasoline* also relied on the core product-process—or, more precisely in those cases, the product-producer distinction—to disqualify features of product-regulating programs that focus on certain nonproduct considerations. As you read the cases, ask whether the country imposing the environmental measure had a discriminatory intent. Further, ask whether the panels construed Article III faithfully. Are these interpretations consistent with the text of Article III and Ad Note Article III? Did they look at the impact on production? Should countries be able to distinguish products based on the way they are produced? Can Article III be interpreted in a manner that permits PPM trade measures without arousing the fears of free trade advocates?

A. The *Tuna/Dolphin* Disputes

1. Tuna/Dolphin I

In some areas of the world, particularly in the eastern tropical Pacific Ocean (ETP), an area about as large as North America, a particular association between dolphins and tuna

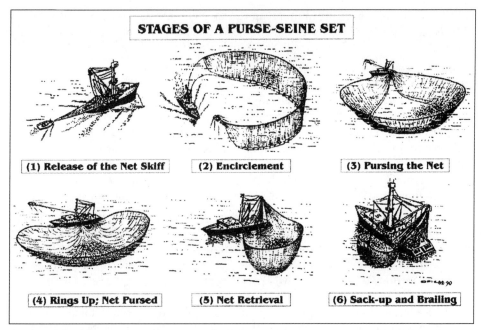

Figure 1. Les différentes phases d'une opération de pêche à la senne. Dessins d'Opic 82–90, inspirés de JAMET (J.) et coll., in STEQUERT B. et MARSAC F., Pêche thonnière à la senne, COI, ORSTOM Éditions, collection Didactiques, Paris, 1991. JAMET (J.) et coll., 1981—Manuel des pêches maritimes tropicales. SCET-International, Ministère de la Coopération et du Développement.

has long been observed, such that fishers locate schools of underwater tuna by finding and chasing dolphins on the ocean surface and intentionally encircling them with nets to catch the tuna below. In this tuna fishery, fishers use "purse-seine" nets. A fishing vessel locates dolphins and a school of fish and sends out a motorboat (a "seine skiff") to hold one end of the purse-seine net. The vessel speeds around the perimeter of the school of fish, unfurling the net and encircling the fish and dolphins, and the seine skiff then attaches its end of the net to the fishing vessel. The fishing vessel then purses the net by winching in a cable at the bottom edge of the net and draws in the top cables of the net to gather its entire contents. *See* Figure 1.

Because more than 400,000 dolphins were drowning (dolphins are air-breathing mammals) in tuna nets each year in the early 1970s, the United States took action to stop this mortality. The U.S. Marine Mammal Protection Act (MMPA) prohibits the "taking" (harassment, hunting, capture, killing, or attempt thereof) and importation into the United States of marine mammals, unless an exception is applied. 16 U.S.C. §§ 1631, 1371. In addition, it seeks to reduce the incidental kill or serious injury of marine mammals in the course of commercial fishing to insignificant levels approaching zero. With regard to the ETP tuna fishery, Section 101(a)(2) of the MMPA authorizes limited incidental taking of marine mammals by U.S. fishers in the course of commercial fishing pursuant to a permit issued by the National Marine Fisheries Service (NMFS) in conformity with and governed by certain statutory criteria in Sections 103 and 104 and implementing regulations. At the time of the GATT dispute in the late 1980s, only one such permit had been issued, to the American Tunaboat Association, covering all domestic tuna fishing operations in the ETP. Under the general permit issued to this Association, no more than 20,500 dolphins could be incidentally killed or injured each year by the U.S. fleet fishing in the ETP.

Within this dolphin mortality limit, no more than 250 could be coastal spotted dolphins (*Stenella attenuata*) and no more than 2,750 could be Eastern spinner dolphins (*Stenella longirostris*).

Also at the time of the dispute, Section 101(a)(2) of the MMPA banned the importation of commercial fish or fish products caught with commercial fishing technology that results in the incidental kill or serious injury of ocean mammals in excess of U.S. standards. It specifically prohibited the importation of yellowfin tuna harvested with purse-seine nets in the ETP unless the Secretary of Commerce certified that: 1) the government of the harvesting country has a program regulating the taking of marine mammals that is comparable to that of the United States, and 2) the average rate of incidental taking of marine mammals by vessels of the harvesting nation is comparable to, but must not exceed 1.25 times, the actual taking by U.S. vessels during the same period.

On August 28, 1990, pursuant to a court order, the United States imposed an embargo on imports of commercial yellowfin tuna and yellowfin tuna products harvested with purse-seine nets in the ETP from Mexico, Venezuela, Vanuatu, Panama, and Ecuador. The embargo would remain in place until the Secretary of Commerce made positive findings under Section 101(a)(2) of the MMPA. On September 7, 1990, the Secretary of Commerce lifted the embargo for Mexico, Venezuela, and Vanuatu, pursuant to positive Commerce Department findings; also, Panama and Ecuador later prohibited their fleets from setting purse seines on dolphin and were exempted from the embargo. However, on October 10, 1990, the United States, pursuant to another court order, reimposed an embargo on imports of such tuna from Mexico, an embargo later extended to Venezuela and Vanuatu. Mexico challenged the embargo as inconsistent with Article XI of the GATT, whereas the United States argued that the measure was consistent with Article III, because it treated all tuna the same and was enforced at the border.

United States-Restrictions on Imports of Tuna

GATT Panel Report, DS21/R (Sept. 3, 1991) (unadopted),
reprinted in 30 I.L.M. 1594 (1991) [hereinafter *Tuna/Dolphin I*]

5.8. The Panel noted that Mexico had argued that the measures prohibiting imports of certain yellowfin tuna and yellowfin tuna products from Mexico imposed by the United States were quantitative restrictions on importation under Article XI, while the United States had argued that these measures were internal regulations enforced at the time or point of importation under Article III:4 and the Note Ad Article III, namely that the prohibition of imports of tuna and tuna products from Mexico constituted an enforcement of the regulations of the MMPA relating to the harvesting of domestic tuna.

5.9. The Panel examined the distinction between quantitative restrictions on importation and internal measures applied at the time or point of importation, and noted the following. While restrictions on importation are prohibited by Article XI:1, contracting parties are permitted by Article III:4 and the Note Ad Article III to impose an internal regulation on products imported from other contracting parties provided that it: does not discriminate between products of other countries in violation of the most-favoured-nation principle of Article I:1; is not applied so as to afford protection to domestic production, in violation of the national treatment principle of Article III:1; and accords to imported products treatment no less favourable than that accorded to like products of national origin, consistent with Article III:4....

5.10. The Panel noted that the United States had claimed that the direct import embargo on certain yellowfin tuna and certain yellowfin tuna products of Mexico constituted an enforcement at the time or point of importation of the requirements of the MMPA that yellowfin tuna in the ETP be harvested with fishing techniques designed to reduce the incidental taking of dolphins. The MMPA did not regulate tuna products as such, and in particular did not regulate the sale of tuna or tuna products. Nor did it prescribe fishing techniques that could have an effect on tuna as a product. This raised in the Panel's view the question of whether the tuna harvesting regulations could be regarded as a measure that "applies to" imported and domestic tuna within the meaning of the Note Ad Article III and consequently as a measure which the United States could enforce consistently with that Note in the case of imported tuna at the time or point of importation. The Panel examined this question in detail and found the following.

5.11. The text of Article III:1 refers to the application to imported or domestic *products* of "laws, regulations and requirements affecting the internal sale … of *products"* and "internal quantitative regulations requiring the mixture, processing or use of *products"*; it sets forth the principle that such regulations on *products* not be applied so as to afford protection to domestic production. Article III:4 refers solely to laws, regulations and requirements affecting the internal sale, etc. of *products*. This suggests that Article III covers only measures affecting products as such. Furthermore, the text of the Note Ad Article III refers to a measure "which applies to an imported *product* and the like domestic *product* and is collected or enforced in the case of the imported *product* at the time or point of importation." This suggests that this Note covers only measures applied to imported products that are of the same nature as those applied to the domestic products, such as a prohibition on importation of a product which enforces at the border an internal sales prohibition applied to both imported and like domestic products.

5.12. [The *Superfund*] panel had found that Article III:2, first sentence, "obliges contracting parties to establish certain competitive conditions for imported *products* in relation to domestic *products.*" [The *Section 337*] panel had found that the words "treatment no less favourable" in Article III:4 call for effective equality of opportunities for imported *products* in respect of the application of laws, regulations or requirements affecting the sale, offering for sale, purchase, transportation, distribution or use of *products*, and that this standard has to be understood as applicable to each individual case of imported *products*. It was apparent to the Panel that the comparison implied was necessarily one between the measures applied to imported products and the measures applied to like domestic products.

5.13. The Panel considered that, as Article III applied the national treatment principle to both regulations and internal taxes, the provisions of Article III:4 applicable to regulations should be interpreted taking into account interpretations by the CONTRACTING PARTIES of the provisions of Article III:2 applicable to taxes. The Panel noted in this context that the Working Party Report on Border Tax Adjustments, adopted by the CONTRACTING PARTIES in 1970, had concluded that

> "… there was convergence of views to the effect that *taxes directly levied on products were eligible for tax adjustment.*… Furthermore, the Working Party concluded that there was convergence of views to the effect that cer-

tain taxes that were not directly levied on products were not eligible for adjustment, [such as] social security charges whether on employers or employees and payroll taxes." [B.I.S.D. 18S/97, 100–101, para. 14.].

Thus, under the national treatment principle of Article III, contracting parties may apply border tax adjustments with regard to those taxes that are borne by products, but not for domestic taxes not directly levied on products (such as corporate income taxes). Consequently, the Note Ad Article III covers only internal taxes that are borne by products. The Panel considered that it would be inconsistent to limit the application of this Note to taxes that are borne by products while permitting its application to regulations not applied to the product as such.

5.14. The Panel concluded from the above considerations that the Note Ad Article III covers only those measures that are applied to the product as such. The Panel noted that the MMPA regulates the domestic harvesting of yellowfin tuna to reduce the incidental taking of dolphin, but that these regulations could not be regarded as being applied to tuna products as such because they would not directly regulate the sale of tuna and could not possibly affect tuna as a product. Therefore, the Panel found that the import prohibition on certain yellowfin tuna and certain yellowfin tuna products of Mexico and the provisions of the MMPA under which it is imposed did not constitute internal regulations covered by the Note Ad Article III.

5.15. The Panel further concluded that, even if the provisions of the MMPA enforcing the tuna harvesting regulations (in particular those providing for the seizure of cargo as a penalty for violation of the Act) were regarded as regulating the sale of tuna as a product, the United States import prohibition would not meet the requirements of Article III. As pointed out in paragraph 5.12 above, Article III:4 calls for a comparison of the treatment of imported tuna *as a product* with that of domestic tuna *as a product*. Regulations governing the taking of dolphins incidental to the taking of tuna could not possibly affect tuna as a product. Article III:4 therefore obliges the United States to accord treatment to Mexican tuna no less favourable than that accorded to United States tuna, whether or not the incidental taking of dolphins by Mexican vessels corresponds to that of United States vessels. * * *

Discussion: Border Measures and Internal Measures Revisited

The conclusion of the *Tuna/Dolphin I* Panel is clear: WTO members may not distinguish products for tax and regulatory purposes based on the way the products are produced. A regulation that distinguishes products based on the way the products are produced does not affect the physical characteristics of the product; these products remain "like" products. Thus, a WTO member cannot regulate like products differently based on the way they are produced.

In this case, the United States essentially argued that its tuna embargo could be reviewed under Article III because it established essentially the same conditions for Mexican fishers as for U.S. fishers. Tuna caught using certain procedures, regardless of national origin, could be imported into the United States; tuna caught using other procedures could not be imported into the United States. The Panel does not describe it this way though. Instead, it concludes that certain *classes of measures* can never be reviewed under Article III.

In reaching that conclusion, the Panel refers to the interpretative note, Note Ad Article III. Note Ad Article III is triggered because the United States claimed that the tuna embargo was enforced at the time or point of importation. Do you see why that triggers a discussion of Note Ad Article III? As a result of the U.S. argument, the Panel states that it must determine whether the MMPA provisions relating to the manner in which tuna is harvested "could be regarded as a measure that 'applies to' imported and domestic tuna within the meaning of the Note Ad Article III." Contrast this view with the minority in the *Lobsters* case (Chapter 3.III.A (pages 151–54)):

> This note holds that the fact that a measure is enforced at the border is not dispositive of whether it is a border or an internal measure. This does not mean that a measure falls within Article III as soon as it is applied to both imported and domestic products, no matter if it is enforced at the border or internally. The interpretative note does not define what is an internal measure covered by Article III; it only says that an internal measure does not stop being one simply by being enforced at the border.

Id. at 8.2.14. Which analysis is more persuasive?

In fact, the interpretive note simply clarifies that the common administrative practice of collecting internal charges or enforcing other internal regulations at the point of importation will not transform a measure into a prohibited quantitative restriction. *See* the negotiating history found in U.N. Doc. EPCT/A/PV.43, at 26–28 (1947). The GATT parties felt it necessary to make this clarification because of the common reference to Article III measures as "internal measures" enforced once the product has entered the stream of commerce and Article XI quantitative restrictions as "border measures" enforced at the point of importation. Because Article XI includes an outright ban on quantitative restrictions, the GATT parties wanted to ensure that taxes and other regulations that truly were internal measures and subject to GATT's nondiscrimination obligation would not become subject to Article XI's prohibition simply because they are collected and enforced at the border.

In the final analysis, the *Tuna/Dolphin* Panel focuses on whether the measure is applied to the product at all, as opposed to whether the measure is on the importation of a product or affects the internal sale of an imported product. This approach raises further questions when the Panel compares taxes eligible for border tax adjustments with regulations in paragraph 5.13. The border tax adjustment rule allows a WTO member to rebate certain taxes imposed on an exported product and to impose certain taxes on imported products, provided that a like domestic product is assessed the same tax. The Working Party Report cited by the Panel explains which taxes are eligible for border tax adjustments. It concludes that taxes applied directly to a product, such as sales taxes, are eligible for border tax adjustments. Taxes applied indirectly to products, such as corporate income taxes, are not eligible. The *Tuna/Dolphin* Panel concludes from this report that "Note Ad Article III covers only internal taxes that are borne by products" and that only such taxes fall within the scope of Article III. By analogy, the *Tuna/Dolphin* Panel then argues that "it would be inconsistent to limit application of this Note to taxes that are borne by products while permitting application to regulations not applied to the product as such." In other words, an entire class of measures, those that do not apply to a product "as such" or affect the product "as a product," do not fall within the scope of Article III. Do you find the analogy between tax adjustments and regulations persuasive? Does the tax policy distinction between "indirect taxes" on products and "direct" taxes on producers have a parallel in the realm of environmental regulation? Do nations "adjust" their regulations? Does a tax imposed directly on a product affect the product as a product?

In any event, the Working Party on Border Tax Adjustments and the GATT parties made a political decision to categorize taxes for border tax adjustment purposes as they did. The parties recognized that a world of taxes exists, such as sales taxes, income taxes, and value added taxes, and that parties would try to impose all kinds of taxes on imported products and rebate taxes on products exported. As discussed further beginning at page 232, the parties distinguished taxes eligible for border tax adjustments based on an assumption that some taxes, such as valued added and sales taxes, could be easily carried forward into the price of the product, whereas income and other taxes could not. So as to allow the rebate and imposition of those taxes that would level the playing field for taxes borne by a product in international trade, the parties agreed that only taxes imposed directly on products were eligible for border tax adjustments. With this background, how do you think the Working Party Report should factor into determining the scope of Article III?

---

2. *Tuna/Dolphin II*

The *Tuna/Dolphin I* Panel also found that U.S. restrictions on tuna products from intermediary countries—those countries buying tuna from countries against whom the United States had imposed primary tuna embargoes—violated Article XI of the GATT for the same reasons as the primary embargo. Prior to the creation of the WTO, GATT panel decisions were not binding unless all the GATT Contracting Parties adopted the findings of the panel. Neither Mexico nor the United States requested that the Contracting Parties adopt the decision in *Tuna/Dolphin I*. As a result, the EU and the Netherlands requested a GATT panel to review the intermediary embargo provisions of the MMPA. In this case, *Tuna/Dolphin II*, the Panel declared more specifically that certain classes of measures—regulations relating to the way a product is produced—do not relate to the product as a product and do not fall within the scope of Article III:

> 5.8 … The Panel noted that Article III calls for a comparison between the treatment accorded to domestic and imported like *products*, not for a comparison of the policies or practices of the country of origin with those of the country of importation. The Panel found therefore that the Note Ad Article III could only permit the enforcement, at the time or point of importation, of those laws, regulations and requirements that affected or were applied to the imported and domestic products considered *as products*. The Note therefore could not apply to the enforcement at the time or point of importation of laws, regulations or requirements that related to policies or practices that could not affect the product as such, and that accorded less favourable treatment to like products not produced in conformity with the domestic policies of the importing country.
>
> 5.9 The Panel then examined in this light the measures taken by the United States. It noted that the import embargoes distinguished between tuna products according to harvesting practices and tuna import policies of the exporting countries; that the measures imposed by the United States in respect of domestic tuna similarly distinguished between tuna and tuna products according to tuna harvesting methods; and that none of these practices, policies and methods could

have any impact on the inherent character of tuna as a product. The Panel therefore concluded that the Note ad Article III was not applicable.

United States-Restrictions on Imports of Tuna, GATT Panel Report, DS29/R (June 16, 1994) (unadopted), *reprinted in* 33 I.L.M. 839 (1994) (italics in original).

This rejection of the legitimacy of trade restrictions based on PPMs led trade advocates and developing countries to champion the *Tuna/Dolphin* reports as vindications of national autonomy over environmental policy. As they see it, it is a matter for the exporting country—the home of the producer of the goods—to determine the PPM measures that are appropriate to its circumstances, rather than being pressured to meet some mandatory environmental "standard" of a distant consuming country. In contrast, environmentalists deplored the *Tuna/Dolphin* rulings because they refused to recognize another kind of national environmental policy autonomy: the right to choose which products may be sold in the nation based on *bona fide* environmental considerations.

Questions and Discussion

1. Article III:4 of the GATT requires no less favorable treatment with respect to laws and regulations "affecting [a product's] internal sale, offering for sale, purchase, transportation, distribution or use." Does the use of the word "product" throughout Article III and the GATT more generally tell us anything about the *classes of measures* that fall within Article III? Or does the overall language of Articles III and XI suggest that the principal distinction between Article III measures and Article XI measures is their *effect*? For example, does an outright ban on the importation of a product, whether based on product characteristics or not, affect the internal sale of a product? If not, then the analysis should be over; Article III does not apply and the measure constitutes an Article XI restriction. To elaborate on this point, assume that the United States enforces the measure after the tuna clears customs. Is it really plausible that the measure is permissible as an Article III measure because enforcement after importation affects the internal sale of the tuna? Is the better analysis that the *Tuna/Dolphin* regulations alter behavior even before a vessel catches the tuna and well before the tuna enters U.S. territory, because it directs fishers to use particular gear as a condition of access to the U.S. market? Suppose, though, that both the domestic manufacture and marketing of a product is prohibited, as well as its importation. Does this change your analysis at all? Aren't domestic and foreign products treated exactly the same? Shouldn't that invoke Article III?

2. The *Tuna/Dolphin I* Panel concluded by stating:

> [The GATT] impose[s] few constraints on a contracting party's implementation of domestic environmental policies.... [A] contracting party is free to tax or regulate imported products and like domestic products as long as its taxes or regulations do not discriminate against imported products or afford protection to domestic producers, and a contracting party is also free to tax or regulate domestic production for environmental purposes. As a corollary to these rights, a contracting party may not restrict imports of a product merely because it originates in a country with environmental policies different from its own.

Tuna/Dolphin I, para. 6.2. Do you agree that the disallowance of import restrictions based on different "environmental policies" is a "corollary" of the inherent right of governments to tax and regulate internally for environmental protection purposes?

3. Why did the Panel not assess the U.S. tuna embargo and the MMPA provisions on which it is based under the traditional four-part test for "like products": physical characteristics, end use of the product, consumer preferences, and tariff classification? The panel could have simply said that tuna, regardless of the method of capture, have the same physical characteristics and end uses, and thus all tuna are "like products." That approach would not have saved the U.S. embargo, which afforded less favorable treatment to Mexican tuna, but would have been more consistent with rulings before (and since) on the scope of Article III.

4. The MMPA regulations still allowed substantial dolphin mortality by U.S. tuna boats but banned all Mexican yellowfin tuna unless the entire Mexican fleet had mortality figures comparable to the U.S. fleet. This comparison was done *ex post facto*, at the end of the annual fishing season. The *Tuna/Dolphin I* Panel found that this element of the tuna/dolphin regulations "could give rise to legitimate concern." *Tuna/Dolphin I*, para. 5.16. What problem does that approach present for the Mexican tuna fleet wishing to sell its catch on the U.S. market? Regardless, the Panel states that "a finding on this point was not required" under its view of Article III. Do you see why?

5. The cases are sometimes portrayed as an effort by the United States to insist on "dolphin safe" tuna and keep "dolphin unsafe" tuna off the market. But in another section of its report, the Panel upheld the U.S. labeling system and the criteria for the "dolphin safe" label. The embargo at issue was not based on the safe/unsafe distinction. U.S. fishermen were allowed to continue to use fishing practices that would not meet the requirements for the dolphin safe label as long as total fleet mortality stayed below regulated limits (and even then, their tuna would not have become contraband), but individual Mexican fishermen were not given an opportunity to use "dolphin safe" practices and market their tuna in the United States. The question of ecolabeling is covered in Chapter 6.

6. Much has been made that this decision illustrates the anti-environment perspective of the GATT and WTO. However, one unpublished study shows that bycatch of marine species by weight actually increases through the use of dolphin-friendly techniques. While the catch of dolphins is significantly reduced, the catch of birds, turtles, and other marine fish increases. That is, the effort to reduce dolphin mortality may have little to do with protection of the marine environment and more to do with the emotional appeal of saving Flipper. If true, the U.S. requirements to protect dolphins could be viewed as a classic case of one country imposing its ethical preferences on others. Does this change your view of the *Tuna/Dolphin* decisions?

7. Subsequently, in a case reminiscent of the *Tuna/Dolphin* dispute, the United States imposed embargos on shrimp imports from countries who failed to follow the U.S. approach to reducing the incidental mortality of endangered sea turtles. The U.S. law and its implementing guidelines were designed to get all shrimp trawlers to place turtle excluder devices (TEDs) on their nets, because TEDs greatly diminish incidental mortality of sea turtles in shrimping operations. In the WTO dispute, the United States conceded the points at issue in *Tuna/Dolphin*—that the measure did not meet the criteria of Article III and that it violated Article XI's prohibition against the use of quantitative restrictions. It only argued that the measure was justified under Article XX. United States-Import Prohibition of Certain Shrimp and Shrimp Products, Panel Report, WT/DS58/R (adopted Nov. 6, 1998), *reprinted in* 37 I.L.M. 834 (1998). This case is covered in detail in Chapter 5, Sections IV.B and V.B.

B. Corporate Average Fuel Economy

Two subsequent trade disputes involving U.S. measures under resource conservation or environmental protection programs follow much the same line of reasoning as the *Tuna/Dolphin* reports. In each of these later cases, the issue was not environmental PPMs, but analogous considerations about the ownership and operation of production facilities — in other words, characteristics unrelated to the product as a product. Nevertheless, the reports rely on and reinforce the distinctions drawn in the *Tuna/Dolphin* reports.

In Section III above, we considered the "like products" analysis of the *Auto Taxes* panel report. That report also addressed a third component of the U.S. fuel conservation policy. One part of the Energy Policy and Conservation Act of 1975 (EPCA), 15 U.S.C. §§ 2001 *et seq.*, established "Corporate Average Fuel Economy" (or CAFE) benchmarks for automobile manufacturers. The CAFE program requires an average fuel economy for each manufacturer's and importer's entire fleet of passenger vehicles sold in the United States. If the manufacturer falls short of the requirement, it must pay a civil penalty of US$5 multiplied by the number of vehicles produced by the manufacturer during the model year, multiplied by the number of tenths of a mile per gallon by which the manufacturer's fleet is below the requirement. For example, if the CAFE requirement is 27.5 mpg, and if a manufacturer's CAFE is 26.5 mpg, with 3.5 million passenger vehicles produced for domestic sale, then the penalty to the manufacturer will be 5×3.5 million $\times$ 10 = US$175 million.

The vehicles of all manufacturers within a control relationship are grouped together for CAFE purposes. The term "automobiles manufactured by a manufacturer" includes all automobiles manufactured by persons who control, are controlled by, or are under common control with, such manufacturer, excluding all exported automobiles. When an importer imports vehicles from more than one foreign producer, the importer is the "manufacturer" of all the vehicles that it imports. If a foreign producer were to import vehicles into the United States through two or more importers, the treatment of those vehicles under CAFE would depend on whether the importers are under common control. If, however, the importers were not under common control, their fleets would be treated separately under CAFE. For companies that are both importers and domestic manufacturers, average fuel economy is calculated separately for imported passenger automobiles and for those manufactured domestically. The CAFE fuel economy test methodology, the average fuel economy requirements, and the penalties for noncompliance applied to a "domestic" fleet are identical to those applied to an "imported" fleet.

United States-Taxes on Automobiles
GATT Panel Report, DS31/R (Oct. 11, 1994) (unadopted),
reprinted in 33 I.L.M. 1397 (1994)

C. Corporate Average Fuel Economy (CAFE) Regulation * * *

[The Panel determined that the separate foreign fleet accounting provisions of CAFE put foreign producers at a competitive disadvantage in certain respects, in violation of Article III.]

(b) Fleet averaging

5.52 * * * The Panel noted that the domestic taxes mentioned in the Working Party report that could be applied also to foreign products (i.e., border adjusted) were based on factors directly related to the product, for example its sale within the importing country. Those that could not be so applied were not directly related to the product, but to other factors such as the income of the producer.

5.53 The Panel considered that this limitation on the range of domestic policy measures that may be applied also to imported products reflected one of the central purposes of Article III: to ensure the security of tariff bindings. Contracting parties could not be expected to negotiate tariff commitments if these could be frustrated through the application of measures affecting imported products subject to tariff commitments and triggered by factors unrelated to the products as such. If it were permissible to justify under Article III less favourable treatment to an imported product on the basis of factors not related to the product as such, Article III would not serve its intended purpose. Equally important, the right to unconditional most-favoured nation treatment in the application of Article III:4, which is specifically mentioned in Article I:1, would not be assured.

5.54 These considerations confirmed in the view of the Panel that Article III:4 does not permit treatment of an imported product less favourable than that accorded to a like domestic product, based on factors not directly relating to the product as such. The Panel found therefore that, to the extent that treatment under the CAFE measure was based on factors relating to the control or ownership of producers/importers, it could not in accordance with Article III:4 be applied in a manner that also accorded less favourable treatment to products of foreign origin. It was therefore not necessary to examine whether treatment based on these factors was also applied so as to afford protection to domestic production.

5.55 The Panel concluded that the fleet averaging requirement based on the ownership or control relationship of the car manufacturer did not relate to cars as products. This requirement could thus result in treatment less favourable than that accorded to like domestic products. Therefore it could not be imposed consistently with Article III:4 so as to affect also cars of foreign origin.

––––––––––

Questions and Discussion

1. Based on the *Auto Taxes* reasoning, reconsider the issue of PPMs and the U.S. restrictions on tuna. Does the CAFE penalties section close the door on tax and regulatory distinctions based on the way products are produced? Or does the whole report, by emphasizing the "aim and effect" of a measure, provide a way to balance trade and environmental concerns in determining whether a PPM measure violates GATT rules? In paragraph 5.52, the Panel states that the measures referred to in Article III:4, "affecting the internal sale, offering for sale, purchase, transportation, distribution or use of products," include all measures that "relate to the product as a product, from its introduction into the market to its final consumption." How does this language affect your answer?

––––––––––

C. *Reformulated Gasoline*

Venezuela and Brazil brought the first case to the new WTO Dispute Settlement Body—a trade and environment dispute against the United States involving intricate rules for determining acceptable levels of pollutants in gasoline under the Clean Air Act. All realized that the stakes were much higher now, because a ruling would become binding unless the WTO members unanimously agreed not to adopt the decision.

In the Clean Air Act Amendments of 1990, Congress set numerical standards for the concentration of certain constituents in gasoline that were intended to reduce air pollution caused by motor vehicle emissions. The statute also required that only gasoline of a specified cleanliness ("reformulated gasoline") be sold in areas of high air pollution as of January 1, 1995. In other areas, only gasoline no dirtier than that sold in the base year of 1990 ("conventional gasoline") could be sold.

For an interim period of years, the statute required the gasoline of refiners, blenders, and importers to meet, on an annual average basis, defined levels for certain chemicals/pollutants. The resulting improvement in gasoline quality was to be measured against the "baseline" of the quality of all the gasoline sold in the United States in 1990. This baseline is known as the "statutory baseline." In devising the specific regulations to implement the gasoline provisions of the 1990 amendments, the U.S. Environmental Protection Agency (EPA), in agreement with the major U.S. refiners, determined that it would be fairer if the reformulated gasoline quality for each refiner were measured with respect to the "individual" baseline gasoline quality provided by that refiner in 1990. This is because the constituents of refined gasoline depend on the chemical composition of the particular petroleum being refined and on the configuration of the refinery. Under the individual baseline approach, every refiner would need to make the same proportionate improvements in gasoline quality, and the nationwide result would be the same as under the statutory baseline approach. EPA rule required all U.S. refiners to provide the necessary data to establish their 1990 baselines.

EPA considered how to regulate foreign refiners of gasoline in light of three problems of legal jurisdiction with respect to individual baselines. First, EPA had no legal authority to require a foreign refiner to submit refinery operations and gasoline quality data. Second, even if the foreign refiner submitted the data, EPA had no authority to inspect the refinery and to review refinery records to audit the accuracy of the submitted information. Finally, if a foreign refiner were determined to have submitted false data, EPA would have no jurisdiction to assess penalties or take enforcement action. EPA also did not want to allow a foreign refiner the option of using an individual baseline or the statutory baseline, because refiners could "game" such an optional system based on their individual circumstances. Thus, EPA concluded that the only reasonable approach was to make all foreign refiners subject to the statutory baseline.

Importers were also allowed to use an individual baseline but only in the case (unlikely, according to the parties to the dispute) that they were able to establish it using actual 1990 data. Unlike domestic refiners, importers were not allowed to establish an individual baseline by using alternative methods based on alternative data. If an importer could not produce the 1990 gasoline quality data for its imports, then it had to use the statutory baseline. A small number of domestic entities (such as refiners with only partial or no 1990 operations and blenders with insufficient 1990 data) were also assigned the statutory baseline. Exceptionally, importers that imported in 1990 at least 75 percent of the production of an affiliated foreign refinery were treated as domestic refiners for the purpose of establishing baselines; this provision accommodated key Canadian refineries.

Venezuela is a major exporter of refined gasoline to the East Coast of the United States through the operations of its subsidiary, Citgo. Its U.S. market region has a high concentration of urban areas where reformulated gasoline is required. Venezuelan crude petroleum has high concentrations of two of the constituents regulated under the reformulated gasoline rule. Because the statutory baseline reflects average gasoline quality, Venezuela would have been required to make disproportionately larger improvements in its refined gasoline quality to bring it below the statutory baseline. If it had the option of establishing its individual baseline, then it would only need to make the same proportionate improvements as other refiners.

Venezuela, along with Brazil, challenged the baseline calculation methodology on the claim that it provided less favorable treatment to foreign gasoline in violation of Article III. The WTO Panel made detailed findings on this point. The United States appealed the Panel's rulings on other issues to the Appellate Body (see Chapter 5.IV.B.1), but it did not contest the following Article III analysis.

United States-Standards for Reformulated and Conventional Gasoline

Panel Report, WT/DS2/R (adopted May 20, 1996),
reprinted in 35 I.L.M. 276 (1996)

6.6 The Panel noted the arguments of Venezuela and Brazil that imported gasoline was "like" domestic gasoline, but received treatment less favourable because imported gasoline was subjected to more demanding quality requirements than gasoline of US origin. The United States replied that gasoline from similarly-situated parties was treated in the same manner under the Gasoline Rule. Gasoline from importers was treated no less favourably than that from other domestic non-refiners such as blenders, or refiners who had only limited or no operations in 1990. * * *

6.9 ... The Panel ... noted that chemically-identical imported and domestic gasoline by definition have exactly the same physical characteristics, end-uses, tariff classification, and are perfectly substitutable. The Panel found therefore that chemically-identical imported and domestic gasoline are like products under Article III:4.6.11. The Panel then examined the US argument that the requirements of Article III:4 are met because imported gasoline is treated similarly to gasoline from similarly situated domestic parties—domestic refiners with limited 1990 operations and blenders. According to the United States, the difference in treatment between imported and domestic gasoline was justified because importers, like domestic refiners with limited 1990 operations and blenders, could not reliably establish their 1990 gasoline quality, lacked consistent sources and quality of gasoline, or had the flexibility to meet a statutory baseline since they were not constrained by refinery equipment and crude supplies. The Panel observed that the distinction in the Gasoline Rule between refiners on the one hand, and importers and blenders on the other, which affected the treatment of imported gasoline with respect to domestic gasoline, was related to certain differences in the characteristics of refiners, blenders and importers, and the nature of the data held by them. However, Article III:4 of the General Agreement deals with the treatment to be accorded to like products; its wording does not allow less favourable treatment dependent on the characteristics of the producer and the nature of the data held by it. The Panel noted that in the Malt Beverages case, a tax regulation according less favourable treatment to beer on the basis of the size of the producer was rejected. Although this finding was made under Article III:2 concerning fiscal measures, the Panel considered that the same principle applied to regulations under Article III:4. Accordingly, the Panel rejected the US argument that the requirements of Article III:4 are met because imported gasoline is treated similarly to gasoline from similarly situated domestic parties.

6.12 Apart from being contrary to the ordinary meaning of the terms of Article III:4, any interpretation of Article III:4 in this manner would mean that the treatment of imported and domestic goods concerned could no longer be assured on the objective basis of their likeness as products. Rather, imported goods would be exposed to a highly subjective and variable treatment according to extraneous factors. This would thereby create great instability and uncertainty in the conditions of competition as between domestic and imported goods in a manner fundamentally inconsistent with the object and purpose of Article III.

6.13 The Panel considered that the foregoing was sufficient to dispose of the US argument. It noted, however, that even if the US approach were to be followed, under any approach based on "similarly situated parties" the comparison could just as readily focus on whether imported gasoline from an identifiable foreign refiner was treated more or less favourably than gasoline from an identifiable US refiner. There were, in the Panel's view, many key respects in which these refineries could be deemed to be the relevant similarly situated parties, and the Panel could find no inherently objective criteria by means of which to distinguish which of the many factors were relevant in making a determination that any particular parties were "similarly situated." Thus, although these refineries were similarly situated, the Gasoline Rule treated the products of these refineries differently by allowing only gasoline produced by the domestic entity to benefit from the advantages of an individual baseline. This consequential uncertainty and indeterminacy of the basis of treatment underlined, in the view of the Panel, the rationale of remaining within the terms of the clear language, object and purpose of Article III:4 as outlined above in paragraph 6.12.

6.14 The Panel then noted the argument of the United States that the treatment accorded to gasoline imported under a statutory baseline was on the whole no less favourable than that accorded to domestic gasoline under individual refiner baselines. The United States claimed that the Gasoline Rule did not discriminate against imported gasoline, since the statutory baseline (by the nature of its calculation) and the average of the sum of the individual baselines both corresponded to average gasoline quality in 1990, and that domestic and imported gasoline was treated equally overall. The Panel noted that, in these circumstances, the argument that on average the treatment provided was equivalent amounted to arguing that less favourable treatment in one instance could be offset provided that there was correspondingly more favourable treatment in another. This amounted to claiming that less favourable treatment of particular imported products in some instances would be balanced by more favourable treatment of particular products in others. [The panel then quoted from the *Section 337* report.] The Panel concurred with this reasoning that under Article III:4 less favourable treatment of particular imported products in some instances could not be balanced by more favourable treatment of other imported products in other instances. The Panel therefore rejected the US argument. * * *

6.16 The Panel found that imported and domestic gasoline were like products, and that since, under the baseline establishment methods, imported gasoline was effectively prevented from benefitting from as favourable sales conditions as were afforded domestic gasoline by an individual baseline tied to the producer of a product, imported gasoline was treated less favourably than domestic gasoline.

Questions and Discussion

1. Consider the following additional facts about the prelude to *Reformulated Gasoline*: The EPA rule was developed through negotiated rulemaking; major refiners and users of gasoline and environmental groups all participated, but neither Venezuela nor its subsidiary, Citgo, was invited to participate. After the rule was promulgated, Venezuela brought its trade concerns to the U.S. Trade Representative, who conveyed these concerns to EPA. After a period of internal deliberation within the U.S. government, Venezuela decided to exert some pressure by initiating a dispute in the GATT. Consultations between the Venezuela and the United States (including EPA officials) resulted in an agreed settlement under which EPA would propose, and ultimately adopt, certain changes to the Gasoline Rule to address Venezuela's concerns. These changes were then proposed in the *Federal Register*. After the comment period on the proposal closed, but before EPA could develop the final rule, members of Congress, including the representative from the home district of Sun Oil Company, a major competitor of Citgo in the U.S. East Coast, inserted a provision into the appropriations bill prohibiting EPA from expending any funds to complete this rulemaking. EPA stopped all work on the rule; Venezuela (and Brazil) waited several months until the new WTO Dispute Settlement Understanding came into effect and then reinstituted their trade complaint under the new system.

2. The United States appealed other parts of the *Reformulated Gasoline* panel report. Why do you think the United States decided not to appeal the rulings on Article III?

3. The effect of *Reformulated Gasoline* on trade-environment jurisprudence was limited by the fact that the competing foreign and domestic products at issue — gasoline — were, in principle, chemically identical. Do you think that the decision left open the possibility for distinguishing between products that are almost but not quite identical, such as food products containing genetically-modified organisms versus food with no GMOs, or paper made from recycled fibers versus paper made from virgin fibers? *See* paras. 6.11–6.12 of the Panel's decision. Do those latter situations involve distinctions between products as such or distinctions based on PPMs? What type of factors might help identify when treatment of products is based on the "objective basis of their likeness as products"? In an earlier adopted panel decision, a GATT panel stated: "Likeness of products must be examined taking into account not only object criteria (such as composition and manufacturing processes of products) but also the more subjective consumers' viewpoint (such as consumption and use by consumers)." Japan-Customs Duties, Taxes and Labelling Practices on Imported Wines and Alcoholic Beverages, GATT Panel Report, L/6216, B.I.S.D. 34th Supp. 83, para. 5.7 (1988) (adopted Nov. 10, 1987).

4. *Problem Exercise.* Reread Articles III and XI of the GATT, as well as the Interpretative Note to Article III. Draft a rule that defines when a measure falls within Article III or XI. Then determine whether the laws at issue in *Lobsters, Tuna/Dolphin,* and *Asbestos* fall within your interpretation of Article III or Article XI.

D. Proposals for New Approaches to PPM-Based Trade Measures

For now, at least, the chance that the WTO will allow products to be distinguished under Article III based on the manner in which they are produced or the characteristics of the producer seems remote. But that has not deterred commentators from suggesting principled legal and policy arguments to give scope to trade restrictions based on PPM considerations. This section reviews the leading proposals and some of the counterarguments they have generated. We begin with an overview of PPM-based trade measures.

1. Defining and Classifying PPMs and PPM-Based Trade Measures

Sanford E. Gaines, *Processes and Production Methods: How to Produce Sound Policy for Environmental PPM-Based Trade Measures?*

27 Colum. J. Envtl. L. 383, 388–99 (2002)

From some of the environmental commentary on trade and environment one gets the impression that PPMs is the single most important point at which trade law interferes with or constrains the free implementation of effective national environmental policy. Yet the number of PPM-based trade measures that have been applied (outside the special, highly-regulated realm of food safety) seems to be extremely small and limited almost exclusively to one type of PPM regulation — the regulation of methods of harvesting natural goods such as fish or timber. Before one delves into analysis of the pros and cons of different trade law provisions or their proper interpretation and application with respect to PPMs, the nature and scope of the policy "problem" to be fixed should be clearly delineated.
* * *

[Gaines classifies environmental regulations, for trade purposes, into three broad categories: product regulations; resource access regulations; and PPM regulations.]

Product regulations regulate the design, characteristics, and use of particular products. They include everything from pollution-control systems on automobiles to the prohibition on the manufacture of PCBs, to pesticide residue limits on fruits and vegetables. Resource allocation regulations are exemplified by the conditions on private access to and removal of publicly-owned or commons resources such as timber, petroleum, or fish. PPM regulations include the statutes and regulations, familiar to any environmental lawyer in any country, that set standards on the release of pollutants to air, water, or soil from manufacturing facilities. To begin to understand the nature of the problem of trade measures based on PPMs, it will be helpful to review how trade law affects each of the three main types of environmental regulation.

1. Product Regulations

International trade rules grant broad authority to governments to set standards for products, to tax products, and even to prohibit the import of products that are banned under national law. The propriety of environmental product regulations has repeatedly been affirmed in trade disputes. * * *

2. Resource Access Regulations

* * * Because of the deep governmental involvement in these systems, because they often involve a byzantine process of bids or concessions or qualifications for access, and because governments supervise private operators, a number of trade disputes have arisen over such regulations. What is at stake in these trade disputes, however, is not the government's sovereign right to exercise control, but whether that control was exercised in a way that treats foreign nationals unfairly or distorts the national or international market for the resource.

3. PPM Regulations * * *

As a matter of trade policy, one should note that almost none of these [national] PPM measures have anything to do with the regulation of trade. The steel mill that must control its air pollution emissions under national and state clean air regulation can import raw materials and export its products without regard to its compliance or non-compliance with those requirements. Likewise, international trade in pulp and paper continues unaffected by the effluent limitations guidelines and permit requirements of the Clean Water Act that dictate for paper mills in the United States the steps they must take to control their wastewater discharges of different substances. The strict requirements for chemical plants for treatment and final disposal of hazardous wastes have no direct bearing on the substantial import and export of chemical products. * * *

[Non-Product-Related PPMs]

The more typical environmental regulation ... is a PPM not related to the product. U.S. air emissions standards and wastewater discharges standards, for example, typically specify a maximum quantity of a pollutant allowed for each unit of production of the particular good: 0.951 kilograms of chlorinated compounds per thousand kilograms of kraft paper, for example. This kind of regulation strongly influences the technologies and raw materials used by the manufacturer, but has no direct effect on the quality or character of the final product, nor does marketing of the product depend on compliance or noncompliance with the indicated PPM.

Not surprisingly, then, out of the vast panoply of national PPM measures only an isolated few have attempted to prevent the export or import of goods because of the processes and production methods associated with them. Within this tiny fraction of laws and regulations, almost every one adopted or proposed has restricted import of natural goods—fish, furs, wood, agricultural products—based on how those goods were harvested from the wild or grown. How can we account for this unexpected result?

The OECD PPMs Paper* offers a few theories for the asymmetry [of scientific uncertainty and competitiveness concerns]. My own explanation emphasizes the political economy of trade restrictions. It has two prongs. The first prong deals with the absence of pollution-control PPM-based trade measures. In this context several pragmatic factors restrain the expected environmental impulse to adopt such measures. Pressure for environmentally-motivated trade measures usually comes from an alliance of affected industries and environmental activists.

---

* Organisation for Economic Co-operation and Development, *Processes and Production Methods (PPMs): Conceptual Framework and Considerations on the Use of PPM-Based Trade Measures*, OCDE/GD (97)137 (Aug. 11, 1997).

In most industries, pollution control costs are a minor factor in the cost of production for most products, so there is little competitive advantage to be gained (or recouped) from a PPM-based trade restriction, and thus little pressure from that quarter for government action. Environmental activists in major market countries would also be hard-pressed to generate political support to restrict access to consumer products because companies in Mexico or Indonesia are not doing "enough" to clean up the air and water of Mexico City or Jakarta. Finally, the variation among pollution standards from country to country—indeed *within* many larger countries—makes political leaders (and businesses) wary of imposing their own PPM as a condition of import for fear that trading partners will be willing and able to retaliate. Thus, there is no effective domestic constituency for extrapolating "our" controls to "their" countries. The exceptional case is long-range or global pollution, which is tackled directly through international pollution-abatement agreements.

The second prong of my explanation tries to account for the relative frequency (though absolute rarity) of PPM-based trade measures for natural goods or resources. In this context, the political economy more easily leads to trade-restricting measures. Resource management or extraction techniques may have a more significant bearing on the costs of production, relate to products that will be differentiated only by price, and in businesses where producers operate on small profit margins. U.S. tuna boat owners and shrimp trawlers, for example, were important constituents supporting the tuna and shrimp embargoes. Environmentally, the global vulnerability of certain resources and sectors (such as endangered species, charismatic animals, tropical forests, and small-scale agriculturalists) mobilizes a large and passionate domestic constituency in many developed countries. While there is diversity in pollution standards from nation to nation, resources management, especially for transboundary resources, tends toward definable and generalizable norms of conduct. Turtle excluder devices work equally well in the Bay of Bengal and in the Gulf of Mexico.

In conclusion, although there is a great universe of environmental laws and regulations that sets specifications for imported (and domestic) products and an even greater universe of regulations that specify PPMs, these two universes function side-by-side and scarcely impinge on each other. Few non-product PPM measures have consequences for product marketing, so the predicted collision between trade law and environmental PPM measures has not happened outside the few infamous cases. For several decades, trade liberalization has coexisted peacefully with the proliferation of environmental laws and regulations. Within the very small ambit of plausible PPM-based trade measures that environmental activists seriously promote and that governments might be interested in adopting, almost all involve methods that primary producers—fishermen, farmers, loggers, miners, and hunters—use to acquire "wild" or cultivated natural goods. This dramatically narrows the scope of the environmental policy "problem" to be addressed through trade policy reform. At the same time, it would be a mistake to ignore the high political profile of the PPM issues that do arise or are likely to arise in the future. The next volatile issue will be trade restrictions on the products of bioengineering. The PPMs issue may be limited in scope, then, but not in political impact. It must be addressed for the WTO and other multilateral trade regimes to maintain their political legitimacy.

Questions and Discussion

1. In an article in which he sets out to demonstrate that WTO law does not make PPM measures illegal, Steve Charnovitz suggests another classification of such measures: 1) the how-produced standard; 2) the government policy standard; and 3) the producer characteristics standard. Steve Charnovitz, *The Law of Environmental "PPMs" in the WTO: Debunking the Myth of Illegality*, 27 YALE J. INT'L L. 59 (2002). A how-produced standard specifies the processing method used for making the product, such as a law banning the importation of driftnet-caught fish. The U.S. measures in *Tuna/Dolphin* are an example of the government policy standard, in that they prohibited imports of tuna from particular countries based on national practices without regard to the performance of particular fishing boats. The measures reviewed in the *Auto Taxes* and *Reformulated Gasoline* reports are examples of standards determined by producer characteristics. Charnovitz then offers the following policy prescription:

> The WTO should discourage the most troublesome types of PPM. The government policy standard should be disfavored because it is coercive and abides origin-based discrimination. The producer characteristics standard should be disfavored because such a standard is too easy to tilt against foreign producers. Thus, if a unilateral PPM is to be used, it should be crafted as a how-produced standard aimed directly at the odious production practice. In other words, rather than specifying a type of turtle-excluder device, the importing government might set a maximum tolerance for incidental turtle deaths during shrimping. This could be policed by observers and product certifications.

Id. at 106–07. Are there practical differences between the how-produced and government policy standards?

2. The OECD PPMs paper to which Gaines refers begins with the traditional distinction between product-related and nonproduct-related PPMs. (A requirement for pasteurization of milk is a classic example of a product-related PPM.) For nonproduct-related PPMs, the OECD then subclassifies them according to the location and nature of the environmental concern being targeted: transboundary pollution; effects on management of transboundary resources; global environmental concerns; and effects limited to the territory of the country or countries targeted by the PPM measure. Do you see how the locus and nature of the environmental problem being addressed is relevant to an evaluation of the legitimacy of a PPM-based trade measure? The OECD paper then explores five possible considerations in assessing a PPM-based trade measure: 1) the motivation for the measure; 2) technical, economic, and legal feasibility; 3) effectiveness; 4) efficiency; and 5) availability of alternatives. Should these five considerations be used as legal criteria in a WTO review of an environmental PPM-based trade restriction?

---

2. Re-Reading GATT Article III to Permit PPM-Based Trade Measures

The trade-environment debate over PPMs arises because the standard interpretation of the GATT, as reflected in the dispute settlement reports excerpted earlier in this chapter, leaves no room for discrimination in national treatment on grounds other than product characteristics. In a provocative article, Robert Howse and Donald Regan contested this standard interpretation of GATT Article III, arguing that it is neither textually correct nor indicated by policy considerations. Another commentator, David Driesen, comes to the same conclusion as Howse and Regan but on the basis of a more theoretical argument. If their views were to gain acceptance, GATT law would be reinterpreted to allow product-specific PPM-based trade measures that are origin neutral and not patently protectionist. Subsequently, Sanford Gaines has criticized both the Howse and Regan and the Driesen analyses on both textual and policy grounds. He believes that a more generous interpretation of the GATT Article XX exceptions would meet the key environmental objectives to be achieved through PPM trade measures.

Robert Howse & Donald Regan,
The Product/Process Distinction — An Illusory Basis for Disciplining "Unilateralism" in Trade Policy
11 Eur. J. Int'l L. 249, 254, 258–61, 276–77 (2000)

Despite the [*Tuna/Dolphin I*] panel, it should be obvious that the repeated reference to "products" tells us nothing about the product/process distinction. It merely reflects the fact that GATT is about trade in goods, not about trade in services or the movement of capital or labour. We could show in detail that none of the panel's three sub-arguments actually applies the text (as opposed to improvising on one of its key terms), but a detailed treatment is unnecessary. The panel's larger argument simply falls under its own weight if we simply compare the conclusion to the text the argument purports to analyse. The text of Article III(4) says it applies to "internal laws, regulations and requirements affecting the internal sale ... of products." Who could doubt that, giving terms their ordinary meaning, process-based measures "affect the sale of products"? This is true even of the ban on the use of dolphin-unsafe fishing techniques by United States fishermen (the panel's prime example of a regulation not affecting "tuna as a product"), since the ban almost certainly affects the price and quantity of tuna sold. But more important, the whole complaint about the United States' regime is that it affects the sale of products by reducing the sales of foreign tuna.

[Howse and Regan go on to argue that the *Tuna/Dolphin I* and *II* panels were wrong to conclude that the fact that the trade measure did not address the product as such meant that it did not qualify for consideration under Article III. They cite other GATT and WTO cases, including *Auto Taxes*, for the proposition that it is standard procedure to consider nonproduct issues in the Article III context.]

We have established that Article III applies to process-based measures. What does it say about their legality, or more specifically, about the legality of origin-neutral process measures? Most people who think origin-neutral process measures are prohibited by Article III probably have in mind something like the following argument ... : (1) "Like products" means products which are alike in their physical properties. (2) Hence, products which differ only in their processing histories (where the difference in process does not cause any difference in the physical constitution of the product are "like." Therefore, (3) foreign products, even if made with the disfavoured process, are entitled to the same treatment as domestic products made with the favoured process.

Even granting for the moment that products which differ only in their processing histories are "like," the conclusion of this argument is a non sequitur. * * *

The root of the problem lies in the claim that physically identical products that differ only in their processing histories are "like" products. The opponent of processing measures thinks this follows from the ordinary meaning of "like." We disagree. "Likeness" in this context is not primarily a matter of physical similarity. * * *

If physical similarity is not the issue, what is? The real issue is the existence of differences between the products that justify different regulation. Regulatory distinctions must have a rational relation to some non-protectionist regulatory purpose; and therefore products must be treated the same (that is to say, they are "like"), if and only if they do not differ in any respect relevant to an actual non-protectionist regulatory policy. This gives us the meaning of "like" in Article III. "Like" means roughly "not differing in any respect relevant to an actual non-protectionist policy." This is not a recondite interpretation; it is the ordinary meaning of "like" in this context. The context is a provision aimed at preventing a certain kind of discrimination. Any lawyer and any thoughtful non-lawyer (and these are the people for whom Article III was written) knows that in the context of a discussion of discrimination, what "like" standard[] means something like "not differing in any way which justifies different treatment." * * *

[Shifting to policy arguments, Howse and Regan address the argument that refusal to import products made with disfavored processes amounts to an effort by the importing country to impose its environmental standards or moral preferences on other countries, infringing their sovereign right to determine their own environmental policies. They respond, in part, that one also has to consider the sovereign interest of the importing country in not contributing to or benefitting from the disfavored process. They suggest that the sovereignty argument reflects a widely held view that WTO members have a right of access to the markets of other countries.]

... We have bumped up against the deepest divide between competing understandings of GATT.... One view is that GATT creates a general right of market access, which right may only be denied for internationally certified reasons (where international certification might involve anything from inclusion in a multilateral treaty to *substantive* endorsement by a WTO dispute settlement tribunal). The other view is that GATT creates no such general right of access, but creates only a negative right that access shall not be denied by rules that discriminate between countries. * * *

The difference between the two views of GATT (the "general right of access view" and the "nondiscrimination view") explains many more specific divergences of perception. It explains, for example, why opponents of process-based restrictions see them as "coercive," while defenders see them as at most attempts to influence foreigners' behaviour by permissible, non-coercive means. Not all attempts to influence amount to coercion. Denying someone something they have a right to (such as market access, on the first view of GATT) is a way of coercing them; whereas merely choosing not to deal with them, when that violates no right (as on the second view of GATT), and especially when one thinks that to deal with them would be to involve oneself in wickedness, is not.

David Driesen elaborates on some of the points raised by Howse and Regan in their discussion of the two views of GATT at the end of the preceding excerpt. *What is Free Trade?: The Real Issue Lurking Behind the Trade and Environment Debate*, 41 Va. J. Int'l L. 279, 287–312 (2001). Driesen argues that those who speak of GATT as protecting "free trade" are really arguing for an international version of laissez-faire capitalism free from any regulatory restraints. For the WTO not to become rhetorically trapped into a defense of laissez-fair policies, Driesen argues, it should apply a "bright line" nondiscrimination test under Article III. By this argument, Driesen would have the WTO disallow only facially discriminatory measures and tolerate measures that are facially origin-neutral even if they might actually serve as disguised or de facto discriminatory restraints on trade. *Id.*

Although Gaines questions much of the legal analysis offered by Howse and Regan, the following excerpt from his article focuses on some practical difficulties in the legal approaches suggested by the preceding authors, difficulties that have legal and political ramifications.

Sanford E. Gaines, *Processes and Production Methods: How to Produce Sound Policy for Environmental PPM-Based Trade Measures?*
27 Colum. J. Envtl. L. 383, 419–21 (2002)

A central feature of the approach that Howse and Regan propose is their firm distinction between trade measures based on the national PPM laws and enforcement actions of the country and trade measures based on observance of the PPMs by the individual producer of the good. They consider country-based PPM measures impermissible because they would unfairly discriminate between PPM-compliant goods from a noncomplying country and like PPM-compliant domestic goods or like goods from another foreign country deemed to be in compliance. By the same token, a trade measure focused on the PPMs used in making the particular good, regardless of the country of origin, would be permissible because it would treat all "like"—that is, PPM-compliant—goods equally.

The effort by Howse and Regan to distinguish between country-based environmental PPM measures and origin-neutral PPM measures, though intellectually elegant, avails little in the real world of environmental policy. Environmental PPM-based trade restrictions have relatively few effective uses. (If they had more uses, they would be more prevalent.) In some cases they are used to reinforce a treaty regime that has already outlawed the offending PPM; U.S. legislation relating to products of driftnet fisheries is one example. In some cases, they are used to promote the adoption by many foreign governments of a PPM that is generally accepted on scientific grounds as an improvement over previous PPMs associated with the same product; the U.S. shrimp-turtle trade embargoes exemplify this approach. In still other cases, PPM-based trade restrictions might be used as a vindication of a national preference for one PPM versus another. Several examples fall into this category: the U.S. Marine Mammal Protection Act with respect to reducing dolphin mortality; the proposed E.U. ban on furs from animals caught with leg-hold traps; and the E.U. ban on beef from cattle treated with growth hormones.

Among these three situations, only the use of PPM-based measures in support of a treaty regime can be naturally construed to be origin-neutral. In the second situation, the precise purpose is to get other national governments, not simply individual firms, to adopt the preferred PPM. The problem in these situations is that effective assurance of compliance with the PPM depends on national enforcement, a situation that also comes up with respect to food safety and pesticide use. The third type, the market vindication measure, while origin-neutral in principle, tends not to be in practice. By definition, the domestic producers are already in compliance or prepared to comply. But even on most-favored-nation grounds, discriminatory effects are often embedded in the circumstances leading to the measure. The MMPA embargo was targeted primarily at Latin American fleets operating in the Eastern Tropical Pacific Ocean fishery; the E.U.'s leg-hold trap directive and the ban on hormones in beef production affected primarily the United States. Other PPM-based measures that have been advocated also tend to be geographic in their orientation because the products come predominantly from one country or region (e.g., PPM-linked restrictions on tropical wood products).

Another real and often overlooked complication with non-product-related PPMs in terms of the "like product" question is how to establish that the domestic producers themselves have complied with the specified PPM. In the tuna-dolphin context, this is accomplished be placing independent observers on every tuna boat, an expensive procedure. In the shrimp-turtle context, though, it is a matter of spot-check enforcement by the Coast Guard or state fisheries authorities on the water. There is no assurance that every U.S. boat is using its TED on every trawling run. Shrimp caught out of compliance may, and probably do, end up on the U.S. market, and there is no control at the point of sale to preclude that. Two legally significant observations follow from the potential discrepancy between what the law may require and what actually occurs. First, if one applied a "like product" analysis, one would have to argue, possibly contrary to fact, that *only* PPM-compliant products, domestic or foreign, are in the market. To the extent that non-compliant domestic products are in the market, you have a "like products" discrimination problem, because the enforcement at the border on foreign products may be stricter than the domestic environmental enforcement. The second observation is a corollary to the first. Since enforcement of the PPM must be a major concern with respect to PPMs that do not affect observable product characteristics, then it becomes almost impossible to avoid country-based design of the trade measure, because the effectiveness of the measure depends on the enforcement effort of foreign governments. Moreover, from an administrative and foreign relations point of view, it is usually easier to evaluate and monitor a government enforcement program than it is to identify the actual PPM practices of every foreign producer. These practical problems may be one reason that environmental PPM-based measures are relatively rare and occur most often with respect to products that are already closely monitored for commercial or other reasons.

Finally, as Howse and Regan and all other commentators note, the acceptability in trade of a regulatory distinction based on PPMs between otherwise identical products depends on some assurance or some test for judging that it is free of protectionist motivation. The trader's suspicion of protectionism is not unreasonable. Why would a country adopt a rule about CFC or chlorine use in foreign manufacturing processes other than to create a market advantage for the CFC-free or chlorine-free product? Do countries adopt such measures if their own producers are not in a position to benefit from that market advantage? It is just such practical questions that have discouraged the parties to the Montreal Protocol from acting on treaty-based trade restrictions on products *made with* but not *containing* ozone-depleting substances. Moreover, just such practical concerns about market advantages probably prompted the E.U. to plan to include chlorine use in production as a heavily-weighted negative factor in its eco-labeling criteria [for paper] (E.U. producers have largely ceased using chlorine) and caused chlorine-using U.S. and Canadian paper companies to protest the criteria vehemently as improper restrictions on trade.

Questions and Discussion

1. Professors Howse and Regan argue that nonproduct-related PPMs affect the internal sale of products and thus fall within Article III provided that they are applied in a nondiscriminatory way. This argument assumes that compliance with an importing country's PPM requirements will increase the price of an imported product and thus "affect" the internal sale of that product. Do you agree that increased price alone should be the basis for stating that a measure "affects" the internal sale of a product? Is the Howse and Regan position supported by *Italian Agricultural Machinery*?

2. In fact, a substantial body of empirical evidence with respect to pollution control suggests that compliance with PPMs is not likely to increase the price of a good, because the costs of pollution control represent a small percentage of the overall production costs for most products. *See, e.g.*, ORGANIZATION FOR ECONOMIC COOPERATION AND DEVELOPMENT, PROCESSES AND PRODUCTION METHODS (PPMs): CONCEPTUAL FRAMEWORK AND CONSIDERATIONS ON USE OF PPM-BASED TRADE MEASURES, OCDE/GD(97)137 (1997); Sanford Gaines, *Rethinking Environmental Regulation, International Trade, and Competitiveness*, 1997 U. CHI. LEGAL F. 231 (reviewing the economics literature). Do the empirical data undercut the theoretical basis of the Howse and Regan position?

3. Howse and Regan, as well as Driesen, stress the policy objective of Article III:1. Might that reliance undercut their argument? How does the Appellate Body apply Article III:1?

4. The difference between origin-neutral measures and country-based measures is easy to state in principle but may be difficult to apply in practice. To take the tuna-dolphin situation as an example, a rule that allowed the sale only of tuna caught without encircling dolphins ("dolphin safe" tuna) and permitted the import of all dolphin-safe tuna would be origin-neutral. But the real U.S. measure was country-based, not origin neutral. It allowed U.S.-caught tuna onto the market even if some dolphins were killed, and it prohibited the import of tuna, even if from a boat following "dolphin safe" practices, if that boat was registered in a country without a government program to reduce dolphin mortality. Howse and Regan would establish a strict prohibition on country-based PPM measures because they invite trade discrimination. As they note, Howard Chang has advanced a defense of country-based measures because they may be necessary to achieve the process-based restriction. Robert Howse & Donald Regan, *The Product/Process Distinction*, at 270, (citing Howard Chang, *An Economic Analysis of Trade Measures to Protect the Global Environment*, 83 GEO. L.J. 2131 (1995)). Driesen follows Chang's position. What conditions might be imposed on country-based PPM measures to make their trade discrimination acceptable to the WTO?

5. Among the three purposes for which PPM-based measures are adopted, Gaines believes that "only the use of PPM-based measures in support of a treaty regime can be naturally construed to be origin-neutral." Do you agree?

6. *Problem Exercise*: Leather tanning uses a number of noxious chemicals, such as sodium sulfide, sulfuric acid, and chromium salts, all of which end up in the wastewater from the tannery. Under modern environmental regulations, such as the U.S. Environmental Protection Agency's (EPA) effluent guidelines and standards for the leather tanning and finishing point source category, 40 C.F.R. Part 425, tanneries must undertake

extensive treatment of their wastewater before discharge to a waterway or to a municipal sewage treatment system. Leather tanneries in many developing countries are not as well controlled, leading to serious water pollution and air pollution problems affecting the health of people in local communities and killing many fish and birds. Imports of leather and leather goods into developed countries have been rising steeply in recent years, and the leather industries in those countries have suffered serious declines. Design a rule for your country to adopt that governs trade in leather and leather products so as to ensure that all leather goods sold in the country are made with leather from tanneries that observe the best wastewater treatment practices. How would your rule affect domestic tanneries? How would it regulate or restrict imports? Would it control exports? Is your rule origin-neutral or country-based? If your rule is based in some way on the EPA regulations, how would the trade measures change if EPA decided to relax the restriction on the pH of alkaline wastes being discharged to municipal sewage systems? How would it change if the EU adopted a more stringent wastewater standard for chromium discharges than the United States? Suppose that tannery wastes are blamed for a major kill of migratory birds in a neighboring country; can the PPM-based trade rules be defended in the WTO, under current WTO jurisprudence, on the grounds that they are intended to protect your country's seasonal populations of these migratory birds?

---

3. Broader Models for Policy Reform

Instead of classifying PPMs and reinterpreting Article III to allow certain types of PPMs, some commentators have offered proposals for rethinking the PPM issue entirely. In the first reading below, Steve Charnovitz proposes that the WTO handle the PPMs question through a multilateral model based on "convergence"—establishing a range of possibilities for regulating particular products. In the second reading, Bill Snape and Naomi Lefkowitz propose a unilateral model based on "fairness." Do these ideas provide reasonable methods for incorporating PPMs within a trade-oriented process?

Steve Charnovitz,
Environmental Harmonization and Trade Policy

in TRADE AND THE ENVIRONMENT: LAW, ECONOMICS, AND POLICY
280–82 (Durwood Zaelke et al., eds. 1993)

PROCESS STANDARDS

It is dogma in trade policy circles that unilateral import standards should relate to products only—not processes. Defenders of this position argue that process standards are intrinsic to a country and should not be anyone else's concern. Thus, what Brazil does with biodiversity is solely its business. Whether China burns more fossil fuel is its business. But this doctrine of insularity is already obsolete from an ecological perspective, and is becoming less acceptable from the perspective of international law.

It may be true that there is a category of issues that are purely internal, where no country has a valid interest in another's process standards. Although much of the analytical writing on trade and environment has sought to use this category as a basis for deriving general principles, the important issues are the ones in which other countries believe they do have an interest. That is where the debate needs to focus.

Those who deny that process standards should be the subject of international negotiations do not have history on their side. Process standards on fishing go back to 19th Century treaties. Throughout the 20th Century, there have been plurilateral or multilateral negotiations on many environmental or health issues such as bird conservation, marine pollution, whale protection, workplace health, and disease control. The point is not that all of these negotiations resulted in international standards (yet many of them did), or that they resulted in trade controls (yet many of them did). The point is that international regulation of process standards is neither a new idea or a radical one.

Another common argument against process standards is that they are "protectionist" and "imperialist." But process standards are not inherently protectionist. There is a clear difference between a local-content requirement and an environmental-content requirement. Furthermore, many process standards are no more imperialist than product standards are. For instance, a requirement that all tuna sold be dolphin-safe is functionally equivalent to a requirement that all soft drinks sold be in recyclable bottles. In both cases, foreign exporters have to meet certain specifications if they want to sell to the regulated market. The customer is always right.

Any unilateral standard, product or process, may seem unfair or coercive to an exporter who does not meet it. Yet convenience to exporters is not a criterion GATT utilizes to judge product standards. GATT uses criteria such as national treatment, non-discrimination, and non-protectionism.

Why should GATT not utilize these same criteria to judge process standards? Nations ought to be able to extend their domestic product and process standards to imports. This points to where the tuna-dolphin panel went wrong. If it had applied the normal GATT rules to the U.S. Marine Mammal Protection Act (MMPA), the decision would have been quite different. Instead, the panel invented new rules and new interpretations in order to erect a GATT bulwark against recent progress in environmental standards.

Carrots, Sticks, and Standards

Conducting international negotiations is one thing. Attaining a consensus is another. How can an agreement on minimum standards be achieved among a hundred countries with different values and resources? One approach is to devise a clever mix of carrots and sticks from a diverse enough issue garden to allow a cross-fertilization of concerns. The goal is not only to obtain an agreement, but also to maintain its stability.

The carrots are the basic tool. Because countries face different economic trade-offs (for example, some countries may benefit from global warming), an assistance mechanism can be developed to enable gainers to compensate losers and rich nations to "bribe" poor ones. This assistance could be in the form of financial aid or technology transfer, as provided under the Montreal Protocol on Substances that Deplete the Ozone Layer (Montreal Protocol), or it could be trade concessions.

But carrots alone may not be sufficient. Uncooperative countries might attempt to extract more assistance or concessions than the global community is willing to provide. During the past decade, for example, American diplomats attempting to negotiate a dolphin-safe fishing agreement were frustrated by the unwillingness of countries like Mexico to undertake any responsibility for marine mammals. In such cases, sticks like trade sanctions may be needed to force free-riding countries to enter multilateral agreements.

In between carrots and sticks are environmental product and process standards applied equally to both domestic production and imports. Such standards are not carrots because they provide no additional benefit to foreign countries. Yet they are not sticks either so long as such standards are applied to all countries in an evenhanded manner. The characterization of such process standards as "sanctions" is an all too common misnomer.

By taking their own product and process standards to the bargaining table, countries will be better able to strike mutually beneficial deals....

ESTABLISHING A RANGE

The first step in negotiation would be to obtain a worldwide minimum standard that may be exceeded but not undercut. (The terminology gets a little confusing. By a minimum standard, I mean a minimum level of protection. Such a standard might operate by setting a maximum exposure level.) For example, there are no internationally recognized norms on dolphin safety while fishing for tuna. Establishing such a minimum is the first step toward delegitimizing the practices of countries like Mexico who claim that their dolphin-lethal techniques are irrelevant to the acceptability of tuna.

The second step would be a maximum standard to establish the highest level of protection. For example, the MMPA sets a dolphin-protection goal "approaching a zero mortality and serious injury rate." An international maximum might set a more reasonable level. If the United States insists upon zero, it should perhaps compensate other countries whenever the zero standard distorts tuna sales in favor of American suppliers. Ideally, this compensation would take the form of a cash transfer rather than an agreement to allow other countries to impose higher tariffs on imports from the United States.

Once the range of minimum and maximum standards is set, periodic discussions can be held on further convergence. There might be a presumption of upward convergence only, but the goal should not generally be the attainment of a single standard. Just as the world benefits from environmental cooperation (for example, the negotiated range), the world also gains from the competition made possible by a variability in standards.

Although it would not work for product standards, a two-tiered approach may be possible for many process standards. For instance, the United States might establish a stringent process standard for its domestic commerce, but then accept imports produced under lower standards so long as such imports meet the international minimum. A two-tiered approach is currently used in the MMPA that allows imports to have a 25 percent higher dolphin kill than America tuna producers have.

––––––––––

William J. Snape, III & Naomi Lefkovitz,
Searching for GATT's Environmental Miranda:
Are "Process Standards" Getting "Due Process?"
27 CORNELL L.J. 777, 805–07 (1994)

Global PPM Leadership

[M]uch of the world remains skeptical of either the need to integrate trade and the environment or U.S. leadership or unilateralism on the issue. This will probably have a chilling effect on the U.S. government's desire to apply PPM trade measures to items like driftnet-caught fish or to utilize related non-PPM environmental trade sanctions. In the face of identifying and correcting severe or acute environmental problems, and consequent trade-distorting PPM externalities, the question of how to enforce responsible behavior in an international vacuum remains unanswered.

A. Green 301

If the world recognizes responsible U.S. leadership on trade and the environment, one possible solution is a "Green 301" provision, which could be added to the U.S. Trade Act. [Editors' Note: If the U.S. Trade Representative determines that a country's action "is unjustifiable and burdens or restricts U.S. commerce," Section 301, 19 U.S.C. § 2242, gives the President discretionary authority to impose unilateral trade measures against that country.] ... A Green 301 proposal would essentially stipulate that certain foreign production methods constitute an unfair international trading practice.

Once the notion of a Green 301 was accepted, drafters would need to identify a legal "trigger" for its application, as well as an equitable "compensatory mechanism;" in other words, when would Green 301 be utilized and how much would it cost the offending country? Although a plethora of options exist, a Green 301 should probably be based on an environmental injury related to trade, not on a trade injury related to environmental competitiveness. This environmental emphasis not only addresses the primary issue at hand, but it also helps avoid disguised green protectionism. Thus, when an environmental PPM of another country is directly harming the United States or a "global interest" (defined as a global common entity or a resource protected by international agreement), the United States should be able to levy a duty equal to the approximated cost of the environmental injury caused by the PPM in question.

While a Green 301 might seem radical or heavy handed to some, it is really only an extension of several existing international trends. First, if based on unsustainable PPMs, a Green 301 would merely expand allowable product bans or tariffs to cover the product's full life cycle. Also, to the extent that duties are levied against products from offending PPMs, such tariffication is consistent with GATT Article XI. Most importantly, once a goal of preventing or controlling damaging PPMs was established and accepted, strong standards would enhance international competitiveness. Green 301, therefore, could become the catalyst for environmental and economic forces already underway.

B. Precautionary 1901

A variant on the Green 301 approach would more fully embrace the "precautionary approach" in international trade negotiations and implementation. Such an approach, which we will call "Precautionary 1901," could combine the best elements of unilateral and multilateral trade actions. If an international agreement on a particular environmental problem cannot be reached, the United States (or any other country) should be permitted to impose unilateral quantitative or added-duty trade measures for a set period of time (e.g., eight to ten years). Then, after that time, if no international agreement was struck, the country using the trade measure must either compensate the complaining party(ies) or rescind the offending trade measure. Significantly, some unilateral PPMs and certain sanctions should be automatically protected without resorting to the Precautionary 1901 approach. Nonetheless, this approach could solve the large bulk of potential PPM and trade problems.

C. An International Commerce Clause?

Trade pressure should only be a means to a greater end. Ideally, political leverage by environmentalists will eventually enable the United States and other like-minded countries to negotiate reasonable trade and environment rules that would make unilateral trade measures unnecessary. What would this global policy look like? Only clues exist. A particularly intriguing analogue is the U.S. Commerce Clause, which, inter alia, governs the trade rules between the states and the federal government. Under this framework, the GATT's dispute settlement procedures and legal tests would be central, with three basic legal principles guiding the panels. First, a country challenging a facially non-discriminatory environmental law would have the burden of proving that the law has a discriminatory effect. Second, if a country challenging an environmental law demonstrated a discriminatory effect, then the defending country could still justify the law by showing that it served a legitimate public interest and that there are no available less-discriminatory alternatives. Third, even in cases where there is discriminatory intent in the questioned law, the defending country could nonetheless still show that it serves a legitimate environmental purpose and is the only means available to achieve that purpose. Although it might be dangerous to carry the analogy too far, U.S. law could at the very least assist the GATT in instituting environmental (and PPM) deference by more fully deferring to democratically accountable decision-makers.

D. Foreign Environmental Practices Act [FEPA]

Other countries, particularly developing countries, have begun to react with increasing consternation to the U.S. use of unilateral trade measures. However, for reasons already outlined, countries sometimes need to resort to unilateral measures for effective environmental protection. In the trade area, these unilateral measures have generally followed a pattern whereby other countries are sanctioned for proscribed actions. Yet this kind of action is not the only type of unilateral measure available that countries can employ. Countries could also control their own actions or those of their own citizens abroad. The United States, for example, could pass a law requiring that its transnational corporations (TNCs) comply with U.S. environmental regulations, including PPM requirements while operating abroad.

Briefly, the principal sections of a FEPA would include a provision providing that in the event of a conflict of laws between the United States and the host country, U.S. TNCs must comply with whichever of the laws of the host country or the United States that gives the greatest level of protection to the host country's environment, although in no case would compliance infringe upon a foreign country's sovereign authority to enforce its own laws. Other provisions would set out the criminal penalties and civil actions for violations of the act and establish the regulatory structure for the administration of the act.

FEPA raises a number of political and legal issues such as defining a U.S. TNC, enforcement of the act, and questions of sovereignty and competitiveness. Although these issues are important, an in-depth discussion of them is beyond the scope of this article. Nevertheless, there are two fundamental objectives that are central to potential passage of FEPA by the Congress.

First, at its core, FEPA is about regulating TNCs. TNCs are by far the greatest participants in trade. Thus, where trade negatively impacts the environment, TNCs are likely to be in a position to take responsibility for some of those effects. Indeed, agreements such as NAFTA and the Uruguay Round of the GATT have manifestly served to increase the power and rights of TNCs, at the expense of individuals and sovereign governments. Now it is only fitting that these enterprises begin to take on some of the responsibilities that go along with those rights.

Second, FEPA is a way for the United States to maintain a leading role in global environmental protection. FEPA demonstrates the U.S. sincerity of commitment to doing its part in taking care of the environment. In light of the North-South rift, it also shows goodwill and may help developing countries to continue developing without contributing to greater destruction of their environment. FEPA also encourages the spread of "enviro-technology" and PPM standards without the harshness of sanctions, which are the hallmarks of other unilateral trade measures. At the very least, FEPA can be a tool to spark greater dialogue at both the national and international levels about how to handle the subject of sustainable development and the role commercial enterprises should play in that process.

Questions and Discussion

1. Charnovitz proposes a model for convergence that differs greatly from the several proposals of Snape and Lefkovitz. Principally, Charnovitz's model calls for a multilateral process, while Snape and Lefkovitz propose unilateral measures. Which approach do you think would be more effective? Which has a greater chance of being implemented? For example, Charnovitz's approach would require a major technical and diplomatic effort to negotiate the maximum and minimum standards for different PPMs. Is that a significant drawback? Could existing international agreements, such as the Montreal Protocol, be used as a forum to establish these ranges?

2. Another alternative proposes that WTO members negotiate the meaning of "like product" for specific products. The negotiated "like product" approach would have the WTO members determine, for example, that paper bleached with chlorine is "not like" paper bleached with ozone, or that tuna caught without setting nets on dolphins is "not like" tuna caught with nets set on dolphins. Is this proposal worth considering? What products and PPMs should be included in such an approach? How many countries would have to agree for the approach to work?

3. Yet another approach is to negotiate tariff differentials based on PPMs. Consider the following tariff classifications:

Heading/ Subheading	Article Description	Unit of Quantity	Rate of Due General
1604	prepared or preserved fish …		
	Fish, whole or in pieces, but not minced:		
1604.14	Tunas, skipjack and bonito (*Sarda* spp.): Tunas and skipjack In airtight containers		
1604.14.10	In oil...	kg	35%
1604.14.20	Not in oil...	....	6%
	Albacore (*Thunnus alalunga*)...........................	kg	
	Other..		
1604.14.30	Other..	....	12.5%
	Albacore (*Thunnus alalunga*)...........................	kg	
	Other	kg	
	Bonita (*Sarda* spp.)		
1604.14.70	In Oil...	kg	4.9%
1604.14.80	Not in Oil...	kg	6%

Given the different tariff classifications, would a separate tariff classification for "tuna: caught with nets setting on dolphins," with a tariff of, say, 300 percent be difficult to administer? If countries are willing to create separate tariff classifications for tuna and albacore, two species of "tuna" as well as create different tariffs for tuna "in oil" and "not in oil," should the panels really be so concerned about distinguishing products based on their production and process methods (PPMs) or based on their carcinogenicity? After *Asbestos*, do you think a panel would find "tuna in oil" and "tuna not in oil" to be like products? With "tuna in oil" carrying a tariff of 35 percent and "tuna not in oil" carrying a tariff of just 6 percent, why hasn't a country challenged this large tariff differential?

Another consideration with respect to negotiated tariffs on PPMs is that the world trading system uses fewer and fewer tariffs. If the basic product can enter a market without any tariff, the only way to establish a tariff "differential" would be to impose a new tariff based on the product made with the disfavored PPM.

4. *Problem Exercise.* Based on the WTO law found in Chapters 3 and 4, create a list of the type of tax and regulatory measures that you think a WTO panel would find acceptable. For example, although the *Asbestos* case turned on human health concerns, is there an analogous environmental situation? After *Asbestos,* do you think a car with a hybrid engine and a car with a traditional gas-powered engine will be considered "like products"? Is beef from cattle raised with hormones the same as beef from cattle never treated with hormones? What about recycled fiber paper and virgin fiber paper? Organic and nonorganic bananas? Genetically modified and heirloom tomatoes? Could the United States impose trade sanctions on the tuna catch from individual boats for failure to comply with the Marine Mammal Protection Act? In any of the above cases, even if the products are deemed not to be "like," are they nevertheless "directly competitive or substitutable"? What would that mean for differing regulatory measures? For differing tax treatment?

5. *Problem Exercise.* In some cases, the environmental and human health objectives seem legitimate (*Asbestos*); in some cases, the supposed environmental and human health

benefits of the trade discrimination seem dubious (*Reformulated Gasoline, Salmon and Herring*) or at least debatable (*Tuna/Dolphin*). Is it good policy to leave judgments about the legitimacy of the underlying objectives to dispute settlement panels? If not, what kind of rules-based system can be created to permit product distinctions that strike a reasonable balance between trade concerns and environmental concerns? Is this possible using the "like product" language of Articles I and III? If yes, how can that be accomplished? If not, what rules and/or factors must we create? In particular, consider how PPMs should be treated.

V. Border Tax Adjustments

A. Environmental Taxes

Economic productivity can be reduced by a variety of environmental problems, including water and air pollution, contamination of ground water resources from solid and hazardous wastes, soil degradation, and soil erosion. *See* THE WORLD BANK, WORLD DEVELOPMENT REPORT 1992: DEVELOPMENT AND THE ENVIRONMENT (1992). To ensure higher economic productivity, as well as to protect human, animal, and plant life and health, governments impose pollution control standards, taxes, and other regulatory restrictions on economic activity. While environmental requirements may increase production costs in the short term, they often reduce costs and increase profits in the long term. UNCTAD, *Environmental Policies, Trade and Competitiveness: Conceptual and Empirical Issues*, TD/B/WG.6/6 (Mar. 29, 1995).

Yet, some businesses complain that strict regulation can make them less competitive in the global marketplace. Small and medium sized enterprises report difficulties in meeting environmental regulations due to their high fixed and variable costs and the difficulty of gaining access to information, finance, technology, and environment-friendly input materials. *Id.* Businesses, and many economists, also contend that market incentives, such as taxes and tradable emissions permits, will more efficiently achieve environmental goals.

Environmental taxes can discourage the consumption of goods and services with higher environmental costs (e.g., high-sulfur fuel) and encourage environmentally sound products and production methods (e.g., taxes on discharges of wastewater). The basic theory of environmental taxes is to more accurately price underpriced and thus overused environmental resources or amenities. Market prices of natural resources such as petroleum and water typically fail to capture the environmental costs associated with their production and use. Perversely, governments often provide access to natural resources at less than the economic cost of their production. Environmental taxes are an attractive alternative for achieving both economic efficiency and environmental protection. However, they may not necessarily be fair, because the poor will spend a larger share of their incomes than the rich for some environmental taxes, especially consumption taxes, such as gasoline taxes. *Greenery and Poverty*, THE ECONOMIST, Sept. 18, 1993, at 80.

Governments may enact three different kinds of environmental taxes. First, taxes can be imposed directly on the sale of a product with undesirable environmental characteristics, such as toxic chemicals, ozone-depleting substances, or gasoline. Second, taxes can be imposed on the use of a natural resource, such as pollution charges for air emissions and water discharges. Third, taxes can be imposed on inputs into products that are either physically incorporated into a product, such as CFCs in a refrigerator, or physically consumed during their production, such as energy to operate machinery and heat a factory. *See* Thomas J. Schoenbaum, *International Trade and Protection of the Environment: The Continuing Search for Reconciliation*, 91 AM. J. INT'L. L. 268, 306 (1997). Whether they are attractive policy options for businesses may depend on whether they are eligible for border tax adjustment under the GATT.

B. An Introduction to Border Tax Adjustments

Border tax adjustments under the GATT allow countries to rebate environmental taxes and fees (although not costs) imposed on products to be exported and assess taxes on imported products equivalent to those imposed on domestic products. Thus, the GATT permits a country to rebate a tax imposed on biofuels or ozone depleting substances destined for export and impose equivalent taxes on imported biofuels and ozone depleting substances. Such border tax adjustments have the potential to maximize each country's environmental policy options while also making their products competitive in the global marketplace. *See* Frieder Roessler, *Diverging Domestic Policies and Multilateral Trade Integration*, *in* 2 FAIR TRADE AND HARMONIZATION 21, 50 (Jagdish Bhagwati & Robert E. Hudec eds., 1997). If a country unloads internal taxes on products prior to export, then those products enter international trade untaxed. If an importing country then imposes a tax on imported goods similar to those assessed on domestic goods, then the imported product does not carry the burden of being taxed by both the importing and exporting country. Moreover, by allowing the importing country to impose a tax, on an imported product equivalent to a tax on like domestic products, the imported product does not receive an advantage in the importing country's market.

The rules on border tax adjustments are scattered within the MFN, national treatment, and subsidies sections of the GATT. For adjustments imposed on imports, Article II:2(a) allows an importing country to assess a "charge equivalent to an internal tax imposed consistently with the provisions of paragraph 2 of Article III in respect of the like domestic product or in respect of an article from which the imported product has been manufactured or produced in whole or in part."

For rebates made to exports, an interpretative note to Article XVI:4 declares that rebates of internal taxes on products shall not be deemed a "subsidy." Article VI:4 further clarifies that rebates of product taxes on exported products do not constitute grounds for antidumping or countervailing duties in the country of import.

GATT Provisions on Border Tax Adjustments

Article II:2(a)—Nothing in this Article shall prevent any Member from imposing at any time on the importation of any product: (a) a charge equivalent to an internal tax imposed consistently with the provisions of paragraph 2 of Article III in respect of the like domestic product or in respect of an article from which the imported product has been manufactured or produced in whole or in part.

Article III:2, first sentence—The products of the territory of any Member imported into the territory of any other Member shall not be subject, directly or indirectly, to internal taxes or other internal charges of any kind in excess of those applied, directly or indirectly, to like domestic products.

Article VI:4—No product of the territory of any contracting party imported into the territory of any other Member shall be subject to anti-dumping or countervailing duty by reason of the exemption of such product from duties or taxes borne by the like product when destined for consumption in the country of origin or exportation, or by reason of the refund of such duties or taxes.

Note Ad Article XVI—The exemption of an exported product from duties or taxes borne by the like product when destined for domestic consumption, or the remission of such duties or taxes in amounts not in excess of those which have accrued, shall not be deemed to be a subsidy.

The GATT parties long ago agreed that only product taxes (also called "indirect taxes"), such as sales, excise, value-added, and other taxes on a product, are eligible for border tax adjustment. Taxes not directly levied on products (called "direct taxes"), such as income, social security, payroll, or corporate taxes, are ineligible. Report of the Working Party on Border Tax Adjustments, Nov. 20, 1970, L/3464, B.I.S.D. 18th Supp. 97, para. 18 (1972). Despite this relatively straightforward set of rules, border tax adjustments remain "[o]ne of the more perplexing trade-policy problems" and subject to significant controversy. JOHN JACKSON, THE WORLD TRADING SYSTEM 218 (2d ed. 1998).

Tension arises because major trading partners rely on different types of taxes. The EU and many other major trading countries rely heavily on value-added taxes that are eligible for border tax adjustment. In contrast, the United States relies heavily on corporate income taxes, including income from sales abroad, that are ineligible for border tax adjustment. As a result, the EU can raise the price of imports significantly and reduce the price of exports through border tax adjustment. The United States and other countries relying on direct taxes cannot. Assuming that EU exporters do not pay income taxes equivalent to U.S. manufacturers, the portion of their export price associated with taxes should be lower and their goods correspondingly cheaper.

The disparity in treatment of taxes is sometimes defended with the argument that indirect taxes can be more readily calculated and thus "shifted forward" to the purchaser. In contrast, direct taxes such as income taxes are borne primarily by the suppliers of capital investment ("origin" based) and shifted "backward." Of course, both direct and indirect taxes can impose burdens on both the purchaser and the provider of capital. *See* Report of the Working Party on Border Tax Adjustments, Nov. 20, 1970, L/3464, B.I.S.D. 18th Supp. 97 (1972); GARY C. HUFBAUER & J.S. ERB, SUBSIDIES IN INTERNATIONAL TRADE 23 (1984). For example, a producer may decide not to shift the burden of paying a value-added tax to the consumer to be more competitive, even if it means lower profits. Similarly, manufacturers in "income tax" countries can increase the cost of a product and shift the costs of an income tax to the purchaser. Economists suggest that as much as 20 percent of corporate tax is shifted forward to consumers in the short term and as much as 60 to 75 percent in the long term. *See* JOHN JACKSON, THE WORLD TRADING SYSTEM, at 220. The GATT's continued distinction between direct and indirect taxes for border tax adjustment thus appears based more on "tradition and practicality" than economics. Thomas J. Schoenbaum, *International Trade and Protection of the Environment,* at 307.

More critically for environmentalists, border tax adjustments cannot be made for taxes imposed on processes and production methods, because these are nonproduct direct taxes. Economists claim that taxes on products are less efficient than taxes on externalities from processes and production methods, because the export price will not equal social costs. Charles S. Pearson & Robert Repetto, *Reconciling Trade and Environment: The Next Steps, in* TRADE AND ENVIRONMENT COMMITTEE OF THE NATIONAL ADVISORY COUN-

CIL FOR ENVIRONMENTAL POLICY AND TECHNOLOGY, THE GREENING OF WORLD TRADE 83, 96 (1993). Moreover, border tax adjustments may be more efficient than trade bans. By favoring indirect product taxes, the GATT rules discourage an economically efficient means for addressing environmental problems at their source.

Moreover, it is not clear to what extent border tax adjustments can be used to offset taxes on certain inputs, such as the amount of energy consumed in the production of a product. Such taxes, known as *taxes occultes*, are generally defined as consumption taxes on capital equipment, auxiliary materials, and services used in transportation and protection of other taxable goods. They also include taxes on advertising, energy, machinery, and transport. Working Party on Border Tax Adjustments, at para. 15(a). As the *Superfund* case demonstrates, border tax adjustments are permissible for environment-related purposes, including certain inputs, provided that the inputs remain in the product itself.

C. The Superfund Case

The GATT Panel in *Superfund* reviewed three taxes levied under the U.S. Superfund Amendments and Reauthorization Act of 1986 (hereinafter referred to as the "Superfund Act"): a tax on petroleum, a tax on certain chemicals ("feedstock chemicals"), and a tax on certain imported substances produced with or manufactured from taxable feedstock chemicals. The Superfund, a fund to clean up hazardous waste sites, was financed by these taxes. The Panel's discussion of the tax on products produced with the listed feedstock chemicals (final products containing more than 50% by weight of feedstock chemicals) has particular relevance for the types of energy consumption taxes that may be eligible for border tax adjustment because that tax was not imposed on the imported product itself but rather on an intermediate product contained in the imported product. The possible use of energy taxes or marketable emissions rights regimes, especially to implement national climate mitigation programs, is discussed after the *Superfund* case.

United States-Taxes on Petroleum and Certain Imported Substances

GATT Panel Report, L/6175, B.I.S.D. 34th Supp. 136 (1988)
(adopted June 17, 1987)

2. Factual aspects * * *

2.2 The tax on petroleum, which had been imposed at the rate of 0.79 cent per barrel for both domestic and imported products, was increased to 8.2 cents per barrel for "crude oil received at a United States refinery" and 11.7 cents a barrel for "petroleum products entered into the United States for consumption, use or warehousing." The term "crude oil" is defined to include crude oil condensate and natural gasoline. The term "petroleum products" is defined to comprise not only the products defined as "crude oil" but also refined gasoline, refined and residual oil, and certain other liquid hydrocarbon products....

2.3 The Superfund Act reimposed a tax on certain chemicals with effect from 1 January 1987.... The tax is borne by the chemicals whether they are sold by the manufacturer, producer or importer thereof. The tax is not imposed if the manufacturer or producer of the taxable chemical sells it for export or for resale by the purchaser to a second purchaser for export.

2.4 The Superfund Act further imposes a new tax on certain imported substances sold or used by the importer thereof.... The taxable substances are derivatives of the chemicals subject to the tax on certain chemicals described in the preceding paragraph. A substance shall be added to the list if the Secretary of the Treasury, in consultation with the Administrator of the Environmental Protection Agency and the Commissioner of Customs, determined that chemicals subject to the tax on certain chemicals constitute more than 50 per cent of the weight of the materials used to produce such substance (determined on the basis of the predominant method of production). He may also, to the extent necessary to carry out the purposes of the legislation, add any substance to the list if the value of the taxable chemicals constitutes more than 50 per cent of the total value of the materials used to produce the substance....

2.5 The amount of tax on any of the imported substances equals in principle the amount of the tax which would have been imposed under the Superfund Act on the chemicals used as materials in the manufacture or production of the imported substance if the taxable chemicals had been sold in the United States for use in the manufacture or production of the imported substance. * * *

5. Findings and Conclusions

5.1 Tax on petroleum

[As discussed on page 177, the Panel concluded that the tax on petroleum products was inconsistent with Article III:2, because foreign petroleum products paid a tax 3.5 cents per barrel higher than the rate applied to the like domestic products. Any difference in the tax that favors domestic producers constitutes a *prima facie* case of nullification and impairment.].

5.2 Tax on certain imported substances * * *

5.2.3 The Panel noted that the United States justified the tax on certain imported substances as a border tax adjustment corresponding in its effect to the internal tax on certain chemicals from which these substances were derived (paragraph 3.2.5 above). The Panel further noted that the EEC [European Economic Community] considered the tax on certain chemicals not to be eligible for border tax adjustment because it was designed to tax polluting activities that occurred in the United States and to finance environmental programmes benefiting only United States producers. Consistent with the Polluter-Pays Principle, the United States should have taxed only products of domestic origin because only their production gave rise to environmental problems in the United States. The United States denied the legal relevance of EEC's arguments and their applicability to the tax on certain chemicals.... The Panel therefore first examined whether the tax on certain chemicals was eligible for border tax adjustments.

5.2.4 * * * As these conclusions of the CONTRACTING PARTIES [as noted in the report of the Working Party on Border Tax Adjustments] clearly indicate, the tax adjustment rules of the General Agreement distinguish between taxes on products and taxes not directly levied on products; they do not distinguish between taxes with different policy purposes. Whether a sales tax is levied on a product for general revenue purposes or to encourage the rational use of environmental resources, is therefore not relevant for the determination of the eligibility of a tax for border tax adjustment. For these reasons the Panel concluded that the tax on certain chemicals, being a tax directly imposed on products, was eligible for border tax adjustment independent of the purpose it served. The Panel therefore did not examine whether the tax on chemicals served environmental purposes and, if so, whether a border tax adjustment would be consistent with these purposes.

5.2.5 The Panel wishes to point out, however, that the Working Party on Border Tax Adjustment agreed that the provisions of the General Agreement on tax adjustment

> "set maxima limits for adjustment (compensation) which were not to be exceeded, but below which every contracting party was free to differentiate in the degree of compensation applied, provided that such action was in conformity with other provisions of the General Agreement."

Consequently, if a contracting party wishes to tax the sale of certain domestic products (because their production pollutes the domestic environment) and to impose a lower tax or no tax at all on like imported products (because their consumption or use causes fewer or no environmental problems), it is in principle free to do so. The General Agreement's rules on tax adjustment thus give the contracting party in such a case the possibility to follow the Polluter-Pays Principle, but they do not oblige it to do so.

5.2.6 The mandate of the Panel is to examine the case before it "in the light of the relevant GATT provisions" (paragraph 1.4 above). The Panel therefore did not examine the consistency of the revenue provisions in the Superfund Act with the environmental objectives of that Act or with the Polluter-Pays Principle. * * *

5.2.7 The Panel, having concluded that the tax on certain chemicals was in principle eligible for border tax adjustment, then examined whether the tax on certain imported substances meets the national treatment requirement of Article III:2, first sentence. This provision permits the imposition of an internal tax on imported products provided the like domestic products are taxed, directly or indirectly, at the same or a higher rate. Such internal taxes may be levied on imported products at the time or point of importation (Note ad Article III). Paragraph 2(a) of Article II therefore clarifies that a tariff concession does not prevent the levying of

> "a charge equivalent to an internal tax imposed consistently with the provisions of paragraph 2 of Article III in respect of the like domestic product or in respect of an article from which the imported product has been manufactured or produced in whole or in part."

The drafters of the General Agreement explained the word "equivalent" used in this provision with the following example:

> "If a charge is imposed on perfume because it contains alcohol, the charge to be imposed must take into consideration the value of the alcohol and not the value of the perfume, that is to say the value of the content and not the value of the whole."

5.2.8 The tax on certain imported substances equals in principle the amount of the tax which would have been imposed under the Superfund Act on the chemicals used as materials in the manufacture or production of the imported substance if these chemicals had been sold in the United States for use in the manufacture or production of the imported substance. In the words which the drafters of the General Agreement used in the above perfume-alcohol example: The tax is imposed on the imported substances because they are produced from chemicals subject to an excise tax in the United States and the tax rate is determined in principle in relation to the amount of these chemicals used and not in relation to the value of the imported substance. The Panel therefore concluded that, to the extent that the tax on certain imported substances was equivalent to the tax borne by like domestic substances as a result of the tax on certain chemicals, the tax met the national treatment requirement of Article III:2, first sentence.

5.2.10 The Panel concluded that the tax on certain imported substances constituted a tax adjustment corresponding to the tax on certain chemicals that was in principle consistent with Article III:2, first sentence, and that the existence of the penalty rate provisions as such did not constitute an infringement of Article III:2, first sentence, since the tax authorities had regulatory power to eliminate the need for the imposition of the penalty rate. The Panel recommends that the CONTRACTING PARTIES take note of the statement by the United States that the penalty rate would in all probability never be applied.

———————

Questions and Discussion

1. *The Polluter Pays Principle.* The *Superfund* case mixes domestic and international environmental policy with international trade law because the EU invoked the Polluter Pays Principle to try to invalidate the U.S. taxes on petroleum and chemicals. The Polluter Pays Principle is an important principle of international environmental law designed to ensure that polluters pay the full environmental and social costs of their activities and internalize their costs. *See supra* pages 24–27.

The Panel refused to consider whether the tax on certain chemicals was inconsistent with the Polluter Pays Principle. In paragraph 3.2.8 of *Superfund*, the Panel notes that the EU argued: "What the United States was in fact doing under the label of border tax adjustments was to ask foreign producers to help defray the costs of cleaning up the environment for the United States industries." According to the United States (see paragraph 3.2.9), the Polluter Pays Principle was not part of GATT law, and thus "irrelevant" to the case at hand:

> Environmental policy principles related to trade could conceivably be incorporated into the GATT legal system, but such a far-reaching step required the cooperation of all contracting parties and could be taken only after considerable study and discussion. A reinterpretation of the existing GATT rules on border tax adjustments would not be the proper vehicle to introduce such principles.

In the end, the *Superfund* panel simply refused to consider the Polluter Pays Principle. Was that the right result? At least one court, the Indian Supreme Court, has ruled that the Polluter Pays Principle constitutes a norm of customary international law. Vellore Citizens Welfare Forum v. Union of India & Ors., PIL 1981–97, p.703, *available at* http://www.elaw.org/node/2555. Another Indian court found that companies conducting hazardous or inherently dangerous activities are:

> absolutely liable to compensate for the harm caused by them to villagers in the affected area, to the soil and to the underground water and hence, they are bound

to take all necessary measures to remove sludge and other pollutants lying in the affected areas.' The "Polluter Pays" principle as interpreted by this Court means that the absolute liability for harm to the environment extends not only to compensate the victims of pollution but also the cost of restoring the environmental degradation. Remediation of the damaged environment is part of the process of "Sustainable Development" and as such polluter is liable to pay the cost to the individual suffers as well as the cost of reversing the damaged ecology.

Indian Council for Enviro-Legal Action vs. Union of India, J.T. 1996 (2) 196, *available at* http:// www.elaw.org/note/2749. Is a tax on hazardous and toxic substances a reasonable way to ensure that those costs can be paid?

2. Dan Esty argues that, as a matter of equity, the GATT's border tax adjustments mechanism should cover taxes imposed on processes and production methods. That small change would "minimize the unfairness of border tax adjustments and create an incentive for governments to shift environmental regulation toward the use of pollution charges to internalize costs. This would at the same time move environmental regulation toward more efficient and less trade-restrictive market mechanisms." DANIEL ESTY, GREENING THE GATT: TRADE ENVIRONMENT AND THE FUTURE 169 (1994). Do you agree?

3. Is a pollution tax a product tax (indirect) or a nonproduct (direct) tax? Most concur that it is a nonproduct tax. However, at least one author has argued that an "effluent tax [is] not a tax, but the pricing of an input into product environmental services which previously had been supplied at less than cost. From that perspective, the effluent tax would be viewed as simply another payment to a factor of production." Charles Pearson, *Environmental Control Costs and Border Adjustments*, 27 NAT'L TAX J. 599, 604 (1974). Is this argument persuasive? For a discussion of pre-GATT treaties that appear to permit border tax adjustments for taxes on processing, see Steve Charnovitz, *Free Trade, Fair Trade, Green Trade: Defogging the Debate*, 27 CORNELL INT'L L.J. 459, 502 (1994).

––––––––––

D. National Climate Legislation and Border Adjustments

Global warming—the earth's average surface temperature has increased by about 0.75 degrees Celsius in the last 100 years—is "unequivocal." INTERGOVERNMENTAL PANEL ON CLIMATE CHANGE (IPCC), FOURTH ASSESSMENT REPORT: CLIMATE CHANGE 2007, SYNTHESIS REPORT, 1.1. Studies show that "many natural systems are [already] being affected by regional climate changes." *Id.* at 1.2. Climate change is being driven in large part by increases in atmospheric concentrations of long-lived greenhouse gases (GHGs), such as carbon dioxide, methane, nitrous oxides, and halocarbons. According to the IPCC's 2007 assessment, "Most of the observed increase in global average temperatures since the mid-20th century is very likely due to the observed increase in anthropogenic GHG concentrations." *Id.* at 2.4.

Carbon dioxide (CO_2) emissions from the combustion of fossil fuels are the dominant human factor contributing to climate change. Such combustion added nearly 32 gigatons of CO_2 (8.7 Gt of carbon) to the atmosphere in 2008. To reduce emissions of GHGs, more than 190 countries have ratified the United Nations Framework Convention on Climate Change (UNFCCC), a product of the 1992 United Nations Conference on Environment and Development. In 1997, the parties to the UNFCCC signed the Kyoto Protocol, which establishes targets and timetables (technically called quantified emissions limitation and reduction objectives) for developed countries through 2012. The Kyoto Protocol created framework mechanisms for reducing GHGs, including tradable emissions permits. Parties may also use "joint implementation" projects through which countries or their companies reduce GHG emissions through investments in other countries and get "carbon credits" for reducing emissions from those investments. The United States is not a party to the Kyoto Protocol. After the less-than-definitive outcome of the 15th Conference of the Parties to the UNFCCC (COP15) in Copenhagen in December 2009, the future of the Kyoto Protocol beyond 2012 is unclear. Nonetheless, governments, including the United States, are taking action or contemplating action to address climate change through domestic legislation. Many of these proposals contemplate some form of border adjustment to ensure that domestic companies are not placed at a competitive disadvantage against their foreign counterparts.

1. Carbon or Energy Taxes

a. Carbon Taxes

Carbon taxes are one strategy for creating economic incentives for privately controlled sources to reduce their GHG emissions. Sweden, for example, has had carbon taxes in place for some time, the Canadian province of British Columbia instituted them in 2008, and France is implementing them in 2010. Many of these taxes are calculated according to the carbon content of energy products, such as coal, crude oil, or gasoline. Because taxes on energy products are indirect taxes relating to the product, they are eligible for border tax adjustment. Thus, countries may place domestic producers of energy products on equal footing with foreign producers by taxing imported energy products, provided that the taxes on imported energy products are not in excess of those imposed on domestic energy products. Further, to ensure that domestic sources are not placed at a competitive disadvantage in international markets, countries may rebate the tax for exported energy products. Taxes on imported energy products are similar to the taxes on certain imported substances at issue in *Superfund*. Recall the Panel's legal conclusion that the tax on certain chemicals was consistent with the GATT's rules on border tax adjustments:

> The tax is imposed on the imported substances because they are produced from chemicals subject to an excise tax in the United States and the tax rate is determined in principle in relation to the amount of these chemicals used and not in relation to the value of the imported substance. The Panel therefore concluded that, to the extent that the tax on certain imported substances was equivalent to the tax borne by like domestic substances as a result of the tax on certain chemicals, the tax met the national treatment requirement of Article III:2, first sentence.

Superfund, at para. 5.2.8. *See also* Thomas J. Schoenbaum, *International Trade and Protection of the Environment*, at 308.

In practice, however, the border tax question does not arise for most carbon taxes. Typically, carbon taxes are collected at the point of sale to consumers, not from the producers of the fuels themselves, so there is no distinction in the marketplace between domestic and imported fuel sources.

----

b. Taxes on Carbon Emissions

While taxes based on the energy content of energy products are eligible for border tax adjustment, any taxes or charges on emitting sources based on their calculated carbon emissions are not. Such taxes, like taxes on other pollution discharges, constitute direct taxes on the manufacturing process. Barring an international agreement on emissions taxes, the inability to adjust these taxes has been a major disincentive to their adoption by individual nations.

––––––––––

c. Taxes on Energy Inputs to Products

There are some products, such as plastics or paints, where the energy input is physically incorporated into the product. As with taxes on the energy content of energy products and taxes on certain chemicals in *Superfund*, these taxes are indirect taxes imposed on a constituent element of the product, and would therefore be eligible for border tax adjustments.

With relation to national efforts to reduce carbon emissions, the more widespread situation is one where energy is consumed in making the product, but is not contained in or incorporated into the product itself. The products of so-called energy intensive industries, such as iron and steel, glass, chemicals, or paper, are in this class. How do the GATT rules apply to these products?

Recall that indirect taxes, such as sales, excise, turnover, and value added taxes, are product related and eligible for border tax adjustment. Direct taxes, such as taxes on wages, profits, and income, are not eligible for border tax adjustment. However, governments have never clearly determined the eligibility for border tax adjustment of *taxes occultes*: taxes on energy, transportation, and equipment used in production. Although the GATT has discussed these taxes, it has concluded only that there is a "divergence of views" on whether *taxes occultes* are eligible for border tax adjustment. Working Party on Border Tax Adjustments, at para. 15.

In light of this failure to make a definitive ruling, some argue that taxes on energy consumption are not eligible for border tax adjustment with respect to *imports*. They argue that Article II:2(a) allows for border tax adjustment only with respect to inputs "from which the imported product has been manufactured." It does not refer to inputs "with the help of which" the imported products are produced. Thomas J. Schoenbaum, *International Trade and Protection of the Environment*, at 310 (citing Kristina Havercamp, The GATT and Environmental Protection 107 (1993) (unpublished LL.M. thesis)). See *also* Daniel C. Esty, Greening the GATT, at 168; Paul Demaret & Raoul Stewardson, *Border Tax Adjustments under GATT and EC Law and General Implications for Environmental Taxes*, 28 J. World Trade 5 (1994).

Nonetheless, some support can be found in *Superfund* that such taxes on imported products may be eligible for border tax adjustment for energy consumed. That Panel interpreted the phrase in Article II:2(a) relating to taxes in respect of "an article from which the imported product has been manufactured or produced in whole or in part" as permitting border tax adjustments for taxes on products "*used as materials in*" the production or manufacture of a final product. Superfund, at para. 5.2.8 (emphasis added). This language could be read to broaden the plain language of Article II:2(a) to include materials not physically incorporated in the final product. Which is the better argument?

With respect to rebates of consumption taxes on energy inputs not physically incorporated into an *exported* product, the rules are, if not more ambiguous, then certainly more complex. Paragraph (h) of Annex I and Annex II of the Agreement on Subsidies and Countervailing Measures (the SCM Agreement) permit rebates of prior stage cumulative indirect taxes "levied on inputs that are consumed in the production of the exported product." Such language covers, for example, value added taxes on product inputs. Are consumption taxes on energy products among the covered "inputs"? Are they in the class of "prior stage cumulative indirect taxes"?

Footnote 61 of Annex II appears to expressly answer the first question. It states that inputs consumed in the production process include inputs physically incorporated in the product as well as "energy fuels and oil used in the production process."

On the second question, a consumption tax must be 1) indirect, 2) prior-stage, and 3) cumulative. Energy taxes are indirect, because Footnote 58 defines indirect taxes as all those that are not direct taxes. Direct taxes include "taxes on wages, profits, interests, rents, royalties and all other forms of income, and taxes on the ownership of property." Taxes on inputs consumed in the production process do not fall into any of the categories of direct taxes.

Such taxes are also arguably "prior stage indirect taxes." Footnote 58 of Annex I defines "prior stage indirect taxes" as "those levied on goods or services used *directly or indirectly* in making a product" (emphasis added). One example of a prior-stage tax is a tax on diodes, resistors, and other parts used to make a computer. Although energy does not become a constituent element of a resulting product as a resistor becomes a part of a computer, energy is a good used to make a product. Footnote 58 may thus encompass taxes on energy consumed in the production of an exported product as prior-stage taxes eligible for border tax adjustment.

Whether energy taxes are "cumulative" is more debatable. Footnote 58 of the SCM Agreement defines "cumulative indirect taxes" as "multi-staged taxes levied where there is no subsequent crediting of the tax if the goods or services subject to tax at one stage of production are used in a succeeding stage of production." A multi-stage tax is a tax assessed on different stages of production and distribution of the same product. Value-added taxes are the classic example, because a product is taxed each time value is added to it. Value-added taxes are noncumulative, however, because the tax previously paid is offset against the amount of value-added tax payable on the resulting product. Demaret & Stewardson, at 21. Cumulative taxes are taxes imposed on each sale of a product during its entire manufacturing process. The tax is assessed based on the value of the product at the time of sale and no offsets are made for taxed paid at earlier stages. *Id.* at 22.

Schoenbaum concludes that environmental taxes such as carbon and energy taxes are generally cumulative. Thomas J. Schoenbaum, *International Trade and Protection of the Environment,* at 311. Steve Charnovitz, however, believes they are indirect, noncumulative, specific (single-stage) taxes that would fall under paragraph (g), not paragraph (h), of Annex I of the SCM Agreement. Steve Charnovitz, *Free Trade, Fair Trade, Green Trade,* at 504. The SCM Agreement in Annex I, paragraph (g) permits rebates of indirect taxes "in respect of the production and distribution of exported products." Because paragraph (h) is intended to address taxes on inputs into products, it is unlikely that the phrase "in respect of production ... of exported products" in paragraph (g) can also refer to inputs into the production process.

These provisions have already caused anxiety among the United States, the European Union, and others, who apparently have negotiated a "gentlemen's agreement" not to interpret these provisions as permitting border tax adjustments for energy taxes. The agreement apparently states that Footnote 61 applies only to a limited number of countries that use a system of cumulative indirect taxes. Demaret & Stewardson, at 30; *U.S. Secures Agreement Not to Use GATT to Allow Energy Tax Rebate,* Inside U.S. Trade

(Inside Washington, Washington, D.C.), Jan. 28, 1994, at 19. Nonetheless, as Schoenbaum writes, "This 'gentlemen's agreement' is not, however, part of the public record. It also countermands the plain meaning of the text of the agreement; under recognized principles of treaty interpretation, it should be disregarded." Thus, Schoenbaum concludes that, with respect to rebates of consumption taxes on exported products, border tax adjustment:

> is permissible for certain *taxes occultes*, environmental taxes on energy and other inputs that are consumed in the production process. This conclusion is supported by the literal language of the cited Subsidies [Agreement] provisions. In addition, as Henry Thaggart points out, both the VAT and the cascade (or turnover) tax include, in effect, taxes on inputs that are not physically incorporated in the final product. A tax on the energy input of a product is clearly an indirect tax.

Thomas J. Schoenbaum, *International Trade and Protection of the Environment*, at 311.

–––––––––––

Questions and Discussion

1. While rebating energy taxes on exports may help sell an energy tax, such rebates may not provide any environmental benefit because the rebate externalizes environmental costs that were otherwise internalized. However, as Steve Charnovitz argues, border tax adjustments of energy taxes could have an environmental benefit:

> In the absence of a border adjustment for factor taxes [*taxes occultes*] a country that imposes energy taxes will feel that similar, but untaxed imports have an unfair advantage. Less expensive imports have no direct impact on the environment, of course. But, if a country is politically unable to levy appropriate taxes on domestic production because of the competitive effects of untaxed imports, that inability can have environmental significance.

Steve Charnovitz, *Free Trade, Fair Trade, Green Trade*, at 504.

–––––––––––

2. Emissions Trading Systems, "Leakage," and Border Adjustments

Although carbon or energy taxes are viewed by many economists as the best means of raising the price of fossil fuels and thus motivating reductions in GHG emissions, many politicians are loath to raise taxes. In the 1990 amendments to its Clean Air Act, the United States addressed another emissions problem—sulfur dioxide emissions and acid rain—with a different form of economic incentive, known since then as cap-and-trade. The law set a cap on the total emissions of sulfur dioxide, declining over time, along with an allocation to existing sources of tradable rights to emit sulfur dioxide. The rights, good for one year, would become increasingly scarce as the emissions cap declined. The economic principle behind such a cap-and-trade system is that those sources able to reduce emissions cheaply would cut their emissions more than required and sell the rights they would not need to other sources who need extra rights because they were not able to reduce their emissions efficiently. The cap would assure that the overall environmental target would be met, but the average cost of emission reductions would be much lower than in a normal command approach requiring proportionally equal reductions from all.

The acid rain cap-and-trade program is generally considered a success, achieving reductions in a timely manner at far below estimated costs. With that positive experience, the United States persuaded other countries to allow a similar approach to reducing GHG emissions under the Kyoto Protocol. In the end, although the United States did not become a party to the Protocol, other countries that accepted obligations to reduce GHG emissions have used cap-and-trade systems. The most notable example is the European Union's Emissions Trading System.

The U.S. Congress has seriously debated climate legislation in recent years, and all the current bills are based on an emissions trading approach to reducing U.S. GHG emissions. But another issue has entered the debate: leakage. In climate mitigation terminology, "leakage" refers to the possibility that emissions reduction mandates in a developed country like the United States might force some industries to curtail production, but the resulting reduction in emissions would "leak" to a developing country through increased production at industries not subject to GHG controls. Since the international goal is to reduce GHG emissions worldwide, the leakage would offset the control efforts in developed countries and give industries in developing countries a competitive advantage as well. There is special concern in connection with energy-intensive industries that would presumably face relatively high emissions control costs.

Careful analyses of energy-intensive industries, emissions, and international trade suggest that the leakage-competitiveness linkage might be more apparent than real. A U.S. Environmental Protection Agency analysis of proposed legislation concluded that only 8 to 11 percent of emissions reductions in the United States would be offset by emission increases in other countries. US EPA, ANALYSIS OF THE LIEBERMAN-WARNER CLIMATE SECURITY ACT OF 2008 (2008). Another analysis found that the sources of energy-intensive goods imported into the U.S. "are, in many industries, less carbon-intensive than the United States." TREVOR HOUSER ET AL., LEVELING THE CARBON PLAYING FIELD 46 (2008). On the other hand, U.S. imports from China in energy-intensive products could increase by about 7 percent if the United States controlled GHG emissions and China did not.

Regardless of the true magnitude of the leakage problem, the comprehensive climate change legislation currently pending in the U.S. Congress, H.R. 2998, known as the Waxman-Markey bill, addresses the leakage issue through explicit border adjustment trade measures. How do those border adjustments stack up under WTO law?

Sanford E. Gaines, *Considering WTO Law in the Design of Climate Change Regimes beyond Kyoto*

IOP CONF. SERIES: EARTH AND ENVIRONMENTAL SCIENCE,
vol. 8, 012002, pp. 12–13 (2009)

The most-discussed border adjustment mechanism ... is included in section 401 of H.R. 2998, the bill passed by the U.S. House on 25 June 2009. In proposed amendments that would add sections 765–68 to the U.S. Clean Air Act, H.R. 2998 would establish some GHG emission allowances in an "international reserve," and then would require importers of energy-intensive products to acquire such allowances in sufficient quantity to equal the emission reduction credits associated with a like product from a US firm subject to cap-and-trade emission reductions, at a price equal to the US market price for domestic emission reduction credits. Under H.R. 2998, this carbon-based border adjustment would begin operating in 2020, giving other countries time to adopt equivalent carbon reduction requirements and thereby avoid the border adjustments for their producers. The expressed preference for a multilateral approach and the allowance of time to negotiate it before applying the border adjustments are clearly designed to conform to WTO interpretations of the GATT Article XX environmental exceptions.

Commentators have noted that this international reserve allowance mechanism raises numerous trade law issues. [Editors' note: *see, e.g.,* HOUSER ET AL. cited above.] How many allowances the product would need at the time of import would depend on a system for determining or estimating the GHG emissions associated with the product in comparison to the GHG emissions for the like US product. There is a substantial possibility that any GHG calculation methodology would be skewed by political pressures from US producers. H.R. 2998, for example, assumes that the comparison would be done on a country average basis, not for each producer individually. No matter what system could be devised for assigning or determining GHG emissions related to the product (and just about any system would have comparability and fairness problems because of variation among individual firms and among countries in production facilities and energy sources), the system is inherently designed to distinguish among products based on how they are produced, and to discriminate between products of different countries. The anti-discrimination provisions of GATT Articles I and III prohibit discrimination based on country of origin, and trade law generally does not permit regulation of products based on their method of production.

The only way to save such a trade provision from violation of trade law would be through the exception offered for many environmental measures under GATT Article XX. But the chapeau of Article XX itself prohibits "arbitrary or unjustifiable discrimination" between imported products from two different countries, or between imported and domestic products. It is difficult to say whether such a system would avoid such discrimination; much would depend on the details of the legislation and the way in which the law would be administered. At the very least, the border adjustment mechanism is highly controversial as a matter of trade policy, and might be found in violation of WTO obligations. It has also aroused strong political opposition from key developing countries such as India and China. A proposal by France to add a similar border adjustment in the EU ETS has met resistance from many other European governments.

Questions and Discussion

1. Recall the issues raised in section IV.D.2 of this chapter on PPM-based trade measures. Howse and Regan favor the opportunity to differentiate products based on their PPMs but oppose country-based measures. Is there a practical way for Congress to meet the carbon leakage concern through border adjustments without basing the adjustments on country of origin?

2. In another excerpt in IV.D.2, Steve Charnovitz appealed for an international negotiation approach to PPM-based product standards. Is that a better way to go? Suppose that a new protocol to the UNFCCC or an extension and expansion of the Kyoto Protocol is negotiated that includes emissions reduction commitments for the major developing countries but ones that are less stringent than those for the developed countries. Should

U.S. legislation accept that compliance with such an internationally-agreed range of commitments would displace the "equivalent to the U.S." approach to border adjustments in Waxman-Markey? Would U.S. industry accept such an arrangement? How would a WTO dispute settlement panel likely use such an international agreement in deciding on the trade legality of the Waxman-Markey approach?

VI. Trade Discrimination in the Domestic Law of Federal Systems

A. The "Dormant" Commerce Clause in the United States

The first federated government of the independent United States under the Articles of Confederation experienced numerous governance failures that led to the drafting and adoption of the United States Constitution. One of the governance failures under the Articles of Confederation was that each of the 13 states adopted tariffs and other barriers to trade with the other states; the consequent disruption of trade among the states contributed to the economic maladies of the period. Thus, one of the key objectives of the new constitution was to establish a truly national economy. Article I, Section 8 grants exclusive authority to the U.S. Congress to "lay and collect Taxes, Duties, Imposts and Excises," and specifies that "all Duties, Imposts and Excises shall be uniform throughout the United States." This clause of the Constitution thus establishes the United States as what we would now call a "customs union"—a group of states that has uniform tariffs with respect to the rest of the world. As we will see in the next section, the European Union is built on the same model.

In further support of a national economy, Article I, Section 8 also contains what is known as the Commerce Clause: "The Congress shall have Power ... [t]o regulate Commerce with foreign Nations, and among the several States, and with the Indian Tribes." While the Commerce Clause relates to both foreign commerce and commerce within the United States, this section focuses on the latter. We examine the consequences of the Commerce Clause on the tax and regulatory autonomy of the 50 American states—an autonomy expressly "reserved to the States" by the Tenth Amendment—when the exercise of that autonomy has effects on "commerce among the several states," that is, interstate commerce.

The Commerce Clause is clear about the power of Congress to make laws regulating interstate commerce. Over time, an enormous body of national regulatory law has been enacted under this authority, including regulation of railroads, trucking, and aviation; regulation of agricultural production and pricing; consumer protection legislation; food safety and drug regulation; and environmental regulation. The Commerce Clause, however, says nothing about any constraints on the reserved authority of states to tax and to regulate in areas where Congress has not exercised its power.

What has emerged to fill this gap is a judicially-formulated doctrine of the "negative" or "dormant" Commerce Clause. Consider the following three Supreme Court cases. What are the key considerations the Court invokes in reaching its decisions. Does the Court define clear boundaries for the "dormant" Commerce Clause? How does U.S. doctrine differ from WTO law? Is it more protective or less protective of local choice in matters of environmental protection?

City of Philadelphia v. New Jersey
437 U.S. 617; 98 S. Ct. 2531; 57 L. Ed. 2d 47 (1978)

JUSTICE STEWART delivered the opinion of the Court.

[The City of Philadelphia challenged the constitutionality of a New Jersey state law that prohibited the import of almost all waste originating outside New Jersey. The lower court had upheld the New Jersey law as consistent with the Commerce Clause.]

The opinions of the Court through the years have reflected an alertness to the evils of "economic isolation" and protectionism, while at the same time recognizing that incidental burdens on interstate commerce may be unavoidable when a State legislates to safeguard the health and safety of its people.... The crucial inquiry, therefore, must be directed to determining whether ch. 363 [the New Jersey law being challenged] is basically a protectionist measure, or whether it can fairly be viewed as a law directed to legitimate local concerns, with effects upon interstate commerce that are only incidental.

[The Court then considered the competing arguments of the parties. New Jersey claimed that the law was necessary to conserve landfill space and protect the environment from pollution until such time as better waste disposal technologies become available. Philadelphia argued that the real purpose of the law was to protect economic interests in New Jersey by keeping waste disposal costs low.]

This dispute about ultimate legislative purpose need not be resolved, because its resolution would not be relevant to the constitutional issue to be decided by this case. Contrary to the evident assumption of the state court and the parties, the evils of protectionism can reside in legislative means as well as legislative ends. Thus, it does not matter whether the ultimate aim of ch. 363 is to reduce the waste disposal costs of New Jersey residents or to save remaining open lands from pollution, for we assume New Jersey has every right to protect its residents' pocketbooks as well as their environment. And it may be assumed as well that New Jersey may pursue those ends by slowing the flow of *all* waste into the State's remaining landfills, even though interstate commerce may be incidentally affected. But whatever New Jersey's ultimate purpose, it may not be accomplished by discriminating against articles of commerce coming from outside the State unless there is some reason, apart from their origin, to treat them differently. Both on its face and in its plain effect, ch. 363 violates this principle of nondiscrimination. * * *

The appellees argue that not all laws which facially discriminate against out-of-state commerce are forbidden protectionist regulations. * * *

It is true that certain quarantine laws have not been considered protectionist measures, even though they were directed against out-of-state commerce. But those quarantine laws banned the importation of articles such as diseased livestock that required destruction as soon as possible because their very movement risked contagion and other evils. Those laws thus did not discriminate against interstate commerce as such but simply prevented traffic in noxious articles, whatever their origin.

The New Jersey statute is not such a quarantine law. There has been no claim here that the very movement of waste into or through New Jersey endangers health, or that waste must be disposed of as soon and as close to its point of generation as possible. The harms caused by waste are said to arise after its disposal in landfill sites, and at that point, as New Jersey concedes, there is no basis to distinguish out-of-state waste from domestic waste. If one is inherently harmful, so is the other. Yet New Jersey has banned the former while leaving its landfill sites open to the latter. The New Jersey law blocks the importation of waste in an obvious effort to saddle those outside the State with the entire burden of slowing the flow of refuse into New Jersey's remaining landfill sites. That legislative effort is clearly impermissible under the Commerce Clause of the Constitution.

JUSTICE REHNQUIST, with whom the Chief Justice joins, dissenting. * * *

The health and safety hazards associated with landfills present the appellees with a currently unsolvable dilemma. Other, hopefully safer, methods of disposing of solid wastes are still in the development stage and cannot presently be used. But appellees obviously cannot completely stop the tide of solid waste that its citizens will produce in the interim. For the moment, therefore, appellees must continue to use sanitary landfills to dispose of New Jersey's own solid waste despite the critical environmental problems thereby created.

The question presented in this case is whether New Jersey must also continue to receive and dispose of solid waste from neighboring States, even though those will inexorably increase the health problems discussed above. The Court answers this question in the affirmative. New Jersey must either prohibit *all* landfill operations, leaving itself to cast about for a presently nonexistent solution to the serious problem of disposing of the waste generated within its own borders, or it must accept waste from every portion of the United States, thereby multiplying the health and safety problems which would result if it dealt only with such wastes generated within the State. Because past precedents [the quarantine cases] establish that the Commerce Clause does not present appellees with such a Hobson's choice, I dissent.

The following case could be thought of as a GATT Article III:2 case. The State of Alabama agreed to accept the hazardous waste of other states, but it wanted to tax the disposal of that out-of-state waste at a higher rate than the disposal of Alabama waste. Consider the parallels with WTO jurisprudence. In what ways does the Supreme Court's analysis of these questions differ from that of the WTO Appellate Body?

Chemical Waste Management, Inc. v. Hunt

504 U.S. 334; 112 S. Ct. 2009; 119 L. Ed. 2d 121 (1992)

JUSTICE WHITE delivered the opinion of the Court.

[Since 1978, Chemical Waste Management, Inc. has owned and operated a hazardous waste treatment, storage, and disposal facility in Emelle, Alabama. Alabama was one of only 16 States with commercial hazardous waste landfills, and the Emelle facility was the largest of the 21 landfills of this kind located in these 16 States. Increasing amounts of out-of-state hazardous wastes were being shipped to the Emelle facility for permanent storage each year. From 1985 through 1989, the tonnage of hazardous waste received per year more than doubled, from 341,000 tons in 1985 to 788,000 tons by 1989. Of this, up to 90 percent of the tonnage permanently buried each year was shipped in from other states.]

Against this backdrop Alabama enacted Act No. 90-326 (Act).... Among other provisions, the Act includes a "cap" that generally limits the amount of hazardous wastes or substances that may be disposed of in any 1-year period, and the amount of hazardous waste disposed of during the first year under the Act's new fees becomes the permanent ceiling in subsequent years. The cap applies to commercial facilities that dispose of over 100,000 tons of hazardous wastes or substances per year, but only the Emelle facility, as the only commercial facility operating within Alabama, meets this description. The Act also imposes a "base fee" of $25.60 per ton on all hazardous wastes and substances disposed of at commercial facilities, to be paid by the operator of the facility. Finally, the Act imposes the "additional fee" at issue here, which states in full:

> For waste and substances which are generated outside of Alabama and disposed of at a commercial site for the disposal of hazardous waste or hazardous substances in Alabama, an additional fee shall be levied at the rate of $72.00 per ton.

* * *

No State may attempt to isolate itself from a problem common to the several States by raising barriers to the free flow of interstate trade.[3] Today, in *Fort Gratiot Sanitary Landfill, Inc. v. Michigan Dept. of Natural Resources,* we have also considered a Commerce Clause challenge to a Michigan law prohibiting private landfill operators from accepting solid waste originating outside the county in which their facilities operate. In striking down that law, we adhered to our decision in *Philadelphia v. New Jersey,* where we found New Jersey's prohibition of solid waste from outside that State to amount to economic protectionism barred by the Commerce Clause. * * *

The Court has consistently found parochial legislation of this kind to be constitutionally invalid, whether the ultimate aim of the legislation was to assure a steady supply of milk by erecting barriers to allegedly ruinous outside competition, or to create jobs by keeping industry within the State, or to preserve the State's financial resources from depletion by fencing out indigent immigrants.

---

3. The Alabama Supreme Court assumed that the disposal of hazardous waste constituted an article of commerce, and the State does not explicitly argue here to the contrary. In *Fort Gratiot Sanitary Landfill, Inc.* v. *Michigan Dept. of Natural Resources, post,* at 359, we have reaffirmed the idea that "solid waste, even if it has no value, is an article of commerce." As stated in *Philadelphia v. New Jersey, 437 U.S. 617, 622–623, 57 L. Ed. 2d 475, 98 S. Ct. 2531 (1978):* "All objects of interstate trade merit Commerce Clause protection; none is excluded by definition at the outset.... Just as Congress has power to regulate the interstate movement of these wastes, States are not free from constitutional scrutiny when they restrict that movement." The definition of "hazardous waste" makes clear that it is simply a grade of solid waste, albeit one of particularly noxious and dangerous propensities, see n. 1, *supra,* but whether the business arrangements between out-of-state generators of hazardous waste and the Alabama operator of a hazardous waste landfill are viewed as "sales" of hazardous waste or "purchases" of transportation and disposal services, "the commercial transactions unquestionably have an interstate character. The Commerce Clause thus imposes some constraints on [Alabama's] ability to regulate these transactions." *Fort Gratiot Sanitary Landfill, post,* at 359. See *National Solid Wastes Management Assn. v. Alabama Dept. of Environmental Mgmt., 910 F.2d 713, 718–719 (CA11 1990),* modified, *924 F.2d 1001,* cert. denied, *501 U.S. 1206 (1991).*

To this list may be added cases striking down a tax discriminating against interstate commerce, even where such tax was designed to encourage the use of ethanol and thereby reduce harmful exhaust emissions, or to support inspection of foreign cement to ensure structural integrity. For in all of these cases, "a presumably legitimate goal was sought to be achieved by the illegitimate means of isolating the State from the national economy."

The Act's additional fee facially discriminates against hazardous waste generated in States other than Alabama, and the Act overall has plainly discouraged the full operation of petitioner's Emelle facility. Such burdensome taxes imposed on interstate commerce alone are generally forbidden: "[A] State may not tax a transaction or incident more heavily when it crosses state lines than when it occurs entirely within the State." Once a state tax is found to discriminate against out-of-state commerce, it is typically struck down without further inquiry.

The State, however, argues that the additional fee imposed on out-of-state hazardous waste serves legitimate local purposes related to its citizens' health and safety. Because the additional fee discriminates both on its face and in practical effect, the burden falls on the State "to justify it both in terms of the local benefits flowing from the statute and the unavailability of nondiscriminatory alternatives adequate to preserve the local interests at stake." "At a minimum such facial discrimination invokes the strictest scrutiny of any purported legitimate local purpose and of the absence of nondiscriminatory alternatives." * * *

These may all be legitimate local interests, and petitioner has not attacked them. But only rhetoric, and not explanation, emerges as to why Alabama targets *only* interstate hazardous waste to meet these goals. As found by the trial court, "although the Legislature imposed an additional fee of $72.00 per ton on waste generated outside Alabama, there is absolutely no evidence before this Court that waste generated outside Alabama is more dangerous than waste generated in Alabama. The Court finds under the facts of this case that the only basis for the additional fee is the origin of the waste." In the face of such findings, invalidity under the Commerce Clause necessarily follows, for "whatever [Alabama's] ultimate purpose, it may not be accomplished by discriminating against articles of commerce coming from outside the State unless there is some reason, apart from their origin, to treat them differently." *Philadelphia v. New Jersey, 437 U.S. at 626–627;* see *New Energy Co., 486 U.S. at 279–280.* The burden is on the State to show that "the *discrimination* is demonstrably justified by a valid factor unrelated to economic protectionism," *Wyoming v. Oklahoma, 502 U.S. 437, 454 (1992)* (emphasis added), and it has not carried this burden. Cf. *Fort Gratiot Sanitary Landfill, post,* at 361.

... To the extent Alabama's concern touches environmental conservation and the health and safety of its citizens, such concern does not vary with the point of origin of the waste, and it remains within the State's power to monitor and regulate more closely the transportation and disposal of *all* hazardous waste within its borders. Even with the possible future financial and environmental risks to be borne by Alabama, such risks likewise do not vary with the waste's State of origin in a way allowing foreign, but not local, waste to be burdened. In sum, we find the additional fee to be "an obvious effort to saddle those outside the State" with most of the burden of slowing the flow of waste into the Emelle facility. *Philadelphia v. New Jersey, 437 U.S. at 629.* "That legislative effort is clearly impermissible under the Commerce Clause of the Constitution." *Ibid.*

Our decisions regarding quarantine laws do not counsel a different conclusion. The Act's additional fee may not legitimately be deemed a quarantine law because Alabama permits both the generation and landfilling of hazardous waste within its borders and the importation of still more hazardous waste subject to payment of the additional fee. In any event, while it is true that certain quarantine laws have not been considered forbidden protectionist measures, even though directed against out-of-state commerce, those laws "did not discriminate against interstate commerce as such, but simply prevented traffic in noxious articles, whatever their origin." Philadelphia v. New Jersey, supra, at 629. * * *

Maine v. Taylor, 477 U.S. 131 (1986), provides no additional justification. Maine there demonstrated that the out-of-state baitfish were subject to parasites foreign to in-state baitfish. This difference posed a threat to the State's natural resources, and absent a less discriminatory means of protecting the environment— and none was available— the importation of baitfish could properly be banned. *Id., at 140.* To the contrary, the record establishes that the hazardous waste at issue in this case is the same regardless of its point of origin. As noted in *Fort Gratiot Sanitary Landfill*, "our conclusion would be different if the imported waste raised health or other concerns not presented by [Alabama] waste." *Post*, at 367. Because no unique threat is posed, and because adequate means other than overt discrimination meet Alabama's concerns, *Maine v. Taylor* provides the State no respite.

The decision of the Alabama Supreme Court is reversed, and the cause is remanded for proceedings not inconsistent with this opinion, including consideration of the appropriate relief to petitioner.

So ordered.

CHIEF JUSTICE REHNQUIST, dissenting.

I have already had occasion to set out my view that States need not ban all waste disposal as a precondition to protecting themselves from hazardous or noxious materials brought across the State's borders. See Philadelphia v. New Jersey, 437 U.S. 617 (1978) (REHNQUIST, J., dissenting). In a case also decided today, I express my further view that States may take actions legitimately directed at the preservation of the State's natural resources, even if those actions incidentally work to disadvantage some out-of-state waste generators. See Fort Gratiot Sanitary Landfill, Inc. v. Michigan Dept. of Natural Resources, post, p. 368 (REHNQUIST, C. J., dissenting). I dissent today, largely for the reasons I have set out in those two cases. Several additional comments that pertain specifically to this case, though, are in order.

Taxes are a recognized and effective means for discouraging the consumption of scarce commodities—in this case the safe environment that attends appropriate disposal of hazardous wastes. Cf. 26 U.S.C. §§ 4681, 4682 (1988 ed., Supp. III) (tax on ozone-depleting chemicals); 26 U.S.C. § 4064 (gas guzzler excise tax). I therefore see nothing unconstitutional in Alabama's use of a tax to discourage the export of this commodity to other States, when the commodity is a public good that Alabama has helped to produce. Nor do I see any significance in the fact that Alabama has chosen to adopt a differential tax rather than an outright ban. Nothing in the Commerce Clause requires Alabama to adopt an "all or nothing" regulatory approach to noxious materials coming from without the State. See Mintz v. Baldwin, 289 U.S. 346 (1933) (upholding State's *partial* ban on cattle importation). * * *

There is some solace to be taken in the Court's conclusion, that Alabama may impose a substantial fee on the disposal of all hazardous waste, or a per-mile fee on all vehicles transporting such waste, or a cap on total disposals at the Emelle facility. None of these approaches provide Alabama the ability to tailor its regulations in a way that the State will be solving only that portion of the problem that it has created. But they do at least give Alabama some mechanisms for requiring waste-generating States to compensate Alabama for the risks the Court declares Alabama must run.

Of course, the costs of any of the proposals that the Court today approves will be less than fairly apportioned. For example, should Alabama adopt a flat transportation or disposal tax, Alabama citizens will be forced to pay a disposal tax equal to that faced by dumpers from outside the State. As the Court acknowledges, such taxes are a permissible effort to recoup compensation for the risks imposed on the State. Yet Alabama's general tax revenues presumably already support the State's various inspection and regulatory efforts designed to ensure the Emelle facility's safe operation. Thus, Alabamians will be made to pay twice, once through general taxation and a second time through a specific disposal fee. Permitting differential taxation would, in part, do no more than recognize that, having been made to bear all the risks from such hazardous waste sites, Alabama should not in addition be made to pay *more* than others in supporting activities that will help to minimize the risk. * * *

For the foregoing reasons, I respectfully dissent.

Minnesota v. Clover Leaf Creamery Co.

449 U.S. 456, 470–474; 101 S. Ct. 715; 66 L. Ed. 2d 659 (1981)

JUSTICE BRENNAN delivered the opinion of the Court.

In 1977, the Minnesota Legislature enacted a statute banning the retail sale of milk in plastic nonreturnable, nonrefillable containers, but permitting such sale in other nonreturnable, nonrefillable containers, such as paperboard milk cartons. Respondents contend that the statute violates the ... Commerce Clause[] of the Constitution.

[In Part I, the Court discusses the history of the case. It notes that the Minnesota legislature declared that the purpose of the statute was to reduce solid waste, conserve energy, and slow the depletion of natural resources. A Minnesota District Court determined that the law would not achieve its stated goals and that the actual purpose of the law "was to promote the economic interests of certain segments of the local dairy and pulpwood industries at the expense of other segments of the dairy industry and the plastics industry." On this basis, the lower court held the state law to be in violation of the Commerce Clause.

Part II of the opinion considered challenges to the statute under the Equal Protection Clause.]

III

The District Court also held that the Minnesota statute is unconstitutional under the Commerce Clause because it imposes an unreasonable burden on interstate commerce. We cannot agree.

When legislating in areas of legitimate local concern, such as environmental protection and resource conservation, States are nonetheless limited by the Commerce Clause. If a state law purporting to promote environmental purposes is in reality "simple economic protectionism," we have applied a "virtually *per se* rule of invalidity." *Philadelphia v. New Jersey*.[15] Even if a statute regulates "evenhandedly," and imposes only "incidental" burdens on interstate commerce, the courts must nevertheless strike it down if "the burden imposed on such commerce is clearly excessive in relation to the putative local benefits." *Pike v. Bruce Church, Inc.*, 397 U.S. 137, 142 (1970). Moreover, "the extent of the burden that will be tolerated will of course depend on the nature of the local interest involved, and on whether it could be promoted as well with a lesser impact on interstate activities." *Ibid.*

Minnesota's statute does not effect "simple protectionism," but "regulates evenhandedly" by prohibiting all milk retailers from selling their products in plastic, nonreturnable milk containers, without regard to whether the milk, the containers, or the sellers are from outside the State. This statute is therefore unlike statutes discriminating against interstate commerce, which we have consistently struck down.

Since the statute does not discriminate between interstate and intrastate commerce, the controlling question is whether the incidental burden imposed on interstate commerce by the Minnesota Act is "clearly excessive in relation to the putative local benefits." *Pike v. Bruce Church, Inc., supra*, at 142. We conclude that it is not.

The burden imposed on interstate commerce by the statute is relatively minor. Milk products may continue to move freely across the Minnesota border, and since most dairies package their products in more than one type of containers, the inconvenience of having to conform to different packaging requirements in Minnesota and the surrounding States should be slight. Within Minnesota, business will presumably shift from manufacturers of plastic nonreturnable containers to producers of paperboard cartons, refillable bottles, and plastic pouches, but there is no reason to suspect that the gainers will be Minnesota firms, or the losers out-of-state firms. Indeed, two of the three dairies, the sole milk retailer, and the sole milk container producer challenging the statute in this litigation are Minnesota firms.

Pulpwood producers are the only Minnesota industry likely to benefit significantly from the Act at the expense of out-of-state firms. Respondents point out that plastic resin, the raw material used for making plastic nonreturnable milk jugs, is produced entirely by non-Minnesota firms, while pulpwood, used for making paperboard, is a major Minnesota product. Nevertheless, it is clear that respondents exaggerate the degree of burden on out-of-state interests, both because plastics will continue to be used in the production of plastic pouches, plas-

---

15. A court may find that a state law constitutes "economic protectionism" on proof either of discriminatory effect, see *Philadelphia v. New Jersey*, or of discriminatory purpose, see *Hunt v. Washington Apple Advertising Comm'n*, 432 U.S., at 352–353, 97 S.Ct., at 2446. Respondents advance a "discriminatory purpose" argument, relying on a finding by the District Court that the Act's "actual basis was to promote the economic interests of certain segments of the local dairy and pulpwood industries at the expense of the economic interests of other segments of the dairy industry and the plastics industry." App. A-19. We have already considered and rejected this argument in the equal protection context, see n. 7, *supra*, and do so in this context as well.

tic returnable bottles, and paperboard itself, and because out-of-state pulpwood producers will presumably absorb some of the business generated by the Act.

Even granting that the out-of-state plastics industry is burdened relatively more heavily than the Minnesota pulpwood industry, we find that this burden is not "clearly excessive" in light of the substantial state interest in promoting conservation of energy and other natural resources and easing solid waste disposal problems, which we have already reviewed in the context of equal protection analysis. We find these local benefits ample to support Minnesota's decision under the Commerce Clause. Moreover, we find that no approach with "a lesser impact on interstate activities," *Pike v. Bruce Church, Inc., supra,* at 142, is available. Respondents have suggested several alternative statutory schemes, but these alternatives are either more burdensome on commerce than the Act (as, for example, banning all nonreturnables) or less likely to be effective (as, for example, providing incentives for recycling).

In *Exxon Corp. v. Governor of Maryland,* 437 U.S. 117 (1978), we upheld a Maryland statute barring producers and refiners of petroleum products—all of which were out-of-state businesses—from retailing gasoline in the State. We stressed that the Commerce Clause "protects the interstate market, not particular interstate firms, from prohibitive or burdensome regulations." *Id.,* at 127–128. A nondiscriminatory regulation serving substantial state purposes is not invalid simply because it causes some business to shift from a predominantly out-of-state industry to a predominantly in-state industry. Only if the burden on interstate commerce clearly outweighs the State's legitimate purposes does such a regulation violate the Commerce Clause.

The judgment of the Minnesota Supreme Court is *Reversed.*

Questions and Discussion

1. As these cases suggest, the legal doctrines surrounding the Dormant Commerce Clause are far from clear in their application, prompting sharp disagreements among members of the Supreme Court. Nevertheless, the basic principles are fairly clear. The following brief discussion draws from Chapter 6 of LAURENCE H. TRIBE, AMERICAN CONSTITUTIONAL LAW (3d ed. 2000), and from Daniel A. Farber & Robert E. Hudec, *GATT Legal Restraints on Domestic Environmental Regulations, in* 1 FAIR TRADE AND HARMONIZATION: PREREQUISITES FOR FREE TRADE 59–94 (Jagdish Bhagwati & Robert E. Hudec eds., 1996).

At the threshold, any state law that imposes a burden on interstate commerce must be taken in pursuit of a legitimate end of state regulation. Without doubt, environmental regulation meets this threshold test (though a state regulation may always be held to have been preempted by a comprehensive federal regulatory program addressing the same issues). As with international trade cases, there are then two basic classes of measures that come in for judicial scrutiny: 1) measures that are facially discriminatory in their treatment of local products or businesses as compared with out-of-state products or businesses, and 2) measures that are facially neutral, but which may nevertheless have a different effect on out-of-state interests as compared with local interests. The general U.S. rule is that measures that are facially discriminatory are at least subject to strict scrutiny. However, the courts have applied the strict scrutiny test in a way that verges on a doctrine that discriminatory measures are invalid *per se*. *Philadelphia v. New Jersey*, excerpted above, is a leading example of this approach. If the measure is designed in such a way that it does not clearly treat intra-state interests differently from interstate or out-of-state interests, then the courts will normally inquire whether it imposes a burden on interstate commerce that is "clearly excessive" in relation to the supposed local benefits to be achieved. This second test is often referred to as the *Pike* test because it was mostly clearly articulated in the case of *Pike v. Bruce Church, Inc.*, 397 U.S. 137 (1970). Notably, though, *Pike* itself phrases the test as one applying to even-handed measures whose "effects on interstate commerce are only incidental." That leaves open for debate whether a particular even-handed measure may have more than merely "incidental" effects on interstate commerce. Indeed, Farber and Hudec identify regulations with "incidental" effects as a third category, with the following caveat:

> Although this three-part scheme has the appearance of tidiness, in practice it involves difficult line drawing. Indeed, a recent Supreme Court decision [*Fort Gratiot*] rather casually lumps the first two categories together as involving "clearly discriminatory" statutes. Similarly, the line between the second two categories has proved permeable, as the Supreme Court has also observed.

Daniel A. Farber & Robert E. Hudec, *GATT Legal Restraints on Domestic Environmental Regulations,* at 65.

As a final general comment linking the Dormant Commerce Clause cases back to international trade law, Farber and Hudec come to the following conclusion:

> There are two important conclusions to be drawn from the U.S. experience. The first is that a commitment to free trade almost inevitably requires scrutiny of local regulations for signs of protectionism. Thus, it is not surprising that GATT has embarked on a similar venture, nor can GATT reasonably be expected to abandon the field. The second lesson is that, particularly absent any explicit discrimination against foreign commerce, this judicial task may not be at all easy to accomplish. It requires a delicate balance between concern for free trade and deference to legislative prerogatives.

Id. at 67.

2. In what ways is the Supreme Court's explanation of its holdings similar to the reasoning of GATT and WTO panels? But consider the following statement from the *Chemical Waste Management* opinion: "No state may attempt to isolate itself from a problem common to the several states by raising barriers to the free flow of interstate trade." Would a WTO panel ever make such a statement in applying GATT Article III? Why or why not?

3. In *Chemical Waste Management*, the Supreme Court refused to look at actual trade data. It considered the tax differential to be *prima facie* discriminatory. Compare that approach with the *Superfund* Panel and other taxation cases in this chapter, at pages 184–90, 234–37. In addition, the Supreme Court ruled in *Minnesota v. Clover Leaf Creamery* that the Dormant Commerce Clause "protects the interstate market, not particular interstate firms, from prohibitive or burdensome regulations." What aspects of GATT jurisprudence does that ruling echo?

4. Americans may be surprised to see Chief Justice Rehnquist defending a state's right to take environmental measures such as the New Jersey import ban and the Alabama tax. What is his view of the issues at stake in these cases? Do you agree with him that the Court's decisions will thwart sound state policy of conservation of land and protection from pollution from waste? Suppose a small state, because of prevalent soil characteris-

tics, has no environmentally suitable location for a landfill? Under Rehnquist's approach, what options does such a state have if its neighbors refuse to accept its waste?

5. Chemical Waste Management located its hazardous waste landfill in Alabama because the local clay soils made it easier to meet Environmental Protection Agency requirements for prevention of leachate from the landfill that might contaminate groundwater. Thus, in a sense, Alabama has a "comparative advantage" in waste disposal. Yet waste disposal has associated environmental and health risks. Does the Court's holding prevent Alabama from taxing out-of-state waste to collect the revenue to protect against and compensate for those environmental and health risks?

6. In *Fort Gratiot*, the Court struck down a state law that allowed a county to prohibit waste from other counties (and states), reaffirming that the state could not isolate itself or allow one of its local jurisdictions to isolate itself from the waste of others. What about international waste trade? Suppose the nearby city of Windsor, Ontario wanted to send its garbage to the Fort Gratiot landfill. Could the county or the State of Michigan bar that shipment? Suppose now that the Supreme Court had upheld the Michigan law. Acting under the state law, the local county allows the Fort Gratiot landfill to accept only waste from the local county. Again, Windsor seeks to send its garbage to Fort Gratiot. Under GATT Article III, can the county refuse to accept the Canadian waste?

7. Some states have urged the U.S. Congress to authorize states to ban imports of out-of-state waste or to establish higher fees for out-of-state waste disposal. Why has Congress not enacted such legislation? Does Congress have the constitutional power to enact such legislation? What effect would such legislation have on the GATT rights of Canadian municipalities to arrange for waste disposal in a state with such congressionally-authorized restrictions?

B. The Free Movement of Goods and National Regulation in Europe

Under the Treaty of Lisbon, which came into force on December 1, 2009, the treaty provisions governing the free movement of goods and national regulation among the 27 members of the European Union (EU) are now governed primarily by one of the EU's two core treaties, the Treaty on the Functioning of the European Union, May 9, 2008, 2008/C 115/47, hereafter the TFEU. Articles 26–37 of the TFEU are similar in some respects to the WTO Agreements and in other respects to the U.S. Constitution. Like the U.S. Commerce Clause, Article 28(1) of the TFEU establishes the EU as a customs union, "which shall involve the prohibition between Member States of customs duties on imports and exports and of all charges having equivalent effect, and the adoption of a common customs tariff in their relations with third countries." The EU has a more ambitious purpose however. It traces its origins to the reconstruction of Europe after two world wars, when an "economic community" was established to bind the countries of Europe together economically (and later politically) in ways that would give them a common purpose and thus forestall international conflict. With this vision in mind, European law with respect to internal commerce rests on an overarching conception of an internal market.

The second core treaty is the new Treaty on European Union, May 9, 2008, 2008/C 115/13. In Article 3(3), this treaty makes establishing the internal market one of the principal purposes of the EU. The idea of the "internal market" is articulated in Article 26(2) of the TFEU: "The internal market shall comprise an area without internal frontiers in which the free movement of goods, persons, services and capital is ensured...." Everything that follows must be read against the paramount principle of free movement.

The provisions of Articles 26–33 of the TFEU establishing the internal market and customs union are followed by three GATT-like articles that extend to restrictions on trade other than tariffs.

Treaty on the Functioning of the European Union
May 9, 2008, 2008/C 115/13

Article 34

Quantitative restrictions on imports and all measures having equivalent effect shall be prohibited between Member States.

Article 35

Quantitative restrictions on exports, and all measures having equivalent effect, shall be prohibited between Member States.

Article 36

The provisions of Articles 34 and 35 shall not preclude prohibitions or restrictions on imports, exports or goods in transit justified on grounds of public morality, public policy or public security; the protection of health and life of humans, animals or plants; the protection of national treasures possessing artistic, historic or archaeological value; or the protection of industrial and commercial property. Such prohibitions or restrictions shall not, however, constitute a means of arbitrary discrimination or a disguised restriction on trade between Member States.

Articles 34 and 35 of the TFEU correspond quite directly to Article XI of the GATT. Article 36 is analogous to Article XX of the GATT, though if you compare the two there is a clear difference that is important to the treatment of national environmental regulations as barriers to trade in EU law, as two leading European commentators explain.

Jan H. Jans & Hans H.B. Vedder,
European Environmental Law
242–44 (3d ed. 2008)

[T]he early case law of the [European] Court of Justice has clearly shown that the scope of Article [36], as an exception to a fundamental Treaty provision, had to be interpreted narrowly. As the protection of the environment is not included in the exhaustive list of exceptions contained in Article [36], a restriction on imports or exports to protect the living environment, without there being a real and actual threat to health or life of humans, animals or plants, was not capable of being justified by Article [36].

Import prohibitions of non-harmful wastes, which do not directly threaten life or health, cannot be justified on the grounds of Article [36], as was made clear in the Court's judgment in the *Walloon Waste* case [Case C-2/90 *Commission v. Belgium* [1992] ECR I-4331]:

So far as the environment is concerned, it should be observed that waste has a special characteristic. The accumulation of waste, even before it becomes a health hazard, constitutes a threat to the environment because of the limited capacity of each region or locality for receiving it.

This case clearly makes a distinction between the environment and protecting health.... In view of this restrictive approach, it was doubtful whether measures not addressing a demonstrable direct health interest will be covered by Article [36].

––––––––––

Article 36, however, is not the only law applicable to national environmental measures that may interfere with the free movement of goods. There is also the so-called "rule of reason" exception, which derives from the first of the following decisions of the European Court of Justice. In the second case below, *Danish Bottles*, the European Court of Justice extends the "rule of reason" to environmental measures and elaborates some elements of that rule that recall similar considerations in WTO law. In the excerpts, and throughout this section, the new TFEU article numbers have been inserted.

Rewe-Zentral AG v. Bundesmonopolverwaltung für Branntwein
(Cassis de Dijon), Case 120/78, [1979] ECR 649 (1979)

[An importer sought a license to import into Germany Cassis de Dijon, manufactured in France. The German regulatory authority denied the license on the grounds that Cassis de Dijon had insufficient alcohol content to be marketed in Germany. German rules for alcoholic beverages required a minimum alcohol content of 25 percent for fruit liqueurs. Cassis de Dijon, a French fruit liqueur which is marketed freely in France, has an alcohol content of between 15 and 20 percent.]

8. In the absence of common [EU] rules relating to the production and marketing of alcohol ... it is for the Member States to regulate all matters relating to the production and marketing of alcohol and alcoholic beverages on their own territory.

Obstacles to movement within the Community resulting from disparities between national laws relating to the marketing of the products in question must be accepted in so far as those provisions may be recognized as being necessary in order to satisfy mandatory requirements relating in particular to the effectiveness of fiscal supervision, the protection of public health, the fairness of commercial transactions and the defense of the consumer.

9. The Government of the Federal Republic of Germany, intervening in the proceedings, put forward various arguments which, in its view, justify the application of provisions relating to the minimum alcohol content of alcoholic beverages, adducing considerations relating on the one hand to the protection of public health and on the other to the protection of the consumer against unfair commercial practices.

[The Court then examined and rejected the arguments of the German government.]

14. It is clear from the foregoing that the requirements relating to the minimum alcohol content of alcoholic beverages do not serve a purpose which is in the

general interest and such as to take precedence over the requirements of the free movement of goods, which constitutes one of the fundamental rules of the Community.

In practice, the principle effect of requirements of this nature is to promote alcoholic beverages having a high alcohol content by excluding from the national market products of other Member States which do not answer that description.

It therefore appears that the unilateral requirement imposed by the rules of a Member State of a minimum alcohol content for the purposes of the sale of alcoholic beverages constitutes an obstacle to trade which is incompatible with the provisions of Article [34] of the Treaty.

There is therefore no valid reason why, provided that they have been lawfully produced and marketed in one of the Member States, alcoholic beverages should not be introduced into any other Member State; the sale of such products may not be subject to a legal prohibition on the marketing of beverages with an alcohol content lower than the limit set by national rules.

———————

Commission v. Denmark (Danish Bottles)
Case No. 302/86, [1988] ECR 4607

2. The main feature of the system which the Commission challenges as incompatible with Community law is that manufacturers must market beer and soft drinks only in re-usable containers. The containers must be approved by the National Agency for the Protection of the Environment, which may refuse approval of new kinds of container, especially if it considers that a container is not technically suitable for a system for returning containers or that the return system envisaged does not ensure that a sufficient proportion of containers are actually re-used or if a container of equal capacity, which is both available and suitable for the same use, has already been approved.

3. Order No 95 of 16 March 1984 amended the aforementioned rules in such a way that, provided that a deposit-and-return system is established, non-approved containers, except for any form of metal container, may be used for quantities not exceeding 3000 hectolitres a year per producer and for drinks which are sold by foreign producers in order to test the market. * * *

6. The first point which must be made in resolving this dispute is that, according to an established body of case-law of the Court [citing *Cassis de Dijon*] in the absence of common rules relating to the marketing of the products in question, obstacles to free movement within the Community resulting from disparities between the national laws must be accepted in so far as such rules, applicable to domestic and imported products without distinction, may be recognized as being necessary in order to satisfy mandatory requirements recognized by Community law. Such rules must also be proportionate to the aim in view. If a Member State has a choice between various measures for achieving the same aim, it should choose the means which least restricts the free movement of goods.

7. In the present case the Danish Government contends that the mandatory collection system for containers of beer and soft drinks applied in Denmark is justified by a mandatory requirement related to the protection of the environment.

8. The Court has already held in its judgment of 7 February 1985 in Case 240/83 Procureur de la République v. Association de défense des brûleurs d' huiles usagées ((1985)) ECR 531 that the protection of the environment is "one of the Community's essential objectives," which may as such justify certain limitations of the principle of the free movement of goods. That view is moreover confirmed by the Single European Act [Editors' note: The Single European Act added to the expressed purposes of the EU, the pursuit of "a high level of protection and improvement in the quality of the environment."]

9. In view of the foregoing, it must therefore be stated that the protection of the environment is a mandatory requirement which may limit the application of Article [34] of the Treaty.

10. The Commission submits that the Danish rules are contrary to the principle of proportionality in so far as the aim of the protection of the environment may be achieved by means less restrictive of intra-Community trade.

11. In that regard, it must be pointed out that in its aforementioned judgment of 7 February 1985 the Court stated that measures adopted to protect the environment must not "go beyond the inevitable restrictions which are justified by the pursuit of the objective of environmental protection."

12. It is therefore necessary to examine whether all the restrictions which the contested rules impose on the free movement of goods are necessary to achieve the objectives pursued by those rules.

13. First of all, as regards the obligation to establish a deposit-and-return system for empty containers, it must be observed that this requirement is an indispensable element of a system intended to ensure the re-use of containers and therefore appears necessary to achieve the aims pursued by the contested rules. That being so, the restrictions which it imposes on the free movement of goods cannot be regarded as disproportionate.

14. Next, it is necessary to consider the requirement that producers and importers must use only containers approved by the National Agency for the Protection of the Environment.

15. The Danish Government stated in the proceedings before the Court that the present deposit-and-return system would not work if the number of approved containers were to exceed 30 or so, since the retailers taking part in the system would not be prepared to accept too many types of bottles owing to the higher handling costs and the need for more storage space. For that reason the Agency has hitherto followed the practice of ensuring that fresh approvals are normally accompanied by the withdrawal of existing approvals.

16. Even though there is some force in that argument, it must nevertheless be observed that under the system at present in force in Denmark the Danish authorities may refuse approval to a foreign producer even if he is prepared to ensure that returned containers are re-used.

17. In those circumstances, a foreign producer who still wished to sell his products in Denmark would be obliged to manufacture or purchase containers of a type already approved, which would involve substantial additional costs for that producer and therefore make the importation of his products into Denmark very difficult.

18. To overcome that obstacle the Danish Government altered its rules by the aforementioned Order No 95 of 16 March 1984, which allows a producer to mar-

ket up to 3000 hectolitres of beer and soft drinks a year in non-approved containers, provided that a deposit-and-return system is established

19. The provision in Order No 95 restricting the quantity of beer and soft drinks which may be marketed by a producer in non-approved containers to 3,000 hectolitres a year is challenged by the Commission on the ground that it is unnecessary to achieve the objectives pursued by the system.

20. It is undoubtedly true that the existing system for returning approved containers ensures a maximum rate of re-use and therefore a very considerable degree of protection of the environment since empty containers can be returned to any retailer of beverages. Non-approved containers, on the other hand, can be returned only to the retailer who sold the beverages, since it is impossible to set up such a comprehensive system for those containers as well.

21. Nevertheless, the system for returning non-approved containers is capable of protecting the environment and, as far as imports are concerned, affects only limited quantities of beverages compared with the quantity of beverages consumed in Denmark owing to the restrictive effect which the requirement that containers should be returnable has on imports. In those circumstances, a restriction of the quantity of products which may be marketed by importers is disproportionate to the objective pursued.

22. It must therefore be held that by restricting, by Order No 95 of 16 March 1984, the quantity of beer and soft drinks which may be marketed by a single producer in non-approved containers to 3000 hectolitres a year, the Kingdom of Denmark has failed, as regards imports of those products from other Member States, to fulfil its obligations under Article [34] of the EEC Treaty.

There are a number of terms embedded in these two European Court of Justice decisions that may be new to people unfamiliar with the European system, but which reflect common principles and concepts. For example, a "mandatory requirement" in European law is an objective, such as environmental protection, which is identified as one of the objectives for creating the European Union. (This objective is now enshrined in Article 191 of the TFEU.) As such, there is a shared legal responsibility for it. The European Commission and the Council, the executive bodies of the EU, may adopt legislation establishing Europe-wide requirements for environmental protection. Alternatively, and more commonly, the Commission may adopt "directives," calling on each of the Member States to enact national laws on a particular environmental issue in order to achieve a certain standard of performance or other objective described in the directive. But as with the U.S. Commerce Clause, the mere fact that the Commission may legislate in the environmental area does not preclude each Member State from enacting its own national and local legislation. Indeed, as the expression "mandatory requirement" suggests, it is incumbent upon each Member State to adopt such laws and regulations as are necessary to fill in all the many gaps in the Europe-wide legislation, so that all Members are acting to achieve and maintain a high quality of environmental protection. This obligation is spelled out in TFEU Article 192. Moreover, as made clear in TFEU Article 193, Member States are free to have more protective or more stringent policies than required by EU law. The tricky part, again reminiscent of issues under the U.S. Commerce Clause, comes when the national legislation may present an obstacle to that other "fundamental" objective of the EU — the free movement of goods. How are these twin goals reconciled when they come into apparent conflict? The following commentary gives some guidance. Note that the terms "with distinction" and "without distinction" refer to existence or nonexistence of legal distinctions between domestic goods and foreign goods in the national regulations.

Jan H. Jans & Hans H.B. Vedder,
European Environmental Law
247–49 (3d ed. 2008)

It could be asked to what extent a national import restriction for environmental reasons should be regarded as a ground for justification in the sense of Article [36], or as a "mandatory requirement" in the sense of *Cassis de Dijon* and the *Danish Bottles* judgments? As the material scope of the rule of reason is wider and offers the Member States more leeway to take protective measures one could even argue that there is hardly any need to rely on Article [36] if the rule of reason is available to the Member States.

However, on the basis of older case law the rule of reason seemed more limited than Article [36] in a different respect. In principle, Article [36] allows an exemption for national measures which relate in particular to imported products only. In other words, it offers some room for "measures applicable *with* distinction." Such specific import restrictions may not, however, constitute an arbitrary discrimination. And prohibition of the importation of a harmful product will constitute an arbitrary discrimination if no restriction whatever is imposed on the domestic use of that product. It is not arbitrary, however, if there is a valid and objective reason why the imported product is to be treated differently. In other words under Article [36] *differentiation* is allowed, but *discrimination* is not.

As far as the rule of reason is concerned, the measure in question had to be applied without distinction to domestic and foreign products. It was well-established case law that the rule of reason doctrine could not be relied on to justify national measures which were not applicable to domestic products and imported products *without* distinction. This mean that national protective measures which might be justified on environmental grounds, but do not fall within the more limited scope of Article [36], are only allowed if they can be regarded as measures applicable without distinction.

However, the judgement in the *Walloon Waste* case [Case C-2/90, *Commission v. Belgium* [1992] ECR I-4331] was the first case which caused some confusion as to the degree to which a measure must be applicable without distinction for the rule of reason to apply. In that case, the lawfulness of a Walloon prohibition on the disposal of foreign waste was at issue. The Commission argued that these mandatory requirements of environmental protection could not be relied on to allow the Walloon restrictions. The Commission insisted that the measures at issue discriminated against waste coming from other Member States though that waste was no more harmful than that produced in Wallonia.... The Court of Justice first confirmed that the mandatory requirements are to be taken into account only with regard to measures which apply to national and imported products without distinction. However, in order to determine whether the obstacle in question is discriminatory, the particular type of waste must be taken into account. The principle that environmental damage should as a priority be rectified at source—a principle laid down by Article 174(2) for action by the [EU] relating to the environment—means that it is for each region, commune or other local entity to take appropriate measures to receive, process and dispose of its own waste. Consequently waste should be disposed of as close as possible to the place where it is produced. It then observed that this principle is in conformity with the principles of self-sufficiency and proximity set out in the Basle Convention [on Transboundary Movements of Hazardous Waste and Their Disposal]. The Court therefore concluded that, having regard to the differences between waste produced in one place and that in another and its connection with the place where it is produced, the Belgian measures could not be considered to be discriminatory.

What is interesting is, in the first place, that the Court has *de facto* equated the fact that a measure applies without distinction to the absence of discrimination. By thus equating the two, the Court has made the test of whether or not a measure applies without distinction a test of whether or not it is discriminatory. The relevance of this discussion could be that, for a national measure to benefit from the rule of reason exception, it no longer has to be framed as a measure applicable without distinction. Apparently, differential measures can also be excepted using the rule of reason, as long as there is an objective justification. * * *

Taken together with indications in the Court's case law outside the field of the environment that the rule of reason will be applied where measures do make a distinction, it cannot be ruled out that the relevance of the distinction between Article [36] interests and rule of reason exceptions has ceased to exist.

Questions and Discussion

1. As noted at the beginning of this section, Article 34 of the TFEU is analogous to GATT Article XI, and Article 36 plays the role of a general exception similar to GATT Article XX. As the commentary by Jans and Vedder explains, however, Article 36 of the TFEU has been narrowly construed to cover only measures to protect health and life and not measures to protect the natural environment. But measures to protect the natural environment can, in European law, also escape the strictures of Article 34 under the so-called "rule of reason." Do you understand the connection between the "rule of reason" and the concept of "mandatory requirements"? Where does the Court find these "mandatory requirements"? Is there an overlap between "mandatory requirements" and the national objectives listed in Article 36?

2. What is the difference between an exception from Article 34 under Article 36 and a "limit [on] the application of Article 34" for mandatory requirements? The Jans and Vedder excerpt uses the terminology familiar in Europe, classifying some measures as "measures applied with distinction" and other measures as ones "applied without distinction." Was the German rule in the *Cassis de Dijon* applied with or without "distinction"? What about the *Danish Bottles* regulation?

3. As Jans and Vedder note, the European Court's decision in the *Walloon Waste* case muddies the doctrinal waters. Compare the viewpoint argued, unsuccessfully, by the European Commission in that case (as described by Jans and Vedder) with the views of the U.S. Supreme Court in the Commerce Clause waste cases. Do they see the issues the same way? How does the European Court of Justice slip the noose of the *prima facie* discrimination/applied with distinction argument? Is the European Court essentially making a "like product" argument? Consider, for example, the "like products" analysis in *Auto Taxes* and *EC-Asbestos*? Do you see any similarities? Differences? How would you distinguish

the argument of the European Court in the *Walloon Waste* case from the position taken by Justice Rehnquist in his dissents from the U.S. waste decisions?

4. In a sequel to *Danish Bottles*, the European Commission targeted the Danish prohibition on the marketing of beer in cans. The Commission argued that the ban on cans interfered with the free movement of goods and the equal opportunity for any producer of beer in Europe to market its product in Denmark. (Aluminum cans are much lighter than bottles, reducing transportation costs.) Denmark argued in response that even if aluminum cans are recycled, the "re-use" of returnable beer bottles is environmentally preferable to recycling and that Denmark had the right to determine its own environmental preferences. Who is right? *See Packaging: Denmark Cancels Beverage Can Ban*, DANISH ENV'T NEWSL. (Ministry of the Env't, Copenhagen, Den.), Feb. 2002, *available at* http://www.mex.dk/uk/vis_nyhed_uk.asp?id=3277&nyhedsbrev_id=395; *Can Ban Lifted in Denmark*, PACKAGING WORLD MAG., Apr. 2, 2002, at 90, *available at* http://www.packworld.com/articles/Departments/14380.html.

A Note on Proportionality

In the excerpt that follows, Jan Jans and Hans Vedder break the "proportionality principle" into two or perhaps three elements. The first element is whether the measure in question is actually suitable to its stated purposes. There must be a causal link between the measure and, in environmental cases, the protection of the environment. As an added element in Europe, the precautionary principle may be used to bridge any scientific uncertainties about the environmental protection needed for the measure.

The second element in the proportionality principle is that the measure "must be *necessary* in the sense that it restricts trade as little as possible." JAN H. JANS & HANS H.B. VEDDER, EUROPEAN ENVIRONMENTAL LAW 254 (3d ed. 2008) (emphasis in original). As the European Court said in *Danish Bottles*, citing an earlier case, "Measures adopted to protect the environment must not 'go beyond the inevitable restrictions which are justified by the pursuit of the objective of environmental protection.'" Note the Court's distinction, in *Danish Bottles*, between the proportionality of the deposit-and-refund system and the lack of proportionality in the Danish restrictions on the size and shape of bottles that could be marketed.

The possible third element in a determination of proportionality goes to the question of "proportional to what?" As Jans and Vedder explain, this issue was addressed by the arguments before the court in *Danish Bottles*.

Jan H. Jans & Hans H.B. Vedder,
European Environmental Law
256–57 (3d ed. 2008)

Some authors argue that there is a third criterion to the application of the principle of proportionality. The Commission considered that it follows from the principle of proportionality that the level of protection should not be fixed exaggeratedly high and that other solutions should be accepted even if they are a little less effective in assuring the aim pursued. By implication, this means that interests such as the environment and public health must be weighed in the same balance as the interest of free movement of goods. The United Kingdom supported this view. Protection of the environment is indeed one of the important objectives of the EC, but it does not follow that every measure adopted for the protection of the environment is *prima facie* justified and that it only remains to examine whether the same results could be achieved by alternative means. The effect of such a view would be that measures to eliminate all forms of pollution would always be justified, since it would be obvious that very often similarly effective results could not be obtained by other means.... Advocate General Slynn expressed a similar view:

> There has to be a balancing of interests between the free movement of goods and environmental protection, even if in achieving the balance the high standard of the protection sought has to be reduced. The level of protection sought must be a reasonable level.

* * *

There is much to be said for applying the principle of proportionality only in the form of the suitability and necessity tests. This view receives support from considerations of the Court that, in the absence of common or harmonized rules on health and/or the environment, it was for the Member States to decide upon the level at which they wished to protect the health and life of animals, and the environment. The precautionary principle also points in this direction. In its guidelines on the precautionary principle the Commission argues that the EU has the right to establish the level of protection of the environment, human, animal and plant health that it deems appropriate. If the EU is entitled to set its own level of protection, in particular vis-a-vis the other WTO members, it is hard to see how this right can be denied the Member States.

Questions and Discussion

1. Subsequent to the Danish law, but before this decision, the Single European Act amended the European treaties to make preservation, protection, and improvement of the quality of the environmental protection a "mandatory requirement." Article 3(3) of the new Treaty on European Union updates the explicit European environmental commitment and puts it in a broad economic context: "[The EU] shall work for the sustainable development of Europe based on balanced economic growth and price stability, a highly competitive social market economy, aiming at full employment and social progress, and a high level of protection and improvement of the quality of the environment."

2. In paragraph 13 of *Danish Bottles*, the European Court of Justice determined that the Danish deposit-and-return system was "necessary" to achieve the objectives of the bottle bill and was "not disproportionate" to that objective. In paragraph 21, though, it found the system for "non-approved countries" to be "disproportionate to the objective." How does the proportionality test differ from the "least trade restrictive" approach developed by GATT and WTO panels? To the extent that it differs, is the Court's analysis useful for devising an Article XX test, or is the decision unique to trade law of the EU?

3. What does "proportionality" mean? Is there any real difference between the European "proportionality principle" and the U.S. concept of unreasonable burdens on interstate commerce, particularly the "rational relationship" test? *See* pages 245–55 for a discussion of the Dormant Commerce Clause.

4. The decision of the European Court of Justice in *Danish Bottles* spurred many European legislatures, particularly Germany's, to adopt new legislation relating to recycling

of products. Subsequently, the European Commission promulgated a directive mandating that all EU members adopt comprehensive programs to reduce packaging waste by specified percentages through specification of materials, recycling, and other measures. An important part of the Europe-wide effort was the harmonization of differing national requirements for packaging. After this directive, another dispute arose between the Commission and Denmark over Denmark's prohibition on the use of aluminum cans for beer. Denmark argued that cans, unlike bottles, cannot be reused but must be recycled, a less preferable environmental approach. Ultimately, Denmark yielded to the Commission's argument that, since Denmark had already exceeded the packaging waste reduction objectives of the directive, the ban on cans was not necessary, and it impermissibly interfered with the free movement of goods under a harmonized packaging system. Given the EU-wide objective of harmonizing standards while achieving environmental goals, is this a positive outcome?

C. Canada's Agreement on Internal Trade

Canada, like many other nations, has a federal system of government, with one national government and separate governments for each of its provinces and territories. Unlike most other federal governments, however, primary law-making power in Canada resides in the provincial and territorial governments. The authority of the national government is limited with respect to internal affairs. In this sense, the Canadian constitutional regime is somewhat akin to the Articles of Confederation system in the United States that preceded the Constitution.

One of the hazards of a system with strong provincial governments and a weak central government is that each province will seek economic advantage even at the expense of other provinces or of the nation as a whole. With Canada's increasing involvement in international trade and with greater ease of transportation of goods and people, the economic autonomy of the provinces came to be seen as an obstacle to national welfare. In 1995, the national government of Canada, the 10 provinces, and the two territories entered into an Agreement on Internal Trade (AIT). The preamble to the AIT declares that the government parties are resolved, among other objectives, to "promote an open, efficient, and stable market for long-term job creation, economic growth and stability," to "reduce and eliminate, to the extent possible, barriers to the free movement of persons, goods, services and investments within Canada," and to "promote sustainable and environmentally sound development." As the following selected articles of the AIT demonstrate, the new Canadian effort to establish a truly national economic system reflects concepts and language drawn from international trade agreements. Following the articles of the AIT is the decision of a panel interpreting the AIT in an early environment-related case.

Agreement on Internal Trade

signed Sept. 1994, entered into force July 1, 1995, *available at*
http://www.ait-aci.ca/en/ait/AIT%20Original%20with%20signatures.pdf

Article 100

It is the objective of the Parties to reduce and eliminate, to the extent possible, barriers to the free movement of persons, goods, services and investments within

Canada and to establish an open, efficient and stable domestic market. All Parties recognize and agree that enhancing trade and mobility within Canada would contribute to the attainment of this goal. * * *

Article 401

1. Subject to Article 404, each Party shall accord to goods of any other Party treatment no less favourable than the best treatment it accords to:

(a) its own like, directly competitive or substitutable goods; and

(b) like, directly competitive or substitutable goods of any other Party or non-Party. * * *

3. With respect to the Federal Government, paragraphs 1 and 2 mean that, subject to Article 404, it shall accord to:

(a) goods of a Province treatment no less favourable than the best treatment it accords to like, directly competitive or substitutable goods of any other Province or non-Party; and

(b) the persons, services and investments of a Province treatment no less favourable than the best treatment it accords, in like circumstances, to persons, services and investments of any other Province or non-Party.

4. The Parties agree that according identical treatment may not necessarily result in compliance with paragraph 1, 2 or 3.

Article 402

Subject to Article 404, no Party shall adopt or maintain any measure that restricts or prevents the movement of persons, goods, services or investments across provincial boundaries.

Article 403

Subject to Article 404, each Party shall ensure that any measure it adopts or maintains does not operate to create an obstacle to internal trade.

Article 404

Where it is established that a measure is inconsistent with Article 401, 402 or 403, that measure is still permissible under this Agreement where it can be demonstrated that:

(a) the purpose of the measure is to achieve a legitimate objective;

(b) the measure does not operate to impair unduly the access of persons, goods, services or investments of a Party that meet that legitimate objective;

(c) the measure is not more trade restrictive than necessary to achieve that legitimate objective; and

(d) the measure does not create a disguised restriction on trade.

Report of the Article 1704 Panel Concerning a
Dispute between Alberta and Canada Regarding the
Manganese-Based Fuel Additives Act

File No. 97/98-15-MMT-P058 (June 12, 1998)

1. NATURE OF THE COMPLAINT

On April 25, 1997, Royal Assent was granted to the *Manganese-based Fuel Additives Act (the Act)*, an Act of the Parliament of Canada. The purpose of the *Act* is to prohibit the importation into Canada of, and interprovincial trade in, certain manganese-based automotive fuel additives as listed by schedule. The only substance listed in the schedule is Methylcyclopentadienyl Manganese Tricarbonyl (MMT). The *Act* came into force on June 24, 1997.

The Government of Alberta (the Complainant) contends that the *Act* fails to comply with Canada's (the Respondent) obligations under the *Agreement on Internal Trade* (the *Agreement*), and that the inconsistencies cannot be justified by reference to the *Agreement's* provisions for measures associated with legitimate objectives. The Complainant contends that the *Act* has impaired internal trade, caused injury to Alberta refiners, and is inconsistent with general and specific provisions of the Agreement. The Governments of Québec, Nova Scotia and Saskatchewan (also Complainants) intervened in support of Alberta. The Government of Nova Scotia did not file a written submission or present oral arguments. * * *

The Respondent maintains that the *Act* is consistent with the provisions of the *Agreement* governing permissible exceptions for legitimate objectives, such as health, environmental protection or consumer protection. * * *

3. BACKGROUND

MMT is used primarily to increase the octane levels in unleaded gasoline. It is produced in the United States by a single company, and imported, blended and distributed for sale to refiners in Canada by a wholly-owned subsidiary.

MMT has been used in unleaded gasoline in Canada since 1977. Motor vehicle manufacturers contend that the use of MMT negatively impacts on the emissions control devices incorporated into vehicles, particularly on the effectiveness of the next generation of on-board diagnostic equipment (OBD-II).

Motor vehicle manufacturers express concern that stricter emissions standards and narrower compliance margins cannot be attained without sophisticated emissions control systems, which are sensitive to MMT damage.

The manufacturer of MMT and Canadian refiners dispute any link between MMT and OBD-II system damage and refer to the 1993 determination of the United States Environmental Protection Agency to allow MMT use in unleaded gasoline in certain areas of the United States, which is based on the absence of any evidence that MMT use would cause or contribute to the failure of any emissions control device. * * *

6. OPERATIONAL PRINCIPLES

In developing this *Agreement*, the federal, provincial and territorial governments were determined to enhance and expand the domestic market and thereby strengthen the economic union. This process required both the reduction and eventual elimination of existing barriers and an undertaking not to introduce new barriers to internal trade.

Article 100 reflects this undertaking. Article 101.2 emphasizes that the mutually agreed balance of rights and obligations of the Parties to the *Agreement* are reciprocal, while Article 101.3 contains a commitment that new barriers will not be established. Article 101.4 recognizes factors that the Parties should consider in pursuing the objectives.

Article 100 provides a broad statement of principles, modified by several factors. While the principles are a guide to policy-makers and dispute resolution panels, the rules governing this dispute are set out in Chapters Four through Fifteen. * * *

8. SUBSTANCE AND PROCESS

The Respondent submits that the issue in dispute is one of substance, and beyond specific provisions of the *Agreement*, the Panel should not consider whether the process was "good" or "bad" from a federal-provincial relations perspective.

It is the Panel's view that process is an integral part of the *Agreement*. In addition to the process obligations contained in specific Part IV chapters, especially Articles 1508 and 1509 (Canadian Council of Ministers of the Environment), and Article 1702 (Consultations), there are a number of general process commitments provided in the Preamble, the Operating Principles and the General Rules of the *Agreement*.

The general emphasis of the *Agreement* is on cooperative resolution of outstanding issues, including an obligation to consult and seek joint action where appropriate. The *Agreement* has in fact changed the policy context facing governments by requiring a greater level of consultation or "process" when introducing measures affecting internal trade.

Articles 1705 and 1707 state that the mandate of a Panel is to determine if the measure under review is consistent with the *Agreement*. Therefore, the question is not whether the *Act* is consistent with a specific chapter, or even with Parts III (General Rules) and IV (Specific Rules), but whether the *Act* conforms to the *Agreement*, including the principles and process contained therein.

On the matter of process, reference was made to the inherent authority of Parliament and the deference due the Parliamentary process. In our view there is no issue relative to Parliamentary authority or Panel deference. The Parliament of Canada and the legislatures of the provinces and territories are not subservient to each other or to the Panel in the exercise of their Constitutional powers. However, they are Parties to this *Agreement*, and it is the *Agreement* which must prevail.

9. ARTICLE 401 (RECIPROCAL NON-DISCRIMINATION)

The basic issue as to whether the *Act* is inconsistent with Article 401 should be addressed in two stages:

1. Does the *Act* discriminate against the goods of one Party to the benefit of the goods of another Party?

2. Are the goods discriminated against "like, directly competitive or substitutable" with the goods of another Party?

In dealing with measures introduced by the Respondent, there must be a geographical component to the discrimination for a measure to be inconsistent with Article 401.3. This geographical component can be direct, where goods from one Party are favoured over identical goods from another Party, or indirect, where goods produced predominately in the territory of one Party are favoured over directly competitive or substitutable goods produced predominately in the territory of another Party.

The *Act* treats MMT less favourably than other octane enhancers, and MMT-enhanced gasoline less favourably than MMT-free gasoline. The intent of Article 401.3 is to prevent the Respondent from favouring goods from one province over the goods of another province. The Panel finds that there is no geographical discrimination in the Act. MMT-enhanced gasoline was produced in all provinces with refineries when the Act came into force, and all refineries in Canada could produce MMT-free gasoline with the proper equipment and process adjustments. Accordingly, market discrimination is more appropriately addressed under Article 403.

The *Act* is consistent with Article 401. The Panel is not required to weigh the scientific evidence presented to determine whether MMT-free gasoline and MMT-enhanced gasoline are like goods, or whether MMT and other octane enhancers are like, directly competitive or substitutable goods.

10. ARTICLES 402 (RIGHT OF ENTRY AND EXIT) AND 403 (NO OBSTACLES)

The Panel agrees with the Respondent and finds that the *Act* is inconsistent with Articles 402 and 403.

11. ARTICLE 405 (RECONCILIATION)

The *Act* does not restrict or make the manufacture or use of MMT illegal. In fact, it in no way restricts the use of MMT. MMT is a legal commodity. The *Act* prohibits the importation and internal trade in MMT.

The *Act* does not restrict the intraprovincial use of, or trade in, MMT-enhanced gasoline on environmental grounds, yet interprovincial trade is prohibited on environmental grounds. The Respondent argues that the intraprovincial use was beyond the legislative authority of Parliament. That factor underscores the need for consultation or joint action as reflected in the *Agreement*. Although there is no requirement for consensus, if the environment and the consumer are to be protected, and internal trade is to be enhanced, unilateral action at the federal level can be counterproductive and ineffective.

It is clear from the submissions that it was the automobile manufacturers who were the driving force behind the elimination of MMT. They claimed that the on-board monitoring equipment in new vehicles would be impaired by the use of MMT-enhanced gasoline. The evidence as to the impact of MMT on the environment is, at best, inconclusive. * * *

12. ARTICLE 404 (LEGITIMATE OBJECTIVES)

The Respondent has conceded that the *Act* is inconsistent with Article 402 and Article 403, but maintains that the *Act* is permissible under Article 404. The Respondent acknowledges that it bears the onus to demonstrate that the Act meets each of the four tests under Article 404.

The Party introducing an inconsistent measure must demonstrate that the purpose of the measure is to achieve a legitimate objective. The Panel does not agree that the requirement of Article 404(a) is a simple requirement to show that legislators or policy makers had declared the purpose to be a legitimate objective. Such an interpretation would open the door to Parties using the legitimate objectives justification to adopt trade restricting measures, by a simple declaration that the measure was in pursuit of a legitimate objective.

The Panel has considered the Respondent's willingness to tolerate the continued use of MMT, both through its suggestion of a two-pump system and the *Act's* tolerance of intraprovincial use. Despite the Respondent's assurance that economics would not support a MMT manufacturing facility in a single province, the fact is that under the *Act* MMT can be produced and used within each province with obvious impact on the environment and vehicle emission monitoring systems.

While the evidence on the effects of MMT is not conclusive, there was sufficient evidence to determine that the Respondent had a reasonable basis for believing that the *Act* would achieve a legitimate objective, and therefore meets the requirements of Article 404(a).

The evidence provided has focussed on: whether MMT affects the performance of the latest generation of emissions control devices in the newest vehicles; debate over the environmental and health effects, particularly in urban areas where smog is a problem; and the major concern of automobile manufacturers regarding the impact of MMT-enhanced gasoline on monitoring equipment in new vehicles.

In the recent past, a similar situation existed in the case of leaded gasoline. At that time, automobile manufacturers designed vehicles to operate on unleaded gasoline, while older vehicles could still use leaded gasoline. Even though it was established that lead was directly toxic, the phased elimination of this substance from gasoline took place over a number of years.

The Respondent has not demonstrated that there existed a matter of such urgency or a risk so widespread as to warrant such comprehensive restrictions as the *Act* provides on internal trade. If the legitimate objective of the *Act* is as stated, to prevent MMT from being used in newer model vehicles in major urban areas, then total elimination of MMT was unduly restrictive.

In light of these factors, the Panel has determined that the Act is inconsistent with Article 404(b).

Article 1505.7 qualifies Article 404(c):

Further to Article 404(c) (Legitimate Objectives) and Annexes 405.1(5) and 405.2(5), an environmental measure shall not be considered to be more trade restrictive than necessary to achieve a legitimate objective if the Party adopting or maintaining the measure takes into account the need to minimize negative trade effects when choosing among equally effective and reasonably available means of achieving that legitimate objective.

Article 404(c) and Article 1505.7 have three requirements: "take into account the need to minimize negative trade effects," "equally effective" means, and "reasonably available" means. The onus is on the Respondent to demonstrate, on balance of probabilities, that it has met these requirements, and to demonstrate that no other available option would have met the legitimate objective.

Several options were identified as equally effective and reasonably available. From the evidence and the submissions of the Complainants, three of those options, namely tradable permits, taxation, and direct regulation under section 46 of CEPA, did not require further study on the effects of MMT.

Not all measures that eliminate MMT are equally trade restrictive. The intention of the Agreement is to limit the use of trade restrictions to achieve other objectives, rather than the objectives themselves.

Therefore the Panel determines that the Respondent has not discharged the requirements of 404(c), as modified by 1505.7.

The Panel finds that the *Act* is transparent, and does not create a disguised restriction on trade [under 404(d)]. * * *

15. PANEL DETERMINATION

The Panel finds that the *Act* is inconsistent with the Articles 402 and 403 of the *Agreement*, and the inconsistency is not justified by the legitimate objectives test contained in Article 404.

Since the restriction on importation into Canada of MMT is not subject to the *Agreement*, and since the Panel does not believe that the object of the *Act* was a disguised restriction on internal trade, the Panel does not recommend repeal of the *Act*.

It may well be that the current structure of MMT supply is such that the *Act's* international trade restriction is an effective barrier to internal trade in what is otherwise a legal product. However, this impediment must be dealt with in another forum.

The Panel recommends that the Respondent remove the inconsistency of the Act with the Agreement. Pending such action, the Panel recommends that the Respondent suspend the operation of the Act with respect to interprovincial trade. * * *

16. DISSENTING OPINION

I disagree with my colleagues.

The Respondent has been faced with a genuine dilemma. It has received the clearest of indications from the car manufacturers that further use of MMT is incompatible with the most up to date pollution control equipment. At the same time, the Respondent has entered into a series of agreements, both nationally and internationally, to control fuel emissions.

The evidence before us clearly showed that the Respondent spent a great deal of time and effort attempting to get a consensus between the fuel industry and the car manufacturers. This effort was not rewarded with success, and the Respondent felt that in these circumstances it had no serious alternative but to introduce legislation.

The path of a simple ban on the substance MMT was not possible, because on the evidence MMT, while noxious in large amounts, did not appear to be dangerous in small quantities. The environmental effects of MMT are cumulative and indirect, in that it appears to affect the operations of fuel control equipment in the latest model vehicles.

For these reasons, I disagree with my colleagues that the *Act* does not meet the tests outlined in 404(b) and 404(c) of the *Agreement on Internal Trade*. There is no doubt that the legislation is by itself an impairment of internal trade. However, it is equally clear to me that the legislation satisfies the test set out in article 404. The purpose and effect of the legislation will be to get rid of MMT as a substance in gasoline. No other substances are so named or restricted, and therefore I would find that there has been "no undue impairment of access of goods," and I would also find that the measure is "not more trade restrictive than necessary to achieve the legitimate objective."

I would also disagree with my colleagues that insofar as the process followed has been less than perfect, the entire blame for this should be placed at the door of the Respondent. This legislation was before the Parliament of Canada for over a year, and there was ample opportunity for other governments to put forward alternative measures. I note that the so-called "two pump solution" was rejected by the petroleum industry itself. We have no basis upon which to find that the differences between the parties would have been resolved if this issue had been discussed further.

In short, the Respondent took action that it concluded was necessary for air quality and the improvement of the environment. The purpose of the *Agreement on Internal Trade* was not to dilute the ability of responsible governments to improve the environment of Canadians, provided these measures meet the tests set out in the *Agreement*. I would therefore have dismissed the application.

––––––––––

Questions and Discussion

1. Compare the provisions of the AIT with the TFEU. What are the points of similarity? What are the points of difference? Which tracks GATT provisions and concepts more closely?

2. Does the Panel's ruling represent an application of the "proportionality principle"? To the extent that it does, consider the Panel's decision in light of Jans's and Vedder's three elements of the proportionality test: 1) suitability of the measure to achieve the objective, 2) necessity of the measure, and 3) whether achievement of the objective is proportionate to the burden imposed on internal trade. The AIT Panel says that the federal government of Canada "has not demonstrated that there existed a matter of such urgency or a risk so widespread as to warrant such comprehensive restrictions as the *Act* provides on internal trade." Is that an argument about necessity of the measure or about a disproportion between benefits and burdens?

––––––––––

If, at the end of this section and this whole chapter, you feel frustrated by the ambiguity of the legal doctrines applied in the most sensitive cases, perhaps you will find comfort in the following thoughts from Farber and Hudec. Their conclusion speaks to U.S. Supreme Court and GATT doctrine but is equally applicable to the jurisprudence of the European Court of Justice and the law of the Canadian AIT.

Daniel A. Farber & Robert E. Hudec, *GATT Legal Restraints on Domestic Environmental Regulations,*

in 1 Fair Trade and Harmonization: Prerequisites for Free Trade 84
(Jagdish Bhagwati & Robert E. Hudec eds., 1996)

The general problem we have addressed in this study has resisted the best efforts of the [U.S.] Supreme Court (for over 150 years), GATT tribunals, international negotiators, and a host of talented legal scholars. The reason, we believe, is that in some ultimate sense the problem is unsolvable. Taken to their logical conclusion, either free trade or local autonomy could virtually eliminate the other, and negotiating a workable border between the two depends as much on history, politics, and local terrain as on any overarching vision. No matter how a legal test is articulated, it cannot satisfactorily resolve the tensions between local autonomy and free trade in all conceivable cases. In the end, the law must have a certain irreducible messiness in dealing with such fundamental tensions.

Messiness is not, however, the same as chaos. Both the Supreme Court and GATT do have fairly adequate ways of dealing with facially discriminatory measures. Both place a heavy burden on the regulating government to justify the measure.... Both run into trouble with facially neutral measures, which run the spectrum from devious bad faith on the one hand and innocent run-of-the-mill regulation on the other. Even here, however, there are a considerable number of easy cases. The difficult cases are those in the middle of the spectrum—where a clear but limited benefit exists, or the benefit is hard to predict (perhaps because of scientific uncertainty), or assessing the benefit requires a difficult and possibly culturally based value judgment.

Chapter 5

The Article XX Exceptions

I. Introduction

In the last two chapters, we saw dispute settlement panels find a number of environmental protection provisions to be inconsistent with the national treatment obligation of GATT Article III or the prohibition against quantitative restrictions of Article XI. These included: a tax to fund an environmental cleanup program that facially discriminated against foreign products (*Superfund*); an environmental regulation of gasoline quality that applied different standards to "like products" (*Reformulated Gasoline*); an export restriction on fish catches (*Salmon and Herring*); and import controls that distinguished between products from different countries based on the way the product was produced (*Tuna/Dolphin I* and *II*, *Shrimp/Turtle*). Could any of these measures that violated Articles III or XI be saved from GATT inconsistency by the exceptions from GATT rules found in Article XX?

GATT Article XX grants governments a "general exception" from GATT rules for certain listed purposes. Two of the specified purposes have a significant relationship to environmental policy. In other words, if an environmental trade measure violates a core GATT obligation, it may nonetheless constitute a valid measure provided that it meets the requirements of one of the two environmental exceptions of Article XX.

Article XX provides, in pertinent part:

Subject to the requirement that such measures are not applied in a manner which would constitute a means of arbitrary or unjustifiable discrimination between countries where the same conditions prevail, or a disguised restriction on international trade, nothing in this Agreement shall be construed to prevent the adoption or enforcement by any Member of measures ...

(b) necessary to protect human, animal or plant life or health ... [or]

(g) relating to the conservation of exhaustible natural resources if such measures are made effective in conjunction with restrictions on domestic production or consumption.

The broadly written environmental exceptions in paragraphs XX(b) and (g) might appear, on first reading, to permit many of the trade restrictions encountered in previous chapters. The conditions in the introductory clause, or chapeau, of Article XX also appear to be broadly written. While they seek to prevent abusive discrimination, they do not prohibit discrimination altogether. Moreover, according to the plain language of the article, if the chapeau conditions are met, *nothing* in GATT should preclude a government from adopting and enforcing measures to protect human, animal, and plant life or health or to conserve natural resources.

Nonetheless, although every trade and environment dispute has resulted in an analysis of Article XX(b) or XX(g), dispute settlement panels have found only two environmental trade restriction to meet the requirements of Article XX—a French ban on asbestos and the U.S. shrimp/turtle regulations. How has this narrow application of Article XX come about? As you read the cases, consider the following questions:

- In many cases, the panels appear afraid that environmental exceptions could swallow the GATT's core rules. Do panels have a legitimate fear? Could rules be drafted that ensure that such fears do not become reality?

- The decisions of dispute settlement panels show the difficulty in distinguishing measures that have a true environmental purpose from measures masquerading as environmental measures. How should panels determine whether a trade restriction has a *bona fide* environmental purpose?

- Has the interpretation of Article XX evolved over time to provide opportunity for countries to invoke Article XX successfully?

II. The Scope of Article XX

Prior to the GATT, the international trading regime was based on what are now considered the GATT's core obligations: the most favored nation and national treatment obligations and the prohibition against quantitative restrictions. In his excellent history of Article XX, Steve Charnovitz traces the particular language of Article XX to one of those pre-GATT trade treaties: the 1927 International Convention for the Abolition of Import and Export Prohibitions and Restrictions. That treaty allowed exceptions to import and export rules "for the protection of public health or for the protection of animals or plants against disease, insects and harmful parasites." Steve Charnovitz, *Exploring the Environmental Exceptions in GATT Article XX*, J. WORLD TRADE, Oct. 1991, at 37. An addendum to that convention clarifies that the drafters intended this exception to apply to "the protection of animals and plants against disease" as well as "to measures taken to preserve them from degeneration or extinction." Still, the treaty precluded this and other exceptions from being "applied in such a manner as to constitute a means of arbitrary discrimination between foreign countries where the same conditions prevail, or a disguised restriction on international trade." As Charnovitz notes, this convention is noteworthy because even though its goal was "achieving the 'final suppression' of import prohibitions, there was general agreement that legitimate action to protect public health, animal or plants was entirely proper." *Id.* at 42.

The 1947 Draft Charter of the International Trade Organization carried forward the idea that environmental restrictions could be exempt from trade rules. It originally provided that "Nothing in Chapter IV [on commercial policy] of this Charter shall be construed to prevent the adoption or enforcement by any Member of measures: … b) necessary to protect human, animal or plant life or health." A subsequent draft read: "For the purpose of protecting human, animal or plant life or health, *if corresponding domestic safeguards under similar conditions exist in the importing country.*" The drafters added the italicized language due to concerns regarding the abuse of sanitary regulations by importing countries. Later, this language was deemed unnecessary and deleted. Exactly why it was unnecessary, however, is subject to debate.

While the history shows that the GATT drafters viewed certain exceptions as proper, it does not give a clear indication of the breadth of permissible exceptions or provide any guidelines for applying them. GATT and WTO dispute settlement panels have thus been tasked with giving detailed meaning to Article XX. For example, although Articles I and III prohibit all discrimination, when is discrimination "arbitrary or unjustifiable" under Article XX? Can countries impose import restrictions to protect plants and animals outside their own borders or are the exceptions limited to protecting their domestic environment? Can countries impose trade restrictions based on processes and production methods (PPMs)?

To help identify the scope of Article XX, dispute settlement panels have asked first whether a measure falls within one of Article XX's enumerated exceptions. Only if the measure falls within one of the exceptions would the analysis proceed to look for impermissible discrimination or a disguised trade restriction under the chapeau. The *Tuna/Dolphin II* Panel described the following three-part test for analyzing Article XX questions:

1. Does the policy for which the disputed trade measure is invoked fall within the range of policies relating to the specific exception, such as the Article XX(g) provision for conservation measures relating to exhaustible natural resources?

2. Does the disputed trade measure meet the requirements of the specific exception; i.e., is it "necessary" to protect human, animal, or plant life or health or does it "relate to" the conservation of exhaustible natural resources made effective "in conjunction" with restrictions on domestic production or consumption?

3. Does the disputed measure conform to the chapeau of Article XX, namely that the measure is not applied in a manner that constitutes a means of arbitrary or unjustifiable discrimination between countries where the same conditions prevail or in a manner that constitutes a disguised restriction on international trade?

United States-Restrictions on Imports of Tuna, GATT Panel Report, DS29/R, paras. 5.12, 5.28 (June 16, 1994) (unadopted), *reprinted in* 33 I.L.M. 839 (1994) [hereinafter *Tuna/Dolphin II*].

Starting with the *Tuna/Dolphin* dispute, panels have used this three-part test to construct a rich body of jurisprudence to shape the scope of Article XX. The first two steps of the *Tuna/Dolphin II* framework may be more easily understood as a single test: does the measure being challenged come within one of the enumerated exceptions? Whether the measure is of the type meant to be covered by the exception (step 1 above) is a distinct issue in some cases, but in others it is either assumed or uncontested. Step 2 above, which involves construing the language of the relevant Article XX paragraph, is more often the focus of the analysis in dispute settlement reports. The WTO Appellate Body has specified this analytical sequence as the only proper approach to Article XX. *See* United States-Standards for Reformulated and Conventional Gasoline, Panel Report, WT/DS2/R, para. 6.20 (adopted May 20, 1996), *reprinted in* 35 I.L.M. 276 (1996) [hereinafter *Reformulated Gasoline*] (expressly adopting this test); United States-Import Prohibition of Certain Shrimp and Shrimp Products, Appellate Body Report, WT/DS58/AB/R, para. 117 (criticizing the Panel for disregarding "the sequence of steps essential for carrying out such an analysis." (adopted Nov. 6, 1998), *reprinted in* 38 I.L.M. 121 (1999) [hereinafter *Shrimp/Turtle*]. After the initial overview in this section, the structure of this chapter will follow the same sequence.

The GATT contracting parties never adopted either *Tuna/Dolphin* report, and WTO panels and the Appellate Body scarcely refer to them. Thus, as guides to interpretation in future disputes, they have limited value. Nevertheless, they offer a good introduction to Article XX, and the approach that they take toward unilateral measures and Article XX remains important for several reasons. First, the two decisions established in the minds of many environmental organizations the hostility of trade rules to environmental concerns. Second, they continue to represent the thinking of many WTO member governments on trade and environment. In 1992, these views became embodied in Principle 12 of the Rio Declaration, which states that unilateral trade measures should be "avoided." Third, while the analyses of these panels have not been directly adopted by the parties or by the Appellate Body, their analyses have been adopted indirectly. For example, the Panel in *Reformulated Gasoline*, the first WTO case to go to a dispute settlement panel, began its analysis of Article XX(b) by stating the three-step test enunciated in *Tuna/Dolphin II*, quoted earlier. It then adopted the interpretation of "necessary" in *Section 337* and *Thai Cigarettes*, which the *Tuna/Dolphin II* Panel also embraced. *Reformulated Gasoline*, Panel Report, at paras. 6.20, 6.24.

Recall from Chapter 4 that the *Tuna/Dolphin I* and *II* Panels (pages 200–08) both found that the U.S. embargoes on tuna violated Article XI of GATT. The Marine Mammal Protection Act (MMPA) required the United States to prohibit the importation of tuna from countries that failed to take measures to limit dolphin mortality when catching tuna by "setting" on dolphins. It also required the United States to prohibit the importation of tuna from countries that purchased tuna from embargoed countries—the "intermediary embargo." The Panels found that these restrictions did not relate to the tuna as a product, but instead related to the process by which the tuna was caught. Thus, even though the United States imposed similar obligations on U.S. fishers, the import restrictions could not be considered under Article III. Instead, they violated Article XI's prohibition against import restrictions. Both Panels then assessed whether the import restrictions met the requirements of Article XX(b) or Article XX(g).

United States-Restrictions on Imports of Tuna (*Tuna/Dolphin I*)

GATT Panel Report, DS21/R (Sept. 3, 1991) (unadopted),
reprinted in 30 I.L.M. 1594 (1991) [hereinafter *Tuna/Dolphin I*]

5.22.... The Panel recalled that previous panels had established that Article XX is a limited and conditional exception from obligations under other provisions of the General Agreement, and not a positive rule establishing obligations in itself. Therefore, the practice of panels has been to interpret Article XX narrowly, to place the burden on the party invoking Article XX to justify its invocation, and not to examine Article XX exceptions unless invoked. Nevertheless, the Panel considered that a party to a dispute could argue in the alternative that Article XX might apply, without this argument constituting ipso facto an admission that the measures in question would otherwise be inconsistent with the General Agreement. Indeed, the efficient operation of the dispute settlement process required that such arguments in the alternative be possible. * * *

Article XX(b)

5.24. The Panel noted that the United States considered the prohibition of imports of certain yellowfin tuna and certain yellowfin tuna products from Mexico, and the provisions of the MMPA on which this prohibition is based, to be justified by Article XX(b) because they served solely the purpose of protecting dolphin life and health and were "necessary" within the meaning of that provision because, in respect of the protection of dolphin life and health outside its jurisdiction, there was no alternative measure reasonably available to the United States to achieve this objective. Mexico considered that Article XX(b) was not applicable to a measure imposed to protect the life or health of animals outside the jurisdiction of the contracting party taking it and that the import prohibition imposed by the United States was not necessary because alternative means consistent with the General Agreement were available to it to protect dolphin lives or health, namely international co-operation between the countries concerned.

5.25. The Panel noted that the basic question raised by these arguments, namely whether Article XX(b) covers measures necessary to protect human, animal or plant life or health outside the jurisdiction of the contracting party taking the measure, is not clearly answered by the text of that provision. It refers to life and health protection generally without expressly limiting that protection to the jurisdiction of the contracting party concerned. The Panel therefore decided to analyze this issue in the light of the drafting history of Article XX(b), the purpose of this provision, and the consequences that the interpretations proposed by the parties would have for the operation of the General Agreement as a whole.

5.26. The Panel noted that the proposal for Article XX(b) dated from the Draft Charter of the International Trade Organization (ITO) proposed by the United States, which stated in Article 32, "Nothing in Chapter IV [on commercial policy] of this Charter shall be construed to prevent the adoption or enforcement by any Member of measures: ... (b) necessary to protect human, animal or plant life or health". In the New York Draft of the ITO Charter, the preamble had been revised to read as it does at present, and exception (b) read: "For the purpose of protecting human, animal or plant life or health, if corresponding domestic safeguards under similar conditions exist in the importing country". This added proviso reflected concerns regarding the abuse of sanitary regulations by importing countries. Later, Commission A of the Second Session of the Preparatory Committee in Geneva agreed to drop this proviso as unnecessary. Thus, the record indicates that the concerns of the drafters of Article XX(b) focused on the use of sanitary measures to safeguard life or health of humans, animals or plants within the jurisdiction of the importing country.

5.27. The Panel further noted that Article XX(b) allows each contracting party to set its human, animal or plant life or health standards. The conditions set out in Article XX(b) which limit resort to this exception, namely that the measure taken must be "necessary" and not "constitute a means of arbitrary or unjustifiable discrimination or a disguised restriction on international trade", refer to the trade measure requiring justification under Article XX(b), not however to the life or health standard chosen by the contracting party. The Panel recalled the finding of a previous panel that this paragraph of Article XX was intended to allow contracting parties to impose trade restrictive measures inconsistent with the General Agreement to pursue overriding public policy goals to the extent that such inconsistencies were unavoidable. The Panel considered that if the broad interpretation of Article XX(b) suggested by the United States were accepted, each contracting party could unilaterally determine the life or health protection policies from which other contracting parties could not deviate without jeopardizing their rights under the General Agreement. The General Agreement would then no longer constitute a multilateral framework for trade among all contracting parties but would provide legal security only in respect of trade between a limited number of contracting parties with identical internal regulations.

5.28. The Panel considered that the United States' measures, even if Article XX(b) were interpreted to permit extrajurisdictional protection of life and health, would not meet the requirement of necessity set out in that provision. The United States had not demonstrated to the Panel—as required of the party invoking an Article XX exception—that it had exhausted all options reasonably available to it to pursue its dolphin protection objectives through measures consistent with the General Agreement, in particular through the negotiation of international cooperative arrangements, which would seem to be desirable in view of the fact that dolphins roam the waters of many states and the high seas. Moreover, even assuming that an import prohibition were the only resort reasonably available to the United States, the particular measure chosen by the United States could in the Panel's view not be considered to be necessary within the meaning of Article XX(b). The United States linked the maximum incidental dolphin taking rate which Mexico had to meet during a particular period in order to be able to export tuna to the United States to the taking rate actually recorded for United States fishermen during the same period. Consequently, the Mexican authorities could not know whether, at a given point of time, their policies conformed to the United States' dolphin protection standards. The Panel considered that a limitation on trade based on such unpredictable conditions could not be regarded as necessary to protect the health or life of dolphins.

5.29. On the basis of the above considerations, the Panel found that the United States' direct import prohibition imposed on certain yellowfin tuna and certain yellowfin tuna products of Mexico and the provisions of the MMPA under which it is imposed could not be justified under the exception in Article XX(b). * * *

Article XX(g)

5.30. The Panel proceeded to examine whether the prohibition on imports of certain yellowfin tuna and certain yellowfin tuna products from Mexico and the MMPA provisions under which it was imposed could be justified under the exception in Article XX(g)....

5.31. The Panel noted that Article XX(g) required that the measures relating to the conservation of exhaustible natural resources be taken "in conjunction with restrictions on domestic production or consumption". A previous panel had found that a measure could only be considered to have been taken "in conjunction with" production restrictions "if it was primarily aimed at rendering effective these restrictions". A country can effectively control the production or consumption of an exhaustible natural resource only to the extent that the production or consumption is under its jurisdiction. This suggests that Article XX(g) was intended to permit contracting parties to take trade measures primarily aimed at rendering effective restrictions on production or consumption within their jurisdiction.

5.32. The Panel further noted that Article XX(g) allows each contracting party to adopt its own conservation policies. The conditions set out in Article XX(g) which limit resort to this exception, namely that the measures taken must be related to the conservation of exhaustible natural resources, and that they not "constitute a means of arbitrary or unjustifiable discrimination ... or a disguised restriction on international trade" refer to the trade measure requiring justification under Article XX(g), not however to the conservation policies adopted by the contracting party. The Panel considered that if the extrajurisdictional interpretation of Article XX(g) suggested by the United States were accepted, each contracting party could unilaterally determine the conservation policies from which other contracting parties could not deviate without jeopardizing their rights under the General Agreement. The considerations that led the Panel to reject an extrajurisdictional application of Article XX(b) therefore apply also to Article XX(g).

5.33. The Panel did not consider that the United States measures, even if Article XX(g) could be applied extrajurisdictionally, would meet the conditions set out in that provision. A previous panel found that a measure could be considered as "relating to the conservation of exhaustible natural resources" within the meaning of Article XX(g) only if it was primarily aimed at such conservation. (Canada-Measures Affecting Exports of Unprocessed Herring and Salmon," GATT Panel Report, para. 4.6, L/6268, BISD, 35th Supp. 98 (1988) (adopted Mar. 22, 1988). The Panel recalled that the United States linked the maximum incidental dolphin-taking rate which Mexico had to meet during a particular period in order to be able to export tuna to the United States to the taking rate actually recorded for United States fishermen during the same period. Consequently, the Mexican authorities could not know whether, at a given point of time, their conservation policies conformed to the United States conservation standards. The Panel considered that a limitation on trade based on such unpredictable conditions could not be regarded as being primarily aimed at the conservation of dolphins.

5.34. On the basis of the above considerations, the Panel found that the United States direct import prohibition on certain yellowfin tuna and certain yellowfin tuna products of Mexico directly imported from Mexico, and the provisions of the MMPA under which it is imposed, could not be justified under Article XX(g).

Questions and Discussion

1. *Who Has the Burden of Proof?* In designating the party invoking the exception as having the burden of proof, the *Tuna/Dolphin I* Panel was merely following many previously adopted GATT panel decisions; subsequent WTO panels have also followed this general rule. Canada-Administration of the Foreign Investment Review Act, GATT Panel Report, L/5504, BISD, 30th Supp. 140, para. 5.20 (1984) (adopted Feb. 7, 1984); United States-Section 337 of the Tariff Act of 1930, GATT Panel Report, L/6439, BISD, 36th Supp. 345, para. 5.27 (1990) (adopted Nov. 7, 1989). In *Brazil-Retreaded Tyres*, the Panel declared that once the party invoking the exception has produced "sufficient evidence to raise a presumption that its defence is justified, then the burden shifts to the [challenging party] to rebut the presumption." Brazil–Measures Affecting Imports of Retreaded Tyres, Panel Report, WT/DS332/R, para. 7.36 (adopted Dec. 17, 2007) [hereinafter *Brazil-Retreaded Tyres*]. *See also Reformulated Gasoline*, Panel Report, at para. 6.20.

2. *The "Extraterritorial" Issue.* The U.S. tuna/dolphin regulations sought to protect dolphins in the eastern tropical Pacific Ocean—far beyond U.S. waters. May a country invoke Article XX to justify trade restrictions to protect a species found outside its territory? This is the so-called "extraterritorial" or "extrajurisdictional" issue. On what basis does the *Tuna/Dolphin I* Panel conclude that neither Article XX(b) nor XX(g) applies extrajurisdictionally? The *Tuna/Dolphin II* Panel rejected these arguments, finding nothing in Articles XX(b) or XX(g) or the chapeau that suggests any territorial limitation. In addition, the *Tuna/Dolphin II* Panel noted that the very decision relied upon by the *Tuna/Dolphin I* Panel to impose a territorial limitation, *Canada-Measures Affecting Exports*

of Unprocessed Herring and Salmon, actually related to species found inside and outside the territory of Canada, the country invoking the exception. The Panel also noted, among other things, that at least one Article XX exception—Article XX(e) relating to products of prison labor—specifically relates to things located, or actions occurring, outside the territorial jurisdiction of the party imposing the measure. The Panel also found that the statements and drafting changes made during the negotiation of the Havana Charter and the GATT cited by the parties and the *Tuna/Dolphin I* Panel failed to support any particular conclusion on the extraterritorial question. For all these reasons, the Panel determined that "no valid reason" supported the conclusion that Article XX(g) applied only to exhaustible natural resources located within the territory of the contracting party invoking the exception. Thus, a policy to conserve dolphins in the eastern tropical Pacific Ocean fell within the range of policies covered by Article XX(g). *Tuna/Dolphin,* at paras. 5.16–5.20. Which Panel's analysis do you find more persuasive?

While the Appellate Body had a chance to resolve this issue in the *Shrimp/Turtle* dispute, it explicitly declined to do so. The dispute arose from a U.S. ban on shrimp imports from countries that did not, in the opinion of the United States, adequately protect sea turtles in the exporting countries' shrimp fisheries. Sea turtles are highly migratory with large ranges. While the sea turtle species at issue in the dispute could be found in both the United States and the countries of the challenging Southeast Asian parties, the United States did not claim that individuals from these species occurred in both places. After noting that all of the species involved occur in waters subject to U.S. jurisdiction, the Appellate Body states: "We do not pass upon the question of whether there is an implied jurisdictional limitation in Article XX(g), and if so, the nature or extent of that limitation. We note only that in the specific circumstances of the case before us, there is a sufficient nexus between the migratory and endangered marine populations involved and the United States for purposes of Article XX(g)." *Shrimp/Turtle,* para. 133. Based on *Shrimp/Turtle,* it is clear that Article XX(g) may be invoked to justify measures to protect those resources that exist, at least for some part of the resource's life history, in the territory of the party invoking the Article XX exception. It may also be possible to interpret the decision more broadly to permit measures protecting resources wholly outside the territory of another country based on some evidence of a "nexus" of interests. Nonetheless, Robert Howse advises to take a narrower reading of the Appellate Body's findings, concluding that the Appellate Body's:

> failure to resolve the question of whether Article XX(g) has jurisdictional or territorial limits must be understood in light of [Article XX(g)'s] condition that unilateral trade measures be taken in conjunction with restrictions on domestic resource production or consumption. By virtue of this condition, Article XX(g) already requires a link between the environmental trade measures and domestic regulation dealing with the same conservation problem. Were a WTO Member to target its conservation concerns solely at the policies of other countries, without putting its own house in order, then it would not be able to meet this condition of XX(g). The question, then, of whether there is an implicit territorial or jurisdictional limitation in XX(g) may therefore be largely moot, since Article XX(g) by its explicit language only applies to environmental trade measures that are coupled with domestic environmental regulation.... The purpose of a territorial nexus is to prevent a state that lacks a legitimate concern from using a global environmental problem as a pretext for protectionist interventionism.

Robert Howse, *The Appellate Body Rulings in the* Shrimp/Turtle *Case: A New Legal Baseline for the Trade and Environment Debate*, 27 Colum. J. Envtl. L. 491, 504 (2002). What if the United States bans the importation of red kangaroos, a species endemic to Australia, and also bans domestic production and consumption of products made from red kangaroos? Should the domestic restrictions save the import restrictions? Under European Union law, the answer appears to be no. *See* Case C-169/89, Criminal Proceedings against Gourmetterie Van den Burg, 1990 E.C.J. I-2143 (1990) (striking down a Dutch law that banned the importation of red grouse, a species endemic to the United Kingdom and for which no U.K.-based restrictions existed). Does it matter, as Howse suggests, that the importing country justifies the measure under Article XX(g) instead of Article XX(b)?

3. *Unilateral Measures and PPMs.* The *Tuna/Dolphin I* Panel remarked negatively on the unilateral nature of the tuna import restriction. *See* para. 5.32 above. The U.S. measures in *Shrimp/Turtle* were also adopted unilaterally—that is, in the absence of a multilateral decision or framework. Can Article XX be invoked to justify such measures? The *Shrimp/Turtle* Panel made the following observations:

> In our view, if an interpretation of the chapeau of Article XX were to be followed which would allow a Member to adopt measures conditioning access to its market for a given product upon the adoption by the exporting Members of certain policies, including conservation policies, GATT 1994 and the WTO Agreement could no longer serve as a multilateral framework for trade among Members as security and predictability of trade relations under those agreements would be threatened. This follows because, if one WTO Member were allowed to adopt such measures, then other Members would also have the right to adopt similar measures on the same subject but with differing, or even conflicting, requirements.... Market access for goods could become subject to an increasing number of conflicting policy requirements for the same product and this would rapidly lead to the end of the WTO multilateral trading system.

Shrimp/Turtle, Panel Report, at para. 7.44.

The Appellate Body sharply criticized the reasoning of the Panel, observing that "[m]aintaining, rather than undermining, the multilateral trading system is necessarily a fundamental and pervasive premise underlying the WTO Agreement; but it is not a right or an obligation, nor is it an interpretative rule which can be employed in the appraisal of a given measure under the chapeau of Article XX." *Shrimp/Turtle*, Appellate Body Report, at para. 116. Perhaps most critically, the Appellate Body made the following conclusion in paragraph 121 of its report:

> It appears to us, however, that conditioning access to a Member's domestic market on whether exporting Members comply with, or adopt, a policy or policies unilaterally prescribed by the importing Member, may, to some degree, be a common aspect of measures falling within the scope of one or another of the exceptions (a) to (j) of Article XX. Paragraphs (a) to (j) comprise measures that are recognized as exceptions to substantive obligations established in the GATT 1994, because the domestic policies embodied in such measures have been recognized as important and legitimate in character. It is not necessary to assume that requiring from exporting countries compliance with, or adoption of, certain policies (although covered in principle by one or another of the exceptions) prescribed by the importing country, renders a measure a priori incapable of justification under Article XX. Such an interpretation renders most, if not all, of the specific exceptions of Article XX inutile, a result abhorrent to the principles of interpretation we are bound to apply.

Shrimp/Turtle thus opens the door to unilateral measures under Article XX(g). Are there legitimate reasons for believing that the scope of Article XX(b) does not encompass unilateral measures or justify discrimination based on nonproduct related PPMs? *See* JOHN JACKSON, THE WORLD TRADING SYSTEM 236 (2d ed. 1997) (arguing that, although Article XX(b) does not expressly limit itself to human, animal, or plant concerns in the importing country, "it can be argued that this is what Article XX means").What factors may warrant the use of unilateral measures?

4. *The "Necessity" Test of Article XX(b)*. In paragraph 5.28 of its report, the *Tuna/Dolphin I* Panel established a test for "necessity" under Article XX(b). What is it? The *Tuna/Dolphin II* Panel took a slightly different approach by expressly adopting the analysis of previous panels:

United States-Restrictions on Imports of Tuna (*Tuna/Dolphin II*)
GATT Panel Report, DS29/R (June 16, 1994) (unadopted),
reprinted in 33 I.L.M. 839 (1994)

5.34 ... The United States argued that its measures met [the "necessary"] requirement, since "necessary" in this sense simply meant "needed". The EEC disagreed, stating that the normal meaning of the term "necessary" was "indispensable" or "unavoidable". The EEC further argued that adopted panel reports had stated that a measure otherwise inconsistent with the General Agreement could only be justified as necessary under Article XX (b) if no other consistent measure, or more consistent measure, were reasonably available to fulfil the policy objective.

5.35 The Panel proceeded first to examine the relationship established by Article XX (b) between the trade measure and the policy of protecting living things. It noted that, in the ordinary meaning of the term, "necessary" meant that no alternative existed. A previous panel, in discussing the use of the same term in Article XX(d), stated that

> "a contracting party cannot justify a measure inconsistent with another GATT provision as "necessary" in terms of Article XX(d) if an alternative measure which it could reasonably be expected to employ and which is not inconsistent with other GATT provisions is available to it. By the same token, in cases where a measure consistent with other GATT provisions is not reasonably available, a contracting party is bound to use, among the measures reasonably available to it, that which entails the least degree of inconsistency with other GATT provisions." (United States-Section 337 of the Tariff Act of 1930, GATT Panel Report, L/6439, BISD, 36th Supp. 345, para. 5.26 (1990) (adopted Nov. 7, 1989)).

This interpretation had also been accepted by another panel specifically examining Article XX(b). (Thailand-Restrictions on importation of and internal taxes on cigarettes, GATT Panel Report, DS10/R, BISD, 37th Supp. 200, 223, para. 73 (1991) (adopted Nov. 7, 1990). The Panel agreed with the reasoning of these previous panels. The Panel then proceeded to examine whether the trade embargoes imposed by the United States could be considered to be "necessary" in this sense to protect the life or health of dolphins.

5.36 ... The Panel observed that the prohibition on imports of tuna into the United States taken under the intermediary nation embargo could not, by itself, further the United States conservation objectives. The intermediary nation embargo would achieve its intended effect only if it were followed by changes in policies or practices, not in the country exporting tuna to the United States, but in third countries from which the exporting country imported tuna.

5.37 The Panel also recalled that measures taken under the primary nation embargo prohibited imports from a country of any tuna, whether or not the particular tuna was harvested in a way that harmed or could harm dolphins, as long as the country's tuna harvesting practices and policies were not comparable to those of the United States. The Panel observed that, as in the case of the intermediary nation embargo, the prohibition on imports of tuna into the United States taken under the primary nation embargo could not possibly, by itself, further the United States objective of protecting the life and health of dolphins. The primary nation embargo could achieve its desired effect only if it were followed by changes in policies and practices in the exporting countries. In view of the foregoing, the Panel observed that both the primary and intermediary nation embargo on tuna were taken by the United States so as to force other countries to change their policies with respect to persons and things within their own jurisdiction, since the embargoes required such changes in order to have any effect on the protection of the life or health of dolphins.

Both *Tuna/Dolphin* Panels underscored the need to find alternatives consistent with the GATT as an element of "necessity." As described in *Tuna/Dolphin II*, when GATT-consistent alternatives are not reasonably available to a country, it must choose "among the measures reasonably available to it that ... entails the least degree of inconsistency with other GATT provisions." This is known as the "least trade restrictive" test. What components are included within the "least trade restrictive" test"? Are there legitimate reasons why a measure should be the "least trade restrictive" in order to be "necessary to protect human, animal, or plant life or health"? As will be seen in Section III, the "least trade restrictive" test remains a central component of the Article XX(b) test.

5. The *Tuna/Dolphin II* Panel found the U.S. tuna/dolphin restrictions inconsistent with Article XX(b) because they could be made effective only if foreign countries changed their policies and practices. Kevin Kennedy argues just the opposite: "The question that needs to be asked and answered in the affirmative before unilateral trade sanctions are imposed is whether the imposition of sanctions will cause the exporting country to change its environmental practices. The effectiveness of trade sanctions ought to be the initial focus and, ultimately, the bottom line." Kevin C. Kennedy, *The Illegality of Unilateral Trade Measures to Resolve Trade-Environment Disputes*, 22 Wm. & Mary Envtl. L. & Pol'y 375, 504 (1998). Do you agree? The WTO's consistent concern with coerciveness has now shifted from XX(b) to the chapeau; we will come back to it when we consider the chapeau language.

6. *The Scope of Article XX(g)*. As noted above, the *Tuna/Dolphin I* Panel relied on the *Herring and Salmon* case for its narrow interpretation of Article XX(g). In that dispute, Canada prohibited the export of unprocessed herring and pink and sockeye salmon. (This case is the precursor to *Salmon and Herring*, pages 155–59, in which a trade panel wrestled with the distinction between Articles III and XI.) Before herring and salmon could be exported, Canada required that the fish be canned, salted, smoked, dried, pickled or frozen. This measure so clearly violated Article XI's prohibition against measures restricting the exportation or sale for export of products that Canada never defended against that charge. Instead, Canada argued that the measure was consistent with Article XX(g). Because the United States conceded that salmon and herring were "exhaustible natural re-

sources" and that Canada's harvest limitations constituted "restrictions on domestic production" within the meaning of Article XX(g), the Panel quickly moved to the questions of whether the export prohibitions "relat[e] to" the conservation of salmon and herring stocks and whether they are made effective "in conjunction with" the domestic restrictions on the harvesting of salmon and herring. The Panel made the following conclusions:

> 4.7 … The Panel noted Canada's contention that the export prohibitions were not conservation measures per se but had an effect on conservation because they helped provide the statistical foundation for the harvesting restrictions and increase the benefits to the Canadian economy arising from the Salmonid Enhancement Program. The Panel carefully examined this contention and noted the following: Canada collects statistical data on many different species of fish, including certain salmon species, without imposing export prohibitions on them. Canada maintains statistics on all fish exports. If certain unprocessed salmon and unprocessed herring were exported, statistics on these exports would therefore be collected. The Salmonid Enhancement Program covers salmon species for which export prohibitions apply and other species not subject to export prohibitions. The export prohibitions do not limit access to salmon and herring supplies in general but only to certain salmon and herring supplies in unprocessed form. Canada limits purchases of these unprocessed fish only by foreign processors and consumers and not by domestic processors and consumers. In light of all these factors taken together, the Panel found that these prohibitions could not be deemed to be primarily aimed at the conservation of salmon and herring stocks and at rendering effective the restrictions on the harvesting of these fish. The Panel therefore concluded that the export prohibitions were not justified by Article XX(g).

Canada-Measures Affecting Exports of Unprocessed Herring and Salmon, GATT Panel Report, L/6268, B.I.S.D. 35th Supp. 98 (1988) (adopted Mar. 22, 1988). How do the *Herring and Salmon* Panel and the *Tuna/Dolphin* panels define "relating to" and "make effective in conjunction with"? Are these interpretations justified? As we will in Section IV below, the WTO's Appellate Body has interpreted Article XX(g) very differently from these early panels.

7. The *Tuna/Dolphin* Panel seems terrified that environmental measures could create a slippery slope that totally destroys the multilateral trading system. Are the fears of the Panel reasonable? Do you think Canada's export restrictions on unprocessed herring and salmon were conservation or protectionist measures? How do we reconcile the concerns of the Panel with concerns of environmentalists who see the need for distinguishing products based on the way they are produced?

Note—The Tuna/Dolphin *Aftermath*

Tuna/dolphin issues remain controversial and complex. In the aftermath of the *Tuna/Dolphin* decisions, the United States refused to repeal the embargoes or change the MMPA. Only after Mexico and other members of the Inter-American Tropical Tuna Commission (IATTC), the regional fisheries management organization with jurisdiction over the tuna fishery in the Eastern Tropical Pacific (ETP), agreed to dolphin mortality limits, the use of observers on tuna vessels, and other measures, did the U.S. Congress amend the MMPA to reflect those changes. The MMPA now permits the importation of tuna caught with purse seine nets if the harvesting nation is 1) meeting the obligations established by the Agreement on International Dolphin Conservation Program (AIDCP), negotiated under the auspices of the IATTC, and 2) the harvesting nation's vessels have not exceeded their dolphin mortality limits on a per-stock, per-year basis. Marine Mammal Protection Act, 16 U.S.C. § 1371(a)(2)(B) (as amended 1997). As a result, importation of tuna is no longer tied to dolphin mortality of the U.S. fleet or fishing practices dictated by U.S. law. The United States has determined that Mexico meets these new standards and may import tuna into the United States. Taking and Importing of Marine Mammals, 65 Fed. Reg. 26585 (May 8, 2000). A federal court upheld the government's decision. Defenders of Wildlife v. Hogarth, 177 F. Supp. 2d 1336 (Ct. Int'l Trade 2001). Separate litigation concerning the "dolphin-safe" label is discussed in Chapter 6 at pages 398–406.

III. The Evolution of Article XX(b) Analysis

For environmentalists, the interpretations of Article XX(b) by the *Tuna/Dolphin* Panels seemed insurmountable. How could governments show that measures were "indispensable" as opposed to "needed" to meet the *Tuna/Dolphin II* Panel interpretation of "necessary"? In the first WTO dispute, *Reformulated Gasoline*, environmentalists felt that the Panel again rebuffed legitimate environmental regulation by declaring that U.S. gasoline standards violated GATT Article III and could not be justified pursuant to Article XX(b). As in the *Tuna/Dolphin* disputes, the *Reformulated Gasoline* Panel concluded that the U.S. measures were not the "least trade restrictive" alternative reasonably available to it. *Reformulated Gasoline,* Panel Report, at paras. 6.26–6.29. Finally, however, the dispute settlement panel hearing Canada's case against a French regulation prohibiting the import and most uses of asbestos, a well known and potent carcinogen, became the first panel to rule that an environmental measure met the "necessary" test.

A. The *Asbestos* Panel Report: A Breakthrough?

Asbestos is a naturally occurring mineral fiber that has been used in a number of building construction materials for insulation and as a fire-retardant. Because of its fiber strength and heat resistant properties, asbestos has also been used as an ingredient in a range of manufactured goods, such as roofing shingles, ceiling and floor tiles, and cement products, as well as automobile clutches, brakes, and transmission parts. Exposure to asbestos in most forms, specifically including the chrysotile form at issue in the WTO dispute, has proven to result in a wide range of health conditions, including mesothelioma, a deadly cancer that attacks the lining of the lungs, heart, or abdomen.

To protect workers and consumers from these health risks, France enacted Decree No. 96-1133 in 1997 to ban the manufacture, processing, sale, import, and export of all varieties of asbestos fibers. The Decree allowed, on an exceptional and temporary basis, an exemption for certain existing materials, products, or devices containing chrysotile fiber (a particular kind of asbestos) when, to perform an equivalent function, no substitute is available that poses less risk to workers handling those materials, products, or devices.

The trade dispute arose when Canada argued that France's ban was not "necessary" to protect human life or health because high-density chrysotile asbestos in products does not pose any detectable risk, especially once enclosed in cement. Consistent with *Tuna/Dolphin* and other decisions, Canada argued that France must show that no other less trade restrictive measures existed. In particular, Canada argued that "controlled use indisputably constitutes an alternative to a total ban that is significantly less restrictive for international trade." European Communities-Measures Affecting Asbestos and Asbestos Containing Products, Panel Report, WT/DS135/R, para. 8.165 (adopted Apr. 5, 2001), *reprinted in* 40 I.L.M. 258 (2001) [hereinafter *Asbestos*].

Before addressing Canada's claim, the Panel described how it would assess the relevant risks and scientific evidence to determine if less trade restrictive measures in fact existed. The Panel noted that its role was not to assess "the choice made by France to protect its population against certain risks, nor the level of protection of public health that France wishes to achieve. We must simply determine if the French policy of prohibiting the use of chrysotile-asbestos falls within the range of policies designed to protect human life or health." *Id.* at para. 8.171. Nevertheless, noting that the parties disagreed on the extent of the health risk from chrysotile-cement products, the Panel decided that it "shall have to take expressly into account the extent of the health problem in assessing the necessity of the measure." *Id.* at para. 8.176.

European Communities-Measures Affecting Asbestos and Asbestos Containing Products

Panel Report, WT/DS135/R (adopted Apr. 5, 2001),
reprinted in 40 I.L.M. 258 (2001)

8.182 [The Panel's] role, taking into account the burden of proof, is to determine whether there is sufficient scientific evidence to conclude that there exists a risk for human life or health and that the measures taken by France are necessary in relation to the objectives pursued. The Panel therefore considers that it should base its conclusions with respect to the existence of a public health risk on the scientific evidence put forward by the parties and the comments of the experts consulted within the context of the present case. The opinions expressed by the experts we have consulted will help us to understand and evaluate the evidence submitted and the arguments advanced by the parties. The same approach will be adopted with respect to the necessity of the measure concerned.

8.183 In proceeding with this exercise, the Panel will have to make a pragmatic assessment of the scientific situation and the measures available, as would the decision-makers responsible for the adoption of a health policy. In this connection, it notes that the determination of the existence of other measures consistent or less inconsistent with the GATT largely depends on a scientific assessment of the risk. In any event, this determination cannot be interpreted as restricting the freedom of Members to take certain measures rather than others under Article XX(b), in the absence of a measure that would be consistent or less inconsistent with the GATT 1994.

(c) Application of Article XX(b) of the GATT 1994 to the Decree

(i) "Protection of human life and health"

8.184 In accordance with the approach defined by the Panel in *United States-Gasoline*, we must first establish whether the policy in respect of the measure for

which the provisions of Article XX(b) were invoked falls within the range of policies designed to protect human life or health. As we have already pointed out, the
use of the word "protection" implies the existence of a risk. Accordingly, we must
begin by identifying a risk for public health. In the light of the comments of the
panel in *United States-Gasoline* and our own remarks in paragraph 8.182, we
must also take into account the fact that it is a public health policy that we have
to assess.

8.185 First of all, we note that the EC argue that in prohibiting the placing on
the market and use of asbestos and products containing it, the Decree seeks to
halt the spread of the risks due to asbestos, particularly for those exposed occasionally and very often unwittingly to asbestos when working on asbestos-containing products. France considers that it can thereby reduce the number of
deaths due to exposure to asbestos fibres among the French population, whether
by asbestosis, lung cancer or mesothelioma.

8.186 In principle, a policy that seeks to reduce exposure to a risk should fall
within the range of policies designed to protect human life or health, insofar as
a risk exists....

8.187 Canada does not dispute that chrysotile asbestos causes lung cancer. However, Canada argues that the mechanism that could give rise to an increased risk
of lung cancer has not yet been fully explained and that the link with chrysotile
might only be indirect. This risk depends on the intensity and duration of the
exposure. On the other hand, according to Canada, there is a great deal of scientific evidence to support the thesis according to which chrysotile does not
cause mesotheliomas. In particular, the mesotheliomas linked to asbestos could
be the result of exposure to low-density products containing amphiboles. It has
not been established that, in their uses, chrysotile fibres pose the same risk as
amphiboles, whose chemical composition, in particular, is different. [The experts consulted by the Panel confirmed that chrysotile was carcinogenic, that the
types of cancer concerned had a mortality rate of close to 100 percent, and that
there was a "serious carcinogenic risk associated with the inhalation of chrysotile
fibres." Regarding chrysotile-cement products, the scientific experts agreed that
the risks of fibres being dispersed due to the degradation of chrysotile-cement
were limited, but that working with such products might result in the disper-
sion of large quantities of fibres and that those fibres pose a definite health risk.
While those risks might be lower than for production or processing workers, it
concerned a much larger group, including do-it-yourself (DIY) enthusiasts. The
scientists consulted by the Panel also agreed that a threshold below which exposure does not present any risks had not been established for any of the diseases attributable to chrysotile, except perhaps for asbestosis.]

8.193 The Panel therefore considers that the evidence before it tends to show
that handling chrysotile-cement products constitutes a risk to health rather than
the opposite. Accordingly, a decision-maker responsible for taking public health
measures might reasonably conclude that the presence of chrysotile-cement products posed a risk because of the risks involved in working with those products.

8.194 Accordingly, the Panel concludes that the EC has made a prima facie case
for the existence of a health risk in connection with the use of chrysotile, in particular as regards lung cancer and mesothelioma in the occupational sectors
downstream of production and processing and for the public in general in rela-

tion to chrysotile-cement products. This prima facie case has not been rebutted by Canada. Moreover, the Panel considers that the comments by the experts confirm the health risk associated with exposure to chrysotile in its various uses. The Panel therefore considers that the EC have shown that the policy of prohibiting chrysotile asbestos implemented by the Decree falls within the range of policies designed to protect human life or health. On the other hand, Canada has not succeeded in rebutting the presumption established on the basis of the evidence submitted by the EC and confirmed by the experts. The Panel concludes therefore that the French policy of prohibiting chrysotile asbestos falls within the range of policies designed to protect human life or health, within the meaning of Article XX(b) of the GATT 1994. * * *

(ii) "necessary"

8.198 We note that in *Thailand-Cigarettes* the Panel defined the test of necessity applicable under Article XX(b):

> "The import restrictions imposed by Thailand could be considered to be 'necessary' in terms of Article XX(b) only if there were no alternative measure consistent with the General Agreement, or less inconsistent with it, which Thailand could reasonably be expected to employ to achieve its health policy objectives."

8.199 ... [I]n order to apply the test defined in *Thailand-Cigarettes,* we must (a) establish *the scope* of the health policy objectives pursued by France and (b) consider the existence of measures consistent, or less inconsistent, with the GATT 1994.

8.200 First of all, we note that the risk due to chrysotile is important to the extent that, as confirmed in the previous section, it can generate lung cancers and mesotheliomas which are still difficult to cure or even incurable. The populations potentially at risk in France are very numerous, since products containing chrysotile, in particular, chrysotile-cement, have many applications in industrial, commercial and residential buildings. The fields of activity concerned include building workers (several hundred thousand) and DIY enthusiasts. These are areas in which health controls are difficult to apply, as the comments of the experts have shown.

8.201 The experts also confirmed that the intensive use of asbestos (in France, mainly chrysotile) over several decades has resulted in the risks of exposure being displaced from the mining and processing industry towards other sectors further downstream and, indeed, the general public. In this context, the Panel finds that the European Communities have shown that a risk exists for a very broad sector of the French population.

8.202 The Panel notes that the exposure of these groups is generally lower. However, the experts confirm the position of the European Communities according to which it has not been possible to identify any threshold below which exposure to chrysotile would have no effect. The experts are also agreed that the linear relationship model, which does not identify any minimum exposure threshold, is appropriate for assessing the existence of a risk. We find therefore that no minimum threshold of level of exposure or duration of exposure has been identified with regard to the risk of pathologies associated with chrysotile, except for asbestosis. Consequently, the possibility remains that low exposure over a fairly long period of time could lead to lung cancer or mesothelioma. Similarly, high-level exposure over a short period could also result in lung cancer or mesothelioma. These two possibilities were confirmed by the experts. The Panel therefore concludes that even though some trades or the French population in general are only intermittently exposed to low levels of asbestos, a decision-maker responsible for public health policy might reasonably conclude that there was nevertheless a real risk for these categories.

8.203 In the light of the above, the Panel concludes that, in addition to the risk presented by low-density friable products, there is an undeniable public health risk in relation to the chrysotile contained in high-density chrysotile-cement products. This risk exists even at low or intermittent exposure levels and can affect a broad section of the population.

8.207 ... [I]n order to determine whether a measure is necessary it is important to assess whether consistent or less inconsistent measures are *reasonably* available. The term "reasonably" has not been defined as such by the panels that have referred to it in the context of Article XX. It suggests, however, that the availability of a measure should not be examined theoretically or in absolute terms. Nevertheless, in the light of the reasoning of these panels, we find the word "reasonably" should not be interpreted loosely either. The fact that, administratively, one measure may be easier to implement than another does not mean that the other measure is not reasonably available. We consider that the existence of a reasonably available measure must be assessed in the light of the economic and administrative realities facing the Member concerned but also by taking into account the fact that the State must provide itself with the means of implementing its policies. Thus, the Panel considers that it is legitimate to expect a country such as France with advanced labour legislation and specialized administrative services to deploy administrative resources proportionate to its public health objectives and to be prepared to incur the necessary expenditure.

8.208 After clarifying this point, we will now proceed to examine whether controlled use (a) is sufficiently effective in the light of France's health policy objectives and (b) whether it constitutes a reasonably available measure.

8.209 In relation to the first of these considerations, we note, first of all, that although controlled use is applied in some countries, such as the United States or Canada, and has also been applied by France, in general in certain sectors its efficacy still remains to be demonstrated. This is confirmed by a number of studies, as well as by the comments of the experts. Thus, even though it seems possible to apply controlled use successfully upstream (mining and manufacturing) or downstream (removal and destruction) of product use, it would seem to be much less easy to apply it in the building sector, which is one of the areas more particularly targeted by the measures contained in the Decree. The Panel therefore concludes that, in view of the difficulties of application of controlled use, an official in charge of public health policy might reasonably consider that controlled use did not provide protection that was adequate in relation to the policy objectives.

8.210 Moreover, Canada refers to the existence of international standards for the protection of workers in contact with chrysotile. First of all, we find that the international standards cover only the precautions to be taken if a worker has to handle asbestos. They contain neither a guarantee of free access for asbestos nor an incentive to use asbestos. On the contrary, the international conventions suggest that, as far as possible, asbestos should be replaced by less hazardous materials. Next, we note that the levels of protection obtained by following international standards, whether it be the ISO standard or the WHO Convention, are lower than those established by France, including those applicable before the introduction of the Decree. Considering the high level of risk identified, France's objective—which the Panel cannot question—justifies the adoption of exposure ceilings lower than those for which the international conventions provide. We therefore find that controlled use based on international standards would not seem to make it possible to achieve the level of protection sought by France.

8.211 The Panel is aware that in some sectors controlled or safe use could be envisaged with greater certainty that it would prove effective. However, as confirmed by the experts, the circumstances of use must be controllable. These circumstances are extremely varied and we note that the safety measures that would make possible results at least equivalent to the exposure level (0.1 f/ml) applied by France before the ban (restrictions on the number of workers and working areas and total containment of the product) exceed the requirements of the international standards and considerably limit the number of industrial sectors that could apply them. Even in these cases, according to one of the experts, the level of exposure is still high enough for there to be a significant residual risk of developing asbestos-related diseases. According to another, it is not possible to guarantee that fibre concentrations will never exceed 0.1 f/ml. In addition, we note that for the application of controlled use to satisfy France's public health objectives, mined or processed products should never be handled by anyone outside the mining and processing industries. If these products were subsequently to be handled by unprotected persons, the fact that they could be mined and processed and then destroyed using controlled use techniques would not be sufficient to meet those objectives. We therefore find that a decision-maker responsible for establishing a health policy might have reasonable doubts about the possibility of ensuring the achievement of France's health policy objectives by relying on controlled use, even in sectors which might lend themselves more readily to these practices.

8.212 *A fortiori* and for the following reasons, we consider that controlled use is not a reasonably available alternative in all the other sectors in which workers may be exposed to chrysotile.

Questions and Discussion

1. The *Asbestos* Panel breaks new ground by introducing a scientific component to Article XX(b). In paragraph 8.170, the Panel analyzes whether or not France's goal to protect human health from chrysotile asbestos falls within the range of policies to protect human life or health. The Panel states that the words "'policies designed to protect human health or life' imply the existence of a *health risk*" (emphasis in original). Thus, to determine whether or not a measure falls within the range of policies designed to protect human life or health, the Panel was required to determine if asbestos poses a risk to human life or health. This requires it to assess whether France's claim is scientifically valid. Is the Panel's ruling reasonable?

2. Consider that France attempted to protect its citizens from any asbestos exposure through a complete ban, with minor exceptions, on the domestic use and manufacture

of asbestos products. Quite clearly, France is not attempting to protect domestic production or consumption of asbestos—it has destroyed it. Should a country be required to import products for which it completely prohibits the use and manufacture unless it has strong scientific evidence to support a total ban? In these circumstances, what is the trade concern? Could such a ban still be protectionist? Perhaps. Other products were needed to serve the same uses as asbestos. The Panel reached its conclusions notwithstanding Canada's argument that the alternatives to asbestos that remained on the market in France, such as fiberglass and cellulose fibers (many produced in France), carried their own health risks. The Panel demanded a rigorous scientific justification for the asbestos measure, but it declined to engage in a comparative risk analysis.

3. Consider hazardous waste. Hazardous waste can be disposed of safely, but expensive facilities are required to do so. Does *Asbestos* allow a country to prohibit the importation of hazardous waste? What must it show in order to do so? What if the country also bans the disposal of domestically-generated hazardous waste? Can a country ban disposal of domestically-generated waste? Does your answer differ from the U.S. Supreme Court's in *Philadelphia v. New Jersey? See* pages 246–47.

4. The Panel notes Canada's argument that controlled uses of asbestos are allowed in the United States (para. 8.209). The U.S. Environmental Protection Agency (EPA) had promulgated broad prohibitions on asbestos under the Toxic Substances Control Act, but those rules were struck down in *Corrosion Proof Fittings.* Corrosion Proof Fittings v. EPA, 947 F.2d 1201 (5th Cir. 1991). The court picked apart EPA's determinations of risk for specific uses and of reasonable availability of substitute materials. In this matter at least, the WTO panel was less intrusive and more deferential to regulatory choices than the Fifth Circuit.

B. The *Brazil-Retreaded Tyres* Case

Although France was allowed to maintain its ban on asbestos products under *Asbestos*, environmentalists did not rest easy. Indeed, the Panel required the EU on behalf of France to marshal a significant body of evidence, and then supported by an expert panel of scientists, simply to prove that asbestos, a well known deadly carcinogen, in fact posed a risk. The EU also had to demonstrate that other alternatives were not as effective for meeting France's policy objectives.

Perhaps attuned to these criticisms, the Appellate Body began to elaborate a more nuanced view of "necessary." The Appellate Body synthesized its evolving views in—*Brazil-Retreaded Tyres*—when the EU challenged Brazil's import restrictions on retreaded tires. The dispute received widespread attention from environmentalists. In addition to providing the dispute settlement panels with the opportunity to redraw the lines of "necessity" in an environmental dispute, the dispute also marked the first time a developed country challenged an environmental restriction of a developing country.

Retreaded tires are produced by reconditioning used tires. The worn tread is stripped from a used tire's skeleton (casing) and replaced with a new tread and, sometimes, new material covering parts or all of the sidewalls. Retreaded tires can be produced through a number of different methods all encompassed by the generic term "retreading." There are different types of retreaded tires which correspond to the different types of casings used to produce them: passenger car retreaded tires, commercial vehicle retreaded tires, aircraft retreaded tires, and others. Under international standards, passenger car tires may be retreaded only once. By contrast, commercial vehicle and aircraft tires may be retreaded more than once. In addition, for international trade purposes, retreaded tires differ from both used tires and new tires.

Brazil allows the use of retreaded tires. Indeed, one of the motivations for its import restriction was to try to increase the retreading of used tires in Brazil in order to cut down the number of discarded tires. In that way, it claimed that the ban on the issuance of import licenses for retreaded tires was designed to protect human, animal, and plant life and health from the effects of dengue, yellow fever, malaria, and other diseases spread by mosquitoes that breed in pools of water that collect in discarded tires. It also claimed that the accumulation of waste tires creates a risk of tire fires and toxic leaching and that this risk has substantial adverse effects on human health and the environment. The EU, however, contended that Brazil's restrictions were designed to protect domestic retreading industries from foreign competition. It noted that since the Brazilian restrictions were imposed in 2000, Brazilian imports of *retreaded* tires dropped to zero whereas imports of *used* tires increased from 5,000 metric tons to 70,000 tons in 2005. According to the EU, imports of used tires increased so that Brazilian companies could manufacture and sell the higher value retreaded tires.

The Panel agreed with the EU that Brazil's ban on the issuance of import licenses for retreaded tires constituted an import ban in violation of GATT Article XI:1. Brazil then sought to justify its measure under Article XX(b).

1. Is There a Risk?

Brazil–Measures Affecting Imports of Retreaded Tyres

Panel Report, WT/DS332/R (adopted Dec. 17, 2007)

7.60 The European Communities does not contest that these [mosquito-borne] diseases pose health risks that potentially fall within the scope of Article XX(b). However, the European Communities considers that health risks may arise from waste tyres only in case of incorrect management. * * *

7.63 ... The European Communities submits that waste tyres themselves are considered inert in Brazilian legislation and non-hazardous in the European Communities' legislation and that only abandoned tyres or tyres negligently placed in monofills may become breeding places for mosquitoes....

7.64 The Panel recalls in this regard the Appellate Body's observation in *EC–Hormones* that the risk being addressed encompasses "risk in human societies as they actually exist, in other words, the actual potential for adverse effects on human health in the real world, where people live and work and die." We believe that the observation, although made in the context of the SPS Agreement, is also applicable to the situation in the present case. * * *

7.67 ... [I]t may be that health risks associated with waste tyres can be significantly reduced with proper management of waste tyres. However, that does not negate the reality that waste tyres get abandoned and accumulated and that risks associated with accumulated waste tyres exist in Brazil.

7.68 Moreover, the evidence before the Panel does not suggest that only illegally dumped or mismanaged waste tyres can cause mosquito-borne diseases. The risk of mosquito-borne diseases, albeit to different extents, seems to exist in relation to all types of accumulated waste tyres. Indeed, this situation does not appear to be limited to Brazil, as some of the evidence presented to the Panel makes clear. * * *

7.71 Therefore, the Panel finds that Brazil has demonstrated that risks posed by mosquito-borne diseases such as dengue, yellow fever and malaria to human health and life exist in Brazil in relation to the accumulation as well as transportation of waste tyres.

[Concerning toxic emissions from tire fires, the Panel concluded that Brazil had demonstrated that highly toxic and mutagenic emissions produced by tire fires result in a number of health problems, including, inter alia, the loss of short-term memory, learning disabilities, immune system suppression, and cardiovascular problems, and that a noxious plume comprising dioxins emitted by tire fires produces significant short- and long-term health hazards, including inter alia, cancer, premature mortality, reduced lung function, suppression of the immune system, respiratory effects, and heart and chest problems.

Nonetheless, the European Communities argued that Brazil had not met its burden of proof because it had not demonstrated the existence of any risks posed by tire fires *within* Brazil. The Panel disagreed with the EC's statement as a factual matter—Brazil had submitted such information—but also rejected the EC's legal argument concerning Brazil's burden:]

7.77 The question before us therefore is whether Brazil was required to present more detailed information on tyre fires in Brazil such as their location, causes, dimension and duration as suggested by the European Communities as well as specific evidence of the actual negative health effects of tyre fires within Brazil. There may be situations in which such specific evidence would be required to demonstrate the existence of a risk. In this case, however, accepting the European Communities' argument would imply that a WTO Member can never prove the existence of health risks from a tyre fire until a tyre fire does in fact take place and the government of that country conducts its own assessment of the consequences of such a fire. The Panel does not consider that detailed proof of actual tyre fires and associated negative impact on health within the territory of Brazil is required in this case. This is because potential harmful effects caused by tyre fires on human health can be assessed on the basis of incidents that have occurred in other countries. The Panel is thus of the view that the incidence of such fires in Brazil, when considered in combination with evidence of the harmful impact of tyre fires on human health and the evidence of specific incidents of such fires in other countries, is sufficient in this case to prove the existence of potential health risks relating to tyre fires in Brazil.

7.78 The European Communities also argues that even if the negative consequences on health were important in the case of a tyre fire, the fire risk arising from waste tyres is low, given that tyres are very difficult to ignite. In the Panel's view however, the low probability of tyre fires occurring negates neither the fact that tyre fires do actually occur, as shown by the evidence presented in relation to tyre fires that have occurred in other countries, nor the fact that health risks exist in relation to tyre fires and that once they occur, tyre fires are very difficult to extinguish

[As with mosquito-borne diseases, the Panel rejected the EC's argument that the risk from tire fires did not fall within the risk contemplated by Article XX(b) because the risk arose only from improperly managed waste tires. In addition, it found that the risk for tire fires is not necessarily limited to improper management.

The Panel also concluded that Brazil had demonstrated a risk to animal or plant life or health from tire fires and mosquito-borne diseases. The Panel particularly noted that "[a]lthough the evidence is less explicit in explaining the risk to animal and plant life or health than that to human health or life, the evidence before us suggests that contamination of water and soil leads to an inevitable negative impact on animal and plant life and health." *Id.* at para 7.88.

In light of the above, the Panel concluded that Brazil had demonstrated the existence of risks to animal life or health in relation to dengue and risks to animal and plant life or health in relation to toxic emissions caused by tire fires. The Panel also concluded that Brazil's measures fell within the range of policies covered by Article XX(b), because Brazil's policy objective was to reduce exposure to the risks to human, animal or plant life or health arising from the accumulation of waste tires: "Measures specifically designed to avoid the generation of further risk, thereby contributing to the reduction of exposure to the risk, fall, in our view, within [Article XX(b)]." *Id.* at para. 7.98.]

2. Is the Measure "Necessary"?

Brazil-Measures Affecting Imports of Retreaded Tyres

Appellate Body Report, WT/DS332/AB/R (adopted Dec. 17, 2007)

1.   The Panel's Analysis of the Contribution of the Import Ban to the Achievement of the Objective * * *

141. Article XX(b) of the GATT 1994 refers to measures "necessary to protect human, animal or plant life or health". The term "necessary" is mentioned not only in Article XX(b) of the GATT 1994, but also in Articles XX(a) and XX(d) of the GATT 1994, as well as in Article XIV(a), (b), and (c) of the GATS. In *Korea–Various Measures on Beef*, the Appellate Body underscored that "the word 'necessary' is not limited to that which is 'indispensable'". The Appellate Body added:

> Measures which are indispensable or of absolute necessity or inevitable to secure compliance certainly fulfil the requirements of Article XX(d). But other measures, too, may fall within the ambit of this exception. As used in Article XX(d), the term "necessary" refers, in our view, to a range of degrees of necessity. At one end of this continuum lies "necessary" understood as "indispensable"; at the other end, is "necessary" taken to mean as "making a contribution to." We consider that a "necessary" measure is, in this continuum, located significantly closer to the pole of "indispensable" than to the opposite pole of simply "making a contribution to". (footnote omitted)

142. In *Korea–Various Measures on Beef*, the Appellate Body explained that determining whether a measure is "necessary" within the meaning of Article XX(d):

> … involves in every case a process of weighing and balancing a series of factors which prominently include the contribution made by the compliance measure to the enforcement of the law or regulation at issue, the importance of the common interests or values protected by that law or regulation, and the accompanying impact of the law or regulation on imports or exports.

143. *US–Gambling*, the Appellate Body addressed the "necessity" test in the context of Article XIV of the GATS [General Agreement on Trade in Services]. The

Appellate Body stated that the weighing and balancing process inherent in the necessity analysis "begins with an assessment of the 'relative importance' of the interests or values furthered by the challenged measure", and also involves an assessment of other factors, which will usually include "the contribution of the measure to the realization of the ends pursued by it" and "the restrictive impact of the measure on international commerce".

144. It is against this background that we must determine whether the Panel erred in assessing the contribution of the Import Ban to the realization of the objective pursued by it, and in the manner in which it weighed this contribution in its analysis of the necessity of the Import Ban. We begin by identifying the objective pursued by the Import Ban. The Panel found that the objective of the Import Ban is the reduction of the "exposure to the risks to human, animal or plant life or health arising from the accumulation of waste tyres", and noted that "few interests are more 'vital' and 'important' than protecting human beings from health risks, and that protecting the environment is no less important." The Panel also observed that "Brazil's chosen level of protection is the reduction of the risks of waste tyre accumulation to the maximum extent possible." Regarding the trade restrictiveness of the measure, the Panel noted that it is "as trade-restrictive as can be, as far as retreaded tyres from non-MERCOSUR countries are concerned, since it aims to halt completely their entry into Brazil."

145. We turn to the methodology used by the Panel in analyzing the contribution of the Import Ban to the achievement of its objective. Such a contribution exists when there is a genuine relationship of ends and means between the objective pursued and the measure at issue. The selection of a methodology to assess a measure's contribution is a function of the nature of the risk, the objective pursued, and the level of protection sought. It ultimately also depends on the nature, quantity, and quality of evidence existing at the time the analysis is made....

146. We note that the Panel chose to conduct a qualitative analysis of the contribution of the Import Ban to the achievement of its objective. In previous cases, the Appellate Body has not established a requirement that such a contribution be quantified. To the contrary, in *EC–Asbestos*, the Appellate Body emphasized that there is "no requirement under Article XX(b) of the GATT 1994 to *quantify*, as such, the risk to human life or health". In other words, "[a] risk may be evaluated either in quantitative or qualitative terms." Although the reference by the Appellate Body to the quantification of a risk is not the same as the quantification of the contribution of a measure to the realization of the objective pursued by it (which could be, as it is in this case, the reduction of a risk), it appears to us that the same line of reasoning applies to the analysis of the contribution, which can be done either in quantitative or in qualitative terms.

147. Accordingly, we do not accept the European Communities' contention that the Panel was under an obligation to quantify the contribution of the Import Ban to the reduction in the number of waste tyres and to determine the number of waste tyres that would be reduced as a result of the Import Ban. In our view, the Panel's choice of a qualitative analysis was within the bounds of the latitude it enjoys in choosing a methodology for the analysis of the contribution. * * *

150. As the Panel recognized, an import ban is "by design as trade-restrictive as can be". We agree with the Panel that there may be circumstances where such a

measure can nevertheless be necessary, within the meaning of Article XX(b). We also recall that, in *Korea–Various Measures on Beef*, the Appellate Body indicated that "the word 'necessary' is not limited to that which is 'indispensable'". Having said that, when a measure produces restrictive effects on international trade as severe as those resulting from an import ban, it appears to us that it would be difficult for a panel to find that measure necessary unless it is satisfied that the measure is apt to make a material contribution to the achievement of its objective. Thus, we disagree with Brazil's suggestion that, because it aims to reduce risk exposure to the maximum extent possible, an import ban that brings a marginal or insignificant contribution can nevertheless be considered necessary.

151. This does not mean that an import ban, or another trade-restrictive measure, the contribution of which is not immediately observable, cannot be justified under Article XX(b). We recognize that certain complex public health or environmental problems may be tackled only with a comprehensive policy comprising a multiplicity of interacting measures. In the short-term, it may prove difficult to isolate the contribution to public health or environmental objectives of one specific measure from those attributable to the other measures that are part of the same comprehensive policy. Moreover, the results obtained from certain actions—for instance, measures adopted in order to attenuate global warming and climate change, or certain preventive actions to reduce the incidence of diseases that may manifest themselves only after a certain period of time—can only be evaluated with the benefit of time. In order to justify an import ban under Article XX(b), a panel must be satisfied that it brings about a material contribution to the achievement of its objective. Such a demonstration can of course be made by resorting to evidence or data, pertaining to the past or the present, that establish that the import ban at issue makes a material contribution to the protection of public health or environmental objectives pursued. This is not, however, the only type of demonstration that could establish such a contribution. Thus, a panel might conclude that an import ban is necessary on the basis of a demonstration that the import ban at issue is apt to produce a material contribution to the achievement of its objective. This demonstration could consist of quantitative projections in the future, or qualitative reasoning based on a set of hypotheses that are tested and supported by sufficient evidence.

152. We have now to assess whether the qualitative analysis provided by the Panel establishes that the Import Ban is apt to produce a material contribution to the achievement of the objective of reducing exposure to the risks arising from the accumulation of waste tyres.

153. … In the light of the evidence adduced by the parties, the Panel was of the view that the Import Ban would lead to imported retreaded tyres being replaced with retreaded tyres made from local casings, or with new tyres that are retreadable. As concerns new tyres, the Panel observed, and we agree, that retreaded tyres "have by definition a shorter lifespan than new tyres" and that, accordingly, the Import Ban "may lead to a reduction in the total number of waste tyres because imported retreaded tyres may be substituted for by new tyres which have a longer lifespan." As concerns tyres retreaded in Brazil from local casings, the Panel was satisfied that Brazil had the production capacity to retread domestic used tyres and that "at least some domestic used tyres are being retreaded in Brazil." The Panel also agreed that Brazil has taken a series of measures to facilitate the access of domestic retreaders to good-quality used tyres, and that

new tyres sold in Brazil are high-quality tyres that comply with international standards and have the potential to be retreaded. The Panel's conclusion with which we agree was that, "if the domestic retreading industry retreads more domestic used tyres, the overall number of waste tyres will be reduced by giving a second life to some used tyres, which otherwise would have become waste immediately after their first and only life." For these reasons, the Panel found that a reduction of waste tyres would result from the Import Ban and that, therefore, the Import Ban would contribute to reducing exposure to the risks associated with the accumulation of waste tyres. As the Panel's analysis was qualitative, the Panel did not seek to estimate, in quantitative terms, the reduction of waste tyres that would result from the Import Ban, or the time horizon of such a reduction. Such estimates would have been very useful and, undoubtedly, would have strengthened the foundation of the Panel's findings. Having said that, it does not appear to us erroneous to conclude, on the basis of the hypotheses made, tested, and accepted by the Panel, that fewer waste tyres will be generated with the Import Ban than otherwise.

154. Moreover, we wish to underscore that the Import Ban must be viewed in the broader context of the comprehensive strategy designed and implemented by Brazil to deal with waste tyres. This comprehensive strategy includes not only the Import Ban but also the import ban on used tyres, as well as the collection and disposal scheme adopted by CONAMA Resolution 258/1999, as amended in 2002, which makes it mandatory for domestic manufacturers and importers of new tyres to provide for the safe disposal of waste tyres in specified proportions. For its part, CONAMA Resolution 258/1999, as amended in 2002, aims to reduce the exposure to risks arising from the accumulation of waste tyres by forcing manufacturers and importers of new tyres to collect and dispose of waste tyres at a ratio of five waste tyres for every four new tyres. This measure also encourages Brazilian retreaders to retread more domestic used tyres by exempting domestic retreaders from disposal obligations as long as they process tyres consumed within Brazil. Thus, the CONAMA scheme provides additional support for and is consistent with the design of Brazil's strategy for reducing the number of waste tyres. The two mutually enforcing pillars of Brazil's overall strategy—the Import Ban and the import ban on used tyres—imply that the demand for retreaded tyres in Brazil must be met by the domestic retreaders, and that these retreaders, in principle, can use only domestic used tyres for raw material. Over time, this comprehensive regulatory scheme is apt to induce sustainable changes in the practices and behaviour of the domestic retreaders, as well as other actors, and result in an increase in the number of retreadable tyres in Brazil and a higher rate of retreading of domestic casings in Brazil. Thus, the Import Ban appears to us as one of the key elements of the comprehensive strategy designed by Brazil to deal with waste tyres, along with the import ban on used tyres and the collection and disposal scheme established by CONAMA Resolution 258/1999, as amended in 2002.

155. As we explained above, we agree with the Panel's reasoning suggesting that fewer waste tyres will be generated with the Import Ban in place. In addition, Brazil has developed and implemented a comprehensive strategy to deal with waste tyres. As a *key element* of this strategy, the Import Ban is likely to bring a material contribution to the achievement of its objective of reducing the exposure to risks arising from the accumulation of waste tyres. On the basis of these con-

siderations, we are of the view that the Panel did not err in finding that the Import Ban contributes to the achievement of its objective.

2.   The Panel's Analysis of Possible Alternatives to the Import Ban

156. In order to determine whether a measure is "necessary" within the meaning of Article XX(b) of the GATT 1994, a panel must assess all the relevant factors, particularly the extent of the contribution to the achievement of a measure's objective and its trade restrictiveness, in the light of the importance of the interests or values at stake. If this analysis yields a preliminary conclusion that the measure is necessary, this result must be confirmed by comparing the measure with its possible alternatives, which may be less trade restrictive while providing an equivalent contribution to the achievement of the objective pursued. It rests upon the complaining Member to identify possible alternatives to the measure at issue that the responding Member could have taken.... We recall that, in order to qualify as an alternative, a measure proposed by the complaining Member must be not only less trade restrictive than the measure at issue, but should also "preserve for the responding Member its right to achieve its desired level of protection with respect to the objective pursued". If the complaining Member has put forward a possible alternative measure, the responding Member may seek to show that the proposed measure does not allow it to achieve the level of protection it has chosen and, therefore, is not a genuine alternative. The responding Member may also seek to demonstrate that the proposed alternative is not, in fact, "reasonably available". As the Appellate Body indicated in *US–Gambling*, "[a]n alternative measure may be found not to be 'reasonably available'... where it is merely theoretical in nature, for instance, where the responding Member is not capable of taking it, or where the measure imposes an undue burden on that Member, such as prohibitive costs or substantial technical difficulties." If the responding Member demonstrates that the measure proposed by the complaining Member is not a genuine alternative or is not "reasonably available", taking into account the interests or values being pursued and the responding Member's desired level of protection, it follows that the measure at issue is necessary.

157. Before the Panel, the European Communities put forward two types of possible alternative measures or practices: (i) measures to reduce the number of waste tyres accumulating in Brazil; and (ii) measures or practices to improve the management of waste tyres in Brazil. The Panel examined the alternative measures proposed by the European Communities in some detail, and in each case found that the proposed measure did not constitute a reasonably available alternative to the Import Ban. Among the reasons that the Panel gave for its rejections were that the proposed alternatives were already in place, would not allow Brazil to achieve its chosen level of protection, or would carry their own risks and hazards. * * *

174. In evaluating whether the measures or practices proposed by the European Communities were "alternatives", the Panel sought to determine whether they would achieve Brazil's policy objective and chosen level of protection, that is to say, reducing the "exposure to the risks to human, animal or plant life or health arising from the accumulation of waste tyres" to the maximum extent possible. In this respect, we believe, like the Panel, that non-generation measures are more apt to achieve this objective because they prevent the accumulation of waste tyres, while waste management measures dispose of waste tyres only once they have accumulated. Furthermore, we note that, in comparing a proposed alter-

native to the Import Ban, the Panel took into account specific risks attached to the proposed alternative, such as the risk of leaching of toxic substances that might be associated to landfilling, or the risk of toxic emissions that might arise from the incineration of waste tyres. In our view, the Panel did not err in so doing. Indeed, we do not see how a panel could undertake a meaningful comparison of the measure at issue with a possible alternative while disregarding the risks arising out of the implementation of the possible alternative. In this case, the Panel examined as proposed alternatives landfilling, stockpiling, and waste tyre incineration, and considered that, even if these disposal methods were performed under controlled conditions, they nevertheless pose risks to human health similar or additional to those Brazil seeks to reduce through the Import Ban. Because these practices carry their own risks, and these risks do not arise from non-generation measures such as the Import Ban, we believe, like the Panel, that these practices are not reasonably available alternatives.

175. With respect to material recycling, we share the Panel's view that this practice is not as effective as the Import Ban in reducing the exposure to the risks arising from the accumulation of waste tyres. Material recycling applications are costly, and hence capable of disposing of only a limited number of waste tyres. We also note that some of them might require advanced technologies and know-how that are not readily available on a large scale. Accordingly, we are of the view that the Panel did not err in concluding that material recycling is not a reasonably available alternative to the Import Ban.

3.   The Weighing and Balancing of Relevant Factors by the Panel

176. ... According to the European Communities, although the Appellate Body has not defined the term "weighing and balancing", "this language refers clearly to a process where, in the first place, the importance of each element is assessed individually and, then, its role and relative importance is taken into consideration together with the other elements for the purposes of deciding whether the challenged measure is necessary to attain the objective pursued." The European Communities reasons that, "since the Panel failed to establish ... the extent of the actual contribution the [Import Ban] makes to the reduction of the number of waste tyres arising in Brazil, ... it was incapable of 'weighing and balancing' this contribution against any of the other relevant factors." In addition, the European Communities contends that "the Panel base[d] ... its 'weighing and balancing' exercise on the wrong analysis it ... made of the alternatives". In sum, the European Communities argues that the Panel conducted a "superficial analysis" that is not a real weighing and balancing of the different factors and alternatives, because it did not balance "its arguments about the measure and the alternatives with the absolute trade-restrictiveness of the import ban and with a real evaluation of the contribution of the import ban to the objective pursued."
* * *

179. In this case, the Panel identified the objective of the Import Ban as being the reduction of the exposure to risks arising from the accumulation of waste tyres. It assessed the importance of the interests underlying this objective. It found that risks of dengue fever and malaria arise from the accumulation of waste tyres and that the objective of protecting human life and health against such diseases "is both vital and important in the highest degree". The Panel noted that the objective of the Import Ban also relates to the protection of the environment, a value that it considered—correctly, in our view—important. Then, the Panel

analyzed the trade restrictiveness of the Import Ban and its contribution to the achievement of its objective. It appears from the Panel's reasoning that it considered that, in the light of the importance of the interests protected by the objective of the Import Ban, the contribution of the Import Ban to the achievement of its objective outweighs its trade restrictiveness. This finding of the Panel does not appear erroneous to us.

180. The Panel then proceeded to examine the alternatives to the Import Ban proposed by the European Communities. The Panel explained that some of them could not be viewed as alternatives to the Import Ban because they were complementary to it and were already included in Brazil's comprehensive policy.[324] Next, the Panel compared the other alternatives proposed by the European Communities—landfilling, stockpiling, incineration, and material recycling—with the Import Ban, taking into consideration the specific risks associated with these proposed alternatives. The Panel concluded from this comparative assessment that none of the proposed options was a reasonably available alternative to the Import Ban.181. The European Communities argues that the Panel failed to make a proper collective assessment of all the proposed alternatives, a contention that does not stand for the following reasons. First, the Panel did refer to its collective examination of these alternatives in concluding that "none of these, either individually *or collectively*, would be such that the risks arising from waste tyres in Brazil would be safely eliminated, as is intended by the current import ban." Secondly, as noted by the Panel and discussed above, some of the proposed alternatives are not real substitutes for the Import Ban since they complement each other as part of Brazil's comprehensive policy. Finally, having found that other proposed alternatives were not reasonably available or carried their own risks, these alternatives would not have weighed differently in a collective assessment of alternatives.

182. In sum, the Panel's conclusion that the Import Ban is necessary was the result of a process involving, first, the examination of the contribution of the Import Ban to the achievement of its objective against its trade restrictiveness in the light of the interests at stake, and, secondly, the comparison of the possible alternatives, including associated risks, with the Import Ban. The analytical process followed by the Panel is consistent with the approach previously defined by the Appellate Body. The weighing and balancing is a holistic operation that involves putting all the variables of the equation together and evaluating them in relation to each other after having examined them individually, in order to reach an overall judgement. We therefore do not share the European Communities' view that the Panel did not "actually" weigh and balance the relevant factors, or that the Panel made a methodological error in comparing the alternative options proposed by the European Communities with the Import Ban.

Questions and Discussion

1. Both the Appellate Body in *Retreaded Tyres* and the Panel in *Asbestos* emphasized the Panel's task was *not* to examine the desirability of the declared policy goal, because Arti-

---

324. For example, measures to encourage domestic retreading and improve the retreadability of domestic used tyres, a better implementation of the import ban on used tyres, and a better implementation of existing collection and disposal schemes. See also Panel Report, paras. 7.169, 7.171, and 7.178.

cle XX(b) embodies "the fundamental principle" that WTO members have "the right . . . to determine the level of protection that they consider appropriate in a given context." *Brazil–Retreaded Tyres*, Appellate Body Report, at para. 210. In light of this fundamental principle, do you think WTO members will have difficulty defending a measure under the new balancing test of Article XX(b)?

2. In *Retreaded Tyres*, the EU argued that Brazil did not show specific health risks from tire fires in Brazil and that, in any event, the probability of adverse health effects is small. The EU also argued that Brazil needed to quantify the contribution of the import ban to a reduction in waste tires. How does the Appellate Body respond? How much evidence and what kind of evidence should the responding party need to demonstrate risk under Article XX(b)?

3. The new "necessary" test allows panels to balance many different factors, including the economic resources available to the country implementing the trade restriction and the environmental problem being addressed. Kevin Gray argues that "the *Brazil-Retreaded Tyres* decision demonstrates that a WTO member's level of economic development and available resources need to be taken into account in assessing the relevance of that member's environmental problems to WTO disputes." Kevin Gray, *Brazil-Measures Affecting Imports of Retreaded Tyres*, 102 AM. J. INT'L L. 610, 613 (2008). In what ways does it do so? Do you think that the new test gives greater weight to environmental considerations?

4. An important conclusion in both *Asbestos* and *Retreaded Tyres* is that the chosen level of protection has an important relationship to whether a particular measure is "necessary." As the Appellate Body stated in *Asbestos*, France "could not be reasonably expected to employ any alternative measure if that measure would involve a continuation of the very risk that the Decree seeks to 'halt.' Such an alternative would, in effect, prevent France from achieving its chosen level of health protection." *Asbestos*, Appellate Body Report, at para. 174. In affirming the Panel, the Appellate Body rejected Canada's argument that an alternative measure is not reasonable only if it is impossible to implement. The Appellate Body concluded that controlled use was not impossible to implement, but it was unreasonable to implement in light of France's goal to stop the spread of asbestos-related human health risks and the scientific consensus that controlled use could still result in health risks. Does *Asbestos* support the view that a country could seek to prevent all risk from a product by banning it, even if the risk to human health from a product is very low? How does the Appellate Body in *Retreaded Tyres* respond to this issue?

5. Which party has the burden to show that alternative measures are not reasonably available? Do you agree that this is where the burden belongs? Does the complaining party have to establish a prima facie case that certain reasonable alternatives meet the objective established by the responding party? In a recent case, the Appellate Body indicated that the responding party may need to show that implementing the alternative proposed by the complaining party is too costly to implement. China-Measures Affecting Trading Rights and Distribution Services for Certain Publications and Audiovisual Entertainment Products, WT/DS363/AB/R, para. 334 (adopted Jan. 19, 2010) (acknowledging that the Panel considered that additional resources might be required to adopt an alternative approach in this dispute interpreting measures "necessary to protect public morals" under Article XX(a)).

6. In *Asbestos*, the Panel concludes that France was not required to use international standards for setting its health protection standards. Even before the ban at issue in this case, France had a statutory exposure limit that was twice as stringent as the World Health Organization exposure limit. The Panel not only rejects Canada's suggestion that an in-

ternational standard should be applied (para. 8.205), but implicitly accepts that France can go beyond its already more stringent level in seeking to reduce health risks from asbestos exposure. This acceptance of national choice may seem inescapable under Article XX, which makes no reference to international standards. However, the Agreement on Technical Barriers to Trade (TBT Agreement) and the Agreement on the Application of Sanitary and Phytosanitary Measures (SPS Agreement) both require WTO members to "base" their relevant standards on international standards. The trend in international trade law toward the use of international standards rather than domestic standards is known as harmonization and is discussed in more detail in Chapters 6 and 7.

7. In *Retreaded Tyres*, Brazil justified its ban on *retreaded* tires even though *waste* tires (as opposed to properly used retreaded tires) caused the risks that Brazil sought to reduce. In other words, the product posing the health risk differed from the product subject to trade restrictions. Similarly, in *Reformulated Gasoline*, the United States imposed trade restrictions on gasoline even through, strictly speaking, the health risks did not directly relate to gasoline itself but rather to air pollution caused by the combustion of gasoline. In *Shrimp/Turtle*, the Appellate Body also found that restrictions on the importation of shrimp to protect sea turtles fell within the scope of measures allowable under Article XX(g). In our discussion of Article XX(g), we will return to the question of just how tight the link must be between the regulated product and the resource to be protected or the risk to be avoided.

IV. The Evolution of Article XX(g) Analysis

Article XX(g) creates an exception for measures "relating to the conservation of exhaustible natural resources if such measures are made effective in conjunction with restrictions on domestic production or consumption." The applicability of Article XX(g) requires an interpretation of three distinct phrases in the paragraph: 1) "exhaustible natural resources," 2) "relating to," and 3) "made effective in conjunction with restrictions on domestic production or consumption." As we saw from the *Tuna/Dolphin* and *Herring and Salmon* cases (pages 278–86), GATT panels had interpreted the second and third elements of Article XX(g) very narrowly. These panels interpreted the phrase "relating to" as "primarily aimed at" and more or less equated "primarily aimed at" with the Article XX(b) "necessary" test. As we will see, the WTO's Appellate Body in the first WTO dispute, *Reformulated Gasoline,* reinterpreted Article XX(g) more consistently with its plain language. As a consequence, the relative importance of Article XX(g) has grown substantially as the hurdles for consistency with Article XX(b) remain high and the interpretation of Article XX(g)'s three phrases has embraced a broader range of environmental and conservation measures.

A. The *Reformulated Gasoline* Case

As we saw in Chapter 4 (pages 210–14), the U.S. Environmental Protection Agency (EPA) required gasoline refineries to reduce levels of contaminants in gasoline as compared to the individual refiner's "baseline" level of contaminants in its gasoline in 1990. The EPA's rule implemented provisions of the Clean Air Act that set the average of all gasoline quality in 1990 as the "statutory baseline," but which also allowed the EPA to devise other baseline approaches that would meet the same objective. The EPA decided to require domestic refiners to establish and use an "individual 1990 baseline" for each refiner, but required foreign refiners to meet gasoline quality goals with reference to the statutory baseline, which, for Venezuela in particular, was substantially lower (stricter) than its own 1990 levels. When Venezuela and Brazil challenged these rules as inconsistent with Articles I and III of the GATT, the Panel agreed.

The Panel then proceeded to consider the U.S. claim that the rule was, nevertheless, permissible under Article XX(b) or XX(g) of the GATT. The Panel concluded that the discriminatory elements of the EPA's rule were not "necessary" within the meaning of Article XX(b), because, among other reasons, the United States had not demonstrated that other measures consistent, or less inconsistent, with Article III:4 were not reasonably available to enforce compliance with foreign refiner baselines. Turning to Article XX(g), it also held that clean air was an "exhaustible natural resource" but that "the less favourable baseline establishment methods were not primarily aimed at conservation of clean air." The United States appealed the Panel's Article XX(g) finding to the WTO's Appellate Body.

United States-Standards for Reformulated and Conventional Gasoline

Appellate Body Report, WT/DS2/AB/R (adopted May 20, 1996),
reprinted in 35 I.L.M. 603 (1996)

[The Appellate Body acknowledged the Panel's conclusions that clean air was a "natural resource" that could be "depleted" and that a policy to reduce the depletion of clean air was thus a policy to conserve an exhaustible natural resource within the meaning of Article XX(g). Because Venezuela and Brazil had not properly appealed this issue, the Appellate Body ruled that it could not address it.]

The Panel Report then went on to apply the 1987 *Herring and Salmon* reasoning and conclusion to the baseline establishment rules of the Gasoline Rule in the following manner:

> The Panel then considered whether the precise aspects of the Gasoline Rule that it had found to violate Article III—the less favourable baseline establishments methods that adversely affected the conditions of competition for imported gasoline—were primarily aimed at the conservation of natural resources. The Panel saw no direct connection between less favourable treatment of imported gasoline that was chemically identical to domestic gasoline, and the US objective of improving air quality in the United States. Indeed, in the view of the Panel, being consistent with the obligation to provide no less favourable treatment would not prevent the attainment of the desired level of conservation of natural resources under the Gasoline Rule. Accordingly, it could not be said that the baseline establishment methods that afforded less favourable treatment to imported gasoline were primarily aimed at the conservation of natural resources. In the Panel's view, the above-noted lack of connection was underscored by the fact that affording treatment of imported gasoline consistent with its Article III:4 obligations would not in any way hinder the United States in its pursuit of its conservation policies under the Gasoline Rule. Indeed, the United States remained free to regulate in order to obtain whatever air quality it wished. The Panel

therefore concluded that the less favourable baseline establishments methods at issue in this case were not primarily aimed at the conservation of natural resources.

It is not easy to follow the reasoning in the above paragraph of the Panel Report. In our view, there is a certain amount of opaqueness in that reasoning. The Panel starts with positing that there was *"no direct connection"* between the baseline establishment rules which it characterized as "less favourable treatment" of imported gasoline that was chemically identical to the domestic gasoline and "the US objective of improving air quality in the United States." Shortly thereafter, the Panel went on to conclude that *"accordingly, it could not be said that* the baseline establishment rules that afforded less favourable treatment to imported gasoline *were primarily aimed at* the conservation of natural resources" (emphasis added). The Panel did not try to clarify whether the phrase "direct connection" was being used as a synonym for "primarily aimed at" or whether a new and additional element (on top of "primarily aimed at") was being demanded.

One problem with the reasoning in that paragraph is that the Panel asked itself whether the "less favourable treatment" of imported gasoline was "primarily aimed at" the conservation of natural resources, rather than whether the "measure," i.e. the baseline establishment rules, were "primarily aimed at" conservation of clean air. In our view, the Panel here was in error in referring to its legal conclusion on Article III:4 instead of the measure in issue. The result of this analysis is to turn Article XX on its head. Obviously, there had to be a finding that the measure provided "less favourable treatment" under Article III:4 before the Panel examined the "General Exceptions" contained in Article XX. That, however, is a conclusion of law. The chapeau of Article XX makes it clear that it is the "measures" which are to be examined under Article XX(g), and not the legal finding of "less favourable treatment."

Furthermore, the Panel Report appears to have utilized a conclusion it had reached earlier in holding that the baseline establishment rules did not fall within the justifying terms of Articles XX(b); i.e. that the baseline establishment rules were not "necessary" for the protection of human, animal or plant life. The Panel Report, it will be recalled, found that the baseline establishment rules had not been shown by the United States to be "necessary" under Article XX(b) since alternative measures either consistent or less inconsistent with the *General Agreement* were reasonably available to the United States for achieving its aim of protecting human, animal or plant life. In other words, the Panel Report appears to have applied the "necessary" test not only in examining the baseline establishment rules under Article XX(b), but also in the course of applying Article XX(g).

[The Appellate Body then concluded that the Panel failed to apply Article 31 of the Vienna Convention on the Law of Treaties, which provides that "A treaty shall be interpreted in good faith in accordance with the ordinary meaning to be given to the terms of the treaty in their context and in the light of its object and purpose." The rule forms part of the "customary rules of interpretation of public international law" which Article 3(2) of the DSU directs panels and the Appellate Body to apply. The Appellate Body recognized that Article XX uses different terms in respect of different categories: "necessary"—in paragraphs (a), (b), and (d); "relating to"—in paragraphs (c), (e), and (g); "in pursuance of"—in paragraph (h); "essential"—in paragraph (j); "for the protection of"—in paragraph (f); and "involving"—in paragraph (i).]

It does not seem reasonable to suppose that the WTO Members intended to require, in respect of each and every category, the same kind or degree of connection or relationship between the measure under appraisal and the state interest or policy sought to be promoted or realized. * * *

All the participants and the third participants in this appeal accept the propriety and applicability of the view of the *Herring and Salmon* report and the Panel Report that a measure must be "primarily aimed at" the conservation of exhaustible natural resources in order to fall within the scope of Article XX(g). Accordingly, we see no need to examine this point further, save, perhaps, to note that the phrase "primarily aimed at" is not itself treaty language and was not designed as a simple litmus test for inclusion or exclusion from Article XX(g).

Against this background, we turn to the specific question of whether the baseline establishment rules are appropriately regarded as "primarily aimed at" the conservation of natural resources for the purposes of Article XX(g). We consider that this question must be answered in the affirmative.

The baseline establishment rules, taken as a whole (that is, the provisions relating to establishment of baselines for domestic refiners, along with the provisions relating to baselines for blenders and importers of gasoline), need to be related to the "non-degradation" requirements set out elsewhere in the Gasoline Rule. Those provisions can scarcely be understood if scrutinized strictly by themselves, totally divorced from other sections of the Gasoline Rule which certainly constitute part of the context of these provisions. The baseline establishment rules whether individual or statutory, were designed to permit scrutiny and monitoring of the level of compliance of refiners, importers and blenders with the "non-degradation" requirements. Without baselines of some kind, such scrutiny would not be possible and the Gasoline Rule's objective of stabilizing and preventing further deterioration of the level of air pollution prevailing in 1990, would be substantially frustrated. The relationship between the baseline establishment rules and the "non-degradation" requirements of the Gasoline Rule is not negated by the inconsistency, found by the Panel, of the baseline establishment rules with the terms of Article III:4. We consider that, given that substantial relationship, the baseline establishment rules cannot be regarded as merely incidentally or inadvertently aimed at the conservation of clean air in the United States for the purposes of Article XX(g).

The Panel did not find it necessary to deal with the issue of whether the baseline establishment rules "are made effective in conjunction with restrictions on domestic production or consumption," since it had earlier concluded that those rules had not even satisfied the preceding requirement of "relating to" in the sense of being "primarily aimed at" the conservation of clean air. Having been unable to concur with that earlier conclusion of the Panel, we must now address this second requirement of Article XX(g), the United States having, in effect, appealed from the failure of the Panel to proceed further with its inquiry into the availability of Article XX(g) as a justification for the baseline establishment rules.

The claim of the United States is that the second clause of Article XX(g) requires that the burdens entailed by regulating the level of pollutants in the air emitted in the course of combustion of gasoline, must not be imposed solely on, or in respect of, imported gasoline.

On the other hand, Venezuela and Brazil refer to prior panel reports which include statements to the effect that to be deemed as "made effective in conjunction with restrictions on domestic production or consumption," a measure must be "primarily aimed at" making effective certain restrictions on domestic production or consumption. Venezuela and Brazil also argue that the United States has failed to show the existence of restrictions on domestic production or consumption of a natural resource under the Gasoline Rule since clean air was not an exhaustible natural resource within the meaning of Article XX(g). Venezuela contends, finally, that the United States has not discharged its burden of showing that the baseline establishment rules make the United States' regulatory scheme "effective." The claim of Venezuela is, in effect, that to be properly regarded as "primarily aimed at" the conservation of natural resources, the baseline establishment rules must not only "reflect a conservation purpose" but also be shown to have had "some positive conservation effect."

The Appellate Body considers that the basic international law rule of treaty interpretation, discussed earlier, that the terms of a treaty are to be given their ordinary meaning, in context, so as to effectuate its object and purpose, is applicable here, too. Viewed in this light, the ordinary or natural meaning of "made effective" when used in connection with a measure—a governmental act or regulation—may be seen to refer to such measure being "operative," as "in force," or as having "come into effect." Similarly, the phrase "in conjunction with" may be read quite plainly as "together with" or "jointly with." Taken together, the second clause of Article XX(g) appears to us to refer to governmental measures like the baseline establishment rules being promulgated or brought into effect together with restrictions on domestic production or consumption of natural resources. Put in a slightly different manner, we believe that the clause "if such measures are made effective in conjunction with restrictions on domestic product or consumption" is appropriately read as a requirement that the measures concerned impose restrictions, not just in respect of imported gasoline but also with respect to domestic gasoline. The clause is a requirement of *even-handedness* in the imposition of restrictions, in the name of conservation, upon the production or consumption of exhaustible natural resources.

There is, of course, no textual basis for requiring identical treatment of domestic and imported products. Indeed, where there is identity of treatment—constituting real, not merely formal, equality of treatment—it is difficult to see how inconsistency with Article III:4 would have arisen in the first place. On the other hand, if no restrictions on domestically-produced like products are imposed at all, and all limitations are placed upon imported products *alone*, the measure cannot be accepted as primarily or even substantially designed for implementing conservationist goals. The measure would simply be naked discrimination for protecting locally-produced goods.

In the present appeal, the baseline establishment rules affect both domestic gasoline and imported gasoline, providing for—generally speaking—individual baselines for domestic refiners and blenders and statutory baselines for importers. Thus, restrictions on the consumption or depletion of clean air by regulating the domestic production of "dirty" gasoline are established jointly with corresponding restrictions with respect to imported gasoline. That imported gasoline has been determined to have been accorded "less favourable treatment" than the domestic gasoline in terms of Article III:4, is not material for purposes of analysis under Article XX(g). It might also be noted that the second clause of Article XX(g) speaks disjunctively of "domestic production *or* consumption."

We do not believe, finally, that the clause "if made effective in conjunction with restrictions on domestic production or consumption" was intended to establish an empirical "effects test" for the availability of the Article XX(g) exception. In the first place, the problem of determining causation, well-known in both domestic and international law, is always a difficult one. In the second place, in the field of conservation of exhaustible natural resources, a substantial period of time, perhaps years, may have to elapse before the effects attributable to implementation of a given measure may be observable. The legal characterization of such a measure is not reasonably made contingent upon occurrence of subsequent events. We are not, however, suggesting that consideration of the predictable effects of a measure is never relevant. In a particular case, should it become clear that realistically, a specific measure cannot in any possible situation have any positive effect on conservation goals, it would very probably be because that measure was not designed as a conservation regulation to begin with. In other words, it would not have been "primarily aimed at" conservation of natural resources at all. * * *

Questions and Discussion

1. The Appellate Body in *Reformulated Gasoline* put distance between the "primarily aimed at" test of Article XX(g) and the "necessary" test under Article XX(b). In doing so, it halted the growing panel practice of cutting and pasting their Article XX(b) analysis into their Article XX(g) conclusions. The Appellate Body also recast the "relating to" test and the "made effective in conjunction with" test. What are the new tests? Are these more reasonable interpretations of Article XX(g)?

2. According to two trade scholars:

> The most striking difference between the [Appellate Body's opinion in *Reformulated Gasoline*] and those of most GATT Panels that had preceded it was the clear legal analysis—word by word, clause by clause, and sentence by sentence. There were leaps neither of logic nor of faith. The decision announces with authority that dispute settlement for trade rules is no longer a diplomatic process, as it had been under the GATT, but an unmistakably judicial one.

BERTA ESPERANZA HERNÁNDEZ-TRUYOL & STEPHEN J. POWELL, JUST TRADE: A NEW COVENANT LINKING TRADE AND HUMAN RIGHTS 100 (2009).

B. *Shrimp/Turtle*

The next trade and environment dispute, *Shrimp/Turtle,* provided the Appellate Body with the opportunity to consolidate its Article XX(g) analysis. In this case, four Southeast Asian countries challenged U.S. import restrictions on shrimp from countries not requiring the use of a Turtle Excluder Device (TED), a device that permits air-breathing sea turtles to escape from shrimp nets and avoid being drowned. Sea turtles frequently swim in areas where shrimpers trawl for shrimp. The loss of turtles trapped in shrimp nets is a major cause of sea turtle mortality in all parts of the world, as are habitat destruction, egg collection, trade, and other factors. All seven species of sea turtles receive the highest level of protection by every international treaty or organization that addresses sea turtle conservation, and the United States lists all but the flatback sea turtle as threatened or endangered under the U.S. Endangered Species Act. *See* Chris Wold *The Status of Sea Turtles under International Environmental Law and International Environmental Agreements,* 5 J. INT'L WILDLIFE L. & POL'Y 11 (2002). Sea turtles are highly migratory, sometimes traveling thousands of miles. The females, however, return to the same beach where they were born to lay their eggs.

How TEDs Work

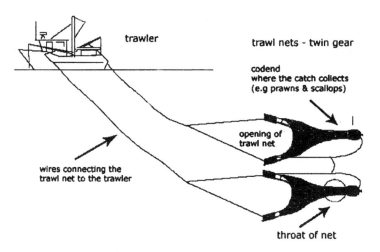

Figure 1. A trawl net without TEDs. As the boat moves forward, anything caught in the net will collect in the codend, because turtles, sharks, and other bycatch have no means to escape the net. Reprinted with the permission of The State of Queensland, Australia (Department of Primary Industries and Fisheries).

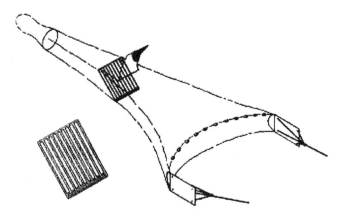

Figure 2. This TED, named the matagorda TED, deflects turtles, sharks, and other species larger than the width of the grid installed in the net out of the net. Illustration courtesy of the National Marine Fisheries Service. 50 C.F.R. § 223.207.

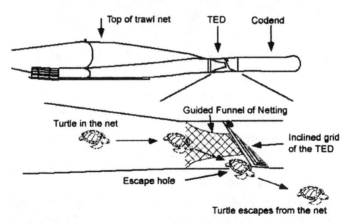

Figure 3. This diagram illustrates how a TED is fitted to a net and deflects turtles out of the net. Reprinted with the permission of The State of Queensland, Australia (Department of Primary Industries and Fisheries).

To reduce sea turtle mortality caused by U.S. shrimp fishing, the United States established requirements under the Endangered Species Act for U.S. shrimpers to use TEDs. Studies have shown that the use of TEDs greatly reduces turtle mortality and may actually reduce costs for shrimpers. While applauding this step, environmentalists and scientists warned that far-ranging and widely dispersed turtle populations would continue to decline if foreign fleets did not also reduce turtle mortality. The U.S. shrimping fleet, believing that foreign fleets would have a competitive advantage if not required to use TEDs, supported efforts to change foreign fishing practices. As a result, the U.S. Congress enacted a law known as "Section 609," which bans shrimp imports from countries that harvest shrimp with "commercial fishing technology" that may adversely affect sea turtles. The import ban would not apply to countries that were "certified" as having a regulatory program that was "comparable" to that of the United States and an average rate of incidental take that was "comparable" to the U.S. average. To implement this congressional mandate, the U.S. State Department issued rules that allowed a country with sea turtle habitat to be "certified" as having a comparable regulatory program only if it adopted a comprehensive TED program. Revised Guidelines for Determining Comparability of Foreign Programs for the Protection of Turtles in Shrimp Trawl Fishing Operations, 58 Fed. Reg. 9015 (Feb. 18, 1993). In other words, the United States required foreign countries to have "essentially the same" TED requirements as the United States. For a more complete discussion of Section 609, see Sanford Gaines, *The WTO's Reading of the GATT Article XX Chapeau: A Disguised Restriction on Environmental Measures*, 22 U. Pa. J. Int'l Econ. L. 739, 762–70 (2001).

Not surprisingly, the Panel found that the U.S. restrictions, which closely resembled the measures at issue in the *Tuna/Dolphin* disputes, violated Article XI of the GATT, because the law distinguished shrimp based on the way shrimp is produced, not on the physical characteristics of shrimp. The United States did not appeal this decision. The Panel also ruled that Section 609 did not meet the requirements of Article XX(g). On appeal of this ruling, the Appellate Body engaged in an exhaustive analysis of Article XX(g). The Appellate Body began its analysis be restating the analytical framework it announced in *Reformulated Gasoline* for assessing measures under Article XX(g): 1) does the measure concern an exhaustible natural resource?, 2) does the trade measure relate to the conservation of that resource?, and 3) is the trade measure made effective in conjunction with restrictions on domestic production or consumption?

United States-Import Prohibition of Certain Shrimp and Shrimp Products

Appellate Body Report, WT/DS58/AB/R (adopted Nov. 6, 1998),
reprinted in 38 I.L.M. 121 (1999)

127. ... India, Pakistan and Thailand contended that a "reasonable interpretation" of the term "exhaustible" is that the term refers to "finite resources such as minerals, rather than biological or renewable resources." In their view, such finite resources were exhaustible "because there was a limited supply which could and would be depleted unit for unit as the resources were consumed." Moreover, they argued, if "all" natural resources were considered to be exhaustible, the term "exhaustible" would become superfluous.... For its part, Malaysia added that sea turtles, being living creatures, could only be considered under Article XX(b), since Article XX(g) was meant for "nonliving exhaustible natural resources". It followed, according to Malaysia, that the United States cannot invoke both the Article XX(b) and the Article XX(g) exceptions simultaneously.

128. We are not convinced by these arguments. Textually, Article XX(g) is *not* limited to the conservation of "mineral" or "non-living" natural resources. The complainants' principal argument is rooted in the notion that "living" natural resources are "renewable" and therefore cannot be "exhaustible" natural resources. We do not believe that "exhaustible" natural resources and "renewable" natural resources are mutually exclusive. One lesson that modern biological sciences teach us is that living species, though in principle, capable of reproduction and, in that sense, "renewable", are in certain circumstances indeed susceptible of depletion, exhaustion and extinction, frequently because of human activities. Living resources are just as "finite" as petroleum, iron ore and other non-living resources.

[The Appellate Body also noted that several widely accepted instruments of international law specifically recognized the "exhaustible" nature of threatened and endangered species and committed governments, including the four complainants, to various steps to prevent further endangerment or extinction of such species.]

135. Article XX(g) requires that the measure sought to be justified be one which "relat[es] to" the conservation of exhaustible natural resources. In making this determination, the treaty interpreter essentially looks into the relationship between the measure at stake and the legitimate policy of conserving exhaustible natural resources. It is well to bear in mind that the policy of protecting and conserving the endangered sea turtles here involved is shared by all participants and third participants in this appeal, indeed, by the vast majority of the nations of the world. None of the parties to this dispute question the genuineness of the commitment of the others to that policy.

136. In *United States-Gasoline*, we inquired into the relationship between the baseline establishment rules of the United States Environmental Protection Agency (the "EPA") and the conservation of natural resources for the purposes of Article XX(g). There, we answered in the affirmative the question posed before the

panel of whether the baseline establishment rules were "primarily aimed at" the conservation of clean air. We held that:

> ... The baseline establishment rules whether individual or statutory, were designed to permit scrutiny and monitoring of the level of compliance of refiners, importers and blenders with the "non-degradation" requirements. Without baselines of some kind, such scrutiny would not be possible and the Gasoline Rule's objective of stabilizing and preventing further deterioration of the level of air pollution prevailing in 1990, would be substantially frustrated.... We consider that, given that substantial relationship, the baseline establishment rules cannot be regarded as merely incidentally or inadvertently aimed at the conservation of clean air in the United States for the purposes of Article XX(g).

The substantial relationship we found there between the EPA baseline establishment rules and the conservation of clean air in the United States was a close and genuine relationship of ends and means.

137. In the present case, we must examine the relationship between the general structure and design of the measure here at stake, Section 609, and the policy goal it purports to serve, that is, the conservation of sea turtles.

138. Section 609(b)(1) imposes an import ban on shrimp that have been harvested with commercial fishing technology which may adversely affect sea turtles. This provision is designed to influence countries to adopt national regulatory programs requiring the use of TEDs by their shrimp fishermen. In this connection, it is important to note that the general structure and design of Section 609 *cum* implementing guidelines is fairly narrowly focused. There are two basic exemptions from the import ban, both of which relate clearly and directly to the policy goal of conserving sea turtles. First, Section 609, as elaborated in the 1996 Guidelines, excludes from the import ban shrimp harvested "under conditions that do not adversely affect sea turtles." Thus, the measure, by its terms, excludes from the import ban: aquaculture shrimp; shrimp species (such as *pandalid* shrimp) harvested in water areas where sea turtles do not normally occur; and shrimp harvested exclusively by artisanal methods, even from non-certified countries. The harvesting of such shrimp clearly does not affect sea turtles. Second, under Section 609(b)(2), the measure exempts from the import ban shrimp caught in waters subject to the jurisdiction of certified countries.

139. There are two types of certification for countries under Section 609(b)(2). First, under Section 609(b)(2)(C), a country may be certified as having a fishing environment that does not pose a threat of incidental taking of sea turtles in the course of commercial shrimp trawl harvesting. There is no risk, or only a negligible risk, that sea turtles will be harmed by shrimp trawling in such an environment.

140. The second type of certification is provided by Section 609(b)(2)(A) and (B). Under these provisions, as further elaborated in the 1996 Guidelines, a country wishing to export shrimp to the United States is required to adopt a regulatory program that is comparable to that of the United States program and to have a rate of incidental take of sea turtles that is comparable to the average rate of United States' vessels. This is, essentially, a requirement that a country adopt a regulatory program requiring the use of TEDs by commercial shrimp trawling vessels in areas where there is a likelihood of intercepting sea turtles. This re-

quirement is, in our view, directly connected with the policy of conservation of sea turtles. It is undisputed among the participants, and recognized by the experts consulted by the Panel, that the harvesting of shrimp by commercial shrimp trawling vessels with mechanical retrieval devices in waters where shrimp and sea turtles coincide is a significant cause of sea turtle mortality. Moreover, the Panel did "not question … the fact generally acknowledged by the experts that TEDs, when properly installed and adapted to the local area, would be an effective tool for the preservation of sea turtles."

141. In its general design and structure, therefore, Section 609 is not a simple, blanket prohibition of the importation of shrimp imposed without regard to the consequences (or lack thereof) of the mode of harvesting employed upon the incidental capture and mortality of sea turtles. Focusing on the design of the measure here at stake, it appears to us that Section 609, *cum* implementing guidelines, is not disproportionately wide in its scope and reach in relation to the policy objective of protection and conservation of sea turtle species. The means are, in principle, reasonably related to the ends. The means and ends relationship between Section 609 and the legitimate policy of conserving an exhaustible, and, in fact, endangered species, is observably a close and real one, a relationship that is every bit as substantial as that which we found in *United States-Gasoline* between the EPA baseline establishment rules and the conservation of clean air in the United States.

142. In our view, therefore, Section 609 is a measure "relating to" the conservation of an exhaustible natural resource within the meaning of Article XX(g) of the GATT 1994. * * *

144. We earlier noted that Section 609, enacted in 1989, addresses the mode of harvesting of imported shrimp only. However, two years earlier, in 1987, the United States issued regulations pursuant to the Endangered Species Act requiring all United States shrimp trawl vessels to use approved TEDs, or to restrict the duration of tow-times, in specified areas where there was significant incidental mortality of sea turtles in shrimp trawls. These regulations … require United States shrimp trawlers to use approved TEDs "in areas and at times when there is a likelihood of intercepting sea turtles", with certain limited exceptions. Penalties for violation of the Endangered Species Act, or the regulations issued thereunder, include civil and criminal sanctions. The United States government currently relies on monetary sanctions and civil penalties for enforcement. The government has the ability to seize shrimp catch from trawl vessels fishing in United States waters and has done so in cases of egregious violations. We believe that, in principle, Section 609 is an even-handed measure.

145. Accordingly, we hold that Section 609 is a measure made effective in conjunction with the restrictions on domestic harvesting of shrimp, as required by Article XX(g).

Questions and Discussion

1. The *Tuna/Dolphin* Panels created an "effects" test under Article XX(g) by rephrasing "made effective in conjunction with" domestic measures to mean "rendering effective" domestic restrictions. *Tuna/Dolphin I*, GATT Panel Report, at para. 5.31;

Tuna/Dolphin II, GATT Panel Report, at para. 5.23. The Appellate Body in *Reformulated Gasoline* and *Shrimp/Turtle* rejected this test. What is the significance of this change for countries that might be considering trade restrictions to conserve natural resources?

2. Based on the ordinary meaning of the words used in Article XX, the Appellate Body in *Reformulated Gasoline* rejected an interpretation of "relating to" that equated with "necessary." Yet, it still defined "relating to" as meaning "primarily aimed at." Why?

3. The Panel in *Reformulated Gasoline* asked whether the "less favorable treatment" related to the conservation of exhaustible natural resources. The Appellate Body stated that the Panel had turned Article XX "on its head.... The chapeau of Article XX makes it clear that it is the 'measures' which are to be examined under Article XX(g), and not the legal finding of 'less favourable treatment.'" The Panel also concluded that under Article XX(b), any discrimination must be "necessary," although the United States did not appeal this conclusion. Consider the following, written by a member of the WTO Secretariat, which supports this view:

> One can safely assume that the drafters of the General Agreement, had they considered that only 'necessary' health policies could be implemented through trade restrictions, would have given some guidance on the criteria to be used in assessing the necessity of the contracting parties' health policies. The significant differences between the health policies of the contracting parties, the conflicts of values that have to be resolved when a health policy is adopted, the enormous difficult of agreeing among the now 128 contracting parties on the common criteria for judging health policies, and the inappropriateness of undertaking such a task in a body not composed of representatives of health ministries should convince anyone of the wisdom of the panels when they interpreted the term 'necessary' to refer to the GATT inconsistency rather than the health policy.

Frieder Roessler, *Diverging Domestic Policies and Multilateral Trade Integration, in* 2 Fair Trade and Harmonization 21, 34–35 (Jagdish Bhagwati & Robert E. Hudec eds., 1997); *see also* Aaditya Mattoo & Petros C. Mavroidis, *Trade, Environment and the WTO: The Dispute Settlement Practice Relating to Article XX of GATT, in* 11 International Trade Law and the GATT/WTO Dispute Settlement System 327, 338 (Ernst-Ulrich Petersmann ed., 1997) ("Article XX does not require that the measure be necessary for the attainment of the objective, but that the inconsistency with the GATT be necessary for the attainment of the objective."). Who has the better argument, the Appellate Body or the Panel and Roessler? In other words, does Article XX ask whether the measure or discrimination/less favorable treatment must be "necessary" or "relate to conservation"? How might the approach of the Panel and Roessler change the analysis under Article XX? Would this approach balance trade and environmental concerns effectively?

4. Although the *Tuna/Dolphin II* Panel articulated a three-part framework for analyzing Article XX(b) and Article XX(g) that subsequent panels have followed, none of the panels have constructed a list of the various elements that must be met under each analytical component. Construct a "hornbook" test for Articles XX(b) and XX(g) based on the decisions included in these materials. Do you think that these tests are sensible from a trade perspective? An environmental perspective? Have the panels and Appellate Body found the right balance between trade and environmental goals?

———————

C. A Closer Look at "Relating To": The U.S. Pelly Amendment

The Appellate Body in *Reformulated Gasoline* expressly refused to review the discriminatory (Article III-inconsistent) baseline establishment provisions "totally divorced from other sections of the Gasoline Rule which certainly constitute part of the context of these provisions." It affirmed this analysis in *Shrimp/Turtle* by stating that it must examine the "relationship between the general structure and design of the measure" and the policy goal it purports to serve. Moreover, it looked beyond the import bans, finding that the "general structure and design of Section 609 *cum* implementing guidelines," were "fairly narrowly focused" and "reasonably related" to the conservation goals. In light of these decisions, how close must the relationship be between the trade measure and the conservation goal? The *Shrimp/Turtle* dispute perhaps provided an easy test, because turtles clearly die in shrimp trawlers' nets. Thus, regulating the harvest of shrimp will protect turtles.

Other cases may not provide such clear ecological or cause-and-effect relationships. Consider the Pelly Amendment to the Fishermen's Protective Act. 22 U.S.C. § 1978. The Pelly Amendment is intended to reduce the alarming international trade in endangered and threatened species by providing the President with authority to encourage other nations to comply with international programs relating to the conservation of fisheries and endangered and threatened species. To accomplish this goal, the Pelly Amendment establishes a two-step general structure to conserve species at risk due to fishing and trade that diminish the effectiveness of international fisheries or endangered or threatened species programs. First, it requires the Secretary of Commerce or Interior to determine that nationals of a country are in fact diminishing the effectiveness of such a program. Only after this finding is made may the relevant Secretary recommend trade sanctions to the President. Second, the President may then impose trade sanctions consistent with the GATT and other U.S. trade obligations against such countries.

In September 2000, the United States determined that nationals of Japan were diminishing the effectiveness of the International Whaling Commission (IWC) by whaling for scientific purposes. Although the International Convention for the Regulation of Whaling (ICRW) permits scientific whaling, a global moratorium on commercial whaling has been in effect since 1986 and the IWC has repeatedly concluded that Japan's scientific whaling does not meet the IWC's conditions for such whaling. Because the United States complies with the Convention on International Trade in Endangered Species of Wild Fauna and Flora (CITES), which currently prohibits all commercial trade in whales and parts thereof, it already completely prohibits the importation of such products. Endangered Species Act, 16 U.S.C. § 1538(a), (c); Whaling Convention Act, 14 U.S.C. § 916c. Regardless of CITES, the United States bars importation of all whale products subject to the Marine Mammal Protection Act, 16 U.S.C. §§ 1371, 1372. If the United States prohibits the importation of Japanese fish products or non-whale products produced by those companies engaged in whaling, would such restrictions be considered "relating to the conservation of exhaustible natural resources"? Consider the following analysis prepared by the Humane Society of the United States, the Whale and Dolphin Conservation Society, and more than 60 other groups trying to halt Japan's whaling activities.

Petition to the Department of Interior to Certify Japan Pursuant to 22 U.S.C. § 1978 for Trading in the Meat of Minke, Bryde's, and Sperm Whales from the North Pacific and the Southern Hemisphere

(November 14, 2000), *available at*
http://www.lclark.edu/org/ielp/whales.html

In the present case, Japan's program to kill 440 minkes in the Southern Hemisphere and 100 minke whales, 50 Bryde's whales, and 10 sperm whales in the North Pacific clearly diminishes the effectiveness of the ICRW's moratorium on the killing of all whales as well as its efforts to control scientific whaling.... Japan's killing places these species at substantial risk. The commercial trade in whale meat keeps markets open for these at risk species, which diminishes CITES efforts to protect species at risk due to trade.

Thus, both steps in the Pelly process relate to the conservation of whales. The finding that a country is diminishing the effectiveness of the ICRW and IWC is directly related to the conservation of exhaustible natural resources. If nationals are diminishing the effectiveness of the ICRW, IWC, and CITES, they jeopardize exhaustible natural resources—whales—because the regimes of these international agreements are designed expressly to conserve and protect the species from the detrimental effects of whaling (ICRW/IWC) and trade (CITES). In many cases, certification alone encourages countries to implement their international obligations.

The sanctions themselves become just one element of this process to encourage a country to comply with its international obligations. A unique aspect of the Pelly Amendment is that it cannot target its sanctions in the same way that the Shrimp/Turtle regulations linked the conservation of sea turtles to the product that causes sea turtle mortality. In the case of whales, no member of the IWC may kill any whale for commercial purposes. CITES prohibits all trade in whale products. Thus, import restrictions on whale products would be totally ineffectual, because U.S. and Japanese obligations under CITES already prohibit trade in whale products. In fact, these are the very international obligations that the Pelly Amendment seeks to enforce.

So long as sanctions under the Pelly Amendment target products that bear some relationship to the activity that diminishes the effectiveness of an international fisheries or endangered or threatened species program, the Pelly Amendment as a whole—the "measure"—constitutes a "means ... reasonably related to the ends."

Petitioners recognize that the United States may wish to tailor trade restrictions to products relating to whaling and products from those companies engaged in whaling or the whale meat trade, as this may tend to encourage compliance with international agreements more effectively. For that reason, we proposed in Section II that sanctions target those products that may include whale parts and those products produced by those companies involved in the scientific whaling program and the trade in whale meat. By closely linking the sanctions to the industry and companies involved in the activity that diminishes the effectiveness of the ICRW/IWC and CITES, the Pelly Amendment ensures that it is a measure relating to the conservation of exhaustible natural resources. This would be true even under a more restrictive reading of *Shrimp/Turtle*.

Questions and Discussion

1. Do you agree that trade restrictions on fish products of companies engaged in whaling activities relate to the conservation of whales? What if the United States imposed trade restrictions on Japanese automobiles? The purpose of the restrictions would still be to compel Japan to withdraw its scientific research whaling program. Is the purpose of the trade restrictions sufficient, regardless of its direct connection to the species a country seeks to conserve?

2. No other country has imposed trade restrictions against Japan for its scientific research whaling program and the IWC has never recommended trade sanctions against Japan. Yet, the IWC has condemned Japan's scientific research whaling program more than 20 times as failing to meet the IWC's criteria for research whaling. In light of these condemnations, is the United States acting unilaterally or multilaterally if the United States adopts trade sanctions against Japan pursuant to the Pelly Amendment?

3. While the Pelly Amendment process has been invoked many times, the President has applied trade sanctions just twice. In 1993, the World Wildlife Fund petitioned the Department of Interior to certify that China, South Korea, Taiwan, and Yemen were diminishing the effectiveness of CITES by failing to implement and enforce CITES adequately with respect to trade in tiger parts and rhino horn. Pelly Amendment to the Fisherman's Protective Act, 59 Fed. Reg. 8998 (Feb. 24, 1994). After consultations with the four governments, the United States imposed sanctions on all CITES-listed products against Taiwan only. Proposed Import Prohibitions on Wildlife Specimens, 59 Fed. Reg. 22043 (Apr. 28, 1994). Trade sanctions against Taiwan were GATT-consistent because Taiwan was not a member of the GATT. (It is now a WTO member). Yet, it could not be a member of the GATT or CITES due to the intractable issue of Taiwan's statehood. If a country is not even able to join a treaty, should it be subject to trade restrictions for failing to implement it? What if Taiwan was a State but chose not to join CITES? Would that change your answer?

4. Of the thirteen Pelly certifications between 1971 and 1994, more than 50 percent led to policy reforms or commitments to reform policies — without sanctions ever being imposed. For example, in 1986, Norway suspended its commercial whaling operations after certification but before the President imposed trade sanctions. After being certified, Japan withdrew its reservation under CITES to the ban on international commercial trade in hawksbill turtles and their parts. In 1992, South Korea and Yemen improved their CITES implementation and avoided certification for failing to implement CITES effectively for tiger and rhino trade. Steve Charnovitz, *Environmental Trade Sanctions and the GATT: An Analysis of the Pelly Amendment on Foreign Environmental Practices*, 9 Am. U. J. Int'l L. & Pol'y 751 (1994) (reviewing the success of the Pelly Amendment up to 1994); *see also*, Gene S. Martin, Jr., & James W. Brennan, *Enforcing the International Convention for the Regulation of Whaling: The Pelly and Packwood-Magnuson Amendments*, 17 Denv. J. Int'l L. & Pol'y 293, 298–308 (1989). Since 1994, the use of the Pelly Amendment has been much less effective. Despite a number of certifications, most environmentalists would agree that very little has changed. Japan and Iceland, both certified for their whaling activities, continue to whale, with Japan increasing its research whaling program from 540 in 2000 to more than 1,200 in 2010. Discussions with government officials make clear that the threat of a WTO dispute is one reason that the United States has refused to impose trade sanctions. How should the United States proceed: Should it risk a WTO dispute, should

it simply stop certifying countries, or should it continue with the practice of certifying even without any likelihood of follow-up trade action?

V. Application of the Article XX Chapeau

The Appellate Body's more relaxed interpretation of Article XX(g), and to a lesser extent Article XX(b), has allowed some disputed environmental measures, such as the U.S. shrimp/turtle regulations, to reach the third step of the Article XX analysis: consistency with the chapeau. The chapeau reads:

> Subject to the requirement that such measures are not applied in a manner which would constitute a means of arbitrary or unjustifiable discrimination between countries where the same conditions prevail, or a disguised restriction on international trade, nothing in this Agreement shall be construed to prevent the adoption or enforcement by any Member of measures [such as those covered by paragraphs (b) and (g)].

Although the chapeau ends by stating that the enumerated exceptions of Article XX may apply notwithstanding any other provision of the GATT, it begins by imposing three distinct limitations:

- measures must not be applied in a manner that constitutes arbitrary discrimination between countries where the same conditions prevail;
- measures must not be applied in a manner that constitutes unjustifiable discrimination between countries where the same conditions prevail; and
- measures must not constitute a disguised trade restriction.

In *Reformulated Gasoline,* the WTO Appellate Body began the process of interpreting these provisions. The Appellate Body made clear its view that the object and purpose of the chapeau are to prevent the abuse of the Article XX exceptions. While a WTO member has a legal right to use the exceptions, they should not be applied to frustrate or defeat another member's basic rights under the GATT. The Appellate Body in *Shrimp/Turtle* expanded this reasoning, calling the chapeau an "expression of the principle of good faith" and an application of the doctrine known as *abus de droit*, which prohibits the abusive exercise of a member's valid legal rights and requires the reasonable exercise of those rights. As such, the Appellate Body concluded that it must interpret and apply the chapeau by:

> locating and marking out a line of equilibrium between the right of a Member to invoke an exception under Article XX and the rights of the other Members under varying substantive provisions (e.g., Article XI) of the GATT 1994, so that neither of the competing rights will cancel out the other and thereby distort and nullify or impair the balance of rights and obligations constructed by the Members themselves in that Agreement. The location of the line of equilibrium, as expressed in the chapeau, is not fixed and unchanging; the line moves as the kind and the shape of the measures at stake vary and as the facts making up specific cases differ.

Shrimp/Turtle, Appellate Body Report, at para. 159. While the Appellate Body has clearly stated the purpose of the chapeau and that the country invoking Article XX has the burden to show that it applies the measure consistently with the chapeau, it has been far less clear in defining and interpreting the meaning of the chapeau's three requirements.

As you read the excerpts from the cases, consider the following questions:

- What is the difference between "arbitrary" discrimination, "unjustifiable" discrimination, and a disguised restriction on international trade?
- What factors should be considered when determining what constitutes "arbitrary" or "unjustifiable" discrimination"?
- What does the phrase "countries where the same conditions prevail" mean? Does it mean environmental conditions?

A. The *Reformulated Gasoline* Case

We first revisit *Reformulated Gasoline*, in which the Appellate Body ruled that U.S. regulations establishing 1990 baseline pollutant levels in gasoline relate to the conservation of an exhaustible natural resource, namely clean air. *See* pages 304–09 for additional facts. The Appellate Body then asked whether those regulations, which imposed a statutory baseline for gasoline pollutant levels on foreign producers but allowed U.S. producers to use an individual baseline for each refinery, were consistent with the chapeau.

United States-Standards for Reformulated and Conventional Gasoline
Appellate Body Report, pages 25–31
WT/DS2/AB/R (adopted May 20, 1996)

"Arbitrary discrimination," "unjustifiable discrimination" and "disguised restriction" on international trade may ... be read side-by-side; they impart meaning to one another. It is clear to us that "disguised restriction" includes disguised discrimination in international trade. It is equally clear that concealed or unannounced restriction or discrimination in international trade does not exhaust the meaning of "disguised restriction." We consider that "disguised restriction," whatever else it covers, may properly be read as embracing restrictions amounting to arbitrary or unjustifiable discrimination in international trade taken under the guise of a measure formally within the terms of an exception listed in Article XX. Put in a somewhat different manner, the kinds of considerations pertinent in deciding whether the application of a particular measure amounts to "arbitrary or unjustifiable discrimination," may also be taken into account in determining the presence of a "disguised restriction" on international trade. The fundamental theme is to be found in the purpose and object of avoiding abuse or illegitimate use of the exceptions to substantive rules available in Article XX.

There was more than one alternative course of action available to the United States in promulgating regulations implementing the CAA [Clean Air Act]. These included the imposition of statutory baselines without differentiation as between domestic and imported gasoline. This approach, if properly implemented, could have avoided any discrimination at all. Among the other options open to the United States was to make available individual baselines to foreign refiners as well as domestic refiners. The United States has put forward a series of reasons why either of these courses was not, in its view, realistically open to it and why, instead, it had to devise and apply the baseline establishment rules contained in the Gasoline Rule.

In explaining why individual baselines for foreign refiners had not been put in place, the United States laid heavy stress upon the difficulties which the EPA [Environmental Protection Agency] would have had to face. These difficulties related to anticipated administrative problems that individual baselines for foreign refiners would have generated. This argument was made succinctly by the United States in the following terms:

> Verification on foreign soil of foreign baselines, and subsequent enforcement actions, present substantial difficulties relating to problems arising whenever a country exercises enforcement jurisdiction over foreign persons. In addition, even if individual baselines were established for several foreign refiners, the importer would be tempted to claim the refinery of origin that presented the most benefits in terms of baseline restrictions, and tracking the refinery or origin would be very difficult because gasoline is a fungible commodity. The United States should not have to prove that it cannot verify information and enforce its regulations in every instance in order to show that the same enforcement conditions do not prevail in the United States and other countries.... The impracticability of verification and enforcement of foreign refiner baselines in this instance shows that the "discrimination" is based on serious, not arbitrary or unjustifiable, concerns stemming from different conditions between enforcement of its laws in the United States and abroad.

Thus, according to the United States, imported gasoline was relegated to the more exacting statutory baseline requirement because of these difficulties of verification and enforcement. The United States stated that verification and enforcement of the Gasoline Rule's requirements for imported gasoline are "much easier when the statutory baseline is used" and that there would be a "dramatic difference" in the burden of administering requirements for imported gasoline if individual baselines were allowed. While the anticipated difficulties concerning verification and subsequent enforcement are doubtless real to some degree, the Panel viewed them as insufficient to justify the denial to foreign refiners of individual baselines permitted to domestic refiners. * * *

[A]s the Panel Report found, established techniques for checking, verification, assessment and enforcement of data relating to imported goods, techniques which in many contexts are accepted as adequate to permit international trade — trade between territorial sovereigns — to go on and grow. The United States must have been aware that for these established techniques and procedures to work, cooperative arrangements with both foreign refiners and the foreign governments concerned would have been necessary and appropriate. At the oral hearing, in the course of responding to an enquiry as to whether the EPA could have adapted, for purposes of establishing individual refinery baselines for foreign refiners, procedures for verification of information found in U.S. antidumping laws, the United States said that "in the absence of refinery cooperation and the possible absence of foreign government cooperation as well," it was unlikely that the EPA auditors would be able to conduct the on-site audit reviews necessary to establish even the overall quality of refineries' 1990 gasoline. From this statement, there arises a strong implication, it appears to the Appellate Body, that the United States had not pursued the possibility of entering into cooperative arrangements with the governments of Venezuela and Brazil or, if it had, not to the point where it encountered governments that were unwilling to cooperate. The record of this case sets out the detailed justifications put forward by the United States. But it does not reveal what, if any, efforts had been taken by the United States to enter into appropriate procedures in cooperation with the governments of Venezuela and Brazil so as to mitigate the administrative problems pleaded by the United States. The fact that the United States Congress might have intervened, as it did later intervene, in the process by denying funding, is beside the point: the United States, of course, carries responsibility for actions of both the executive and legislative departments of government.

In its submissions, the United States also explained why the statutory baseline requirement was not imposed on domestic refiners as well. Here, the United States stressed the problems that domestic refineries would have faced had they been required to comply with the statutory baseline. The Panel Report summarized the United States' argument in the following terms:

> The United States concluded that, contrary to Venezuela's and Brazil's claim, Article XX did not require adoption of the statutory baseline as a national standard even if the difficulties associated with the establishment of individual baselines for importers were insurmountable. Application of the statutory baseline to domestic producers of reformulated and conventional gasoline in 1995 would have been *physically and financially impossible because of the magnitude of the changes required in almost all US refineries; it thus would have caused a substantial delay in the programme.* Weighing the feasibility of policy options in economic or technical terms in order to meet an environmental objective was a legitimate consideration, and did not, in itself, constitute protectionism, as alleged by Venezuela and Brazil. Article XX did not require a government to choose the most expensive possible way to regulate its environment (emphasis added).

Clearly, the United States did not feel it feasible to require its domestic refiners to incur the physical and financial costs and burdens entailed by immediate compliance with a statutory baseline. The United States wished to give domestic refiners time to restructure their operations and adjust to the requirements in the Gasoline Rule. This may very well have constituted sound domestic policy from the viewpoint of the EPA and U.S. refiners. At the same time we are bound to note that, while the United States counted the costs for its domestic refiners of statutory baselines, there is nothing in the record to indicate that it did other than disregard that kind of consideration when it came to foreign refiners.

We have above located two omissions on the part of the United States: to explore adequately means, including in particular cooperation with the governments of Venezuela and Brazil, of mitigating the administrative problems relied on as justification by the United States for rejecting individual baselines for foreign refiners; and to count the costs for foreign refiners that would result from the imposition of statutory baselines. In our view, these two omissions go well beyond what was necessary for the Panel to determine that a violation of Article III:4 had occurred in the first place. The resulting discrimination must have been foreseen, and was not merely inadvertent or unavoidable. In the light of the foregoing, our conclusion is that the baseline establishment rules in the Gasoline Rule, in their application, constitute "unjustifiable discrimination" and a "disguised restriction on international trade." We hold, in sum, that the baseline establishment rules, although within the terms of Article XX(g), are not entitled to the justifying protection afforded by Article XX as a whole.

Questions and Discussion

1. *Disguised Restriction on Trade.* How has the Appellate Body defined "disguised restriction on international trade"? Do you agree with its interpretation of this phrase? Two previous GATT panels declared that if a measure was published, that is, not concealed, it was not a disguised trade restriction. United States-Prohibition of Imports of Tuna and Tuna Products, B.I.S.D. 29th Supp. 91, para. 4.8 (1982) (adopted Feb. 22, 1982); *see also* United States-Automotive Spring Assemblies, BISD 30th Supp. 107, para. 56 (1984) (adopted May 26, 1983). The history of this provision suggests that it was intended to prevent GATT parties from disguising protectionist measures as environmental measures. Steve Charnovitz, *Exploring the Environmental Exceptions in GATT Article XX*, at 47–48. In *Canada-Salmon and Herring*, the Panel concluded that the prohibition against disguised restrictions on international trade "is an acknowledgment by the Parties that they will submit the *purposes* of trade-restricting conservation measures to third-party scrutiny." In the Matter of Canada's Landing Requirement for Pacific Coast Salmon and Herring, U.S.-Canada Free Trade Agreement Panel Report, No. CDA-89-1807-01, 1989 FTAPD LEXIS 6, at para. 7.11 (Oct. 16, 1989) (emphasis added). How would you distinguish "disguised restriction on trade" from "arbitrary or unjustifiable discrimination"? In answering this question, recall that a measure may violate the GATT without discriminating against products from other countries. The principal trade and environment cases, *Tuna/Dolphin* and *Shrimp/Turtle*, involved not discrimination against imported products as such but import restrictions targeted to selected countries to support the desired policies. Do panel and Appellate Body reports that find "discrimination" nonetheless incorrectly interpret "discrimination"?

2. The Appellate Body cites "two omissions" by the United States: failing to adequately explore means of mitigating the administrative problems and failing to "count the costs for foreign refiners" of using the statutory baselines. Do those omissions, in your view, make the U.S. gasoline rule a "disguised restriction on international trade"? "Unjustifiable discrimination"?

3. The United States admitted that the gasoline rule was discriminatory but argued that verification of foreign data made separate baseline rules appropriate. Do EPA's concerns justify a different approach for foreign refiners? In light of these concerns and the omissions cited by the Appellate Body, do you agree with the Appellate Body that the separate baseline rules constitute "unjustifiable discrimination between countries where the same conditions prevail"?

4. As with many court decisions, unspoken or barely mentioned facts may have shaped the views of the Appellate Body on the U.S. measure. When Venezuela, and later Brazil, protested the discriminatory aspects of the rule, EPA negotiated with them and proposed a modification to the rule that addressed their concerns. The two countries agreed to drop their trade dispute if this proposal were adopted. Before EPA could issue a final revised rule, however, the U.S. Congress passed a rider on EPA's appropriations that prohibited the agency from any further work on the rule (the Appellate Body alludes to this). The rider was advocated by a congresswoman from the Philadelphia area whose district included the main refinery of Sun Oil Company (Sunoco). Sunoco is a competitor of

Citgo (a subsidiary of the Venezuelan oil company) in the U.S. east coast market where reformulated gasoline is required. Are these facts relevant? Jeffrey L. Dunoff, *Rethinking International Trade*, 19 U. Pa. J. Int'l Econ. L. 347, 368–69 (1998).

B. The *Shrimp/Turtle* Case

As discussed above (pages 312–14) in the discussion of Article XX(g), the Appellate Body in *Shrimp/Turtle* reversed the Panel's conclusion that the U.S. shrimp/turtle regulations of Section 609 fell outside the scope of measures permitted under Article XX(g). It concluded that Section 609 and its implementing regulations, which conditioned the importation of shrimp on the adoption of "essentially the same" sea turtle conservation measures including the use of turtle excluder devices (TEDs), related to the conservation of an exhaustible natural resource. The Appellate Body then undertook the first detailed analysis of the chapeau. Perhaps reflecting the nature of the trade and environment debate itself, the Appellate Body's decision has been hailed by some as opening the door to greater use of environmental trade restrictions, particularly unilateral restrictions, and by others as closing the door to any real-world unilateral use of trade leverage to further environmental goals. As you read the Appellate Body decision, ask yourself whether the Appellate Body is:

- making any meaningful distinction between arbitrary discrimination and unjustifiable discrimination.
- defining "countries where the same conditions prevail" appropriately.
- moving the Article XX(b) test for "necessity" into the chapeau.
- defining any real "line of equilibrium" between one member's right to a predictable trading regime and another member's right to invoke Article XX.

---

1. The Report on the Original Claim
United States-Import Prohibition of Certain Shrimp and Shrimp Products

Appellate Body Report, WT/DS58/AB/R (adopted Nov. 6, 1998), reprinted in 38 I.L.M. 121 (1999)

2. "Unjustifiable Discrimination"

161. We scrutinize first whether Section 609 has been applied in a manner constituting "unjustifiable discrimination between countries where the same conditions prevail." Perhaps the most conspicuous flaw in this measure's application relates to its intended and actual coercive effect on the specific policy decisions made by foreign governments, Members of the WTO. Section 609, in its application, is, in effect, an economic embargo which requires *all other exporting Members*, if they wish to exercise their GATT rights, to adopt *essentially the same* policy (together with an approved enforcement program) as that applied to, and enforced on, United States domestic shrimp trawlers. As enacted by the Congress of the United States, the *statutory* provisions of Section 609(b)(2)(A) and (B) do not, in themselves, *require* that other WTO Members adopt *essentially*

the same policies and enforcement practices as the United States. Viewed alone, the statute appears to permit a degree of discretion or flexibility in how the standards for determining comparability might be applied, in practice, to other countries. However, any flexibility that may have been intended by Congress when it enacted the statutory provision has been effectively eliminated in the implementation of that policy through the 1996 Guidelines promulgated by the Department of State and through the practice of the administrators in making certification determinations.

162. According to the 1996 Guidelines, certification "shall be made" under Section 609(b)(2)(A) and (B) if an exporting country's program includes a requirement that all commercial shrimp trawl vessels operating in waters in which there is a likelihood of intercepting sea turtles use, at all times, TEDs comparable in effectiveness to those used in the United States. Under these Guidelines, any exceptions to the requirement of the use of TEDs must be comparable to those of the United States program. Furthermore, the harvesting country must have in place a "credible enforcement effort." The language in the 1996 Guidelines is mandatory: certification "shall be made" if these conditions are fulfilled. However, we understand that these rules are also applied in an *exclusive* manner. That is, the 1996 Guidelines specify the *only* way that a harvesting country's regulatory program can be deemed "comparable" to the United States' program, and, therefore, they define the *only* way that a harvesting nation can be certified under Section 609(b)(2)(A) and (B). Although the 1996 Guidelines state that, in making a comparability determination, the Department of State "shall also take into account other measures the harvesting nation undertakes to protect sea turtles," in practice, the competent government officials only look to see whether there is a regulatory program requiring the use of TEDs or one that comes within one of the extremely limited exceptions available to United States shrimp trawl vessels.

163. The actual *application* of the measure, through the implementation of the 1996 Guidelines and the regulatory practice of administrators, *requires* other WTO Members to adopt a regulatory program that is not merely *comparable*, but rather *essentially the same*, as that applied to the United States shrimp trawl vessels. Thus, the effect of the application of Section 609 is to establish a rigid and unbending standard by which United States officials determine whether or not countries will be certified, thus granting or refusing other countries the right to export shrimp to the United States. Other specific policies and measures that an exporting country may have adopted for the protection and conservation of sea turtles are not taken into account, in practice, by the administrators making the comparability determination.

164. We understand that the United States also applies a uniform standard throughout its territory, regardless of the particular conditions existing in certain parts of the country. The United States requires the use of approved TEDs at all times by domestic, commercial shrimp trawl vessels operating in waters where there is any likelihood that they may interact with sea turtles, regardless of the actual incidence of sea turtles in those waters, the species of those sea turtles, or other differences or disparities that may exist in different parts of the United States. It may be quite acceptable for a government, in adopting and implementing a domestic policy, to adopt a single standard applicable to all its citizens throughout that country. However, it is not acceptable, in international

trade relations, for one WTO Member to use an economic embargo to *require* other Members to adopt essentially the same comprehensive regulatory program, to achieve a certain policy goal, as that in force within that Member's territory, *without* taking into consideration different conditions which may occur in the territories of those other Members.

165. Furthermore, when this dispute was before the Panel and before us, the United States did not permit imports of shrimp harvested by commercial shrimp trawl vessels using TEDs comparable in effectiveness to those required in the United States if those shrimp originated in waters of countries not certified under Section 609. In other words, *shrimp caught using methods identical to those employed in the United States* have been excluded from the United States market solely because they have been caught in waters of *countries that have not been certified by the United States*. The resulting situation is difficult to reconcile with the declared policy objective of protecting and conserving sea turtles. This suggests to us that this measure, in its application, is more concerned with effectively influencing WTO Members to adopt essentially the same comprehensive regulatory regime as that applied by the United States to its domestic shrimp trawlers, even though many of those Members may be differently situated. We believe that discrimination results not only when countries in which the same conditions prevail are differently treated, but also when the application of the measure at issue does not allow for any inquiry into the appropriateness of the regulatory program for the conditions prevailing in those exporting countries.

166. Another aspect of the application of Section 609 that bears heavily in any appraisal of justifiable or unjustifiable discrimination is the failure of the United States to engage the appellees, as well as other Members exporting shrimp to the United States, in serious, across-the-board negotiations with the objective of concluding bilateral or multilateral agreements for the protection and conservation of sea turtles, before enforcing the import prohibition against the shrimp exports of those other Members....

167. *A propos* this failure to have prior consistent recourse to diplomacy as an instrument of environmental protection policy, which produces discriminatory impacts on countries exporting shrimp to the United States with which no international agreements are reached or even seriously attempted, a number of points must be made. First, the Congress of the United States expressly recognized the importance of securing international agreements for the protection and conservation of the sea turtle species in enacting this law. Section 609(a) *directs* the Secretary of State to:

> 1) *initiate negotiations as soon as possible for the development of bilateral or multilateral agreements with other nations* for the protection and conservation of such species of sea turtles;

> 2) *initiate negotiations as soon as possible* with all foreign governments which are engaged in, or which have persons or companies engaged in, commercial fishing operations which, as determined by the Secretary of Commerce, may affect adversely such species of sea turtles, *for the purpose of entering into bilateral and multilateral treaties with such countries to protect such species of sea turtles*; ... (emphasis added).

Apart from the negotiation of the Inter-American Convention for the Protection and Conservation of Sea Turtles (the "Inter-American Convention") which concluded in 1996, the record before the Panel does not indicate any serious, substantial efforts to carry out these express directions of Congress.

168. Second, the protection and conservation of highly migratory species of sea turtles, that is, the very policy objective of the measure, demands concerted and cooperative efforts on the part of the many countries whose waters are traversed in the course of recurrent sea turtle migrations. The need for, and the appropriateness of, such efforts have been recognized in the WTO itself as well as in a significant number of other international instruments and declarations. As stated earlier, the Decision on Trade and Environment, which provided for the establishment of the CTE [Committee on Trade and the Environment] and set out its terms of reference, refers to both the Rio Declaration on Environment and Development and Agenda 21. Of particular relevance is Principle 12 of the Rio Declaration on Environment and Development, which states, in part:

> Unilateral actions to deal with environmental challenges outside the jurisdiction of the importing country should be avoided. *Environmental measures addressing transboundary or global environmental problems should, as far as possible, be based on international consensus* (emphasis added).

In almost identical language, paragraph 2.22(i) of Agenda 21 provides:

> Governments should encourage GATT, UNCTAD and other relevant international and regional economic institutions to examine, in accordance with their respective mandates and competences, the following propositions and principles: ...
>
> (i) Avoid unilateral action to deal with environmental challenges outside the jurisdiction of the importing country. *Environmental measures addressing transborder problems should, as far as possible, be based on an international consensus.* (emphasis added)

Moreover, we note that Article 5 of the Convention on Biological Diversity states:

> ... each contracting party shall, as far as possible and as appropriate, cooperate with other contracting parties directly or, where appropriate, through competent international organizations, in respect of areas beyond national jurisdiction and on other matters of mutual interest, for the conservation and sustainable use of biological diversity.

The Convention on the Conservation of Migratory Species of Wild Animals, which classifies the relevant species of sea turtles in its Annex I as "Endangered Migratory Species," states:

> The contracting parties [are] convinced that conservation and effective management of migratory species of wild animals requires the concerted action of all States within the national boundaries of which such species spend any part of their life cycle.

Furthermore, we note that WTO Members in the Report of the CTE, forming part of the Report of the General Council to Ministers on the occasion of the Singapore Ministerial Conference, endorsed and supported:

> ... *multilateral solutions based on international cooperation and consensus as the best and most effective way for governments to tackle environmental problems of a transboundary or global nature.* WTO Agreements and multilateral environmental agreements (MEAs) are representative of efforts of the international community to pursue *shared goals*, and in the develop-

ment of a mutually supportive relationship between them, *due respect must be afforded to both.* (emphasis added)

169. Third, the United States did negotiate and conclude one regional international agreement for the protection and conservation of sea turtles: The Inter-American Convention. This Convention was opened for signature on 1 December 1996 and has been signed by five countries, in addition to the United States, and four of these countries are currently certified under Section 609. This Convention has not yet been ratified by any of its signatories. The Inter-American Convention provides that each party shall take "appropriate and necessary measures" for the protection, conservation and recovery of sea turtle populations and their habitats within such party's land territory and in maritime areas with respect to which it exercises sovereign rights or jurisdiction. Such measures include, notably,

> [t]he reduction, to the greatest extent practicable, of the incidental capture, retention, harm or mortality of sea turtles in the course of fishing activities, through the appropriate regulation of such activities, as well as the development, improvement and use of appropriate gear, devices or techniques, including the use of turtle excluder devices (TEDs) pursuant to the provisions of Annex III [of the Convention].

Article XV of the Inter-American Convention also provides, in part:

> Article XV — Trade Measures

> 1. *In implementing this Convention, the Parties shall act in accordance with the provisions of the Agreement establishing the World Trade Organization* (WTO), as adopted at Marrakesh in 1994, including its annexes.

> 2. In particular, and *with respect to the subject-matter of this Convention, the Parties shall act in accordance with the provisions of* the Agreement on Technical Barriers to Trade contained in Annex 1 of the WTO Agreement, as well as *Article XI of the General Agreement on Tariffs and Trade of 1994* (emphasis added)....

170. The juxtaposition of (a) the *consensual* undertakings to put in place regulations providing for, *inter alia*, use of TEDs *jointly determined* to be suitable for a particular party's maritime areas, with (b) the reaffirmation of the parties' obligations under the *WTO Agreement*, including the *Agreement on Technical Barriers to Trade* and Article XI of the GATT 1994, suggests that the parties to the Inter-American Convention together marked out the equilibrium line to which we referred earlier. The Inter-American Convention demonstrates the conviction of its signatories, including the United States, that consensual and multilateral procedures are available and feasible for the establishment of programs for the conservation of sea turtles. Moreover, the Inter-American Convention emphasizes the continuing validity and significance of Article XI of the GATT 1994, and of the obligations of the *WTO Agreement* generally, in maintaining the balance of rights and obligations under the *WTO Agreement* among the signatories of that Convention.

171. The Inter-American Convention thus provides convincing demonstration that an alternative course of action was reasonably open to the United States for securing the legitimate policy goal of its measure, a course of action other than the unilateral and non-consensual procedures of the import prohibition under Section 609. It is relevant to observe that an import prohibition is, ordinarily, the heaviest "weapon" in a Member's armoury of trade measures. The record does not, however, show that serious efforts were made by the United States to negotiate similar agree-

ments with any other country or group of countries before (and, as far as the record shows, after) Section 609 was enforced on a world-wide basis on 1 May 1996. Finally, the record also does not show that the appellant, the United States, attempted to have recourse to such international mechanisms as exist to achieve cooperative efforts to protect and conserve sea turtles before imposing the import ban.

172. Clearly, the United States negotiated seriously with some, but not with other Members (including the appellees), that export shrimp to the United States. The effect is plainly discriminatory and, in our view, unjustifiable. The unjustifiable nature of this discrimination emerges clearly when we consider the cumulative effects of the failure of the United States to pursue negotiations for establishing consensual means of protection and conservation of the living marine resources here involved, notwithstanding the explicit statutory direction in Section 609 itself to initiate negotiations as soon as possible for the development of bilateral and multilateral agreements. The principal consequence of this failure may be seen in the resulting unilateralism evident in the application of Section 609. As we have emphasized earlier, the policies relating to the necessity for use of particular kinds of TEDs in various maritime areas, and the operating details of these policies, are all shaped by the Department of State, without the participation of the exporting Members. The system and processes of certification are established and administered by the United States agencies alone. The decision-making involved in the grant, denial or withdrawal of certification to the exporting Members, is, accordingly, also unilateral. The unilateral character of the application of Section 609 heightens the disruptive and discriminatory influence of the import prohibition and underscores its unjustifiability.

173. The application of Section 609, through the implementing guidelines together with administrative practice, also resulted in other differential treatment among various countries desiring certification. Under the 1991 and 1993 Guidelines, to be certifiable, fourteen countries in the wider Caribbean/western Atlantic region had to commit themselves to require the use of TEDs on all commercial shrimp trawling vessels by 1 May 1994. These fourteen countries had a "phase-in" period of three years during which their respective shrimp trawling sectors could adjust to the requirement of the use of TEDs. With respect to all other countries exporting shrimp to the United States (including the appellees, India, Malaysia, Pakistan and Thailand), on 29 December 1995, the United States Court of International Trade directed the Department of State to apply the import ban on a world-wide basis not later than 1 May 1996. On 19 April 1996, the 1996 Guidelines were issued by the Department of State bringing shrimp harvested in all foreign countries within the scope of Section 609, effective 1 May 1996. Thus, all countries that were not among the fourteen in the wider Caribbean/western Atlantic region had only four months to implement the requirement of compulsory use of TEDs. We acknowledge that the greatly differing periods for putting into operation the requirement for use of TEDs resulted from decisions of the Court of International Trade. Even so, this does not relieve the United States of the legal consequences of the discriminatory impact of the decisions of that Court. The United States, like all other Members of the WTO and of the general community of states, bears responsibility for acts of all its departments of government, including its judiciary.

174. The length of the "phase-in" period is not inconsequential for exporting countries desiring certification. That period relates directly to the onerousness of the burdens of complying with the requisites of certification and the practi-

cal feasibility of locating and developing alternative export markets for shrimp. The shorter that period, the heavier the burdens of compliance, particularly where an applicant has a large number of trawler vessels, and the greater the difficulties of re-orienting the harvesting country's shrimp exports. The shorter that period, in net effect, the heavier the influence of the import ban. The United States sought to explain the marked difference between "phase-in" periods granted to the fourteen wider Caribbean/western Atlantic countries and those allowed the rest of the shrimp exporting countries. The United States asserted that the longer time-period was justified by the then undeveloped character of TED technology, while the shorter period was later made possible by the improvements in that technology. This explanation is less than persuasive, for it does not address the administrative and financial costs and the difficulties of governments in putting together and enacting the necessary regulatory programs and "credible enforcement effort," and in implementing the compulsory use of TEDs on hundreds, if not thousands, of shrimp trawl vessels.

175. Differing treatment of different countries desiring certification is also observable in the differences in the levels of effort made by the United States in transferring the required TED technology to specific countries. Far greater efforts to transfer that technology successfully were made to certain exporting countries—basically the fourteen wider Caribbean/western Atlantic countries cited earlier—than to other exporting countries, including the appellees. The level of these efforts is probably related to the length of the "phase-in" periods granted—the longer the "phase-in" period, the higher the possible level of efforts at technology transfer. Because compliance with the requirements of certification realistically assumes successful TED technology transfer, low or merely nominal efforts at achieving that transfer will, in all probability, result in fewer countries being able to satisfy the certification requirements under Section 609, within the very limited "phase-in" periods allowed them.

176. When the foregoing differences in the means of application of Section 609 to various shrimp exporting countries are considered in their cumulative effect, we find, and so hold, that those differences in treatment constitute "unjustifiable discrimination" between exporting countries desiring certification in order to gain access to the United States shrimp market within the meaning of the chapeau of Article XX.

3. "Arbitrary Discrimination"

177. We next consider whether Section 609 has been applied in a manner constituting "arbitrary discrimination between countries where the same conditions prevail." We have already observed that Section 609, in its application, imposes a single, rigid and unbending requirement that countries applying for certification under Section 609(b)(2)(A) and (B) adopt a comprehensive regulatory program that is essentially the same as the United States' program, without inquiring into the appropriateness of that program for the conditions prevailing in the exporting countries. Furthermore, there is little or no flexibility in how officials make the determination for certification pursuant to these provisions. In our view, this rigidity and inflexibility also constitute "arbitrary discrimination" within the meaning of the chapeau.

178. Moreover, the description of the administration of Section 609 provided by the United States in the course of these proceedings highlights certain prob-

lematic aspects of the certification processes applied under Section 609(b). With respect to the first type of certification, under Section 609(b)(2)(A) and (B), the 1996 Guidelines set out certain elements of the procedures for acquiring certification, including the requirement to submit documentary evidence of the regulatory program adopted by the applicant country. This certification process also generally includes a visit by United States officials to the applicant country.

179. With respect to certifications under Section 609(b)(2)(C), the 1996 Guidelines state that the Department of State "shall certify" any harvesting nation under Section 609(b)(2)(C) if it meets the criteria in the 1996 Guidelines "without the need for action on the part of the government of the harvesting nation...." Nevertheless, the United States informed us that, in all cases where a country has not previously been certified under Section 609, it waits for an application to be made before making a determination on certification. In the case of certifications under Section 609(b)(2)(C), there appear to be certain opportunities for the submission of written evidence, such as scientific documentation, in the course of the certification process.

180. However, with respect to neither type of certification under Section 609(b)(2) is there a transparent, predictable certification process that is followed by the competent United States government officials. The certification processes under Section 609 consist principally of administrative *ex parte* inquiry or verification by staff of the Office of Marine Conservation in the Department of State with staff of the United States National Marine Fisheries Service. With respect to both types of certification, there is no formal opportunity for an applicant country to be heard, or to respond to any arguments that may be made against it, in the course of the certification process before a decision to grant or to deny certification is made. Moreover, no formal written, reasoned decision, whether of acceptance or rejection, is rendered on applications for either type of certification, whether under Section 609(b)(2)(A) and (B) or under Section 609(b)(2)(C). Countries which are granted certification are included in a list of approved applications published in the Federal Register; however, they are not notified specifically. Countries whose applications are denied also do not receive notice of such denial (other than by omission from the list of approved applications) or of the reasons for the denial. No procedure for review of, or appeal from, a denial of an application is provided.

181. The certification processes followed by the United States thus appear to be singularly informal and casual, and to be conducted in a manner such that these processes could result in the negation of rights of Members. There appears to be no way that exporting Members can be certain whether the terms of Section 609, in particular, the 1996 Guidelines, are being applied in a fair and just manner by the appropriate governmental agencies of the United States. It appears to us that, effectively, exporting Members applying for certification whose applications are rejected are denied basic fairness and due process, and are discriminated against, vis-a-vis those Members which are granted certification.

182. The provisions of Article X:3 of the GATT 1994 bear upon this matter. In our view, Section 609 falls within the "laws, regulations, judicial decisions and administrative rulings of general application" described in Article X:1. Inasmuch as there are due process requirements generally for measures that are otherwise imposed in compliance with WTO obligations, it is only reasonable that rigorous compliance with the fundamental requirements of due process should be

required in the application and administration of a measure which purports to be an exception to the treaty obligations of the Member imposing the measure and which effectively results in a suspension *pro hac vice* of the treaty rights of other Members.

183. It is also clear to us that Article X:3 of the GATT 1994 establishes certain minimum standards for transparency and procedural fairness in the administration of trade regulations which, in our view, are not met here. The non-transparent and *ex parte* nature of the internal governmental procedures applied by the competent officials in the Office of Marine Conservation, the Department of State, and the United States National Marine Fisheries Service throughout the certification processes under Section 609, as well as the fact that countries whose applications are denied do not receive formal notice of such denial, nor of the reasons for the denial, and the fact, too, that there is no formal legal procedure for review of, or appeal from, a denial of an application, are all contrary to the spirit, if not the letter, of Article X:3 of the GATT 1994.

184. We find, accordingly, that the United States measure is applied in a manner which amounts to a means not just of "unjustifiable discrimination," but also of "arbitrary discrimination" between countries where the same conditions prevail, contrary to the requirements of the chapeau of Article XX. The measure, therefore, is not entitled to the justifying protection of Article XX of the GATT 1994. Having made this finding, it is not necessary for us to examine also whether the United States measure is applied in a manner that constitutes a "disguised restriction on international trade" under the chapeau of Article XX.

---

2. The Recourse Report

Although the Appellate Body's ruling that U.S. regulations to protect endangered sea turtles were inconsistent with the GATT was widely publicized by newspapers and environmental groups, very little attention was given to two important facts. First, the United States never amended or repealed Section 609. Instead, the U.S. Department of State issued revised guidelines for implementing Section 609 that it hoped met the concerns of the Appellate Body. Second, when Malaysia challenged these revisions as failing to comply with the GATT, the Appellate Body upheld a panel's determination that the revised guidelines were justifiable under Article XX of the GATT. In doing so, the Appellate Body clarified the nature of the obligation to negotiate international agreements. It did not, however, clarify the meaning of the phrase "countries where the same conditions prevail," a key phrase for determining whether a WTO member's measure constitutes arbitrary or unjustifiable discrimination.

Under the original shrimp/turtle guidelines, the Department of State certified countries as "turtle safe" *only after* they had shown that they required the use of TEDs. Under the Revised Guidelines, countries may apply for certification even if they do not require the use of TEDs. In such cases, a harvesting country must demonstrate that it has implemented, and is enforcing, a regulatory program that is *comparable in effectiveness* to the U.S. regulatory program. The Department of State must "take fully into account any demonstrated differences between the shrimp fishing conditions in the United States and those in other nations, as well as information available from other sources." Revised Guidelines for the Implementation of Section 609 of Public Law 101-162 Relating to the Protection of Sea Turtles in Shrimp Trawl Fishing Operations (the "Revised Guidelines"), 64 Fed. Reg. 36946 (July 8, 1999).

An exporting country may also be certified if its shrimp fishing environment does not pose a threat of incidental capture of sea turtles. The Revised Guidelines provide that the Department of State shall certify a harvesting country pursuant to Section 609 if it meets any of the following criteria: the relevant species of sea turtles do not occur in waters subject to that country's jurisdiction; in that country's waters, shrimp is harvested exclusively by means that do not pose a threat to sea turtles, for example, any country that harvests shrimp exclusively by artisanal means; or, commercial shrimp trawling operations take place exclusively in waters in which sea turtles do not occur. *Id.*

The United States did not certify Malaysia under the Revised Guidelines and thus maintained an import restriction on Malaysian shrimp. Unhappy with that determination, and using the expedited procedures of Article 21.5 of the Dispute Settlement Understanding, Malaysia challenged the Revised Guidelines and import ban as a failure to comply with Appellate Body's earlier ruling.

United States-Import Prohibition of Certain Shrimp and Shrimp Products: Recourse to Article 21.5 of the DSU by Malaysia

Appellate Body Report, WT/DS58/AB/RW (adopted Nov. 21, 2001),
reprinted in 41 I.L.M. 149 (2002)

[Malaysia raised two fundamental objections to the revised U.S. program in its complaint under the DSU Article 21.5 recourse process. First, it argued that the United States had not followed the mandate to seek a multilateral solution before resorting to a unilateral trade restriction. Second, it argued that the U.S. regulations still essentially compelled a country to require the use of TEDs as a condition of certification for shrimp exports to the United States.

On the issue of seeking a multilateral solution, Malaysia claimed that the Appellate Body imposed an obligation on the United States to *conclude* an international agreement, not simply *negotiate* one. According to Malaysia, to rule otherwise would lead to an "incongruous" result: a WTO Member could offer to negotiate in good faith an agreement incorporating its "unilaterally defined standards" and if a WTO Member refuses to *conclude* such an agreement, the member could then claim that its application of a unilateral measure does not constitute "unjustifiable discrimination." The Appellate Body's responded]:

122.... Given the specific mandate contained in Section 609, and given the decided preference for multilateral approaches voiced by WTO Members and others in the international community in various international agreements for the protection and conservation of endangered sea turtles that were cited in our previous Report, the United States, in our view, would be expected to make good faith efforts to reach international agreements that are comparable from one forum of negotiation to the other. The negotiations need not be identical. Indeed, no two negotiations can ever be identical, or lead to identical results. Yet the negotiations must be *comparable* in the sense that comparable efforts are made, comparable resources are invested, and comparable energies are devoted to securing an international agreement. So long as such comparable efforts are made, it is more likely that "arbitrary or unjustifiable discrimination" will be avoided between countries where an importing Member concludes an agreement with one group of countries, but fails to do so with another group of countries.

123. Under the chapeau of Article XX, an importing Member may not treat its trading partners in a manner that would constitute "arbitrary or unjustifiable discrimination." With respect to this measure, the United States could conceivably respect this obligation, and the conclusion of an international agreement might nevertheless not be possible despite the serious, good faith efforts of the United States. Requiring that a multilateral agreement be *concluded* by the United States in order to avoid "arbitrary or unjustifiable discrimination" in applying its measure would mean that any country party to the negotiations with the United States, whether a WTO Member or not, would have, in effect, a veto over whether the United States could fulfill its WTO obligations. Such a requirement would not be reasonable. For a variety of reasons, it may be possible to conclude an agreement with one group of countries but not another. The conclusion of a multilateral agreement requires the cooperation and commitment of many countries. In our view, the United States cannot be held to have engaged in "arbitrary or unjustifiable discrimination" under Article XX solely because one international negotiation resulted in an agreement while another did not.

[The Appellate Body then upheld the Recourse Panel's decision that the United States had undertaken serious, good faith efforts to negotiate an international agreement by supporting and attending a number of meetings and negotiations on sea turtle conservation. *Id.* at para. 134.

Malaysia also disagreed with the Recourse Panel's finding that a measure meets the newly-defined requirements of the chapeau of Article XX if it is flexible enough, both in design and application, to permit certification of an exporting country with a sea turtle protection and conservation program "comparable" to that of the United States. According to Malaysia, even if the measure at issue allows certification of countries having regulatory programs "comparable" to that of the United States, and even if the measure is applied in such a manner, the requirement results in "arbitrary or unjustifiable discrimination" because it conditions access to the United States market on compliance with policies and standards "unilaterally" prescribed by the United States.

The Appellate Body first recalled its conclusion from its previous decision in *Shrimp/Turtle* that a measure requiring exporters to meet "a single, rigid and unbending requirement" to "adopt essentially the same policies and enforcement practices as those applied to, and enforced on, domestic producers" would not meet the requirements of the chapeau of Article XX. *Id.* at para. 140. In contrast, a requirement that U.S. and foreign programs be "comparable in effectiveness" would meet the requirements of the chapeau]:

144. In our view, there is an important difference between conditioning market access on the adoption of essentially the same programme, and conditioning market access on the adoption of a programme *comparable in effectiveness*. Authorizing an importing Member to condition market access on exporting Members putting in place regulatory programmes *comparable in effectiveness* to that of the importing Member gives sufficient latitude to the exporting Member with respect to the programme it may adopt to achieve the level of effectiveness required. It allows the exporting Member to adopt a regulatory programme that is suitable to the specific conditions prevailing in its territory. As we see it, the Panel correctly reasoned and concluded that conditioning market access on the adoption of a programme *comparable in effectiveness*, allows for sufficient flexibility in the application of the measure so as to avoid "arbitrary or unjustifiable

discrimination." We, therefore, agree with the conclusion of the Panel on "comparable effectiveness."

[Malaysia then argued that the U.S. regulations themselves should be tailored to address the specific conditions in Malaysia and all other countries affected by the regulations]:

149. We need only say here that, in our view, a measure should be designed in such a manner that there is sufficient flexibility to take into account the specific conditions prevailing in *any* exporting Member, including, of course, Malaysia. Yet this is not the same as saying that there must be specific provisions in the measure aimed at addressing specifically the particular conditions prevailing in *every individual* exporting Member. Article XX of the GATT 1994 does not require a Member to anticipate and provide explicitly for the specific conditions prevailing and evolving in *every individual* Member.

[The Appellate Body ruled that the Revised Guidelines allowed U.S. officials to take into account the specific conditions of Malaysian shrimp production and any demonstrated differences between U.S. and foreign shrimp fishing conditions. As such, the Appellate Body concluded that the revised guidelines provided sufficient flexibility to account for the prevailing conditions in other countries, including Malaysia, and met the requirements of the chapeau of Article XX. *Id.* at para. 150.]

Questions and Discussion

1. *Arbitrary versus Unjustifiable Discrimination.* The Appellate Body's analyses in *Shrimp/Turtle* and *Reformulated Gasoline* separate "arbitrary discrimination" from "unjustifiable discrimination." Which actions of the United States did it determine were "arbitrary" or "unjustifiable"? Does it articulate a clear distinction between the two? As is probably clear from your answer to the previous question, the distinction between arbitrary and unjustifiable discrimination is difficult to discern. According to the Oxford English Dictionary, "arbitrary" means "derived from mere opinion or preference; not based on the nature of things; hence, capricious, uncertain, varying." On the other hand, "unjustifiable" means not defensible. Do the Appellate Body conclusions fit within these definitions?

With respect to "arbitrary or unjustifiable discrimination," perhaps panels have incorrectly assumed that this constitutes two distinct findings. Under the U.S. Administrative Procedure Act, for example, courts may overturn agency actions if those actions are "arbitrary, capricious an abuse of discretion, or otherwise not in accordance with law." Courts have always ruled that "arbitrary" and "capricious" constitute a single standard, not two. *See* Citizens to Preserve Overton Park v. Volpe, 401 U.S. 402, 414, 91 S.Ct. 814, 822 (1971). In the scheme of the chapeau, what should arbitrary and unjustifiable mean? Is it one standard or two?

2. *Unjustifiable Discrimination: When Is a Measure Coercive?* The Appellate Body, asserting that the U.S. regulations were applied with "intended and actual coercive effect on the specific policy decisions made by foreign governments," called this coercive effect "[p]erhaps the most conspicuous flaw" in the U.S. shrimp/turtle policy. *Shrimp/Turtle*, Appellate Body Report, at para. 161. *See also Tuna/Dolphin II*, GATT Panel Report, at para. 5.27. Both of these statements reflect a deep-seated WTO antipathy to the use of trade mea-

sures as means of dictating domestic policy to other governments. Nonetheless, the Appellate Body in the *Shrimp/Turtle* recourse proceeding remarked that "conditioning access to a member's domestic market on whether exporting members comply with, or adopt, a policy or policies unilaterally prescribed by the importing member may, to some degree, be a common aspect of measures" under the enumerated Article XX exceptions. *Shrimp/Turtle-Recourse to Article 21.5*, Appellate Body Report, at para. 138. The Appellate Body balanced these concerns by rejecting the original U.S. shrimp/turtle regulations as "rigid and unbending," requiring target countries to adopt "essentially the same" turtle protection program as the United States. On the other hand, it approved the revised regulations, which required importing countries to have a sea turtle conservation program "comparable in effectiveness" to the U.S. program. *Shrimp/Turtle*, Appellate Body Report, at para. 144. Do you find the distinction between an "essentially the same" program and a "comparable in effectiveness" program to be a meaningful distinction for interpreting the discrimination elements of Article XX?

3. *Countries Where the Same Conditions Prevail. Shrimp/Turtle* gives some attention to the other part of the discrimination test in Article XX: different treatment is discrimination for Article XX purposes only "if the same conditions prevail" in the countries being treated differently. But which "conditions" must be the same? One obvious criterion would be to interpret "same conditions" in light of the specific exception invoked. For example, it would do little good to consider environmental conditions if the measure at issue relates to the protection of artistic treasures under Article XX(f). In the case of *Shrimp/Turtle*, however, the ecological conditions affecting sea turtle conservation and shrimp harvesting seem highly relevant. In *Shrimp/Turtle*, the United States argued for such a test: "In context, an alleged 'discrimination between countries where the same conditions prevail' is not 'unjustifiable' where the policy goal of the Article XX exception being applied provides the rationale for the justification." The Appellate Body rejected that approach: "The policy goal of a measure at issue cannot provide its rationale or justification under the standards of the chapeau of Article XX." *Shrimp/Turtle*, Appellate Body Report, at para. 149. But if the policy objective and the measure at issue do not frame the relevant conditions that must be the same, then what conditions must the same? Consider the following analysis.

Sanford Gaines, *The WTO's Reading of the GATT Article XX Chapeau, A Disguised Restriction on Environmental Measures*

22 U. Pa. J. Int'l. Econ. L. 739, 779–82 (2001). Reprinted with permission of the Pennsylvania Journal of International Economic Law

At the threshold, then, the WTO needs a jurisprudence to decide which "conditions" are pertinent and when they can be deemed to be "the same." Each nation in the world is unique; it is impossible that all conditions might be the same in any two countries. In the trade context, however, it would be preposterous to argue from that premise that the "same conditions" never prevail.... It would be senseless for the comparison to focus on conditions that have no relationship to the purposes for which the trade measure was instituted. For example, the United States should not be allowed to discriminate between two countries under Section 609 on the basis of the number of television sets per household. The only principled basis on which to select the relevant conditions for comparison is that they should have something to do with the declared objectives of the measure—in this case, something to do with shrimp fishing and sea turtle protection. The Appellate Body's provisional acceptance of Section 609 under Article XX(g) depended on its finding a rational relationship between the operation of Section 609 and its turtle-protection objective. The test for discrimination under the chapeau ought to be congruent with that rational relationship, looking at the similarity of those conditions in each country that have some relevance to the environmental policy objectives of the measure in question.

[Gaines then notes that the WTO Agreement on the Application of Sanitary and Phytosanitary Measures uses the identical language and is well understood to refer to differences in agricultural or sanitary conditions.]

Using the same analytical approach to discrimination under Article XX(g), a trade measure to conserve an exhaustible natural resource should be able to discriminate between different nations depending on such conservation-relevant factors as whether the resource exists in the nation and whether its conservation programs and practices for the resource are consistent with the policies for conserving the same resource in the country taking the measure. Indeed, the better argument is that such conservation-relevant factors should be the only permissible bases for differentiation. No other conceivable similarities or differences in conditions from one country to the next, including social values or economic conditions, bear a direct relationship to the conservation purposes of the measure. A turtle-protective shrimp embargo that discriminated, for example, between shrimp from Malaysia and shrimp from the Dominican Republic on the basis of their different economic conditions would be "unjustifiable." That is not to say that international environmental policy should not, as the Rio Declaration puts it, consider the "differentiated responsibilities" of countries based on their developmental status. Certain aspects of trade policy also make or permit distinctions between countries in terms of economic development. But an economically-based discrimination should be virtually impossible to justify for an environmental trade measure under the chapeau of Article XX.

Instead of adopting this approach, the Appellate Body turned the analysis on its head: it found that the inflexible approach first adopted by the United States failed the test because it "*refused to discriminate* in trade treatment between countries where *different* conditions may prevail." It concluded that "discrimination results not only when countries in which the same conditions prevail are differently treated, but also when the application of the measure does not allow for any inquiry into the appropriateness of the regulatory program for the conditions prevailing in those exporting countries." *Shrimp/Turtle*, Appellate Body Report, at 165. Is the Appellate Body right?

Given a chance to revisit this question in the Article 21.5 recourse proceeding, the Appellate Body refused to analyze which conditions must be the same. Instead, it stated that "[w]e need only say here that, in our view, a measure should be designed in such a manner that there is sufficient flexibility to take into account the specific conditions prevailing in any exporting member, including, of course, Malaysia." *Shrimp/Turtle-Recourse to Article 21.5*, Appellate Body Report, at para. 149.

4. *Is There a Duty to Negotiate a Bilateral or Multilateral Agreement?* One of the most hotly contested issues after *Shrimp/Turtle* is whether countries must initiate international negotiations before invoking Article XX. In *Reformulated Gasoline*, the Appellate Body found unjustifiable discrimination and a disguised restriction on international trade because the United States "had not pursued the possibility of entering into cooperative

arrangements" with foreign governments and failed "to explore adequately means, including in particular cooperation with the governments of Venezuela and Brazil, of mitigating the administrative problems" identified by the United States. In the main *Shrimp/Turtle* report, the Appellate Body said that failure of the United States to engage in "serious across-the-board negotiations" on a sea turtle conservation regime with the Southeast Asian countries "bears heavily in any appraisal of justifiable or unjustifiable discrimination."

Did the Appellate Body merely indicate that the failure to negotiate contributed to its finding of unjustifiable discrimination, or does a country have an affirmative duty to negotiate before it can successfully invoke an Article XX exception? Although the Appellate Body seems to articulate the failure to negotiate as a consideration itself, it also raises the point that the United States had negotiated a sea turtle conservation convention with countries in the Western Hemisphere in this same period. Given that context, Professor Robert Howse clearly believes that the Appellate Body did not establish a stand-alone requirement to negotiate:

> [T]he AB never held that the requirements of the chapeau, in and of themselves, impose a *sui generis* duty to negotiate. Rather, the AB's *Shrimp/Turtle* ruling stands for the more limited propositions that 1) undertaking serious negotiations with some countries and not with others is, in circumstances such as these, "unjustifiable discrimination," and 2) that a failure to undertake serious negotiations may be closely connected with, and indeed part and parcel of, various discriminatory effects of a scheme, and may reinforce or perhaps even tip the balance towards a finding that those discriminatory effects amount to "unjustifiable discrimination" within the meaning of the chapeau. By taking each of these propositions separately and carefully examining them in context, we can discern the extent to which the AB actually infers a duty to negotiate from the requirements of the chapeau, and the extent and nature of that duty.

> Within GATT/WTO jurisprudence, offering different terms of market access to some Members and not others will almost always constitute "discrimination." Thus, it is hardly controversial that by offering negotiated market access to some Members and not others, the U.S. was engaging in "discrimination." One does not need to infer any self-standing duty to negotiate in order to arrive at this conclusion. However, the AB had to consider not only whether there was discrimination, but also whether that discrimination was unjustifiable. In other words, could it be justified in terms of the objective of the United States, the protection of endangered species of sea turtles?

Robert Howse, *The Appellate Body Rulings in the Shrimp/Turtle Case*, at 507. Howse concludes that the Appellate Body's findings are appropriate in light of the numerous international declarations and agreements indicating an international bias to use multilateral measures to protect sea turtles. Does this analysis take into account the failure-to-negotiate aspect of *Reformulated Gasoline*? In that case, there was no claim that the United States negotiated cooperative agreements with some foreign producers or countries and not with others.

In contrast to Howse, Sanford Gaines argues that the Appellate Body by "[e]stablishing international negotiation as a precondition to the invocation of Article XX unreasonably stretches the concept of 'justifiability' into sensitive areas of national policy discretion. Multilateralism may be preferable, but it is not obligatory.... *Shrimp/Turtle* articulates no historical foundation or legal basis for the conclusion that failure to make bona fide efforts to negotiate a treaty comes within the chapeau's concept of 'unjustifiable' discrimi-nation." Sanford Gaines, *The WTO's Reading of the GATT Article XX Chapeau*, at 805.

Gaines also comments on the report of the panel in the recourse proceeding. The Panel, while stopping short of construing multilateralism as an absolute requirement, notes that the migratory nature and worldwide distribution of sea turtles "significantly moves the line of equilibrium [between unilateral approaches and multilateral approaches] to-wards a bilaterally or multilaterally negotiated solution, thus rendering recourse to uni-lateral measures less acceptable." It then holds that the standard is "whether the United States made serious good faith efforts to negotiate an international agreement, taking into account the situations of the other negotiating countries." United States-Import Pro-hibition of Certain Shrimp and Shrimp Products, Recourse to Article 21.5 of the DSU by Malaysia, Panel Report, WT/DS58/RW, paras. 5.59, 5.73 (adopted Nov. 21, 2001).

Gaines applauds the Appellate Body's clarification in the recourse proceeding that the negotiations for the Southeast Asian countries, as compared with the Western Hemi-sphere countries, need only be "comparable in the sense that comparable energies are de-voted to securing an international agreement" and that the Inter-American Convention should only be used as an example for analysis of comparability, not as a substantive benchmark. Nonetheless, Gaines believes this is not enough:

> While this new gloss on *Shrimp-Turtle* is helpful in understanding the criteria for establishing discrimination when comparing different negotiating contexts, it still leaves open the problematic issue … about the threshold of efforts, re-sources, and energies needed to satisfy the implicit more general requirement, which the Appellate Body's recourse report does not question, that there must always be a good faith effort at negotiations before invoking Article XX rights. On that question, the only point that the Appellate Body makes absolutely clear is that the obligation is one to negotiate, not to reach agreement.
>
> > [I]t is one thing to prefer a multilateral approach in the application of a mea-sure that is provisionally justified under one of the subparagraphs of Arti-cle XX of the GATT 1994; it is another to require the conclusion of a multilateral agreement as a condition of avoiding "arbitrary or unjustifiable discrimination" under the chapeau of Article XX. We see, in this case, no such requirement.
>
> That last qualifier, "in this case," leaves one with the uneasy feeling that the pref-erence for multilateralism remains so strong that unilateral measures affecting transnational or global resources outside the context of any systematic effort to promote a multilateral solution will, *ipso facto*, not qualify under Article XX. Al-though it never so holds explicitly, the Appellate Body's language suggests that it would not have found Section 609 qualified if it had not contained the Section 609(a) congressional instruction for the pursuit of international negotiations. The carrot of Section 609(a) was a desirable expression of policy, but nothing in the GATT suggests that it should be a necessary precondition to invoking the shelter of Article XX for the embargo stick of Section 609(b).

Sanford Gaines, *The WTO's Reading of the GATT Article XX Chapeau*, at 819–20. Do you agree with Gaines's concerns? Compare his "uneasy feeling" with Howse's level of com-fort in the *Shrimp/Turtle* result. Is Gaines being alarmist?

If Howse is right that the failure to negotiate with all countries equally constituted unjustifiable discrimination, does that create a perverse incentive *not* to negotiate at all? Similarly, if a duty to negotiate in *Shrimp/Turtle* derives from a legislative mandate to negotiate, does that not also create a perverse incentive for legislatures to avoid such statutory requirements? If a duty to negotiate derives from a preference in international agreements for multilateral efforts to conserve global resources, is the corollary that no duty to negotiate exists when an importing country imposes trade restrictions to protect endemic species of an exporting country? Based on *Shrimp/Turtle*, what grounds exist to mandate international negotiations prior to imposing trade restrictions on endemic species? What happens if international consensus is not possible in an environmentally relevant timeframe? Should "good faith" be interpreted in light of a species' endangered status or a chemical's toxic effects on human health?

Finally, is the duty to negotiate a mere legal abstraction? As the Appellate Body notes (para. 169), the Inter-American Convention had not been ratified by *any* of its signatories. So what significance does it have beyond being words on paper? Compliance or noncompliance with the Convention had absolutely no bearing—could not have had any bearing—on U.S. decisions about certification of country programs, and thus no bearing on the right to have shrimp accepted into the U.S. market.

5. The Appellate Body in *Shrimp/Turtle* found that Section 609 constituted unjustifiable discrimination because a shrimper using methods identical to those employed in the United States could not sell his shrimp in the United States, because the shrimper's country had not been certified as in compliance with Section 609. While the Appellate Body did not suggest that an individualized approach would always make a measure permissible under Article XX, it showed a preference for such an approach. Is it reasonable to expect a country to enforce a law on a boat-by-boat basis? How would such a law be implemented and enforced? Even if difficult to implement and enforce, is it fairer—especially in light of a country's WTO obligations?

6. *Shrimp/Turtle Aftermath.* On April 30, 2010, the Department of State certified 13 nations as maintaining regulations for the protection of sea turtles that are comparable to those of the United States: Belize, Colombia, Ecuador, El Salvador, Guatemala, Guyana, Honduras, Madagascar, Nicaragua, Nigeria, Pakistan, Panama and Suriname. The Department also certified 25 shrimp harvesting nations and one economy as having fishing environments that do not pose a danger to sea turtles and another sixteen nations as having shrimping grounds only in cold waters where the risk of taking sea turtles is negligible. It also concluded that nine nations and one economy only harvest shrimp using small boats with crews of less than five that use manual rather than mechanical means to retrieve nets or catch shrimp using other methods that do not threaten sea turtles, and that use of such small-scale technology does not adversely affect sea turtles. The nine nations and one economy are: The Bahamas, China, the Dominican Republic, Fiji, Hong Kong, Jamaica, Oman, Peru, Sri Lanka and Venezuela. However, effective as of April 20, 2010, the United States withdrew Mexico's certification after it concluded that Mexico's TED program no longer met standards established under Section 609. The United States has provided Mexico with detailed technical recommendations and capacity-building support to improve its program and will seek further opportunities help Mexico toward reinstatement of certification. Certifications Pursuant to Section 609 of Public Law 101-162 75 Fed. Reg. 27855 (May. 18, 2010).

C. The *Brazil–Retreaded Tyres* Case

Recall that the Panel found that Brazil's ban on the issuance of licenses to import retreaded tires was provisionally justified pursuant to Article XX(b) (pages 293–304). It then assessed whether that ban was consistent with the chapeau of Article XX. The Panel, and then the Appellate Body, focused on the discrimination caused by two measures. First, Brazil allowed retreaded tires to be imported from countries participating in MERCOSUR, (a customs union called (in Spanish) the Mercado Común del Sur, or Southern Common Market). Brazil implemented the exemption only after Uruguay successfully challenged Brazil's ban in a MERCOSUR dispute. Second, Brazil allowed imports of used tires, despite a general ban on such imports, because importers obtained an injunction from a Brazilian court requiring Brazil to allow such imports. Do you think these measures create conditions of "arbitrary" or "unjustifiable" discrimination?

Brazil–Measures Affecting Imports of Retreaded Tyres
Appellate Body Report, WT/DS332/AB/R
(adopted Dec. 17, 2007)

1.   The MERCOSUR Exemption and Arbitrary or Unjustifiable Discrimination

* * *

226. The Appellate Body Reports in *US–Gasoline*, *US–Shrimp*, and *US–Shrimp (Article 21.5–Malaysia)* show that the analysis of whether the application of a measure results in arbitrary or unjustifiable discrimination should focus on the cause of the discrimination, or the rationale put forward to explain its existence. In this case, Brazil explained that it introduced the MERCOSUR exemption to comply with a ruling issued by a MERCOSUR arbitral tribunal. This ruling arose in the context of a challenge initiated by Uruguay against Brazil's import ban on remoulded tyres, on the grounds that it constituted a new restriction on trade prohibited under MERCOSUR. The MERCOSUR arbitral tribunal found Brazil's restrictions on the importation of remoulded tyres to be a violation of its obligations under MERCOSUR. These facts are undisputed.

227. We have to assess whether this explanation provided by Brazil is acceptable as a justification for discrimination between MERCOSUR countries and non-MERCOSUR countries in relation to retreaded tyres. In doing so, we are mindful of the function of the chapeau of Article XX, which is to prevent abuse of the exceptions specified in the paragraphs of that provision. In our view, there is such an abuse, and, therefore, there is arbitrary or unjustifiable discrimination when a measure provisionally justified under a paragraph of Article XX is applied in a discriminatory manner "between countries where the same conditions prevail", and when the reasons given for this discrimination bear no rational connection to the objective falling within the purview of a paragraph of Article XX, or would go against that objective. The assessment of whether discrimination is arbitrary or unjustifiable should be made in the light of the objective of the measure. We note, for example, that one of the bases on which the Appellate Body relied in *US–Shrimp* for concluding that the operation of the measure at issue resulted in unjustifiable discrimination was that one particular aspect of the application of the measure (the measure implied that, in certain circumstances, shrimp caught abroad using methods identical to those employed in the United States would be excluded from the United States market) was "difficult to reconcile with the declared objective of protecting and conserving sea turtles". Accordingly, we have difficulty understanding how discrimination might be viewed as complying with the chapeau of Article XX when the alleged rationale for discriminating does not relate to the pursuit of or would go against the objective

that was provisionally found to justify a measure under a paragraph of Article XX.

228. In this case, the discrimination between MERCOSUR countries and other WTO Members in the application of the Import Ban was introduced as a consequence of a ruling by a MERCOSUR tribunal. The tribunal found against Brazil because the restriction on imports of remoulded tyres was inconsistent with the prohibition of new trade restrictions under MERCOSUR law. In our view, the ruling issued by the MERCOSUR arbitral tribunal is not an acceptable rationale for the discrimination, because it bears no relationship to the legitimate objective pursued by the Import Ban that falls within the purview of Article XX(b), and even goes against this objective, to however small a degree. Accordingly, we are of the view that the MERCOSUR exemption has resulted in the Import Ban being applied in a manner that constitutes arbitrary or unjustifiable discrimination.

229. The Panel considered that the MERCOSUR exemption resulted in discrimination between MERCOSUR countries and other WTO Members, but that this discrimination would be "unjustifiable" only if imports of retreaded tyres entering into Brazil "were to take place in such amounts that the achievement of the objective of the measure at issue would be significantly undermined". The Panel's interpretation implies that the determination of whether discrimination is unjustifiable depends on the quantitative impact of this discrimination on the achievement of the objective of the measure at issue. As we indicated above, analyzing whether discrimination is "unjustifiable" will usually involve an analysis that relates primarily to the cause or the rationale of the discrimination. By contrast, the Panel's interpretation of the term "unjustifiable" does not depend on the cause or rationale of the discrimination but, rather, is focused exclusively on the assessment of the *effects* of the discrimination. The Panel's approach has no support in the text of Article XX and appears to us inconsistent with the manner the Appellate Body has interpreted and applied the concept of "arbitrary or unjustifiable discrimination" in previous cases.[437]

230. Having said that, we recognize that in certain cases the effects of the discrimination may be a relevant factor, among others, for determining whether the cause or rationale of the discrimination is acceptable or defensible and, ultimately, whether the discrimination is justifiable. The effects of discrimination might be relevant, depending on the circumstances of the case, because, as we indicated above , the chapeau of Article XX deals with the manner of application of the measure at issue. Taking into account as a relevant factor, among others, the effects of the discrimination for determining whether the rationale of the discrimination is acceptable is, however, fundamentally different from the Panel's approach, which focused exclusively on the relationship between the effects of the discrimination and its justifiable or unjustifiable character.

---

437 ... We also observe that the Panel's approach was based on a logic that is different in nature from that followed by the Appellate Body when it addressed the national treatment principle under Article III:4 of the GATT 1994 in *Japan–Alcoholic Beverages II*. In that case, the Appellate Body stated that Article III aims to ensure "equality of competitive conditions for imported products in relation to domestic products". (Appellate Body Report, *Japan–Alcoholic Beverages II*, p. 16, DSR 1996:I, 97, at 109) The Appellate Body added that "it is irrelevant that 'the trade effects' of the [measure at issue], as reflected in the volumes of imports, are insignificant or even non-existent". (*Ibid.*, at 110) For the Appellate Body, "Article III protects expectations not of any particular trade volume but rather of the equal competitive relationship between imported and domestic products." (*Ibid.* (footnote omitted)).

231. We also note that the Panel found that the discrimination resulting from the MERCOSUR exemption is not arbitrary. The Panel explained that this discrimination cannot be said to be "capricious" or "random" because it was adopted further to a ruling within the framework of MERCOSUR.

232. Like the Panel, we believe that Brazil's decision to act in order to comply with the MERCOSUR ruling cannot be viewed as "capricious" or "random". Acts implementing a decision of a judicial or quasi-judicial body—such as the MERCOSUR arbitral tribunal—can hardly be characterized as a decision that is "capricious" or "random". However, discrimination can result from a rational decision or behaviour, and still be "arbitrary or unjustifiable", because it is explained by a rationale that bears no relationship to the objective of a measure provisionally justified under one of the paragraphs of Article XX, or goes against that objective.

233. Accordingly, we *find* that the MERCOSUR exemption has resulted in the Import Ban being applied in a manner that constitutes arbitrary or unjustifiable discrimination....

234. This being said, we observe, like the Panel, that, before the arbitral tribunal established under MERCOSUR, Brazil could have sought to justify the challenged Import Ban on the grounds of human, animal, and plant health under Article 50(d) of the Treaty of Montevideo. Brazil, however, decided not to do so. It is not appropriate for us to second-guess Brazil's decision not to invoke Article 50(d), which serves a function similar to that of Article XX(b) of the GATT 1994. However, Article 50(d) of the Treaty of Montevideo, as well as the fact that Brazil might have raised this defence in the MERCOSUR arbitral proceedings, show, in our view, that the discrimination associated with the MERCOSUR exemption does not necessarily result from a conflict between provisions under MERCOSUR and the GATT 1994. * * *

2. The MERCOSUR Exemption and Disguised Restriction on International Trade

236. When examining whether the Import Ban was applied in a manner that constitutes a disguised restriction on international trade, the Panel was not persuaded by the European Communities' contention that Brazil adopted the prohibition on the importation of retreaded tyres as "a disguise to conceal the pursuit of trade-restrictive objectives".

[In reaching its conclusion, the Panel referred to its reasoning with respect to arbitrary or unjustifiable discrimination: if imports from MERCOSUR countries were to occur in significant amounts, then the Import Ban would be applied in a manner that constitutes a disguised restriction on international trade. The Panel concluded that, as of the time of its examination, "the volume of imports of remoulded tyres that has actually taken place under the MERCOSUR exemption has not been significant."]

239. We agree with the European Communities' observation that the reasoning developed by the Panel to reach the challenged conclusion was the same as that made in respect of arbitrary or unjustifiable discrimination. Indeed, the Panel conditioned a finding of a disguised restriction on international trade on the existence of significant imports of retreaded tyres that would undermine the achievement of the objective of the Import Ban. We explained above why we believe that the Panel erred in finding that the MERCOSUR exemption would result in

arbitrary or unjustifiable discrimination only if the imports of retreaded tyres from MERCOSUR countries were to take place in such amounts that the achievement of the objective of the Import Ban would be significantly undermined. As the Panel's conclusion that the MERCOSUR exemption has not resulted in a disguised restriction on international trade was based on an interpretation that we have reversed, this finding cannot stand. Therefore, we also *reverse* the Panel's findings ... that "the MERCOSUR exemption ... has not been shown to date to result in the [Import Ban] being applied in a manner that would constitute ... a disguised restriction on international trade."

[As with the exception based on the MERCOSUR decision, the Panel found that the exception for imports of used tires due to court injunctions was not arbitrary. However, because imports of used tires were taking place under the injunctions in significant amounts to the benefit of the domestic industry, the Panel concluded that the imports constituted unjustifiable discrimination and a disguised restriction on international trade. The Appellate Body, for the same reasons that it reversed the Panel's legal analysis concerning the MERCOSUR decision, reversed the Panel's analysis concerning imports of used tires through court injunctions.]

Questions and Discussion

1. The *Brazil–Retreaded Tyre* Panel resorted to a dictionary to distinguish "arbitrary" from "unjustifiable" discrimination. It began by referring to *The Shorter Oxford English Dictionary* to discern the ordinary meaning of these terms:

> "*arbitrary*   1 Dependent on will or pleasure; 2 Based on mere opinion or preference as opp. to the real nature of things; capricious, unpredictable, inconsistent; 3 Unrestrained in the exercise of will or authority; despotic, tyrannical."

> "*unjustifiable* Not justifiable, indefensible."

> "*justifiable*   2 Able to be legally or morally justified; able to be shown to be just, reasonable, or correct; defensible."

Brazil–Retreaded Tyres, Panel Report, at paras. 7.257, 7.259. The Appellate Body did not reverse the Panel's conclusions that these definitions should guide interpretation of Article XX's chapeau. Did the Appellate Body adhere to these definitions? Are these useful definitions for interpreting arbitrary and unjustifiable discrimination?

2. Using the definitions above, the Panel declared that the exception for the importation of retreaded tires from MERCOSUR members did not constitute arbitrary discrimination because the exception resulted from the decision of a MERCOSUR Tribunal; Brazil's exception was not capricious. On the other hand, the Panel concluded that the exception could result in unjustifiable discrimination if the volume of imports that took place under the discriminatory measure would "significantly undermine[]" Brazil's objective. The Appellate Body, however, concluded at paragraph 227 that a discriminatory measure could not be justified under Article XX if "the reasons for the discrimination bear no rational connection to the objective falling within the purview of a paragraph of Article XX, or would go against that objective." Did the Panel establish a useful way to distinguish "arbitrary" from "unjustifiable" discrimination, or did the Appellate Body rightfully reverse the Panel?

3. Some scholars maintain that even the recent decisions "unduly privileged trade considerations, showed little understanding of how environmental policy works, and give

little ground for hope that the WTO will tolerate *any* real-world unilateral use of trade leverage in furtherance of environmental protection objectives reaching beyond national
boundaries." Sanford Gaines, *The WTO's Reading of the GATT Article XX Chapeau*, at
743–44. Others see real openings for countries to adopt environmental trade restrictions
so long as they are based on environmental performance rather than the country of origin of the goods. Robert Howse, *The Appellate Body Rulings in the* Shrimp/Turtle *Case:
A New Legal Baseline for the Trade and Environment Debate*, 27 COLUM. J. ENVTL. L. 491
(2002). What do you think: Do *Shrimp/Turtle* and *Brazil–Retreaded Tyres* usher in the
WTO's acceptance of trade restrictions to protect the environment or do they so tightly
guard the door to Article XX acceptance that only the rare environmental measure will
pass through?

4. *Small Group Project.* Devise a test that permits trade-related measures under the Article XX(b) and XX(g) exceptions without putting the WTO on the slippery slope toward
renewed protectionism that would undermine the world trading system. Specifically, assume that the U.S. measures prohibiting imports of tuna and shrimp are legitimate exercises of unilateral authority for the conservation of dolphins and sea turtles. How can
they be justified under Article XX(b) or XX(g) without allowing protectionist measures
disguised as environmental measures from being accepted under Article XX? Try to make
your test as "objective" as possible. Can you avoid subjective judgments about the intent
behind the measure?

5. *Class Exercise: Mock Dispute Settlement Proceeding.* In September 2009, the European
Union (EU) enacted a binding regulation that prohibits the importation and the placing
on the market in the customs territory of the EU of all seal products. The regulation defines "seal" as all species of pinnipeds. It further defines "seal product" as "all products,
either processed or unprocessed, deriving or obtained from seals, including meat, oil,
blubber, organs, raw fur skins and fur skins, tanned or dressed, including fur skins assembled
in plates, crosses and similar forms, and articles made from fur skins." The Regulation
does allow the importation and placing on the market of seal products where they result
from traditional hunts conducted by Inuit and other indigenous communities and where
the products contribute to their subsistence. Regulation (EC) No. 1007/2009 of the European Parliament and of the EC Council of 16 September 2009 on trade in seal products.

The regulation is clearly a reaction to the clubbing of seals in Canada and elsewhere.
The EU acknowledges that "[t]he seal populations that are hunted for commercial purposes—an estimated 15 million animals—are generally not endangered." European Commission, Seal Hunting, http://ec.europa.eu/environment/biodiversity/animal_welfare/
seals/seal_hunting.htm. In addition, the EU expressly states that it "is concerned about
the animal welfare aspects of the seal hunt. Doubts have been expressed about some of
the methods used for hunting seals, such as shooting, netting and clubbing, that can
cause avoidable pain and distress." *Id.*

In November 2009, Canada and Norway requested consultations with the EU. They claim,
among other things, that the regulation violates Articles I:1, III:4 and XI:1 of the GATT.
WT/DS400/1 (Nov. 4, 2009); WT/DS401/1 (Nov. 5, 2009). The EU counters that the regulation is justified under Articles XX(b) and XX(g). (The EU also claims that the measure is consistent with Article XX(a), a measure "necessary to protect public morals.")

For this mock dispute settlement proceeding, divide into three groups: 1) Canada and
Norway, 2) the European Union, and 3) the dispute settlement panel. Research the factual and legal issues surrounding the hunt and regulation. In making your arguments,

consider in particular the following facts: 1) the regulation applies to seal products produced in the EU and to imported products, 2) the aim of the regulation is to ensure that products derived from seals are no longer found on the European market, 3) about 900,000 seals are hunted each year around the globe, with the commercial hunt in Canada, Greenland and Namibia accounting for some 60% of the seals killed each year, and 4) seal hunting within the EU is marginal, but about one third of world trade in seal products either passes through or ends up in the EU market.

VI. Alternative Approaches to Interpreting the Environmental Exceptions

In light of these decisions, scholars and environmentalists have proposed alternative tests for analyzing whether a trade-related measure can be justified on environmental grounds under Article XX. Sanford Gaines and Daniel Esty, for example, have asked that the inquiry focus on discrimination and protection—core concepts of the GATT and Article XX. They acknowledge that the benefits of trade should not be undermined by protectionist motives. At the same time, they insist that Article XX must be interpreted in accordance with its plain meaning to permit legitimate environmental measures that may affect economic activity and international trade. Finding an appropriate balance between these two interests presents the central challenge to avoid the "slippery slope" that panels have feared would destroy the multilateral trading regime. What principles can provide that balance?

Sanford Gaines, for example, makes the following proposal:

> To infuse this spirit of mutual accommodation into the multilateral trading system will require a shift away from the current presumption against the trade-legitimacy of any PPM measure toward a presumption that PPM measures within the categories marked out by Article XX(b) and (g) are legitimate exercises of national rights unless complaining Members can demonstrate obviously discriminatory treatment of traded goods or a clear effort to disguise trade restrictions behind a green mask. WTO determinations that environmental trade measures are abusively discriminatory should not be lightly made. The complaining Members should be required to put forward at least a prima facie case that each element of the chapeau conditions has been breached: there is trade discrimination; the relevant conditions in the nations are the same; and the discrimination cannot be justified or is arbitrary. As in national legal systems, even if some discrimination in application of the measure can be established there should be a presumption of legitimacy for the national environmental measure and a deference to the responding nation's explanation or justification for the observed discrimination.

Sanford Gaines, *The WTO's Reading of the GATT Article XX Chapeau*, at 852–53.

Daniel Esty's reworking of Article XX specifically balances two principles of international environmental law. As with the Appellate Body in *Shrimp/Turtle*, Esty is cognizant of Principle 12 of the Rio Declaration on Environment and Development, which states that "[u]nilateral actions to deal with environmental challenges outside the jurisdiction of the importing country should be avoided. Environmental measures addressing transboundary or global environmental problems should, as far as possible, be based on an international consensus." He balances that admonition with Principle 3 of the Rio Declaration (and Principle 21 of the Stockholm Declaration), which provides that States have "the sovereign right to exploit their own resources pursuant to their own environmental and developmental policies, and the responsibility to ensure that activities within their jurisdiction or control do not cause damage to the environment of other States or of areas beyond the limits of national jurisdiction." Rio Declaration, June 14, 1992, U.N. Doc. A/CONF.151/5/Rev. 1, *reprinted in* 31 I.L.M. 874 (1992).

Daniel C. Esty, *Greening the GATT: Trade, Environment, and the Future*
234–36 (1994)

Using the U.S. Commerce clause jurisprudence as a base, this study argues for adoption of a three-pronged test to weight competing trade and environment claims. In particular, when a challenge has been made to the use of trade restrictions in support of an environmental program, a review panel would examine:

- the intent or effect of the challenged policy or regulation;

- the legitimacy of the underlying environmental policy or claim of environmental injury;

- the justification for the disruption to trade.

Regulations that intentionally discriminate against foreign products may constitute blatant protectionism and should be subject to careful scrutiny. Strict scrutiny should also be applied to requirements that have a disproportionate effect on imported products—perhaps indicating that the "environmental" standard was surreptitiously designed as a hidden trade barrier.

The second prong of the new balancing test for trade and environment disputes—the environmental legitimacy or injury examination—represents an entirely new concept for the GATT. It recognizes two fundamental bases for establishing the legitimacy of environmental policies with trade effects:

- multilateral agreement; or

- environmental injury to the country imposing trade measures.

This second prong provides a basis for separating "real" environmental programs from those in protectionist guises.

Internationally agreed standards offer the most secure foundation for environmental trade measures. To the maximum extent possible, nations should be encouraged to obtain multilateral support for any environmental program with an impact on trade.

In the absence of a multilateral agreement that expressly sanctions trade measures to combat noncompliance, the legitimacy of an environmental policy should be judged by reference to the presence of a bona fide environmental issue or injury and the nexus of the party using the trade measures to the environmental harm they wish to stop. In this context, a claim of legitimacy implicitly derives from the general commitments not to cause transboundary or global environmental harm that are embedded in the Stockholm and Rio Declarations and in customary international law. The bona fides of an environmental claim should be established by the scientific underpinnings of the policy in question and the significance of the harm addressed. The significance of an environmental injury should be calculated by reference to the importance of the species or ecosystem at risk, the strength of the scientific analysis of harm, the speed at which the harm is occurring, the irreversibility of the potential damage, and the breadth of the threatened harm.

In cases where the use of environmental trade measures rests on the implicit multilateral obligations found in the Stockholm and Rio Declarations, the connection of the party imposing the environmental trade measures to the injury should be a central factor in the legitimacy assessment. This study separates five possible "locations" of environmental harms:

- domestic

- transboundary

- global

- foreign resulting in a loss of global "positive externalities"

- foreign

Countries should have the greatest leeway to use regulatory policies with trade effects when addressing environmental problems that arise within their own territories. Thus, domestic environmental regulations such as product standards should be given considerable deference, as they currently are under existing GATT rules.

Policies designed to curb transboundary pollution should also be generally considered legitimate insofar as they respond to established violations of international law—that is, multilaterally determined norms. Trade actions penalizing a neighboring country polluting a shared waterway therefore might well be appropriate. Environmental trade measures aimed at harm to the global commons affecting the sustainability of an important species or ecosystem should also benefit from a presumption of legitimacy based on the established international obligation not to cause harm.

The most difficult cases are those in which the direct harm per se affects only a foreign country but there are indirect negative effects on others, or, as economists would say, a loss of positive externalities. For example, deforestation directly affects the country whose trees are cut or burned, causing erosion and other local environmental damage. But the loss of forests also has climate change and other biodiversity impacts that affect other countries. In such cases, if outsiders who benefit from (but do not pay for) the "positive externalities" demand the forests' preservation, there is a strong argument for them to compensate the country with the forest.

Environmental trade measures that attempt to address an injury that is entirely "local" to a foreign country should not be considered legitimate if undertaken unilaterally. This study argues, however, that nations should always retain the right, in a "soft" sense, to impose unilateral trade restrictions in support of their own environmental policies or values so long as they are willing to compensate those who trading opportunities are impaired.

Once the legitimacy of an environmental policy has been established, the remaining question—and the third prong of the proposed trade and environment balancing test—is whether the trade remedy chosen to support the policy is appropriate. The severity of the measure applied should vary with the significance and locus of the environmental harm. Respecting the prior determination of environmental legitimacy, the chosen trade restriction should generally be accepted as long as the burden imposed on trade is not clearly disproportionate to the environmental benefits to be obtained in light of alternative policies that are reasonably available and equally effective.

Questions and Discussion

1. Esty calls the second prong of his test "an entirely new concept" for the GATT. Why? Even so, can his entire approach fit within the existing language of the chapeau?

2. Esty's approach to Article XX would allow a WTO member to impose unilateral trade restrictions to reinforce its environmental values, but only if it is willing to compensate trading partners affected by such value choices. Is this the right approach? Esty also claims that his test does not include a requirement that the measure chosen be the "least GATT-inconsistent" or "least trade-restrictive." Yet, his "clearly disproportionate" test asks whether an equally effective policy mechanism was reasonably available. What is the difference between the two requirements? A more detailed version of Esty's argument can be found in DANIEL C. ESTY, GREENING THE GATT, at 116–30.

3. Do the approaches of Gaines and Esty provide better models for balancing trade and environmental interests than the approaches taken in WTO cases? In particular, are they able to identify protectionist measures disguised as environmental measures while at the same time allowing real environmental measures to pass GATT scrutiny?

4. Gaines argues that under his proposal, which preceded the *Retreaded Tyres* case, only one case—*Tuna-Dolphin*—would come out differently. Do you agree? What about under Esty's approach?

5. In the 1980s, poaching of elephants to fuel the international trade in ivory decimated African elephant populations throughout most of Africa. Populations fell from 1.2 million in 1979 to between 400,000 and 600,000 by 1989. More than 20 years later, scientists estimate that between 470,000 and 690,000 elephants survive in Africa. Before governments imposed a ban on commercial trade in ivory under the Convention on International Trade in Endangered Species of Wild Fauna and Flora (CITES), the United States, Japan, and the European Union unilaterally banned ivory imports. Those unilateral bans are credited with spurring CITES Parties to ban all international commercial trade in ivory, an action which has helped stabilize African elephant populations. Would those unilateral bans be acceptable under Esty's approach? The International Whaling Commission (IWC) has imposed a moratorium on commercial whaling. Nonetheless, Japan issues permits to kill more than 1,200 whales per year pursuant to an exception for scientific research whaling. Norway kills about 600 whales per year pursuant to an objection (reservation) to the moratorium. Could a member of the IWC ban the importation of products from Japan or Norway pursuant to Esty's approach? Could a nonmember?

6. Recall from Chapter 4, pages 258–60, that the European Court of Justice in the *Danish Bottles* case asked if the trade impacts are disproportionate to the conservation objectives achieved. Can the European concept of proportionality be used to interpret any aspects of Article XX?

7. Farber and Hudec question Esty's two-prong analysis of the U.S. Dormant Commerce Clause cases. Daniel A. Farber & Robert E. Hudec, *GATT Legal Restraint on Domestic Environmental Regulations, in* 2 Fair Trade and Harmonization 59, 65 (Jagdish Bhagwati & Robert E. Hudec eds., 1996). In their more complex view, current U.S. doctrine distinguishes three categories of cases: 1) facially discriminatory measures, which are subject to "strict scrutiny" and almost never tolerated; 2) facially neutral measures with discriminatory effect, which puts the burden on the state to justify benefits of the regulation and the lack of nondiscriminatory alternatives; and 3) measures with an "incidental" or "indirect" discriminatory effect, to which the U.S. courts apply a balancing test. Farber and Hudec further emphasize that these categories are not neatly separated.

Chapter 6

The Agreement on Technical Barriers to Trade, Ecolabeling, and the Question of Harmonization

I. Introduction

As GATT fulfilled its promise to reduce tariffs (average tariffs have fallen from about 40 percent of the cost of the good to less than 4 percent), countries found new, nontariff barriers to protect their domestic markets. These nontariff barriers include standards defining product characteristics relating to the quality, shape, and size of a product. Product standards abound; they are essential in a modern economy for guarding against risks to health, environmental quality, and many other important social values. Familiar standards include motor vehicle safety regulations, building codes to ensure structural and fire safety of construction materials, and requirements for appliances related to electrical safety. Product standards for environmental objectives include automobile fuel efficiency standards, energy efficiency requirements for appliances, and regulations setting requirements for "green" product labels such as "post-consumer waste recycled paper" or "organic" foods.

To minimize trade distortions arising from different national product standards beyond what the GATT's core nondiscrimination obligations already required, the GATT Contracting Parties negotiated the Agreement on Technical Barriers to Trade, often called the "Standards Code." This Tokyo Round agreement from 1979 disciplined parties' mandatory specifications ("technical regulations") for products by requiring them to use multilaterally agreed standards as a basis for national measures. It also included nondiscrimination provisions similar to the GATT's most favored nation and national treatment obligations. Parties were also required to ensure that any technical regulation or standard did not constitute an "unnecessary obstacle to international trade." This test, however, was not clearly articulated. Moreover, the Standards Code only applied to those parties that adopted it, and only 45 parties, including the European Union, did so. To bring more coherency to the control of product standards, the Uruguay Round negotiators added a substantially revised Agreement on Technical Barriers to Trade—the TBT Agreement, as it is now known—to the package of WTO agreements that are binding on all WTO members.

Because national product standards are ubiquitous but often not uniform from one country to another, the challenge of making a product for multiple markets with slightly vary-

351

ing standards pervades industry. A single product, such as an electric cable, may require compliance with numerous product standards, including the cable's flammability, flexibility, and permeability to water, as well as the insulating material that may be used, the thickness of the insulation, the electrical properties of the insulation, and the chemicals that may be released into the air when the cable burns. Several of these product standards have obvious importance to public safety and welfare, such as flammability and the chemicals released into the air. At the same time, costs to manufacturers increase dramatically if these product standards differ among even a few countries, because meeting different specifications requires different production runs and more complex logistics must then assure that the differing products reach the proper markets. In the face of these costs, manufacturers may choose to avoid markets with unusual or substantially different product standards. As a result, product standards can greatly affect market access and competitiveness. Clever domestic businesses and government bureaucrats can use this market effect to craft product standards according to local manufacturing practices in ways designed to discourage foreign competitors.

To ward off such protectionist strategies and capture market efficiencies, the TBT Agreement encourages harmonization of standards. International harmonization facilitates trade and enhances market efficiencies by avoiding the costs of producing slightly different goods for diverse markets. Instead of adjusting production to meet the product standards of two, or a dozen, countries, full harmonization would give manufacturers just one set of product standards to meet. Consumers will benefit from the reduced costs associated with market efficiencies. They also benefit from the harmonization of the features and parts of competing products, such as screw threads or DVDs, because harmonization widens competition and facilitates the availability and interchangeability of products or parts.

Despite these benefits, harmonization is not a panacea. As discussed more fully in Chapter 1, a variety of differences in ecological, economic, and social circumstances explain why different countries establish different environmental laws and regulations. In addition, those economists who assess global trade flows and economic welfare note that harmonization may be inefficient if it relates to geographic or other factors that give countries a comparative advantage in certain products. Environmental advocates, for their part, worry that the move toward international standards will drive environmental and human health standards downward, at least in their countries.

This chapter introduces the TBT Agreement and the harmonization of product standards. It also explores the implications of the TBT Agreement for the use of ecolabels. The TBT Agreement specifically covers packaging and labeling specifications, which are considered product standards because they identify products based on their characteristics. A variety of legal questions arise about ecolabels, many of which are voluntary and many of which focus on the way the product was produced rather than the intrinsic characteristics of the product.

II. The Agreement on Technical Barriers to Trade

The most favored nation (MFN) and national treatment obligations of the General Agreement on Tariffs and Trade (GATT) limit the use of many nontariff barriers by ensuring that all foreign products are treated equally and that foreign products are treated no less favorably than domestic products. However, strict adherence to GATT's nondiscrimination obligations could still produce unwanted market inefficiencies of the kind described in the introduction above. The TBT Agreement disciplines the use of product standards to help maintain GATT protections against discriminatory national measures.

A. The Purpose and Structure of the TBT Agreement

The TBT Agreement extends its substantive and procedural requirements to both "technical regulations" and "standards." In this usage, "technical regulations" are mandatory, "standards" are voluntary. Both are defined as documents that lay down product characteristics or their related processes and production methods. They may also relate to labeling, packaging, and other product characteristics. (The remainder of this chapter uses "technical regulation" and "standard" as defined by the TBT Agreement. However, it sometimes uses, as do the authors of the excerpts in this chapter, the word "standard" in its general sense of either a mandatory rule or voluntary guideline relating to product characteristics.)

Beyond its application to both technical regulations and standards, the TBT Agreement extends its reach throughout the entire standard setting process. The provisions of the TBT Agreement can be placed in the following categories:

1. Foremost, the TBT Agreement adopts rules regarding the preparation, adoption, and application of technical regulations (found in Articles 2 and 3) and standards (found in the "Code of Good Practice" of Annex 3 of the TBT Agreement). The majority of this chapter focuses on these rules.

2. *Conformity Assessment.* The TBT Agreement establishes rules for *conformity assessment*—those procedures used to determine whether a product complies with relevant technical regulations or standards (Articles 5 to 8).

3. *Transparency.* The TBT Agreement establishes requirements for sharing information about technical regulations, standards, and conformity assessment procedures (Article 10). These requirements, including notification and publication of technical regulations and standards, provide WTO members and producers with extensive information about the technical regulations and standards of member governments. For example, a search of the WTO's TBT Information Management System of technical regulations and standards relating to fish yielded 14,251 responses.

4. *Equivalence.* Because the technical regulations and standards of many countries may be similar but not the same, the TBT Agreement requires WTO members to give "positive consideration" to accepting as equivalent the technical regulations from other members. This concept is known as "equivalence."

5. *Mutual Recognition.* Similarly, the conformity assessment procedures of various countries may be the same or similar. As a result, the TBT Agreement requires WTO members to accept the results of conformity assessment procedures from other members, even when those procedures differ from their own, provided they are satisfied that those procedures offer an assurance of conformity with applicable technical regulations or standards equivalent to their own procedures. Equivalence and mutual recognition are designed to promote consistency with the technical regulations and standards of other members.

A few points are worth noting by way of introduction. First, despite the voluntary nature of standards, the TBT Agreement applies similar, mandatory rules to the adoption of both technical regulations and standards and to the conformity assessment procedures that are used to ensure compliance with technical regulations and standards. These rules blend core GATT concepts with new harmonization concepts. For example, in the preparation and application of technical regulations, standards, and conformity assessment procedures, members must act consistently with most favored nation and national treatment principles. In addition, technical regulations, standards, and conformity assessment procedures "shall not be more trade-restrictive than necessary to fulfill a legitimate objective, taking account of the risks nonfulfillment would create."

Second, consistent with the goal of harmonization, the TBT Agreement requires WTO members to base their technical regulations on international standards adopted by international standardizing bodies. Nonetheless, when a member determines that the relevant international standard will be "ineffective or inappropriate" for fulfilling legitimate objectives, it does not need to use that standard. Importantly, the TBT Agreement defines "legitimate objectives" broadly to include environmental and human health objectives, giving members a wide range of possible reasons for adopting technical regulations that differ from the international standard. In any case, a member must ensure that its technical regulation does not constitute an unnecessary obstacle to trade.

Third, the applicability of these obligations with respect to standards varies depending on the governmental or nongovernmental nature of the standard setting body. For governmental standard setting bodies and those bodies "subject to the control" of the central government, the TBT Agreement's requirements apply directly. They do not apply directly to local government and nongovernmental bodies. WTO members, however, must "take such reasonable measures as may be available" to ensure that local governmental and nongovernmental bodies adopt the TBT Agreement's Code of Good Practice.

The materials that follow emphasize those rules that apply to technical regulations. Nonetheless, because many governments frequently adopt voluntary standards, we highlight any differences between the rules that apply to standards. In addition, the disputes that have arisen under the TBT Agreement have all related to the adoption of technical regulations. Thus, we focus on those rules as opposed to those applying to conformity assessment procedures, despite the obvious importance of those procedures.

The Agreement on Technical Barriers to Trade

Members, * * *

Recognizing the important contribution that international standards and conformity assessment systems can make ... by improving efficiency of production and facilitating the conduct of international trade; * * *

Desiring however to ensure that technical regulations and standards, including packaging, marking and labelling requirements, and procedures for assessment of conformity with technical regulations and standards do not create unnecessary obstacles to international trade;

Recognizing that no country should be prevented from taking measures necessary to ensure the quality of its exports, or for the protection of human, animal or plant life or health, of the environment, or for the prevention of deceptive practices, at the levels it considers appropriate, subject to the requirement that they are not applied in a manner which would constitute a means of arbitrary or unjustifiable discrimination between countries where the same conditions prevail or a disguised restriction on international trade, and are otherwise in accordance with the provisions of this Agreement; * * *

Hereby agree as follows:

Article 1 — General Provisions * * *

1.3 All products, including industrial and agricultural products, shall be subject to the provisions of this Agreement. * * *

1.5 The provisions of this Agreement do not apply to sanitary and phytosanitary measures as defined in Annex A of the Agreement on the Application of Sanitary and Phytosanitary Measures. * * *

Article 2 — Preparation, Adoption and Application of Technical Regulations by Central Government Bodies

With respect to their central government bodies:

2.1 Members shall ensure that in respect of technical regulations, products imported from the territory of any Member shall be accorded treatment no less favourable than that accorded to like products of national origin and to like products originating in any other country.

2.2 Members shall ensure that technical regulations are not prepared, adopted or applied with a view to or with the effect of creating unnecessary obstacles to international trade. For this purpose, technical regulations shall not be more trade-restrictive than necessary to fulfill a legitimate objective, taking account of the risks non-fulfillment would create. Such legitimate objectives are, *inter alia*: national security requirements; the prevention of deceptive practices; protection of human health or safety, animal or plant life or health, or the environment. In assessing such risks, relevant elements of consideration are, *inter alia*: available scientific and technical information, related processing technology or intended end-uses of products.

2.3 Technical regulations shall not be maintained if the circumstances or objectives giving rise to their adoption no longer exist or if the changed circumstances or objectives can be addressed in a less trade-restrictive manner.

2.4 Where technical regulations are required and relevant international standards exist or their completion is imminent, Members shall use them, or the relevant parts of them, as a basis for their technical regulations except when such international standards or relevant parts would be an ineffective or inappropriate means for the fulfillment of the legitimate objectives pursued, for instance because of fundamental climatic or geographical factors or fundamental technological problems.

2.5 A Member preparing, adopting or applying a technical regulation which may have a significant effect on trade of other Members shall, upon the request of another Member, explain the justification for that technical regulation in terms of the provisions of paragraphs 2 to 4. Whenever a technical regulation is prepared, adopted or applied for one of the legitimate objectives explicitly mentioned in paragraph 2, and is in accordance with relevant international standards, it shall be rebuttably presumed not to create an unnecessary obstacle to international trade. * * *

Annex 1—Terms and Their Definitions for the Purpose of This Agreement * * *

For the purpose of this Agreement, however, the following definitions shall apply:

1. Technical regulation

Document which lays down product characteristics or their related processes and production methods, including the applicable administrative provisions, with which compliance is mandatory. It may also include or deal exclusively with terminology, symbols, packaging, marking or labelling requirements as they apply to a product, process or production method. * * *

2. Standard

Document approved by a recognized body, that provides, for common and repeated use, rules, guidelines or characteristics for products or related processes and production methods, with which compliance is not mandatory. It may also include or deal exclusively with terminology, symbols, packaging, marking or labeling requirements as they apply to a product, process or production method.

Explanatory note

The terms as defined in ISO/IEC Guide 2 cover products, processes and services. This Agreement deals only with technical regulations, standards and conformity assessment procedures related to products or processes and production methods. Standards as defined by ISO/IEC Guide 2 may be mandatory or voluntary. For the purpose of this Agreement standards are defined as voluntary and technical regulations as mandatory documents. Standards prepared by the international standardization community are based on consensus. This Agreement covers also documents that are not based on consensus.

Questions and Discussion

1. Familiarize yourself with the basics of the TBT Agreement. What is the distinction between a "standard" and a "regulation"? What substantive obligations of the TBT Agreement differ significantly from the GATT? What triggers the TBT Agreement? Do we need a comparison between "like products"?

B. The Scope of the TBT Agreement

Environmental advocates quickly recognized the potential relevance of the TBT Agreement to environmental matters. First, they feared that the TBT Agreement's call for harmonization would threaten to strip governments of another component of their regulatory autonomy with respect to technical regulations. The *Tuna/Dolphin* and *Shrimp/Turtle* decisions had already limited a country's authority to impose import restrictions on a product based on the way it was produced, but those decisions made clear that governments could regulate industries and products produced within their own territories as they saw fit. Now the TBT Agreement seemed to take away that right. For example, if an appropriate international body defined "organic," would a WTO member need to bring its definition of "organic" into conformity with those international definitions or otherwise meet the requirements of the TBT Agreement? What if the international standard was less strict than the domestic standard?

Second, environmental advocates worried that the scope of the TBT Agreement would affect the use of ecolabels. Many WTO members had turned to ecolabeling as a way to inform consumers of the environmental soundness of various products. Because these labels did not restrict trade, environmental advocates and some WTO members believed that they complied with the GATT's nondiscrimination requirements and prohibition against quantitative restrictions. The TBT Agreement, however, clearly applied to labeling requirements (although we will see it is not clear which labeling requirements). Now ecolabels could run afoul not only of the TBT Agreement's GATT-like nondiscrimination obligations, but also its requirement to base technical requirements on international standards.

The broad application of the TBT Agreement relating to environmental matters other than labels did not become apparent until the *EC-Asbestos* case, in which Canada challenged France's ban on the importation and domestic sale of asbestos fibers and certain products containing asbestos. Although the Appellate Body decided this case on Article III grounds (*see* pages 191–199), it also made some important conclusions concerning the scope of the TBT Agreement. The broad scope of the TBT Agreement was affirmed in *EC-Sardines,* when Peru successfully challenged a labeling regulation of the European Communities that limited the use of the term "sardines" when marketing certain fish products.

European Communities-Measures Affecting Asbestos and Asbestos-Containing Products

Appellate Body Report, WT/DS135/AB/R (adopted Apr. 5, 2001)

67. The heart of the definition of a "technical regulation" is that a "document" must "lay down"—that is, set forth, stipulate or provide—"product *characteristics*." The word "characteristic" has a number of synonyms that are helpful in understanding the ordinary meaning of that word, in this context. Thus, the "characteristics" of a product include, in our view, any objectively definable "features," "qualities," "attributes," or other "distinguishing mark" of a product. Such "characteristics" might relate, *inter alia*, to a product's composition, size, shape, colour, texture, hardness, tensile strength, flammability, conductivity, density, or viscosity. In the definition of a "technical regulation" in Annex 1.1, the *TBT Agreement* itself gives certain examples of "product characteristics"— "terminology, symbols, packaging, marking or labelling requirements." These examples indicate that "product characteristics" include, not only features and qualities intrinsic to the product itself, but also related "characteristics," such as the means of identification, the presentation and the appearance of a product. In addition, according to the definition in Annex 1.1 of the *TBT Agreement*, a "technical regulation" may set forth the "applicable administrative provisions" for products which have certain "characteristics." Further, we note that the definition of a "technical regulation" provides that such a regulation "may also include or deal *exclusively* with terminology, symbols, packaging, marking, or labelling requirements." (emphasis added) The use here of the word "exclusively" and the disjunctive word "or" indicates that a "technical regulation" may be confined to laying down only one or a few "product characteristics."

68. The definition of a "technical regulation" in Annex 1.1 of the *TBT Agreement* also states that "*compliance*" with the "product characteristics" laid down in the

"document" must be "*mandatory.*" A "technical regulation" must, in other words, regulate the "characteristics" of products in a binding or compulsory fashion. It follows that, with respect to products, a "technical regulation" has the effect of *prescribing* or *imposing* one or more "characteristics" — "features," "qualities," "attributes," or other "distinguishing mark."

69. "Product characteristics" may, in our view, be prescribed or imposed with respect to products in either a positive or a negative form. That is, the document may provide, positively, that products *must possess* certain "characteristics," or the document may require, negatively, that products *must not possess* certain "characteristics." In both cases, the legal result is the same: the document "lays down" certain binding "characteristics" for products, in one case affirmatively, and in the other by negative implication.

70. A "technical regulation" must, of course, be applicable to an *identifiable* product, or group of products. Otherwise, enforcement of the regulation will, in practical terms, be impossible. This consideration also underlies the formal obligation, in Article 2.9.2 of the *TBT Agreement*, for Members to notify other Members, through the WTO Secretariat, "of the *products to be covered*" by a proposed "technical regulation." (emphasis added) Clearly, compliance with this obligation requires identification of the product coverage of a technical regulation. However, in contrast to what the Panel suggested, this does not mean that a "technical regulation" must apply to "*given*" products which are actually *named*, *identified* or *specified* in the regulation. (emphasis added) Although the *TBT Agreement* clearly applies to "products" generally, nothing in the text of that Agreement suggests that those products need be named or otherwise *expressly* identified in a "technical regulation." Moreover, there may be perfectly sound administrative reasons for formulating a "technical regulation" in a way that does *not* expressly identify products by name, but simply makes them identifiable — for instance, through the "characteristic" that is the subject of regulation.

71. With these considerations in mind, we examine whether the measure at issue is a "technical regulation." Decree 96-1133 aims primarily at the regulation of a named product, asbestos. The first and second paragraphs of Article 1 of the Decree impose a prohibition on asbestos *fibres*, as such. This prohibition on these *fibres* does not, *in itself*, prescribe or impose any "characteristics" on asbestos fibres, but simply bans them in their natural state. Accordingly, if this measure consisted *only* of a prohibition on asbestos *fibres*, it might not constitute a "technical regulation."

72. There is, however, more to the measure than this prohibition on asbestos *fibres*. It is not contested that asbestos fibres have no known use in their raw mineral form. Thus, the regulation of asbestos can *only* be achieved through the regulation of *products that contain asbestos fibres*. This, too, is addressed by the Decree before us. An integral and essential aspect of the measure is the regulation of "*products containing asbestos fibres*," which are also prohibited by Article 1, paragraphs I and II of the Decree. It is important to note here that, although formulated *negatively* — products containing asbestos are prohibited — the measure, in this respect, effectively prescribes or imposes certain objective features, qualities or "characteristics" on *all* products. That is, in effect, the measure provides that *all* products must *not* contain asbestos fibres. Although this prohibition against products containing asbestos applies to a large number of products, and although it is, indeed, true that the products to which this prohibition ap-

plies cannot be determined from the terms of the measure itself, it seems to us that the products covered by the measure are *identifiable*: all products must be asbestos free; any products containing asbestos are prohibited. We also observe that compliance with the prohibition against products containing asbestos is mandatory and is, indeed, enforceable through criminal sanctions.

73. Articles 2, 3 and 4 of the Decree also contain certain exceptions to the prohibitions found in Article 1 of the Decree. As we have already noted, these exceptions would have no meaning in the absence of the rest of the measure because they define the scope of the prohibitions in the measure. The nature of these exceptions is to *permit* the use of certain products containing chrysotile asbestos fibres, subject to compliance with strict administrative requirements. The scope of the exceptions is determined by an "exhaustive list" of products that are permitted to contain chrysotile asbestos fibres, which is promulgated and reviewed annually by a government Minister. The inclusion of a product in the list of exceptions depends on the absence of an acceptable alternative fibre for incorporation into a particular product, and the demonstrable provision of "all technical guarantees of safety." Any person seeking to avail himself of these limited exceptions must provide a detailed justification to the authorities, complete with necessary supporting documentation concerning "the state of scientific and technological progress." Compliance with these administrative requirements is mandatory.

74. Like the Panel, we consider that, through these exceptions, the measure sets out the "applicable administrative provisions, with which compliance is mandatory" for products with certain objective "characteristics." The exceptions apply to a narrowly defined group of products with particular "characteristics." Although these products are not named, the measure provides criteria which permit their identification, both by reference to the qualities the excepted products must possess and by reference to the list promulgated by the Minister.

75. Viewing the measure as an integrated whole, we see that it lays down "characteristics" for all products that might contain asbestos, and we see also that it lays down the "applicable administrative provisions" for certain products containing chrysotile asbestos fibres which are excluded from the prohibitions in the measure. Accordingly, we find that the measure is a "document" which "lays down product characteristics ... including the applicable administrative provisions, with which compliance is mandatory." For these reasons, we conclude that the measure constitutes a "technical regulation" under the *TBT Agreement*. * * *

77. We note, however—and we emphasize—that this does not mean that *all* internal measures covered by Article III:4 of the GATT 1994 "affecting" the "sale, offering for sale, purchase, transportation, distribution or use" of a product are, necessarily, "technical regulations" under the *TBT Agreement*. Rather, we rule only that this particular measure, the Decree at stake, falls within the definition of a "technical regulation" given in Annex 1.1 of that Agreement.

European Communities-Trade Description of Sardines

Appellate Body Report, WT/DS231/AB/R (adopted Oct. 23, 2002)

[In this case, the European Communities defended European Council Regulation (EEC) No. 2136/89, which established marketing standards for preserved sardines and permitted the term "sardines" to apply only to the species *Sardina pilchardus Walbaum*. The Regulation also required that "sardines" be sterilized and pre-packaged in a hermetically sealed container. Peru, supported by the United States, Venezuela, and other countries, challenged the labelling requirement as inconsistent with the TBT Agreement.

Peru argued that Codex Alimentarius, an international standards organization, had established an international standard for preserved sardines and sardine-type products that regulated presentation, hygiene, and labelling, among other things. This standard, CODEX STAN 94-1981, Rev.1-1995 ("Codex Stan 94"), covers preserved sardines or sardine-type products prepared from 21 fish species. Codex Stan 94 limits the use of the term "sardines" to preserved *Sardina pilchardus Walbaum*. However, it allowed similar species, such as preserved *Sardinops sagax sagax,* to be labeled as "sardines" provided that the label also indicates where the species was caught. Thus, *Sardinops sagax sagax* caught in Peruvian waters could be labeled "Peruvian sardines" or "Pacific sardines."

The European Communities defended its regulation by distinguishing "naming" from labeling requirements; as a naming regulation, it did not constitute a document that lays down product characteristics. It also contended that the EC Regulation is a "technical regulation" only for preserved *Sardina pilchardus*, and that preserved *Sardinops sagax* is not an identifiable product under the EC Regulation.]

176. [I]n *EC-Asbestos* ... we set out *three criteria* that a document must meet to fall within the definition of "technical regulation" in the *TBT Agreement. First,* the document must apply to an identifiable product or group of products. The *identifiable* product or group of products need not, however, be expressly *identified* in the document. *Second,* the document must lay down one or more characteristics of the product. These product characteristics may be intrinsic, or they may be related to the product. They may be prescribed or imposed in either a positive or a negative form. *Third,* compliance with the product characteristics must be mandatory. * * *

181. The European Communities argues that the Panel erred in failing to acknowledge that the EC Regulation uses the term "preserved sardines" to mean — exclusively — preserved *Sardina pilchardus*. The European Communities is of the view that preserved *Sardina pilchardus* and preserved *Sardinops sagax* are not like products. The European Communities reasons that preserved *Sardinops sagax* can neither be an identified nor an identifiable product under the EC Regulation.

182. In our view, the Panel correctly found that the EC Regulation is applicable to an identified product, and that the identified product is "preserved sardines." This is abundantly clear from a plain reading of the EC Regulation itself. The EC Regulation is entitled "Council Regulation (EEC) 2136/89 of 21 June 1989 Laying Down Common Marketing Standards for *Preserved Sardines*." (emphasis added) Article 1, which sets forth the scope of the EC Regulation, states that "[t]his Regulation defines the standards governing the marketing of *preserved sardines* in the Community." (emphasis added) Article 2 states that "[o]nly products meeting the following requirements may be marketed as *preserved sardines*." (emphasis added)

183. This alone, however, does not dispose of the European Communities' argument, as the European Communities reproaches the Panel for failing to ac-

knowledge that the EC Regulation uses the term "preserved sardines" to mean—exclusively—preserved *Sardina pilchardus*. We observe that the EC Regulation does not expressly identify *Sardinops sagax*. However, this does not necessarily mean that *Sardinops sagax* is not an *identifiable* product. As we stated in *EC-Asbestos*, a product need not be expressly identified in the document for it to be *identifiable*.

184. Even if we were to accept, for the sake of argument, the European Communities' contention that the term "preserved sardines" in the EC Regulation refers exclusively to preserved *Sardina pilchardus*, the EC Regulation would still be applicable to a range of *identifiable* products beyond *Sardina pilchardus*. This is because preserved products made, for example, of *Sardinops sagax* are, by virtue of the EC Regulation, *prohibited* from being identified and marketed under an appellation including the term "sardines."

185. As we explained in *EC-Asbestos*, the requirement that a "technical regulation" be applicable to *identifiable* products relates to aspects of compliance and enforcement, because it would be impossible to comply with or enforce a "technical regulation" without knowing to what the regulation applied. As the Panel record shows, the EC Regulation has been enforced against preserved fish products imported into Germany containing *Sardinops sagax*. This confirms that the EC Regulation is applicable to preserved *Sardinops sagax*, and demonstrates that preserved *Sardinops sagax* is an *identifiable product* for purposes of the EC Regulation. Indeed, the European Communities admits that the EC Regulation is applicable to *Sardinops sagax*, when it states in its appellant's submission that "[T]he only legal consequence of the [EC] Regulation for preserved *Sardinops sagax* is that they may not be called 'preserved sardines.'"

186. Therefore, we reject the contention of the European Communities that preserved *Sardinops sagax* is not an identifiable product under the EC Regulation.

187. Next, we examine whether the EC Regulation meets the second criterion of a "technical regulation," which is that it must be a document that lays down product characteristics. According to the European Communities, Article 2 of the EC Regulation does not lay down product characteristics; rather, it sets out a "naming" rule. The European Communities argues that, although the definition of "technical regulation" in the *TBT Agreement* covers labelling requirements, it does not extend to "naming" rules. Therefore, the European Communities asserts that Article 2 of the EC Regulation is not a "technical regulation." * * *

190. We do not find it necessary, in this case, to decide whether the definition of "technical regulation" in the *TBT Agreement* makes a distinction between "naming" and labelling. This question is irrelevant to the issue before us. As we stated earlier, the EC Regulation expressly identifies a product, namely "preserved sardines." Further, Article 2 of the EC Regulation provides that, to be marketed as "preserved sardines," products must be prepared exclusively from fish of the species *Sardina pilchardus*. We are of the view that this requirement—to be prepared exclusively from fish of the species *Sardina pilchardus*—is a product characteristic "intrinsic to" preserved sardines that is laid down by the EC Regulation. Thus, we agree with the Panel's finding in this regard that:

> ... one product characteristic required by Article 2 of the EC Regulation is that preserved sardines must be prepared exclusively from fish of the species *Sardina pilchardus*. This product characteristic must be met for the

product to be "marketed as preserved sardines and under the trade description referred to in Article 7" of the EC Regulation. We consider that the requirement to use exclusively *Sardina pilchardus* is a product characteristic as it objectively defines features and qualities of preserved sardines for the purposes of their "market[ing] as preserved sardines and under the trade description referred to in Article 7" of the EC Regulation.

191. In any event, as we said in *EC-Asbestos*, a "means of identification" *is* a product characteristic. A name clearly identifies a product; indeed, the European Communities concedes that a name is a "means of identification." As the following excerpt from the Panel Report illustrates, the European Communities itself underscored the important role that a "name" plays as a "means of identification" when it argued before the Panel that one of the objectives pursued by the European Communities through the EC Regulation is to provide precise information to avoid misleading the consumer:

> The European Communities argues that the provisions of its Regulation laying down minimum quality standards, harmonizing the ways in which the product may be presented and regulating the indications to be contained on the label, all serve to facilitate comparisons between competing products. It further submits that some of these objectives are pursued by the Regulation at issue in conjunction with EC Directive 2000/13. The European Communities argues that this is particularly true of the name; *accurate and precise names allow products to be compared with their true equivalents rather than with substitutes and imitations whereas inaccurate and imprecise names reduce transparency, cause confusion, mislead the consumer*, allow products to benefit from the reputation of other different products, give rise to unfair competition and reduce the quality and variety of products available in trade and ultimately for the consumer. (emphasis added)

192. Before concluding on this second criterion and proceeding to the third criterion in the definition of "technical regulation," we observe that, although the European Communities argued before the Panel that Article 2 of the EC Regulation could not be analyzed in isolation, on appeal, the European Communities asks us to focus our attention exclusively on whether Article 2, taken by itself, lays down product characteristics. As the Panel correctly points out, in *EC-Asbestos*, we stated that "the proper legal character of the measure at issue cannot be determined unless the measure is examined as a whole." With this in mind, we observe that the Panel analyzed other articles of the EC Regulation and found that those, too, lay down product characteristics. * * *

194. The third and final criterion that a document must fulfill to meet the definition of "technical regulation" in the *TBT Agreement* is that compliance must be mandatory. The European Communities does not contest that compliance with the EC Regulation is mandatory. We also find that it is mandatory.

195. We, therefore, uphold the Panel's finding, in paragraph 7.35 of the Panel Report, that the EC Regulation is a "technical regulation" for purposes of the *TBT Agreement*, because it meets the three criteria we set out in *EC-Asbestos* as necessary to satisfy the definition of a "technical regulation" under the *TBT Agreement*.

Questions and Discussion

1. Evaluate the reasoning of the Appellate Body in both *Asbestos* and *Sardines*. Which aspects of a law or regulation will be evaluated to determine whether it constitutes a "technical regulation"?

2. What is the effect of interpreting "technical regulation" broadly as the Appellate Body did in *Asbestos* and *Sardines*? The Appellate Body in *Asbestos* says that not all prohibitions will constitute a technical regulation. Perhaps that is so, but in light of *Asbestos* and *Sardines*, which prohibitions or restrictions are *not* technical regulations? For example, could the U.S. requirements for establishing baseline pollutant levels for gasoline at issue in *Reformulated Gasoline* have been analyzed under the TBT Agreement?

3. Can a product in its natural state be a "product characteristic," and thus a technical regulation, once it becomes subject to regulation? The Appellate Body in *Asbestos* (para. 71) suggests no, but the Appellate Body in *Sardines* (para. 190) concludes that, because the EC Regulation defines "preserved sardines" to mean only *Sardina pilchardus*, then *Sardina pilchardus* is a product characteristic "intrinsic to" preserved sardines. A law regulating a product in its natural state presumably must identify that product. For example, the U.S. Endangered Species Act prohibits the importation for commercial purposes of African elephants and parts thereof, such as ivory (noncommercial imports for hunting trophies, among other things, are permissible subject to certain management and/or scientific findings). The product has been identified — *Loxodonta africana*. What more, if anything, is needed for the prohibition against imports of African elephants and ivory to be deemed a technical regulation? Does it matter that two other species of elephant exist, the Asian elephant (*Elephas maximus*) and the Forest elephant (*Loxodonta cyclotis*)?

4. The Appellate Body in *Sardines* affirmed the Panel's conclusion that the TBT Agreement applied to technical regulations adopted before but which continue in force after the TBT Agreement entered into force. Thus, the TBT Agreement does not apply retroactively *per se*, but WTO members have an obligation to monitor their technical regulations for consistency with the TBT Agreement. *Sardines*, Appellate Body Report, at paras. 196–216.

5. The Appellate Body defined "technical regulation" in *Sardines* and *Asbestos*, but presumably its conclusions also apply to the definition of "standard", due to the nearly identical language used to define them (other than technical regulations being mandatory and standards being voluntary). Thus, a "standard," while being voluntary, must identify a product and may prescribe or impose product characteristics in a positive or a negative form. A second issue, what constitutes a "relevant international standard" upon which a member must base its technical regulation, is a question addressed in the excerpt from *EC-Sardines* that follows in Section C.

6. *Processes and Production Methods (PPMs)*. The definitions of "technical regulation" and "standard" clearly include product-related PPMs. Solely in the context of ecolabeling, whether they also include nonproduct-related PPMs is a matter of intense debate. This issue will be addressed in Section III.C.2.b below (pages 403–05).

C. Toward Harmonization

Look again at Article 2.4 of the TBT Agreement and its requirement for WTO members to base their technical regulations on international standards. Paragraph F of the

Code of Good Practice imposes the same obligation on standardizing bodies when adopting standards. These provisions clearly point toward harmonization. Yet, these provisions leave a number of questions unanswered concerning the degree to which members must harmonize their technical regulations and standards. Which organizations can adopt relevant international standards that members must use? What is a relevant international standard? What is the full range of "legitimate objectives" that permits a member to deviate from international standards? How can a member show that the international standard is "ineffective or inappropriate to achieve a legitimate objective"? We return to the *Sardines* dispute to answer some of these questions.

1. The Sardines Case and Relevant International Standards

Recall that the *Sardines* dispute involved an EC Regulation that allowed only *Sardina pilchardus Walbaum* to be marketed as "sardines." In contrast, Codex Stan 94, an international standard approved by Codex Alimentarius, allowed some other species to be labeled as sardines if combined with the name of a country, geographic area, species, or common name of the species in accordance with the law and custom of that country in which the product is sold. Thus, *Sardinops sagax* could be marketed as "Peruvian sardines" or perhaps "Pacific sardines."

The EC did not contest that Codex Alimentarius is an international standardization body, and that it is a "recognized body" for TBT Agreement purposes. The EU challenged the *Sardines* Panel finding that Codex Stan 94 was a "relevant international standard" and asserted that only standards adopted by international bodies by consensus are "relevant international standards" under Article 2.4 of the TBT Agreement. In the alternative, the EU argued that, even if Codex Stan 94 were considered an international standard, it is not a "*relevant* international standard" because its product coverage is different from that of the EU Regulation. The EU contended that the EU Regulation covers only preserved sardines, while Codex Stan 94 covers that product as well as "sardine-type" products.

European Communities-Trade Description of Sardines
Appellate Body Report, WT/DS231/AB/R (adopted Oct. 23, 2002)

VII. The Characterization of Codex Stan 94 as a "Relevant International Standard"

[The Appellate Body affirmed the Panel's decision that a standard does not need to be approved by consensus, because the explanatory note to the definition of "standard" explicitly recognizes that the TBT Agreement covers "documents that are not based on consensus."]

228. We turn now to examine the European Communities' argument that Codex Stan 94 is not a "relevant international standard" because its product coverage is different from that of the EC Regulation.

229. In analyzing the merits of this argument, the Panel first noted that the ordinary meaning of the term "relevant" is "bearing upon or relating to the matter in hand; pertinent." The Panel reasoned that, to be a "relevant international standard," Codex Stan 94 would have to bear upon, relate to, or be pertinent to the EC Regulation....

230. We do not disagree with the Panel's interpretation of the ordinary meaning of the term "relevant." Nor does the European Communities. Instead, the

European Communities argues that, although the EC Regulation deals *only* with preserved sardines — understood to mean exclusively preserved *Sardina pilchardus* — Codex Stan 94 *also covers* other preserved fish that are "sardine-type."

231. We are not persuaded by this argument. First, even if we accepted that the EC Regulation relates only to preserved *Sardina pilchardus*, which we do not, the fact remains that section 6.1.1(i) of Codex Stan 94 also relates to preserved *Sardina pilchardus*. Therefore, Codex Stan 94 can be said to bear upon, relate to, or be pertinent to the EC Regulation because both refer to preserved *Sardina pilchardus*.

232. Second, we have already concluded that, although the EC Regulation expressly mentions only *Sardina pilchardus*, it has legal consequences for other fish species that could be sold as preserved sardines, including preserved *Sardinops sagax*. Codex Stan 94 covers 20 fish species in addition to *Sardina pilchardus*. These other species also are legally affected by the exclusion in the EC Regulation. Therefore, we conclude that Codex Stan 94 bears upon, relates to, or is pertinent to the EC Regulation.

233. For all these reasons, we uphold the Panel's finding, in paragraph 7.70 of the Panel Report, that Codex Stan 94 is a "relevant international standard" for purposes of Article 2.4 of the *TBT Agreement*.

VIII. Whether Codex Stan 94 Was Used "As a Basis For" the EC Regulation

[The Appellate Body then turned to whether the European Communities used Codex Stan 94 "as a basis for" its Regulation, as required by Article 2.4 of the TBT Agreement. Section 6.1.1(ii) of Codex Stan 94 provides: "The name of the product shall be: ... (ii) "X sardines" of a country, a geographic area, the species, or the common name of the species in accordance with the law and custom of the country in which the product is sold, and in a manner not to mislead the consumer." The European Communities argued that the phrase "the common name of the species in accordance with the law and custom of the country in which the product is sold" is a self-standing option for "naming," independent of the formula "X sardines" and that each country has the option of choosing between "X sardines" and the common name of the species.

The Panel and the Appellate Body, however, agreed with Peru that this provision contains four alternatives and that each alternative envisaged the use of the term "sardines" combined with the (1) name of a country; (2) name of a geographic area; (3) name of the species; or (4) the common name of the species in accordance with the law and custom of the country in which the product is sold.]

241. On appeal, the European Communities contends that the Panel erred in finding that Codex Stan 94 was not used "as a basis for" the EC Regulation. The European Communities submits that the EC Regulation is "based on" Codex Stan 94 "because it used as a basis paragraph 6.1.1(i) of the Codex standard", and because this paragraph reserves the term "sardines" exclusively for *Sardina pilchardus*. According to the European Communities, the term "'as a basis' should involve a consideration of the texts as a whole, examining the basic structure of the domestic measure and deciding whether the international standard has been used in its preparation and adoption." The European Communities adds that, in order to determine whether a relevant international standard, or a part of it,

is used "as a basis for" a technical regulation, the criterion to apply is not, as the Panel suggested, whether the standard is the principal constituent or the fundamental principle of the technical regulation, but, rather, whether there is a "rational relationship" between the standard and the technical regulation on the substantive aspects of the standard in question.

242. ... In *EC–Hormones*, we stated that "based on" does not mean the same thing as "conform to". In that appeal, we articulated the ordinary meaning of the term "based on", as used in Article 3.1 of the *SPS Agreement* in the following terms:

> A thing is commonly said to be "based on" another thing when the former "stands" or is "founded" or "built" upon or "is supported by" the latter.[150]

> [150] L. Brown (ed.), *The New Shorter Oxford English Dictionary on Historical Principles* (Clarendon Press), Vol. I, p. 187.

The Panel here referred to this conclusion in its analysis of Article 2.4 of the *TBT Agreement*. In our view, the Panel did so correctly, because our approach in *EC–Hormones* is also relevant for the interpretation of Article 2.4 of the *TBT Agreement*.

243. In addition, as we stated earlier, the Panel here used the following definition to establish the ordinary meaning of the term "basis":

> The word "basis" means "the principal constituent of anything, the fundamental principle or theory, as of a system of knowledge".[90]

> [90] [*Webster's New World Dictionary*, (William Collins & World Publishing Co., Inc., 1976)], p. 117.

Informed by our ruling in *EC – Hormones*, and relying on this meaning of the term "basis", the Panel concluded that an international standard is used "as a basis for" a technical regulation when it is used as the principal constituent or fundamental principle for the purpose of enacting the technical regulation.

244. We agree with the Panel's approach. In relying on the ordinary meaning of the term "basis", the Panel rightly followed an approach similar to ours in determining the ordinary meaning of "based on" in *EC – Hormones*. In addition to the definition of "basis" in *Webster's New World Dictionary* that was used by the Panel, we note, as well, the similar definitions for "basis" that are set out in the *The New Shorter Oxford English Dictionary*, and also provide guidance as to the ordinary meaning of the term:

> 3 [t]he main constituent.... 5 [a] thing on which anything is constructed and by which its constitution or operation is determined; a determining principle; a set of underlying or agreed principles.

245. From these various definitions, we would highlight the similar terms "principal constituent", "fundamental principle", "main constituent", and "determining principle" — all of which lend credence to the conclusion that there must be a very strong and very close relationship between two things in order to be able to say that one is "the basis for" the other.

246. The European Communities, however, seems to suggest the need for something different. The European Communities maintains that a "rational relationship" between an international standard and a technical regulation is sufficient to conclude that the former is used "as a basis for" the latter. According to the

European Communities, an examination based on the criterion of the existence of a "rational relationship" focuses on "the qualitative aspect of the substantive relationship that should exist between the relevant international standard and the technical regulation." In response to questioning at the oral hearing, the European Communities added that a "rational relationship" exists when the technical regulation is informed in its overall scope by the international standard.

247. Yet, we see nothing in the text of Article 2.4 to support the European Communities' view, nor has the European Communities pointed to any such support. Moreover, the European Communities does not offer any arguments relating to the context or the object and purpose of that provision that would support its argument that the existence of a "rational relationship" is the appropriate criterion for determining whether something has been used "as a basis for" something else.

248. We see no need here to define in general the nature of the relationship that must exist for an international standard to serve "as a basis for" a technical regulation. Here we need only examine this measure to determine if it fulfils this obligation. In our view, it can certainly be said—at a minimum—that something cannot be considered a "basis" for something else if the two are *contradictory*. Therefore, under Article 2.4, if the technical regulation and the international standard *contradict* each other, it cannot properly be concluded that the international standard has been used "as a basis for" the technical regulation.

249. Thus, we need only determine here whether there is a *contradiction* between Codex Stan 94 and the EC Regulation. If there is, we are justified in concluding our analysis with that determination, as the only appropriate conclusion from such a determination would be that the Codex Stan 94 has not been used "as a basis for" the EC Regulation. * * *

257. The effect of Article 2 of the EC Regulation is to prohibit preserved fish products prepared from the 20 species of fish other than *Sardina pilchardus* to which Codex Stan 94 refers—including *Sardinops sagax*—from being identified and marketed under the appellation "sardines," even with one of the four qualifiers set out in the standard. Codex Stan 94, by contrast, permits the use of the term "sardines" with any one of four qualifiers for the identification and marketing of preserved fish products prepared from 20 species of fish other than *Sardina pilchardus*. Thus, the EC Regulation and Codex Stan 94 are manifestly contradictory. To us, the existence of this contradiction confirms that Codex Stan 94 was not used "as a basis for" the EC Regulation. * * *

IX. The Question of the "Ineffectiveness or Inappropriateness" of Codex Stan 94

259. We turn now to the second part of Article 2.4 of the *TBT Agreement*, which provides that members need not use international standards as a basis for their technical regulations "when such international standards or relevant parts would be an ineffective or inappropriate means for the fulfillment of the legitimate objectives pursued." * * *

266. The European Communities appeals the Panel's assignment of the burden of proof under Article 2.4 of the *TBT Agreement*. The European Communities disputes the Panel's conclusion that the burden rests with the European Communities to demonstrate that Codex Stan 94 is an "ineffective or inappropriate" means to fulfill the "legitimate objectives" of the EC Regulation. The European Commu-

nities maintains that the burden of proof rests rather with Peru, as Peru is the party claiming that the measure at issue is inconsistent with WTO obligations.

267. The European Communities also appeals the finding of the Panel that Codex Stan 94 is not "ineffective or inappropriate" to fulfill the "legitimate objectives" of the EC Regulation. In particular, the European Communities argues that the Panel erred in founding its analysis on the factual premise that consumers in the European Communities associate "sardines" exclusively with *Sardina pilchardus*. Furthermore, the European Communities contends that the Panel erred in concluding that the term "sardines," either by itself or when combined with the name of a country or geographic area, is a common name for *Sardinops sagax* in the European Communities. The European Communities also objects to the decision by the Panel to take this conclusion into account in its assessment of whether consumers in the European Communities associate the term "sardines" exclusively with *Sardina pilchardus*.

268. In considering these claims of the European Communities, we will address, first, the question of the burden of proof, and, next, the substantive content of the second part of Article 2.4 of the *TBT Agreement*....

[The Appellate Body reversed the Panel's finding that the European Communities has the burden to demonstrate that Codex Stan 94 is an "ineffective or inappropriate" means to fulfill the "legitimate objectives." The Appellate Body recognized the right of every WTO member to establish for itself the objectives of its technical regulations; this was not an exception to the rules of the TBT Agreement. It also acknowledged that complainant members may face difficulties obtaining information to meet its burden, but that the Article 2.5 affords every other member adequate opportunities to obtain information about these objectives upon request. As such, it held that Peru bears the burden of demonstrating that Codex Stan 94 is an effective and appropriate means to fulfill the "legitimate objectives" pursued by the European Communities through the EC Regulation.]

284. We recall that the second part of Article 2.4 of the *TBT Agreement* reads as follows:

> ... except when such international standards or relevant parts would be an ineffective or inappropriate means for the fulfillment of the legitimate objectives pursued ...

Before ruling on whether Peru met its burden of proof in this case, we must address, successively, the interpretation and the application of the second part of Article 2.4.

1. *The Interpretation of the Second Part of Article 2.4*

285. The interpretation of the second part of Article 2.4 raises two questions: first, the meaning of the term "ineffective or inappropriate means;" and, second, the meaning of the term "legitimate objectives." As to the first question, we noted earlier the Panel's view that the term "ineffective or inappropriate means" refers to two questions—the question of the *effectiveness* of the measure and the question of the *appropriateness* of the measure—and that these two questions, although closely related, are different in nature. The Panel pointed out that the term "ineffective" "refers to something which is not 'having the function of accomplishing,' 'having a result,' or 'brought to bear,' whereas [the term] 'inappro-

priate' refers to something which is not 'specially suitable,' 'proper,' or 'fitting.'"
The Panel also stated that: Thus, in the context of Article 2.4, an ineffective
means is a means which does not have the function of accomplishing the legitimate objective pursued, whereas an inappropriate means is a means which is
not specially suitable for the fulfillment of the legitimate objective pursued.... The
question of effectiveness bears upon the *results* of the means employed, whereas
the question of appropriateness relates more to the *nature* of the means employed. (original emphasis) We agree with the Panel's interpretation.

286. As to the second question, we are of the view that the Panel was also correct in concluding that "the 'legitimate objectives' referred to in Article 2.4 must
be interpreted in the context of Article 2.2," which refers also to "legitimate objectives," and includes a description of what the nature of some such objectives
can be. Two implications flow from the Panel's interpretation. First, the term
"legitimate objectives" in Article 2.4, as the Panel concluded, must cover the objectives explicitly mentioned in Article 2.2, namely: "national security requirements; the prevention of deceptive practices; protection of human health or
safety, animal or plant life or health, or the environment." Second, given the use
of the term "*inter alia*" in Article 2.2, the objectives covered by the term "legitimate objectives" in Article 2.4 extend beyond the list of the objectives specifically mentioned in Article 2.2. Furthermore, we share the view of the Panel that
the second part of Article 2.4 implies that there must be an examination and a
determination on the legitimacy of the objectives of the measure.

2. *The Application of the Second Part of Article 2.4*

287. With respect to the application of the second part of Article 2.4, we begin
by recalling that Peru has the burden of establishing that Codex Stan 94 is an
effective *and* appropriate means for the fulfillment of the "legitimate objectives"
pursued by the European Communities through the EC Regulation. Those "legitimate objectives" are market transparency, consumer protection, and fair
competition. To satisfy this burden of proof, Peru must, at least, have established a *prima facie* case of this claim. If Peru has succeeded in doing so, then
a presumption will have been raised which the European Communities must
have rebutted in order to succeed in its defence. If Peru has established a *prima
facie* case, and if the European Communities has failed to rebut Peru's case effectively, then Peru will have discharged its burden of proof under Article 2.4.
In such an event, Codex Stan 94 must, consistent with the European Communities' obligation under the *TBT Agreement*, be used "as a basis for" any European Communities regulation on the marketing of preserved sardines, because
Codex Stan 94 will have been shown to be both effective and appropriate to fulfill the "legitimate objectives" pursued by the European Communities. Further,
in such an event, as we have already determined that Codex Stan 94 was not
used "as a basis for" the EC Regulation, we would then have to find as a consequence that the European Communities has acted inconsistently with Article
2.4 of the *TBT Agreement*.

288. This being so, our task is to assess whether Peru discharged its burden of
showing that Codex Stan 94 is appropriate and effective to fulfill these same three
"legitimate objectives." In the light of our reasoning thus far, Codex Stan 94
would be *effective* if it had the capacity to accomplish all three of these objectives, and it would be *appropriate* if it were suitable for the fulfillment of all three
of these objectives.

289. We share the Panel's view that the terms "ineffective" and "inappropriate" have different meanings, and that it is conceptually possible that a measure could be effective but inappropriate, or appropriate but ineffective. This is why Peru has the burden of showing that Codex Stan 94 is both *effective* and *appropriate*. We note, however, that, in this case, a consideration of the *appropriateness* of Codex Stan 94 and a consideration of the *effectiveness* of Codex Stan 94 are interrelated—as a consequence of the nature of the objectives of the EC Regulation. The capacity of a measure to accomplish the stated objectives—its *effectiveness*—and the suitability of a measure for the fulfilment of the stated objectives—its *appropriateness*—are *both* decisively influenced by the perceptions and expectations of consumers in the European Communities relating to preserved sardine products.

290. We note that the Panel concluded that "Peru has adduced sufficient evidence and legal arguments to demonstrate that Codex Stan 94 is not ineffective or inappropriate to fulfil the legitimate objectives pursued by the EC Regulation." We have examined the analysis which led the Panel to this conclusion. We note, in particular, that the Panel made the factual finding that "it has not been established that consumers in most member States of the European Communities have always associated the common name "sardines" exclusively with *Sardina pilchardus*." We also note that the Panel gave consideration to the contentions of Peru that, under Codex Stan 94, fish from the species *Sardinops sagax* bear a denomination that is distinct from that of *Sardina pilchardus*, and that "the very purpose of the labelling regulations set out in Codex Stan 94 for sardines of species other than *Sardina pilchardus* is to ensure market transparency."

We agree with the analysis made by the Panel. Accordingly, we see no reason to interfere with the Panel's finding that Peru has adduced sufficient evidence and legal arguments to demonstrate that Codex Stan 94 meets the legal requirements of effectiveness and appropriateness set out in Article 2.4 of the *TBT Agreement*.

291. We, therefore, uphold the finding of the Panel ... that Peru has adduced sufficient evidence and legal arguments to demonstrate that Codex Stan 94 is not "ineffective or inappropriate" to fulfil the "legitimate objectives" of the EC Regulation.

––––––––––

Some of the evidence produced by Peru concluded that Europeans did not identify "sardines" exclusively with *Sardina pilchardus* before the Sardines Regulation. The Panel found, among other things, that the United Kingdom, an EU Member State, imported 97 percent of Peruvian exports of *Sardinops sagax* to the EU, and labeled them as "Pacific pilchards." Meanwhile *Sardina pilchardus* was also labeled as "pilchards." The Panel concluded that this indicated that consumers could distinguish species if provided the proper geographic or other qualifying terms, such as "Pacific." Moreover, publications published in close association with the European Commission listed *Sardinops sagax* in nine European languages as "sardines." *Sardines*, Panel Report, at paras. 7.130–7.131.

––––––––––

Questions and Discussion

1. *Burden of Proof.* Re-read Article 2.4 as well as the preamble to the TBT Agreement. Do you agree with the Appellate Body that the TBT Agreement creates a right for mem-

bers to adopt technical regulations that are different from international standards? What are the effects of the Appellate Body's decision for WTO members establishing technical regulations and those challenging technical regulations? Because the TBT Agreement does not require upward harmonization (harmonization to higher or the highest standard), is this decision a compromise between harmonization and regulatory autonomy?

2. The TBT Agreement states that members "shall use" international standards where they exist as the basis for their technical regulations. After *Sardines*, are we able to say with any authority whether a member's right to adopt its own technical regulations is a broad one? Or was this simply an easy case to find protectionism? Do you think the EU was really concerned about misleading consumers or was it worried about its fishermen? Assuming that the EU was trying to protect its fishermen, how could the EU have achieved that goal consistently with the Codex standard?

3. The EU argued that Codex Stan 94 was ineffective and inappropriate because the EC's own regulation created consumer expectations in some EU Member States that "sardines" only applied to *Sardina pilchardus*. The Panel rejected this as a basis for establishing that an international standard was ineffective or inappropriate for the fulfillment of legitimate objectives:

> 7.127 ... If we were to accept that a WTO Member can "create" consumer ex-
> pectations and thereafter find justification for the trade-restrictive measure which
> created those consumer expectations, we would be endorsing the permissibility
> of "self-justifying" regulatory trade barriers. Indeed, the danger is that Mem-
> bers, by shaping consumer expectations through regulatory intervention in the
> market, would be able to justify thereafter the legitimacy of that very same reg-
> ulatory intervention on the basis of the governmentally created consumer ex-
> pectations. Mindful of this concern, we will proceed to examine whether the
> evidence and legal arguments before us demonstrate that consumers in most
> member States of the European Communities have always associated the com-
> mon name "sardines" exclusively with *Sardina pilchardus* and that the use of "sar-
> dines" in conjunction with "Pacific," "Peruvian" or "*sardinops sagax*" would
> therefore not enable European consumers to distinguish between products made
> from *Sardinops sagax* and *Sardina pilchardus*.

The Appellate Body stated that the Panel made this statement *in abstracto* and not as a definitive ruling with respect to Article 2.4's requirement to ensure that technical regulations are not more trade-restrictive than necessary to fulfill a legitimate objective. Nevertheless, what does this say about a government's ability to direct its market toward "green" products or other products a government wishes to promote?

4. Does the TBT Agreement allow members to adopt technical regulations that are *less* strict than the international standard without meeting the requirements of Article 2? The *Sardines* dispute did not address that question, because the sardines regulation contradicted the relevant international standard.

5. The EU stated (see paragraph 267) that the Panel erred in basing its analysis on the factual premise that consumers in the EU associate "sardines" exclusively with *Sardina pilchardus*. However, the EU itself argued that its consumers expect that products of the same nature and characteristics will always have the same trade description, and that consumers in most EU Member States have always, and in some Member States have for at least 13 years, associated "sardines" exclusively with *Sardina pilchardus*. Sardines, Panel Report, at paras. 4.79, 7.113. In other words, the three objectives of the sardines regulation were based on that factual premise. As such, the Panel stated that "the persuasive-

ness of European Communities' argument will be affected by the extent to which this factual premise is supported by the evidence and established to be valid." *Id.* at para. 7.123. What effect does this conclusion have on determining whether a technical regulation is consistent with the TBT Agreement?

6. Did the Appellate Body defer too quickly to the Codex standard? What should the obligation of panels and the Appellate Body be in determining whether or not a standard setting body complied with requirements of the TBT Agreement in setting the relevant international standard? Some scholars have written that the WTO is essentially delegating regulatory power from the WTO to these bodies and consequently creating oversight problems to ensure that the WTO's "agents" are faithfully executing the TBT Agreement. *See* Jan McDonald, *Domestic Regulation, Harmonization, and Technical Barriers to Trade* 18–19 (2004), *available at* http://www.iibel.adelaide.edu.au/docs/Jan%20McDonald.pdf. Should a panel consult with the standardizing body and undertake an inquiry into the decisionmaking process for that particular standard before it makes a determination as to its "relevance"? Is it troubling that in the absence of such consultation, a WTO panel can unilaterally determine "the meaning" of international instruments created outside the WTO system? How would you resolve this potential problem?

7. Would the result of this case have been different had it been brought under the GATT? Are *Sardina pilchardus* and *Sardinops sagax* "like products" under GATT Article III:4?

8. Environmental advocates worry that harmonization will be downward, because countries with lower standards will not agree to higher standards. Many people in developing countries worry about upward harmonization, because they believe that their businesses will not be able to meet higher standards or that the cost of doing so will make developing country businesses uncompetitive. Consequently, they view environmental standards as a means to impose protectionist trade barriers. Does the TBT Agreement call for upward or downward harmonization? Does it balance the concerns of developed country environmentalists and developing country trade officials?

———————

2. Recognized International Organizations

The TBT Agreement does not specifically identify organizations that have competence to adopt standards upon which members must base their technical regulations. Instead, Annex 1 of the TBT Agreement defines a standard as a document "approved by a recognized body" and an "international body or system" as one whose "membership is open to the relevant bodies of at least all Members." The WTO Committee on Technical Barriers to Trade (TBT Committee) identified criteria for determining whether an international standard can be used for compliance with the TBT Agreement, including: 1) transparency; 2) openness without discrimination as to participation at the policy development level and at every stage of standards development; 3) impartiality and consensus so that WTO members are provided with meaningful opportunities to contribute to the elaboration of an international standard; 4) effectiveness and relevance, meaning taking into account relevant regulatory or market needs, as well as scientific and technological developments in the elaboration of standards; 5) coherence, meaning coordination with other standardizing bodies to avoid duplication of efforts; and 6) concerns of developing countries. These criteria, while not directed to the decisionmaking processes of standard setting bodies, will surely influence the range of organizations relevant for TBT Agreement purposes. TBT Committee, G/TBT/9, Annex 4; TBT Committee, *Decision On Principles For*

The Development of International Standards, Guides and Recommendations with Relation To Articles 2, 5 and Annex 3 of The Agreement, G/TBT/5, para. 22(a) (Nov. 19, 1997).

A range of international organizations are qualified to set standards, including Codex Alimentarius, which sets various standards for food. It is the organization that established the standard for labeling "sardines" at issue in the *Sardines* dispute. Its work is described more fully in Chapter 7. For TBT Agreement purposes, the most important international body is the International Organization for Standardization (ISO), an international federation of national standardization bodies. The ISO emerged from discussions in 1946 when delegates from 25 countries met in London to create a new organization "to facilitate the international coordination and unification of industrial standards." The new organization, ISO, began operations in 1947 and now includes members from 161 countries. Its Central Secretariat in Geneva, Switzerland coordinates the system.

Each country is represented in ISO by one member. However, ISO is a nongovernmental organization. The U.S. representative is the American National Standards Institute (ANSI), not the federal government or one of its agencies. The United States and other governments are not excluded from the process of establishing standards through ANSI and the ISO. Instead, governmental agencies frequently participate in meetings of their national members, alongside representatives from businesses, consumer welfare, and other organizations.

ISO standards are developed by ISO technical committees (TC) and subcommittees (SC) (known collectively as "TC/SC") through a six-stage process, although a "fast-track" procedure is available for well developed proposed standards. Without going into the details, the process allows the members with the most interest in a particular standard to develop a proposal, but final approval requires a super-majority voting procedure that assures broad, though not unanimous, agreement.

The technical work of ISO is highly decentralized, with hundreds of technical committees, subcommittees, and working groups responsible for development of an international standard within its area of work. In the United States, Technical Advisory Groups (TAGs) develop and transmit, through ANSI, U.S. positions on activities and votes of the international TC. As a result, representation on these TAGs is critical for establishing not only the U.S. position but also the substantive standards embodied in any resulting international standard.

ANSI procedures for the development of ISO standards state that membership "shall be open to all U.S. national interested parties who indicate that they are directly and materially affected by the activity of the U.S. TAG." Moreover, the "process of developing U.S. positions shall provide an opportunity for fair and equitable participation without dominance by any single interest." According to ANSI procedures, the requirement implicit in the phrase "without dominance by any single interest" normally will be satisfied if a reasonable balance among interests can be achieved. ANSI Executive Standards Council, ANSI Procedures for U.S. Participation in the International Standards Activities of ISO 24 (Jan. 2004), http://publicaa.ansi.org/sites/apdl/isodocs/ANSI_Procedures_for_US_Participation_in_the_International_Standards_Activities_of_ISO_2004_edition.doc.

With these ANSI rules in mind, who should be included on a TAG that is developing standards for humane trapping? The chair of the U.S. TAG, a representative of the National Trappers Association, denied TAG membership to animal welfare organizations, because they refused to agree in writing that they did not oppose all use of steel jaw leghold traps, even though 78 percent of the American public is reported to be opposed to steel jaw leghold traps. Even after some welfare interests successfully used ANSI's appeal process to gain membership to the TAG, they remained in the minority. According to the Animal Welfare Institute, the TAG included 11 members with an interest in traps, four members with animal welfare interests, and two neutral members. Is that balanced? What kind of expertise is needed for this TAG? *See* Letter from Cathy A. Liss, Executive Director, Animal Welfare Institute, to Kalya Serotte, Recording Secretary, ANSI, (Nov. 4, 1993); In the Matter of the Appeal of Animal Welfare Institute, Findings of Fact, Conclusions of Law and Decision (May 10, 1994) (rejecting the composition of the TAG as unbalanced).

Questions and Discussion

1. Where should harmonization occur? The TBT Agreement does not designate the ISO (or any other organization) as a relevant international standard setting body, but ISO is internationally recognized as such a body. In practice, though, such technical work is dominated by industry representatives; public interest organizations are scarcely represented. *See, e.g.*, Natalie Avery, *Diet for a Corporate Planet: Industry Sets World Food Standards*, *available at* http://multinationalmonitor.org/hyper/issues/1993/08/mm0-893_07.html (citing NATALIE AVERY ET AL., CRACKING THE CODEX: AN ANALYSIS OF WHO SETS WORLD STANDARDS (1993)). If you do not think that ISO or Codex are appropriate international standard setting bodies, then which organization(s) might be? How might you change the process for setting standards? Is more or less governmental involvement needed? Is the process for setting technical standards domestically much different?

2. Professor Jan McDonald sees another risk in delegating standard setting to international organizations:

> Codex objectives involve the development of international standards for food and food products to protect the health of consumers and to ensure "fair trade practices." … Codex underwent an independent review in 2002 which recommended that the organisation's highest priority should be food safety. This recommendation was endorsed by FAO management, with the proviso that it was necessary to "bear[] in mind the expectation of members that international food trade issues also need to be given due consideration as required by existing WTO Agreement, especially the TBT." The FAO's logic is somewhat circular. The TBTA recognises the need for product standards, and says that the best way to set standards that every Member can live with is through these international bodies. It is the fact of delegation to international bodies, and the compromises that take place therein, that ensures their trade-compatibility. It should not, therefore, be necessary for organisations like Codex to have explicit regard to trade considerations — Member delegations will do that anyway. That said, the objectives of Codex still emphasise the trade facilitation aspects of harmonization.

Jan McDonald, *Domestic Regulation, Harmonization, and Technical Barriers to Trade*, at 19.

On the other hand, ISO has also promulgated important quality management standards that include environmental safety aspects (ISO 9,000 series) and standards for good environmental management practices (ISO 14,000 series). Neither set of standards is legally obligatory in the United States, but virtually all corporations require that their suppliers of parts or materials be certified under both standards *and* that those suppliers include similar requirements in their contracts for goods and materials. Thus, these ISO standards reach deep into production supply chains, covering most businesses engaged in international trade.

3. An important, yet unanswered, question is whether the rules of multilateral environmental agreements (MEAs) constitute "standards" created by a relevant international standard setting body for TBT Agreement purposes. The Convention on International Trade in Endangered Species of Wild Fauna and Flora (CITES), for example, establishes rules for marking crocodile and leopard skins, ivory, and other plant and animal products entering trade. CITES, like other major MEAs, also has procedures for standard setting that meet the criteria established by the TBT Committee. The meetings are transparent and open to all countries of the world. Decisions are made by consensus and, where consensus cannot be achieved, by a vote. Due to the participatory nature of the meetings, the concerns of developing countries are taken into account.

4. The Code of Good Practice of the TBT Agreement also establishes rules for standard setting by governmental — including local governmental — and nongovernmental bodies. While compliance with the Code is not required in order to produce a "relevant international standard," standardizing bodies may choose to adopt it. In addition, Article 4.1 of the TBT Agreement directs members to ensure that central governmental standardizing bodies accept and comply with the Code of Good Practice. With respect to local government and nongovernmental standardizing bodies, it directs members to take "such reasonable measures as may be available" to ensure compliance. The Code of Good Practice includes provisions similar to those that apply to the adoption of technical regulations. That is, standardizing bodies must adopt standards consistent with most favored nation and national treatment principles. In addition, they must ensure that standards do not create "unnecessary obstacles to trade." Moreover, if another international standard already exists, the standardizing body must use it as a basis for its standard, except where it would be ineffective or inappropriate. TBT Agreement, Annex 3, paras. D–F.

What does it mean for governments to "take such reasonable measures as may be available to them" to ensure compliance with the Code of Good Practice? Guidance can perhaps be taken from jurisprudence relating to GATT Article XXIV:12, which requires WTO members to "take such reasonable measures as may be available to it to ensure observance of the [GATT] by the regional and local governments and authorities within its territory." One Panel interpreted the requirement as applying when regional or State action "fall[s] outside its jurisdiction under the constitutional distribution of power." United States-Measures Affecting Alcoholic and Malt Beverages, GATT Panel Report, para. 5.79, DS23/R, B.I.S.D. 39th Supp. 206 (1993) (adopted June 19, 1992). In other words, central governments are expected to take all measures within their constitutional authority. Another Panel has interpreted "reasonable" to require only a balancing test, that the "consequences of … nonobservance … for trade relations with other parties … be weighed against the domestic difficulties of securing observance." Canada-Measures Affecting the Sale of Gold Coins, GATT Panel Report, para. 69, L/5863 (Sept. 17, 1985) (unadopted). Yet another Panel found this provision to require a country to make "serious, persistent and convincing efforts" to secure compliance by subnational governments with GATT rules. Canada-Import, Distribution and Sale of Certain Alcoholic Drinks by Provincial Marketing Agencies, GATT Panel Report, para. 5.37, L/6304, B.I.S.D. 39th Supp. 27 (1993) (adopted Feb. 18, 1992). Do these decisions suggest that a central government must withhold, for example, highway funds in order to compel observance by a state government with the TBT Agreement? What other powers might a government reasonably employ?

5. Would humane trapping standards fall within the scope of the TBT Agreement? The EU adopted humane trapping legislation that banned the use of leghold traps. European

Commission Regulation EEC 1771/94, 1994 O.J. (L 184/3). It also called for a ban on the importation of animals caught using leghold traps. Many of these animals inhabited the United States and Canada, where the governments had no intention of banning the use of leghold traps. When the two countries threatened to bring a GATT dispute, the EU postponed the ban. The international standards that Europe hoped would result from its unilateral action never materialized, but it did successfully negotiate two agreements between the principal fur trading countries: 1) the Agreement on International Humane Trapping Standards between the European Community, Canada, and the Russian Federation, Feb. 14, 1998, 1998 O.J. (L 042) 0043-0057, and 2) the International Agreement in the form of an Agreed Minute between the European Community and the United States of America on humane trapping standards. Standards for the Humane Trapping of Specified Terrestrial and Semi-aquatic Mammals, Aug. 7, 1998, 1998 O.J. (L 219) 0026-0037. For a short history of this dispute, see Stuart R. Harrop, *The Agreements on International Humane Trapping Standards: Background, Critique and the Texts*, 3 J. Int'l Wildlife L. & Pol'y 387 (1998).

D. The Prohibitions against Discrimination and Obstacles to Trade

Article 2 of the TBT Agreement and the Code of Good Practice set out several obligations that share many characteristics with the GATT. These obligations apply to the preparation and adoption of technical regulations and standards as well as to conformity assessment procedures. As summarized below, there are some minor differences in language that may result in interpretative challenges.

1. MFN and National Treatment

With respect to agencies of central government bodies and any body subject to the control of the central government, technical regulations and standards must be adopted consistent with most favored nation and national treatment obligations. Article 2.1 and Paragraph D of the Code of Good Practice require members to ensure that, in respect of technical regulations and standards, products imported from the territory of any member are accorded treatment no less favourable than that accorded to like products of national origin and to like products originating in any other country. Article 5.1.1 also applies the most favored nation and national treatment obligations to conformity assessment procedures for technical regulations and standards relating to "like products" in "comparable situations."

2. No Unnecessary Obstacles to Trade

The TBT Agreement also requires members to ensure that their technical regulations and standards do not create "unnecessary obstacles to international trade." The TBT Agreement does not use this phrase consistently. For technical regulations, standards, and conformity assessment procedures, each test is slightly different.

- For *standards*, this obligation in Paragraph E of the Code of Good Practice is not further qualified.

- For *technical regulations*, Article 2.2 provides that for the purposes of defining "unnecessary obstacle to international trade," a technical regulation "shall not be more trade-restrictive than necessary to fulfill that legitimate objective, taking account of the risks non-fulfillment would create." When assessing the risks created by nonfulfillment of the legitimate objective, relevant elements to consider include "available scientific and technical information, related processing technology or intended end uses of products."

- For *conformity assessment procedures*, Article 5.1.2 defines "unnecessary obstacles to trade" to mean that conformity assessment procedures "shall not be more strict than necessary to give the importing Member adequate confidence that products conform with applicable technical regulations or standards, taking into account the risk non-conformity would create."

What is an interpreter to make of these differences? Although the obligations with respect to standards and conformity assessment procedures omit any reference to trade-restrictiveness, some commentators wonder whether a "trade-restrictiveness" test will be incorporated into it, just as one has been incorporated into a determination of "necessary" under Article XX(b). GARY COOK ET AL., APPLYING TRADE RULES TO TIMBER ECOLABELING: A REVIEW OF TIMBER ECOLABELING INITIATIVES AND THE WTO AGREEMENT ON TECHNICAL BARRIERS TO TRADE, 33, 36 (CIEL Discussion Paper, Draft: Feb. 1997). The Appellate Body's frequent resort to the plain meaning of treaty terms would suggest a different outcome; since an express reference to a less-trade restrictive test is included for technical regulations, drafters meant to exclude such a test for standards and conformity assessment procedures. This seems especially true with respect to conformity assessment procedures:

> Article 5 gives an example of a situation in which conformity assessment procedures constitute unnecessary obstacles: when they are more strict than necessary to give "adequate confidence" that the product conforms. This seems to reflect a deliberate decision not to have the Article 2 definition apply to conformity assessment procedures. Instead, this example is offered, as a basis for interpretation, in place of a full-blown definition. This is significant, first, because this example leaves room for finding procedures to be unnecessary obstacles to trade for other, additional reasons not mentioned in the Agreement. Second, an overly inclusive interpretation of "adequate" would diminish the strength of the "adequate confidence" standard. This could impair the ability of Members to ensure compliance with the standards they set for products and the methods by which they are produced.

GARY COOK ET AL., APPLYING TRADE RULES TO TIMBER ECOLABELING, at 36.

Turning to the obligation as it applies to technical regulations, how should the phrase "not more trade-restrictive than necessary" be defined? Focusing solely on the "necessary" language brings obvious parallels to Article XX of the GATT. Recall from Chapter 5 that the Appellate Body has defined a measure as "necessary" if no other less trade-restrictive alternative is "reasonably" available and could be employed to achieve the member's goals but only after weighing and balancing other factors, including the contribution to achieving the measure's objective and its trade restrictiveness, in light of the importance of the interests or values at stake. Brazil–Measures Affecting Imports of Retreaded Tyres, Appellate Body Report, WT/DS332/AB/R para. 156 (adopted Dec. 17, 2007). However, Article XX provides an exception to the GATT's core obligations whereas Article 2.2 describes the nature of a member's right to adopt technical regulations. Does this suggest Article 2.2's "not more trade-restrictive" test is less stringent than Article XX(b)'s "less trade-restrictive" test?

The WTO Secretariat has interpreted the least trade-restrictive alternative test of Article 2.2 to mean "that those standards which have the least degree of trade restrictiveness should be used. Consideration of the degree of restrictiveness should be proportional to the risk of non-fulfillment of the legitimate objectives in the case of TBT." WTO Secretariat, TER/W/16 and corr. 1, para. 12 (Sept. 2, 1993). Gabrielle Marceau and Joel Trachtman take a different approach. They argue that a necessity test—as a search for the least trade-restrictive alternative as under Article XX(b)—does not make sense as part of an inquiry into the risks of non-fulfillment of a country's legitimate objectives. They argue that taking account of the risk of nonfulfillment is part of a balancing test, or cost-benefit analysis. Cost-benefit analysis would ordinarily discount risk by its probability in order to calculate its "cost." In addition, if the necessity test under this provision is thought of as proportionality testing, which would evaluate whether the costs are disproportionate to the benefits, the magnitude and probability of risk become relevant. Gabrielle Marceau & Joel P. Trachtman, *The Technical Barriers to Trade Agreement, the Sanitary and Phytosanitary Measures Agreement, and the General Agreement on Tariffs and Trade: A Map of the World Trade Organization Law of Domestic Regulation of Goods*, 36 J. World Trade 811, 831 (2002).

Other aspects of the obligation are more clearly defined, particularly the term "legitimate objective" as Article 2.2 applies to technical regulations. Article 2.2 lists the range of legitimate objectives as including, "*inter alia*: national security requirements; the prevention of deceptive practices; protection of human health or safety, animal or plant life or health, or the environment." But as the Appellate Body in *Sardines* noted (para. 286), the list is not exclusive, and the *Sardines* Panel and Appellate Body readily accepted the EU's legitimate objectives of market transparency, consumer protection, and fair competition by noting that Article 2.2 includes an illustrative list of legitimate objectives. While the Appellate Body did state that "there must be an examination and a determination on the legitimacy of the objectives of the measure," it also acknowledged that the Preamble to the TBT Agreement affirms a member's right to decide which policy objectives it wishes to pursue and at what level. *Sardines*, Appellate Body Report, at para. 286. While members may pursue legitimate objectives not included in Article 2.2, Article 2.5 gives special consideration to a technical regulation prepared, adopted, or applied for one of the legitimate objectives explicitly included in Article 2.2 that is "in accordance with" relevant international standards: the technical regulation shall be rebuttably presumed not to create an unnecessary obstacle to international trade.

————————

Questions and Discussion

1. *"Like Product."* A question remains as to whether the phrase "like product" in Article 2.1 has the same meaning as under the GATT. Considering the "accordion" of likeness, how do you think it should be defined? Should it be similar to "like product" under Article III:4 of the GATT? Or should it explicitly include "directly competitive or substitutable products" under the Note to Article III:2, second sentence? If "like product" is defined quite differently in the two agreements, it is conceivable that a technical regulation could fulfill a legitimate objective of market transparency and be applied consistently with most favored nation and national treatment obligations. Yet because of the different definition of "like product," that same technical regulation could violate GATT's national treatment obligation and not be exempted under Article XX, because market transparency is not an enumerated exception to GATT.

Problems could also arise if the scope of like products under the TBT Agreement is the same as under Article III:4 of the GATT, because the TBT Agreement has no equivalent to the exceptions of Article XX of the GATT. For example, an environmental-based technical regulation could be inconsistent with the national treatment obligation of Article 2.1 of the TBT Agreement and thus violate the TBT, while the same regulation, even though it might violate Article III:4, could nevertheless be justified under Article XX. Does the ability of a member to define most any objective as legitimate under the TBT Agreement and the lack of exceptions to GATT Article XX for these legitimate objectives argue for either a broad or narrow interpretation of "like products"? Is a product produced in nonconformity with a technical regulation "unlike" a product made in conformity with it?

In addition, the most favored nation and national treatment obligations for conformity assessment procedures apply only to conformity assessment undertaken "in a comparable situation." Does the phrase "in a comparable situation" broaden or narrow the range of "like products" for which conformity assessment procedures must be prepared, adopted, and applied consistently with MFN and national treatment obligations?

2. Note that under the GATT the least trade-restrictive test applies only in the context of an Article XX exception. Under the TBT Agreement (as well as the SPS Agreement), the "not more trade-restrictive" test forms part of a member's obligation when adopting a technical regulation. Interpreted in this light, who has the more persuasive interpretation of Article 2.2, the WTO Secretariat or Marceau and Trachtman? More generally, how do you think the three different standards of "unnecessary obstacle to international trade" should be interpreted?

3. Consider the following examples. Are they discriminatory? Do they create "unnecessary obstacles to trade"? What evidence would be needed to find these technical regulations in violation of the TBT Agreement?

- In *Lobsters*, the United States imposed size restrictions on lobsters to ensure that lobsters reached breeding age before they were caught. Is the U.S. size restriction for lobsters a technical regulation? The United States set its size restriction of 3-3/8 inches based on the size of lobsters at sexual maturity in waters of a particular temperature. In some Canadian waters, however, lobsters reach sexual maturity at a much smaller size. Nonetheless, the United States chose a single size requirement to ensure that undersized U.S. lobsters would not be marketed illegally as "Canadian" lobsters.

- In 2009, the European Union adopted a regulation that prohibits the importation and the placing on the market of all seal products in the EC customs territory. "Seal product" is defined in the Regulation as "all products, either processed or unprocessed, deriving or obtained from seals, including meat, oil, blubber, organs, raw fur skins and fur skins, tanned or dressed, including fur skins assembled in plates, crosses and similar forms, and articles made from fur skins." The Regulation allows the importation and placing on the market of seal products where they result from traditional hunts conducted by Inuit and other indigenous communities and where the products contribute to their subsistence. Regulation (EC) No. 1007/2009 of the European Parliament and of the Council of 16 September 2009 on trade in seal products, 2009 O.J. (286/36). The Regulation is clearly a reaction to the clubbing of seals in Canada and elsewhere. The EU acknowledges that "[t]he seal populations that are hunted for commercial purposes—an estimated 15 million animals—are generally not endangered." European Commission, Seal Hunting, http://ec.europa.eu/environment/biodiversity/animal_welfare/seals/

seal_hunting.htm. In addition, the European Union expressly states that it "is concerned about the animal welfare aspects of the seal hunt. Doubts have been expressed about some of the methods used for hunting seals, such as shooting, netting and clubbing, that can cause avoidable pain and distress." *Id.* No international standards exist for seal hunting. Canada and Norway claim that these measures violate Articles 2.1 and 2.2 of the TBT Agreement.

- Country A has extensive northern forests very far from population centers, so that for its paper mills to source recycled paper would involve expensive and energy-consuming shipment of recycled paper over long distances. For many years, firms in A have supplied newsprint to purchasers in Country B. Country B newly requires newspapers to use only newsprint that contains at least 50 percent recycled material.

- In an effort to reduce packaging waste, Country X, which has a strong greenhouse vegetable industry, requires vegetables to be transported and sold only in heavy packaging suitable for at least 20 roundtrips. A foreign vegetable grower claims that the cost of purchasing and obtaining such heavy packaging, and then shipping it with the vegetables to Country X, makes her vegetables uncompetitive.

4. Prior to completion of the TBT Agreement, some environmental critics of the TBT Agreement (as well as the SPS Agreement) proposed that challenges to a technical regulation should be limited to whether the technical regulation was discriminatory or a disguised barrier to trade. Letter from Seven Environmental NGOs, to Ambassador Michael Kantor (May 4, 1993). How does this approach differ from the one actually taken in the TBT Agreement? If it does differ, do you think this is a better approach than the one adopted in the TBT Agreement?

5. *Differential and More Favourable Treatment.* Article 12 of the TBT Agreement requires members to provide differential and more favourable treatment to developing country members. In particular, members must prepare and apply technical regulations, standards, and conformity assessment procedures that "take account of the special development, financial and trade needs of developing country Members, with a view to ensuring that such technical regulations, standards and conformity assessment procedures do not create unnecessary obstacles to exports from developing country Members." Members also "recognize" that developing country members should not be expected to use international standards as a basis for their technical regulations or standards, including test methods, which are not appropriate to their development, financial, and trade needs. The TBT Committee may also grant developing countries specified, time-limited exceptions from the obligations of the TBT Agreement. What special problems do you think developing countries might have with respect to technical regulations, standards, and conformity assessment procedures? Section III.B of this chapter reviews this question in the context of ecolabels.

E. The Relationship of the TBT Agreement to the GATT

Another perplexing question involving interpretation of the TBT Agreement concerns its relationship to the GATT. Does the TBT Agreement replace the GATT with respect to technical regulations or does it impose rules in addition to GATT rules?

The TBT Agreement has several provisions that overlap with the GATT. First, Article 2.1 includes the most favored nation and national treatment obligations. Second, Article

2.2 provides that technical regulations should not be more trade-restrictive than necessary to fulfill a legitimate objective. That language echoes panel interpretations of Article XX that were known to negotiators when they were drafting the TBT Agreement. Similarly, the sixth preambular paragraph to the TBT Agreement borrows heavily from the chapeau of Article XX. There, the WTO members:

> Recogniz[e] that no country should be prevented from taking measures necessary to ensure the quality of its exports, or for the protection of human, animal or plant life or health, of the environment, or for the prevention of deceptive practices, at the levels it considers appropriate, subject to the requirement that they are not applied in a manner which would constitute a means of arbitrary or unjustifiable discrimination between countries where the same conditions prevail or a disguised restriction on international trade, and are otherwise in accordance with the provisions of this Agreement[.]

Moreover, the TBT Agreement was negotiated because the GATT contracting parties believed that the GATT was ineffectively controlling product standards. Do these factors suggest that the TBT Agreement was intended to replace the GATT with respect to technical regulations?

The Appellate Body in *Asbestos* and *EC-Bananas* made clear that the separate WTO agreements such as the TBT Agreement and the General Agreement on Trade in Services are independent and may overlap with the GATT. European Communities-Regime for the Importation, Sale and Distribution of Bananas, Appellate Body Report, WT/DS27/AB/R, paras. 221–22 (adopted Sept. 25, 1997). In *Asbestos*, the Appellate Body acknowledged that the TBT Agreement represented a "specialized regime" but that it was different from and "additional to" the obligations of the GATT. *Asbestos*, Appellate Body Report, at para. 80. As discussed in the first discussion note on page 378 above, this additive approach could pose some significant problems.

Marceau and Trachtman recommend treating the TBT Agreement as more specific—*lex specialis*—and thus as prevailing over the provisions of the GATT. Marceau & Trachtman, *A Map of the World Trade Organization Law of Domestic Regulation of Goods*, at 869–70, 875. Is this a sensible approach? Nevertheless, not only has the Appellate Body deemed the TBT Agreement to impose obligations in addition to the GATT, it has been unable to decide which agreement should be analyzed first. In *Asbestos*, it found that the French ban on asbestos fibers constituted a technical regulation but then found the measure consistent with GATT Article III. It never returned to the question of whether the measure violated the TBT Agreement. In *Sardines*, the Appellate Body first ruled on the question of whether the EU's measure violated the TBT Agreement. In the SPS Agreement, another specialized WTO agreement (in fact, it covers a subset of technical regulations), Article 2.4 states that measures conforming to the SPS Agreement shall be presumed to be in accordance with the GATT, in particular the provisions of Article XX(b). The TBT Agreement includes no equivalent provision. How should these provisions be interpreted?

III. Ecolabeling and International Trade Law

When Germany introduced the "Blue Angel" ecolabel in 1977, it became the first country in the world to use an ecolabel. It started a global trend. Hundreds, if not thousands, of ecolabels now identify products according to various "green" standards. Typical labels give consumers information about the impacts of harvesting natural resources on other species (dolphin-safe tuna; bird-friendly coffee), the energy efficiency of appliances (the U.S. "energy star" program), and whether a product or its packaging is recyclable (Germany's "green dot" program). Many of these labels are government sponsored, including Germany's "Blue Angel" and "green dot" ecolabels. Many others are supported by non-governmental organizations. In the Pacific Northwest, for example, a local environmental organization certifies wine as "salmon safe" if the producer has, among other things, undertaken measures to prevent fertilizers and pesticides from entering salmon habitat.

Ecolabels can play an important role in providing consumers with environmental and health and safety information about a product. They help consumers exercise preferences for products based on certain product characteristics, such as the way the product is produced, used, and disposed. Consumers receive better information about the impacts of the products they buy, allowing them to use their purchasing power to encourage environmental protection. Manufacturers of "green" products may also benefit by garnering greater market share and potentially higher prices.

From a trade perspective, advocates of ecolabels consider ecolabels to be a nondiscriminatory way for consumers to increase demand for environmentally sound products. Further, they argue that ecolabels do not constitute a trade restriction because a label merely provides information; it does not prevent the entry of a product into a country and it does not prevent the sale of a product once it enters a market. On the other hand, many countries, especially developing countries, have raised economic concerns about the use of ecolabels. They fear that their producers may not be able to meet the requirements for obtaining a label, especially when labels relate to processes and production methods (PPMs). Further, they argue that ecolabels have the potential to be biased toward environmental or manufacturing conditions in the country designing the ecolabel.

The world's leaders, meeting at the United Nations Conference on Environment and Development in 1992, adopted *Agenda 21*, a blueprint for sustainable development. *Agenda 21* recommends that, "Governments, in cooperation with industry and other relevant groups, should encourage expansion of environmental labeling and other environmentally related product information programs designed to assist consumers to make informed choices." *Agenda 21*, Annex II, Chapter 4.21, U.N. Doc. A/Conf.151.26 (June 3–14, 1992). In 2005, the World Summit on Sustainable Development (WSSD) Plan of Implementation directed governments to "[d]evelop and adopt, where appropriate, on a voluntary basis, effective, transparent, verifiable, non-misleading and non-discriminatory consumer information tools to provide information relating to sustainable consumption and production, including human health and safety aspects. These tools should not be used as disguised trade barriers." UN Department of Economic and Social Affairs, Division for Sustainable Development, *Johannesburg Plan of Implementation*, para. 15(e) (Aug. 11, 2005), http://www.un.org/esa/sustdev/documents/WSSD_POI_PD/English/WSSD_PlanImpl.pdf.

The WSSD statement is far more nuanced than *Agenda 21*. While recognizing the value of ecolabels, the WSSD also took note of the growing discontent among developing countries about the potential discriminatory effects of ecolabels. It also took note of the different types of ecolabels, the potential to mislead consumers, and the need for ecolabels to be effective.

In a global economy, consumers need to know that the information they receive from labels is accurate and meaningful. Similarly, producers need clear ecolabeling standards to identify which environmental criteria to meet. They also need widely recognized ecolabeling programs to inform consumers of the green values of their products and to prevent unfair competition from less scrupulous producers that make misleading or deceptive environmental claims about their products. Ideally, ecolabel criteria would transcend particular conditions in a particular geographic area so that timber products from tropical Brazil and temperate Sweden may be eligible for the same ecolabel. How should trade law account for these needs and concerns?

A. Ecolabel Types

Ecolabels come in many different types. Some relate specifically to product characteristics. Products subject to the U.S. Federal Insecticide, Fungicide, and Rodenticide Act must carry labels that list the active ingredients in the product, first aid statements, environmental, physical, and chemical hazards, directions for use, and instructions for storage and disposal. 7 U.S.C. §§ 136–136y (2000). Other products may carry voluntary labels specific only to environmental attributes, such as the percent of postconsumer recycled content of the product or its packaging.

Other labels, rather than describing particular product characteristics, provide information about a product's PPMs. Many of these ecolabels rely on life-cycle analysis (LCA) — an assessment of the resource consumption, energy use, pollutant releases to the environment, and workplace and ecosystem effects, as well as the product's packaging, use, and disposal. In this way, a product is evaluated from "cradle to grave" — from the raw materials needed to produce it to its disposal. For example, ecolabel criteria for paper products would consider not only the amount of recycled material in the product, but also the manner in which the paper was produced. Does the company log virgin forests or does it use recycled paper? Does it bleach the paper with chlorine, thus adding chlorinated compounds to the environment? How much and what type of energy is used to operate the machinery? Can the paper be recycled or will it be disposed in a landfill?

Labels also vary in format. Many labels provide a "seal of approval" indicating that the product has met specific standards for the issuance of that label, such as Germany's Blue Angel and the U.S. dolphin-safe labels. Such labels typically require a means to establish relevant criteria as well as a system for certifying that the relevant criteria have been met. Other information-based labels may provide an environmental report card or checklist that provides raw data on a variety of environmental factors about the product. A report card could also rank a product on certain environmental factors, such as levels of pollution, and give the product a scaled score ranging from 1 (best) to 5 (worst).

Ecolabels may also be mandatory or voluntary. Currently, very few ecolabels are mandatory. Those labels that are mandatory often focus on characteristics of the products themselves, such as the information requirements for insecticides mentioned above. Many governments also require producers of processed foods to list the ingredients and nutritional value of foods and identify a medicine's recommended dosage and side effects. Voluntary labels, whether issued by a governmental or a nongovernmental body, are far more common. With voluntary labels, producers are not required to label their products, but if they choose to label their product as, for example, "dolphin safe," they must meet the conditions imposed by the issuing body.

In addition, ecolabels differ with respect to who issues them and who certifies that the relevant labeling criteria have been met. With "*first-party*" ecolabels, the producer of the product proclaims that the product meets environmental criteria or attributes that the producer itself has established. "*Second-party*" ecolabels are developed by a trade association for the products of its business members. Generally, the establishment of eligibility criteria and the awarding of the ecolabel are left to the membership of the trade association. "*Third-party*" ecolabels are awarded by institutions or organizations that are fully independent from the product's manufacturer and that certify that a product has met the standards established for that label.

Questions and Discussion

1. Might the lack of independent verification and criteria with first-party labels lead to "greenwash," where the producer's environmental claims are either misleading or false? How would you challenge such claims? In the United States, the Federal Trade Commission (FTC), acting under federal truth in advertising laws, has brought enforcement actions against manufacturers for misleading claims made through ecolabels. For example, the FTC recently accused companies of making false claims that their rayon fabrics were made from "bamboo" and that they were falsely labeled as "biodegradable." Press Release, Federal Trade Commission, FTC Charges Companies with 'Bamboo-zling' Consumers with False Product Claims (Aug. 11, 2009). However, disciplining of voluntary ecolabels has proven difficult in the absence of detailed criteria to evaluate the accuracy of claims involving specific products. In 1992, the FTC established guidelines for making environmental claims to assist manufacturers in developing acceptable ecolabels. The most recent versions of the Guides for the Use of Environmental Marketing Claims can be found at 16 C.F.R § 260. Are there any benefits to first-party labels?

2. For an exhaustive list of ecolabels, see the websites of Ecolabelling.org (http://www.ecolabelling.org) and the Global Ecolabelling Network (http://www.global ecolabelling.net). The U.S. Environmental Protection Agency also maintains a very useful website for making environmentally preferable purchases at http://www.epa.gov/epp/ index.htm.

B. Concerns about Ecolabels

Despite its many champions, ecolabeling also has many detractors. They raise three core questions concerning ecolabels. The first two questions relate to methodology. First, by what criteria should a product's "greenness" be identified? Second, how can we ensure products are uniformly labeled so that the consumer receives valuable information? The third question invokes trade concerns: if the methodology for identifying green products is flawed, does a label discriminate against products in the marketplace?

1. Methodological Concerns

Identifying "green" products or the "greenest" products is an incredibly difficult and vexing task. Roger Wynne explores the problems associated with LCA by assessing the lifecycle inventory (LCI) and impact analysis components of LCA. LCI quantifies the amounts of resources consumed as well as emissions and wastes released throughout the lifecycle of a given product or process. Impact analysis seeks to identify, characterize, and value the potential environmental and health impacts associated with the quantities calculated in the LCI.

Roger D. Wynne, *The Emperor's New Eco-Logos?:* *A Critical Review of the Scientific Certification Systems Environmental Report Card and the Green Seal Certification Mark Programs*
14 Va. Envtl. L.J. 51, 64–71 (1994)

A vital premise for discussing eco-logos is understanding that no empirical, judgment-free arbiter of "greenness" exists. Some would like to elevate lifecycle assessment (LCA) methodology to the status of the most principled, quantitative means of determining which products impose the least environmental burden. Although LCA methodology can assist and inform many decisions very effectively, it is not now, nor might it ever be, a tool for answering the fundamental question green consumers want an eco-logo to answer: "What product will serve a particular need and minimize my environmental impact?" Understanding why LCA methodology cannot generate an answer that is susceptible to proof or verification merely by observation and calculation underscores the quandary facing eco-logo organizations. * * *

1. Life-Cycle Inventory

Using ... an inventory analysis[] to discern the "greenest" product is a problematic venture. As an initial task, one must define the boundaries of the life-cycle for the product system in question. The analyst must resolve several issues. As for inputs, should she consider all of the system's raw and intermediate material requirements at the risk of becoming mired in an "endless exercise," or limit the scope of the investigation at the risk of ignoring important elements? For example, should she consider all of the specific environmental impacts of locating, drilling, and transporting the particular barrels of oil used to manufacture a certain batch of plastic, or should she simply treat all batches of that type of plastic as environmentally equivalent and therefore omit oil production from the scope of the study? The former option requires a tremendous, perhaps prohibitive, amount of site-specific data, but the latter option risks ignoring potentially significant differences in the actual environmental burdens posed by different methods of oil production. As for outputs, if the analyst decides not to account for all emitted pollutants, what method should she employ? Should she consider only regulated emissions, for which data more readily exist, or all regular and fugitive emissions and wastes, regardless of data availability? None of these boundary questions are susceptible to purely empirical answers. The analyst must make judgment calls, each of which shapes the ultimate result of the study.

Once the analyst defines the system's boundaries, her next challenge is to collect all of the relevant data for all of the environmental inputs and outputs that cross those boundaries. Unfortunately, such data are lacking for many products, and much of the available information is often of poor quality. For example, plant-specific data would certainly be most desirable, but even those plants (and their suppliers' plants) that maintain such records may hesitate to disclose them because of confidentiality concerns. Other sources of information might include aggregated or statistical data from across an industry, but that data, even if historically relevant, could mask elements that distinguish the individual product under study. These data-quality issues are challenging enough for the LCI of one product alone. They become only more so as one attempts to compare LCIs over a range of products.

Even if one could collect accurate data for all of the relevant products, one must still decide what to do with it. The computational models used to perform LCIs involve many assumptions. For example, when a plant produces three products, environmental data from that plant will not likely be allocated to each product. If the plant uses X amount of electrical energy, how much was used for Product 1, for Product 2, and for Product 3? The analyst might resolve this issue of co-product allocation by employing a technique based simply on the relative weight of each product. Yet other techniques exist, and choosing among them is an exercise of professional judgment, not an empirical determination mandated purely by observation or logic.

The challenges involved in conducting an LCI do not necessarily render LCIs inapplicable to all product comparisons. One can reasonably assume that LCI methodology will evolve so that every analyst at least makes the same assumptions and uses the same techniques for generating, evaluating, and supplementing data. When that day arrives, it may be possible to use LCIs to compare products that are virtually identical and that involve the exact same types of inputs and outputs. One would only have to compare the products across each input and output. If one product were equal or superior to all the others in every category, one would simply invoke the "less is best" rule to declare that product the winner.

Yet reality is not so accommodating. A clear environmental winner likely will not emerge under the "less is best" rule, because a product that is superior in some categories may be inferior in others. Imagine that one product incorporates pre-consumer, recycled paper (scrap from the manufacturing process that is reintroduced into the feed stock). When compared with a product that uses only virgin stock, the recycled product may require less material and produce less solid waste, but it might produce more hazardous liquid waste because of its internal recycling activity. Which is the winner? Again, the choice involves judgment.

Reality intrudes even more critically when one considers the most relevant choice facing consumers. They do not necessarily want to know, for instance, which large Kraft paper grocery sack is the least environmentally burdensome. They probably want to know what is the "greenest" way to get their groceries home. Is paper better than plastic? Are reusable cotton bags better than both? The relative environmental burdens associated with these functionally equivalent products differ not only in degree, but also in type. Thus, consumers may not simply apply the "less is best" rule to pick a winner. They must compare disparate elements and judge for themselves which elements render a product superior. * * *

2. Impact Analysis

LCA practitioners have relegated the task of comparing disparate units of environmental burdens to the realm of impact analysis. Yet impact analysis methodology has evolved even less than LCI methodology. As envisioned by LCA practitioners, an impact assessment framework consists broadly of three phases.

First, in the classification phase, the analyst examines the LCI data and attempts to identify relatively homogeneous groupings of impacts that those LCI items might cause, such as depletion of atmospheric ozone, increased human cancer risk, or depletion of fossil fuel reserves, within the primary impact categories of ecosystem, human health, natural resources, and other human welfare effects. Second, the analyst characterizes the relative contribution of each LCI item to each impact group by converting all of the relevant LCI data within each group to a common unit. For example, the analyst must convert amounts of nitrogen oxides and carbon dioxide emissions into some unit of atmospheric ozone depleted per pound of pollutant released, or convert volumes of various toxic wastes into a unit of increased cancer risk per liter of pollutant. Finally, the analyst engages in some explicit process of assigning relative values or weights to the various groups' disparate units, deciding, for instance, whether a decrease of X amount of atmospheric ozone is more troubling than an increase of Y number of potential cancer cases.

This framework is deceptively simple because it masks the complex, qualitative choices each phase involves. In the classification phase, for example, the analyst must make a qualitative assessment of potential impacts of each item of the life-cycle inventory, searching literature to identify impacts that may not yet be fully identified and that may be influenced by a host of factors. Furthermore, unless the analyst is prepared to assess every impact that she identifies, she must make some qualitative decisions about which ones to exclude from the study. In the second phase, characterization, models that convert disparate data within a given impact group into common units of environmental harm are based on a number of qualitative assumptions and, more importantly, the more sophisticated models require data that is currently very difficult to obtain.

Finally, the crucial valuation-of-disparate-impacts phase is inherently subjective because "developing a truly objective method for [assigning relative values to impact groups] is both impossible and inappropriate…." Although one might be able to articulate such value judgments qualitatively or quantitatively, one cannot escape the judgments that permeate those valuations.

––––––––––

2. Uniformity Concerns

Because of the methodological difficulties associated with LCA, Roger Wynne and others have questioned whether ecolabels are an effective means for providing information to consumers. Any methodological problems are exacerbated by the large number of labels. For example, there are more than 40 labels and standards for coffee, with the following general labeling approaches: organic, sustainable, bird/biodiversity-friendly, shade-grown, and fair trade. Even within these general groupings, the labels vary. Consider the following standards for growing coffee:

- Demeter's "Biodynamic" farm standard for coffee includes soil fertility management, crop protection, greenhouse management, and animal welfare. Biological diversity within the farm landscape is emphasized; ten percent of the total farm acreage must be set aside as a preserve and genetically modified seeds are prohibited. The farm must be viewed as a living "holistic organism." Demeter Association, Inc., Biodynamic Farm Standard (Mar. 18, 2010), http://demeter-usa.org/files/DemeterFarmStandardsm2.pdf.

- Thanksgiving Coffee, a roaster/retailer in Fort Bragg, California, defines its coffee as "Not Just a Cup, but a Just Cup." It emphasizes sustainable agriculture, including shade-grown coffee, combining the concepts of organic agriculture, maintenance of the growing environment, support of local producing communities (i.e., fair trade), and consumer satisfaction. *See* Thanksgiving Coffee Company, http://www.thanksgivingcoffee.com.

- The Smithsonian Migratory Bird Center's "Bird Friendly®" seal of approval is the only 100% organic shade-grown coffee: that is, the coffee plantation must have at least 40% canopy cover, even after pruning. The shade trees must belong to a minimum of 10 different species, of which each species must constitute at least 1% of the total shade trees present. It also requires, among other things, vegetational buffer zones to protect rivers, streams, lakes, and areas exposed to erosion. The label does not require any social or other "fair trade" criteria. Smithsonian Migratory Bird Center, Norms for Production, Processing and Marketing of "Bird Friendly®" Coffee (Apr. 4, 2002), http://nationalzoo.si.edu/SCBI/MigratoryBirds/Coffee/Certification/Norms-English_1.pdf.

- The Sustainable Coffee Program (SCP) of the Merchants of Green Coffee combines socio-economic factors, as certified under criteria established by the Fairtrade Labeling Organization (FLO), organic production under criteria established and certified by the International Foundation for Organic Agriculture, biodiversity conservation criteria, as established by Smithsonian Migratory Bird Center or other organizations, as well as the use of ecologically sustainable technologies and methods to process coffee in a way that eliminates water pollution and deforestation. Merchants of Green Coffee, Sustainable Coffee Program, http://www.merchantsofgreencoffee.com/4_About_the_Merchants/sustainable_coffee_program.html.

For more on coffee ecolabels and standards, see TerraChoice Environmental Services, *Environmental and Other Labeling of Coffee: The Role of Mutual Recognition Supporting Cooperative Action* 12 (Feb. 22, 2000), http://www.cec.org/Storage/39/3160_Terra-e_EN.pdf.

Questions and Discussion

1. Should attempts be made to harmonize these definitions? If terms are not clearly defined, or if terms are used differently by different ecolabeling programs, can the ecolabel achieve its goal of providing the consumer with useful information about a product's characteristics? If one company's version of "sustainable" includes living wages as well as environmental sustainability factors, would you want to know about that distinction? How should that information be conveyed to the consumer? Does the presence of so many labels create "label fatigue"?

---

3. Trade Concerns

WTO members remain deeply divided about labeling generally and ecolabeling specifically. On the one hand, ecolabels are specifically designed to influence consumer purchasing habits, which may then affect the decisions of producers and suppliers to make and supply goods that meet the environmental standards of the ecolabels. In this way, ecolabels rely on market forces rather than government intervention to protect domestic industries from protection.

On the other hand, developing countries particularly oppose ecolabels directed at identifying environmentally sound nonproduct related PPMs, such as sustainable management or dolphin-safe fishing. They worry that they do not have the capital and technical capacity to meet PPM- or LCA-based criteria. They have other trade, environmental, and economic concerns as well.

Arthur E. Appleton, *Environmental Labelling Schemes Revisited: WTO Law and Developing Country Implications*

in TRADE, ENVIRONMENT, AND THE MILLENNIUM 240, 240–43
(Gary P. Sampson & W. Bradnee Chambers eds., 2d ed. 2002)

Developing countries fear the potential discriminatory implications of these schemes. Providing consumers with the ability to discriminate against products perceived to be less environmentally sound is a source of worry for developing countries for the technical and financial reasons.... Producers in developing countries may also lack the resources and political expertise to influence the development of foreign labelling criteria, and may find it difficult from a linguistic and cultural perspective to inform themselves about the requirements of foreign labelling schemes and to participate in these schemes. In other words, information asymmetries may influence participation in particular schemes. Local manufacturers are more likely to be aware of the criteria being applied in a particular scheme, and are often better positioned politically to influence the selection of applicable criteria.

Developing countries are also concerned because of the perceived tendency of developed countries to formulate eco-labelling criteria based on conditions in the developed world, or only in the labelling state. Flexibility is necessary to assure that labelling criteria also reflect conditions prevailing in developing countries, particularly with respect to PPMs. This flexibility may be lacking in certain developed country programmes, particularly when protectionist interests influence the drafting of labelling criteria.

Complicating the problem are questions of comparative advantage. Wage considerations, regulatory requirements, and the lax enforcement of regulations are often viewed as sources of comparative advantage. Labelling schemes that alert consumers to serious discrepancies in the above may disadvantage developing countries that benefit from low wages or a less rigorous regulatory environment.

Another potential criticism is that eco-labelling schemes are likely to be of greater interest to the residents of developed countries—from the perspective of both demand and supply. From the demand perspective, increased discretionary income brings the luxury of selecting products based on factors other than price, including social and moral considerations. Assuming that many labeled products are more expensive to produce, and that they may command a premium price, it is probable that labelled products will be more expensive than competing unlabelled products, and as a result less likely to attract consumer interest in developing countries that have labelling schemes. On the supply side, to the extent that the market for a product labelled by a developed country is of interest to a developing country (often not the case because primary goods and agricultural products are frequently not labelled), for reasons mentioned above it may be difficult for developing countries to participate in foreign labelling programs.

From the developing country perspective, eco-labelling schemes give rise to serious economic concerns. This is because, by definition, eco-labelling programmes evaluate environmental aspects of production processes—an area of potential weakness for some developing countries. Although the overall goal of such labelling schemes (using market forces to improve the environment) is laudable, producers face risks which can result from very subjective factors. For example:

- What should receive a greater weighting in a life-cycle analysis—factors associated with a product's production, use, or disposal?

- Should one evaluate transport-related criteria, given that this would seem to discriminate against many imports?

- How do you evaluate products produced using dirty or dangerous sources of energy?

- How do you evaluate foreign production processes that may be more suitable given a particular country's geographical, climatic, and other circumstances?

- More specifically, how do you evaluate products coming from countries at different levels of development and with different levels of technology?

Accounting for differing ecological conditions and PPMs is a serious challenge for ecolabels. What looks reasonable in one locale may be completely unreasonable in another due to differences in environmental conditions among regions. As Appleton mentions, ecolabels sometimes reflect local environmental conditions or production methods. For example, an ecolabel that penalizes harvesting from old growth forests will favor European and U.S. producers, because the once vast old growth forests of those regions were cut long ago. In contrast, Brazil and other places have abundant old growth forests. Yet, U.S. or European logging may not be environmentally preferable if logging there occurs on steep slopes causing serious erosion and the loss of important ecological attributes.

Many of the issues identified by Wynne and Appleton bear on the complaints registered by Colombia, whose flower cultivation industry faced market access problems due to ecolabels. The ecolabels at issue were voluntary labels issued by nongovernmental environmental organizations, and thus no TBT Agreement dispute arose. Nonetheless, the underlying trade concerns could apply to any kind of ecolabel, which is why Colombia prepared this case study for the WTO's Committee on Trade and Environment.

Colombia, *Environmental Labels and Market Access: Case Study on the Colombian Flower-Growing Industry*
WT/CTE/W/76, G/TBT/W/60 (Mar. 9, 1998)

B. The FLORVERDE Programme

10. Environmental protection is a priority for floriculturists in Colombia. This led ASOCOLFLORES—the association of Colombia's principal flower exporters—to commit itself to carrying out major environmental protection activities.

11. The first action undertaken by the association was to review and document all the environmental initiatives that have been under way in the Colombian

flower growing industry for many years now. It then made study of the various sectoral environmental management schemes existing both nationally and internationally.

The association then drafted a proposal tailored to suit the industry and which encouraged and motivated each flower grower to strive towards eco-efficiency and constant improvement. Thus was born the Environmental Self-Management Programme (Programa de Autogestión Ambiental) for floriculturists in Colombia.

12. This initiative takes the form of the FLORVERDE programme, which aims to procure immediate benefits for the 76 participating companies and for the association as a whole. FLORVERDE is a systematic and comprehensive proposal for developing an environmental management style that will reorient attitudes towards cleaner production.

13. The FLORVERDE programme is based on the principle of self-management and continual and gradual improvement. It comprises five instruments:

- A registration system;
- case studies;
- a Code of Good Practice (Manual de Mejores Prácticas);
- An environmental management system;
- regional committees.

* * *

Registration system

15. The registration system entails the collection, processing, storage and the dissemination of environmental management indicators. The areas for which indicators are determined and which are subject to periodic monitoring are: human resource management, soils, water, phytosanitary inputs, energy and wastes.

16. The participating companies agree to be classified into category A, B or C, depending on the evaluation of their performance indicators. The 20 per cent of companies with the best performance are given an A-rating. The following 40 per cent a B-rating, and the remaining 40 per cent a C-rating.

17. The level attained in category A during the first evaluation becomes the industry's target for the following three years. During that time, companies continue to submit and receive reports on trends in their historical performance and how they stand in relation to the rest of the industry. This enables them to strive for improved management by gradually moving their indicators towards the desired goal.

18. At the end of the three years, a new evaluation of performance indicators will set a new level for category A (the best 20 per cent at that time). This new level A becomes the new target for the next three years. Thus, it is the industry that sets itself realistic goals and a gradual pace for sustained improvement. * * *

Code of good practice and manual of procedures

20. This is a document that can be updated and, in addition to being a guide, lists generic environmental practices that are desirable and presently available.

Environmental management systems

21. At company level, the FLORVERDE programme supports the adoption of an ISO 14001-type environmental management system, with specific reference to the following elements:

(a) Initial review or diagnosis;

(b) elaboration of the plan of action and;

(c) follow-up of the commitments undertaken therein.

22. It is intended in each case to set up an environmental committee within the company as part of its administrative structure, enabling it to approach environmental matters preventively.

23. When a company commits itself to environmental management, it examines its production processes and identifies obsolete practices and technologies that could be causing higher costs. In setting the objective of cleaner production, that is, producing more using less resources (inputs, energy and water), the company is aiming simultaneously at environmental efficiencies and lower costs. Thus, the concept "eco-efficiency" which embodies a dual objective, becomes an excellent opportunity for promoting competitiveness within the flower-growing industry. * * *

C. Private eco-labels

25. Despite the efforts described to improve environmental protection, the Colombian flower-growing sector has encountered restrictions on its exports by means of environmental measures. These restrictions have not taken the form of laws or labelling or packaging regulations, but have resulted from the proliferation of private environmental labels being proposed by a variety of organizations.

(a) The origin of the problem

26. Roughly since 1990, campaigns have been waged to discredit Colombian flowers on some international markets. FirstFood Information and Action Network (FIAN) an NGO founded in Germany, launched a "Flower Campaign" with the sole aim of denouncing, inter alia, the environmental aspects of flower production in Colombia.

27. The attacks against flowers from Colombia have not been based on serious, objective and representative studies from the industry. Despite the good intentions of some of these pressure groups, the accusing studies and documents take isolated and not necessarily verified cases as being representative of Colombia's flower-growing industry.

(b) Eco-labelling by private organizations

28. In 1995, at the height of these campaigns, the German importers association (BGI) proposed to ASOCOLFLORES the programme known as the "Colombia Flower Declaration." The aim of this initiative was to produce a voluntary declaration in which Colombian floriculturists would acknowledge compliance with environmental standards in force in Colombia and accordingly agree to submit to an environmental audit by a commission of Colombian and German experts. The BGI also sent a checklist of several requirements that would be verified by the monitoring committee.

29. The proposal also envisaged that a committee of German experts would visit Colombia to verify compliance by each farm with the requirements set out in

the checklist. The experts proposed were basically private consultants and persons linked to universities, but who had no form of accreditation as international certifiers or verifiers.

30. Faced with the threat of exclusion from the European market and bearing in mind that they had no problems of compliance with labour and environmental or occupational health and safety standards in Colombia, the Colombian floriculturists were prepared to go along with the Colombia Flower Declaration and hence to submit to an audit by private consultants from Germany.

31. Nevertheless, ASOCOLFLORES decided not to subscribe to the proposed system of certification, owing to considerations such as the following:

- The programme was very costly and any company agreeing to the scheme would have to pay an additional amount for the label, while there was no mechanism for recovering the investment should the consumer have to pay a surcharge on account of the certification. The proceeds from a so-called green surcharge paid by the consumer would go towards the operation of the labelling scheme in the importing country;

- the approach used was coercive, as anyone who did not accept the labelling scheme was subjected to negative pressure from the Flower Campaign. In other words, the proposal was not consistent with the leading worldwide environmental management initiatives for the private sector, such as those within UNEP, the proposals of the Rio Summit for businessmen who would make up the World Business Council for Sustainable Development, or with current international environmental legislation which envisages voluntary and therefore real commitment by the production sector;

- the scheme proposed by the German importers was discriminatory, as it had not been proposed to any other country exporting flowers to Germany, but was aimed solely at Colombia.

32. Furthermore, the Government of Colombia disapproved of the scheme on the ground that it amounted to an eco-labelling programme in which compliance was subject to verification by foreign experts. It was inadmissible for a foreign committee to be responsible for verifying compliance with Colombian environmental regulations, as that task fell within the exclusive competence of the National Government.

33. In the wake of this refusal, the activities of the Flower Campaign have multiplied, as have the certification initiatives.

34. Indeed, proposals have been received of more than three different types of private environmental labels:

(i) A new proposal from Germany called the "Flower Label Programme" (FLP), which is the being offered only to flower exporters from Colombia and Ecuador, and not to other flower-producing countries. Again, the programme involves a checklist and an audit committee comprised of German experts.

The checklist proposed under the programme seems arbitrary, as it is not clear regarding the terms of compliance with some of its demands, for example, in the following cases:

- The proposed programme states that "only active pesticide ingredients registered in countries with stringent registration laws may be used. Registration procedures in force in the country where the company is located will be given due consideration at the time of evaluation." What is meant by stringent registration laws? How objective is that criterion?

- It further states that "products with toxicological classification (1a) Extremely Toxic and (1b) Highly Toxic, according to the WHO toxicological classification, should only be used in duly justified cases of extreme necessity." What is meant by extreme necessity? How is it defined? That would surely depend on each cultivation and its specific circumstances.

- "Only biodegradable products may be used for post-harvest treatments." No alternative biodegradable products for this type of treatment are as yet commercially available to producers who need to export their products over great distances. What is more, the programme seems very costly to exporters and does not guarantee the gradual process of continual improvement which is being incorporated into the FLORVERDE environmental management programme. It would cost a minimum of US$2,500 per year to defray the expenses arising from the verification visit, plus a price of US$1 per label sold, which must be affixed to each box of exported flowers. In other words, if 20,000 boxes of flowers are sold per year, that would imply US$20,000 in addition to the US$2,500 in verification expenses.

The programme's advocates also said that this extra cost would be met from the premium to be paid by the consumer, though they have no way of guaranteeing that all retailers in Germany will buy FLP flowers exclusively:

(ii) FIAN, the NGO that launched the Flower Campaign, has been working on the design of its own environmental label for flowers from Colombia, in cooperation with the Colombian NGO Fundación Cactus.

(iii) The Max Haveelar Foundation in Switzerland is designing its own generic label, and even though it has not been specifically offered to Colombian flower exporters, there is no doubt that the hope is for it to become the label allowing flowers to be sold on the Swiss market.

35. The experiences described with the BGI's Columbia Flower Declaration and with the private labels proposed to Colombian floriculturists demonstrate the serious threats facing the industry. There is the risk that private organizations with no qualification as international certifiers and without being subject to any kind of international standards, will be in a position to issue environmental product labels.

D. Inherent Dangers of Private Eco-Labelling Schemes

36. Private environmental labels can significantly affect trade flows in that they inform consumers about flowers in a potentially discriminatory manner, depending on whether or not the flowers display the label.

37. The proliferation of private labels sold by private organizations based on divergent and dissimilar criteria would lead to significant trade diversion by favouring demand for flowers displaying those labels, without adequately informing the consumer as to the nature of the labels, the way they are supervised or even how they actually come about. This could lead to market disruption which would then be very difficult to correct.

38. In the case of the Colombian flower industry, for example, a look at its export volumes for the period 1992–1996 shows that while global flower exports

showed an upward trend, exports to Germany declined markedly. One of the possible causes of this is the proliferation of unjustified environmental labels and campaigns in respect of Colombian flowers.

Percentage Change in Volume of Flower Exports from Colombia
Flower Exports from Colombia to Germany 1992–1996

	1992–1993	1993–1994	1994–1995	1995–1996
Global	6.32%	4.15%	0.53%	1.47%
To Germany	-14.93%	-4.85%	-4.15%	-21.80%

Questions and Discussion

1. A major element of Colombia's complaint concerned the discriminatory nature of Germany's flower ecolabels. In what ways were Colombian producers discriminated against? In light of the Colombian flower industry's efforts to improve the environmental performance of its members, shouldn't Germany's ecolabel organizations defer to those efforts? To the extent you find the German labels discriminatory, how could that discrimination have been avoided?

2. Ecuador also exports large quantities of cut flowers. A 1999 International Labor Organization study and a 2003 Catholic University study showed that women in the Ecuadoran flower industry had more miscarriages than average and that more than 60 percent of all workers suffered headaches, nausea, blurred vision, or fatigue. One farm involved in the Catholic University study used several pesticides restricted as health hazards in other countries, including the United States, and labeled as highly toxic by the World Health Organization. One researcher described workers "fumigating in street clothes without protective equipment, pesticides stored in poorly sealed containers and fumes wafting over the workers' dining halls." Ginger Thompson, *Behind Roses' Beauty, Poor and Ill Workers,* N.Y. TIMES, Feb. 13, 2003 (reporting on comments from Dr. Cesar Paz-y-Mino, a geneticist at the Catholic University). These circumstances continue today; the U.S. Labor Education in the Americas Project (USLEAP), a nonprofit organization, found that 66 percent of flower workers in Colombia and Ecuador—the two largest flower exporters to the United States—suffer work-related health problems, as pesticide use and abuse is rampant. USLEAP, More Information on the Flower Industry, http://www.usleap.org/usleap-campaigns/flower-workers-and-economic-justice/more-information-flower-industry. Do these circumstances change your response to whether German organizations should establish ecolabels for flowers produced in specific foreign countries?

3. All the ecolabels referred to in Colombia's complaint were private, voluntary labels. How should the international trading system regulate private, voluntary ecolabels, if at all? Even if you believe it should not regulate these ecolabels, are there principles that might prove valuable for developing them?

4. Claims of discrimination featured in a 1992 dispute, when the Austrian parliament enacted legislation that required all tropical timber and tropical timber products to be labeled "Made From Tropical Timber" or "Containing Tropical Timber." The legislation also imposed a 70 percent tariff increase on the importation of tropical timber, with tar-

iff proceeds pre-designated for projects promoting sustainable forest management of trop-ical timber. The law also called for a voluntary ecolabel to identify the quality of the wood in terms of sustainable management. Many tropical timber producing countries hotly contested Austria's proposals, arguing that they were protectionist and inconsistent with the GATT because the law did not define "sustainably harvested" and, more importantly, because only tropical timber was subject to the labeling requirement. Can you see why de-veloping countries might object to this ecolabel and to ecolabels in general? In this case, they argued that both the mandatory and voluntary aspects of the law violated the dis-crimination provisions of the TBT. Do you agree? Austria has no tropical forests. Does that affect your analysis? Ignoring the tariff increase for the moment, does the Austrian label, merely by identifying products as containing tropical timber, violate Article I or III of the GATT? Are tropical timber and temperate timber "like products"?

Under threat of a WTO dispute by developing countries, Austria repealed both the tariff and mandatory labeling scheme. In its place, it enacted a voluntary ecolabeling pro-gram that included all timber, not just tropical timber. The government also established an advisory board, including environmental NGOs, with the mission of developing prin-ciples and criteria for sustainable forest management certification. *See* Lilly Sucharipa-Behrmann, *Eco-Labels for Tropical Timber: The Austrian Experience, in* OECD, Life-Cycle Management and Trade (1994). Do you think this is an example of trade law having positive regulatory effects — when the threat of a trade dispute resulted in a net environ-mental gain?

5. Daniel Esty says that ecolabels should be the "default" trade restriction. He argues that ecolabels provide information to consumers while also allowing products to be sold, which "strikes a useful balance between trade and environmental goals in many situa-tions where the appropriateness of more severe restrictions is uncertain." Daniel C. Esty: Greening the GATT: Trade, Environment, and the Future 134 (1994). Are ecola-bels an alternative to trade restrictions? For example, would the "dolphin-safe" label in-dicating zero dolphin mortality in a tuna fishery adequately protect dolphins if not supplemented with an import ban on tuna caught using dolphin unsafe fishing meth-ods? The United Nations Environment Programme (UNEP) has drawn the following conclusions:

> The anecdotal evidence ... seems to support the view that most successful eco-labels do not just address individual consumer preferences, but are designed as a complement to other policy initiatives. Potter and Hinnells, for example, state that product labelling 'needs to be integrated with other environmental policy in-struments, and to be part of a coherent policy-making structure.' This suggests that ecolabelling is not effective in itself, but that its overall impact depends on the effectiveness of these other complementary policies. In effect, the establish-ment of an ecolabel should not be seen as a policy initiative in its own right. In-stead, some types of ecolabels should perhaps be considered as — in a general sense — communication tools that enable the creation of incentive mechanisms through other policy initiatives. These can be public or private initiatives.

UNEP, The Trade and Environmental Effects of Ecolabels: Assessment and Re-sponse 8 (2005). Among the other incentive mechanisms that UNEP found most useful for leveraging the effects of ecolabels was government procurement and strategies that focus on suppliers of products. *Id.*

6. More than 30 years have passed since Germany first introduced the Blue Angel eco-label, presumably enough time to gauge the effectiveness of ecolabels. Are ecolabels ef-

fective at producing environmental and economic benefits? At altering production to more environmentally sound processes and production methods? Consider the following:

> Evaluating the effects of policies in the real world is difficult. Ecolabelling policies are no exception to this rule. There is no easily accessible, independent body of data on the environmental effectiveness of ecolabelling. Despite the relatively high profile of the five labels [Editors' note: including Germany's Blue Angel Program and programs associated with the Forest Stewardship Council and "fair trade" labeling] that are the focus of this study, adequate data does not even exist on them. Anecdotal evidence and proxy indicators (many of which are imperfect) are not a sufficient basis for evaluating the environmental usefulness or desirability of ecolabelling programmes. In addition, it is currently difficult to isolate the effects of labelling from other variables that could lead to more sustainable production and consumption. There remains an urgent need to collect additional, reliable scientific data on the environmental effects of existing ecolabelling programmes.

> Neither is reliable, quantified evidence available concerning changes in trade flows—positive or negative—related to ecolabelling. Until trade statistics differentiate between labelled and non-labelled products, the only basis for discussion will be anecdotal evidence and imperfect proxies, such as percentage growth of a labeled market segment. It is currently difficult to evaluate the effects of ecolabelling among all the other variables that affect trade flows. This is particularly the case in regard to developing countries, about which less information is generally available. Thus there is an urgent need to collect additional reliable economic data on the trade effects of ecolabelling programmes. * * *

> To date, much has been made of consumers' willingness to pay for environmentally preferable products. While most ecolabels have not existed long enough for markets to reach maturity, anecdotal evidence generally suggests that price premia (where they exist) are often not sustained. It is unclear why this is the case. It may be due to a transformative impact on the market leading to overall shifts in production patterns (e.g. an increasing supply of ecolabelled products), which satisfies demand and thus reduces prices. However, it may also indicate that consumers are generally unwilling to pay higher prices for ecolabelled products.

> Where price premia do exist, and do accrue to the producer, they can be very important in helping to pay for investments in cleaner technology or production processes. This is another potential effect of ecolabelling that requires further examination. Other economic incentives, including long-term supply contracts, may prove more important than a price premium. Initial analysis suggests that access to markets and (perhaps even more important) the *predictability* of future access to markets is of greater consequence. In this respect, the extent to which ecolabelling could help to create stronger relationships between buyers and suppliers should be investigated.

> Another key factor in assessing the impacts of ecolabelling on sustainable development is: Who receives the economic benefits derived from ecolabelling if these benefits exist? Is it the producers, middlemen or retailers, and in what proportions? Although the data is inadequate for firm conclusions to be drawn, it appears likely that the producer (who bears most of the costs of shifting to more sustainable production techniques) is not the main benefactor of these investments.

In some cases, the spread of ecolabelling may be facilitated by inequitable power dynamics within the supply chain.

UNEP, THE TRADE AND ENVIRONMENTAL EFFECTS OF ECOLABELS, at v, vii. Are you surprised by these conclusions? UNEP concluded that proxies for environmental effectiveness, such as market share and adoption of the label, were inadequate. Why do you think this is so? While recognizing significant data limitations, Professor Errol Meidinger is more optimistic:

> Forest certification, for example, clearly has shifted a multitude of practices in many places around the world. These include not only the environmental practices of forestry firms, but also their dealings with local communities, labor, and other stakeholder groups. The increased consultation and participation spurred by certification also seems to have rippled out into other local institutions in many cases.

Errol Meidinger, *Multi-Interest Self-Governance through Global Product Certification Programs*, 27 (Buffalo Legal Studies Research Paper Series, Paper No. 2006-016, Buffalo, N.Y.) (July 2006).

C. Ecolabels and the WTO

The WTO's Committee on Trade and Environment (CTE) has stated that "[w]ell-designed eco-labelling schemes/programmes can be effective instruments of environmental policy to encourage the development of an environmentally-conscious consumer public." Due to some of the problems raised in the preceding section, however, ecolabeling can sometimes constitute a disguised protectionist measure or discriminate against imported products. Even absent protectionist intent, the use of local criteria can advantage domestic or regional producers. The CTE has noted that "eco-labelling schemes/programmes have raised, in certain cases, significant concerns about their possible trade effects." Report (1996) of the Committee on Trade and Environment, WT/CTE/W/40, para. 183 (Nov. 12, 1996).

Whether those trade effects cause violations of the GATT or the TBT Agreement is another matter. In April 2010, a panel was established to hear renewed complaints by Mexico of the U.S. tuna/dolphin label. The issues are certainly compelling—41 WTO members reserved their right to participate in the dispute. The panel will be looking at several critical issues for the first time. These issues are taken up in Section 2 below. Until then, the only guide remains the unadopted decision in *Tuna/Dolphin I*.

1. Tuna/Dolphin I

In Chapter 4 (pages 200–08) we saw that the *Tuna/Dolphin I* GATT Panel found that a U.S. import ban on tuna caught inconsistently with regulations designed to protect dolphins violated GATT Article XI. That Panel, like the *Tuna/Dolphin II* and *Shrimp/Turtle* Panels that followed, concluded that the criteria for triggering the import ban related to PPMs and that such criteria could not justify distinctions in how a product is treated. In other words, tuna caught using "dolphin-friendly" techniques was "like" tuna caught using other techniques. The *Tuna/Dolphin I* Panel also addressed the question of whether the U.S.'s dolphin-safe ecolabel was consistent with the GATT.

United States-Restrictions on Imports of Tuna

GATT Panel Report, DS21/R (Sept. 3, 1991) (unadopted),
reprinted in 30 I.L.M. 1594 (1991) [hereinafter *Tuna/Dolphin I*]

2.12. The Dolphin Protection Consumer Information Act (DPCIA) specifies a labelling standard for any tuna product exported from or offered for sale in the United States. "Tuna products" covered include any tuna-containing food product processed for retail sale, except perishable items with a shelf life of less than three days. Under this statute, it is a violation of section 5 of the Federal Trade Commission Act (FTCA) for any producer, importer, exporter, distributor or seller of such tuna products to include on the label of that product the term "Dolphin Safe" or any other term falsely suggesting that the tuna contained therein was fished in a manner not harmful to dolphins, if it contains tuna harvested in either of two situations. The two situations are (1) harvesting in the Eastern Tropical Pacific Ocean [ETP] by a vessel using purse-seine nets which does not meet certain specified conditions for being considered dolphin safe, and (2) harvesting on the high seas by a vessel engaged in driftnet fishing. Violations of Section 5 of the FTCA are subject to civil penalties. The DPCIA provided that its labelling standard and civil penalty provisions for tuna products would take effect on 28 May 1991. Regulations to implement the DPCIA had not yet been issued at the time of the Panel's consideration. * * *

5.41. The Panel noted that Mexico considered the labelling provisions of the DPCIA to be marking requirements falling under Article IX:1, which reads: "Each contracting party shall accord to the products of the territories of other contracting parties treatment with regard to marking requirements no less favourable than the treatment accorded to like products of any third country."

The United States considered that the labelling provisions were subject not to Article IX but to the most-favoured-nation and national-treatment provisions of Articles I:1 and III:4. The Panel noted that the title of Article IX is "Marks of Origin" and its text refers to marking of origin of imported products. The Panel further noted that Article IX does not contain a national-treatment but only a most-favoured-nation requirement, which indicates that this provision was intended to regulate marking of origin of imported products but not marking of products generally. The Panel therefore found that the labeling provisions of the DPCIA did not fall under Article IX:1.

5.42. The Panel proceeded to examine the subsidiary argument by Mexico that the labelling provisions of the DPCIA were inconsistent with Article I:1 because they discriminated against Mexico as a country fishing in the ETP. The Panel noted that the labelling provisions of the DPCIA do not restrict the sale of tuna products; tuna products can be sold freely both with and without the "Dolphin Safe" label. Nor do these provisions establish requirements that have to be met in order to obtain an advantage from the government. Any advantage which might possibly result from access to this label depends on the free choice by consumers to give preference to tuna carrying the "Dolphin Safe" label. The labeling provisions therefore did not make the right to sell tuna or tuna products, nor the access to a government-conferred advantage affecting the sale of tuna or tuna products, conditional upon the use of tuna harvesting methods. The only issue before the Panel was therefore whether the provisions of the DPCIA governing the right of access to the label met the requirements of Article I:1.

5.43. The Panel noted that the DPCIA is based *inter alia* on a finding that dolphins are frequently killed in the course of tuna-fishing operations in the ETP through the use of purse-seine nets intentionally deployed to encircle dolphins. The DPCIA therefore accords the right to use the label "Dolphin Safe" for tuna harvested in the ETP only if such tuna is accompanied by documentary evidence showing that it was not harvested with purse-seine nets intentionally deployed to encircle dolphins. The Panel examined whether this requirement applied to tuna from the ETP was consistent with Article I:1. According to the information presented to the Panel, the harvesting of tuna by intentionally encircling dolphins with purse-seine nets was practised only in the ETP because of the particular nature of the association between dolphins and tuna observed only in that area. By imposing the requirement to provide evidence that this fishing technique had not been used in respect of tuna caught in the ETP the United States therefore did not discriminate against countries fishing in this area. The Panel noted that, under United States customs law, the country of origin of fish was determined by the country of registry of the vessel that had caught the fish; the geographical area where the fish was caught was irrelevant for the determination of origin. The labelling regulations governing tuna caught in the ETP thus applied to all countries whose vessels fished in this geographical area and thus did not distinguish between products originating in Mexico and products originating in other countries.

5.44. The Panel found for these reasons that the tuna products labelling provisions of the DPCIA relating to tuna caught in the ETP were not inconsistent with the obligations of the United States under Article I:1 of the General Agreement.

Questions and Discussion

1. Recall that the *Tuna/Dolphin I* Panel had earlier ruled that measures must relate to the product as a product and that nonproduct-related PPMs could not be used to discriminate among otherwise like products. Why do you think the Panel abandoned that logic? Do you think that the decision would have been different if the "dolphin-safe" label was required?

2. *Rules of Origin*. The Agreement on Rules of Origin defines a rule of origin as a criterion applied by a country to determine the country of origin of goods. It is through such rules that products are labeled "Made in Thailand." *Preferential rules of origin* determine whether a product comes from a country that gets preferential treatment, such as reduced duty rates. Each country may set whatever preferential rules it likes. *Nonpreferential rules of origin* determine the country of origin for all other purposes (for whatever policy and practical reasons, including trade restrictions). The lack of rules of origin in GATT 1947 allowed each country to determine its own preferential and nonpreferential rules and led to substantial differences in approaches. As a result, the Agreement on Rules of Origin established the Committee on Rules of Origin to develop harmonized rules and a Technical Committee on Rules of Origin to undertake the necessary technical work. According to the 2003 minutes of the Rules Committee, G/L/656, 94 core policy issues have been identified that must be resolved before a harmonized set of rules is possible. Until those rules are completed, the Agreement on Rules of Origin provides guidance during this "transition period." Under Article 2, the rules of origin must not be

used as trade policy instruments, may not "create restrictive, distorting or disruptive effects on international trade," and must be based on a "positive standard" based on what is required rather than what is not required. Any administrative actions taken in relation to the determination of origin must be available for prompt, independent review. Nevertheless, the work plan identifies two basic principles for harmonization. First, if a product is wholly produced in one country, it originates from that country. Second, if a product is produced in more than one country, its country of origin is where it was "last substantially transformed." The Rules Committee and Technical Committee will ultimately define "substantial transformation" in more detail. For more on rules of origin, see Joseph A. LaNasa, *Rules of Origin and the Uruguay Round's Effectiveness in Harmonizing and Regulating Them,* 90 Am. J. Int'l L. 625, 626 (1996); Raj Bhala & Kevin Kennedy, World Trade Law 267–91 (1998); Philippe G. Nell, *WTO Negotiations on the Harmonization of Rules of Origin: A First Critical Appraisal,* 33 J. World Trade 45 (1999).

3. *Marks of Origin.* Marks of origin are those symbols and other marks that identify the origin of the product. Article IX of the GATT prohibits discrimination among marks from different countries. Thus, a member may not require a disfavored country to mark its products with a skull and crossbones, while allowing a favored country to mark its products with flowers. It also requires, among other things, that marking requirements not "seriously damage" the product, "materially reduce" its value, or "unreasonably increase" its cost. It further requires members to cooperate to prevent the use of trade names to misrepresent the true origin of the product to the detriment of distinctive regional or geographic names, such as Champagne or Bordeaux.

---

2. Tuna/Dolphin III

As a result of the *Tuna/Dolphin* dispute, U.S. domestic and international developments led to new rules—and litigation—for labeling tuna as "dolphin safe." First, the members of the Inter-American Tropical Tuna Commission (IATTC), which has jurisdiction over the tuna fishery at issue in the dispute, adopted the Agreement for an International Dolphin Conservation Program (AIDCP). The AIDCP sets dolphin mortality limits for each vessel fishing for tuna in the eastern tropical Pacific Ocean (ETP). It further establishes requirements for tracking tuna into the marketplace to ensure that dolphin-safe tuna does not get mixed with other tuna. It also requires each vessel fishing for tuna to have an internationally trained observer on board to document that catches meet the requirements of the AIDCP. AIDCP Parties and individual vessels that fail to comply with these requirements are subject to a compliance regime that can impose sanctions—including the loss of dolphin mortality limits.

Due to the import restrictions of the U.S. Marine Mammal Protection Act and developments within the IATTC and AIDCP, dolphin mortality has dropped from more than 420,000 per year in the 1970s to fewer than 1,000 per year today. In light of the AIDCP, the U.S. Congress enacted the International Dolphin Conservation Program Act (IDCPA), Pub. L. No. 105-42, 111 Stat. 1122 (1997), which conditionally amended the dolphin-safe labeling standard of the DPCIA. The IDCPA directed the Secretary of Commerce to make initial and final findings of "whether the intentional deployment on or encirclement of dolphin with purse seine nets is having a significant adverse impact on any depleted dolphin stock in the eastern tropical Pacific Ocean." Dolphin Protection Consumer Information Act, 16 U.S.C. § 1385(d)(2) (1999). These findings would determine the requirements for labeling tuna as "dolphin safe":

If the Secretary determines that purse seine fishing in the ETP *has no* significant adverse impact on any depleted dolphin stock, then tuna from there may be labeled as "dolphin safe" if:

1) the tuna was caught in compliance with rules established by the IATTC/AIDCP; and

2) if purse seine nets were used, if the captain and a qualified observer certify that no dolphins were killed or seriously injured during the sets in which the tuna were caught.

If the Secretary finds that purse seine fishing *does have* a significant adverse impact on any depleted dolphin stock, then tuna may not be labeled as "dolphin safe" only if the captain and a qualified observer certify:

1) that no tuna were caught *on the trip* in which such tuna were harvested using a purse seine net intentionally deployed on or to encircle dolphins, and

2) that no dolphins were killed or seriously injured *during the sets* in which the tuna were caught.

16 U.S.C. § 1385(d)(2)(B), § 1385(h)(1999) (emphasis added).

Congress required the Secretary to conduct the so-called "stress" studies to determine whether purse seine fishing was having a significant adverse impact on any depleted dolphin stock. Although the MMPA and efforts within the IATTC had reduced dolphin mortality from an estimate of 423,678 in 1972 to perhaps fewer than 1,000 today, three populations of dolphin—eastern spinner dolphin, northeastern offshore spotted dolphin and coastal spotted dolphin—associated with the tuna fishery remained "depleted." Indeed, these studies reported that:

> [w]ith this dramatic reduction in mortality, indications of the initial stages of a recovery of the affected populations to pre-exploitation abundance levels would be expected. Despite considerable scientific effort by fishery scientists, there is little evidence of recovery, and concerns remain that the practice of chasing and encircling dolphins somehow is adversely affecting the ability of these depleted stocks to recover.

SOUTHWEST FISHERIES SCIENCE CENTER, NATIONAL OCEANIC AND ATMOSPHERIC ADMINISTRATION, REPORT OF THE SCIENTIFIC RESEARCH PROGRAM UNDER THE INTERNATIONAL DOLPHIN CONSERVATION PROGRAM ACT (Sept. 17, 2002). Nonetheless, the Department of Commerce determined that "the chase and intentional deployment on or encirclement of dolphins with purse seine nets is not having a significant adverse impact on depleted dolphin stocks." Taking and Importing of Marine Mammals, 68 Fed. Reg. 2010–11 (Jan. 15, 2003).

In August 2004, a federal district court agreed with environmental groups that the Secretary's decision was arbitrary and capricious. The court found that, while the record was hampered by the limited data obtained from the studies, virtually all of the best available scientific evidence pointed toward the fishery having a significant adverse impact on the dolphin stocks. Earth Island Inst. v. Evans, 2004 U.S. Dist. LEXIS 15729 (N.D. Cal. Aug. 9, 2004), *aff'd* Earth Island Inst. v. Hogarth, 494 F.3d 757 (9th Cir. 2007). As a result, the "dolphin-safe" label continues to mean that the tuna was not harvested with purse seine nets and that no dolphins were killed or seriously injured when the tuna were caught.

Mexico, whose fishermen export large amounts of tuna to the United States, has objected to the U.S. labeling requirements, alleging that they "have the effect of prohibiting the labelling of Mexican tuna and tuna products as "dolphin-safe", even when the tuna has been harvested by means that comply with the multilaterally agreed "dolphin-safe" standard established by the Inter-American Tropical Tuna Commission." United States-Measures Concerning the Importation, Marketing and Sale of Tuna and Tuna Products, Request for the Establishment of a Panel by Mexico, WT/DS381/4 (Mar. 10, 2009). Mexico specifically considers the U.S. labeling requirements to be inconsistent with Articles I:1 and III:4 of the GATT. It also claims that the requirements violate Article 2 of the TBT Agreement for the following reasons:

1. Mexican products are accorded treatment less favourable than like products of US origin and like products originating in any other country, contrary to Article 2.1 of the TBT Agreement;

2. The measures have the effect of creating unnecessary obstacles to trade, contrary to Article 2.2 of the TBT Agreement;

3. The measures are maintained although their objectives can be addressed in a less trade-restrictive manner, contrary to Article 2.3 of the TBT Agreement; and

4. The measures do not use as their basis an existing international standard, contrary to Article 2.4 of the TBT Agreement.

As noted above, the Panel will be asked to interpret for the first time several critical issues relating to the TBT Agreement. These include the following issues:

a. Relevant International Organization

The following States and regional economic organizations have ratified or acceded to the Agreement: Costa Rica, Ecuador, El Salvador, European Union, Guatemala, Honduras, Mexico, Nicaragua, Panama, Peru, United States, Vanuatu, and Venezuela. Reread the material from pages 372–76. Is the AIDCP a "relevant international organization" competent to make "international standards"? On what basis should the Panel make its decision?

b. Ecolabels and the TBT Agreement — PPMs Revisited

Because ecolabels can identify product characteristics, they implicate the TBT Agreement. The question is not whether the TBT Agreement applies to ecolabels generally; the Appellate Body in *Sardines* made clear that the simple act of naming a product brings it within the scope of the TBT Agreement. The question is whether the TBT Agreement covers ecolabels based on nonproduct-related PPMs, such as the "dolphin-safe" label. Because the point of many ecolabels is to identify "green" PPMs, this issue remains critical.

After ten years of discussion in the WTO, the members cannot agree on the TBT Agreement's coverage of PPM-based ecolabels. Two idiosyncrasies of the TBT Agreement text are at the root of the difficulty. First, the TBT Agreement defines mandatory "technical regulations" and voluntary "standards" slightly differently. A "technical regulation" is a document setting forth "product characteristics or their related processes and production methods." A voluntary "standard" is a document providing "rules, guidelines, or characteristics for products or related processes and production methods."

An authoritative review of the negotiating history of this text by the WTO Secretariat indicates substantial ambiguity about whether the relevant distinction between the two definitions—namely, the single word "their" before "related"—was inadvertent or indicated some intention that the scope of the two definitions be different. WTO Secretariat, *Negotiating History of the Coverage of the Agreement on Technical Barriers to Trade with Regard to Labelling Requirements, Voluntary Standards and Processes and Production Methods Unrelated to Product Characteristics,* WT/CTE/W/10, G/TBT/W/11, paras. 145–151 (Aug. 29, 1995). All agree that the TBT Agreement applies to technical regulations and standards regarding PPMs related to the quality or character of the final product, such as the sterilization requirements in the EU's sardines regulation. Whether harvesting methods, pollution controls, and other PPMs not related to product characteristics are covered is much less clear. Based on the first sentence of the definitions of both "technical regulation" and "standard," one possibility is that such PPM measures are covered if the measure is a mandatory technical regulation, but they are *not* covered if the measure is a voluntary standard. Since most ecolabeling regimes are voluntary in nature, such a differentiation in the scope of the TBT Agreement is a central issue of dispute.

This brings us to the second textual idiosyncrasy: for both a "technical regulation" and a "standard," the second sentence of each definition provides that "It may also include … marking or labelling requirements as they apply to a product, process or production method." Curiously, this phrasing omits language indicating that the process or production method should be "related to" the characteristics of the product. How might these textual discrepancies be resolved? Does the open-ended nature of the reference to PPMs in the second sentence overcome or supersede the apparent limits of the "related" test in the first sentence?

The EU and many developing countries, among others, have argued that nonproduct-related PPM technical regulations are not covered. These members focus on the first sentence of the definition, which defines a technical regulation as a "document" laying down "product characteristics or *their related* processes and production methods." The first sentence, they claim, covers *only* product-related PPMs. Then, they define "it" in the second sentence to mean "a document laying down product characteristics or their related processes and production methods." As a result, any PPM covered by the TBT Agreement must relate to product characteristics. The second sentence's reference to PPMs is simply a shorthand for the formulation already expressed in the first sentence; the second sentence cannot reasonably be interpreted as broadening the scope of requirements for labeling and other concerns beyond the scope of the first sentence.

The debate appears more politically motivated than legally based. The EU, as an advocate of ecolabels, believes that ecolabels based on nonproduct-related PPMs are permissible under the GATT and therefore does not want them to be covered by the TBT Agreement. The EU already has a broad range of ecolabels, some required by regulations and directives of the EU itself, rather than individual countries. Its interpretation will ensure that it and its members have the right to use ecolabels. Developing countries, while adopting the legal analysis of the EU concerning "technical regulation," are not guided solely by concerns for existing ecolabels; they do not want to legitimate the use of nonproduct-related criteria for any purpose. Based on decisions such as *Shrimp/Turtle,* they believe that nonproduct-related criteria for ecolabels would be inconsistent with the GATT. Although the WTO's Committee on Trade and Environment (CTE) has discussed the issue of whether nonproduct-related standards may be legitimate criteria for ecolabels, no proposal has come close to consensus. In addition, despite an exhaustive analysis by the WTO Secretariat of the negotiating history of the Standards Code as well as the TBT Agreement, it could only conclude that the negotiating history "suggests that many participants were of the view that standards based *inter alia* on PPMs unrelated to a product's characteristics" fell outside the scope of the

TBT Agreement. WTO Secretariat, *Negotiating History*, WT/CTE/W/10, G/TBT/W/11, at para. 3(c).

The political aspect to this debate is highlighted by the often opposite views of the members with respect to voluntary standards: because the TBT Agreement calls for notification of actions affecting trade in products and sets certain procedural requirements and legal standards designed to ensure fairness in such standards, governments with voluntary programs frequently argue that the TBT Agreement does not apply. In essence, their position is that they have no binding trade obligations with respect to such ecolabeling. This has been the position of the EU, among others. The EU prevailed on Denmark to withdraw its notification of certain ecolabeling standards so as to maintain its view that notification is not required. Developing countries and others skeptical of ecolabeling programs, however, argue that the TBT does apply, because that is their only hope of persuading countries to do a better job of making the voluntary labeling systems more transparent and more even-handed in their effect. Canada, which has an ecolabeling program, has also taken this view, putting forward a proposal that the WTO should confirm that the provisions of the TBT Agreement and its Code of Good Practice apply to all ecolabeling schemes, whether voluntary or mandatory, and whether administered by governmental or nongovernmental bodies. Ellen Margrethe Basse & Sanford E. Gaines, *How Thinking About Trade Can Improve Environmental Performance: Trade Issues in Environmental Labelling Systems*, 8 ENVTL. LIABILITY 71, 79 (2000).

Canada has sought a middle ground in hopes of resolving the issue. It recognizes both the TBT Agreement's ambiguous definition of "technical regulation" as compared to the definition of "standard" but also the growing importance of ecolabeling. As such, it recommends that the members interpret the TBT Agreement to cover the use of certain standards based on nonproduct-related PPMs, provided that the standards adhere strictly to multilaterally-agreed ecolabeling guidelines, including nondiscrimination; national treatment; transparency and consultation; use of relevant international standards when they exist; and consideration given to available scientific and technical information. Canada made clear that its proposal "should not be interpreted as providing any scope or safe haven for the use of standards based on unilaterally-determined nonproduct-related PPMs that do not strictly adhere to multilaterally-agreed eco-labelling guidelines" and that consideration should be given to equivalency of standards and mutual recognition based on a case-by-case approach. Canada, Committee on Technical Barriers to Trade, G/TBT/W/21, WT/CTE/W/21, para. 19 (Feb. 21, 1996).

c. Voluntary Labels and the GATT

The dolphin-safe label is voluntary. In other words, U.S. law does not require that tuna be labeled as "dolphin safe" if it meets the applicable requirements. However, only tuna that meets the requirements may be labeled as "dolphin safe."

Arthur Appleton argues that *voluntary* labels like the "dolphin safe" label do not violate Article XI of the GATT except "when there are sufficient government incentives to discourage the import of goods that do not bear [on] the label in question—perhaps in the form of a government programme that stigmatizes the import of unlabelled goods." Appleton, *Environmental Labelling Schemes Revisited*, at 255; *see also* COOK ET AL., APPLYING TRADE RULES TO TIMBER LABELING, at 29. Others believe that *mandatory* labels are covered by Articles I and III of the GATT but that it is not clear whether voluntary labels implemented by governments are. Ellen Margrethe Basse & Sanford E. Gaines, *How Thinking About Trade Can Improve Environmental Performance*, at 78.

Are labels covered by the nondiscrimination obligations or are they covered by Article XI? Analyses vary as to whether the exceptions of Article XX of the GATT will save specific labels, but many argue that, assuming a label violates Article XI of the GATT, it will be justifiable under Article XX. To the extent that the label is reviewed for trade-restrictiveness under Article XX(b) or the chapeau of Article XX, labels should constitute the least trade-restrictive alternative reasonably available. Nevertheless, the *Shrimp/Turtle* decisions require flexibility in the application of a measure so that differing conditions can be accounted for. Review the Article XX analyses of the Appellate Body in *Asbestos, Reformulated Gasoline,* and *Shrimp/Turtle.* Do you think the dolphin-safe label is consistent with those decisions?

Questions and Discussion

1. *Classroom Exercise.* Review the materials concerning *Tuna/Dolphin III* as well as Section II of this chapter. Divide the class into the following groups: 1) the United States, 2) Mexico, 3) the European Union, 4) Brazil (representing Latin American countries that do not fish in the ETP), and 5) Panel members. Debate the issues presented by Mexico's complaint.

2. Given that the TBT Agreement was designed to discipline product standards and was negotiated in the wake of (although not because of) the *Tuna/Dolphin* disputes, do you think it odd that the TBT Agreement is not clear as to whether it covers nonproduct-related PPMs? Would their omission from the TBT Agreement be consistent with the idea that trade rules do not discipline characteristics unrelated to the product? Professor Jan McDonald supports an interpretation that ensures that all the labeling schemes, regardless of whether based on PPMs, fall within the scope of the TBT Agreement. This approach, she says, "acknowledges that a label (or packaging) is attached to and therefore *necessarily part of* the product itself, regardless of the criteria by which the label is awarded or the warnings/statements it makes." Jan McDonald, *Domestic Regulation, Harmonization, and Technical Barriers to Trade,* at 14. Does the definition of technical regulation suggest that a label is *part of* the product itself?

3. The EU and many developing countries argue that voluntary ecolabels concerning nonproduct-related PPMs are not covered by the TBT Agreement. The EU takes the position that such labels are permissible under the GATT because they are not covered by any of the GATT articles. On what basis might voluntary labeling systems lie outside WTO jurisdiction? Does the same argument hold if the labeling system is determined to be mandatory? The developing countries take the opposite position on voluntary PPM-based ecolabeling systems, arguing that such ecolabels are not allowed under the TBT Agreement and are not permissible under relevant GATT articles either. What article or articles do the developing countries have in mind? Are voluntary ecolabels vulnerable to GATT challenge? If so, would Article XX be available to save an ecolabeling system from being found GATT-inconsistent?

4. Are ecolabels trade-restrictive within the meaning of the TBT Agreement? According to Arthur Appleton, they are not:

> By their very nature, labelling requirements that simply provide product-related information, even if mandatory, are not a particularly trade-restrictive measure. Instead, product-related labelling tends to play an informative role. Despite the fact that labelling may result in consumers choosing not to purchase certain

products based on the information provided, … such product discrimination is indirect and, for many people (particularly those in the developed world), well within what they would view as necessary for informed decisionmaking and consumer choice.

Arthur Appleton, *Environmental Labelling Schemes Revisited*, at 259. Appleton's comment above only considers the requirement not to create an "unnecessary obstacle to trade." Nevertheless, do you think it is so easy to categorize all labeling requirements as informative? As not trade-restrictive? Moreover, when the MFN and national treatment obligations are added, do ecolabels encounter problems? Are the following ecolabels consistent with the TBT Agreement? What information, if any, might you need to answer whether any of these labels are consistent with the TBT Agreement?

- Austria's former requirement to label all tropical timber and tropical timber products as "Made From Tropical Timber" or "Containing Tropical Timber."

- Austria's voluntary ecolabel identifying timber in terms of sustainable forest management practices.

- Under the voluntary "Energy Star" program of the United States, dishwashers can be labeled with the Energy Star if they are at least 25 percent more efficient than minimum federal government standards. DVD players receive the Energy Star if they consume three watts of power or less when switched off.

5. Environmental advocates, as well as advocates for worker's rights, have difficulty accepting that Article XI of the GATT prevents trade restrictions based on PPMs and that the TBT Agreement may also prevent ecolabels based on PPMs. Unless an Article XX exception applies, then not only must a member import products that may be environmentally or socially undesirable from the perspective of that member, but consumers will have no means to identify undesirable from desirable products. You can see why ecolabeling issues draw passionate discussion. What is the solution?

———

D. The Way Forward?

As the WTO members continue to wrestle over the coverage of ecolabels, including nonproduct-related PPMs, some headway has been made on other ways to improve the use of ecolabels. Within the framework of the TBT Agreement, members are identifying strategies for increased use of equivalence or mutual recognition, as well as greater transparency. Outside the TBT Agreement, organizations such as the ISO are developing harmonized guidelines for ecolabeling. Other organizations, such as the Forest Stewardship Council, have developed elaborate institutional structures and universally applicable ecolabeling criteria capable of addressing local ecological conditions.

1. Transparency

Increased transparency of ecolabeling programs has been a significant goal of the Committee on Technical Barriers to Trade. Article 2 of the TBT Agreement provides a number of provisions requiring members to notify other members of their technical regulations. It also allows members to obtain information concerning the technical regulations of other members. The Code of Good Practice requires standardizing bodies to publish their work programs, make standards available for comment, take into account any comments received, and publish the final standard. Article 10 requires members to establish an "enquiry point" to answer questions about their technical regulations, standards, and conformity assessment procedures.

Nevertheless, foreign producers often have difficulties obtaining information concerning mandatory and voluntary ecolabeling programs of other countries. To address transparency concerns, the Committee on Technical Barriers to Trade made the following recommendation:

> In order to improve transparency, acceptance of, and compliance with the Code [of Good Practice], the Committee agreed to the following: ... (e) without prejudice to the views of Members concerning the coverage and application of the [TBT] Agreement, the obligation to publish notices of draft standards containing voluntary labelling requirements under paragraph L of the Code is not dependent upon the kind of information provided on the label.

Committee on Technical Barriers to Trade, *First Triennial Review of the Operation and Implementation of the Agreement on Technical Barriers to Trade*, G/TBT/5, para. 12 (Nov. 5, 1997).

Questions and Discussion

1. What goal did the Committee on Technical Barriers to Trade hope to achieve with its recommendation? How did the Committee handle the PPM issue?

2. Do you think any adverse trade effects and obstacles to market entry resulting from ecolabels can be overcome by promoting transparency, consultation, and disseminating adequate and timely information?

3. Earlier in the chapter, the claim was made that ecolabel criteria were biased toward local production or ecological factors. Can greater transparency resolve those problems?

4. To promote transparency, the WTO has established the TBT Information Management System (TBT IMS). The TBT IMS is "a 'one-stop' system to allow users to track and obtain information on TBT measures that Member governments have notified to the WTO, on Member governments' enquiry points, on standardizing bodies having accepted the Code of Good Practice on publications used to provide information on technical regulations, standards and conformity assessment procedures and on statements on implementation and administration of the TBT Agreement." WTO, TBT Information Management System, http://tbtims.wto.org.

---

2. Equivalence and Mutual Recognition

In the TBT Agreement context, "equivalence" describes the process of recognizing another member's technical regulations and standards. "Mutual recognition" describes the recognition of another member's conformity assessment procedures.

With respect to equivalence, Article 2.7 of the TBT Agreement provides that:

> Members shall give positive consideration to accepting as equivalent technical regulations of other Members, even if these regulations differ from their own, pro-

vided that they are satisfied that these regulations adequately fulfill the objectives of their own regulations.

With respect to mutual recognition, Article 6.1 provides that:

Members shall ensure, whenever possible, that results of conformity assessment procedures in other Members are accepted, even when those procedures differ from their own, provided they are satisfied that those procedures offer an assurance of conformity with applicable technical regulations or standards equivalent to their own procedures.

Article 6.3 also encourages members to engage in negotiations toward "mutual recognition" of each other's conformity assessment procedures. In contrast, the Code of Good Practice does not contain an "equivalence" or "mutual recognition" provision for standards. Given the large number of voluntary standards, members have asked for an examination of this issue.

During the First Triennial Review of the TBT Agreement, WTO members called for greater acceptance of other members' technical regulations as "equivalent." If the members embrace equivalence and mutual recognition, an ecolabel issued in one country pursuant to that member's criteria and conformity assessment procedures would be deemed to satisfy the criteria and procedures of the other member. Mexico, for example, could grant "dolphin-safe" labels for use in the U.S. market, assuming of course that the legitimate objectives of the U.S. tuna/dolphin policy are met.

The move toward equivalence and mutual recognition is not likely to be easy. First, some claim that differences in economic development pose challenges to equivalence because that generally foreshadows discrepancies in the stringency of standards. Second:

many participants are concerned about undermining the credibility of their own labels if products that meet less stringent criteria are awarded the corresponding domestic label through mutual recognition. Concessions made to implement mutual recognition are also likely to inflame any tension on the issue of competitiveness between domestic producers and exporting producers. Nevertheless, some criteria, such as those based on PPMs focusing on domestic environmental conditions, are more easily coordinated through mutual recognition. Mutual recognition allows exporting producers to use the criteria of exporting countries and thereby benefit from standards that reflect the environmental conditions where the product was made.

Atsuko Okubo, *Environmental Labeling Programs and the GATT/WTO Regime*, 11 GEO. INT'L ENVTL. L. REV. 599, 641–42 (1999).

Beyond the issue of credibility, further difficulties arise in ascertaining whether or not another country has the same legitimate objective and whether criteria are equivalent. As described in the next section, the development of criteria capable of addressing regional differences can help overcome this problem. If comparable environmental objectives can be achieved in different ways and also take into account specific environmental conditions of each country, then equivalency and mutual recognition can encourage regulatory efficiency and autonomy while achieving the environmental goals of the label. The next section pursues this challenge.

----

3. Harmonizing Ecolabels

At least two paths could lead to greater equivalencies of standards for ecolabeling. First, various definitions could be harmonized in the same way that Codex and ISO develop standards for product characteristics. In fact, Codex and ISO have initiated such processes. In addition, programs could universalize ecological and other criteria for issuing ecolabels. The Forest Stewardship Council provides a model for doing so.

a. Codex and ISO Efforts

Both Codex Alimentarius and ISO have initiated projects to establish international standards that could affect labeling programs. Codex has drafted rules for defining and labeling organic foods. In addition to defining "organic" to exclude genetically modified foods, Codex has proposed rules for labeling processed foods whose ingredients are not completely organic. Moreover, it has proposed rules for inspection and monitoring (i.e., conformity assessment). Codex Alimentarius Commission, *Guidelines for the Production, Processing, Labelling and Marketing of Organically Produced Food*, GL 32-1999, Rev. 1-2001 (last amended in 2009). A separate Codex committee has been developing guidelines for labeling foods derived from biotechnology, but after nearly two decades it has failed to reach a consensus on definitions, the scope of the guidelines, the provisions of the guidelines, threshold levels, exemptions, label declarations, and implementation. Many countries now oppose the establishment of such guidelines altogether. Codex Alimentarius Commission, Report of the Thirty-Eighth Session of the Codex Committee on Food Labelling, ALINORM 10/03/22, at 134–61 (May 3–7, 2010).

More generally, ISO is developing standards specifically governing ecolabeling. ISO 14020 defines the scope of its labeling provisions to include multi-issue third-party labeling ("Type I"), single-issue first party labels ("Type II"), and ecolabels based on LCA ("Type III"). ISO 14020 establishes nine general principles that apply not only to labeling schemes but to all environmental claims, designed to promote accurate, verifiable, and relevant information. ISO 14021 and 14022 establish requirements for self-declared first-party labels and define key terms and symbols used in ecolabels, such as "recycled content." ISO 14024 establishes standardized criteria for evaluating multi-issue ecolabels. Meanwhile, ISO 14040–14043 establish principles for LCA, although there is no requirement to perform LCA according to these guidelines.

---

b. Universal Ecolabel Criteria: The Forest Stewardship Council

Rather than harmonize the underlying terminology for ecolabels as the ISO 14000 series proposes or harmonizing definitions as Codex proposes, commentators, including Daniel Esty, have proposed the use of labels based on several broad principles that can address differences in natural endowments. First, ecolabeling programs must reflect the spectrum of issues relating to the product being labeled. When labeling timber, for example, the criteria should account for water pollution, mitigation of climate change, soil erosion, and biodiversity loss. Second, the label should incorporate life-cycle analysis so that a product is not given a "green" rating based on a single variable. Third, criteria should be sensitive to differences in natural and geographic variables. Fourth, draft criteria should be made available for comment by all interested parties and they should be given a chance to comment. ESTY, GREENING THE GATT, at 135; *see also* Rene Vossenaar, *Eco-Labelling and International Trade: The Main Issues*, *in* ECO-LABELLING AND INTERNATIONAL TRADE 21, 32 (Simonetta Zarrilli et al. eds., 1997).

The Forest Stewardship Council (FSC) provides an interesting example of how those principles can be put into practice on a global scale. FSC is a nonprofit, nongovernmental organization established in 1993 to promote environmentally responsible, socially beneficial, and economically viable management of the world's forests. FSC, like ecolabels generally, seeks to harness public concern about the environmental impacts of logging into a market force. FSC thus developed international principles criteria for sustainable forest management (SFM). These Principles and Criteria apply to all tropical, temperate, and boreal forests and address legal issues, indigenous rights, labor rights, multiple benefits, and environmental impacts surrounding forest management. They were developed through an extensive international consultation involving a diverse and large number of interest groups.

The FSC's 10 Principles include: 1) compliance with laws; 2) tenure and use rights; 3) recognition of legal and customary rights of indigenous peoples to own, use and manage their lands, territories, and resources; 4) maintenance of high conservation value forests; and 5) the development of written management plans appropriate to the scale and intensity of operations. Based on these Principles and Criteria, approved by FSC International, the roughly 50 national initiatives of FSC then develop National Indicators or regional criteria to account for local conditions. For example, FSC-United States has adopted National Indicators as well as standards for nine regions covering specific forest types in the continental United States that are applied "above and beyond" the Principles and Criteria. Forest Stewardship Council–United States, Standards and Policies, http://www.fscus.org/standards_criteria.

Through this process, a principle to conserve biological diversity and its associated values, water resources, soils, and unique and fragile ecosystems gets translated into a number of much more specific standards, including the following:

6.3. Ecological functions and values shall be maintained intact, enhanced, or restored, including:

  a) Forest regeneration and succession.

  b) Genetic, species, and ecosystem diversity.

  c) Natural cycles that affect the productivity of the forest ecosystem.

  d) Old-growth stands and forests

  e) Retention

  f) Even-aged silvicultural systems

6.3.a.1. Forest owners or managers use the following information to make management decisions regarding regeneration: landscape patterns (e.g., successional processes, land use/land cover, non-forest uses, habitat types); ecological characteristics of adjacent forested stands (e.g., age, productivity, health); species' requirements; and frequency, distribution, and intensity of natural disturbances.

Revised Final Pacific Coast (USA) Regional Forest Stewardship Standard Version 9.0, Approved by FSC-US Board Aug. 12, 2002, Accredited by FSC International, July 26, 2003, http://www.scscertified.com/docs/pcwg_9.0_NTC.pdf.

In the end, certification organizations conduct certification to FSC standards and give written assurance that a product, process, or service conforms to specified requirements. A number of certification organizations have received FSC accreditation, including Rainforest Alliance's Smartwood Program (U.S.); Scientific Certification System's Forest Conservation Program SGS-Forestry Qualifor Programme (U.K.); Soil Association's Responsible Forestry Programme (U.K.). As of March 2010, more than 125 million hectares of forest in more than 80 countries have been certified to FSC standards, and several thousand products now carry the FSC trademark. For more details, *see* http://www.fscus.org/certifiers; http://www.fsc.org.

––––––––––

Questions and Discussion

1. The approaches of Codex, ISO, and FSC offer three distinct options for harmonizing ecolabels. Which approach do you think best meets environmental goals? Which best resolves trade concerns? Which approach makes equivalency and mutual recognition findings more readily accepted, while at the same time ensuring the integrity of the ecolabel?

2. Do the four principles described by Esty and Vossenaar provide a sound basis for ecolabeling at the global scale? Is it possible that implementation of these principles instead will dilute ecolabeling criteria and make them meaningless? Consider, for example, the FSC criteria quoted above. Are the criteria robust enough to provide meaningful information to consumers about timber products and to treat timber products from various parts of the world in a fair, nondiscriminatory way? If not, do you think a better ecolabel would use a scorecard with numerical scores in three areas: sustainable management; ecosystem health; and community benefit? An overall score could be awarded to the forest manager, say from 1 to 5, with a score of 1 signifying noncertifiable and 5 indicating that the forest is "well managed."

3. The FSC criteria and standards do not establish specific water pollution standards or harvesting practices. They do, however, describe particular actions that forest managers must undertake under various circumstances. Thus, if a rare species is present, then the forest manager must make modifications to a management plan "to maintain, improve, or restore the species and its habitat," but the exact modifications are left to the discretion of the forest manager. Conservation zones must be established but the criteria do not mandate a minimum size for the area or population sizes for any species that must be maintained. Do you think that this approach to labeling provides sufficient specificity to be meaningful?

4. Do equivalence and mutual recognition promote trade liberalization at the expense of local regulatory autonomy, or do they promote regulatory autonomy?

––––––––––

IV. Harmonization in the Environmental Context

As stated at the beginning of this chapter, harmonization is an attempt to overcome market access and competitiveness problems associated with differences in national regulatory standards by moving toward the use of international standards. Yet, many environmental advocates remain troubled by harmonization. Some of their concerns mirror those they have about free trade generally. For example, they fear the loss of regulatory sovereignty and the loss of strict environmental requirements. Harmonization magnifies those fears, because deference is given to the product standards developed by an international organization. These concerns, and the responses to them, are briefly described in Section A. Section B explores the question of when harmonizing environmental standards might be appropriate.

The TBT Agreement's focus on harmonization of design and performance characteristics of product standards is just one approach to harmonization. Harmonization can also relate to process standards—the way in which a good is produced or harvested—and other laws and regulations, such as those relating to intellectual property or the regulation of services. In addition, harmonization need not focus on a single standard. Harmonization can also be based on maximum standards or minimum standards. Section C reviews the different approaches to harmonization and the environmental costs and benefits of those different approaches.

A. Environmental Concerns and Benefits of Harmonization

Daniel C. Esty, *Greening the GATT: Trade, Environment and the Future*
172–74 (1994)

[M]any environmentalists object to standards harmonized in a trade context. They fear that standards will sink to baseline or average requirements or that the common standards will preclude individual jurisdictions from adopting more protective standards. The answer to the environmentalists' fear is to negotiate international environmental agreements that set floors that parties are free to exceed so long as they do so in ways that do not unduly burden trade. The prospect of losing control over environmental regulations to international standard-setting organizations is another major source of concern. Environmentalists worry about this loss of sovereignty because, in many cases, international bodies provide fewer opportunities for public participation than the domestic political process and in some cases are clearly dominated by business perspectives.

Moreover, as a matter of political theory, some environmentalists argue that decisions should be made at the most decentralized level possible, giving maximum scope to local citizens' priorities and preferences. Of course, their enthusiasm for local decision making wanes when locales choose low standards. Nonetheless, this philosophy has considerable resonance in both the United States, with its strong federalist tradition, and in Europe, where the similar concept of "subsidiarity" has become a rallying cry. Those who argue for decentralized decision making believe that access to policymakers and the ability to hold elected officials accountable for their actions is sacrosanct—and lacking in international bodies.

Environmentalists, in addition, have historically cared very little about the economic efficiencies of standardized market-access requirements. This gives added force to the conclusion to which many environmentalists still cling: that the right to promulgate environmental regulations exceeding international levels is a central element of political sovereignty that should never be surrendered, regardless of the disruption to commerce. The strength of this argument is that environmental conditions and health risk exposures, as well as public priorities and preferences, vary from place to place, particularly with regard to factors such as risk tolerances. If preferences vary considerably and the cost of having varying standards is small, different standards are not only legitimate but welfare-maximizing from an economic perspective.

If, however, every nation and all their political subdivisions have complete autonomy to set their own radically different environmental standards, trade could grind to a halt. Inconsistent production, testing, labeling, packaging, and disposal requirements could become serious trade barriers, reducing the opportunities for producers to achieve scale economies and gain market access—economic virtues that translate into broader product choice, better service, and lower prices for consumers.

Environmentalists often overlook the fact that harmonized standards can yield environmental as well as economic benefits. With proper attention to environmental needs, good science, and open decision making, common standards often result in a high degree of environmental protection, not infrequently higher than any individual country would have been willing to adopt on its own. The Montreal Protocol's worldwide phaseout of CFCs is a classic example of upward harmonization beyond the existing regulations of any country. Reciprocal commitments allow nations to escape the "prisoners' dilemma" fear that others will take advantage of them if they alone adopt strict environmental standards.

In focusing excessively on their fear of downward harmonization, environmentalists tend to ignore the fact that it is the lack of any coordinated policies that exacerbates competitiveness concerns and depresses the level of standards. The European Community, for example, made implementation of new energy taxes to combat greenhouse gas emissions explicitly contingent on comparable new taxes being introduced in the United States. Joint action would, in this case, strengthen worldwide environmental efforts. Similarly, ... US national environmental standards (e.g., the US Clean Air Act and Clean Water Act) have allowed for rigorous approaches to air and water pollution that might otherwise have been impossible to achieve or enforce if individual states were free to maintain lower standards.

Questions and Discussion

1. The Prisoners' Dilemma can be more fully described as follows: "Each nation, acting independently, fears that other nations will adopt lax environmental requirements, and that it will therefore suffer serious competitive disadvantage by adopting the more stringent requirements that it prefers. Since each nation reasons in the same way, all adopt less stringent requirements than they would prefer individually. This is the 'race to the bottom.'" Richard B. Stewart, *Environmental Regulation and International Competitiveness*, 102 YALE L.J. 2039, 2058 (1993). How does the Prisoners' Dilemma relate to harmonization? Are you surprised that very little evidence exists to support the conclusion that lax environmental regulations attract industry? *See* Richard L. Revesz, *Rehabilitating Interstate Competition: Rethinking the "Race to the Bottom" Rationale for Federal Environmental Regulation*, 68 N.Y.U. L. REV. 1210 (1992).

2. Assume that you live in a country with strict requirements for fuel efficiency. On a scale of 1 to 10, your country's laws are rated a 10. Most countries of the world have low standards, let's say 4. Those countries refuse to harmonize to 10, because they believe such standards would be too costly, but they would agree to 7. Yet, businesses in your

country are asking for harmonized levels of fuel efficiency to facilitate international trade in automobiles. The effect of harmonization, while based on competition and market efficiency concerns, will reduce fuel consumption and the adverse impacts of fossil fuel combustion on a global scale. However, those levels will rise in your country. Is that an acceptable trade off? What factors, other than the fuel efficiency standard, should be considered before answering whether the trade off is acceptable?

B. When to Harmonize Environmental Requirements

As discussed in Chapter 1, assimilative, as well as social, cultural, political, and historical factors may lead some societies to enact stricter environmental laws than others. Far from undermining free trade, many argue that the use of different environmental standards in fact fuels comparative advantage and international trade while also adequately protecting the environment:

> Economists would argue that investment in polluting industry should flow to nations with lower standards and greater assimilative capacity. This flow of investment benefits the residents of these nations, who place a higher priority on expanding the output of public and private goods and services or can assimilate pollution with less environmental damage. It also benefits residents of nations with higher standards and lower assimilative capacity, who would suffer greater welfare loss if polluting industries were located in their country. This beneficial flow of investment is driven by variations in relative competitive advantage attributable to the differences in national standards. Adoption of uniform standards would lead to inappropriately high standards in nations with higher assimilative capacity, forcing them to devote too few resources to nonenvironmental goods and services which they would otherwise prefer. It might also lead to inappropriately low standards in other nations. Unilateral measures would reduce welfare by restraining trade without producing compensating benefits.

Richard B. Stewart, *Environmental Regulation and International Competitiveness*, 102 YALE L.J. 2039, 2057–58 (1993). Because of the benefits that flow from differences in standards, many free trade advocates are reluctant supporters of harmonization. Yet, harmonization may be desirable in some circumstances. What criteria should we use to determine when harmonization is desirable?

Daniel Esty and Damien Geradin acknowledge the legitimacy of differences in environmental requirements based on natural ecological advantages such as assimilative capacity. Yet, they recognize that differences in environmental or other requirements may create competitiveness concerns as well, particularly with respect to differences in PPMs. They offer at least three circumstances when harmonization may be an appropriate response to these competitiveness concerns. Daniel C. Esty & Damien Geradin, *Market Access, Competitiveness, and Harmonization: Environmental Protection in Regional Trade Agreements*, 21 HARV. ENVTL. L. REV. 265, 271–73 (1997).

First, while recognizing that governments rarely lower standards in a "race to the bottom" in response to economic competition, such competition may result in "regulatory chill," making it difficult for governments to move toward optimal environmental policies. Second, Esty and Geradin acknowledge that differences in process standards are unlikely to induce industrial relocation to jurisdictions with lower environmental standards;

little empirical evidence supports the "pollution havens" hypothesis. Yet, as capital, labor, and other costs equalize across jurisdictions, small differences in environmental costs may create environmental competitiveness concerns. In certain industries (e.g., refining) environmental costs already represent a significant share (more than 10 percent) of total costs. In most industries, moreover, pollution prevention and control expenditures are rising.

Lastly, they recognize that cost advantages obtained by producers facing lower pollution control expenditures might be unfair "in cases where less strict requirements are not based on any comparative advantage. Policy intervention may be appropriate where the choice of suboptimal standards in one jurisdiction threatens to erode the competitive position of producers in other places." *Id.* at 271.

Steve Charnovitz looks at the environmental case for harmonization from a different perspective. He suggests that by examining spillovers we can identify when environmental competition is "bad" and that harmonization is one potential solution to these spillovers:

> There are four types. An *economic* spillover is the financial loss to a high-standard country from competition with a country having lower environmental standards. For example, jobs and investment can migrate to the country with lower standards. A *political* spillover is the negative repercussion on the regulatory regime of the high-standard country.... [T]hat is, international competition can serve as a pretext for lowering domestic standards. A *physical* spillover is the environmental harm that the trade causes directly (like hazardous waste spills) or indirectly, that is, by allowing one's own consumer market to propagate the environmental harm (like killing rare tortoises to make eyeglass frames). A *psychological* spillover is the moral cost associated with participating in environmentally unfriendly commerce. For instance, knowing that the tuna is not dolphin-safe could lower a consumer's utility from eating it.

Steve Charnovitz, *Environmental Harmonization and Trade Policy, in* TRADE AND THE ENVIRONMENT: LAW, ECONOMICS AND POLICY 267, 269–72 (Durwood Zaelke et al. eds., 1993). Do these spillovers represent situations in which comparative advantage is illegitimate or advantages are not based on comparative advantage, as Esty and Geradin suggest? In any event, would the presence of these four spillovers provide the basis for harmonization? What other circumstances might lead to the conclusion that harmonization is warranted?

Professor Stewart, who is a much more reluctant supporter of harmonization, finds a narrower range of situations for when harmonization might be an appropriate policy response.

Richard B. Stewart, *Environmental Regulation and International Competitiveness*
102 YALE L.J. 2039, 2099–100 (1993)

Efforts at international harmonization should focus on those areas such as product standards, where most nations may benefit economically from common standards, or on environmental problems that create especially serious externalities. In many cases, it may be appropriate to recognize variations in assimilative capacity by narrowing rather than eliminating differences in national standards. In this respect, any efforts at harmonization should accord sufficient attention to the special problems faced by the developing countries in achieving higher levels of environmental protection.

In the area of product regulation, harmonization would benefit consumers in all nations by eliminating differences in environmental standards that undercut producers' ability to achieve economies of scale, increase the transaction costs of complying with different state regulations, and hinder trade and its attendant benefits. But here, too, differences among nations in assimilative capacity and the social value placed on environmental protection create impediments to common standards. Work to harmonize regulatory and labelling standards for chemicals is proceeding under the auspices of the GATT, OECD, and international environmental and health organizations. Understandably, it has been much more difficult to harmonize environmental standards for other products, such as automobiles, where differences in assimilative capacity are often much more important. Thus, it makes little sense to have the same automotive emission controls in Mali as in Japan. Harmonization has also been impeded by the insistence of nations, such as the U.S., that others adopt their relatively stringent standards ("harmonization up") or that they retain the right to set standards more stringent than those adopted by international agreement.

Differing national requirements for resource exploitation and manufacturing processes present other considerations. Harmonization of process measures cannot be justified on the ground that it promotes consumer welfare by removing impediments to trade. Indeed, to the extent that existing variations in national standards appropriately reflect national differences in assimilative capacity and social values, eliminating those differences would reduce consumer welfare. Existing standards are often too low, however, because of two types of externality problems. In the first type of problem, exemplified by transboundary pollution and the destruction within a given country of rare ecosystems and endangered species, part of the costs of environmental degradation are borne by those in other jurisdictions. In the second type of problem, exemplified by stratospheric ozone depletion, climate changes threatened by greenhouse gas emissions, and over-exploitation of the ocean's resources, all nations face a potential tragedy of the commons. Some form of collective agreement is necessary to deal with these externalities and to prevent environmental degradation that reduces total welfare. These externalities would exist even without trade, although economic growth resulting from trade liberalization might make these externalities more severe.

It is difficult to reach such agreements for many reasons. Because of their more urgent need for economic development, citizens of developing countries often place a lower value on reducing environmental externalities than citizens of developed countries. Moreover, these countries often have very limited administrative and technical, as well as general economic, resources. A relatively modest infusion of additional resources from the developed nations could make it possible to strengthen the standards of the developing countries, which would obtain economic and environmental benefits as a result of such transfers. Both developed and developing nations would benefit from the protection of ecologically valuable resources, such as tropical rain forests, that are located in developing countries. Developed nations might also benefit from the creation of markets for exports of environmentally superior technologies. They could also benefit by reducing transboundary pollution and other forms of environmental spillovers. The developing countries have some responsibility to deal with these spillovers, but at most only in relation to standards appropriate to their own as-similative capacities as well as to their proportionate contribution to common environmental problems. Once it is acknowledged that differences in national standards are appropriate, such transfers ought not to be dismissed as mere "bribes" to induce other nations to cease improper behavior. Rather, they may be an essential element in arrangements of mutual advantage and common responsibility.

———————

Questions and Discussion

1. Under what circumstances should harmonization be used? Should some kind of cost-benefit analysis be prepared before deciding to harmonize? Professor Stewart argues that transfers of funds and technology may provide a catalyst for strengthening developing country environmental standards. Do you agree?

2. The short description in Section A of the benefits of regulatory differences summarizes some of the main themes introduced in Chapter 1. For additional insight into the justifications for such regulatory differences, as well as the arguments for and against harmonization, see David W. Leebron, *Lying Down with Procrustes: An Analysis of Harmonization Claims, in* 1 FAIR TRADE AND HARMONIZATION: PREREQUISITES FOR FREE TRADE 41 (Jagdish Bhagwati & Robert E. Hudec eds., 1996); Richard B. Stewart, *Environmental Regulation and International Competitiveness*, at 2039.

———————

C. Approaches to Harmonization

While harmonization is generally described as a move toward the same regulatory requirements, harmonization is not a single, inflexible process that demands, for example, that all countries regulate arsenic emissions identically. While harmonization can seek uniform standards, it can involve other forms of integration as well.

Daniel C. Esty & Damien Geradin, *Market Access, Competitiveness, and Harmonization: Environmental Protection in Regional Trade Agreements*
21 HARV. ENVTL. L. REV. 265, 283–94 (1997)

1. Market Access

Market access can be promoted through various forms of harmonization. These include: (a) uniform standards; (b) maximum standards; (c) international standards; (d) essential requirements harmonization; (e) pre-standard harmonization; and (f) public information harmonization.

a. Uniformity of Standards or Total Harmonization

Total harmonization suggests the adoption of uniform standards across all jurisdictions. Each regulating authority implements exactly the same environmental requirements. Neither higher nor lower standards are permitted. There are several advantages to total harmonization. First, uniform product standards prevent market fragmentation and allow producers to realize economies of scale in design and production. Second, total harmonization prevents confusion about which rules apply. Because everyone must adhere to the same standards, any deviation can be detected easily. Third, this form of harmonization also facilitates regulatory economies of scale, allowing officials in different jurisdictions to share data, policy strategies, and enforcement techniques. Finally, there may be some administrative gains from "network effects" that arise where adherence to a common standard allows efficiency in developing control technologies, training programs, legal systems, or any other aspect of an environmental regime that would otherwise consume resources in each jurisdiction individually.

These advantages, however, come at a high price. A single standard across all jurisdictions does not allow governments to tailor requirements to local needs, circumstances, or preferences. To the extent that the world is heterogeneous, single standards have a tendency to reduce welfare. Under conditions of relative homogeneity, however, the efficiency advantages of uniform standards may outweigh the losses that arise from ignoring diversity in conditions and values.

b. Maximum Standards

In contrast to uniform rules, maximum standards impose a ceiling on the stringency of environmental requirements. Maximum *product* standards promote freer trade because diminished variations in product requirements facilitate the entry of companies into new markets. Exporting companies are assured, moreover, that national rules will not be contorted to the advantage of domestic producers. Because governments are free to apply more lax standards, however, maximum standards provide no guarantee against environmental degradation arising because some jurisdictions adopt suboptimal standards. * * *

c. International Standards

Another way of ensuring that governments do not engage in regulatory mischief to advantage domestic producers is by establishing the principle that any imported product meeting identified international standards, such as the International Organization for Standardization ("ISO") or Codex Alimentarius standards, must be permitted entry to the marketplace. A softer version of this same principle would establish a rebuttable presumption that products which conform to international standards should be allowed entry. A jurisdiction might then be allowed to set higher standards only if it could demonstrate an environmental purpose and a scientific basis for the level of protection selected, and it could show that there was no intent to discriminate against imported products. There are a number of advantages to using international benchmarks. Notably, the rules are clear. Regulators do not have to gather data, analyze harms, or establish standards; they simply borrow the existing requirements. But there are some disadvantages as well. Because of the difficulties of reaching agreement in a multilateral setting, international standards often represent the lowest common denominator. They may not be entirely appropriate for the jurisdictions that "borrow" them. In some cases, they will be too permissive; in others, too restrictive. In addition, international standards are generally adopted without adequate public input.

d. Essential Requirements Harmonization

By limiting coordination efforts to a core set of essential environmental requirements, trade regimes gain much of the benefit of harmonization with less administrative burden. The creation of the detailed technical regulations necessary to achieve those basic requirements is generally left to individual jurisdictions or, as in the EC context, standardization organizations. The principal advantage of this approach is that it permits some regulatory diversity and yields some of the benefits of uniform standards. This form of partial harmonization may promote consensus among states on key environmental goals and thus lead to an optimal degree of harmonization.

e. Pre-Standard Harmonization

Many of the benefits of product standard harmonization can be achieved if jurisdictions coordinate their regulatory systems so that they use common data collection processes, testing protocols, scientific methodologies, and risk assessment procedures. The OECD Chemicals group, for example, coordinates the exchange of data and test results on potentially hazardous chemicals, facilitating national standard setting. This type of harmonization may offer cost savings for companies operating in multiple jurisdictions. For example, a pesticide maker that has met the testing requirements for selling its product in the German market would be able to have regulatory judgments made by French authorities on the basis of the data from Germany. With adequate quality controls, such an inter-jurisdictional system of mutual recognition ensures that the company does not need to go through additional years of product testing and re-proving, thereby speeding market entry and reducing the cost of regulatory review. Because one of the stumbling blocks to good environmental protection is the dearth of good science and analytic work upon which to base regulations, ensuring that the technical efforts of one country are made available to other countries is an important step forward. Because pre-standard harmonization makes sense for both regulators and regulated entities, it offers one of the most promising avenues for responding to market access pressures.

f. Public Information Harmonization

A final type of harmonization focuses on the information that the public is provided about the environmental qualities of products. If a common "eco-label" were developed for all states that are parties to a trade agreement, companies would not have to go through separate analysis and label-development processes for each market. In addition, consumers would become well-versed in a specific set of environmental criteria and better able to make informed judgments. In fact, efforts are underway in the EU to set up a common eco-labelling scheme.

2. Competitiveness

Harmonization is also available as a tool to respond to competitiveness tensions that arise when jurisdictions within a free trade agreement have varying environmental requirements, especially differing PPM standards that translate into differences in cost structures for industry. Again, a diverse set of harmonization techniques are available including: (a) minimum standards; (b) multilateral agreements; (c) multi-tier requirements; (d) convergence of standards; (e) differentiated standards; (f) goal harmonization; (g) standardization of options; and (h) systems harmonization.

a. Minimum Standards

Minimum production process or method standards set a regulatory floor below which no jurisdiction can go. Such standards ensure that all governments require at least a baseline level of environmental protection from their industries. Under a program of minimum standards, jurisdictions remain free to impose more stringent requirements. By reducing environmental compliance cost differentials across jurisdictions, minimum standards constrain the possibility of distortions of competition, industrial relocation, and a race toward the bottom. Indeed, game theory suggests that mechanisms which promote cooperation, such as minimum standards, may diminish strategic behavior and thereby reduce the risk that interjurisdictional competition will yield suboptimal results. A regime of minimum standards allows for some tailoring to meet local conditions, but does not allow for unlimited variations in environmental requirements. This approach provides some of the benefits of uniform standards, such as opportunities for scale economies in the administration of environmental regulations, without surrendering all of the welfare gains of standards that match local requirements.

b. Multilateral Agreement

Requiring all countries to meet public health or ecological standards established by multilateral environmental agreements ("MEAs") also serves to prevent a race toward the bottom in environmental policy. Mandatory standards established by MEAs, more importantly, prevent "free riding" by some countries on the environmental efforts of others. The Montreal Protocol, for example, mandates a phase-out of chlorofluorocarbons ("CFCs") and other chemicals that deplete the ozone layer. In doing so, it ensures that producers who follow the phase-out and employ more expensive CFC substitutes are not disadvantaged in the marketplace by having to compete with other producers whose costs are lower because they are not following the ozone protection scheme. Such disciplines are especially important where harms might spill across national boundaries or where contested resources represent a "global commons."

c. Multi-Tier Harmonization

Multi-tier regulatory regimes with different standards for different groups of states also obtain some of the benefits of standards tailored to local conditions without losing all of the advantages of uniform requirements. Because one of the most important variables determining the optimal level of environmental protection is a state's wealth and level of economic development, a system of unified standards for those states at comparable levels of development may prove quite valuable. One could imagine, for example, a set of environmental standards developed for the most economically advanced states that would require quite a high degree of environmental protection. A second set of standards, with more modest requirements, might be established for industrializing countries that have a great need for environmental protection but cannot afford high-level standards. Finally, a baseline set of standards could be defined for the least developed nations whose economic positions are so modest that they could not meet anything more than a limited set of environmental goals, and whose capacity to develop their own regulatory regimes is limited. Such a multi-tier system would provide for economies of scale and network effects among the countries within each regulatory tier. At the same time, the existence of multiple tiers would ensure that standards would at least roughly correspond to countries' individualized needs.

Such a program would also allow states to "graduate" into higher degrees of environmental protection as they develop. Because of their capacity to respond to some degree to diversity in circumstances without losing all of the benefits of harmonization, multi-tier standards offer particular promise as a tool for environmental policy in the international domain. The Montreal Protocol provides for two tiers of compliance. OECD countries phased out their production of CFCs in 1995, but developing countries have an extra ten years to complete their phase-outs. The Dutch government has proposed a similar multi-tier approach to address the difficult issue of the allocation of greenhouse gas emissions reductions in the EC.

d. Convergence of Standards

Another response to harmful competitive pressures created by varying environmental standards would be to promote a negotiated convergence of standards across jurisdictions. Eliminating wide variations in environmental standards would limit the risk of a race toward the bottom because the capacity to lure investment with very low standards is constrained. This "convergence" of requirements—perhaps through a regime of both maximum and minimum standards—would provide for some administrative efficiency while still permitting environmental programs to be tailored to local conditions. For example, establishing minimum requirements on tuna fishing methods that prevent dolphin deaths, combined with a guarantee that countries will not insist on collateral dolphin death limits more stringent than some agreed threshold, might offer a basis for resolving the longstanding "tuna-dolphin" controversy.

Again, the hope is that by narrowing the gap between environmental compliance costs in high-standard and low-standard jurisdictions, regulatory convergence will minimize distortions in competition, incentives to relocate, and competitiveness pressure on environmental standards, all of which might lead to sub-optimal policy choices. By combining minimum standards aimed at race-toward-the-bottom concerns with maximum standards geared to market access, environmental protection and trade facilitation goals can be pursued simultaneously.

e. Differentiated Standards

A regulatory program that sets standards *centrally* but not *uniformly* represents another approach to the uniformity-versus-diversity dilemma. Under such a regime, authorities at the level of a free trade agreement would identify environmental targets common to all countries but would provide for different degrees of stringency—for example, in time tables for achieving the target or in the level of accomplishment itself—depending on the circumstances present in each separate jurisdiction. The United States uses this sort of differentiated approach in its Clean Air Act. Metropolitan areas are ranked as extreme, severe, serious, moderate, and marginal based on the severity of their air pollution problems. The more severe an area's "non-attainment" problem, the more time the jurisdiction is given to comply with national clean air goals; the worst cities have seventeen extra years to meet the established National Ambient Air Quality Standards.

Differential standards are more economically efficient than total harmonization because they better match regulatory requirements to localized needs. Yet the presence of common long-term goals ensures that wide variations in the rigor of environmental protection efforts do not persist over time as countries converge on the jointly defined goal. This mechanism serves to balance the advantages of regulatory diversity with the benefits of reduced competitiveness stresses obtained by more centralized standards.

f. Goal Harmonization

Harmonization can be limited to the environmental goals that must be achieved by each jurisdiction. Under this approach, states are free to choose the environmental strategies they deem most appropriate to attain the centrally-defined goals. A team of Dutch and Belgian academics have proposed such a regulatory approach for the EC. They suggest that creating an "environmental margin," within which standards may fluctuate, offers the best balance between the benefits of standards that are purely tailored to local conditions and the advantages of uniform controls. Specifically, van den Bergh and his coauthors argue for broad environmental quality standards and goals to be set at the EC-wide level. Each Member State would determine for itself how to achieve the target. In effect, the goals are harmonized, but the implementation of specific environmental programs and the identification of precise emission standards would be decentralized.

In the United States, goal harmonization takes the form of federal ambient standards. The National Ambient Air Quality Standards of the Clean Air Act specify the acceptable levels of various pollutants. If a certain level of exposure to a specified type of pollution is identified as the safe threshold, this standard can be established as the baseline requirement in all jurisdictions. Of course, the difficulty of attaining this standard will vary across jurisdictions, depending on local conditions.

g. Standardization of Options

An alternative to goal harmonization is to limit policy coordination to the identification of a set of options from which jurisdictions can choose their own regulatory approach. With respect to solid waste, for example, jurisdictions would select from such policy options as landfilling under specified conditions, incineration with defined controls, or various recycling strategies. This approach offers two advantages. It facilitates consensus across jurisdictions with varying requirements and, hence, the adoption of harmonization legislation.

Further, it allows a degree of experimentation that may yield improved results over time. The weakness of the "options" approach is that implementation may suffer. In particular, environmental authorities may find it difficult to assess whether parties are in compliance because of the range of ways of meeting one's legal obligations.

h. Systems Harmonization

Another approach to the issue of divergent regulatory standards is to mandate conformity with certain established environmental systems or procedures, but not to insist that all jurisdictions adopt identical substantive standards. The development of environmental management requirements by the ISO provides an example of systems harmonization. Known as "ISO 14000," these requirements would impose basic management standards on participating companies, such as environmental audit and reporting requirements, but not a strict set of substantive requirements. Another example of systems harmonization is the EC Eco-Management and Audit Scheme (also known as "EMAs"), which provides for a number of environmental management requirements that must be fulfilled by the companies that want to participate in the scheme.

By guaranteeing that at least a rudimentary environmental management structure is in place in all companies, such an approach might help to reduce the number of cases where divergent standards arise from "public choice" distortions—that is, where political decisions do not reflect the will of the people—or "regulatory" failure rather than variations in local needs and conditions. The disadvantage of relying on environmental systems is that there may be little convergence in the substantive requirements that are imposed from jurisdiction to jurisdiction. As a result, wide variations in environmental compliance costs may persist and competitiveness tensions may endure. A harmonized approach to environmental systems would reduce the risk of a race toward the bottom. In addition, when harmonization is directed by entities outside of government, as in the case of the ISO or the Codex Alimentarius, questions of legitimacy and accountability may arise.

Questions and Discussion

1. What are the primary economic and environmental benefits of harmonization? Is harmonization inherently anti-environmental? How can we ensure that harmonization is not harmful to the environment?

2. According to Esty and Geradin, environmental *product* standards create barriers to market entry, whereas *process* standards cause competitiveness concerns. Why? In addition, why would certain harmonization strategies help resolve market entry barriers while others would overcome competitiveness issues? For example, why would maximum standards resolve market access problems while minimum standards would resolve competitiveness concerns? After weighing the costs and benefits of each of the various approaches, which offer the best trade and economic solutions? Which seem to offer the best environmental solutions? Are they the same?

3. Charnovitz and Stewart admit that harmonizing up or harmonizing down to a rigid standard would generally be too high for some countries and too low for others. As a result, Charnovitz argues for policy convergence rather than full harmonization. In his view, the degree of spillover would determine how much convergence is desirable. For instance, when dealing with high physical spillover problems such as the spread of disease, a consistency in quarantines, testing, and disinfecting techniques may be highly advantageous. Is convergence a better approach to international standard-setting than other forms of harmonization? *See* Charnovitz, *Environmental Harmonization and Trade Policy*, at 272–73.

4. Esty believes that a multilateral agreement on baseline environmental performance standards would be the best long-term response to environmentalists' competitiveness concerns. He would initially limit harmonization to address physical transboundary or global pollution spillovers that cannot be argued to be legitimate bases for comparative advantage. In stage two, he envisions harmonization of standards that relate to production issues that do not result in physical spillovers, but only among developed countries with a common interest in reducing political spillovers—both downward pressure on high standards and general anti-free trade sentiment created by fears about loss of competitiveness. Esty, Greening the GATT, at 172. How does his view differ from Charnovitz's?

D. Rethinking Harmonization

1. Values and Harmonization

In the preceding section, Daniel Esty and Damien Geradin outlined several forms of harmonization to promote market access and competitiveness. Broadly categorized, these forms of harmonization relate to specific or convergent harmonization of characteristics or performance, general policy objectives which set broad standards, agreed principles which influence or constrain factors taken into account in making specific rules, and harmonization of institutional structures and procedures. Using both this general taxonomy and the more specific forms of harmonization outlined by Esty and Geradin, what kind of harmonization best describes the TBT Agreement? Does the TBT Agreement take a market access or competitiveness approach to harmonization?

Professor Daniel Kalderimis takes a distinctly different approach to harmonization that focuses not on its external form but rather on its underlying purpose with respect to the international trading system. In his classification, *progressive harmonization agreements* seek to attain some nontrade value, thus expanding the reach of trade disciplines. These agreements, such as the Agreement on Trade-Related Aspects of Intellectual Property Rights, use nontrade values as swords in the sense that breach of a relevant nontrade value becomes a breach of the relevant WTO agreement. According to Kalderimis, progressive harmonization shifts the institutional locus of the WTO from a uni-polar concentration on trade values to a multi-polar balancing of multiple values. The mark of a progressive harmonization agreement is the stipulation of minimum standards with respect to the nontrade value at issue.

In contrast, *defensive harmonization agreements* seek to restrain nontrade values from interfering with free trade. These agreements, including the TBT and SPS agreements, prevent nontrade values such as health protection, environmental standards, and consumer safety from being used as shields against WTO discipline, and they expand the reach of trade values into nontrade areas.

While finding fault with both progressive and defensive harmonization, Kalderimis finds a "troubling double-standard at the heart of defensive harmonization." Whereas health and environmental standards must be carefully justified and drafted on the basis of nonbinding international standards, trade and economic agendas are not subject to the same discipline. Further, countries may be sanctioned for adopting "faulty" health or environmental regulations, but they will not be sanctioned for deciding not to regulate at all.

To overcome these problems, he recommends that both defensive and progressive harmonization cease "until, if ever, the WTO acquires sufficient legitimacy to move its locus of balance from trade issues to a comprehensive economic (or even global) agenda." With respect to the TBT Agreement, he recommends creating a rebuttable presumption that measures based on international standards are consistent with the Article XX of the GATT. Daniel Kalderimis, *Problems of WTO Harmonization and the Virtues of Shields and Swords*, 13 Minn. J. Global Trade 305, 346–49 (2004).

Questions and Discussion

1. Do you agree that harmonization within the WTO needs to be reconsidered? In ten years, only one case has been decided on the basis of the TBT Agreement, although five

have been decided in favor of the challenging party under the SPS Agreement. Does this indicate a serious problem? What other information might help you answer that question? Do we need the existence of a problem to recognize that the WTO may not be the appropriate forum for restraining nontrade values? How can the "troubling double-standard" be remedied?

---

2. The "New Approach" to Harmonization in the EU

The European Union (EU) has taken a much different approach to harmonization than the TBT Agreement. Under Article 115 of the Treaty on the Functioning of the European Union (TFEU) the European Council may adopt Directives for the "the approximation of such laws, regulations or administrative provisions of the Member States as directly affect the establishment or functioning of the internal market." Under the EU's "New Approach" to approximation—that is, harmonization—the Council enacts framework directives that establish the "essential requirements" that products must meet relating to health, safety, environmental protection, and consumer protection, among other things. Voluntary standards established by European standards organizations complement the Directive's binding requirements.

As described in Chapter 4 on pages 255–66, Articles 34 and 36 of the TFEU prohibit quantitative restrictions or measures having equivalent effect. The technical regulations of the EU Member States are subject to these provisions, as well as the decision of the European Court of Justice in the *Cassis de Dijon* case. That case set out the main elements for the application of technical regulations and for mutual recognition, including the following:

1. Products legally manufactured or marketed in one country should in principle move freely throughout the Community, where such products meet equivalent levels of protection to those imposed by the Member State of exportation and where they are marketed in the territory of the exporting country.

2. In the absence of Community measures, Member States are free to legislate on their territory.

3. Barriers to trade, which result from differences between national legislations, may only be accepted if national measures:

   a. are necessary to satisfy mandatory requirements (such as health, safety, consumer protection and environmental protection);

   b. serve a legitimate purpose justifying the breach of the principle of free movement of goods; and

   c. can be justified with regard to the legitimate purpose and are proportionate with the aims.

In the wake of the *Cassis de Dijon* case, the EU set out to harmonize technical regulations across the EU Member States to avoid or eliminate barriers to trade. In 1985, the EU adopted a new regulatory approach known as the New Approach to Technical Harmonization and Standards, or more simply as the New Approach. Council Resolution 85/C 136/01 of 7 May 1985 on a New Approach to Technical Harmonization and Standards O.J. (C 136). The New Approach directs the Council to adopt New Approach directives for a range of products (e.g., gas appliances, packaging and packaging waste, recreational craft, among many others). The New Approach directives, however, do not comprehensively establish detailed product standards but rather lay down technical standards for "essential requirements"—those "necessary elements for protecting the public interest." Only products complying with essential requirements may be placed on the market and put into service. The essential requirements are distinguished from "technical specifications." Technical specifications are those standards needed for the production and placing on the market of products conforming to the essential requirements. Meeting the essential requirements is mandatory; only products fulfilling the essential requirements may be placed on the market and put into service. However, use of the technical specifications established by EU standardizing bodies is voluntary. *Id.* at Annex II. Products made in conformity with harmonized technical specifications are presumed to conform to the "essential requirements" established by the relevant directive setting out essential requirements for that product. When a manufacturer decides to use other standards, it must prove that its product conforms to the essential requirements of the relevant directive. *Id.*

The essential requirements are quite general. For example, the directive relating to gas-burning appliances provides the following two essential requirements (among many others):

- Appliances must be so designed and built as to operate safely and present no danger to persons, domestic animals or property when normally used as defined in Article 1(3) of this Directive.

- Appliances must be so constructed that, when used normally, flame stability is assured and combustion products do not contain unacceptable concentrations of substances harmful to health.

Council Directive No. 2009/142/EC of the European Parliament and of the Council of 30 November 2009 Relating to Appliances Burning Gaseous Fuels, 2009 O.J. (L 330/10). The European Committee for Standardization (CEN) was then charged with developing a wide variety of more specific standards relating to gas-burning stoves, water storage tanks, pressure regulators, and other appliances and devices. (The European Committee for Electrotechnical Standardization (CENELEC) is the other EU standardizing body charged with developing technical specifications under New Approach directives).

New Approach directives have a significant effect on national measures, and, of course, this was a major purpose of the New Approach as a means to eliminate barriers to trade. Once a New Approach directive is adopted, its provisions supersede all corresponding national provisions. The Member States must transpose these directives into their national legislation, as appropriate, and repeal all contradictory national legislation. As a general rule, Member States may not maintain or introduce more stringent measures than foreseen in the directive. They must then notify the European Commission of national laws, regulations, or administrative provisions adopted and published to implement the directive.

The EU has also adopted rules for conformity assessment known as the Global Approach. Council Resolution of 21 December 1989 on a Global Approach to Conformity Assessment, O.J. (C 010). Before placing a product on the Community market, the manufacturer must subject the product to a conformity assessment procedure provided for in the applicable directive to demonstrate that the product actually meets a directive's essential requirements. Manufacturers may choose between different conformity assessment procedures provided for in the applicable directive.

The Global Approach is an important complement to the New Approach:

Under what is termed the EC's "global approach" to regulation, products may be tested and certified within any Member State in order to receive a "CE" marking (which indicates that they comply with "Communauté Européenne" norms). All Member States must recognize these certifications (i.e. mandatory mutual recognition), such that certified products may circulate freely throughout the EC market. In 1990, the Member States formed the European Organization for Testing and Certification (EOTC) to coordinate national bodies engaged in the certification process and thereby help assure national authorities of the reliability of tests conducted in other Member States. Each Member State must approve and is responsible for overseeing the certification bodies within its jurisdiction and must notify the Commission's Enterprise Directorate-General (DG) of its approvals. These testing and certification laboratories consequently are referred to as "notified bodies." Member State authorities periodically meet and exchange information about the process' operation through working groups and committees created pursuant to the respective directives. They thereby attempt to build and retain confidence in the system. This EC system can be characterized as governance by coordinated cross-border public-private networks. The system permits for significant national regulatory diversity to achieve broader EC regulatory goals within an increasingly integrated European economy.

Gregory Shaffer, *Reconciling Trade and Regulatory Goals: The Prospects and Limits of New Approaches to Transatlantic Governance through Mutual Recognition and Safe Harbor Agreements*, 9 COLUM. J. EUR. L. 29, 34–35 (2002).

Because New Approach directives are designed to ensure the free movement of products that comply with applicable directives, Member States generally may not prohibit, restrict, or impede the placing on the market of such products. Nevertheless, Member States may adopt additional national requirements to protect, in particular, workers, consumers, or the environment. These additional requirements, however, must be in compliance with the TFEU, in particular Articles 34 and 36, and may not require modification of the product or influence the conditions for placing the product on the EU market. *See* European Commission, Guide to the Implementation of Directives Based on the New Approach and the Global Approach 18 (2000).

Questions and Discussion

1. The New Approach was designed to "develop flexible and technology-neutral legislation by moving from detailed product specific technical requirements to defining the essential requirements for types of products, thus promoting innovation and competitiveness." European Commission, Communication from the Commission to the Council and the European Parliament: Enhancing the Implementation of the New Approach Directives 4 (May 7, 2003). Does the EU approach provide a legal framework more capable of achieving that goal than the TBT Agreement?

2. Compare the harmonization of standards of the EU's New Approach with that of the TBT Agreement through international organizations such as the ISO. How do they differ, if at all? Why is harmonization in Europe widely accepted and strongly implemented? What lessons should we draw from this experience for harmonization under the TBT Agreement?

3. *EU and Harmonization of PPMs.* The EU has also harmonized PPMs, but has done so through various approaches. In some cases, such as for water quality standards, the EU

has set minimum standards that eliminate the lowest possible standards, but also allow Member States to adopt stricter standards. With respect to air pollution from large combustion plants, the EU set different standards for sulfur dioxide (SO_2) and nitrogen oxides (NO_x) for new and existing facilities, and also allowed some Member States, including Greece, Ireland, and Portugal, to increase their emissions. At other times, the EU has developed standards based on differences in an ecosystem's assimilative capacity, such as with water pollution caused by certain dangerous substances. Here, the EU has established specific effluent standards for dangerous substances, but it allows Member States to opt for ambient water quality standards in certain circumstances. Council Directive No. 76/464 on Pollution Caused by Certain Dangerous Substances Discharged into the Aquatic Environment of the Community, 1976 O.J. (L 129) 23.

The EU has adopted other approaches for harmonizing PPMs. Directive 96/61/EC on Integrated Pollution Prevention and Control establishes a framework for minimizing pollution from various industrial point sources. All installations covered by the Directive must obtain a permit from the authorities in the EU countries. Unless they have a permit, they are not allowed to operate. The permits must include emissions limits based on "Best Available Techniques" (BAT). BAT does not require the use of any technique or specific technology, but must "tak[e] into account the technical characteristics of the installation concerned, its geographical location and the local environmental conditions." Council Directive No. 96/61/EC of 24 September 1996 concerning Integrated Pollution Prevention and Control, art. 9.4, 1996 O.J. (L 257) 266.

The development of these various directives has not come without significant debate. Member States with high environmental standards such as Germany have often sought more rigorous standards to protect the competitive position of their industries. Other Member States have sought lower or ambient standards to obtain competitive advantages for their companies. What are the costs and benefits of the various approaches to harmonization of PPMs in the EU? Could any of these approaches apply in the global context? Why or why not?

4. For more on EU harmonization efforts, see Esty & Geradin, *Market Access, Competitiveness, and Harmonization*, at 307–10. For more on the Directive on Integrated Pollution Prevention and Control, see European Integrated Pollution Prevention and Control Bureau, http://eippcb.jrc.es; European Commission, *The IPPC Directive*, http://europa.eu.int/comm/environment/ippc/index.htm; Uwe M. Erling, *Approaches to Integrated Pollution Control in the United States and the European Union*, 15 TUL. ENVTL. L.J. 1 (2001). For the texts of the legislation implementing the New Approach and the Global Approach, see http://ec.europa.eu/enterprise/policies/single-market-goods/documents/blue-guide. The EU maintains a website on the New Approach, http://www.newapproach.org, and a more general website including information on the Global Approach and the 2008 New Legislative Framework for the marketing of products, which is intended to facilitate harmonization and make the system easier for small and medium enterprises, http://ec.europa.eu/enterprise/policies/single-market-goods/regulatory-policies-common-rules-for-products/index_en.htm.

For the original text of the EU resolution on the New Approach to Technical Harmonisation and Standards, and subsequent Council Decisions, see 1985 O.J. (C 136) 1; Council Resolution of 7 May 1985, Annex II A. 1, New Approach to Technical Harmonization and Standards, 1985 O.J. (C 136) 1. For the Global Approach to Conformity Assessment, see Council Resolution of 21 December 1989 on a Global Approach to Conformity Assessment, 1990 O.J. (L 10) 1; Council Decision 90/683/EEC Concerning the Modules for the Various Phases of the Conformity Assessment Procedures which are Intended to be Used in the Technical Harmonization Directives, 1990 O.J. (L 380) 13, amended by Council Decision 93/465/EEC of 22 July 1993, 1993 O.J. (L 220) 23.

————————

Chapter 7

Sanitary and Phytosanitary Measures: Science, Risk Assessment, and Risk Management

I. Introduction

The WTO's Agreement on the Application of Sanitary and Phytosanitary Measures (SPS Agreement) governs the many measures, such as product standards, that governments apply to protect human, animal, or plant life or health, especially agriculture, from the risk of introduction or spread of pests and diseases, and to protect human and animal life or health from risks from additives, contaminants, toxins, or disease-causing organisms in foods, beverages, or feedstuffs. SPS measures include such common regulations as limits on pesticide residues on fresh fruits and vegetables, quarantine requirements on animals to prevent the introduction of diseases, restrictions on imports of certain fruits from certain countries to prevent introduction of insects threatening to domestic agriculture, and food safety laws prohibiting certain additives in food products. The WTO's SPS Agreement (as well as the very similar SPS provisions of the North American Free Trade Agreement) are intended to assure that governments have good reasons for such health or agricultural measures that create barriers to trade. In so doing, the WTO members have made science the "neutral" arbiter of whether an SPS measure is permissible. This chapter explores some of the difficult issues that arise at the interface of law, science, and policy.

At the very outset, it is important to understand the particular nature of SPS measures that prompted the detailed provisions of the SPS Agreement. Take, for example, some of the trade restrictions that resulted from recent concern about outbreaks of bovine spongiform encephalopathy (BSE, often called "mad cow disease") and the human health concern that exposure to BSE contamination can lead to a neurological disease known as new variant Creutzfeldt-Jakob disease, which is in many instances fatal. The recent outbreak of BSE first became apparent on a large scale in the United Kingdom in the late 1980s. In response, many European countries and others adopted special requirements for British beef products, including prohibitions on imports. Later studies revealed that mixing cow bones into cattle feed could spread BSE. By this route, in the early 2000s some BSE cases showed up in U.S. cattle, prompting some 65 countries, prominently including Korea and Japan, to impose prohibitions on import of beef from the United States, cutting total U.S. beef exports by more than 75 percent. There are many, many other examples showing that SPS measures often, and quite properly, target a specific product from a specific country.

Until now, we have emphasized the core GATT nondiscrimination obligations of most favored nation and national treatment found in GATT Articles I and III. For manufactured products, domestic taxation and regulation for many purposes is permissible so long as the rules apply equally to domestic and foreign products and to imported products from different countries. SPS measures, however, are often discriminatory by nature; that is, they inherently violate either or both of GATT Articles I and III and are thus justifiable under the GATT, if it all, only under Article XX. It is noteworthy that the SPS Agreement describes itself in part as an elaboration of the provisions of Article XX(b), including the chapeau. Naturally, the SPS Agreement itself contains no nondiscrimination obligations.

Because the possible spread of pests or diseases or the possible human health effects from food contaminants or additives are fundamentally scientific questions, it is not illogical that the SPS Agreement disciplines SPS trade measures through a set of scientific principles and requirements. But because the scientific evidence in this field can be unclear or indefinite, the same issues of food or environmental safety and human health protection are often hotly contested regulatory issues within countries. Many consumer and environmental advocates vehemently criticize the elements of the SPS Agreement that give the WTO authority to review and possibly overrule such national decisions at the behest of a foreign government in the name of removing barriers to trade. For one interesting analysis of the influence of consumer and environmental interests, see Tim Josling et al., The Beef-Hormone Dispute and its Implications for Trade Policy (undated), available at http://iis-db.stanford.edu/pubs/11379/HORMrev.pdf.

Part of the continuing controversy about the SPS Agreement arises both from the frequently complex and disputed science involved and from the subtle interplay between the essentially scientific process of assessing risk and the more policy-influenced decisionmaking about whether or how to manage the risk. Therefore, Section II begins with an introduction to risk assessment and risk management and the classic distinction between them. Section III summarizes the key elements of the SPS Agreement. Section IV examines the interpretations of risk assessment requirements and risk management discretion in the very important Appellate Body reports in the long-running dispute over regulation of the use of growth hormones in beef production between the United States, Canada, and other beef producers on the one hand, and the European Union on the other. Subsequent parts of the chapter take up other specific issues arising under the SPS Agreement.

II. An Introduction to Risk Assessment and Risk Management

The process of establishing health-based regulations or plant protection regulations is frequently split into two phases. In the first phase, "risk assessment," experts review and evaluate the scientific evidence that would be the basis for regulatory action, often but not always summarizing their conclusions through a best effort quantification of the risk. In the second phase, "risk management," a government official or committee with appropriate authority decides what regulatory or other measures should be promulgated in light of the scientific information revealed in the risk assessment. The decisionmaker is often required by statute or policy direction to take into consideration nonscientific matters such as cost or a policy to completely prevent certain kinds of risks. For example, the U.S. Environmental Protection Agency may establish a tolerance for a pesticide chemical residue on a food only if it determines that the tolerance is "safe"—"that there is a reasonable certainty that no harm will result from aggregate exposure to the pesticide chemical residue, including all anticipated dietary exposures and all other exposures for which there is reliable information." U.S. Food, Drug, and Cosmetic Act, 21 U.S.C. §346a(b)(2). Australia's Quarantine and Inspection Service may quarantine, test, or destroy any imported ornamental fish indicating the presence of an infectious disease agent or pest. Australia's Quarantine and Inspection Service, Import Case Details—Public Listing, Condition C8592 (June 4, 2010). An examination of the scientific evidence in the risk assessment may make some policy choices more reasonable than others, and most regulatory systems do not allow a risk management decision that is contrary to or lacks any support from the available evidence.

Even so, scientific certainty about human health or environmental effects is rare. Many scientific determinations and policy choices regarding SPS measures require judgments about differing scientific views. While some scientific questions can be isolated and assessed in an objective matter through risk assessment methodologies, "risk assessment necessarily requires inferences, choices, and assumptions that themselves reflect policy preferences." David A. Wirth, *The Role of Science in the Uruguay Round and NAFTA Trade Disciplines*, 27 CORNELL INT'L L.J. 817, 834 (1994). The following excerpt explains these inferences, choices, and assumptions in more detail. The Questions and Discussion touch briefly on some issues for further consideration, some of which we return to in Section IV.B.5. below.

Adapted from Vern R. Walker, *Keeping the WTO from Becoming the "World Trans-Science Organization": Scientific Uncertainty, Science Policy, and Factfinding in the Growth Hormones Dispute*
31 CORNELL INT'L L. J. 251, 257, 263–67 (1998)

Hazard Identification involves a qualitative judgment about which substances are capable of causing adverse health effects, and the types of adverse health effects they may cause. This step requires scientists to choose among scientifically plausible options, and inferences may be necessary. Thus, according to the guidelines on cancer risk assessment of the U.S. Environmental Protection Agency (EPA), the EPA uses the default assumption (absent specific data to the contrary), that positive effects in animal cancer studies indicate carcinogenic potential in humans. Also, a carcinogenic substance may also be associated with neurological effects or reproductive effects, but the risk assessment may evaluate only one of these effects. The hazard identification stage is where the scientists make clear which of the possible and plausible effects are being assessed

Dose-Response Assessment evaluates the quantitative and qualitative aspects of the causal relationship between a dose—that is, a level of exposure—and the incidence or severity of the adverse health effect. The challenge here is that there is seldom any specific information relating human exposures to human health effects. EPA's cancer assessment guidelines provide that effects seen in animals at the highest dose tested (the maximum tolerated dose) are appropriate to use in carcinogenicity assessment; that concordance among target organs of carcinogenicity is not a prerequisite; that benign tumors observed in the animal studies should be included in assessing animal tumor incidence if the tumors have the capacity to progress to malignancies; that there is a similarity of the basic pathways of metabolism that are relevant to species-to-species extrapolation of cancer hazard; and that a human dose that is equivalent to an animal dose can be estimated by using a scaling factor based on body weight (in the case of oral exposure), default estimates of lung deposition and of internal dose (for inhalation exposure), or internal dose (for a route-to-route of exposure extrapolation). Unless such default rules were used to bridge large gaps in fundamental knowledge or smaller gaps in agent-specific knowledge, the dose-response analysis could not be completed.

An especially critical regulatory task is to determine the shape of the dose-response curve at the low doses typical of many human exposures. For non-carcinogenic effects, regulators try to determine whether there is a "no-effect threshold" specific to the agent and the adverse effect—that is, a dose or exposure level below which the adverse effect does not occur and above which it can occur. If the agent is carcinogenic, however, there are often plausible scientific grounds for acting as though no threshold exists or for inferring that, if it exists, it is very low and cannot be identified reliably. Where the causal mechanism for cancer is unclear or the agent is genotoxic, the traditional regulatory approach has been to treat carcinogens as not having a no-effect threshold. Such carcinogens are treated as though any level of exposure poses some positive risk.

In extrapolating from high-dose effects to low-dose effects, from laboratory animals to humans, and from healthy individuals to more sensitive individuals, many choices have to be made among scientifically plausible options. Uncertainties arise repeatedly along the chains of inference, and science policies are adopted to guide the choices of scientists performing risk assessment. Sometimes those choices are made by legislative institutions. Whether those choices are made in statutes or regulations, or whether they are made in the form of generic guidelines for all decisions or on a purely ad-hoc and case-specific basis, they are essential to completing dose-response assessment.

Exposure Assessment evaluates the probability, magnitude, duration, and timing of the doses that people might receive as the result of the various pathways of exposure to the agent. Risk is a function not only of the toxicity of the agent, but also of the likelihood that a dose will be received, the likely magnitude of the maximum short-term dose, and the frequency and duration of exposure. Once again, agencies such as EPA often have to make assumptions to bridge gaps in available empirical data. They also have to use computer models to predict the environmental fate of chemicals in air, water, and soil. Science policy informs the choice of such assumptions and models and thus can play a role in exposure assessment as it does in dose-response assessment.

Risk Characterization integrates information on hazard identification, dose-response assessment, and exposure assessment to develop a qualitative or quantitative estimate of the total risk of the identified adverse health effects. At this stage, it may be important to present information about the risk of adverse effects for the most exposed persons (for example, workers in a particular industry, or children) as well as the level of risk for the nation as a whole. In short, the idea is to present the integrated risk information in a form useful to decision-makers, the risk managers. EPA has been careful to emphasize that risk characterizations should also describe "the constraints of available data and the state of knowledge, significant scientific issues, and significant science and science policy choices that were made when alternative interpretations of data existed." Unless a risk characterization acknowledges that "risk assessment is an iterative process" and that "default assumptions are used at every stage because no database is ever complete," then risk assessment as a process is less likely to achieve its goals of "transparency in environmental decisionmaking, clarity in communication, consistency in core assumptions and science policies from case to case, and reasonableness."

Risk management is the process by which an agency chooses what action, if any, to take based on the risk assessment. Risk management "entails consideration of political, social, economic, and engineering information with risk-related information to develop, analyze, and compare regulatory options and to select the appropriate regulatory response to a potential chronic health hazard. The selection process necessarily requires the use of value judgments on such issues as the acceptability of risk and the reasonableness of the costs of control." The Presidential/Congressional Commission on Risk Assessment and Risk Management, 1 FRAMEWORK FOR ENVIRONMENTAL HEALTH RISK MANAGEMENT 1, 18–19 (1997), *available at* http://www.riskworld.com/riskcommission/Default.html. *See also* REPORT OF A JOINT FAO/WHO CONSULTATION, RISK MANAGEMENT AND FOOD SAFETY (Jan. 27–31, 1997) *available at* http://www.fao.org/documents/show_cdr.asp?url_file=/docrep/W4982E/w4982e00.htm. In practice, the boundaries between risk assessment and risk management are not clear cut:

> One fundamental axiom admonishes that regulations to protect public health involve social policy choices. Because the regulatory process is not wholly scientific, science does not have all the answers. There is no way to infer regulatory outcomes solely on the basis of scientific data, especially when most regulations are implicitly or explicitly crafted to respond to a particular social, economic, or political context. While scientific analysis can provide assistance in attaining a given public health goal, the choice of that goal reflects societal values as to which science may provide little, if any, guidance. In other words, science may inform the regulatory process but cannot, by itself, determine the result with particularity. For instance, a risk assessment may help in setting a standard designed to limit the probability that an individual will develop cancer after a lifetime of exposure to a particular chemical substance to no more than one chance in a million. By contrast, the choice of the one-in-a-million goal — as opposed to, say, zero or one-in-a-thousand — is one of public policy.

David A. Wirth, *The Role of Science in the Uruguay Round and NAFTA Trade Disciplines*, 27 CORNELL INT'L L.J. 833 (1994).

Questions and Discussion

1. Are you surprised at how many assumptions are made in the development of a risk assessment? If uncertainty permeates the risk assessment, what is its value?

2. Both Walker and Wirth emphasize the policy choices that are embedded in the "scientific" process of risk assessment. Does that mean that risk assessment and risk management cannot be separated? Even if they are separated, how do they relate to each other? These are subtle questions that have been the subject of academic and public debate for many years. For a detailed review of much of the literature in the SPS context, see Tracey Epps, International Trade and Health Protection: A Critical Assessment of the WTO's SPS Agreement (2008). See how the Appellate Body addresses these questions in the Parts IV and V of this chapter. We consider these issues further in Section IV.B.5 below.

3. *Dose-response* relationships. The graph below shows different dose-response relationships. Lines A and B show a *linear response*. That is, an observed response is proportional to the dose. Line C illustrates a *nonlinear response*. That is, an observed response is not directly proportional to the dose. Line A differs from Lines B and C by illustrating a *non-threshold response*. In other words, any dose produces an effect. Lines B and C show a *threshold response* in which there is a dose below which there would be no effects observed. Whether a threshold can be identified is a major issue in the *Hormones* dispute discussed in Section IV below.

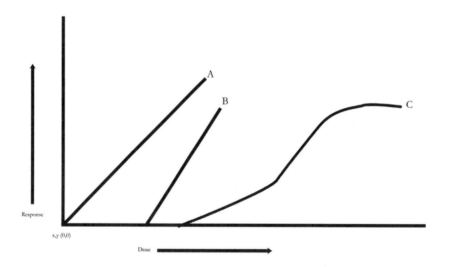

4. Risk assessment itself is an evolving art. The U.S. EPA updated its cancer assessment guidelines in light of developments in science. Guidelines for Carcinogen Risk Assessment 2005, 70 Fed. Reg. 17,765 (2005), *available at* http://www.epa.gov/cancerguidelines/. Thus the specific statements made in the Walker excerpt, which are based on the earlier guidelines, may not reflect the latest science, but they are nevertheless accurate indicators of the kinds of assumptions and inferences risk assessors must make.

5. Of international and trade relevance, risk assessments are done for many substances by the World Health Organization's (WHO) International Agency for Research on Cancer (http://www.iarc.fr) and by the WHO/Food and Agricultural Organization Joint Experts Committee on Food Additives (JECFA) (http://www.who.int/ipcs/food/jefca/en/index.html).

III. The Scope of the SPS Agreement

A. What Is an SPS Measure?

By its terms (Article 1.1), the SPS Agreement applies to "all sanitary and phytosanitary measures which may, directly or indirectly, affect international trade." Paragraph 1 of Annex A defines "sanitary or phytosanitary measures" as any measure applied:

    (a) to protect animal or plant life or health within the territory of the Member from risks arising from the entry, establishment or spread of pests, diseases, disease-carrying organisms or disease-causing organisms;

    (b) to protect human or animal life or health within the territory of the Member from risks arising from additives, contaminants, toxins or disease-causing organisms in foods, beverages or feedstuffs;

    (c) to protect human life or health within the territory of the Member from risks arising from diseases carried by animals, plants or products thereof, or from the entry, establishment or spread of pests; or

    (d) to prevent or limit other damage within the territory of the Member from the entry, establishment or spread of pests.

Sanitary or phytosanitary measures include all relevant laws, decrees, regulations, requirements and procedures including, inter alia, end product criteria; processes and production methods; testing, inspection, certification and approval procedures; quarantine treatments including relevant requirements associated with the transport of animals or plants, or with the materials necessary for their survival during transport; provisions on relevant statistical methods, sampling procedures and methods of risk assessment; and packaging and labeling requirements directly related to food safety.

The exact scope of an SPS measure remains uncertain, but the Panel's report in *EC-Biotech*, which the DSB adopted, indicates that it is broad. European Communities-Measures Affecting the Approval and Marketing of Biotech Products, Report of the Panel, WT/DS291/R, WT/DS292/R, & WT/DS293/R (Sept. 29, 2006) (adopted Nov. 21, 2006). The Panel noted that the phrase "risks arising from," found in the definition of an SPS measure in Annex A(1), "is broad and unqualified" and includes "not just measures which are applied to protect against risks that *will* invariably and inevitably arise from, *e.g.*, the spread of a pest, but also measures applied to protect against risks which *might* arise from, *e.g.*, the spread of a pest." EC-Biotech, para. 7.225 (emphasis added). In addition, the Panel concluded that the SPS Agreement covers measures taken to protect against indirect or long-term risks arising from, for example, pests.

The Panel then analyzed the separate enumerated paragraphs of Annex A(1). With respect to the SPS measures covered by Annex A(1)(a), the Panel concluded that the development of resistance to herbicides in target pests constitutes the "entry, establishment or spread" of a pest. *Id.* at para. 7.232. The term "pest" includes any "animal or plant that is destructive or causes harm to the health of other animals, plants or humans, or other harm, or a troublesome or annoying animal or plant." *Id.* at para. 7.240. Thus, the growth of genetically modified plants where they are undesired constitutes the spread of a pest. So, too, does the unintentional gene flow or transfer from a GM plant to other plants. *Id.* at para. 7.257. To the extent that a law seeks to prevent GM plants from impacting non-target populations and biogeochemical cycles, introducing or spreading diseases, or al-

tering susceptibility to pathogens that facilitate the dissemination of infectious diseases
and/or creating new reservoirs or vectors, that law constitutes a measure applied to protect animal or plant life or health from risks arising from the entry, establishment or
spread of pests, diseases, disease-carrying organisms (*e.g.*, vectors) and disease-causing
organisms (*e.g.*, pathogens). The Panel reached these findings in part by first concluding
that "there is nothing in the text of Annex A(1) to suggest that the product subject to an
SPS measure—in this case, a GM plant to be released into the environment—need itself be the pest which gives rise to the risks from which the measure seeks to protect." It
is for that reason "that even if the GM plant or the [antibiotic resistance marker genes]
were not viewed as a "disease-causing organisms" in and of themselves, the pathogen
which develops resistance to the antibiotic in question could be regarded as a 'disease-
causing organism' for the purposes of Annex A(1)." *Id.* at para. 7.282.

With respect to the SPS measures covered by Annex A(1)(b), the Panel concluded that
a GM crop grown for one purpose, for example as a feedstuff for farm animals, but is
eaten by animals, including wild fauna, can be considered a "food" for that animal. According to the Panel, this would include pollen of the GM crop consumed by insects and
GM plants consumed by nontarget insects, deer, rabbits, or other wild fauna. GM seeds
used for growing crops could also be considered animal "food" if the seeds are spilled and
subsequently eaten by birds. *Id.* at para. 7.292. Genes, including antibiotic resistance
marker genes, that are intentionally added to a product for a technological purpose are
"additives" within the meaning of Annex A(1)(b). *Id.* at paras. 7.301, 7.303.

The Panel also distinguished the terms "additive," "contaminant," and "toxin" in Annex
A(1)(b). A "contaminant" is the "unintentional" presence of a substance that is said to
"infect or pollute." *Id.* at para. 7.313. Thus, if a GM plant produces an intended protein,
then it is not a "contaminant," although the gene inserted to create that protein would
still be an "additive." However, "proteins produced through the *unintended* expression of
modified genes in agricultural crops may be considered 'contaminants' within the meaning of Annex A(1)(b), if these proteins 'infect or pollute' the food product." *Id.* Moreover, the introduction of herbicide-resistant GM crops might lead to a higher level of
contaminants, specifically herbicide residues, in foods or feedstuffs. The Panel concluded
that the term "contaminants" encompasses herbicide residues present in foods or feedstuffs,
even though the herbicide residues are the direct result of applying herbicides, not the introduction of the herbicide-resistant GM plant. Meanwhile, "toxin" means "a substance
that causes death or harm when introduced into or absorbed by a living organism," such
as a poison. *Id.* at para. 7.336. It thus encompasses allergens, which the Panel considered
to be poisons.

The Panel similarly interpreted Annex A(1)(c) and (d) broadly. For example, possible
human health effects from increased herbicide use associated with a regulated product—
in this case GMOs—may fall within the scope of Annex A(1)(c). The phrase "other damage" in subparagraph (d) includes impacts on nonliving components of the environment,
including effects on the dynamics of populations and effects on biogeochemistry.

B. The Science-Based Rules of the SPS Agreement

Generally speaking, the SPS Agreement (Article 5) calls on WTO members to base
their SPS measures on a risk assessment and disallows measures that are more trade-restrictive than necessary to achieve the government's "appropriate level of protection." The

Agreement strongly prefers international harmonization of SPS measures (Article 3), requiring members to "base" their SPS measures on international standards, guidelines, or recommendations where they exist. Moreover, if the measure "conforms to" the international standard, then it is deemed consistent with the relevant provisions of the GATT and the SPS Agreement. The key provisions are excerpted below, and are discussed in more detail in the *EC-Hormones* case in the next section.

There is a considerable array of international SPS standard-setting organizations. Annex A to the Agreement, in paragraph 3, designates several of these organizations as the relevant international standard setting bodies, depending on the nature of the SPS measure: the Codex Alimentarius Commission for most food safety and veterinary practice standards and guidelines and related monitoring and sampling methodology issues; the International Office of Epizootics for SPS measures relating to animal health and zoonoses; and the International Plant Protection Convention for plant health SPS measures. For other matters, paragraph 3 provides that the WTO SPS Committee may identify "other relevant international organizations open for membership to all members."

The Codex Alimentarius Commission has a central role. It was created in 1962 by the United Nations Food and Agriculture Organization (FAO) and the World Health Organization (WHO). With 182 member countries currently, the Codex, as it is often called, establishes standards and guidelines for protecting the health of consumers and ensuring fair practices in the food trade. *See* ftp://ftp.fao.org/codex/publications/understanding/understanding_en.pdf. It adopts advisory commodity standards for specific foods or classes of foods such as sugars, fats and oils, fish and fishery products, milk and milk products, as well as general standards (not product-specific) on such matters as the composition of food products, food additives, food labeling, food processing techniques, contaminants, methods of analysis and sampling, food hygiene, nutrition and foods for special dietary uses, food import and export inspection and certification systems, residues of veterinary drugs in foods, and pesticide residues in foods. *See Understanding the Codex Alimentarius: The Codex System: FAO, WHO and the Codex Alimentarius Commission— The Commission's Operations* (FAO Information Division, 2004), *available at* http://www.fao.org/docrep/w9114e/W9114e04.htm#TopOfPage. As of 2006, the Codex had evaluated 185 pesticides, 54 veterinary drugs, and 1,005 food additives, and established 186 food standards for commodities, 2,930 limits for residues of 218 pesticides, and 1,112 provisions on 292 different food additives. *Id.* at 11. For an excellent discussion of the Codex, as well as the International Office of Epizootics and the International Plant Protection Convention, *see* David G. Victor, *The Sanitary and Phytosanitary Agreement of the World Trade Organization: An Assessment after Five Years*, 32 INT'L L. & POL. 865 (2000).

A WTO member may adopt an SPS measure stricter than an applicable international standard if there is "scientific justification" or as a consequence of the level of protection the member determines to be appropriate in light of the risk assessment provisions in Article 5. Members must ensure that the chosen measures are based on—have some rational relationship to—the risk assessment. Moreover, where an acceptable level of risk can be achieved in various ways, members must choose the regulatory alternative that meets health objectives in the least trade restrictive way possible and that does not arbitrarily or unjustifiably discriminate among members.

Under Article 2, whether a WTO member establishes its own SPS measure or bases the measure on an international standard, it must ensure that the SPS measure is applied only to the extent necessary to protect human, animal, or plant life or health, is based on scientific principles, and is not maintained without sufficient scientific evidence. Moreover, the SPS measure must not constitute arbitrary or unjustifiable discrimination between members where identical or similar conditions prevail, or a disguised restriction on international trade.

––––––––––

Agreement on the Application of Sanitary and Phytosanitary Measures

Members,

Reaffirming that no Member should be prevented from adopting or enforcing measures necessary to protect human, animal or plant life or health, subject to the requirement that these measures are not applied in a manner which would constitute a means of arbitrary or unjustifiable discrimination between Members where the same conditions prevail or a disguised restriction on international trade; * * *

Desiring the establishment of a multilateral framework of rules and disciplines to guide the development, adoption and enforcement of sanitary and phytosanitary measures in order to minimize their negative effects on trade; * * *

Desiring therefore to elaborate rules for the application of the provisions of GATT 1994 which relate to the use of sanitary or phytosanitary measures, in particular the provisions of Article XX(b) [including the Art. XX chapeau];

Hereby agree as follows:

* * *

Article 2-Basic Rights and Obligations

1. Members have the right to take sanitary and phytosanitary measures necessary for the protection of human, animal or plant life or health, provided that such measures are not inconsistent with the provisions of this Agreement.

2. Members shall ensure that any sanitary or phytosanitary measure is applied only to the extent necessary to protect human, animal or plant life or health, is based on scientific principles and is not maintained without sufficient scientific evidence, except as provided for in paragraph 7 of Article 5.

3. Members shall ensure that their sanitary and phytosanitary measures do not arbitrarily or unjustifiably discriminate between Members where identical or similar conditions prevail, including between their own territory and that of other Members. Sanitary and phytosanitary measures shall not be applied in a manner which would constitute a disguised restriction on international trade.

4. Sanitary or phytosanitary measures which conform to the relevant provisions of this Agreement shall be presumed to be in accordance with the obligations of the Members under the provisions of GATT 1994 which relate to the use of sanitary or phytosanitary measures, in particular the provisions of Article XX(b).

Article 3-Harmonization

1. To harmonize sanitary and phytosanitary measures on as wide a basis as possible, Members shall base their sanitary or phytosanitary measures on international standards, guidelines or recommendations, where they exist, except as otherwise provided for in this Agreement, and in particular in paragraph 3.

2. Sanitary or phytosanitary measures which conform to international standards, guidelines or recommendations shall be deemed to be necessary to protect human, animal or plant life or health, and presumed to be consistent with the relevant provisions of this Agreement and of GATT 1994.

3. Members may introduce or maintain sanitary or phytosanitary measures which result in a higher level of sanitary or phytosanitary protection than would be achieved by measures based on the relevant international standards, guidelines or recommendations, if there is a scientific justification, or as a consequence of the level of sanitary or phytosanitary protection a Member determines to be appropriate in accordance with the relevant provisions of paragraphs 1 through 8 of Article 5.[2]

Notwithstanding the above, all measures which result in a level of sanitary or phytosanitary protection different from that which would be achieved by measures based on international standards, guidelines or recommendations shall not be inconsistent with any other provision of this Agreement.

4. Members shall play a full part, within the limits of their resources, in the relevant international organizations and their subsidiary bodies, in particular the Codex Alimentarius Commission, the International Office of Epizootics, and the international and regional organizations operating within the framework of the International Plant Protection Convention, to promote within these organizations the development and periodic review of standards, guidelines and recommendations with respect to all aspects of sanitary and phytosanitary measures. * * *

Article 5-Assessment of Risk and Determination of the Appropriate Level of Sanitary or Phytosanitary Protection

1. Members shall ensure that their sanitary or phytosanitary measures are based on an assessment, as appropriate to the circumstances, of the risks to human, animal or plant life or health, taking into account risk assessment techniques developed by the relevant international organizations.

2. In the assessment of risks, Members shall take into account available scientific evidence; relevant processes and production methods; relevant inspection, sampling and testing methods; prevalence of specific diseases or pests; existence of pest- or disease-free areas; relevant ecological and environmental conditions; and quarantine or other treatment.

3. In assessing the risk to animal or plant life or health and determining the measure to be applied for achieving the appropriate level of sanitary or phytosanitary protection from such risk, Members shall take into account as relevant economic factors: the potential damage in terms of loss of production or sales in the event of the entry, establishment or spread of a pest or disease; the costs of control or eradication in the territory of the importing Member; and the relative cost-effectiveness of alternative approaches to limiting risks.

4. Members should, when determining the appropriate level of sanitary or phytosanitary protection, take into account the objective of minimizing negative trade effects.

---

2. For the purposes of paragraph 3 of Article 3, there is a scientific justification if, on the basis of an examination and evaluation of available scientific information in conformity with the relevant provisions of this Agreement, a Member determines that the relevant international standards, guidelines or recommendations are not sufficient to achieve its appropriate level of sanitary or phytosanitary protection.

5. With the objective of achieving consistency in the application of the concept of appropriate level of sanitary or phytosanitary protection against risks to human life or health, or to animal and plant life or health, each Member shall avoid arbitrary or unjustifiable distinctions in the levels it considers to be appropriate in different situations, if such distinctions result in discrimination or a disguised restriction on international trade. Members shall cooperate in the Committee, in accordance with paragraphs 1, 2 and 3 of Article 12, to develop guidelines to further the practical implementation of this provision. In developing the guidelines, the Committee shall take into account all relevant factors, including the exceptional character of human health risks to which people voluntarily expose themselves.

6. Without prejudice to paragraph 2 of Article 3, when establishing or maintaining sanitary or phytosanitary measures to achieve the appropriate level of sanitary or phytosanitary protection, Members shall ensure that such measures are not more trade-restrictive than required to achieve their appropriate level of sanitary or phytosanitary protection, taking into account technical and economic feasibility.[3]

7. In cases where relevant scientific evidence is insufficient, a Member may provisionally adopt sanitary or phytosanitary measures on the basis of available pertinent information, including that from the relevant international organizations as well as from sanitary or phytosanitary measures applied by other Members. In such circumstances, Members shall seek to obtain the additional information necessary for a more objective assessment of risk and review the sanitary or phytosanitary measure accordingly within a reasonable period of time.

8. When a Member has reason to believe that a specific sanitary or phytosanitary measure introduced or maintained by another Member is constraining, or has the potential to constrain, its exports and the measure is not based on the relevant international standards, guidelines or recommendations, or such standards, guidelines or recommendations do not exist, an explanation of the reasons for such sanitary or phytosanitary measure may be requested and shall be provided by the Member maintaining the measure.

* * *

Annex A-Definitions

* * *

4. Risk assessment—The evaluation of the likelihood of entry, establishment or spread of a pest or disease within the territory of an importing Member according to the sanitary or phytosanitary measures which might be applied, and of the associated potential biological and economic consequences; or the evaluation of the potential for adverse effects on human or animal health arising from the presence of additives, contaminants, toxins or disease-causing organisms in food, beverages or feedstuffs.

5. Appropriate level of sanitary or phytosanitary protection—The level of protection deemed appropriate by the Member establishing a sanitary or phytosanitary measure to protect human, animal or plant life or health within its territory.

---

3. For purposes of paragraph 6 of Article 5, a measure is not more trade-restrictive than required unless there is another measure, reasonably available taking into account technical and economic feasibility, that achieves the appropriate level of sanitary or phytosanitary protection and is significantly less restrictive to trade.

NOTE: Many Members otherwise refer to this concept as the "acceptable level of risk."

Questions and Discussion

1. Review the provisions of the SPS Agreement. What are its basic obligations? Notwithstanding its rather detailed provisions, the SPS Agreement text leaves many questions open, including the following:

- Does the definition of SPS measures apply to regulation of genetically modified foods regulated for human health reasons? Is a flounder gene in a tomato an "additive" or a "contaminant"? *See* the description of the *EC-Biotech* Panel report above.

- Under what conditions may a WTO member choose its own level of protection when an international standard exists? What if the results of a risk assessment show very little risk? Is a zero risk goal an "appropriate level" of risk?

- Do individual governments determine what constitutes scientific evidence and scientific principles under Article 2?

- What is "sufficient scientific evidence"? Based on the negotiating history of the SPS Agreement, David Wirth says that it should be a "minimal level of scientific evidence." David A. Wirth, *The Role of Science in the Uruguay Round and NAFTA Trade Disciplines,* 27 CORNELL INT'L L.J. 854–58 (1994). What would be the effect of such a threshold? When the provisions of Articles 2, 3, and 5 are considered together, do you believe that Wirth offers an appropriate threshold?

- What must be included in the risk assessment? How must the risk assessment relate to the measure chosen by the member to attain its appropriate level of risk?

- Are the scientific requirements of Articles 2 and 5 procedural or are they substantive? Wirth describes the science requirements of the SPS Agreement as procedural, which might require, for example, scientifically sound peer review. Review Articles 5.1 and 5.2 of the SPS Agreement before answering this question.

- On these questions of science, how much deference should the panels grant the environmental authorities of the member adopting an SPS measure, especially if that judgment reflects minority or controversial views within the scientific community? Based on your evaluation of the components of risk assessment and risk management as articulated by Walker, and the provisions of the SPS Agreement, how much deference should be given to national authorities?

- What questions should panels ask to determine if a member has "based" its measure on a risk assessment or if the measure is scientifically justifiable?

2. The SPS Agreement covers import restrictions or quarantine measures to prevent harm to commercially important plants and animals as well as product regulations based on human health concerns, such as pesticide residues on food. Note that of the cases that follow, *EC-Hormones* concerns a food safety measure, while the measures in *Japan-Apples* and *Australia-Salmon* were for protection of agricultural or fisheries production. Do you think it is appropriate to bring such disparate measures within the same legal framework? In that regard, notice the precise wording of the definition of risk assessment in paragraph 4 of Annex A. What differences are intended? We return to that issue in Section IV.D below.

3. Must an SPS measure apply to a traded product? Re-read Article 1.1 and consider the following measure. In July 2004, the United States adopted a rule regulating discharges

of ship ballast water. Typically, ocean-going vessels take on ballast water in one coastal marine ecosystem and discharge it into another coastal marine ecosystem, thus releasing various marine species into new ecosystems. The introduction of alien species by ballast water has caused significant problems around the world. Does the SPS Agreement apply to this measure? Are invasive or nonnative species "pests"? Does the ballast measure, which controls operation of freighters, tankers, and container vessels, "directly or indirectly affect international trade"?

4. *Relationship to the GATT.* An interpretative note to the SPS Agreement provides that the SPS Agreement prevails in the event of a conflict between it and provisions of the GATT. As noted earlier, the preamble to the Agreement also states that it "elaborate[s] rules for the application of the provisions of GATT 1994 which relate to the use of sanitary or phytosanitary measures, in particular the provisions of Article XX(b)," including the chapeau of Article XX. How much of Article XX do you see reflected in the text of the SPS Agreement? Should Article XX jurisprudence of the Appellate Body guide the interpretation of the SPS Agreement?

5. *Grandfather Rights.* The Appellate Body in *EC-Hormones* found that the SPS Agreement applies to measures enacted before the WTO Agreement came into force. The Appellate Body said that, unlike the GATT 1947, the WTO Agreement was accepted definitively by members, and therefore "existing legislation" exceptions (so-called "grandfather rights") have been eliminated. It acknowledged that the retroactive application of the risk assessment provisions of the SPS Agreement may impose burdens on members.

6. *Special and Differential Treatment.* Article 10 of the SPS Agreement requires members to "take account of the special needs of developing country Members, and in particular of the least-developed country Members." When the appropriate level of protection allows for phased introduction of new SPS measures, members should allow developing country members a longer period to achieve compliance. In addition, the SPS Committee may grant developing countries specified, time-limited exceptions from the obligations of the SPS Agreement, "taking into account their financial, trade and development needs."

7. *NAFTA's SPS Provisions.* The SPS chapter of the North American Free Trade Agreement (NAFTA) was modeled on the WTO draft text as of 1992. While most of the provisions of the two agreements are identical, there are some differences, which the United States negotiated for during the NAFTA negotiations. Subsequently, the United States tried in the final stage of the Uruguay Round negotiations to have the final WTO text conform to the NAFTA. Although the U.S. proposals were broadly resisted, they did result in footnotes 2 and 3 in the SPS text excerpted above. Compare the following NAFTA provisions with their WTO SPS Agreement counterparts. What differences do you see? Why do you suppose the United States asked for the changes in wording? Are the textual differences mere optics, or do they change the substance of the obligations?

- NAFTA Article 712 requires parties to ensure that an SPS measure is 1) based on "scientific principles" and 2) not maintained "where there is no longer a scientific basis for it."

- Article 712 also provides that each party must ensure that its SPS measures do not create a disguised restriction on trade and do not arbitrarily or unjustifiably discriminate between its goods and "like goods" of another party, or between like goods of other parties, "where identical or similar conditions prevail."

- Article 712.5 requires that a country apply an SPS measure "only to the extent necessary to achieve its appropriate level of protection taking into account technical and economic feasibility."

- Article 713.1 provides that parties "shall use" international standards, guidelines or recommendations as the basis for SPS measures, with the objective of making their SPS measures "equivalent, or where appropriate, identical to those of other Parties."

- An SPS measure that conforms to the international standard is presumed consistent with Article 712.

- Article 713.3 emphasizes that parties may adopt, maintain, or apply SPS measures that are more stringent than the relevant international standard, guideline or recommendation, but the SPS measures must be consistent with article 712.

- If a party is conducting a risk assessment and finds that the scientific information needed to complete it is unavailable, Article 715.4 permits a provisional SPS measure "on the basis of available relevant information."

For a detailed comparison of the NAFTA and WTO provisions, *see* David A. Wirth, *The Role of Science in the Uruguay Round and NAFTA Trade Disciplines*, at 835–37.

IV. The *EC-Hormones* Dispute

A. Introduction

The history of the *EC-Hormones* dispute begins with a "scare" about the artificial animal growth hormone diethylstilbestrol (DES) in French veal and veal-based baby foods in the 1970s. An aroused European public and their political leaders pressed for controls on use of hormones in livestock production, leading to a first directive from the European Council in 1981 banning the use of five hormones in Europe. After further administrative and legislative inquiries and reports, the Council issued a new directive in 1985 (re-promulgated in 1988 after correcting procedural deficiencies), which included a ban on imports of beef from livestock treated with hormones effective January 1, 1989. The addition of the import ban is not hard to understand. Use of growth hormones is widespread in large-scale cattle production in the United States, Canada, and other beef-exporting countries. As a French cattle grower recently explained: "Baudot says he has nothing against the American cattle farming system. What is not right, he says, is having to compete internationally with a product made using methods that are outlawed in your own country. Using hormones to grow cows is kind of like doping in sports, Baudot says, and that creates an unlevel playing field." Eleanor Beardsley, *In Europe, A Cow over Hormone-Treated U.S. Beef* (National Public Radio broadcast Sept. 29, 2009).

In what is now known as *Hormones I*, The United States challenged Europe's import ban under the GATT's TBT "standards code." The GATT declined to convene an experts group to review the matter, so the United States imposed retaliatory tariffs on some European goods, and then denied the EU's request for a GATT dispute panel with respect to those tariffs. In 1996, with the WTO's Dispute Settlement Understanding (DSU) now in force, Europe renewed its request for a panel on the U.S. retaliatory tariffs (WT/DS39), at which point the United States removed the tariffs. Meanwhile, the United States had initiated its own WTO dispute over the European import ban (WT/DS/26), joined later by Canada (WT/DS48), along with some other countries as third parties.

The measure in dispute was a 1988 European Council directive, as revised in European Council Directive of April 29, 1996, 96/22/EC ("Directive 96/22"). The directive prohibited the importation of meat and meat products derived from cattle to which either certain natural hormones (oestradiol-17β, progesterone, or testosterone), or synthetic hormones (trenbolone acetate, zeranol, or melengestrol acetate ("MGA")) had been administered for growth promotion purposes. Because some of the same hormones continued to be authorized for administration in Europe under certain conditions for therapeutic and zootechnical purposes, Directive 96/22 allowed the placing on the market, and the importation from third countries, of meat and meat products from animals to which these substances have been administered for those purposes. Notably, Directive 96/22 did not correspond to international standards. The Codex Alimentarius Commission had adopted standards allowing use in livestock of five of the hormones, although it had not adopted any standards for the use of MGA.

The WTO disputes initiated by the United States and Canada resulted in lengthy proceedings, including panel consultations with experts. In August 1997, the Panel ruled that Europe 1) violated Article 5.1 of the SPS Agreement by maintaining sanitary measures which were not based on a risk assessment; 2) violated Article 5.5 by adopting arbitrary or unjustifiable distinctions in the levels of sanitary protection it considers to be appropriate in different situations, resulting in discrimination or disguised restriction on international trade; and 3) violated Article 3.1 by not basing their measures on existing international standards without justification under Article 3.3. European Communities-Measures Concerning Meat and Meat Products (Hormones), Panel Report, WT/DS26/R/USA, WT/DS48/R/CAN (adopted Feb. 13, 1998).

Each of the parties appealed certain aspects of the panel decision, leading to an important report by the Appellate Body giving its first interpretation of the SPS Agreement. EC-Measures Concerning Meat and Meat Products (Hormones), Appellate Body Report, WT/DS26/AB/R, WT/DS48/AB/R (adopted Feb. 13, 1998). The Appellate Body upheld some of the Panel's conclusions, most notably on the lack of an adequate Article 5.1 risk assessment.

Europe was now under an obligation to remove the hormones trade measure or to correct the deficiencies identified in the Appellate Body's report. Europe chose the latter course, undertaking a variety of new research and risk assessment studies. Based on the new studies and assessments, the European Council issued a new directive, 2003/74/EC, to take the place of Directive 96/22. Directive 2003/74 maintained the import bans, but gave new legal grounds for some of them. As to oestradiol-17β, Europe maintained that its new risk assessment provided a scientific basis for the import restriction. For the other five hormones, Europe invoked Article 5.7 of the SPS Agreement to maintain the import restriction "provisionally," arguing (as it had explicitly declined to do in the earlier proceeding) that there was insufficient scientific information to complete a risk assessment under the other paragraphs of Article 5.

The United States and Canada had meanwhile received authority from the Dispute Settlement Body (DSB) to impose compensatory tariffs on European goods, but held those in abeyance while Europe completed its studies. After Directive 2003/74 was promulgated, however, they imposed compensatory tariffs on the ground that Europe had not complied with the Appellate Body's requirements. After negotiations failed to resolve the continuing differences of opinion, the EU brought a WTO complaint against the United States and Canada under DSU Article 22.8, asking the Dispute Settlement Body to find them acting inconsistently with their WTO obligations by maintaining restrictions on imports from Europe even though the EU had complied with the requirements of the Appellate Body report. The United States and Canada defended on the grounds that the EU had in fact not corrected the deficiencies in its risk assessments for the hormones and was thus maintaining its ban on hormone-treated beef in violation of the SPS Agreement. Another lengthy dispute settlement proceeding ensued, including the convening of a new group of experts to advise the Panel. Once again, the panel found violations of the SPS Agreement on Europe's part. Once again the Panel's report was appealed to the Appellate Body, resulting in a new report, issued almost exactly 10 years after the first report. United States-Continued Suspension of Obligations in the EC-Hormones Dispute, Appellate Body Report, WT/DS320/AB/R (adopted Nov. 14, 2008), which we refer to as *Hormones II*.

In *Hormones II*, the Appellate Body reconfirms many of the legal conclusions of its first report, but often with additional reasoning and in slightly different, often more precise, phraseology. More importantly, even though it reversed the Panel on several critical legal issues, it declined to "complete the analysis" because of the complex facts involved, leaving *Hormones I* in place as the governing determination. Effectively, Europe was allowed to keep its import ban in place. After further negotiations, the United States and Europe entered into a Memorandum of Understanding (MOU) to resolve the dispute. *See* 74 Fed. Reg. 22626 (May 13, 2009). Under the MOU, the United States essentially accepts the validity of the European import restrictions and agrees to phase out retaliatory tariffs. In return, the EU grants duty-free access to specified quantities of hormone-free U.S. beef. This 20-year saga seems to have come to an end.

Hormones I, the Appellate Body's first report, was the first detailed interpretation of the SPS Agreement. Between *Hormones I* and *Hormones II*, the Appellate Body issued several other reports concerning SPS measures. We take up a few of these later in the chapter, but because *Hormones II* refers to them, we introduce them here. In *Australia-Salmon*, the Appellate Body found Australia's prohibition on imports of salmon on the basis of concern about introduction of pests or diseases, compared with allowance of imports of other fish such as herring and cod presenting similar risks, to constitute arbitrary and unjustifiable discrimination under Article 5.5 of the SPS Agreement. Australia-Measures Affecting the Importation of Salmon, Appellate Body Report, WT/DS18/AB/R (adopted Nov. 6, 1998). In *Japan-Agricultural Products II*, the Appellate Body concluded that Japan had maintained varietal testing requirements for various fruit products without sufficient scientific evidence as required by Article 2.2 and the risk assessments it cited did not meet the requirements of Article 5.1 or 5.7. Japan-Measures Affecting Agricultural Products, Appellate Body Report, WT/DS76/AB/R (adopted Mar. 19, 1999). Finally, the Appellate Body's report in *Japan-Apples* examined some of the issues about risk assessment that arose in *Hormones I*, disapproving a ban on import of apples from the United States supposedly intended to prevent the introduction into Japan of fire blight, a pest that affects apple production because it found Japan's risk assessment inadequate. Japan-Measures Affecting the Importation of Apples, Appellate Body Report, WT/DS245/AB/R (adopted Dec. 10, 2003).

We conclude this introduction with a short excerpt from *Hormones II* that offers an overview of the science-related issues to be considered under the SPS Agreement.

United States-Continued Suspension of Obligations in the EC-Hormones Dispute (*Hormones II*)

Appellate Body Report, WT/DS320/AB/R (adopted Nov. 14, 2008)

E. *The Panel's Assessment of Directive 2003/74/EC under Article 5.1 of the SPS Agreement*

1. General Disciplines Applicable to the Adoption of an SPS Measure

522. The *SPS Agreement* recognizes the right of WTO Members to take measures necessary to protect human, animal or plant life or health. The right to take a protective measure must be exercised consistently with a series of obligations that are set forth in that Agreement, and that seek to ensure that such measures are properly justified.

523. There are several concepts that are defined in the *SPS Agreement* and that describe aspects of a WTO Member's decision-making process when taking an SPS measure. The "appropriate level of protection" is defined in paragraph 5 of Annex A to the *SPS Agreement* as "[t]he level of protection deemed appropriate by the Member establishing a sanitary or phytosanitary measure to protect human, animal or plant life or health within its territory." It is the "prerogative" of a WTO Member to determine the level of protection that it deems appropriate.[1088] The SPS measure is the "instrument" chosen by the WTO Member to implement its sanitary or phytosanitary objective. Based on the wording of Article 5.6 of the *SPS Agreement*, the Appellate Body has explained that the "determination of the level of protection is an element in the decision-making process which logically precedes and is separate from the establishment or maintenance of the SPS measure". In other words, the appropriate level of protection determines the SPS measure to be introduced or maintained, rather than the appropriate level of protection being determined by the SPS measure. The Appellate Body has also found that "the *SPS Agreement* contains an implicit obligation to determine the appropriate level of protection." Although it need not be determined in quantitative terms, the level of protection cannot be determined "with such vagueness or equivocation that the application of the relevant provisions of the *SPS Agreement* ... becomes impossible" [quoting from *Australia-Salmon*].

524. Another important aspect of the decision-making process is the "risk assessment". Pursuant to Article 5.1 of the *SPS Agreement*, an SPS measure must be "based on an assessment, as appropriate to the circumstances, of the risks to human, animal or plant life or health". Under Article 5.7 of the *SPS Agreement*, WTO Members are also allowed to take an SPS measure, on a provisional basis, where certain conditions are fulfilled, including where the relevant scientific evidence is insufficient to perform a risk assessment. We examine Article 5.7 in more detail in section VII. * * *

1088. Although it is for a WTO Member to choose its level of protection, the *SPS Agreement* provides for disciplines that a Member must respect when it has done so. Pursuant to Article 5.5, a WTO Member "shall avoid arbitrary or unjustifiable distinctions in the levels it considers to be appropriate in different situations, if such distinctions result in discrimination or a disguised restriction on international trade." Article 5.6 states that Members "shall ensure that [SPS] measures are not more trade-restrictive than required to achieve their appropriate level of sanitary or phytosanitary protection, taking into account technical and economic feasibility". In addition, Article 5.4 provides that "Members should, when determining the appropriate level of sanitary or phytosanitary protection, take into account the objective of minimizing negative trade effects."

526. Article 5.1 is a "specific application of the basic obligations contained in Article 2.2 of the *SPS Agreement*." Article 2.2 focuses on the need for an SPS measure to be based on scientific principles and sufficient scientific evidence.... The Appellate Body has observed that "Articles 2.2 and 5.1 should constantly be read together" because "Article 2.2 informs Articles 5.1: the elements that define the basic obligation set out in Article 2.2 impart meaning to Article 5.1."[quoting from *Hormones I*, para. 180].

527. A list of factors that must be taken into account in a risk assessment is provided in Article 5.2. The list begins with "available scientific evidence" and also includes: "relevant processes and production methods; relevant inspection, sampling and testing methods; prevalence of specific diseases or pests; existence of pest- or disease-free areas; relevant ecological and environmental conditions; and quarantine or other treatment." In *EC–Hormones*, the panel described a "risk assessment" as a "scientific process aimed at establishing the scientific basis" for the SPS measure. The Appellate Body understood the panel to refer to "a process characterized by systematic, disciplined and objective enquiry and analysis, that is, a mode of studying and sorting out facts and opinions". Science therefore plays a central role in a risk assessment. However, the Appellate Body has cautioned against taking too narrow an approach to a risk assessment:

> It is essential to bear in mind that the risk that is to be evaluated in a risk assessment under Article 5.1 is not only risk ascertainable in a science laboratory operating under strictly controlled conditions, but also risk in human societies as they actually exist, in other words, the actual potential for adverse effects on human health in the real world where people live and work and die. [*Hormones I*, para. 187.]

528. As we noted earlier, Article 5.1 requires that SPS measures be "based on" a risk assessment. This does not mean that the SPS measures have to "conform to" the risk assessment. Instead, "the results of the risk assessment must sufficiently warrant—that is to say, reasonably support—the SPS measure at stake". Put differently, there must be a "rational relationship" between the SPS measure and the risk assessment. [*Hormones I*, para. 193.]

529. Moreover, the risk assessment need not "come to a monolithic conclusion that coincides with the scientific conclusion or view implicit in the SPS measure", nor does the risk assessment have to "embody only the view of a majority of the relevant scientific community." While recognizing that, in most cases, WTO Members "tend to base their legislative and administrative measures on 'mainstream' scientific opinion", the Appellate Body has observed that, "[i]n other cases, equally responsible and representative governments may act in good faith on the basis of what, at a given time, may be a divergent opinion coming from qualified and respected sources." The Appellate Body added that an approach based on a divergent opinion from a qualified and respected source, "does not necessarily signal the absence of a reasonable relationship between the SPS measure and the risk assessment, especially where the risk involved is life-threatening in character and is perceived to constitute a clear and imminent threat to public health and safety." [*Hormones I*, para. 194.]

530. An SPS measure need not be based on a risk assessment performed by the WTO Member taking the measure. It can be based on a risk assessment performed by a relevant international organization or by another WTO Member.

The risk assessment can be quantitative or qualitative in nature. Nevertheless, the Appellate Body has noted that "theoretical uncertainty" is not the kind of risk to be assessed under Article 5.1; instead, the risk to be assessed must be an "ascertainable" risk. In addition, the risk assessment must have the requisite degree of specificity. The assessment must be "sufficiently specific" in terms of the harm concerned and the precise agent that may possibly cause the harm. [citing *Hormones I* and *Japan-Apples*]

531. Whilst WTO Members have the right to take SPS measures, they are not required to do so. The risk assessment may conclude that there is no ascertainable risk, in which case no SPS measure can be taken. Alternatively, a WTO Member may conclude that an SPS measure is not necessary in the light of the risks determined in the risk assessment and the acceptable level of protection determined by that WTO Member.

532. International standards are given a prominent role under the SPS Agreement, particularly in furthering the objective of promoting the harmonization of sanitary and phytosanitary standards between WTO Members. This is to be achieved by encouraging WTO Members to base their SPS measures on international standards, guidelines or recommendations, where they exist. There is a rebuttable presumption that SPS measures that conform to international standards, guidelines or recommendations are "necessary to protect human, animal or plant life or health, and ... [are] consistent with the relevant provisions of this Agreement and of GATT 1994". While use of international standards is encouraged, the *SPS Agreement* recognizes the right of WTO Members to introduce or maintain an SPS measure which results in a higher level of protection than would be achieved by measures based on such international standards. Where a Member exercises its right to adopt an SPS measure that results in a higher level of protection, that right is qualified in that the SPS measure must comply with the other requirements of the *SPS Agreement*, including the requirement to perform a risk assessment. However, the Appellate Body has found that the adoption of an SPS measure that does not conform to an international standard and results in a higher level of protection does not give rise to a more exacting burden of proof under the SPS Agreement:

> The presumption of consistency with relevant provisions of the *SPS Agreement* that arises under Article 3.2 in respect of measures that conform to international standards may well be an *incentive* for Members so to conform their SPS measures with such standards. It is clear, however, that a decision of a Member not to conform a particular measure with an international standard does not authorize imposition of a special or generalized burden of proof upon that Member, which may, more often than not, amount to a *penalty*. (original emphasis)[*Hormones I*, para. 102]

533. At the oral hearing, we explored the relationship between the appropriate level of protection and the risk assessment. The European Communities considers that the appropriate level of protection can clearly be taken into account in a risk assessment and may, in some cases, be reflected in the mandate and parameters given to the risk assessors. The United States and Canada recognize that the acceptable level of risk may sometimes play a role, albeit a limited one, in respect of the risk assessment. The United States and Canada, however, caution about the need to maintain the objectivity of the risk assessment process and reject the notion that subjective policy choices have a role to play in a risk

assessment. In their view, these policy choices may be taken into account by a WTO Member in determining its appropriate level of risk and in selecting the SPS measure, but should not be part of the risk assessment process, which must remain an objective and scientific evaluation.

534. The risk assessment cannot be entirely isolated from the appropriate level of protection. There may be circumstances in which the appropriate level of protection chosen by a Member affects the scope or method of the risk assessment. This may be the case where a WTO Member decides not to adopt an SPS measure based on an international standard because it seeks to achieve a higher level of protection. In such a situation, the fact that the WTO Member has chosen to set a higher level of protection may require it to perform certain research as part of its risk assessment that is different from the parameters considered and the research carried out in the risk assessment underlying the international standard. However, the chosen level of protection must not affect the rigour or objective nature of the risk assessment, which must remain, in its essence, a process in which possible adverse effects are evaluated using scientific methods. Likewise, whatever the level of protection a Member chooses does not pre-determine the results of the risk assessment. Otherwise, the purpose of performing the risk assessment would be defeated.

535. We understand that Codex draws a distinction between "risk assessment" and "risk management". It defines "risk management" as "the process, *distinct from risk assessment*, of weighing policy alternatives ... considering risk assessment and other factors relevant for the health protection of consumers and for the promotion of fair trade practices, and, if needed, selecting appropriate prevention and control options." In *EC–Hormones*, the Appellate Body noted that the *SPS Agreement* does not refer to the concept of "risk management" and it rejected the panel's restrictive interpretation of a "risk assessment" based on that distinction. The Appellate Body has not provided a clear demarcation of the factors that may be considered in a "risk assessment" under the *SPS Agreement*, but it has held that the list of factors provided in Article 5.2 is not a closed list and, in particular, that abuse or misuse and difficulties of control in the administration of hormones may be considered in the context of a risk assessment.

Questions and Discussion

1. One basic question not fully clarified by the Appellate Body's summary of principles is what it means for an SPS measure to be "based on" a risk assessment. Note the language of paragraph 528, above. In *Hormones I*, the panel had purported to find a minimum procedural requirement in the "based on" phrase, namely that the government needed to take the risk assessment into account when adopting its measure. The Appellate Body disagreed, finding no textual basis for such a procedural requirement. Absent a requirement for the government to consider the risk assessment, what does it mean for the measure to be "based on" a risk assessment? In paragraph 189 of *Hormones I*, the Appellate Body stated: "We believe that 'based on' is appropriately taken to refer to a certain *objective relationship* between two elements, that is to say, to an *objective situation* that persists and is observable between an SPS measure and a risk assessment." (Emphasis in the original.) Why is the Appellate Body wary of implying a "take account of" requirement? Is its reasoning consistent with the purposes of a risk assessment as discussed by Vernon

Walker and David Wirth earlier in this chapter? If a government does not take account of the risk assessment to choose its measure, then what is the point of a risk assessment?

Consider the elements of the SPS Agreement requirements in the order that the Appellate Body presented them in the excerpt above. First, it is for each government to choose, for each measure, its "appropriate level of protection." As a second step, the government must undertake (or adopt) a risk assessment "appropriate to the circumstances" as a basis for selecting SPS measures to achieve the desired level of protection. Third, Article 5.7 nevertheless allows "provisional" SPS measures in cases when there is not enough scientific information to complete a risk assessment. Finally, the Agreement has a declared preference for adoption of international standards or guidelines where they exist, which lies in the background of the first three elements. In the *EC-Hormones* dispute, it became obvious that these four elements are intertwined in complex ways.

Section B below begins with a focus on the requirements for a risk assessment. Section C begins with a lengthy excerpt from *Hormones II* that connects the appropriate level of protection, insufficiency of evidence, provisional measures, and international standards. The remainder of Section C explores each of those elements.

B. Risk Assessment

There are two basic questions about risk assessment in the WTO SPS Agreement. First, under what circumstances do the risk assessment provisions of Article 5 apply? Second, exactly what kinds of scientific analysis and assessment of other factors are allowed or required to meet the Article 5 requirements?

In the Appellate Body's view, the answer to the first question is straightforward. As it says in paragraph 526 of the excerpt above, it views Article 5.1 as a "specific application" of the general obligation under Article 2.2 to base measures on "scientific principles" and not maintain them "without sufficient scientific evidence." By the same token, it says that Article 2.2 "imparts meaning to Article 5.1" These legal conclusions, originally stated in *Hormones I*, have been repeated in almost every SPS dispute since then and have not drawn any adverse commentary. In short, every SPS measure must have as its basis an assessment of the risk that the measure is designed to protect against.

The Appellate Body has also made it clear from the outset that risk assessment is not a purely academic exercise. *See* paragraph 527 above. But these statements leave plenty of room for argument about just what kind of analysis constitutes a suitable "assessment ... of the risks." We excerpt extensively from *Hormones II*, the Appellate Body's most recent comprehensive discussion of the scientific and legal questions involved. The excerpts contain a number of acronyms; here is a short glossary of the references:

JECFA: Joint FAO/WHO Expert Committee on Food Additives (advisory to the Codex)

SCVPH: The Scientific Committee on Veterinary Measures relating to Public Health of the European Communities

1999 Opinion: SCVPH Assessment of Potential Risks to Human Health from Hormone Residues in Bovine Meat and Meat Products

2000 Opinion: SCVPH review of its 1999 Opinion, making no alteration to its conclusions

2002 Opinion: SCVPH second review and revision of its 1999 Opinion on the basis of
scientific data collected since the 2000 review

---

1. *Allowable Factors for Consideration in Risk Assessments*

United States-Continued Suspension of Obligations in the EC-Hormones Dispute (*Hormones II*)

Appellate Body Report, WT/DS320/AB/R (adopted Nov. 14, 2008)

536. Before we proceed to examine the European Communities' claims, we briefly summarize some of the relevant facts of this case. We note that Codex has adopted an international standard for oestradiol-17β, based on evaluations carried out by JECFA. The European Communities asserts that it has determined a higher level of protection than that which would be achieved under Codex's standard. According to the European Communities, its level of protection is "no (avoidable) risk, that is a level of protection that does not allow any unnecessary addition from exposure to genotoxic chemical substances that are intended to be added deliberately to food." The European Communities also notes that it has performed a risk assessment for meat from cattle treated with oestradiol-17β for growth-promotion purposes. This risk assessment consists of the 1999, 2000, and 2002 Opinions, as supported by 17 studies conducted between 1998 and 2001. The European Communities further explains that its SPS measure—that is, the import and marketing ban applied pursuant to Directive 2003/74/EC—was taken in the light of the higher level of protection that it determined for itself and is properly based on its risk assessment.

2. The Panel's Interpretation and Application of Articles 5.1 and 5.2 of the SPS Agreement

537. We examine, first, the European Communities' claim that the Panel erred by adopting "an extremely narrow and consequently erroneous interpretation of Article 5.1 and failed to take into account that risk assessment and risk management partly overlap in the SPS Agreement". The European Communities argues that the Panel's restrictive interpretation of risk assessment led it to wrongfully exclude from the scope of its analysis under Article 5.1 evidence concerning misuse or abuse and difficulties of control in the administration of hormones to cattle for growth promotion.

538. [The Appellate Body quotes two paragraphs from the Panel Report, concluding with the following statement:] However, the Panel finds that neither that finding nor the text of the Agreement includes within the definition of a risk assessment the concepts put forward by the European Communities as "risk management."

539. Therefore, the Panel stated that it would ask questions of the experts relating to whether the SCVPH Opinions identified the potential for adverse effects on human health of residues of oestradiol 17β in the meat of cattle treated with this hormone when applied in accordance with good veterinary practice.

540. At the interim review stage, the European Communities asserted that the Panel "misinterpret[ed]" what the Appellate Body had said in *EC–Hormones*. In response, the Panel explained:

> The Appellate Body disapproved of the panel's use in the original *EC–Hormones* dispute of the distinction between "risk assessment" and "risk management" because it had no textual basis. However, this did not mean that the Appellate Body endorsed an interpretation of Article 5.1 or Annex A(4) of the *SPS Agreement* that included a risk management stage. In fact, it emphatically stated that the term "risk management" is not to be found in Article 5 or any other provision of the *SPS Agreement*. The Panel, therefore, finds no basis for the European Communities' assertion that the Appellate Body "confirmed that a risk assessment within the meaning of Article 5.1 includes a risk management stage which is the responsibility of the regulator to carry out and not of the scientific bodies." (footnote omitted)

541. We find it difficult to reconcile the Panel's understanding of *EC–Hormones* with what the Appellate Body held in that Report. As we noted above, in that case, the Appellate Body rejected the rigid distinction drawn by the panel between "risk assessment" and "risk management", explaining:

> We must stress, in this connection, that Article 5 and Annex A of the *SPS Agreement* speak of "risk assessment" only and that the term "risk management" is not to be found either in Article 5 or in any other provision of the *SPS Agreement*. Thus, the Panel's distinction, which it apparently employs to achieve or support what appears to be a restrictive notion of risk assessment, has no textual basis.

Subsequently in the same Report, the Appellate Body reiterated its view that "the concept of 'risk management' is not mentioned in any provision of the *SPS Agreement* and, as such, cannot be used to sustain a more *restrictive* interpretation of 'risk assessment' than is justified by the actual terms of Article 5.2, Article 8 and Annex C of the *SPS Agreement*".

542. Therefore, in our view, the Panel's interpretation of "risk assessment" resulted in the same "restrictive notion of risk assessment" that the Appellate Body found to be erroneous in *EC–Hormones*. The Panel sought in this case to rewrite the Appellate Body Report in *EC–Hormones* and to re-establish the rigid distinction between "risk assessment" and "risk management" that the Appellate Body had rejected in that case.

543. We set out above our understanding of the Appellate Body's finding in *EC–Hormones* in so far as the distinction between "risk assessment" and "risk management" is concerned. We now turn to the European Communities' argument that the distinction that the Panel drew between "risk assessment" and "risk management" resulted in the exclusion of certain factors from the Panel's analysis under Article 5.1 of the *SPS Agreement*. In particular, the European Communities asserts that the Panel improperly excluded the evidence concerning misuse or abuse and difficulties of control in the administration of hormones to cattle for growth promotion.

544. The relevance of the risks relating to abuse or misuse in the administration of hormones was also addressed in *EC–Hormones*. In that case, the Appellate Body noted that "[s]ome of the kinds of factors listed in Article 5.2 such as 'relevant processes and production methods' and 'relevant inspection, sampling and testing

methods' are not necessarily or wholly susceptible of investigation according to laboratory methods of, for example, biochemistry or pharmacology" and that "there is nothing to indicate that the listing of factors that may be taken into account in a risk assessment of Article 5.2 was intended to be a closed list." It then specifically examined whether risks relating to misuse or abuse in the administration of the hormones could be considered as part of the "risk assessment":

> Where the condition of observance of good veterinary practice (which is much the same condition attached to the standards, guidelines and recommendations of Codex with respect to the use of the five hormones for growth promotion) is *not* followed, the logical inference is that the use of such hormones for growth promotion purposes may or may not be "safe". The *SPS Agreement* requires assessment of the potential for adverse effects on human health arising from the presence of contaminants and toxins in food. We consider that the object and purpose of the *SPS Agreement* justify the examination and evaluation of all such risks for human health whatever their precise and immediate origin may be. We do not mean to suggest that risks arising from potential abuse in the administration of controlled substances and from control problems need to be, or should be, evaluated by risk assessors in each and every case. When and if risks of these types do in fact arise, risk assessors may examine and evaluate them. Clearly, the necessity or propriety of examination and evaluation of such risks would have to be addressed on a case-by-case basis. What, in our view, is a fundamental legal error is to exclude, on an *a priori* basis, any such risks from the scope of application of Articles 5.1 and 5.2. We disagree with the Panel's suggestion that exclusion of risks resulting from the combination of potential abuse and difficulties of control is justified by distinguishing between "risk assessment" and "risk management". As earlier noted, the concept of "risk management" is not mentioned in any provision of the *SPS Agreement* and, as such, cannot be used to sustain a more restrictive interpretation of "risk assessment" than is justified by the actual terms of Article 5.2, Article 8 and Annex C of the *SPS Agreement*. (original emphasis; footnote omitted)

545. Thus, the risks arising from the abuse or misuse in the administration of hormones can properly be considered as part of a risk assessment. Where a WTO Member has taken such risks into account, they must be considered by a panel reviewing that Member's risk assessment. Any suggestion that such risks cannot form part of a risk assessment would constitute legal error.

546. At the interim review stage, the Panel dismissed the relevance of the evidence concerning misuse or abuse in the administration of hormones under Article 5.1 for the following reasons:

> The Panel agrees with the European Communities that the question of misuse and abuse in the administration of hormones may apply to all six hormones at issue and is an element that can be taken into account in risk assessment, as set forth in Article 5.2 of the *SPS Agreement* and confirmed by the Appellate Body in *EC–Hormones*. However, the Panel did not deem it necessary to address this question in the section regarding the conformity with Article 5.1 of the definitive ban on oestradiol 17β, to the extent that the question whether misuse or abuse exists in the administration of hormones did not have an impact on the issues addressed by the Panel under

Article 5.1. Indeed, the question of misuse or abuse in the administration of hormones is relevant to the extent that it can lead to higher concentrations of hormone residues in meat and meat products than would occur if good veterinary practices were applied. As stated by the 1999 Opinion, it is an aspect of exposure assessment. In this case, the Panel found that the European Communities had not evaluated specifically the possibility that the adverse effect[s] that it had identified in its risk assessment come into being, originate, or result from the consumption of meat or meat products which contain veterinary residues of oestradiol-17β as a result of the cattle being treated with this hormone for growth promotion purposes. Therefore, whether the concentrations of hormone residues in meat and meat products could be higher as a result of misuse or abuse did not have to be addressed. The Panel does not deem it necessary to move this section to another part of its findings. (footnote omitted)

547. The United States and Canada consider that this statement indicates that the Panel did address the European Communities' arguments relating to misuse or abuse. We note that in this statement, the Panel acknowledges that those risks are "an element that can be taken into account in risk assessment, as set forth in Article 5.2 of the *SPS Agreement* and confirmed by the Appellate Body in *EC–Hormones*." Although the Panel does not seem to reject *a priori* the relevance of the potential risks of misuse or abuse, it then states that it was not necessary to address this question in its analysis, to the extent that it did not have an impact on the issues addressed by the Panel under Article 5.1. However, some of the scientific experts consulted by the Panel indicated that risks arising from residues of oestradiol-17β in bovine meat are likely to increase where good veterinary practices in the administration of this hormone are not followed. Indeed, these experts agreed that their conclusions in relation to the risks posed by oestradiol-17β were predicated on good veterinary practices being followed. Accordingly, the abuse or misuse in the administration of oestradiol-17β has a bearing on the particular risks being assessed by the European Communities. The Panel's conclusion was thus premature because the Panel could not have decided whether the European Communities failed to evaluate specifically the possible adverse effects of residues of oestradiol-17β in meat before considering the evidence on abuse or misuse. The Panel's summary dismissal of the relevance of the evidence on misuse or abuse at the interim review stage gives the appearance of being an *ex post* rationalization of an earlier decision to exclude such risks from consideration.

548. The risks of abuse or misuse of the hormones at issue were examined by the European Communities as part of its risk assessment. * * *

553. The Panel does not address the evidence on misuse or abuse referred to in the 1999 and 2002 Opinions in its analysis under Article 5.1 of the *SPS Agreement*. Neither does the Panel discuss the testimony of the scientific experts that recognized the relevance of this evidence and the potential adverse effects of the misuse or abuse in the administration of the hormones. The Panel summarily dismissed the relevance of the evidence on misuse or abuse stating that it relates to exposure assessment and adding that it is not necessary to address it given the finding that the European Communities had not evaluated *specifically* the possibility that the adverse effects arise from the consumption of meat from cattle treated with oestradiol-17β for growth-promotion purposes. We recognize that the 1999 Opinion examines the risks of misuse or abuse under the heading "Ex-

posure considerations upon misuse". After discussing the evidence on misuse and abuse, the 2002 Opinion states that "these data have to be considered in any quantitative exposure assessment exercise." This, however, cannot justify the Panel's failure to address the evidence on misuse or abuse. The European Communities made it clear that the risks of abuse or misuse were a relevant consideration in its risk assessment. This is confirmed in the 1999 and 2002 Opinions. At least two of the scientific experts consulted by the Panel recognized that the misuse or abuse in the administration of the hormones could give rise to adverse effects. The Panel had a duty to engage with this evidence and with the discussion of this evidence in the SCVPH Opinions. By summarily dismissing the evidence on the misuse or abuse in the administration of the hormones and the consequent conclusions in the SCVPH Opinions in the manner that it did, the Panel incorrectly applied Article 5.1 and the definition of "risk assessment" in Annex A of the *SPS Agreement*, as interpreted by the Appellate Body.

554. The United States and Canada submit that there are no economic incentives to fail to observe good veterinary practices by, for example, giving higher doses of hormones to the cattle. This is something the Panel could have examined, but it did not. Therefore, it cannot justify the Panel's inadequate treatment of the issue.

555. Accordingly, we <u>find</u> that the Panel erred in its interpretation and application of Article 5.1 of the *SPS Agreement* in relation to risks of misuse and abuse in the administration of hormones to cattle for growth-promoting purposes.

Questions and Discussion

1. What is the distinction between the Appellate Body's legal conclusion that abuse or misuse of hormones "can properly be considered as part of the risk assessment" (paragraph 545, above) and the Panel's (improper) insistence that any increase in risk from abuse or misuse should have been part of the EU's exposure assessment in its risk assessment? Where did the Panel go off the legal track identified by the Appellate Body?

2. The Appellate Body cites the testimony of two experts (paragraph 553; omitted paragraphs quote the experts' testimony). What legal conclusions does the Appellate Body draw from their testimony? How had the Panel come to a different legal result?

3. Is it appropriate for WTO panels and the Appellate Body to delve into the scientific issues in this detail? What are the risks? What are the benefits?

---

2. Specificity of the Risk Assessment in Relation to the SPS Measure

United States-Continued Suspension of Obligations in the EC-Hormones Dispute (*Hormones II*)

Appellate Body Report, WT/DS320/AB/R (adopted Nov. 14, 2008)

3. The Panel's Specificity Requirement

556. The European Communities claims that the Panel erred in finding that the European Communities had acted inconsistently with Article 5.1 of the *SPS Agree-*

ment by failing to evaluate specifically the risks arising from residues of oestradiol-17β in meat from cattle treated with this hormone for growth promotion. The European Communities argues that "[a]t no stage did the Panel[] correctly identify what the Appellate Body found to be wanting in the risk assessments carried out for the purposes of Directive 96/22/EC in the original hormones dispute."

557. Relying on the Appellate Body's findings in *EC–Hormones*, the Panel observed that "a risk assessment in this instance required not a general evaluation of the carcinogenic potential of entire categories of hormones, but rather should include an examination of residues of those hormones found in meat derived from cattle to which the hormones had been administered for growth promotion purposes." The Panel also noted the Appellate Body's finding in *Japan–Apples* that "a risk assessment should refer in general to the harm concerned as well as to the precise agent that may possibly cause the harm", and its explanation that "an evaluation of risk must connect the possibility of adverse effects with an antecedent or cause." The Panel concluded:

> [T]he European Communities was required to evaluate the possibility that the identified adverse effect came into being, originated, or resulted from the presence of residues of oestradiol-17β in meat or meat products as a result of the cattle being treated with the hormone for growth promoting purposes.

558. The European Communities alleges that the Panel improperly required demonstration of *actual* effects while the Appellate Body had required mere demonstration of the *possibility of adverse effects*. The European Communities' allegation is unfounded. In the statement quoted above, the Panel focused on the *possibility* that the adverse effects could arise from the consumption of meat from cattle treated with oestradiol-17β. The test articulated by the Panel is compatible with the definition of the term "risk assessment" in paragraph 4 of Annex A of the *SPS Agreement* and with the interpretation developed by the Appellate Body in *EC–Hormones*. In that dispute, the European Communities presented a number of scientific studies and opinions of individual scientists indicating that the hormones at issue in that case had "carcinogenic potential". Yet, the Appellate Body found that those studies fell short of the requirements of paragraph 4 of Annex A of the *SPS Agreement*, because:

> The 1987 IARC Monographs and the articles and opinions of individual scientists submitted by the European Communities constitute general studies which do indeed show the existence of a general risk of cancer; but they do not focus on and do not address the particular kind of risk here at stake— the carcinogenic or genotoxic potential of the residues of those hormones found in meat derived from cattle to which the hormones had been administered for growth promotion purposes—as is required by paragraph 4 of Annex A of the *SPS Agreement*. Those general studies, are in other words, relevant but do not appear to be sufficiently specific to the case at hand.

559. The definition of a risk assessment in paragraph 4 of Annex A, as interpreted by the Appellate Body, required the European Communities to conduct a risk assessment that addresses the specific risk at issue. The particular risk being evaluated by the European Communities in this case was the potential for neurobiological, developmental, reproductive, and immunological effects, as well as immunotoxic, genotoxic and carcinogenic effects from the residues

of oestradiol-17β found in meat derived from cattle to which this hormone was administered for growth-promoting purposes. Although the European Communities is correct in arguing that it was not required to demonstrate that these adverse health effects would actually arise, it was nevertheless required to demonstrate that these adverse effects could arise from the presence of residues of oestradiol-17β in meat from treated cattle. In our view, this is what the Panel required when it examined whether the European Communities had "evaluate[d] the possibility that the identified adverse effect ... resulted from the presence of residues of oestradiol-17β in meat or meat products as a result of the cattle being treated with the hormone for growth promoting purposes."

560. The European Communities also argues that the Panel erred by requiring a demonstration of "direct causality", which the European Communities posits constitutes "a very narrow reading" by the Panel of the definition of risk assessment in paragraph 4 of Annex A.

561. The Appellate Body explained in *Japan–Apples* that:

> Indeed, we are of the view that, as a general matter, "risk" cannot usually be understood only in terms of the disease or adverse effects that may result. Rather, an evaluation of risk must connect the possibility of adverse effects with an antecedent or cause. For example, the abstract reference to the "risk of cancer" has no significance, in and of itself, under the *SPS Agreement*; but when one refers to the "risk of cancer from smoking cigarettes", the particular risk is given content.

562. The particular risk being assessed by the European Communities is the possibility of adverse health effects from the consumption of residues of oestradiol-17β in meat treated with this hormone for growth promotion. In *EC–Hormones*, the Appellate Body required evaluation of "the carcinogenic or genotoxic potential of the residues of [the] hormones" at issue found in meat from treated cattle. In this case, the European Communities had to evaluate whether a causal connection exists between the consumption of meat from cattle treated with oestradiol-17β and the possibility of adverse health effects. This does not mean that the European Communities was required to establish a direct causal relationship between the possibility of adverse health effects and the residues of oestradiol-17β in bovine meat. In order to meet the requirements of Article 5.1 and Annex A of the SPS Agreement, it was sufficient for the European Communities to demonstrate that the additional human exposure to residues of oestradiol-17β in meat from treated cattle is one of the factors contributing to the possible adverse health effects. The European Communities was not required to isolate the contribution made by residues of oestradiol-17β in meat from cattle treated with the hormone for growth promotion from the contributions made by other sources. Where multiple factors may contribute to a particular risk, a risk assessor is not required to differentiate the individual contribution made by each factor. Article 5.1 requires that SPS measures be based on a risk assessment "as appropriate to the circumstances", which suggests that the scientific inquiry involved in a risk assessment must take due account of particular methodological difficulties posed by the nature and characteristics of the particular substance and risk being evaluated. However, that does not excuse the risk assessor from evaluating whether there is a connection between the particular substance being evaluated and the possibility that adverse health effects may arise.

563. Finally, we are not persuaded by the European Communities suggestion that the Panel required testing in humans in order to specifically evaluate the risks associated with the consumption of meat from cattle treated with oestradiol-17β. We do not see this as a necessary implication of the Panel's analysis. There is no indication in the Panel Report to suggest that the evaluation could not proceed on the basis of experimentation in laboratory animals and extrapolating the results to humans, or by other means. Certainly, where a substance may be potentially toxic, requiring a WTO Member to evaluate specifically the risks through actual human consumption of the substance would be unethical and would not be "appropriate to the circumstances" within the meaning of Article 5.1.

564. For these reasons, we <u>find</u> that the Panel did not err in requiring a specific evaluation of the risks arising from the presence of residues of oestradiol-17β in meat or meat products from cattle treated with the hormone for growth-promoting purposes.

Questions and Discussion

1. Perhaps the most important conclusion of the Appellate Body in *Hormones I* concerned the specificity of information that must be included in the risk assessment. The Appellate Body noted (and reiterates in *Hormones II* (see para. 529 in the first excerpt on page 449)) that a risk assessment does not need "to come to a monolithic conclusion that coincides with the scientific conclusion or view implicit in the SPS measure" adopted by a member. The Appellate Body embraced the idea that an SPS measure could be based on a minority view. Yet, in *Hormones I* at para. 198, the Appellate Body said that the views of one scientist, Dr. Lucier, which were based on a general assessment of carcinogenicity of the hormones, were "not reasonably sufficient" to overturn contrary studies showing the use of hormones in beef production to be safe, even while noting Dr. Lucier's estimates of a 1 in 1 million lifetime risk for women of breast cancer as a result of ingesting meat containing oestrogens as a growth promoter when used as prescribed. Why was that scientific opinion not "sufficient"? Now re-read para. 562 of *Hormones II*, above. Is the Appellate Body quietly moving toward a position more tolerant of views like Dr. Lucier's?

2. Moreover, the Appellate Body in *Hormones I* stated that general information about a class of chemicals was insufficient to identify risk associated with a specific chemical within that class of chemicals. The Appellate Body declared (para. 200) that these general studies "do not focus on and do not address the particular kind of risk here at stake—the carcinogenic or genotoxic potential of the residues of those hormones found in meat derived from cattle to which the hormones had been administered for growth promotion purposes—as is required by paragraph 4 of Annex A of the SPS Agreement." Re-read paragraph 4 of Annex A. Where is the Appellate Body finding the "specificity" requirement? After *Hormones I*, some commentators suggested that the Appellate Body was *sub rosa* attacking the level of protection set by the EU. *See, e.g.,* Fiona Macmillan, WTO and the Environment 153 (2001). David Wirth argued that the SPS Agreement does not "speak to whether empirical data must correlate with regulated exposures, to whether uses from data are obtained must be identified with a high degree of particularity, or to the specificity with which uses or exposures might be regulated based on particular effects." David A. Wirth, *The Role of Science in the Uruguay Round and NAFTA Trade Disciplines*, at 857. Do these same concerns apply after *Hormones II*? Consider these same questions after reading Section IV.C starting on page 476 on the EU's provisional measures.

3. To what extent does the specificity requirement arise from the language of Article 2.2 requiring *"any"* SPS measure to be scientifically based? Consider the following discussion from *Japan-Apples*. In this dispute, the United States challenged import restrictions on U.S. apples intended, so Japan claimed, to safeguard Japanese apple production from fire blight, a well-known agricultural pest.

Japan-Measures Affecting the Importation of Apples

Appellate Body Report, WT/DS245/AB/R (adopted Dec. 10, 2003)

200. In this case, the Panel, relying on the Appellate Body's finding in *EC-Hormones*, concluded that the 1999 PRA [Pest Risk Analysis] was not sufficiently specific to constitute a "risk assessment" in accordance with the *SPS Agreement*. The Panel based this conclusion on its finding that, although the 1999 PRA makes determinations as to the entry, establishment and spread of fire blight through a collection of various hosts (including apple fruit), it failed to evaluate the entry, establishment or spread of fire blight through apple fruit as a separate and distinct vector. As the Panel stated in response to Japan's comments during the Interim Review, "Japan evaluated the risks associated with all possible hosts taken together, not sufficiently considering the risks specifically associated with the commodity at issue: US apple fruit exported to Japan."

201. Japan does not contest the Panel's characterization of the risk assessment as one that did not analyze the risks of apple fruit separately from risks posed by other hosts. Rather, Japan claims that the Panel's reasoning relates to a "matter of methodology," which lies within the discretion of the importing Member. Japan contends that the requirement of "specificity" explained in *EC-Hormones* refers to the specificity of the risk and not to the methodology of the risk assessment.

202. We disagree with Japan. Under the *SPS Agreement*, the obligation to conduct an assessment of "risk" is not satisfied merely by a general discussion of the disease sought to be avoided by the imposition of a phytosanitary measure.... Therefore, when discussing the risk to be specified in the risk assessment in *EC-Hormones*, the Appellate Body referred in general to the harm concerned (cancer or genetic damage) *as well as* to the precise agent that may possibly cause the harm (that is, the specific hormones when used in a specific manner and for specific purposes).

203. In this case, the Panel found that the conclusion of the 1999 PRA with respect to fire blight was "based on an overall assessment of possible modes of contamination, where apple fruit is only one of the possible hosts/vectors considered." The Panel further found, on the basis of the scientific evidence, that the risk of entry, establishment or spread of the disease varies significantly depending on the vector, or specific host plant, being evaluated. Given that the measure at issue relates to the risk of transmission of fire blight through apple fruit, in an evaluation of whether the risk assessment is "sufficiently specific to the case at hand," the nature of the risk addressed by the measure at issue is a factor to be taken into account. In the light of these considerations, we are of the view that the Panel properly determined that the 1999 PRA "evaluat[ion of] the risks associated with all possible hosts taken together" was not sufficiently specific to qualify as a "risk assessment" under the *SPS Agreement* for the evaluation of the likelihood of entry, establishment or spread of fire blight in Japan through apple fruit.

204. Japan contends that the "methodology" of the risk assessment is not directly addressed by the *SPS Agreement*. In particular, Japan suggests that, whether to analyze the risk on the basis of the particular pest or disease, or on the basis of a particular commodity, is a "matter of methodology" not directly addressed by the *SPS Agreement*. We agree. Contrary to Japan's submission, however, the Panel's reading of *EC-Hormones* does not suggest that there is an obligation to follow any particular methodology for conducting a risk assessment. In other words, even though, in a given context, a risk assessment must consider a specific agent or pathway through which contamination might occur, Members are not precluded from organizing their risk assessments along the lines of the disease or pest at issue, or of the commodity to be imported. Thus, Members are free to consider in their risk analysis multiple agents in relation to one disease, provided that the risk assessment attribute a likelihood of entry, establishment or spread of the disease to each agent specifically. Members are also free to follow the other "methodology" identified by Japan and focus on a particular commodity, subject to the same proviso.

205. Indeed, the relevant international standards, which, Japan claims, "adopt both methodologies" expressly contemplate examining risk in relation to particular pathways. Those standards call for that specific examination even when the risk analysis is initiated on the basis of the particular pest or disease at issue as was the 1999 PRA. Therefore, our conclusion that the Panel properly found Japan's risk assessment not to be sufficiently specific, does not limit an importing Member's right to adopt any appropriate "methodology," consistent with the definition of "risk assessment" in paragraph 4 of Annex A to the *SPS Agreement*.

206. We therefore uphold the Panel's finding, in paragraph 8.271 of the Panel Report, that Japan's 1999 Pest Risk Analysis does not satisfy the definition of "risk assessment" in paragraph 4 of Annex A to the *SPS Agreement*, because it fails to evaluate the likelihood of entry, establishment or spread of fire blight specifically through apple fruit.

---

4. *Invasive Alien Species.* In the words of the Appellate Body in *Japan-Apples*, a risk assessment "must consider a specific agent or pathway through which contamination might occur." Can the "specific agent or pathway" requirement be applied to measures to prevent the introduction of alien invasive species, which pose significant threats to biodiversity, agriculture, forestry, and fisheries? There are two imponderable factors: 1) What species need to be controlled? and 2) What reasonable or "proportionate" measures are available to prevent their entry? As to the first question, is there any reliable scientific way to predict that a particular nonnative species will become a damaging pest in a particular country? As to the second question, what is the likely route or means of entry of a particular species? Are there multiple routes? For example, the Asian long-horned beetle is believed to have hitchhiked into the United States in the early 1990s in wooden crates of a cargo ship, but on what kind of ship carrying what type of product is not known. It has since become a major pest in North America, especially affecting maple (Acer) species.

Much of the potential for trade disputes regarding defensive measures against invasive alien species is mitigated by a substantial and growing network of international agreements and cooperation. Under the auspices of the FAO, countries negotiated an International Plant Protection Convention (IPPC), revised in 1997, which has 172 parties. See https://www.ippc.int. Paragraph 1(a) of Article VII of the IPPC expressly allows phytosanitary trade measures to prevent introduction of alien species and pests, including inspection at the border, treatment requirements, quarantine procedures, and prohibitions on imports. The IPPC has established a Commission on Phytosanitary Measures, which has promulgated 32 International Standards for Phytosanitary Measures (ISPMs). A prime illustration is ISPM-15, Regulation of Wood Packaging Material in International Trade, revised in 2009. ISPM-15 sets standards for debarking and treatment of unprocessed wood used in crates, pallets and other forms of packaging, and includes a stamping procedure for marking the packaging as in compliance with the standard. ISPM-15 has drastically reduced the transfer of species like the Asian long-horned beetle. International associations of forestry officials and horticultural organizations are also actively engaged in the battle against invasive species.

---

3. Quantitative vs. Qualitative Risk Assessment

United States-Continued Suspension of Obligations in the EC-Hormones Dispute (*Hormones II*)

Appellate Body Report, WT/DS320/AB/R (adopted Nov. 14, 2008)

4. Quantification of Risk

566. Next, we turn to the European Communities' claim that the Panel erred in requiring the quantification of the risks arising from the consumption of meat containing residues of oestradiol-17β. The European Communities asserts that, by referring to "potential occurrence" of adverse effects when asking questions to the experts, the Panel incorrectly "imposed a quantitative method of risk assessment on the European Communities borrowed from Codex Alimentarius and JECFA."

567. In *EC–Hormones*, the Appellate Body held that:

> What needs to be pointed out at this stage is that the Panel's use of "probability" as an alternative term for "potential" creates a significant concern. The ordinary meaning of "potential" relates to "possibility" and is different from the ordinary meaning of "probability". "Probability" implies a higher degree or a threshold of potentiality or possibility. It thus appears that here the Panel introduces a quantitative dimension to the notion of risk. (footnote omitted)

568. The Appellate Body further stated that:

> It is not clear in what sense the Panel uses the term "scientifically identified risk." The Panel also frequently uses the term "identifiable risk", and does not define this term either. The Panel might arguably have used the terms "scientifically identified risk" and "identifiable risk" simply to refer to an ascertainable risk: if a risk is not ascertainable, how does a Member ever know or demonstrate that it exists? In one part of its Reports, the Panel opposes a requirement of an "identifiable risk" to the uncertainty that theoretically always remains since science can *never* provide *absolute* certainty that a given substance will not *ever* have adverse health effects. We agree with the Panel that this theoretical uncertainty is not the kind of risk which, under Article 5.1, is to be assessed. In another part of its Reports, however, the Panel appeared to be using the term scientifically identified risk" to prescribe im-

plicitly that a certain *magnitude* or threshold level of risk be demonstrated in a risk assessment if an SPS measure based thereon is to be regarded as consistent with Article 5.1. To the extent that the Panel purported to require a risk assessment to establish a minimum magnitude of risk, we must note that imposition of such a quantitative requirement finds no basis in the *SPS Agreement*. (original emphasis; footnotes omitted)

569. Although the definition of a risk assessment does not require WTO Members to establish a minimum magnitude of risk, it is nevertheless difficult to understand the concept of risk as being devoid of any indication of potentiality. A risk assessment is intended to identify adverse effects and evaluate the possibility that such adverse effects might arise. This distinguishes an ascertainable risk from theoretical uncertainty. However, the assessment of risk need not be expressed in numerical terms or as a minimum quantification of the level of risk. We are also mindful that the risk assessment at issue in this case concerns the *potential* for adverse effects under the second sentence of paragraph 4 of Annex A and not an evaluation of likelihood under the first sentence of paragraph 4.

570. The European Communities' challenge in this case is directed at the following question that the Panel posed to the scientific experts:

> The Panel specifically asked the experts whether the [European Communities] Opinions identified the potential for adverse effects on human health, including the carcinogenic or genotoxic potential, of the residues of oestradiol-17β found in meat derived from cattle to which this hormone had been administered for growth promotion purposes in accordance with good veterinary practice and to what extent the Opinions evaluated the potential occurrence of these adverse effects.

571. The European Communities does not consider this formulation to be "problematic" as such. The European Communities argues, however, that if this formulation is understood as requiring a Member to specify in quantitative terms "to what extent [it] evaluated the *potential occurrence* of these adverse effects", it would lead to an error in law. The European Communities submits that this is precisely how the Panel addressed the issue and how it invited the experts to analyse the SCVPH Opinions.

572. As the European Communities acknowledges, "a quantitative dimension may not be immediately evident from the ordinary meaning of the words 'potential occurrence.'" The terms "potential occurrence of adverse effects" can be understood as referring to the possibility that the adverse effects might occur, without necessarily requiring that this be expressed in numerical terms. This would be consistent with the definition of "risk assessment" in paragraph 4 of Annex A of the *SPS Agreement*, as interpreted by the Appellate Body. Moreover, it would be consistent with the Appellate Body's view that "theoretical uncertainty" is not the kind of risk to be assessed under Article 5.1, but rather the risk to be assessed must be an "ascertainable" risk. In this sense, we agree with Canada that "to examine the 'potential' for adverse effects is to ask whether those adverse effects could <u>ever occur</u>".

573. Other statements by the Panel confirm that it did not require that the possibility of the risks arising be expressed in numerical terms. For example, the Panel took note of the Appellate Body's finding that a risk assessment can take into account "matters not susceptible of quantitative analysis by the empirical

or experimental laboratory methods commonly associated with the physical sciences." The Panel also stated that "it must determine whether the European Communities evaluated the *possibility* that the identified adverse effects came into being, originated, or resulted from the presence of residues of oestradiol-17β in meat or meat products as a result of the cattle being treated with the hormone for growth promotion purposes." * * *

575. For these reasons, we consider that the Panel's reference to "potential occurrence" of adverse health effects could be read consistently with the definition of a risk assessment in paragraph 4 of Annex A of the *SPS Agreement*, as interpreted by the Appellate Body. Accordingly, we <u>dismiss</u> the European Communities' claim that the Panel incorrectly interpreted Article 5.1 and paragraph 4 of Annex A of the *SPS Agreement* as requiring quantification of risk.

Questions and Discussion

1. Recall the issue of abuse or misuse of hormones in Section 1 above. Is that another case where the Appellate Body accepted an unquantified assessment of risk?

2. If the risk assessment does not quantify the risk, isn't there the possibility that risk management factors will influence the risk assessment? If so, is that a problem?

---

4. Standard of Review and Deference to National Decisions

United States-Continued Suspension of Obligations in the EC-Hormones Dispute (*Hormones II*)

Appellate Body Report, WT/DS320/AB/R (adopted Nov. 14, 2008)

6. <u>The Panel's Articulation and Application of the Standard of Review under Article 5.1 of the *SPS Agreement*</u>

585. We turn next to the European Communities' claim that the Panel erred in the standard that it applied to review whether Directive 2003/74/EC was based on a risk assessment within the meaning of Article 5.1 of the *SPS Agreement*. * * *

... The European Communities claims that the appropriate standard of review is one which limits a panel's mandate to determining whether there is any "reasonable scientific basis" for the SPS measure. The United States and Canada object to such a standard. We recall that in *EC–Hormones*, the Appellate Body rejected the European Communities' argument that a "deferential 'reasonableness' standard" is applicable under the *SPS Agreement* to "all highly complex factual situations, including the assessment of the risks to human health arising from toxins and contaminants". The Appellate Body cautioned that the applicable standard of review "must reflect the balance established in [the *SPS Agreement*] between the jurisdictional competences conceded by the Members to the WTO and the jurisdictional competences retained by the Members for themselves" and concluded that Article 11 of the DSU "articulates with great succinctness but with sufficient clarity the appropriate standard of review for panels" reviewing the assessment of facts under the SPS Agreement.

588. Article 11 of the DSU states, in relevant part:

> [A] panel should make an objective assessment of the matter before it, including an objective assessment of the facts of the case and the applicability of and conformity with the relevant covered agreements.

589. The Appellate Body has observed that, so far as fact-finding by panels is concerned, the applicable standard is "neither *de novo* review as such, nor 'total deference', but rather the 'objective assessment of facts'". It further explained that, while panels are "poorly suited to engage in [a *de novo*] review", "'total deference to the findings of the national authorities' ...'could not ensure an "objective assessment" as foreseen by Article 11 of the DSU."

590. A panel reviewing the consistency of an SPS measure with Article 5.1 must determine whether that SPS measure is "based on" a risk assessment. It is the WTO Member's task to perform the risk assessment. The panel's task is to review that risk assessment. Where a panel goes beyond this limited mandate and acts as a risk assessor, it would be substituting its own scientific judgement for that of the risk assessor and making a *de novo* review and, consequently, would exceed its functions under Article 11 of the DSU. Therefore, the review power of a panel is not to determine whether the risk assessment undertaken by a WTO Member is correct, but rather to determine whether that risk assessment is supported by coherent reasoning and respectable scientific evidence and is, in this sense, objectively justifiable.

591. The Appellate Body has observed that a WTO Member may properly base an SPS measure on divergent or minority views, as long as these views are from qualified and respected sources. This must be taken into account in defining a panel's standard of review. Accordingly, a panel reviewing the consistency of an SPS measure with Article 5.1 of the *SPS Agreement* must, first, identify the scientific basis upon which the SPS measure was adopted. This scientific basis need not reflect the majority view within the scientific community but may reflect divergent or minority views. Having identified the scientific basis underlying the SPS measure, the panel must then verify that the scientific basis comes from a respected and qualified source. Although the scientific basis need not represent the majority view within the scientific community, it must nevertheless have the necessary scientific and methodological rigour to be considered reputable science. In other words, while the correctness of the views need not have been accepted by the broader scientific community, the views must be considered to be legitimate science according to the standards of the relevant scientific community. A panel should also assess whether the reasoning articulated on the basis of the scientific evidence is objective and coherent. In other words, a panel should review whether the particular conclusions drawn by the Member assessing the risk find sufficient support in the scientific evidence relied upon. Finally, the panel must determine whether the results of the risk assessment "sufficiently warrant" the SPS measure at issue. Here, again, the scientific basis cited as warranting the SPS measure need not reflect the majority view of the scientific community provided that it comes from a qualified and respected source.

592. A panel may and should rely on the advice of experts in reviewing a WTO Member's SPS measure, in accordance with Article 11.2 of the *SPS Agreement* and Article 13.1 of the DSU. In doing so, however, a panel must respect the due process rights of the parties. Moreover, a panel may not rely on the experts to

go beyond its limited mandate of review. The purpose of a panel consulting with experts is not to perform its own risk assessment. The role of the experts must reflect the limited task of a panel. The panel may seek the experts' assistance in order to identify the scientific basis of the SPS measure and to verify that this scientific basis comes from a qualified and respected source, irrespective of whether it represents minority or majority scientific views. It may also rely on the experts to review whether the reasoning articulated on the basis of the scientific evidence is objective and coherent, and whether the particular conclusions drawn by the Member assessing the risk find sufficient support in the evidence. The experts may also be consulted on the relationship between the risk assessment and the SPS measure in order to assist the panel in determining whether the risk assessment "sufficiently warrants" the SPS measure. The consultations with the experts, however, should not seek to test whether the experts would have done a risk assessment in the same way and would have reached the same conclusions as the risk assessor. In other words, the assistance of the experts is constrained by the kind of review that the panel is required to undertake.

593. In this case, the Panel correctly identified Article 11 of the DSU as setting out the standard of review applicable to its examination of the consistency of the European Communities' risk assessment with Article 5.1 of the *SPS Agreement*. The Panel also referred to the guidance provided by the Appellate Body in *EC–Hormones* concerning the standard of review. Moreover, the Panel made reference to the interpretation of Article 5.1 of the *SPS Agreement* developed by the Appellate Body in *EC–Hormones* and acknowledged that a risk assessment may be based on divergent or minority views.

594. Next, the Panel referred to its consultations with scientific experts, noting that it had consulted six scientific experts individually, and not as an expert review group. The Panel stated that:

> Although the Panel is not carrying out its own risk assessment, its situation is similar in that it may benefit from hearing the full spectrum of experts' views and thus obtain a more complete picture both of the mainstream scientific opinion and of any divergent views.

595. The analogy that the Panel draws between its situation and that of a risk assessor is unfortunate, but is not in itself a sufficient indication that the Panel incorrectly understood the applicable standard of review. We do not think that the Panel meant to suggest that it saw its task under Article 5.1 as requiring it to perform a risk assessment. At the beginning of the statement, the Panel expressly recognizes that it "is not carrying out its own risk assessment".

596. The Panel then elaborated on the approach it would take in respect of the testimony of the experts:

> We note that, in some circumstances, only one or two experts have expressed their views on an issue. Sometimes these views were similar or complemented each other. In other circumstances, a larger number of experts expressed opinions and, sometimes, they expressed diverging opinions. While, on some occasions, we followed the majority of experts expressing concurrent views, in some others the divergence of views were such that we could not follow that approach and decided to accept the position(s) which appeared, in our view, to be the most specific in relation to the question at issue and to be best supported by arguments and evidence. (footnotes omitted)

597. The European Communities submits that "the majority view is not probative simply because it represents the majority". We agree that automatically giving more weight to the testimony of the majority of experts would be too rigid an approach. The fact that a majority in the spectrum of the scientific experts consulted by the Panel had a particular view is not a proper basis for determining whether a WTO Member's risk assessment complies with the requirements of Article 5.1 and Annex A of the *SPS Agreement*.

598. Looking at the Panel's analysis of whether the European Communities specifically assessed the risks arising from the consumption of meat from cattle treated with oestradiol-17β, we note that a significant portion of the Panel's reasoning consists of summaries of the responses of the experts. It is only after summarizing the experts' responses that the Panel describes some of the issues discussed in the 1999 Opinion. Given the applicable standard of review and the role of the Panel that is determined by it, the Panel's analysis should have proceeded differently. The Panel should have first looked at the European Communities' risk assessment. It should then have determined whether the scientific basis relied upon in that risk assessment came from a respected and qualified source. The Panel should have sought assistance from the scientific experts in confirming that it had properly identified the scientific basis underlying the European Communities' risk assessment or to determine whether that scientific basis originated in a respected and qualified source. The Panel should also have sought the experts' assistance in determining whether the reasoning articulated by the European Communities on the basis of the scientific evidence is objective and coherent, so that the conclusions reached in the risk assessment sufficiently warrant the SPS measure. Instead, the Panel seems to have conducted a survey of the advice presented by the scientific experts and based its decisions on whether the majority of the experts, or the opinion that was most thoroughly reasoned or specific to the question at issue, agreed with the conclusion drawn in the European Communities' risk assessment. This approach is not consistent with the applicable standard of review under the *SPS Agreement*.

599. The Panel's flawed approach is evident in its analysis of the genotoxicity of oestradiol 17β, one of the central issues in the European Communities' risk assessment. * * *

602. Rather than turning first to the European Communities' risk assessment in order to identify the scientific basis for the conclusions on the genotoxicity of oestradiol-17β, the Panel begins with a survey of the views of the scientific experts on this issue in general. The Panel tries to justify its approach on its inability to evaluate the evidence itself:

> The Panel is not in a position to evaluate the scientific data the SCVPH reviewed in drawing its conclusions. For this reason, the Panel consulted a group of scientific experts and asked them to evaluate the [European Communities'] Opinions as well as the underlying science.

However, under the applicable standard of review, neither the Panel nor the experts it consulted were called upon to evaluate the correctness of the European Communities' risk assessment. The Panel's role was more limited and consisted, as we explained earlier, of identifying the scientific basis and evidence relied upon in the risk assessment; verifying that the scientific evidence comes from respected and qualified sources; and determining whether the reasoning articulated by the European Communities on the basis of the scientific evidence is objective and coherent.

603. The summary of the experts' opinions, which constitutes the lengthiest portion of the Panel's reasoning, often appears to be a general discussion as to whether the genotoxicity of oestradiol-17β is widely accepted by the broader scientific community, rather than a discussion of the evidence relied upon in the European Communities' risk assessment. The Panel concludes that the "scientific evidence referred to in the Opinions does not support the European Communities' conclusion that for oestradiol-17β genotoxicity had already been demonstrated explicitly." The Panel's conclusion appropriately focuses on the scientific evidence in the SCVPH Opinions. Yet, the Panel's reasoning reveals several flaws. First, some of the experts seemed to accept the European Communities' position on the genotoxicity of oestradiol-17β. For example, the Panel quotes the following opinion of Dr. Cogliano in its reasoning:

> Dr. Cogliano explained that "the [European Communities'] statement that a threshold cannot be identified reflects their view of genotoxic mechanisms, just as the contrary statement that there is a threshold and that this threshold is above the levels found in meat residues reflects how Canada and the [United States] view genotoxic mechanisms. Neither statement has been demonstrated by the scientific evidence, rather, they are different assumptions that each party uses in their interpretation of the available evidence." * * *

605. The Panel should have addressed whether Dr. Cogliano's statements provided evidence that the European Communities' position on the genotoxicity of oestradiol-17β had some acceptance in the scientific community, even if it did not constitute the majority view. At the interim review, the Panel rejected the relevance of Dr. Cogliano's statement, explaining that "the SPS Agreement requires an analysis that goes beyond the identification of a potential adverse effect". According to the Panel, "[t]he analysis must include an examination of the potential for that adverse affect to come into being, originate, or result from the presence of the specific substance under review in food, beverages, or feedstuffs, in this case oestradiol-17β in meat and meat products derived from cattle treated with the hormone for growth promotion purposes."

606. There is no indication in the Panel's reasoning about how to reconcile Dr. Cogliano's statements with the Panel's conclusion that the scientific evidence in the SCVPH Opinions do not support the European Communities' conclusions that "for oestradiol-17β genotoxicity had already been demonstrated explicitly" or that the "presence of residues of oestradiol 17β in meat and meat products as a result of the cattle being treated with the hormone for growth promotion purposes leads to increased cancer risk."

607. The genotoxicity of oestradiol-17β also comes up in connection with the European Communities' conclusion that a threshold could not be established for oestradiol-17β. As with genotoxicity, the risk assessment would need to provide a scientific basis for the conclusion that a threshold could not be established for oestradiol-17β. The Panel does not identify what was the scientific basis for this conclusion, as it should have done. Rather, the Panel's reasoning reproduces the views of the experts on the issue of genotoxicity, with some of them mentioning the distinction between in vivo and in vitro genotoxicity. The discussion seeks to establish whether the genotoxicity in vivo of oestradiol-17β had been accepted

by the general scientific community, rather than whether the European Communities' risk assessment provided scientific evidence of the genotoxicity *in vivo* of oestradiol-17β and whether this evidence came from a respected and qualified source. * * *

610. We reiterate that the Panel was not called upon to determine whether there is general acceptance that oestradiol-17β is genotoxic *in vivo* or that it causes cancer by a genotoxic mechanism. Instead, the focus should have been on the evidence relied upon by the European Communities in its risk assessment. As we noted earlier, the 1999 Opinion refers to several studies on the genotoxicity of oestradiol-17β. Additional studies are discussed in the 2002 Opinion. These studies should have been the focus of the Panel's analysis, yet they are not mentioned in the Panel's analysis. The Panel does not give any reasons why it did not consider them relevant. * * *

612. We have identified above how the Panel approached its task without proper regard to the standard of review and the limitations this places upon the appraisal of expert testimony. Ultimately, the Panel reviewed the scientific experts' opinions and somewhat peremptorily decided what it considered to be the best science, rather than following the more limited exercise that its mandate required. In addition, the European Communities has drawn our attention to the following response provided by Dr. Guttenplan to the Panel's question on the specificity of the European Communities' risk analysis:

> I believe the [European Communities] has done a thorough job in identifying the potential for adverse effects on human health of oestradiol-17β found in meat derived from cattle to which this hormone had been administered. They have identified a number of potential adverse effects of oestradiol-17β in humans. They have established metabolic pathways relevant to these effects, and have examined mechanisms of these effects. In addition they have performed thorough studies of residue levels in cattle, and the environment. The evidence evaluating the occurrence of adverse effects is weak. Animal models are very limited and the target organs do not coincide well with the target organs in humans. There are basically no epidemiological studies comparing matched populations consuming meat from untreated and hormone-treated cattle. Thus, little can be inferred about the potential occurrence of the adverse effects, the potential for adverse effects seems reasonable.

613. In his response, Dr. Guttenplan seems to recognize that the European Communities' risk assessment did specifically examine the potential for adverse effects from the consumption of meat from cattle treated with oestradiol-17β. Dr. Guttenplan's response is summarized in the Panel's reasoning. Yet, the Panel does not address that response any further. Given that the European Communities was entitled to rely on minority views, the Panel was required to explain why it did not consider that Dr. Guttenplan's testimony supported the European Communities' position.

614. An additional flaw in the Panel's reasoning relates to the following remark at the end of Panel's summary of the experts' responses:

> Additionally, in response to direct questioning during the Panel meeting with the experts, Drs. Boobis, Boisseau, and Guttenplan all agreed that there is no appreciable risk of cancer from residues of oestradiol-17β in

meat and meat products from cattle treated with the hormone for growth promotion purposes. While all the experts who responded to the question agreed that a zero risk could not be guaranteed, the actual level of risk was in their view so small as to not be calculable.

It was not the Panel's task, much less that of the experts that the Panel consulted, to determine whether there is an appreciable risk of cancer arising from the consumption of meat from cattle treated with oestradiol-17β. Instead, the Panel was called upon to review the European Communities' risk assessment.

615. The United States and Canada argue that the Panel properly exercised its discretion as the trier of facts. We have found that the Panel did not apply the proper standard of review. This is a legal error and does not fall within the authority of the Panel as the trier of facts. Moreover, we have found instances in which the Panel exceeded its authority in the assessment of the testimony of the scientific experts. By merely reproducing testimony of some experts that would appear to be favourable to the European Communities' position, without addressing its significance, the Panel effectively disregarded evidence that was potentially relevant for the European Communities' case. This cannot be reconciled with the Panel's duty to make an "objective assessment of the facts of the case" pursuant to Article 11 of the DSU.

616. For these reasons, we <u>find</u> that the Panel failed to conduct an objective assessment of the facts of the case, as required by Article 11 of the DSU, in determining whether the European Communities' risk assessment satisfied the requirements of Article 5.1 and Annex A of the *SPS Agreement*.

F. *Conclusion*

* * *

620. Having reversed the Panel, we must now determine whether we can complete the analysis by reviewing ourselves the consistency of the European Communities' risk assessment relating to oestradiol-17β with Article 5.1 of the *SPS Agreement*. In the past, the Appellate Body has completed the analysis when there were sufficient factual findings by the panel or undisputed facts on the Panel record to enable it to do so. In light of the numerous flaws we have found in the Panel's analysis, and the highly contested nature of the facts, we do not consider it possible to complete the analysis in this case. Thus, we make no findings on the consistency or inconsistency of the European Communities' import ban relating to oestradiol-17β.

A Note on Deference to National Decisions

At the conclusion of this very long section on risk assessment, with its many details of the *Hormones* dispute, we come back to one of the fundamental policy questions about the SPS risk assessment requirement: In light of the ambiguity and complexity of the science involved in many cases, to what extent should the WTO defer to national choices, which may, and arguably should, reflect the (nonscientific) policy preferences of the government taking the measure?

David Wirth and others have called on WTO panels and the Appellate Body to grant national authorities deference with respect to SPS measures. In practice, panels have found fault with many national SPS measures. The Appellate Body has frequently overruled panels on their disposition of subsidiary legal issues, but has generally upheld their ultimate judgments about the measures in question. In reviewing SPS measures based on an "objective assessment of the facts" in accordance with the DSU, panels and the Appellate Body have asked many of the same questions posed by Wirth, but reached different conclusions.

Panels and the Appellate Body have addressed two important procedural issues relating to deference: the burden of proof and the standard of review. In so doing, they have shown no fear in critically examining a WTO member's assessment of scientific evidence or its scientific methodology. But some larger policy considerations are also involved that go beyond the evaluation of scientific evidence

a. The Burden of Proof

The Appellate Body has made clear that the WTO member defending an SPS measure may face a burden of proving its compliance with the Agreement. In *Hormones I*, the Appellate Body ruled that the Panel erred in absolving the United States and Canada of the obligation to establish a *prima facie* case showing the absence of the risk assessment required by Article 5.1 and the EU's failure to comply with the requirements of Article 3.3. The Appellate Body ruled that a complaining party must present a *prima facie* case of noncompliance, which it defined as "one which, in the absence of effective refutation by the defending party, requires a panel, as a matter of law, to rule in favour of the complaining party presenting the *prima facie* case." Hormones I, at para. 104. Thus, the complaining party has the initial burden to present evidence and legal arguments sufficient to demonstrate that the SPS measure at issue is inconsistent with the SPS Agreement. The evidence "required to demonstrate a *prima facie* case is necessarily influenced by the nature and the scope of the claim pursued by the complainant." Japan-Apples, Appellate Body Report, at para.166.

What are the elements of a *prima facie* case? One commentator has proposed the following:

> [T]he complaining member should produce a prima facie case that the Agreement has been violated. In disputes involving article 2.2, for example, a complaining member should have both the burden of production and the burden of persuasion in proving that there is no reasonable scientific basis for the adopted sanitary measure. Under article 2.2, the complaining member should also have the burden of proving that the challenged measure is not necessary to achieve the defendant member's selected level of protection. In complaints alleging a violation of article 3, the complaining member should have the burden to prove which of the three options provided in articles 3.1, 3.2, and 3.3 applies and has been violated. This allocation of burdens is consistent not only with the general principles discussed above, but also with other SPS provisions.

Vern R. Walker, *Keeping the WTO from Becoming the "World Trans-science Organization"* at 295–96. Do the statements of the Appellate Body in *Hormones II* above comport with Walker's views? Walker also argues that the "proper standard of proof should be a matter of law binding upon all panels, not decided by individual panels on a case-by-case or issue-by-issue basis." *Id.* at 312. Do you think the Appellate Body agrees? Consider the following language from *Japan-Apples*:

> [The Panel's approach] does not exhaust the range of methodologies available to determine whether a measure is maintained "without sufficient scientific evidence." ... Whether or not a particular approach is appropriate will depend on the "particular circumstances of the case." The methodology adopted by the Panel

was appropriate to the particular circumstances of the case before it, and therefore, we see no error in the Panel's reliance on it.

Japan-Apples, Appellate Body Report, at para. 164.)

Only after a panel determines that the complaining party has made a *prima facie* case does the burden shift to the defending party to show its compliance with the requirements of the SPS Agreement. While the defending member may need to provide rebuttal evidence, does the Appellate Body's approach give the defending member the burden of production? Of persuasion?

b. The Standard of Review

Closely related to the burden of proof is the standard of review applied to the challenged measure. WTO members defending SPS measures have argued vigorously for deference. Embracing Wirth's arguments, the EU claimed that a panel should not redo the investigation conducted by the national authority but instead should limit itself to examining whether the "procedures" required by the relevant WTO rules had been followed. It specifically argues against *de novo* review by panels, which would give them discretion to reach a different conclusion than the competent authority of the member whose act or determination was under review. *See, e.g.*, Hormones II, Appellate Body Report, paras. 585–87 above.

The Appellate Body in *Hormones II*, as we have seen, rejected *de novo* review, but declined to accept an explicitly deferential standard of review, citing the "objective assessment of the facts ... and conformity with the relevant covered agreements" charge to panels under Article 11 of the DSU. *See* paragraph 588 above. It goes on to quote its own statements in *Hormones I* that panels are, on the one hand "poorly suited to engage in [a *de novo*] review" and, on the other hand, "total deference to the findings of the national authorities ... could not ensure an 'objective assessment' as foreseen by Article 11 of the DSU." What does the Appellate Body's middle way entail? Is the following formulation in paragraph 590 above illuminating?: "[T]he review power of a panel is not to determine whether the risk assessment undertaken by a WTO Member is correct, but rather to determine whether that risk assessment is supported by coherent reasoning and respectable scientific evidence and is, in this sense, objectively justifiable."

Consider the treatment of the conclusions of scientific experts in *Hormones II*. The Panel seemed to select certain statements by the scientists that supported its view that the EU had failed to meet Article 5 requirements. By the same token, the Appellate Body quotes the statements of other scientists that tend to give support to the EU's conclusions. Is either the Panel or the Appellate Body justified in making such detailed reference to scientific evidence? Is the Appellate Body's approach any more "objective" than the Panel's? Is it more deferential to the EU's judgment of the evidence?

In the end, the Appellate Body uses the testimony of some of the scientific experts to overrule certain Panel findings on the ground that the Panel had not objectively considered all the evidence. Notably, however, the Appellate Body explicitly declined to reach its own conclusions on the adequacy of the scientific basis for the EU risk assessment. Given that result, does *Hormones II* provide adequate guidance about how to properly evaluate the science underpinning public policy choices?

c. Policy Considerations

Legalistic analysis of burden of proof and standard of review may obscure the larger issues at stake. The most sensitive questions arise precisely in those cases where the science involved does not provide clear answers, so that the policy preferences and nonscientific values that are to some extent embedded in risk assessment are part of the foundation of the national measure. What deference should the WTO accord to these values and preferences?

The difficulty for the WTO is that the SPS Agreement itself expresses an overly simplified view of the objective rationality of science as opposed to the potentially protectionist distortions that might arise if nonscientific considerations are explicitly allowed to come into play. But the large science policy literature on risk assessment makes clear that this sharp dividing line cannot really be maintained. Many years ago, Alvin Weinberg coined the term "trans-science" for those situations in which public policy poses "questions which can be asked of science yet cannot be answered by science." *Science and Trans-science,* 10 MINERVA 209 (1972). Joanne Scott notes that there will be circumstances for which "science neither proves the existence of the risk, nor proves that there is no risk, [when] there is scope for 'rational' debate as to whether this risk should be tolerated." But she comments about the SPS Agreement: "This is a world in which the law is the servant of science in the name of free trade. A world in which law as an instrument of other values—social order, public confidence, trust, community rights, democracy or deliberation—has no role." *On Kith and Kine (and Crustaceans): Trade and the Environment in the EU and WTO, in* THE EU, THE WTO AND THE NAFTA—TOWARDS A COMMON LAW OF INTERNATIONAL TRADE? 157, 160 (J.H.H. Weiler ed., 2000). None other than Pascal Lamy, then in charge of trade for the EU and now the director-general of the WTO, proposed a "safeguards" clause for trade restrictive measures based on "collective preferences." Steve Charnovitz, *An Analysis of Pascal Lamy's Proposal on Collective Preferences,* 8 J. INT'L ECON. L. 449 (2005). Reviewing these and other comments and proposals, Tracey Epps, observing that "it would be extremely difficult and likely impossible to get to the bottom of what drives public opinion in any given case," offers the following suggestion:

> [S]o long as public sentiment—as self-identified by a government—can fit within the bounds of scientific rationality, then it should have a place in domestic risk analysis and panels should recognize the validity of it when they review those processes. That is, so long as scientific rationality is present, the fact that the decision made reflects a view of the evidence that would not have been taken by the complaining party (or indeed, perhaps even by the majority of scientific opinion) should not render the measure illegitimate in WTO law.

TRACEY EPPS, INTERNATIONAL TRADE AND HEALTH PROTECTION: A CRITICAL ASSESSMENT OF THE WTO's SPS AGREEMENT 200, 201 (2008).

Jacqueline Peel has compared the use of deference in the United States and the European Union with the WTO and concludes that panels and the Appellate Body have shown little if any deference to national decisionmaking. She argues that the judicial deference to expert agencies in the case of scientific uncertainty is "effectively deference to the capacity (and legitimacy) of agencies to make policy and value choices in such situations that will reflect a normative perspective on the risks involved which is acceptable to American society as a whole." In the EU, the Treaty on the Functioning of the European Union establishes reference points for a high level of health and environmental protection and expressly adopts the precautionary principle, which reflects a value choice in favor of erring on the side of health and environmental protection in circumstances of scientific uncertainty. She argues that comparable normative yardsticks are absent from the SPS Agreement and consequently there is nothing upon which to balance deference. Perhaps that is the inevitable result in shifting from national judicial bodies reviewing national decisions to an international dispute context where there is no common set of policies and values. In the absence of normative yardsticks, she ponders the use of "science" for determining the validity of national SPS measures.

Jacqueline Peel, *Risk Regulation under the WTO SPS Agreement: Science as an International Normative Yardstick?*
93–97 (Jean Monnet Working Paper 02/04, 2004)

In most cases then, WTO decision-makers reviewing national SPS measures will be operating in a 'normative vacuum' where the only criterion available to guide the 'balance' struck between competing risk regulatory policies of Members is that of science. Without the option of being able to defer to a regulatory authority whose policy judgments and value choices have global legitimacy, or to adjust the stringency of judicial review of risk regulatory measures according to an agreed normative goal, decision-makers will fall back on the advice of scientists and the opinions they offer about the available evidence of risk. In the absence of a true normative yardstick for evaluating national decisions to address risks in circumstances where no conclusive evidence of harm exists, science becomes a default criterion for determining whether measures pursuing the level of risk chosen by Members receive international endorsement or not.

The irony of constituting science as a default normative yardstick, is that choices about competing risk regulatory policies are thereby yielded to a body of knowledge which [doesn't have] (or is not purported to have) any normative content. Science's only adherence is to the notion of progress, narrowly defined in terms of the improvement of existing levels of scientific understanding about the natural and physical world. Post-modern critiques of science notwithstanding, science's vision is not one which offers value judgments about whether certain forms of progress are right or wrong, a task which it leaves to the community and politicians. In a global 'risk society,' where questions concerning the normativity of international health and environmental policy are often viewed in scientific terms, notions of what is possible and what is desirable may sometimes be aligned. But the history of nuclear power for one, and more recent international debates over agricultural uses of biotechnology, are evidence that this is not always the case.

Questions and Discussion

1. As a matter of law and policy, the Appellate Body sees interpretation of the SPS Agreement as an exercise in finding the right balance. In paragraph 177 of *Hormones I*, the Appellate Body described the requirement for SPS measures to be based on science in the following terms: "The requirements of a risk assessment under Article 5.1, as well as of 'sufficient scientific evidence' under Article 2.2, are essential for the maintenance of the delicate and carefully negotiated balance in the *SPS Agreement* between the shared, but sometimes competing, interests of promoting international trade and of protecting the life and health of human beings."

2. Robert Hudec calls the SPS Agreement "post-discriminatory," because its scientific requirements diverge from the basic nondiscrimination principles at the core of trade rules. For example, a food safety measure that is not based on scientific principles vio-

lates Article 2 of the SPS Agreement, even if applied equally to foreign and domestic products. This is the case with the measures in *EC-Hormones*. Similarly, the lack of a risk assessment, as in *Hormones I*, violates Article 5.1 of the SPS Agreement even in the absence of discrimination. Hudec concludes that legal criteria that do not require proof of discrimination allow a dispute resolution panel to second-guess the rationality of a regulatory judgment at the national level, thereby opening the trade regime's decisionmaking to legitimate criticism. Robert E. Hudec, *Science and "Post-Discriminatory" WTO Law*, 26 B.C. Int'l & Comp. L. Rev. 185, 187 (2003). Do you agree? How much second-guessing of national measures occurs under other WTO agreements, including the nondiscrimination rules of Articles I and III?

3. In reading the Appellate Body's analysis in *Hormones II*, including its discussion of the relationship between "appropriate level of protection" and risk assessment (in paragraphs 684–686 in the next section of this chapter), consider whether the Appellate Body is doing just what Epps suggests in the short excerpt above—accepting nonscientific national preferences that are within the bounds of "scientific rationality."

4. Finally, it is noteworthy that WTO panels have ruled against the validity of domestic SPS measures in four of the five main cases. Some would take this as confirmation of expectations that the SPS Agreement will cause "'downward harmonization' of health and safety standards." Bruce A. Silverglade, *The Impact of International Trade Agreements on U.S. Food Safety and Labeling Standards*, 53 Food & Drug L.J. 537, 539 (1998); *see also* Martin Wagner, *The WTO's Interpretation of the SPS Agreement Has Undermined the Right of Governments to Establish Appropriate Levels of Protection Against Risk*, 31 Law & Pol'y Int'l Bus. 855 (2000). But *Hormones II*, while not affirmatively finding compliance with the SPS Agreement, leaves the EU measures in place. Does that lend support to another view, that the "latitude afforded to nations in setting their own food safety standards is so large that nearly all bona fide attempts to protect food safety will be consistent with the SPS Agreement"? David Victor, *The Sanitary and Phytosanitary Agreement of the World Trade Organization*, at 872.

―――――――

C. Provisional Measures, Levels of Protection, and International Standards

As noted earlier, many of the legal questions about the SPS Agreement are intertwined. In *Hormones I*, the EC explicitly declined to invoke Article 5.7, which allows WTO members to adopt SPS "provisional measures" in the absence of sufficient scientific evidence for a risk assessment, arguing instead for an interpretation of the SPS Agreement *in toto* that incorporated the precautionary principle. The Appellate Body's response was controversial; we will touch on that controversy in the *Questions and Discussion* following the excerpt below. For now, it is noteworthy that the EU, in the *Hormones II* dispute, changed legal course and specifically referred to Article 5.7 as the basis for its measures relating to five hormones.

1. Hormones II *and the Intertwined Issues*

The following long excerpt from *Hormones II* focuses the issue of provisional SPS measures under Article 5.7. In the course of its analysis, however, issues of the "appropriate level of protection" and the use of international standards as a "basis" for SPS measures come into play.

United States-Continued Suspension of Obligations in the EC-Hormones Dispute (*Hormones II*)

Appellate Body Report, WT/DS320/AB/R (adopted Nov. 14, 2008)

VII. The Consistency with Article 5.7 of the *SPS Agreement* of the European Communities' Provisional Import Ban ...

A. *Introduction*

621. We turn finally to the European Communities' appeal of the Panel's finding that the European Communities' provisional ban on meat from cattle treated with testosterone, progesterone, trenbolone acetate, zeranol, and MGA failed to meet the requirements of Article 5.7 of the SPS Agreement because the relevant scientific evidence was not "insufficient" within the meaning of that provision....

B. *The European Communities' Evaluation of the Five Hormones Subject to the Provisional Ban*

622.... [F]ollowing the adoption of the DSB's recommendations and rulings in *EC–Hormones*, the European Communities initiated 17 scientific studies aimed at evaluating, inter alia, the potential for adverse effects to human health from residues in bovine meat and meat products resulting from the use of oestradiol-17β, testosterone, progesterone, zeranol, trenbolone acetate, and MGA. The results of these studies, as well as other publicly available information, were reviewed by the SCVPH. On 30 April 1999, the SCVPH issued the 1999 Opinion, in which it concluded that "in view of the intrinsic properties of hormones and epidemiological findings, a risk to the consumer has been identified with different levels of conclusive evidence for the six hormones in question." As regards the five hormones, the 1999 Opinion further provided that "in spite of the individual toxicological and epidemiological data described in the report, the current state of knowledge did not allow a quantitative estimate of the risk." The European Communities concluded that "the currently available information for testosterone, progesterone and the synthetic hormones zeranol, trenbolone and particularly MGA has been considered inadequate to complete [a risk] assessment." The 1999 Opinion also states that "no final conclusions can be drawn with respect to the safety" of the five hormones.

[The Appellate Body then quotes extensively from the 2002 Opinion, which uses such phrases as "data needed further clarification" and "[f]urther experiments should clarify the toxicological significance of these impurities."]

624. The European Communities enacted Directive 2003/74/EC, which provides for a *provisional* ban on meat and meat products from cattle treated with progesterone, testosterone, zeranol, trenbolone acetate and MGA for growth-promotion purposes. Before the Panel, the European Communities argued that the SCVPH Opinions and supporting studies provided the "available pertinent information" within the meaning of Article 5.7 on the basis of which the provisional ban on the five hormones had been enacted. * * *

E. The Panel's Finding that the Relevant Scientific Evidence in Relation to the Five Hormones Was Not "Insufficient" Within the Meaning of Article 5.7 of the SPS Agreement

674. Under Article 2.2 of the *SPS Agreement*, WTO Members are required to "ensure that any sanitary or phytosanitary measure is applied only to the extent necessary to protect human, animal or plant life or health, is based on scientific principles and is not maintained without sufficient scientific evidence, except as provided for in paragraph 7 of Article 5." This requirement is made operative in other provisions of the *SPS Agreement*, including Article 5.1, which requires SPS measures to be "based on" a risk assessment. At the same time, Article 2.2 excludes from its scope of application situations in which the relevant scientific evidence is insufficient. In such situations, the applicable provision is Article 5.7 of the SPS Agreement. Thus, the applicability of Articles 2.2 and 5.1, on the one hand, and of Article 5.7, on the other hand, will depend on the sufficiency of the scientific evidence. The Appellate Body has explained that the relevant scientific evidence will be considered "insufficient" for purposes of Article 5.7 "if the body of available scientific evidence does not allow, in quantitative or qualitative terms, the performance of an adequate assessment of risks as required under Article 5.1 and as defined in Annex A to the *SPS Agreement*." This means that where the relevant scientific evidence is sufficient to perform a risk assessment, as defined in Annex A of the *SPS Agreement*, a WTO Member may take an SPS measure only if it is "based on" a risk assessment in accordance with Article 5.1 and that SPS measure is also subject to the obligations in Article 2.2. If the relevant scientific evidence is insufficient to perform a risk assessment, a WTO Member may take a provisional SPS measure on the basis provided in Article 5.7, but that Member must meet the obligations set out in that provision.

675. Having discussed the relationship between Articles 2.2, 5.1 and 5.7, we now focus on the conditions for the application of a provisional SPS measure pursuant to the latter provision. Article 5.7 provides:

> In cases where relevant scientific evidence is insufficient, a Member may provisionally adopt sanitary or phytosanitary measures on the basis of available pertinent information, including that from the relevant international organizations as well as from sanitary or phytosanitary measures applied by other Members. In such circumstances, Members shall seek to obtain the additional information necessary for a more objective assessment of risk and review the sanitary or phytosanitary measure accordingly within a reasonable period of time.

676. The Appellate Body has explained that Article 5.7 sets out four obligations. Two of these obligations set conditions that must be met before a provisional SPS measure is adopted. The other two obligations are conditions for maintaining the provisional SPS measure once it has been taken. These four obligations are:

(1) [the measure is] imposed in respect of a situation where "relevant scientific information is insufficient";

(2) [the measure is] adopted "on the basis of available pertinent information";

(3) [the Member that adopted the measure] "seek[s] to obtain the additional information necessary for a more objective assessment of risk"; and

(4) [the Member that adopted the measure] "review[s] the … measure accordingly within a reasonable period of time."

677. Article 5.7 begins with the requirement that the "relevant scientific evidence" be "insufficient". As explained earlier, the relevant scientific evidence is "insufficient" where "the body of available scientific evidence does not allow, in quantitative or qualitative terms, the performance of an adequate assessment of risks as required under Article 5.1 and as defined in Annex A to the *SPS Agreement*." Under Article 5.1, WTO Members are allowed to base SPS measures on divergent or minority views provided they are from a respected and qualified source. Thus the existence of scientific controversy in itself is not enough to conclude that the relevant scientific evidence is "insufficient". It may be possible to perform a risk assessment that meets the requirements of Article 5.1 even when there are divergent views in the scientific community in relation to a particular risk. By contrast, Article 5.7 is concerned with situations where deficiencies in the body of scientific evidence do not allow a WTO Member to arrive at a sufficiently objective conclusion in relation to risk. When determining whether such deficiencies exist, a Member must not exclude from consideration relevant scientific evidence from any qualified and respected source. Where there is, among other opinions, a qualified and respected scientific view that puts into question the relationship between the relevant scientific evidence and the conclusions in relation to risk, thereby not permitting the performance of a sufficiently objective assessment of risk on the basis of the existing scientific evidence, then a Member may adopt provisional measures under Article 5.7 on the basis of that qualified and respected view.

678. WTO Members' right to take provisional measures in circumstances where the relevant scientific information is "insufficient" is also subject to the requirement that such measures be adopted "on the basis of available pertinent information". Such information may include information from "the relevant international organizations" or deriving from SPS measures applied by other WTO Members. Thus, Article 5.7 contemplates situations where there is some evidentiary basis indicating the possible existence of a risk, but not enough to permit the performance of a risk assessment. Moreover, there must be a rational and objective relationship between the information concerning a certain risk and a Member's provisional SPS measure. In this sense, Article 5.7 provides a "temporary 'safety valve' in situations where some evidence of a risk exists but not enough to complete a full risk assessment, thus making it impossible to meet the more rigorous standards set by Articles 2.2 and 5.1."

679. The second sentence of Article 5.7 requires that the available pertinent information which provides a basis for a Member's provisional SPS measure be supplemented with "the additional information necessary for a more objective assessment of risk" within a "reasonable period of time". As the Appellate Body noted, these two conditions "relate to the *maintenance* of a provisional [SPS] measure and highlight the *provisional* nature of measures adopted pursuant to Article 5.7." The requirement that the WTO Member "shall seek to obtain the additional information necessary for a more objective assessment of risk" implies that, as of the adoption of the provisional measure, a WTO Member must make best efforts to remedy the insufficiencies in the relevant scientific evidence with additional scientific research or by gathering information from relevant international organizations or other sources. Otherwise, the provisional nature of

measures taken pursuant to Article 5.7 would lose meaning. The "insufficiency" of the scientific evidence is not a perennial state, but rather a transitory one, which lasts only until such time as the imposing Member procures the additional scientific evidence which allows the performance of a more objective assessment of risk. The Appellate Body has noted that Article 5.7 does not set out "explicit prerequisites regarding the additional information to be collected or a specific collection procedure". Nevertheless, the WTO Member adopting a provisional SPS measure should be able to identify the insufficiencies in the relevant scientific evidence, and the steps that it intends to take to obtain the additional information that will be necessary to address these deficiencies in order to make a more objective assessment and review the provisional measure within a reasonable period of time. The additional information to be collected must be "germane" to conducting the assessment of the specific risk. A Member is required under Article 5.7 to seek to obtain additional information but is not expected to guarantee specific results. Nor is it expected to predict the actual results of its efforts to collect additional information at the time when it adopts the SPS measure. Finally, the Member taking the provisional SPS measure must review it within a reasonable period of time.

680. These four conditions set out in Article 5.7, however, must be interpreted keeping in mind that the precautionary principle finds reflection in this provision. As the Appellate Body has emphasized:

> a panel charged with determining, for instance, whether "sufficient scientific evidence" exists to warrant the maintenance by a Member of a particular SPS measure may, of course, and should, bear in mind that responsible, representative governments commonly act from the perspectives of prudence and precaution where risks of irreversible, e.g. life-terminating, damage to human health are concerned.

In emergency situations, for example, a WTO Member will take a provisional SPS measure on the basis of limited information and the steps it takes to comply with its obligations to seek to obtain additional information and review the measure will be assessed in the light of the exigencies of the emergency.

681. The European Communities argues that SPS measures are either "based on" a risk assessment under Article 5.1, or otherwise the relevant scientific evidence will be "insufficient" within the meaning of Article 5.7, so that provisional SPS measures may be justified. We do not agree. There may be situations where the relevant scientific evidence is sufficient to perform a risk assessment, a WTO Member performs such a risk assessment, but does not adopt an SPS measure either because the risk assessment did not confirm the risk, or the risk identified did not exceed that Member's chosen level of protection. Also, there may be situations where there is no pertinent scientific information available indicating a risk such that an SPS measure would be unwarranted even on a provisional basis.

1. Insufficiency and the Acceptable Level of Protection

682. The European Communities argues that the Panel failed to take into account that the European Communities had chosen a higher level of protection when determining whether the relevant scientific evidence is "insufficient" within the meaning of Article 5.7 of the *SPS Agreement*. According to the European Communities, the context provided by Article 3.3 of the *SPS Agreement*, and the cross-reference to Article 5 contained therein, compels a panel to consider a

Member's chosen level of protection in examining whether the requirements of Article 5.7 have been met. As we noted earlier, Article 3.3 permits that WTO Members adopt measures which result in a higher level of protection than the one achieved by measures based on the relevant international standards.

683. In their appellee's submissions, both the United States and Canada emphasize that risk assessment is an "objective" process aimed at identifying and evaluating a certain risk, and that a Member's appropriate level of protection is therefore entirely separate from the question of whether scientific evidence is "insufficient" to perform a risk assessment. At the oral hearing, however, the United States and Canada recognized that the chosen level of protection may have a role to play in framing the scope and methods of a risk assessment in the particular circumstances where a WTO Member chooses a higher level of protection than that which would be achieved by a measure based on the international standard.

684. The Panel noted that the terms of Article 5.1 and Annex A of the *SPS Agreement* "do not indicate that a Member's level of protection is pertinent to determine whether a risk assessment can be performed or not." The Panel quoted approvingly the reasoning of the panel in *EC–Approval and Marketing of Biotech Products*, which stated that "[t]he protection goals of a legislator may have a bearing on the question of which risks a Member decides to assess ... [a]nd are certainly relevant to the determination of the measure ... to be taken for achieving a Member's level of protection against risk. Yet there is no apparent link between a legislator's protection goals and the task of assessing the existence and magnitude of potential risks." The Panel concluded that:

> The assessment [of] whether there is sufficient scientific evidence or not to perform a risk assessment should be an objective process. The level of protection defined by each Member may be relevant to determine the measure to be selected to address the assessed risk, but it should not influence the performance of the risk assessment as such.
>
> Indeed, whether a Member considers that its population should be exposed or not to a particular risk, or at what level, is not relevant to determining whether a risk exists and what its magnitude is. *A fortiori*, it should have no effect on whether there is sufficient evidence of the existence and magnitude of this risk.
>
> A risk-averse Member may be inclined to take a protective position when considering the measure to be adopted. However, the determination of whether scientific evidence is sufficient to assess the existence and magnitude of a risk must be disconnected from the intended level of protection.

685. A WTO Member that adopts an SPS measure resulting in a higher level of protection than would be achieved by measures based on international standards must nevertheless ensure that its SPS measure complies with the other requirements of the *SPS Agreement*, in particular Article 5. This includes the requirement to perform a risk assessment. At the same time, we recognize that, in order to perform a risk assessment, a WTO Member may need scientific information that was not examined in the process leading to the adoption of the international standard. We see no basis in Articles 3.3 and 5.1 of the *SPS Agreement* to conclude that WTO Members choosing a higher level of protection than would be achieved by a measure based on an international standard must frame the

scope and methods of its risk assessment, including the scientific information to be examined, in the same manner as the international body that performed the risk assessment underlying the international standard. Thus, where the chosen level of protection is higher than would be achieved by a measure based on an international standard, this may have some bearing on the scope or method of the risk assessment. In such a situation, the fact that the WTO Member has chosen to set a higher level of protection may require it to perform certain research as part of its risk assessment that is different from the parameters considered and the research carried out in the risk assessment underlying the international standard.

686. For these reasons, we disagree with the Panel's finding that "the determination of whether scientific evidence is sufficient to assess the existence and magnitude of a risk must be disconnected from the intended level of protection." We emphasize, however, that whatever level of protection a WTO Member chooses does not pre-determine the outcome of its determination of the sufficiency of the relevant scientific evidence. The determination as to whether available scientific evidence is sufficient to perform a risk assessment must remain, in essence, a rigorous and objective process.

687. The European Communities refers to the chosen level of protection to support its argument that the existence of JECFA risk assessments for the five hormones does not necessarily mean that the relevant scientific evidence was sufficient for the European Communities to perform its own risk assessment. Before the Panel, the European Communities explained that "the evidence which served as the basis for the 1988 and 1999–2000 JECFA evaluations is not sufficient 'to perform a definitive risk assessment within the meaning of Article 5.7, in particular by the WTO Members applying a high level of health protection of no risk from exposure to unnecessary additional residues in meat of animals treated with hormones for growth promotion.'" We turn to this issue next.

2. Relevance of International Standards under Article 5.7 of the SPS Agreement

[The Appellate Body reviews the arguments of the parties.]

692. As the preamble of the *SPS Agreement* recognizes, one of the primary objectives of the *SPS Agreement* is to "further the use of harmonized sanitary and phytosanitary measures between Members, on the basis of international standards, guidelines and recommendations developed by the relevant international organizations". This objective finds reflection in Article 3 of the *SPS Agreement*, which encourages the harmonization of SPS measures on the basis of international standards, while at the same time recognizing the WTO Members' right to determine their appropriate level of protection. Article 3.1 of the *SPS Agreement* establishes that Members shall "base their [SPS] measures on international standards, guidelines or recommendations, where they exist, except as otherwise provided in this Agreement, and in particular in paragraph 3."

693. The relevant "international standards, guidelines or recommendations" that are referred to in Articles 3.1 and 3.2 are those set by the international organizations listed in Annex A, paragraph 3 of the *SPS Agreement*, which includes Codex as the relevant standard-setting organization for matters of food safety. As we noted above, Codex adopts international standards for veterinary drug residues based on evaluations performed by JECFA. In this case, Codex has adopted international standards for testosterone, progesterone, trenbolone ac-

etate, and zeranol, on the basis of evaluation performed by JECFA. In addition, Codex has initiated a standard-setting process for MGA, also on the basis of JECFA's evaluation, but this process has not yet been concluded.

694. It is therefore undisputed that JECFA has performed risk assessments for the six hormones at issue and that Codex has adopted international standards for five of these hormones on the basis of JECFA's risk assessments. The fact that JECFA has performed risk assessments for all six hormones means that the relevant scientific evidence was in its estimation sufficient to do so. Article 3.2 provides that SPS measures which conform to international standards shall be deemed necessary to protect human, animal or plant life or health, and shall be presumed to be consistent with the relevant provisions of the *SPS Agreement* and of the GATT 1994. This presumption, however, does not apply where a Member has not adopted a measure that conforms with an international standard. Article 3.2 is inapplicable where a Member chooses a level of protection that is higher than would be achieved by a measure based on an international standard. The presumption in Article 3.2 cannot be interpreted to imply that there is sufficient scientific evidence to perform a risk assessment where a Member chooses a higher level of protection.

695. This is borne out by Article 5.7, which provides that WTO Members may adopt provisional SPS measures "on the basis of available pertinent information, including that from the relevant international organizations as well as from sanitary or phytosanitary measures applied by other Members". There is no indication in Article 5.7 that a WTO Member may not take a provisional SPS measure wherever a relevant international organization or another Member has performed a risk assessment. Information from relevant international organizations may not necessarily be considered "sufficient" to perform a risk assessment, as it may be part of the "available pertinent information" which provides the basis for a provisional SPS measure under Article 5.7. Moreover, scientific evidence that may have been relied upon by an international body when performing the risk assessment that led to the adoption of an international standard at a certain point in time may no longer be valid, or may become insufficient in the light of subsequent scientific developments. Therefore, the existence of a risk assessment performed by JECFA does not mean that scientific evidence underlying it must be considered to be sufficient within the meaning of Article 5.7.

696. In our view, it is reasonable for a WTO Member challenging the consistency with Article 5.7 of a provisional SPS measure adopted by another Member to submit JECFA's risk assessments and supporting studies leading to the adoption of international standards as evidence that the scientific evidence is not insufficient to perform a risk assessment. However, such evidence is not dispositive and may be rebutted by the Member taking the provisional SPS measure.

697. The European Communities argues that the Panel considered the existence of international standards as establishing an "irrebuttable presumption" that the relevant scientific evidence in this case is not "insufficient" for the purposes of Article 5.7. As we pointed out above, the existence of an international standard does not create a legal presumption of sufficiency for purposes of Article 5.7. The Panel recognized that "[i]t cannot be excluded that new scientific evidence or information call into question existing evidence", and acknowledged the possibility that "different risk assessments reach different interpretations of the same scientific evidence." The Panel examined the specific points raised by the Euro-

pean Communities concerning the insufficiencies it saw in the scientific evidence considered in JECFA's risk assessment. There would not have been a need for the Panel to undertake such an assessment if it had considered that the existence of international standards established an irrebuttable presumption that the relevant scientific evidence was not insufficient within the meaning of Article 5.7. Thus we find no fault with the Panel to the extent that it treated the evidence underlying JECFA's risk assessment as having probative value for determining whether the relevant scientific evidence was insufficient. In our view, the existence of risk assessments conducted by JECFA in relation to the five hormones at issue has probative value, but is not dispositive, of the question of whether the relevant scientific evidence on those hormones is "insufficient" within the meaning of Article 5.7.

698. The Panel relied on the existence of international standards to adopt a "critical mass" test for determining when scientific information that was previously considered sufficient becomes insufficient for purposes of Article 5.7 of the *SPS Agreement*. The European Communities also challenges this test on appeal. We examine this issue in the section that follows.

3. The Panel's "Critical Mass" Standard for Determining "Insufficiency" under Article 5.7 of the *SPS Agreement*

699. The European Communities asserts that the Panel's "critical mass" standard imposed an excessively "high quantitative and qualitative threshold" with respect to the new evidence that is required to render "insufficient" scientific evidence that was previously considered sufficient. According to the European Communities, the quality of the scientific evidence is more important than the quantity, and therefore even a single study could be considered *a priori* sufficient to question the sufficiency of previous scientific evidence. The European Communities adds that the Panel's "critical mass" standard effectively precluded the application of the precautionary principle in the interpretation of Articles 5.1 and 5.7, because the scientific evidence would pass immediately from a state of insufficiency under Article 5.7 to a state of sufficiency under Article 5.1.

700. Both the United States and Canada accept that evidence which at some point in time was sufficient to perform a risk assessment could become insufficient at a later point in time. The United States said this could happen, for example, if there was new pathway for a risk for which the information was insufficient. Canada gave as an example the situation in which there is new scientific data that identifies new adverse effects or adverse effects at lower exposure levels. Another example given by Canada is the identification of new sources of exposure. The Panel also recognized that:

> ... there could be situations where existing scientific evidence can be put in question by new studies and information. There could even be situations where evidence which supported a risk assessment is unsettled by new studies which do not constitute sufficient relevant scientific evidence as such to support a risk assessment but are sufficient to make the existing, previously relevant scientific evidence insufficient. (footnote omitted)

701. We agree that scientific progress may lead a WTO Member and international organizations to reconsider the risk assessment underlying an SPS measure. In some cases, new scientific developments will permit a WTO Member to conduct a new risk assessment with the sufficient degree of objectivity. There

may be situations, however, where the new scientific developments themselves do not permit the performance of a new risk assessment that is sufficiently objective. Such a situation would fall within the scope of Article 5.7 of the *SPS Agreement*.

702. The Appellate Body has explained that " 'relevant scientific evidence' will be 'insufficient' within the meaning of Article 5.7 if the body of available scientific evidence does not allow, in quantitative or qualitative terms, the performance of an adequate assessment of risks as required under Article 5.1 and as defined in Annex A to the *SPS Agreement*." The body of scientific evidence underlying a risk assessment can always be supplemented with additional information. Indeed, the nature of scientific inquiry is such that it is always possible to conduct more research or obtain additional information. The possibility of conducting further research or of analyzing additional information, by itself, should not mean that the relevant scientific evidence is or becomes insufficient.

703. Moreover, as the Panel noted, science continuously evolves. It may be useful to think of the degree of change as a spectrum. On one extreme of this spectrum lies the incremental advance of science. Where these scientific advances are at the margins, they would not support the conclusion that previously sufficient evidence has become insufficient. At the other extreme lie the more radical scientific changes that lead to a paradigm shift. Such radical change is not frequent. Limiting the application of Article 5.7 to situations where scientific advances lead to a paradigm shift would be too inflexible an approach. WTO Members should be permitted to take a provisional measure where new evidence from a qualified and respected source puts into question the relationship between the pre-existing body of scientific evidence and the conclusions regarding the risks. We are referring to circumstances where new scientific evidence casts doubts as to whether the previously existing body of scientific evidence still permits of a sufficiently objective assessment of risk.

704. The Panel next discussed its understanding of "insufficiency" in the specific circumstances where international standards exist for the particular substance. It concluded:

> We therefore conclude that if relevant evidence already exists, not any degree of insufficiency will satisfy the criterion under Article 5.7 that "relevant scientific evidence is insufficient". Having regard to our reasoning above, particularly with respect to scientific uncertainty and the existence of international standards, we consider that, depending on the existing relevant evidence, there must be a *critical mass* of new evidence and/or information that calls into question the fundamental precepts of previous knowledge and evidence so as to make relevant, previously sufficient, evidence now insufficient. In the present case where risk assessments have been performed and a large body of quality evidence has been accumulated, this would be possible only if it put into question existing relevant evidence *to the point that* this evidence is no longer sufficient to support the conclusions of existing risks assessments. (original emphasis; footnote omitted)

705. The Panel's statement that "there must be a *critical mass* of new evidence and/or information that calls into question the fundamental precepts of previous knowledge and evidence so as to make relevant, previously sufficient, evidence now insufficient" could be understood as requiring that the new scientific evidence lead

to a paradigm shift. As we have said, such an approach is too inflexible. Although the new evidence must call into question the relationship between the body of scientific evidence and the conclusions concerning risk, it need not rise to the level of a paradigm shift.

706. Some of the Panel's statements intended to explain what it meant by "critical mass" similarly can be understood as requiring a paradigm shift, which is too high a threshold. At the interim review stage, the European Communities requested that the Panel identify the provenance of the "critical mass" standard and explain how it should be reconciled with the Appellate Body's findings in *EC–Hormones*. The Panel responded as follows:

> The Panel used the term "critical mass" in full knowledge of its meaning.[294] It used it in the sense of a situation where evidence becomes quantitatively and qualitatively sufficient to call into question the fundamental precepts of previous knowledge and evidence. The Panel does not mean that there must be sufficient evidence to perform a new risk assessment. Otherwise, Article 5.7 of the *SPS Agreement* would become meaningless. It used the term "critical mass" very much in its common scientific usage, i.e. the new scientific information and evidence must be such that they are *at the origin* of a change in the understanding of a scientific issue. We do not see in what respect this approach by the Panel, which applies to the specific situation in this case (i.e. one where a party alleges that previously sufficient scientific evidence has become insufficient) would be contrary to the findings of the Appellate Body in *EC–Hormones*. (original emphasis)

---

[294] In mathematics and physics "critical" is defined as "constituting or relating to a point of transition from one state, etc. to another". "Critical size" or "critical mass" are defined as the minimum size or mass of a body of a given fissile material which is capable of sustaining a nuclear chain reaction (Shorter Oxford English Dictionary, 5th edition (1993), p. 558). In other words, the Panel assessed whether it had been provided with the minimum evidence necessary to conclude that knowledge has become quantitatively and qualitatively sufficient to call into question the fundamental precepts of previous knowledge and evidence.

707. In the reasoning quoted above, the Panel again required that the scientific evidence be "sufficient to call into question the fundamental precepts of previous knowledge and evidence". The Panel's explanation that "the new scientific information and evidence must be such that they are at the origin of a change in the understanding of a scientific issue" also connotes a paradigm shift.

708. We earlier observed that the existence of an international standard for which a risk assessment was conducted could be offered as evidence in support of an assertion that the relevant scientific evidence is not insufficient within the meaning of Article 5.7 of the SPS Agreement. It is an evidentiary issue in the sense that the scientific information underlying the international standard has probative value as to the sufficiency of the scientific evidence needed for conducting a risk assessment at a discrete point in time. However, in circumstances where a Member adopts a higher level of protection than that reflected in the international standard, the legal test that applies to the "insufficiency" of the evidence under Article 5.7 is not made stricter. Thus, it is incorrect to use JECFA's risk assessments as a legal benchmark for assessing insufficiency as the Panel did in this case.

709. In the interim review, the Panel expressly recognized that it used JECFA's risk assessments as a "benchmark":

[I]t is correct that the Panel considered that, in order to determine whether relevant scientific evidence was insufficient within the meaning of Article 5.7 of the SPS Agreement, it had to take the results of the risk assessments made by JECFA as a "benchmark" of the existence of sufficient scientific evidence. This is in line with the findings of the Appellate Body in *Japan–Apples* that the relevant scientific evidence will be insufficient within the meaning of Article 5.7 if the body of available scientific evidence does not allow, in quantitative or qualitative terms, the performance of an adequate assessment of risks as required under Article 5.1 and as defined in Annex A to the *SPS Agreement*, as well as with the presumption of compliance under Article 3.2 of the *SPS Agreement*. (footnote omitted)

710. We recall that the presumption in Article 3.2 is inapplicable where a WTO Member adopts an SPS measure that results in a higher level of protection than that reflected in an international standard. For this reason, Article 3.2 did not provide a basis for the Panel's use of the JECFA risk assessments as the legal benchmark against which the insufficiencies in the relevant scientific evidence identified by the European Communities had to be evaluated. As the Appellate Body explained in *EC–Hormones*:

The presumption of consistency with relevant provisions of the SPS Agreement that arises under Article 3.2 in respect of measures that conform to international standards may well be an *incentive* for Members so to conform their SPS measures with such standards. It is clear, however, that a decision of a Member not to conform a particular measure with an international standard does not authorize imposition of a special or generalized burden of proof upon that Member, which may, more often than not, amount to a *penalty*. (original emphasis)

711. The particular insufficiencies in the relevant scientific evidence identified by the European Communities had to be evaluated on their own terms. As indicated earlier, the scientific evidence underlying the risk assessments conducted by JECFA has probative value as to the sufficiency of the scientific evidence needed to perform an assessment of risks in relation to the five hormones; however, it was by no means dispositive of that question, in particular where a WTO Member has elected to adopt an SPS measure that does not conform to the international standard.

712. For these reasons, we reverse the Panel's finding that, where international standards exist, "there must be a *critical mass* of new evidence and/or information that calls into question the fundamental precepts of previous knowledge and evidence so as to make relevant, previously sufficient, evidence now insufficient" within the meaning of Article 5.7. * * *

5. The Panel's Application of Article 5.7 of the *SPS Agreement*

719. We turn finally to the European Communities' claim that the Panel incorrectly applied Article 5.7 of the *SPS Agreement*. On appeal, the European Communities asserts that the Panel "systematically downplay[ed]" and ignored "highly relevant scientific evidence" which "go[es] against the evaluations of the JECFA or support the position of the European Communities and that in fact the scientific evidence was indeed insufficient" to perform a risk assessment, particularly in the following areas: (a) effects of hormones on certain population groups; (b) dose response; (c) bioavailability; (d) long latency periods for cancer and

confounding factors; and (e) adverse effects on growth and reproduction. The European Communities also points to several errors committed by the Panel when determining whether the evidence concerning the risks posed by each of the five hormones individually was insufficient to conduct a risk assessment under Article 5.7. * * *

721. As we noted in subsection 3, the Panel's "critical mass" test imposed an excessively high threshold in terms of the change in the scientific evidence that would make previously sufficient evidence insufficient.... One such example is the Panel's analysis of the European Communities' contention that the relevant scientific evidence concerning the effects of the hormones on certain categories of the population, in particular pre-pubertal children, was "insufficient" within the meaning of Article 5.7 of the *SPS Agreement*.

722. Before the Panel, the European Communities argued that the development of more sensitive detection methods had identified lower endogenous levels of oestradiol in pre-pubertal children than previously assumed by the detection method referred to in JECFA's risk assessments. According to the European Communities, this suggested that individuals that have the lowest endogenous levels of sex hormones, such as pre-pubertal children and post-menopausal women, might be at an increased risk for adverse health effects that might be associated with exposure to exogenous sources of both oestrogens and testosterone.

723. The new detection method was examined in a scientific study conducted by Klein et al. (1994), and was reviewed by the European Communities in the 1999 Opinion. * * *

726. The Panel seemed to rely on two pieces of evidence in coming to the conclusion that the ultra-sensitive detection method discussed in the Klein study had not yet been validated: a statement to that effect in the 2002 Opinion, and the testimony of Dr. Boobis, who questioned the validity of the Klein study. However, the Panel record shows that at least some of the scientific experts considered that the Klein study could possibly cast doubt as to whether the body of scientific evidence relied on by JECFA still permitted of a sufficiently objective assessment of risks posed by the five hormones in relation to pre-pubertal children.

727. Dr. Sippell seemed to agree with the European Communities' position that the relevant scientific evidence on the effects of hormones in pre-pubertal children was not "sufficient" to conduct a risk assessment under Article 5.1. Dr. Sippell observed that "[w]e just don't have yet everywhere where it would be necessary the methodology, the analytical tools to measure as sensitively as we should do it, and therefore I think that the data available are insufficient." Dr. Sippell also explained that:

> ... it is difficult to calculate the exact [hormone] production rates in pre-pubertal children.... [JECFA values] have been based on the, so to speak, traditional levels measured by radio immuno assays, and usually by radio immuno assays without prior extraction. We all know that the sensitivity of such procedures is not enough compared with more modern techniques ... the extractive procedures involving radio immuno assays, but even more modern molecular base techniques like recombinant cell bioassays, of oestrogen, oestradiol or oestrogen activity. And these ... are significantly below the levels previously thought, and by that the production

rate is now significantly lower. And this of course implies that any risk from exogenous sources, for example, beef treated with hormones, treated with oestradiol-17β, is much higher.

728. Dr. De Brabander concurred, stating that "I cannot say that the [JECFA] data are bad ... I just say you don't know that they are good, and you have to check them with modern analytical methods." Dr. Guttenplan espoused a similar view, noting that "more accurate methods of analysis could now be used to measure the effect of eating hormone-treated beef on blood levels of estrogen in children and post-menopausal women." He also observed that "in boys the [oestrogen] levels are even lower, and there I think we have to worry about developmental effects ... I still think that these could be investigated epidemiologically or in or some type of study. We might ... need a surrogate, perhaps saliva or urine, but I think it is perhaps the most important issue to address is the sensitivity of children."

729. Dr. Boobis, who as the Panel noted questioned the validity of the ultra-sensitive recombinant assay used in the Klein study, also testified that the levels of oestradiol endogenously produced in pre-pubertal children may be lower than previously thought. In response to direct questioning by the United States, Dr. Boobis explained that:

> ... having looked at these data is that, first of all, the recombinant assay has not yet been validated adequately, but secondly there is evidence, when one looks at these data, to suggest that the circulating levels of oestradiol in male children are lower than previously thought, I would accept that, but I would not think they are as low as in the original publication by Klein et al, because there have been numerous publications since then using a variety of assays .which suggest that the levels are certainly higher than those very low levels first reported.

730. Although the Panel was correct in observing that the Klein study only examined endogenous levels of oestradiol, lower levels of endogenous production of hormones in humans played a key role in the European Communities' conclusion that no safe threshold level or ADI could be established for any of the six hormones assessed. The 1999 Opinion states that, in the light of "uncertainties in the estimates of endogenous hormone production rates and metabolic clearance capacity, particularly in prepubertal children, no threshold level and therefore no ADI can be established for any of the [six] hormones." For this reason, the Panel should have explored further the question of what relevance, if any, the study relied on by the European Communities examining endogenous levels of oestradiol could have in relation to potential adverse health effects relating to the other five hormones. During the course of the oral hearing, the European Communities argued that some scientists agree with its position that measurements of the endogenous levels of natural hormones are relevant for synthetic hormones that share similar toxicological properties and effects.

731. In sum, the Panel erred in its interpretation and application of Article 5.7 of the *SPS Agreement* by adopting an incorrect legal test to assess the European Communities' explanations concerning the insufficiencies in the relevant scientific evidence.

732. The European Communities argues further that the Panel failed to conduct an objective assessment of the facts of the case, as required by Article 11 of the

DSU, in its analysis under Article 5.7. Having determined that the Panel incorrectly interpreted and applied Article 5.7 of the *SPS Agreement*, we do not find it necessary to address the European Communities' claim that the Panel acted inconsistently with Article 11 of the DSU.

* * *

737. Because we have been unable to complete the analysis as to whether Directive 2003/74/EC has brought the European Communities into substantive compliance within the meaning of Article 22.8 of the DSU, the recommendations and rulings adopted by the DSB in *EC–Hormones* remain operative.

---

2. *"Sufficient Evidence," "Insufficient Evidence," and Precaution*

a. *The Link between Article 2.2 and Article 5.7: "Sufficient Scientific Evidence" and "Where Relevant Scientific Evidence is Insufficient"*

Earlier we noted that the Appellate Body has concluded that Article 5 is a "particular application" of Article 2.2, and that Article 2.2 "informs" the understanding of Article 5. This becomes absolutely clear in the bright-line distinction the Appellate Body draws between requiring a risk assessment to support an SPS measure on the one hand and the allowance in Article 5.7 for provisional measures to be maintained for a period of time "where the relevant scientific information is insufficient," on the other. The explicit reference in the text of Article 2.2 to Article 5.7 as an exception to its rule supports this bright line distinction.

Before *Hormones II*, the Appellate Body had addressed the issue of "sufficient" and "insufficient" scientific evidence in two cases involving Japan and the United States.

In *Japan-Agricultural Products II*, the measure for varietal testing of certain agricultural products had been in effect for nearly 30 years. The Panel concluded that the testing requirement could not be considered as a provisional SPS measure, because Japan had not sought to obtain the information necessary for a more objective assessment of risk and had not sought to review the measure within a reasonable period of time. Japan-Measures Affecting Agricultural Products, Panel Report, WT/DS76/R, paras. 8.57, 8.59 (Oct. 27, 1998). The Appellate Body upheld the Panel's decision, stating that what constitutes a "reasonable period of time" must "be established on a case-by-case basis and depends on the specific circumstances of each case, including the difficulty of obtaining the additional information necessary for the review and the characteristics of the provisional SPS measure."

In the second case, *Japan-Apples*, the United States challenged Japan's restrictions on the importation of apples to protect against the transmission of fire blight. After years of different studies, there was a substantial body of "high quality" scientific evidence showing that the risk of introduction of fire blight to Japan from apples was negligible. Japan insisted, nevertheless, that there were "unresolved" scientific uncertainties warranting continued provisional measures. The Appellate Body first stated the general principle behind section 5.7 as follows: "The question is whether the relevant evidence, be it 'general' or 'specific,'... is sufficient to permit the evaluation of the likelihood of entry, establishment or spread of, in this case, fire blight in Japan." Japan-Measures Affecting the Importation of Apples, Appellate Body Report, WT/DS245/AB/R, para. 179 (Dec. 16,

2003). As to Japan's argument about "unresolved scientific uncertainties, the Appellate Body held:

> We disagree with Japan. The application of Article 5.7 is triggered not by the existence of scientific uncertainty, but rather by the insufficiency of scientific evidence. The text of Article 5.7 is clear: it refers to "cases where relevant scientific evidence is insufficient," not to "scientific uncertainty." The two concepts are not interchangeable. Therefore, we are unable to endorse Japan's approach of interpreting Article 5.7 through the prism of "scientific uncertainty."

Id. at para. 184.

Questions and Discussion

1. The Appellate Body concludes that the phrase "cases where relevant scientific evidence is insufficient" is not interchangeable with "scientific uncertainty." What distinction is the Appellate Body making? Recall the Appellate Body's criticism of the Panel's "critical mass" test in *Hormones II* above. Is the sufficiency of evidence a matter of quantity? Of quality? Where is the line between "insufficient evidence" and "scientific uncertainty" in *Hormones II*?

2. Article 5.7 allows the application of provisional measures based on "available *pertinent* information" when "*relevant* scientific evidence is insufficient." What is "pertinent information"? What is "relevant scientific evidence"? How does the Appellate Body interpret "pertinent" and "relevant" in *Hormones II* above?

3. In light of questions 1 and 2, consider rulings on these matters by the panel in *European Communities-Measures Affecting the Approval and Marketing of Biotech Products*, WT/DS 291, 292, 293/R (adopted Nov. 2006). In that case, as allowed by the European system, Austria had taken a "safeguard" measure to prohibit the use of a genetically modified crop variety that had been approved at the EU level, citing some studies that had not been part of the EU approval process. Austria argued that, based on the new studies, it had reassessed the risk. It also made the argument that the new studies called into question the sufficiency of the evidence to assess the risk of release of GMOs into the environment. The panel found the new studies insufficient to meet the requirements for a risk assessment under Article 5.1. Furthermore, noting that the EU itself had done a risk assessment on these products, the panel said that this created a "presumption" that the "relevant scientific evidence was not insufficient." Howse and Horn suggest that these rulings create a system that ignores the scientific process, because Article 5.1 requires a completely new risk assessment to support a divergent measure, and under Article 5.7 once a risk assessment has been done the "sufficiency" of the evidence to support it can never be questioned. Robert L. Howse & Henrik Horn, *European Communities-Measures Affecting the Approval and Marketing of Biotech Products*, 8 WORLD TRADE REV. No. 1, 49, 72–82 (2009). Does *Hormones II* effectively overrule *EC-Biotech* on these points?

4. Consider that the Appellate Body also said that "there is a 'scientific justification' for an SPS measure, within the meaning of Article 3.3, if there is a rational relationship between the SPS measure and the available scientific information." *Japan-Agricultural Products II*, Appellate Body Report, at para. 79. How does that statement fit with its interpretation of Article 5.7?

b. The Relationship between the Precautionary Principle and Article 5.7

The idea of precaution for environmental issues is stated as follows in Principle 15 of the Rio Declaration on Environment and Development, U.N. Doc. A/CONF.151/26 (June 3–14, 1992): "Where there are threats of serious or irreversible damage, lack of full scientific certainty shall not be used as a reason for postponing cost-effective measures to prevent environmental degradation." The Rio Declaration refers to this idea as the precautionary "approach." In European law and in many writings on international environmental law, it is known as the precautionary "principle." In short, while the basic idea of acting to avoid serious risk even in the absence of persuasive scientific evidence is widely accepted, scholars and governments differ on its exact legal status in international law.

The SPS Agreement's requirement for a risk assessment, qualified by the allowance of Article 5.7 for temporary measures "where relevant scientific evidence is insufficient," calls into question the relationship between the SPS Agreement and the precautionary principle. In the *Hormones I* proceeding, the EC declined to invoke Article 5.7. Rather, it argued that its permanent import restrictions on hormone-treated beef to prevent health risks, even if the scientific evidence did not necessarily show a link between eating those beef products and human health problems, was a proper circumstance for the application of the precautionary principle. This line of argument presented the Appellate Body with the need to define the relationship between the precautionary principle, the risk assessment provisions of Article 5, and the allowance for provisional measures in Article 5.7.

European Communities-Measures Concerning Meat and Meat Products (Hormones) [*Hormones I*]

Appellate Body Report, WT/DS26/AB/R, WT/DS48/AB/R (Feb. 13, 1998)

120. We are asked by the European Communities to reverse the finding of the Panel relating to the precautionary principle. The Panel's finding and its supporting statements are set out in the Panel Reports in the following terms:

> The European Communities also invokes the precautionary principle in support of its claim that its measures in dispute are based on a risk assessment. To the extent that this principle could be considered as part of customary international law and be used to interpret Article 5.1 and 5.2 on the assessment of risks as a customary rule of interpretation of public international law (as that phrase is used in Article 3.2 of the DSU), we consider that *this principle would not override the explicit wording of Articles 5.1 and 5.2 outlined above*, in particular since the precautionary principle has been incorporated and given a specific meaning in Article 5.7 of the *SPS Agreement*. We note, however, that the European Communities has explicitly stated in this case that it is not invoking Article 5.7.

> We thus find that *the precautionary principle cannot override our findings made above*, namely that the EC import ban of meat and meat products from animals treated with any of the five hormones at issue for growth promotion purposes, in so far as it also applies to meat and meat products from animals treated with any of these hormones in accordance with good practice, is, from a substantive point of view, not based on a risk assessment. [underlining added by Appellate Body]

121. The basic submission of the European Communities is that the precautionary principle is, or has become, "a general customary rule of international law" or at least "a general principle of law." Referring more specifically to Articles 5.1 and 5.2 of the *SPS Agreement*, applying the precautionary principle means, in the view of the European Communities, that it is not necessary for all scientists around the world to agree on the "possibility and magnitude" of the risk, nor for all or most of the WTO Members to perceive and evaluate the risk in the same way. It is also stressed that Articles 5.1 and 5.2 do not prescribe a particular type of risk assessment and do not prevent Members from being cautious in their risk assessment exercise. The European Communities goes on to state that its measures here at stake were precautionary in nature and satisfied the requirements of Articles 2.2 and 2.3, as well as of Articles 5.1, 5.2, 5.4, 5.5 and 5.6 of the *SPS Agreement*. * * *

123. The status of the precautionary principle in international law continues to be the subject of debate among academics, law practitioners, regulators and judges. The precautionary principle is regarded by some as having crystallized into a general principle of customary international environmental law. Whether it has been widely accepted by Members as a principle of general or customary international law appears less than clear. We consider, however, that it is unnecessary, and probably imprudent, for the Appellate Body in this appeal to take a position on this important, but abstract, question. We note that the Panel itself did not make any definitive finding with regard to the status of the precautionary principle in international law and that the precautionary principle, at least outside the field of international environmental law, still awaits authoritative formulation.

124. It appears to us important, nevertheless, to note some aspects of the relationship of the precautionary principle to the *SPS Agreement*. First, the principle has not been written into the SPS Agreement as a ground for justifying SPS measures that are otherwise inconsistent with the obligations of Members set out in particular provisions of that Agreement. Secondly, the precautionary principle indeed finds reflection in Article 5.7 of the *SPS Agreement*. We agree, at the same time, with the European Communities, that there is no need to assume that Article 5.7 exhausts the relevance of a precautionary principle. It is reflected also in the sixth paragraph of the preamble and in Article 3.3. These explicitly recognize the right of Members to establish their own appropriate level of sanitary protection, which level may be higher (i.e., more cautious) than that implied in existing international standards, guidelines and recommendations. Thirdly, a panel charged with determining, for instance, whether "sufficient scientific evidence" exists to warrant the maintenance by a Member of a particular SPS measure may, of course, and should, bear in mind that responsible, representative governments commonly act from perspectives of prudence and precaution where risks of irreversible, e.g. life-terminating, damage to human health are concerned. Lastly, however, the precautionary principle does not, by itself, and without a clear textual directive to that effect, relieve a panel from the duty of applying the normal (i.e. customary international law) principles of treaty interpretation in reading the provisions of the *SPS Agreement*.

125. We accordingly agree with the finding of the Panel that the precautionary principle does not override the provisions of Articles 5.1 and 5.2 of the *SPS Agreement*.

Questions and Discussion

1. How would you characterize the Appellate Body's treatment of the precautionary principle and public international law? Has it dismissed public international law as irrelevant to WTO decisionmaking? Is its analysis consistent with the following reasoning from a subsequent WTO panel?

> We take note that Article 3.2 of the DSU requires that we seek within the context of a particular dispute to clarify the existing provisions of the WTO agreements in accordance with customary rules of interpretation of public international law. However, the relationship of the WTO Agreements to customary international law is broader than this. Customary international law applies generally to the economic relations between the WTO Members. Such international law applies to the extent that the WTO treaty agreements do not "contract out" from it. To put it another way, to the extent there is no conflict or inconsistency, or an expression in a covered WTO agreement that implies differently, we are of the view that the customary rules of international law apply to the WTO treaties and to the process of treaty formation under the WTO.

Korea-Measures Affecting Government Procurement, WT/DS163/R, para. 7.96 (June 19, 2000).

2. The Appellate Body concluded that "it is unnecessary, and probably imprudent" to clarify the "abstract question" of whether the precautionary principle constitutes customary international law. If, however, a member raises the precautionary principle as a defense on the grounds that the precautionary principle is customary international law, shouldn't the Appellate Body need to determine whether or not that is the case? If the precautionary principle is customary international law, then it could prevail over treaty provisions, if, using typical rules of treaty interpretation, it is later in time (*lex posterior*) or more specific than the treaty rule (*lex specialis*). Joost Pauwelyn thinks that the Appellate Body reached the right decision but through faulty legal reasoning:

> [T]here was no need for the SPS Agreement to refer explicitly to the precautionary principle for this principle to be a possible defense in WTO dispute settlement, nor a fortiori for it to be a rule of general international law to be referred to in the interpretation of SPS provisions pursuant to Article 31(3)(c) of the Vienna Convention. I believe that the Appellate Body was obliged to rule on whether this principle is part of customary law binding on the disputing parties. Had this been the case, the Appellate Body should have acknowledged that a rule of customary law, if later in time and in conflict with an earlier (SPS) treaty rule, must prevail over the treaty rule (no inherent hierarchy existing between treaty and custom), unless it found an intention to continue applying the (SPS) treaty rule as *lex specialis*. In the circumstances, however, it was difficult to establish 1) that the "precautionary principle" is a rule of customary international law; 2) that it emerged subsequent to the WTO treaty; 3) that it indeed conflicted with SPS rules (the European Community, for example, had not invoked SPS Article 5.7, which explicitly provides for a form of precautionary approach); and 4) that WTO members did not want the SPS Agreement to continue as *lex specialis* (in particular, given the "continuing" nature of the WTO treaty). Hence, the Appellate Body was correct in concluding that "the precautionary principle does

not override the provisions of Articles 5.1 and 5.2 of the SPS Agreement." But it did so too categorically and without deciding certain crucial questions it should have answered before coming to that conclusion.

Joost Pauwelyn, *The Role of Public International Law in the WTO: How Far Can We Go?*, 95 AM. J. INT'L L. 535, 570 (2001). Do you agree?

3. The Appellate Body in *Hormones I* stated that the precautionary principle finds reflection in Article 5.7. Review the definition of the precautionary principle at the beginning of this section and Article 5.7. Do you agree that the precautionary principle finds reflection in Article 5.7? Does the Appellate Body contradict itself in paragraph 184 of *Japan-Apples* when it declares:

> The application of Article 5.7 is triggered not by the existence of scientific uncertainty, but rather by the insufficiency of scientific evidence. The text of Article 5.7 is clear: it refers to "cases where relevant scientific evidence is insufficient," not to "scientific uncertainty." The two concepts are not interchangeable.

Do you agree with this analysis? What is the difference between "scientific uncertainty" and "cases where relevant scientific evidence is insufficient"? To which situation does the Rio Declaration's formulation, "lack of full scientific certainty," apply?

4. If the EU had prevailed with its precautionary principle argument, what would have been the impact on the SPS Agreement? Would the risk assessment provisions of Article 5 have any meaning? Would that undermine the object and purpose of SPS Agreement? If the Appellate Body attempted to read the SPS Agreement and the precautionary principle as mutually compatible, would panels and the Appellate Body need to give greater deference to national regulatory decisions?

5. Would the ability to use the precautionary principle as a defense in SPS disputes help or hinder developing countries? Principle 15 of the Rio Declaration also provides, "In order to protect the environment, the precautionary approach shall be widely applied by States according to their capabilities." Does that change your answer?

---

3. Choosing the Appropriate Level of Protection

a. The Role of International Standards

To recap, Article 2 of the SPS Agreement grants WTO members the right to impose SPS measures for the protection of human, animal, or plant life or health. Article 3 provides them with options for choosing the level of sanitary and phytosanitary protection they want. Article 3.1 requires that SPS measures be "based on" international standards, guidelines, or recommendations where they exist. Article 3.2 further provides that, if a member's SPS measure "conforms to" the international standard, it will be deemed "necessary" for the protection of human, animal, or plant life or health and thus presumptively in compliance with the SPS Agreement and the GATT.

The panel in *Hormones I* interpreted the phrase "based on" to mean essentially the same as "conform to," reasoning that "measures which *are* based on a given international standard should in principle achieve the *same* level of sanitary protection" as the international standard. In its *Hormones I* report, the Appellate Body rejected that analysis. The Appellate Body reasoned that a measure "based on" a standard might not "conform to" to it — for example where only some, but not all, of the elements of the international standard are incorporated into the measure. Moreover, the panel's interpretation would vest Codex standards, which are recommendatory in form and nature, "with *obligatory* force and effect." *Hormones I*, Appellate Body Report, at para. 165. The Appellate Body was unwilling to transform those standards, guidelines and recommendations into binding norms.

The Appellate Body also explained that Article 3.3 grants a member the right to set a level of protection different from, and higher than, the level of protection implicit in the international standard. This does not establish an exception from the requirement to "base" a measure on an applicable international standard. Article 3.2 simply confers on SPS measures that "conform to" an international standard a rebuttable presumption of consistency with the SPS Agreement and the GATT 1994. In contrast, measures merely "based on" international standards, as well as those unilaterally chosen by a member, do not enjoy such a presumption. *Id.*, paras. 170–72.

In *Hormones II*, the Appellate Body tackles another aspect of international standards, namely the legal significance of risk assessments on which such standards are based. Here the Panel fell into much the same logical trap as in *Hormones I*: it assumed the sufficiency of the science supporting an international standard (barring a "critical mass" of new evidence indicating otherwise), and ruled that even if the member had a higher appropriate level of protection, that was not a pertinent factor in judging the sufficiency of the scientific information. The Appellate Body rejected that stringent reading of the SPS Agreement in favor of a more nuanced view that an Article 5.1 risk assessment to support a measure to meet a member's chosen level of protection may require more or different scientific data than the science supporting the more relaxed international standard. *See* paragraphs 682–87. In that sense, at least, the appropriate level of protection may reasonably influence the member's evaluation of the sufficiency of the available scientific information for doing a risk assessment vis-à-vis its decision about whether it is obliged to perform a risk assessment or might instead opt for a provisional measure under Article 5.7.

Questions and Discussion

1. Do the risk assessment provisions of Article 5 also apply to SPS measures that are weaker than the international standard? Article 3 suggests that only stricter standards are subject to risk assessment. However, the interpretations of Article 2 by panels and Appellate Body suggest that any SPS measure that deviates from the international standard will be subject to risk assessment. Do you agree? David Victor notes that weaker standards can also have trade effects, especially with processed foods where "there is often a substantial premium in efficiency for producers that can export to a market governed by a single standard. Lax standards, even if applied equally to local and imported products, could favor local producers and harm imports that are produced according to more expensive standards that prevail in the rest of the world market." He argues that such an argument could be used to "pry open local markets that are 'distorted' by weak SPS standards and force a higher level of SPS protection." David Victor, *The Sanitary and Phytosanitary Agreement of the World Trade Organization*, at 883–84.

---

b. The Requirements of Article 3.3

The Appellate Body has noted that the right of a member to define its appropriate level of protection is not an absolute or unqualified right. In the *Hormones I* proceeding, the

EC argued that Article 3.3 included two separate situations for the introduction or maintenance of SPS measures that result in a higher level of protection:

(a) "if there is a scientific justification"; or

(b) "as a consequence of the level of ... protection a Member determines to be appropriate in accordance with the relevant provisions of paragraphs 1 through 8 of Article 5."

The EC explicitly argued that situation (a) does not refer to the risk assessment and risk management provisions of Articles 5.1 through 5.8. In its *Hormones I* report, the Appellate Body disagreed:

175. First, the last sentence of Article 3.3 requires that "all measures which result in a [higher] level of ... protection," that is to say, measures falling within situation (a) as well as those falling within situation (b), be "not inconsistent with any other provision of [the SPS] Agreement." "Any other provision of this Agreement" textually includes Article 5. Secondly, the footnote to Article 3.3, while attached to the end of the first sentence, defines "scientific justification" as an "examination and evaluation of available scientific information in conformity with relevant provisions of this Agreement...." This examination and evaluation would appear to partake of the nature of the risk assessment required in Article 5.1 and defined in paragraph 4 of Annex A of the *SPS Agreement*. * * *

177. Consideration of the object and purpose of Article 3 and of the *SPS Agreement* as a whole reinforces our belief that compliance with Article 5.1 was intended as a countervailing factor in respect of the right of Members to set their appropriate level of protection. In generalized terms, the object and purpose of Article 3 is to promote the harmonization of the SPS measures of Members on as wide a basis as possible, while recognizing and safeguarding, at the same time, the right and duty of Members to protect the life and health of their people. The ultimate goal of the harmonization of SPS measures is to prevent the use of such measures for arbitrary or unjustifiable discrimination between Members or as a disguised restriction on international trade, without preventing members from adopting or enforcing measures which are both "necessary to protect" human life or health and "based on scientific principles," and without requiring them to change their appropriate level of protection. The requirements of a risk assessment under Article 5.1, as well as of "sufficient scientific evidence" under Article 2.2, are essential for the maintenance of the delicate and carefully negotiated balance in the *SPS Agreement* between the shared, but sometimes competing, interests of promoting international trade and of protecting the life and health of human beings. We conclude that the Panel's finding that the European Communities is required by Article 3.3 to comply with the requirements of Article 5.1 is correct and, accordingly, dismiss the appeal of the European Communities from that ruling of the Panel.

Questions and Discussion

1. Review the provisions of Articles 2, 3, and 5. How do they relate? For example, Article 2 requires members to adopt SPS measures based on "scientific principles" which cannot be maintained without "sufficient scientific evidence." Article 3 provides that a member that wishes to adopt an SPS measure stricter than the international standard

may do so if there is "scientific justification" or based on the risk assessment provisions of Article 5. How do these scientific requirements differ? If a measure is based on a review consistent with Article 5's risk assessment provisions, could it fail to be based on "scientific principles"?

2. Do you agree that Article 3.3 requires a risk assessment for *any* SPS measure that includes a higher level of protection than the international standard? If the drafters intended the second sentence of Article 3.3 to require the application of the provisions of Article 5 to all measures achieving a higher level of protection, then why did they create the elaborate architecture of Article 3.3? In particular, if the drafters wanted all measures to be justified pursuant to the risk assessment provisions of Article 5, what becomes of the phrase "if there is scientific justification"? Has the Appellate Body departed from its own oft-repeated interpretive principle that all of the provisions of the WTO agreements should be given effect and read according to their ordinary meaning? To be fair, the Appellate Body was "not unaware that this finding tends to suggest that the distinction made in Article 3.3 between two situations may have very limited effects and may, to that extent, be more apparent than real." Is there another interpretation that would have avoided this result?

3. Along similar lines, does footnote 2 suggest that "scientific justification" means something different from risk assessment under Article 5? Is it fair to argue that "an examination and evaluation of available scientific information in conformity with relevant provisions of this Agreement" means something different from "in accordance with the provisions of paragraphs 1 through 8 of Article 5"?

4. Note that footnote 2 refers to a determination of a member that "relevant international standards, guidelines or recommendations are not sufficient to achieve its appropriate level of sanitary or phytosanitary protection." Is that finding different from the allowance in Article 3.3 for more stringent SPS measures adopted "as a consequence of the level of sanitary or phytosanitary protection a Member determines to be appropriate"? The Appellate Body comes back to this question in *Hormones II*.

D. Risk Assessment for the Spread of Pests and Diseases

The SPS Agreement establishes two different types of risk assessment in Annex A, paragraph 4. The *Hormones* cases involved a risk assessment relating to additives, contaminants, toxins, or disease-causing organisms in food, beverages, or feedstuffs. The SPS Agreement defines risk assessments relating to these risks as follows:

> [T]he evaluation of the potential for adverse effects on human or animal health arising from the presence of additives, contaminants, toxins or disease-causing organisms in food, beverages or feedstuffs.

The other four disputes—*Japan-Apples, Japan-Agricultural Products II, Australia-Salmon,* and *EC-Biotech*—all related to the risk of spread of a pest or disease. For these risks, the SPS Agreement requires:

> The evaluation of the likelihood of entry, establishment or spread of a pest or disease within the territory of an importing Member according to the sanitary and phytosanitary measures which might be applied, and of the associated potential biological and economic consequences[.]

Panels and the Appellate Body had an opportunity to analyze the similarities and differences of these two risk assessments in *Australia-Salmon* and *Japan-Apples*.

1. Scope of the Risk Assessment

In *Australia-Salmon*, Canada challenged Australia's Quarantine Proclamation 86A (QP86A), which prohibited the importation into Australia of salmon in any form unless the fish or parts of fish have been treated in a way, such as by heat treatment, that prevents the introduction of any infectious or contagious disease or pest affecting persons, animals, or plants. Australia was particularly concerned about the spread of certain diseases from salmon to other fish species in Australian waters. It performed a risk analysis of Pacific salmon in a document called the "1996 Report," which concluded that the importation of Pacific salmon should be prohibited. Australia-Measures Affecting Importation of Salmon: Recourse to Article 21.5 by Canada, Panel Report, WT/DS18/RW (Feb. 18, 2000).

The Appellate Body ruled that a risk assessment relating to the spread of diseases must accomplish the following three goals:

1. *identify* the diseases whose entry, establishment or spread a Member wants to prevent within its territory, as well as the potential biological and economic consequences associated with the entry, establishment or spread of these diseases;

2. *evaluate the likelihood* of entry, establishment or spread of these diseases, as well as the associated potential biological and economic consequences; and

3. evaluate the likelihood of entry, establishment or spread of these diseases *according to the SPS measures which might be applied.*

Australia-Measures Affecting Importation of Salmon, Appellate Body Report, WT/DS18/AB/R, para. 121 (Nov. 6, 1998) (emphasis in original).

The Appellate Body specifically noted that this type of risk assessment differs from the risk assessment evaluated in *Hormones I*. Although the EU argued that no substantial differences exist between the two definitions of risk assessment, the Appellate Body disagreed:

123. Before taking up the question of whether the 1996 Final Report satisfies these requirements, we note that the first definition in paragraph 4 of Annex A speaks about the evaluation of "likelihood." In our report in *European Communities-Hormones,* we referred to the dictionary meaning of "probability" as "degrees of likelihood" and "a thing that is judged likely to be true," for the purpose of distinguishing the terms "potential" and "probability." For the present purpose, we refer in the same manner to the ordinary meaning of "likelihood", and we consider that it has the same meaning as "probability". On this basis, as well as on the basis of the definition of "risk" and "risk assessment" developed by the Office international des épizooties ("OIE") and the OIE *Guidelines for Risk Assessment,* we maintain that for a risk assessment to fall within the meaning of Article 5.1 and the first definition in paragraph 4 of Annex A, it is not sufficient that a risk assessment conclude that there is a *possibility* of entry, establishment or spread of diseases and associated biological and economic consequences. A proper risk assessment of this type must evaluate the "likelihood," i.e., the "probability," of entry, establishment or spread of diseases and associated biological and economic consequences as well as the "likelihood," i.e., "probability," of entry, establishment or spread of diseases *according to the SPS measures which might be applied.*

According to the Appellate Body, a member must do more than show "*some* evaluation of the likelihood or probability." The evaluation of the likelihood may be expressed either quantitatively or qualitatively, but the risk assessment need not establish a certain magnitude or threshold level of degree of risk. The risk evaluated in a risk assessment must be an ascertainable risk, but a member may ultimately determine that its appropriate level of protection is "zero risk." *Id.* at paras. 124–25.

The Appellate Body found that the 1996 Report identified the risks but that it did not evaluate the likelihood—the probability—of entry, establishment or spread of diseases, because it only evaluated some possible adverse effects through vague statements. It ruled that these vague statements did not constitute either a quantitative or qualitative assessment of probability. It further stated that the existence of unknown and uncertain elements does not justify a departure from the requirements of a risk assessment, because members must take into account "available scientific evidence" under Article 5.2 and they must base their measures on "scientific principles" under Article 2.2. *Id.* at paras. 128–30. The Appellate Body did not tell members, however, how they could adequately account for uncertainty in a risk assessment without running afoul of the requirements of the SPS Agreement.

2. Alternatives Analysis

Risk assessments relating to the spread of pests and diseases must also evaluate the likelihood of entry, establishment, or spread "according to the SPS measures which might be applied." This provision requires a member to conduct an alternatives analysis to determine the level of risk under other regulatory regimes.

The Appellate Body in *Australia-Salmon* concluded that the 1996 Report did not assess the likelihood of entry, establishment, or spread of diseases according to measures that might be applied. The 1996 Report identified several different approaches to eliminate the potential threats posed by salmon imports, but it did not evaluate the relative effectiveness of these different approaches in reducing overall disease risk. *Id.* at paras. 133–34.

The Appellate Body revisited this issue in *Japan-Apples*, in which it was asked to determine the validity of Japan's import restrictions on apples to avoid fire blight, a bacterial disease of apples and pears that kills blossoms, shoots, limbs, and, sometimes, entire trees.

Japan-Measures Affecting the Importation of Apples
Appellate Body Report, WT/DS245/AB/R (Dec. 16, 2003)

207. According to the Panel, the terms in the definition of "risk assessment" set out in paragraph 4 of Annex A to the *SPS Agreement*—more specifically, the phrase "according to the sanitary or phytosanitary measures which might be applied"—suggest that "consideration should be given not just to those specific measures which are currently in application, but at least to a potential range of relevant measures." Japan acknowledged that it did not consider policies other than the measure already applied. However, according to Japan, this "again relates to the matter of methodology," which is left to the discretion of the importing Member.

208. The definition of "risk assessment" in the *SPS Agreement* requires that the evaluation of the entry, establishment or spread of a disease be conducted "according to the sanitary or phytosanitary measures which might be applied." We

agree with the Panel that this phrase "refers to the measures *which might* be applied, not merely to the measures which *are being* applied." The phrase "which might be applied" is used in the conditional tense. In this sense, "might" means: "were or would be or have been able to, were or would be or have been allowed to, were or would perhaps." We understand this phrase to imply that a risk assessment should not be limited to an examination of the measure already in place or favoured by the importing Member. In other words, the evaluation contemplated in paragraph 4 of Annex A to the *SPS Agreement* should not be distorted by preconceived views on the nature and the content of the measure to be taken; nor should it develop into an exercise tailored to and carried out for the purpose of justifying decisions *ex post facto*.

209. In this case, the Panel found that the 1999 PRA dealt exclusively with the "'plant quarantine measures against *E. amylovora* concerning US fresh apple fruit,' which have been taken by Japan based on the proposal by the US government since 1994." The Panel also found that, in the 1999 PRA, no attempts were made "to assess the "relative effectiveness" of the various individual requirements applied, [that] the assessment appears to be based on the assumption from the outset that all these measures would apply cumulatively," and that no analysis was made "of their relative effectiveness and whether and why all of them in combination are required in order to reduce or eliminate the possibility of entry, establishment or spread of the disease." Moreover, the Panel referred to "the opinions of Dr Hale and Dr Smith that the 1999 PRA 'appeared to prejudge the outcome of its risk assessment' and that 'it was principally concerned to show that each of the measures already in place was effective in some respect, and concluded that all should therefore be applied'." In our opinion, these findings of fact of the Panel leave no room for doubt that the 1999 PRA was designed and conducted in such a manner that *no* phytosanitary policy other than the regulatory scheme *already in place* was considered. Accordingly, we uphold the Panel's finding, in paragraph 8.285 of the Panel Report, that "Japan has not ... properly evaluated the likelihood of entry "according to the SPS measures that might be applied"."

Questions and Discussion

1. Does this alternatives analysis restrict the range of SPS measures that a member can use to protect the environment or human health from pests and diseases? Or is it a valuable method for providing information to decisionmakers for evaluating which option may best protect the environment? Under the environmental impact assessment (EIA) laws of most countries, an agency responsible for a development project must assess the environmental impacts of the proposed project and "reasonable alternatives" to the project. The alternatives analysis has been considered the "heart" of the EIA process under the U.S. National Environmental Policy Act, 16 U.S.C. § 4371 *et seq.*; 40 C.F.R. § 1502.14. Are there valid reasons for requiring an alternatives analysis in the environmental context but not in the environment-trade context?

2. The alternatives analysis establishes a very high threshold for a risk assessment, because a member must determine the effectiveness of each alternative. A member may attempt to meet this test by minimizing the number of alternative SPS measures, and thus the number of measures that it must evaluate. But, if a member does that, it runs the

risk of running afoul of the "least trade restrictive alternative" language of Article 5.6 of the SPS Agreement, described in Section V (pages 508–11).

3. Even after Australia made several adjustments to its salmon importation rules, a Panel found that Australia's application of SPS measures to "consumer ready" products, such as cutlets less than 450 grams, was not supported by a risk assessment. The Panel concluded that Australia's risk assessment failed to explain "in any of its disease-specific assessments what should be considered as 'consumer-ready product,' on what basis and for what reasons." *Australia-Salmon: Recourse to Article 21.5*, at para. 7.81 The Panel, in many respects, is requiring decisions to be made "on the record," as is required under the U.S. Administrative Procedure Act.

Final Questions and Discussion for Part IV

1. One perspective on SPS disputes is that they represent a struggle between agricultural exporters (U.S. apple growers or Canadian cattlemen) and perhaps overly-cautious citizens or bureaucrats in importing countries. Steve Charnovitz creatively proposed that countries challenging SPS measures should post bonds or insurance against the health or agricultural risks that might materialize if their challenges are successful. "It would be an interesting market test of WTO dispute settlement to see how costly such disease insurance would be." Steve Charnovitz, *Improving the Agreement on Sanitary and Phytosanitary Standards, in* TRADE, ENVIRONMENT, AND THE MILLENNIUM 223–24 (Gary P. Sampson & W. Bradnee Chambers eds., 2d ed. 2002). Is this a feasible approach? How would an insurer calculate the risk potential?

2. In the real world, governments ultimately find ways to accommodate their interests. After *Japan-Apples* and *Japan-Agricultural Products II*, the United States and Japan reached agreement on adjustments to Japan's SPS measures. As noted earlier, the United States and the EU have negotiated a resolution of the *Hormones* dispute that leaves Europe's import restrictions in place but allows duty-free import of substantial quantities of U.S. beef produced without growth hormones, as certified under a U.S. Department of Agriculture program.

V. The Application of Risk Management in Trade Disputes

Just as the panels and the Appellate Body have analyzed the requirements of the SPS Agreement for risk assessments in each of the four SPS disputes, they have also explored the risk management provisions of the SPS Agreement. While the SPS Agreement does not expressly use the term "risk management," it includes the following risk management requirements:

- when determining the SPS measure, members shall take into account relevant economic factors (Article 5.3) and the objective of minimizing negative trade effects (Article 5.4);

- members shall avoid arbitrary and unjustifiable distinctions in protection with respect to different situations, if such distinctions result in discrimination or a disguised restriction on trade (Article 5.5); and

- members shall ensure that measures are not more trade-restrictive than required to achieve their appropriate level of protection (Article 5.6).

The elements of Articles 5.3 and 5.4 have not been adjudicated. As described below, Articles 5.5 and 5.6 have been at issue in several of the SPS disputes.

A. Article 5.5: Regulating Comparable Situations Similarly

In *Australia-Salmon,* Canada invoked Article 5.5 by claiming that Australia regulated risks from wild, ocean-caught salmon differently from similar risks from other fish, such as herring and cod. Article 5.5 provides that "each Member shall avoid arbitrary or unjustifiable distinctions in the levels it considers to be appropriate in different situations, if such distinctions result in discrimination or a disguised restriction on international trade." Affirming *Hormones I,* the Panel in *Australia-Salmon* found that a measure violates Article 5.5 if:

1. the member adopts different appropriate levels of sanitary protection in several "different situations";

2. those levels of protection exhibit differences which are "arbitrary or unjustifiable"; and

3. the measure embodying those differences results in "discrimination or a disguised restriction on international trade."

This aspect of the Appellate Body's decision is unremarkable. The remaining aspects of the Appellate Body's decision are less obvious.

Australia-Measures Affecting the Importation of Salmon
Appellate Body Report, WT/DS18/AB/R (adopted Nov. 6, 1998)

143. With regard to the first element of Article 5.5, namely, the existence of distinctions in appropriate levels of protection in different situations, the Panel cited our Report in *European Communities-Hormones,* where we stated that "situations ... cannot, of course, be compared, unless they are comparable, that is, unless they present some common element or elements sufficient to render them comparable." The Panel found that:

> ... in the circumstances of this dispute, we can compare situations under Article 5.5 if these situations involve either a risk of "entry, establishment or spread" of the same or a similar disease *or* of the same or similar "associated biological and economic consequences" and this irrespective of whether they arise from the same product or other products. (emphasis added)

144. On this basis, the Panel determined that the import prohibition on fresh, chilled or frozen salmon for human consumption *and* the admission of imports of (i) uncooked Pacific herring, cod, haddock, Japanese eel and plaice for human consumption; (ii) uncooked Pacific herring, Atlantic and Pacific cod, haddock, European and Japanese eel and Dover sole for human consumption; (iii) herring in whole, frozen form used as bait ("herring used as bait"); and (iv) live ornamental finfish, are "different" situations which can be compared under Article 5.5 of the *SPS Agreement.* * * *

145. Situations which involve a risk of entry, establishment or spread of the same or a similar disease have some common elements sufficient to render them comparable under Article 5.5. Likewise, situations with a risk of the same or similar associated potential biological and economic consequences also have some common elements sufficient to render them comparable under Article 5.5. We, therefore, consider that for "different" situations to be comparable under Article 5.5, there is no need for both the disease *and* the biological and economic consequences to be the same or similar. We recognize that, as pointed out by Australia, the risk which needs to be examined in a risk assessment, pursuant to Article 5.1 and the first definition of risk assessment of paragraph 4 of Annex A, is the risk of *both* the entry, establishment or spread of a disease *and* the associated potential biological and economic consequences. However, we fail to see how this can be of relevance to the question of comparability of different situations under Article 5.5 which is the issue addressed by the Panel. We, therefore, conclude that the Panel was correct in stating that situations can be compared under Article 5.5 if these situations involve *either* a risk of entry, establishment or spread of the same or a similar disease, *or* a risk of the same or similar "associated potential biological and economic consequences."

The Appellate Body in *Australia-Salmon* then affirmed the Panel's decision that the importation of other fish, such as herring and cod, constituted a comparable situation. The Appellate Body quickly affirmed the Panel's finding that Australia's different levels of sanitary protection for comparable situations were "arbitrary or unjustifiable." Because Australia allowed the importation of those fish products, and prohibited the importation of salmon, Australia was treating comparable situations differently. In fact, these other fish posed a risk of entry of certain diseases at least as high as salmon, according to the Appellate Body. *Id.* at paras. 154–58.

With respect to the third element — the determination of whether the arbitrary or unjustifiable distinctions in levels of protection results in discrimination or a disguised restriction on trade — panels have evaluated several "warning signals." The first warning signal is whether the measure is arbitrary or unjustifiable. In *Australia-Salmon*, Australia argued that this logic was flawed, because the second element of Article 5.5, whether the measure is arbitrary or discriminatory, is separate and distinct from the third, whether the measure is a disguised restriction. Australia argued that the Panel was in fact using the same legal conclusion to make two different legal findings. The Appellate Body rejected Australia's argument, because the Panel used this factor only as a "warning signal" for, and not as "evidence" of, a disguised restriction on trade. *Id.* at para. 162. The Appellate Body, however, did not distinguish a "warning signal" from "evidence."

The second warning signal is whether there is a "rather substantial difference" in levels of protection. In *Australia-Salmon*, the Appellate Body accepted the Panel's conclusion that the difference between an import prohibition for salmon and a tolerance for imports of herring and other fish was "rather substantial" and a legitimate warning signal. *Id.* at paras. 164.

The third warning signal is whether the measure is inconsistent with Articles 5.1 and 2.2 of the SPS Agreement. Australia objected to this factor in *Australia-Salmon*, because these were separate and distinct legal findings, but again the Appellate Body rejected its claim. The Appellate Body concluded that an SPS measure that is not based on a risk assessment in accordance with Article 5.1 "is a strong indication that this measure is not really concerned with the protection of human, animal, or plant life or health but is instead a trade-restrictive measure taken in the guise of an SPS measure, i.e., a 'disguised restriction on international trade.'" *Id.* at para. 166.

While these first three "warning signals" were considered in both *Australia-Salmon* and *Hormones I*, the *Australia-Salmon* Panel included additional warning signals. First, it considered the differences between the draft risk Report, which would have permitted the importation of salmon under certain circumstances, and the final risk assessment included in the 1996 Report, which omitted this possibility. From this information, the Panel speculated, unsupported by any evidence, that this change "might well have been inspired by domestic pressures to protect the Australian salmon industry against import competition." *Id.* at para. 170.

Australia complained that this was pure speculation, that decisions evolve during the decisionmaking process, that a government should not be held accountable to a draft rule, and that a draft rule could not be considered an SPS measure. The Appellate Body considered Australia's arguments to be "without merit." *Id.* at para. 172. It restated the definition of an SPS measure and concluded, without analysis, that the draft was in fact an SPS measure.

Further, the Appellate Body found that the Panel never obliged members to implement draft recommendations absent new scientific evidence. Again, because the Panel ruled that this was not conclusive "evidence" of a disguised restriction, only a "warning signal," the Appellate Body considered the change in the recommendation relevant.

The last warning signal considered by the Panel was the absence of control on the internal movement of salmon products in Australia compared to the prohibition against importation of Pacific salmon, which the Appellate Body affirmed. *Id.* at para. 174. Considered cumulatively, the Appellate Body affirmed the Panel's finding that the distinctions in the levels of protection imposed by Australia constitute a disguised restriction on trade.

Questions and Discussion

1. With respect to Article 5.5, the Appellate Body interpreted the phrase "different situations" to mean "comparable" or "similar" situations. Is this interpretation correct? While Article 5.5 clearly calls for "comparability" among different SPS levels, is inconsistency between SPS levels really so "bad" that the trading regime should prevent it? Does it relate to core trade concerns, such as discrimination or protectionism? That is, does the fact that Australia imposes different levels of protection for salmon and herring indicate that Australia is discriminating among trading partners or between domestic and foreign products with respect to either salmon or herring? Is this notion of regulatory comparability the way agencies or legislatures normally operate?

2. According to the Appellate Body, which situations can be compared for determining consistency with Article 5.5? Do you agree? In *Hormones I*, the Appellate Body reversed the Panel's findings that the EU had treated comparable situations differently. The Panel found that the difference between levels of permissible natural and synthetic hormones when used for growth promotion was "arbitrary" and "unjustifiable" because the EU had not provided any reason other than the difference between added hormones and hormones naturally occurring in meat and other foods that have formed part of the human diet for centuries. Further, the Panel said that the EU had not submitted any ev-

idence that the risk relating to natural hormones used as growth promoters is higher than the risk relating to endogenous hormones and that the residue level of natural hormones in some natural products (such as eggs and broccoli) is higher than the residue level of hormones administered for growth promotion in treated meat. The Panel also noted the very marked gap between a "no-residue" level of protection against natural hormones used for growth promotion and the "unlimited-residue" level of protection with regard to hormones occurring naturally in meat and other foods. Hormones I, Appellate Body Report, at para. 220 (citing both Panel reports). The Appellate Body disagreed, stating that:

> 221. We do not share the Panel's conclusions that the above differences in levels of protection in respect of added hormones in treated meat and in respect of naturally-occurring hormones in food, are merely arbitrary and unjustifiable. To the contrary, we consider there is a fundamental distinction between added hormones (natural or synthetic) and naturally-occurring hormones in meat and other foods. In respect of the latter, the European Communities simply takes no regulatory action; to require it to prohibit totally the production and consumption of such foods or to limit the residues of naturally-occurring hormones in food, entails such a comprehensive and massive governmental intervention in nature and in the ordinary lives of people as to reduce the comparison itself to an absurdity. The other considerations cited by the Panel, whether taken separately or grouped together, do not justify the Panel's finding of arbitrariness in the difference in the level of protection between added hormones for growth promotion and naturally-occurring hormones in meat and other foods.

However, the Appellate Body affirmed the Panel's finding that the EU's treatment of natural and synthetic growth hormones on the one hand and carbadox and olaquindox on the other was arbitrary and unjustifiable. While the EU regulated all these substances because of their carcinogenic potential, carbadox and olaquindox are anti-microbial agents, not hormones. The Panel responded that the EU had not explained why this difference would justify a different regulatory treatment in light of the carcinogenic potential of both kinds of substances. Hormones I, Appellate Body Report, at paras. 228, 235. Do you agree with the Panel's conclusion? What must be "comparable" under Article 5.5—the substance or agent being regulated or the human health affect that a member seeks to prevent?

3. Do these "warning signals" provide a reasonable method for determining whether a measure results in discrimination or a disguised restriction on trade? For example, should panels use inconsistencies with *other* requirements of the SPS Agreement as "warning signals" under Article 5.5? Do you agree, for example, that the failure to meet the requirements of Article 5.1 is a "strong indication" that the SPS measure adopted is a disguised restriction on trade?

Steve Charnovitz calls the Appellate Body's approach to Article 5.5:

> confounding in its analytical weakness and in its potential for mischief. Accusing a government of trade discrimination or a disguised restriction is a serious charge that should not be hurled lightly. As the Australian representative explained to the Appellate Body, it cannot possibly be a violation of the WTO for a government to change a recommendation between a draft and a final report. Similarly, it cannot possibly be a violation of the WTO for a government to lack internal controls on commerce equivalent to border controls. Yet, according to the Appellate Body, such innocent acts can aggregate into a WTO violation. It

is unclear why the Appellate Body did not realize that an island nation might need stricter health controls at the perimeter than internally. According to the Australian government, there are at least 20 diseases of salmon not currently found in Australia.

Steve Charnovitz, *Improving the Agreement on Sanitary and Phytosanitary Standards*, at 218.

4. By comparing the draft risk assessment to the final risk assessment, the Appellate Body draws the intent of regulators into its conclusion of whether differences in protection were discriminatory or a disguised restriction on trade. Is the Appellate Body reviving the "aim and effect" test of the *Auto Taxes* decision (Chapter 4, Section III.A pages 181–83)? If so, is that consistent with Article 5.5? Is it consistent with the overall goal of the SPS Agreement to ensure that decisions are based on science?

5. A Panel in a recourse proceeding later found that Australia's amendments to its rules for various species of fish provided the same or similar levels of protection. In addition, it found that, where differential treatment was granted, Australia had based such differential treatment on scientifically justifiable reasons, such as different levels of risk from certain diseases. That Panel also found that Australia's changes to its salmon importation rules did not constitute a disguised restriction on trade, largely because it had earlier found that the measure was not arbitrary or unjustifiable, but also because differences in treatment were not substantial. Australia-Salmon: Recourse to Article 21, at paras. 7.90–7.107. In light of the SPS Agreement's focus on science as a means to justify SPS measures, is this a satisfying conclusion to this case?

6. *Relationship to GATT*. What is the link between Article 5.5 and the preamble of Article XX of the GATT? Recall that the preamble allows a member to impose measures that are otherwise inconsistent with the GATT if they are applied in a manner that does not constitute "arbitrary or unjustifiable discrimination between countries where the same conditions prevail." This language is repeated *verbatim* in the preamble to the SPS Agreement. The preamble to the SPS Agreement further provides that one purpose of the SPS Agreement is to "elaborate rules for the application of the provisions of GATT 1994 which relate to the use of sanitary and phytosanitary measures, in particular the provisions of Article XX(b)" and the preamble to Article XX. Moreover, Article 2.4 of the SPS Agreement declares that SPS measures that conform to the SPS Agreement are presumed to be in accordance with Article XX(b) and the preamble to Article XX. Keeping in mind that SPS Agreement Article 5.5 specifically addresses "distinctions in the levels [of protection] it considers to be appropriate in different situations," should the legal conclusions in *Reformulated Gasoline, Asbestos,* and *Shrimp-Turtle* be used to interpret Article 5.5 of the SPS Agreement? The Appellate Body in *Hormones I* said "yes," but with a caveat: given the "structural differences" between Article XX and Article 5.5 of the SPS Agreement, Article XX jurisprudence "cannot be casually imported" into an SPS Agreement case. *Hormones I*, Appellate Body Report, at para. 239.

If the SPS Agreement is intended to elaborate on provisions of the GATT, in particular Article XX(b), does that mean the SPS Agreement applies only when a panel first finds a violation of the GATT? The *Hormones I* Panel said "no," because Article 1.1 sets out the two requirements for application of the SPS Agreement: the measure in dispute is an SPS measure and the measure may, directly or indirectly, affect international trade. It concluded that the SPS Agreement contains "no explicit requirement of a prior violation of a provision of GATT." Hormones I, Panel Report, at para. 8.36. Does application of the SPS Agreement preclude application of the GATT? The Panels in *Hormones I* and *Australia-*

Salmon both said "no." Neither addressed GATT issues, however, because they first found violations of the SPS Agreement. They reviewed the consistency of the SPS measure with the SPS Agreement first, because "if a violation of GATT were found, we would need to consider whether Article XX(b) could be invoked and would then necessarily need to examine the SPS Agreement; if on the other hand, no GATT violation were found, we would still need to examine the consistency of the measure with the SPS Agreement since nowhere is consistency with GATT presumed to be consistency with the SPS Agreement." *Hormones I*, Panel Report (Canada), at para. 8.45; *Hormones I*, Panel Report (U.S.), at para. 8.42; *see also*, *Australia-Salmon*, Panel Report, at para. 8.29, Corr. 1.

B. Article 5.6: "Not more trade-restrictive than required"

Article 5.6 of the SPS Agreement requires a member to choose an SPS measure that is "not more trade-restrictive than required to achieve their appropriate level of sanitary or phytosanitary protection, taking into account technical and economic feasibility." According to the footnote in Article 5.6, a measure is more trade restrictive than necessary, if another measure meets each of the following three elements:

1. it is "reasonably available taking into account technical and economic feasibility";

2. it "achieves [the Member's] appropriate level of sanitary or phytosanitary protection"; and

3. it is "significantly less restrictive to trade."

With respect to the first part of the test, the Panel and Appellate Body in *Australia-Salmon* analyzed each of the three "least trade restrictive" factors. In deciding the first factor, both the Panel and the Appellate Body relied on the alternatives expressed by Australia in their 1996 Report and did not suggest that other alternatives were reasonably available to Australia. The fact that the Panel relied on the alternatives proposed by Australia is significant. Panels interpreting the meaning of "least trade restrictive" under Article XX of the GATT have stated that other less trade restrictive alternatives exist without identifying what those alternatives might be. They have also identified their own alternatives without explaining how those alternatives are less trade restrictive. Nonetheless, Canada came better prepared for its recourse case. There, the Panel agreed with Canada that Australia could adopt less trade restrictive measures, such as those adopted by New Zealand. Instead of applying quarantine requirements for salmon cutlets based on weight, as Australia required, New Zealand allowed imports of larger cutlets provided they were individually and commercially packaged to make it unattractive for commercial processors to prefer buying it. According to the Panel, not only was this less trade restrictive, but it also was "significantly less trade-restrictive." Australia-Salmon: Recourse to Article 21.5, Panel Report, at paras. 7.146–7.152. That decision makes clear that the range of alternatives to review is not limited to those analyzed by the member defending the measure. Nonetheless, the alternative must actually exist and not be theoretical or merely a possible measure.

On the second element of the test, the Appellate Body iterated that the member could choose its own appropriate level of protection. The Appellate Body said, "It is the appropriate level of protection which determines the SPS Measure to be introduced or maintained." Australia-Salmon, Appellate Body Report, para. 203. Further, the level may be different from that reflected in the measure. *Id.* at para. 197. For Australia, the complete import prohibition was higher than its chosen level of protection. Although the total ban amounted to a zero-risk level of protection, Australia was aiming for a very conservative level of sanitary protection aimed at reducing risk to "very low levels," although "not based on a zero-risk approach." *Id.* at para. 197. The Appellate Body further stated, however, that where a member does not state its chosen level of protection with sufficient precision, the Panel may ascertain the chosen level by reviewing the measure actually chosen. *Id.* at para. 207.

In *Australia-Salmon*, the Appellate Body could not determine whether the import restriction was in fact the least trade restrictive measure, because Australia had not properly evaluated the risks under the alternatives. *Id.* at para. 212. In *Japan-Agricultural Products II*, the Panel and Appellate Body noted that other less trade restrictive measures may be available, but that they would not achieve Japan's desired level of protection. *See, e.g.,* Japan-Agricultural Products II, Appellate Body Report, at paras. 96–97.

Questions and Discussion

1. Article 2.3 requires members to ensure that their SPS measures do not arbitrarily or unjustifiably discriminate between members where identical or similar conditions prevail and are not applied in a manner that would constitute a disguised restriction on international trade. Article 5.5 requires members to avoid arbitrary or unjustifiable distinctions in the levels of SPS protection it considers appropriate in different situations, "if such distinctions result in discrimination or a disguised restriction on international trade." Is a violation of Article 2.3 also a violation of Article 5.5, or vice-versa? The Appellate Body in *Australia-Salmon* said yes. Nonetheless, it said that arbitrary or unjustifiable discrimination in the sense of Article 2.3 can be found to exist without any examination under Article 5.5. Australia-Salmon, Appellate Body Report, at para. 252. Do you agree with these conclusions?

2. Article 2.2 requires a member to apply an SPS measure "only to the extent necessary to protect human, animal, or plant life or health." Is this different from the requirement in Article 5.6 to ensure that SPS measures "are not more trade-restrictive than required to achieve [a Member's] appropriate level" of protection"? Does Article 2.2 impose a "least trade restrictive" test? The U.S. Trade Representative has said that the provision would prevent a country from imposing a two-year quarantine when a two-week quarantine would suffice. The provision thus focuses on the application of the measure. According to the USTR, it does not restrict a Member's choice of measures to attain an "appropriate level of protection." Letter from Michael Kantor, U.S. Trade Representative, to Henry A. Waxman, Chairman, House Committee on Energy and Commerce (Sept. 7, 1993). Do you agree?

3. *Hormones I* did not address Article 5.6 directly. However, the Appellate Body said that the EU had not provided any evidence that a system of controlling the importation of hormone-treated meat products would be more difficult than a total ban on using hormones for beef production. Hormones I, Appellate Body Report, at para. 203.

4. Is a science-based test a useful tool for deciding which SPS measures are valid? Steve Charnovitz suggests that such science-based rules should be used to justify rules for themselves:

> In mandating science-based analysis, the WTO will promote global economic welfare. So it is unfortunate that this respect for science does not permeate other

areas of the WTO law. Aside from the SPS Agreement and the review of environmental measures under GATT Article XX, the scientific basis for government regulations is not being scrutinized elsewhere in the WTO system. For example, is there a scientific justification for the WTO to condemn "dumping" in a broad definition that includes the practice of selling a product at less than its cost of production when that prevents price increases in the country of importation? Is there a scientific basis for the WTO to require governments to issue patents for at least 20 years?

Steve Charnovitz, *Improving the Agreement on Sanitary and Phytosanitary Standards*, at 223. Do you agree with Charnovitz? Others also see a "troubling double-standard," where health and environmental rules must be carefully justified and drafted to meet international standards while trade rules do not. Daniel Kalderimis, *Problems of WTO Harmonization and the Virtues of Shields and Swords*, 13 Minn. J. Global Trade 305, 338 (2004).

5. Consider the following U.S. laws or proposals to determine whether or not they are consistent with the SPS Agreement:

a. *Pesticides and the Delaney Clause.* Under the "Delaney Clause," before it was revised, the Food and Drug Administration (FDA) could not approve a food additive, including pesticide chemical residues on food, found to induce cancer when ingested by animals; under such circumstances, the FDA had no discretion to approve that additive as safe. Food, Drug, and Cosmetic Act, 21 U.S.C. §348(c)(3)(A). (Two other "Delaney Clauses" relate to color additives and new animal drugs. 21 U.S.C. §§379e(b)(5)(B), 360b(d)(1)(I)). Whether on raw food commodities or in processed foods, the food additive Delaney Clause was triggered. Essentially, the food additive Delaney Clause called for "zero tolerance," even if the level of pesticide chemical residue might be considered "safe" when compared to other food contaminant standards. Eventually, Congress amended this Delaney Clause for carcinogenic pesticide chemical residues from zero tolerance to "a reasonable certainty that no harm will result." Food Quality Protection Act of 1996, Pub. L. No. 104-170, 110 Stat. 1489, 1514-35, §405; 21 U.S.C. §346a(b)(2)(A)(ii). Still, the law does not permit regulators to balance the benefits of the pesticide or assess whether impermissible levels of pesticides in processed foods can be prevented through governmental monitoring. Does the food additive Delaney Clause, in either form, violate the SPS Agreement?

b. *Risk Benefit Analysis.* The EPA may limit the distribution and sale of a pesticide "to prevent unreasonable adverse effects on the environment." Federal Insecticide, Fungicide, and Rodenticide Act (FIFRA), 7 U.S.C. §§136a(a). The EPA uses a risk-benefit standard to determine whether or not a pesticide causes unreasonable adverse effects on the environment. FIFRA defines "unreasonable adverse effects on the environment" to mean:

(1) any unreasonable risk to man or the environment, taking into account the economic, social, and environmental costs and benefits of the use of any pesticide, or (2) a human dietary risk from residues that result from a use of a pesticide in or on any food inconsistent with the standard under Section 346a of Title 21. The [EPA] Administrator shall consider the risks and benefits of public health pesticides separate from the risks and benefits of other pesticides. In weighing any regulatory action concerning a public health pesticide under this subchapter, the Administrator shall weigh the risks of the pesticide against the health risks such as the diseases transmitted by the vector to be controlled by the pesticide.

7 U.S.C. §§ 136(bb) (1996).

Is this provision governed by the TBT Agreement or the SPS Agreement? Is the provision consistent with whichever agreement applies?

VI. Genetically Modified Organisms and Living Modified Organisms

Modern biotechnology uses genetic modification, genetic engineering, or recombinant-DNA technology to transfer traits carried on genetic material in one organism to another organism that does not naturally have that trait. Genetically modified organisms (GMOs) can be defined as organisms (and microorganisms) in which the genetic material (DNA) has been altered in a way that does not occur naturally by mating or natural recombination. Living modified organisms (LMOs), a subcategory of GMOs, are regulated under the Cartagena Protocol on Biosafety to the Convention on Biological Diversity (Biosafety Protocol). This section addresses some issues that have been raised under the SPS Agreement for national regulation of GMOs in general and Biosafety Protocol regulation of LMOs.

The question for many governments and citizens is whether GMOs, especially those used in food production and processing, are safe for human consumption and whether they can be released safely into the environment. Despite many studies showing no ill effects on people or the environment, other studies tend to support the concerns of GM opponents, in particular with respect to potential environmental harms. Whatever the scientific merits of concern over GM foods and crops, their use is politically sensitive in many parts of the world. For many people, including many Europeans governed by the regime for regulation of biotechnology at issue in the leading WTO dispute on GMO regulation, genetic modification raises profound ethical, religious, or spiritual questions, and governments are properly responsive to these moral considerations.

Notwithstanding these concerns, the United States and other major agricultural exporting countries believed that restrictions on GMOs undermine the development and use of agricultural biotechnology to improve agricultural production and food processing. The use of GMOs in agriculture grows year by year. According to the U.S. Department of Agriculture, in 2010 about 93 percent of soybeans, 86 percent of corn (maize), and 93 percent of cotton plantings in the United States were genetically modified varieties. A private biotech organization, the International Service for the Acquisition of Agri-Biotech Applications, estimates that 77% of soybeans, 26% of maize, and 49% of cotton planted throughout the world in 2009 were biotech plantings. James Clive, Global Status of Commercialized Biotech 6M Crops: 2009 (2009), at http://www.isaaa.org/resources/publications/briefs/41/executive/default.asp.

By its strict terms, however, the SPS Agreement appears to bar trade-related regulation of GMO products absent an "objective" evaluation of the scientific evidence, regardless of social or moral concerns. Consequently, the regulation of GMOs raises in particularly acute form a question that the WTO would rather not address definitively: Can an SPS measure that is inconsistent with the SPS Agreement nevertheless be accepted as a legitimate exercise of national rights by reference to other WTO agreements, such as GATT

Article XX or the TBT Agreement? Put another way, is there a principled way for the WTO to legitimate member government measures responsive to public opinion without upsetting the "careful balance" between scope for national action and the interest of other governments in maintaining the scientific rigor of the SPS system?

A. EU Regulation of GMOs and a WTO Dispute

Since the late 1990s, the EU has pursued policies to regulate the release of GMOs into the environment, the marketing of GMO-derived products, and the labeling of genetically modified foods (GMFs). The most recent form of this regulation is European Council Directive 2001/18 "on the deliberate release into the environment of genetically modified organisms". Among many other things, the directive requires the competent national authority of the Member State where the product is to be first placed on the market to approve the GMO prior to its release into the environment. A company intending to market a GMO must first submit a risk assessment with its application. If the national authority gives a favorable opinion on the placing on the market of the GMO concerned, this Member State must inform the other Member States through the European Commission. If the other Member States or the European Commission do not object, then the competent authority that carried out the original evaluation grants the consent for the placing on the market of the product. The product may then be placed on the market throughout the European Union in conformity with any conditions required in that consent. Approvals under this scheme are good for 10 years, after which they must be renewed.

If objections are raised, the Commission will seek the opinion of its Scientific Panels. If the scientific opinion is favorable, the Commission then solicits the opinion of the Regulatory Committee composed of representatives of Member States on a draft legislative Decision. If the Regulatory Committee gives a favorable opinion, the Commission adopts the Decision. If not, the draft Decision is submitted to the Council of Ministers for adoption or rejection by qualified majority. If the Council does not act within three months, the Commission shall adopt the decision.

The EU regulatory scheme also allows for national exceptions based on scientific considerations. In the late 1990s, six EU member States — Austria, France, Germany, Greece, Italy and Luxembourg — banned imports of genetically modified corn and rapeseed approved by the European Union. Although these actions arguably did not have the scientific basis required under European law, the European Commission declined to challenge the bans. In 1998, Member States began blocking EU regulatory approval for new agricultural biotech products. In 2003, the United States, Argentina, and Canada, three countries that make extensive use of biotechnology in agriculture and food processing, requested the establishment of a WTO dispute settlement panel to determine whether the EU's continuing failure to act on applications for use of GMOs under EU Directive 2001/18 and other EU law constituted a violation of the SPS Agreement and other WTO agreements. The complainants claimed that the EU's inaction effectively prohibited most corn exports to Europe and violated the SPS Agreement's requirement to base SPS measures on "sufficient scientific evidence" and risk assessments.

The Panel's report concluded that the inaction by the European authorities amounted to a general *de facto* moratorium, causing "undue delays" in final decisions on 24 out of 27 biotech products seeking approval from 1999–2003. The undue delays were inconsistent with SPS Agreement Article 8 and the first clause of Annex C, paragraph 1(a). European Communities-Measures Affecting the Approval and Marketing of Biotech Products, WT/DS291/R (adopted Nov. 21, 2006).

To some extent, the Panel's judgment is unexceptional. Governments that have regulatory systems for products have an obligation to consider and rule on applications for product approval by foreign suppliers within a reasonable period of time. Moreover, federal governments cannot permit sub-federal units of government to nullify the effect of the federal regulatory system. But other aspects of the panel report are troubling. We have already raised the question of how to allow consideration of nonscientific values and preferences into the system. There is also an element of the report that concerns nondiscrimination and like product analysis. *See* the Question and Discussion at the end of this section on these points. We have also earlier noted the panel's handling of scientific evidence and precautionary measures in Section IV.C above. Taking those and other issues into account, including the Panel's handling of the testimony of scientific experts, at least one commentator states bluntly: "The panel's performance was disappointing and ultimately unacceptable." Trish Kelly, The Impact of the WTO: The Environment, Public Health and Sovereignty 180 (2007).

In practical terms, after further struggles within the EU to come up with a WTO-compatible and politically acceptable approach to GMO approvals and marketing, the logjam has broken in recent years. Under Directive 2001/18 and related European regulations 1829/2003 and 1830/2003, 31 different GMOs are approved for use as of the end of 2009— some for cultivation, some for import and processing, some as feed, and some as food. Approved GM crop species include maize, oil seed rape, soybean, cotton, and sugar beet.

Despite these approvals, some Member States have continued to invoke the so-called "safeguard clause," now in Article 23 of Directive 2001/18, which allows a Member State to restrict or prohibit the use and/or sale of that product in its territory if it has "grounds for considering" that the GMO poses a risk to human health or the environment "as a result of new or additional information." National bans are in place for some of the approved GMOs in Austria, France, Germany, Hungary, Luxembourg, and Greece. Moreover, these countries maintain their import bans despite the opinion of various EU Scientific Committees that there was no new evidence that would justify overturning the original decision to authorize these GMOs. As commented on in Question and Discussion note 3 in Section IV.C.2. of this chapter (page 491), the WTO dispute settlement panel determined that these "safeguards" were not based on risk assessments meeting the requirements of Articles 2.2, 5.1, or 5.7, but so far the European Commission has not taken any action to have them overturned.

In 2003, the EU revamped its GMO regulation system. The key requirements are found in Regulation 1829/2003, with implementing details for applicants in Regulation 641/2004. Regulation 1829/2003 governs the placing on the market, the labeling, and the tracking of GM food and feed products. Article 4(1) for food (and similar language in Article 16(1) for feed) provides that GM food "must not: a) have adverse effects on human health, animal health or the environment; b) mislead the consumer; or c) differ from the food which it is intended to replace to such an extent that its normal consumption would be nutritionally disadvantageous for the consumer." Under the criteria of Directive 2001/18, the Regulation establishes a single procedure for approval of deliberate release of GMOs into the environment, with scientific review by the European Food Safety Authority and 10-year (renewable) authorization. As of October 2010, 129 applications have been made under this regulation, of which 13 were determined to be pre-existing (pre-2003). Of the remaining 116, 32 have been approved, 6 denied, 6 withdrawn, and the rest are still under review. GMO Compass, GMO Database, at http://www.gmo-compass.org/eng/gmo/db.

A final element of the European scheme is a Novel Food Regulation, EC 258/97. Under this regulation, Europe has received, through November 2009, 111 applications for approval, of which it has approved 47. Only three applications have been refused so far, but 18 were withdrawn and some others were handled under other regulations. This Novel Foods Regulation also includes a safeguard clause, which Italy invoked to suspend trade in and use of products derived from four GM maize varieties. After Europe's Scientific Committee for Food concluded that the information provided by the Italian authorities did not provide scientific justification that the use of the GM foods in question endangered human health, Italy relented and removed its national restriction.

Questions and Discussion

1. Are the EU's GMO rules or the Member State safeguard findings on selected GMOs "sanitary or phytosanitary measures"? If the SPS Agreement does not govern, which WTO agreement does? Can this question be answered without resurrecting the "aim and effect" test discussed in Chapter 4, Section 3.A (pages 181–83)? That is, suppose a regulation is driven in part by scientific concern over environmental effects of release of GMOs. Does that make it an SPS measure? But suppose the record of the decision also explicitly refers to morally-driven public sentiment against allowing GMO products in foods. Can that nonscientific explanation for the measure justify it, and thus "trump" the SPS Agreement? Should a government be advised (required?) to apply legally separate (even if practically equivalent) measures to vindicate these separate grounds for decision? Would such an approach turn national regulation into a meaningless game? *See* Robert L. Howse & Henrik Horn, *European Communities-Measures Affecting the Approval and Marketing of Biotech Products*, 8 WORLD TRADE REV. No. 1, 2009, at 49, 66–72.

2. Argentina made a GATT Article III national treatment claim in *EC-Biotech*: it argued that the process for approval of genetically engineered crops and products was more burdensome than the processes for approval of non-GMO crop varieties used by European farmers. In a manner reminiscent of the *Auto Taxes* case, the Panel focused its analysis on the issue of "less favourable treatment" and found that the EU regulatory system did not make any distinction based on national origin. It did so, however, without first determining whether GMO varieties and non-GMO varieties of the same crop are "like products." Howse and Horn see here an effort to return to issues of "aim and effect" and "so as to afford protection." Although each of them has advocated some reforms along these lines, they find it "extraordinary ... that the Panel should make such a large jurisprudential step without in any way engaging these larger issues, or the rationales of the AB's rejection of aims and effects in the first place." Howse & Horn, *EC-Measures*, at 66.

B. The SPS Agreement and the Biosafety Protocol

The Cartagena Protocol on Biosafety (Biosafety Protocol), concluded on January 29, 2000, and entered into force on September 11, 2003. There are now 160 parties to the Protocol. The text and other information is available at: http://www.cbd.int/biosafety. The Protocol addresses the transboundary movement, handling, and use of "all living modified organisms [LMOs] that may have adverse effects on the conservation and sustainable use of biological diversity, taking also into account risks to human health." Protocol,

Art. 4. In general, the parties must comply with the Protocol's "advanced informed agreement" (AIA) procedure for any transboundary movements of LMOs. LMOs are defined as "any living organism that possesses a novel combination of genetic material obtained through the use of modern biotechnology." Protocol, Art. 3(g).

The AIA procedure most importantly requires an exporter to notify the competent national authority of the party of import, in writing, prior to exporting an LMO to that country. The notification must include, among other things, a risk assessment that is "carried out in a scientifically sound and transparent manner" and which evaluates, as appropriate, the likelihood and consequences of any potential adverse effects. Protocol, Annex III. The importing country then must determine whether or not to allow the import. The importing country may grant its consent (with or without conditions), prohibit the import, or request additional information. An importing country may base its decision regarding transboundary movements of LMOs on socio-economic considerations arising from the impact of LMOs on the conservation and sustainable use of biological diversity.

The AIA procedure actually applies to a relatively small number of LMOs. First, the AIA procedure applies only to the "first intentional transboundary movement of living modified organisms for intentional introduction into the environment." It excludes LMOs that are pharmaceuticals, in transit, and for "contained use." The Protocol also applies rules that are less stringent than the AIA procedure to LMOs "for direct use as food or feed, or for processing." The parties may also exclude LMOs from the AIA procedure that they identify as "not likely to have adverse effects on the conservation and sustainable use of biological diversity, taking into account risk to human health." Nonetheless, the AIA procedure still applies to this smaller subset of LMOs, including seeds or live fish, assuming that they do not fall within one of the exceptions.

The Protocol establishes a separate procedure for LMOs intended for direct use as food or feed, or for processing (FFP LMOs). For these LMOs, a party may establish conditions regarding domestic use, including conditions for placing the LMO on the market. The party must make this decision based on a risk assessment and inform the other parties of this decision through the Biosafety Clearinghouse. In addition, the documentation required for these LMOs must state that the shipment "may contain" LMOs, declare that the shipment is not intended for introduction into the environment, and specify a point of contact.

Given the negotiating history of the Protocol against the backdrop of the SPS Agreement, several flashpoints exist between the Biosafety Protocol and the SPS Agreement.

1. Food Safety and Human Health Concerns

The first flashpoint is whether the Protocol applies to food safety and human health. While it may seem obvious that an international agreement addressing LMOs would relate to food safety and human health, the Biosafety Protocol has its origins in Article 19.3 of the Convention on Biological Diversity (CBD), which calls on its parties to develop a protocol for LMOs "that may have adverse effect on the conservation and sustainable use of biological diversity." Article 4 of the Protocol amends the CBD's environment-oriented scope with the phrase "taking also into account risks to human health." May a party to the Protocol impose restrictions on the importation of an LMO based on human health concerns alone or is it limited to the human health concerns associated with any LMO that may potentially affect biodiversity? The European Union clearly believes that the Protocol covers possible threats posed by LMOs to human health as well as biodiversity. The United States has a different view: "The Protocol does not address food safety issues. Experts in other international fora, such as Codex Alimentarius, address food safety." Statement of July 21, 2003, written by the U.S. Department of State, Bureau of Oceans and International Environmental and Scientific Affairs, *at* http://www.fas.usda.gov/info/fact sheets/biosafety.asp. Note that the United States is not a party to the Biosafety Protocol because it is not a party to the underlying CBD.

---

2. The Precautionary Principle

A second flashpoint concerns the application of the precautionary principle. The drafters of the Biosafety Protocol spent considerable energy negotiating the language concerning the precaution. Some wanted a definition similar to Principle 15 of the Rio Declaration (which calls it the precautionary "approach" rather than "principle") to focus the Protocol on the "central question of safety." Some wanted to specifically mention the precautionary principle in the risk assessment article of the Protocol, while others wanted to adhere closely to the language of Article 5.7 of the SPS Agreement. Terence P. Stewart & David S. Johanson, *A Nexus of Trade and the Environment: The Relationship between the Cartagena Protocol on Biosafety and the SPS Agreement of the World Trade Organization*, 14 Colo. J. Int'l Envtl. L. & Pol'y 1, 16–20 (2003); Sean D. Murphy, *Biotechnology and International Law*, 42 Harv. Int'l L. J. 47 (2001).

The final language of the Protocol attempts to satisfy all points of view. The Preamble reaffirms the "precautionary approach" of Rio Principle 15. In operative legal terms, Articles 10.6 and 11.8 of the Protocol then state:

> Lack of scientific certainty due to insufficient relevant scientific information and knowledge regarding the extent of the potential adverse effects of a living modified organism on the conservation and sustainable use of biological diversity in the Party of import, taking also into account risks to human health, shall not prevent that Party from taking a decision, as appropriate, with regard to the import of [the living modified organism in question ... in order to avoid or minimize such potential adverse effects (Art. 10.6][that living modified organism intended for direct use as food or feed, or for processing, in order to avoid or minimize such potential adverse effects (Art. 11.8)].

While this language resembles Article 5.7 of the SPS Agreement, it is not identical. How do they differ? If a country adopts a precautionary measure deemed consistent with the Biosafety Protocol but arguably not consistent with the SPS Agreement, which treaty prevails?

---

3. The Savings Clause

At a more fundamental level, what is the relationship between the Biosafety Protocol and the SPS Agreement? The Biosafety Protocol language perhaps satisfied everyone with its ambiguity but left challenging questions for lawyers. The final recitals in the Preamble to the Protocol provide as follows:

> *Recognizing* that trade and environment agreements should be mutually supportive with a view to achieving sustainable development,
> *Emphasizing* that this Protocol shall not be interpreted as implying a change in the rights and obligations of a Party under any existing international agreements,

Understanding that the above recital is not intended to subordinate this Protocol to other international agreements....

To say that it is challenging to decipher the full import of these statements may be an understatement. The United States has attempted to dismiss the phrases "mutually supportive" and "subordinate" as mere "political statements" and that the relationship between the Protocol and the SPS Agreement is "clarified" in the clause that begins with "Emphasizing." The "Recognizing" clause reflects Principle 12 of the Rio Declaration. What, then, to make of the final "Understanding" clause? Which treaty is meant to prevail in case of a conflict? If both countries are WTO members but only one is a party to the Protocol, the SPS Agreement applies, because a country cannot be bound by a treaty to which it has not consented. A gray area emerges potentially when both disputing WTO members are also parties to the Protocol; with 160 parties to the Protocol and 153 members of the WTO, this situation is likely to be the most common.

As discussed in Chapter 9 in more detail (pages 654–59; 673–84), the Vienna Convention on the Law of Treaties (Vienna Convention) provides the basic rules for resolving conflicts between treaties. Article 30 of the Vienna Convention on the application of successive treaties relating to the same subject matter would not seem to apply, because the preamble indicates that both treaties are to be treated equally and that neither prevails over the other. Here are two contrasting perspectives on the interpretive challenge:

Claire R. Kelly, *Power, Linkage and Accommodation: The WTO as an International Actor and Its Influence on Other Actors and Regimes*
24 BERKELEY J. INT'L L. 79, 125–26 (2006).

[t]he Preamble to the Protocol also attempted to accommodate WTO objectives and rules, noting that "this Protocol shall not be interpreted as implying a change in the rights and obligations of a party under any existing international agreement," but then adding that "the above recital is not intended to subordinate this Protocol to other international agreements." The effect of this language is unclear. It does not appear to be a savings clause such that it would clearly except it from the later-in-time rule of lex posterior. If it were not for the contradictory phrases in the preamble, then under a preemption model, Article 30 of the Vienna Convention would indicate which treaty should prevail.... [U]nder the Vienna Convention, where two parties were signatories to the WTO and the Protocol, then the Protocol's terms would apply, but where one party signed only one of the treaties, that treaty would take precedence. Although the preamble indicates that the Protocol is not meant to displace existing rights, it immediately qualifies this statement, indicating that the Protocol will not be deemed subservient to other treaties. This language would seem to preclude a clear preemption argument....

Although the negotiators rejected accommodation through preemption or a conflicts rule, all the circumstances suggest that the Protocol should at least be considered when evaluating WTO disputes and that the WTO should likewise acknowledge the existence of the Protocol in its disputes. Article 31.3(a) of the Vienna Convention further provides that "there shall be taken into account, together with the context: (a) any subsequent agreement between the parties regarding the interpretation of the treaty or the application of its provisions." The Protocol failed to provide for conflict rules or to allow for a preemption argument and instead seems to have settled for accommodation through a general sense of comity. Of course, comity may lead to other forms of accommodation at a later time, particularly explicit deference through conflict resolution. The general exercise of comity in this sense seems less troubling than implicit deference, although less helpful than a clear rule via the choice of law/forum or preemption model. However, it may lead to comity through accommodation, which may undermine transparency and predictability.

———————

Terence P. Stewart & David S. Johanson, *A Nexus of Trade and the Environment: The Relationship between the Cartagena Protocol on Biosafety and the SPS Agreement of the World Trade Organization*
14 Colo. J. Int'l Envtl. L. & Pol'y 1, 35, 36–38 (2003)

The panel or the Appellate Body would likely refer to the Vienna Convention's Article 30 * * *

The Vienna Convention's provision for such a situation is somewhat difficult to follow. Article 30(4)(a) of the Vienna Convention provides that if two treaties exist, and all of the parties to the two agreements are not the same, then "as between States parties to both treaties the same rule applies as in paragraph 3." Paragraph 3 reads:

> When all the parties to the earlier treaty are parties also to the later treaty but the earlier treaty is not terminated or suspended in operation under article 59, the earlier treaty applies only to the extent that its provisions are compatible with those of the latter treaty.

Thus, if a dispute involving LMOs were settled at the WTO, and both parties to the WTO dispute were also parties to the Protocol, the provisions of the later treaty, the Protocol, would apply in situations in which certain provisions are not "compatible." In such a case, the panelists or the Appellate Body members would presumably inform themselves of the terms of the Protocol, including its more expansive interpretation of the precautionary principle, when settling the dispute.

Further, another provision of the Vienna Convention might apply in situations in which all parties in a WTO dispute involving LMOs are also parties to the Protocol. Article 31(3)(c) of the Vienna Convention provides that, in interpreting a treaty, "there shall be taken into account, together with the context, … any relevant rules of international law applicable in the relations between the parties." Accordingly, in LMO disputes that reach the WTO in which both parties to the dispute are also parties to the Protocol, panelists and Appellate Body members might refer to other "relevant rules of international law" that apply to the parties, namely, those of the Protocol.

As noted, Article 30(4)(a) of the Vienna Convention provides that the terms of a later treaty apply in situations in which provisions of two treaties are incompatible. Thus, at some point, a WTO panel or the Appellate Body might evaluate whether the versions of the precautionary principle as found in the Protocol and the SPS Agreement are incompatible. It is not clear that they are. Article 5.7 of the SPS Agreement provides that WTO members may provisionally adopt SPS measures in situations in which scientific evidence is lacking. Alternatively, the Protocol states that import decisions regarding certain LMOs may be based upon the precautionary principle. Nothing in the Protocol provides that such measures may not be provisional. Even if an LMO measure were based upon the precautionary principle per the Protocol, it would be reasonable for a country to revisit its regulation in light of new evidence of possible risks posed by the LMO. Thus, in the end, the precautionary principle as found in the Protocol and the SPS Agreement might both in effect be provisional.

Questions and Discussion

1. With whom do you agree? Perhaps Kristin Dawkins is correct when she notes, "the compromise struck ... is so delicate, lawyers may never be able to sort out whether one or the other treaty should prevail." Kristin Dawkins, *Biotech—From Seattle to Montreal and Beyond, The Battle Royale of the 21st Century*, SEEDLING, Mar. 2000, http://www.biotech-info.net/ montreal_beyond.html.

2. Article 2(4) of the Biosafety Protocol states:

Nothing in this Protocol shall be interpreted as restricting the right of a Party to take action that is more protective of the conservation and sustainable use of biological diversity than that called for in this Protocol, provided that such action is consistent with the objective and the provisions of this Protocol and is in accordance with its other obligations under international law.

Does this alter your analysis of which agreement might prevail in a dispute?

3. At the conclusion of the Biosafety Protocol negotiations, all sides claimed victory. The biotechnology industry interpreted the Protocol as requiring strong scientific support to prohibit the importation of LMOs. Interpreting the risk assessment and precautionary provisions, one Biotech representative stated that "[s]hipments of anything can't be blocked on the suspicion of harm—there must be probable evidence." Patricia Ware, *Biosafety Protocol Provides for Labeling of Modified Foods, House Member Says*, 24 CHEMICAL REP. 280 (Feb. 21, 2000). Others, especially Europeans who strongly supported the precautionary principle, expressed their pleasure with the Protocol, because they believe that the Protocol supports the use of the precautionary principle to reject imports of LMOs. What do you think?

4. For the most comprehensive assessment of the Biosafety Protocol, *see* RUTH MACKENZIE ET AL., AN EXPLANATORY GUIDE TO THE CARTAGENA PROTOCOL ON BIOSAFETY (2003). A large number of articles analyze the relationship between the Biosafety Protocol and the SPS Agreement. *See, e.g.*, Paul E. Hagen & John Barlow Weiner, *The Cartagena Protocol on Biosafety: New Rules for International Trade in Living Organisms*, 12 GEO. INT'L L. REV. 697 (2000); Olivette Rivera-Torres, *The Biosafety Protocol and the WTO*, B.C. INT'L & COMP. L. REV. 263 (2003); Steve Charnovitz, *The Supervision of Health and Biosafety by World Trade Rules*, 13 TUL. ENVTL. L.J. 271 (2000).

C. The Role of Codex Alimentarius in Biotechnology

To provide a framework for evaluating the safety and nutritional concerns of GM foods, the Codex established an Ad Hoc Intergovernmental Task Force on Food Derived from Biotechnology to create principles for risk analysis of foods derived from biotechnology, which produced guidelines for Food Safety Assessments for foods derived from recombinant-DNA plants and for foods produced using recombinant-DNA microorganisms. Codex Alimentarius Commission, *Principles for the Risk Analysis of Foods Derived from Modern Biotechnology*, CAC/GL 44-2003 (2003, amended in 2008) (Codex *GMO Principles*). These *GMO Principles* are to be read in conjunction with guidelines specific to safety assessments for foods derived from animals, plants, and microorganisms. For all of these documents, see World Health Organization, Codex Work on Foods Derived from Biotechnology, http://www.who.int/foodsafety/biotech/codex_taskforce/en/index.html.

The scope of the Codex *GMO Principles* is at once broad and limited. The principles cover animals, plants, and microorganisms derived from modern biotechnology and used as food for human consumption and feed. They include provisions for risk assessment, risk management, and labeling of such products. The risk assessment principles provide that a safety assessment should be conducted of the intended and unintended effects to evaluate whether the new food is as safe as the conventional counterpart. *Id.* at paras. 10–15. The risk assessment principles also include a pre-market safety assessment undertaken on a case-by-case basis, based on sound science, obtained using appropriate methods, and analyzed using appropriate statistical techniques that should be of the quality that would withstand scientific peer review. *Id.* at para. 12. Post-market monitoring may also be considered on a case-by-case basis during risk assessment and assessed for practicability during risk management. *Id.* at para. 20.

The safety assessment for foods derived from GM plants requires, among other things, a description of the recombinant-DNA plant, the host plant and its use as food, genetic modifications, a characterization of the genetic modifications, and an assessment of possible toxicity and allergenicity. Guideline for the Conduct of Food Safety Assessment of Foods Derived from Recombinant-DNA Plants, CAC/GL 45-2003, para. 23 (2003). The assessment of possible allergenicity recommends an "integrated, stepwise, case-by-case approach" and includes an initial assessment of the source of the protein, the amino acid sequence homology, and the pepsin resistance. *Id.* at para. 41. In addition, specific serum screening is required for those proteins known to be allergenic or similar in sequence to allergens. *Id.* at para. 14–15. Other considerations to be taken into account are the potential accumulation of substances significant to human health and the use of antibiotic resistance marker genes. *Id.* at para. 46, 55–58. Similar information is required for recombinant-DNA microorganisms. Guideline for the Conduct of Food Safety Assessment of Foods Derived from Recombinant-DNA Microorganisms, CAC/GL 46-2003 (2003) (Microorganism Guideline).

Nonetheless, the *GMO Principles* exclude a number of important factors. For example, the guidelines for GM plants do not address environmental, ethical, moral, and socio-economic aspects of the research, development, production, and marketing of GM foods. Nor do they address animal feed or animals fed such feed except insofar as the animals have been developed by using modern biotechnology. GMO Principles, at para. 7. The *GMO Principles* do not address the safety of foods produced using recombinant-DNA microorganisms in agriculture, risks relating to environmental releases of such microorganisms used in food production, or issues relating to the safety of food production workers handling these organisms. Microorganism Guideline, at para. 2.

Finding consensus on labeling of GM foods has eluded Codex and its Committee on Food Labelling. Governments have had difficulty finding agreement on definitions, the scope of the guidelines, the provisions of the guidelines, threshold levels, exemptions, label declarations, and implementation. Codex Alimentarius Commission, Report of the Thirtieth Session of the Codex Committee on Food Labelling, ALINORM 03/22 (May 6–10, 2002), at paras. 27–62 & Appendix III, IV. For example, many delegations and observers supported using the phrase "genetically modified/engineered" because this terminology is more familiar to consumers. Others, such as the United States, supported "modern biotechnology" in order to maintain consistency with other Codex texts and the Biosafety Protocol, stressing that this terminology is more understandable to consumers in their countries. Eventually, governments agreed to define "genetically modified/engineered organism" as one changed through "modern biotechnology." *Id.* at paras. 29–30. Delegations also clashed over whether labeling should be required or voluntary, whether labeling, if required, should only be so if certain threshold levels of GM content are found in the food product, and whether certain exemptions should apply for processed food ingredients, flavors, and food additives.

Unable to reach consensus on these and other issues, the Committee on Food Labelling is now working from a greatly simplified text. The key proposal to date provides that:

> When the physical, chemical, or functional characteristics of a food are significantly altered through any means (production or processing), the labelling of such food be appropriately modified from its traditional labelling to ensure that the food is described or presented in a manner that is truthful and not misleading and not likely to create an erroneous impression regarding its character in any respect.

ALINORM 10/33/22 (May 3–7, 2010), at Appendix X, para. 6. For further commentary and the remainder of the proposals, see *id.* at paras. 159–161 and Appendix X.

Questions and Discussion

1. What is the effect of the failure of the Codex *GMO Principles* to include provisions for assessing the environmental impacts of intentional releases of GM foods and microorganisms? Does this mean that there is no relevant international standard on which WTO members must base their SPS measures relating to environmental impacts? Or does it mean the opposite: that the relevant international standard for GM foods and microorganisms does not include such a requirement? Does the answer to this question have any impact on whether a WTO member must base an SPS measure for intentional releases into the environment on a risk assessment?

2. Since 1995, Codex has failed to muster consensus on several important issues. For example, votes on proposed standards for bovine growth hormones to promote the production of meat and milk were adopted by simple majority votes. Terence P. Stewart & David S. Johanson, *Cartagena Protocol and the SPS Agreement*, at 48. Votes on risk assessments for GM foods and feed as well as labeling of GM foods and feed have been by consensus. Does a simple majority vote mean that the standard does not constitute an "international standard" for the purposes of Article 3 of the SPS Agreement?

VII. Equivalence

A. Equivalence and the SPS Agreement

Although the issue of equivalence has received little public or scholarly attention, it is a major issue for all WTO members, especially developing country members. The doctrine of equivalence is intended to facilitate trade in a world filled with ubiquitous and technically complex SPS measures by requiring countries to accept goods that do not satisfy the particular technical configuration of their own SPS measures if the exporting country can demonstrate that its own SPS practices achieve the importing country's level of protection. No WTO disputes to date have involved equivalence issues, but the members have been active on them through the WTO's Committee on Sanitary and Phytosanitary Measures (SPS Committee).

Article 4 of the SPS Agreement addresses equivalence. Article 4.1 provides:

> Members shall accept the sanitary or phytosanitary measures of other Members as equivalent, even if these measures differ from their own or from those used by other Members trading in the same product, if the exporting Member objectively demonstrates to the importing Member that its measures achieve the importing Member's appropriate level of sanitary or phytosanitary protection. For this purpose, reasonable access shall be given, upon request, to the importing Member for inspection, testing and other relevant procedures.

One important question is whether Article 4 focuses on equivalent "measures" or equivalent "appropriate levels of protection." Some importing countries may actually have lower "appropriate levels of protection" but different SPS measures than the exporting country. It appears that some of these importing countries were not accepting the requests for equivalence determinations from exporting countries with higher levels of protection on the grounds that the exporting country's SPS "measures" were not equivalent. To eliminate any ambiguity, the SPS Committee issued a "decision" clarifying that the inquiry should focus on the level of protection:

> When considering a request for recognition of equivalence, the importing Member should analyze the science-based and technical information provided by the exporting Member on its sanitary or phytosanitary measures with a view to determining whether these measures achieve the level of protection provided by its own relevant sanitary or phytosanitary measures.

Committee on Sanitary and Phytosanitary Measures, *Decision on the Implementation of Article 4 of the Agreement on the Application of Sanitary and Phytosanitary Measures*, G/SPS/19, para. 7 (Sept. 26, 2001). Despite this clarification, some problems persist. Suppose the importing member's SPS measures do not actually achieve that member's own appropriate level of protection. For example, a member's appropriate level of protection for a certain health concern may be "zero risk" but its SPS measures do not achieve zero risk. Due to such circumstances, Argentina has asked that the importing member not compare the exporting country's SPS measures to the importing country's appropriate level of protection, but rather to the level of protection actually attained by the importing member's own measure. Committee on Sanitary and Phytosanitary Measures, *Clarification of Paragraph 7 of the Decision on Equivalence*, G/SPS/W/128/Rev.2 (June 10, 2003).

The more common problem is that each country has its own approach to food safety or agricultural protection measures, and it is often tricky to judge whether an exporting member's SPS measures reliably achieve the importing country's appropriate level of protection. Developing countries especially suffer from this kind of question about equivalency for their agricultural exports. *Id.* at para. 6; Committee on Sanitary and Phytosanitary Measures, *Decision on the Implementation of Article 4*, G/SPS/19, preamble (Oct. 26 2001). But the problem can arise anywhere. The United States expended considerable effort to reach bilateral agreements with its Latin American trading partners to have them agree that U.S. sanitary standards for meat are equivalent to their own. *See, e.g,* the 2006 agreement with Panama at http://www.ustr.gov/sites/default/files/uploads/reports/2009/ NTE/asset_upload_file26_15497.pdf. In early 2010, the United States. and Europe have an unresolved question about equivalency of measures to guard against E. coli contamination of shellfish such as oysters and mussels. Europe tests for E. coli in the flesh of the mollusks, while the U.S. requires growers to test for E. coli in the water in which the mollusks are raised. Are these two approaches "equivalent" in their level of protection?

An older dispute between the United States and Canada over Ultra High Temperature (UHT) milk under the U.S.-Canada Free Trade Agreement illustrates the difficulties. UHT is a milk sterilization process that allows milk to be distributed and marketed at room temperature for months. UHT milk is almost unknown in the United States, where pasteurization of fresh milk, which then requires refrigeration, is the standard practice. A producer of UHT milk from Quebec, Canada, had a significant share of the market in Puerto Rico. The U.S. FDA prevailed on Puerto Rico to change their regulations to conform to U.S. mainland requirements for milk. This change meant that the Canadian milk could no longer be marketed in Puerto Rico absent a determination by U.S. authorities that the Quebec UHT process was equivalent to U.S. pasteurization. Here is one view of the resulting trade dispute.

Patti Goldman, *The Democratization of the Development of United States Trade Policy*
27 Cornell Int'l L.J. 631, 684–86 (1994)

The concept of "equivalence" has led to controversy under the U.S.-Canada Free Trade Agreement (USCFTA) in the area of meat and milk inspection. Prior to the USCFTA, USDA [the U.S. Department of Agriculture] conducted random inspections of meat imported to the United States from Canada. Under the USCFTA, USDA conducted an equivalence study and determined that the Canadian meat inspection procedures were equivalent to U.S. ones.

The General Accounting Office has criticized this equivalence determination for overlooking important considerations and for reaching certain conclusions without outside review. The equivalence study did not assess the Canadian system's control of, or testing for, drugs approved for use in Canada but not in the United States. In addition, the study made professional judgments about the scientific and health implications of differences in the two systems, such as the U.S. testing of end products for listeria contamination, in contrast to the Canadian testing of workers and the work environment in which the food is processed. These professional assessments were not peer reviewed.

Pursuant to its equivalence determination, USDA ceased inspecting all Canadian meat imports in 1989. Instead, it instituted a cursory reinspection system designed not to ensure that the meat imports met U.S. standards, but rather to ensure that Canada maintained its equivalent inspection system. Only certain shipments were inspected; USDA would give Canadian plants advance notice when a shipment was selected for inspection and allow Canadian inspectors to select the samples to be inspected.

The General Accounting Office criticized the relaxed border inspections, contending that USDA documentation did not support the conclusion that the Canadian meat inspection was equivalent to the U.S. system. Meat inspectors complained that Canadian producers were taking advantage of the cursory reinspections and shipping contaminated meat. Under this system, the rejection rate for Canadian imports dropped by half, even though the Canadian rejection rate for U.S. meat doubled over the same time period.

The Canadian meat inspection example illustrates the controversial public health issues that underlie equivalence determinations. Nonetheless, NAFTA, like the USCFTA and the Uruguay Round of GATT, entitles countries to such a determination without requiring the assessment of every potentially significant public health issue or every inspection process. Applying the concept of equivalence to performance standards and good manufacturing practice requirements will present an array of difficult problems, similar to those presented by the different regulatory approaches to the detection of listeria contamination.

The concept of equivalence also fueled a formal trade challenge under the USCFTA to Puerto Rico's restrictions of Canadian exports of ultra-high temperature milk. In 1990, responding to FDA pressure, Puerto Rico adopted the standards and inspection procedures that are in place throughout the rest of the United States. This milk inspection system is preventive in nature, designed to ensure milk industry compliance with safe sanitation standards and practices. It relies heavily on inspections and certifications by state and local agencies. The Canadian UHT milk did not comply with the Puerto Rican standards, and neither Canada nor Quebec had joined the inspection and certification system used by Puerto Rico and the rest of the United States.

Although the Puerto Rican authorities were involved at the outset, the FDA soon took the lead role in trying to work out a solution. It urged Quebec to participate in the inspection system, in which case the FDA would certify its rating officers, but, because of the large expense involved, it agreed to do so only if Canada would participate fully in the system. As an alternative, the FDA suggested that Quebec contract with a northern state (such as Vermont) to have its authorized inspectors, laboratory officials, and rating officers carry out the required inspections and ratings. Canada rejected these options and argued that its standards were substantially equivalent, and thus its milk had to be accepted. In response, imports of Canadian UHT milk were barred at the end of 1991.

Canada demanded an equivalence study, but the two countries could not agree on the parameters of the study. In September of 1992, Canada requested establishment of a dispute settlement panel. The USTR then indicated that it would be too costly to conduct an equivalence study and participate in the dispute settlement process at the same time.

The panel convened under the USCFTA concluded that the United States had nullified and impaired Canada's expectations under the USCFTA by closing the Puerto Rican market to UHT milk during the course of negotiations on equivalence, and it recommended the expeditious completion of an equivalence study. The FDA is now conducting the equivalence study, but the study is quite costly and has required the FDA to divert funds from its other statutorily-mandated public health missions.

Questions and Discussion

1. To clarify what Goldman describes, the USCFTA panel found that the United States. had not violated the trade agreement in either changing the standards in Puerto Rico or

in not carrying out an expeditious equivalency study, but that the delay in resolving the matter amounted to a nonviolation nullification and impairment of Canada's benefits under the agreement. And as a follow-up to Goldman's account, the equivalency study was eventually completed late in 1995 and found that Quebec's practices were indeed equivalent to the U.S. practices. But by then it was too late for the Quebec producer to re-establish itself in the Puerto Rico market.

2. Does equivalence seem to be a reasonable attempt to reconcile differences in SPS measures of different countries? How does a member "objectively demonstrate[]" that its SPS measures achieve the importing member's appropriate level of protection? Do the nondiscrimination provisions of Articles 2.3 and 5.5 of the SPS Agreement apply to equivalence determinations?

3. One way for exporting firms to get their products certified by an importing country is to allow that country's inspectors to visit the production facilities and conduct tests. The United States was anxious to get its agreements on meat product equivalency with Latin American countries in order to save U.S. firms the hassles and expenses associated with inspections by foreign teams.

4. Meeting international standards for international food safety and quality standards poses significant challenges for developing countries. To do so, they must make significant investments in physical and institutional infrastructure. The least developed countries "lack data as well as the capacity and technical expertise to fully participate in Codex standard-setting processes and other fora relevant to food safety issues and quality issues," such as the World Health Organization and the International Organization for Standardization. World Health Organization & World Trade Organization, *WTO Agreements & Public Health* 69 (2002). Article 9 of the SPS Agreement calls on members to provide technical assistance to developing countries. Article 10 allows the SPS Committee to grant "specified, timelimited exceptions" to the SPS Agreement's rules and provides that members "should encourage and facilitate" the active participation of developing country members in relevant international organizations. Because developing countries often have a comparative advantage in the production of food, their participation in the development of SPS rules is critical. Do developed countries have a legal or moral obligation to ensure the participation of developing countries?

5. Consider the following equivalence provisions from Article 714 of the NAFTA:

2. Each importing Party:

   a) shall treat a sanitary or phytosanitary measure adopted or maintained by an exporting Party as equivalent to its own where the exporting Party, in cooperation with the importing Party, provides to the importing Party scientific evidence or other information, in accordance with risk assessment methodologies agreed on by those Parties, to demonstrate objectively, subject to subparagraph (b), that the exporting Party's measure achieves the importing Party's appropriate level of protection;

   b) may, where it has a scientific basis, determine that the exporting Party's measure does not achieve the importing Party's appropriate level of protection; and

   c) shall provide to the exporting Party, on request, its reasons in writing for a determination under subparagraph (b).

3. For purposes of establishing equivalence, each exporting Party shall, on the request of an importing Party, take such reasonable measures as may be available

to it to facilitate access in its territory for inspection, testing and other relevant procedures.

How do the NAFTA provisions differ from the WTO's SPS Agreement? Did NAFTA strike a better balance between the rights of the exporting country to have access to the importing country's market and the rights of the importing country to ensure that its level of protection is not easily subverted through equivalence requirements?

6. Patti Goldman, a leading lawyer-advocate for public participation in trade processes, argues that the United States should adhere to notice-and-comment rulemaking requirements when making equivalence determinations and that Congress should prescribe additional procedural and substantive rules for making equivalence determinations. For example, she believes that an equivalence determination should be made only if the following conditions are met: 1) the other country's standard meets or exceeds the goal of each procedural or substantive requirement of the standard; 2) the equivalence determination does not lead to a reduction in the level of protection provided to the public, nor should they lead to less effective means of implementing or enforcing a level of protection or other goal; 3) the agency responsible for the domestic standard makes the equivalence determination; 4) the process requires that equivalence requests be made public and that they lead to the creation of an official docket on the matter; 5) the lead agency publishes the request in the Federal Register, solicits public comments, and takes those comments into account in making its determination because it is promulgating the equivalent of a rule; 6) equivalence determinations are subjected to extensive peer review when issues arise concerning scientific, health, safety, or policy issues on which there is any substantial difference of opinion; and 7) the equivalence determination identifies precisely which requirements are waived for particular imports and prescribe a system of rigid monitoring to ensure that the equivalence determination continues to be valid. Patti Goldman, *The Democratization of the Development of United States Trade Policy*, at 688–90. Are these sensible suggestions? In at least one respect, the U.S. Congress agreed. The legislation implementing the Uruguay Round agreements requires the Food and Drug Administration (FDA) to follow notice-and-comment procedures in making equivalence determinations. 103 Pub. L. No. 465, § 432 (Dec. 8, 1994), *amending* Uruguay Round Agreements Act, 19 U.S.C. § 2578. It is unclear why Congress subjected only the FDA to this requirement, and not the U.S. Department of Agriculture, which has been involved in the most controversial equivalence determination thus far.

B. Equivalence and SPS Protection in the EU

The European Union has laws relating to SPS measures, including equivalence and the recognition of SPS measures of other EU Member States. A case in the European Court of Justice illustrates the similarities and differences between the SPS Agreement and EU law. In *European Commission v. France*, Case C-24/00 (February 5, 2004), the European Commission challenged France's failure to adopt legislation to allow the importation of foodstuffs manufactured and/or marketed in other Member States but which contain additives, such as vitamins, minerals, amino acids, and other nitrogenous compounds.

The court recognized that France's measure hindered the free movement of goods between Member States and was inconsistent with Article 34 of the Treaty on the Functioning of the European Union (TFEU), which prohibits measures having an effect equivalent to quantitative restrictions. France's legislation requires vitamins and nutrients to be included in an authorized list before foodstuffs fortified with those vitamins and minerals can be marketed. This requirement makes marketing of such foodstuffs more difficult and more expensive, and consequently hinders trade between the Member States.

However, the Court has held that national legislation which makes the addition of a nutrient to a foodstuff lawfully manufactured and/or marketed in other Member States subject to prior authorization is not, in principle, contrary to EU law, provided that 1) such legislation provides a readily accessible procedure that can be completed within a reasonable time enabling economic operators to have that nutrient included on the national list of authorized substances; and 2) national authorities can reject an application only if the substance at issue poses a genuine risk to public health.

The court found that the absence of a law that recognizes the legitimacy of products legally produced and marketed in other Member States was not in and of itself a violation of EU law. It found, however, that France did not process applications either as a matter of law or as the law was applied within a reasonable period or according to a procedure which was sufficiently transparent as regards to the possibility of challenging refusal to authorize before the courts. In evaluating whether France had legally refused to authorize certain foodstuffs, the court made the following findings:

European Commission v. France
Case C-24/00 (Feb. 5, 2004)

49. It must be borne in mind, first, that it is for the Member States, in the absence of harmonisation and to the extent that there is still uncertainty in the current state of scientific research, to decide on the level of protection of human health and life they wish to ensure and whether to require prior authorization for the marketing of foodstuffs, taking into account the requirements of the free movement of goods within the Community.

50. Moreover, the discretion relating to the protection of public health is particularly wide where it is shown that there is still uncertainty in the current state of scientific research as to certain substances, such as vitamins, which are not as a general rule harmful in themselves but may have special harmful effects solely if taken to excess as part of the general diet, the composition of which cannot be foreseen or monitored.

51. It follows, as is clear from paragraph 25 of this judgment, that Community law does not, in principle, preclude legislation of a Member State which prohibits, save with prior authorization, possession with a view to sale or the putting on sale of foodstuffs intended for human consumption where nutrients other than those whose addition is lawful under the said legislation have been added thereto.

52. However, in exercising their discretion relating to the protection of public health, the Member States must comply with the principle of proportionality. The means which they choose must therefore be confined to what is actually necessary to ensure the safeguarding of public health or to satisfy overriding requirements regarding, for example, consumer protection, and they must be proportional to the objective thus pursued, which could not have been attained by measures less restrictive of intra-Community trade.

53. Furthermore, since [Article 36 of the TFEU] provides for an exception, to be interpreted strictly, to the rule of free movement of goods within the Commu-

nity, it is for the national authorities which invoke it to show in each case, in the light of national nutritional habits and in the light of the results of international scientific research, that their rules are necessary to give effective protection to the interests referred to in that provision and, in particular, that the marketing of the products in question poses a real risk to public health.

54. A prohibition on the marketing of foodstuffs to which nutrients have been added must therefore be based on a detailed assessment of the risk alleged by the Member State invoking Article 36 of the [TFEU].

55. A decision to prohibit the marketing of a fortified foodstuff, which is in fact the most restrictive obstacle to trade in products lawfully manufactured and marketed in other Member States, can be adopted only if the alleged real risk for public health appears to be sufficiently established on the basis of the latest scientific data available at the date of the adoption of such decision. In such a context, the object of the risk assessment to be carried out by the Member State is to appraise the degree of probability of harmful effects on human health from the addition of certain nutrients to foodstuffs and the seriousness of those potential effects.

56. It is clear that such an assessment of the risk could reveal that scientific uncertainty persists as regards the existence or extent of real risks to human health. In such circumstances, it must be accepted that a Member State may, in accordance with the precautionary principle, take protective measures without having to wait until the existence and gravity of those risks are fully demonstrated. However, the risk assessment cannot be based on purely hypothetical considerations.

The European Court of Justice found that France had impermissibly rejected applications for confectionery and vitamin-enriched drinks. The Court accepted France's argument that it could refuse such vitamin-enriched drinks because of an absence of a nutritional need necessitating the addition of nutrients to the foodstuffs concerned, but that the "absence of such a need cannot, by itself, justify a total prohibition, on the basis of Article 36 of the TFEU, on marketing foodstuffs lawfully manufactured and/or marketed in other Member States." *European Commission v. France*, at para. 60.

In this case, the risk assessment solely relied upon by France "merely refers vaguely to the possibility of a general risk of excessive intake, without specifying the vitamins concerned, the extent to which those limits would be exceeded or the risks incurred thereby." Similarly, the scientific opinion upon which France relied concerning the addition of L-tartrate and of L-carnitine to food supplements and dietary products was not specific enough to warrant a prohibition on marketing them:

65. [The] Opinion cites digestive problems which affect 13% of the population, without specifying their nature, and mentions the absence of proof of the claims as to the usefulness or benefits of adding L-tartrate and L-carnitine, which does not amount to a detailed assessment of the effects which the addition to foodstuffs of such substances could have on public health and is not sufficient, therefore, to justify under Article 36 of the Treaty a prohibition on marketing them.

Nonetheless, the Court upheld France's ban on energy drinks such as "Red Bull," where those drinks had caffeine levels higher than those authorized in France. While France may decide at what level it wishes to ensure the protection of human life and health, it must still show why the prohibition on marketing energy drinks containing caffeine in excess of a certain limit is necessary and proportionate for public health.

France's scientific committee had found that excessive caffeine consumption posed risks to pregnant women and that the labeling of these drinks as "energy enhancing" was misleading. Moreover, the Scientific Committee on Human Nutrition gave an adverse opinion on the presence in those drinks of certain nutrients such as taurine and glucurunolactone.

The Court found that the Commission had failed to explain why these opinions were insufficient to justify a prohibition, under Article 36 of the TFEU, on marketing energy drinks with a caffeine content higher than that authorized in France. Nor had the Commission adduced evidence sufficient to call into question the French authorities' analysis as regards the dangers which those drinks pose to public health.

Questions and Discussion

1. Compare this case to the WTO cases. What similarities do you see between the SPS Agreement and EU law concerning the adoption of an SPS measure?

2. In a similar case, the European Court of Justice found that Italy's law requiring prior authorization for the marketing of food products for sportsmen and women lawfully manufactured and marketed in other Member States violated the EC Treaty's prohibition against quantitative restrictions on imports and that the authorization could not be justified on grounds of the protection of health and life of humans, animals, or plants. The Court found that Italy had not shown that the prior authorization procedure for the marketing of sports foods was justified by, and proportionate to, one of the public-interest grounds set out in Article 36 of the TFEU, namely protection of public health. Further, Italy failed to show in what way that procedure is necessary and proportionate to its objective and that less restrictive measures existed, such as notification and labeling, to prevent misleading consumers about the products at issue. European Commission v. Italy, Case C-270/02 (Feb. 5, 2004). The concept of proportionality is also used to justify non-SPS measures otherwise found to be inconsistent with EU trade laws. *See* Chapter 4, Section VI.B (pages 258–65). Is proportionality a useful, all-purpose concept for balancing trade and nontrade interests, even in the SPS context? If a risk assessment is still required prior to adoption of an SPS measure, at what point should proportionality come into play? Should we ensure that the SPS measure chosen is proportional to the scientific evidence, the appropriate level of protection desired, or the goal of protecting human, animal, or plant life or health?

Chapter 8

Subsidies and Countervailing Duties

I. Introduction

The treatment of subsidies within the WTO has generated significant interest among governments and environmental organizations, because they see subsidies as both a means to encourage environmentally beneficial activities and behavior and a contributing factor in environmentally harmful activities, depending on how they are used. For example, fisheries subsidies have helped to overcapitalize an industry that now depletes valuable fish populations. At the same time, subsidies have helped fishermen switch to less destructive gear types, including turtle excluder devices that save the lives of sea turtles. They have also made China a leader in manufacturing solar panels that will help reduce carbon dioxide emissions causing climate change. Can a global trading regime like the WTO establish rules that permit the environmentally positive subsidies but discourage the environmentally harmful ones? If so, how can the trading system distinguish "good" subsidies from "bad" subsidies? Consider a program that provides support to small-town sawmills and unemployed loggers adjusting to new restrictions on timber harvesting. This subsidies program could be considered a worthwhile social welfare program to maintain employment in small towns and to soften the blow to rural communities during economic hard times. It could also be deemed an unnecessary subsidy to an overcapitalized industry. It may well be both.

Whether or not we can identify "good" and "bad" subsidies, economists agree that subsidies in general distort markets by underpricing goods. As Professor John Jackson explains, subsidies produce three different trade related effects:

> [S]ubsidies of country A can enhance the exportability of products into an importing nation, country B. In such a case, nation B may wish to respond with countervailing duties. Second, subsidies from country A can enhance the exportation of its products to a third-country, C, where they compete with similar products that are exported from country B. In such a case, country B does not have easy recourse to a response. Its own countervailing duties are not effective. It may not wish to competitively subsidize its exports. Thus it must somehow induce the importing country, country C in this case, to respond to the subsidized imports. However, country C may be quite happy to receive such subsidized goods. Consequently, country B's grievance against country A may have to be aided by some other technique, such as recourse to an international forum like the [WTO].

> A third effect of subsidies can be to restrain imports into the subsidizing country. Thus, if country A subsidizes its bicycles even when all of those bicycles are

sold in its home market, one effect is to make it harder for other countries such as B or C to export bicycles to country A. The subsidy in this situation has become an import barrier, and economists can demonstrate that the effect is in some ways similar to a tariff. Once again, countervailing duties will not provide a remedy, since the country which is "harmed" is not receiving subsidized imports.

JOHN JACKSON, THE WORLD TRADING SYSTEM 280 (2d ed. 1997). These trade-related effects make subsidies an issue for international trade.

Professor Jackson alludes to countervailing duties as a means to counteract the trade effects of subsidies. Countervailing duties are special tariff surcharges imposed by the importing country on the subsidized products, calibrated to offset the price effect of the subsidy. The WTO Agreement on Subsidies and Countervailing Measures (SCM Agreement) establishes the rules for determining whether a particular government program constitutes a "subsidy," and the specific findings that an importing country must make with respect to the trade effects of a subsidy before it may levy countervailing duties or take other countermeasures in response to a subsidy. The process for such national determinations is quite elaborate. In the United States, for example, an affected industry can petition for countervailing duties to the International Trade Administration (ITA) of the U.S. Department of Commerce. The ITA conducts a preliminary investigation to determine if the foreign goods are benefiting from a subsidy as defined by WTO law, what the value of that benefit is, and whether the U.S. industry appears to be suffering "material injury" because of the presence of the subsidized goods in the U.S. market. If the ITA's preliminary investigation leads to affirmative findings on these points, the matter is referred to the bipartisan International Trade Commission (ITC). ITC economists and analysts conduct a more thorough investigation into the economic effect of the subsidy and whether the U.S. industry has been materially injured by competition from the subsidized imports (as opposed to other conditions in the marketplace). If the ITC finds material injury attributable to the subsidized imports, then the case goes back to the ITA for the final calculation of the countervailing duty to be applied to the imports to offset the price effect of the subsidy in the U.S. market. The business of initiating claims for countervailing duties and then providing the market evidence and economic analysis to support (or rebut) both the claim that there is a subsidy and that the U.S. industry is being materially injured by the subsidized imports provides substantial work for trade lawyers and economic consultants.

Despite agreement among economists that subsidies distort markets, almost every WTO member continues to use subsidies as a tool of national economic policy, specifically including subsidies for the production of natural resources and agricultural products. With respect to natural resource subsidies, underpricing of natural resources may cause extensive environmental damage by encouraging the overuse of natural resources. The United States and Canada battled for nearly three decades as to whether Canada's low fees for access to softwood timber constitute a subsidy and, if so, what countervailing duties the United States could assess on wood products imported from Canada.

Agricultural subsidies raise special issues. For example, the United States government subsidizes irrigation water at 85 to 90 percent of its value, thereby not only affecting the prices for agricultural products, but also increasing soil salinity, contaminating wetlands, and harming fish and bird populations. Robert Repetto, *Complementarities between Trade and Environment Policies*, in TRADE AND THE ENVIRONMENT: LAW, ECONOMICS, AND POLICY 244 (Durwood Zaelke et al. eds., 1993). Jessica Tuchman Mathews has cogently summarized the cascade of problems associated with agricultural subsidies that:

encourage farmers in the developed countries to overproduce at unnecessary environmental cost. Governments then dump the surpluses on the international market, forcing down prices. This in turn reduces production by farmers in developing countries whose crops are taxed, not subsidized, by their governments. To partially make up for low prices, these governments heavily subsidize irrigation, pesticides, and fertilizer, causing their overuse and consequent water pollution, health problems, and land degradation.

Jessica Tuchman Mathews, *A Retreat on Trade?*, WASH. POST, Jan. 17, 1992, at A21.

The atmosphere is particularly charged with respect to agricultural subsidies due to the expiration of the Agriculture Agreement's "peace clause," which exempted from countervailing duties certain support measures that comply with the Agriculture Agreement. Fights over agricultural subsidies have stalled the Doha Development Round negotiations since 2003, with the United States and other developed country members refusing to reduce agricultural subsidies that often depress global prices and create barriers to agricultural imports from developing countries. At the same time, developing countries are unwilling to curtail their own agricultural subsidies that burden South-South trade.

Many countries have targeted U.S. subsidies to cotton farmers—about $3 billion annually—for particular scorn. Instead of committing to remove these subsidies to benefit poor African farmers who grow cotton more cheaply than U.S. producers, the United States offered to study cotton and suggested that African farmers grow something else. Elizabeth Becker, *U.S. Subsidizes Companies to Buy Subsidized Cotton*, N.Y. TIMES, Nov. 4, 2003, at C1. Brazil and other countries successfully challenged these U.S. price supports to cotton producers as a subsidy, but the United States has failed so far to substantially alter its cotton subsidies. This chapter examines key issues and WTO rulings in this trade dispute. Appellate Body Report, WT/DS267/AB/R (adopted March 21, 2005); United States-Subsidies on Upland Cotton Recourse to Article 21.5 of the DSU by Brazil, WT/DS267/AB/RW (adopted June 20, 2008) (concluding that the United States remains in noncompliance with respect to a number of cotton subsidies); United States-Subsidies on Upland Cotton Recourse to Arbitration by the United States under Article 22.6 of the DSU and Article 4.11 of the *SCM Agreement*, WT/DS267/ARB/1 (Aug. 31, 2009) (allowing Brazil to request authorization from the DSB to suspend concessions with the United States, because the United States had not repealed prohibited cotton subsidies, which may run as high as $1 billion per year).

Before you read the following sections on the WTO's rules for restraining subsidies, consider the following:

- What is a subsidy? Is it any kind of government grant of funds? Could it include the failure of the government to recoup debt? The failure to enact or enforce environmental law could allow domestic producers to produce goods more cheaply and have the effect of keeping imported goods from countries that have substantial environmental rules. Is the lack of environmental rules a subsidy?

- In the late 1990s, the United States exempted two logging programs from the requirements of the Endangered Species Act and other environmental laws. All other industries and private individuals remained subject to these laws. Should this constitute a subsidy?

- For which subsidies should the WTO allow the imposition of countervailing duties? If the WTO restrains subsidies for unsustainable extraction of natural resources because they distort trade, should it not also restrain subsidies that pay for pollution control technology or promote green technologies if they too distort trade?

- How should WTO members penalize subsidies? Should they increase tariffs on subsidized products? Should they be allowed to increase tariffs on nonsubsidized products?

II. The Definition of "Subsidy"

A. General Considerations

At the most basic level, a subsidy is a grant or gift of money. In economic and international trade terms, however, "subsidy" carries a more specific meaning relating to a certain kind of benefit provided by the government. As John Jackson explains below, governments have several choices in how they define "subsidy." They could define it as a government financial contribution, as a benefit conferred by the government regardless of whether the government provided some financial contribution, or based on harm to the international trading system.

At the outset, it is important to define different types of subsidies, because trade law has traditionally made distinctions based on these classifications. *Export subsidies* are those subsidies granted only when products are exported or based on a certain number of products exported. *Domestic* or *production subsidies* are subsidies granted regardless of whether the product is exported. Export subsidies have always been considered to have a greater impact on trade than domestic subsidies, because they directly affect the price of traded goods.

John Jackson, *The World Trading System*
293–96 (2d ed. 1997)

The definition of "subsidy" has always perplexed policymakers, partly because the word "subsidy" can mean so many things and be so generic. If the term "subsidy" is defined in a rather broad way, as is sometimes the case, it can include an enormous range of government activities. For example, if an economic definition of subsidy contends that it is deemed to mean a benefit conferred on a firm or product by action of a government, then the concept of subsidy could include such typical and universal governmental activities as providing fire and police protection, roads, and even schools or education. Highly effective fire and police protection would obviously reduce the insurance costs of producing firms, and thus reduce part of their costs of production. Likewise, other types of societal infrastructure can reduce the costs which are "internalized" in the accounting of a firm evaluating the price of its goods. The problem is that if such a broad definition were used, and international rules permitted governments to respond with countervailing duties against such subsidies, the whole system of post-World War II GATT liberal trade (including the reduction in tariffs) would be undermined: governments would be able to impose many countervailing duties, since virtually every product would benefit from these kinds of governmental assistance.

Therefore, the problem becomes one of defining "subsidy" in such a way as to avoid these broad, damaging effects on international trade. * * *

A basic approach is to recognize that there is a vast universe of governmental activity which can be called "subsidy" under broad definitions, but to recognize that the international system should not be concerned about all of the contents of this vast universe. Rather, the international system should be trying to define a subset of a certain type of "subsidy" with which it will be concerned.

Behind all this it must be recognized that subsidies are an exceedingly important, even crucial, tool of national governments in order to act in their sovereign capacities to promote legitimate governmental policies to serve their constituents. There is no way that a government can "give up subsidies" under any broad definition of the term "subsidies." One needs only to recall a variety of different kinds of subsidies to realize this, including: aid to the poor, aid for technological development, special aids for education, aid to handicapped persons, aid to disadvantaged groups and regions, aid to offset certain disadvantages that have been created by other government policies, national security policies, etc.

Although many subsidies, particularly the so called production or general subsidies, have legitimate government policies behind them, as implemented these subsidies may transgress on foreign governments' legitimate aspirations on behalf of their own producing interests. Thus we may have a clash of competing policy goals: on the one hand, governments have legitimate reasons for implementing subsidies; on the other hand, importing nations have legitimate reasons for being concerned about the importation of subsidized goods when those goods cause distress to their own industries. The basic problem is how to balance these competing interests. It is in this connection that the material injury test is crucial: it acts as a sort of "mediating principle" to help governments accommodate these diametrically opposed competing interests. If the subsidized goods are not harming or causing material injury in the importing country, then why bother with any response? On the other hand, if the subsidized imports create sufficient distress in the importing country to rise to some threshold level of "material injury," or "serious prejudice," perhaps at that point a response such as a countervailing duty is justified. * * *

With these caveats in mind, we can turn to some of the concepts that are currently being used to constrain the breadth of a definition of "subsidy," and also think a bit about other concepts that could be likewise used. * * *

[A]n initial question is sometimes asked by policymakers, namely: does the subsidy impose a cost on the granting government, and/or a benefit on the production of a particular product which moves in international trade? According to one approach, in order for a subsidy to be brought under the GATT rules, it must be established that the government has incurred a cost. According to a different viewpoint (that prevailing in the United States administration), "cost" is not the relevant consideration. Instead, the key question is whether the subsidy activity has conferred a benefit on a firm, compared to what that firm would receive under normal market conditions without the government intervention.

An example is useful to illustrate this difference in approach. Suppose that the government is prepared to make special loans to a particular industry sector at a cost of 8 percent interest. Suppose, at the same time, the government can borrow its own funds at a cost of about 6 percent. On the other hand, suppose that the normal private-market lending would require an interest rate of 10 percent. In this situation, it might be argued that there has been no cost to the government for its 8 percent loans, since the government receives its funds for 6 percent. It will be further noted that the recipient firm is receiving a benefit because it obtains the loan at 8 percent, instead of the market rate of 10 percent. Under United States administration of its countervailing duty law, it is very clear that the benefit approach is being used and that the loan would be considered a "subsidy." Arguably, the U.S. approach is the correct one, if one of the basic policies of the international discipline on subsidies is to prevent "distortions." The benefit conferred on the firm by a lower interest rate than that of the market induces that firm to produce goods that it might not otherwise produce, and induces a certain allocation of resources that is not "fine tuned" to economic principles and to the needs of society or the world.

Of course, if one wanted to push the frontiers of this concept, it would be possible to note that when the government lends at 8 percent (even though it borrows at 6 percent), it has incurred an "opportunity cost" by giving up a portion of the interest it *could* obtain. If the "cost approach" includes this opportunity cost, then we see the opposing approaches converge. Perhaps this is another reason why the benefit approach seems to be preferable.

Questions and Discussion

1. For purposes of defining a subsidy, what is the practical difference between whether the government has incurred a cost or has conferred a benefit? Which definition is narrower? Which definition might reach typical natural resource subsidies, such as underpriced water or timber?

2. Jackson mentions a number of concepts, including countervailing duties (the domestic remedy to offset the impacts of a subsidy) and material injury (the test to determine whether a domestic industry has been harmed and countervailing duties may be imposed). These issues are discussed later in this chapter.

B. The SCM Agreement's Definition of Subsidy

As Jackson notes above, the challenge for the trading regime is to balance legitimate government interests to promote public welfare with the goal of avoiding the damaging effects of subsidies on international trade. The GATT and the GATT's 1979 Subsidies Code made initial efforts to restrain the use of subsidies. Because neither agreement defined "subsidy" and the language of some obligations was "relatively tortured and ambiguous," it is no surprise that many governments sought a new agreement as part of the Uruguay Round negotiations. Jackson, The World Trading System, at 189.

The WTO Agreement on Subsidies and Countervailing Measures (SCM Agreement) sets out to find that balance between domestic interests and international trade concerns. As seen below, it defines subsidy with a three-tiered approach. First, it defines subsidy in terms of the "benefit conferred" and "financial contribution" granted. Second, it distinguishes between general and specific subsidies. Third, it classifies subsidies according to their acceptability, with certain subsidies, such as export subsidies, considered "prohibited" while "actionable" subsidies may be subject to countervailing duties or countermeasures if the importing country finds that they distort trade sufficiently to injure competing domestic producers.

WTO Agreement on Subsidies and Countervailing Measures
Article 1 — Definition of a Subsidy

1.1 For the purpose of this Agreement, a subsidy shall be deemed to exist if:

(a)(1) there is a financial contribution by a government or any public body within the territory of a Member (referred to in this Agreement as "government"), i.e. where:

(i) a government practice involves a direct transfer of funds (e.g. grants, loans, and equity infusion), potential direct transfers of funds or liabilities (e.g. loan guarantees);

(ii) government revenue that is otherwise due is foregone or not collected (e.g. fiscal incentives such as tax credits);[1]

(iii) a government provides goods or services other than general infrastructure, or purchases goods;

(iv) a government makes payments to a funding mechanism, or entrusts or directs a private body to carry out one or more of the type of functions illustrated in (i) to (iii) above which would normally be vested in the government and the practice, in no real sense, differs from practices normally followed by governments;

or

(a)(2) there is any form of income or price support in the sense of Article XVI of GATT 1994;

and

(b) a benefit is thereby conferred.

Article 2 — Specificity

2.1 In order to determine whether a subsidy, as defined in paragraph 1 of Article 1, is specific to an enterprise or industry or group of enterprises or industries (referred to in this Agreement as "certain enterprises") within the jurisdiction of the granting authority, the following principles shall apply:

(a) Where the granting authority, or the legislation pursuant to which the granting authority operates, explicitly limits access to a subsidy to certain enterprises, such subsidy shall be specific.

(b) Where the granting authority, or the legislation pursuant to which the granting authority operates, establishes objective criteria or conditions[2] gov-

---

1. In accordance with the provisions of Article XVI of GATT 1994 (Note to Article XVI) and the provisions of Annexes I through III of this Agreement, the exemption of an exported product from duties or taxes borne by the like product when destined for domestic consumption, or the remission of such duties or taxes in amounts not in excess of those which have accrued, shall not be deemed to be a subsidy.

2. Objective criteria or conditions, as used herein, mean criteria or conditions which are neutral, which do not favour certain enterprises over others, and which are economic in nature and horizontal in application, such as number of employees or size of enterprise.

erning the eligibility for, and the amount of, a subsidy, specificity shall not exist, provided that the eligibility is automatic and that such criteria and conditions are strictly adhered to. The criteria or conditions must be clearly spelled out in law, regulation, or other official document, so as to be capable of verification.

(c) If, notwithstanding any appearance of non-specificity resulting from the application of the principles laid down in subparagraphs (a) and (b), there are reasons to believe that the subsidy may in fact be specific, other factors may be considered. Such factors are: use of a subsidy programme by a limited number of certain enterprises, predominant use by certain enterprises, the granting of disproportionately large amounts of subsidy to certain enterprises, and the manner in which discretion has been exercised by the granting authority in the decision to grant a subsidy.[3] In applying this subparagraph, account shall be taken of the extent of diversification of economic activities within the jurisdiction of the granting authority, as well as of the length of time during which the subsidy programme has been in operation.

2.2 A subsidy which is limited to certain enterprises located within a designated geographical region within the jurisdiction of the granting authority shall be specific. It is understood that the setting or change of generally applicable tax rates by all levels of government entitled to do so shall not be deemed to be a specific subsidy for the purposes of this Agreement.

2.3 Any subsidy falling under the provisions of Article 3 [subsidies contingent on export performance or use of domestic over imported goods] shall be deemed to be specific.

2.4 Any determination of specificity under the provisions of this Article shall be clearly substantiated on the basis of positive evidence.

---

1. "Financial Contribution" and "Benefit Conferred"

To define "subsidy," the SCM Agreement combines elements of both financial contribution and benefit conferred.

a. Financial Contribution

Article 1.1(a) of the SCM Agreement defines a subsidy, in part, as a financial contribution by a government or public body or an income or price support. The negotiating history of the SCM Agreement makes plain that defining "subsidy" to include a "financial contribution" was intended specifically "to prevent the countervailing of *benefits* from any sort of (formal, enforceable) government measures, by restricting to a finite list the *kinds* of government measures that would, if they conferred benefits, constitute subsidies." United States-Measures Treating Exports Restraints as Subsidies, Panel Report, WT/DS194/R, paras. 8.65, 8.73 (adopted Aug. 23, 2001) (emphasis in original). That finite list is included in subparagraphs (i)–(iii) of Article 1.1(a)(1). Under subparagraphs (i)–(iii), the government acting on its own behalf is effecting that transfer by directly providing something of value—either money, goods, or services—to a private entity. Sub-

---

3. In this regard, in particular, information on the frequency with which applications for a subsidy are refused or approved and the reasons for such decisions shall be considered.

paragraph (iv) ensures that the same kinds of government transfers of economic resources, when delegated to a private entity, do not escape the requirements of the SCM Agreement.

Each of these subparagraphs has been subject to interpretation by WTO panels and the Appellate Body, although only subparagraph (iii) has been subject to a trade–environment dispute. Both in and outside the natural resources context, the Appellate Body has embraced a broad definition of financial contribution. For example, one panel concluded that certain payments made in the form of bonds constituted direct transfers of funds under subparagraph (i). Brazil-Export Financing Programme for Aircraft: Second Recourse by Canada to Article 21.5 of the DSU, Panel Report, WT/DS46/RW2, para. 5.22 (adopted Aug. 23, 2001) (hereinafter Brazil-Aircraft).

Under subparagraph (ii) — "government revenue that is otherwise due is foregone or not collected" — the Appellate Body has concluded that a "financial contribution" does not arise simply because a government does not raise revenue when it could have done so. Instead, the Appellate Body stated that the phrase "otherwise due" implies some comparison:

> [T]he "*foregoing*" of revenue "*otherwise* due" implies that less revenue has been raised by the government than would have been raised in a different situation, or, that is, "otherwise." Moreover, the word "foregone" suggests that the government has given up an entitlement to raise revenue that it could "otherwise" have raised. This cannot, however, be an entitlement in the abstract, because governments, in theory, could tax *all* revenues. There must, therefore, be some defined, normative benchmark against which a comparison can be made between the revenue actually raised and the revenue that would have been raised "otherwise." We, therefore, agree with the Panel that the term "otherwise due" implies some kind of comparison between the revenues due under the contested measure and revenues that would be due in some other situation. We also agree with the Panel that the basis of comparison must be the tax rules applied by the Member in question.... What is "otherwise due," therefore, depends on the rules of taxation that each Member, by its own choice, establishes for itself.

United States-Tax Treatment for Foreign Sales Corporations, Appellate Body Report, WT/DS108/AB/R, para. 90 (adopted March 20, 2000) (emphasis in original); *see also* United States-Tax Treatment for Foreign Sales Corporations: Recourse to Article 21.5 of the DSU, Appellate Body Report, WT/DS108/AB/R, paras. 88–92 (adopted Jan. 29, 2002). The Appellate Body also found that, in most cases, the term "otherwise due" establishes a "but for" test. That is, the appropriate basis of comparison for determining whether revenues are "otherwise due" is "the situation that would prevail but for the measures in question." *Id.* at para. 91. The Appellate Body cautioned, however, that the "but for" test may not work all the time and that other methods may be needed.

In the discussion of the *Softwood Lumber* dispute in Subsection 3 below (pages 545–58), we ask whether below-cost timber sales constitute a financial contribution "where a government provides goods or services" within the meaning of Article 1.1(a)(1)(iii).

---

b. Benefit Conferred

A financial contribution alone does not constitute a "subsidy." That financial contribution must also confer a benefit to the recipient. While the SCM Agreement does not expressly define "benefit conferred," the Appellate Body has made clear that the beneficiary must "in fact receive[] something," such as an advantage. It is not merely a "cost to the government," which is covered by the "financial contribution" component of Article 1. Rather, the word "benefit" "is concerned with the 'benefit to the recipient' and not with the 'cost to government.'" Canada-Measures Affecting Exports of Civilian Aircraft, Appellate Body Report, WT/DS70/AB/R, para. 155 (adopted August 20, 1999) (hereinafter Canada-Aircraft). The Appellate Body further stated that the word "benefit":

> [I]mplies some kind of comparison. This must be so, for there can be no "benefit" to the recipient unless the "financial contribution" makes the recipient "better off" than it would otherwise have been, absent that contribution. In our view, the marketplace provides an appropriate basis for comparison in determining whether a "benefit" has been "conferred," because the trade-distorting potential of a "financial contribution" can be identified by determining whether the recipient has received a "financial contribution" on terms more favourable than those available to the recipient in the market.

Id. at para. 157. *See also* United States-Imposition of Countervailing Duties on Certain Hot-Rolled Lead and Bismuth Carbon Steel Products Originating in the United Kingdom, Appellate Body Report, WT/DS138/AB/R, paras. 57–58 (adopted June 7, 2000).

Moreover, a given law may constitute a "subsidy" even if it does not always confer a benefit on a recipient. So long as a law confers a benefit in *some* situations, the law confers a benefit within the meaning of the SCM Agreement. Brazil-Aircraft (Article 21.5-Canada II), Panel Report, at paras. 5.32 and 5.37.

Panels and the Appellate Body have declared that there is a distinction between a financial benefit and a benefit conferred. For example, the government may provide a financial contribution that does not confer a benefit over what is available on the market. They have also stated that there is a distinction between the existence of a benefit and its calculation. Nonetheless, they ultimately have been using methods for calculating a benefit found in Article 14 of the SCM Agreement to identify the existence of a benefit. *See, e.g.*, European Communities-Countervailing Duty on Dynamic Random Access Memory Chips from Korea, Panel Report, WT/DS299/R (adopted Aug. 3, 2005). Article 14 establishes "guidelines" for calculating benefits conferred with respect to equity investments, loans, loan guarantees, the provision of goods or services by a government, and the purchase of goods by a government. The guidelines assess, for example, whether a company receives a government loan at below commercial rates or whether the government provides goods or services "for less than adequate remuneration." Generally speaking, a "benefit" arises under each guideline if the recipient has received a "financial contribution" on terms more favourable than those available to the recipient in the market. This is sometimes referred to as the private-investor test. We will see in Section II.B.3.a the heavy reliance the Appellate Body in *Softwood Lumber* placed on these guidelines to define a benefit conferred for the provision of goods or services.

Questions and Discussion

1. According to the Appellate Body, a subsidy is "granted" "when the unconditional legal right of the beneficiary to receive the payments has arisen, even if the payments themselves have not yet occurred." In this case, *Brazil-Aircraft*, the export subsidies were not granted when the letter of commitment to provide the subsidy was issued, because

the export sales contract had not yet been concluded at that time and the export shipments had not yet occurred. However, the payments would be considered "granted" "when all the legal conditions have been fulfilled that entitle the beneficiary to receive the subsidies." Brazil-Export Financing Programme for Aircraft, Appellate Body Report, WT/DS46/AB/R, para. 158 (August 20, 1999).

2. The SCM Agreement definition of a subsidy, and the Appellate Body's interpretation of it, appears to eliminate the possibility that the failure to enforce or implement adequate environmental legislation could be deemed a subsidy. This issue will be taken up in more detail in Section IV.A (pages 575–82).

---

2. "Specificity"

In addition to defining "subsidy," the SCM Agreement also introduces a key screening device to limit the Agreement's applicability—the concept of "specificity." If the SCM Agreement disciplined every financial contribution or income support that "confers a benefit," it would quickly restrain government efforts to fund roads, schools, police and fire protection, and other essential components of a country's basic infrastructure. The WTO would no doubt lose political support as well.

As a result, Article 1.2 of the SCM Agreement limits its applicability by distinguishing subsidies of general applicability from those that are "specific." To be "specific," the subsidy must be conferred on an identifiable enterprise or group of enterprises. Thus, subsidies that are generally available to the public, such as public education and fire protection, are not subject to trade discipline and cannot be countervailed. From an economic perspective, subsidies that are generally available to all sectors of society do not distort trade, or at least they do not distort trade to the same extent as "specific" subsidies.

The SCM Agreement presumes nonspecificity: Article 2.4 requires clear substantiation of specificity based on positive evidence. Nevertheless, Article 2.1(a) allows that presumption to be rebutted by a showing of *de jure* specificity, that the law expressly limits access to the subsidy to certain enterprises.

The specificity test becomes much more difficult to apply where the subsidy is facially neutral and theoretically generally available but in reality only a few are able to take advantage of it. As discussed in greater detail in the next subsection in the context of the *Softwood Lumber* dispute, Canadian provinces offer "stumpage," the right to remove trees from government property, to anyone. One of the questions underlying that dispute is whether such an offer is really generally available when only a limited number of timber companies can actually take advantage of this offer.

Article 2.1(c) of the SCM Agreement embraces this notion of *de facto* specificity by declaring that, notwithstanding the appearance of nonspecificity, a subsidy may be specific if "there are reasons to believe that the subsidy may in fact be specific." *De facto* specificity may be found where: 1) the actual recipients are limited in number; 2) an enterprise or industry is a predominant user of the subsidy; 3) certain enterprises receive a disproportionately large amount of the subsidy; and 4) the manner in which the granting authority exercises discretion to grant a subsidy indicates that an enterprise or industry is "favored over others." These four factors have their origins in U.S. subsidies law. *See* Cabot Corp. v. United States, 620 F. Supp. 722 (Ct. Int'l Trade 1985).

Unfortunately, the difficulties of implementing the *de facto* specificity test are not abstract: all the factors raise difficult questions of interpretation. For example, if a subsidy is available to any industry, but that country has only one dominant industry, should that subsidy be deemed specific, because the actual recipients are limited in number or because one industry would be the predominant user? Article 2:1(c) says that the level of economic diversification should be taken into account. Does that help answer the preceding question? Is something which is available to the entire agricultural products sector non-specific because there are a large number of agricultural subsectors (grains, beef, fruits, etc.)?

In the United States, the Department of Commerce treats subsidies limited to the "agricultural sector" or to "small- and medium-sized businesses" as "nonspecific." 19 C.F.R. § 351.502(d)-(e). *See also* PPG Industries v. United States, 928 F.2d 1568 (Fed. Cir. 1991) (rejecting an argument that "energy-intensive" industries should be considered a "specific" category benefitting from subsidized natural gas prices). When Brazil challenged several U.S. cotton subsidies, a WTO Panel had the opportunity to decide whether the components of the agricultural sector were "specific."

United States-Subsidies on Upland Cotton
Panel Report, WT/DS267/R (Mar. 21, 2005)

7.1142 [A]n industry, or group of "industries," may be generally referred to by the type of products they produce. To us, the concept of an "industry" relates to producers of certain products. The breadth of this concept of "industry" may depend on several factors in a given case. At some point that is not made precise in the text of the agreement, and which may modulate according to the particular circumstances of a given case, a subsidy would cease to be specific because it is sufficiently broadly available throughout an economy as not to benefit a particular limited group of producers of certain products. The plain words of Article 2.1 indicate that specificity is a general concept, and the breadth or narrowness of specificity is not susceptible to rigid quantitative definition. Whether a subsidy is specific can only be assessed on a case-by-case basis.

7.1143 We see merit in the shared view of the parties that the concept of "specificity" in Article 2 of the SCM Agreement serves to acknowledge that some subsidies are broadly available and widely used throughout an economy and are therefore not subject to the Agreement's subsidy disciplines. The footnote to Article 2.1 defines the nature of "objective criteria or conditions" which, if used to determine eligibility, would preclude an affirmative conclusion of specificity. Such criteria are "neutral, which do not favour certain enterprises over others, and which are economic in nature and horizontal in application, such as number of employees or size of enterprise."

7.1144 Furthermore, the concept of specificity in Article 2 of the SCM Agreement is germane to the disciplines imposed by the SCM Agreement. The SCM Agreement is an agreement on trade in goods, in Annex 1A of the WTO Agreement. By its own terms, subject to considerations reflected in the text of some of its provisions, it applies in respect of *all* goods. The concept of specificity must be considered within the legal framework and frame of reference of that agreement as a whole. * * *

7.1146 [A] textual analysis of "the legislation pursuant to which the granting authority operates," to discern whether or not it "explicitly limits access to a subsidy to certain enterprises" leads us to conclude that [certain cotton] subsidies are "specific" within the meaning of Article 2.1(a).

7.1147 Certain of the measures at issue were or are available specifically in respect of upland cotton: user marketing (Step 2) payments depend on the domestic use or export of upland cotton. Other products or industries are not eligible for the subsidy. Cottonseed payments went to first handlers, while also, to some extent, benefiting producers of upland cotton. We believe that a subsidy that is limited to a small proportion of industries, such as those producing one or two individual United States products would be limited and thus "specific" within the meaning of Article 2 of the SCM Agreement. These subsidies are "specific" as they are not even available in respect of a number of commodities.

7.1148 Other measures before us pertain to a restricted number of agricultural products, but are not widely or generally available in respect of all agricultural production, let alone the entire universe of United States production of goods. These measures include the marketing loan programme payments. They also include the measures available in respect of upland cotton as part of a restricted basket of agricultural commodities. These are the four types of domestic support which permit production flexibility ... that were or are provided in respect of certain agricultural production in a base period which satisfies certain eligibility criteria. These criteria have the effect of limiting eligibility to a subset of basic agricultural products, including upland cotton or certain other programme crops. We therefore find that these subsidies are "specific" within the meaning of Article 2. The fact that some of the subsidies go to farmers who may produce different commodities, or, in theory, may not produce a given commodity does not mean, by some process of reverse reasoning, that the specificity that is apparent from the face of the grant instrument no longer exists.

7.1149 The United States disagrees with Brazil's allegation that crop insurance subsidies are "specific."

7.1150 Crop insurance subsidies are, generally, available for most crops but they are not generally available in respect of the entire agricultural sector in all areas. Each insurance plan is available for a defined list of crops to which the FCIC determines that it is adapted. The proportion of the premium borne by the FCIC [Federal Crop Insurance Corporation] is set out in each plan. The major plan type (actual production history) is available for approximately 100 agricultural commodities, and specifies upland cotton as one of them. The other four plan types (group risk, crop revenue coverage, income protection and revenue assurance) are available only for a limited number of eight commodities or less and they each specify upland cotton as one of them. Certain sample policy provisions specify "cotton." There are no subsidized crop insurance policies on the record available to all agricultural producers. They are therefore, in fact, not even generally available to the industry which can be categorized as the agricultural industry.

7.1151 In our view, the industry represented by a portion of United States agricultural production that is growing and producing certain agricultural crops (and certain livestock in certain regions under restricted conditions) is a sufficiently discrete segment of the United States economy in order to qualify as "specific" within the meaning of Article 2 of the SCM Agreement.

Questions and Discussion

1. Note that Article 2.3 makes *all* subsidies contingent on export performance or use of domestic over imported goods "specific." Why?

2. John Jackson advises that:

> the issue is not so much an abstract one of what is or is not "specific," but is one that must be understood as an administrative tool which can assist even low-level officials to determine "actionability." ... National government administrators need some leeway in making these determinations, which will allow them to provide some guideposts for lower-level officials. Otherwise, the processes become so expensive that they themselves are "non-tariff barriers" to liberal world trade.

JACKSON, THE WORLD TRADING SYSTEM, at 298. Does the definition of specificity in the SCM Agreement and its interpretation in *US-Cotton* provide enough leeway for administrators to avoid lengthy and expensive determinations of whether or not a subsidy is specific? Consider the following questions:

- What percentage of the subsidy must the industry receive to be the "predominant" user of the subsidy? Is 50.01 percent the cut off?

- How does one determine whether the government exercises discretion in the allocation of a resource in a manner that in fact limits the resource's availability to a specific industry or group of industries? At least one commentator believes that the "government discretion" factor in Article 2.1(c) could be interpreted to effectively eliminate the requirement of specificity with respect to government-owned natural resources, because a government must be able to use discretion in the allocation of natural resources. Christian G. Yoder, *The Canadian Forest Products Industry and U.S. Trade Laws*, RESOURCES: NEWSLETTER CAN. INST. RESOURCES L. No. 17, at 2 (Winter 1987). Others contend that this provision calls for an inquiry into the degree of government discretion to favor a group of enterprises. In this regard, footnote 3 of the SCM Agreement provides that the frequency with which applications for a subsidy are refused or approved and the reasons for such decisions must be considered in determining whether the use of discretion establishes specificity. Thus, "if government officials exercise discretion to increase the subsidy allocation to the industry under investigation, a finding of specificity is appropriate." John A. Ragosta, *Natural Resource Subsidies and the Free Trade Agreement: Economic Justice and the Need for Subsidy Discipline*, 24 GEO. WASH. J. INT'L L. & ECON. 255, 279 (1990).

- Is the ambiguity embedded in these key phrases apt to give administrators the discretion to make specificity determinations easily or will it encourage claims that certain subsidies are specific? Should the SCM Agreement define specificity less ambiguously? If yes, how would you define it?

3. Panels have found measures to violate Article III's national treatment obligation if they change the "conditions of competition." Rather than employ a vague specificity test, should the SCM Agreement ask whether a subsidy changes the conditions of competition between domestic and foreign producers or distorts the international market? Under such a scheme, export subsidies would not be *per se* prohibited subsidies. Instead, the question would be whether export and other subsidies actually distort market conditions. What are the costs and benefits of such a scheme? Or should export subsidies be seen as more akin to the *per se* determination under GATT Article III:2, first sentence, that tax-

ation of imported goods "in excess of" the taxation of like domestic goods violates national treatment?

---

3. *"Subsidy" in Context: The* Softwood Lumber *Dispute*

The dispute between the United States and Canada over softwood lumber is perhaps the most acrimonious trade dispute on record. The dispute has led to multiple opinions from the U.S. Department of Commerce, a U.S.-Canada Free Trade Agreement panel, a GATT panel, a special NAFTA panel, a NAFTA investment panel, and the WTO's DSB.

In Canada, timber companies pay a "stumpage fee," a fee based on the volume of timber cut on "crown" lands, to the provincial government. Arguing that stumpage fees were set well below fair market value, the U.S. Coalition for Fair Canadian Lumber Imports (U.S. Coalition) initiated a trade dispute in 1982 by bringing a countervailing duty claim (*Lumber I*). In 1983, the Department of Commerce ruled against the U.S. Coalition, holding that the subsidy was generally available, nonpreferential, and thus noncountervailable. Certain Softwood Lumber Products from Canada 48 Fed. Reg. 24,159 (May 31, 1983). Based on a change in the law regarding interpretation of subsidies and armed with better factual information concerning the use and value of timber in Canada, the U.S. Coalition initiated another countervailing duty case in 1986 (*Lumber II*). This time, the Department of Commerce made a preliminary determination that the low stumpage fees constituted a subsidy and were specific. Certain Softwood Lumber Products from Canada, 51 Fed. Reg. 37,453 (Oct. 22 1986). It instituted a 15 percent countervailing duty against Canadian lumber imports. Just before the Department's deadline for making a final determination on the amount of the duty, the parties settled the dispute, with Canada agreeing to collect a 15 percent charge on exports of softwood lumber to the United States. Memorandum of Understanding [MoU] on Trade in Softwood Lumber, Dec. 30, 1986, United-States-Canada (as amended Oct. 31, 1990).

The dispute resumed in October 1991, when Canada terminated that 1986 MoU. The United States responded by picking up where it left off: it imposed a bonding requirement of 15 percent of the value of Canadian softwood lumber exported after the MoU was terminated and resumed the countervailing duty investigations that had been suspended by the MoU. However, a GATT Panel found that Canada's termination of the MoU did not meet the requirements of the Subsidies Code for resuming a suspended investigation, and ruled that the United States was not justified in imposing duties without a new investigation. United States-Measures Affecting Imports of Softwood Lumber from Canada, GATT Panel Report, SCM/162, B.I.S.D., 40th Supp. 358, 480–86, paras. 308–25 (1993) (adopted Oct. 27–28, 1993).

Subsequently, the Department of Commerce determined that a Canadian export restriction on raw logs, which effectively reduced the price of raw logs to Canadian lumber mills, was an actionable subsidy to those mills. A binational panel constituted under Chapter 19 of the U.S.-Canada Free Trade Agreement accepted the U.S.'s definition of "subsidy" but, in a second appeal, failed to find that the subsidy was specific. In re Certain Softwood Lumber Products from Canada, No. ECC-94-1904-01 USA; 1993 FTAPD LEXIS 10 (Sept. 17, 1993); 1993 FTAPD LEXIS 15 (Dec. 17, 1993); Extraordinary Challenge Committee, Panel No. ECC-94-1904-01 USA, 1994 FTAPD LEXIS 11 (Aug. 3, 1994). As a result, the countervailing duty order was dismissed. Certain Softwood Lumber Products from Canada, 59 Fed. Reg. 42,029 (Aug. 16, 1994) (rev. countervailing duty order).

The United States and Canada then agreed to the Softwood Lumber Agreement which required Canada to set fees for exporting softwood lumber, although it exempted certain provinces from those export fees. Softwood Lumber Agreement, May 29, 1996, *reprinted in* 35 I.L.M. 1195 (1996). Pope & Talbot, a U.S. lumber company operating in British Columbia, brought a NAFTA case against Canada, alleging that Canada's implementation of the Softwood Lumber Agreement violated its investment rights under Chapter 11 of the NAFTA. Pope & Talbot, Inc. v. Canada (Notice of Arbitration), (Mar. 25, 1999), at 2, *available at* http://www.naftaclaims.com. While that aspect of Pope & Talbot's claim failed (*see* Chapter 10), it highlighted that any resolution of the subsidies question may fuel different types of trade-related challenges.

Lumber III began after the Softwood Lumber Agreement expired without renewal on April 1, 2001, and the U.S. Coalition brought another countervailing duty claim before the Department of Commerce on April 2. This time, the Department of Commerce found that Canada subsidized timber and assessed a final subsidy rate of 18.79 percent. Notice of Final Affirmative Countervailing Duty Determination and Final Negative Critical Circumstances Determination: Certain Softwood Lumber Products from Canada, 67 Fed. Reg. 15545 (April 2, 2002). Canada challenged the preliminary findings of the United States under the WTO Dispute Settlement Understanding. United States-Preliminary Determinations with Respect to Certain Softwood Lumber from Canada, Panel Report, WT/DS236/R (adopted Nov. 1, 2002). In *Lumber IV*, Canada challenged the final determination that Canada provided a subsidy to timber producers. United States-Final Countervailing Duty Determination with respect to Softwood Lumber from Canada, Appellate Body Report, WT/DS257/AB/R (adopted Feb. 17, 2004).

Throughout the dispute, several issues continued to emerge. For example, was Canada's stumpage fee even a subsidy? Within the meaning of the SCM Agreement, did Canada provide a financial contribution? Did access to timber on public land at less than market prices confer a benefit? If the underpriced stumpage constituted a subsidy, was it specific or generally available? In answering these questions, WTO Panels and the Appellate Body have greatly clarified the extent to which other types of natural resource subsidies may be actionable under the SCM Agreement.

a. Do the Stumpage Fees Constitute a "Subsidy"?

United States-Final Countervailing Duty Determination with Respect to Softwood Lumber from Canada

Appellate Body Report, WT/DS257/AB/R (Feb. 23, 2004)

[Canada argued that stumpage programs do not constitute a financial contribution through which a government "provides goods or services other than general infrastructure" within the meaning of Article 1.1(a)(1)(iii) of the SCM Agreement. Canada claimed that stumpage program did not relate to "goods" and that the provincial governments, which operate the stumpage programs, do not *provide* goods to harvesters merely by virtue of conferring, through stumpage arrangements, an intangible right to harvest.

The Appellate Body first concluded that standing timber constitutes "goods" within the meaning of Article 1.1(a)(1)(iii). After reviewing the definition of "goods" in various legal and other dictionaries, the Appellate Body concluded that the term "goods" includes a wide range of property, including "items that are tangible and capable of being possessed." In addition, after reviewing the meaning of "goods" in French and Spanish, the other working languages of the WTO, it found that "goods" could include immovable property, and that the definitions corresponded more closely to "property or possessions" generally. As such, it held that "goods" "should not be read so as to exclude tangible items of property, like trees, that are severable from land."

The Appellate Body also rejected Canada's argument that specific trees are not "identified" in stumpage contracts and therefore are not "goods," because stumpage contracts concern a specified area of land containing a predictable quantity of timber that may be harvested. Harvesters pay a volumetric "stumpage fee" only for that volume of timber actually harvested. The Appellate Body compared the identification of trees by reference to a general area of forest to fungible goods, such as milk, that are identifiable only by number, volume, value or weight. The Appellate Body thus concluded that standing timber — trees — are "goods" within the meaning of Article 1.1(a)(1)(iii) of the *SCM Agreement.*]

68. Having considered the meaning of the term "goods," we now turn to consider what it means to "provide" goods, for purposes of Article 1.1(a)(1)(iii) of the *SCM Agreement.* Canada argues that stumpage arrangements do not "provide" standing timber. According to Canada, all that is provided by these arrangements is an intangible right to harvest. At best, this intangible right "makes available" standing timber. But, in Canada's submission, the connotation "makes available" is not an appropriate reading of the term "provides" in Article 1.1(a)(1)(iii). In contrast, the United States argues that the Panel's interpretation that stumpage arrangements "provide" standing timber is correct. The United States contends that, where a government transfers ownership in goods by giving enterprises a right to take them, the government "provides" those goods, within the meaning of Article1.1(a)(1)(iii).

69. Again, we begin with the ordinary meaning of the term. Before the Panel, the United States pointed to a definition of the term "provides," which suggested that the term means, *inter alia*, to "supply or furnish for use; make available." This definition is the same as that relied upon by USDOC [U.S. Department of Commerce] in making its determination that "regardless of whether the Provinces are supplying timber or making it available through a right of access, they are providing timber" within the meaning of the provision of United States countervailing duty law that corresponds to Article 1.1(a)(1)(iii) of the *SCM Agreement.* We note that another definition of "provides" is "to put at the disposal of."

70. Notwithstanding these definitions, Canada submits that the meaning of the term "provides" in Article 1.1(a)(1)(iii) of the *SCM Agreement* should be limited to the supplying or giving of goods or services. Canada raises two arguments to support this view. First, Canada suggests that the terms "provides goods" and "provides services" cannot be read to include the mere "making available" of goods or services, because "[t]o '*make available* services'… would include any circumstance in which a government action makes possible a later receipt of services and to '*make available* goods' would capture every property law in a jurisdiction." Secondly, Canada points to the use of the term "provide" in Articles 3.2 and 8 of the *Agreement on Agriculture* and in Article XV:1 of the *General Agreement on Trade in Services* (the "GATS") to suggest that "provides," when used in the context of the granting of subsidies, requires the actual *giving* of a subsidy.

71. With respect to Canada's first argument, we do not see how the general governmental acts referred to by Canada would necessarily fall within the concept of a government "making available" services or goods. In our view, such actions would be too remote from the concept of "making available" or "putting at the disposal of," which requires there to be a reasonably proximate relationship between the action of the government providing the good or service on the one hand, and the use or enjoyment of the good or service by the recipient on the other. Indeed, a government must have some control over the *availability* of a specific thing being "made available."

72. Moreover, Canada's argument in this respect seems to disregard the fact that, in order to be subject to the disciplines of the *SCM Agreement*, or countervailing measures under Part V of that Agreement, a government action would also need to meet all other elements of the subsidy definition. Under Article 1.1(a)(1)(iii) of the *SCM Agreement*, not all government actions providing goods and services are necessarily financial contributions. If a government provides goods and services that are "general infrastructure," no financial contribution will exist. Furthermore, not all financial contributions are subsidies. The definition of subsidy includes further elements, in particular, that a financial contribution by a government must confer a "benefit." Finally, in accordance with Articles 1.2 and 2 of the *SCM Agreement*, a subsidy must be "specific" in order to be subject to the disciplines of the Agreement.

73. In any event, in our view, it does not make a difference, for purposes of applying the requirements of Article 1.1(a)(1)(iii) of the *SCM Agreement* to the facts of this case, if "provides" is interpreted as "supplies," "makes available" or "puts at the disposal of." What matters for determining the existence of a subsidy is whether all elements of the subsidy definition are fulfilled as a result of the transaction, irrespective of whether all elements are fulfilled *simultaneously*. * * *

75. Turning to the Panel's finding regarding what is provided by provincial stumpage programs, we note that the Panel found that stumpage arrangements give tenure holders a right to enter onto government lands, cut standing timber, and enjoy exclusive rights over the timber that is harvested. Like the Panel, we conclude that such arrangements represent a situation in which provincial governments provide standing timber. Thus, we disagree with Canada's submission that the granting of an intangible right to harvest standing timber cannot be equated with the act of providing that standing timber. By granting a right to harvest, the provincial governments put particular stands of timber at the disposal of timber harvesters and allow those enterprises, exclusively, to make use of those resources. Canada asserts that governments do not supply felled trees, logs, or lumber through stumpage transactions. In our view, this assertion misses the point, because felled trees, logs and lumber are all distinct from the "standing timber" on which the Panel based its conclusions. Moreover, what matters, for purposes of determining whether a government "provides goods" in the sense of Article 1.1(a)(1)(iii), is the consequence of the transaction. Rights over felled trees or logs crystallize as a natural and inevitable consequence of the harvesters' exercise of their harvesting rights.[72] Indeed, as the Panel indicated, the evidence

---

72. The Panel found, at paragraph 7.14 of the Panel Report, that:
    In light of Canada's answers, it appears that the United States is correct when it argues that "there is no record evidence of stumpage contracts under which the contracting party

suggests that making available timber is the *raison d'être* of the stumpage arrangements.[73] Accordingly, like the Panel, we believe that, by granting a right to harvest standing timber, governments provide that standing timber to timber harvesters. We therefore agree with the Panel that, through stumpage arrangements, the provincial governments "provide" such goods, within the meaning of Article 1.1(a)(1)(iii) of the *SCM Agreement*.

76. For these reasons, we *uphold* the Panel's finding, in paragraph 7.30 of the Panel Report, that USDOC's "[d]etermination that the Canadian provinces are providing a financial contribution in the form of the provision of a good by providing standing timber to timber harvesters through the stumpage programmes" is not inconsistent with Article 1.1(a)(1)(iii) of the *SCM Agreement*.

77. We turn next to the issue whether the Panel erred in its interpretation of Article 14(d) of the *SCM Agreement*, which relates, *inter alia*, to the calculation of benefit when goods are provided by a government. In the countervailing duty investigation underlying this dispute, USDOC determined that there were "no useable market-determined prices between Canadian buyers and sellers" that could be used to determine whether provincial stumpage programmes provide goods for less than adequate remuneration. Therefore, USDOC used as a benchmark prices of stumpage in certain bordering states in the northern United States, making adjustments purportedly to account for differences in conditions between those states and Canadian provinces.

* * *

82. The initial issue before us is whether an investigating authority may use a benchmark, under Article 14(d) of the *SCM Agreement*, other than private prices in the country of provision for determining if goods have been provided by a government for less than adequate remuneration. If our answer were to be in the affirmative, two additional questions would arise: (i) what are the specific circumstances under Article 14(d) in which an investigating authority may use a benchmark other than private prices in the country of provision; and (ii) assuming such circumstances exist, what alternative benchmarks may an investigating authority use to determine whether goods were provided by a government for less than adequate remuneration.

* * *

84. As we observed earlier in this Report, not every financial contribution by a government in the form of provision of goods constitutes a subsidy, because a "benefit" must be conferred by virtue of that provision of goods. Article 14(d)

(tenureholder or licensee) does not have ownership rights to the harvested timber." (footnote omitted).

73. In this regard, we note that the Panel cited with approval a finding by the panel in *US-Softwood Lumber III* that "from the perspective of the tenure holder, the *only reason* to enter into tenure agreements with the provincial governments is to obtain the timber." (Panel Report, para.7.16 (emphasis added)). In footnote 97 to that paragraph, the Panel continued, noting "that Canada acknowledged before that Panel that the main interest of tenure holders is the *end-product* of the harvest." (emphasis added) Indeed, the panel record in these proceedings shows that timber harvesters pay a "stumpage fee" only on the basis of the volume of timber that is *actually harvested*. Moreover, the record shows that, at least in Quebec, Ontario and Alberta, the provincial governments retain a residual interest in the timber harvested until such time as the harvester has paid this volumetric fee. These considerations indicate that it is *standing timber*, as opposed to a mere right to harvest trees, that is the thing of value contracted for in a stumpage contract.

establishes that the provision of goods by a government shall not be considered as conferring a benefit unless the provision is made for less than adequate remuneration. As the Panel observed, the term "adequate" in this context means "sufficient, satisfactory". "Remuneration" is defined as "reward, recompense; payment, pay". Thus, a benefit is conferred when a government provides goods to a recipient and, in return, receives insufficient payment or compensation for those goods.

85. The question then becomes how to determine whether adequate remuneration was paid for the goods provided by the government. This is dealt with in the second sentence of Article 14(d), which provides that "[t]he adequacy of remuneration shall be determined *in relation to prevailing market conditions* for the good or service in question *in the country of provision* or purchase (including price, quality, availability, marketability, transportation and other conditions of purchase or sale)". (emphasis added)

* * *

87. Turning first to the text of Article 14(d), we consider the submission of the United States that the term "market conditions" necessarily implies a market undistorted by the government's financial contribution. In our view, the United States' approach goes too far. We agree with the Panel that "[t]he text of Article 14 (d) [of the] SCM Agreement does not qualify in any way the 'market' conditions which are to be used as the benchmark ... [a]s such, the text does not explicitly refer to a 'pure' market, to a market 'undistorted by government intervention', or to a 'fair market value'." This is confirmed by the Spanish and French versions of Article 14(d), neither of which supports the contention that the term "market" qualifies the term "conditions" so as to exclude situations in which there is government involvement.

88. We now examine the meaning of the phrase "in relation to" in Article 14(d). We are of the view that the Panel failed to give proper meaning and effect to the phrase "in relation to" as it is used in Article 14(d). The Panel reasoned that the phrase "in relation to" in the context of Article 14(d) means "in comparison with". Hence, the Panel concluded that the determination of the adequacy of remuneration has to be made "in comparison with" prevailing market conditions for the goods in the country of provision, and thus no other comparison will do when private market prices exist. We do not agree.

89. Thus, the use of the phrase "in relation to" in Article 14(d) suggests that, contrary to the Panel's understanding, the drafters did not intend to exclude any possibility of using as a benchmark something other than private prices in the market of the country of provision. This is not to say, however, that private prices in the market of provision may be disregarded. Rather, it must be demonstrated that, based on the facts of the case, the benchmark chosen relates or refers to, or is connected with, the conditions prevailing in the market of the country of provision.

90. Although Article 14(d) does not dictate that private prices are to be used as the *exclusive* benchmark in all situations, it does emphasize by its terms that prices of similar goods sold by private suppliers in the country of provision are the primary benchmark that investigating authorities must use when determining whether goods have been provided by a government for less than adequate remuneration. In this case, both participants and the third participants agree

that the starting-point, when determining adequacy of remuneration, is the prices at which the same or similar goods are sold by private suppliers in arm's length transactions in the country of provision. This approach reflects the fact that private prices in the market of provision will generally represent an appropriate measure of the "adequacy of remuneration" for the provision of goods. However, this may not always be the case. As will be explained below, investigating authorities may use a benchmark other than private prices in the country of provision under Article 14(d), if it is first established that private prices in that country are distorted because of the government's predominant role in providing those goods.

[The Appellate Body also concluded that the Panel's singular focus on prevailing market conditions does not give due consideration to the chapeau of Article 14. The chapeau of Article 14 requires that "any" method used by investigating authorities to calculate the benefit to the recipient shall be provided for in a WTO Member's legislation or regulations. The reference to "any" method "clearly implies that more than one method" is available to calculate the benefit to the recipient. In addition, the chapeau of Article 14 provides that any method used by an investigating authority in calculating benefit "shall be consistent with the ... guidelines" set out in paragraphs (a) through (d). Taken together, "these terms establish mandatory parameters within which the benefit must be calculated," but "paragraphs (a) through (d) should not be interpreted as 'rigid rules that purport to contemplate every conceivable factual circumstance.'"]

93. Furthermore, ... in *Canada-Aircraft*, the Appellate Body stated that the "there can be no 'benefit' to the recipient unless the 'financial contribution' makes the recipient 'better off' than it would otherwise have been, absent that contribution." According to Article 14(d), this benefit is to be found when a recipient obtains goods from the government for "less than adequate remuneration," and such adequacy is to be evaluated in relation to prevailing market conditions in the country of provision. Under the approach advocated by the Panel (that is, private prices in the country of provision must be used whenever they exist), however, there may be situations in which there is no way of telling whether the recipient is "better off" *absent the financial contribution*. This is because the government's role in providing the financial contribution is so predominant that it effectively determines the price at which private suppliers sell the same or similar goods, so that the comparison contemplated by Article 14 would become circular. * * *

97. Having established that prices in the market of the country of provision are the primary, but not the exclusive, benchmark for calculating benefit, we come to the next question that arises in our analysis, namely, when an investigating authority may use a benchmark other than private prices in the country of provision for purposes of calculating the benefit under Article 14(d).

98. Despite the Panel's finding that Article 14(d) requires the use of private prices in the country of provision as the benchmark whenever they exist, the Panel nevertheless acknowledged that "it will in certain situations not be possible to use in-country prices" as a benchmark, and gave two examples of such situations, neither of which it found to be present in the underlying countervailing duty investigation: (i) where the government is the only supplier of the particular goods in the country; and, (ii) where the government administratively controls all of the prices for those goods in the country. In these situations, the Panel reasoned

that the "only remaining possibility would appear to be the construction of some sort of a proxy for, or estimate of, the market price for the good in that country."

99. The United States claims, on appeal, that the Panel erred in not recognizing that Article 14(d) also allows investigating authorities to use a benchmark other than private prices in a third situation: where private prices are "substantially influenced" or "effectively determined" by the government's financial contribution. We understand that by "substantially influenced" or "effectively determined," the United States refers to a situation where the government has such a predominant role in the market, as a provider of certain goods, that private suppliers will align their prices with those of the government-provided goods; in other words, a situation where the government effectively acts as a "price-setter" and private suppliers are "price-takers." Considering that the situation of government predominance in the market, as a provider of certain goods, is the only one raised on appeal by the United States, we will limit our examination to whether an investigating authority may use a benchmark other than private prices in the country of provision in that particular situation.

100. In analyzing this question, we have some difficulty with the Panel's approach of treating a situation in which the government is the sole supplier of certain goods differently from a situation in which the government is the predominant supplier of those goods. In terms of market distortion and effect on prices, there may be little difference between situations where the government is the sole provider of certain goods and situations where the government has a predominant role in the market as a provider of those goods. Whenever the government is the predominant provider of certain goods, even if not the sole provider, it is likely that it can affect through its own pricing strategy the prices of private providers for those goods, inducing the latter to align their prices to the point where there may be little difference, if any, between the government price and the private prices. This would be so even if the government price does not represent adequate remuneration. The resulting comparison of prices carried out under the Panel's approach to interpreting Article 14(d) would indicate a "benefit" that is artificially low, or even zero, such that the full extent of the subsidy would not be captured, as the Panel itself acknowledged. As a result, the subsidy disciplines in the *SCM Agreement* and the right of Members to countervail subsidies could be undermined or circumvented when the government is a predominant provider of certain goods.

101. It appears to us that the language found in Article 14(d) ensures that the provision's purposes are not frustrated in such situations. Thus, while requiring investigating authorities to calculate benefit "in relation to" prevailing conditions in the market of the country of provision, Article 14(d) permits investigating authorities to use a benchmark other than private prices in that market. When private prices are distorted because the government's participation in the market as a provider of the same or similar goods is so predominant that private suppliers will align their prices with those of the government-provided goods, it will not be possible to calculate benefit having regard exclusively to such prices.

* * *

103.... [A]n allegation that a government is a significant supplier would not, on its own, prove distortion and allow an investigating authority to choose a benchmark other than private prices in the country of provision. The determination of whether private prices are distorted because of the government's predominant role in the market, as a provider of certain goods, must be made on a case-by-case basis, according to the particular facts underlying each countervailing duty investigation.

104. For these reasons, we *reverse* the Panel's finding, in paragraph 7.64 of the Panel Report, with respect to the interpretation of Article 14(d) of the *SCM Agreement*. We find, instead, that an investigating authority may use a benchmark other than private prices of the goods in question in the country of provision, when it has been established that those private prices are distorted, because of the predominant role of the government in the market as a provider of the same or similar goods. When an investigating authority resorts, in such a situation, to a benchmark other than private prices in the country of provision, the benchmark chosen must, nevertheless, relate or refer to, or be connected with, the prevailing market conditions in that country, and must reflect price, quality, availability, marketability, transportation and other conditions of purchase or sale, as required by Article 14(d).

Questions and Discussion

1. Recall that Article 1 defines a financial contribution as a direct transfer of funds, revenue otherwise foregone, or the provision of goods or services. After reading the Appellate Body's decision, in what way does "financial contribution," as defined by the SCM Agreement, limit the scope of a subsidy? What types of government activities would not constitute a "financial contribution"?

2. The need for a benefit to be conferred provides a significant screen for identifying subsidies. According to the Appellate Body, what is the difference between a financial contribution and a benefit conferred?

3. The Appellate Body, in order to ensure that the objectives of the SCM Agreement are not undermined, has defined benefit conferred broadly and permitted the use of other than private prices in the country providing the subsidy to determine whether a benefit has been conferred. When can a country use other than private prices or fair market value in the country providing the subsidy to determine whether a benefit has been conferred? Do you understand why the Appellate Body's interpretation of "benefit conferred" is especially important with respect to government controlled resources, such as access to fish, minerals, and timber?

4. The Appellate Body is not the only tribunal to define "goods" broadly. In 1994, the European Court of Justice ruled that electricity is a good. Case C-393/92, Municipality of Almelo v. NV Energiebedrijf Ijsselmij, 1994 E.C.R. I-1477 (1994).

---

b. Was the Subsidy Specific?

United States-Final Countervailing Duty Determination with Respect to Softwood Lumber from Canada
Panel Report, WT/DS257/R (adopted Feb. 17, 2004)

7.115 [W]e understand Canada to argue that for a subsidy to be specific under Article 2.1(c) SCM Agreement, the granting authority must have *deliberately*

limited access to the subsidy to a group of *enterprises producing similar products.*
In particular, Canada argues that a subsidy which consists of the provision of a
good which can only be used as an input by a particular industry should not
be considered to be specific unless the granting authority has deliberately limited its use to a certain subgroup of enterprises in that industry. Under the facts
of this case, Canada moreover argues that the USDOC finding that there were
only a limited number of users of the stumpage programmes was flawed. In addition, Canada considers that the USDOC should have analysed the end-products of the industries it alleged were the users of the programme in order to
determine whether they constituted a group of industries producing similar
products.

7.116 We first address Canada's argument that a subsidy is specific only when
the authority deliberately limits access of this subsidy to certain enterprises within
the group of enterprises eligible or naturally apt to use the subsidy. In our view,
Article 2 SCM Agreement is concerned with the distortion that is created by a subsidy which either in law or in fact is not broadly available.[179] While deliberate action by a government to restrict access to a subsidy that is in principle broadly
available, through the use of discretion, could well be the basis for a finding of
de facto specificity, we see no basis in the text of Article 2, and 2.1(c) SCM Agreement in particular, for Canada's argument that if the inherent characteristics of
the good provided limit the possible use of the subsidy to a certain industry, the
subsidy will not be specific unless access to this subsidy is limited to a sub-set of
this industry, i.e. to certain enterprises within the potential users of the subsidy
engaged in the manufacture of similar products. Article 2 speaks of the use by a
limited number of certain enterprises or the predominant use by certain enterprises, not of the use by a limited number of certain *eligible* enterprises. In the
case of a *good* that is provided by the government—and not just money, which
is fungible—and that has utility only for certain enterprises (because of its inherent characteristics), it is all the more likely that a subsidy conferred via the provision of that good is specifically provided to certain enterprises only. We do not
consider that this would imply that any provision of a good in the form of a natural resource automatically would be specific, precisely because in some cases,
the goods provided (such as for example oil, gas, water, etc.) may be used by an
indefinite number of industries. This is not the situation before us. As Canada
acknowledges, the inherent characteristics of the good provided, standing timber, limit its possible use to "certain enterprises" only.

7.117 We now turn to Canada's argument that the USDOC failed to properly
determine that the stumpage programmes were used by only a limited number
of industries. On the basis of the facts of this case, Canada argues that specificity should have been analyzed based on the end-products sold by the industry or industries using the programme. Canada argues that more than 200 separate
products are manufactured by companies holding harvesting rights, together

---

179. We note that the availability of a subsidy which is limited by the inherent characteristics of
the good cannot be considered to have been limited by "objective" criteria in the sense of footnote 2
to Article 2.1(b) SCM Agreement, i.e. "criteria or conditions which are neutral, which do not favour
certain enterprises over others, and which are economic in nature and horizontal in application, such
as number of employees or size of enterprise."

forming about 23 separate industries.[180] This, according to Canada, is hardly a "limited number of industries."

7.118 We note that the USDOC determined that

> Benefits under these Provincial stumpage [programmes] are limited to those companies and individuals specifically authorized to cut timber on Crown lands. These companies are pulp and paper mills and the saw mills and remanufacturers which are producing the subject merchandise. This limited group of wood product industries is specific under section 771 (5A)(D)(iii)(I) of the Act."[181]

7.119 We recall that a subsidy is specific under Article 2 SCM Agreement, if it is specific to an enterprise or industry or group of enterprises or industries (referred to in the SCM Agreement as "certain enterprises"). The SCM Agreement does not define an "industry" nor does it provide for any other rules concerning which enterprises could be considered to form an industry for the purposes of Article 2 SCM Agreement or whether a group of industries have to produce certain similar products in order to be considered a "group."

7.120 The *New Shorter Oxford Dictionary* defines an industry as "a particular form or branch of productive labour; a trade, a manufacture." Both parties seem to agree that the common practice is to refer to industries by the type of products they produce. It seems therefore that the term "industry" in Article 2 SCM Agreement is not used to refer to enterprises producing specific goods or end-products. Indeed, even Canada agrees that a single industry may make a broad range of end products and still remain a "industry" within the meaning of Article 2 SCM Agreement. We note in this respect that Canada considers that "it may be completely appropriate to find that producers of a wide variety of steel products (or automobile products or textile products, etc) are a group of "steel industries" (or "automobile industries," "textile industries," etc.) because of the similarity and the relatedness of their output products." Canada also does not dispute that a subsidy limited to a single large industry (such as "steel," "autos," "textiles," "telecommunications," or the like) could be found specific, even though the producers make a diversity of products.

7.121 The USDOC Determination considered that only a group of wood product industries, consisting of the pulp and paper mills and the sawmills and remanufacturers which are producing the subject merchandise used the stumpage programmes. It does not seem that USDOC simply labelled an aggregation of producers as a group of industries merely because they use a particular programme. In our view, the opposite was the case. As Canada recognized, the stumpage programme can clearly only benefit certain enterprises in the wood product indus-

---

180. Exhibit CDA-73 provides an overview of these 23 allegedly separate industries and the 201 products. produced by these industries. We note that Canada considers as separate industries such industries as the "wooden kitchen cabinet and bathroom vanity industry" and the "wooden door and window industry" to mention just two.

181. USDOC Determination, p. 52. (CDA-1). According to the USDOC, "whether we classify the users of the stumpage programs as sawmills and pulp mills, the primary timber processing group, the wood products industry, the forest products industries, the wood fibre user industry, the 'industries' suggested by respondents, or any combination thereof, the subsidies provided by these stumpage programs are not 'broadly available and widely used.' The vast majority of companies and industries in Canada does not receive benefits under these programs." USDOC Determination, p. 52. (CDA-1).

tries which can harvest and/or process the good provided, standing timber. In sum, the text of Article 2 SCM Agreement does not require a detailed analysis of the end-products produced by the enterprises involved, nor does Article 2.1(c) SCM Agreement provide that only a limited number of *products* should benefit from the subsidy. In our view, it was reasonable of the USDOC to reach the conclusion that the use of the alleged subsidy was limited to an industry or a group of industries. We consider that the "wood products industries" constitutes at most only a limited group of industries—the pulp industry, the paper industry, the lumber industry and the lumber remanufacturing industry—under any definition of the term "limited." We do not consider determinative in this respect the fact that these industries may be producing many different end-products. As we discussed above, specificity under Article 2 SCM is to be determined at the enterprise or industry level, not at the product level.[188] * * *

7.123 Canada also argues that an authority is required to examine all four factors mentioned in Article 2.1(c) SCM Agreement in order to determine *de facto* specificity. We note in this respect that Article 2.1(c) SCM Agreement provides that if there are reasons to believe that the subsidy may in fact be specific, other factors *may* be considered. The use of the verb "may" rather than "shall," in our view, indicates that if there are reasons to believe that the subsidy may in fact be specific, an authority *may* want to look at any of the four factors or indicators of specificity. We note the difference in language between Article 2.1(c) SCM Agreement and, for example, Article 15.4 SCM Agreement concerning injury which provides that "the examination of the impact of the subsidized imports on the domestic industry *shall include* an evaluation of all relevant economic factors and indices having a bearing on the state of the industry *including ...*", and then lists the factors which have to be included in the evaluation. Article 15.4 SCM Agreement is almost identical in language to Article 3.4 Anti-Dumping Agreement, which it is well established, contains an obligation on the part of the investigating authority to at a minimum examine and evaluate all factors listed in the provision. In our view, if the drafters had wanted to impose a formalistic requirement to examine and evaluate all four factors mentioned in Article 2.1(c) SCM Agreement in all cases, they would have equally explicitly provided so as they have done elsewhere in the SCM Agreement.[190] They did not do so. We conclude therefore that there was no obligation on the USDOC to examine whether disproportionately large amounts of the subsidy were granted to certain enter-

---

188. We consider therefore not determinative either the fact that a distinction may be made on the basis of the specific products produced into 23 industries, as Canada is suggesting. Irrespective of the question whether 23 industries could still be considered to be a limited number in absolute or relative terms, we are of the view that for the purposes of Article 2 SCM Agreement, it was entirely legitimate of the USDOC to group such alleged separate industries as the "wooden kitchen cabinet and bathroom vanity industry" and the "wooden door and window industry" together with other similar industries into a group of wood products industries. In a similar vein, it appears to us that, whether a "group" is required to produce similar products or not in order to be considered a "group" under Article 2 SCM Agreement, an issue which we need not and do not decide, the industries producing wood products are, in our view, obviously producing sufficiently similar products to be considered as a "group" of industries for the purposes of Article 2 SCM Agreement.

190. We note that it appears that on the basis of the facts before the USDOC, it was reasonable to conclude that certain of these factors, such as the granting of disproportionately large amounts of the subsidy to certain enterprises or the manner in which discretion has been exercised by the granting authority in the decision to grant a subsidy, were not relevant in this situation, and thus did not have to be examined.

prises or the manner in which discretion has been exercised by the granting authority in the decision to grant a subsidy, the two factors mentioned in Article 2.1(c) SCM Agreement which the USDOC did not explicitly examine.

7.124 We finally note that Article 2.1(c) SCM Agreement provides that "[I]n applying this subparagraph, *account shall be taken of* the extent of diversification of economic activities within the jurisdiction of the granting authority, as well as of the length of time during which the subsidy programme has been in operation." While it is clear that the USDOC did not explicitly and as such address the extent of economic diversification in its Final Determination, we consider that in noting that "the vast majority of companies and industries in Canada does not receive benefits under these programmes," the USDOC showed that it had *taken account of* the extent of economic diversification in Canada and its provinces, i.e. the publicly known fact that the Canadian economy and the Canadian provincial economies in particular are diversified economies. Although we understand the wood product industry to be an important industry for Canada, it is clear that the Canadian economy is more than just wood products alone. In light of the fact that, in our view, all that is required under the last sentence of Article 2.1(c) SCM Agreement is that "account be taken of" the extent of economic diversification, we find that USDOC Determination complied with this obligation.

7.125 We find therefore that the USDOC determination that the stumpage programmes which are used only by a limited group of wood product industries are in fact specific, is not inconsistent with Article 2.1(c) SCM Agreement and reject all of Canada's claims in this respect.

Questions and Discussion

1. Because of the inherent characteristics of timber, Canada's low-cost stumpage is only used by a certain industry, the wood products industry. How does the Panel respond to Canada's argument that in these situations a subsidy is specific only if the subsidy is provided to a sub-set of enterprises within the wood products industry?

2. In *Lumber I*, the Department of Commerce adopted an "inherent characteristics" test to determine whether a subsidy was specific. Under this test, if the use of a subsidy was limited by the inherent characteristics of the subsidized resource, then the subsidy would be deemed generally available and not countervailable. In *Lumber I*, the Department of Commerce found that Canadian timber subsidies were generally available because their use was not limited by law, but rather by the inherent characteristics of the timber resource. What did the Panel say when Canada sought to revitalize this argument? Does the "inherent characteristics" standard make sense? John Ragosta argues that it does not:

> Suppose a government provides iron ore at a small fraction of its value, and almost all of the ore is "coincidentally" purchased by steel manufacturers. Following the inherent characteristics analysis, this subsidy would be considered generally available because the inherent characteristics of the ore, rather than specific legislation or regulations, limit its use. Under this inherent characteristics test, a government interested in subsidizing a resource-intensive industry could simply rely on the inherent characteristics of a resource to make a resource subsidy immune from a countervailing duty.

Ragosta, *Natural Resource Subsidies*, at 276. The Department of Commerce apparently agreed. In a subsequent case, it did not use the inherent characteristics test and found a Brazilian iron ore subsidy countervailable. Certain Carbon Steel Products from Brazil (final affirm. countervailing duty determination), 49 Fed. Reg. 5157 (Feb. 10, 1984) [hereinafter Steel Products], *rev'd on other grounds*, 49 Fed. Reg. 17,988 (Apr. 26, 1984).

3. Canada defines "stumpage" as the right of a harvester to enter into a forest owned by a province, select a tree, and harvest it. *Softwood Lumber*, Panel Report, WT/DS257/R, at para. 4.106. Yet, the Panel in *Lumber IV* defines "industry" for purposes of Article 2 as the "wood products industries," which includes both producers and some processors of wood, such as the lumber remanufacturing industry (which produces decking, finger joints, lumber specialties, fencing, siding, and panels). Why is this larger category of entities considered a beneficiary of the stumpage fee subsidy?

4. *The End of the Softwood Lumber Dispute?* Yet another string of cases in the *Softwood Lumber* dispute addresses the threat of material injury. On August 31, 2004, a NAFTA Panel issued a decision finding that the "record does not support a finding of threat of material injury." This Panel determined that a further remand is not warranted and would be an "idle and useless formality." In the Matter of Certain Softwood Lumber Products from Canada-Final Affirmative Threat of Injury Determination, Second Remand Decision of the Panel (Aug. 31, 2004). Other aspects of this case were decided in *Lumber V*. United States-Final Dumping Determination on Softwood Lumber from Canada, Appellate Body Report, WT/DS264/AB/R (adopted Aug. 31, 2004) (*Lumber V*).

Lumber VI related to the determination by the U.S. International Trade Commission that there was a threat of material injury to the U.S. softwood lumber industry caused by imports of Canadian softwood lumber sold at less than fair market value (i.e., subsidized timber). A WTO Panel concluded that the U.S. methodology for calculating material injury was inconsistent with Article 15.7 of the SCM Agreement. United States-Investigation of the International Trade Commission in Softwood Lumber from Canada, Panel Report, WT/DS277/R (adopted Apr. 26, 2004) (*Lumber VI*). Nonetheless, the United States maintained a combined countervailing and anti-dumping duty of 27% on imports of Canadian softwood lumber. The fees declined to 20 percent and then fell to 10.81 percent on December 12, 2005. Finally, on October 12, 2006, Canada and the United States implemented the 2006 Softwood Lumber Agreement in which the duties were replaced by an export tax collected by Canada and the United States agreed to return more than US$4 billion in duties collected since 2002. Softwood Lumber Agreement (Canada-United States), Sept. 12, 2006. The agreement is valid for seven years. Despite winning many aspects of the case, the Government of British Columbia has commented that "This agreement ends the costly litigation, secures the return to Canadian companies of the bulk of the duties paid to date, and provides some certainty for softwood lumber trade in the future." The Ministry of Environment of British Columbia maintains a website relating to the *Softwood Lumber* dispute. *See* http://www.for.gov.bc.ca/het/softwood/ index.htm.

5. The irony of the countervailing duties and other charges imposed on Canadian timber is that many U.S. companies are paying a sizable portion of those duties. Weyerhauser, for example, operates on about 35 million acres in five Canadian provinces and produces about 2.4 billion board feet of lumber per year. This represents about one-third of its total annual production. The countervailing duties have cost it about $100 million per year. Matthew Daly, *Northwest Timber Firm Backs Idea of Tariff Cuts*, OREGONIAN, June 12, 2004, at E1. What does this suggest about the effectiveness of countervailing duties?

III. The Restraint of Subsidies in the Trading Regime

A. Early Restraints on Subsidies

The GATT began the process of addressing the effects of subsidies. Article XVI of the GATT stated that the parties "should avoid" export subsidies—those subsidies contingent on the export of products—and that export subsidies should not be applied to primary products in a manner that gives the subsidizing country "more than an equitable share" of world export in that product. The limitations of this provision are obvious: Article XVI restrains only export subsidies on primary products, thus excluding a large number of subsidies that distort international trade. Moreover, determining whether a subsidy leads to more than an equitable share of world trade is difficult to prove. If such obstacles could be overcome, Article VI of the GATT allows governments to impose countervailing duties to offset the effects of subsidies where the subsidy causes or threatens material injury.

The 1979 Subsidies Code remedied some of the problems of Article XVI of the GATT. For example, it moved to restrain domestic, production, or general subsidies—those granted regardless of whether the product is exported—although it merely asked parties to "avoid" their use. As a separate code, however, GATT parties needed to ratify it before it applied to them. Only 24 parties did so.

B. The SCM Agreement's Traffic Light System

In establishing rules for restraining the use of subsidies, the SCM Agreement continues the same balance it struck in defining a subsidy: on one hand it carves out space for legitimate needs of governments to grant subsidies; on the other hand, it attempts to prevent subsidies from causing a trade injury to competing industries in the importing country. For this reason, the SCM Agreement absolutely prohibits members from granting certain subsidies. Meanwhile, other subsidies are permitted but may be offset if injury can be proven, and yet others may be granted free of any sanction. As discussed in Section C below, depending on the circumstances of the subsidy, relief may be sought from two different sources—countermeasures under the WTO dispute settlement system or countervailing duties under the laws of the importing country.

The tiered system described above for evaluating subsidies has been unofficially color-coded to match a traffic light. Prohibited subsidies (red light) are always prohibited and countermeasures (as distinct from countervailing duties) may be taken even in the absence of explicit proof of injury or prejudice to a domestic industry of the nonsubsidizing country. Actionable subsidies (yellow or amber light) include domestic subsidies and may be sanctioned if material injury to a domestic industry or serious prejudice to the interests of another member is found. Nonactionable subsidies (green light) were freely permitted, but that exception to the normal rules has expired.

1. Prohibited Subsidies

Prohibited subsidies under Article 3 of the SCM Agreement comprise export subsidies and import substitution subsidies (subsidies contingent upon the use of domestic over imported goods), unless covered by the Agreement on Agriculture. *See* Section V.D, starting on page 621. The trading regime has always considered export subsidies as particularly trade distorting. Article 3.1 defines export subsidies as those contingent "in law or fact, whether solely or as one of several other conditions, upon export performance." Annex I of the SCM Agreement provides an illustrative list of export subsidies that are prohibited, including payments that are contingent upon export levels, export financing at below commercial rates, internal freight rates that are more favorable for exports than for domestic shipments, and inputs or materials for export products at rates more favorable than those for products destined for domestic sale, among others.

Two points show the extent to which the SCM Agreement seeks to eliminate export and import substitution subsidies. First, while such subsidies must meet the Article 1 definition of a subsidy, a "specificity" determination is not needed, because Article 2.3 irrebuttably presumes them to be specific. Second, if the subsidizing country does not withdraw the prohibited subsidy, a WTO member may seek "countermeasures" that are not disproportionate to the subsidies without showing an injury or serious prejudice to its producers, as it must with respect to actionable subsidies. SCM Agreement, art. 5. By making export and import substitution subsidies prohibited subsidies, the SCM Agreement takes the view that these subsidies clearly impose unacceptable burdens on producers from countries that compete with the subsidized products. In addition, subsidies contingent upon the use of domestic products are clearly discriminatory. As a result, the SCM Agreement prohibits them completely.

2. Actionable Subsidies

Actionable subsidies are more difficult to identify. They may include a range of domestic or production subsidies granted for the benefit of producers. The SCM Agreement draws some lines for determining which of these subsidies may be identified as actionable and thus subject to countermeasures or countervailing duties.

First, actionable subsidies must meet the definition of a subsidy and be specific. Second, actionable subsidies are defined not as a type, such as an export subsidy; subsidies become actionable based on their adverse trade impacts. Actionable subsidies are those that: 1) cause "injury" to the domestic industry of another member; 2) cause "serious prejudice to the interests" of another member, including a threat of serious prejudice; or 3) nullify or impair benefits accruing directly or indirectly to another member. SCM Agreement, art. 5.

With respect to actionable subsidies, a member or a domestic industry alleging injury from the subsidy may bring an action for countervailing duties under the domestic laws of the country where the injury is alleged to occur. Only claims of "injury" may be brought as countervailing duty actions. The rules for determining injury and calculating countervailing duties are provided in Articles 10–23 of the SCM Agreement and are discussed briefly in Section C below.

A member may also seek a remedy within the WTO's dispute resolution system for any of the three types of harm that may arise: injury, serious prejudice, or nullification and impairment. Where a panel or the Appellate Body rules that a subsidy causes one of these harms, Article 7.8 directs the member granting or maintaining the subsidy to "with-draw the subsidy" or, in the alternative, to "remove the adverse effects" of the subsidy, which presumably allows the subsidizing country to retain the subsidy but in a way that eliminates the adverse effects on trade. If the member has not complied with Article 7.8 within six months of the issuance of the decision, then the Dispute Settlement Body "shall grant" the complaining member the right to take countermeasures commensurate with the degree and nature of the adverse effects and a member.

Both "injury" and "serious" prejudice are difficult concepts to apply. "Injury," which is discussed in Section C below, relates to an injury to the domestic industry caused by a sub-sidy granted to a foreign industry. The injured industry and the subsidized industry must produce "like" products. "Serious prejudice," on the other hand, covers a broader range of impacts, including impacts in the subsidizing country or a third country. Article 6 of the SCM Agreement defines "serious prejudice" to include one or more of the following trade effects of the subsidized goods: 1) they displace or impede the imports of a like product of another member into the market of the subsidizing member; 2) they displace or impede the exports of a like product of another member from a third country mar-ket; 3) they significantly undercut prices of the subsidized product as compared with the price of a like product of another member in the same market or cause a significant price suppression, price depression or lost sales in the same market; or 4) they increase world market share of the subsidizing member in a particular subsidized primary product or com-modity as compared to the average share it had during the previous period of three years and this increase follows a consistent trend over a period when subsidies have been granted.

Because of the potential difficulty of proving "serious prejudice" under these factors, the SCM Agreement created several categories of actionable subsidies with a rebuttable presumption of serious prejudice, e.g., in the case of total *ad valorem* subsidization of a product exceeding 5 percent. However, these *per se* categories expired on December 31, 1999 when the Subsidies and Countervailing Measures Committee of the WTO could not reach consensus on a decision to extend their effect.

---

3. Nonactionable Subsidies

The SCM Agreement originally had a category of nonactionable subsidies, that is, sub-sidies for which other members were prohibited from applying any countervailing duties. This "green light" category only applied provisionally for five years ending December 31, 1999. The Subsidies and Countervailing Measures Committee could have extended this category but it could not reach consensus to do so, as required by Article 31 of the SCM Agreement.

Even so, this category of nonactionable subsidies did not provide much room for using subsidies to encourage environmentally sound activities. Article 8 created a small list of exceptions, including assistance for a limited range of certain research activities and as-sistance to disadvantaged regions, provided certain conditions were met. It also included one "environmental exception" for one-time nonrecurring assistance to adapt existing fa-cilities to new environmental requirements. This assistance, however, could not exceed 20 percent of the cost of adaptation. Nor could it cover the cost of replacing and operating the assisted investment, which must be fully borne by firms. Moreover, the assistance was required to be linked directly to and proportionate to a firm's planned reduction of nui-sances and pollution, and not cover any manufacturing cost savings which could be achieved. The subsidy also had to be available to all firms which could adopt the new equipment and/or production processes.

C. Countermeasures and Countervailing Duties

1. Economic Impacts of Countervailing Duties

As noted in the introduction to this chapter, subsidies distort markets by underpricing goods. Although economists agree that subsidies distort markets in ways that affect trade, the appropriate remedy for a subsidy has been the subject of much debate. The SCM Agreement authorizes "countervailing duties" and "countermeasures," special offsetting import duties that are charged on products from those countries providing the subsidy, but many question whether a response is warranted at all.

Countervailing duties are controversial for a couple of reasons. First, a country that subsidizes production of exports or domestic products "loses in net national economic welfare, while the rest of the world gains." JACKSON, THE WORLD TRADING SYSTEM, at 281. Thus, while the specific company or group of companies may benefit from the subsidy, the subsidizing country ultimately pays the cost of the subsidy while consumers everywhere benefit from the lower cost of the subsidized goods. Second, imposing a countervailing duty on the subsidized product (or any other product) will make those products more expensive for consumers in the importing country. Moreover, there are underlying questions as to whether subsidized imports uniquely distort markets in ways that domestic market distortions do not and whether more effective responses than countervailing duties exist.

Alan O. Sykes, *Countervailing Duty Law: An Economic Perspective*
89 COLUM. L. REV. 199, 210–14 (1989)

Beyond question, domestic firms that compete with subsidized imports may suffer financial difficulties as a result of such competition, resulting in lost profits and unemployment in the workforce. Thus, competition from subsidized imports may lead to serious economic hardship for workers and their families, a hardship that society may wish to ameliorate. The hardship that results from competition with subsidized imports, however, is no different from the hardship that can result from competition with unsubsidized imports or indeed from competition with domestic firms; the burdens of unemployment and economic dislocation are the same whatever causes them. For this reason, individuals dislocated by import competition, "subsidized" or not, arguably should enjoy no greater entitlement to government assistance than the victims of other competition; they should enjoy the benefits of the public safety net programs available to all displaced workers, and no more.

But a counterargument exists. Many workers displaced by import competition, particularly those with skills not readily transferable to other industries, may suffer greater hardship than other displaced workers. When domestic firms fail as a result of competition from other domestic firms, for example, the demise of one domestic firm is typically accompanied by the expansion or creation of another (more competitive) domestic firm in the same line of business. Displaced workers may then have an opportunity to secure alternative employment that draws upon their existing skills and training, perhaps even in the same geographic area. The same cannot be said of workers displaced by import competition since relocation to find employment overseas is rarely an attractive or a viable option.

Similarly, when workers are displaced by cyclical downturns in the domestic economy, they may at least anticipate that the displacement is temporary and that they will eventually be able to return to work in a position that draws upon their existing human capital. In the interim, the public safety net program that typically pays the greatest benefits, unemployment insurance, will provide assistance. Workers displaced by import competition, by contrast, may have less hope of returning to work in the same industry, and thus confront a choice between retraining themselves for a new line of work or accepting employment in unskilled positions.

This observation perhaps justifies programs of special assistance for workers who are displaced by import competition and whose skills are not readily transferable to other industries. The more difficult question is whether trade restrictions are ever the best way to deliver such assistance.

Conventional economic wisdom suggests that the hardship of economic dislocation is usually better alleviated with tools other than restrictive trade policies. Retraining programs, public employment agencies, and the like can often reduce periods of unemployment and move workers to alternative positions in which their services can be utilized efficiently. Special "adjustment assistance" programs can and do provide added relocation and retraining assistance to workers displaced by import competition. Economists have long maintained that such programs can reduce the hardships of economic dislocation at lower cost to the economy than protectionist policies. Such programs not only create fewer short run allocative inefficiencies than do restrictive trade policies, but they also encourage the movement of resources to higher valued uses in the long run.

Protection, by contrast, impedes the efficient reallocation of resources. Furthermore, protection is an exceptionally clumsy method of redistribution. Many of the benefits are captured not by the displaced workers, but by wealthy stockholders in the companies that receive protection and workers who would have retained their jobs in the absence of protection. Other methods of redistribution are superior because they provide aid directly to needy individuals.

Thus, the proposition that trade policy should pursue economic efficiency without regard to distributional consequences does not necessarily imply that the government should leave dislocated workers to fend for themselves. Rather, it implies an assumption, well-supported in the economic literature, that policies other than protection can alleviate any distributional inequities more effectively and more cheaply.

But again, a plausible counterargument exists. Although duties or other forms of protection assuredly impose net costs on the economy, the taxes to finance alternative means of redistribution can themselves create considerable distortions. More importantly, the federal, state and local bureaucracies that administer other redistributive programs may be relatively expensive to operate and may themselves consume much of the budget for redistribution. The administrative costs of imposing additional duties at the border through the Customs Service, coupled with the attendant deadweight losses in the protected markets, might be modest by comparison and thus in some cases tip the balance in favor of redistribution through protection.

In the end, therefore, theory alone cannot establish conclusively that protection is an inefficient means of redistribution, at least in relation to the politically and bureaucratically feasible alternatives. That proposition can only be established through empirical research into the actual costs associated with the viable options for redistribution. Yet definitive empirical evidence is lacking. Consequently, the analysis to follow will briefly consider whether countervailing duties might reasonably be used to accomplish distributional goals, assuming arguendo that protection is sometimes a sensible policy instrument for that purpose. The remainder of the analysis is limited to the question whether countervailing duties can be used to enhance the efficiency of resource allocation.

Subsidies arise for a variety of reasons and have a variety of consequences for the subsidizing country. Subsidies can correct market failures and enhance economic welfare in the subsidizing country, or can distort resource allocation and reduce the subsidizing country's economic welfare. They can also enhance or reduce worldwide economic welfare. Much of the existing literature on the international discipline of subsidy practices devotes considerable attention to the question whether these various categories of subsidies can be reliably distinguished. From the perspective of a country that imports the subsidized merchandise, however, these distinctions are often of no consequence. Specifically, if product and input markets in the importing country are perfectly competitive and adjust quickly to any disequilibrium, a subsidy will enhance the economic welfare of the importing country whatever the effect of the subsidy on the welfare of the subsidizing country or on the welfare of the world as a whole.

Despite these arguments, producers that are disadvantaged by subsidies do not generally take a global perspective; when viewed from the perspective of an individual producer, countervailing duties are economically supportable. Some view the matter as one of "economic justice" and support the use of countervailing duties to offset natural resource and other subsidies:

> [Economic justice] arises out of concerns for the economic well-being of a specific sector and the individuals working in that sector, rather than a focus on general efficiency. In other words, as a matter of "economic justice," we expect that a person should have to compete against other persons at home and abroad, but should not have to compete against a government, whether domestic or foreign. At the root of this concept is the ardent support in the United States for market-based allocation of human and capital resources and a belief in individual rights and economic justice, rather than collective concerns for overall efficiency. If a firm would be more competitive in a fully open market without government intervention, then it is unfair for government interference to change that situation.

Ragosta, *Natural Resource Subsidies*, at 263.

---

2. Thresholds for Imposing Countervailing Duties and Countermeasures

Regardless of the adverse economic effects of countervailing duties, their absence in the global trading regime would be difficult for governments to defend politically. As a result, countervailing duties, which apply to products from specific countries, are an accepted departure from the GATT's core nondiscrimination obligations.

The SCM Agreement establishes two different adjudicatory mechanisms for challenging subsidies. First, a private party or the government on behalf of a domestic industry may seek countervailing duties under the domestic law of the country in which producers allege injury due to the subsidized imports, provided those domestic proceedings are consistent with the SCM Agreement. SCM Agreement, arts. 10, 11. Footnote 36 of the SCM Agreement defines countervailing duties as "a special duty levied for the purpose of offsetting any subsidy bestowed directly or indirectly upon the manufacture, production or export of any merchandise."

Second, a WTO member may bring a challenge to the WTO's DSB for subsidies alleged to cause "injury" to the domestic industry of that member or "serious prejudice to the interests" of that member, including a threat of serious prejudice. It may also allege that a subsidy nullifies or impairs a member's benefits. As stated above, such actions may end with the removal of the subsidy or its adverse effects, or, if the subsidizing member takes no action to remove the subsidy or its effects, "countermeasures." The SCM Agreement does not define "countermeasures" but they include tariff increases and other restrictions on trade with the offending member, including a suspension of benefits under the General Agreement on Trade in Services and the Agreement on Trade-related Aspects of Intellectual Property Rights. *See* United States-Subsidies on Upland Cotton Recourse to Arbitration by the United States under Article 22.6 of the DSU and Article 4.11 of the SCM Agreement, WT/DS267/ARB/1, paras. 5.1–5.32 (Aug. 31, 2009).

While footnote 35 specifically provides that an action for countervailing duties "may be invoked in parallel" with an action for countermeasures, only one form of relief is available to remedy the effects of a subsidy in the domestic market of the importing member. There are advantages and disadvantages to each approach. The domestic industry harmed by a subsidy may find countervailing duty actions preferable because Article 10 of the SCM Agreement allows private actions for countervailing duties.

Nevertheless, a number of other advantages may make disputes within the WTO dispute resolution system more attractive, even though such claims may be brought only by a member. First, a WTO action regarding prohibited subsidies requires neither a showing of injury nor of specificity. Second, a "serious prejudice" claim could challenge a foreign subsidy to local manufacturers that significantly suppresses prices "in the same market," or that displaces or impedes a member's exports to a third country market or the market of the subsidizing member. In contrast, a countervailing duty action will only address a foreign subsidy that injures a domestic industry within the market of that domestic industry.

Third, a potential benefit of bringing a serious prejudice claim may be a lower threshold of evidence that the challenging member must present. With respect to any action for countervailing duties, a subsidy must cause "injury." Footnote 45 of the SCM Agreement defines "injury" to mean "material injury to a domestic industry, threat of material injury to a domestic industry or material retardation of the establishment of such an industry." *See also* SCM Agreement, arts. 10, 11; GATT, art. VI:6(a). The "injury" determination cannot be subjective or mere conjecture, but must be based on "positive evidence" and involve an "objective examination" of the volume of the subsidized imports and the effect of the subsidized imports on prices in the domestic market for "like products" and the consequent impact of these imports on the domestic producers of such products. In the very complex case involving U.S. cotton subsidies, the Panel suggested that the finding of "injury" may be more difficult than a finding of "serious prejudice."

United States-Subsidies on Upland Cotton
Panel Report, WT/DS267/R (adopted Mar. 21, 2005)

7.1166 ... [C]ertain ... arguments by the United States raise the question of the appropriateness of applying certain relatively precise quantitative and/or "countervailing duty" methodologies and concepts, found in Part V of (or elsewhere in) the SCM Agreement, when conducting a "serious prejudice" analysis under Part III of the SCM Agreement. * * *

7.1169 ... Article XVI of the GATT 1994 contains certain rights and obligations concerning subsidies, as do Parts II and III of the SCM Agreement. Under the multilateral "actionable subsidies" disciplines in Part III of the SCM Agreement, a WTO panel established by the DSB assesses the extent to which a Member's subsidy causes "adverse effects" to the "interests" of other Members. Pursuant to Article 5(c), one form of adverse effects is "serious prejudice to the interests of another Member." Pursuant to Article 6.3(c), such serious prejudice may arise where the effect of the subsidy is significant price suppression in the same market.

7.1170 The remedies available in a Member's unilateral countervailing duty action under Part V of the SCM Agreement also contrast sharply with the remedies available for successful multilateral actions under Part III of the SCM Agreement. Footnote 35 of the SCM Agreement sets out rules pertaining to the relationship between these two sets of obligations and remedies. The role of the WTO dispute settlement system is different than the role of a national investigating authority imposing countervailing duties: where a claim under Part III prevails, the subsidizing Member concerned is obligated to take appropriate steps to remove the adverse effects or withdraw the subsidy.

7.1171 Other aspects of the current text of the provisions of Part III of the SCM Agreement further support the view that the focus of an "adverse effects"/"serious prejudice" analysis does not call for any precise quantification of the subsidy at issue.

7.1172 Articles 7.2–7.10 of the SCM Agreement are "special or additional rules and procedures" identified in Appendix 2 to the DSU. Entitled "Remedies," Article 7 sets out procedures and remedies pertaining to dispute settlement proceedings involving actionable subsidy claims. Article 7.2 requires that a request for consultations in an actionable subsidies dispute include a statement of available evidence with regard to (a) "the existence and nature of the subsidy in question; and (b) ... the serious prejudice caused to the interests of the member requesting consultations." (emphasis added)

7.1173 This provision does not explicitly refer to the "magnitude" or "amount" or "value" of the subsidy, let alone to any precise quantitative methodologies pertaining to its breakdown or allocation. Rather, while it may not preclude consideration of the general order of magnitude of a subsidy where this information may be relevant and readily available, we understand it to call for a qualitative and, to some extent, quantitative analysis of the existence and nature of the subsidy and the serious prejudice caused. Allocating absolutely precise proportions of the subsidy to the product concerned, or trying to trace with precision where each subsidy dollar may be spent by a recipient, is not a necessary exercise on the part of the Panel. Broader considerations are at play in a serious prejudice analysis than those involved in a countervailing duty sense.

7.1174 If a request for consultations in an actionable subsidies case must set out a statement of available evidence with regard to "the existence and nature of the subsidy in question", and need not focus on its amount or value (let alone any more precise quantitative concepts or methodologies) then the focus of the claims in an actionable subsidies dispute may also logically be the existence and nature of the subsidy in question.

7.1175 Pursuant to Article 7.3 of the SCM Agreement: "The purpose of the consultations shall be to clarify the facts of the situation and to arrive at a mutually agreed solution." (emphasis added) These facts would necessarily pertain to the subject of the request for consultations, including the statement of available evidence. They would thus logically pertain to the existence and nature of the subsidy. We see no requirement in Article 7.3 that the consultations clarify the facts of the situation, including facts relating to the precise quantification of the amount of the subsidy.

7.1176 This contrasts with the text of Part V of the SCM Agreement, dealing with countervailing duty investigations. There, Article 19.4 provides that "no countervailing duty shall be levied on any import in excess of the amount of the subsidy found to exist, calculated in terms of subsidization per unit of the subsidized and exported product." Therefore, the general rationale of a unilateral countervailing duty investigation is to determine whether or not a countervailable subsidy exists and, if so, to ensure that any countervailing duty levied on any import is not in excess of the amount of the subsidy found to exist, calculated in terms of subsidization per unit of the subsidized and exported product. Logically, should a Member make an affirmative determination that a countervailable subsidy exists, these provisions in Part V necessitate calculation of the amount of the subsidy before a countervailing duty may be imposed. Moreover, they require the calculation of that amount to be performed in a certain way: "in terms of subsidization per unit of the subsidized and exported product."

7.1177 In view of the contrast in the text, context, legal nature and rationale of the provisions in Part III of the SCM Agreement relating to a multilateral assessment as to whether a Member is causing, through the use of any subsidy, "adverse effects" in the form of "serious prejudice to the interests of another Member" and Part V of the Agreement relating to obligations of a Member in conducting a unilateral countervailing duty investigations, we decline to transpose directly the quantitative focus and more detailed methodological obligations of Part V into the provisions of Part III of the SCM Agreement.

———

Rather than quantify the amount of price suppression that Brazil alleged caused serious prejudice, the Panel examined: 1) the relative magnitude of the U.S. exports on the world upland cotton market; 2) general price trends; and 3) the nature of the subsidies at issue, and in particular, whether or not the nature of these subsidies is such as to have discernible price suppressing effects. *Id.* at 7.1280. With respect to several of the U.S. subsidies, such as the programs that compensate producers when the world market price falls below a price set by the U.S. government, the Panel concluded, "We have no doubt that the payments stimulate production and exports and result in lower world market prices than would prevail in their absence." *Id.* at paras. 7.1291; *see also id.* at paras. 7.1299, 7.1309. Although the Panel did not require any quantification of serious prejudice, it did require a causal link between a subsidy and the significant price suppression. With respect to four separate U.S. cotton subsidies, the Panel found that causal link and that the subsidies violated Article 5(c) of the SCM Agreement. *Id.* at para. 7.1355. The Appellate Body upheld these findings of the Panel. United States-Subsidies on Upland Cotton, Appellate Body Report, WT/DS267/AB/R, paras. 434–35, 461–67 (Mar. 21, 2005).

---

3. Threshold Issues: "Like Product" and "Domestic Industry"

Whether the claim is for "injury" or "serious prejudice," the relevant harm must occur between "like products." The SCM Agreement appears to define "like product" more narrowly than in the GATT Article III context. Rather than the Article III four-part test based on a product's end uses, physical characteristics, tariff classification, and consumer preferences, the SCM Agreement defines "like product" to mean "a product which is identical, i.e. alike in all respects to the product under consideration, or in the absence of such a product, another product which, although not alike in all respects, has characteristics closely resembling those of the product under consideration." Despite the narrower definition, a Panel concluded that cars assembled by consumers from kits were like finished cars. Indonesia-Certain Measures Affecting the Automobile Industry, Panel Report, WT/DS54/R, WT/DS54/R, WT/DS59/R, WT/DS64/R (adopted July 23, 1998).

Assuming a finding of "like product" has been made, Article 15.7 directs the investigating authorities to make a determination regarding the existence of a threat of material injury based on, *inter alia,* such factors as:

(i) nature of the subsidy or subsidies in question and the trade effects likely to arise therefrom;

(ii) a significant rate of increase of subsidized imports into the domestic market indicating the likelihood of substantially increased importation;

(iii) sufficient freely disposable, or an imminent, substantial increase in, capacity of the exporter indicating the likelihood of substantially increased subsidized exports to the importing Member's market, taking into account the availability of other export markets to absorb any additional exports;

(iv) whether imports are entering at prices that will have a significant depressing or suppressing effect on domestic prices, and would likely increase demand for further imports; and

(v) inventories of the product being investigated.

Because a countervailing duty action must involve injury to a domestic injury of a WTO member, another threshold issue is what constitutes a "domestic industry." Article 16.1 of the SCM Agreement defines "domestic industry" as referring to the "domestic producers as a whole of the like products or to those of them whose collective output of the products constitutes a major proportion of the total domestic production of those products." The Appellate Body defined "domestic industry" in a case under the Agreement on Safeguards, which allows a member to impose temporary trade restrictions otherwise in violation of a WTO agreement when increased imports threaten to cause serious injury to a domestic industry. The Agreement on Safeguards defines "domestic industry" similarly to the SCM Agreement, except that it applies to producers of a "like or directly competitive product." In a case involving lamb meat, the United States argued that the "domestic industry" included growers and feeders of live lambs because there is a 1) continuous line of production from the raw product (live lambs) to the end-product (lamb meat) and 2) there is a substantial coincidence of economic interests between the producers of the raw product and the producers of the end-product. The Appellate Body found no basis for this interpretation:

> If an input product and an end-product are not "like" or "directly competitive," then it is irrelevant, under the Agreement on Safeguards, that there is a continuous line of production between an input product and an end-product, that the input product represents a high proportion of the value of the end-product, that there is no use for the input product other than as an input for the particular end-product, or that there is a substantial coincidence of economic interests between the producers of these products. In the absence of a "like or directly competitive" relationship, we see no justification, in Article 4.1(c) or any other provision of the Agreement on Safeguards, for giving credence to any of these criteria in defining a "domestic industry."

United States-Safeguard Measures on Imports of Fresh, Chilled or Frozen Lamb Meat from New Zealand and Australia, Appellate Body Report, WT/DS177/AB/R, WT/DS178/AB/R, para. 90 (adopted May 16, 2001) [hereinafter United States-Lamb].

In determining what constituted the "domestic industry" in this case, the Panel considered the importance to be attached to the degree of integration of the production process. For the Panel, if the process of production for one "like product" can be separately identified, it will be treated as a separate industry whether or not it is owned in common with parallel, earlier, or subsequent production lines. Because the Appellate Body had reservations about examining the degree of integration of production processes for the products at issue for defining the "domestic industry," it made a point to conclude that "the determination of the 'domestic industry' is based on the 'producers ... of the like or directly competitive products.' The focus must, therefore, be on the identification of the *products*, and their 'like or directly competitive' relationship, and not on the *processes* by which those products are produced." *Id.* at para. 94 (emphasis in original). As such, it concluded that the United States had acted inconsistently with the Agreement on Safeguards by expanding the "domestic industry" to include producers of live lambs, rather than restricting its findings to producers of lamb meat.

Questions and Discussion

1. Why might quantification be required for countervailing duties but not countermeasures?

2. On what basis should countermeasures or countervailing duties be calculated: the amount of the subsidy or the amount of injury incurred by the industry in the challenging country? Consider the following decision concerning Brazilian export subsidies for aircraft producers:

> [T]he level of countermeasures simply corresponds to the amount of subsidy which has to be withdrawn. Actually, given that export subsidies usually operate with a multiplying effect (a given amount allows a company to make a number of sales, thus gaining a foothold in a given market with the possibility to expand and gain market shares), we are of the view that a calculation based on the level of nullification or impairment would, as suggested by the calculation of Canada based on the harm caused to its industry, produce higher figures than one based exclusively on the amount of the subsidy. On the other hand, if the actual level of nullification or impairment is substantially lower than the sub-

sidy, a countermeasure based on the actual level of nullification or impairment will have less or no inducement effect and the subsidizing country may not withdraw the measure at issue.

Brazil-Aircraft: Recourse to Arbitration under Article 22.6 of the DSU and Article 4.11 of the SCM Agreement by Brazil, Decision by the Arbitrators, WT/DS46/ARB, para. 3.54 (Aug. 28, 2000). Do you agree that the challenging party should be able to impose countermeasures that are more than the actual harm to its industries? What if Brazil refuses to eliminate its subsidy and another WTO member successfully challenges Brazil's subsidies? If the same reasoning is used again, won't Brazil be paying double the subsidy in countermeasures? Panels and arbitrators have not had to consider this. In dicta, however, one arbitrator noted that the presence of multiple complainants "would certainly have been a consideration to take into account in evaluating whether such countermeasures might be considered 'appropriate' in the circumstances." United States-Tax Treatment for Foreign Sales Corporations: Recourse to Arbitration by the United States under Article 22.6 of the DSU and Article 4.11 of the SCM Agreement, Decision by the Arbitrator, WT/DS108/ARB, para. 6.27 (Aug. 30, 2002).

3. In the biggest case under the SCM Agreement to date, an arbitrator authorized the European Union (EU) to impose $4 billion in countermeasures in the form of tariffs on imports of certain goods from the United States to offset an export subsidy granted by the United States to certain U.S. exporters. The tariffs can be up to 100 percent *ad valorem*. *Id*. In March 2004, the EU began imposing an additional 5 percent tariff on a broad range of goods across a variety of industries, and is increasing the tariffs by 1 percent per month until reaching a maximum of 17 percent by March 2005. After years of delays, the United States amended its legislation to remove the subsidy in October 2004, but the EU successfully challenged the new legislation for failing to implement fully the recommendations from the original dispute. United States-Tax Treatment for Foreign Sales Corporations-Second Recourse to Article 21.5 of the DSU by the European Communities, Appellate Body Report, WT/DS108/AB/RW2 (adopted Mar. 14, 2006). The United States finally repealed the offending subsidies and the EU terminated its countermeasures.

4. Although the United States provides massive natural resource subsidies, such as water and grazing rights, they largely redistribute wealth within the U.S. economy and are not contingent upon the export of a product. As a result, many U.S. natural resource subsidies would need to be evaluated as "actionable subsidies" rather than prohibited subsidies. Moreover, subsidies for irrigated water are granted to many different water users and thus are not specific. Grazing rights, which are sold far below fair market value, have a more discrete group of beneficiaries: ranchers. In the United States, grazing rights are based on an "animal unit month" (AUM) which is the price of hay times the quality of the pasture. While grazing fees vary from region to region, the fair market value in the western United States is currently about US$11.10 to US$12.30, but may run as high as US$120 in the Northern Rockies, and US$40–$75 in other parts of the west. In contrast, the Bureau of Land Management and the Forest Service charge $1.35 per AUM on lands they administer. *See* CAROL HARDY VINCENT, GRAZING FEES: AN OVERVIEW AND CURRENT ISSUES (Congressional Research Service, updated March 10, 2008); http://www.publiclandsranching.org/htmlres/fs_buy_the_numbers.htm; 43 C.F.R. § 4130.8-1 (2004). In 2004, these two agencies spent about $132.5 million on grazing management, but collected just $17.5 million in grazing fees. U.S. GOVERNMENT ACCOUNTABILITY OFFICE, LIVESTOCK GRAZING: FEDERAL EXPENDITURES AND RECEIPTS VARY, DEPENDING ON THE AGENCY AND THE PURPOSE OF THE FEE CHARGED,

GAO-05-869, 47 (Sept. 2005). Do you think such grazing fees constitute a subsidy? If yes, what would a country need to show before imposing countervailing duties or countermeasures?

5. *Like Product.* Compare the definition of like product for Article III purposes with that of the SCM Agreement. *See* Chapter 4, Section III (pages 180–99) for a more detailed discussion of "like product" under the GATT. Now reconsider the Panel's conclusion that kit cars are like finished cars under the SCM Agreement. Do you agree? Would they be under the GATT? What about big screen and small screen televisions made with the same technology? The broad interpretation of "like product" under the SCM Agreement by panels has led one group of scholars to conclude that "[i]t seems that the tendency across panel reports is to avoid, in the name of technicalities, interpreting the term *like product* in a manner that would prejudice the right of WTO Members to counteract subsidies which were, undeniably, granted." MITSUO MATSUSHITA, THOMAS J. SCHOENBAUM & PETROS C. MAVROIDIS, THE WORLD TRADE ORGANIZATION: LAW, PRACTICE, AND POLICY 379 (2d ed. 2006). If these scholars are correct, have the panels upset the balance established in the SCM Agreement between domestic interests in providing certain types of subsidies and international interests in avoiding trade distortions?

6. *Domestic Industry.* Reconsider the Appellate Body's decision in *United States-Lamb.* If producers of live lambs are threatened with serious injury as a result of increasing imports of lamb meat, why should their injury be ignored? Aren't they part of the "industry" that produces lamb meat, even if not owned or controlled by the meat processors? Based on the definition of domestic industry under the SCM Agreement, should we assume a similar interpretation of that term?

7. Governments and industries may be able to avail themselves of potentially more attractive dispute resolution processes of regional free trade agreements. Under Chapter 19 of the North American Free Trade Agreement, private parties in antidumping and countervailing duty administrative proceedings may appeal decisions of those agencies to special "binational panels" rather than national courts. Although the cases are resolved under the national law of the importing country, the private actor may view the binational panel, where panelists are chosen from a roster of individuals with trade expertise, as more attractive than national courts. For a comparison of the procedures for bringing countervailing duty actions under the WTO and NAFTA, see David A. Gantz, *Government-to-Government Dispute Resolution Under NAFTA's Chapter 20: A Commentary on the Process,* 11 AM. REV. INT'L ARB. 481 (2000).

8. This issue of subsidies is often paired with "dumping," because both involve market distortions caused by incorrectly priced goods. Whereas subsidies involve a government financial contribution that results in a benefit conferred to a specific industry, dumping is defined in general terms as an unfair trade practice due to international price discrimination. More specifically, Article 2.1 of the WTO's Antidumping Agreement, formally known as the Agreement on Implementation of Article VI of the General Agreement on Tariffs and Trade 1994, provides: "a product is to be considered as being dumped, i.e. introduced into the commerce of another country at less than its normal value, if the export price of the product exported from one country to another is less than the comparable price, in the ordinary course of trade, for the like product when destined for consumption in the exporting country." The remedy for dumping, antidumping measures, may be imposed after a WTO member determines that the dumping causes or threatens material injury to a domestic industry or materially retards the establishment of a domestic industry. Antidumping Agreement, art. 3, note 9; GATT, art. VI. Mem-

bers may invoke the WTO's dispute settlement provisions for the review of domestic antidumping decisions. Antidumping Agreement, art. 17.

9. There is extensive U.S. case law on many of the issues raised here arising from challenges by domestic industry or other parties to the determinations of the Department of Commerce International Trade Administration on countervailing duties and/or the determinations of the International Trade Commission on injury to the domestic industry.

IV. Environmental and Natural Resource Subsidies

Environmental advocates have turned their attention to the SCM Agreement as a potential tool for eliminating environmentally harmful subsidies and promoting environmentally beneficial subsidies. As noted in the introduction to this chapter, subsidies can have positive, neutral, or negative impacts on the environment. This chapter takes a closer look at these subsidies. Section A reviews "brown" subsidies—those that harm the environment—primarily to determine whether the SCM Agreement can be used to eliminate them. Section B takes a look at "green" subsidies—those that benefit the environment—and whether they actually promote economic and environmental benefits. Section C assesses the difficulties of promoting "green" subsidies and discouraging "brown" subsidies within the fisheries sector, where the elimination of vast brown subsidies and promotion of green subsidies could help restore the world's severely depleted fish populations.

A. Brown Subsidies

1. Introduction

At the moment, there is no universally agreed definition of a "brown" subsidy—perhaps more frequently called environmentally harmful subsidies. Just as defining "subsidy" more generally plagued trade ministers for many years, so too problems persist in defining environmentally harmful subsidies. Just how broad should the definition be? Should it include government action as well as inaction? Should it relate to trade distorting subsidies like the SCM definition or should it encompass a broader range of subsidies? Should it include direct and indirect impacts?

The Organization for Economic Cooperation and Development (OECD) has established an extensive body of work on environmentally harmful subsidies. In one of its more recent reports, it defined an environmentally harmful subsidy as follows:

> A subsidy is harmful to the environment if it leads to higher levels of waste and emissions, including those in the earlier states of production and consumption, than what would be the case without the support measure. This includes high levels of resource extraction than is socially optimal as well impacts on biodiversity. Removing the subsidy would result in an improvement in environmental outcomes, as the benefits from removing the subsidy would be expected to exceed the cost of removing the subsidy.

OECD, Environmentally Harmful Subsidies: Challenges for Reform 33 (2005)

This definition is notably broad. In contrast to the SCM Agreement, it includes subsidies that may not affect trade. It also includes so-called off-budget subsidies—tax exemptions, revenue foregone, preferential market access, and other subsidies that do not require the actual provision of goods, services, or funds from the government. On the other hand, it requires some governmental action, thereby excluding failures to regulate that lead to environmental degradation. It also attempts to address the fact that all production and consumption activities have some environmental impact. Thus, it excludes those impacts that would occur even in the absence of the subsidy. Of course, that only introduces the problem of measuring the counterfactual scenario—that is, what would the impacts be without the subsidy? Moreover, by not restricting the definition to direct impacts—those resulting from the subsidy—it may also cover indirect impacts—for example, increased waste problems due to subsidies to boost tourism.

Environmentally harmful subsidies have two general forms. First, governments may underprice natural resources, which may cause environmental damage by encouraging the oversupply and overuse of natural resources. This was the issue at the heart of the *Softwood Lumber* dispute, but the practice of underpricing natural resources is widespread. Governments around the world underprice water, minerals, and forage for grazing, among many other natural resources to support agricultural and other interests. Second, the government may provide support for activities that directly or indirectly cause environmental degradation. Subsidies for oil and gas exploration that increase emissions of the greenhouse gas carbon dioxide are a common example. The OECD definition, like the SCM Agreement, specifically excludes what many consider to be a third category of subsidies—subsidies occurring when a government sets artificially low environmental protection regulations. Although the SCM Agreement and other definitions make clear that the failure to regulate or enforce environmental law is not a subsidy, some analysts argue that such action *ought* to constitute a subsidy. These issues are discussed in Subsection 2 below.

Each of these governmental policies may cause environmental degradation to the producing country, a neighboring country, or perhaps the international community or the global commons, depending on the nature of the activity. The following excerpt illustrates how this may occur:

> Subsidies are rarely designed to harm the environment, but often harm will result from a poorly designed subsidy programme. For example, subsidies to promote offshore fishing are generally intended to develop or maintain a fishing industry, particularly one that may benefit coastal communities. Unfortunately, as has been observed globally, the subsidisation of this sector has also contributed to the reduction of important fishery stocks and an increase in the mortality of non-target species, reducing the resiliency and integrity of the ecosystem. Not only have these subsidies contributed to ecosystem failures, they have also necessitated expenditure on new programmes—notably vessel or license retirement schemes—to mitigate the negative externalities. Likewise, subsidies intended to help lower the costs of farming inputs, such as irrigation water, fertilizers and pesticides, have helped raise agricultural productivity and profitability. But the subsidization of irrigation water (or the electricity required to pump it out of the ground) at below-market prices has often resulted in depletion of groundwater aquifers and, more generally, the inefficient use of a scarce and critical resource.

The environmental effects of consumption or production induced by subsidies also can include higher volumes of waste or emissions. For example, subsidies to promote irrigation often encourage the growing of crops that are farmed intensively, leading to higher levels of fertilizer use than would occur otherwise; drainage water from irrigated crops typically contains high levels of nitrates, as well as dissolved salts. In countries that subsidize local coal production, that coal is often higher in sulphur content than imported coal; removing the sulphur from the flue gases of power plants that burn that coal can, depending on the technology used, create sludges that must be disposed of.

Stephan Barg et al, *A Sustainable Development Framework for Assessing the Benefits of Subsidy Reform*, *in* OECD, SUBSIDY REFORM AND SUSTAINABLE DEVELOPMENT: POLITICAL ECONOMY ASPECTS 35–36 (2007).

In fact, one analysis paints a gloomy picture concerning the impacts of subsidies on the environment, making two important conclusions:

1. There is a prima facie case for supposing that subsidies that encourage more production will be environmentally harmful. Subsidies that try to decouple payment from output levels are less environmentally harmful, but still have the effect of keeping production in existence when the optimal solution may be for it to cease altogether.

2. Subsidies that seek to insulate domestic production from international competition are likely to have further environmentally harmful effects in the countries facing trade barriers.

David Pearce, *Environmentally Harmful Subsidies: Barriers to Sustainable Development*, *in*, OECD, ENVIRONMENTALLY HARMFUL SUBSIDIES: POLICY ISSUES AND CHALLENGES 9, 13 (2003). Pearce further concludes that while historically subsidies were often introduced to support vulnerable groups, many subsidies actually harm them. For example, subsidies for irrigation water may cause environmental damage, making water cheaper but also increasing water logging and salinization of soils which reduces agricultural potential. *Id.* at 17–19.

In Pearce's calculation, environmentally harmful subsidies are a "ubiquitous feature of the economic landscape," totaling a staggering US$557 billion for fossil fuel consumption alone in 2008. *Id.* at 113; see also, INTERNATIONAL ENERGY AGENCY, Energy Subsidies: Getting the Prices Right 1 (June 7, 2010). In addition to their environmental costs, these same energy subsidies result in substantial net welfare losses — US$275 billion according to one study, a time when energy subsidies were closer to US$245 billion. INTERNATIONAL ENERGY AGENCY, ENERGY SUBSIDY REFORM AND SUSTAINABLE DEVELOPMENT: CHALLENGES FOR POLICY MAKERS (2001).

Despite the growing body of evidence pointing to the environmentally and socially harmful impacts of many subsidies, governments are unwilling to dismantle them. Frequently, users of a subsidy argue forcefully for the subsidy's "need." Subsidies for technology may have "locked in" users to that technology, making transition to another technology costly (provided another subsidy is not granted). This is particularly true where capital assets have long life spans. The lack of transparency may also make it difficult for opponents of a subsidy to gain public support to eliminate an environmentally harmful subsidy. OECD, ENVIRONMENTALLY HARMFUL SUBSIDIES: CHALLENGES FOR REFORM, at 61–62.

So what is to be done? Can the SCM Agreement provide a potential remedy? The use of subsidies disciplines to countervail underpriced access to natural resources hews closely to traditional subsidies law, because underpricing natural resources is frequently designed to promote exports, protect domestic markets, or maintain low prices to benefit domestic producers. For example, the United States provides extraordinarily cheap water from federal water projects to farmers, thereby allowing them to produce fruit and vegetables at artificially low prices. As we saw in the previous section, certain Canadian provinces charge very low fees for access to timber, which provides additional opportunities for Canadian softwood lumber in export markets. Low resource prices often encourage unsustainable harvesting and discourage governments from paying for adequate environmental protection measures.

The challenge under the SCM Agreement will be showing that a subsidy actually exists and that a domestic industry has been injured or prejudiced. Some argue that underpricing natural resources does not distort trade and should not be countervailed, because the subsidized resource can be easily transported out of the country before it is processed into the final product. According to this argument, if "the subsidy is freely available to foreign manufacturers, and the harvested resource is reasonably transportable, then the subsidy does not distort trade in the manufactured product and arguably should not be countervailed." Ragosta, *Natural Resource Subsidies*, at 272. Under this scenario, the foreign harvester has equal access to the subsidized resource and can produce value added products in that harvester's market of choice. This argument, however, does not address other scenarios that are equally likely. For example, while natural resources may be underpriced, access to underpriced natural resources may be restricted to domestic producers. Thus, unsubsidized imports from foreign producers into the market of the subsidizing country may be at a competitive disadvantage. What are some other obstacles to using the SCM Agreement to challenge environmentally harmful subsidies?

---

2. Does the Failure to Regulate Constitute a Subsidy?

For more than 20 years, environmentalists and others have sought to use the remedies of trade law as a means to prevent environmental harm. In particular, they have argued that low environmental standards constitute a subsidy because producers in those countries are not bearing the full costs of production. In other words, they are externalizing the full costs of production. As such, these subsidies should be countervailable. To combat climate change, the Nobel Prize-winning economist, Joseph Stiglitz, recently called for countervailing duties on products not subject to a carbon tax based on the idea that such products are "subsidized." Joseph E. Stiglitz, *A New Agenda for Global Warming*, Economists' Voice 3 (July 2006). (That would, of course, include U.S. manufacturers.)

When these claims about "green" countervailing duties first arose, the GATT Secretariat took note and sought to dispel them:

> [I]n principle there is no difference between the competitive implications of the type raised by different environmental standards and the competitive consequences of many other policy differences between countries. Differences between countries in tax and other policies toward savings and investment affect the capital stock, which means that countries encouraging capital formation may be enhancing their competitive advantage in capital-intensive industries. Large expenditures on education and immigration policies which selectively encourage the immigration of skilled labour, will encourage competitive advantage in skill-intensive industries.... The extent of government support for science education can influence competitive advantage in high-tech industries.

GATT Secretariat, *Trade and the Environment*, GATT Doc. GATT/1529, at 20 (Feb. 3, 1991). A 1971 GATT study stated more succinctly that lower product prices resulting from the absence of environmental regulations are a form of competitive advantage and not an "unfair" trade practice. *International Pollution Control and International Trade*, GATT Studies in International Trade No. 1, at 23 (1971). Do you agree? As Jeffrey Dunoff asks, "Where is the line to be drawn if the competitive implications of differences in so many government policies are to become a source of demands for the neutralization of the consequences for trade?" Jeffrey L. Dunoff, *Institutional Misfits: The GATT, the ICJ & Trade-Environment Disputes*, 15 Mich. J. Int'l L. 1043, 1061 (1994).

Article 1 of the SCM Agreement clearly states that products subject to low or no environmental standards are not subsidized, because the government has not provided any financial contribution, i.e., there is no transfer of funds or provision of goods or services. Even if the failure to regulate certain products was somehow construed as a subsidy, it would likely not be "specific," because the subsidy would be generally available to everyone.

Nonetheless, the question remains whether the failure to provide adequate environmental protection *should* be considered an actionable subsidy. Had the negotiators eliminated the "financial contribution" component of the definition and focused solely on whether a "benefit was conferred" to an enterprise or industry or on a "market distortion," then it might have been possible to identify certain cases in which the failure to regulate amounted to a subsidy.

In addition, international environmental law provides a possible basis for some form of remedy. Under customary international law, countries have affirmative obligations not to cause significant environmental harm to the territory of others. *See* Stockholm Declaration, June 16, 1972, UN Doc. A/CONF.48/14, at Principle 21, *reprinted in* 11 I.L.M. 1416 (1972); Rio Declaration, at Principle 2. Despite this duty, countries do not agree on its nature and scope. In fact, many international environmental obligations are qualified. For example, the Convention on Biological Diversity requires each party, "in accordance with its particular conditions and capabilities," to develop national strategies for the conservation and sustainable use of biological diversity. It also requires each party, "as far as possible and as appropriate," to rehabilitate and restore degraded ecosystems and promote the recovery of threatened species. Convention on Biological Diversity, signed June 5, 1992, entered into force Dec. 29, 1993, arts. 6(a), 8(f), *reprinted in* 31 I.L.M. 818 (1992). How much threatened species protection is appropriate for the United States? For Mozambique? These questions have relevance in the trade context because some countries have conditioned access to their markets based on the level of environmental protection afforded by the exporting country. The U.S. tuna/dolphin and shrimp/turtle rules are examples.

Rather than bar the export of products subject to low standards, would a less trade restrictive option be the imposition of countervailing duties on such products? The following articles, one by Thomas Plofchan and the other by Charles Pearson and Robert Repetto, investigate the use of countervailing duties to offset low environmental standards. Are they convincing?

Thomas K. Plofchan, *Recognizing and Countervailing Environmental Subsidies*

26 Int'l Law. 763, 768–80 (1992)

[S]everal questions immediately arise when considering whether the lack of an environmental policy in an exporting country is a subsidy that is countervailable by an importing country whose industries are required to conform to strict environmental laws. First, do industries that operate in countries without strict environmental laws adequately recognize costs of production? Second, does a policy that does not require the recognition of environmental costs of production add another factor to supply, demand, and scarcity—thereby distorting market efficiency and the efficient determination of price and resource allocation?

If the answers to the first two questions are in the affirmative, is the lack of strict environmental controls on production an export subsidy? If not, does the lack of controls qualify as a domestic subsidy that may be countervailed against by an importing country? Next, if lack of environmental controls is considered a subsidy, how does one determine material injury, and how should the subsidy be valued? Finally, even if the lack of strict environmental controls on production is a subsidy, material injury is determined, and the subsidy is valued, is the use of countervailing duty laws the best way to address the problem?

In answering the first two questions a hypothetical is useful. *Country E* is a developing nation and has only one industry, *X*. *X* produces widgets in its only factory at a cost of $1 per widget. Production by *X* is in accordance with the laws of *E*. However, *E* is known for its lax environmental controls of production, and *X* in its manufacturing process, pollutes the only river in *E*: the same river that is used for drinking water. In order to provide adequate drinking water, *E* cleans up the river. Thus, for each widget sold in *E*, the citizens of *E* must pay $1 per widget plus the cost of cleaning the water. If *X* produced 100 widgets and the water cleanup costs $100, then the cost of cleanup per widget would be an additional $1 per widget. Consequently, one may fairly argue that *X* has erred in its determination of the cost of producing widgets as the true cost is at least $1 per widget plus $1 for water cleanup per widget.[30]

Given the true cost of $2 per widget, the answer to the first question becomes obvious. Industries that produce goods in countries without strict environmental controls on production may not adequately assess the cost of production. Thus, the answer to the second question also appears obvious. If producers do not incorporate all costs of production, they cannot adequately measure demand because they do not include the increasing scarcity of environmental resources in their equation. Consequently, producers can neither properly price nor properly allocate resources. In short, improper cost recognition distorts the view of market efficiency, resulting in the perception of efficiency when none exists.

Given that the lack of environmental controls on a specific industry results in a distortion of market efficiency, conceivably a governmental policy that rejects these controls or fails to incorporate them can constitute a subsidy in the broadest definition of the term. * * *

In order for a subsidy to be countervailable, it must be an export subsidy or a countervailable domestic subsidy [eds. Note: which the SCM Agreement calls an ac-

---

30. The value of the subsidy is not necessarily the cost of the widget plus the cost of cleaning up the water. The value of the subsidy includes the foregoing value to the victims of the externalities. In other words, it must include the cost the citizens must expend to get water, including the importation of water if necessary. This hypothetical assumes that cleaning the water is the cheapest way for the citizens to get water. If the citizens could import water for $.50 per widget per unit of water, that price would define the subsidy, not the price of cleaning the water, as it is the real measure of the foregone value of not having clean water in the country.

tionable subsidy].... To qualify as an export subsidy the government would have to provide a policy that lowers the cost of exported goods without similarly affecting domestic goods. It seems possible, but not very likely, that the lack of government-required environmental controls will qualify as an export subsidy. Recalling the production scenario of country *E,* an export subsidy would exist if the government of *E* required industry *X* to incorporate the cost of water cleanup into its price for domestic sales only. In this case widgets could be sold domestically for $2 per widget and in foreign markets for $1 per widget. *E* would thus create a strong incentive for *X* to send most of its widgets across its border.

Unfortunately, this scenario, though possible, seems highly unlikely. *X* would find it difficult to separate the cost of environmental controls between its domestic sales and foreign sales since *X* probably would not run separate production lines for each market. Because allocation to different markets is not usually made until after production, a separate production costing for both domestic and foreign markets is unlikely. What is more likely is that if *X* is forced to incorporate the cost of environmental controls for some widgets, it will incorporate the cost over the entire production. By incorporating the cost of environmental controls into the cost of the entire production process, *X* will thereby be raising the marginal production cost of each widget, regardless of eventual market. Thus, if the government does not require environmental controls over the production process, the price of both domestic and foreign products will reflect the subsidy. Because there will be no difference between these two markets, no export subsidy will exist.

Although no export subsidy exists, a domestic subsidy may possibly exist. As mentioned earlier, a domestic subsidy results from governmental programs designed to provide an advantage to producers in the marketplace. What makes domestic subsidy countervailable is best explained by another reference to the hypothetical.

If country *E* does not require strict environmental controls of domestic production, *X* industry can sell its goods for anything more than $1 per widget and still make a profit. In country *I,* industry *R* also produces widgets under the same conditions as industry *X,* but the government of *I* has instituted requirements for environmental controls that make the marginal cost of production $2 per widget. Therefore, to make a profit, industry *R* must sell widgets for any price above $2 per widget — a difference of $1 per widget between the price that *X* must command to make a profit. If *X* exports widgets to *I,* it will enjoy a competitive price advantage over industry *R* as long as the cost of shipment is less than the $1 per widget selling price differential.

Consequently, although the domestic and foreign sales price of *X* made widgets may be the same, *E*'s governmental policy that fails to include a provision for properly assessing the costs of environmental usage to the producer, *X,* will still result in a subsidy for the production of widgets. This subsidy is a domestic one that should be countervailable if the other requirements of countervailing duties are met. * * *

[It will also be difficult to identify whether the government provides this subsidy to a specifically targeted industry.]

U.S. trade law [and the SCM Agreement] adopts a multifactored test for material injury that incorporates a wide variety of economic factors. "Such analysis relies heavily upon information about the size of the subsidies, the elasticity of import supply, the elasticities of domestic demand and supply, and so on." Part of this test focuses on determining the impact of the subsidy on a specific domestic industry or group of industries, relative to the impact of other domestic industries on the specific domestic industry claiming "material injury."

Thus, … for a subsidy to qualify for countervailing measures, material injury requires that domestic industry be harmed by reason of the subsidized imports. Consequently, a causal link must be established between the presence of a subsidy on imported goods and a negative trend in domestic industry performance. The causal link is better explained by referring again to the hypothetical.

Industry X exports widgets from country E to country I. Country E has relaxed environmental control requirements and consequently subsidizes the production of X's widgets. In country I, industry R also produces widgets. Because of the environmental subsidy by country E, X is able to sell its widgets at the same price in country I as industry R. However, R controls 90 percent of the widget market in country I and is able to sell all the widgets it can make. X is also able to sell all the widgets it can make to buyers in country I. and X controls the remaining 10 percent of the widget industry in country I. Widgets are an important and necessary part of all automobiles manufactured in country I.

Unfortunately, country I is experiencing a mild economic downturn and its automobile production has dropped by 5 percent. Both R and X experience a drop in sales relative to the slowdown in automobile production. Thus, R is only able to sell the number of widgets equal to 85.5 percent of the preeconomic downturn market capacity, and X is only able to sell the number of widgets equal to 9.5 percent of the preeconomic downturn market capacity. R argues that the subsidy enjoyed by X has materially injured it. R argues that if no subsidy existed, it would be able to sell at the same level as before, despite the downturn in the economy.

In the preceding situation, industry X and country E can argue that the injury to industry R is not the result of E's environmental subsidy. Instead, the injury experienced by R is the result of demand elasticity. Furthermore, E's subsidy provides no advantage to X, the subsidy merely allows X to price its widgets competitively in I's market. Consequently, the injury to R is not causally connected to the E's subsidy. The subsidy, therefore, may not be countervailed. * * *

The need for the adoption of policies that move the world economy to a point of maximum efficiency is indisputable. That normal subsidies are often more counterproductive than helpful is also indisputable. However, what occurs with environmental subsidies is most probably not predation or some other form of deliberate market distortion, but merely the failure of adequate cost assessment.

The growing environmental movement has publicly demonstrated that most economic industrial decisions treat environmental costs as externalities not subsequently incorporated into production cost assessments. The countervailing of environmental subsidies should produce the beginning of worldwide internalization of environmental costs into calculations of production costs. To rely merely on an inefficient market to eventually internalize these costs may prove to be an inadequate response.

Charles S. Pearson & Robert Repetto,
Reconciling Trade and Environment: The Next Steps

in THE GREENING OF WORLD TRADE 83, 93–95
(Environmental Protection Agency ed., 1993)

From a trade perspective (and setting aside short-run industry adjustment costs), the main issue is whether such differences in environmental control costs represent a distortion in international trade leading to an inefficient allocation of productive resources (including, in the present context, environmental resources). A trade distortion arises when product prices do not reflect their full social costs of protection. Thus the trade question boils down to whether environmental control cost differences are accurate reflections of differences in social production costs among countries. To the extent that such cost differences accurately reflect differences in the implicit value of environmental services, due to differences in physical assimilative capacity, economic structure, availability of pollution abatement technology, income levels, or social preferences, no trade distortion is present. Cost differences are the basis for trade and the source of gains from trade. * * *

The preceding analysis allows us to refine the subsidy question as it relates to the environment.... [G]overnments may set artificially low environmental protection regulations in the expectation of some trade advantage, or fail to enforce their own standards. The "subsidy" in this case takes the form of excessive environmental degradation, borne by the producing country or, in the event of transnational pollution, the international community. But, because conditions differ among countries, a low standard in and of itself is not evidence of a subsidy. * * *

From the environmental policy perspective, something looks amiss. A country that takes strong environmental protection measures may bear a trade loss, at least in high [EU] cost industries, whereas a country that does not may enjoy a trade gain. It should be noted at this point that the empirical evidence to be discussed below gives little support to this possibility. Not only are environmental control costs insignificant in most industries relative to international differences in other input costs and productivities, but there may be offsetting gains to the industry from higher environmental control, in the form of less wastage and high quality.

Questions and Discussion

1. On what basis does Plofchan argue that the failure to regulate constitutes a subsidy? Plofchan prefaces his argument by noting that the GATT is intended to increase market efficiency so that each country may "specialize by exporting those goods it can produce most efficiently and importing those goods that it can produce only at a higher cost." If the use of countervailing duties can help ensure that costs are properly recognized so that only supply, demand, and scarcity determine price and resource allocation, why do you think that the negotiators of the SCM Agreement defined subsidy so as to preclude "regulatory" subsidies? Is the answer found in the argument of Pearson and Repetto?

2. In a separate article, Charles Pearson argues that three possible grounds may exist to support a change in the rules of the SCM Agreement so as to allow countries to coun-

tervail artificially low standards or weak enforcement: 1) to offset a trade distortion caused by this implicit subsidy; 2) to contribute to a perception of fairness in international trade; or 3) to induce stronger environmental standards in the delinquent exporting country. In addition to the absence of empirical evidence to suggest that low environmental standards have serious trade distortive effects, he is also unsure how to determine what constitutes an inappropriate standard. He also worries that the use of countervailing duties for these purposes could invite covert protectionism and bullying. Charles S. Pearson, *Testing the System: GATT + PPP = ?*, 27 CORNELL INT'L L. J. 553, 570–71 (1994). How might we decide what constitutes an inappropriate or artificially low environmental standard?

3. In the United States, pollution abatement costs are generally small compared to total operating costs. For example, pollution abatement costs for the tobacco products industry were just 0.12 percent of total costs; for the fabricated metals products, 0.42 percent; for petroleum and coal products, 1.93 percent; and for all industries evaluated, an average of 0.62 percent. Håkan Nordström & Scott Vaughan, *Trade and Environment* 37 (1999), *available at* http://www.wto.org/english/news_e/pres99_e/environment.pdf. What does this tell us about the appropriateness of countervailing low environmental standards?

4. If a country does not have effective environmental law, can the failure to regulate ever be specific? What if a country's economic base centers on the production of industrial products along the country's one major river? The country has enacted wildlife and habitat conservation laws but few if any pollution control requirements. Might we now find the failure to enact pollution control requirements a specific subsidy? What if a government fails to enforce a law to protect migratory birds, which disproportionately benefits loggers? Is that specific? Does the Appellate Body's decision in *Softwood Lumber* help at all?

5. The OECD has made its views on this subject very clear: "OECD Governments firmly reject demands sometimes made to introduce so-called 'green countervailing duties,' or other protectionist or WTO inconsistent trade measures, to compensate for negative competitiveness effects, whether real or perceived, of environmental policies." OECD, Report on Trade and Environment to the OECD Council at Ministerial Level, OCDE/GD(95)63, at 5 (May 24,1995).

6. Plofchan acknowledges that valuation of these "regulatory environmental subsidies" poses additional difficulties. What might some of those difficulties be? Are those difficulties really any different from valuing other types of subsidies? Recall that under Article 14 of the SCM Agreement that the benefit conferred with respect to the provision of goods or services is calculated in relation to prevailing market conditions. How would you construct a methodology to identify the "fair market value" of such subsidies?

7. Although the SCM Agreement clearly defines "subsidy" so as to exclude low environmental standards, other free trade agreements (FTAs) have included provisions to restrain trading partners from lowering environmental standards to attract trade and investment. For example, in the North American Free Trade Agreement and subsequent FTAs, including DR-CAFTA, the parties recognize that it is "inappropriate to encourage trade and investment by weakening or reducing the protections afforded in domestic environmental laws." *See, e.g.*, DR-CAFTA, art. 17.2, para. 2. Most FTAs make disputes arising out of this obligation subject to consultations, as under DR-CAFTA, although at least one FTA, U.S.-Peru FTA, makes this obligation subject to dispute settlement. U.S.-Peru FTA, art. 18.12. These FTAs also provide that a party "shall not fail to effectively enforce its environmental laws, through a sustained or recurring course of action or inaction, in a manner affecting trade between the Parties." This obligation is also subject to dispute settlement. See, *e.g.*, DR-CAFTA, arts. 17.2, para. 1(a), 17.10. What are the strengths and weaknesses of this approach?

8. Principle 2 of the Rio Declaration on Environment and Development provides that "State[s] have, in accordance with the Charter of the United Nations and the principles of international law, the sovereign right to exploit their own resources pursuant to their own environmental and developmental policies, and the responsibility to ensure that activities within their jurisdiction or control do not cause damage to the environment of other States or of areas beyond the limits of national jurisdiction." This principle is widely regarded as customary international law. Does this principle of international environmental law insulate natural resource subsidies from SCM Agreement scrutiny?

B. Green Subsidies

"Green" subsidies are typically subsidies designed to mitigate an environmental problem or increase the supply of an environmental good. Economists use different terminology to describe these two kinds of "green" subsidies. First, a government may seek to eliminate a negative externality (also called an "external cost") such as pollution. A negative externality exists when an economic actor produces an economic cost (for example, the health care and clean up costs associated with pollution) but does not fully pay that cost. To eliminate that negative externality, the government may offer direct financial subsidies for environmental control technology to reduce pollution and for health care and clean up costs.

Second, a government may want to capture a positive externality (also called an "external benefit"). A positive externality exists when an economic actor produces an economic benefit but does not reap the full reward from that benefit. For example, it may want to encourage reforestation as a means to capture carbon dioxide, a principal greenhouse gas, and abate global warming (plants consume carbon dioxide and release oxygen through photosynthesis). In this way, a landowner that reforests her land reduces carbon dioxide concentrations in the atmosphere but that benefit is shared by everyone. A government may offer a financial contribution to capture this positive externality. Subsidies are also used to overcome obstacles (like high up-front costs) to the adoption by private parties of environmentally desired behaviors like improved energy efficiency or installation of renewable energy sources.

To many environmental advocates, both types of green subsidies are "good," because they seek to improve the environment. Nonetheless, businesses fear that foreign competitors will obtain subsidies whose real purpose is to improve production more so than the environment. In addition, some environmental advocates and economists argue that they are "bad" because they are inefficient and distort markets. Moreover, subsidies to eliminate pollution will typically be inconsistent with the Polluter Pays Principle, a cost allocation rule of environmental law designed to make polluters bear the costs of measures to maintain the environment at the level public officials declare "acceptable."

1. Are Green Subsidies Efficient?

Some consider green subsidies as correcting a market distortion (the externalized cost). For example, because the use of "dirty" fuels pollutes the environment, a subsidy that promotes switching to cleaner fuels would correct that market distortion. Similarly, a subsidy for recycling would reduce the environmental harm caused by a reliance on virgin materials to produce goods. As such, these subsidies would not be considered as creating inefficiencies in trade.

Others, however, view such subsidies as distorting prices despite their environmental benefits. If a company receives a subsidy for pollution abatement equipment, for example, the price of its product will not reflect all social production costs. That in turn distorts the market by making its products less expensive relative to the same products from a firm that pays for the pollution abatement equipment.

In addition to asking whether subsidies distort markets, economists have also asked whether subsidies are the most economically efficient instrument to achieve the desired goal. For activities that have external benefits, subsidies more efficiently capture the external benefit than taxes. Because the subsidy decreases the private cost of an activity and brings the cost into agreement with the social cost, it encourages an efficient increase in the activity. Thus, a subsidy for recycling or afforestation would reduce the costs of those activities but increase the activities to the optimal level.

Conversely, subsidies may not be the most efficient policy option for limiting activities with external costs. Economists generally agree that incentive instruments such as taxes and tradeable allowances are superior to subsidies or command and control strategies for abating pollution. First, taxes to abate pollution (Pigouvian taxes) raise private costs to the same level as the social cost, and thus move the activity back toward its optimal level. Thus, a polluter pays a tax that raises the private cost of polluting to the social cost tax on pollution. Second, economists argue that incentive instruments are more cost effective, spur innovation, lower administrative cost, and are fairer. Taxes to abate pollution are considered cost-effective and nondistorting, because each source abates up to the point that its marginal cost of abatement equals the tax on the next unit of emissions. While high-cost abaters may abate less and pay more taxes, low-cost abaters compensate by reducing greater amounts of pollution abatement and paying fewer taxes. In contrast, subsidies to abate pollution (such as by subsidizing pollution control equipment) may actually increase pollution, because polluters "may behave *ex ante* as if they are insured against the cost of risk-making and increase their risk-making activities" and "capital markets may respond to abatement subsidies by increasing investment in the polluting industry." *See, e.g.*, Jonathan Baert Wiener, *Global Environmental Regulation: Instrument Choice in Legal Context*, 108 YALE L. J. 677, 726–27 (1999).

---

2. Green Subsidies and the Polluter Pays Principle

Despite the potential value of "green" subsidies, they underscore a fundamental tension in environmentalism and its desire for cost internalization. The excerpts that follow assess these subsidies against a foundational element of international environmental policy: the Polluter Pays Principle.

Steve Charnovitz, *Free Trade, Fair Trade, Green Trade: Defogging the Debate*
27 CORNELL INT'L L. J. 459, 505–06 (1994)

On the one hand, a core tenet of environmental economics is that a pricing system reflective of social costs will produce more efficient and ecologically-sound outcomes. Therefore, tax and regulatory policies that lead to internalization of true environmental costs are desirable because they reflect prices correctly. Conversely, subsidies, which pay certain costs, are undesirable because they do not send the proper signal to producers (to use cleaner methods) or to consumers (to conserve).

On the other hand, subsidies are a direct way to finance environmental improvements. They are particularly well-suited to deal with past environmental degradation. Subsidies may also have a useful role in instances of market failure. For example, environmental subsidies may be justified in promoting new pollution control technologies because the private sector is not making a sufficient investment for society's future needs. * * *

When the issue of pollution control subsidies first came to international attention two decades ago, the Organization for Economic Co-operation and Development (OECD) recommended that nations follow a cost allocation rule known as the "Polluter-Pays Principle" (PPP). Because it was badly (or cleverly) named, the PPP is sometimes misunderstood. The PPP says the following: "The polluter should bear the expenses of carrying out … measures decided by public authorities to ensure that the environment is in an acceptable state." The PPP also states that public measures should not include "subsidies that would create significant distortions in international trade and investment" [OECD, Guiding Principles Concerning International Economic Aspects of Environmental Policies, May 26, 1972, 11 I.L.M. 1172, 1175 (1972)].

––––––––––

Like the Polluter Pays Principle, Principle 16 of the Rio Declaration on Environment and Development calls on governments "to promote the internalization of environmental costs … taking into account the approach that the polluter should, in principle, bear the cost of pollution … without distorting international trade and investment." Rio Declaration on Environment and Development, June 14, 1992, UN Doc. A/CONF.151/5/Rev. 1, at Principle 16, *reprinted in* 31 I.L.M. 874 (1992).

As discussed in more detail in Chapter 1, Section III.A.2.a (pages 24–27), the Polluter Pays Principle does not require that abatement costs be paid either by the polluter or the consumer. Instead, it calls for abatement costs to be included in the cost of production. Thus, depending on market conditions, abatement costs could be partly or completely passed through to consumers or may be borne by producers and their shareholders. Moreover, it only requires pollution reductions to an "acceptable" state. Can subsidies for pollution abatement be used consistently with the Polluter Pays Principle? Can subsidies that pay for damages be consistent with the Polluter Pays Principle if the damages are caused by an "acceptable" level of pollution? If these subsidies do not internalize costs or if they significantly distort trade, then they will be difficult for environmental advocates to support as nonactionable subsidies under the SCM Agreement.

Charles S. Pearson, *Testing the System: GATT = PPP = ?*
27 CORNELL INT'L L. J. 553, 560–61, 573 (1994)

Are subsidies to reduce pollution consistent with the PPP? At first glance, the obvious answer would be no. Indeed the PPP is said to be a "no subsidy" principle. On second glance, however, one is not so sure. Consider a subsidy paid to a firm for each unit by which the firm reduces its pollution below a target level. Such a subsidy induces the firm to reduce pollution up to the point where its marginal abatement costs, either in reduced output and profits or in pollution abatement expenditures, are just equal to the subsidy. The firm's opportunity cost for continued pollution is the subsidy forgone, whereas in the pollution charges system its cost is the tax. Both, however, have the effect of increasing the firm's marginal costs. In this sense, pollution costs are internalized to the firm, and the PPP does not appear violated. This led Beckerman to conclude that "it is for this reason that the widespread view to the effect that [pollution abatement subsidies] distort[ ] international trade and constitute[ ] a subsidy to the output of the polluting product happens to be mistaken, at least in the context of a static analysis."

Pearce and Turner provide the basis for a third glance. They note that while both the tax and the subsidy will increase the firm's marginal cost, the tax increases average costs while the subsidy decreases average costs. In the long run, at the industry level, with free entry and exit, we can therefore expect a tax to increase product price and reduce output, whereas the subsidy may attract firms, reduce product price, increase output, and increase pollution. For this reason, pollution abatement subsidies should be considered inconsistent with the PPP. * * *

[Nonetheless,] the apparent move toward interpreting the PPP to include payment for residual damages or indeed "rent" for assimilative capacity has little economic justification. In general, payment for residual damages is not necessary for economic efficiency if, on the margin, environmental damages are equal to abatement costs. Nor is such payment necessary to avoid trade distortions. If one country were to allege infraction of the PPP because residual damages were not paid by a second and ask for trade relief, the result would be trade chaos. The OECD should adhere to its original interpretation that the PPP requires polluters to pay for abatement but not necessarily for residual damages.

----

3. Green Subsidies and the SCM Agreement

The SCM Agreement contained only one short-lived provision that allowed governmental assistance to promote the adaptation of existing facilities to new environmental requirements. Even so, this nonactionable subsidy was required to be nonrecurring and limited to 20 percent of the costs of adaptation. This "green light" subsidy expired in 1999 when developing countries refused to extend it, because WTO members could not agree on extensions for developing country compliance grace periods under several key WTO agreements. *Developing Countries Block Extension of Green Subsidies Rules*, INSIDE U.S. TRADE, Dec. 24, 1999, at 7.

That does not mean that green subsidies are impermissible. Such subsidies may be permissible provided that they are not 1) prohibited export or import substitution subsidies or 2) actionable subsidies because they cause material injury to a domestic industry or serious prejudice to the interests of another member or nullify or impair benefits to another member.

Questions and Discussion

1. Do the environmental benefits of green subsidies outweigh their trade distorting effects (assuming you agree that they distort trade) and inefficient aspects such that they should be considered nonactionable, or are the existing rules for prohibited and actionable subsidies sufficient? If they should be classified as nonactionable, how should nonactionable green subsidies be defined? Would a subsidy for retraining fishermen to become

laboratory technicians, loggers, and steel workers be considered "green" because it removes them from a fishery? Rather than creating a general category of nonactionable green subsidies, should such subsidies be limited to specific countries, such as developing countries, and for specific purposes, such as compliance with technical regulations under the Agreement on Technical Barriers to Trade? If we create nonactionable green subsidies, then what other types of subsidies might be considered worthy of similar treatment? Are you concerned that classifying certain subsidies as nonactionable will lead to advocacy for a larger number of categories of nonactionable subsidies? If yes, how should the range of nonactionable subsidies be defined?

2. While many economists and environmentalists alike consider green subsidies to be antithetical to the Polluter Pays Principle, Daniel Esty argues that the Polluter Pays Principle must not become dogma. Instead, the focus must be on "environmental efficiency— optimal investment in pollution controls—[which] can be achieved either by imposing costs on polluters or by subsidizing their emission reduction expenditures." DANIEL C. ESTY, GREENING THE GATT: TRADE, ENVIRONMENT, AND THE FUTURE 170–71 (1994). What is the difference between environmental efficiency and economic efficiency? Do you agree with Esty?

3. Esty recognized that government could abuse subsidies for environmental purposes. Consider the following. Solar energy remains more expensive to generate than energy from coal, oil, natural gas, or even wind. It nonetheless presents an opportunity to significantly reduce emissions of carbon dioxide, which cause climate change. For years, Germany has been the leader in making solar panels. One reason Germany became the world leader in solar technology was that the German government required utilities to buy back energy from consumers that used solar energy—at 8 times the average price of electricity. These feed-in tariffs, as they are called, generated significant demand for solar energy, a demand that German and other European manufacturers were eager to meet. China responded to the growing demand for solar energy by lavishing generous subsidies on its own producers, making China the world leader. The German subsidies are now used to buy Chinese solar panels, because they are substantially cheaper than similar German panels: Chinese companies sell modules at about 1.20 euros per watt, while European panels sell at nearly 2 euros per watt. In 2009, China's largest producer of solar panels, Suntech Power Holdings, admitted that it is selling solar panels on the U.S. market for less than the cost of the materials, assembly, and shipping to build market share. Subsidy cuts throughout Europe promise more business for Chinese solar companies at the expense of European and American peers as customers seek lower cost products. Chinese subsidies are clearly affecting businesses in Germany, the United States, and elsewhere. In light of these Chinese subsidies, many worry that Germany's solar cell and module manufacturers will not survive. Chinese subsidies have also led Peter Morici, a former chief economist of the U.S. International Trade Commission, to say: "It's absolutely disgraceful that [U.S. President Barack] Obama is going around the world saying we will not resort to protectionist measures against China when they're stealing the solar-panel business out from under us." Dean Calbreath, SAN DIEGO UNION-TRIBUNE (Aug. 30, 2009). What do you think—are these subsidies promoting environmental efficiency or are they an unfair trade practice?

4. If taxes are more economically efficient than subsidies, why might subsidies be more politically attractive? In the WTO context, why might subsidies be more attractive than taxes?

5. For additional articles on green taxes, and the sources for the paragraphs in this section comparing taxes and subsidies, *see* WILLIAM J. BAUMOL & WALLACE E. OATES, THE THEORY OF ENVIRONMENTAL POLICY: EXTERNALITIES, PUBLIC OUTLAYS, AND THE QUAL-

ITY OF LIFE 212–34 (Cambridge 2d ed. 1988); Charles S. Pearson & Robert Repetto, *Reconciling Trade and Environment: The Next Steps, in* THE GREENING OF WORLD TRADE 83, 94 (Environmental Protection Agency ed., 1993); ESTY, GREENING THE GATT, at 84, 169–71; Pearson, *Testing the System*, at 553–75.

C. Fishery Subsidies

Some environmental advocates have shifted their attention to affirmatively using trade rules, such as those found in the SCM Agreement, for environmental purposes. The SCM Agreement holds promise to correct market distortions and serious environmental problems where subsidies to certain economic sectors encourage significant impacts on the environment. The fisheries sector, with its enormous subsidies, has become a target for using the new rules of the SCM Agreement for environmental purposes.

1. The Environmental and Economic Effects of Fisheries Subsidies

The United Nations Food and Agriculture Organization (FAO) estimates that 52 percent of marine fisheries are fully exploited and another 19 percent are overexploited. Catches from these stocks will decrease if remedial action is not taken to reduce or reverse overfishing conditions. Only then will sustained higher catches be possible. Another 9 percent of stocks have become "significantly depleted" or are recovering from depletion. U.N. FOOD AND AGRICULTURE ORGANIZATION, WORLD REVIEW OF WORLD FISHERIES AND AQUACULTURE 7 (2008). In addition, about 37 percent of freshwater fish are threatened with extinction. Press Release, IUCN, Extinction Crisis Continues Apace (2009), http://iucn.org/?4143/Extinction-crisis-continues-apace.

Fisheries subsidies are a principal reason for the state of global fisheries. In 1993, the FAO estimated that total costs in world fisheries at US$124 billion per year but gross revenues of only $70 billion per year. The FAO estimated that subsidies covered the remaining $54 billion annually, representing 77 percent of the gross revenue from fish harvested by the world's fishing fleet. FAO Fisheries Department, *Marine Fisheries and the Law of the Sea: A Decade of Change. Special Chapter (revised) of The State of Food and Agriculture 1992*, FAO Fisheries Circular No. 853 (1993). In 2006, a global study of the period from 1995–2005 estimated fisheries subsidies at US$30–34 billion. CATCHING MORE BAIT: A BOTTOM-UP RE-ESTIMATION OF GLOBAL FISHERIES SUBSIDIES, Fisheries Centre Research Reports, Vol.14 No. 6, 2 (2d vers. Ussif Rashid Sumaila & Daniel Pauly eds. 2007). A recent UNEP report values fisheries subsidies at $27 billion, with "only around $8 billion ... classed as 'good' with the rest classed as 'bad' and 'ugly' as they contribute to over-exploitation of stocks." Press Release, UNEP, Turning the Tide on Falling Fish Stocks— UNEP-Led Green Economy Charts Sustainable Investment Path, 2 (May 17, 2010).

Due in part to subsidies, total fishing capacity may be 250 percent bigger than needed to harvest available fish stocks in an economically and environmentally sustainably manner. Gareth Porter, *Estimating Overcapacity in the Global Fishing Fleet* (1998). Overfishing has wide-ranging environmental consequences that affect target and nontarget species. For example, if canary rockfish harvests were completely halted in U.S. waters off the west coast, it would take 57 years for the fish to return to 40 percent of its historic population. The bocaccio needs 111 years to recover. Nontarget species are also adversely affected by overfishing. Bycatch, which includes birds, dolphins, sea turtles as well as fish, accounts for 25 percent of the total fish catch in the United States and it is discarded, usually dead. John Heilprin, *Wasted Bycatch Detailed in Study*, SEATTLE PI, Dec. 1, 2005, *available at* http://www.seattlepi.com/national/250412_fish01.html. Bottom trawling can turn rich, biodiverse coral reefs in tropical and temperate waters into biological deserts. Global figures are a bit harder to estimate, given the number of international fisheries and difficulty determining what exactly constitutes "bycatch." Figures range between 8 percent (discards only) and 40 percent (including both unmanaged and discarded fish), with the FAO estimating global bycatch at 23 percent of the total catch in 2008. FAO Fisheries Department, *Discards in the World,* FAO Fisheries Technical Paper 470 (2005), *available at* ftp://ftp.fao.org/docrep/fao/008/y5936e/y5936e00.pdf; R.W.D. Davies, et al., *Defining and Estimating Global Marine Fisheries Bycatch,* 33 MARINE POLICY 661 (2009); FAO, THE STATE OF WORLD FISHERIES AND AQUACULTURE 68 (2008).

Overfishing also has significant economic consequences beyond the cost of subsidies. Investing US$8 billion in sustainable management could increase total harvests by 112 million metric tons and gross revenues by $1.7 trillion over the next 40 years. Turning the Tide on Falling Fish Stocks, at 1. But the costs of reducing overcapacity, if borne by the public through publicly-funded vessel buyback programs, can be substantial as well. The cost of seven of ten U.S. buyback programs cost a totaled of US$397 million from 1995 to 2007. U.S. DEPT. OF COMMERCE, FISHERIES ECONOMICS IN THE UNITED STATES 2007 5 (Jan. 2010).

---

2. Are Fisheries Subsidies Actionable?

In addition to the environmental and economic consequences of fisheries subsidies, the United States and others believe that fisheries subsidies distort markets by supporting marginal, often economically unviable fishing fleets. When subsidized fleets harvest resources that are shared, transboundary, or on the high seas, these subsidies displace more efficient producers. In a submission to the Committee on Trade and Environment, the United States succinctly stated its market-based objections to fisheries subsidies.

United States, *Environmental and Trade Benefits of Removing Subsidies in the Fisheries Sector*
WT/CTE/W/51, para. 18 (May 19, 1997)

(a) *Fisheries subsidies promote a misallocation of economic resources.* They encourage over-production and hinder market exit. Subsidized fleets thus tend to be too big and fish too much. Subsidies represent resources that could be more efficiently used elsewhere in the economy. Eliminating them can provide an advantage for strapped budgets.

(b) *Subsidies induce a distorted market equilibrium.* They usually lower costs and tend to encourage fishing activity, lower prices and stimulate demand. Since these distortions tend to push short-term production beyond yield levels which are sustainable over the longer term, the inevitable market correction is delayed and risks are much more severe (e.g., the collapse of a fishery as an economic resource).

(c) *Subsidies promote structural overcapacity by delaying exit from the market.* In a situation of structural excess fishing capacity, the rationally expected response would be exit from the market by the least efficient producers. However, subsidies can serve to keep these producers from exiting the market, thus sustaining chronically inefficient fleets. This creates a permanent lobby for continued assistance.

(d) *Subsidies affect trade by shifting the burden of adjustment onto non-subsidized producers.* By removing market pressures to equate revenues with long term average costs, domestic subsidies tend to shift the burden of adjustment in overcapacity situations to foreign suppliers. This response further exacerbates the market distortions listed above.

(e) *Subsidies can make it more difficult for developing countries to take full economic advantage of the fish resources in their own EEZs.* When paid to distant water fleets, subsidies promote operations that often target highly migratory and straddling stocks. As a result, stocks that straddle the EEZ of a country but also exist in the high seas may be exploited on the high seas by a subsidized distant water fleet. These subsidized operations thus take resources that would be taken by other unsubsidized fleets, often of developing countries, operating in their own EEZs. [An EEZ is an Exclusive Economic Zone, an area up to 200 nautical miles from a country's coastline, in which the coastal State has authority to regulate the harvest of natural resources, among other things. eds.]

Environmental advocates believe that the WTO can be instrumental in righting the environmental, economic, and market consequences of overfishing caused by fishery subsidies. A potential problem, however, is that some remedies for overfishing and overcapacity, such as buyback programs, may also be actionable subsidies. The variety of fishery subsidies in part explains why fishery subsidies have been difficult to address.

David K. Schorr, *Fishery Subsidies and the* WTO

in Trade, Environment, and the Millennium 175, 176–92
(eds. Gary P. Sampson & W. Bradnee Chambers, 2d. ed. 2002)

Naturally, not all [fisheries] subsidies should be considered harmful or illegitimate. The key distinction is between those subsidies that promote unsustainable fishing (especially by encouraging overcapacity or excess effort) and those that promote a transition to sustainable fisheries (especially by encouraging reductions in capacity and effort, by encouraging environmentally responsible fishing techniques, or by promoting sustainable community development). This distinction is not always easy to apply. Is an income support programme helping a depressed fishing community adjust to new limits on the available resource, or is it artificially maintaining the work force for an oversized national fleet? Is a vessel buy-back programme truly reducing total effective capacity, or is it just a shell game that moves boats around while promoting additional investments in fishing capital? Is a gear modernization programme helping fleets adopt cleaner fishing practices, or is it just underwriting operating costs? Questions of this kind will have to be confronted in detail by any serious scheme to reduce harmful fishery subsidies. But in assessing the adequacy of current international rules, it is enough to begin with the widely accepted fact that "capacity-enhancing" subsidies greatly outweigh "capacity reducing" or "conservation" subsidies in the fishery sector. * * *

Subsidization on the scale described unavoidably raises the level of industry-wide capitalization and fishing effort, with consequent pressures on the resources base. A stark fact suggests that subsidies are playing a significant role in fisheries depletion: the world's most depleted fisheries are often those that are dominated by fleets from countries with the largest fishery subsidy programmes. Despite occasional voices to the contrary, the conclusion that subsidies help drive fishing overcapacity pervades the literature from both official and non-governmental sources.

Still, in the debate over how best to address the world's fisheries crises, there are some who argue that subsidies should not be considered a problem in themselves. Rather, they hold, the fundamental cause of both overcapacity and overfishing is the failure of governments to impose proper limits on permissible catches of fish. According to this view, if you limit legal takes of fish, excess levels of capacity and subsidization become the financial problems of businesses and governments, but not the cause of overfishing. This argument merely begs the question, however. Even if the fundamental cause of overfishing is the failure to limit access and otherwise manage fishing effort, this hardly means that subsidies on the order of 20–25 percent of industry revenues ought to be ignored. The scope of the fisheries crisis requires the use of every tool reasonably available to reduce unsustainable fishing effort. Fisheries management regimes will not reach their full potential overnight. And even the best management regimes will be subject to problems of compliance and long-term political stability. Capacity-enhancing subsidies will only serve to maintain artificially large constituencies whose interests do not always lie with the smooth functioning or longevity of management regimes. * * *

The trade impacts of fishery subsidies have also been the focus of increasing attention. Although the fishery sector is not especially large in comparison with the global economy, its economic and social importance are not slight. Fish trade represents a significant source of foreign currency earnings for many developing countries—a dependency that is increasing steadily. Unfortunately, current empirical knowledge about the trade consequences of fishery subsidies is thin. But it has been broadly accepted that subsidies as large as those now granted in various national fishing industries must have significant impacts on the international market. In any case, concern with the trade implications of fishery subsidies has been rising.

* * *

[F]or most fishery subsidies, the question is whether they can be successfully challenged under the "amber [yellow] light" rules. The stakes are relatively high—a successful challenge can lead to a WTO recommendation calling for the removal of the challenged subsidy or, alternatively, to the imposition of countervailing duties against the offending member.

* * *

Does it cause a cognizable harm?

A party complaining against an actionable subsidy must also generally show that it has suffered some kind of trade-related harm (such as international market displacement or price undercutting). The rapid depletion of the world's fisheries obviously causes international economic injuries. However, these may not be expressed in classic distortions of international trade, for two reasons. First, the fisheries game is more of a race for access to resources than a race for access to markets. If subsidies in country X prevent fishermen from country Y ever having access to a particular breed of fish, it will be difficult to discuss the problem in terms of the underpricing of product from country Y. Secondly, the multilateral trading system has traditionally focused on creating and enforcing trade obligations that run between national governments. But, in the case of fishery subsidies, the interests run more fundamentally between individual nations and the shared interests of the international community. Harms to such common interests are not likely to be cognizable by traditional WTO rules, even if they are precipitated in part by the kind of irrational governmental market meddling that the WTO was designed to help prevent.

So if the WTO "amber light" category were fully restricted to addressing proven "trade" harms, the applicability of the Agreement to fishery subsidies would be greatly reduced.

Questions and Discussion

1. Most fishery subsidies are unlikely to be prohibited "red light" subsidies, because they are not provided for export or other prohibited purposes. Yet, many undeniably distort trade as well as promote unsustainable fishing practices. Why aren't WTO members using the SCM Agreement to stop those subsidies?

2. Developed countries sometimes negotiate agreements for access to the fisheries of developing countries on behalf of their fishers. Many developing countries provide access at bargain rates, because they fear they will lose the contract to another country and lose financial resources that can help repay crushing national debt or fund other needs. For example, the European Union (EU) has negotiated agreements with African countries in which the EU pays most of the cost for access of private EU vessels to African fisheries. EU tuna vessels paid less than 15 percent of the total cost of access to fishing grounds under the EU's fishing agreements with African countries; the EU paid more than 85 percent of the costs of access under seven of the eight agreements. Shrimp trawlers paid just 24–32 percent of the total cost under five of the agreements, with the EU paying the rest. More remarkable, EU vessels paid just 0.18 percent to 0.73 percent of the value of estimated catches under EU agreements with Guinea, Guinea-Bissau, Senegal, Mauritania, and Morocco. Gareth Porter, *Fishing Subsidies, Overfishing and Trade*, at 29 (1997); Gareth Porter, *The Euro-African Fishing Agreements: Subsidizing Overfishing in African Waters*, 10 (1997). After *Softwood Lumber*, can these payments be considered a subsidy? If yes, who is providing the subsidy, the EU or the African countries? *See* UNEP, Towards sustainable Fisheries Access Agreements: Issues and Options at the World Trade Organization (2008) (arguing that access agreements may violate the SCM Agreement depending on how they are structured).

3. What kinds of subsidies would help make fisheries sustainable? What changes must be made to the SCM Agreement to make subsidies that support sustainability nonactionable and subsidies that promote unsustainable practices actionable?

4. Will the elimination of fisheries subsidies harm developing country coastal states? Some commentators believe that the prohibition against many fisheries subsidies could "seriously retard the development effort of many coastal states as they attempt to domesticate their fisheries sector and increase down-stream processing." Roman Grynberg & Martin Tsamenyi, *Fisheries Subsidies, the WTO and the Pacific Island Tuna Fisheries*, 32 J. World Trade 127, 139 (1998). In fact, although approximately 60 percent of the world's

skipjack tuna live within the jurisdictions of Pacific Island countries, they harvest comparatively little of the total catch. These countries catch so little of the total catch because they lack a comparative advantage in production and processing due to high costs of operation, low levels of development, and isolation from principal sources of supply and markets. *Id.* at 143. How should any resolution to fisheries subsidies account for this situation, if at all?

---

3. The Way Forward?

Trade officials took note of the many arguments to reform fisheries subsidies made by environmentalists and others. Responding to the problems associated with fisheries subsidies and to make trade law and environmental law mutually supportive, WTO members agreed in 2001 as part of the Doha Development Agenda to "clarify and improve WTO disciplines on fisheries subsidies, taking into account the importance of this sector to developing countries." World Trade Organization, Ministerial Declaration of 20 November 2001, WT/MIN(01)/DEC/1, para. 28 (Nov. 20, 2001). Yet, substantial questions remained, including the following:

- How broadly should the current definition of "subsidy" be expanded to include certain subsidies that promote overcapacity and excess fishing effort?

- To what extent, if at all, should current distinctions between legitimate and illegitimate fisheries subsidies relate to economic harm and trade distortions?

- Should developing countries be treated differently from developed countries?

- How will existing harmful subsidies be phased out?

See David Schorr, *Fishery Subsidies and the WTO*, 191–92.

The negotiations, taking place within the WTO Negotiating Group on Rules and not the Committee on Trade and the Environment, quickly gained momentum, if not consensus, with three main approaches emerging. First, countries such as Japan and South Korea with substantial fisheries subsidies and large distant water fishing fleets saw no reason to treat fisheries subsidies differently from any other subsidy. They view the SCM Agreement as adequate for addressing fisheries subsidies. A second group of countries favored a "traffic light" approach inspired by the SCM Agreement. There was significant divergence in this group, however, about which subsidies to include in the "red," "amber," and "green" categories. In some proposals, prohibited red light subsidies would include fisheries subsidies that directly promote overcapacity and overfishing or have other direct trade-distorting effects. The United States also proposed an "amber" category of actionable subsidies that would be presumed harmful unless the subsidizing government could affirmatively demonstrate that no overcapacity/overfishing or other adverse trade effects have resulted from the subsidy. The proposals of the United States and Chile failed to include a permissible "green" light category. The European Union did not include an "amber" light category. The third approach focused on "special and differential treatment" for developing countries. This approach would permit a range of subsidies for small vulnerable coastal states, such as those for artisanal fisheries, access fees and development assistance provided by developed countries, and incentives applied by for the development and domestication of their fisheries. For an excellent review of the early proposals, see Marc Benitah, *Ongoing WTO Negotiations on Fisheries Subsidies*, ASIL INSIGHTS (June 2004), *available at* http://www.asil.org/insights/insigh136.htm.

At the Hong Kong Ministerial meeting in December 2005, members reaffirmed their commitment to address fisheries subsidies. In a Ministerial Declaration, the WTO members stated that they:

> ... *note* that there is broad agreement that the [Rules] Group should strengthen disciplines on subsidies in the fisheries sector, including through the prohibition of certain forms of fisheries subsidies that contribute to overcapacity and overfishing, and *call on* Participants promptly to undertake further detailed work to, *inter alia*, establish the nature and extent of those disciplines, including transparency and enforceability. Appropriate and effective special and differential treatment for developing and least-developed Members should be an integral part of the fisheries subsidies negotiations, taking into account the importance of this sector to development priorities, poverty reduction, and livelihood and food security concerns.

World Trade Organization, Doha Work Programme Ministerial Declaration of 18 December 2005, Annex D, para 9, WT/MIN(05)/DEC (2005).

Recognizing that the WTO members needed some assistance to fulfill the goals of the Doha Development Agenda and the Hong Kong Ministerial Declaration, the Chair responsible for the fisheries negotiations, Uruguay's Guillermo Valles Galmés, undertook the difficult task of placing these divergent positions (other than the "no need" approach), into a single "Chair's Text." As you read the Chair's Text, note how he has married environmental and economic aspects of subsidies as well as elements of the traffic light and special and differential treatment approaches. Nonetheless, several WTO members believe that the Chair's Text does not address environmental issues adequately. In addition, a group of powerful developing countries believe that the Chair's Text on special and differential treatment is inadequate. When reading the following proposals, bear in mind that article numbers using Roman numerals (I, II, etc.) refer to provisions of the fisheries subsidies text while article numbers using Hindu-Arabic numerals (1, 2, etc.) refer to the SCM Agreement.

Draft Consolidated Chair Texts of the AD and SCM Agreements
TN/RL/W/213, Annex VIII (Nov. 30, 2007)

Article I—Prohibition of Certain Fisheries Subsidies

I.1 Except as provided for in Articles II and III, or in the exceptional case of natural disaster relief, the following subsidies within the meaning of paragraph 1 of Article 1, to the extent they are specific within the meaning of paragraph 2 of Article 1, shall be prohibited:

(a) Subsidies the benefits of which are conferred on the acquisition, construction, repair, renewal, renovation, modernization, or any other modification of fishing vessels or service vessels [eds. note: e.g., those used for transhipment and refueling], including subsidies to boat building or shipbuilding facilities for these purposes.

(b) Subsidies the benefits of which are conferred on transfer of fishing or service vessels to third countries, including through the creation of joint enterprises with third country partners.

(c) Subsidies the benefits of which are conferred on operating costs of fishing or service vessels (including licence fees or similar charges, fuel, ice, bait, personnel, social charges, insurance, gear, and at-sea support); or of landing, handling or in- or near-port processing activities for products of marine wild capture fishing; or subsidies to cover operating losses of such vessels or activities.

(d) Subsidies in respect of, or in the form of, port infrastructure or other physical port facilities exclusively or predominantly for activities related to marine wild capture fishing (for example, fish landing facilities, fish storage facilities, and in- or near-port fish processing facilities).

(e) Income support for natural or legal persons engaged in marine wild capture fishing.

(f) Price support for products of marine wild capture fishing.

(g) Subsidies arising from the further transfer, by a payer Member government, of access rights that it has acquired from another Member government to fisheries within the jurisdiction of such other Member.[80]

(h) Subsidies the benefits of which are conferred on any vessel engaged in illegal, unreported or unregulated fishing.[81]

I.2 In addition to the prohibitions listed in paragraph 1, any subsidy referred to in paragraphs 1 and 2 of Article 1 the benefits of which are conferred on any fishing vessel or fishing activity affecting fish stocks that are in an unequivocally overfished condition shall be prohibited.

Article II — General Exceptions

Notwithstanding the provisions of Article I, and subject to the provision of Article V:

(a) For the purposes of Article I.1(a), subsidies exclusively for improving fishing or service vessel and crew safety shall not be prohibited, provided that:

(1) such subsidies do not involve new vessel construction or vessel acquisition;

(2) such subsidies do not give rise to any increase in marine wild capture fishing capacity of any fishing or service vessel, on the basis of gross tonnage, volume of fish hold, engine power, or on any other basis, and do not have the effect of maintaining in operation any such vessel that otherwise would be withdrawn; and

(3) the improvements are undertaken to comply with safety standards.

(b) For the purposes of Articles I.1(a) and I.1(c) the following subsidies shall not be prohibited:

subsidies exclusively for: (1) the adoption of gear for selective fishing techniques; (2) the adoption of other techniques aimed at reducing the environmental impact of marine wild capture fishing; (3) compliance with fisheries management regimes aimed at sustainable use and conservation (e.g., devices for Vessel Monitoring Systems); provided that the subsidies do not give rise to any increase in the marine wild cap-

---

80. Government-to-government payments for access to marine fisheries shall not be deemed to be subsidies within the meaning of this Agreement

81. The terms "illegal fishing", "unreported fishing" and "unregulated fishing" shall have the same meaning as in paragraph 3 of the International Plan of Action to Prevent, Deter and Eliminate Illegal Unreported and Unregulated Fishing of the United Nations Food and Agricultural Organization.

ture fishing capacity of any fishing or service vessel, on the basis of gross tonnage, volume of fish hold, engine power, or on any other basis, and do not have the effect of maintaining in operation any such vessel that otherwise would be withdrawn.

(c) For the purposes of Article I.1(c), subsidies to cover personnel costs shall not be interpreted as including:

(1) subsidies exclusively for re-education, retraining or redeployment of fishworkers into occupations unrelated to marine wild capture fishing or directly associated activities; and

(2) subsidies exclusively for early retirement or permanent cessation of employment of fishworkers as a result of government policies to reduce marine wild capture fishing capacity or effort.

(d) Nothing in Article I shall prevent subsidies for vessel decommissioning or capacity reduction programmes, provided that:

(1) the vessels subject to such programmes are scrapped or otherwise permanently and effectively prevented from being used for fishing anywhere in the world;

(2) the fish harvesting rights associated with such vessels, whether they are permits, licences, fish quotas or any other form of harvesting rights, are permanently revoked and may not be reassigned;

(3) the owners of such vessels, and the holders of such fish harvesting rights, are required to relinquish any claim associated with such vessels and harvesting rights that could qualify such owners and holders for any present or future harvesting rights in such fisheries; and

(4) the fisheries management system in place includes management control measures and enforcement mechanisms designed to prevent overfishing in the targeted fishery. Such fishery-specific measures may include limited entry systems, catch quotas, limits on fishing effort or allocation of exclusive quotas to vessels, individuals and/or groups, such as individual transferable quotas.

(e) Nothing in Article I shall prevent governments from making user-specific allocations to individuals and groups under limited access privileges and other exclusive quota programmes.

Article III—Special and Differential Treatment of Developing Country Members

III.1 The prohibition of Article 3.1(c) [eds. note: a proposed new set of prohibited subsidies incorporating this annex on Fisheries subsidies] and Article I shall not apply to least-developed country ("LDC") Members.

III.2 For developing country Members other than LDC Members:

(a) Subsidies referred to in Article I.1 shall not be prohibited where they relate exclusively to marine wild capture fishing performed on an inshore basis (i.e., within the territorial waters of the Member) with non-mechanized net-retrieval, provided that (1) the activities are carried out on their own behalf by fishworkers, on an individual basis which may include family members, or organized in associations; (2) the catch is consumed principally by the fishworkers and their families and the activities do not go beyond a small profit trade; and (3) there is no major employer-employee relationship in the activities carried out. Fisheries management measures aimed at ensuring sustainability, such as the measures referred to in Article V, should be implemented in respect of the fisheries in question, adapted as necessary to the particular situation, including by making use of indigenous fisheries management institutions and measures.

(b) In addition, subject to the provisions of Article V:

    (1) Subsidies referred to in Articles I.1(d), I.1(e) and I.1(f) shall not be prohibited.

    (2) Subsidies referred to in Article I.1(a) and I.1(c) shall not be prohibited provided that they are used exclusively for marine wild capture fishing employing decked vessels not greater than 10 meters or 34 feet in length overall, or undecked vessels of any length.

    (3) For fishing and service vessels of such Members other than the vessels referred to in paragraph (b)(2), subsidies referred to in Article I.1(a) shall not be prohibited provided that (i) the vessels are used exclusively for marine wild capture fishing activities of such Members in respect of particular, identified target stocks within their Exclusive Economic Zones ("EEZ"); (ii) those stocks have been subject to prior scientific status assessment conducted in accordance with relevant international standards, aimed at ensuring that the resulting capacity does not exceed a sustainable level; and (iii) that assessment has been subject to peer review in the relevant body of the United Nations Food and Agriculture Organization ("FAO").[83]

III.3 Subsidies referred to in Article I.1(g) shall not be prohibited where the fishery in question is within the EEZ of a developing country Member, provided that the agreement pursuant to which the rights have been acquired is made public, and contains provisions designed to prevent overfishing in the area covered by the agreement based on internationally-recognized best practices for fisheries management and conservation as reflected in the relevant provisions of international instruments aimed at ensuring the sustainable use and conservation of marine species … and technical guidelines and plans of action (including criteria and precautionary reference points) for the implementation of these instruments, or other related or successor instruments. These provisions shall include requirements and support for science-based stock assessment before fishing is undertaken pursuant to the agreement and for regular assessments thereafter, for management and control measures, for vessel registries, for reporting of effort, catches and discards to the national authorities of the host Member and to relevant international organizations, and for such other measures as may be appropriate.

III.4 Members shall give due regard to the needs of developing country Members in complying with the requirements of this Annex, including the conditions and criteria set forth in this Article and in Article V, and shall establish mechanisms for, and facilitate, the provision of technical assistance in this regard, bilaterally and/or through the appropriate international organizations.

---

83. If the Member in question is not a member of the FAO, the peer review shall take place in another recognized and competent international organization.

Article IV—General Discipline on the Use of Subsidies

IV.1 No Member shall cause, through the use of any subsidy referred to in paragraphs 1 and 2 of Article 1, depletion of or harm to, or creation of overcapacity in respect of, (a) straddling or highly migratory fish stocks whose range extends into the EEZ of another Member; or (b) stocks in which another Member has identifiable fishing interests, including through user-specific quota allocations to individuals and groups under limited access privileges and other exclusive quota programmes. The existence of such situations shall be determined taking into account available pertinent information, including from other relevant international organizations. Such information shall include the status of the subsidizing Member's implementation of internationally-recognized best practices for fisheries management and conservation as reflected in the relevant provisions of international instruments aimed at the sustainable use and conservation of marine species ... and technical guidelines and plans of action (including criteria and precautionary reference points) for the implementation of these instruments, or other related or successor instruments.

IV.2 Any subsidy referred to in this Annex shall be attributable to the Member conferring it, regardless of the flag(s) of the vessel(s) involved or the application of rules of origin to the fish involved.

Article V—Fisheries Management

V.1 Any Member granting or maintaining any subsidy as referred to in Article II or Article III.2(b) shall operate a fisheries management system regulating marine wild capture fishing within its jurisdiction, designed to prevent overfishing. Such management system shall be based on internationally-recognized best practices for fisheries management and conservation as reflected in the relevant provisions of international instruments aimed at ensuring the sustainable use and conservation of marine species, such as, *inter alia*, the *Fish Stocks Agreement*, the *Code of Conduct*, the *Compliance Agreement*, technical guidelines and plans of action (including criteria and precautionary reference points) for the implementation of these instruments, or other related or successor instruments. The system shall include regular science-based stock assessment, as well as capacity and effort management measures, including harvesting licences or fees; vessel registries; establishment and allocation of fishing rights, or allocation of exclusive quotas to vessels, individuals and/or groups, and related enforcement mechanisms; species-specific quotas, seasons and other stock management measures; vessel monitoring which could include electronic tracking and on-board observers; systems for reporting in a timely and reliable manner to the competent national authorities and relevant international organizations data on effort, catch and discards in sufficient detail to allow sound analysis; and research and other measures related to conservation and stock maintenance and replenishment. To this end, the Member shall adopt and implement pertinent domestic legislation and administrative or judicial enforcement mechanisms. It is desirable that such fisheries management systems be based on limited access privileges.[85] Informa-

---

85. Limited access privileges could include, as appropriate to a given fishery, community-based rights systems, spatial or territorial rights systems, or individual quota systems, including individual transferable quotas.

tion as to the nature and operation of these systems, including the results of the stock assessments performed, shall be notified to the relevant body of the FAO, where it shall be subject to peer review prior to the granting of the subsidy.[86] References for such legislation and mechanism, including for any modifications thereto, shall be notified to the Committee on Subsidies and Countervailing Measures ("the Committee") pursuant to the provisions of Article VI.4.

V.2 Each Member shall maintain an enquiry point to answer all reasonable enquiries from other Members and from interested parties in other Members concerning its fisheries management system, including measures in place to address fishing capacity and fishing effort, and the biological status of the fisheries in question. Each Member shall notify to the Committee contact information for this enquiry point.

Communication from the United States, Fisheries Subsidies: Articles I.2, II, IV, and V
TN/RL/GEN/165 (Apr. 22, 2010)

I.2 In addition to the subsidies prohibited in paragraph 1, any subsidy referred to in paragraphs 1 and 2 of Article 1 [of the SCM Agreement] that is provided or used for fishing activity affecting marine wild capture fish stocks that are manifestly overfished[3] shall be prohibited.

Article II—General Exceptions

Subject to compliance with Article V, the following subsidies shall not be prohibited under Article I:

(a) A subsidy exclusively for improving the safety of a fishing or service vessel or its crew, such as a subsidy for life boats, other life saving equipment or safety training, provided that:

(1) the subsidy is not used for new vessel construction or vessel acquisition;

(2) the subsidy does not result in an increase in fishing capacity of any fishing or service vessel;

(3) the subsidy does not result in the continuation in operation of any fishing or service vessel where such continued operation otherwise is inconsistent with generally accepted commercial practices within the relevant industry; and

(4) the subsidy is used to further compliance with safety requirements imposed by law.

(b) A subsidy exclusively for one of the following purposes:

---

86. If the Member in question is not a member of the FAO, the notification for peer review shall be to another relevant international organization. The specific information to be notified shall be determined by the relevant body of the FAO or such other organization.

3. A fish stock is manifestly overfished if the stock is at such a low level of abundance that mortality from fishing needs to be restricted to allow the stock to rebuild to sustainable levels. Manifestly overfished stocks include cases in which: (a) the stock has significantly reduced spawning biomass or reproductive capacity; or (b) the stock is recovering from such a low level of abundance or potential for collapse, but further expansion of exploitation would adversely affect recovery.

(1) adopting gear for selective fishing techniques;

(2) reducing the impact of fishing activity on the marine habitat, such as incentives to avoid bycatch or fishing that harms vulnerable marine ecosystems; or

(3) covering expenses for actions taken towards complying with a fishery conservation and management regime, such as the costs of equipment for providing electronic catch reports, vessel monitoring systems, and observers;

provided that the subsidy results in neither an increase in the fishing capacity of any fishing or service vessel, nor the continuation in operation of any such vessel where such continued operation otherwise is inconsistent with generally accepted commercial practices within the relevant industry.

(c) A subsidy provided or used for a vessel decommissioning programme, provided that:

(1) any vessel subject to the programme is scrapped or otherwise permanently and effectively prevented from being used for fishing anywhere in the world;

(2) any fish harvesting rights associated with such a vessel in the fishery that is the subject of the programme are permanently revoked and may not be reassigned;

(3) the owner of such a vessel and the holder of any such fish harvesting rights are required to relinquish

(i)   any claim associated with that vessel; and

(ii) any harvesting rights that could qualify the owner or holder for any present or future harvesting rights in the fishery to which the programme applies; and

(4) the fisheries management system in place in the fishery to which the programme applies includes management control measures and enforcement mechanisms designed to prevent overfishing in the fishery.

(d) A subsidy provided to an individual or a group for the purpose of acquiring user-specific allocations under limited access privileges.

Article IV—General Discipline on the Use of Fisheries Subsidies

IV.1. No Member shall cause, through the use of any subsidy referred to in paragraphs 1 and 2 of Article 1 [of the ASCM], harm to a fish stock in which another Member has a demonstrable interest.[10]

IV.2. Harm in the sense of paragraph 1 exists where:

(a) The capacity of the subsidizing Member's fleet actively fishing the relevant stock is above the level necessary to harvest a sustainable allowable catch;[11] or

---

10. A Member shall be deemed to have a demonstrable interest where: (1) it has a substantial trade interest in fish from the relevant stock or in any directly competitive or substitutable product; (2) it is a party or cooperating non-party to a relevant fisheries agreement; or (3) the range of the relevant stock includes waters under that Member's national fisheries jurisdiction.

11. The term "sustainable allowable catch" means the annual catch level that represents the optimal current use of the resource to ensure its long-term conservation. The sustainable allowable catch

(b) The subsidizing Member's rate of harvest of the relevant stock is above the level necessary to harvest a sustainable allowable catch.

In determining the presence of such situations, the following factors may be considered: (i) a significant decrease in catches or landings; (ii) a significant decline in catches per unit of fishing effort; (iii) a significant increase in the percentage of juvenile or smaller fish in the composition of the catch of all vessels; or (iv) a significant decrease in the length of the fishing season.

IV.3. Harm in the sense of paragraph 1 shall be deemed to have been caused by the subsidy in question where:

(a) Neither the subsidizing Member nor an international fisheries organization has conducted a scientific assessment, within a reasonable period prior to granting the subsidy, that establishes a sustainable allowable catch for the relevant stock; or

(b) The subsidizing Member has not implemented a management plan for the relevant stock that includes measures to control fishing effort and capacity and is designed to achieve a sustainable allowable catch throughout the duration of subsidization of the stock.

IV.4. Notwithstanding paragraph 3, a subsidy shall not be found to have caused harm if the subsidizing Member demonstrates that the subsidy has not resulted in the situations identified in paragraphs 2 (a) and (b).

Article IV bis—Attribution of Subsidy to the Member Conferring It

Any subsidy referred to in this Annex shall be attributable to the Member conferring it, regardless of the flag of the vessel that the subsidy recipient uses or the origin of the fish that are harvested by that vessel.

Article V—Fisheries Management

V.1 Any Member granting or maintaining any subsidy referred to in Article II or Article III.2(b) shall operate a fisheries management system that regulates marine wild capture fishing subject to its national fisheries jurisdiction,[12] and that is designed to prevent overfishing and overcapacity and to promote the recovery of overfished stocks.

(a) The management system shall be based on internationally-recognized best practices for fisheries management and conservation as reflected in the relevant provisions of international instruments aimed at ensuring the sustainable use and conservation of marine species.[13]

(b) The management system shall include, at a minimum:

(i) regular scientific assessments of fish stocks;

---

is based on the best available scientific information and is set at a level reduced from the maximum sustainable yield (the maximum long-term average catch that can be achieved from the resource) to allow for scientific and management uncertainty.

12. Such fishing includes all fishing conducted by that Member's flag vessels, including on the high seas.

13. These instruments include the United Nations Convention on the Law of the Sea, the *UN Fish Stocks Agreement*, the *FAO Code of Conduct for Responsible Fisheries*, and the *1993 FAO Compliance Agreement*.

(ii) regular assessments of the capacity of the Member's fishing fleets, and a plan for managing capacity consistent with the FAO International Plan of Action for the Management of Fishing Capacity;

(iii) legally binding measures regulating fishing effort that are designed to maintain populations of harvested species at levels no lower than necessary to produce a sustainable allowable catch, taking into account ecosystem interactions where applicable;

(iv) mechanisms for the regular collection of and readily available public access to data on catches (including discards) in sufficient detail to allow sound analysis of trends in fishing effort and stock health;

(v) requirements that all vessels have licenses and be registered in a national registry and, where applicable, international registry, that are readily available to the public; and

(vi) in the case of shared, straddling, highly migratory and discrete high seas stocks, measures requiring cooperation with other parties and co-operating non-parties in the fishery and the relevant regional fisheries management organization.

(c) A Member referred to in paragraph 1 shall ensure that judicial, quasi-judicial or administrative proceedings, in accordance with its law, are available to ensure compliance with its management system.

V.2.(a) Each Member shall notify to the Committee any laws, regulations, and administrative procedures relating to marine fisheries management, including any modifications thereto, in accordance with the provisions of Article VI.4.

(b) A Member referred to in paragraph 1 shall notify to the Committee information as to the operation of its management system, including the results of fish stock and fleet capacity assessments performed. The Committee shall conduct an examination of the management system within six months of such notification. To facilitate this examination, the Committee shall seek the views of the relevant bodies of the FAO, the International Council for the Exploration of the Sea (ICES) or the relevant regional fisheries management organization concerning scientific and technical matters, unless the Committee decides not to seek such views.

V.3. A Member referred to in paragraph 1 shall maintain an enquiry point to answer all reasonable enquiries from another Member and from interested person of another Member concerning its fisheries management systems, including measures in place or proposed to address fishing capacity and fishing effort; size, landings and catch rates of that Member's fleet; and the biological status of the relevant fish stock. Each Member shall notify to the Committee contact information for this enquiry point.

―――――――

Communication from Brazil, China, India, and Mexico, Fisheries Subsidies: Special and Differential Treatment
TN/RL/GEN/163 (Feb. 11, 2010)

III.2 For developing country Members other than LDC Members, the subsidies referred to in Article I.1 shall not be prohibited where the benefits of those subsidies are conferred on low income, resource poor or livelihood fishing activities, provided that these activities are performed by fishworkers on an individual or family basis or employed by associations or micro-enterprises or individual boat owners. Fisheries management measures aimed at ensuring a sustainable level, such as the measures referred to in Article V, should be implemented in respect of the fisheries in question, adapted as necessary to the particular situation, including by making use of indigenous fisheries management institutions and measures.

Questions and Discussion

1. A driving force behind the fisheries subsidies negotiations has been the well known adverse environmental impacts resulting from those subsidies. Moreover, even if subsidies are eliminated but governments fail to adopt sustainable catch quotas and other appropriate fisheries management measures, the reduction in subsidies will be seriously undermined. For that reason, the relationship between subsidies and fisheries management has been an important aspect of the negotiations. Do the Chair's Text and the U.S. proposal establish adequate linkages between prohibited/permissible subsidies and fisheries management?

2. The United States claims that its proposal clarifies the biological conditions of the fish stock in question that would trigger application of the prohibition under Article I:2 by removing the implication (in the term "unequivocally" overfished) that there can be no scientific ambiguity concerning the stock conditions. It further believes that its proposal prevents unintended loopholes in Article II. In its view, a subsidy to lessen the "environmental impact" of fishing, as in the Chair's Text, could be read as covering subsidies for energy-efficient engines, which would enhance fishing capacity. Do you believe that these changes, as well as others proposed by the United States, are an improvement on the Chair's Text?

3. The SCM Agreement ignores harm to the commons (areas beyond national jurisdiction, such as on the high seas), because the definitions of "serious prejudice" and "injury" are trade terms that focus on harm to domestic industries or otherwise relate to market distortions. How do the Chair's Text and the U.S. proposal address fishing on the high seas? Given the member-against-member or industry-against-member nature of actions for countermeasures and countervailing duties, how would dispute resolution work and who would represent the commons if the SCM Agreement were amended to cover harm to the commons?

4. The group of developing countries proposing changes to the Chair's Text on special and differentiated treatment believes their proposal better allows "developing countries to achieve development priorities, poverty reduction, and address their livelihood and food security concerns." TN/RL/GEN/163, at 1. The World Wildlife Fund (WWF) worries that this proposal "offers a very ambiguous reply" to the question of whether it provides meaningful sustainable criteria. WWF, One Step Forward, Three Steps Back: Comment on TN/RL/GEN/163, 3 (Apr. 28, 2010). Compare the language of Article III.2 in the Chair's Text with that of the developing countries. How do the two proposals differ with respect to the following criteria: 1) poverty level, 2) location of fishing, 3) technical fishing capacity, 4) level of commerce/trade, and 5) enterprise structure (i.e., to whom the subsidy is provided). WWF concludes that the developing countries' Article

III.2 text "offers a blank cheque for the subsidies that it covers." *Id.* Do you agree that the developing countries' proposal grants developing countries great latitude to provide environmentally harmful fisheries subsidies?

5. Many in the environmental community are skeptical of the WTO getting more involved in environmental matters. They worry that using the SCM Agreement to address fisheries and other natural resource subsidies will entangle the WTO in environmental matters beyond its trade-related mandate or expertise. For that reason, David Downes and Brennan Van Dyke recommend that the WTO and FAO co-sponsor the negotiations. David R. Downes & Brennan Van Dyke, Fisheries Conservation and Trade Rules 41 (1998). In that regard, consider the number of scientific concepts introduced by the U.S. proposal. Do you think that these concepts raise issues beyond the expertise of trade ministers and dispute settlement panelists? If so, in which forum should issues involving trade and environmental matters be discussed and resolved?

V. Agriculture, Subsidies, and Development

A. Introduction

Every country in the world supports its agricultural sector through subsidies, price supports, tariffs, and quotas. Virtually everyone agrees that agriculture is among the most distorted sectors, affecting major staples such as cotton, sugar, wheat, peanuts, and bananas. In fact, the OECD estimated total support to the agricultural sector from OECD countries alone at almost $376 billion in 2008 with $265 billion going directly to producers. OECD, Agricultural Policies in OECD Countries: Monitoring and Evaluation 5, 14 (2009). Critics of these subsidies make a provocative comparison: 3 billion people live on less than $2 per day, yet each European cow receives about $2.50 per day in subsidies.

Most agree that developing country farmers are most affected by these subsidies and other protectionist measures, because those distorting practices increase supply from the developed world and drive down prices globally. The World Bank estimates that developed-country agricultural policies cost developing countries about US$17 billion each year—roughly five times current levels of development assistance to agriculture. World Bank, World Development Report 2008: Agriculture for Development 103 (2007). Full liberalization of the agricultural sector would allow developing countries to increase their share of global agricultural exports by nine percent. *Id.* at 105. For some crops, however, the differences are staggering. If cotton subsidies were removed, including the US$120,000 on average paid to a U.S. cotton producer, the price of cotton would increase 20.8 percent and the developing country share of global exports would increase 27 percent. *Id.* at 99, 106. In fact, removing U.S. cotton subsidies alone is estimated to increase the incomes of West African cotton producers by 8 to 20 percent. *Id.* at 106. Production in OECD countries would correspondingly decline in the absence of current producer subsidies. Mexican farmers reduced their corn prices below costs of production to compete with U.S. corn farmers, who benefited from subsidies as high as 47 percent of farm income. Timothy A. Wise, *The Paradox of Agricultural Subsidies: Measurement Issues, Agricultural Dumping and Policy Reform* (Feb. 2004), *available at* http://ase.tufts.edu/ gdae/Pubs/wp/04-02AgSubsidies.pdf. Overall, both developing and developed countries win from removing agricultural subsidies and other barriers to trade. In one study, removing all agricultural barriers to trade would yield global gains of US$287 billion per year by 2015, but high-income countries would receive more than two-thirds of those dollars. Kym Anderson et al., *Distortions to World Trade: Impacts on Agricultural Markets and Farm Incomes*, 28 Review of Agricultural Economics 168, 174–75 (2006). A World Bank estimate, however, claims that liberalizing trade, largely through the elimination of agricultural barriers to trade, would fuel a US$350 billion welfare gain for developing countries and another US$170 billion for developed countries. World Bank, Global Economic Prospects 2004, at xxix. Under either scenario, however, developing countries would gain more as a share of national income, with an average increase of 0.8 percent compared with 0.6 percent for high-income countries. Anderson et al., at 174.

Not all developing countries would be winners if price-distorting agricultural policies were eliminated. Many of the poorest countries—the least developed countries—are net importers of important staple crops. For example, some countries—Benin, Burundi, Ethiopia, Mozambique, Niger, Rwanda—already spend more than 10 percent of their export earnings to import cereals. Agriculture for Development, at 106–07. Removing subsidies would result in higher prices for these staples and thus negatively affect such countries. At the individual level, trade liberalization may help reduce poverty for the 8 percent of the world's poor who are net sellers, but most poor are net buyers of food and are expected to be worse off as they spend more money to pay for higher-priced food. *Id.* at 108–09. While consumers may benefit from these price-lowering subsidies, the subsidies harm the ability of farmers from the developing world to improve their economic conditions. Agriculture provides livelihoods for about 86 percent of rural people in the developing world. About 2.5 billion of the developing world's 5.5 billion people are involved in agriculture. Agriculture for Development, at 3.

Despite the widespread recognition that subsidy reform is needed and the bounty promised by liberalizing trade in agricultural products, the WTO negotiations over the entire Doha Development Agenda have foundered over the failure of members to agree on a path for reducing agricultural subsidies. Section B of this chapter begins by describing key elements and terms of farm policy that frame the ongoing negotiations. Section C describes some of the environmental consequences of these policies. Section D summarizes the Agreement on Agriculture (Agriculture Agreement), which emerged during the Uruguay Round and which began the process of reducing certain types of agriculture support programs. Section D takes a look at the differences that currently divide WTO members and possible directions for agricultural policy negotiations within the WTO.

Questions and Discussion

1. Removing agricultural trade barriers has substantial economic ripple effects. According to the WTO, developing countries could earn at least three times more in exports than all the official development assistance put together if developed countries drop domestic agricultural subsidies. Those funds would increase employment and reduce poverty in Africa. It would also reduce developed country taxpayer expenditures for two programs: subsidies and development assistance. Tom Maliti, *Developing Countries Could Earn Three Times the Aid They Receive if Subsidies Are Removed, WTO Says*, Associated Press (Feb. 11, 2002).

2. As noted above, several studies report that that the elimination or reduction in agricultural trade barriers will benefit developing country producers in the aggregate. They argue that these barriers will make developing country products more competitive and thus increase exports. An increasing concern for trade policy is how to balance aggregate trade gains for developing countries with significant welfare losses for some of the world's poorest people. Professor Arvind Panagariya challenges the notion that the least developed countries will become net exporters of food with the removal of these barriers, unless they become a sufficiently large exporter to offset losses caused by higher food prices. He further argues that many least developing countries benefit from preferential export treatment, especially in the EU where African, Caribbean, and Pacific Island nations receive premium prices or preferential tariff or quota treatment on sugar and other agricultural goods. Arvind Panagariya, *The Tide of Free Trade Will Not Float All Boats*, FINANCIAL TIMES, Aug. 3, 2004, at 17.

William Cline, a Senior Fellow with the Center for Global Development and Institute for International Economics, has directly challenged Professor Panagariya's claims. Cline argues that those least developed countries with a comparative advantage in food production and with food trade surpluses will unambiguously benefit from more liberalized trade in agricultural products. He also estimates that another one-fifth of the world's poorest who live in countries that have a comparative advantage in food production but have small food trade deficits (amounting to an average of 4 percent of total nonfood imports) will benefit from eliminating agricultural subsidies, provided that a small reduction of 0.5 percent in world prices of manufactures and other nonfood goods occurs. William R. Cline, *Global Agricultural Free Trade Would Benefit, Not Harm, LDCs*, FINANCIAL TIMES, Aug. 9, 2004, at 16.

3. Consumers around the world feel the effects of agricultural subsidies. The price of food in the EU is 45 percent higher than it would be without the subsidies, according to the Organization for Economic Cooperation and Development (OECD).

B. Governmental Farm Policies

At first glance, the farm policies of the world's nations appear so fantastically out of synch with trade disciplines that they would appear to be easy targets for reform. However, with food shortages a war time legacy for Japan and Europe, and famine an everyday experience for hundreds of millions of people primarily in the developing world, the use of market restrictions, production subsidies, and export subsidies to fulfill the desire for self-sufficiency and food security is easily understood. In addition, many farm support programs are designed to help stabilize income for farmers and avoid the harsh economic consequences of year-to-year weather variables affecting both production and commodity prices.

To fulfill these needs, governments have designed an array of farm policies to support agriculture. Farm policies can be lumped into three main types of instruments, each considered to distort trade: market access, export subsidies, and domestic support. *Domestic support measures* include direct support to farmers linked to the type, price, and volume of production. Depending on the level of support, local production is usually higher and competing imports lower than in the absence of subsidies. *Export subsidies* include government payments that cover some of the costs of exporters such as marketing expenses, special domestic transport charges, and payments to domestic exporters to make sourcing products from domestic producers competitive. *Market access instruments* include import tariffs and quotas that protect local producers from competing imports. Protection induces local production to be higher than would be the case at market prices, at the expense of international producers and exporters. The following excerpt takes a closer look at some of these mechanisms.

1. Domestic Support Measures

Market price support, deficiency payments, production quotas, and direct income support are four major production-related agricultural policy instruments used to support a variety of agricultural products. Jussi Lankoski introduces these policy instruments.

Jussi Lankoski, *Environmental Effects of Agricultural Trade Liberalization and Domestic Agricultural Policy Reforms*
UNCTAD/OSG/DP/126, 4–5 (Apr. 1997)

In the *market price support system* the domestic market price is fixed at a level higher than the equivalent world market price. For a traded commodity, market price support requires the use of border measures to provide import protection, and if domestic surpluses are generated, the use of export subsidies. Market price support raises domestic producer and consumer prices, thus increasing production and decreasing consumption, implying a transfer from consumers to producers. Hence, the market price support system distorts both production and consumption decisions.

Deficiency payments guarantee producers a per unit payment on output equal to the difference between the market price and an administrative target price. This policy instrument raises the effective producer price through direct payments by taxpayers rather than transfers from consumers, as consumers pay the lower market price.

Under the *production quota* system the government sets a support price and restricts production to a level below that which would otherwise occur at the support price. Production quotas are usually used in combination with support price or deficiency payments. According to [the] OECD, the main quantitative restrictions in OECD countries include quotas on output (e.g. the EU quotas for milk and sugar) and set-aside of agricultural land, and it is increasingly the case that farmers receiving market price support or direct payments must comply with specific input or output constraints. Quantitative restrictions lead to economic efficiency losses, can create significant market distortions for the commodity controlled and have negative "spillover" effects on competing products or on factors of production. In addition, the long term supply controls may reduce the competitiveness of controlled sector by slowing structural change and technological innovation.

The term *direct income payment/support* refers to transfers that are financed by budgets and paid directly to farmers, and are independent of current and future production levels, whereas the term *direct payments* refers to budgetary measures with no judgement as to their linkage with production or factors of production. The latter category includes a wide range of different types of payments, such as deficiency payments, area and headage payments. These payments may be based on past farm or regional production data, and can generate economic distortions to varying degrees.

There are many variations on these mechanisms. For example, *counter-cyclical payments* ensure a minimum price for farmers by increasing payments to producers as market prices fall. Most view these payments as trade distorting because they interfere with the market signal to grow less as prices fall. As Lankoski says, some of these mechanisms are also made effective through *import bans* and *quotas*. Countries commonly use import bans and quotas to protect their domestic industries or to help ensure self-sufficiency. Japan, for example, maintains a complex system of tariff-free import quotas, over-quota tariffs and fees, and purchasing arrangements that limit the quantities and types of rice that can compete in the Japanese market.

Beyond these programs for agricultural products themselves, governments also subsidize inputs. Developing countries heavily subsidize agrichemicals and irrigation water to offset the negative impacts of price limits and to improve international competitiveness. Odin Knudsen et al., *Redefining the Role of Government in Agriculture for the 1990s*, 70–76 (World Bank Paper No. 105, 1990). The United States, too, is no stranger to subsidized irrigation water, providing it at 10 to 15 percent of its value, a subsidy that increases soil salinity, contaminates wetlands, and harms fish and bird populations. Robert Repetto, *Complementarities Between Trade and Environment Policies, in* Trade and the Environment: Law, Economics, and Policy 244 (Durwood Zaelke et al. eds., 1993).

2. Export Subsidies

Export subsidies take a variety of forms, but all are essentially payments to increase the export of agricultural products. For example, government programs not directly tied to the production of crops may be classified as export subsidies. Through *export credit* practices, an importer arranges to defer payment of the contract price to the exporter over an agreed period of time. The financial terms may include credit or conditions relating to the length of repayment, interest rates, down payments, and other conditions of purchase. Thus, in addition to competing on the basis of quality and price of their products and delivery times, exporting firms may need to offer attractive financing arrangements if they are to compete successfully. Because of the way these arrangements are structured, and because governments often assist these arrangements through export credit agencies, they have been called "subsidies by any other name." Kym Anderson, *Agriculture and the WTO into the 21st Century* (Center for International Economic Studies: Oct. 1998).

Whether these arrangements are financed by commercial banks, governmental agencies, or by other means, the lender will likely guard against risks by obtaining insurance through financial institutions specialized in trade financing and insurance. Export credit insurance policies enable lenders to be reimbursed for losses arising from payment delays or nonpayment resulting from "commercial" and or "country" risks. Commercial risks include default, insolvency, or other business related problems, whereas country risks include borrower/importer country government actions that prevent, or delay, the repayment of export credits (*e.g.*, foreign exchange restrictions, sometimes referred to as "transfer risk") and other borrower country risks (*e.g.*, civil war, physical disaster, etc.).

Export credit "guarantees" are commitments by specialized export credit institutions in the exporting country to reimburse a lender if the borrower fails to repay a loan. The lender pays a guarantee fee. While guarantees could be unconditional, they usually have conditions attached to them, so that in practice there is little distinction between credits that are guaranteed and credits that are subject to insurance. The premiums for such insurance (and guarantees) vary according to the terms and conditions of the export, such as their duration, but more importantly according to the credit rating or risk status of the importer, the importer's bank, or the importing country. Again, either private institutions or government export credit agencies can provide export credit guarantees and insurance guarantees.

Export credit agencies conduct much of their business on a commercial basis, with their income deriving from premiums. However, the WTO reports that export credit agencies, "having regard to the risks inherent in the nature of longer term export credits and insurance, and to the fact that in many cases export credit agencies have been established to promote national exports," actually conduct business on a "break-even" basis. To the extent their premium rates do not cover long-term operating costs and losses, their guarantees could constitute a subsidy.

The support that export credit agencies provide, whether in the form of export credit insurance and guarantees in respect of supplier and buyer credits, or in the form of, for example, export credits ("direct financing"), is referred to as "official support." Thus when an exporting firm arranges credit or line of credit with a private bank to finance an export transaction and this export financing arrangement is then insured by the national export credit agency, it is referred to as an "officially supported export credit." As a result, the export credit agency may assume or cover the risks involved at premiums that may not be risk- or market-based. In addition, export credit agencies, because of their governmental status and associated credit ratings, may offer interest rates on the export credit transaction that are lower than commercial banks can offer.

Exports of agricultural products may also benefit from export credits on terms which, directly or indirectly, are influenced by some form of government action or assistance, through state trading export enterprises or export marketing bodies. These institutions have access to funds at special rates, or at rates close to government cost of borrowing from commercial sources, and are able to finance exports on credit/deferred payment terms that are more competitive than would otherwise be the case.

The WTO has estimated that about 90 percent of total world trade is conducted on a cash basis or with short-term credits of up to 180 days, suggesting that about 10 percent of world trade is conducted on the basis of export credits whose terms are longer than six months. WTO Secretariat, *Trade, Finance and Financial Crises* (1999). Preliminary statistics published by the OECD show total officially supported export credit for agricultural commodity allocations for those participating in the OECD's Export Credit Arrangement increasing from $11 billion in 1995 to $18 billion in 1998. For more on export credits, and the basis for this discussion, *see* WTO Secretariat, *Export Credits and Related Facilities*, G/AG/NG/13 (June 26, 2000).

---

3. Tariffs

In addition to production and export subsidies, governments also protect their agricultural industries with tariffs, which on average are much higher than tariffs for manufactured goods. For example, EU tariffs average 19 percent for agricultural goods versus 4.2 percent for manufactured goods. Moreover, more than 90 percent of the global costs of agricultural policies are estimated to come from tariffs rather than from export subsidies or domestic support. AGRICULTURE FOR DEVELOPMENT, at 104. Developing countries show similar bias. Also on average, developing countries have higher agricultural tariffs than developed countries. For example, among a group of countries analyzed by the World Bank, Morocco had average agricultural tariffs of 64 percent, Korea 42 percent, and Turkey 49.5 percent. However, some developing countries had extremely low average tariffs, such as Indonesia (8.5 percent) and Malaysia (2.8 percent). At the same time, developing country tariffs have declined more rapidly than OECD countries. The World Bank reports that developing country agricultural tariffs declined from an average of almost 30 percent in 1990 to about 18 percent in 2000, a decline of 35 percent. WORLD BANK, GLOBAL ECONOMIC PROSPECTS 2004, at 119. As Table 1 indicates, not only do high average tariffs persist, but some countries have extreme tariff peaks—a country's highest agricultural tariff.

Table 1. Agricultural Tariffs: High Peaks and Deep Valleys
Tariff peaks and variance in selected countries; MFN, out of quota, applied duties (percent and standard deviation)

	Average Tariff	Maximum Tariff	Standard Deviation	Percentage of Tariff Lines Covered
Canada	3.8	238.0	12.9	76.0
European Union	19.0	506.3	27.3	85.9
Japan	10.3	50.0	10.0	85.5
United States	9.5	350.0	26.2	99.3
Korea, Rep. of	42.2	917.0	119.2	98.0
Brazil	12.4	55.0	5.9	100.0
Costa Rica	13.2	154.0	17.4	100.0
Indonesia	8.5	170.0	24.1	100.0
Malawi	15.3	25.0	9.1	100.0
Morocco	63.9	376.5	68.2	100.0
Togo	14.7	20.0	6.5	99.9
Uganda	12.9	15.0	3.7	100.0

Source: WTO Integrated Database; From: World Bank, *Global Economic Prospects 2004*, at 119.

---

4. Environmental Subsidies

A number of countries provide subsidies or employ other strategies to counter the effects of overproduction caused by other farm policies. The following excerpt takes a look at U.S. agricultural programs to benefit the environment.

David E. Adelman & John H. Barton,
Environmental Regulation for Agriculture: Towards a Framework to Promote Sustainable Intensive Agriculture
21 STAN. ENVTL. L.J. 3, 27–28, 37–38 (2002)

The United States has increasingly adopted incentive programs to safeguard water resources and wetlands. Initiated in 1990, the Water Quality Incentives Program (WQIP) is a voluntary program that provides incentives in the form of crop subsidies for farmers to adopt environmentally and economically sound management practices to prevent soil erosion, protect wildlife habitat, and conserve water resources. The benefits of the program have been minimal, though, because of Congress's failure to fund it adequately. The 1996 Farm Bill merged the WQIP with USDA's Environmental Quality Incentives Program (EQIP), which has boosted funding for the program substantially. These incentive programs should be expanded and leveraged by conditioning receipt of other agricultural subsidies like loan deficiency payments on compliance with the EQIP's requirements.

In place of a traditional regulatory scheme, the U.S. government has established two incentive programs to protect wetlands, the Wetlands Reserve and Swampbuster programs. Under the 1990 Wetlands Reserve program the USDA compensates landowners for restoring wetlands through either permanent or thirty-year easements. Despite high farmer interest, low funding has seriously limited restoration efforts. It will have taken more than ten years for the program to enroll 975,000 acres (about ten percent of current agricultural wetlands). The Swampbuster program creates a disincentive to alter wetlands by denying USDA benefits to farmers if they produce a commodity crop on converted wetlands. The benefits of this program also have been limited, though, because the restrictions have been severely diluted by an array of exceptions. In spite of the enormous resources for other programs, USDA implementation and support of these incentive programs, as a general rule, have been meager; this parsimony is reflected in their limited success. * * *

The U.S. has two primary agricultural conservation incentive programs, the Conservation Compliance Program (CCP) and the Conservation Reserve Program (CRP). The Conservation Compliance Program fosters sustainable soil management practices using educational programs and, more importantly, conditions certain agricultural benefits on the adoption of farming practices that meet designated conservation standards. Predictably, the USDA has not uniformly enforced the requirements under this program and often has failed to promote erosion control effectively.

The largest U.S. agroenvironmental program is the CRP, under which the government "rents" agricultural land for a term of years (usually ten) during which time the owner must take the land out of agricultural production and plant it with soil-fixing grasses or trees. Land is selected using an "environmental benefits index," which ranks factors such as benefits to wildlife, water quality, air quality, and erosion reduction. The CRP's impact, however, derives more from its size—thirty-three million acres (ten percent of U.S. farmland) and an average annual budget of $1.7 billion—than from its structure. The USDA needs to prioritize programs effectively based on environmental criteria. Oversight in the CCP and CRP, and thus, the environmental benefit per dollar, has been relatively low.

Questions and Discussion

1. Beginning with an enrollment of 2 million acres in 1985, the CRP in 2007 included just under 37 million acres (more than eight percent of all cropland in the United States), although the 2008 Farm Bill capped maximum total acreage at 32 million. By 2007, the CRP had reduced soil erosion by an estimated 470 million tons. With a 2007 budget of almost $2 billion, the CRP is the largest federally funded conservation program. While

the program remains popular with both farmers and conservationists, many worry about the program's effectiveness. For example, one study found that "a great majority of the benefits of all CRP lands could have been realized with only a small fraction of the land enrolled, suggesting that the benefits from the enrollment of the rest of the acres are marginal." Jeffrey Ferris & Juha Siikamäki, Conservation Reserve Program and Wetland Reserve Program: Primary Land Retirement Programs for Promoting Farmland Conservation 27 (Aug. 2009) (citing B.A. Babcock et al., *The Economic, Environmental, and Fiscal Impacts of a Targeted Renewal of Conservation Reserve Program Contracts* (Working paper 95-WP 129, 1995)).

2. Why would a government subsidize a farmer to produce crops and at the same time not produce crops in order to protect the environment? This has been called the taxpayers' double burden. The Wilderness Society and the Environmental Defense Fund report that subsidies for natural resource extraction on federal lands resulted in the annual loss of billions of dollars in revenue. At the same time, federal funds spent for the recovery of species endangered by extractive activities on public lands exceeded $118 million in 1991. The Wilderness Society, The Taxpayers' Double Burden: Federal Resource Subsidies and Endangered Species (1993).

3. How should the international community address agricultural subsidies that have environmental benefits? Should these be exempt from subsidies disciplines? These types of subsidies provide income to farmers that may allow them to sell their crops more cheaply than other farmers. Do the social benefits outweigh the economic distortions created by the subsidy? The WTO's Agriculture Agreement addresses these subsidies through its "green" and "blue" subsidies. *See* Section D.2, below (pages 623–24). In addition, countries such as Japan, Norway, and Switzerland, among others, continue to advocate for "multifunctionality," a concept that attempts to account for social benefits of subsidies. Their views are described in Section D.4, below (pages 630–34).

4. For more information on U.S. programs to reduce the impacts of agricultural subsidies, see Natural Resources Conservation Service, *at* http://www.nrcs.usda.gov/programs.

C. Environmental Consequences

1. Scale of the Consequences

In addition to distorting markets, the agricultural trade barriers mentioned above have significant adverse environmental impacts. The adverse environmental impacts of agricultural programs are difficult to dissociate from the adverse environmental impacts of agriculture generally, largely due to the vast scale of global agricultural production. The World Resources Institute estimates that 36 percent of the earth's land surface, excluding Antarctica, is used for growing crops and grazing animals. World Resources Institute, World Resources 1994–95, 182 (1994). As summarized by Professors Adelman and Barton:

> Agriculture is the largest consumer of freshwater resources, the largest contributor to a doubling of the earth's level of fixed nitrogen, and a significant source of global warming gases and ground-level-ozone-generating chemicals. In the United States, agricultural practices are implicated in almost a third of the species listings under the Endangered Species Act and have been the single most significant cause of habitat destruction. Agricultural production is believed to be

the primary contributor to surface water deterioration in the United States, predominantly through sedimentation and agrichemical runoff. A 1990 study by the U.S. Environmental Protection Agency (EPA) ranking the severity of environmental threats in the United States concluded that pesticides, nonpoint-source water pollution, physical degradation of terrestrial ecosystems, and degradation of water and wetlands were among the top five most urgent environmental threats. Each of these problems is linked to agriculture.

David E. Adelman & John H. Barton, *Environmental Regulation for Agriculture: Towards a Framework to Promote Sustainable Intensive Agriculture*, 21 STAN. ENVTL. L.J. 3, 4–5 (2002). The environmental impacts of agriculture are clearly not only local or national issues. Agriculture is responsible for about 14 percent of total worldwide annual emissions of greenhouse gases. T. Barker et al., *Technical Summary, in* CLIMATE CHANGE 2007: MITIGATION: CONTRIBUTION OF WORKING GROUP III TO THE FOURTH ASSESSMENT REPORT OF THE INTERGOVERNMENTAL PANEL ON CLIMATE CHANGE 27 (B. Metz et al. eds., 2007). When livestock are included, the numbers soar. Two more recent studies attribute 18 percent and 51 percent of *total* global greenhouse gas emissions to livestock production (including use of grains to feed livestock). HENNING STEINFELD, LIVESTOCK'S LONG SHADOW: ENVIRONMENTAL ISSUES AND OPTIONS (Food and Agriculture Organization, 2006); Robert Goodland & Jeff Anhang, *Livestock and Climate Change*, WORLD WATCH 10, 11 (Nov./Dec. 2009).

By creating economic and market distortions, agricultural subsidies and programs likely exacerbate these adverse environmental impacts from agricultural production. Agricultural support policies often influence levels of inputs, such as fertilizers and pesticides. The World Bank has concluded that agricultural subsidies and protection can lead to excessive use of chemicals and fertilizers that can harm the environment. In Japan, for example, the high price paid to rice farmers encouraged overuse of insecticides to protect crops. In 1993, although Japan produced only 3 percent of the world's rice, its farmers' share of global expenditure on rice insecticides was 34 percent. World Bank, *Agriculture Investment Note: Reform of Agriculture Subsidy and Protection Policy, available at* http://www-esd.worldbank.org/ais/index.cfm?Page=mdisp&m=1&p=03.

Jussi Lankoski, *Environmental Effects of Agricultural Trade Liberalization and Domestic Agricultural Policy Reforms*
UNCTAD/OSG/DP/126, 6–8 (Apr. 1997)

The same agricultural policies that have distorted production decisions and trade have also reinforced environmental damages in agriculture.... [A]gricultural policies are composed of a complex set of measures that interact with one another in determining farmers' decisions on the extensive and intensive margins simultaneously.

It can be argued that agricultural production subsidies have increased incentives that have led, for instance, to water and soil pollution. Market price support has an effect on the price-ratio between a product and a production input like fertilizer or pesticide. Market price support increases the producer prices, which in turn increases the economically optimal rate of input use. Farmers try to apply fertilizers at the economically optimal rate in order to maximize profits. This economically optimal level of fertilization, however, may exceed the rate that is optimal for crop growth (depending, for example, on weather conditions), thus exceeding also the environmentally optimal rate. Excessive use of fertilizers has led to eutrophication in surface waters and nitrate accumulation in ground waters; agriculture has indeed been the main source of both nitrogen and phosphorus leakages into surface waters in many countries. In other words, the growth in fertilizer intensity has resulted in external costs. These external costs can be internalized through appropriate environmental policy instruments. However, monitoring and controlling agricultural pollution encounters enormous problems owing to the characteristics of nonpoint source pollution.... [T]he dilemma faced by the agricultural sector is that the policy failures due to government intervention in agricultural markets tend to reinforce rather than mitigate market failures in agriculture.

Because commodity-specific policies alter the relative prices of crops that can be grown in rotation, they lead to an increased use of fertilizers to maintain soil productivity. These policies have encouraged the intensive cultivation of "programme" crops and reduced rotation. The chosen crop mix has important implications for environmental quality as some crops are more pollution intensive than others. Adverse environmental impacts are reinforced if programme crops are highly polluting. Tobey (1991) has analysed the pollution intensity of different crops using data from the United States. The rankings of different crops were mainly based on chemical input requirements and the rate of soil erosion. The most pollution intensive grains were (in descending order) corn, rice, wheat, oats and barley.

Moreover, differential support levels distort relative crop and livestock prices and may produce environmental strain through reduced production diversity. The pattern of relative production subsidies also encourages higher spatial concentration of specific production lines. For example, intensive pig and poultry production is often located in geographically concentrated areas near EU ports where imported feeds are cheaper due to lower transportation costs. As a result, the volume of manure produced in areas where livestock production is concentrated has exceeded the area of cropland available on which to apply manure. Thus, manure surpluses and nutrient pollution of surface and groundwaters have increased.

Price support policies are usually combined with other measures like supply controls, and their environmental impacts depend on the form of these combinations. Open-ended price support will result in more input use than price support that is supplemented by quotas. Another combination is price support that is supplemented by restrictions on input use like a set-aside of arable land. While the purpose of set-aside programmes is to limit the output-increasing effects of price supports, the reduction of available arable land can induce input intensification on lands remaining on cultivation. The environmental effects of set-aside as a supply control measure are, however, complex depending on the way the set-aside programme is implemented (e.g. plant cover) and input use intensity on the remaining production base.

... [T]he concentration of farms, land and livestock, the specialization in a narrow range of products and the intensification of the use of fertilizers, pesticides, feedstuffs and energy have been responsible for the greatest environmental damage due to agricultural production in EU. These factors have composed part of an adjustment process to technological and economic developments which has been reinforced by agricultural policies. However, the most important effects on environment have resulted from distorted prices and cost structures. These distorted price relationships exist between the EU market and the world market, between output and input, between domestic and imported products, and between products with market regulation and those without intervention.

Subsidies for the purchase of fertilizers and pesticides, as well as supply of natural resources below their marginal cost (e.g. irrigation water) distort the real price of these inputs and encourage their enhanced use due to lower effective prices. Subsidies may contribute to over-application of these inputs, thus increasing pollution. Furthermore, these subsidies also discourage farmers to practise soil conservation and use organic manure more efficiently. Lower production input costs also induce greater overall production on the natural resource base. Correspondingly, interest subsidies provide incentive to invest in farm capital which encourages a shift to capital- and stock-intensive farming practises.

In developing countries, as a partial compensation for policies which usually tax agricultural production, the use of fertilizers and pesticides has often been subsidized by governments. Sometimes fertilizer subsidies are justified in order to maintain soil fertility and they may play an important role in combating soil erosion and deforestation. However, pesticide subsidies also contribute to the low application efficiency, probably under 50 per cent, in those countries, thus resulting in environmental pollution. By contrast, fertilizer and pesticide subsidies have not been common in OECD countries. However, irrigation water is commonly subsidized, and where soils are saline, this tends to exacerbate salinity problems. Some Latin American countries have subsidized livestock production on large estates through tax incentives, thus increasing the clearing of tropical forests for grazing purposes.

---

2. Agricultural Policy, Environmental Impacts and the Everglades

In southern Florida, slow moving waters flow south from Lake Okeechobee through the Everglades. This unique and fragile ecosystem contains hundreds of species of plants and animals. It is also home to the sugar industry and a striking case study concerning the effects of agricultural policy on the environment. This "river of grass," as the Everglades are popularly known, has been devastated primarily by agricultural activities that have filled it with fertilizers and other agricultural chemicals and by human habitation that has sucked its water for green lawns and potable water. By 1929, scientists were lamenting "the wholesale devastation" of the Everglades. How did this come to be?

Aaron Schwabach, *How Free Trade Can Save the Everglades*

14 Geo. Int'l Envtl. L. Rev. 301, 303–11, 316 (2001),
reprinted with permission of the publisher, Georgetown International
Environmental Law Review © 2001

Flooding caused by the 1926 hurricane claimed more than 300 lives in the area around Moore Haven, and destroyed existing flood-control works. In the aftermath of the flood, it became apparent that the residents of the Everglades Drainage District, who by then lived largely by agriculture, could not afford adequate flood control. At this point a rational, market-based response would have been to conclude that the proceeds from agriculture in the area could not exceed the cost of making the land safe and suitable for agriculture, and to allow the land to return to a natural state.

Instead, the federal government stepped in, creating the expensive and ecologically disastrous Hoover Dike around the southern shore of Lake Okeechobee and turning over control of most drainage projects to the Army Corps of Engineers. The Corps of Engineers created a network of drainage canals to lower water levels. Since the peat soils of the Everglades are largely water, lowering the level of fresh water created problems of saltwater intrusion, soil fires, and soil subsidence. In Moore Haven, for example, thirteen years of agriculture resulted in a subsidence of "approximately 45 per cent of the original depth of the soil."

During the Depression, though, Everglades drainage control represented a way to bring needed federal dollars and jobs into Florida. Even if the state government had possessed the will or the common sense to abandon the idea of making the Everglades into farmland, the federal government was providing a financial counterincentive to economic and ecological good sense. At the same time, the general unprofitability of Everglades farming and the economic collapse of family farming during the late 1920s and early 1930s allowed a few large landowners to take over much of the agricultural land south of Lake Okeechobee. By 1929, the Southern Sugar Company controlled over 100,000 acres of this land; by 1940 its successor, U.S. Sugar, produced eighty-six percent of the region's sugar. * * *

The greatest harm to the Everglades ecosystem is done by through drainage. Sugar[*] production also harms the Everglades through habitat destruction and through run-off of agricultural chemicals. Biochemical oxidation of muck soils leads to increased nutrient discharge, in turn leading to eutrophication of the Everglades and Florida Bay. All agriculture in the EAA [Everglades Agricultural Area] contributes to these problems to some extent, but sugar is the biggest culprit. * * *

Over the last two decades, a protectionist quota/tariff regime and loan program have also kept sugar prices high. The price support regime, itself only a part of the total system of subsidies to Everglades sugar growers, is a structure of truly astonishing complexity. For those who appreciate administrative complexity for its own sake, it is a work of art. The price support system has two main components: a loan program that guarantees a support price of eighteen cents per pound for cane sugar produced in the United States, and a tariff/quota regime that prevents world prices from being reflected in United States markets by excluding foreign competitors.

1. The Loan Program

There are more direct subsidies, as well. The U.S. Department of Agriculture loans money to sugar farmers through its Commodity Credit Corporation (CCC). The CCC makes both "recourse" and "nonrecourse" loans. Recourse loans are

---

* As used in this article, "sugar" means sucrose derived from sugar cane or sugar beets. The Harmonized Tariff Schedule of the United States (HTSUS) lists sucrose in chapter 17, along with glucose, fructose, lactose, and maltose. U.S. Int'l Trade Comm'n Pub. No. 3378, Harmonized Tariffs Schedule of the United States § 1701, 1702 (2001) [hereinafter HTSUS]. Syrups containing these sugars are listed in chapter 21. HTSUS § 2106.90.42. Some chemically pure sugars are also listed in chapter 29.

straightforward business loans, with the borrower responsible for repayment of all money borrowed. When imports in a given fiscal year reach 1.5 million tons, nonrecourse loans also become available. Nonrecourse loans are actually a commodity purchase program, giving borrowers the option to "sell" the sugar at a set price. Nonrecourse loans are secured only by the sugar pledged as collateral; forfeiture of the sugar satisfies the loan, even if the value of the sugar is less than the value of the money borrowed. Forfeiture of collateral during a crop year carries a penalty of one cent per pound, but does not disqualify a borrower from receiving additional loans in subsequent years.

Although most CCC nonrecourse loans are made to growers, sugar loans are made to processors, because sugar cane and sugar beets must be processed before they can be stored. However, to receive the loans, processors must purchase sugar cane and sugar beets from farmers at set support prices. In the case of U.S. Sugar, at least, there is sufficient vertical integration that the distinction between grower and processor is irrelevant.

The nonrecourse loans thus function as a price support program, guaranteeing farmers a minimum price for their crop. The price of raw cane sugar is supported by the nonrecourse loans at eighteen cents per pound; the price of refined beet sugar is supported at 22.9 cents per pound. By comparison, raw cane sugar outside the United States sells for about eight cents a pound.

If the sugar price in the United States falls below the support level, the sugar standing as collateral for the loans can be forfeited, leaving the government with sugar that the market doesn't want. This happened on a large scale last year [in 2000]: In 1999, because of overproduction, sugar prices in the United States dropped to eighteen cents per pound. By June 2000, the CCC was buying sugar at twenty cents per pound to support sugar prices. The federal government then provided a payment-in-kind (PIK) program, as yet another bailout to the sugar industry. Under the PIK program, sugar farmers could remove a portion of their crop from production and receive in exchange sugar warehoused by the government. The maximum PIK payment to any farmer would be the equivalent of U.S.$20,000 in sugar. The PIK program would thus provide only limited direct benefit to the two giant Everglades sugar growers; rather, it was designed to help smaller sugar-beet farmers. As part of a continuing program of price supports, though, the PIK helps Everglades growers by continuing to ensure an inflated price for their output.

2. The Quota/Tariff Regime

Restrictive quotas on sugar imports keep prices high, so that Americans often pay twice the world price for sugar. For years prior to the overproduction crisis of 1999–2000, growers were able to sell raw cane sugar for 22.5 cents per pound, 4.5 cents above the support price.

Prior to 1982, the United States still imported about half of its sugar. Sugar imports had risen from 3.7 million short tons in 1955 to 6.1 million short tons by 1977. During the 1980s the Reagan administration, ostensibly committed to free trade and market solutions, oversaw a tightening of the quota/tariff regime. Imports continued to average about five million short tons per year through 1981, but by 1987 had fallen to just over one million short tons.

The current quota/tariff portion of the overall price support system is itself extraordinarily complex. It keeps prices high by restricting the entry of sugar imports, preventing foreign sugar from competing with domestically produced sugar. Defenders of subsidies point out that at the same time that United States subsidies artificially inflate the U.S. price, the actions of other governments (especially within the European Union) artificially deflate the world price. A free-market price would still be lower than the U.S. price. In addition, the quota scheme does not serve to counteract these subsidies; antidumping and countervailing duties against several countries serve this purpose.

Presidential Proclamation 6179 sets out the basic framework of the current quota/tariff regime. It sets up a two-tiered tariff system, replacing the previous absolute quota system. * * *

In addition to being strictly limited in quantity, sugar imports are also taxed. Raw cane sugar from most countries imported within the quota is taxed at between .94 and 1.46 cents per kilogram; beet sugar from these countries is taxed at 3.14 to 3.66 cents per kilogram, as is cane sugar containing added coloring matter. The exact amount of the tariff depends on the polarity of the sugar. Cane and beet sugar from Canada, Mexico and a few other countries imported within the quota is not taxed at all. One of these countries is the Dominican Republic. Half of the sugar producing capacity in the Dominican Republic, and thus half of that country's import quota, belongs to the Fanjul family. Raw cane sugar imported within the quota (if any) from the handful of countries that do not enjoy what used to be called "most favored nation" treatment is taxed at a much steeper 2.83 to 4.38 cents per kilogram, while beet sugar from these countries is taxed at between 5.03 and 6.58 cents per kilo.

Cane sugar imported in excess of the quota limits is taxed at 18.26 to 28.25 cents per kilo (for sugar from Mexico), 33.87 cents per kilo (for sugar from most other countries), and 39.85 cents per kilo (from a handful of countries). These tariffs are often greater than the value of the sugar itself, and effectively prohibit the import of sugar in excess of the quotas. Beet sugar in excess of the quota is taxed at the same rate as cane sugar if originating in Mexico, at 35.74 cents for most other countries, and at 42.05 cents per kilo for the handful of least-favored nations.

These direct subsidies cost American consumers nearly U.S.$2 billion dollars per year. In addition to propping up the sugar-cane industry, they have created a still-expanding sugar-beet industry. The United States enjoys no particular competitive advantage in the production of sugar beets, yet the existing protectionist regime is luring farmers into an industry that, as soon as the price supports are removed, must surely fail. One sugar processor says "The U.S. sugar program is the most efficient tax we have.... It comes directly from the consumers and goes directly to the growers, who turn around and give some of the money to the politicians." Similarly, an editorial in the *Washington Post* declares, "Billions of dollars have been transferred to producers, but the money hasn't been sluiced through the Treasury. Rather, the public has paid at the checkout counter." This hidden tax is also regressive, since lower-income families spend a proportionately higher amount of their income on food. * * *

Environmentalists have a distressing tendency to view economists as enemies. Yet many environmental problems, such as pollution, result from the simple absence of an effective mechanism to compel the problem-causer to internalize externalities. Others, such as the ongoing destruction of the Everglades, are the result of government intervention to prevent the market from removing the destructive businesses. Without the existing protectionist regime, sugar industry revenues would fall by up to U.S.$2 billion per year. Without the construction and continuing operation of the elaborate and costly EAA drainage system, sugar cane could not be grown in the EAA at all. The federal government can solve a large part of the Everglades problem through inaction. Simple passivity—that is, refusal to impose and enforce price supports and a protectionist quota/tariff regime—will bring about the gradual demise of sugar production in the Everglades. An active solution—undoing the EAA drainage project—would have a one-time cost, but would speed that demise and eliminate the danger that some other crop might replace sugar cane in the EAA.

Jonathan Tolman, *Federal Agricultural Policy: A Harvest of Environmental Abuse*
4–6 (Competitive Enterprise Institute, Aug. 1995)

In 1948, Congress authorized the Army Corps of Engineers to construct 1,500 miles of canals and levees throughout the area of southern Florida. This was done in an attempt to control flooding in the region and promote the farming of sugarcane in the Everglades, a locality whose soil was uniquely suited to this crop. The Corps completed its task several years later. Over 700,000 acres of land was turned into the Everglades Agricultural Area (EAA). Through a series of pumps, canals, and levees, the Corps now diverts over 2.5 million acre-feet of water every year into the Atlantic Ocean and Gulf of Mexico.

The drainage project itself has caused several severe environmental problems, including a shrinking water base for wildlife in the region. In the twenty year period from 1953 to 1973, when much of the Corps draining program was in operation, the state of Florida lost 1.44 million acres of wetlands, almost entirely in the Everglades region. Furthermore, the state has lost over fifty percent of the Everglades' original area to drainage and pollution in the past two hundred years, with much of that loss occurring over the last fifty years. While there have been some legitimate concerns about flooding in the area, this drainage would, for the most part, be unnecessary if the land was not used for agriculture.

In addition to the environmental damage caused by the drainage, agricultural policies encouraging intensive sugar production have exacerbated the environmental degradation. * * *

As already noted, the USDA's price supports provide an incentive for farmers to produce more of their crop than they would if no such subsidies existed. To take advantage of this incentive, growers are forced into overusing non-land inputs such as fertilizers, chemicals which cause extensive harm to the Everglades ecosystem.

A major component of fertilizer is phosphorus, a chemical not abundantly found in the natural water supply of the Everglades. Due to the extensive use of fertilizers in farming, a great deal of phosphorus leaches into the groundwater, which is then pumped out to the Everglades National Park and Loxahatchee Wildlife Refuge. A recent study found that up to 80 percent of phosphorus used in fertilizing sugarcane crops is transferred with drainage water into the Everglades. Once there, the phosphorus allows many nonnative plants to outgrow and crowd out naturally occurring species. A prime example of this phenomenon is the vast replacement of native sawgrass with non-native cattails in nutrient rich waters.

Unfortunately, the consequences of overproduction are not only related to compositional changes in plant life, but extend higher up the food chain. The plants that are appearing as a result of this pattern change cannot support many kinds of animal life. Without a ready supply of food, many animals once common to the Everglades are shrinking in number. This is not just affecting certain classes of animals, but the entire food chain. Bird populations have been reduced dramatically due to the striking drop in habitat as well as fish and other aquatic species on which they feed. One study suggests that the present number of birds in the Everglades National Park area is only 10 percent of what it used to be at the turn of the century.

Changes in the U.S. sugar policy have accelerated the domestic production of sugarcane in recent years. Sugar consumption in the U.S. was 9 million tons in 1981, a level which has seen no overall growth in the past thirteen years. Sugarcane production in the U.S., however, has increased approximately 26 percent from 1981 to 1991, from 2.7 million tons to 3.4 million tons. This is due to the increasingly strict tariff barriers set up by the USDA in an effort to maintain the domestic price of sugar. In 1977, the U.S. imported 6.1 million tons of sugar. By 1993 that amount had dropped 77 percent to only 1.35 million tons.

This increase in production has been accompanied by both increases in land use and the application of non-land inputs such as fertilizer. In Florida, for example, the acreage that was farmed and harvested for sugar went from 233,000 acres in the early 1970s to 346,000 in the early 1980s to a high mark of 420,000 acres in 1990. Phosphorus concentrations in agricultural runoff water pumped into Lake Okeechobee from the Everglades Agricultural Area (EAA) also increased during this time, from a level of 0.095 to 0.314 milligrams per liter (mg/l) between the years 1973 to 1979 to a level of 0.188 to 0.573 mg/l for the years for 1983 to 1985.

———————

World Bank, *Global Economic Prospects 2004*
128

The benefits of sugar policy reform are substantial—particularly with multilateral reform. Presently, developed countries are protecting their sugar producers at great cost to themselves and to developing countries with export potential. A recent study of the global sugar and sweetener markets estimated that removing all trade protection and support would bring annual global welfare gains of $4.7 billion. In countries with the highest protection—Europe, Indonesia, Japan, and the United States—net imports would increase by 15 million tons per year. World sugar prices would rise about 40 percent, while prices in heavily protected countries would decline: in Japan by 65 percent, in Western Europe by 40 percent, and in the United States by 25 percent. Brazilian producers would gain the most from liberalization—about $2.6 billion per year—but this gain would be partially offset by higher consumer prices. Japan's net gain from lower consumer prices would more than offset lower producer prices on the 40 percent of sugar that is domestically produced. In the United States, producer losses would be some $200 million greater than consumer gains. Western Europe would show a net gain of $1.5 billion, with consumer gains of $4.3 billion exceeding producer losses of $3.3 billion. Exporting countries that presently enjoy preferential access to the European Union and the United States now collect some $800 million by selling into protected markets at high prices. However, the value of this preferential access is less than it appears, because many of these producers have high production costs and would not produce at all at world-market prices. The rise of world sugar prices following full liberalization would partially offset the loss of preferences and allow some preferred producers to compete. The net loss to preferred producers from full liberalization is estimated to total about $450 million per year.

Questions and Discussion

1. In the mid-1990s, Heartland By-Products began shipping sugar cane from Brazil to Ontario where it processed the cane into a molasses-like syrup. The U.S. Beet-Sugar Association protested the action as an evasion of U.S. import restrictions and petitioned the Customs Service to reclassify the molasses as sugar, which the Customs Service did. The Court of International Trade, however, overturned the decision of the Customs Service. If Heartland produces only about 1 percent of sugar produced in the United States, why would the Beet-Sugar Association mount a vigorous defense of the import restrictions? Professor Schwabach describes the association's reaction as "not excessive." Why? *See* Schwabach, *How Free Trade Can Save the Everglades*, at 351.

2. Due to the poor health of the Everglades ecosystem, federal and state officials, working with stakeholders, have developed the Comprehensive Everglades Restoration Plan to restore, protect, and preserve the water resources of central and southern Florida, including the Everglades. The Plan will restore natural flows of water and water quality by removing more than 240 miles of internal levees and canals, among other things. Because the health of the Everglades is dependent on capturing water, the Plan also calls for water to be stored in more than 217,000 acres of new reservoirs and wetlands-based treatment areas, and about 300 underground Aquifer Storage and Recovery wells. Planners hope these features of the Plan will ensure a reliable, adequate supply of fresh water for the environment, as well as urban and agricultural users. Approximately 80 percent of the new water captured by the Plan will go to the environment and 20 percent will be used to enhance urban and agricultural supplies. The original 1998 estimate indicated that implementation of the Plan would cost $7.8 billion with an additional $182 million needed annually to operate, maintain and monitor the plan. In general, the Federal government will pay half the cost. The State of Florida will pay the other half. For more information, *see* http://www.evergladesplan.org. Implementation has been slow, however. *See Two Bushes and the Everglades*, N.Y. Times, Nov. 10, 2004, at A24. For the latest on the Everglades saga, see Don Van Natta, Jr. & Damien Cave, *Deal to Save Everglades May Help Sugar Firm*, N.Y. Times, Mar. 7, 2010.

3. As the World Bank report makes clear, the United States is not the only sugar subsidizer. Oxfam, a nongovernmental organization dedicated to alleviating poverty, reports that the EU currently spends 3.30 Euros (€) in subsidies to export sugar worth 1 Euro.

In addition to the €1.3 billion in export subsidies recorded annually in its budgets, the EU provides hidden support amounting to around €833 million on nominally unsubsidized sugar exports. These hidden dumping subsidies reflect the gap between EU production costs and export prices. Oxfam estimates that market distortions associated with EU sugar policies cost Brazil US$494 million, Thailand US$151 million, and South Africa and India around US$60 million each in 2002—large losses for countries with significant populations living in poverty, acute balance-of-payments pressures, and limited budget resources. Oxfam International, *Dumping on the World: How EU Sugar Policies Hurt Poor Countries* (Oxfam Briefing Paper No. 61: March 2004). The EU also sets quotas for sugar production for the European market, and farmers must export any surplus sugar at lower prices. Todd Benson, *W.T.O. Rules for Brazil in Sugar Dispute*, N.Y. TIMES, Aug. 5, 2004, at W1, col. 4.

In August 2004, a WTO panel ruled that the EU's sugar subsidies violate the SCM Agreement. The challenge, brought by Brazil, Australia, and Thailand, argued, among other things, that the EU's subsidies artificially depressed international prices. Brazil estimated that global sugar prices would rise almost 20 percent if Brussels scrapped its subsidies. Brazilian sugar producers claim they lose $500 million to $700 million in exports a year because of European subsidies. European Communities-Export Subsidies on Sugar, WT/DS265, WT/DS266 and WT/DS283. The Appellate Body upheld the Panel's conclusions. European Communities-Export Subsidies on Sugar, WT/DS265/AB/R, WT/DS266/AB/R, WT/DS283/AB/R (adopted May 19, 2005). In light of these decisions, Europe is dramatically reforming its sugar policies.

4. For a history of the Everglades canal projects, *see* David G. Guest, *"This Time for Sure"—A Political and Legal History of Water Control Projects in Lake Okeechobee and the Everglades*, 13 ST. THOMAS L. REV. 645 (2001); John J. Fumero & Keith W. Rizzardi, *The Everglades Ecosystem: From Engineering to Litigation to Consensus-based Restoration*, 13 ST. THOMAS L. REV. 667 (2001).

D. The Agreement on Agriculture

The WTO's Agreement on Agriculture begins the process of reducing the variety of farm policies that distort trade in agricultural products. Like the SCM Agreement, it adopts a color coded system to identify measures covered by the Agreement: amber box, blue box, and green box. This is, indeed, just the beginning. Article 20 of the Agriculture Agreement recognizes that further commitments are necessary in an "ongoing process" to achieve the long-term objective of "substantial progressive reductions in support and protection resulting in fundamental reform...."

1. Negotiations

The negotiations of the Agriculture Agreement led to the creation of interest blocs that sometimes overlapped. Because negotiations over agricultural subsidies continue, these interest blocs remain largely intact. The 18-country "Cairns Group" consists of developing and developed country agricultural exporters and has included such diverse countries as Australia, Brazil, Guatemala, Malaysia, New Zealand, Pakistan, Paraguay, South Africa, and others. As exporters of agricultural products, they want to liberalize trade even if they themselves have substantial subsidies and other trade restraints.

The EU has in many respects stood alone and certainly in opposition to the United States. The EU has sought to protect the Common Agricultural Policy and its preferences for EU producers over all other producers. The "Like-Minded Group" (also called the Group of 33, or G33) includes developing countries such as Haiti, Kenya, Pakistan, and Zimbabwe. They want more liberalized trade from the developed world while maintaining additional protection for themselves. The "Quad" countries—Canada, the European Union, Japan, and the United States—often have similar trade interests but are frequently divided on agricultural reform. These fault lines have been in place for some time, as the following discussion of the Uruguay Round negotiations shows.

Raj Bhala & Kevin Kennedy, *World Trade Law*
1188–90 (1998)

The hot button issue during the Uruguay Round that split the Quad Members down the middle, with Japan and the EU aligned against Canada and the United States, was trade in agricultural products. Calls for protectionism from the agricultural sector within the EU and Japan nearly derailed the Uruguay Round.

The United States, with its 3.5 million farmers, together with the Cairns Group, began the negotiations with a "zero-zero" position, i.e., all agricultural subsidies and quotas were to be eliminated over a ten-year period. In the face of stiff resistance from the EU, the U.S. negotiators gradually retreated to a position that called for the elimination of all export subsidies and a 90 percent reduction of all domestic farm subsidies over ten years, with "tariffication" of all other nontrade barriers. The United States backpedalled even more by later demanding that domestic farm subsidies be lowered by 75 percent and export subsidies slashed by 90 percent over ten years.

The farm lobby in the EU and Japan exerted tremendous pressure on their negotiators to protect them from import competition from food-exporting nations. The EU, with 10 million farmers, refused to budge from a 30 percent reduction in domestic subsidies. In Japan, the domestic rice market was completely closed to imports, precisely the way rice farmers preferred it.

Against this backdrop, the prospects of successfully achieving any reform of agricultural trade rules appeared dim in the closing months of the Uruguay Round. It is no exaggeration that without a successful conclusion of an agricultural agreement, the Uruguay Round would have failed because reform of agricultural trade was the *raison d'etre* of the Uruguay Round.

After repeatedly failing to meet deadline after deadline for concluding the Uruguay Round negotiations, in November 1992, the United States and the EU were able to compromise on the major stumbling blocks to an agricultural agreement. The Blair House Accord broke the negotiation logjam. Working to the advantage of the negotiators were domestic budgetary pressures many WTO members were feeling that would have forced some agricultural reforms with or without an Uruguay Round Agreement. By agreeing to undertake agricultural reforms simultaneously and in the context of a comprehensive, multilateral trade negotiations round, the negotiators were able to clear the political hurdles to an agreement. The Agreement on Agriculture represents a modest first step toward serious reform of international rules governing trade in agricultural products.

2. The Basics of the Agriculture Agreement

The Agriculture Agreement applies to both primary and processed agricultural products, although it excludes fish and fish products, and addresses three main issues that have become known as the "three pillars": decreased domestic support measures, decreased export subsidies, and increased market access (i.e., decreased tariffs). The Agriculture Agreement subdivided domestic support measures into amber, blue, and green boxes, and established separate rules for treating measures within those boxes. It also established separate obligations for market access and export subsidies.

a. Domestic Support Measures

The Agriculture Agreement does not prohibit amber box measures. Instead, all domestic support measures that favor agricultural producers are subject to reduction commitments, unless they are specifically exempted. Green box and blue box measures are exempted as are *de minimis* supports.

Green Box. The green box, found in Annex 2 of the Agriculture Agreement, allows payments without limits for environmental programs, pest and disease control, infrastructure development, and domestic food aid, provided they have "no, or at most minimal, trade-distorting effects or effects on production." To be eligible, the program must be government-funded and not involve a price support (that is, they are "decoupled payments" because they are not tied to price or production). Annex 2 imposes additional criteria for specific types of green box subsidies. For example, payments for environmental programs are permitted provided they are "part of a clearly-defined government environmental or conservation programme and … dependent on the fulfilment of specific conditions under the government programme, including conditions related to production methods or inputs." In addition, the amount of payment is "limited to the extra costs or loss of income involved in complying with the government programme." Agriculture Agreement, Annex 2, para. 12.

Blue Box. The blue box of Article 6.5 includes direct payments to producers for production-limiting programs, such as deficiency payments, and imposes no limits on spending. Whereas green box measures cover decoupled payments, blue box measures require production in order to receive the payments, but the actual payments do not relate directly to the current quantity of that production. Even if a measure would otherwise be classified as an amber box measure (see below), it will nonetheless, be placed in the blue box if the support also requires farmers to limit production.

De Minimis *Measures.* The Agriculture Agreement expressly exempts "*de minimis*" product-specific supports from reductions if the support represents less than 5 percent of that commodity's total production value for developed countries or 10 percent for developing countries. In addition, developed countries are not required to reduce non-product specific supports that are less than 5 percent of the value of total agricultural production. Developing countries have the same obligations, except that their *de minimis* limits for product and nonproduct supports are less than 10 percent. Unless a member has made a commitment to reduce *de minimis* levels of support in a separate schedule, the Agriculture Agreement simply requires that a member not exceed the caps placed on *de minimis* levels of support.

Amber Box. The amber box includes all domestic support measures considered to distort production and trade. Article 6 of the Agriculture Agreement defines amber box measures as all domestic support measures except those in the blue and green boxes. Generally speaking, amber box measures include payments to farmers that are directly linked to prices or quantities, such as price supports, subsidies to produce specific quantities, and input subsidies.

The Agriculture Agreement requires reductions of amber box measures above *de minimis* levels. A total of 28 members (counting the EU as one) had nonexempt domestic support during the base period of 1986 to 1988, which they were required to reduce. Developed countries had until the end of 2000 to reduce total support by 20 percent, while developing countries had until the end of 2004 to reduce their amber box support by 13.3 percent. Least developed countries did not incur any reduction targets.

These reduction commitments are calculated based on a member's "Total Aggregate Measurement of Support" (Total AMS). AMS includes all support for specified products together with support that is not for specific products, in one single figure. AMS can be thought of as the cash equivalent of all programs subject to reductions. However, *de minimis* and green box supports are excluded from the AMS calculation. The Agriculture Agreement sets a baseline for measuring reductions based on the average expenditures from 1986 to 1988, a period of very high trade-distorting support programs. Thomas C. Beierle, *Agricultural Trade Liberalization — Uruguay, Doha, and Beyond*, 36 J. WORLD TRADE 1089, 1100 (2002). As a result, most countries had little difficulty meeting their targets and timetables. For example, the United States, with expenditures between $6 and $11 billion, easily met its cap of $19 billion.

---

b. Export Subsidies

Agricultural surpluses stimulated by export subsidies harm the efforts of even the most efficient producers to participate in global markets, because the surpluses, once domestic markets are sated, are usually dumped on other markets below world market prices. Although the SCM Agreement outright prohibited export subsidies for nonagricultural goods, the Agriculture Agreement allows them, at least for a nine-year transition period, even when they result in massive surpluses.

The Agriculture Agreement takes some first steps to eliminate export subsidies. In Article 9, developed countries were required to reduce their export subsidies by the end of 2000 by 36 percent in financial value and 21 percent in volume of products subsidized. Developing countries were required to reduce their export subsidies by 24 percent in value and 14 percent in volume by the end of 2004. Least developing countries were not required to reduce their export subsidies but were required to bind them.

Article 9 specifies the types of subsidies covered by the reductions; all other export subsidies are prohibited, including export subsidies for products that did not receive export subsidies in the 1986 to 1990 base period. Permissible export subsidies include, among others: 1) direct subsidies, including payments-in-kind, contingent on export performance; 2) the sale or disposal for export by governments or their agencies of noncommercial stocks of agricultural products at a price lower than the comparable price charged for the like product to buyers in the domestic market; 3) subsidies to reduce the costs of marketing exports of agricultural products; 4) internal transport and freight charges on export shipments on terms more favourable than for domestic shipments; and 5) subsidies on agricultural products contingent on their incorporation in exported products.

Aware that members may seek to circumvent the restrictions on export subsidies, Article 10 prohibits members from tying food aid directly or indirectly to commercial exports. In addition, members may not adopt new export subsidies and the Agreement restricts the use of export subsidies for processed foods.

---

c. Market Access

Whereas reductions in domestic support programs and export subsidies are intended to eliminate trade distortions in agricultural products, the market access provisions are designed to liberalize trade by reducing tariffs, variable import levies, and voluntary and other import and export restraints. The Agriculture Agreement thus required developed countries to reduce tariffs over five years by an average of 36 percent, with a minimum reduction of 15 percent for each tariff line (e.g., live poultry). Developing countries, too, are required to reduce their tariffs over nine years by 24 percent overall, with a minimum reduction of 10 percent for each tariff line. Least developed countries were exempted from tariff reductions, but were required either to convert nontariff barriers to tariffs — "tariffication" — or bind their tariffs at a ceiling that future tariffs could not exceed.

Article 4 prohibits all other members from maintaining nontariff barriers and requires them to convert nontariff barriers to tariffs. Tariffs are preferred to nontariff barriers, because they are transparent and quantifiable. It is also easier to negotiate a lower tariff than a less trade restrictive nontariff barrier. Members have largely submitted to tariffication by implementing "tariff-rate quotas" — setting one tariff rate for a set quantity of imports and a higher tariff for imports above that quantity. In this way, the tariff-rate quota does not prohibit imports above the quota limit, as a typical product quota would, but it does substantially increase the cost of imported products over the quota.

Because the members felt that tariffication could lead to sudden surges in imports, the Agriculture Agreement permits a member to employ special safeguard (SSG) measures — an additional duty on products that a member has identified in its Schedule of Concessions. These so-called "snapback" duties may be assessed only if 1) a surge in imports exceeds a "trigger level" or 2) import prices fall below a "trigger price." The WTO reports that 39 members have adopted 6,156 special safeguard measures. WTO, WTO Agriculture Negotiations: The Issues, and Where We Are Now 39 (updated Dec. 1, 2004).

---

d. Nontrade Concerns

The preamble to the Agriculture Agreement includes food security and the environment as nontrade issues that reform of the agricultural sector should take into account. The green box provides one outlet for environmental measures. In addition, Article 12 requires a member imposing a temporary export restriction "to prevent or relieve critical shortages of foodstuffs or other products essential to the exporting contracting party" subject to Article XI:2(a) of the GATT to give "due consideration" to that measure's effect on the food security of importing members. Nontrade concerns have become a more prominent element of agricultural negotiations, especially as members attempt to include other issues, such as animal welfare and ecolabeling, within its rubric for the purpose of exempting them from reductions.

---

e. The "Due Restraints" Clause

The "due restraints" clause of Article 13, frequently called the "peace clause," strictly limited the circumstances under which legal challenges could be brought pursuant to the SCM Agreement during the nine-year implementation period of the Agriculture Agreement. For example, members could not challenge green box subsidies provided those subsidies met the criteria of Annex 2 of the Agriculture Agreement. Other domestic measures (amber and blue boxes) that conform to the requirements of Article 6 are exempt from countervailing duty actions of a member unless they injure or threaten to injure a like product. Such conforming measures are exempt from "serious prejudice" and "non-violation" nullification and impairment claims provided that they do not support a specific commodity in excess of the amount given during the 1992 marketing year.

Export subsidies that conform to the requirements of the Agriculture Agreement are exempt from actions under the SCM Agreement, but they are subject to "nullification and impairment" claims. In addition, if an export subsidy injures or threatens to injure a like product, then it is subject to an importing member's countervailing duty law.

The specificity of the allowable claims for each type of subsidy gives some sense of the delicate balance negotiators sought between maintaining and eliminating subsidies. The peace clause did in fact limit the number of claims brought, although the United States and New Zealand successfully challenged Canada's export subsidies on milk and other dairy products. Canada-Measures Affecting the Importation of Milk and the Exportation of Dairy Products, WT/DS103, WT/DS113 (Oct. 27, 1999). Whatever the value of the peace clause, its effect has been diminished for two reasons. First, it expired in 2004 without renewal. Second, Brazil breached the bulwark with its claims that U.S. cotton subsidies and EU sugar subsidies violated the Agriculture Agreement and the SCM Agreement with or without the peace clause.

Questions and Discussion

1. The requirement to reduce tariffs by an average of 36 percent appears to be a substantial achievement. However, the World Bank reports that some countries merely reduced already low tariffs to meet their goals. For example, a 2 percent tariff would be cut to 1 percent in order to achieve a 50 percent reduction. World Bank, Global Economic Prospects 2004, at 117. In addition, because the baseline period for amber box subsidies was 1986–1988, the EU was able to take credit for converting many amber box subsidies to exempted blue box subsidies in 1992 when it adopted its Common Agricultural Policy. It was also able to include those subsidies in their Total AMS, because they were amber box subsidies during the baseline period. Is it possible to avoid such "gaming" of the rules?

2. While the continuation of export subsidies is easy to understand as a political compromise, is there any economic or food security justification for them?

3. Should there be limits to or additional criteria for green box subsidies to ensure that green box subsidies are not used to circumvent restrictions on export and production subsidies? Does an open-ended green box simply perpetuate problems caused by export and production subsidies? At least one author concludes that current green box subsidies are production neutral in the sense that they do not distort production decisions, but that new criteria are needed to ensure that abuse does not occur. James Rude, *Under the Green Box: The WTO and Farm Subsidies*, 35 J. World Trade 1015 (2001). Paul Faeth

has argued that cutting in half the U.S. $10 billion subsidy program that existed in 1995 (when he completed his assessment) would protect the environment almost as well as payments to farmers to adopt "greener" production methods, thereby saving taxpayers billions of dollars. Paul Faeth, *Growing Green: Enhancing the Economic and Environmental Performance of U.S. Agriculture* (1995).

4. The Agriculture Agreement has had some impact on agricultural subsidies, but not as much as hoped. The World Bank reports "relatively little progress" in the overall decline in producer support in OECD countries, with producer support declining from 37 percent of gross value of farm receipts in 1986–1988 (the beginning of the Uruguay Round) to 30 percent in 2003–2005. Agriculture for Development, at 97. The level of subsidy as a percentage of total farm receipts varies substantially in OECD countries, with Australia at 5 percent, the United States at 16 percent, the EU at 34 percent, and Japan at 58 percent, all reductions from the years 1986–1988. While producer support declined, the World Bank calculated an increase in aggregate support over the same period from $242 billion a year to $273 billion. *Id.* The OECD, meanwhile, reported changes in the composition of agricultural support: the most trade distorting policies (amber box) decreased, while blue box (support under production limiting programs) and green box (only minimally trade distortive support) measures increased. OECD, *Agricultural Policies in OECD Countries: At a Glance—2004 Edition* (2004).

---

3. The U.S.-Brazil Cotton Dispute

On June 18, 2004, a WTO Panel ruled that some U.S. subsidies on upland cotton violated the Agriculture Agreement and the SCM Agreement—the first case in which a developing country challenged a developed country agricultural subsidy. The Appellate Body upheld the Panel's conclusions. United States-Subsidies on Upland Cotton, Panel Report, WT/DS267/R (adopted Mar. 21, 2005); Appellate Body Report, WT/DS267/AB/R (adopted Mar. 21, 2005).

The Panel's massive 350-page, 1576-footnote decision covers an array of measures the United States uses to support cotton users, producers, and exporters that raised issues with respect to export subsidies, import substitution subsidies, and actionable subsidies. These measures include export credit guarantees, grants, and any other assistance to U.S. producers, users, and exporters of upland cotton, as well as marketing loan program payments (including marketing loan gains and loan deficiency payments (LDPs)), user marketing payments, production flexibility contract payments, market loss assistance payments, direct payments, counter-cyclical payments, and crop insurance payments.

Each of these measures has its own nuances and complexities that do not directly affect the trade and environment debate (except the Panel's findings with respect to specificity discussed in Section II.B.2 of this chapter at pages 542–43). The decision, however, illuminates the difficulties a country faces when challenging agricultural subsidies.

As mentioned above, the Agriculture Agreement's peace clause insulated most agricultural subsidies from challenge under the SCM Agreement provided that members capped their subsidies at their 1992 levels. Brazil challenged U.S. subsidies as exceeding those limits. In 1992, the United States paid cotton producers US$1.62 billion, but it was paying its 25,000 cotton farmers US$2.3 billion in 1999 and US$2.06 billion in 2001, according to the Department of Agriculture. When all cotton-related programs are considered, Brazil estimated that U.S. producers received US$12.47 billion in subsidies between August 1999 and July 2003.

The Panel found that many, but not all, of the various U.S. cotton subsidies were granted in excess of the 1992 limits or that the peace clause did not apply to them because the United States had not included them in its schedule of reduction commitments. The Panel also found that the United States provided export credit guarantees under three separate programs at rates inadequate to cover long-term operating costs and losses. They thus constituted *per se* export subsidies prohibited by Article 3 of the SCM Agreement. The Panel also ruled that direct payments to cotton exporters constituted prohibited export subsidies, even though similar subsidies were granted under the same law to cotton producers. Contrary to U.S. claims, the Panel ruled that this program comprised two distinct users of the subsidy with those payments to exporters being "contingent upon export performance" within the meaning of Article 9.1 of the Agriculture Agreement. *Id.* at paras. 7.692–7.735.

Brazil also argued that several of these subsidies caused "serious prejudice" to the interests of Brazil by depressing world cotton prices and affecting export markets. For example, Brazilian cotton producers claim they lost out on sales worth $600 million in the 2001–2002 season alone. But between August 1999 and July 2003, when cotton prices reached a record low of US 29 cents per pound in spring 2002 (far below the 20-year average of 72 U.S. cents), the International Cotton Advisory Committee estimated that the U.S. share of world cotton exports rose from under 20 percent in 1999 to more than 40 percent in 2004. According to Brazil, U.S. cotton production would have fallen by at least 29 percent between 1999 and 2002 and world prices would have risen by 12.6 percent, but for the U.S. cotton subsidies. However, U.S. export share did not fall, because U.S. subsidies allowed U.S. cotton producers to sell their cotton during this four-year period at prices on average 77 percent below production costs.

Despite the availability of these statistics, the Panel did not explicitly use them. As discussed in Section III.C.2 of this Chapter at pages 566–68, the Panel found that an action for countermeasures alleging "serious prejudice" brought under Article 7 of the SCM Agreement does not require quantification of the amount of the subsidy, as is required for countervailing duty claims alleging injury. *Id.* at paras. 7.1167–7.1190. Instead, the Panel examined: 1) the relative magnitude of the U.S. exports on the world upland cotton market; 2) general price trends; and 3) the nature of the subsidies at issue, and in particular, whether or not the nature of these subsidies is such as to have discernable price suppressive effects. *Id.* at 7.1280. With respect to several of the U.S. subsidies, such as the programs that compensate producers when the world market price falls below a price set by the U.S. government, the Panel concluded, "We have no doubt that the payments stimulate production and exports and result in lower world market prices than would prevail in their absence." *Id.* at paras. 7.1291; *see also id.* at paras. 7.1299, 7.1309. Ultimately, the Panel found a causal link between four separate U.S. cotton subsidies and significant price suppression in violation of Article 5(c) of the SCM Agreement. *Id.* at para. 7.1355.

Questions and Discussion

1. The United States has been very slow to comply with the recommendations of the Panel and Appellate Body. As a result, Brazil received authorization from the DSB to impose countermeasures against the United States. With Brazil set to impose up to US$829 million in countermeasures, which included higher tariffs on goods as well as lifting patent protection on pharmaceuticals and chemicals, the United States and Brazil reached an

agreement. Under the deal, the United States pledged to revise its export credit guarantees and give Brazil about $147 million a year in "technical assistance" for Brazil's cotton growers. The United States also agreed to: 1) modify its export credit guarantee program, 2) recognize the State of Santa Catarina as free of foot-and-mouth disease, rinderpest, classical swine fever, African swine fever, and swine vesicular disease, based on World Organization for Animal Health Guidelines, and 3) complete a risk evaluation and identify appropriate risk mitigation measures to determine whether fresh beef can be imported from Brazil while preventing the introduction of foot-and-mouth disease in the United States. Press Release, U.S. Trade Rep., U.S., Brazil Agree on Framework Regarding WTO Cotton Dispute (June 17, 2010).

2. To the extent that the U.S. cannot find some means to continue its cotton subsidies, cotton farmers may need to shift to other crops. Without the lavish subsidies, U.S. cotton farmers will find it difficult to compete with West African farmers. According to economists and many other critics of developed country agricultural subsidies, that is exactly what should happen.

---

4. The Doha Development Agenda

The Agriculture Agreement recognized the need for greater reform of the agricultural sector, with Article 20 requiring members to begin new negotiations one year before the end of the implementation period. These negotiations were to consider further commitments to achieve the long-term objective of "substantial progressive reductions in support and protection resulting in fundamental reform," as well as commitments on nontrade concerns, special and differential treatment to developing country members, and the objective of establishing a fair and market-oriented agricultural trading system.

In paragraph 13 of the 2001 Doha Ministerial Declaration, the members further committed to comprehensive negotiations aimed at "substantial improvements in market access; reductions of, with a view to phasing out, all forms of export subsidies; and substantial reductions in trade-distorting domestic support." Moreover, they agreed that special and differential treatment for developing countries must be "an integral part of all elements of the negotiations ... so as to be operationally effective and to enable developing countries to effectively take account of their development needs, including food security and rural development."

Despite agreement in Doha on the basic framework for new agriculture negotiations, every other aspect of the negotiations has been contentious. With little agreement over the content of the new agriculture negotiations, the entire Doha round of negotiations was suspended.

The United States and the EU remain at the heart of the impasse, but developing countries and other negotiating blocs have positions that are difficult to reconcile. The excerpt by Sophia Murphy below, describes the competing interests and positions of the various negotiating blocs that have made the agriculture negotiations particularly intractable. While the specific percentages being offered may have changed, the basic positions remain largely intact, thus providing an excellent primer to these negotiations.

Sophia Murphy, *The World Trade Organization Agreement on Agriculture Basics*

8–12 (Institute for Agricultural and Trade Policy, 2003)

United States

The U.S. released its proposal for the WTO agriculture negotiations in July 2002.

The main elements of the proposal are:

- to eliminate export subsidies over five years;

- to reduce tariffs on agricultural products over five years such that no tariff will exceed 25 percent after the phase-in period; and,

- to reduce "trade distorting" domestic support to five percent of the total value of agricultural production over five years. In other words, to eliminate all AMS down to the de minimis level. For the U.S., this would create a threshold of some $10 billion, given the current value of its agricultural sector.

The U.S. proposal also proposed to include production-limiting payments (those now categorized in the Blue box) in the AMS reduction commitments. This proposal, with the call to eliminate export subsidies, primarily targets the European Union. Developing countries criticize the U.S. proposal for not addressing U.S. food aid policy, which is used to off-load surplus production. The U.S. has also called for the elimination of the Special Safeguard [eds. note: that would allow importing countries to impose special duties to protect domestic production from import surges] and allowing developing countries to protect certain products from more substantial tariff reduction by self-designating them as products necessary for food security. * * *

The Cairns Group * * *

The Cairns proposal on the AoA includes:

- A reduction of all developed country tariffs to 25 percent or less and an expansion of developed country tariff quotas to 20 percent of domestic consumption. The Group proposed the elimination of the SSG for developed countries. Developing countries were granted lower tariff reductions (a maximum of 50 percent reduction on tariffs of 250 percent or less) and longer implementation periods. Canada, Malaysia and Indonesia did not sign on to this proposal.

- Led by the Philippines and Argentina, the Cairns Group endorsed a proposal to address dumping which suggests that a new special and differential provision be developed granting developing countries access to temporary countervailing duties against subsidized agricultural products from developed countries. The measure would relieve much of the burden of proof of injury, required under the … Agreement on Subsidies and Countervailing Measures. Instead, the proposed rules would allow the presumption of subsidy where a developed country had utilized export subsidies or certain kinds of domestic support.

- On domestic support, the Cairns Group proposed the elimination of all amber box spending over five years for developed and nine years for developing countries. Developed countries would be required to cut amber box spending by half in the first year. Blue box spending would be eliminated immediately. The de minimis provision would be eliminated over time for developed countries, but retained for developing countries. Some suggestions were also made to tighten the criteria for the Green Box, to ensure it is not abused. Canada again did not sign this proposal.

The European Union

The European Commission (which speaks for the EU in trade negotiations) was unable to present an agreed position from its members until January of 2003, long past the deadline agreed by governments to submit proposals. This reticence reflects the internal political differences among EU member states on how to reform the Common Agricultural Policy (CAP). A recent agreement between Germany and France has made it unlikely that there will be any significant reduction in the use of export subsidies before 2007. The EU has just welcomed 10 new members into the Union, including Poland, which has more farmers than all existing EU members combined. The EU cannot afford to leave the CAP unreformed in these circumstances. However, the WTO process is not likely to be the main driver of reform. The EU proposal indicates how little reform they are ready for. It includes:

- a proposal to cut export subsidies by 45 percent, but on average rather than per product line;

- a proposal to cut AMS (amber box) levels by 55 percent. However, its gradual shift of payments to the Green Box means this will not require significant change in current policy;

- on tariffs, a straight 36 percent reduction from existing tariff levels (The EU does not support the U.S. call to "harmonize" tariffs by cutting higher tariffs more than lower tariffs);

- for developing countries, duty-free and quota-free access for all farm exports from LDCs, as well as zero tariff access for at least 50 percent of developed country imports from developing countries. The EU proposed a "food security box" that included measures for rural development and to protect food security crops through a special safeguard;

- New "Non-Trade Concerns" include geographical indicators (GI) regarding food products (so that only wine from Portugal could be called porto, and only ham from Parma could be called Parma ham); and

- strong precautionary measures to guide food safety rules, and the right to provide financial incentives for farmers to implement stringent animal welfare regulations. The United States and the Cairns Group have vigorously rejected these proposals.

Like-Minded Group * * *

The heart of the Like Minded Group (LMG) proposals have been grouped into what is called the Development Box. The Development Box (DB) was first proposed at the WTO agricultural talks in 2000. The LMG was concerned that the liberalization of agricultural trade was jeopardizing their food security and the livelihoods of their producers, especially small farmers, who are among the most vulnerable sectors in their populations. The governments who proposed the DB wanted to create exceptions to the trade rules for countries with scarce resources and significant food security concerns.

Specific proposals include:

- the creation of a simpler special safeguard for developing countries only;
- a proposal that would allow developing countries to raise tariffs on food security crops where experience had shown the existing tariff binding to be too low;
- a joint proposal, submitted by seven members of the group in November, 2002, suggesting that if production of a crop is below an UN FAO determined world average for national production,

and if exports of that crop are less than 3.25 percent of world trade in that crop for five years or more consecutively, then domestic support for that crop should not be included in reduction commitments; and

- a proposal to exclude from domestic support restrictions for money spent on transporting staple foods to food deficit areas within the country.

Friends of Multifunctionality

Multifunctional agriculture (MFA) describes an approach to agriculture that goes beyond production-related measures to consider the broader benefits to society provided by the sector. For example, providing payments to farmers for managing water quality, soil erosion, habitats for particular species or other services that the market does not recognize or reward but that have a clear public value. The MFA framework provides a rationale for such payments, and considers some level of domestic food production in all countries to be an essential component of food security.

The core support for multifunctional agriculture comes from Japan, South Korea, Norway and Switzerland. The EU associates itself with this group, although there are divisions among member countries as to the usefulness, validity and application of multifunctional agriculture.

Japan's comprehensive proposal of November 2002 would leave significant leeway to countries to determine which products to liberalize and how. The proposal leaves domestic support at the levels reached under the existing AoA and seeks to raise market access barriers on rice.

Former Eastern Bloc and Soviet States The former Eastern Bloc and Soviet States have made only a limited number of proposals. They largely reflect two, sometimes overlapping, concerns. The first concern is from the states that hope to accede to the European Union. This group is careful to reflect EU interests in their statements. The second is from those who recently acceded to the WTO. The WTO accession process famously requires much deeper liberalization than existing WTO rules, which leaves new members in a much-weakened negotiating position. Newly acceded countries, with support from China (another new member) proposed that they be credited for their accession commitments and thus avoid further tariff cuts for themselves in the new round of agreements. All of these countries want to increase market access for their exports. Many of them depend on agriculture for a significant share of their foreign exchange earnings. [eds. note: The friends of multifunctionality are also called the Group of 10, or G10.]

Least Developed Countries

While Least Developed Countries (LDCs) are singled out as a group in the AoA for special treatment, they do not work as a group in any formal sense. Their exemption from a number of disciplines under the AoA, as well as their institutional weaknesses, leads larger countries to ignore them in the negotiations. A number of LDCs cannot afford to maintain a mission in Geneva. They have very limited domestic capacity to develop and pursue a trade policy agenda. They are subject to intense bilateral pressures because of their dependence on foreign aid. They are of limited trade interest because their people are relatively few and poor, reducing the interest of traders in their domestic markets, and their production is too limited to create problems in world markets.

On the other hand, LDCs are very much affected by international trade policies. They often depend on only one or two exports for their foreign exchange revenues, and their export markets are usually heavily concentrated. Thus, they have an important stake in the outcome of the negotiations, yet very little bargaining power to ensure an outcome favourable to their interests. Competing interests complicate solidarity even across LDCs countries. There is now a legal center that provides LDCs with help in using the WTO's trade dispute system, but much remains to be done.

Questions and Discussion

1. Why would the United States and the Cairns Group oppose financial incentives for animal welfare regulations? Won't these payments be nontrade distorting measures such as those that already are included in the green box?

2. Do any of the approaches appear to make environmental considerations a priority or are the proposals more related to poverty alleviation or maintaining market dominance? To eliminate the adverse environmental impacts from subsidies, what mechanisms would you propose? Do any of your strategies also help alleviate poverty?

3. The "multifunctional" approach posits that the trade distorting effects of agricultural subsidies must be balanced by the environmental and other benefits derived from the subsidy. In accord with the view that environmental subsidies generally are an inefficient means to accomplish environmental objectives, scholars have noted that agriculture-related environmental subsidies are also inefficient. They argue that compensating farmers directly for landscape preservation would reduce negative externalities (such as pesticide use) that come with production subsidies and would therefore more efficiently protect the landscape. Moreover, if the multifunctional approach is adopted, both positive and negative externalities of the environmental subsidy must be accounted for when balancing the trade distorting and beneficial components of a subsidy. As a result, C. Ford Runge argues that WTO members must clearly define "multifunctionality":

> Specifically, countries asserting the beneficial joint products of agricultural subsidies must be required to demonstrate these empirically. Second, they should not be allowed to "pick and choose" multifunctional benefits without also acknowledging and demonstrating costs, especially to the environment. Third, it must be shown that agricultural subsidies are the least-trade distorting measures among an opportunity set of feasible alternatives to accomplish these goals. Finally, it will be useful to lay bare who benefits from such subsidies in relation to who loses from their budgetary and environmental costs. In the final analysis, much of what is being justified under the rubric of multifunctionality would be better described as "multidysfunctionality," to coin an infelicitous term.

C. Ford Runge, *A Conceptual Framework for the Agricultural Trade and the Environment*, J. WORLD TRADE, 47, 63 (1999). Is this a sensible approach to balancing trade and environmental concerns? Without concrete tests, would a multifunctional approach be unworkable, or perhaps more to the point, would it undermine efforts to reform agricultural policies?

4. How do the various proposals address the concerns of the least developing countries? Should they receive preferential treatment with respect to their exports? With respect to market access, should they be able to use subsidies that others cannot?

5. How should food security issues be addressed? Again, the members have proposed a variety of approaches. Which best meets the concerns of self-sufficiency while also protecting consumers and foreign producers from the effects of a distorted market?

---

5. Current Negotiations

After initially failing to conclude negotiations on the Doha Ministerial Declaration, the members have taken a number of steps that keep negotiations moving forward but which also show how challenging resolutions to this issue will be. First, strenuous negotiations led to a framework agreement in July 2004 to progress discussions. Decision Adopted by the General Council on 1 Aug. 2004, WT/L/579 (Aug. 2, 2004). The framework agreement committed the members to reforms in all three pillars of the negotiations: market access, export subsidies, and domestic measures. The agreement called for overall reductions in domestic support to be at least 20 percent of total AMS, while also calling on members with higher levels of trade-distorting domestic support to make deeper cuts. It further limited blue box subsidies to 5 percent of a member's total value of agricultural production calculated relative to a baseline period to be established later. Green box subsidies will be reviewed and clarified to ensure that they have no, or at most minimal, trade-distorting effects or effects on production. Reductions in *de minimis* domestic support will also be negotiated and members affirmed their commitment to eliminating certain export subsidies, including export credits and export credit guarantees. With respect to market access, the members agreed to a tiered formula for reducing tariffs and that "substantial overall tariff reductions" must be achieved. Members also agreed to make deeper cuts in higher tariffs with "flexibilities for sensitive products," and to make "[s]ubstantial improvements" for all products, but the agreement did not establish any targets and timetables. With respect to all these obligations, developing countries are given "special and differential treatment" through longer implementation periods, greater flexibility to designate "sensitive products," or through other mechanisms. The least developed countries will not be required to make any reduction commitments.

The WTO's Director-General at the time, Dr. Supachai Panitchpakdi, called the framework agreement a "truly historic" achievement. Nevertheless, the United States trumpeted the decision as requiring it to do little, if anything, in the first year. Allen Johnson, the chief agricultural negotiator for the U.S. Trade Representative, noted that the 20 percent cut in trade-distorting amber box subsidies would not require the United States to reduce its spending, because the United States already spent less than 20 percent on subsidies relative to the limits established it the framework. Christopher S. Rugaber, *WTO Framework Makes "Historic" Changes to Farm Trade Talks, Johnson Says*, 21 INT'L TRADE REP. 1340 (Aug. 12, 2004). Negotiations again sputtered and then were resuscitated by the Hong Kong Ministerial Declaration, which reaffirmed the members' commitment to reduce support in all three pillars, including elimination of all forms of export subsidies. WT/MIN(05)/DEC, paras. 5–12 (adopted on Dec. 18, 2005).

Since the Doha and Hong Kong Ministerial Declarations, the members have moved closer to realizing their goal of agricultural reform, although they still have many differences to resolve. In December 2008, the Chairman of the agricultural negotiations submitted his *Revised Draft Modalities for Agriculture*. TN/AG/W/4/Rev.4 (Dec. 6, 2008). The Chairman carefully noted that these Revised Draft Modalities did not constitute a negotiating text and acknowledged that there is still "real divergence" on some issues.

The resulting text is, to say the least, extraordinarily complex. As with the original Doha Ministerial Declaration, it rests on the three pillars of domestic support measures, export subsidies, and market access. To these three pillars are added a variety of formulas and tiers for reducing agricultural support, coupled with exceptions for "sensitive products," "special products," and "special safeguard measures," among many others. In fact, the number of exceptions is so great that, by one estimate, the welfare gains from the proposed reductions in agricultural support decline markedly from US$163 billion to US$93 billion when the exceptions are accounted for, with estimated gains for developing countries dropping by more than half to US$22 billion. David Laborde et al., Implications of the 2008 Doha Draft Agricultural and Non-agricultural Market Access Modalities for Developing Countries 29 (Jan. 22, 2010).

a. Domestic Support Measures

The Chairman's Revised Draft Modalities text establishes ambitious targets to reduce domestic support. For example, the text calls on the EU to reduce its "overall trade distorting domestic support"—amber + *de minimis* + blue box support—by 80%, the United States by 70%, and everyone else by 55%. In addition, it calls on the EU to cut its amber box support by 70%, the United States and Japan by 60%, and everyone else by 45%. The text does not name specific countries—the text establishes a tiered formula for determining percentage cuts (see Tables 1 and 2)—but surely each negotiator is aware that certain countries fall within certain tiers. Revised Draft Modalities, paras. 3–13.

Table 1. Proposed Cuts to Overall Trade Distorting Domestic Support

Base OTDS	Tariff Cut	Key Members in Category
> US$60 billion	80%	EU
US$10–$60 billion	70%	United States
≤ US$10 billion	55%	All Other Members

Table 2. Proposed Cuts to Total AMS

Final Bound Total AMS	Cut	Key Members in Category
> US$40 billion	70%	EU
US$15–$40 billion	60%	United States, Japan
≤ US$15 billion	45%	All Other Members

As with other aspects of the Chairman's text, least developed countries, recently-acceded members (RAMs) (Saudi Arabia, Vietnam, Tonga, and Ukraine), small low-income RAMs with economies in transition (Albania, Armenia, Georgia, and others), and net food-importing developing countries are not subject to these proposals. Regarding AMS cuts, other developing countries would make cuts of two-thirds of the formula amounts. For both Overall Trade-distorting Domestic Support (OTDS) and AMS cuts, developed countries have five years to comply and developing countries have eight years.

Beyond these cuts, the chairman's text then establishes specific rules that apply to each box, each with its own nuances and exceptions. For example, the blue box (for support that minimally distorts trade) adds a new type of support based on payments that do not require production but are based on a fixed amount of production in the past. Moreover, whereas the Agriculture Agreement did not limit blue box support, the Chairman's Revised Draft Modalities text limits them to 2.5 percent of the value of production during the base period (generally, the average spent in 1995–2000). Developed countries must reduce all *de minimis* support by 50 percent, with developing countries subject to different cuts. *Id.* at para. 30.

b. Export Subsidies

The text currently calls for developed countries to eliminate their remaining export subsidies by the end of 2013, with developing countries eliminating theirs by 2016. *Id.* at paras. 162–163. However, export credits, export credit guarantees, and insurance programs would not be considered export subsidies subject to elimination but instead would be subject to separate rules, such as limiting the repayment period to 180 days. *Id.* at Annex J.

c. Market Access

The provisions on market access begin with a tiered formula that requires larger tariff cuts on products protected by higher tariffs, as shown in Table 3. This tiering approach overcomes the deficiencies in the Agriculture Agreement, which only required members to meet an overall average percentage cut in their tariffs. As a result, many countries simply made large percentage cuts in low tariffs, since reducing a tariff from 2% to 1% would equal a 50% cut even if the overall impact on trade was insignificant. The tiering thus requires minimum designated percentage cuts within each tier. Moreover, developed countries' tariff cuts must be no less than 54%, with developing country cuts no more than 36%. *Id.* at paras. 61–65.

Table 3. The Tiered Approach for Cutting Agricultural Tariffs

Developed Countries		Developing Countries	
Current Bound Tariffs	*Tariff Cut*	*Current Bound Tariffs*	*Tariff Cut*
0–20%	50%	0–30%	33.3%
20–50%	57%	30–80%	38%
50–75%	64%	80–130%	42.7%
>75%	70%	>130%	46.7%

The tiered approach only represents a starting point on market access. A number of deviations and exceptions apply, including the following:

- The least developed countries, RAMs, and small low-income RAMs are not required to make any tariff cuts. Small and Vulnerable Economies (SVEs) may undertake reductions 10% smaller than required for developing countries in each tier. *Id.* at paras. 65, 67.

- *Tariff Escalation.* To counter the practice in many countries of raising tariffs in relation to the degree of processing, a practice called tariff escalation (see pages 148–49), the Revised Draft Modalities establishes the following general rule: when a processed product is subject to a higher tariff than their raw or intermediate counterparts, then the product is moved into the next higher tier for tariff cutting. If the product already is in the highest tier, then it will be subject to a cut six percentage points higher than the highest tier. *Id.* at para. 86.

- *Sensitive Products.* All members are permitted to make smaller cuts on "sensitive products," an undefined term. Developed countries may designate up to 4 percent of their tariff lines as "sensitive products," except countries with more than 30 percent of bindings in the top tier may designate 6 percent of tariff lines as sensitive products. Because Japan and Canada oppose the 4 percent figure as unworkable, wanting a higher percentage, this issue remains very much unresolved. Developing countries are entitled to designate one-third more sensitive products than developed countries. *Id.* at paras. 71–72. A large number of other rules add to the complexity of this issue.

- *Special Products.* Developing countries, but not developed countries, may also designate "special products." *Id.* at para. 129. "Special products" is another undefined term but members must use a number of indicators relating to livelihoods security, food security, and rural development in designating them. *Id.* at Annex F. The Revised Draft Modalities allow developing countries to designate 12 percent of their agricultural tariff lines as special products, with up to 5 percent of lines having no cuts. Still, the average cut must be 11 percent. These provisions potentially subject a large number of important staple crops to no or much lower tariff cuts. Developing countries believed that this concept is necessary because "opening markets to competition from cheap and often highly subsidised foreign agriculture imports may affect the livelihood of small and resource-poor farmers, particularly in countries where agriculture still accounts for a large share of gross domestic product (GDP) and employment." Christophe Bellman, et al., *Recent Trends in World Trade and International Negotiations*, Revue Internationale de Politique de Développement 161, para. 29 (2010). These numbers represent a compromise between the 20 percent of tariff lines proposed by developing countries and the U.S. proposal to limit the concept to 5 lines. *Id.*

- *Special Agricultural Safeguard (SSG) and Special Safeguard Mechanism (SSM).* The Revised Draft Modalities indicate some consensus among the members to reduce the use of the SSG; the Agriculture Agreement currently allows members that converted nontariff barriers into tariffs through tariffication (see page 625) to impose duties above their Uruguay Round agreed bound tariffs. The SSM would allow developing countries to impose tariffs above their Doha Round bindings. Because of substantial disagreement concerning the SSM, the chairman has drafted a separate paper to outline different approaches to it. Revised Draft Modalities for Agriculture: Special Safeguard Mechanism, TN/AG/W/7 (Dec. 6, 2008). One group of commentators has noted the following:

Two quite different models are presented as potential alternatives, making it difficult to assess the likely consequences for average tariff levels. The elimination or reduction of the SSG can be expected to increase market access, and to reduce the extent to which domestic prices in the industrial countries are insulated from world market prices (and hence increase the instability of world market prices. The extent to which the introduction of the SSM will lead to higher average tariffs and insulation in developing countries, and hence in world average tariffs and the volatility of world prices will depend on the specific parameters chosen.

David Laborde et al., *Implications of the 2008 Doha Draft Agricultural and Non-agricultural Market Access Modalities for Developing Countries*, 7 (Jan. 22, 2010).

Questions and Discussion

1. Compare the proposals summarized by Sonia Murphy with the Chairman's Revised Draft Modalities. How much progress do you think has been made?

2. A major issue in the negotiations is deciding which products developing countries will designate as "special products." Developing countries, the EU, and others have insisted that the members agree on the modalities before self-designating products as special products. The United States, however, proposed that the list of special products be produced first so that members could better monetize the value of tariff reductions. The United States has failed to convince other members of its approach. What are the advantages and disadvantages of the two approaches?

3. As noted above, the number of exceptions to the rules will significantly reduce welfare gains from the agriculture agreement. Nonetheless, the Chairman's Revised Draft Modalities would result in cuts to U.S. trade-distorting agricultural subsidies of approximately US$14.4 billion, while the EU would make cuts of roughly US$24.7 billion. Are the reduced welfare gains resulting from the various exceptions acceptable in light of the size of reductions required by the United States and EU? On the other hand, the Doha Ministrerial Declaration provides that:

> International trade can play a major role in the promotion of economic development and the alleviation of poverty. We recognize the need for all our peoples to benefit from the increased opportunities and welfare gains that the multilateral trading system generates. The majority of WTO members are developing countries. We seek to place their needs and interests at the heart of the Work Programme adopted in this Declaration. Recalling the Preamble to the Marrakesh Agreement, we shall continue to make positive efforts designed to ensure that developing countries, and especially the least-developed among them, secure a share in the growth of world trade commensurate with the needs of their economic development. In this context, enhanced market access, balanced rules, and well targeted, sustainably financed technical assistance and capacity-building programmes have important roles to play.

WTO, Ministerial Declaration of 14 November 2001, WT/MIN(01)/DEC/1, para. 2 (Nov. 14, 2001). Is the Chairman's Draft Revised Modalities a betrayal of these goals?

4. It has always been clear that subsidies, particularly agricultural subsidies, are potent issues in the free trade debate. Brazil has won significant victories in the cotton and sugar disputes. The WTO's dispute settlement system has generated significant decisions that broadly define "subsidy" and clarify the law of countervailing duties. The members continue to move forward, albeit very slowly, with the negotiations on agricultural reform. How can environmental advocates harness this energy to achieve their goals?

5. In *The Paradox of Agricultural Subsidies*, Timothy Wise argues that developed country agricultural subsidies "are not the primary cause of agricultural dumping or rural poverty," and that attention should be diverted from eliminating agricultural subsidies. He does not deny that the elimination of certain subsidies, such as cotton, could have significant welfare benefits for poor farmers in specific regions. Nonetheless, he claims that these

cases may be the exception. He argues that "the most trade-distorting aspect of international trade may be the oligopolistic nature of the market. Vertically integrated conglomerates are involved in all aspects of production and distribution, and all are internal to the company's operation. This leaves little room for the market to set prices for the different stages of production, since there is limited competition...." As a result, "policy reforms should focus on ending agricultural dumping, reducing global commodity over-production in key crops, and reducing the market power of agribusiness conglomerates." Timothy A. Wise, *The Paradox of Agricultural Subsidies: Measurement Issues, Agricultural Dumping, and Policy Reform* (Feb. 2004).

———————

Chapter 9

Trade Rules and Multilateral Environmental Agreements

I. Introduction

Just as governments have cooperated to develop an international trading regime, so too they have cooperated to address a number of global environmental problems, such as global warming, ozone depletion, and hazardous waste trade, among many others. In many cases, the multilateral environmental agreement (MEA) created to resolve a global environmental problem uses trade restrictions. The Convention on International Trade in Endangered Species of Wild Fauna and Flora (CITES) controls international trade in species of conservation concern because trade in those species for pets, clothing, trinkets, and other products may lead to their overexploitation. The Montreal Protocol on Substances that Deplete the Ozone Layer bars trade in ozone depleting substances between parties and nonparties to encourage broad membership in the treaty and better achieve the Protocol's goal of restoring the ozone layer. Several fisheries treaties use trade bans and deny port privileges to secure compliance with their conservation measures.

Despite these clear trade and environment linkages, the trade community and the environmental community, either separately or collectively, have failed to agree on a framework for addressing the linkages between MEAs and the WTO agreements. Many observers believe such a framework is needed. They point to the following examples to support their view:

- In 1997, to control trade in ivory from African elephants, the CITES Parties approved commercial sales of ivory from Botswana, Namibia, and Zimbabwe only to Japan. Japan did indeed accept shipments from those countries, but during the same year confiscated shipments from other countries, as required by CITES. Did Japan violate its most favored nation obligation? If there is a dispute, should the disputing parties use the WTO's Dispute Settlement Body (DSB) or the dispute settlement procedures of CITES?

- In 2001, the United States threatened to impose trade sanctions on Japan for its so-called scientific research whaling. Members of the International Whaling Commission (IWC) have passed more than 20 resolutions condemning Japan's whaling program as violating IWC resolutions on scientific research whaling. Neither the International Convention for the Regulation of Whaling (ICRW) nor the resolutions of the IWC provide for the use of trade sanctions, but the United States maintains that any trade sanctions would encourage compliance with the rules of the ICRW and IWC. Can the United States adopt trade sanctions in furtherance of the rules of the ICRW and IWC even if not expressly permitted by the ICRW and IWC? Could Japan have recourse to the DSB?

- In 2000, the European Union (EU) invoked GATT law and the WTO's DSB to challenge Chile's prohibition on landing EU-caught swordfish, part of Chile's program to conserve swordfish. Chile responded by initiating a separate proceeding in the International Tribunal for the Law of the Sea (ITLOS) of the United Nations Convention on the Law of Sea (UNCLOS) alleging the EU's failure to comply with UNCLOS provisions. Under which law should the dispute be resolved? In which forum should the dispute be resolved?

- In 1999, the Commission of the International Convention for the Conservation of Atlantic Tuna prohibited the import by parties of bigeye tuna and its products from nonparties, including Belize, Cambodia, Honduras, and St. Vincent and the Grenadines, because longline fishing vessels from those countries were fishing inconsistently with the conservation and management regulations adopted by the Commission. Can Belize, Honduras, and St. Vincent and the Grenadines, which are WTO members, use their WTO rights to challenge the trade restrictions before a WTO panel?

Although no country has formally challenged a trade measure of an MEA as inconsistent with trade rules, all four examples have drawn questions about the applicability of WTO rules to MEAs and about how and in which forum such disputes should be resolved. The EU and Chile settled their dispute, but it underscored that overlaps of jurisdiction and law exist. Indeed, a WTO study identified trade measures in 32 different environmental agreements among the 238 listed by UNEP, though that count includes some subsidiary and regional agreements. WTO, Matrix on Trade Measures Pursuant to Selected Multilateral Environmental Agreements (Note by the Secretariat), WT/CTE/W/160/Rev.4 (Mar. 14, 2007).

The apparent conflicts between the legal obligations of the MEAs and the legal obligations of the same governments under the WTO raise a number of questions that this chapter explores. How should such disputes be resolved? To what extent should MEAs (or any other treaty using trade measures) be subject to trade disciplines? Does the purpose of the trade measure (*e.g.*, to eliminate an environmental threat, encourage membership, or enforce a treaty provision) or whether the measure is required (as opposed to allowed) by an MEA have any bearing on whether such trade restrictions should be permissible? Does Article XX of the GATT offer an appropriate way to resolve apparent conflicts? Perhaps most importantly, who bears the responsibility for clarifying how to avoid or reconcile potential conflicts between WTO and MEA rules?

II. Setting the Stage for Conflict: Trade Restrictions in MEAs

In the trade policy context, "trade measure" means any policy instrument that imposes requirements, conditions, or restrictions on imported or exported products or services themselves, or the process of their importation or exportation. In this broad sense, MEAs employ a range of trade-related measures, including outright trade bans for conservation purposes and as a compliance tool, labeling requirements, import and export licensing systems, notification and prior informed consent requirements, and import or export bans imposed by parties against nonparties unless the nonparties are effectively adhering to the treaty obligations.

This section provides a snapshot of the potential interface between MEAs and the WTO agreements. Because more than 20 MEAs include trade measures, this snapshot is by no means exhaustive. Yet it attempts to provide an introduction into the importance of trade measures in MEAs, as well as the purposes for which such trade measures are used, without suggesting that a dispute is imminent. Trade measures are deeply embedded in MEAs. As a consequence, these global environmental rules engage a wide range of WTO agreements, including the GATT, the General Agreement on Trade in Services, and the Agreement on Trade Related Aspects of Intellectual Property, among others.

A. Import/Export Licensing Schemes

Some international trade has direct, significant environmental impacts, including trade in endangered species and hazardous waste. Rather than ban outright the potentially environmentally dangerous trade, MEAs use international permitting systems to regulate and monitor trade. For example, CITES allows international trade in species that are threatened with extinction if the importing and exporting countries certify through permits that the trade will not be detrimental to the survival of the species in the wild.

CITES regulates international trade in species of conservation concern. Appendix I species are those that "are threatened with extinction [and] which are or may be affected by trade." This list of approximately 900 species includes the black rhinoceros, tiger, orangutan, and monkey-puzzle tree. Appendix II species are those that "although not necessarily now threatened with extinction may become so unless trade in specimens of such species is subject to strict regulation in order to avoid utilization incompatible with their survival." Appendix II contains more than 33,000 species, including the whale shark, American alligator, and several hundred genera of orchids. Species are listed in Appendix III solely on the basis of a decision by the country of origin and are not discussed further here.

To ensure that trade in these species is sustainable, CITES imposes permit requirements as a condition of trade in "specimens," any living or dead animal or plant and readily recognizable parts and derivatives, of the listed species. Trade in an Appendix I species requires both an import and export permit. Before issuing an import permit, the country of import must determine that 1) the import will be for purposes that are not detrimental to the survival of the species for which the permit is sought; 2) the proposed recipient of a living specimen is suitably equipped to house and care for it; and 3) the specimen is not to be used for primarily commercial purposes.

The "primarily commercial purposes" finding is the most important for protecting Appendix I species from overexploitation due to trade. Because of the significant role that trade has played in driving many species toward extinction, the parties have interpreted "primarily commercial purposes" very broadly so that "any transaction which is not wholly 'non-commercial' is considered 'commercial.'" For example, when the Toledo, Ohio, Zoo proposed to display giant pandas from China and charge a separate admission fee to view them, the transaction was considered primarily commercial and prohibited.

An export permit must accompany each export of an Appendix I or Appendix II species. To grant an export permit, the country of export must determine that 1) the export will not be detrimental to the survival of the species; 2) the specimen was not obtained in contravention of the laws of that state; 3) any living specimen will be so prepared and shipped as to minimize the risk of injury, damage to health, or cruel treatment; and 4) an import permit has been granted for an Appendix I species. Various combinations of these permit conditions also apply to trade in species taken on the high seas and Appendix III species.

Any of these permit findings could violate the core obligations of the GATT despite the central importance of preventing trade that is detrimental to the survival of the species and preventing the commercial trade that may be responsible for the species' threatened status. A decision of a CITES party to deny an import permit because the trade is for "primarily commercial purposes" or an export permit because the trade would be "detrimental to the survival of the species" could be challenged as a trade restriction in violation of Article XI of GATT.

Through its implementation of CITES permitting requirements, a party could also violate its most favored nation and national treatment obligations. CITES permits the "split listing" of species. For example, certain populations of vicuña, a relative of the camel that lives throughout much of the Andes, are included in Appendix I and imports for primarily commercial purposes are prohibited; other populations are included in Appendix II because their populations are larger and imports for primarily commercial purposes are permitted. If a party rejects imports of vicuña wool (a very valuable product in international trade) from an Appendix I Chilean population, but allows imports from an Appendix II Peruvian population, that country possibly violates its MFN obligation. Similarly, if Peru rejects imports of Chilean vicuña wool, but allows internal commerce in vicuña wool to continue from its Appendix II populations, then it violates its national treatment obligation, because it would be treating its vicuña products more favorably than Chile's.

Fisheries regimes have also been drawn to licensing schemes to prevent illegal, unreported, and unregulated (IUU) fishing. IUU fishing includes a range of illicit activities by parties and nonparties alike: fishing without permission or out of season; harvesting prohibited species; using outlawed types of fishing gear; disregarding catch quotas; or nonreporting or underreporting of catch weights. The U.N. Food and Agriculture Organization (FAO) has called IUU fishing "[a]n insidious problem with far reaching consequences." Press Release, FAO, Groundbreaking Treaty on Illegal Fishing Approved (Nov. 25, 2009). One widely used strategy to combat IUU fishing is a catch document scheme. For example, bluefin tuna managed by the International Commission for the Conservation of Atlantic Tunas (ICCAT) requires any trade to be accompanied by a catch document. ICCAT, Recommendation 07-10 on an ICCAT Bluefin Tuna Catch Documentation Program (2007).

B. Notice and Consent Requirements

The Basel Convention on the Control of Transboundary Movements of Hazardous Waste and Their Disposal (the Basel Convention) allows international trade in hazardous and other waste through a prior informed consent procedure designed to ensure the safe disposal of waste. Upon receiving notice from an exporter of hazardous or other waste, the importing country may reject trade for any reason. Further, an exporting country "shall prohibit" the export of hazardous wastes to a party that prohibits the import of hazardous and other wastes. In addition, both the importing and exporting countries must ensure that international transfers of hazardous and other wastes are managed in an environmentally sound manner in the state of import. A party also must take "appropriate measures" to prohibit shipments of hazardous and other wastes to a party "if it has reason to believe that the wastes in question will not be managed in an environmentally sound manner." The country of import has a corresponding duty to "prevent" imports of hazardous and other wastes if it believes these wastes will not be managed in an environmentally sound manner. Moreover, a party should only export to another party if the wastes will be used as raw material for recycling or recovery industries in the importing country. In addition, conditions in the country of export might prevent shipments of hazardous waste; a country of export must take "appropriate measures" to allow export of its hazardous and other wastes only if it does not have the technical capacity and the necessary facilities to dispose of the wastes in an "environmentally sound and efficient manner."

The Cartagena Protocol on Biosafety (Biosafety Protocol) and the Rotterdam Convention on the Prior Informed Consent Procedure for Certain Hazardous Chemicals and Pesticides in International Trade contain notice and consent provisions that, while not identical to those of the Basel Convention, pose similar GATT questions. As with CITES, parties that reject shipments of waste from certain countries under the Basel Convention, genetically modified foods under the Biosafety Protocol, or chemicals regulated by the Rotterdam Convention expose themselves to violations of their MFN and national treatment obligations, as well as the prohibition against restrictions on the importation and exportation of goods.

C. Import and Export Bans and Restrictions

Many MEAs use import or export bans and restrictions to protect the environment. For example, CITES uses a quota system to regulate trade in leopard skins. After eight years in Appendix I, the leopard population had increased to the point where some parties felt that limited trade could safely occur, particularly in countries where populations were known not to be endangered. At the same time, countries remembered the reckless slaughter of previous years for furs and trophies and wanted to prohibit commercial trade in leopard skins. As a compromise, the parties retained all populations of leopards in Appendix I but established quotas for sport-hunted trophies based on the leopard's population status in particular countries. The parties have also used quotas to limit trade in elephant ivory, crocodile skins, and other species when transferring these species to Appendix II. The quotas for leopards and crocodiles are considered some of the most successful measures adopted by the parties. Ironically, CITES quotas may actually increase trade; the parties would be extremely reluctant to allow an Appendix II listing for some species without restrictions, because that would permit commercial trade, the very trade that necessitated Appendix I protection in the first place.

In addition, the Basel Convention and the Bamako Convention on the Ban of Import into Africa and the Control of Transboundary Movement and Management of Hazardous Waste within Africa restrict trade in hazardous waste between certain parties. The parties to the Basel Convention have approved an amendment to the Convention—not yet in effect—to prohibit trade in hazardous waste from developed countries to developing countries. The Bamako Convention prohibits the importation of hazardous waste into Africa from nonparties (and only African nations may be party to the convention). Many developing countries believe that these restrictions are necessary because most hazardous waste is produced in developed countries and they fear that their countries will be used as garbage dumps for the developed world.

By their very nature, these quota systems and trade bans are inconsistent with the GATT Article XI prohibition against restrictions on the importation and exportation of goods. Implementation of the hazardous waste bans also violates most favored nation requirements, because, for example, an African party to the Bamako Convention may accept waste from another Bamako Convention party but must prohibit identical waste from non-African countries. Implementation of the Bamako Convention also poses Article III national treatment problems, because parties may allow trade in and disposal of domestic waste while prohibiting the importation of waste for disposal from other countries. Under GATT, a party must treat all waste equally.

D. Trade Bans/Sanctions for Noncompliance

Some MEAs allow parties to impose trade bans with other parties to enforce compliance with the provisions of the convention. Because MEAs rarely provide for trade sanctions within the text of the convention, these procedures have evolved through binding regulations or authoritative resolutions approved by the parties. For example, several fisheries organizations, such as the Commission of the Convention for the Conservation of Antarctic Marine Living Resources (CCAMLR), have adopted binding conservation measures that require its parties to inspect all shipments of toothfish and prohibit toothfish landings and transshipments of parties and nonparties if evidence exists that the vessel fished in contravention of CCAMLR Conservation Measures.

Other MEAs have adopted resolutions that authorize trade sanctions but which are implemented through treaty provisions allowing "stricter domestic measures." While governments retain the right to adopt stricter domestic measures unless a convention expressly excludes that possibility, a large number of MEAs expressly acknowledge a party's right to adopt them, including CITES, the Basel Convention, the Convention on the Conservation of Migratory Species of Wild Animals, and the Convention on the Conservation of European Wildlife and Natural Habitats. For example, Article XIV(1) of CITES authorizes parties to enact stricter domestic measures than required by the provisions of CITES. Pursuant to Article XIV(1), the CITES parties have developed a mechanism to implement trade sanctions at the recommendation of the parties and the CITES Standing Committee. The Standing Committee is a body of CITES charged with carrying out activities of the parties between meetings of the Conference of the Parties. If the Standing Committee finds that the party is not meeting its obligations under the convention, the Standing Committee recommends that the parties take stricter domestic measures, including trade restrictions, against that party. The recommendations of the Standing Committee do not bind the parties, nor does the text of CITES provide for sanctions against individual countries that fail to implement CITES fully. But the parties have interpreted the grant of authority to take stricter measures under Article XIV(1) as authorizing the implementation of sanctions recommended by the Standing Committee, including a total prohibition of trade in CITES-listed species. As with other import and export bans, the measures a country takes pursuant to Article XIV(1) (or other provisions allowing the use of stricter domestic measures) may conflict with GATT rules, in particular a country's MFN obligation and the prohibition against restrictions on the importation and exportation of goods.

E. Trade and Other Restrictions with Nonparties

Many MEAs, including CITES, the Montreal Protocol, the Basel Convention, and several fisheries conventions, bar trade with nonparties unless the nonparty adopts domestic measures comparable to those required by the relevant convention. Such provisions encourage countries to sign and implement the agreement, help ensure effective enforcement of the agreement, and ultimately help resolve a global environmental problem. Because these provisions intentionally discriminate against nonparties, they appear on their face to conflict with GATT provisions.

Similarly, CCAMLR prohibits landings and transshipments of any CCAMLR-regulated fish from a nonparty vessel that has been sighted engaging in fishing activities in the Convention Area because it presumes that such vessels undermine the effectiveness of CCAMLR's Conservation Measures. Other fisheries organizations maintain almost identical landing and transshipment bans for nonparty vessels. *See, e.g.*, International Commission for the Conservation of Atlantic Tuna (ICCAT), Recommendation 02-16 concerning the Importation of Atlantic Bluefin Tuna, Atlantic Swordfish, and Atlantic Bigeye Tuna and their Products from Belize (2002) (lifting trade restrictions in various fish species against Belize, Honduras, and other nonparties).

Questions and Discussion

1. MEAs use the trade measures described above for at least four main purposes. First, MEAs, such as CITES, control trade to discourage or prevent unsustainable exploitation of natural resources, especially where the trade itself constitutes an environmental threat. Second, some MEAs use trade measures to control trade in environmentally harmful substances to protect the environment of the importing country. The prior informed consent provisions of the Basel Convention, the Biosafety Protocol, and others fall within this group. Third, MEAs, including CITES and the Montreal Protocol, among others, control or prohibit trade with nonparties to prevent "free riders" and to discourage the migration of industries to countries with standards lower than those established by the treaty. Fourth, MEAs such as CITES, the Montreal Protocol, and several fisheries treaties, have imposed trade sanctions against parties and nonparties to encourage compliance with the rules of the treaty. Are any of these reasons more compelling than others from an environmental perspective? Should any be automatically exempt from trade rules? More generally, should trade measures in MEAs always be exempt from WTO scrutiny?

2. *MEAs and Article XX.* Under Article XX, would the implementation of any of the above measures taken pursuant to an MEA merit any more deference than they would if taken unilaterally? Based on the Appellate Body's decision in *Shrimp/Turtle* (*see* Chapter 5, Section V.B at pages 324–35), there is reason to think that they do. A more deferential review by a panel may depend on the reason a trade measure was taken. Consider the use of stricter domestic measures under CITES. How much deference should a CITES party receive if it imposes trade restrictions to compel another party's compliance based on a recommendation of the parties? Should that warrant greater deference than a party's unilateral decision to impose the stricter CITES permit requirements applicable to Appendix I species to an Appendix II species?

3. The range of potential disputes is vast, even if no country has ever brought a dispute. Do you think this "issue-spotting" exercise exaggerates the potential for MEA-WTO problems and may actually increase tensions and possible disputes? If it does, then why do you think no party has yet brought a WTO challenge to a trade measure in an MEA?

_____

III. Strategies for Reconciliation

Because of the large number of questions relating to the consistency of MEAs and the WTO Agreements, much attention has been given to the search for reconciliation. In a Ministerial Declaration concluded as part of the Uruguay Round negotiations, the WTO members created the Committee on Trade and Environment (CTE) and instructed it to examine, among other issues, the relationship between the provisions of WTO agreements and trade measures used for environmental purposes, including those in MEAs. It also directed the CTE to examine "the relationship between the dispute settlement mechanisms in the multilateral trading system and those found in [MEAs]." WTO, Ministerial Decision of 15 April 1994 on Trade and Environment (1994), *available at* http://www.wto.org/english/tratop_e/envir_e/issu5_e.htm. In 2001, as part of the Doha Development Agenda, trade ministers agreed to negotiations on:

> the relationship between existing WTO rules and specific trade obligations set out in multilateral environmental agreements (MEAs). The negotiations shall be limited in scope to the applicability of such existing WTO rules as among parties to the MEA in question. The negotiations shall not prejudice the WTO rights of any Member that is not a party to the MEA in question;

World Trade Organization, Ministerial Declaration of Ministerial Conference Fourth Session, Doha, Nov. 9–14 2001, WT/MIN(01)/DEC/W/1, para. 31(i) (adopted Nov. 14, 2001).

One way that WTO and various MEAs have worked to resolve potential conflict is to engage in consultations. Thus, the WTO Secretariat is an observer (nonvoting participant) of the Governing Council of UNEP, and UNEP and several MEA secretariats are official observers of the WTO Committee on Trade and Environment (CBD, CITES, ICCAT, and UNFCCC). Four other MEA secretariats have requests for observer status pending as of 2009—the Montreal Protocol, the International Tropical Timber Organization, the Basel Convention, and the Rotterdam Convention. Committee on Trade and Environment, Report (2009) of the Committee on Trade and Environment, WT/CTE/16, para. 21 (Oct. 30, 2009). This consultation only extends so far, however; when the Committee on Trade and Environment meets for its negotiations pursuant to the Doha Development Agenda, MEA secretariats are excluded as only WTO members can negotiate.

Those consultations, while productive for providing a greater understanding of various international agreements, have not led to concrete rules to resolve future disputes involving a WTO agreement and an MEA. To that end, the CTE, environmental advocates, and scholars have proposed a number of approaches for reconciliation. These proposals focus on three main questions:

- Who will decide how to reconcile any inconsistencies between an MEA and a WTO agreement?

- Which rules will be used to reconcile any inconsistency between an MEA and a WTO agreement?

- Which law applies?

A. Who Reconciles?

The question of which forum has competence to decide how to reconcile the provisions of an MEA and a WTO agreement has obvious importance for the outcome of the dispute. For example, one forum may allow certain defenses and grant additional procedural rights, such as the right to appeal, that are not available in another forum. Success in the WTO's Dispute Settlement Body (DSB) would permit a WTO member to impose trade sanctions against an offending member that refuses to implement the recommendation of the panel or Appellate Body. Panel members in one forum may have expertise that may or may not be more relevant to a particular component of the case.

In fact, the EU considered several of these issues, even noting the "great advantage" offered by the WTO's retaliatory trade sanctions, when it chose the WTO as its forum for challenging Chile's measures to conserve swordfish populations. European Commission, *Report to the Trade Barriers Regulation Committee: TBR Proceedings concerning Chilean Practices Affecting Transit of Swordfish in Chilean Ports*, 43 (Mar. 1999). To protect populations of swordfish, a species considered to be over-exploited, Chile imposed gear restrictions, limited fishing effort by denying new permits, and established minimum size limits for fish. In addition, it banned the operation of factory ships within its Exclusive Economic Zone (EEZ). Because Chile felt that EU vessels were failing to enforce minimum conservation measures, such as failing to report its catches to the Food and Agriculture Organization (FAO) and to prohibit fishing on the swordfish's nesting and spawning grounds, Chile effectively banned EU vessels from using its ports for landing swordfish and for service. Marcos Orellana Cruz, *The Swordfish in Peril: The EU Challenges Chilean Port Access Restrictions at the WTO*, 6 BRIDGES 11–12 (July–Aug. 2000).

After the EU initiated WTO proceedings alleging that Chile's conservation measures violated Article V of the GATT on the free transit of goods among the members' territories, Chile responded by invoking the compulsory dispute settlement provisions of the United Nations Law of the Sea Convention (UNCLOS) and invited the EU to the International Tribunal for the Law of the Sea (ITLOS). Chile alleged that the EU violated UNCLOS's duty to cooperate to conserve a highly migratory species by failing to report its catch to the relevant international organization, the FAO, and by failing to cooperate with the coastal state to ensure the conservation of highly migratory species. Although the EU rejected the ITLOS jurisdiction, it agreed to the formation of an Arbitral Tribunal under UNCLOS provisions. *Id.* at 11–12.

Which forum governs the dispute? Before that question could be answered, the EU and Chile reached an agreement that suspends both the WTO and ITLOS proceedings. Under this agreement, EU vessels may use Chilean ports provided that the fish are caught under a new scientific fisheries program that limits the amount of fish caught and landed in Chile and which requires the use of satellite monitoring systems (VMS) and scientific observers on board fishing vessels. Marcos Orellana, *The EU and Chile Suspend the Swordfish Case Proceedings at the WTO and the International Tribunal of the Law of the Sea*, ASIL

INSIGHTS (Feb. 2001), *available at* http://www.asil.org/insights/insigh60.htm; Chile-Measures Affecting the Transit and Importation of Swordfish, Communication from Chile, WT/DS193/3/add.1 (Apr. 9, 2001). Significantly, the EU has retained its rights to revive the proceedings at any time. Communication from the European Communities, WT/DS193/3/Add.4 (Dec. 17, 2007).

While a political solution avoided a clash of treaties in this case, existing rules of public international law and of the applicable treaties themselves remain unhelpful for deciding whether a dispute involving a trade measure relating to, for example, UNCLOS may be adjudicated only at the WTO, only through the dispute resolution provisions of UNCLOS, or both. Clearly the strength of the WTO's dispute settlement procedures will draw conflicts toward it. In fact, the EU brought its case to the WTO even though it has a policy "to apply, in a first instance, to dispute settlement bodies under the auspices of an MEA rather than revert to WTO proceedings under the Dispute Settlement Understanding (DSU). The political aim is to avoid the undermining and weakening the credibility and effectiveness of MEAs by allowing them to be bypassed or even circumvented via the WTO route." EUROPEAN COMMISSION, TBR PROCEEDINGS CONCERNING CHILEAN PRACTICES AFFECTING TRANSIT OF SWORDFISH IN CHILEAN PORTS, at 42. Similarly, the WTO's CTE stated:

> While WTO Members have the right to bring disputes to the WTO dispute settlement mechanism, if a dispute arises between WTO Members, Parties to an MEA, over the use of trade measures they are applying between themselves pursuant to the MEA, they should consider trying to resolve it through the dispute settlement mechanisms available under the MEA.

Report of the Committee on Trade and Environment, WT/CTE/1, para. 178 (Nov. 12, 1996).

How should such conflicts be resolved? In the WTO? In the MEA? In a neutral forum?

1. Dispute Settlement in MEAs

The dispute settlement processes of MEAs are notable for being uniformly noncompulsory. (Although UNCLOS contains compulsory jurisdiction, it is not strictly speaking an MEA, because it covers a range of issues only some of which concern environmental matters). The typical dispute settlement provisions of MEAs require disputing parties to settle their dispute through negotiation or other peaceful means. If that does not resolve the dispute, they may seek mediation. Assuming no resolution there, then the disputing parties may agree to submit their dispute to the International Court of Justice (ICJ) or to arbitration. In addition, a party "may declare" at the time of ratification that it recognizes the jurisdiction of the ICJ or another identified arbitration panel or process as compulsory. *See* Basel Convention, art. 20; CBD, art. 27.

The use of formal dispute settlement mechanisms in MEAs to resolve disputes is rare and, with the exception of the use of ITLOS to resolve disputes arising under fisheries treaties, the dispute settlement provisions of MEAs have never been tested. The failure to use these dispute settlement provisions may reflect the multilateral effects of noncompliance in MEAs (and thus greater collective efforts to control noncompliance) rather than the more bilateral effect of noncompliance with WTO provisions. It may also reflect the emphasis in MEAs on positive incentives for compliance and processes to address noncompliance through multilateral reviews, recommendations by various treaty bodies, technical and financial assistance, and other forms of international cooperation. Committee on Trade and Environment, *Compliance and Dispute Settlement Provisions in the WTO and in Multilateral Environmental Agreements,* Note by the WTO and UNEP Secretariats, WT/CTE/W/191, para. 26 (June 6, 2001).

This may be changing. CITES, the Montreal Protocol, and the Kyoto Protocol have all developed compliance mechanisms that, while intended to be nonconfrontational, may end in sanctions, such as trade bans in CITES-listed species or loss of funds from the Montreal Protocol's Multilateral Fund. The Inter-American Tropical Tuna Commission's International Review Panel may reduce a vessel's dolphin mortality limits in the tuna fishery well known for its tuna/dolphin interactions. The International Commission for the Conservation of Atlantic Tuna has imposed trade restrictions on parties and nonparties alike for fishing in contravention of the Commission's fishing regulations.

The Non-Compliance Procedure of the Montreal Protocol, which provides the model upon which many compliance procedures are based, relies on discussion, recommendations, and transparency to encourage compliance. The parties created the Non-Compliance Procedure as a nonconfrontational approach for pursuing "amicable solutions" to noncompliance problems. Non-Compliance Procedure, Decision IV/5, Annex IV (1992). The Non-Compliance Procedure establishes an Implementation Committee (IC) consisting of ten parties elected for two years who meet twice each year. It receives complaints initiated by any party to the Protocol that suspects another party of noncompliance, a party self-reporting a default on its obligations, or the Secretariat. Upon receiving a complaint, the IC may collect information relating to a party's compliance in its territory, but only if the party concerned has requested it to do so. Parties send their submissions to the Secretariat, which transmits the submission, including any reply from the party alleged to be in noncompliance, to the IC. The IC reviews the submission and makes its recommendations to the parties. The parties ultimately decide which measures to take against a noncomplying party. Copenhagen Amendments to the Montreal Protocol, 32 I.L.M. 874 (1995).

The Non-Compliance Procedure appears to be successfully achieving compliance through its "nonconfrontational process." The success of the procedure can be attributed to several factors. The IC first engages the noncomplying party in discussions. If those discussions fail, then the IC has shown its willingness to recommend significant actions, such as revocation of a party's Article 5 status, a status that gives such parties grace periods for implementation of the Protocol's obligations and access to funds from the Protocol's Multilateral Fund. For example, because all parties must submit to the Secretariat baseline and annual data on production, imports, and exports of ODS covered by the Montreal Protocol, data reporting remains a prominent feature of the IC's agenda. When parties fail to provide the required information, or if the Secretariat believes that information is incorrect or missing, the Secretariat refers these matters to the IC. The IC has taken an increasingly aggressive role in compelling compliance with the data reporting requirements of the Protocol. For example, Russia refused "repeated requests" for estimates of its production and consumption of ODS and supplied the information only after the IC refused to approve Russia's compliance plan, a prerequisite to obtaining funding from the Global Environment Facility. When the IC publicly invited nine parties to explain their persistent failure to supply their baseline data, five of those countries submitted their data before the meeting. Another 17 parties submitted missing data when the IC recommended that they lose their Article 5 status. David G. Victor, *The Operation and Effectiveness of the Montreal Protocol's Non-Compliance Procedure, in* THE IMPLEMENTATION AND EFFECTIVENESS OF INTERNATIONAL ENVIRONMENTAL COMMITMENTS 137 (David G. Victor et al. eds., 1998).

----

2. Dispute Settlement in the WTO

As with MEAs, dispute settlement in the WTO begins with attempts to resolve the dispute through mandatory consultations and voluntary conciliation or mediation. *See* Chapter 2, Section IV.B at pages 91–100 for a description of the WTO's dispute settlement process. From that point of similarity, the two systems diverge with the WTO proceedings heading to compulsory and binding dispute settlement of the Dispute Settlement Body (DSB).

Article 1.1 of the WTO Dispute Settlement Understanding (DSU) makes clear that the DSU's dispute resolution provisions of the WTO apply to any dispute concerning a member's "rights and obligations" under the WTO agreements. Article 23 elaborates on the types of disputes that fall within the competence of the DSU.

Understanding on Rules and Procedures Governing the Settlement of Disputes
Article 23 Strengthening of the Multilateral System

1. When Members seek the redress of a violation of obligations or other nullification or impairment of benefits under the covered agreements or an impediment to the attainment of any objective of the covered agreements, they shall have recourse to, and abide by, the rules and procedures of this Understanding.

2. In such cases, Members shall: (a) not make a determination to the effect that a violation has occurred, that benefits have been nullified or impaired or that the attainment of any objective of the covered agreements has been impeded, except through recourse to dispute settlement in accordance with the rules and procedures of this Understanding, and shall make any such determination consistent with the findings contained in the panel or Appellate Body report adopted by the DSB or an arbitration award rendered under this Understanding.

Questions and Discussion

1. Do the provisions of Article 23, when read together with Article 1.1, *require* disputes concerning a conflict between an MEA and a WTO agreement to be brought within the WTO system? One commentator believes that Article 23 "exclude[s] ... the competence of any other mechanism to examine the WTO violation" and, if a WTO member pursues a dispute in another forum, "that WTO Member would be violating the WTO Agreement and might become subject to sanctions corresponding to the level of trade benefits nullified or impaired" thereby. Gabrielle Marceau, *Conflicts of Norms and Conflicts of Jurisdictions: The Relationship Between the WTO Agreement and MEAs and other Treaties*, 35 J. WORLD TRADE 1081, 1101 (second quotation), 1115–16 (first quotation) (2001).

Do you agree? CITES has banned international trade in whale meat for many years. It has done so to support the moratorium on commercial whaling imposed by the International Whaling Commission (IWC). Thus, two MEAs are interacting to ensure the protection of whale populations that have been decimated by commercial whaling. If Japan were to challenge the CITES ban, must it bring its challenge to the WTO? Does it matter that Japan is a party to both CITES and the IWC and subject to the decisionmaking rules of those MEAs? Does your analysis change in light of calls in other parts of the DSU to examine the dispute or make decisions concerning the dispute based on the relevant provision included in any covered agreement or agreements? *See* DSU, arts. 1.1, 4.2, 4.4, 4.7, 11. For a description of "covered agreement," see pages 73–75.

2. Marceau concludes that the dispute settlement mechanisms of MEAs "cannot be viewed as a limitation on WTO panels and the Appellate Body to examine the content of relevant MEAs when this is necessary to perform their DSU functions," but that "the right, and sometimes the obligation, of panels and the Appellate Body to interpret a relevant MEA should not be viewed as usurpation of the authority of MEA Secretariats (or other MEA bodies) to supervise and administer the enforcement of such MEAs." Marceau, *Conflicts of Norms and Conflicts of Jurisdictions*, at 1124. Do you agree? If the Conference of the Parties to CITES adopts quotas for the export and import of leopard skins, and then a WTO panel rules that such quotas violate Article XI's prohibition against quantitative restrictions, is that not a usurpation of the role of the Conference of the Parties? She would not exclude the use of the MEA's dispute resolution process, however, and finds no obstacle to concurrent jurisdiction and contradictory results. How would a country comply with contradictory opinions?

3. In *Mexico-Soft Drinks*, the Appellate Body found that once the WTO's jurisdiction has been validly established, a WTO panel may not decline to exercise it, even though the defendant in this case described the WTO claims as "inextricably linked" to dispute settlement proceedings before another international tribunal. With respect to Mexico's alternative argument, the Appellate Body found that Article XX(d) of the GATT concerned measures to secure compliance with *domestic* laws or regulations—not to secure compliance with international laws. Mexico-Tax Measures on Soft Drinks and other Beverages, Appellate Body Report, WT/DS308/AB/R, paras. 46–57. (adopted Mar. 24, 2006). In its key passage, the Appellate Body states:

> A decision by a panel to decline to exercise validly established jurisdiction would seem to "diminish" the right of a complaining Member to "seek the redress of a violation of obligations" within the meaning of Article 23 of the DSU, and to bring a dispute pursuant to Article 3.3 of the DSU. This would not be consistent with a panel's obligations under Articles 3.2 and 19.2 of the DSU. We see no reason, therefore, to disagree with the Panel's statement that a WTO panel "would seem … not to be in a position to choose freely whether or not to exercise its jurisdiction."

Id. at para. 53.

4. The compliance mechanisms of MEAs have proven to be robust and effective. What advantages might they have over the WTO's dispute settlement procedures?

5. As noted above, many MEAs have compliance regimes that, like the Montreal Protocol's procedure, rely on substantial communication between the relevant MEA committee and the noncomplying party. For more on the CITES compliance mechanism, see CITES, Resolution Conf. 14.3, CITES Compliance Procedures (2007); ROSALIND REEVE, POLICING INTERNATIONAL TRADE IN ENDANGERED SPECIES: THE CITES TREATY AND COMPLIANCE (2002); Marceil Yeater & Juan Vasquez, *Demystifying the Relationship Between CITES and the WTO*, 10 RECEIL 271, 274–75 (2000). For more on the compliance mechanism of the Kyoto Protocol, see Decision 27/CMP.1, Annex, Procedures and Mechanisms Relating to Compliance under the Kyoto Protocol (2005); CHRIS WOLD, DAVID HUNTER & MELISSA POWERS, CLIMATE CHANGE AND THE LAW 305–24 (2009).

B. The Rules of Reconciliation

The international trade community has been wrestling with the relationship between trade law and MEAs for some time. During the negotiations of CITES, and thus long before the modern trade and environment debate, the drafters of CITES solicited an opinion from the GATT Secretariat on the GATT-consistency of CITES trade measures. The GATT Secretariat replied that the draft "seems consistent with the preamble of article XX." Letter from Gardner Patterson, Assistant Director-General, Department of Trade Policy, GATT, to F.G. Nichols, Deputy Director-General, IUCN (Feb. 24, 1971). Montreal Protocol negotiators received a similar opinion. UNEP/WG.172/2, Report of the Ad Hoc Working Group on the Work of its Third Session, 18 (May 8, 1987).

These Secretariat interpretations, however, were far from reassuring. Not only are GATT Secretariat opinions nonbinding just as WTO Secretariat opinions are nonbinding, but it is clear that the members have divergent views on how to resolve tensions between MEAs and trade law.

To move toward a consistent approach for addressing MEA-WTO concerns, the WTO ministers directed the WTO's Committee on Trade and Environment to negotiate, as part of the Doha agenda, an outcome to "the relationship between existing WTO rules and specific trade obligations" of MEAs. Ministerial Declaration, WTO Ministerial Conference, Fourth Session, Doha, Nov. 9–14 2001, WT/MIN(01)/DEC/W/1, para. 31 (Nov. 14, 2001).

Ideas to reconcile MEA and trade law have taken diverse paths. These efforts have focused on the provisions of the Vienna Convention on the Law of Treaties, the establishment of binding or nonbinding criteria for identifying "acceptable" trade measures in MEAs, and the use of existing trade rules such as Article XX to filter acceptable from unacceptable trade measures. A fourth approach has looked to resolution of these issues through MEAs, rather than trade bodies.

1. The Rules of Treaty Interpretation

The rules of treaty interpretation under the Vienna Convention on the Law of Treaties (the Vienna Convention) and general rules of interpretation are standard tools for interpreting treaties and resolving disputes between conflicting treaties. Often, parties will include provisions that describe the relationship of an agreement to other treaties. In addition, the *travaux preparatoires* (the preparatory work) might provide useful insights into the intent of the negotiators, though like their domestic counterpart, legislative history, they cannot be used to contradict the plain meaning of the text.

Vienna Convention on the Law of Treaties
May 23, 1969, U.N. Doc. A/CONF. 39/27, 1155 U.N.T.S. 331
(entered into force Jan. 27, 1980)

Article 30 — Application of successive treaties relating to the same subject-matter

1. Subject to Article 103 of the Charter of the United Nations, the rights and obligations of States parties to successive treaties relating to the same subject-matter shall be determined in accordance with the following paragraphs.

2. When a treaty specifies that it is subject to, or that it is not to be considered as incompatible with, an earlier or later treaty, the provisions of that other treaty prevail.

3. When all the parties to the earlier treaty are parties also to the later treaty but the earlier treaty is not terminated or suspended in operation under article 59, the earlier treaty applies only to the extent that its provisions are compatible with those of the later treaty.

4. When the parties to the later treaty do not include all the parties to the earlier one:

(a) as between States parties to both treaties the same rule applies as in paragraph 3;

(b) as between a State party to both treaties and a State party to only one of the treaties, the treaty to which both States are parties governs their mutual rights and obligations. * * *

———————

Article 30 of the Vienna Convention provides a number of rules that would appear to be useful for reconciling potential conflicts between MEAs and the WTO agreements. Article 30(2) acknowledges that a treaty can simply specify which treaty prevails in the event of a conflict. Article 30(3) declares that a treaty that is later in time prevails over earlier treaties (*lex posterior*). A related rule of treaty interpretation provided by customary international law, *lex specialis*, holds that a more specific treaty or provision prevails over the more general treaty or provision.

These rules, however, may only be applied to successive treaties relating to the "same subject-matter." The history of the Vienna Convention indicates that the parties established rules for interpreting successive treaties, such as GATT 1947 and GATT 1994, rather than for completely separate agreements, such as GATT 1994 and the Basel Convention, that address entirely different fields of law but have some provisions that overlap in some respects. Christopher J. Borgen, *Resolving Treaty Conflicts*, 37 GEORGE WASH. INT'L L. REV. 573, 604–05 (2005); IAN M. SINCLAIR, THE VIENNA CONVENTION ON THE LAW OF TREATIES 98 (2d ed. 1984). If this interpretation is correct, then the Vienna Convention would have no relevance for defining the relationship between WTO agreements and MEAs.

However, the International Law Commission (ILC) and others have articulated a broader approach. The ILC, for example, has declared that:

[T]he test of whether two treaties deal with the "same subject matter" is resolved through the assessment of whether the fulfilment of the obligation under one treaty affects the fulfilment of the obligation of another. This "affecting" might then take place either as strictly preventing the fulfilment of the other obligation or undermining its object and purpose in one or another way.

International Law Commission, Fragmentation of International Law: Difficulties Arising from the Diversification and Expansion of International Law, U.N. Doc A/CN.4/L.682, para. 254 (Apr. 13, 2006) (finalized by Martti Koskenniemi). Others have stated the test more simply: "If an attempted simultaneous application of two rules to one set of facts or actions leads to incompatible results it can safely be assumed that the test of sameness is satisfied." E.W. Vierdag, *The Time of the 'Conclusion' of a Multilateral Treaty: Article 30 of the Vienna Convention on the Law of Treaties and Related Provisions*, 59 BRIT. Y.B. INT'L. L. 100 (1988). Even assuming that a less strict test applies, one must still determine whether the GATT or another WTO agreement and the MEA at issue actually relate to the same subject matter. The existence of trade measures in MEAs and the existence of environmental exceptions in GATT suggest that certain provisions of the agreements relate to the same subject matter. Also, the interest of the GATT Secretariat in the negotiations of the Climate Change Convention and the Convention on Biological Diversity (CBD) indicate that, at a minimum, the provisions of those agreements may overlap provisions of the GATT or other WTO agreements. Of course, one also could argue that such treaties relate to different topics, because the subject of an environmental agreement relates to a particular environmental problem, whereas GATT and the WTO agreements relate to eliminating trade barriers.

If the "same subject matter" hurdle is overcome, then one must try to apply one of the Vienna Convention's specific rules. As described below, this is not a straightforward task.

a. Primacy Clauses

A number of MEAs, including CITES, the CBD, and the Biosafety Protocol, have "primacy," or savings, clauses that attempt to clarify the relationship between that MEA and other treaties. The preamble to the Biosafety Protocol, for example, provides that its parties:

> *Emphasiz[e]* that this Protocol shall not be interpreted as implying a change in the rights and obligations of a Party under any existing international agreements,
>
> *Understand[]* that the above recital is not intended to subordinate this Protocol to other international agreements[.]

Article XIV(2) of CITES provides:

> The provisions of the present Convention shall in no way affect the provisions of any domestic measures or the obligations of Parties deriving from any treaty, convention, or international agreement relating to other aspects of trade, taking, possession or transport of specimens which is in force or subsequently may enter into force for any Party.

Theoretically, these provisions apply Article 30(2) of the Vienna Convention by seeking to ensure that one treaty prevails over another. However, "they potentially reinforce the uncertainty inherent in a mutually supportive relationship." Duncan Brack & Kevin Gray, Int'l Inst. for Sustainable Development Report, Multilateral Environmental Agreements and the WTO 30 (Sept. 2003). Reread Article XIV(2) of CITES. Does it resolve disputes between CITES and a WTO agreement? In addition, these primacy clauses are often the result of intense debate leading to compromises that leave the meaning of the provision in doubt. The Biosafety Protocol illustrates this point all too well; its provisions state both that the Protocol does not imply a change in the rights and obligations under any existing agreement, and that the Protocol is not subordinate to other international agreements. *See* Chapter 7, Section VI.B.3 at pages 516–17. Due to this ambiguity, commentators believe that interpretation of such clauses by WTO dispute settlement bodies could lead "to unpredictable results." *Id.*

b. Lex Posterior *and* Lex Specialis

Chris Wold, *Multilateral Environmental Agreements and Trade Rules: Conflict and Resolution*
26 Envtl. L. 841, 911–13 (1996)

Lex Posterior

If a multilateral environmental agreement and GATT relate to the same subject matter, then the Vienna Convention mandates that the later in time treaty prevails, a rule known as *lex posterior*. The application of this simple rule is not easy. First, the Vienna Convention does not state when a treaty is "dated," and scholars are not in agreement. Some argue that a treaty is dated from the time of its adoption, others from the time of its entry into force. The order of priority is confused further by amendments to agreements, and, in the case of GATT, by the negotiation of entirely new codes and a subsequent treaty.

Regarding GATT, the Final Act of the Uruguay Round does not clearly specify how different aspects of GATT relate to each other. For example, GATT 1947 is an integral part of GATT 1994, but the two documents are considered legally distinct. Thus, whether GATT 1947, with its core obligations of most-favored-nation (MFN), national treatment, and prohibitions against quantitative restrictions, carries forward or retains its original date is uncertain. If GATT 1947 retains its earlier date, the provisions of multilateral environmental agreements trump GATT 1947 but not the newly created TBT, Subsidies, and TRIPs Agreements.

CITES and the Montreal Protocol are examples of frequently amended agreements. Parties to the Montreal Protocol have accelerated the schedules for phasing out ozone depleting chemicals. The parties to CITES amend the appendices at each conference of the parties. The relevant date for treaty interpretation should be the date the amendments are adopted or entered into force. Such a situation would create absurd administrative hassles, however, if amendments to the Montreal Protocol schedules or the CITES appendices are later in time than the relevant GATT provisions. For example, assume that the core obligations of GATT carry a 1994 date for the purposes of treaty interpretation. If the parties to CITES add the bluefin tuna to Appendix I at the next conference of the parties in 1997, a party's import ban on bluefin tuna would be GATT-consistent because the CITES amendment would be later in time. On the other hand, the import bans on Javan rhinos, which number about fifty total individuals, would violate GATT because the parties protected Javan rhinos in 1975. In this case, GATT is later in time and prevails. For a split listed species, trade restrictions for populations in one country might be consistent with GATT while those from another country might be inconsistent. Similar silliness would result if parties added to or accelerated the schedules of the Montreal Protocol. In the latter case, restrictions to reduce consumption by fifty percent might be consistent with GATT while amended consumption percentages would be inconsistent.

Lex Specialis

Although not stated in the Vienna Convention, specific treaties or provisions control general treaties or provisions under the rule of *lex specialis*, even if the general provisions are later in time. As with *lex posterior*, *lex specialis* requires the treaties to relate to the same subject matter. Arguably, the provisions of multilateral environmental agreements are more specific than GATT and its codes. Whereas the subject matter of GATT applies to the entire universe of products, with the goal of reducing tariffs and nontariff restrictions such as quotas and technical barriers to trade, a multilateral environmental agreement focuses on one environmental problem and tailors its measures, including its trade measures, to reducing or eliminating that problem. Moreover, in interpreting a treaty, its total context must be considered, including any subsequent practice of the parties in applying the treaty. This includes the practice of the parties, and any institutions established under an agreement, in implementing the agreement.... In short, because GATT is a more general international agreement than are multilateral environmental agreements, the latter should control if there is a conflict.

_____

c. Parties versus Nonparties

Article 30(4) of the Vienna Convention appears to establish at least one rule that allows resolution to the MEA-WTO conflict: as between a State party to both the WTO and the MEA and a State party to only one of those treaties, the treaty to which both States are parties governs their mutual rights and obligations. Thus, because the United States is party to both the WTO and CITES, but Russia is party only to CITES, then CITES prevails in any dispute between the two countries concerning the trade obligations of CITES. Alternatively, because the United States is not a party to the Biosafety Protocol and Venezuela is, then the WTO should prevail in a dispute between these two WTO members relating to trade in genetically modified organisms.

The utility of Article 30(4) is questionable for practical as well as legal reasons. First, the most prominent MEAs that include trade restrictions, such as CITES, the Montreal Protocol, the Basel Convention, among others, have memberships that overlap almost entirely with the membership of the WTO. As such, very few possibilities exist to use the rule. In addition, Article 30(4) assumes that a treaty can be separated into at least two sets of legal relations and that it can become a series of different bilateral arrangements. PAUL REUTER, AN INTRODUCTION TO THE LAW OF TREATIES 102–03 (1st ed. 1989).

_____

Questions and Discussion

1. What factors should be considered when evaluating whether or not one treaty is more specific than another? Could a tribunal evaluate the decisionmaking process of a treaty, in addition to its underlying purpose? Consider these arguments:

First, CITES trade measures do not implicate the concerns underlying the GATT's non-discrimination provisions. The national treatment principle of GATT is intended to prohibit measures that discriminate against imports so as to afford protection to domestic production. Similarly, the MFN obligation is intended to prohibit protectionist measures that provide unfair advantages or privileges to the products of another country. The CITES Parties, however, do not apply trade measures to a wildlife specimen for the purpose of affording protection to domestic production or conferring competitive advantages and privileges to producers from another country. Instead, the CITES Parties evaluate biological and ecological criteria and then apply trade measures to a species or certain populations that most accurately reflect the conservation status of the species or populations.... [W]ildlife specimens from a particular population ... are regulated on the basis of that population's conservation status, not on the basis of the specimens' production within the political borders of any particular country.

The deliberate, science-based, multilateral, decision of two-thirds or more of the CITES Parties (which include a significant number of developed and developed countries from different regions), shows how unlikely it is that CITES measures are motivated by protectionist motivations or by arbitrary discrimination among nations. WTO rules are designed to prevent the unfair use of economic power to impose trade measures.... As a matter of common sense, WTO concerns would not generally be implicated when two-thirds or more of CITES' [175] Parties agree to restrict trade in a species.

Chris Wold, *An Analysis of the Relationship between CITES and the WTO* (May 31, 1997).

2. Do you agree with the view of commentators that the rules of "the Vienna Convention are unlikely to resolve any dispute between provisions of a multilateral environmental agreement and GATT and WTO rules?" Wold, *Multilateral Environmental Agreements and Trade Rules*, at 910; *see also* Richard G. Tarasofsky, *Ensuring Compatibility between Multilateral Environmental Agreements and the GATT/WTO*, 7 Y.B. Int'l Envtl. L. 52, 65 (1996).

---

2. Waivers

Some members of the CTE believe that existing WTO mechanisms, such as waivers under Article IX of the WTO Agreement, can accommodate MEAs effectively. Waivers provide the opportunity for members to seek, in exceptional circumstances, a waiver from a WTO obligation, subject to approval by at least three-fourths of the WTO membership. A waiver is time-limited and must be renewed periodically.

Some WTO members have viewed these limitations on the use of waivers to resolve conflicts between MEAs and WTO agreements favorably, especially where MEA parties apply WTO-inconsistent discriminatory trade measures against nonparties. Hong Kong suggested all measures taken under MEAs would be eligible for a waiver, provided they meet specified criteria. With respect to trade measures specifically required by an MEA, these criteria could include, for example, (i) the negotiation of and participation in the MEA reflect a genuine international consensus; (ii) the MEA meets the criteria set out in the chapeau to GATT Article XX; and (iii) the grant of the waiver does not prejudice WTO members' rights and obligations under the DSU, irrespective of whether they are parties to the MEA in question. For trade measures allowed but not required, or for trade measures taken in furtherance of an MEA, proposed additional criteria included the measure's necessity, least trade-restrictiveness, effectiveness, and proportionality. Report (1996) of the Committee on Trade and Environment, WT/CTE/1, para. 13 (Nov. 12, 1996).

Richard Tarasofsky and Alice Palmer, two frequent writers on trade and environment issues, have other ideas for waivers:

> Yet another variation on the proposal to exempt MEA trade measures from WTO rules relates to who carries the "burden of proof" in disputes. Under WTO exceptions, such as GATT article XX, the evidentiary burden of persuading the arbitrators that the challenged measure qualifies for the exemption falls on the member defending that measure. Some proposals to accommodate MEA trade measures have suggested reversing the burden of proof under article XX. By reversing the burden of proof for MEA trade measures, the WTO members would be requiring the members that complain that an MEA trade measure violates one of the primary WTO rules—such as the ban on quotas under GATT article XI—to show that it does not qualify as an exception under article XX. * * *
>
> WTO members could [also] expressly require WTO members to exhaust all options for resolving disputes over MEA trade measures under MEA dispute settlement procedures before initiating a dispute in the WTO. The rationale for this

is that MEAs are best able to assess measures aimed at implementing their objectives. This outcome would, however, depend on there being effective dispute settlement procedures available under the MEA. WTO arbitrators could be required to seek and follow advice from MEA authorities in the course of disputes. Under current WTO rules, WTO arbitrators may seek advice from MEA bodies on the question of whether a challenged measure has been validly taken pursuant to an MEA. However, without an express requirement for WTO arbitrators to seek and follow the advice of an MEA body authorized to determine whether a given measure is a valid MEA trade measure, WTO arbitrators might make assessments on MEA compliance that are beyond their area of competence.

Richard Tarasofsky & Alice Palmer, *The WTO in Crisis: Lessons Learned from the Doha Negotiations on the Environment*, 82 Int'l Affairs 899, 907–08 (2006).

Questions and Discussion

1. Does Hong Kong's waiver proposal provide useful criteria for balancing trade and environmental considerations? Does its criteria differ significantly from those developed by the Appellate Body in *Shrimp/Turtle* and other decisions for meeting the requirements of Article XX? If yes, are the waiver criteria stricter than the criteria developed by the Appellate Body? If no, then what is the value of a waiver? Do these proposals grant a minority of WTO members a kind of veto over the use of trade measures in MEAs?

2. Whereas the Hong Kong proposal would exempt certain MEAs from dispute settlement, the proposals of Tarasofsky and Palmer establish procedural rules that would be applied if a dispute were to arise. What do you think of their approach?

---

3. Rules-Based Approaches

Some WTO members, as well as environmental advocates, have searched for *ex ante* approaches that seek to avoid conflicts before they arise, rather than through *ex post* approaches under the WTO dispute settlement or waiver provisions. These proposals seek greater certainty that trade measures of MEAs meeting specific conditions will benefit from special treatment under WTO provisions.

Report (1996) of the Committee on Trade and Environment
WT/CTE/1 (Nov. 12, 1996)

17. One proposal [EU] elaborates two options. The first is to include measures taken pursuant to specific provisions of MEAs in GATT Article XX. The second is to introduce a reference not only to these measures but, also in more general terms, to measures necessary to protect the "environment;" and to improve the consistency of the rules of the multilateral trading system taking into account both the commitment expressed in the first preambular paragraph of the Agreement establishing the WTO and the fact that the environment is already mentioned in several WTO Agreements. Both options suggest the development of an Understanding under the provisions of GATT Article XX that in the event a

trade measure applied pursuant to an MEA is challenged in the WTO, subject to certain procedural criteria being met[19] the dispute settlement panel would examine only whether the measure has been applied in conformity with the requirements in the headnote language of Article XX and would not consider its necessity. The aim is to send a political signal of the WTO's support for multilateral measures as a means of discouraging the use of more trade-disruptive and less-environmentally efficient unilateral ones, and so to strengthen the multilateral trading system by establishing a framework to deal with problems that arise. The WTO would not judge the legitimacy of the environmental objectives or the necessity of the measures taken to achieve these objectives because the multilateral character of the trade measures would be the best guarantee against abuse. At the same time, the WTO would retain its power to counter protectionist implementation of a multilaterally-agreed measure through the headnote language in Article XX.

18. A second proposal [New Zealand] is to develop an Understanding, applicable across all WTO Annex 1 Agreements, on differentiated treatment for trade measures applied pursuant to MEAs, depending on whether they apply between Parties or against non-parties and whether they are specifically mandated in an MEA. Specific and jointly notified trade measures applied among MEA Parties would prevail over their WTO obligations to the extent of the mandated inconsistency, and WTO dispute settlement would not be available to them for trade action within the terms of the notified measures. Non-consensual measures (those applied among Parties but not specifically mandated in an MEA, and those applied against non-parties which are specifically mandated in an MEA) could be tested through WTO dispute settlement against procedural and substantive criteria which would be set out in the Understanding. The Understanding would not apply to trade measures taken against non-parties to an MEA that were not specifically mandated in the MEA; nor would it apply to unilateral measures. These would continue to be subject to existing WTO provisions. The proposed procedural criteria aim at ensuring that an MEA reflects a genuine "multilateral" consensus through requiring: (i) negotiation of and participation in an MEA to be open on equitable terms to all interested countries; (ii) broad participation of interested countries in both geographical terms and representing varying levels of development; and (iii) adequate representation of consumer and producer nations of the products covered by the MEA. The proposed substantive criteria aim at ensuring that the trade measure is necessary to achieve the environmental objective of the MEA, including through consideration of: (i) the effectiveness of the trade measure in achieving the environmental objective; (ii) whether the measure is the least trade-restrictive or distorting; and (iii) the proportionality of the measure to the need for trade restriction to achieve the environmental objective.

19. A third proposal [Switzerland] is to introduce "a coherence clause." It would provide that in case of a WTO dispute over a trade measure mandated under an MEA, the dispute panel would examine whether the measure was applied in a manner that constitutes arbitrary discrimination between coun-

---

19. Those terms would be whether the MEA was open to participation by all parties concerned with the environmental objectives of the MEA, and reflected, through adequate participation, their interests, including significant trade and economic interests.

tries where the same conditions prevail or with a view to achieving trade advantages, but it would not examine the legitimacy of the environmental objective nor the measure's necessity. A list of MEAs benefiting from the coherence clause would be established. Two possible approaches were identified to establish the list: either the General Council could make a decision concerning the inclusion of each MEA on the list, or each MEA could be notified to the WTO Director-General by its depositary in which case the General Council would be asked to reach a decision only if a WTO member objected to a proposed listing.

20. Another approach [Korea] proposes the "possibility of setting differentiated WTO disciplines" for trade measures applied pursuant to MEAs based on whether the trade measures are specifically mandated by an MEA and whether they are applied among Parties or against non-parties.... Trade measures taken among Parties would be eligible for qualified codification on a lapse of time basis, subject to them meeting appropriate conditions which would be less strict for measures specifically mandated in an MEA than for those simply authorized by the MEA. Under this proposal it would be premature to consider the accommodation of any other type of trade measures taken pursuant to an MEA (for example, against a non-party) that goes beyond the scope of existing WTO disciplines.

21. A different approach suggested by some Members is to develop guidelines to provide more predictability than exists at present over the treatment of certain trade measures applied pursuant to MEAs and allow for the development of mutually supportive trade and environment policies, as envisaged in *Agenda 21.* One proposal [Japan] made in this regard is to draw up non-binding interpretative guidelines, with the possibility of making them legally-binding with appropriate modifications as necessary. Guidelines could be used by MEA negotiators to provide them with an authoritative point of reference on the application of WTO provisions when they are considering the use of trade measures pursuant to MEAs, they could be used by WTO dispute panels when examining the compatibility with WTO rules of trade measures applied pursuant to MEAs, or they could serve as a basis on which the WTO Secretariat would provide technical advice on WTO provisions to MEA Secretariats and environmental negotiators. The proposed guidelines are not intended to be used directly in a panel examination, although they could have a certain impact on the scrutiny of panels. Formal decisions concerning substantive criteria made by the relevant MEA authority should be taken into sufficient account on the condition that the MEA meets procedural criteria that would reflect its consensual basis.[24] These substantive criteria could incorporate characteristics of MEA trade measures such as their necessity, effectiveness, and proportionality.[25]

---

24. Examples of procedural criteria are: (i) negotiation of the MEA is open to all countries, and takes place preferably under the UN aegis; (ii) countries from different geographical regions and at different stages of economic and social development which are Parties to the MEA have participated in the negotiations and must be reflected in the membership of the agreement; and (iii) the MEA deals with environmental protection of a transboundary or global nature.

25. Substantive criteria are, for example: (i) trade measures are chosen only when effective and when alternative measures are ineffective in achieving the environmental objective, or when other measures are inefficient without trade measures as part of the MEA; (ii) trade measures are not more trade-restrictive than required to achieve the environmental objective; (iii) trade measures do not constitute arbitrary or unjustifiable discrimination; (iv) trade with non-parties is permitted on the same basis

22. One proposal [United States] suggested that the Committee develop an agreed framework for endorsement by the Singapore Ministerial Conference that would include, inter alia, the following points: the strong appreciation among WTO Members of the importance of MEAs; that WTO rules should not hamper the ability of MEAs to achieve their environmental objectives; that trade measures have been and will continue to be an important tool for achieving important environmental objectives; that trade measures will not always be needed, and should be used prudently but should be available when needed, and MEA negotiators are in the best position to determine when this is so; that the WTO should recognize and respect the technical and environmental expertise of MEA negotiators; and that panels can, and should, seek input from relevant MEA bodies in any dispute involving questions relating to an MEA.

Questions and Discussion

1. Developing countries have generally opposed waivers or other modifications to WTO rules for MEAs. Some of this opposition derives from the perception that developed countries, particularly the EU, are pushing this issue. Opposition of some developing countries may also relate to their failure to coordinate trade and environment issues at the national level. One WTO observer claims that this lack of coordination at the national level results from difficulties raising awareness of trade and environment linkages, turf battles, and lack of capacity. As a result, trade representatives from these countries decry the use of discriminatory trade measures while that country's environmental officials demand their use within MEAs, such as the Basel Convention. Doaa Abdel Motall, *Multilateral Environmental Agreements (MEAs) and WTO Rules: Why the "Burden of Accommodation" Should Shift to MEAs*, 35 J. WORLD TRADE 1215, 1220 (2001).

Perhaps most importantly, these countries also fear that an exemption for certain trade measures in MEAs would not guarantee the cessation of unilateral trade measures. For this reason, Southeast Asian countries proposed, "In a *quid pro quo* for the opening of an 'environmental window' in relation to specific measures included in MEAs, WTO Members shall formally agree not to in future resort to the use of … unilateral extra-jurisdictional trade measures to protect extra-jurisdictional environmental resources." Proposal by ASEAN, WT/CTE/W/39 (July 24, 1996). Is that a reasonable compromise?

2. Several of the proposals, including those from Switzerland, New Zealand and the EU, remove the requirement that the measure be "necessary." How do they differ in their approach to evaluating the measures of MEAs pursuant only to the chapeau of Article XX? Do any of these proposals strike a reasonable balance between WTO and MEA concerns?

3. Some WTO members felt that the substantive criteria proposed in footnote 25 of Doc. WT/CTE/1 actually imposed greater hurdles for some trade measures. Others, however, saw the criteria of necessity, effectiveness, least trade restrictiveness, and proportionality as implicitly included in WTO disciplines. Some members stated that the concept of necessity is particularly relevant to Article XX(g). Do you agree?

4. Some of the proposals would require an assessment of the effectiveness of the MEA's trade measure to determine whether it should be exempted from WTO rules. Does that

---

as with Parties if non-parties provide equivalent environmental protection; and (v) trade measures and the circumstances under which they can be taken are clearly defined.

make sense? For at least three reasons, very few studies attempt to assess the effectiveness of trade measures in MEAs. First, the contribution of trade measures to the success of an MEA is extremely difficult to ascertain when trade measures are not the sole means to accomplish the MEA's goals. All MEAs require political will, financial resources, and technical capacity for successful implementation. Second, the contribution of trade measures to the success of an MEA is extremely difficult to ascertain when, as with many MEAs, others factors contribute to the problem that the MEA seeks to redress. For example, even perfect implementation of CITES' trade controls will fail to protect a species from habitat destruction. *See* Brack & Gray, Multilateral Environmental Agreements and the WTO, at 12. Third, many trade measures of MEAs have been invoked infrequently.

Nonetheless, some efforts have been made to assess the effectiveness of trade measures in MEAs. The International Union for the Conservation of Nature (IUCN) examined the wide range of trade measures in CITES. The IUCN cautions that its findings may not accurately reflect CITES success because data is most readily available for those species perceived to have the greatest problems. Nonetheless, its report found that CITES played a role in slowing the declines of several bird species and reversed the decline of African elephants. It also played a role in the "spectacular success" in protecting wild cat species, although this success is probably due in "large measure" to advertising campaigns aimed at consumers. While rhinoceros populations have continued to decline despite CITES protection, the report was unable to determine if CITES slowed or hastened these declines. Ultimately, the IUCN concludes that the trade measures of CITES were "most responsive to trade in species which are associated with high demand elasticities." IUCN, Trade Measures in Multilateral Agreements: A Report on the Effectiveness of Trade Measures Contained in CITES (1999). With respect to the use of trade measures against nonparties and noncomplying parties, lawyers working for the CITES Secretariat report that the threat of trade sanctions often draws high level political attention that "result[s] in action being taken quickly to enact legislation, develop work plans, control legal/illegal trade, or improve the basis for government decision making" to avoid trade sanctions or have them withdrawn. Marceil Yeater & Juan Vasquez, *Demystifying the Relationship Between CITES and the WTO*, 10 RECEIL 271, 274 (2000). In a fascinating study of the Montreal Protocol, the authors were able to correlate trade measures (as well as the Montreal Protocol's positive incentives, such as technology transfer) to ratification and implementation of the Protocol. That in turn led to reductions in the consumption of ODS. Donald L. Goldberg et al., *Effectiveness of Trade & Positive Measures in Multilateral Agreements: Lessons from the Montreal Protocol* (United Nations Environment Programme 1997).

Should MEAs be required to conduct "effectiveness" studies like the ones performed by the IUCN and Goldberg et al. at periodic intervals? If yes, based on what criteria would you decide that a treaty's trade measures should be repealed? Consider the numerous qualifications that the IUCN made concerning the effectiveness of CITES's trade measures. How would you take those qualifications into account in deciding whether a measure is effective?

5. Defining *"specific trade obligation."* In addition to the actual substantive criteria for resolving the MEA-WTO relationship, WTO members have struggled to define "specific trade obligation." Recall that the Doha Ministerial Declaration is limited to an outcome on "the relationship between existing WTO rules and specific trade obligations." The members appear to generally understand the phrase "specific trade obligations" to include mandatory measures that are expressly identified in an MEA. However, few provisions of MEAs unequivocally demand the imposition of trade sanctions in all situations. Instead, MEAs often demand the use of a trade measure but grant the parties a wide range

of discretion to implement the measure. The CITES prohibition against trade for "primarily commercial purposes" mentioned above illustrates this point well. Consider the following submission to the CTE from India.

India, Relationship between Specific Trade Obligations Set Out in MEAs and WTO Rules
TN/TE/W/23 (Feb. 20, 2003)

7. A number of delegations have given their views regarding what constitutes a STO. India believes that the term "*specific trade obligation*" has three elements that must be considered together i.e. the provision must be *specific* with a *trade* element and should be in the nature of an *obligation*. Thus, any provision in an MEA to qualify as an STO must be specific and mandatory in character, and so precise in its direction that there can be no doubt about the action or restraint that a party to the MEA must adopt.

8. MEAs contain a number of trade related measures, which could be categorised as follows:

(i) A trade measure that is both mandatory and specific in its entirety.

Article 4.1 (b), (c) of the Basel Convention according to which Parties are obliged to prohibit export of covered waste to Parties that have banned such imports or do not consent in writing to the specific import.

(ii) only the outcome to be achieved is identified with a list of appropriate measures that Parties could implement to achieve the desired outcome.

Article 6.2 of the Basel Convention requires the State of import to respond to the notifier in writing, by either consenting to the movement with or without conditions, or denying permission for the movement, or requesting additional information.

(iii) the outcome to be achieved is identified, however the measures which could be implemented to achieve that outcome are not specified.

Article 16 of the Cartagena Protocol dealing with "Risk Management" states that the Parties shall, taking into account Article 8 (g) of the Convention, establish and maintain appropriate mechanisms, measures and strategies to regulate, manage and control risks identified in the risk assessment provisions of this Protocol associated with the use, handling and trans-boundary movement of living modified organisms. This provision fails to be specific as to the nature of the measure, although it contains an obligation.

(iv) additional and more stringent measures to achieve the overall objectives of the MEA which are more in the form of a right granted to a Party as opposed to an obligation.

Article XIV.1 of CITES states that the provisions of the Convention shall in no way affect the right of Parties to adopt stricter domestic measures regarding the conditions for trade, taking, possession or transport of specimens of species (whether included in the Appendices or not) or the complete prohibition thereof.

9. India believes that the mandate given under paragraph 31(i) of Doha Declaration refers to only the first category of trade measures that are both mandatory and specific in their entirety. In India's view, non-specific provisions cannot

qualify as an STO. Also if the provision set out in the MEA does not contain the crucial *"obligation"* element, such provisions too would fail to qualify.

10. While identifying STOs several other aspects are also relevant in considering the specificity, as a number of trade obligations are not specific in their entirety, that is, they contain non-specific elements as well. For instance, Article 13.1 of the Rotterdam Convention states that: *"The Conference of the Parties shall encourage the World Customs Organization to assign specific Harmonized System customs codes to the individual chemicals or groups of chemicals listed in Annex III, as appropriate. Each Party shall require that, whenever a code has been assigned to such a chemical, the shipping document for that chemical bears the code when exported."* The second sentence of the provision could qualify as an STO but the first sentence would clearly not. Furthermore, several provisions have to be read with another provision containing a trade obligation to understand whether it is specific or not.

The United States, on the other hand, categorized a provision as a "specific trade obligation" if it is "set out" in the MEA and it "is one that *requires* an MEA party to take, or refrain from taking, a particular action. Such action must be mandatory and not simply permitted or allowed by a provision in an MEA. In other words, it cannot be discretionary." United States, Relationship between Specific Trade Obligations Set Out in MEAs and WTO Rules, TN/TE/W/20, para. 3 (Feb. 10, 2003) (emphasis in original).

Unlike India, the United States claimed that Article 6.2 of the Basel Convention constituted a specific trade obligation. How are the two countries defining specific trade obligation differently? The United States considers permit requirements, such as the CITES finding of primarily commercial purposes, to be specific trade obligations. Would India? If the decisionmaking body of an MEA approves trade sanctions based on a provision of the relevant MEA, or establishes criteria for imposing sanctions, would these measures be considered specific trade obligations?

6. *Defining "MEA."* The WTO members are also debating what constitutes an MEA. India believes that an MEA must have the following elements: 1) the MEA was negotiated under the aegis of the United Nations or specialized agencies like UNEP; 2) the MEA's procedures stipulate that participation in the negotiations is open to all countries; 3) there was effective participation in the negotiations by countries belonging to different geographical regions and by countries at different stages of economic and social development; 4) the MEA provides for procedures for accession of countries which are not its original members and on terms that are equitable in relation to those of its original participants; and 5) the MEA has entered into force. Japan has defined an MEA as one that is open to all countries sharing the environmental objective of the agreement, takes into account participation by a substantial number of parties and "reflects the interests of major Parties concerned, such as Parties with substantial trade interests, actual and potential major producers and consumers of materials concerned." The EU would include agreements with three or more parties, including regional agreements. European Communities, Multilateral Environmental Agreements (MEAs): Implementation of the Doha Development Agenda, TN/TE/W/1 (Mar. 21, 2002). Meanwhile, the United States believes that no definition is needed as the "sense of delegations regarding [MEAs] will come to the surface through a concrete review of the examples they identify in the document." United States, Sub-Paragraph 31(i) of the Doha Declaration, TN/TE/W/20, para. 10 (Feb. 10, 2003). How do these definitions differ? How should

MEA be defined? For a list of all relevant documents related to the CTE deliberations and negotiations on MEAs and the WTO, as of May 2004 (not updated since), see TN/TE/INF/4/Rev.2.

7. The positions of WTO members on the various issues surrounding the relationship between MEAs and the WTO have remained virtually unchanged since at least 2003. Members did act on the proposal of the United States to share national experiences. As a consequence, Australia and Argentina reported that:

> The national experiences discussion revealed that national level coordination between different domestic agencies and stakeholders involved with international agreements is key to achieving compatibility between countries' international obligations and domestic implementation. Several Members noted that effective domestic implementation is not only essential but also the most efficient and direct means of fostering mutual compatibility between STOs set out in MEAs and WTO rules—whether in the development of negotiating positions or the subsequent implementation of agreements. Coordination procedures between various governmental bodies in developing negotiating positions and in drafting MEA implementing legislation were considered useful in both averting and reconciling potential issues at the national level. In addition, procedures that offer opportunities for stakeholders and the public to offer their own views and perspectives were also deemed useful to Members in their efforts to enhance mutual supportiveness. Through such inclusive domestic processes, Members can enhance the mutual supportiveness of trade and environment, as called for in the mandate.

> One important observation is that, at no point during the CTESS' sharing of national experiences or its negotiations under Paragraph 31(i), has any Member identified any evidence to the contrary. Moreover, many delegations consider the relationship between trade and environment to be working well.

Australia and Argentina, Revised Proposal for an Outcome on Trade and Environment Concerning Paragraph 31(i) of the Doha Ministerial Declaration, TN/TE/W/72/Rev.1 (May 7, 2007). What, if anything, does this suggest about the direction that the negotiations on the MEA-WTO relationship should take?

8. Article 104 of the North American Free Trade Agreement (NAFTA) has a rule that combines a "primacy" clause with substantive criteria:

> In the event of any inconsistency between this Agreement and the specific trade obligations set out in [the Basel Convention, CITES, Montreal Protocol, and two bilateral agreements], such obligations shall prevail to the extent of the inconsistency, provided that where a Party has a choice among equally effective and reasonably available means of complying with such obligations, the Party chooses the alternative that is the least inconsistent with the other provisions of this Agreement.

North American Free Trade Agreement, Dec. 17, 1992, art. 104(1), *reprinted in* 32 I.L.M. 289. Article 18.13.4 of the U.S. Peru Free Trade Agreement also provides:

> In the event of any inconsistency between a Party's obligations under this Agreement and a covered agreement, the Party shall seek to balance its obligations under both agreements, but this shall not preclude the Party from taking a particular measure to comply with its obligations under the covered agreement, provided that the primary purpose of the measure is not to impose a disguised restriction on trade.

"Covered agreement" is then defined to include ICCAT, ICRW, CITES, the Montreal Protocol, and other MEAs. What are the differences between Article 104 of NAFTA and Article 18.4 of U.S.–Peru?

Later U.S. free trade agreements take different approaches to the MEA-trade law question. In the Dominican Republic–Central America–United States Free Trade Agreement ("DR-CAFTA"), the parties recognize that MEAs "play an important role in protecting the environment globally and domestically" and that the parties "shall continue to seek means to enhance the mutual supportiveness" of MEAs and trade agreements. DR-CAFTA, art. 17.12. The U.S.-Peru Free Trade Agreement requires each party to "adopt, maintain, and implement laws, regulations, and all other measures to fulfill its obligations under the [MEAs] listed in Annex 18.2," such as CITES, the Montreal Protocol, and others. U.S.–Peru, art. 18.2. What are the strengths and limitations of these approaches?

9. How would any of these ideas be implemented? The WTO members could amend Article XX of the GATT or some other provision of the WTO Agreement. This option is labor-intensive, however. An amendment must be adopted by two-thirds of the members voting at a Ministerial Conference and then ratified by the members' governments before it comes into force, and then only for those countries that have ratified it. The General Council could adopt a formal Interpretation under Article IX:2 of the WTO Agreement by a three-fourths majority vote, but that Article also warns against using this provision "in a manner that would undermine the amendment provisions in Article X." A Plurilateral Agreement could also be negotiated pursuant to Article II:3, although such agreements are binding only on those members who accept them.

10. *Problem Exercise.* Develop your own criteria for resolving the MEA-WTO question. Explain how the interests of trade and the environment are met through your criteria. Also, explain whether you address adequately the interests and concerns of developing countries, who believe that MEAs and environmental trade measures generally will be used as disguised trade restrictions.

---

4. Article XX Strategies

Some WTO members, including India, have relied on the fact that no disputes have actually arisen between an MEA and a WTO agreement to propose the use of Article XX and the WTO's Dispute Settlement Body to resolve any dispute between the trade measures of an MEA and a WTO agreement. These members believe that the only way to prevent nondiscrimination in trading relations is to ensure that any environmental trade measure meets the unqualified conditions of the WTO agreements, including Article XX of the GATT. According to India, restrictive trade measures of MEAs, even if taken for enhancing environmental protection, "must respect the rule-based nature of the multilateral trading system and their costs in terms of trade restriction must be fully taken into account." Report (1996) of the Committee on Trade and Environment, WT/CTE/1, para. 11 (Nov. 12, 1996).

Questions and Discussion

1. Do you agree with India that MEA trade measures must be consistent with the GATT and other WTO agreements? After analyzing more recent WTO jurisprudence with respect

to Article XX, in particular *Shrimp/Turtle*, Professor John Knox appears unconcerned about taking the trade measures of MEAs to the WTO. He writes:

> Measures taken pursuant to an MEA, even if taken against non-parties, appear virtually certain to pass muster. Any multilaterally agreed trade restriction would appear to satisfy concerns about inflexible unilateralism, as long as negotiation and membership of the MEA were open to all nations against which the restriction was directed and did not otherwise discriminate against them. The major MEAs employing trade restrictions—Basel, CITES, and Montreal—all satisfy these requirements.

Professor John Knox, *The Judicial Resolution of Conflicts Between Trade and the Environment*, 28 HARV. ENVTL. L. REV. 1, 42 (2004). Do you agree? Based on existing GATT and WTO jurisprudence, which trade restrictions in MEAs would be consistent with Article XX? Analyze the following trade measures for consistency with Article XX:

- The parties to the Basel Convention have adopted an amendment that bans shipments of hazardous waste from developed to developing country parties. Developing countries have sought this ban since the Basel Convention negotiations began, in part because they want to eliminate the economic pressure to accept such shipments. It is also true that many developing countries do not have the facilities or capacity to dispose of hazardous waste in an environmentally sound way. Assume that the ban is in force, that Ghana and Germany are both party to the Basel Convention, and that this transaction is covered by the GATT. If Ghana refuses to accept hazardous waste from Germany, will Ghana be able to successfully defend its actions under Article XX? Does your answer change if you know that the ban has not entered into force because an insufficient number of parties have ratified the ban?

- In 1997, the parties to CITES first approved exports of elephant ivory from Botswana, Namibia, and Zimbabwe to Japan only. They have subsequently approved sales from South Africa as well, and allowed shipments from these African countries to both Japan and China. The parties have rejected proposals to export ivory from Zambia and Tanzania, because the parties considered their internal controls on trade inadequate. The parties required that Japan and China show that they are capable of effectively enforcing ivory trade before they could import ivory. There was no specific reason that Japan and China were chosen as the only importing countries other than they requested the imports. If Japan rejects a shipment of ivory from Zambia, does Zambia have a legitimate WTO claim? Will Japan be able to successfully defend its actions under Article XX? What if Thailand wants to import ivory from Namibia, but Namibia refuses to grant the export permit? Has Namibia violated Article XI or its MFN obligation? If yes, is the violation justified by Article XX?

- In 1999, the Commission of the International Convention for the Conservation of Atlantic Tuna (ICCAT) prohibited the import of bigeye tuna and its products with nonparties, including Belize, Cambodia, Honduras, and St. Vincent and the Grenadines, because longline fishing vessels from those countries were fishing inconsistently with the conservation and management regulations adopted by the Commission. If an ICCAT party, such as the United States, bans the import of bigeye tuna from Belize, Honduras, or St. Vincent and the Grenadines, which are WTO members, will the United States be able to successfully defend its actions under Article XX?

2. Are there risks to a definitive negotiated answer to the question in paragraph 31 of the Doha Ministerial Declaration on the relationship between the WTO agreements and

MEAs? Some urge caution because any binding clarification under the WTO may be "less supportive of a mutually integrative approach" than seen today. Moreover, they fear that the results could limit the scope for panels and the Appellate Body to interpret and apply WTO rules to avoid conflicts with MEAs, and a definitive legal text may "attract the exact kind of MEA-focused disputes that political pressure continues to prevent." HOWARD MANN & STEVE PORTER, THE STATE OF TRADE AND ENVIRONMENT LAW 2003: IMPLICATIONS FOR DOHA AND BEYOND 25–26 (Int'l Inst. for Sustainable Development and the Center for International Environmental Law 2003). Do you agree?

5. Actions Pursuant to MEAs

As the previous sections have discussed, the trade measures of MEAs pose significant questions concerning their consistency with WTO agreements. An equally relevant question, rarely asked, is whether the rules of GATT and other WTO agreements are consistent with MEAs. After all, many such agreements, such as CITES, the Montreal Protocol, and the Climate Change Convention, have more parties than the WTO, and these parties have agreed to create uniform rules for regulating and resolving a particular environmental problem, such as hazardous waste trade or trade in endangered species. They have agreed that resolution of certain global environmental problems requires a separate set of rules, some trade-related, based on biological and ecological factors. Despite the powerful dispute resolution machinery of the WTO, there is nothing in trade law or public international law that inherently grants the WTO agreements a higher legal status than MEAs. As such, reconciliation can be initiated from within the WTO or individual MEAs.

The parties to MEAs, however, have generally waited for the WTO to act, in effect declaring the preeminence of GATT. At the twelfth meeting of the Conference of the Parties to CITES in 2002, the Secretariat submitted a resolution that attempted to address CITES-WTO issues. The proposed resolution:

> Urge[d] all Parties to avoid where possible the application of stricter domestic measures and to favour multilateral collaboration in the adoption of incentive measures at the international level; [and]

> Call[ed] upon the Parties that decide to take stricter domestic measures to do so in a manner which would not constitute a means of arbitrary or unjustifiable discrimination between Parties, or a disguised restriction on international trade, and to ensure that those measures are appropriately targeted to a specific situation.

After extensive debate and revision, the proposed resolution garnered only a handful of votes and was rejected.

Questions and Discussion

1. Why do you think the proposed CITES resolution attracted so much discussion and so few supporters? What might be a better approach to addressing MEA-WTO issues in the relevant MEA forum?

2. Actions taken by the parties to specific MEAs cannot bind nonparties to those agreements. As a result, do you think action by WTO parties would more effectively resolve tensions between MEAs and the WTO agreements?

6. *Trade and Environment Synergies*

The approaches described above all attempt to reconcile trade and environment goals by highlighting potential MEA-WTO conflicts and resolving those potential conflicts through various legal approaches. Some claim that progress has been limited in resolving the MEA-WTO interface "because discussions have focused on potential conflicts rather than synergies and on theoretical and legal linkages rather than concrete and practical linkages." Matthew Stilwell & Richard Tarasofsky, *Towards Coherent Environmental and Economic Governance: Legal and Practical Approaches to MEA-WTO Linkages* 5 (WWF-CIEL Discussion Paper, Oct. 2001).

As a result, recent action has focused on cooperation, not conflict, between the WTO and MEAs to strengthen the relationships between these institutions. Already, the WTO and UNEP Secretariats have agreed to cooperate through exchanges of relevant nonconfidential information, including access to trade-related environmental databases, and reciprocal representation at meetings. As noted already, the WTO Secretariat is an observer of the Governing Council of UNEP, and UNEP and the secretariats of the CBD, CITES, ICCAT, and UNFCCC are official observers of the WTO Committee on Trade and Environment.

In addition, the CTE and governments party to both the WTO and MEAs have called for coordination between trade and environment officials in national capitals and during the negotiation of MEAs and new trade rules to ensure coherence between MEAs and the WTO. However, observer status for MEA Secretariats remains *ad hoc* and some WTO members still object to their participation. For example, the request of the Secretariat of the CBD to participate in meetings of the Committees on Agriculture and the TRIPS Council, despite the clear relationship between the work of CBD and these WTO bodies, was rejected. Since then, several members have proposed criteria for determining whether MEA Secretariats may become observers. The United States, for example, proposed the following criteria, or indicative questions, to be answered by the relevant WTO body before deciding whether to grant an MEA observer status:

- Does the MEA contain specific trade obligations or other trade-related obligations among parties, and if so, are these specifically relevant to the WTO body's scope of work?

- Is the MEA currently an observer to other WTO bodies, and if so, what is the extent of the MEA's participation in meetings of that body?

- Does the WTO Secretariat participate in the MEA meetings as an observer? If so, does the participation relate to issues addressed by the relevant WTO body?

- Have the WTO Secretariat and the MEA Secretariat worked together on reports or to plan workshops, capacity building events, or seminars?

United States, Continued Work Under Paragraph 31(ii) of the Doha Ministerial Declaration, TN/TE/W/70, para. 18 (Feb. 20, 2007). Canada and New Zealand have proposed similar criteria. TN/TE/W/71, para. 10 (Apr. 30, 2007).

Korea, among others, has suggested that consultation and cooperation between the Secretariats of the WTO and MEAs should be encouraged, especially during initial negotiations and amendments of MEAs. This cooperation could include exchange of information, mutual participation in meetings, mutual access to documents and databases, and briefing sessions, as necessary. Hong Kong has proposed that the WTO Secretariat compile a reference guide containing WTO principles for use by MEA negotiators in their consideration of proposed trade measures.

Certainly additional cooperation is needed, because many MEAs rely on trade-related mechanisms. But how can enhanced communication and exchanging information help avoid conflict? At least five concrete suggestions were made to improve coordination and communication:

UNEP Meeting on Developing Synergies and Enhancing Mutual Supportiveness of Multilateral Environmental Agreements and the World Trade Organization

Session 2: A Practical Approach Towards Developing Synergies in the Implementation of MEAs and the WTO (Oct. 2000)

Cooperating on technical assistance and capacity building. The MEAs and the WTO each have programs of technical assistance and capacity building. There are significant opportunities for synergies in relation to these programs. Capacity building and technical assistance are also cross-cutting and may thus be of relevance in realizing synergies in the following substantive areas.

Streamlining notification requirements. MEAs such as CITES, the Montreal Protocol, the Basel Convention, Convention on the Prior Informed Consent Procedure for Certain Chemicals and Pesticides in the International Trade (PIC) and the Biosafety Protocol require notification of implementing regulations, or contain other reporting requirements. The WTO similarly requires its Members to notify the Secretariat of national regulations that fall under various WTO agreements, such as the TBT and SPS Agreements. Reducing duplication and streamlining these notification requirements could be carefully explored in order to reduce the burden on national officials.

Cooperating on domestically prohibited goods. MEAs such as the Basel Convention, PIC and Protocol on Persistent Organic Pollutants (POPs) have established rules regarding some categories of domestically prohibited goods (DPGs). Other categories of products, such as certain domestically prohibited consumer goods, may not be covered by existing MEA. Many of these may be covered by the WTO's notification system. Given the overlap between these systems, cooperation between the relevant MEAs, which have significant technical expertise on DPG-related matters, and the WTO may help to avoid duplication, and to establish an efficient international framework.

Cooperating in the collection and management of data. Data on trade and environment issues is collected by the WTO, MEAs and UNEP. The WTO through various studies, mandated reviews and, more generally, through the Trade Policy Review mechanism, collects information about the impacts of implementing WTO rules. The MEAs each have detailed national reporting requirements, as well as subsidiary and technical bodies that undertake studies that are relevant to issues at the interface of WTO and MEA rules. And UNEP's methodology for integrated assessment provides an important tool for gathering data on the impacts of trade rules and trade liberalization on environmental rules and environmental protection. Collecting and managing data on the environmental impacts of trade liberalization is a prerequisite to sound, integrated policy-making. To assist their parties and Members, MEAs, UNEP and the WTO could consider how to consolidate this wealth of information, both in relation to specific issues, and more generally about macro-economic and environmental trends related to sustainable development.

Encouraging transfer of environmentally sound technology. Technology transfer promotes greater production efficiency and helps to reduce environmental harm. MEAs such as the Basel Convention include obligations to transfer technology. Similarly, WTO obligations, including those in the TRIPS Agreement, may promote technology transfer.

Questions and Discussion

1. Do you think environmentalists should focus on conflict or cooperation between international trade law and MEAs? What do environmentalists hope to achieve by focusing on synergies and cooperation?

2. To what extent is coordination between WTO and MEA Secretariats and other forms of collaboration useful? Will it prevent disputes from arising?

C. What Law Applies?

Despite the dozens of papers that have been prepared on the subject and intense interest among the members, many remain frustrated at the CTE's efforts over the last decade:

> [T]he CTE has made little progress regarding ways to strengthen and clarify the relationship between MEAs and the WTO. Moreover, despite proposals by a number of WTO Members to amend WTO agreements, the CTE has offered no recommendations to modify the rules of the trading system or other measures to address the tensions between the WTO and the use of trade measures in MEAs. As a result, a number of WTO agreements continue to raise questions about the use of trade measures in MEAs.

Stilwell & Tarasofsky, *Towards Coherent Environmental and Economic Governance,* at 10.

In the meantime, environmental advocates and governments that originally pressed this issue are now a bit more reticent about pursuing it because they believe that the *Shrimp/Turtle* decision, in its final analysis, provides enough policy space for legitimate trade measures of MEAs. Indeed, the Appellate Body in *Shrimp/Turtle* found a *unilateral* measure justifiable under Article XX(g) based, in part, on good faith efforts to negotiate an international agreement. As a result of *Shrimp/Turtle*, many believe that the existence of an MEA, especially one with substantial participation, should provide the basis for justifying a member's implementation of a *multilateral* trade measure, assuming that it is applied in a manner flexible enough to accommodate different ecological conditions in exporting countries.

Due to the impasse and failure to adopt rules, panels and the Appellate Body will be left to decide on their own how to resolve this thorny issue. But how should they do so? If a dispute involving an MEA trade measure must be taken to the WTO, what law may panels and the Appellate Body apply? What is the range of law that panels and the Appellate Body can rely on to make decisions? As the following readings make clear, the answer is anything but clear.

Several provisions of the DSU offer clues as to whether panels can look outside the four corners of the WTO agreements.

- Article 3.2 provides that the dispute settlement system "serves to preserve the rights and obligations of Members under the covered agreements, and to clarify the existing provisions of those agreements in accordance with customary rules of interpretation of public international law."

- Article 3.2 also provides that "recommendations and rulings of the DSB cannot add to or diminish the rights and obligations provided in the covered agreements."

- Under Article 7, the standard terms of reference for a panel are "[t]o examine, in the light of the relevant provisions in (name of the covered agreement(s) cited by the parties to the dispute), the matter referred to the DSB by (name of party) in document ... and to make such findings as will assist the DSB in making the recommendations or in giving the rulings provided for in that/those agreement(s)."

- Article 11 states that the function of panels is to make an objective assessment of the matter before it, including the applicability of and conformity with the covered agreements.

Several questions follow from these provisions concerning the applicability of non-WTO law to WTO disputes.

- First, may panels use rules of treaty interpretation to clarify terms and provisions of a WTO agreement? Article 3.2 makes clear that they must. These principles of treaty interpretation are found largely in the Vienna Convention on the Law of Treaties. As we have seen in *Reformulated Gasoline* and several other decisions, panels and the Appellate Body frequently resort to Article 31(1) of the Vienna Convention, the principle of treaty interpretation that terms should be given their "ordinary meaning." *See* Chapter 2, Section IV.D.5 at pages 118–24.

- Second, may panels use other international law, such as an MEA, to shape the meaning of a term used in a WTO agreement? Can an MEA shape the scope of a WTO obligation, such as the scope of a member's national treatment obligation? Panels and the Appellate Body have had much more difficulty answering this question.

The remainder of this section addresses the second question. We begin with Article 31 of the Vienna Convention on the Law of Treaties, which establishes rules for interpreting treaties in light of subsequent agreement and practice of the parties.

Vienna Convention on the Law of Treaties
May 23, 1969, U.N. Doc. A/CONF. 39/27, 1155 U.N.T.S. 331
(entered into force Jan. 27, 1980)

Article 31 — General rule of interpretation

1. A treaty shall be interpreted in good faith in accordance with the ordinary meaning to be given to the terms of the treaty in their context and in the light of its object and purpose.

2. The context for the purpose of the interpretation of a treaty shall comprise, in addition to the text, including its preamble and annexes:

(a) any agreement relating to the treaty which was made between all the parties in connexion with the conclusion of the treaty;

(b) any instrument which was made by one or more parties in connexion with the conclusion of the treaty and accepted by the other parties as an instrument related to the treaty.

3. There shall be taken into account, together with context:

(a) any subsequent agreement between the parties regarding the interpretation of the treaty or the application of its provisions;

(b) any subsequent practice in the application of the treaty which establishes the agreement of the parties regarding its interpretation;

(c) any relevant rules of international law applicable in the relations between the parties.

4. A special meaning shall be given to a term if it is established that the parties so intended.

---

1. The Early Decisions

Panels and the Appellate Body have suggested that non-WTO law could be applicable in WTO disputes. The Appellate Body in *Reformulated Gasoline* stated that the GATT "is not to be read in clinical isolation from public international law." United States-Standards for Reformulated and Conventional Gasoline, Appellate Body Report, WT/DS2/AB/R, 17 (adopted May 20, 1996). The Appellate Body's focus on public international law suggests that the Appellate Body believed that panels and the Appellate Body could apply a corpus of law broader than the law of treaty interpretation.

A panel later made far-reaching conclusions concerning the role of customary international law. The case involved Korea's obligations under the WTO Agreement on Government Procurement (GPA) with respect to the construction of the Inchon International Airport (IIA). The GPA applies the basic GATT obligations of most favored nation and national treatment, but only if a WTO member specifies that the agreement applies to a particular agency. Korea claimed that the agency responsible for building the IIA is not included in its list and thus not covered by the GPA. The United States lost its argument that the relevant agency building the IIA was under the control of a covered agency and thus subject to the GPA. The United States thus further argued that Korea agreed that the IIA project would be subject to the government procurement rules, regardless of which entity was responsible. The question for the Panel was whether the U.S. belief that the IIA project was covered by the GPA could prevail over Korea's list of covered agencies pursuant to the rule of error in treaty negotiations, a rule of customary international law codified at Article 48 of the Vienna Convention.

To determine first whether the customary rule of error applied, the Panel declared:

> 7.96 We take note that Article 3.2 of the DSU requires that we seek within the context of a particular dispute to clarify the existing provisions of the WTO agreements in accordance with customary rules of interpretation of public international law. However, the relationship of the WTO Agreements to customary international law is broader than this. Customary international law applies generally to the economic relations between the WTO Members. Such international law applies to the extent that the WTO treaty agreements do not "contract out" from it. To put it another way, to the extent there is no conflict or inconsistency, or an expression in a covered WTO agreement that implies differently, we are of

the view that the customary rules of international law apply to the WTO treaties and to the process of treaty formation under the WTO. * * *

7.101 Thus, … we will review the claim of nullification or impairment raised by the United States within the framework of principles of international law which are generally applicable not only to performance of treaties but also to treaty negotiation.[755] To do otherwise potentially would leave a gap in the applicability of the law generally to WTO disputes and we see no evidence in the language of the WTO Agreements that such a gap was intended. If the non-violation remedy were deemed not to provide a relief for such problems as have arisen in the present case regarding good faith and error in the negotiation of [Agreement on Government Procurement] commitments (and one might add, in tariff and services commitments under other WTO Agreements), then nothing could be done about them within the framework of the WTO dispute settlement mechanism if general rules of customary international law on good faith and error in treaty negotiations were ruled not to be applicable. As was argued above, that would not be in conformity with the normal relationship between international law and treaty law or with the WTO Agreements.

Korea-Measures Affecting Government Procurement, Report of the Panel, WT/DS163/R (adopted June 19, 2000).

The Panel concluded that the WTO members had not contracted out of the customary rule of error, even though the United States had not raised it in its request for establishment of a Panel. The Panel's ruling is particularly noteworthy because it clearly changed the scope of the GPA by granting the United States a defense (even though the Panel ultimately concluded that the United States had not demonstrated error successfully as a basis for a claim of non-violation nullification or impairment of benefits).

Similarly, the Appellate Body in *Shrimp/Turtle* noted that its task was to interpret the chapeau of Article XX, "seeking additional interpretive guidance, as appropriate, from general principles of international law." United States-Import Prohibition of Certain Shrimp and Shrimp Products, Appellate Body Report, WT/DS58/AB/R, para. 158 (Nov. 6, 1998), *reprinted in* 38 I.L.M. 121 (1999). Recall from the Appellate Body's discussion in *Shrimp/Turtle*, excerpted at pages 324–332, that it reviewed a wide range of international environmental law. That discussion included reference to nonbinding principles contained in Agenda 21 and the Rio Declaration on Environment and Development, as well as a number of MEAs, including the CBD, the Convention on the Conservation of Migratory Species, CITES, UNCLOS, and the Inter-American Convention for the Protection and Conservation of Sea Turtles. Significantly, the Appellate Body reviewed these documents knowing that not all parties to the *Shrimp/Turtle* dispute were parties to these

---

755. We note that DSU Article 7.1 requires that the relevant covered agreement be cited in the request for a panel and reflected in the terms of reference of a panel. That is not a bar to a broader analysis of the type we are following here, for the [Agreement on Government Procurement] would be the referenced covered agreement and, in our view, we are merely fully examining the issue of non-violation raised by the United States. We are merely doing it within the broader context of customary international law rather than limiting it to the traditional analysis that accords with the extended concept of *pacta sunt servanda*. The purpose of the terms of reference is to properly identify the claims of the party and therefore the scope of a panel's review. We do not see any basis for arguing that the terms of reference are meant to *exclude* reference to the broader rules of customary international law in interpreting a claim properly before the Panel.

MEAs. Moreover, it reviewed these principles and MEAs in order to interpret and apply the terms and tests in Article XX(g) and the chapeau of Article XX:

> 130. From the perspective embodied in the preamble of the *WTO Agreement*, we note that the generic term "natural resources" in Article XX(g) is not "static" in its content or reference but is rather "by definition, evolutionary". It is, therefore, pertinent to note that modern international conventions and declarations make frequent references to natural resources as embracing both living and non-living resources. [The Appellate Body then refers to UNCLOS, which refers to "*natural resources*", *whether living or non-living*"]. The UNCLOS also repeatedly refers in Articles 61 and 62 to "living resources" in specifying rights and duties of states in their exclusive economic zones. The Convention on Biological Diversity uses the concept of "biological resources". Agenda 21 speaks most broadly of "natural resources" and goes into detailed statements about "marine living resources". In addition, the Resolution on Assistance to Developing Countries, adopted in conjunction with the Convention on the Conservation of Migratory Species of Wild Animals, recites:

>> Conscious that an important element of development lies in the conservation and management of *living natural resources* and that migratory species constitute a significant part of these resources; ... (emphasis added)

> 131. Given the recent acknowledgement by the international community of the importance of concerted bilateral or multilateral action to protect living natural resources, and recalling the explicit recognition by WTO Members of the objective of sustainable development in the preamble of the *WTO Agreement*, we believe it is too late in the day to suppose that Article XX(g) of the GATT 1994 may be read as referring only to the conservation of exhaustible mineral or other non-living natural resources. Moreover, two adopted GATT 1947 panel reports previously found fish to be an "exhaustible natural resource" within the meaning of Article XX(g). We hold that, in line with the principle of effectiveness in treaty interpretation, measures to conserve exhaustible natural resources, whether *living* or *non-living*, may fall within Article XX(g).

> 132. We turn next to the issue of whether the living natural resources sought to be conserved by the measure are "exhaustible" under Article XX(g). That this element is present in respect of the five species of sea turtles here involved appears to be conceded by all the participants and third participants in this case. The exhaustibility of sea turtles would in fact have been very difficult to controvert since all of the seven recognized species of sea turtles are today listed in Appendix 1 of the Convention on International Trade in Endangered Species of Wild Fauna and Flora ("CITES"). The list in Appendix 1 includes "all species *threatened with extinction* which are or may be affected by trade." (emphasis added)

For those seeking a broader integration of MEA law into trade law, the *Shrimp/Turtle* decision was a significant step forward. The Appellate Body clearly is using other treaties to interpret provisions of the GATT. *See* Mann & Porter, The State of Trade and Environment Law 2003, at 22–24.

---

2. EC-Biotech

In *EC-Biotech*, the Panel considered the relationship between the Agreement on the Application of Sanitary and Phytosanitary Measures (SPS Agreement) and other international law, including the CBD, the Biosafety Protocol to the CBD and the precautionary principle. The EU argued that, consistent with Article 3.2 of the DSU and the Appellate Body's conclusions in *Shrimp/Turtle*, the WTO agreements must be interpreted and applied by reference to relevant rules of international law arising outside the WTO context. For the EU, it was irrelevant that the United States was not party to the CBD and Biosafety Protocol and that neither Argentina nor Canada had ratified the Biosafety Protocol. In addition, the EU argued that the Biosafety Protocol and the SPS Agreement are complementary and that the Protocol's provisions on precaution and risk assessment inform the meaning and effect of the relevant provisions of the WTO agreements.

In contrast, the United States, Canada, and Argentina argued that Article 7 of the DSU required the Panel to consider only relevant WTO agreements and that Article 3.2 of the DSU allowed reference to non-WTO law only if that law would assist the Panel in interpreting the particular terms of the covered agreements at issue in this dispute. Moreover, they argued that the reference to "parties" in Article 31 of the Vienna Convention refers to parties to the treaty that is being interpreted, not the parties to the dispute.

European Communities-Measures Affecting the Approval and Marketing of Biotech Products
Report of the Panel, WT/DS291-293/R, (Sept. 29, 2006)
(adopted Nov. 21, 2006)

7.67 Article 31(3)(c) [of the Vienna Convention] directly speaks to the issue of the relevance of other rules of international law to the interpretation of a treaty. In considering the provisions of Article 31(3)(c), we note, initially, that it refers to "rules of international law." Textually, this reference seems sufficiently broad to encompass all generally accepted sources of public international law, that is to say, (i) international conventions (treaties), (ii) international custom (customary international law), and (iii) the recognized general principles of law. In our view, there can be no doubt that treaties and customary rules of international law are "rules of international law" within the meaning of Article 31(3)(c). We therefore agree with the European Communities that a treaty like the *Biosafety Protocol* would qualify as a "rule of international law." Regarding the recognized general *principles* of law which are applicable in international law, it may not appear self-evident that they can be considered as "*rules* of international law" within the meaning of Article 31(3)(c). However, the Appellate Body in *US–Shrimp* made it clear that pursuant to Article 31(3)(c) general principles of international law are to be taken into account in the interpretation of WTO provisions. As we mention further below, the European Communities considers that the principle of precaution is a "general principle of international law." Based on the Appellate Body report on *US–Shrimp*, we would agree that if the precautionary principle is a general principle of international law, it could be considered a "rule of international law" within the meaning of Article 31(3)(c).

7.68 Furthermore, and importantly, Article 31(3)(c) indicates that it is only those rules of international law which are "applicable in the relations between the parties" that are to be taken into account in interpreting a treaty. This limitation gives rise to the question of what is meant by the term "the parties." In considering this issue, we note that Article 31(3)(c) does not refer to "one or more parties."[240] Nor does it refer to "the parties to a dispute."[241] We further note that Article 2.1(g) of the *Vienna Convention* defines the meaning of the term "party" for the purposes of the *Vienna Convention*. Thus, "party" means "a State which has consented to be bound by the treaty and for which the treaty is in force." It may be inferred from these elements that the rules of international law applicable in the relations between "the parties" are the rules of international law applicable in the relations between the States which have consented to be bound by the treaty which is being interpreted, and for which that treaty is in force.[242] This understanding of the term "the parties" leads logically to the view that the rules of international law to be taken into account in interpreting the WTO agreements at issue in this dispute are those which are applicable in the relations between the WTO Members. * * *

7.71 ... In relation to the present dispute it can thus be said that if a rule of international law is not applicable to one of the four WTO Members which are parties to the present dispute, the rule is not applicable in the relations between all WTO Members. Accordingly, based on our interpretation of Article 31(3)(c), we do not consider that in interpreting the relevant WTO agreements we are required to take into account other rules of international law which are not applicable to one of the Parties to this dispute. But even independently of our own interpretation, we think Article 31(3)(c) cannot reasonably be interpreted as the European Communities suggests. Indeed, it is not apparent why a sovereign State would agree to a mandatory rule of treaty interpretation which could have as a consequence that the interpretation of a treaty to which that State is a party is affected by other rules of international law which that State has decided not to accept.

[Because the United States is not a party to the CBD and Argentina, Canada, and the United States are not parties to the Biosafety Protocol, the Panel concluded that neither treaty was "applicable" in the relations between these WTO members and all other WTO members and that it was not required to take them into

---

240. We note that, by contrast, Article 31(2)(b) of the *Vienna Convention* refers to "one or more parties."

241. By contrast, Article 66 of the *Vienna Convention*, which deals with procedures for judicial settlement, arbitration and conciliation, refers to "the parties to a dispute." We note that the absence of a reference to "the parties to a dispute" in Article 31 is not surprising given that Article 31 does not purport to lay down rules of interpretation which are applicable solely in the context of international (quasi-)judicial proceedings.

242. We are aware that Article 31(2)(a) of the *Vienna Convention* refers to "all the parties." However, we do not consider that Article 31(2)(a) rules out our interpretation of the term "the parties" in Article 31(3)(c). In our view, the reference to "all the parties" is used in Article 31(2)(a) to make clear the difference between the class of documents at issue in that provision (namely, agreements relating to a treaty which were made between "all the parties") and the class of documents at issue in Article 31(2)(b) (namely, instruments made by "one or more parties" and accepted by "the other parties" as related to a treaty). In other words, we think that the use of the term "all the parties" in Article 31(2)(a) is explained, and necessitated, by the existence of Article 31(2)(b). Consistent with this view, we think that the absence of a reference to "all the parties" in Article 31(3)(c) is explained by the fact that Article 31(3) contains no provision like Article 31(2)(b), *i.e.*, that Article 31(3) contains no provision which refers to "one or more parties" and hence could render unclear or ambiguous the reference to "the parties" in Article 31(3)(c).

It is useful to note, in addition, that the view that the term "the parties" in Article 31(3)(c) should be understood as referring to all the parties to a treaty has also been expressed by Mustafa Yasseen, "L'interprétation des Traités d'après la Convention de Vienne sur le Droit des Traités", in *Recueil des Cours de l'Académie de Droit International* (1976), Vol. III, p. 63, para. 7.

account in interpreting the WTO agreements at issue in this dispute. In addition, the Panel concluded, as in *EC–Hormones*, that the legal status of the precautionary principle remains unsettled and that it would refrain from expressing a view on the issue. See pages 492–93.]

7.90 Up to this point, we have examined whether there are other applicable rules of international law which we are required to take into account, in accordance with Article 31(3)(c) of the *Vienna Convention*, in interpreting the WTO agreements at issue in this dispute. We now turn to examine whether other rules of international law could be considered by us in the interpretation of the WTO agreements at issue even if these rules are not applicable in the relations between the WTO Members and thus do not fall within the category of rules which is at issue in Article 31(3)(c). * * *

7.92 The Panel recalls that pursuant to Article 31(1) of the *Vienna Convention*, the terms of a treaty must be interpreted in accordance with the "ordinary meaning" to be given to these terms in their context and in the light of its object and purpose. The ordinary meaning of treaty terms is often determined on the basis of dictionaries. We think that, in addition to dictionaries, other relevant rules of international law may in some cases aid a treaty interpreter in establishing, or confirming, the ordinary meaning of treaty terms in the specific context in which they are used. Such rules would not be considered because they are legal rules, but rather because they may provide evidence of the ordinary meaning of terms in the same way that dictionaries do. They would be considered for their informative character. It follows that when a treaty interpreter does not consider another rule of international law to be informative, he or she need not rely on it.

7.93 In the light of the foregoing, we consider that a panel may consider other relevant rules of international law when interpreting the terms of WTO agreements if it deems such rules to be informative. But a panel need not necessarily rely on other rules of international law, particularly if it considers that the ordinary meaning of the terms of WTO agreements may be ascertained by reference to other elements.

7.94 This approach is consistent with the Appellate Body's approach in *US–Shrimp*, as we understand it. In that case, the Appellate Body had to interpret the term "exhaustible natural resources" in Article XX(g) of the GATT 1994. The Appellate Body found that this term was by definition evolutionary and therefore found it "pertinent to note that modern international conventions and declarations make frequent references to natural resources as embracing both living and nonliving resources." Thus, as we understand it, the Appellate Body drew on other rules of international law because it considered that they were informative and aided it in establishing the meaning and scope of the term "exhaustible natural resources." The European Communities correctly points out that the Appellate Body referred to conventions which were not applicable to all disputing parties. However, the mere fact that one or more disputing parties are not parties to a convention does not necessarily mean that a convention cannot shed light on the meaning and scope of a treaty term to be interpreted.

7.95 In the present case, in response to a question from the Panel, the European Communities has identified a number of provisions of the *Convention on Biological Diversity* and of the *Biosafety Protocol* which it considers must be taken into account by the Panel. The European Communities has not explained how these provisions are relevant to the interpretation of the WTO agreements at issue in this dispute. We have carefully considered the provisions referred to by the European Communities. Ultimately, however, we did not find it necessary or appropriate to rely on these particular provisions in interpreting the WTO agreements at issue in this dispute.

Questions and Discussion

1. The *EC-Biotech* Panel makes two important distinctions. First, it explicitly answers whether panels *must* use or *may* use non-WTO law in a WTO dispute. Second, in answering the first question, it implicitly answers whether non-WTO law may be used to interpret the terms of WTO agreements only or whether that law may be used more broadly to define the scope of WTO obligations. How does the Panel answer these questions?

2. In answering these questions, do you think that the Panel is interpreting the Appellate Body's jurisprudence accurately? Compare, in particular, the *EC-Biotech* Panel's analysis in paragraph 7.94 with the Appellate Body's analysis in *Shrimp/Turtle* in paragraphs 130–32 excerpted on pages 676–77. At least one trade scholar, Professor Stephen Powell, believes that the Panel is essentially "overruling" the Appellate Body's analysis in *Shrimp/Turtle* (personal communication). Do you agree? In this passage, the Appellate Body notes that Article XX(g) is evolutionary in its content. If that is so, is Article 5.7 of the SPS Agreement also evolutionary and thus capable of being influenced by the Biosafety Protocol?

3. Scholars have been quick to criticize the *EC-Biotech* Panel's conclusions regarding the applicability of international law. The International Law Commission is among those that have criticized the *EC-Biotech* Panel. It has noted that the Appellate Body, in resolving previous disputes such as *Shrimp/Turtle*, *EC-Poultry*, and *Korea-Beef*, among others, has referred to bilateral and regional trade agreements entered into by select parties as a "supplementary means of interpretation" or "for the purpose of interpreting an ambiguous WTO provision." Isn't that what the Panel did?

Concerning the use of other agreements to interpret WTO agreements and provisions of them, the International Law Commission stated:

> 447. One sometimes hears the claim that this might not even be permissible in view of the express prohibition in the DSU according to which the "[r]ecommendations and rulings of the DSB cannot add to or diminish the rights and obligations provided in the covered agreements" (DSU 3:2 *in fine*). Such a view would, however, presume that the covered agreements are "clinically isolated" precisely in the way the AB has denied. Two considerations are relevant here. First, when article 31(3)(c) VCLT [Vienna Convention on the Law of Treaties] is used, it is used with the specific authorization of the DSU itself. But second, and more important, interpretation does not "add" anything to the instrument that is being interpreted. It constructs the meaning of the instrument by a legal technique (a technique specifically approved by the DSU) that involves taking account of its normative environment. Here it appears immaterial whether recourse to other agreements is had under article 31(3)(c), as supplementary means of interpretation, as evidence of party intent or of ordinary meaning or good faith (the presumption that States do not enter agreements with the view of

breaching obligations). The rationale remains that of seeing States when they are acting within the WTO system as identical with themselves as they act in other institutional and normative contexts. Interpretation *does not add or diminish rights or obligations* that would exist in some lawyers' heaven where they could be ascertained "automatically" and independently of interpretation. All instruments receive meaning through interpretation—even the conclusion that a meaning is "ordinary" is an effect of interpretation that cannot have *a priori* precedence over other interpretations.

450.... [The *EC–Biotech* Panel] interpreted article 31(3)(c) so that the treaty to be taken account of must be one to which all parties to the relevant WTO treaty are parties. This latter contention makes it practically impossible ever to find a multilateral context where reference to other multilateral treaties as aids to interpretation under article 31(3)(c) would be allowed. The panel buys what it calls the "consistency" of its interpretation of the WTO Treaty at the cost of the consistency of the multilateral treaty system as a whole. It aims to mitigate this consequence by accepting that other treaties may nevertheless be taken into account as facts elucidating the ordinary meaning of certain terms in the relevant WTO treaty. This is of course always possible and, as pointed out above, has been done in the past as well. However, taking "other treaties" into account as evidence of "ordinary meaning" appears a rather contrived way of preventing the "clinical isolation" as emphasized by the Appellate Body.

International Law Commission, Fragmentation of International Law: Difficulties Arising From the Diversification and Expansion of International Law, U.N. Doc A/CN.4/L.682 (Apr. 13, 2006) (finalized by Martti Koskenniemi). Whose analysis do you find more persuasive, the International Law Commission's or the Panel's?

4. Prior to the *EC-Biotech* case, Professor John Knox argued that "parties" under Article 31 of the Vienna Convention meant all parties bound by a treaty. He then challenged those commentators, such as the International Law Commission, who have resisted this interpretation because they believe that too few extratextual agreements will be able to satisfy it.

[I]t is easier than it may first appear for such agreements to be considered. First, Article 31(3) does not prevent the parties from jointly deciding that subsequent agreements may be relevant to interpretation even if not all of the parties have adopted them. For example, the WTO Agreement allows the General Council to make interpretive decisions on the basis of a three-fourths majority. Second, subsequent agreements, whether reached expressly or through practice, may establish an interpretation of a treaty that is not subject to challenge by states ratifying the treaty later. In other words, new parties have to take the treaty as it is when they join it, including any interpretations of it already established under Article 31(3). Third, rules of customary international law potentially relevant under Article 31(3)(c) may bind nations that have not specifically agreed to them, at least as long as the nations have not persistently objected to their formation.

Fourth, subsequent practice establishing the agreement of the parties under Article 31(3)(b) need not be by every party; the practice need only be accepted by all, and the acceptance can be tacit. MEAs containing trade restrictions provide an example of such subsequent practice. From the early 1970s, when CITES was drafted and adopted, to the present, when it and other major MEAs with trade restrictions have attained close to universal membership, the vast majority of GATT parties have negotiated, signed, and ratified the MEAs without contemporary claims by other GATT parties that the trade restrictions violate GATT. While "negative practice"— i.e., "the absence of action which would have been expected had a certain interpretation of a treaty been the correct one"—should be carefully employed, when coupled with such a long-standing positive practice, there can be little doubt that GATT parties have accepted the MEAs as consistent with GATT. * * *

[A]pplying Article 31(3) would narrow the range of extratextual agreements that the Appellate Body could take into account. In particular, even widely adopted political declarations such as Rio Principle 12, which the Appellate Body cited in *Shrimp-Turtle I* as evidence of the preference of the international community for multilateral approaches to environmental protection, could be taken into account only if they were "regarding" the text under review (in that case, GATT Article XX), or if they reflected relevant customary international law. Principle 12 would not meet either requirement. Political declarations are far more likely to meet the first criterion if they are made in the WTO context. The WTO members' consensus statement in the 1996 CTE Report that they support and endorse "multilateral solutions based on international cooperation and consensus as the best and most effective way for governments to tackle environmental problems of a transboundary or global nature" probably does qualify as a subsequent agreement under Article 31(3)(a), especially since the following sentence of the report specifically refers to the need to ensure a "mutually supportive relationship" between WTO agreements and MEAs.

John H. Knox, *The Judicial Resolution of Conflicts between Trade and the Environment*, 28 HARV. ENVTL. L. REV. 1, 67–69 (2004). Professor Knox says that the requirement of Article 31(3) of the Vienna Convention to have agreement among "all" parties may not be difficult to overcome. Does Knox suggest reasonable responses to overcome these problems?

5. In arguing that the DSU allows consideration of more than WTO covered agreements and does not include a general and automatic conflict clause in favor of WTO covered agreements, Joost Pauwelyn asks us to consider the following provocative example:

Imagine that the WTO treaty included an agreement regulating the slave trade. Would a WTO panel be obliged to apply and enforce this agreement at the request of a WTO member complaining about trade restrictions regarding slaves imposed by another member? If the DSU were read as precluding reference to international law other than WTO covered agreements (i.e., as a mechanism created outside the system of international law) and/or as containing a conflict clause to the effect that WTO rules always prevail, a WTO panel would be so obliged. This example confirms the absurdity of portraying the DSU as some alien mechanism divorced from, and superior to, all other international law. Following the theory put forward in this paper, the defending party in our hypothetical dispute would be allowed to invoke Article 53 of the Vienna Convention as a legal defense against the WTO slave trade agreement (the applicable law for defenses not being inherently limited). Article 53 provides that "[a] treaty is void if, at the time of its conclusion, it conflicts with a peremptory norm of general international law." On that ground, the WTO panel would be obliged to find the WTO slave trade agreement invalid, hence inapplicable to and unenforceable against the WTO member in question. Nevertheless, given the limited jurisdiction of WTO panels (claims under WTO covered agreements only), the WTO member concerned could not itself bring a complaint to the WTO against the WTO member trading in slaves.

Joost Pauwelyn, *Public International Law in the WTO System: How Far Can We Go?*, 95 Am. J. Int'l L. 535, 565 (2002). Has Pauwelyn convinced you that non-WTO law must be considered by panels in a WTO dispute to interpret the scope of a WTO provision?

6. Panels and the Appellate Body have also invoked Article 32 of the Vienna Convention to justify the use of "supplementary means" of interpretation. Thus, they have reviewed the negotiating history of WTO agreements to confirm a conclusion reached on the basis of a textual and contextual analysis of a treaty. *See, e.g.*, EC-Computer Equipment, Appellate Body Report, WT/DS62/AB/R, WT/DS67/AB/R, WT/DS68/AB/R, para. 84 (June 5, 1998). Japan-Alcoholic Beverages II, Appellate Body Report, WT/DS8/AB/R, WT/DS10/AB/R, WT/DS11/AB/R, p.10 (Oct. 4, 1996). United States-Measures Treaty Export Restraints as Subsidies, Report of the Panel, WT/DS194/R, para. 8.64 (June 29, 2001). The Appellate Body in *EC-Computer Equipment* also referred to the EU's classification practice as part of the "circumstances of the conclusion" of the WTO Agreement and that this may be used as a supplementary means of interpretation. EC-Computer Equipment, at paras. 92–95.

7. Is the proper result to leave this crucial issue (among many others that the members cannot resolve) to the panels and Appellate Body? If not, then what is a reasonably available alternative? Consider *Shrimp/Turtle*. The parties had been unable to reach any agreement on the use of unilateral trade measures to protect the environment for at least a decade. Finally, a dispute arose in which the panel and Appellate Body were confronted with the issue but given no direction from the members. Should the panel and Appellate Body have refused to consider the issue or should it attempt to resolve the issue through whatever tools of interpretation are available to it? Are the panels and the Appellate Body resolving important policy decisions for the WTO members and, in doing so, making definitive interpretations of the GATT and other WTO agreements in violation of Article IX:2 of the WTO Agreement which provides that authority only to the Ministerial Conference and the General Council? A substantial body of literature is emerging around these issues. *See, e.g.*, Richard H. Steinberg, *Judicial Lawmaking at the WTO: Discursive, Constitutional, and Political Constraints*, 98 Am. J. Int'l. L. 247 (2004); John Ragosta, et al., *WTO Dispute Settlement: The System Is Flawed and Must Be Fixed*, 37 Int'l Law. 697 (2003); Joseph H. Weiler, The EU, the WTO, and the NAFTA: Towards a Common Law of International Trade? (2000); Knox, *The Judicial Resolution of Conflicts Between Trade and the Environment*, 28 Harv. Envtl. L. Rev. 1 (2004).

IV. MEA Issues Arising under Specialized WTO Agreements

The range of possible MEA-WTO conflicts is not limited to the GATT. As discussed in Chapter 7, the Biosafety Protocol and the SPS Agreement both address aspects of trade in genetically modified organisms, especially genetically modified foods. In addition, two other WTO agreements may have far reaching implications for public policy beyond their relationship to MEAs. The Agreement on Trade-related Aspects of Intellectual Property Rights (TRIPS Agreement) governs the procedures for obtaining and recognizing intellectual property rights. The TRIPS Agreement may affect access to important medicines for the treatment of AIDS and other diseases. In the context of the trade and environment debate, it may determine whether or not governments must recognize intellectual property rights for living organisms or the "traditional knowledge" of local communities and indigenous peoples. It is an issue that deeply divides developed and developing countries. As a result, Paragraph 19 of the Doha Ministerial Declaration instructs the Council for TRIPS to review the relationship between the TRIPS Agreement and the CBD, which includes provisions for the protection of genetic resources and traditional knowledge.

The General Agreement on Trade in Services (GATS) liberalizes trade in services. It has clear implications for the energy sector, including mechanisms to implement the Kyoto Protocol. The use of market instruments such as tradable emissions permits pursuant to the Kyoto Protocol involves services that could come within the scope of the GATS. As described in Section B below, because the GATS is a document of many compromises and discretionary application, its full scope is difficult to ascertain.

A. The TRIPS Agreement and the CBD

1. Overview of the CBD

The CBD seeks to conserve and sustainably use biological diversity. To that end, it established numerous provisions relating to habitat and species conservation. One primary impetus for the CBD, however, was the resolution of intellectual property rights (IPRs) relating to genetic resources. The biotechnology industry and researchers who develop new pharmaceuticals and agricultural products from genetic material believed that they needed the security of IPRs to protect their research and development investments. For many people in the global south, however, the profits derived from genetic material obtained in developing countries amounted to "biopiracy" because those who profited provided little or no compensation to those in the south, often members of indigenous peoples or local communities, whose "traditional knowledge" regarding the uses of local flora and fauna was tapped to develop the new, IPR-protected pharmaceutical or agricultural product.

In light of these problems, the CBD establishes rules for the equitable sharing of benefits from the use of genetic resources. While these rules are intended to provide an economic incentive for protecting habitat and to ensure the equitable distribution of the benefits of biotechnology, they are also intended to protect the interests of communities and others that provide genetic material for biotechnology.

In balancing these two interests, Article 15.1 of the CBD first recognizes that States have "sovereign rights over their natural resources" and "the authority to determine access to genetic resources." Nevertheless, States must "endeavour to create conditions to facilitate access to genetic resources for environmentally sound uses." In addition, those countries obtaining genetic resources from other countries must receive the prior informed consent from the competent authority of the country providing the resources, and the terms of access must be on "mutually agreed terms" (Articles 15.4, 15.5). Any benefit arising from commercial or other use of these resources must be shared on "mutually agreed terms" and in a "fair and equitable way" (Article 15.7).

With these provisions, the CBD rejected the "common heritage" doctrine that had been applied to genetic material. Under the common heritage doctrine, no one owned genetic material and thus it was freely accessible. That rule benefitted biotechnology interests because, while the raw material was free, any subsequent product derived from that raw material was patentable as an "invention," at least in developed countries. As David Downes notes:

> This new approach to control of a previously common resource paves the way for commercial trade that could, in theory at least, provide incentives to preserve biodiverse-rich ecosystems in hopes of realizing economic returns from exploitation of the genetic resources that they contain.
>
> On the other hand, the Convention does not treat genetic resources as a type of property like any other natural resource. The control of a sovereign nation over resources within its own jurisdiction is limited by the obligation under Article 15(2) to facilitate access by other countries to genetic resources. In this respect, the developed countries prevailed against the biodiverse-rich countries' desire to assert complete control over their genetic resources

David Downes, *The New Diplomacy for the Biodiversity Trade: Biodiversity, Biotechnology, and Intellectual Property in the Convention on Biological Diversity*, 4 Touro J. Transnt'l L. 1, 9–10 (1993).

The CBD also requires parties to "provide and/or facilitate access for and transfer to" other parties of technology for conservation purposes as well as biotechnology deriving from genetic resources (Article 16.1). While the transfer of technology to developing countries must be on "fair and most favourable" terms, including "concessional and preferential terms where mutually agreed," the transfer of technology subject to patents and other IPRs must "recognize and [be] consistent with the adequate and effective protection of intellectual property rights." Nevertheless, Article 16.5 recognizes that, because IPRs may influence the implementation of the Convention, the parties must cooperate "to ensure that such rights are supportive of and do not run counter to its objectives."

---

2. Overview of the TRIPS Agreement

The provisions of the CBD, particularly the call to ensure that IPRs do not run counter to the objectives of the CBD, raise potential conflicts with provisions of the TRIPS Agreement. The inclusion of IPRs in the WTO regime has universalized notions of intellectual property rights protection. The TRIPS Agreement has also recognized the need to balance public and private rights. Article 7 provides that the "protection and enforcement of intellectual property rights should contribute to the promotion of technological innovation and to the transfer and dissemination of technology, to the mutual advantage of producers and users of technological knowledge and in a manner conducive to social and economic welfare." Article 8.1 recognizes that members may need to adopt measures to protect public health and nutrition and to promote the public interest in sectors of vital importance to their socio-economic and technological development, provided that such measures are consistent with the TRIPS Agreement. But, Article 8.2 also provides that appropriate measures "consistent with the provisions of this Agreement" may be needed to prevent the abuse of intellectual property rights by right holders or the resort to practices which unreasonably restrain trade or adversely affect the international transfer of technology.

Developing countries have criticized this text for not properly balancing public and private interests in IPRs. This is especially true in the biodiversity context, where many countries believe that patenting of life forms and processes is immoral. The underlying premise of the TRIPS Agreement that IPRs are private rights thus runs head-on into moral considerations as well as the CBD's transformative legal regime which subordinates private rights to public rights in genetic resources. The TRIPS Agreement's divergence from CBD principles, in addition to its underlying premise, rests on Article 27.

Article 27.1 provides that members shall make patents available on a nondiscriminatory basis for "any inventions, whether products or processes, in all fields of technology, provided that they are new, involve an inventive step and are capable of industrial application." Footnote 5 declares that members may define "inventive step" and "capable of industrial application" as synonymous with the terms "non-obvious" and "useful" respectively, requirements found in the patent law of the United States and other countries.

Article 27.2 allows members to exclude from patentability inventions necessary to protect "*ordre public* or morality, including to protect human, animal or plant life or health or to avoid serious prejudice to the environment." Article 27.3(b) also allows members to exclude from patentability

> (b) plants and animals other than micro-organisms, and essentially biological processes for the production of plants or animals other than non-biological and microbiological processes. However, Members shall provide for the protection of plant varieties either by patents or by an effective *sui generis* system or by any combination thereof. The provisions of this subparagraph shall be reviewed four years after the date of entry into force of the WTO Agreement.

Howard Mann & Steve Porter, *The State of Trade and Environment Law 2003: Implications for Doha and Beyond*

39–44 (International Institute for Sustainable Development and the Center for International Environmental Law, 2003)

State of the Law in 1994

The issue of the relationship between the evolving intellectual property regime and the CBD was never expressly addressed in the text of the TRIPS Agreement. Since IPRs were among the most controversial subjects being negotiated in the Uruguay Round, with a number of issues raising profound divergences between the North and the South and even between developed countries, it is not surprising that some of these issues, including the clarification of the legal relationship with the CBD, were not ultimately addressed.

Notwithstanding, several countries did express specific concerns with direct bearing on the subject of biodiversity. Developing countries in general raised concerns about patentable subject matter under the TRIPS Agreement. India, for instance, desired the possibility of excluding patent protection of micro-organisms and plant varieties. In their view, since micro-organisms existed in nature, they were not inventions and thus should not necessarily be patented. Other groups argued that the draft should outlaw patents on all life-forms, rather than simply permit the exclusion, introducing ethical issues in the discussions. Finally, in exchange for transition periods for implementation, countries accepted the compromise reflected in the current text of Article 27.3(b), which allows patent protection of micro-organisms and plant varieties and provides for a review four years after the date of entry into force.

By the end of the Uruguay Round the issue of patentable subject matter was one of a set of concerns that had begun to emerge regarding the relationship between

IPRs and the conservation of biodiversity. These issues would pervade discussions in the coming years and include: i) patentability of life forms; ii) access to and fair and equitable sharing of benefits arising from the use of genetic resources; iii) preservation and respect for the knowledge, innovation and practices of indigenous and local communities; and iv) transfer of technology.

Article 27.3(b) allows WTO Members to exclude plants and animals and processes that are essentially biological from patentability, but requires them to grant patents over micro-organisms and non-biological and micro-biological processes. These "patents on life" allowed by the TRIPS Agreement raise a number of ethical, environmental, economic and social concerns.

For the conservation of biodiversity, the significance of Article 27 lies in the scope of the exclusions. Whether or not the TRIPS Agreement obliges Members to patent plant parts such as cells or genes, for instance, will directly impact the CBD's provisions on the access and benefit sharing of genetic resources. Moreover, the span of the Article 27.3(b) exclusions will affect the range of patent protection for biotechnology, with the potential risks to biodiversity. * * *

The [CBD's] prior informed consent (PIC) requirement is a measure to prevent misappropriation and to facilitate fair benefit sharing. It requires collectors of biological resources or of related knowledge to provide sufficient information on the purpose and nature of their work as well as obtain permission from the holders of such resources or knowledge. Nothing in the TRIPS Agreement explicitly prevents the use of such a PIC mechanism, but the mere omission of the requirement within the TRIPS Agreement may effectively impede its utilization as required by the CBD. If the TRIPS Agreement does not recognize the rights of the community or country in which a biological resource originated, it may facilitate the submission of patent applications over such a resource in other countries without the knowledge or assent of the rightful owners. Such misappropriation has been dubbed "bio-piracy."

Likewise, the TRIPS Agreement does not require that the IPR holder of biological resources or related knowledge share the benefits of its use with the communities or countries of origin. While that omission may leave open the possibility of negotiating benefit-sharing contracts or challenging cases of misappropriation of biological resources and traditional knowledge under the CBD, these are prohibitively complicated and expensive options that may not even ensure adequate protection.

The CBD provides for the preservation and promotion of the traditional knowledge and innovation methods held by indigenous and local communities. Many indigenous and local communities have cultivated and used biological diversity in a sustainable way for thousands of years and the CBD recognizes their skills and techniques as valuable for the conservation of biodiversity. While traditional knowledge also plays a vital role in the commercial development of numerous products and applications, the TRIPS Agreement, does not expressly provide for its protection. As a regime developed to protect formal and systematic knowledge, the TRIPS Agreement emphasizes conventional intellectual property instruments and does not provide any specific mechanisms to grant traditional communities control over their knowledge and innovations.

The TRIPS Agreement, however, only sets minimum standards. Members are still able to adopt supplementary requirements, such as certification of origin or the combination of existing IPRs with benefit-sharing arrangements, which could adequately address the issue of traditional knowledge. Nevertheless, while these methods could result in financial benefits to indigenous and local communities, there is debate over whether they fulfil the CBD's requirement of respect of traditional knowledge, which might demand the recognition of the diverse and complex facets of the subject and the resort to non-IPR based solutions.

The CBD recognizes that "both access to and transfer of technology, including biotechnology, among Contracting Parties are essential elements for the attainment of the objectives" of the agreement. Although the TRIPS Agreement also refers to the transfer and dissemination of technology "to the mutual advantage of producers and users of knowledge and in a manner conducive to social and economic welfare" as one of its objectives, the implementation of these provisions, as mentioned above, has been limited. Moreover, some studies suggest that, in practice, the strength and scope of the IPRs established in TRIPS may seriously be undermining the transfer of technology between developed and developing countries. As an issue high in the list of priorities of developing countries, technology transfer remains a key topic in the discussion of the relationship between the TRIPS Agreement and the CBD.

The issues of patentability of life-forms, access to genetic resources, protection of traditional knowledge and transfer of technology generate concern because it is in these areas that conflicts between the CBD and the TRIPS Agreement may arise. As mentioned, patents over a country's genetic resource granted outside its territory could potentially conflict with the principle of the sovereignty of the Contracting Parties of the CBD over their own genetic resources. In addition, such patents are generally obtained without the prior informed consent of the government or of the traditional community that holds the knowledge on that material. Moreover, there is no requirement in the TRIPS Agreement for the patent holder to establish a fair and equitable sharing of the benefits resulting from the exploitation. * * *

Developments Since 1994 * * *

Discussions on the relationship between the CBD and the TRIPS Agreements, as well as on the issues involved in that interface, have taken place in both the Committee on Trade and Environment (CTE) and the TRIPS Council. Most of the issues raised, however, remain unresolved. Moreover, case law has not much clarified the situation since no claim regarding the TRIPS-CBD relationship has reached the dispute settlement procedure. Notwithstanding, WTO jurisprudence has provided some initial guidance as to how such a case would potentially evolve.

Over 25 dispute settlement proceedings have been brought under the TRIPS Agreement, relating primarily to patent, enforcement, copyright and trademark provisions. While the legal reasoning and interpretative methodology of the emerging jurisprudence may provide a basis for the further clarification of TRIPS obligations, little has been said about the areas of the agreement that directly implicate the CBD and biodiversity.

An examination of TRIPS-related cases does, however, evidence the Panels' and Appellate Body's approach to the interpretation of the agreement's provisions, as well as their understanding of the general TRIPS exceptions in the patent and copyright areas. This is significant because the success or failure of any challenge of measures taken to implement CBD obligations, such as national legislation requiring patent holders to share their profits with the providers of genetic resources or providing for licenses for the use and development of patented products, will largely depend on the interpretation of the scope of exceptions within the TRIPS Agreement.

The *Canada-Patent Protection* case was the first time a Panel was required to interpret one of the TRIPS Agreement's generally-worded exception provisions. The case involved an EC challenge of a Canadian law that created exceptions to the exclusive rights of patent holders. To fall within the scope of Article 30 of the TRIPS Agreement, an exception must be "limited," not "unreasonably conflict with the normal exploitation of the patent," and not "unreasonably prejudice the legitimate interests of the patent owner, taking account of the legitimate interests of third parties." The Panel stated the first step in interpreting Article 30 was to examine its object and purpose, that is, to consider the goals and limitations established in Articles 7 and 8 of the TRIPS Agreement.

Despite the reference to Articles 7 and 8, however, the Panel did not expressly consider these provisions when examining the meaning of Article 30, relying instead on the context provided by national patent laws and the negotiating history. As a result, some commentators consider the decision sets a dangerous precedent by ignoring the public-private interest balance in TRIPS Agreement.

In the *United States-Copyright* case, the European Communities challenged U.S. limitations on certain exclusive rights in copyright works. The Panel thus interpreted Article 13 of the TRIPS Agreement, which establishes limitations and exceptions for copyrights and related rights, but this time made no reference to Articles 7 and 8. A potential trend towards a limited interpretation of exceptions within the TRIPS Agreement raises the question of how this would affect measures taken by Members to implement the CBD, and whether it would increase tensions, rather than synergies, between the two agreements.

———————

In discussions concerning MEAs generally, India has sought to narrow the scope of potential MEA-WTO relationships and thus leave open the possibility that trade measures in MEAs would be found subordinate to the WTO agreements. With respect to the CBD, however, India has shown much more interest in resolving any apparent conflicts with the TRIPS Agreement in favor of the primacy of the CBD in order to protect the traditional knowledge of its citizens.

India, *Item 8: The Relationship between the TRIPS Agreement and the Convention on Biological Diversity*
WT/CTE/W/65 (Sept. 29, 1997)

6. Till the CBD came into force, genetic resources were considered a common heritage of mankind that should be available freely for anyone who wants to access them. Through the CBD, for the first time an international agreement confirmed the sovereign rights of nation states over these resources, and called for the equitable sharing of benefits with prior informed consent and on mutually agreed terms. It further provided for special treatment for countries of origin and for developing countries. Most importantly, the CBD upheld the role of indigenous communities in conservation and protection of genetic resources and

stated that there should be a fair and equitable sharing of benefits arising out of the utilization of knowledge system of such communities.

7. More specifically, the objectives of the CBD as stated in Article I are the conservation of biological diversity, the sustainable use of its components and the fair and equitable sharing of the benefits arising out of the utilization of genetic resources. Genetic resources are defined in the CBD as any material of plant, microbial or other origin containing functional units of heredity, which has actual or potential value. In addition, Article 15 specifically obliges Parties to take necessary measures to share in a fair and equitable way the results of research and development and the benefits arising from the commercial and other utilization of genetic resources with the Party providing such resources, on mutually agreed terms. However, the fair and equitable sharing of benefits arising out of the patenting and commercial exploitation of genetic resources is not dealt with at all in the TRIPS Agreement.

8. Article 3 of the CBD lays down the principle of the sovereign right to exploit such resources. Further, in Article 15 it is unambiguously stated that the authority to determine access to genetic resources rests with national governments and is subject to national legislation and that access, where granted, shall be on mutually agreed terms and shall be subject to the prior informed consent of the Contracting Party providing such resources. * * *

13. The first important contradiction between the TRIPS Agreement and the CBD is the lack of any conditions on patent application (in Article 29 of the TRIPS Agreement) to mention the origin of biological/genetic resources and indigenous/traditional knowledge used in the biotechnological invention. The present mandatory conditions are confined to disclosure of the invention in a manner sufficiently clear and complete for inventions to be carried out by a person skilled in the art. In addition Members may require the applicant to indicate the best mode of carrying out the inventions known to the inventor at the filing date. These conditions were developed in the patent laws of different countries basically with respect to mechanical and chemical inventions. Biotechnological inventions need to be governed by a set of additional specification requirements. It could be considered whether the objectives of the CBD could be incorporated through inclusion in Article 29 of provisions requiring a clear mention of the biological source material by indigenous communities in the country of origin. This part of the patent application should be open to full public scrutiny immediately after filing of the application. Such a reconciliation would permit countries with possible opposition claims to examine the application and stake their claims well in time.

14. The next contradiction is the lack of provisions in the TRIPS Agreement on prior informed consent of the country of origin and the knowledge-holder of the biological raw material meant for usage in a patentable invention. This needs to be reconciled with Article 15.5 of the CBD. Thus, if any inventor wants to develop such biological materials for commercial purpose, he or she would have to get the prior informed consent of the country as well as of the owner and, if required by such owner, enter into agreements with the country of origin.

––––––––––

Originally, India proposed that the TRIPS Agreement require inventors to use a Material Transfer Agreement (MTA) to transfer benefits to the source of the genetic material or knowledge when the invention is based on indigenous or traditional knowledge. India further proposed that national governments would negotiate such MTAs "since individual beneficiaries cannot be expected to negotiate with large multinational companies." *Id.* at para. 15.

India, Brazil, and many other resource-rich developing countries later switched gears, believing that a "fragmented nation-to-nation system" would not achieve their objectives because such a system would entail "high transaction costs" and because "[contractual] arrangements alone cannot suffice to ensure the monitoring and enforcement of these requirements in third countries." The Relationship between the TRIPS Agreement and the Convention on Biological Diversity (CBD) and the Protection of Traditional Knowledge: Technical Observations on Issues Raised in a Communication by the United States, IP/C/W/443, paras. 8, 9, 24 (Mar. 18, 2005). They also worry that patents could be improperly issued if disclosure is not required. Rather than focusing on the benefits deriving from access to genetic resources, they proposed the following amendment to the TRIPS Agreement:

Article 29*bis*

Disclosure of Origin of Biological Resources and/or Associated Traditional Knowledge

1. For the purposes of establishing a mutually supportive relationship between this Agreement and the Convention on Biological Diversity, in implementing their obligations, Members shall have regard to the objectives and principles of this Agreement and the objectives of the Convention on Biological Diversity.

2. Where the subject matter of a patent application concerns, is derived from or developed with biological resources and/or associated traditional knowledge, Members shall require applicants to disclose the country providing the resources and/or associated traditional knowledge, from whom in the providing country they were obtained, and, as known after reasonable inquiry, the country of origin. Members shall also require that applicants provide information including evidence of compliance with the applicable legal requirements in the providing country for prior informed consent for access and fair and equitable benefit-sharing arising from the commercial or other utilization of such resources and/or associated traditional knowledge.

3. Members shall require applicants or patentees to supplement and to correct the information including evidence provided under paragraph 2 of this Article in light of new information of which they become aware.

4. Members shall publish the information disclosed in accordance with paragraphs 2 and 3 of this Article jointly with the application or grant, whichever is made first. Where an applicant or patentee provides further information required under paragraph 3 after publication, the additional information shall also be published without undue delay.

5. Members shall put in place effective enforcement procedures so as to ensure compliance with the obligations set out in paragraphs 2 and 3 of this Article. In particular, Members shall ensure that administrative and/or judicial authorities have the authority to prevent the further processing of an application or the grant of a patent and to revoke, subject to the provisions of Article 32 of this Agreement, or render unenforceable a patent when the applicant has, knowingly

or with reasonable grounds to know, failed to comply with the obligations in paragraphs 2 and 3 of this Article or provided false or fraudulent information.

Brazil, India, Pakistan, Peru, Thailand and Tanzania, Doha Work Programme — The Outstanding Implementation Issue on the Relationship Between the TRIPS Agreement and the Convention on Biological Diversity, WT/GC/W/564/Rev.2 (July 5, 2006).

Variations of this proposal have now garnered the support of more than half of the WTO members, including the European Union, Norway, the African region, the least-developed countries (LDC) Group, and African-Caribbean-Pacific (ACP) Group. *See, e.g.,* Draft Modalities for TRIPS Related Issues, TN/C/W/52 (July 19, 2008). These countries see the proposal as a way to monitor and enforce the access and benefit sharing provisions of the CBD, thus reinforcing the synergy between TRIPS Agreement and the CBD.

The United States, on the other hand, sees no conflict between the TRIPS Agreement and the CBD and notes that the CBD does not include patent disclosure requirements. Article 27.3(b), Relationship Between the TRIPS Agreement and the CBD, and the Protection of Traditional Knowledge and Folklore, IP/C/W/449, paras. 3, 4 (June 10, 2005). Moreover, it argues that a patent disclosure requirement would do nothing to prevent biopiracy and enforce a country's access and benefit sharing regime in the case of herbal medicines and use of plant varieties, which do not require patents. Thus, the United States has presented the following proposal to address concerns of members:

> With respect to access and benefit sharing, we view the best approach to be one involving the implementation of national regimes for prior informed consent and equitable benefit sharing that establishes clear terms and that can be enforced adequately and effectively outside the patent system. Further, when addressing issues regarding the erroneous granting of patents, Members should focus on remedies that directly address that goal. These remedies include the use of organized databases, information material to patentability and the use of post-grant opposition or re-examination systems as an alternative to litigation.

Id. at para. 41.

Questions and Discussion

1. Do you think IPRs benefit conservation? According to David Downes, whether IPRs and the resulting profits from biotechnology create an incentive for conservation depends on four unproven assumptions: "1) the economic value of biotechnology will grow rapidly to a very high level; 2) biodiversity will be a valuable 'raw material' for biotechnology; 3) source countries of biodiversity will be able to capture a significant proportion of the total value of biotechnology through benefit-sharing or as compensation for the contribution of biodiversity to the final product; and 4) compensation or a share of the benefits will flow back to source countries so as to promote conservation of biodiversity." Downes, *New Diplomacy for the Biodiversity Trade,* at 15, 16–20. What is the likelihood that these assumptions are true?

2. That wild species are important for the development of important medicines and food products is well known. Approximately 25 percent of prescriptions, with a value of $15.5 billion in 1990, are filled with drugs whose active ingredients derived or were extracted from plants. When over-the-counter drugs are added to prescription drugs based on plants, the estimated annual value jumps to $43 billion from Europe, Japan, Australia,

Canada, and the United States alone. With profits like these, why does the biotechnology industry need the assurance of a patent as an incentive to invest in research and development of new products? While the profits seem enormous, success rates are extremely low. Only one in 10,000 chemicals yields a potentially valuable lead, much less a new product. As of 1990, a commercially marketed drug cost $231 million and 12 years on average to develop. Walter Reid, et al., *A New Lease on Life*, 6–7, 12–18 *in* Biodiversity Prospecting: Using Genetic Resources for Sustainable Development (Walter Reid et. al. eds, 1993).

3. India identifies two contradictions between the CBD and TRIPS Agreement, both of which relate to protection of traditional knowledge of indigenous and local communities. Intellectual property rights law of developed countries, on which the TRIPS Agreement is based, does not protect knowledge that has developed over generations for at least two reasons. First, this knowledge is often in the public domain, and has been for long periods of time, because local communities have shared knowledge concerning, for example, the pesticidal qualities of a particular crop, with other communities. Once knowledge enters the public domain it is not considered "novel." Second, because traditional knowledge develops over generations, it is not viewed as an "invention" that can be patented. Despite the obvious usefulness of traditional knowledge, why might governments be reluctant to provide patents for such knowledge? Can those problems be overcome?

In addition to not requiring the patentability of such knowledge, the TRIPS Agreement does not require any prior informed consent from holders of traditional knowledge before their knowledge is used to develop an invention that can be patented. Is that fair? Can the TRIPS Agreement accommodate the remedy proposed by India? Unlike the CBD, the TRIPS Agreement does not require any benefit sharing with the providers of genetic material, including providers of traditional knowledge. Should it?

4. The WTO members remain deeply divided over the proposal to amend the TRIPS Agreement to include disclosure requirements. Why do developing countries believe such requirements are essential to the monitoring and enforcement of their access and benefit sharing regimes? Why might they also be useful to countries in which patents are granted? Why do you think the United States opposes the proposal?

5. Are the provisions of the CBD consistent with the TRIPS Agreement? Opinions differ. *See* Shalini Bhutani & Ashish Kothari, *Rio's Decade: Reassessing the 1992 Earth Summit: Reassessing the 1992 Biodiversity Convention: The Biodiversity Rights of Developing Nations: A Perspective from India*, 32 Golden Gate U. L. Rev. 587 (2002) (arguing that the TRIPS Agreement is inconsistent with the CBD, because it would not protect traditional knowledge but would protect innovations of biotechnology companies deriving from traditional knowledge and genetic resources); Jim Chen, *Diversity and Deadlock: Transcending Conventional Wisdom on the Relationship Between Biological Diversity and Intellectual Property*, 31 Envtl. L. Rep. 10625 (2001) (arguing that the CBD and TRIPS Agreement are compatible). For a provocative article on how the provisions of the CBD concerning access and benefit sharing could be a model for trade agreements, *see* David R. Downes, *The Convention on Biological Diversity: Seeds of Green Trade?* 8 Tul. Envtl. L.J. 163 (1994).

B. The GATS, Gas, and Garbage

The General Agreement on Trade in Services (GATS) extends many of the trade liberalization rules of the GATT from products to services. Because of the framework structure of the GATS, its full impact is difficult to gauge. Nonetheless, its scope is readily apparent and broad; it applies to all service sectors, including those relating to transportation, construction, health, education, water, electricity, and energy.

Due to its scope, it captures many of the services that could be used to implement the UN Framework Convention on Climate Change (Climate Change Convention) and the subsequent Kyoto Protocol. It may also cover disposal services under the Basel Convention, provided that the disposal of hazardous waste constitutes a service rather than trade in a good. No doubt as with energy services and energy products, both the GATS and the GATT would apply, depending on the circumstances. In any event, this section focuses on the Climate Change Convention and the Kyoto Protocol, because its use of market incentives differs fundamentally from the approaches taken in other MEAs. It thus offers an opportunity to see the different ways WTO agreements interface with different types of environmental measures.

1. The General Agreement on Trade in Services

The GATS is structured much differently from other WTO agreements. Rather than establish a number of obligations with which all WTO members must comply, the GATS establishes a number of "opt in" and "opt out" provisions. The framework section of the GATS, modeled on the GATT, contains the general rules and disciplines that apply to all services. Nevertheless, parties are allowed to "opt out" of some obligations, such as the most favored nation (MFN) obligation. A second component of the GATS allows parties to establish national "schedules" that list that country's specific commitments on access to their domestic markets by foreign suppliers of services that are additional to those contained in the general obligations applicable to all services. For example, members must provide national treatment with respect to services included in their national schedules but not to those services falling within the general obligations. The national schedules, however, include only those services to which each individual WTO member agrees to guarantee access to foreign suppliers. That is, parties "opt in." While parties are required to comply with MFN and national treatment obligations for these services, they can limit ("opt out") the applicability of those obligations. A third component of the GATS allows the parties to negotiate separate service agreements—some in the form of annexes to the GATS, others embodied in Ministerial decisions—which apply to specific sectoral issues. The United States has been eager to negotiate an agreement that would cover all energy-related services, such as pipelines, tanker and other transport, that would harmonize rules relating to such services. This multifaceted approach to the GATS makes the GATS a very complex document. This section merely highlights those aspects that may relate to the environment or measures affecting trade in environmental services subject to MEAs. For a more thorough discussion of the GATS, *see* Raj Bhala & Kevin Kennedy, World Trade Law 1242–1303 (1998); Mitsuo Matsushita, Thomas J. Schoenbaum, & Petros C. Mavroidis, The World Trade Organization: Law, Practice, and Policy 227–58 (2d. ed. 2006).

a. Defining Measures "Affecting Trade in Services"

The GATS applies to all measures affecting trade in services, except for services provided to the public in the exercise of governmental authority and various components of the air transport sector. The GATS broadly defines "services" as "any service in any sector." While there is no agreed definition for "services," the GATT Secretariat used the United Nations Central Product Classification (CPC) list during the Uruguay Round negotiations to develop the "Services Sectoral Classification List." MTN/GNS/W/120 (July 10, 1991). Most WTO members use this list, which classifies services by sector, to describe and categorize their GATS commitments.

Instead, Article I:2 of the GATS defines "trade in services" as the "supply of a service" through four "modes of supply":

- from the territory of one member into the territory of any other member, such as telephone calls or delivery services (officially called "cross-border supply");

- in the territory of one member to the service consumer of any other member, such as when consumers from one country make use of a service in another country for tourism or to attend a seminar on strategies for reducing pollution (officially called "consumption abroad");

- by a service supplier of one member, through a commercial presence in the territory of any other member, such as a hazardous waste disposal company from one country setting up operations in another country (officially called "commercial presence"); and

- by a service supplier of one member, through the presence of natural persons of a member in the territory of any other member, such as when individuals travel from their own country to repair pollution control equipment (officially called "movement of natural persons").

While most services can be distinguished from goods, and thus applicability of the GATS versus the GATT is clear, some measures may involve a service relating to or supplied in conjunction with a good. As noted in the introduction to this section, it is not readily apparent whether the cross-border transfer of hazardous waste is GATT-regulated trade in goods or whether the disposal of that hazardous waste is a service regulated under the GATS. In these circumstances, the Appellate Body has explained that, while such measures "could be scrutinized under both agreements, the specific aspects of that measure examined under each agreement could be different." European Communities-Regime for the Importation, Sale and Distribution of Bananas, Appellate Body Report, WT/DS27/AB/R, para. 221 (Sept. 25, 1997) [hereinafter *EC-Bananas*]. The determination as to whether the GATT or GATS applies must be made on a case-by-case basis. *Id.* For a more complete discussion of the potential overlap between the GATT and GATS, *see* Matsushita, Schoenbaum, & Mavroidis, The World Trade Organization, at 609–11.

The scope of measures "affecting trade in services" is potentially vast. "Services" is not well defined and "affecting" "indicates a broad scope of application." *EC-Bananas*, at para. 220. The Appellate Body has restricted the scope of "affecting" somewhat by stating that "the focus is on how the measure affects the supply of the service or the service suppliers involved." *Id.* As such, panels must examine whether or how the challenged measure "affects *wholesale trade service suppliers in their capacity as service suppliers.*" Canada-Certain Measures Affecting the Automotive Industry, Appellate Body Report, WT/DS139/AB/R, WT/DS142/AB/R, para. 164 (June 19, 2000) (emphasis in original). That, in turn, requires an examination of "*who* supplies wholesale trade services … and *how* such services are supplied." *Id.* at 165 (emphasis in original).

b. GATS Commitments

Even if a "service" affects international trade in services within the broad meaning of those terms, the GATS does not necessarily apply its obligations to those services. The GATS includes general obligations as well as specific commitments with several "opt out" provisions.

Within the general obligations, Article II:1 of the GATS requires WTO members to accord "immediately and unconditionally to services and service suppliers of any other member treatment no less favourable than that it accords to like services and service suppliers of any other country." Article XIV allows exceptions to this most favored nation obligation that are typical of Article XX of the GATT. However, while it includes an exception for measures necessary to protect human, animal or plant life or health, it does not allow exceptions for measures relating to the conservation of exhaustible natural resources. The Article XIV chapeau mirrors that of Article XX of the GATT, except that whereas Article XX of the GATT prohibits arbitrary or unjustifiable discrimination between countries where the same conditions prevail, Article XIV of the GATS prohibits such discrimination where "like" conditions prevail.

In addition, Article II:2 allows a member to maintain a measure inconsistent with the MFN obligation, provided that the member lists the measure in Annex II. Negotiators designed this exception when they realized that they would not achieve unqualified liberalization in some service sectors and that qualified liberalization was preferable to no liberalization at all. WTO Secretariat, *An Introduction to the GATS* (Mar. 29, 2006), *available at* http://www.wto.org/english/tratop_e/serv_e/gsintr_e.doc. More than 70 WTO members made their scheduled services commitments subject to a further list of exemptions from Article II's MFN obligation. No further exceptions under Article II:1 are permitted unless the member uses the formal waiver provisions of the WTO Agreement and existing exceptions are subject to negotiation in future negotiating rounds. Although Article II exceptions should not exceed 10 years, the obvious advantage of using Article II rather than Article XIV is that no justification is needed. The advantage of this exception is particularly acute, because the MFN obligation otherwise applies to all service sectors and suppliers of services whether or not specific commitments have been made. European Communities-Regime for the Importation, Sale, and Distribution of Bananas: Complaint by the USA, Panel Report, WT/DS27/R/USA, para. 7.298 (adopted May 22, 1997). Because the Appellate Body has reversed two panels that discussed the scope of "like services" as more or less equivalent to "like product" under the GATT, the exact scope of "like services" is still not known. *See* Matsushita, Schoenbaum, & Mavroidis, The World Trade Organization, at 620–21 (discussing "like services").

The second component of the GATS asks WTO members to commit to liberalization beyond that provided in Article II via MFN, national treatment, and other obligations, for services included in that members "Schedule of Specific Commitments." When granting market access through the modes of supply provided by Article I, Article XVI requires each member to "accord services and service suppliers of any other Member treatment no less favourable than that provided for under the terms, limitations and conditions agreed and specified in its Schedule." As in Article II, Article XVI allows deviations from this MFN obligation. Two points are worth mentioning with respect to the MFN obligation. Most important, a member is not required to grant market access for services. Even if it does, it can still opt out of its MFN obligation by limiting the MFN obligation in its schedule.

Where a member makes market access commitments, Article XVI prohibits, unless otherwise specified in its Schedule, a member from adopting or maintaining the following types of measures: 1) limitations on the number of service suppliers; 2) limitations on the total value of services transactions or assets; 3) limitations on the total number of service operations or the total quantity of service output; 4) limitations on the number of persons that may be employed in a particular sector or by a particular supplier; 5) measures that restrict or require supply of the service through specific types of legal entity or joint venture; and 6) percentage limitations on the participation of foreign capital or on the total value of foreign investment.

Pursuant to Article XVII, the national treatment obligation also applies to services specified in a member's Schedule:

> In the sectors inscribed in its Schedule, and subject to any conditions and qualifications set out therein, each Member shall accord to services and service suppliers of any other Member, in respect of all measures affecting the supply of services, treatment no less favourable than that it accords to its own like services and service suppliers.

The GATS national treatment obligation adopts some of the jurisprudence from GATT decisions. The GATS embraces *de facto* and *de jure* discrimination. According to Article XVI:3, a member violates its GATS national treatment obligation, even if treatment is identical, provided that the measure modifies the conditions of competition.

Nevertheless, the GATS national treatment obligation is not nearly as restrictive as in the GATT. First, members are not required to include any services in its commitment Schedule; they have discretion to choose which services to include. Second, a member may condition and qualify its implementation of the national treatment obligation. As such, both the MFN and national treatment obligations under the GATS operate like a GATT bound tariff: the stated conditions or qualifications represent the minimum standards (or worst treatment) that may be given, and members may provide better treatment if they choose. WTO Secretariat, *An Introduction to the GATS*, at 7, 8.

Why allow deviation from national treatment obligation and not under the GATT? According to the WTO Secretariat:

> The reason lies in the nature of trade in services. Universal national treatment for goods is possible, without creating free trade, because the entry of foreign goods into a national market can still be controlled by import duties, quantitative restrictions and other border measures. By contrast, a foreign supplier of most services, particularly if those services are supplied by commercial or personal presence in the importing country's market, will in practice enjoy virtually free access to that market if given national treatment, since this by definition will remove any regulatory advantage enjoyed by the domestic service supplier.

Id.

---

2. Trade Measures in the Kyoto Protocol

The Framework Convention on Climate Change and the subsequent Kyoto Protocol are perhaps the most difficult multilateral environmental agreements to assess for WTO consistency. The Climate Change Convention is, in fact, a framework convention with no binding commitments to reduce emissions of greenhouse gases (GHGs), but it does "require" developed countries to "aim" to return their GHG emissions to 1990 levels by 2000. The Kyoto Protocol establishes very specific targets and timetables, called quantifiable emissions limitations and reductions objectives, for the developed country parties to reduce their emissions of six GHGs (carbon dioxide (CO_2), methane, nitrous oxide, and three other chemicals). The two agreements are also very interesting because they permit the parties to use economic instruments to meet their GHG reductions. Nonetheless, the use of economic instruments, such as energy taxes, tradeable emissions permits, and "joint implementation," could engage several provisions of the GATT and GATS.

Under Article 6 of the Kyoto Protocol, through a program known as joint implementation (JI), a developed country party (an "Annex I" party) or one of its investors may earn "carbon credits"—called "emission reduction units" (ERUs)—by investing in a project that reduces GHG emissions in another Annex I country. A similar program, called the Clean Development Mechanism (CDM), allows Annex I parties to obtain credits—called "certifiable emissions reductions" (CERs)—for emission reductions in non-Annex I countries (i.e., developing countries). For example, if a German electrical utility installs CO_2-removing technology on a facility in Brazil, that facility would obtain CERs for reducing CO_2 emissions that it could use to meet its emissions reduction obligations or sell. Brazil would obtain valuable technology at no cost. Dutch investment in a wind power farm in China that would avoid "business-as-usual" emissions from a new coal-fired plant would generate carbon credits for the Dutch investor. Both JI and the CDM programs are premised on the notion that the removal of a ton of carbon dioxide or any other GHG regardless of geographic origin reduces the threat of global warming the same. As a result, so long as the emissions reductions from these projects are additional to any that would occur in the absence of the project, as required by the Protocol, parties should seek to reduce emissions where it is most efficient. Kyoto Protocol, arts. 6, 12.

While the names of the two programs may be different, the concept is the same: countries, companies, and others that invest in emissions-reducing projects will generate ERUs and CERs that can be exchanged, bought, and sold in a manner that allows a private entity and a party to demonstrate compliance with their commitments to reduce or limit greenhouse gas emissions. "Emissions trading" is the vehicle for buying and selling CERs and ERUs and other forms of carbon credits without the need for a specific project. The CDM and JI, as well as emissions trading more generally, have become accepted, well-used strategies for reducing emissions and for meeting emissions reduction obligations. In 2008, for example, CDM and JI projects generated transactions valued at more than US$6.8 billion; the total value of the carbon market was US$126 billion. KARAN CAPOOR & PHILIPPE AMBROSI, STATE AND TRENDS OF THE CARBON MARKET 2009 1, 2 (2009).

_____

3. The Kyoto Protocol and the WTO Agreements

A full WTO analysis of these market instruments is difficult because the parties can use the Kyoto Protocol's framework in many different ways. For example, a country can invest in pollution control technology, reforest denuded forests, or finance the conversion to cleaner fuels. Generally, however, because JI and the CDM involve projects that lead to ERUs and CERs that represent an amount of carbon or other GHG that may be bought, sold or used to meet obligations to reduce greenhouse gas emissions; countries or investors are not trading emissions. Thus, emissions trading is highly unlikely to be considered trade in goods subject to GATT rules. Recall, however, the definition of "goods" in the *Softwood Lumber* case (Chapter 8, Section III.B at pages 546–53). The Appellate Body embraced a definition of "goods" under the SCM Agreement that included a wide range of property. Without specifically defining "goods," it noted that various definitions would include "items that are tangible and capable of being possessed" as well as "property or possessions" generally. If the GATT definition of "product" is interpreted as broadly as "goods" under the SCM Agreement, it is possible that an emissions credit obtained through JI or CDM projects could be considered a product, and thus subject to the GATT.

More likely, JI and CDM-related services associated with trading emission rights, such as brokerage, financing, legal, accounting, and auditing services, are covered by the GATS.

Certainly, operation of JI and the CDM will require services. Some entity, whether private or governmental, must issue ERUs and CERs. The design of a CDM project will require engineering, architectural and planning services, as well as construction, installation, assembly, finishing and, in some cases, landscaping and real estate services. To monitor and maintain the project, additional services may be required, such as database and accounting, testing and analysis, and consulting services. Securing project funding and executing contracts will necessitate financial, lending, and legal services. If a secondary market exists for ERUs and CERs, brokerage, advisory and ratings services may be needed to buy, sell, or trade them. These activities could be supplied through any of the modes of supply included in Article I of the GATS. For example, a German company that brokers CDM projects may establish an office in Costa Rica (a "commercial presence" service); a Japanese auditing company may send an analyst to Brazil to calculate the reductions produced at a facility (a "movement of natural persons" service); lawyers setting up a CDM project may need to send documents to offices in different countries (a "cross-border supply" service); or executives from an Australian electrical utility may travel to Malaysia to establish a CDM project and in the process avail themselves of Malaysian financiers, lawyers, and auditors (a "consumption abroad" service). Glenn Wiser, an attorney with the Center for International Environmental Law, looks at the various GATT and GATS issues with respect to the CDM, including the distinction between "products" and "services."

Glenn M. Wiser, *Frontiers in Trade: The Clean Development Mechanism and the General Agreement on Trade in Services*

2 Int'l J. Global Envtl. Issues 288, 294–97, 304–05 (2002)

Although some people refer to the "product" or "commodity" of carbon when discussing the CDM, they obviously do not expect CDM investors to receive carbon for their efforts. Rather, CDM investors will acquire allowances or credits that they may be able to sell to a third party or apply toward their own domestic emissions obligations. * * *

CERs might exist as tangible things. They may be paper certificates; alternatively, they may exist only in electronic form in computerized registries or databases. Nonetheless, to the extent paper certificate CERs can be described as things, they will be things in the sense that a printed license is a thing. The holder of the license or CER does not value or use the certificate as a piece of paper, but instead values it for the rights it symbolizes or conveys.

A license is permission by a competent authority to do an act that, without the permission, would be prohibited or illegal. While such permission may be transferable from one holder of the license to another, the permission itself is not created through any kind of production process, and it has no physical attributes that give it value. In the case of the CDM, CERs will represent permission granted to the holder by the [Kyoto parties] and/or Executive Board [of the CDM] to emit one tonne of carbon dioxide equivalent, which the holder would not have been allowed to emit but for its possession of the CER. CERs thus should properly be viewed as a kind of license that confers a right—a *future right to pollute*. Just as a license is not a good but merely a permit to do something, so a CER should not be seen as a good. Because the GATT only covers trade in goods, it is probably unlikely that a country's treatment of CERs would fall under the GATT. * * *

The [United Nations Central Product Classification (CPC)] lists no services directly analogous to the issuance of CERs. However, the CPC does not specifically list all imaginable forms of services, nor does it list as-yet unimagined services that might emerge in coming decades. Accordingly, the fact that a service is not listed in the CPC does not necessarily mean it will not be covered by the GATS in the future. As WTO members periodically reclassify the definitions of specific services to update the CPC in light of economic changes, the CPC could include listings that encompass or are directly relevant to CDM services.

To decide whether CERs are services within the ambit of the GATS, it may be useful to consider the U.S. Clean Air Act's sulfur dioxide (SO_2) emissions trading scheme. Under the SO_2 program, electric power plants are given an emissions target or cap and an equivalent number of emissions allowances. If a utility reduces its emissions below its target, it can sell the excess allowances to another plant, which can raise its own emissions by the amount of allowances it purchased. The Clean Air Act explicitly stipulates that emissions allowances allocated under the plan constitute a "limited authorization to emit sulfur dioxide in accordance with the provisions of [the Act]." Thus, even though allowances can become available for trading because a utility rendered the "service" of reducing its emissions, the allowances themselves are not services, but government-issued "limited authorizations"—licenses—that give their recipients the right to emit a given amount of pollution.

Like SO_2 allowances, CERs will be created not by a power plant or project developer, but by an administrative institution acting under governmental authority—in this case, the CDM Executive Board. The CERs will not be part of the project nor part of the services that created the project and reduced the emissions. Rather, they will be a kind of tradable permit—issued or approved by the Executive Board—that acknowledges a certain amount of greenhouse gas emissions were reduced or avoided and which, in turn, gives the holder of the permit the right to emit an equivalent amount of emissions at a different time and place.

Both CERs and SO_2 allowances play the same kind of role in their respective regimes: Each allows the holder to emit a certain quantity of regulated pollutants that it would not be allowed to emit *but for the allowances.* Each is a form of government-granted permission. Neither CERs nor SO_2 allowances should be considered a form of service under the GATS. By clearly defining CERs (as well as "emissions reduction units" under Article 6 joint implementation and "assigned amount units" under Article 17 emissions trading) as a form of license or permit, Kyoto Protocol Parties could lessen the possibility that a WTO member might try to use the WTO dispute settlement understanding to preempt or redefine the intentions of the [Kyoto parties]. Parties might include language in the CDM implementing decision that paraphrases the U.S. Clean Air Act language: "CERs shall constitute a limited authorization to emit carbon dioxide equivalent in accordance with the rules in and under the Protocol."

A "license view" of CERs would help ensure there was no question that the [Kyoto parties] would have the sole authority to decide whether CER trade with nonparties will be restricted; whether CDM-eligibility criteria might curtail a Party's ability to use CERs; whether a Party might be limited in how many CERs it can tender for compliance purposes during any given time period; or whether the [parties] or a designated authority might respond to a case of noncompliance by suspending the right of a Party to export, import, or redeem CERs. The license view could also protect the right of individual Parties to enact domestic regulations that restrict the use of CERs in ways not specifically articulated under the international rules. This unambiguous authority would, in turn, help Protocol Parties avoid the "chilling effect" that may be present when negotiators—uncertain whether or not their decisions could somehow run afoul of WTO rules—consciously or unconsciously allow their uncertainty to make them refrain from taking needed action. * * *

The GATS applies to measures affecting trade in services ...

In the absence of a generally agreed upon definition of "services" under the GATS, most WTO members have provisionally adopted the Central Product Classification list to describe and categorize their GATS commitments. The list includes general categories covering, *inter alia,* construction and engineering services, environmental services, and business services, the latter of which include professional services of architectural, engineering, and urban planning and landscape architecture. These areas necessarily overlap. However, construction services are generally those that entail the "application of technology to the building of structures (such as houses) and productive facilities (such as factories) by combinations of skilled and unskilled labor, encompassing both public and private activity." They include both design (i.e., architects and engineers developing the conception of the project) and implementation. Professional services involve the "provision of intellectual or specialized skills on a personal, direct basis, based on extensive educational training." All of these services, as noted earlier, may contribute to the development and construction of CDM projects. * * *

[M]any or all of the individual services that collectively constitute CDM project development are services that could be defined as falling under one or more of the categories identified in the list of services covered by the GATS. But two of the most important GATS provisions affecting the treatment of these services—the market access and national treatment obligations—are "opt-in" commitments. Very few WTO members (and nearly all of them industrialized countries) have made commitments for the energy or environmental services sectors, which will arguably be among the most important service sectors for CDM projects. Accordingly, it is likely that non-Annex I host countries would not at this time be required to extend market access or national treatment to CDM project services. This leaves a significant opportunity open for countries acting collectively within the climate and trade regimes—as well as individually when they consider what services they may want to list among their GATS commitments—to take the initiative to ensure that the GATS enhances, rather than interferes with, the CDM's sustainable development objectives.

Parties to the Climate Change Convention and the Kyoto Protocol may trade "carbon credits" without developing a project under the CDM or JI. This allows an emitter of carbon dioxide or other GHGs to reduce emissions by purchasing credits from another emitter of carbon dioxide that has reduced its emissions more than required. This second emitter, by reducing beyond the level required, earns carbon credits, also called emissions allowances, that can be bought and sold. The systems for accounting for transfers of these credits are established by national governments, for example the EU Emission Trading System; the trades typically take place on public exchanges.

Even if TEPs fall outside the scope of GATS, the business of trading TEPs could be covered either under the GATS or through the GATS agreement on financial services as a "negotiable instrument."

Jacob Werksman, *Greenhouse Gas Emissions Trading and the WTO*
8 RECIEL 251, 256 (1999)

GATS disciplines might prohibit those WTO members that have fully liberalized their financial services sector from placing quantitative restrictions on the "import" of emissions allowances. For example, GATS might prohibit such a Member from limiting access of other Members' emissions allowances to its market on the basis of "the total value of ... assets in the form of numerical quotas."

However, GATS rules would not require any Member to recognize the regulatory validity of these allowances, once they had been "imported." In other words, GATS might require that brokers and other financial service providers within Country A be free to buy and sell the emissions allowances issued by any other WTO Member. But Country A could nonetheless refuse to recognize these allowances as valid for the purpose of offsetting emissions with A's territory. A useful analogy is to the trade in government-issued currency. Currency is not itself a "service" or a "product," but the provision of financial services, such as currency exchange, would fall within the scope of the GATS. Depending on Country A's specific GATS commitments, it may be required to guarantee market access to bureaux de change registered in Country B, and it may be prohibited from limiting the volume of currency exchanged through these services. Country A would not, however, under GATS rules, be required to recognize as legal tender for the use within its domestic market, currency issued by Country B.

Questions and Discussion

1. *CO_2 and Energy Taxes.* To meet the schedules for reducing emissions of GHGs, either unilaterally or jointly, the parties can adopt CO_2 and energy taxes based on the amount of energy used or the amount of CO_2 emitted by a product. In addition, they can apply such taxes to a product based on the amount of energy consumed or CO_2 emitted in the product's production. As discussed in Chapter 4, GATT allows a country to tax imported products, provided that the country imposes an equivalent tax on domestic production. In GATT terms, this is a border tax adjustment. A tax on energy products (e.g., coal), or some element of the energy product (such as its carbon content), is an indirect tax imposed directly on the product. As indirect taxes, they are eligible for border tax adjustments. Whether parties also could impose border tax adjustments on imported products based on the amount of energy used to make them is unclear. Because this issue is discussed at length in Chapter 4, simply recall here that legal distinctions may arise with respect to two situations: 1) when the energy product remains a constituent of the final product, such as in the case of plastics that incorporate petroleum products into the finished product, and 2) when the process of making the product consumes energy, for example to make steel or to run machines.

2. The Kyoto Protocol specifically allows discrimination between parties and nonparties and essentially requires discrimination between developed country parties and de-

veloping country parties (under the principle of "common but differentiated responsibility" in the Climate Change Convention). For example, rules for emissions trading between developed and developing countries through the CDM differ from those for trading between developed countries through JI. For example, CDM projects, unlike JI projects, must lead to "[r]eal, measurable, and long-term benefits related to the mitigation of climate change" and contribute to sustainable development in the developing country. *Cf.* Kyoto Protocol, arts. 6, 12. Explain how you would implement the various services required to implement these mechanisms as envisioned by the Kyoto Protocol to ensure you also comply with your MFN and national treatment obligations under the GATS.

3. *Subsidies.* Legislation in the European Union and proposals for climate change legislation in other countries to reduce CO_2 emissions rely on the issuance of "allowances" to facilities that are covered by the legislation. In the EU, for example, legislation provides that at least 95 percent of allowances during the first commitment period and 90 percent during the second commitment period must be allocated free of charge. Directive 2003/87/EC of the European Parliament and of the Council of 13 October 2003 establishing a scheme for greenhouse gas emission allowance trading within the Community and amending Council Directive 96/61/EC, OJ 2003 L 275, arts. 9, 10. These allowances are obviously of great value. Recall the requirements of "financial contribution, "benefit conferred," and specificity from Chapter 8. Do you think the issuance of free allowances constitutes a subsidy? Many economists argue that the allowances are not really "free" and that firms will manage their businesses much as if they had paid for them. But regardless of that, does the issuance of free allowances have a trade effect? Vis-à-vis producers in a country that has no emission reduction program of any kind?

4. Will the provision of services needed to implement the CDM violate the GATS? Most conclude that it depends on how a country organizes those services. *See* Glenn Wiser, *The Clean Development Mechanism Versus The World Trade Organization: Can Free-Market Greenhouse Gas Emissions Abatement Survive Free Trade?*, 11 GEO. INT'L ENVTL. L. REV. 531 (1999); Werksman, *Greenhouse Gas Emissions and the WTO*, at 251, 261.

5. Jacob Werksman argues that no WTO challenge to a trade measure of an MEA has been brought, because 1) WTO members have exercised self-restraint; 2) participation in the MEAs with trade measures is broad; and 3) the scope of economic activity covered by these MEAs is narrow. He is uncertain, however, whether these conditions will hold true for the Kyoto Protocol. Werksman, *Greenhouse Gas Emissions and the WTO*, at 261. Why might conditions under the Kyoto Protocol be different from, for example, CITES and the Montreal Protocol?

6. *Basel Convention.* Similar GATS questions arise under the Basel Convention on the Control of Transboundary Movement of Hazardous Wastes and their Disposal. The waste itself is likely a product whereas the disposal of waste is a service. Consider the prior informed consent provisions of the Basel Convention discussed in Section II.B (pages 644–45). Do notice and consent provisions regulate international shipments of hazardous wastes or the disposal of waste?

7. *Water and Electricity.* Just as with energy services, the GATS potentially applies to the provision of water and electricity. *See* Elisabeth Türk & Markus Krajewski, *The Right to Water and Trade in Services: Assessing the Impact of GATS Negotiations on Water Regulation* (Oct. 2003); Aaron Ostrovksy, et al., *GATS, Water and the Environment: Implications of the General Agreement on Trade in Services for Water Resources* (CIEL-WWF International Discussion Paper: Oct. 2003); Gary Horlick, *NAFTA Provisions and the Electricity Sector* (Background Paper: Council for Environmental Cooperation, 2001).

8. The NAFTA provisions on services differ from the GATS in several ways. One potential distinction the two agreements make relates to the application of most favored nation and national treatment obligations. Whereas the GATS requires nondiscrimination between "like services," the NAFTA requires nondiscrimination between service providers "in like circumstances." Do those phrases mean the same thing? When the United States refused to lift its moratorium on the processing of applications by Mexican-owned trucking firms for authority to operate in U.S. border states, Mexico charged that the United States was failing to provide its trucking services treatment no less favorable than U.S. trucking services, as required by Article 1202 of the NAFTA. The United States argued that U.S. and Mexican trucking services were not in "like circumstances," in part because, according to the United States, Mexican trucks are less safe. The Panel agreed that "like circumstances" may properly include differential treatment, but that such "differential treatment should be no greater than necessary for legitimate regulatory reasons such as safety, and that such different treatment be equivalent to the treatment accorded to domestic service providers." In the Matter of Cross-Border Trucking Services, Final Report of the Panel, Secretariat File No. USA-MEX-98-2008-01, para. 258 (Feb. 6, 2001). The Panel concluded that the "in like circumstances" language could not support a very significant barrier to NAFTA trade, namely a prohibition on cross-border trucking services." *Id.* This decision must be read with caution, however, because the Panel's interpretation of national treatment derives in substantial part from Article 1402 of the U.S.-Canada Free Trade Agreement. Whereas Article 1402 of that agreement specifically includes provisions relating to differential treatment and "least trade restrictiveness," Article 1202 of the NAFTA is completely silent on those matters.

Chapter 10

Investment

I. Introduction

The tectonic forces of globalization—especially the mobility of massive private capital flows—are shaping the frontiers of trade policy by thrusting investment and competition policy into the foreground. This chapter examines the shifting interface between international trade policy and national and international law relating to private investments, exemplified by a large number of investor claims filed under the investment chapter of the North American Free Trade Agreement (NAFTA). We identify some points of friction and uncertainty in environmental policies created by the overlap of trade and investment law, along with the measures taken in response to these concerns. Along the way, some provocative questions will be raised about the application to investors and their investments of trade law principles originally devised for products. In the background, as always, are important policy questions. Even if foreign direct investment is an essential ingredient in the pursuit of sustainable development, as many would argue, is the trade liberalization approach appropriate for a foreign investment regime? *See, e.g.*, KONRAD VON MOLTKE, AN INTERNATIONAL INVESTMENT REGIME? ISSUES OF SUSTAINABILITY v–vi (2000); HOWARD MANN, PRIVATE RIGHTS, PUBLIC PROBLEMS: A GUIDE TO NAFTA'S CONTROVERSIAL CHAPTER ON INVESTOR RIGHTS (International Institute for Sustainable Development, 2001).

II. A First Look at the Economics and Environmental Consequences of Foreign Investment

A. The Economics of Investment

As noted in Chapter 1 (page 10), flows of private foreign direct investment (FDI) were measured at US$1.7 trillion in 2008, already down from nearly $2.0 trillion in 2007 and declining substantially to about $1.0 trillion in 2009. *See* UNCTAD, WORLD INVESTMENT REPORT 2009 1, 4 (2009), *available at* http://www.unctad.org/en/docs/wir2009overview_en.pdf; UNCTAD, GLOBAL INVESTMENT TRENDS MONITOR, No. 2 (Jan. 19, 2010) *available at* http://www.unctad.org/en/docs/webdiaeia20101_en.pdf. This massive amount of capital is supplemented by foreign portfolio investment—for example, American investors buying stocks and bonds of a German or a Malaysian firm. International com-

mercial bank loans are another element of globalized finance, of which we are periodically reminded when one company or another is in danger of defaulting on its debt. And
each day huge quantities of currencies are exchanged to cover cross-border purchases of
everything from steel and televisions to airplane tickets and hotel rooms. In the end,
though, the key element of cross-border financial transactions for trade and environment
policy is FDI. Where does FDI come from, and where is it going?

Some FDI represents transnational corporate mergers and acquisitions, and some is accounted for by un-repatriated profits of foreign business ventures. Most FDI, though,
represents more consequential investments by companies or private investors of one country in the assets of a business in a foreign country. Those assets might be a store or a shipping firm or a bank, but in the classic case involve investment in or ownership of
goods-producing assets like forest products companies, mines, and manufacturing facilities. As we are vividly aware in 2010, FDI flows, by their nature, are more sensitive than
other economic measures to the ups and downs of national, regional, and world economic conditions. Even in the midst of the global economic crisis of 2008–09, however,
FDI flows remained at levels much higher than 10 years earlier.

With sustainable development in mind, investment patterns in developing countries
are of special interest, even though "North-North" FDI (such as between the United States
and Europe) continues to dominate the world picture because of the large size of the
economies involved.

Private capital flows to developing countries now dwarf official government foreign
aid assistance, but it is notoriously difficult to predict FDI levels or the sources and des-
tinations of the flows. For example, the amount of private capital flowing into the emerging markets of the developing world exploded in the early 1990s, rising from US$44 billion
at the beginning of the decade to hundreds of billions by the end of the decade, finally
reaching more than US$620 billion in 2008 before falling back to US$405 billion in 2009.
In percentage terms, inflows to developing and transitional economies rose to 44 percent
of global FDI in 2004, fell to 31 percent in 2007, and rose again to 43 percent in 2008. There
has been more even growth in FDI outflows from developing and transitional economies,
from 10 percent in 2003 to almost 20 percent in 2008. Variations from country to country are substantial. As might be expected, inflows to and outflows from China, and to a
lesser extent India, play an increasing role in the world scene. Inflows to China more than
doubled between 2003 and 2008 (from US$53 billion to US$108 billion), while outflows
mushroomed from a mere US$2.9 billion in 2003 to US$52 billion in 2008. Africa, after
suffering a dramatic decline in FDI inflows from US$19 billion in 2001 to US$11 billion
in 2002, saw FDI increase to US$21 billion in 2003 and US$88 billion in 2008, with much
of the increase in investment coming in the commodities sector. Latin America has seen
a similar investment pattern. UNCTAD, World Investment Report 2009, at 14–22.
Even the "structurally weak" economies of the least-developed countries, landlocked countries, and small island states have seen welcome increases in FDI, but UNCTAD cautions
that their dependence on commodities makes them vulnerable and recommends that
such countries may "wish to consider promoting FDI in industries which are less prone
to cyclical fluctuations, such as agriculture-related industries, particularly food and beverages, as part of a diversification strategy." Id. at 6.

Despite the recent fluctuations in FDI, UNCTAD and the WTO remain bullish on FDI
flows to developing countries, in part because of the trend toward liberalization of investment regulation. UNCTAD notes favorably that most government regulatory changes
in 2008 (85 out of 110) enhanced investment liberalization; the network of international
investment agreements (IIAs) also grew, with 59 new bilateral investment treaties. Id. at

12. In UNCTAD's view, "IIAs have a role to play in ensuring predictability, stability and transparency of national investment regimes. Policymakers should also consider strengthening the investment promotion dimension of IIAs through effective and operational provisions. Investment insurance and other home-country measures that encourage outward investment are cases in point where continued international cooperation can be useful." *Id.* at 13.

Recent decades have also seen a major shift in the modes of foreign direct investment. As recently as the 1970s, commercial bank lending accounted for most foreign investment, often to finance large infrastructure projects such a highways or power plants. In the 21st century, investments by transnational corporations, including merger and acquisition activity and non-repatriation of foreign profits, are major investment factors.

UNCTAD's annual world investment reports and other reports on investments have noted the importance of commodity-related FDI, especially in sub-Saharan Africa, Latin America, and the "structurally weak" economies. In that light, the following perspective is still pertinent.

Hilary F. French, *Assessing Private Capital Flows to Developing Countries*

in STATE OF THE WORLD 152–55 (Worldwatch Institute, 1998)

The quest for natural resources has traditionally drawn international investors into distant ventures in the developing world. Oil has been a particularly strong pull since the dawn of the petroleum age, with oil-producing countries accounting for fully half of all FDI flows to developing countries between 1979 and 1981. But this picture has changed rapidly in recent decades. First, investment in manufacturing began to climb. Now, the services sector, which includes diverse activities such as construction, electricity distribution, finance, and telecommunications, is poised for takeoff. Oil-producing countries, meanwhile accounted for only one fifth of FDI flows into the developing world in 1995 and 1996. The World Bank estimates that the services sector now accounts for more than a third of overall FDI flows to these countries, while manufacturing has declined to less than half of the total. The primary sector, which includes agriculture, forestry, and mining, makes up the remainder roughly 20 percent. * * *

Although primary commodities are receiving a declining share of total international investment in the developing world, these investments continue to increase in absolute terms in many countries. Indeed, international investment in resource extraction is now flowing rapidly into the developing world, with its rich endowments of natural assets, including primary forests, mineral and petroleum reserves, and biological diversity. Among other things, this trend reflects degraded environmental conditions in the countries that are a source of the capital, as well as the greening impact of environmental legislation in these countries aimed at minimizing further destruction. * * *

The flow of funds into natural resources is particularly pronounced within the mining industry. From 1994 to 1997, spending on exploration of nonferrous minerals doubled in Latin America, almost tripled in the Pacific region, and more than tripled in Africa, while leveling off in the traditional mining countries of Australia, Canada, and the United States. * * *

The U.S. mining industry blames environmentalists for the migration. More to the point, perhaps, is the fact that host countries are inviting international investors in with open arms; some 70 countries have rewritten their national mining codes in recent years with the aim of encouraging investment. Yet few are devoting similar energy to strengthening environmental laws and enforcement. And no matter how good the laws are, mining takes a heavy environmental toll. Even in the United States, a country with relatively strong environmental controls, for every kilogram of gold produced, some 3 million kilograms of waste rock are removed from the Earth. The social costs are also high: one out of every five gold prospecting sites over 1995–96 was on land owned or claimed by indigenous peoples. * * *

Multinational oil and gas companies are also continually looking for new horizons, as the most accessible fields in industrial countries have already been tapped. Indeed, more than 90 percent of known gas and oil reserves are now in the developing world.... Uncontrolled logging by international companies poses yet another threat to the world's rapidly dwindling tropical forests and those who inhabit them. * * *

As the pace of natural resource exploitation picks up in many countries, intriguing research is raising questions about whether this is a sound economic strategy—let alone a wise environmental one. Research by Jeffrey Sachs and Andrew Warner of Harvard University demonstrates that countries rich in natural resources have on average actually performed worse economically than resource-poor countries in recent decades. One reason may be that resource extraction often leads to only marginal spin-off benefits when it involves few linkages with other segments of economies. Furthermore, natural resource extraction creates relatively few jobs. The mining and petroleum sectors in Papua New Guinea, for example, employ less than 2 percent of the population, although the sectors' exports provide 25 percent of the country's GDP. A wiser strategy for both the environment and the economy would be to funnel international capital into activities that sustain rather than destroy natural endowments. This is what a number of innovative experiments now under way aim to do.

Questions and Discussion

1. Should we be concerned that private capital flows target a small number of developing countries for natural resource development? Although French indicates that this is problematic, does it also represent a development opportunity? How, if at all, should international investment law respond?

2. Should the home countries of transnational corporations regulate the activities of their corporations abroad? Countries can certainly regulate the activities of persons and corporate entities under their jurisdiction, but they rarely do. Why? Even if countries began to regulate the activities of their corporations when they invest abroad, do you think that would be effective? If you were the chief executive officer of a U.S. corporation that wanted to do business in Guatemala, and the United States decided to regulate the foreign activities of U.S. corporations, what would you do to avoid such U.S. regulations? The United Nations Center for Transnational Corporations attempted to create a draft code for foreign investment based on corporate responsibilities. The "final" draft code—

filled with bracketed (disputed) text—demonstrates the controversial nature of imposing substantive obligations on transnational corporations when they invest abroad. More
telling is the fate of this Center: it no longer exists. The OECD has done slightly better.
Its 2000 "Guidelines for Multinational Enterprises," scheduled for a full review in 2010,
urge enterprises to refrain from seeking or accepting exemptions from environmental
laws and regulations (Part II, para. 5), and more generally provides that "[e]nterprises should,
within the framework of laws, regulations and administrative practices in the countries
in which they operate, and in consideration of relevant international agreements, principles, objectives, and standards, take due account of the need to protect the environment, public health and safety, and generally to conduct their activities in a manner
contributing to the wider goal of sustainable development." (Part V). OECD, OECD
Guidelines for Multinational Enterprises (2008), *available at* http://www.oecd.org/
daf/investment/guidelines.

3. As French reports, a large portion of FDI targets countries rich in natural wealth.
She concludes that countries frequently squander their natural resources by investing in
ill-conceived projects that essentially mine natural resources "for the short-term economic
gain of political elites, at the expense of local peoples and future generations. A wiser
long-term strategy would be to funnel capital into economic activities that preserve natural endowments." Hilary French, Investing in the Future: Harnessing Private
Capital Flows for Environmentally Sustainable Development 19 (1998). How
can they accomplish that? One exemplar is Norway, which has systematically saved a large
fraction of its income from its offshore oil fields and invested some of those savings in domestic infrastructure and programs.

B. The Environmental Consequences of Investment

Countries moving to liberalize their markets to foreign investors clearly believe the
economic benefits outweigh any short-term environmental consequences. The focus of
investment has also affected the types of environmental consequences that can be expected. The excerpts below identify several considerations respecting the environmental
dimensions of foreign investment.

Hilary French, *Investing in the Future: Harnessing Private Capital Flows for Environmentally Sustainable Development*
6–8 (1998)

As investors search the globe for the highest return, they are often drawn to
places endowed with bountiful natural resources but handicapped by weak or
ineffective environmental laws. Many people and communities are harmed as
the environment that sustains them is damaged or destroyed—villagers are displaced by large construction projects, for example, and indigenous peoples watch
their homelands disappear as timber companies level old growth forests. For-
eign-investment-fed growth also promotes western-style consumerism, pushing
car ownership, paper use, and Big Mac consumption rates towards the unten-
able levels found in the United States—with grave potential consequences for the

health of the natural world, the stability of the earth's climate, and the security of food supplies. * * *

Policy reforms are needed to steer private capital flows in a more environmentally sound direction. But the levers of change are shifting: the influence wielded by public aid agencies is waning while private sector clout is on the rise. Over the first half of the 1990s, spending on official development assistance fell by more than a quarter in the face of large government budget deficits in donor countries and declining political support for aid. The shrinking public presence coupled with expanding private flows dramatically changed the complexion of North-South development finance. Whereas in 1990 less than half the international capital moving into the developing world came from private sources, by 1996 this share had risen to 86 percent.

This shift in the sources of capital poses a policy challenge, as the private sector is by definition less accountable to the public interest than government agencies are. * * *

David Hunter, James Salzman, & Durwood Zaelke, *International Environmental Law and Policy*
1342–44 (3d ed. 2007)

Multinational enterprises engage in FDI for a host of reasons that lower their costs of doing business—avoiding tariffs, reducing transport costs, securing access to natural resources, taking advantage of cheap labor, etc. And the attractive benefits offered by FDI to host developing countries are also undeniable. For the host country, FDI can provide needed capital, spur technology transfer, create jobs, and increase domestic competition and foreign exchange. But equally, there are potential downsides, including [the following:]

From Local to Global Control. Globalization of the market economy, and with it the growth of multinational corporations, presents a conflict, at least conceptually, with the goal of sustainable development, which requires local participation and control over development choices. In the global economy, owners who may benefit from environmentally damaging processes typically do not live in or near the local communities that are affected by the environmental harm. Local concerns may thus not be adequately reflected in corporate decision making. Since the political and economic power is vested in people physically separated from the environmental harm, less environmental protection might be expected. Moreover, when States agree to broad investment agreements, ... they may be ceding some of their sovereign power to assert local control over the environmental and social impacts of foreign investment.

Dangerous and Inappropriate Technologies. Just as important as these global environmental issues are the issues raised by foreign investment at the national level. Environmental disasters, such as the 1984 isocyanate gas leak in Bhopal, India, that killed several thousand people, highlight the problems that occur when foreign investment brings environmentally hazardous technologies to countries with neither the environmental law framework nor the technical infrastructure to address the resulting environmental problems. Consequently, some types of investments perhaps should be restricted until adequate environmental and public health controls can reasonably be expected to be in place.

Double-standards and Fairness. The export of technologies and practices that are prohibited in industrialized countries to developing countries also raise issues of fairness and equity. Many chemical products, for example pesticides like DDT, which are illegal in OECD countries are nonetheless produced by subsidiaries of OECD-country companies in developing countries. Practices in certain other industries, for example oil production and gold mining, have repeatedly involved serious allegations of environmental and human rights abuses. Texaco in Ecuador, Shell Oil in Nigeria, Ok Tedi in Papua New Guinea, and Freeport McMoran in Indonesia ... are well known cases. The disparity between how companies operate in developing countries when compared to their industrialized home countries has led to some discussions about controlling the exports of domestically prohibited technologies and goods, or imposing minimum industry operating standards on multinational corporations....

Competitiveness and the Lowest Common Denominator. Some environmentalists fear that competition for foreign investment could lead developing countries to sacrifice environmental standards and public health in a "race to the bottom" to lure foreign investments. Environmental standards and performance have little competitiveness impact for most industries because they represent a small percentage of their operating cost, at least in developed countries, but this does not stop developing countries from resisting stronger environmental policies, at least in part to attract investment (... this is known as a "chilling effect"). As sovereign countries, States clearly are free to choose relatively lower environmental standards than other States, but ... this can encourage foreign investment that harms local populations, provides little or no local participation in the decision, nor local benefits from jobs or profits. NGOs argue that minimum national environmental standards and laws should be a prerequisite for open trade and investment.

Environmental Opportunities. Of course, foreign investment not only presents challenges, but also opportunities, for environmental protection and sustainable development. Official development assistance is declining and has never met the levels required for moving developing countries toward sustainable development. Private sector investments will have to provide the majority of environmentally sustainable investments in the future. The markets for environmental investments are increasing; for example, investments in energy efficiency projects are expected to reach another $250 billion in the next 20 years.

Questions and Discussion

1. Recall the four potential beneficial or adverse effects of trade (and investment) on the environment first introduced on pages 6–9 of Chapter 1: scale effects (including technology and product effects), composition effects, competitive effects, and regulatory effects. Are the environmental effects of investment and private capital flows any different from those associated with trade? Hilary French discusses the potential scale and composition effects of private capital flows most extensively, with particular attention placed on the exploitation or extraction of natural resources. Hunter et al. identify some additional considerations, including the loss of local control and the absence of global environmental standards. Can you think of more examples that highlight these and other potential effects?

2. Consider the following examples in the hypothetical country of Invierte, an equatorial country poor in monetary resources but rich in biodiversity and forest and marine resources. Identify which effects you think might be most prominent, and re-consider these examples as you plunge deeper into this chapter:

- Invierte seeks to attract foreign capital to exploit its comparative advantage in premium coffee production, including bringing new acreage into production. How big a difference does it make if investors prefer shade-grown coffee (grown under the canopy of primary forest), organic, or plantation-style sun grown varieties? Who wins or loses if Invierte courts investors for U.S.-style agribusiness models, characterized by higher inputs of fertilizers and pesticides and larger farming units?

- Invierte recently enacted a modern and comprehensive set of environmental laws and regulations, including environmental impact assessment for projects, policies, or activities that may adversely impact the environment. Nonetheless, the country lacks the environmental infrastructure, technical capacity, and legal culture to expect much in terms of implementation and compliance in the near term. A surge in FDI has quadrupled the volume of projects subject to environmental assessment, though the Ministry of Environment has not budgeted additional resources or assigned additional staff to handle the increase in assessments. Large multinational firms are pressing the Minister of Finance to streamline assessment and expedite the approval process. International and domestic NGOs are partnering to call attention to threats to Invierte's unique ecoregions and biodiversity. On behalf of the Minister of the Environment, you are tasked with preparing a briefing note on how the Ministry should respond to these challenges, including consideration of strategies to "green" FDI.

3. Why does the shift from governmental aid to FDI pose a policy challenge? Are you convinced that governmental agencies are more accountable than corporations? To what extent does the public engage in debate over how its agencies provide bilateral assistance? Is the public really watching how the U.S. Agency for International Development, the U.S. Export-Import Bank, and the Overseas Private Investment Corporation (OPIC) operate? What about Japanese or Canadian development agencies? In fact, few public interest organizations, such as Friends of the Earth, oversee the work of these agencies. Friends of the Earth reports that "[m]ost export credit agencies lack environmental and social standards." *See* http://www.foe.org/camps/intl/institutions/index.html.

4. Under the Kyoto Protocol and the commitments following the December 2009 Copenhagen Accord on climate change, FDI is explicitly encouraged as a means to reduce emissions growth in developing countries under the Clean Development Mechanism and an emerging program to reduce emissions from deforestation known as REDD. Does this affirmative policy to recruit environmentally sound FDI offset some of the concerns expressed in the French and Hunter et al. excerpts?

III. NAFTA's Chapter 11: Investment

We devote the most attention to NAFTA's Chapter 11 because the large number of disputes under Chapter 11 (60 separate investor-State arbitration claims as of early 2010 by one unofficial count, see http://www.naftaclaims.com/disputes.htm) has shifted the debate on investment liberalization from inside the walls of business to the larger public. In the minds of many environmentalists, consumer activists and conservative organizations in North America (the last group unnerved by perceived diminution of national sovereignty), the little-debated NAFTA investment provisions impinge on the ability of local, state, and federal government to enact and implement laws for the public welfare. Investors, on the other hand, welcome the added stability and impartiality of having recourse to a "neutral" forum for adjudicating claims, even though arbitrations can be expensive and take years before a final decision. In the early years of NAFTA, environmental groups were particularly concerned that most of the Chapter 11 claims challenged government conduct in the area of environmental law and regulation, with many such cases against Canada in particular. These environmental concerns were compounded upon discovering that the governments had overlooked transparency considerations when adapting a dispute resolution mechanism designed for private commercial litigation for use in areas touching on vital public policy issues, including public health and safety. The lack of transparency worked against the governments in other ways, fueling sometimes distorted and exaggerated accounts about the effects of the investment provisions. Such charges prove doubly hard to rebut when proceedings are shrouded in secrecy. (Only one international arbitration entity even maintains a public registry listing of disputes).

Although the early wave of environment-related investment claims under NAFTA subsided, a new wave appears to be emerging, especially against Canada. Three pending claims challenge Canadian application of environmental law: a U.S. company is making an unfair and discriminatory treatment claim against Nova Scotia and the federal government of Canada in its application of environmental impact assessment requirements to a proposed quarry project (Bilcon v. Canada); another U.S. company is complaining of unfair treatment by Canada in connection with not allowing an orderly phase-out in the use of the pesticide lindane (Chemtura Corp. v. Canada); and a third U.S. company is complaining about legislation in Ontario that it claims specifically rescinds or negates permits for a municipal waste landfill at the site of a former iron mine (Gallo v. Canada).

A. Chapter 11's Origins in BITs

The NAFTA, which is noteworthy as a free trade agreement between developing and developed countries, was also the first free trade agreement among more than two nations to extend the traditional nondiscrimination rules of trade to investments, along with the right for non-State investors to challenge host government actions through binding arbitration. But these NAFTA provisions were not really novel. Rather, the NAFTA, as well as more recent free trade agreements, more or less replicate the provisions for protection of foreign investment of modern Bilateral Investment Treaties ("BITs").

Germany and Pakistan agreed to the first BIT in 1959. In more recent decades, BITs have proliferated rapidly, numbering 2,676 by the end of 2008. UNCTAD, WORLD INVESTMENT REPORT 2009, at 12. BITs are the modern manifestation of concepts first developed for securing more protection for investments in the developing world in post-colonial treaties of amity, commerce, and navigation (or friendship, commerce, and navigation). *See* AARON COSBEY ET AL., INVESTMENT AND SUSTAINABLE DEVELOPMENT: A GUIDE TO THE USE AND POTENTIAL OF INTERNATIONAL INVESTMENT AGREEMENTS 3 (International Institute for Sustainable Development, 2004) [hereinafter *Investment and Sustainable Development*]. In general, BITs are designed to provide greater legal certainty and protection to foreign investors who otherwise may be reluctant to take their chances with being expropriated or left to the vagaries of domestic judicial or administrative remedies in the host country if difficulties arise. Because BITs provide investors with the security they want, they also meet the economic development interests of developing countries seeking to attract foreign investment. For an excellent short summary of the historical and political economic background to BITs, see Nicholas DiMascio and Joost Pauwelyn, *Nondiscrimination in Trade and Investment Treaties: Worlds Apart or Two Sides of the Same Coin?*, 102 Am. J. Int'l L. 48, 51–58 (2008). See also, Catherine Yannaca-Small, OECD, Fair and Equitable Treatment Standard in International Investment Law (Sept. 2004), *available at* http://www.oecd.org/dataoecd/22/53/33776498.pdf.

While the language in BITs varies, almost all contain protection against uncompensated expropriations and discriminatory behavior by the host government; most also guarantee minimum standards of fair treatment for foreign investors and their investments. Should disputes arise, most BITs allow private investors to initiate arbitration proceedings directly against the host government without any obligation to pursue or exhaust domestic legal remedies before tendering claims. The leading arrangements for arbitration rules and services through ad hoc tribunals for each case are two separate facilities under the World Bank's International Center for Settlement of Investment Disputes (ICSID), as well as the 1976 Arbitration Rules of the UN Commission on International Trade Law (UNCITRAL). NAFTA Chapter 11 makes all three systems available.

Due to persistent controversy surrounding the operation of NAFTA's investment provisions, and the fact that NAFTA investment tribunals sometimes look to BITs for interpretive guidance and as potential sources of customary international law, BITs are being scrutinized anew. UNCTAD reports a total of 317 investor-State arbitrations as of 2008, though the number may be higher because UNCITRAL does not maintain a registry of arbitrations under its rules. UNCTAD, World Investment Report 2009, at 12. Only recently have public policy analysts started examining arbitration decisions to evaluate whether these agreements have constrained or "chilled" the ability of governments to enact or enforce environmental law and policies, though such inquiries are made difficult by standard arbitration rules that, unless waived by the parties to a dispute, impose confidentiality restrictions on documents and decisions. For a comprehensive study of UNCITRAL arbitrations, see David D. Caron, Lee M. Caplan & Matti Pellonpää, The UNCITRAL Arbitration Rules: A Commentary (2006).

Howard Mann, *Private Rights, Public Problems: A Guide to NAFTA's Controversial Chapter on Investor Rights*

7–8 (International Institute for Sustainable Development, 2001)

The main precursor to NAFTA was the Canada-United States Free Trade Agreement, concluded in 1988, which contained provisions on investor protection and on investment liberalization. But since both Canada and the United States had similar legal and economic infrastructures, investor protection was not the key issue. Rather, the main U.S. objective—of such importance that it tied inclusion of an investment chapter to the completion of the overall trade agreement—was investment liberalization in Canada. Canada, for its part, wanted to preserve as many of its foreign investment restrictions as it could. At the end of the day, Canada agreed to significantly reduce its barriers to foreign investments, and both Parties agreed to the types of investor protection provisions generally seen in the BITs at that time. However, the Canada-U.S. Agreement did not include a binding dispute settlement mechanism between the foreign investor and the host state.

With this model in hand, the U.S. sought to expand the investment agreement to the trilateral NAFTA. Of greater importance for the U.S. in the NAFTA case, however, was investor protection in Mexico, given that country's shaky record on treatment of foreign investors. The opportunity to increase FDI into Mexico through vigorous investment liberalization provisions remained an important goal as well. Although Mexican domestic law was changing, U.S. investors wanted a broader range of protections and market access that could not be easily reversed by a subsequent administration.

These objectives were largely supported by Canada for its investors as well. On the other hand, Canada hoped the investment chapter would not lead to any further reduction in its foreign investment management regime, in particular in sectors such as culture and natural resources management.

Mexico, for its part, embraced the goal of attracting new foreign investment. Under the Salinas administration, Mexico had been promoting more open markets and an open investment regime. The inclusion of the investment chapter in NAFTA, while originally opposed by Mexico, became seen as a way to "advertise" that the country was indeed a new, safe place to do business. Five and six years later, Mexico became the most steadfast supporter of the NAFTA investment regime, having seen an exponential increase in investments from its NAFTA partners, as well as from European and Japanese investors eager to have better access to the North American market through a low-cost location they now considered "safe."

B. Overview of NAFTA's Chapter 11

Chapter 11 of the NAFTA commits Canada, Mexico and the United States to investment liberalization and the protection of foreign investors and investments. As we will see, Chapter 11 has expansive scope, covering not only "traditional" investments in companies, but also investments in intangible property, loans, and shareholding, among others. Moreover, it covers all "measures ... relating to" investments and investors, including local, municipal, state, and federal laws and administrative actions, with few exceptions.

With respect to liberalizing investment, Chapter 11 requires the Parties, and in most cases their state and local governments, to apply measures relating to foreign investments and investors in a manner consistent with national treatment and MFN obligations. As in BITs, the Parties must also meet minimum standards of fair and equitable treatment and full protection and security. In addition, Chapter 11 requires compensation for direct expropriations, and also for measures "tantamount" to expropriation. In the rest of this section we will be exploring some of the difficult interpretive questions that arise in environment-related investment disputes.

Chapter 11 applies to all measures adopted before and after NAFTA came into effect, unless specifically included in an Annex of exempted measures or exempted as a nonconforming measure in Article 1108. Article 1108 allows state, provincial, and local governments to maintain measures existing on the date NAFTA entered into force that may violate national treatment and MFN obligations, but not those that violate the minimum standard of treatment obligations. Government procurement is also exempted from the national treatment and MFN obligations.

Article 1106(6), which limits performance requirements (such as use of domestic raw materials) for foreign investors, contains a provision very similar to Article XX(b) and (g) of the GATT. Other national measures or actions that might violate MFN, national treatment, or minimum standards of treatment are not subject to general environmental exceptions. Rather, in Article 1114, the governments promise each other not to lower their environmental standards to attract investment, and expressly declare that environmental conditions on investments that are "otherwise consistent" with Chapter 11 are allowed.

Chapter 11 also borrows from the BITs in terms of arbitration procedures. Most prominently, a NAFTA foreign investor has the right to pursue claims against the host country government for any violation of the substantive obligations imposed on the Parties, without pursuing remedies in the domestic courts or administrative bodies where the investment is established. Although at first all such proceedings were officially confidential, the Parties have, through later official actions, substantially increased the transparency of the arbitration process.

As of February 2010, some 60 notices of intent to file claims under NAFTA Chapter 11 are on record. Two claims were settled before arbitration, three were consolidated into a single proceeding, 20 "awards" (as arbitral panel decisions are called) have been rendered on the merits or in other dispositive rulings, another 15 or so disputes are pending, and about 20 claims have not been pursued after the initial notice of intent or filing of the claim. Just five of the final awards have called for compensation by the responding government, one partial award finds responsibility but leaves compensation undecided, and two other claims have resulted in settlements.

Section C below begins with preliminary but very important jurisdictional issues about the scope of Chapter 11. Section D then briefly describes the procedures for Chapter 11 arbitrations and some of the changes to practice to enhance transparency and citizen participation. Finally, in Section E we examine the key substantive provisions and the interpretive questions they have raised.

C. The Scope of Chapter 11

We begin with the language of NAFTA Article 1101 and the definitions related to it. The opening paragraph of the article uses three words or phrases that we take up in the following sections: "investors or investments"; "measures"; and "relating to".

NAFTA Chapter Eleven: Investment

Article 1101: Scope and Coverage

1. This Chapter applies to measures adopted or maintained by a Party relating to:

   (a) investors of another Party;

   (b) investments of investors of another Party in the territory of the Party; and

   (c) with respect to Articles 1106 and 1114, all investments in the territory of the Party.

* * *

Article 1139: Definitions

For purposes of this Chapter: * * *

equity or debt securities includes voting and non-voting shares, bonds, convertible debentures, stock options and warrants; * * *

investment means:

(a) an enterprise;

(b) an equity security of an enterprise;

(c) a debt security of an enterprise

(i) where the enterprise is an affiliate of the investor, or

(ii) where the original maturity of the debt security is at least three years,

but does not include a debt security, regardless of original maturity, of a state enterprise;

(d) a loan to an enterprise

(i) where the enterprise is an affiliate of the investor, or

(ii) where the original maturity of the loan is at least three years, but does not include a loan, regardless of original maturity, to a state enterprise;

(e) an interest in an enterprise that entitles the owner to share in income or profits of the enterprise;

(f) an interest in an enterprise that entitles the owner to share in the assets of that enterprise on dissolution, other than a debt security or a loan excluded from subparagraph (c) or (d);

(g) real estate or other property, tangible or intangible, acquired in the expectation or used for the purpose of economic benefit or other business purposes; and

(h) interests arising from the commitment of capital or other resources in the territory of a Party to economic activity in such territory, such as under

(i) contracts involving the presence of an investor's property in the territory of the Party, including turnkey or construction contracts, or concessions, or

(ii) contracts where remuneration depends substantially on the production, revenues or profits of an enterprise;

but investment does not mean,

(i) claims to money that arise solely from

(i) commercial contracts for the sale of goods or services by a national or enterprise in the territory of a Party to an enterprise in the territory of another Party, or

(ii) the extension of credit in connection with a commercial transaction, such as trade financing, other than a loan covered by subparagraph (d); or

(j) any other claims to money,

that do not involve the kinds of interests set out in subparagraphs (a) through (h);

investment of an investor of a Party means an investment owned or controlled directly or indirectly by an investor of such Party;

investor of a Party means a Party or state enterprise thereof, or a national or an enterprise of such Party, that seeks to make, is making or has made an investment; * * *

---

1. Defining "Investment"

An early NAFTA arbitration tribunal had the occasion to interpret the term "investment" in connection with the trade dispute between Canada and the United States on softwood lumber. Pope & Talbot, a U.S.-based timber producer with investments in Canadian facilities, challenged Canada's implementation of the Softwood Lumber Agreement (SLA) with the United States, one interim resolution of the long-running dispute between the United States and Canada about low-cost Canadian timber sales. Pursuant to the SLA, Canada was required to collect fees from producers of softwood lumber in certain provinces. Canada accordingly established limits on the amount of fee-free softwood lumber manufactured in certain Canadian provinces that could be exported into the United States, but those same limits did not apply to exports from other provinces. Pope & Talbot complained that Canada's export rules impaired the value of its Canadian investments by limiting its fee-free exports to the United States. The tribunal addressed Canada's contention that Pope & Talbot's business interests did not constitute an "investment":

> 97. … Article 1139(g) defines investment to include, among other things, "property, tangible or intangible, acquired in the expectation or used for the purpose of economic benefit or other business purposes."

> 98. While Canada suggests that the ability to sell softwood lumber from British Columbia to the U.S. is an abstraction, it is, in fact, a very important part of the "business" of the Investment. Interference with that business would necessarily have an adverse effect on the property that the Investor had acquired in Canada, which, of course, constitutes the Investment.… [T]he true interests at stake are the Investment's asset base, the value of which is largely dependent on its export business. The Tribunal concludes that the Investor properly asserts that Canada has taken measures affecting its "investment," as the term is defined in Article 1139 and used in Article 1110.

Pope & Talbot v. Canada (Interim Award) (June 26, 2000). A few months later, the *S.D. Myers* tribunal similarly interpreted investment broadly to include an expectation of income or profit. S.D. Myers, Inc. v. Government of Canada (Partial Award), para. 226 (NAFTA Arb. Trib. Nov. 12, 2000), *reprinted in* 40 I.L.M. 1408 (2001).

On the other hand, other arbitration awards make it clear that Chapter 11 does not apply where the claimant has no property or asset or other investment in the responding country. Thus, for example, the tribunal dismissed claims by Texas farmers against Mexico relating to management of water in the Rio Grande on jurisdictional grounds because the Texas claimants had no investments or plans for investments of any kind in Mexico. Bayview Irrigation District v. United Mexican States (Award), para. 122 (June 19, 2007). Lack of investment by claimants in the United States led to dismissal as well in Canadian Cattlemen for Fair Trade v. United States of America (Award on Jurisdiction) (Jan. 28, 2008).

Questions and Discussion

1. Do you find the interpretations from *Pope & Talbot* and *S.D. Myers* overly broad? In *S.D. Myers*, the claimant's investment consisted of a family-owned "company" in Canada for soliciting Canadian customers to use S.D. Myers's U.S. waste management facilities. Does the definition of "investment" in Article 1139 invite such an expansive interpretation?

---

2. Defining "Measure"

Article 1101 states that Chapter 11 applies to "measures adopted or maintained by a Party." The term "measure," as defined for NAFTA in Article 201, means "any law, regulation, procedure, requirement, or practice." In one interesting case, Loewen, a Canadian businessman with investments in Mississippi, claimed unfair and discriminatory treatment by attorneys and the court in violation of Chapter 11 in their conduct during a trial resulting in a US$500 million jury verdict against Loewen's U.S. business. The *Loewen* tribunal award makes it clear that judicial decisions constitute "measures" (though in that circumstance the claimant must have exhausted his or her judicial remedies for modification or reversal of the verdict). Loewen Group, Inc. v. United States of America (Award on Jurisdiction), ICSID Case No. ARB(AF)/98/3 (Jan. 5, 2001).

Given the applicability of most provisions of Chapter 11 to state and local governments, the term "measures" also encompasses state, county, municipal or other actions of a local character, including those taken by local agencies, zoning boards, commissions, and bodies. In essence, Chapter 11's broad application to "measures" makes clear what was already true under international law—that investment protections reach into many aspects of local governance. The problem is that many states, and almost certainly most local governments, are only vaguely, if at all, aware of the nature of the obligations they have to foreign investors, who may in some situations have certain rights or remedies that local investors do not enjoy.

---

3. Defining "Relating to"

Recall that Chapter 11 applies to "measures adopted or maintained by a Party *relating to*" foreign investors or investments. The meaning of "relating to" became a central legal question in the *Methanex* arbitration.

To combat smog, gasoline in California must contain an oxygenate to improve combustion. For many years, MTBE—methyl tertiary-butyl ether—was the standard oxygenate. In the 1990s, MTBE began showing up in California water supplies because of leaks from gasoline storage tanks. In 1997, the California legislature ordered a study, which confirmed the contamination problem and the difficulty of preventing gasoline leakage. Given these findings, the governor, as required by the legislation, issued an executive order directing a rapid phase-out of MTBE use in gasoline. His order was subsequently implemented by California regulations.

Methanex Corporation, a Canadian corporation, is the world's leading manufacturer and distributor of methanol, with distribution and sales operations in the United States. Methanol is an essential ingredient in the manufacture of MTBE. Methanex itself did not manufacture MTBE, but it sold large quantities of methanol to MTBE manufacturers supplying the California market. Methanex initiated investor-State arbitration, seeking US$970 million in lost value for its investments because California's MTBE ban eliminated a major market for the corporation's U.S. sales of methanol.

Before the tribunal could reach the substantive merits of the claim, it needed to determine its jurisdiction, specifically whether California's measure was one "relating to" Methanex's investments in the United States. The following excerpt is from the tribunal's "preliminary award" on jurisdiction, which is a final ruling on the questions decided. One aspect of that question is how regulation of MTBE relates to the production and sale of methanol. But another aspect the tribunal discusses arose from a motion by Methanex to amend its Chapter 11 claim to add a new allegation: that California Governor Gray Davis specifically intended to discriminate against Methanex and benefit a U.S. company, Archers Daniel Midland (ADM). (ADM is the major producer of ethanol, the only significant and approved alternative to MTBE as a gasoline oxygenate.) Methanex wanted a chance to prove that ADM made political contributions to Governor Davis's election campaign in exchange for his efforts to favor ethanol in California.

Methanex v. United States of America
(Preliminary Award on Jurisdiction and Admissibility) (Aug. 7, 2002)

128. The issue that divides the Disputing Parties is whether these US [i.e., California] measures, on the assumed facts, *"relate to"* Methanex because, as recited above, neither measure was expressly directed at methanol, methanol producers or Methanex. Applying the approach described in the previous chapter, it is necessary first to interpret definitively this phrase; and second to determine on the basis of the assumed facts, whether or not any of these measures *"relate to"* Methanex and its investments. * * *

130. *The USA:* In summary, the USA contends that, in the context of Article 1101(1), the phrase "relating to" requires a legally significant connection between the disputed measure and the investor. It argues that measures of general application, especially measures aimed at the protection of human health and the environment (such as those at issue here), are, by their nature, likely to affect a vast range of actors and economic interests. Given their potential effect on enormous numbers of investors and investments, there must be a legally significant connection between the measure and the claimant investor or its investment. It would not be reasonable to infer that the NAFTA Parties intended to subject themselves to arbitration in the absence of any significant connection between the particular measure and the investor or its investments. Otherwise, untold numbers of local, state and federal measures that merely have an incidental impact on an investor or investment might be treated, quite wrongly, as "relating to" that investor or investment.

131. *Methanex:* In summary, Methanex contends that it is sufficient that the measures "affect" the investor or its investment. It argues that the requirement for a legally significant connection between the measure and the investment is not supported by an interpretation of Article 1101(1) or other legal materials. Methanex relies on various dictionary definitions of the phrase, the separate opinion of Dr Schwartz in the *SD Myers* case (paragraphs 49–59 thereof) and the separate opinion of Judge Shahabuddeen in the *Headquarters Agreement* case, which refers in turn to the dissenting opinion of Judge Schwebel in the *Yakimetz* case (where "relating to" is interpreted as meaning "has reference to" or "is con-

nected with"). Methanex also contends that past statements of the USA and Canada support its interpretation and contradict the USA's current submissions. It cites the USA's interpretation of the words "relating to" put forward before the WTO appellate body in *United States Standards for Reformulated and Conventional Gasoline*. There, the phrase "relating to" was interpreted as merely suggesting "any connection or association existing between two things". Methanex also refers to Canada's reformulation of "related to" as "affecting" in its Statement of Implementation of NATFA. * * *

137. For Methanex, the phrase "relating to" should be interpreted in the context of a treaty chapter concerned with the protection of investors; and hence, a broad interpretation is appropriate. Because of its simple application, it is an attractive interpretation; but it is also a brave submission. If the threshold provided by Article 1101(1) were merely one of "affecting," as Methanex contends, it would be satisfied wherever any economic impact was felt by an investor or an investment. For example, in this case, the test could be met by suppliers to Methanex who suffered as a result of Methanex's alleged losses, suppliers to those suppliers and so on, towards infinity. As such, Article 1101(1) would provide no significant threshold to a NAFTA arbitration. A threshold which could be surmounted by an indeterminate class of investors making a claim alleging loss is no threshold at all; and the attractive simplicity of Methanex's interpretation derives from the fact that it imposes no practical limit. It may be true, to adapt Pascal's statement, that the history of the world would have been much affected if Cleopatra's nose had been different, but by itself that cannot mean that we are all related to the royal nose. The Chaos theory provides no guide to the interpretation of this important phrase; and a strong dose of practical common-sense is required.

138. In a legal instrument such as NAFTA, Methanex's interpretation would produce a surprising, if not an absurd, result. The possible consequences of human conduct are infinite, especially when comprising acts of governmental agencies; but common sense does not require that line to run unbroken towards an endless horizon. In a traditional legal context, somewhere the line is broken; and whether as a matter of logic, social policy or other value judgment, a limit is necessarily imposed restricting the consequences for which that conduct is to be held accountable. For example, in the law of tort, there must be a reasonable connection between the defendant, the complainant, the defendant's conduct and the harm suffered by the complainant; and limits are imposed by legal rules on duty, causation and remoteness of damage well-known in the laws of both the United States and Canada. Likewise, in the law of contract, the contract-breaker is not generally liable for all the consequences of its breach even towards the innocent party, still less to persons not privy to that contract. It is of course possible, by contract or statute, to enlarge towards infinity the legal consequences of human conduct; but against this traditional legal background, it would require clear and explicit language to achieve this result.

139. The approach here can be no different. Methanex's interpretation imposes no practical limitation; and an interpretation imposing a limit is required to give effect to the object and purpose of Chapter 11. The alternative interpretation advanced by the USA does impose a reasonable limitation: there must [be] a legally significant connection between the measure and the investor or the investment. With such an interpretation, it is perhaps not easy to define the exact dividing line, just as it is not easy in twilight to see the divide between night and

day. Nonetheless, whilst the exact line may remain undrawn, it should still be possible to determine on which side of the divide a particular claim must lie. * * *

147. **Conclusion:** We decide that the phrase "relating to" in Article 1101(1) NAFTA signifies something more than the mere effect of a measure on an investor or an investment and that it requires a legally significant connection between them, as the USA contends. Pursuant to the rules of interpretation contained in Article 31(1) of the Vienna Convention, we base that decision upon the ordinary meaning of this phrase within its particular context and in the light of the particular object and purpose in NAFTA's Chapter 11. * * *

151. As to Methanex's Amended Statement of Claim, the answer is potentially different. As regards its allegations surrounding the meeting with ADM on 4th August 1998, Methanex contends, as characterised in its Reply Submission of 27th July 2001 (page 9), "*that Gov. Davis intended to benefit the US ethanol industry and to penalise foreign producers of methanol and MTBE.*" Methanex contends that the "relating to" requirement under Article 1101(1) NAFTA is satisfied where harmful intent is alleged by the claimant against the source of the disputed measure.

152. On this point, subject to an important qualification, there was apparently a measure of common ground between the Disputing Parties. At the jurisdictional hearing of July 2001, the USA accepted with regard to Article 1101 that: "*If the purpose of the measure is an intent to harm foreign owned investors or investments on the basis of nationality, then the measure relates to the foreign-owned investor or investment.*" That qualification relates to the credibility of Methanex's allegations concerning the intent underlying the US measures, to which we turn below. * * *

157. . . . Methanex also alleges that . . . methanol and Methanex were "foreign" in California; and this, it is suggested, explains why anti-foreigner action could be taken against methanol in California which on its face would appear to hurt US producers of methanol. In short, it is contended, as regards Governor Davis, that his constituency was the State of California; a "foreign" product was a product foreign to California, which to him, as influenced by ADM, signified methanol produced by Methanex, a "foreign" product produced by "foreigners"; and his intent was to harm Methanex.

158. In these circumstances, we do not consider the case clear enough to determine whether or not Methanex's allegations based on "intent" are sufficiently credible. Accordingly, it is not possible for us to decide, at this stage, that any measure does or does not relate to Methanex or its investments. In particular, decrees and regulations may be the product of compromises and the balancing of competing interests by a variety of political actors. As a result, it may be difficult to identify a single or predominant purpose underlying a particular measure. Where a single governmental actor is motivated by an improper purpose, it does not necessarily follow that the motive can be attributed to the entire government. Much if not all will depend on the evidential materials adduced in the particular case.

[After lengthy additional proceedings on the "intent" evidence, the tribunal's final award found that Methanex had not established intent to discriminate by the California legislature or the governor. It therefore concluded that there were no violations of national treatment or minimum standards of treatment, and

dismissed the Methanex claim in its entirety. The final award also makes fascinating and instructive reading about how lawyers should, and should not, conduct themselves. The tribunal was clearly displeased with the conduct of Methanex
and its attorneys and assigned all costs of the arbitration to Methanex. Methanex
Corporation v. The United States of America (Final Award) (August 9, 2005),
http://naftaclaims.com.]

Questions and Discussion

1. Are you persuaded by the tribunal's distinction between "affected by" and "relating
to"? In particular, does the phrase "relating to" really have different meanings in different international agreements? Recall that Article XX(g) of the GATT allows an exception
to GATT rules for trade restrictions "relating to" the conservation of exhaustible natural
resources. In *Reformulated Gasoline* and *Shrimp/Turtle*, the Appellate Body looked for a
"substantial relationship" between the trade measure and the conservation of an exhaustible natural resource and asked whether there was a "close and genuine relationship
of ends and means." Should this WTO interpretation inform legal understanding of the
relationship between a measure and an investment or investor for Chapter 11 purposes?
Methanex raised just this question; here is the tribunal's response:

> 144. As to past contentions of the USA, Methanex relies on an interpretation of
> "relating to" advanced before the WTO Appellate Body in *United States Stan-*
> *dards for Reformulated and Conventional Gasoline*, to the effect that "relating to"
> signifies "any connection or association existing between two things". In the Tri-
> bunal's view, this is again of only marginal assistance to Methanex.

> 145. The USA's interpretation was there made in a "normal context"; whereas in
> the context of the specific provision (Article XX(g) of the General Agreement),
> its position was as follows:

>> The phrase "relating to conservation", interpreted in its context and in light
>> of the purpose of the General Agreement, means that the measure being
>> examined has a connection to conservation that is not incidental or tan-
>> gential, but that does not have to be "necessary" or "essential" ...

> The "normal context" interpretation does not appear materially different from
> the dictionary definitions; and the interpretation actually relied on by the USA
> is evidently specific to the particular context. This demonstrates the importance
> attributed by the USA to interpreting a term in its particular context and in the
> light of an instrument's object and purpose, an approach consistent with the
> USA's submissions in the present case. In the event, the WTO Appellate Body
> decided that Article XX(g) of the General Agreement required that a measure
> had to be "primarily related to conservation". That its interpretation in this re-
> spect was quite different from the interpretation in the *Pope & Talbot* case again
> confirms the need to interpret a term in accordance with the particular context,
> object and purpose.

Methanex v. United States of America (Preliminary Award on Jurisdiction and Admissibility), 69 (Aug. 7, 2002).

2. In connection with whether WTO jurisprudence should inform interpretation of
investment provisions of Chapter 11 and investment treaties, DiMascio and Pauwelyn

explain and analyze the different approaches to "national treatment" in the GATT trade context and the investment context. Nicholas DiMascio and Joost Pauwelyn, *Nondiscrimination in Trade and Investment Treaties: Worlds Apart or Two Sides of the Same Coin?*, 102 Am. J. Int'l L. 48 (2008).

3. The *Methanex* tribunal accepted that discriminatory intent alone might supply the necessary "legally significant connection" between a measure taken by a State and the investment or investor. Now comes the hard part. NAFTA tribunals have no power to subpoena documents or compel discovery, though tribunal members can, and sometimes do, draw negative inferences where a party fails to provide evidence supporting its claims and arguments. Methanex sought the assistance of the U.S. federal courts to conduct discovery into the "intent" of the measures taken by California. Can you see where this is leading? How does one ascribe "primary" intent to decisions which may be sustained as a legitimate exercise of government power but which also evince discriminatory intent?

D. The Procedural Requirements

1. The Investor-State Process

To initiate a claim, an investor must submit a notice of intent to submit a claim to arbitration at least 90 days before submitting the claim. The notice must provide the basis for the investor's claims as well as choose one of the three arbitral processes available under Chapter 11: 1) the rules of the ICSID Convention (if both the disputing (challenged) Party and the Party of the investor are parties to the Convention); 2) the Additional Facility Rules of ICSID (if either the disputing Party or the Party of the investor, but not both, is a party to the ICSID Convention); or 3) UNCITRAL rules. Because neither Canada nor Mexico is a party to the ICSID, investors may not use the rules of ICSID in claims against Canada or Mexico, and the Additional Facility Rules of ICSID are available only if the claimant is a U.S. investor or the United States is the challenged government.

During the 90-day period, the disputing parties should attempt to resolve their dispute through consultation and negotiation. Assuming no such resolution, an investor may submit its claim to arbitration any time thereafter, subject to a statute of limitations clause that the investor must submit its claim to arbitration within three years from the date on which it first acquired knowledge, or should have first acquired knowledge, "of the alleged breach and knowledge that the enterprise has incurred loss or damage."

NAFTA stipulates that three arbitrators will hear the dispute. Each disputing party appoints one arbitrator; the disputing parties must agree on the third arbitrator or the ICSID Secretary General chooses the third from the ICSID Panel of Arbitrators. In either case, this third panelist will be the presiding arbitrator. Although many panelists have commercial law or trade law backgrounds and experience, prominent international lawyers and international law scholars have also been appointed.

If the arbitral tribunal's award concludes that a Party has not complied with one or more of the substantive rules of Chapter 11, the tribunal may grant monetary damages with interest or restitution of property. Each Party must provide for the enforcement of the award within its territory; if a Party fails to make payment, the investor may ask its government to compel payment through NAFTA's Free Trade Commission. The investor may also choose to enforce the judgment under international arbitration rules.

ICSID and UNCITRAL rules do not provide for appeals. However, many jurisdictions allow appeals of arbitral decisions before that jurisdiction's courts, provided the arbitration took place there. Thus, the choice of the locus of the arbitration by the disputing parties will determine the forum of any appeal (although the proceedings before the arbitral tribunal do not necessarily have to occur at that location). Any such judicial review is limited, however, to a determination of whether the arbitral tribunal exceeded its jurisdiction. Among the environment-related arbitrations, Mexico appealed the *Metalclad* award to a British Columbia court and Canada appealed the *S.D. Myers* award to the Ontario courts.

In many other respects, UNCITRAL and ICSID operate in a considerably different manner. UNCITRAL consists of a body of rules designed for commercial disputes between private parties. There is no supervisory institution, nor is there a specific location where arbitrations are held. This makes it "particularly elusive for analysts who seek to monitor investor-State disputes." AARON COSBEY ET AL., INVESTMENT AND SUSTAINABLE DEVELOPMENT, at 4. In contrast, ICSID was established as part of the World Bank Group in 1965 to handle investor-state disputes, and maintains a registry of arbitrations under its auspices. As of early 2010, 155 nations have acceded to the ICSID, and its docket has grown steadily in recent years, with 184 cases concluded and 127 pending as of March 2010. *See* http://icsid.worldbank.org.

2. The Investor-State-Citizen Process?

Both ICSID and UNCITRAL lack the transparency and openness features of many of the world's judicial systems—a fact which some countries have sought to remedy in the most recent generation of trade and investment agreements. The NAFTA governments recognized early on that the formal confidentiality of commercial arbitrations and the public controversy surrounding early environment-related disputes under Chapter 11 was creating a crisis of legitimacy. Following a meeting of the three trade ministers, formally constituted as the NAFTA Free Trade Commission (FTC), they issued "Notes of Interpretation of Certain Chapter 11 Provisions" addressing some of the transparency issues. Stating that, with limited exceptions, nothing in NAFTA requires confidentiality or prevents public release of documents in an arbitration, the Parties committed to making publicly available "all documents submitted to, or issued by, a Chapter Eleven tribunal." Confidentiality is retained only for confidential business information, legally privileged information, and other information that the Parties must withhold pursuant to arbitral rules. NAFTA Free Trade Commission, *Notes of Interpretation of Certain Chapter 11 Provisions* (July 31, 2001). In terms of practical access to legal documents in the arbitrations, an American lawyer established and has maintained a website where all the Chapter 11 arbitration documents are posted and available for download, in redacted versions when appropriate. *See* http://www.naftaclaims.com

Another issue of keen interest to environmental NGOs was establishing a right to submit *amicus* briefs to tribunals. In *Methanex*, several organizations, led by the International Institute for Sustainable Development, requested permission to submit an *amicus curiae* brief, to obtain documents generated by the arbitration, and to observe the proceedings. As might be expected, Methanex argued that UNCITRAL rules, under which this dispute was brought, did not provide for submissions by public interest groups or otherwise allow citizens to participate in the arbitration. Moreover, it argued that Article

1128 of the NAFTA adequately protected the public interest; if citizens wanted to address the arbitral tribunal, they could do so by convincing their government to include their arguments in its brief. Mexico filed a third party submission claiming that the tribunal had no authority to allow the participation of citizens in any form, because Chapter 11 only provides for the involvement of the Parties and the investor alleging an infringement of its rights (Mexican courts do not accept *amicus* briefs). Canada urged the disclosure of submissions and decisions. It was unwilling to give general support for *amicus* briefs, but stated that it could support them in this case. The United States argued that neither the UNCITRAL rules nor the NAFTA prohibited the tribunal from accepting *amicus* briefs, so the tribunal had the discretion to accept them. The tribunal adopted the U.S. view. Given confidentiality concerns, however, it ruled that it had no power to receive requests from citizens for documents generated by the arbitration or to allow citizens to observe the proceedings. (The United States had consented to oral hearings, but Methanex had not.) Methanex v. United States of America (Decision on Authority to Accept Amicus Submissions), (Jan. 15, 2001).

In light of the tribunal's conclusions in *Methanex* and the efforts of environmental and other groups, the NAFTA FTC issued a nonbinding document stating that no provision of the NAFTA limits a tribunal's discretion to accept written submissions from a person or entity that is not directly involved in the dispute (a "non-disputing party"). It then recommended that the "Chapter 11 Tribunals" adopt procedures to allow non-disputing parties to submit written *amicus* briefs. The FTC recommended a two-document process. First, *amici* would submit an application of no longer than five pages for leave to file a brief, explaining why the tribunal should accept the submission. If the tribunal granted the leave, the brief itself could be no longer than 20 pages, including any appendices. The FTC also proposed guidelines for a tribunal to follow when determining whether to grant a request to submit an *amicus* brief.

Statement of the Free Trade Commission on Non-Disputing Party Participation
(Oct. 7, 2003)

6. In determining whether to grant leave to file a non-disputing party submission, the Tribunal will consider, among other things, the extent to which:

(a) the non-disputing party submission would assist the Tribunal in the determination of a factual or legal issue related to the arbitration by bringing a perspective, particular knowledge or insight that is different from that of the disputing parties;

(b) the non-disputing party submission would address matters within the scope of the dispute;

(c) the non-disputing party has a significant interest in the arbitration; and

(d) there is a public interest in the subject-matter of the arbitration.

7. The Tribunal will ensure that:

(a) any non-disputing party submission avoids disrupting the proceedings; and

(b) neither disputing party is unduly burdened or unfairly prejudiced by such submissions.

8. The Tribunal will render a decision on whether to grant leave to file a non-disputing party submission. If leave to file a non-disputing party submission is

granted, the Tribunal will set an appropriate date for the disputing parties to respond in writing to the non-disputing party submission. By that date, non-disputing Parties may, pursuant to Article 1128, address any issues of interpretation of the Agreement presented in the non-disputing party submission.

9. The granting of leave to file a non-disputing party submission does not require the Tribunal to address that submission at any point in the arbitration. The granting of leave to file a non-disputing party submission does not entitle the non-disputing party that filed the submission to make further submissions in the arbitration.

10. Access to documents by non-disputing parties that file applications under these procedures will be governed by the FTC's Note of July 31, 2001.

The *Methanex* Tribunal then adopted procedures consistent with the FTC's statement, with the proviso that disputing parties could respond to any claims made by Mexico and Canada and that *amici* identify any groups that have collaborated in the preparation of their brief. ICSID News Release, Methanex v. United States of America (NAFTA/UNCITRAL Arbitration Rules Proceeding), (Jan. 30, 2004). In June 2004, the Tribunal held public hearings in the *Methanex* case.

In the more recent *Glamis Gold* dispute, another claim by a Canadian corporation (a mining concern) protesting U.S. and California regulatory decisions, the tribunal also accepted *amicus* briefs in line with the FTC statement. The tribunal had this to say about the role of such *amicus* briefs in its deliberations:

[I]nasmuch as the State Parties to the NAFTA have agreed to allow *amicus* filings in certain circumstances, it is the Tribunal's view that it should address those filings explicitly in its Award to the degree that they bear on decisions that must be taken. In this case, the Tribunal appreciates the thoughtful submissions made by a varied group of interested non-parties who, in all circumstances, acted with the utmost respect for the proceedings and the Parties. Given the Tribunal's holdings, however, the Tribunal does not reach the particular issues addressed by these submissions.

Glamis Gold, Ltd. v. United States of America (Final Award), para. 8 (ICSID Tribunal June 8, 2009).

A final aspect of public access to the arbitration process is the right of non-participant citizens to observe the proceedings before the tribunals. Beginning with *Methanex*, many tribunals have, with the consent of the parties in each case, exercised their discretion to allow closed-circuit telecast of the proceedings to a nearby location where the public can observe.

E. Chapter 11's Substantive Requirements

1. Overview

Chapter 11 includes several substantive obligations intended to liberalize investment opportunities, and others to protect investors from improper action by the host government. Two obligations—national treatment (Article 1102) and most favored nation treatment (Article 1103)—derive from the GATT, although the language has been modified slightly for the investment context. As discussed below, these national treatment and most favored nation requirements transform GATT's "like product" analysis into a more contextual "like circumstances" analysis.

Foreign investors must also be accorded the "minimum standard of treatment," an international law norm defined in Chapter 11 as "treatment in accordance with international law, including fair and equitable treatment." That is to say, treating foreign investors no less favorably than domestic investors may not be good enough if the domestic procedures were to fall below minimum levels required by international law. The proper meaning of this norm has been the subject of controversy in multiple Chapter 11 disputes, prompting an interpretive clarification by the three governments acting as the NAFTA Free Trade Commission.

Finally, Article 1110 addresses expropriation and measures "tantamount" to expropriation. Prohibitions on direct expropriations are no stranger to international law, but the state of the law surrounding indirect expropriations through regulation is another matter. In the material that follows, consider how well the NAFTA parties have addressed often-voiced concerns that differences between national constitutional law on regulatory takings and the NAFTA counterpart may chill environmental regulation or result in foreigners or their investments receiving better treatment than domestic investors.

NAFTA Chapter Eleven: Investment

Article 1102: National Treatment

1. Each Party shall accord to investors of another Party treatment no less favorable than that it accords, in like circumstances, to its own investors with respect to the establishment, acquisition, expansion, management, conduct, operation, and sale or other disposition of investments.

2. Each Party shall accord to investments of investors of another Party treatment no less favorable than that it accords, in like circumstances, to investments of its own investors with respect to the establishment, acquisition, expansion, management, conduct, operation, and sale or other disposition of investments....

3. The treatment accorded by a Party under paragraphs 1 and 2 means, with respect to a state or province, treatment no less favorable than the most favorable treatment accorded, in like circumstances, by such state or province to investors, and to investments of investors, of the Party of which it forms a part.

Article 1103: Most-Favored-Nation Treatment

1. Each Party shall accord to investors of another Party treatment no less favorable than that it accords, in like circumstances, to investors of any other Party or of a non-Party with respect to the establishment, acquisition, expansion, management, conduct, operation, and sale or other disposition of investments.

2. Each Party shall accord to investments of investors of another Party treatment no less favorable than that it accords, in like circumstances, to investments of investors of any other Party or of a non-Party with respect to the establishment, acquisition, expansion, management, conduct, operation, and sale or other disposition of investments.

Article 1104: Standard of Treatment

Each Party shall accord to investors of another Party and to investments of investors of another Party the better of the treatment required by Articles 1102 and 1103.

Article 1105: Minimum Standard of Treatment

1. Each Party shall accord to investments of investors of another Party treatment in accordance with international law, including fair and equitable treatment and full protection and security. * * *

Article 1110: Expropriation and Compensation

1. No Party may directly or indirectly nationalize or expropriate an investment of an investor of another Party in its territory or take a measure tantamount to nationalization or expropriation of such an investment ("expropriation"), except:

  (a) for a public purpose;

  (b) on a non-discriminatory basis;

  (c) in accordance with due process of law and Article 1105(1); and

  (d) on payment of compensation in accordance with paragraphs 2 through 6.

2. Compensation shall be equivalent to the fair market value of the expropriated investment immediately before the expropriation took place ("date of expropriation"), and shall not reflect any change in value occurring because the intended expropriation had become known earlier. Valuation criteria shall include going concern value, asset value including declared tax value of tangible property, and other criteria, as appropriate, to determine fair market value.

3. Compensation shall be paid without delay and be fully realizable.

---

2. National Treatment

The national treatment obligation is a standard feature of investment treaties. Like its GATT counterpart, how the national treatment obligation applies in the investment context depends on the "likeness" of the domestic and foreign firms and whether the treatment accorded the foreign firm is in some meaningful way less favorable. The counterpart to "like products" under GATT Article III is "like circumstances" under NAFTA Article 1102. The excerpts from tribunal reports focus on the proper interpretation of "like circumstances."

a. The Ethyl Claim

The ramifications of Article 1102 for environmental measures were not evident until the U.S.-based Ethyl Corporation initiated a Chapter 11 claim challenging Canada's ban on the importation of the gasoline additive methylcyclopentadienyl manganese tricarbonyl (MMT), which enhances octane and reduces engine "knocking."

The possible health risks associated with the use of MMT are disputed, to say the least. The U.S. Environmental Protection Agency (EPA) at one time prohibited MMT because it believed it interfered with catalytic converters, but withdrew that regulation when such interference was disproven. EPA also investigated regulation of MMT on public health grounds under the Clean Air Act, but eventually decided it lacked sufficient scientific evidence for health-based regulation. After their own studies, Canadian agencies (Health Canada and Environment Canada) reached similar conclusions about the insufficiency of evidence of health effects from the use of MMT in gasoline to support health-based regulation of this product.

Nevertheless, at the behest of the Canada's Minister for Environment, the Canadian Parliament enacted a ban the importation or inter-provincial sale of MMT, though it remained legal to produce and market MMT entirely within a single province. Because Ethyl Corporation was the sole supplier of MMT to Canadian gasoline refiners and because the gasoline market required inter-provincial movement of the product, Parliament's legislation effectively locked Ethyl out of the Canadian market for what remained, in principle, a legal product. Ethyl initiated a Chapter 11 claim, alleging that the import ban violated Canada's national treatment obligation and expropriated Ethyl's investment in its Canadian sales and distribution infrastructure.

Ethyl did not stand alone in litigating against Parliament's enactment. The provinces of Alberta, Québec, Nova Scotia, and Saskatchewan challenged the ban on inter-provincial trade in MMT as a violation of Canada's Agreement on Internal Trade (AIT), an agreement between the provinces and the federal government. As discussed more fully in Chapter 4 at pages 267–272, the AIT panel found that the trade ban was not justified, in part because MMT could be produced and used within each province and in part because there was insufficient evidence of any health risk to justify the measure. Canada's own AIT panel concluded that the federal government had not demonstrated that "there existed a matter of such urgency or a risk so widespread as to warrant such comprehensive restrictions...." Report of the Article 1704 Panel concerning a Dispute between Alberta and Canada regarding the Manganese-Based Fuel Additives Act, File No. 97/98-15-MMT-P058 (June 12, 1998). After losing the domestic case with the provinces, Canada settled Ethyl's NAFTA claim, paying about US$13 million.

b. S.D. Myers

In the wake of the Ethyl settlement, another U.S. company, S.D. Myers, Incorporated, invoked national treatment in challenging a newly-imposed Canadian ban on the export of polychlorinated biphenyls (PCBs). Again, the facts are quite convoluted. S.D. Myers Incorporated (SDMI) reclaims oil and equipment from waste, including old electrical transformers containing PCBs, and destroys the PCBs through high-temperature incineration at its facility in Ohio prior to disposal of any remaining material. SDMI's facility has served well in the destruction of U.S. PCB wastes. At the time of this dispute, Canada had a large volume of PCB-contaminated electrical equipment to dispose of, most of it located in eastern Canada. SDMI created Myers Canada to arrange contracts for disposal of these PCB wastes by exporting them to SDMI's incineration facility, just 100 miles south of Canadian border in Ohio. SDMI recognized that it had significant cost advantages over its one Canadian competitor, Chem-Security, whose incinerator was in northern Alberta, well over 1000 miles from where most of Canada's PCB-contaminated equipment was stored.

The tricky part for SDMI's business plan was arranging for the transboundary movement of the PCB wastes. The Basel Convention on the Control of Transboundary Movements of Hazardous Wastes and Their Disposal requires Parties to dispose of hazardous waste in an environmentally sound manner and encourages Parties to dispose their own hazardous waste rather than exporting it to other countries. After joining the Basel Convention, Canadian federal and provincial authorities agreed that PCBs of Canadian origin should be destroyed in Canada to the maximum extent possible. Canada prohibited the *export* of PCBs starting in 1990 to all countries *other than* the United States, with which it had a separate bilateral agreement on hazardous waste. Even before the Basel Convention, the United States had banned production of PCBs and both the export and import of PCBs under the Toxic Substances Control Act.

To enter the Canadian PCB disposal business, SDMI lobbied the U.S. EPA to open the U.S. border to PCB imports for the specific purpose of destruction and disposal. Meanwhile, however, the Canadian firm Chem-Security was having business and operational problems, and Canadian political leaders were more concerned than ever with keeping the company operating. In July 1995, Canada's Minister for the Environment stated: "It is still the position of the government that the handling of PCBs should be done in Canada by Canadians." In October 1995, the U.S. EPA issued an "enforcement discretion" letter to SDMI, which allowed it to import PCBs from Canada for incineration and final disposal from November 15, 1995 to December 31, 1997. The very next day, November 16, 1995, Canada's Minister for the Environment issued an Interim Order banning exports of PCBs to the United States; the Order became final on February 26, 1996.

Canada maintained the ban on PCB exports to the United States from November 20, 1995 to February 1997, a period of 16 months, when it rescinded the Order. But in July 1997, under order of a U.S. court, EPA withdrew its "enforcement discretion," again closing the border to imports of PCBs. Thus, SDMI was able to import PCBs from Canada only for the five-month period between February and July 1997. SDMI brought a Chapter 11 claim against Canada, alleging that Canada had not provided it national treatment because the domestic firm Chem-Security was allowed to operate its PCB remediation facilities in Alberta throughout the period of the export ban. SDMI also claimed that Canada's actions violated the minimum standard of treatment provisions of Article 1105.

The NAFTA arbitral tribunal first concluded that the Canadian ban on PCB exports favored Canadian nationals over non-nationals and that "the practical effect of the [ban] was that SDMI and its investment were prevented from carrying out the business they planned to undertake, which was a clear disadvantage in comparison to its Canadian competitors." S.D. Myers and Canada (Partial Award), para. 193, (Nov. 13, 2000). It also concluded that, notwithstanding Canada's adherence to the Basel Convention, "there was no legitimate environmental reason for introducing the ban." *Id.* at para. 195. It based that conclusion in part on evidence of the advice given to the Minister for the Environment by her staff stating that Canada had consistently expressed the view that the Basel Convention did not bar waste exports when those exports would facilitate environmentally sound disposal.

In addition, although members of the Myers family owned Myers Canada in their individual capacities, the tribunal concluded that SDMI could bring this claim because SDMI — which is also owned by members of the Myers family — indirectly controlled Myers Canada. The tribunal concluded that SDMI was an "investor" and Myers Canada constituted an "investment" under Article 1139 of the NAFTA. *Id.* at para. 231. These underlying conclusions provide the bases for the Tribunal's legal findings relating to national treatment and minimum treatment.

S.D. Myers, Inc. v. Government of Canada

(Partial Award), (Nov. 13, 2000)

"Like Circumstances"

243. Articles 1102(1) and 1102(2) refer to treatment that is accorded to a Party's own nationals "in like circumstances." The phrase "like circumstances" is open to a wide variety of interpretations in the abstract and in the context of a particular dispute.

244. WTO dispute resolution panels, and its appellate body, frequently have been required to apply the concept of "like products." The case law has emphasized

that the interpretation of "like" must depend on all the circumstances of each case. The case law also suggests that close attention must be paid to the legal context in which the word "like" appears; the same word "like" may have different meanings in different provisions of the GATT. In *Japan-Alcoholic Beverages*, WT/DS38/ABlR, the Appellate Body stated at paragraphs 8.5 and 8.6:

> [the interpretation and application of "like"] is a discretionary decision that must be made in considering the various characteristics of products in individual cases. No one approach to exercising judgment will be appropriate for all cases. The criteria in [an earlier case], Border Tax Adjustments[,] should be examined, but there can be no one precise and absolute definition of what is "like." The concept of "likeness" is a relative one that evokes the image of an accordion. The accordion of "likeness" stretches and squeezes in different places as different provisions of the WTO Agreement are applied. The width of the accordion in any one of those places must be determined by the particular provision in which the term "like" is encountered as well as by the context and the circumstances that prevail in any given case to which the provisions may apply.

245. In considering the meaning of "like circumstances" under Article 1102 of the NAFTA, it is similarly necessary to keep in mind the overall legal context in which the phrase appears.

246. In the GATT context, a *prima facie* finding of discrimination in "like" cases often takes place within the overall GATT framework, which includes Article XX (General Exceptions). A finding of "likeness" does not dispose of the case. It may set the stage for an inquiry into whether the different treatment of situations found to be "like" is justified by legitimate public policy measures that are pursued in a reasonable manner.

247. The Tribunal considers that the legal context of Article 1102 includes the various provisions of the NAFTA, its companion agreement the NAAEC [the North American Agreement on Environmental Cooperation, otherwise known as the NAFTA environmental side agreement] and principles that are affirmed by the NAAEC (including those of the Rio Declaration). The principles that emerge from that context, to repeat, are as follows:

• states have the right to establish high levels of environmental protection. They are not obliged to compromise their standards merely to satisfy the political or economic interests of other states;

• states should avoid creating distortions to trade;

• environmental protection and economic development can and should be mutually supportive.

248. As SDMI noted in its Memorial, all three NAFTA partners belong to the OECD [the Organisation for Economic Cooperation and Development]. OECD practice suggests that an evaluation of "like situations" in the investment context should take into account policy objectives in determining whether enterprises are in like circumstances. The OECD Declaration on International and Multinational Enterprises, issued on June 21, 1976, states that investors and investments should receive treatment that is no less favorable than that accorded in like situations to domestic enterprises. In 1993 the OECD reviewed the "like situation" test in the following terms:

As regards the expression 'in like situations,' the comparison between foreign-controlled enterprises is only valid if it is made between firms operating in the same sector. More general considerations, such as the policy objectives of Member countries could be taken into account to define the circumstances in which comparison between foreign-controlled and domestic enterprises is permissible inasmuch as those objectives are not contrary to the principle of national treatment.

* * *

250. The Tribunal considers that the interpretation of the phrase "like circumstances" in Article 1102 must take into account the general principles that emerge from the legal context of the NAFTA, including both its concern with the environment and the need to avoid trade distortions that are not justified by environmental concerns. The assessment of "like circumstances" must also take into account circumstances that would justify governmental regulations that treat them differently in order to protect the public interest. The concept of "like circumstances" invites an examination of whether a non-national investor complaining of less favourable treatment is in the same "sector" as the national investor. The Tribunal takes the view that the word "sector" has a wide connotation that includes the concepts of "economic sector" and "business sector."

251. From the business perspective, it is clear that SDMI and Myers Canada were in "like circumstances" with Canadian operators such as Chem-Security and Cintec. They all were engaged in providing PCB waste remediation services. SDMI was in a position to attract customers that might otherwise have gone to the Canadian operators because it could offer more favourable prices and because it had extensive experience and credibility. It was precisely because SDMI was in a position to take business away from its Canadian competitors that Chem-Security and Cintec lobbied the Minister of the Environment to ban exports when the U.S. authorities opened the border.

National treatment and protectionist motive or intent

252. The Tribunal takes the view that, in assessing whether a measure is contrary to a national treatment norm, the following factors should be taken into account:

 • whether the practical effect of the measure is to create a disproportionate benefit for nationals over non-nationals;

 • whether the measure, on its face, appears to favour its nationals over non-nationals who are protected by the relevant treaty.

253. Each of these factors must be explored in the context of all the facts to determine whether there actually has been a denial of national treatment.

254. Intent is important, but protectionist intent is not necessarily decisive on its own. The existence of an intent to favour nationals over non-nationals would not give rise to a breach of Chapter 1102 of the NAFTA if the measure in question were to produced [sic] no adverse effect on the non-national complainant. The word "treatment" suggests that practical impact is required to produce a breach of Article 1102, not merely a motive or intent that is in violation of Chapter 11.

255. CANADA was concerned to ensure the economic strength of the Canadian industry, in part, because it wanted to maintain the ability to process PCBs within

Canada in the future. This was a legitimate goal, consistent with the policy objectives of the Basel Convention. There were a number of legitimate ways by which CANADA could have achieved it, but preventing SDMI from exporting PCBs for processing in the USA by the use of the Interim Order and the Final Order was not one of them. The indirect motive was understandable, but the method contravened CANADA's international commitments under the NAFTA. CANADA's right to source all government requirements and to grant subsidies to the Canadian industry are but two examples of legitimate alternative measures. The fact that the matter was addressed subsequently and the border reopened also shows that CANADA was not constrained in its ability to deal effectively with the situation.

256. The Tribunal concludes that the issuance of the Interim Order and the Final Order was a breach of Article 1102 of the NAFTA. * * *

[The Tribunal awarded SDMI CAN$350,000 plus CAN$500,000 in legal fees. S.D. Myers v. Canada (Final Award), paras. 29, 49 (Dec. 30, 2002).]

----

c. Pope & Talbot

While the *S.D.Myers* arbitration was still in process, another arbitration claim against Canada was initiated by a U.S. lumber company caught up in the maneuverings between the United States and Canada over the production and export from Canada to the United States of large amounts of the softwood lumber that is the staple of U.S. homebuilding.

The United States contended that low Canadian stumpage fees—licensing fees for access to timber—constituted a subsidy and had threatened to impose countervailing duties on imports of Canadian softwood lumber (it later did). The United States and Canada partially settled this dispute through the Softwood Lumber Agreement (SLA), which required Canada to set fees for exporting softwood lumber. The SLA, however, exempted certain provinces from those export fees. It also imposed higher fees on wood harvested from coastal forests than from interior forests. Pope & Talbot, a U.S.-owned company, operated in British Columbia where export fees and export restrictions applied. Pope & Talbot maintained that Canada violated the national treatment obligation by treating investors in non-covered provinces differently from investors, including foreign investors, in provinces covered by the SLA's export fees and export restrictions. Pope & Talbot specifically argued that it was in "like circumstances" to producers in other provinces that were not subject to quotas.

Pope & Talbot v. Canada
(Award on the Merits of Phase 2), (Apr. 10, 2001)

78. In evaluating the implications of the legal context, the Tribunal believes that, as a first step, the treatment accorded a foreign owned investment by Article 1102(2) should be compared with that accorded domestic investments in the same business or economic sector. However, that first step is not the last one. Differences in treatment will presumptively violate Article 1102(2), unless they have a reasonable nexus to rational government policies that (1) do not distinguish, on their face or *de facto*, between foreign-owned and domestic companies, and (2) do not otherwise unduly undermine the investment liberalizing objectives of NAFTA.

79. In one respect, this approach echoes the suggestion by Canada that Article 1102 prohibits treatment that discriminates on the basis of the foreign investment's nationality. The other NAFTA Parties have taken the same position. However, the Tribunal believes that the approach proposed by the NAFTA Parties would tend to excuse discrimination that is not facially directed at foreign owned investments. A formulation focusing on the like circumstances question, on the other hand, will require addressing *any* difference in treatment, demanding that it be justified by showing that it bears a reasonable relationship to rational policies not motivated by preference of domestic over foreign owned investments. That is, once a difference in treatment between a domestic and a foreign-owned investment is discerned, the question becomes, are they in like circumstances? It is in answering that question that the issue of discrimination may arise.

80. For its part, the Investor raises another important question relating to the legal context of the measures to be evaluated:

> If the measure is applied in a manner that has the effect of providing a less satisfactory competitive position to the foreign company, can the state applying the measure use the very same elements of the measure that leads to the discriminatory treatment in question to justify why the competitors are actually not in "like circumstances"? The answer must be no. Otherwise a state could merely manipulate the definition of what is a "like investment" through the design of the measure itself. National treatment would be rendered meaningless as a principle.

81. In other words, does NAFTA permit the Parties to reach an agreement that is not a "measure" under Chapter 11, and then permit one of those Parties to use the substance of that agreement to create an unchallengeable basis for discrimination? The Tribunal believes that if the situation were to arise, it could be evaluated as stated above, i.e., whether there is a reasonable nexus between the measure and a rational, non-discriminatory government policy, whether those policies are embodied in statute, regulation or international agreement.

[The Tribunal then found that implementing the SLA in this way was "reasonably related to the rational policy of removing the threat of [countervailing duty] actions" by the United States, so producers of softwood lumber in provinces not covered by the SLA were *not* in "like circumstances" with producers in covered provinces. *Id*. at para. 88. The Tribunal also found that British Columbia's implementation of the SLA, which imposed higher fees on wood harvested from coastal forests than from interior forests, did not violate Article 1102's national treatment obligation, because those producers from coastal and interior forests were not in "like circumstances." The Tribunal concluded that the "settlement undoubtedly had a greater adverse effect on some producers than others, but there is no convincing evidence that it was based on any distinction between foreign-owned and Canadian owned companies." *Id*. at para. 103.]

Questions and Discussion

1. *National Treatment.* Compare the two tribunals' interpretations of the national treatment obligation. Does the *S.D. Myers* tribunal confuse *de facto* discrimination with an ef-

fects-based inquiry into discrimination? Or are discriminatory effects within the range of factors to be considered for determination of *de facto* discrimination? Does the *Pope & Talbot* Tribunal come to a different conclusion about what constitutes less favorable treatment under Article 1102?

2. The *S.D. Myers* decision also states that the actual impact of the regulation will have some bearing on whether the measure is consistent with the national treatment obligation. The Tribunal specifically concludes that a measure consistent on its face would be considered in violation of national treatment if the "the practical effect of the measure is to create a disproportionate benefit for nationals over non-nationals." S.D. Myers (Partial Award), para. 252 (Nov. 13, 2000). What is the origin of that rule? Is the rule consistent with determinations of "like product" under Article III? Recall that several GATT and WTO panels expressly refused to discuss actual impacts. Even in the *Auto Taxes* case, where the regulator's motive could be considered, the panel did not accept European arguments that the U.S. taxes disproportionately burdened manufacturers of European cars. Instead, the panel, as in other cases, asked whether the measure at issue affected the conditions of competition. Have the investment tribunals misunderstood GATT decisions? If not, do you think that national treatment for investment purposes should be interpreted differently from national treatment under Article III of the GATT?

3. Is *S.D. Myers* a case of the tribunal interfering with Canada's right to regulate toxic waste? Consider the following additional facts:

- The United States and Canada committed to allowing trade in hazardous wastes under the Canada-USA Agreement on the Transboundary Movement of Hazardous Waste.

- Canada had a policy of disposing hazardous waste in other developed countries provided that it could be sure that they would be managed in an environmentally sound manner.

- Due to the location of most Canadian PCB waste in Ontario and Quebec, disposal of the wastes in the United States represented a technically and environmentally sound solution to the destruction of some of Canada's PCBs by minimizing the risk of spills associated with transport of the wastes and reducing transportation costs and pollution.

- A memo from a Canadian official in the Department of Environment suggested that the PCB export ban could not be justified on human health grounds, but it would fulfill the commitment made to the Canadian PCB destruction industry.

How should these facts be balanced? Do you think the *S.D. Myers* tribunal reached its "like circumstances" conclusion because it believed that Canada was just trying to protect its industries? From an environmental perspective, is the outcome positive, negative, or neutral?

4. *Interpreting "Like Circumstances."* Most tribunals, like the *S.D. Myers* and *Pope & Talbot* tribunals, have begun their assessment of whether two investors are in "like circumstances" by asking whether they are in the "same business sector." From this point of consensus, their opinions diverge. In *Methanex*, the foreign investor was a methanol producer and argued it suffered less favorable treatment than the United States ethanol industry. Recall from pages 721–22 that methanol is used to make MTBE, an oxygenate for gasoline. Ethanol can be used directly as an oxygenate. Is Methanex in the same business sector, i.e., in "like circumstances" with ethanol producers? The tribunal rejected Methanex's "like circumstances" claim, because it found identical U.S. domestic investors — other

methanol producers—who were treated the same as Methanex. Methanex Corp. v. U.S. (Final Award of the Tribunal on Jurisdiction and Merits), Part IV, Chapter B, paras. 13–22 (August 3, 2002).

What if there are no identical comparators? In *ADM v. Mexico*, Mexico assessed a tax on high fructose corn syrup (HFCS) but not on sugar. Both HFCS and sugar are used to make a variety of soft drinks, but they are produced with different equipment and processes and raw materials. The *ADM* Tribunal began by defining circumstance as "a condition, fact, or event accompanying, conditioning, or determining another, or the logical surroundings of an action." Turning to the same business sector test, it concluded that the foreign investment in HFCS was in like circumstances with the domestic sugar industry because they "compet[ed] face to face in supplying sweeteners to the soft drink and processed food markets." The tribunal justified its decision to select non-identical comparators, because no identical comparators existed: all HFCS producers were U.S. investors and all sugar producers were Mexican investors. Archer Daniels Midland Co. & Tate & Lyle Ingredients Americas, Inc. v. Mex. (Award), paras. 197–202 (Nov. 21, 2007).

Based on these cases, now reconsider *Methanex* and *S.D. Myers*.

- In *Methanex*, what if there were no U.S. methanol producers. Should a tribunal then compare the treatment of methanol producers like Methanex to ethanol producers? Is the difference between a raw material and a final product still relevant?

- In *S.D. Myers*, recall that Myers Canada was essentially a sales operation to direct business to SDMI's Ohio facility; SDMI never intended to build or operate a remediation facility in Canada. Canada did not deny SDMI or Myers Canada the right to construct PCB remediation facilities in Canada. Chem-Security and Cintec, on the other hand, could both contract and remediate PCBs. Is Myers Canada really in the same business sector as Chem-Security and Cintec? Should that make a difference in the analysis? Does the phrase "foreign-controlled enterprise[] established in a Member country" require a physical, operational presence?

5. The decisions in *S.D. Myers* and *Pope & Talbot* represent another line of analysis. In *S.D. Myers*, the Tribunal asserted that "like circumstances" should take into account justifiable governmental regulations to protect the public interest. Similarly, the *Pope & Talbot* Tribunal concluded that differential treatment reasonably related to a rational policy did not violate the national treatment obligation. *See also* Marvin Feldman v. Mex. (Award), paras. 170–72 (Dec. 16, 2002) (concluding that "[i]n the investment context, ... discrimination has been defined to imply *unreasonable* distinctions between foreign and domestic investors in like circumstances."). Suppose a foreign investor is denied permission to build an industrial facility near a wetland. Is the foreign investor in "like circumstances" to a domestic investor who was allowed to build an identical facility in an already industrialized area? Would the *S.D. Myers* and *Pope & Talbot* tribunals reach the same conclusion on this question? Would it matter if the measure to protect the wetland was pre-existing compared to a measure newly adopted after the foreign investor applied for a construction permit?

6. *"Like Circumstances" and "Like Products."* The *S.D. Myers* Tribunal also related the meaning of "like" in Article 1102 to the meaning of "like" in Articles I and III of the GATT. In another case involving HFCS, the Tribunal in *Corn Products International* expressly drew from the "like products" analysis under the GATT when it concluded that HFCS and sugar producers were in like circumstances because "their products were in direct competition with one another." Corn Prod. Int'l, Inc. v. Mex. (Decision on Responsibility), paras. 120–26 (Jan. 15, 2008). On the other hand, the *Methanex* Tribunal rejected

the use of GATT "like product" jurisprudence, noting that the phrase is a term of art that is not used in some other WTO agreements or in NAFTA's Chapter 11. It further concluded that had the NAFTA negotiators wished to graft a "like products" analysis onto Chapter 11's national treatment obligation, they could have required NAFTA Parties to accord to investors of another Party treatment "no less favorable than it accords its own investors, in like circumstances *with respect to any like, directly competitive or substitutable goods.*" *Methanex* (Final Award of the Tribunal), para. 34 (Aug. 3, 2002) (emphasis in original).

Which Tribunal has the better argument? Given the different contexts and language, is it reasonable to use "like products" analysis to interpret "like circumstances"? The *S.D. Myers* Tribunal recognizes that Chapter 11 includes no general exception provision similar to Article XX. Should that affect whether "like products" jurisprudence should be used to interpret "like circumstances"?

Note also that the *S.D. Myers* Tribunal concluded that a finding of "likeness" under the GATT "often takes place within the overall GATT framework, which includes the Article XX (General Exceptions)." Is it true that findings of "like product" under Articles I and III of the GATT take place within the overall GATT framework? A few months after the *S.D. Myers* award, the WTO Appellate Body in *EC-Asbestos* expressly rejected an interpretation of "like product" that took account of Article XX. According to the *S.D. Myers* Tribunal (paras. 246–252 above), the legal context of the national treatment obligation includes the right to establish high levels of environmental protection, the duty to avoid trade distortions, and the idea that environmental protection and economic development can and should be mutually supportive. Did these objectives factor into the Tribunal's decision?

7. Consider the following proposed "interpretative note" to a draft national treatment clause, from the chairman of the negotiations of the Multilateral Agreement on Investments:

> Governments may have legitimate policy reasons to accord differential treatment to different types of investments. Similarly, governments may have legitimate policy reasons to accord differential treatment as between domestic and foreign investors and their investments in certain circumstances, for example where needed to secure compliance with certain domestic laws that are not inconsistent with national treatment and most-favoured nation treatment. The fact that a measure applied by a government has a different effect on an investment or investor of another Party would not in itself render the measure inconsistent with national treatment and most-favoured nation treatment. The objective of "in like circumstances" is to permit consideration of all relevant circumstances, including those relating to a foreign investor and its investments, in deciding to which domestic and third country investors they should appropriately be compared.

Chairman's Note on Environment and Related Matters and on Labour, March 9, 1998, DAFFE/MAI(98)10, *available at* http://www1.oecd.org/daf/mai/pdf/ng/ng9810e.pdf. Does such an interpretation accomplish its avowed purpose of addressing "concerns about the practical implementation of the 'de facto' discrimination principle and preserv[ing] the necessary scope for nondiscriminatory regulation"? *Id.*

8. Some commentators regard the application of national and most-favored nation treatment for investments and investors to states and provinces as the sleeping giant of NAFTA. State and local governments often engage in discriminatory conduct or conduct which affects the conditions of competition. Consider the following real-life situation: The City of Anaheim, California, denied Wal-Mart authorization to establish a massive "Superstore" in its jurisdiction. Wal-Mart took the issue to the voters by placing a mea-

sure on the local ballot that would have overturned the City's decision and also declared that the project met all environmental and zoning requirements (thus denying the City the power to impose additional conditions or requiring mitigation). The measure lost handily. Had it won, would a Canadian or Mexican-owned big box store similar to Wal-Mart be entitled to the same terms and conditions stipulated in the measure? Before answering, look at the exceptions in NAFTA Article 1108.

---

3. Minimum Standard of Treatment

Article 1105(1) of the NAFTA, entitled "Minimum Standard of Treatment," requires that each Party "accord to investments of investors of another Party treatment in accordance with international law, including fair and equitable treatment and full protection and security." The basic notion of fair and equitable treatment is not hard to comprehend: foreigners who have entered a country legally and are engaged in legal activities, including foreign investors, should at a minimum be secure against abuses of authority by host governments or other grossly unfair or arbitrary treatment. Nonetheless, the contours of fairness and equity are as difficult to define in this context as in any other. NAFTA's extension of "minimum standards of treatment" to a US$7 trillion free trade zone with a vibrant cross-border investment market has sparked renewed interest and examination of "minimum standards." This section describes the so-called *Neer* test, how early NAFTA tribunals such as *S.D. Myers* and *Pope & Talbot* grappled with the issue, and the response of the NAFTA Parties to the early awards. It then presents the 2009 final award in *Glamis Gold*, which gives a more comprehensive analysis.

a. The Neer Test, the Early Cases, and the FTC "Note of Interpretation"

The concept of minimum standards has a long history in international law generally and has been regularly applied in investment agreements. *See, e.g.*, IAN BROWNLIE, PRINCIPLES OF PUBLIC INTERNATIONAL LAW 528 (5th ed. 1998). Central to many analyses of "fair and equitable" is the so-called *Neer* test, a reference to a landmark 1926 decision rendered by the U.S.-Mexico General Claims Commission. United States (L.F. Neer) v. United Mexican States, 4 R.I.A.A. 60 (Mexico-U.S. General Claims Commission 1926) [hereinafter *Neer*]. In oft-quoted language, the Commission stated:

> ... [T]he propriety of government acts should be put to the test of international standards. The treatment of an alien, in order to constitute an international delinquency, should amount to an outrage, to bad faith, to wilful neglect of duty, or to an insufficiency of government actions so far short of international standards that every reasonable and impartial man would readily recognize its insufficiency.

In the early cases, the NAFTA tribunals gave attention to the *Neer* test but declined to apply it as the key to interpretation of Article 1105.

S.D. Myers, Inc. v. Government of Canada
(Partial Award), (Nov. 13, 2000)

259. The minimum standard of treatment provision of the NAFTA is similar to clauses contained in BITs [bilateral investment treaties]. The inclusion of a "minimum standard" provision is necessary to avoid what might otherwise be a gap. A gov-

ernment might treat an investor in a harsh, injurious and unjust manner, but do so in a way that is no different than the treatment inflicted on its own nationals. The "minimum standard" is a floor below which treatment of foreign investors must not fall, even if a government were not acting in a discriminatory manner.

260. The US-Mexican Claims Commission noted in the *Hopkins* case that:

> It not infrequently happens that under the rules of international law applied to controversies of an international aspect a nation is required to accord to aliens broader and more liberal treatment than it accords to its own citizens under its municipal laws.... The citizens of a nation may enjoy many rights which are withheld from aliens, and conversely, under international law, aliens may enjoy rights and remedies which the nation does not accord to its own citizens.

261. When interpreting and applying the "minimum standard," a Chapter 11 tribunal does not have an open-ended mandate to second-guess government decision-making. Governments have to make many potentially controversial choices. In doing so, they may appear to have made mistakes, to have misjudged the facts, proceeded on the basis of a misguided economic or sociological theory, placed too much emphasis on some social values over others and adopted solutions that are ultimately ineffective or counterproductive. The ordinary remedy, if there were one, for errors in modern governments is through internal political and legal processes, including elections.

262. Article 1105(1) expresses an overall concept. The words of the article must be read as a whole. The phrases ... *fair and equitable treatment* ... and ... *full protection and security* ... cannot be read in isolation. They must be read in conjunction with the introductory phrase ... *treatment in accordance with international law*.

263. The Tribunal considers that a breach of Article 1105 occurs only when it is shown that an investor has been treated in such an unjust or arbitrary manner that the treatment rises to the level that is unacceptable from the international perspective. That determination must be made in the light of the high measure of deference that international law generally extends to the right of domestic authorities to regulate matters within their own borders. The determination must also take into account any specific rules of international law that are applicable to the case.

264. In some cases, the breach of a rule of international law by a host Party may not be decisive in determining that a foreign investor has been denied "*fair and equitable treatment,*" but the fact that a host Party has breached a rule of international law that is specifically designed to protect investors will tend to weigh heavily in favour of finding a breach of Article 1105.

265. The breadth of the "*minimum standard,*" including its ability to encompass more particular guarantees, was recognized by Dr. Mann in the following passage:

> it is submitted that the right to fair and equitable treatment goes much further than the right to most-favored-nation and to national treatment ... so general a provision is likely to be almost sufficient to cover all conceivable cases, and it may well be that provisions of the Agreements affording substantive protection are not more than examples of specific instances of this overriding duty.

266. Although modern commentators might consider Dr. Mann's statement to be an over-generalisation, and the Tribunal does not rule out the possibility that

there could be circumstances in which a denial of the national treatment provisions of the NAFTA would not necessarily offend the minimum standard provisions, a majority of the Tribunal determines that on the facts of this particular case the breach of Article 1102 essentially establishes a breach of Article 1105 as well.

267. Mr. Chiasson [one of the three Tribunal members] considers that a finding of a violation of Article 1105 must be based on a demonstrated failure to meet the fair and equitable requirements of international law. Breach of another provision of the NAFTA is not a foundation for such a conclusion. The language of the NAFTA does not support the notion espoused by Dr. Mann insofar as it is considered to support a breach of Article 1105 that is based on a violation of another provision of Chapter 11. On the facts of this case, CANADA's actions come close to the line, but on the evidence no breach of Article 1105 is established.

268. By a majority, the Tribunal determines that the issuance of the Interim and Final Orders was a breach of Article 1105 of the NAFTA. The Tribunal's decision in this respect makes it unnecessary to review SDMI's other submissions in relation to Article 1105.

A year after the *S.D. Myers* Partial Award, Canada argued in *Pope & Talbot* that "all tribunals that have applied or commented on minimum standard have held that a breach may only be found where the facts are extreme and the governmental conduct is egregious." Pope & Talbot v. Canada (Government of Canada Counter-Memorial (Phase Two), para. 281 (Oct. 10, 2000). That much sounds like the *Neer* test. But the Tribunal, focusing on the phrase "fair and equitable treatment," commented that, although the "language of Article 1105 suggests that those [fairness] elements are included in the requirements of international law" they could be "additive" and that investors would be entitled to the international law minimum plus the fairness elements. *Pope & Talbot* (Award on the Merits of Phase 2), para. 111 (Apr. 10, 2001). In other words, if "fair and equitable" adds to the investor's rights, then conduct violating Article 1105 may be less egregious than if only the *Neer* minimum standard applied. The difference would be significant, as tribunals such as *Metalclad* imported NAFTA commitments in areas such as transparency into their interpretation of Article 1105.

Distressed by what the NAFTA governments believed to be overly expansive interpretations of minimum standards in *Metalclad* and *S.D. Myers* (*Pope & Talbot* was pending), the NAFTA Parties sought to bring the tribunals under control. NAFTA Article 1131(2) gives the Parties, acting by consensus, the authority to "interpret" Chapter 11's provisions without triggering the more procedurally onerous task of amending the NAFTA. Such interpretations are binding on tribunals. Under this authority, on July 31, 2001, the Trade Ministers of Canada, Mexico and the United States, acting as the NAFTA Free Trade Commission (FTC), issued *Notes of Interpretation of Certain Chapter 11 Provisions*. The second section of the *Notes of Interpretation* addresses "Minimum Standard of Treatment in Accordance with International Law":

Article 1105(1) prescribes the customary international law minimum standards of treatment of aliens as the minimum standard of treatment to be afforded to investments of investors of another Party.

The concepts of "fair and equitable treatment" and "full protection and security" do not require treatment in addition to or beyond that which is required by the customary international law minimum standard of treatment of aliens.

A breach of other provisions of NAFTA or of a separate international agreement, does not establish that there has been a breach of Article 1105(1).

See http://www.international.gc.ca/trade-agreements-accords-commerciaux/disp-diff/ NAFTA-interpr.aspx?lang=en.

Subsequent NAFTA claimants argued that the FTC exceeded its powers by improperly amending, rather than interpreting, NAFTA Article 1105. Tribunals have entertained these arguments but have generally ruled in a manner consistent with the interpretative note. *See* David A. Gantz, *Contrasting Key Investment Provisions of the NAFTA with the United States-Chile FTA, in* NAFTA INVESTMENT LAW AND ARBITRATION: PAST ISSUES, CURRENT PRACTICE, FUTURE PROSPECTS 408–413 (Todd Weiler ed. 2004). Nonetheless, some tribunals acknowledging the validity of the *Notes of Interpretation* have declined to adopt the *Neer* test for the minimum standard of treatment, instead reiterating the view that customary international law is evolving and expanding beyond its early roots. *Id.* In fact, all three NAFTA Parties also accept that the "minimum standard" is an evolving one, not "frozen in amber at the time of the *Neer* decision." ADF Group Inc. v. United States of America (Second Submission of Canada Pursuant to NAFTA Article 1128), ICSID Case No ARB(AF)/00/1 para. 33 (July 19, 2002). *Glamis Gold*, below, takes up the question of the contours of that evolution.

Questions and Discussion

1. Reconsider the *S.D. Myers* award. The Tribunal closely paraphrases the *Neer* standard in paragraph 263. Did it apply that standard in reaching its result? Note the majority's quotation from Dr. Mann (a noted British scholar) in paragraph 265, and the reaction to it from tribunal member Chiasson. Was the conduct of Canadian officials, who appear to have imposed the export ban in part to aid Canadian companies, unfair or inequitable? Was it below the minimum standard as defined by *Neer*?

2. The *Metalclad* Tribunal found a breach of minimum standards because Mexico failed to provide a transparent, predictable framework for business planning and investment, and demonstrated a lack of orderly process and timely disposition in relation to an investor. In so deciding, however, the Tribunal glossed over complicated questions of jurisdiction (did the local government have authority to deny a permit?) on which even Mexican lawyers could not agree. Was Mexico's behavior unfair and inequitable? Egregious behavior under *Neer*? In any event, a British Columbia court overturned the tribunal's decision with respect to minimum standard of treatment because it found that the tribunal had exceeded its jurisdiction. The United Mexican States v. Metalclad Corp., 2001 B.C.S.C 664 (2001), *available at* http://www.courts.gov.bc.ca/jdb-txt/sc/01/06/2001bcsc0664.htm. This is discussed in more detail on pages 753–55.

3. So, what does minimum standard of treatment mean after the FTC Notes of Interpretation? In *Mondev Int'l Ltd. v. United States of America* (Final Award), ICSID Case No. ARB(AF)/99/2 (Oct. 11, 2001) [hereinafter *Mondev*], the tribunal made clear that, in its judgment, whatever minimum standard of treatment means, it is no longer frozen to the 1926 *Neer* definition:

> [B]oth the substantive and procedural rights of the individual in international law have undergone considerable development. In the light of these developments it is unconvincing to confine the meaning of "fair and equitable treatment" and "full protection and security" of foreign investments to what those

terms — had they been current at the time — might have meant in the 1920s when applied to the physical security of an alien. To the modern eye, what is unfair or inequitable need not equate with the outrageous or the egregious. In particular, a State may treat foreign investment unfairly and inequitably without necessarily acting in bad faith.

Compare this statement with the analysis by the *Glamis Gold* tribunal below.

4. *Mondev* and *Loewen*, both decided after the FTC's July 2001 *Notes of Interpretation*, appear to have applied the same test in determining the boundaries of minimum standards as they apply to judicial "measures" in the country where the investment is made. In both cases the Tribunals determined that a proceeding must clearly be "improper and discreditable" to fall below the floor of minimum standards. Interestingly, the *Loewen* tribunal made just such a finding, emphatically declaring that "[b]y any standard of measurement, the trial involving O'Keefe and Loewen was a disgrace," and was "so flawed that it constituted a miscarriage of justice ... as that expression is understood in international law." The tribunal stated that "manifest injustice" in the sense of "lack of due process leading to an outcome which offends a sense of judicial propriety" is enough to violate guarantees of minimum standards, and that bad faith or malicious intent is not an essential element of the claim. Loewen Group, Inc. v. United States (Final Award), ICSID Case No. ARB(AF)/98/3, paras. 119, 54 (June 26, 2003). (The claim was nevertheless denied on jurisdictional grounds, as well as on a separate finding that the claimant had failed to meet the finality requirement by not exhausting its judicial remedies, in this case by not appealing to the U.S. Supreme Court.)

---

b. The Glamis Gold *Case*

Glamis Gold is the most recent environment-related Chapter 11 arbitration to consider a violation of the minimum standard of treatment (as well as expropriation). As is true of most arbitration claims, the facts are complex and controverted; the Tribunal's statement of the facts in the final award takes 50 pages. The essential facts begin with a decision in 1987 by Glamis Gold, a Canadian mining concern, to explore the feasibility of operating a surface gold mine in Imperial County in the Mojave Desert of far southern California not very far west of the Colorado River. The region is remote and unpopulated; it had seen mining activity in the past. It contains some areas of archaeological and religious significance to the Quechans, a local Indian tribe, and some ecological and recreational value, such as for hunting. After acquiring mining rights and undertaking exploration, in 1994 Glamis filed a preliminary plan of operations and a reclamation plan with the appropriate local and state agencies in California and with the U.S. Bureau of Land Management (BLM), which manages the area where most of the mining would take place. By the time Glamis completed some feasibility studies and began to engage with BLM in the first steps of an environmental impact study, it had invested about $18.7 million in the project.

There followed a period of years in which BLM prepared a draft environmental impact statement, further work was done to assess the archaeological and historical significance of the mining site for the Quechan and other Indian tribes, and Indian opposition to the proposed mine became manifest. In 1999, the solicitor general (chief lawyer) for the Department of the Interior issued a legal opinion opening the way for BLM to deny operating rights to Glamis without payment of compensation. While Glamis contested that decision in court, George W. Bush became president and in 2001, the new officials at Interior rescinded the earlier legal opinion and re-opened consideration of operating rights for Glamis. That process of reconsideration was still under way when Glamis filed its notice of intent to make a claim under NAFTA Chapter 11.

Meanwhile, after the change of administrations in Washington, the legislature of California, aware of local opposition to the Glamis mine project, acted to amend requirements for surface mining operations. In early 2003, the legislature passed and the governor signed legislation establishing a new requirement for backfilling of excavated mining sites. Even before final legislation, the California geological agency issued emergency regulations, which it eventually made permanent, establishing the backfilling requirement.

Backfilling a large mine is an expensive undertaking. Under these new operating conditions, Glamis decided that its proposed mine would no longer be commercially viable. It suspended its efforts to get operational approval, pursuing the Chapter 11 claim instead. Nevertheless, it still owns the mining rights in question, and operation of a mine, albeit with backfilling and with certain protections for archaeological sites and other areas of special interest to the Quechan, could still be permitted. Glamis claimed that this changing legal framework violated the fair and equitable treatment standard of Article 1105 because Article 1105 protects against arbitrariness and discrimination, protects legitimate investment-backed expectations, and requires a transparent and predictable legal and business framework. Glamis Gold v. United States of America (Award of the Tribunal), para. 542.

Glamis Gold, Ltd. v. United States of America

(Award of the Tribunal), (June 8, 2009)

599. There is no disagreement among the State Parties to the NAFTA, nor the Parties to this arbitration, that the requirement of fair and equitable treatment in Article 1105 is to be understood by reference to the customary international law minimum standard of treatment of aliens. Indeed, the Free Trade Commission ("FTC") clearly states, in its binding Notes of Interpretation on July 31, 2001, that "Article 1105(1) prescribes the customary international law minimum standard of treatment of aliens as the minimum standard of treatment to be afforded to investments of investors of another Party."

600. The question thus becomes: what does this customary international law minimum standard of treatment require of a State Party vis-à-vis investors of another State Party? Is it the same as that established in 1926 in *Neer v. Mexico*? Or has Claimant proven that the standard has "evolved"? If it has evolved, what evidence of custom has Claimant provided to the Tribunal to determine its current scope?

601. As a threshold issue, the Tribunal notes that it is Claimant's burden to sufficiently answer each of these questions. The State Parties to the NAFTA (at least Canada and Mexico) agree that "the test in *Neer* does continue to apply," though Mexico "also agrees that the standard is relative and that conduct which may not have violated international law [in] the 1920's might very well be seen to offend internationally accepted principles today." If, as Claimant argues, the customary international law minimum standard of treatment has indeed moved to require something less than the "egregious," "outrageous," or "shocking" standard as elucidated in *Neer*, then the burden of establishing what the standard now requires is upon Claimant.

602. The Tribunal acknowledges that it is difficult to establish a change in customary international law. As Respondent explains, establishment of a rule of

customary international law requires: (1) "a concordant practice of a number of States acquiesced in by others," and (2) "a conception that the practice is required by or consistent with the prevailing law (*opinio juris*)."

603. The evidence of such "concordant practice" undertaken out of a sense of legal obligation is exhibited in very few authoritative sources: treaty ratification language, statements of governments, treaty practice (e.g., Model BITs), and sometimes pleadings. Although one can readily identify the practice of States, it is usually very difficult to determine the intent behind those actions. Looking to a claimant to ascertain custom requires it to ascertain such intent, a complicated and particularly difficult task. In the context of arbitration, however, it is necessarily Claimant's place to establish a change in custom.

604. The Tribunal notes that, although an examination of custom is indeed necessary to determine the scope and bounds of current customary international law, this requirement—repeatedly argued by various State Parties—because of the difficulty in proving a change in custom, effectively freezes the protections provided for in this provision at the 1926 conception of egregiousness.

605. Claimant did provide numerous arbitral decisions in support of its conclusion that fair and equitable treatment encompasses a universe of "fundamental" principles common throughout the world that include "the duty to act in good faith, due process, transparency and candor, and fairness and protection from arbitrariness." Arbitral awards, Respondent rightly notes, do not constitute State practice and thus cannot create or prove customary international law. They can, however, serve as illustrations of customary international law if they involve an examination of customary international law, as opposed to a treaty-based, or autonomous, interpretation.

606. This brings the Tribunal to its first task: ascertaining which of the sources argued by Claimant are properly available to instruct the Tribunal on the bounds of "fair and equitable treatment." As briefly mentioned above, the Tribunal notes that it finds two categories of arbitral awards that examine a fair and equitable treatment standard: those that look to define customary international law and those that examine the autonomous language and nuances of the underlying treaty language. Fundamental to this divide is the treaty underlying the dispute: those treaties and free trade agreements, like the NAFTA, that are to be understood by reference to the customary international law minimum standard of treatment necessarily lead their tribunals to analyze custom; while those treaties with fair and equitable treatment clauses that expand upon, or move beyond, customary international law, lead their reviewing tribunals into an analysis of the treaty language and its meaning, as guided by Article 31(1) of the Vienna Convention.

607. Ascertaining custom is necessarily a factual inquiry, looking to the actions of States and the motives for and consistency of these actions. By applying an autonomous standard, on the other hand, a tribunal may focus solely on the language and nuances of the treaty language itself and, applying the rules of treaty interpretation, require no party proof of State action or *opinio juris*. This latter practice fails to assist in the ascertainment of custom.

608. As Article 1105's fair and equitable treatment standard is, as Respondent phrases it, simply "a shorthand reference to customary international law," the Tribunal finds that arbitral decisions that apply an autonomous standard provide no guidance inasmuch as the entire method of reasoning does not bear on an in-

quiry into custom. The various BITs cited by Claimant may or may not illuminate customary international law; they will prove helpful to this Tribunal's analysis when they seek to provide the same base floor of conduct as the minimum standard of treatment under customary international law; but they will not be of assistance if they include different protections than those provided for in customary international law.

609. Claimant has agreed with this distinction between customary international law and autonomous treaty standards but argues that, with respect to this particular standard, BIT jurisprudence has "converged with customary international law in this area." The Tribunal finds this to be an over-statement. Certainly, it is possible that some BITs converge with the requirements established by customary international law; there are, however, numerous BITs that have been interpreted as going beyond customary international law, and thereby requiring more than that to which the NAFTA State Parties have agreed. It is thus necessary to look to the underlying fair and equitable treatment clause of each treaty, and the reviewing tribunal's analysis of that treaty, to determine whether or not they are drafted with an intent to refer to customary international law.

610. Looking, for instance, to Claimant's reliance on *Tecmed v. Mexico* for various of its arguments, the Tribunal finds that Claimant has not proven that this award, based on a BIT between Spain and Mexico, defines anything other than an autonomous standard and thus an award from which this Tribunal will not find guidance. Article 4(1) of the Spain-Mexico BIT involved in the *Tecmed* proceeding provides that each contracting party guarantees just and equitable treatment conforming with "International Law" to the investments of investors of the other contracting party in its territory. Article 4(2) proceeds to explain that this treatment will not be less favorable than that granted in similar circumstances by each contracting party to the investments in its territory by an investor of a third State. Several interpretations of the requirement espoused in Article 4(2) are indeed possible, but the *Tecmed* tribunal itself states that it "understands that the scope of the undertaking of fair and equitable treatment under Article 4(1) of the Agreement described ... is that resulting from an *autonomous interpretation....*" Thus, this Tribunal finds that the language or analysis of the Tecmed award is not relevant to the Tribunal's consideration.

611. The Tribunal therefore holds that it may look solely to arbitral awards—including BIT awards—that seek to be understood by reference to the customary international law minimum standard of treatment, as opposed to any autonomous standard. The Tribunal thus turns to its second task: determining the scope of the current customary international law minimum standard of treatment, as proven by Claimant.

612. It appears to this Tribunal that the NAFTA State Parties agree that, at a minimum, the fair and equitable treatment standard is that as articulated in *Neer*: "the treatment of an alien, in order to constitute an international delinquency, should amount to an outrage, to bad faith, to wilful neglect of duty, or to an insufficiency of governmental action so far short of international standards that every reasonable and impartial man would readily recognize its insufficiency." Whether this standard has evolved since 1926, however, has not been definitively agreed upon. The Tribunal considers two possible types of evolution: (1) that what the inter-

national community views as "outrageous" may change over time; and (2) that the minimum standard of treatment has moved beyond what it was in 1926.

613. The Tribunal finds apparent agreement that the fair and equitable treatment standard is subject to the first type of evolution: a change in the international view of what is shocking and outrageous. As the *Mondev* tribunal held:

> *Neer* and like arbitral awards were decided in the 1920s, when the status of the individual in international law, and the international protection of foreign investments, were far less developed than they have since come to be. In particular, both the substantive and procedural rights of the individual in international law have undergone considerable development. In light of these developments it is unconvincing to confine the meaning of 'fair and equitable treatment' and 'full protection and security' of foreign investments to what those terms—had they been current at the time—might have meant in the 1920s when applied to the physical security of an alien. To the modern eye, what is unfair or inequitable need not equate with the outrageous or the egregious. In particular, a State may treat foreign investment unfairly and inequitably without necessarily acting in bad faith.

Similarly, this Tribunal holds that the *Neer* standard, when applied with current sentiments and to modern situations, may find shocking and egregious events not considered to reach this level in the past.

614. As regards the second form of evolution—the proposition that customary international law has moved beyond the minimum standard of treatment of aliens as defined in *Neer*—the Tribunal finds that the evidence provided by Claimant does not establish such evolution. This is evident in the abundant and continued use of adjective modifiers throughout arbitral awards, evidencing a strict standard. *International Thunderbird* used the terms "*gross* denial of justice" and "*manifest* arbitrariness" to describe the acts that it viewed would breach the minimum standard of treatment. *S.D. Myers* would find a breach of Article 1105 when an investor was treated "in *such an unjust or arbitrary* manner." The *Mondev* tribunal held: "The test is not whether a particular result is surprising, but whether the *shock or surprise* occasioned to an impartial tribunal leads, on reflection, to justified concerns as to the judicial propriety of the outcome...."

615. The customary international law minimum standard of treatment is just that, a minimum standard. It is meant to serve as a floor, an absolute bottom, below which conduct is not accepted by the international community. Although the circumstances of the case are of course relevant, the standard is not meant to vary from state to state or investor to investor. The protection afforded by Article 1105 must be distinguished from that provided for in Article 1102 on National Treatment. Article 1102(1) states: "Each Party shall accord to investors of another Party treatment no less favorable than that it accords, in like circumstances, to its own investors...." The treatment of investors under Article 1102 is compared to the treatment the State's own investors receive and thus can vary greatly depending on each State and its practices. The fair and equitable treatment promised by Article 1105 is not dynamic; it cannot vary between nations as thus the protection afforded would have no minimum.

616. It therefore appears that, although situations may be more varied and complicated today than in the 1920s, the level of scrutiny is the same. The fundamentals of the *Neer* standard thus still apply today: to violate the customary

international law minimum standard of treatment codified in Article 1105 of the NAFTA, an act must be sufficiently egregious and shocking—a gross denial of justice, manifest arbitrariness, blatant unfairness, a complete lack of due process, evident discrimination, or a manifest lack of reasons—so as to fall below accepted international standards and constitute a breach of Article 1105(1). The Tribunal notes that one aspect of evolution from *Neer* that is generally agreed upon is that bad faith is not required to find a violation of the fair and equitable treatment standard, but its presence is conclusive evidence of such. Thus, an act that is egregious or shocking may also evidence bad faith, but such bad faith is not necessary for the finding of a violation. The standard for finding a breach of the customary international law minimum standard of treatment therefore remains as stringent as it was under *Neer*; it is entirely possible, however that, as an international community, we may be shocked by State actions now that did not offend us previously.

617. Respondent argues below that, in reviewing State agency or departmental decisions and actions, international tribunals as well as domestic judiciaries favor deference to the agency so as not to second guess the primary decision-makers or become "science courts." The Tribunal disagrees that domestic deference in national court systems is necessarily applicable to international tribunals. In the present case, the Tribunal finds the standard of deference to already be present in the standard as stated, rather than being additive to that standard. The idea of deference is found in the modifiers "manifest" and "gross" that make this standard a stringent one; it is found in the idea that a breach requires something greater than mere arbitrariness, something that is surprising, shocking, or exhibits a manifest lack of reasoning.

618. With this thought in mind, the Tribunal turns to the duties that Claimant argues are part of the requirements of a host State per Article 1105: (1) an obligation to protect legitimate expectations through establishment of a transparent and predictable business and legal framework, and (2) an obligation to provide protection from arbitrary measures. As the United States explained in its 1128 submission in *Pope & Talbot*, and as Mexico adopted in its 1128 submission to the *ADF* tribunal: "'fair and equitable treatment' and 'full protection and security' are provided as examples of the customary international law standards incorporated into Article 1105(1).... The international law minimum standard [of treatment] is an umbrella concept incorporating a set of rules that has crystallized over the centuries into customary international law in specific contexts."

[With respect to protection of legitimate expectations, the Tribunal finds that neither the United States nor California gave Glamis any specific assurances that would create "reasonable or justifiable expectations on the part of an investor to act in reliance on said conduct" (quoting from *International Thunderbird*). With respect to protection from arbitrary measures, the Tribunal holds that:

[T]here is an obligation of each of the NAFTA State Parties inherent in the fair and equitable treatment standard of Article 1105 that they do not treat investors of another State in a *manifestly* arbitrary manner. The Tribunal thus determines that Claimant has sufficiently substantiated its arguments that a duty to protect investors from arbitrary measures exists in the customary international law minimum standard of treatment of aliens; though Claimant has not sufficiently rebutted Respondent's assertions that a finding of arbitrariness requires a determination of some act far beyond the measure's mere illegality, an act so manifestly arbitrary, so unjust and surprising as to be unacceptable from an international perspective. (para. 626)

But the Tribunal finds that Glamis failed to show any action by the United States or California that was so arbitrary as to meet that standard. It also finds no impermissible intent to halt the investment behind the actions complained of, while acknowledging that such an intent, if shown, "may elevate individually non-violative acts into a record as a whole that breaches international treaty obligations." (para. 826)]

Questions and Discussion

1. The *Glamis Gold* Tribunal made a major legal point about the distinction between many BIT provisions on "fair and equitable treatment" and the specific reference to international law as the agreed standard in Article 1105. Compare, for example, the minimum standard provision of the US-Czech Republic BIT with the NAFTA:

> U.S.-Czech Republic BIT, Article II.2(a): "Investment shall at all times be accorded fair and equitable treatment, shall enjoy full protection and security and shall in no case be accorded treatment less than required by international law."

> NAFTA, Article 1105(1): "Each Party shall accord to investments of investors of another Party treatment in accordance with international law, including fair and equitable treatment and full protection and security."

In reaction to the NAFTA interpretation controversy, the United States has changed the formulation of the minimum standard of treatment provision in both its model BIT and in later free trade agreements to be even more specific about its international law basis. *See* Section IV.A.

2. It can safely be said that consideration of breaches of minimum standard of treatment will be fact-driven and that its "fairness and equity" elements may come to resemble something akin to "due process" in U.S. constitutional law, at least to the extent that such principles are evidenced as customary international law. What about similar examples of local government decisions on permitting, zoning, or land use where these decisions suffer from serious procedural deficiencies such as lack of notice or opportunity to be heard? How would these government actions fare under a minimum standards analysis? Is *Glamis Gold* sufficiently reassuring?

3. *Glamis Gold* does not attempt to mark the elusive boundary between authorized action by the NAFTA Parties to "interpret" the text and a surreptitious maneuver by trade ministers to "redefine" a term in the text significantly enough to constitute an amendment of the treaty requiring formal ratification.

4. As the case excerpts suggest, tribunals have yet to develop a coherent interpretation of the minimum standard of treatment under NAFTA Article 1105. Most tribunals agree that government conduct does not need to be egregious, outrageous, or shocking, but the threshold for a violation remains high. Is this perhaps an issue on which Justice Potter Stewart's famous dictum applies: "I shall not attempt ... further to define [hard-core pornography ... but] I know it when I see it"? Jacobellis v. Ohio, 378 U.S. 184, 197 (1964).

5. For an analysis of "minimum standard of treatment" and "fair and equitable treatment" in BITs, FTAs, and other international instruments, see OECD, Directorate for Fi-

nancial and Enterprise Affairs, Fair and Equitable Treatment Standard in International Investment Law, Sept. 2004, *available a*t http://www.oecd.org/dataoecd/22/53/33776498.pdf.

---

4. Expropriation

The laws of most countries protect property owners from the "taking" of property by the government without just compensation. U.S. Const. amend. V ("nor shall private property be taken for public use, without just compensation"). NAFTA Chapter 11 places this general obligation in the investment context. NAFTA Article 1110(1) provides:

> No party may directly or indirectly nationalize or expropriate an investment of an investor of another Party in its territory or take a measure tantamount to nationalization or expropriation of such investment ("expropriation"), except:
>
> (a) for a public purpose;
>
> (b) on a nondiscriminatory basis;
>
> (c) in accordance with due process of law and Article 1105(1); and
>
> (d) on payment of compensation in accordance with paragraphs 2 through 6.

International investment law and investment agreements have long protected foreign property from direct expropriation in the form of nationalization or other seizure or confiscation of assets. Under NAFTA Chapter 11, foreign investors have more typically made claims that governmental environmental regulation has operated as a measure "tantamount to ... expropriation", a concept also known as "indirect" or "creeping" expropriation under international law or "regulatory taking" in the United States.

From the beginning, many environmentalists voiced concerns about how investor claims under the expropriation provision of Article 1110 might threaten environmental regulation or intimidate governments from legitimate regulatory activities. Martin Wagner, a lawyer for Earthjustice, tried to provide guidance to future Chapter 11 tribunals by reviewing the state of investment law prior to the NAFTA. He concluded that international law does not make a State liable for economic losses suffered by investors as a consequence of bona fide regulation within the accepted police power of states. In other words, laws and regulations to protect public health or the environment are noncompensable limitations on the value of property (investments). J. Martin Wagner *International Investment, Expropriation and Environmental Protection*, 29 Golden Gate U. L. Rev. 465, 517–26 (1999).

Others reached similar conclusions. *See, e.g.,* Howard Mann & Konrad von Moltke, *NAFTA's Chapter 11 and the Environment: Addressing the Impacts of the Investor-State Process on the Environment* (International Institute for Sustainable Development, 1999). Professor Todd Weiler takes a different approach. Focusing only on the text of NAFTA itself, he concludes, "There is no indication anywhere in the NAFTA text that [Article 1110] does not apply equally to regulatory measures...." Todd Weiler, *Interpreting Substantive Obligations in Relation to Health and Safety Measures, in* Investment Law and Arbitration, at 125. Even if one follows Weiler's approach, it begs the question just *how* Article 1110 applies in any particular case. As you read further, consider to what extent the NAFTA tribunals agree with Wagner or Weiler.

a. The Metalclad Case

When the Tribunal in the *Metalclad* arbitration made its award in 2000, its handling of the expropriation issue caused consternation in many quarters.

Metalclad is a U.S. corporation which, through a subsidiary, purchased the Mexican company Confinamiento Tecnico de Residuos Industriales, SA (COTERIN) to develop COTERIN's hazardous waste transfer station into a hazardous waste landfill in the municipality of Guadalcazar in the Mexican state of San Luis Potosí. In 1993, the National Ecological Institute (INE), a sub-agency of the Mexican environmental agency, granted COTERIN a federal permit to construct a hazardous waste landfill; three months later, Metalclad entered into an agreement to purchase COTERIN. The government of San Luis Potosí granted COTERIN a state land use permit to construct the landfill.

Metalclad also applied for a "construction permit" from the municipality of Guadalcazar, although whether such a permit is required for a federally-permitted facility in Mexico is disputed. Guadalcazar failed to act on the construction permit. Metalclad, on the advice of Mexico's federal environmental officials, proceeded with construction nevertheless. When it came time to obtain an operating permit, Metalclad entered into a 1995 agreement (a "convenio") with the Secretariat of the Mexican Environment, Natural Resources and Fishing (SEMARNAP) to clean up some contamination left behind by COTERIN. Meanwhile, the federal and local governments disputed who had competence over key aspects of the project. After the facility was constructed, Guadalcazar denied Metalclad the municipal construction permit.

After various legal maneuvers, INE issued Metalclad an additional permit to increase landfill capacity from 36,000 to 360,000 tons. But in a final step in this saga, the Governor of San Luis Potosí, one week before his term expired, issued an Ecological Decree declaring a Natural Area of 189,000 hectares (about 700 square miles) to protect several rare species of cactus. The Natural Area encompassed the site of Metalclad's hazardous waste landfill. (The Mexican Supreme Court later nullified this decree because the area it defined by metes and bounds included portions of a neighboring state.) The terms of the decree precluded activities necessary to operate the already-constructed landfill. Metalclad then challenged the actions of San Luis Potosí and Guadalcazar as violations of, *inter alia*, the expropriation provisions of Article 1110.

Metalclad Corp. v. Mexico
ICSID Case No. ARB(AF)/97/1 (Aug. 30, 2000)

76. Prominent in the statement of principles and rules that introduces the [NAFTA] is the reference to transparency (NAFTA Article 102(1)). The Tribunal understands this to include the idea that all relevant legal requirements for the purpose of initiating, completing and successfully operating investments made, or intended to be made, under the Agreement should be capable of being readily known to all affected investors of another Party. There should be no room for doubt or uncertainty on such matters. Once the authorities of the central government of any Party (whose international responsibility in such matters has been identified in the preceding section) become aware of any scope for misunderstanding or confusion in this connection, it is their duty to ensure that the correct position is promptly determined and clearly stated so that investors can proceed with all appropriate expedition in the confident belief that they are acting in accordance with all relevant laws. * * *

103. ... [E]xpropriation under NAFTA includes not only open, deliberate and acknowledged takings of property, such as outright seizure or formal or obligatory transfer of title in favour of the host State, but also covert or incidental interference with the use of property which has the effect of depriving the owner, in whole or in significant part, of the use or reasonably-to-be-expected economic benefit of property even if not necessarily to the obvious benefit of the host State.

104. By permitting or tolerating the conduct of Guadalcazar in relation to Metalclad which the Tribunal has already held amounts to unfair and inequitable treatment breaching Article 1105 and by thus participating or acquiescing in the denial to Metalclad of the right to operate the landfill, notwithstanding the fact that the project was fully approved and endorsed by the federal government, Mexico must be held to have taken a measure tantamount to expropriation in violation of NAFTA Article 1110(1).

105. The Tribunal holds that the exclusive authority for siting and permitting a hazardous waste landfill resides with the Mexican federal government. This finding is consistent with the testimony of the Secretary of SEMARNAP and, as stated above, is consistent with the express language of the LGEEPA [Mexico's General Law of Ecological Equilibrium and Environmental Protection].

106. As determined earlier..., the Municipality denied the local construction permit in part because of the Municipality's perception of the adverse environmental effects of the hazardous waste landfill and the geological unsuitability of the landfill site. In so doing, the Municipality acted outside its authority. As stated above, the Municipality's denial of the construction permit without any basis in the proposed physical construction or any defect in the site, and extended by its subsequent administrative and judicial actions regarding the *Convenio*, effectively and unlawfully prevented the Claimant's operation of the landfill.

107. These measures, taken together with the representations of the Mexican federal government, on which Metalclad relied, and the absence of a timely, orderly or substantive basis for the denial by the Municipality of the local construction permit, amount to an indirect expropriation. * * *

109. Although not strictly necessary for its conclusion, the Tribunal also identifies as a further ground for a finding of expropriation the Ecological Decree issued by the Governor of SLP on September 20, 1997. This Decree covers an area of 188,758 hectares within the "Real de Guadalcazar" that includes the landfill site, and created therein an ecological preserve. This Decree had the effect of barring forever the operation of the landfill. * * *

111. The Tribunal need not decide or consider the motivation or intent of the adoption of the Ecological Decree. Indeed, a finding of expropriation on the basis of the Ecological Decree is not essential to the Tribunal's finding of a violation of NAFTA Article 1110. However, the Tribunal considers that the implementation of the Ecological Decree would, in and of itself, constitute an act tantamount to expropriation.

112. In conclusion, the Tribunal holds that Mexico has indirectly expropriated Metalclad's investment without providing compensation to Metalclad for the expropriation. Mexico has violated Article 1110 of the NAFTA.

Mexico appealed this decision to the British Columbia Supreme Court, the Province's superior trial court. The B.C. Supreme Court ruled that the Tribunal's decision with respect to minimum standard of treatment and expropriation with respect to the municipal construction permit exceeded the Tribunal's jurisdiction because its decision was based on transparency. The Supreme Court found that the tribunal did not simply misinterpret the law, but misstated the applicable law by concluding that international law included a transparency requirement. The Supreme Court nevertheless upheld the Tribunal's decision that the ecological decree constituted an expropriation on the ground that the decree effectively prevented Metalclad from operating the landfill it had constructed. Thus, it upheld the award of $16.8 million to Metalclad less the interest compounded prior to the expropriation arising from the ecological decree. The United Mexican States v. Metalclad Corp., 2001 B.C.S.C 664 (2001), *available at* http://www.courts.gov.bc.ca/jdb-txt/sc/01/06/2001bcsc0664.htm.

Although it generated a great deal of anxiety, *Metalclad* has made little lasting impact. Most legal commentators agree that the issuance of the ecological decree without compensation, which the tribunal dealt with as a makeweight issue but the B.C. court found dispositive, meets the traditional test of an indirect taking. *See* Sanford E. Gaines, *Protecting Investors, Protecting the Environment: The Unexpected Story of NAFTA Chapter 11*, *in*, Greening NAFTA: The North American Commission for Environmental Cooperation 173, 186 (David L. Markell & John H. Knox eds., 2003).

b. The Pope & Talbot *Case*

Pope & Talbot argued that Canada's implementation of the Softwood Lumber Agreement (SLA), which denied Pope & Talbot the ability to export unlimited quantities of softwood lumber, constituted an indirect expropriation by substantially devaluing its investment. It argued that Canada "ha[d] deprived the Investment of its ordinary ability to alienate its product to its traditional and natural market." Pope & Talbot v. Canada (Interim Merits Award), para. 81 (June 26, 2000). Pope & Talbot further argued that international law on expropriation "refers to an act by which governmental authority is used to deny *some* benefit of property" and that NAFTA's phrase "measure tantamount to expropriation" includes "even nondiscriminatory measures of general application which have the effect of substantially interfering with the investments of investors of NAFTA Parties." *Id.* at paras. 83–84. Based on these interpretations of "expropriation," Pope & Talbot claimed Canada expropriated its investment by reducing its fee-free quota for exports of softwood lumber and thereby limiting its ability to run at full capacity and export a larger volume of softwood lumber to the United States.

Despite broadly defining "investment" (*see* page 720), the *Pope & Talbot* tribunal concluded that Canada's restrictions on exports from some provinces did not constitute an expropriation.

Pope & Talbot v. Canada
(Interim Merits Award) (June 26, 2000)

96. [T]he Tribunal concludes that the Investment's access to the U.S. market is a property interest subject to protection under Article 1110 and that the scope of that article does cover nondiscriminatory regulation that might be said to fall within an exercise of a state's so-called police powers. However, the Tribunal

does not believe that those regulatory measures constitute an interference with the Investment's business activities substantial enough to be characterized as an expropriation under international law. Finally the Tribunal does not believe that the phrase "measure tantamount to nationalization or expropriation" in Article 1110 broadens the ordinary concept of expropriation under international law to require compensation for measures affecting property interests without regard to the magnitude or severity of that effect. * * *

99. Canada appears to claim that, because the measures under consideration are cast in the form of regulations, they constitute an exercise of "police powers," which, if nondiscriminatory, are supposedly beyond the reach of the NAFTA rules regarding expropriations. While the exercise of police powers must be analyzed with special care, the Tribunal believes that Canada's formulation goes too far. Regulations can indeed be exercised in a way that would constitute creeping expropriation:

> Subsection (1) [relating to responsibility for injury from improper takings] applies not only to avowed expropriations in which the government formally takes title to property, but also to other actions of the government that have the effect of "taking" the property in whole or in large part, outright or in stages ("creeping expropriation"). A state is responsible as for an expropriation of property under Subsection (1) when it subjects alien property to taxation, *regulation*, or other action that is confiscatory, or that prevents, unreasonably interferes with, or unduly delays, effective enjoyment of an alien's property of its removal from the state's territory.[72]

Indeed, much creeping expropriation could be conducted by regulation, and a blanket exception for regulatory measures would create a gaping loophole in international protections against expropriation. For these reasons, the Tribunal rejects the argument of Canada that the Export Control Regime, as a regulatory measure, is beyond the coverage of Article 1110.

100. The next question is whether the Export Control Regime has caused an expropriation of the Investor's investment, creeping or otherwise. Using the ordinary meaning of those terms under international law, the answer must be negative. First of all, there is no allegation that the Investment has been nationalized or that the Regime is confiscatory. * * *

101. The sole "taking" that the Investor has identified is interference with the Investment's ability to carry on its business of exporting softwood lumber to the U.S. While this interference has, according to the Investor, resulted in reduced profits for the Investment, it continues to export substantial quantities of softwood lumber to the U.S. and to earn substantial profits on those sales.

102. Even accepting (for the purpose of this analysis) the allegations of the Investor concerning diminished profits, the Tribunal concludes that the degree of interference with the Investment's operations due to the Export Control Regime does not rise to an expropriation (creeping or otherwise) within the meaning of Article 1110. While it may sometimes be uncertain whether a particular interference with business activities amounts to expropriation, the test is whether that interference is sufficiently restrictive to support a conclusion that the prop-

---

72. *Third Restatement of the Foreign Relations Law of the U.S.*, §712, comment (g) (emphasis added).

erty has been "taken" from the owner. Thus, the *Harvard Draft* defines the standard as requiring interference that would "justify an inference that the owner * * * will not be able to use, enjoy, or dispose of the property...." The *Restatement*, in addressing the question whether regulation may be considered expropriation, speaks of "action that is confiscatory, or that prevents, unreasonably interferes with, or unduly delays, effective enjoyment of an alien's property." Indeed, at the hearing, the Investor's Counsel conceded, correctly, that under international law, expropriation requires a "substantial deprivation." The Export Control Regime has not restricted the Investment in ways that meet these standards.

103. As noted, the Investor expressly agreed that "the Export Control Regime is a measure not covered by customary international law definitions or interpretations of the term expropriation." It contends that NAFTA goes beyond those customary definitions and interpretations to adopt broader requirements that include under the purview of Article 1110 "measures of general application which have the effect of substantially interfering with the investments of investors of NAFTA Parties." The Investor discerns this additional requirement because of the use of the phrase "measure tantamount to ... expropriation" in Article 1110.

104. The Tribunal is unable to accept the Investor's reading of Article 1110. "Tantamount" means nothing more than equivalent. Something that is equivalent to something else cannot logically encompass more. No authority cited by the Investor supports a contrary conclusion. References to the decisions of the Iran-U.S. Claims Tribunal ignore the fact that tribunal's mandate expressly extends beyond expropriation to include "other measures affecting property rights." And, to the extent the Investor is correct in urging that the comments of Dolzer and Stevens suggest that measures "tantamount" to expropriation can encompass restraints less severe that expropriation itself (creeping or otherwise), those comments would not be well-founded under a reasonable interpretation of the treaties that the authors analyze.

105. Based upon the foregoing, the Tribunal rejects the Investor's claim under Article 1110.

We revisit *Glamis Gold*, this time to see how the tribunal addressed Glamis Gold's claim of expropriation. Recall from the facts on pages 745–46 that Glamis is challenging changes in regulations that Glamis believes have made mining unprofitable. The State of California, the U.S. BLM, and the local Quechans believe the regulations are necessary to protect important environmental, recreational, and religious values.

Glamis Gold, Ltd. v. United States of America

(Final Award), (June 8, 2009)

356. This proceeding involves the particularly thorny issue of what is commonly known as a regulatory taking. More specifically, the question presented in this proceeding is whether the administrative and legislative actions taken individually, or in concert, by the federal government and the State of California constitute an expropriation under Article 1110. The Parties, citing to the *2004 Model Bilateral Investment Treaty*, indicate that tribunals in such instances often assess whether measures of a State constitute a non-compensable regulation or a compensable expropriation by examining, inter alia, (1) the extent to which the mea-

sures interfered with reasonable and investment-backed expectations of a stable regulatory framework, and (2) the purpose and character of the governmental actions taken. There is for all expropriations, however, the foundational threshold inquiry of whether the property or property right was in fact taken. This threshold question is relatively straightforward in the case of a direct taking, for example, by nationalization. In the case of an indirect taking or an act tantamount to expropriation such as by a regulatory taking, however, the threshold examination is an inquiry as to the degree of the interference with the property right. This often dispositive inquiry involves two questions: the severity of the economic impact and the duration of that impact.

357. Several NAFTA tribunals agree on the extent of interference that must occur for the finding of an expropriation, phrasing the test in one instance as, "the affected property must be impaired to such an extent that it must be seen as 'taken'"; and in another instance as, "the test is whether that interference is sufficiently restrictive to support a conclusion that the property has been 'taken' from the owner." Therefore, a panel's analysis should begin with determining whether the economic impact of the complained of measures is sufficient to potentially constitute a taking at all: "[I]t must first be determined if the Claimant was radically deprived of the economical use and enjoyment of its investments, as if the rights related thereto ... had ceased to exist." The Tribunal agrees with these statements and thus begins its analysis of whether a violation of Article 1110 of the NAFTA has occurred by determining whether the federal and California measures "substantially impair[ed] the investor's economic rights, i.e. ownership, use, enjoyment or management of the business, by rendering them useless. Mere restrictions on the property rights do not constitute takings."

358. To determine whether Claimant's investment in the Imperial Project has been so radically deprived of its economic value to Claimant as to potentially constitute an expropriation and violation of Article 1110 of the NAFTA, the Tribunal must assess the impact of the complained of measures on the value of the Project. Claimant has alleged that the federal and California measures acted both individually and together to effect a taking. * * *

360. To the extent that Claimant argues that the delay and temporary denial occasioned by the federal government themselves effected an expropriation, the Tribunal finds Claimant's argument without merit. The Tribunal finds that the federal Record of Decision denying approval of the Imperial Project, even if it presented difficulties to Claimant, was quickly reversed and therefore of short duration. This does not constitute an expropriation under NAFTA Article 1110. The Tribunal therefore denies Claimant's claim that the delay and temporary denial occasioned by the federal government either individually or in combination with subsequent complained of measures of the State of California were violations of Article 1110.

361. To the extent that Claimant is arguing that the federal measures facilitated the expropriation by the California measures, the issue becomes the effect of the California measures. The Tribunal thus focuses upon the effect of the California measures, which Claimant itself has done. The Tribunal necessarily turns its attention to the impact of the California measures—Senate Bill 22 ("SB 22") and the State Mining and Geology Board Regulations ("SMGB Regulations") (collectively referred to as "the backfilling measures" or the "California measures"). Therefore, the Tribunal turns to the determination of whether there has been a radical

diminution in value of the Imperial Project, which is ascertained by the analysis of the entitlements and value that remain with Claimant after the enactment of these measures.

362. The Tribunal begins with Claimant's assertion that the value of the Imperial Project before the adoption of the backfilling measures was $49.1 million and its further assertion that after the adoption of the backfilling measures the value of the Project was negative $8.9 million. The Parties focus on five different elements which, Claimant argues, together lead to this asserted negative value. In making its own evaluation of whether the Imperial Project retained value following the backfilling measures, the Tribunal starts with the values and methodologies offered by Claimant for the several elements of its valuation, reviews them one-by-one with Respondent's objections to each, and makes adjustments that the Tribunal considers appropriate in light of the facts presented.

363. The first of the five contested elements concerns the cost of backfilling and involves weighing the two Parties' contentions as to the appropriate cost of backfilling, which in turn is based on four sub-factors: (a) the calculated cost per ton of backfilling, which includes an analysis of the regulatory requirements for and estimated expenses of pit engineering, (b) the cost of equipment refurbishment, (c) the appropriate swell factors for the two identified mineral groups—ore-containing materials and waste rock—a critical issue for determining how many tons of material would need to be backfilled and thus the ultimate cost of backfilling; and (d) the estimated total tonnage that would need to be backfilled to satisfy the California requirements, which includes evaluating the Parties' disparate views regarding the timing of such movement and the associated costs of performing the various stages of backfilling at different times. The second element examined is the appropriate weight to be given the third pit, the Singer Pit, and Claimant's assertion that its value is too speculative to include in the post-backfilling valuation and Respondent's argument that this assumption is incorrect. The third element that the Tribunal analyzes is the appropriate price of gold: although the Parties agree on the correct price of gold at the alleged date of expropriation, they dispute the relevance of the current price to the value of the Imperial Project. The fourth element the Tribunal analyzes is the Parties' dispute regarding the amount and type of financial assurances that the federal, state and county governments would require to be posted to ensure proper reclamation of the Imperial Project. The Tribunal assesses both the types of financial assurances available to Claimant, as well as the timing for posting these assurances as required by the various responsible governmental entities. In the fifth and final element, the Tribunal determines the appropriate discount rate to be employed in valuing the Imperial Project as of the asserted date of expropriation—December 12, 2002—which includes an assessment of the disparate discount rates offered by the Parties to use in calculating the present value of the Imperial Project. This rate is based on the risk-free rate plus a component that accounts for the specific risks of the particular project and is a critical component of valuing an asset with an uncertain or risky income stream. * * *

365. Thus, to be specific, the Tribunal's goal in this inquiry into Claimant's valuation model is not to determine if there *was* an expropriation, but to determine if there was *not* significant economic impact. These are very different inquiries: the first requires definitive cost calculations and a full revision of the discounted cash flow methodologies to determine exactly the value of the Imperial

Project post-backfilling; while the second requires only sufficient calculation to determine if the Project's value is positive. In this latter endeavor, issues presenting specific complexity, in which the Tribunal is satisfied with neither of the calculations offered by either Party, can be resolved in Claimant's favor, as the question above is not what is the exact value of the Imperial Project following the complained of measures, but is the value of the post-backfilling Imperial Project positive *even* if such an issue is decided in Claimant's favor.

366. The Tribunal, after completing its analysis, concludes that the California backfilling measures did not result in a radical diminution in the value of the Imperial Project. Therefore, it denies Claimant's claim that the actions of the state and federal government resulted in an expropriation under Article 1110....

367. The California measures require complete backfilling of all pits to the extent possible, and spreading and recontouring of any remaining piles to a maximum height of 25 feet. The cost of this required backfilling is central to the determination of whether the value of the Glamis Imperial Project has been so dramatically decreased as to warrant a finding of expropriation under Article 1110. Claimant estimates total reclamation costs at the end of the Project being as much as $98.5 million; Respondent places the total cost of backfilling, spreading and recontouring at approximately $55.4 million, a difference of $43 million.

[The Tribunal then embarks on an exhaustive, often highly technical, analysis of each of the five elements of the valuation claims.]

535. When these adjustments are applied to Claimant's valuation methodology, the post-backfilling valuation of the Imperial Project exceeds $20 million.

536. In light of this significantly positive valuation, the Tribunal holds that the first factor in any expropriation analysis is not met: the complained of measures did not cause a sufficient economic impact to the Imperial Project to effect an expropriation of Claimant's investment. The Tribunal thus holds that Claimant's claim under Article 1110 fails.

Questions and Discussion

1. The award in Waste Management v. Mexico, ICSID Case No. ARB(AF)/00/3, para. 144 (Apr. 30, 2004), reasoned that the use of the phrase "tantamount to expropriation" in Article 1110 in addition to mention of "indirect" expropriation "suggests that the drafters entertained a broad view of what might be 'tantamount to an expropriation.'" In paragraph 355 of *Glamis Gold*, the tribunal explicitly disagrees with the *Waste Management* reasoning: "'Tantamount' means equivalent and thus the concept should not encompass *more* than direct expropriation; it merely differs from direct expropriation which effects a physical taking of property in that no actual transfer of ownership rights occurs."

2. Consider the following hypotheticals and consider whether they might constitute an "indirect expropriation" under Article 1110.

- The U.S. Fish & Wildlife Service lists a forest dwelling species, the purple-spotted goshawk, as an "endangered species." Under the U.S. Endangered Species Act, no person may "take" an endangered species. "Take" is defined broadly to mean harass, harm, pursue, hunt, shoot, would, kill, trap, capture, or collect, or attempt to engage in any such conduct. 16 U.S.C. §§ 1531–1544, § 1538. The definition of "harm" prohibits the adverse modification of the species' habitat. *See* Babbitt v. Sweet Home Chapter of Communities for a Great Oregon, 515 U.S. 687, 115 S. Ct. 2407, 132 L. Ed. 2d 597 (1995). BC Timber, a Canadian logging company, owns land in the United States for logging purposes in the range of the purple-spotted goshawk. The Fish & Wildlife Service, however, has prohibited logging within 300 yards of any goshawk's nest. There are five goshawk nests on BC Timber's property of 1,000 acres. Has BC Timber's investment been indirectly expropriated? In light of *Glamis Gold*, what else would a tribunal want to know about BC Timber's investment, before and after the FWS ruling?

- Waste, Inc., a U.S.-based company enters into a contract with the city of Cancun, Mexico, to be the exclusive hauler of garbage in several Cancun neighborhoods. As part of the contract, Waste, Inc. must build a landfill. Waste, Inc. identifies an arguably suitable site for the landfill, but local citizens object, and the government of the Quintana Roo (where Cancun is) denies Waste, Inc.'s permit application. Because Waste, Inc. has not built a landfill as required under the contract, Cancun cancels the contract with Waste, Inc. and gives the garbage collection contract to a Mexican company. Has Waste, Inc.'s investment been indirectly expropriated?

3. Some commentators believe that a definition of expropriation should be based on international law, because the NAFTA does not define the term. *See* J. Martin Wagner, *International Investment, Expropriation and Environmental Protection*, at 527. Others, however, warn that successful claims under NAFTA's expropriation provision could short-circuit ongoing domestic legal debates to define expropriation, particularly regulatory takings/indirect expropriation. Konrad von Moltke, An International Investment Regime? Issues of Sustainability, at 23–24. If a Canadian investor challenges a U.S. law as an indirect expropriation, should the tribunal defer to U.S. law on regulatory takings or should it opt for an interpretation consistent with international law? Which approach does *Glamis Gold* adopt? A system that defers to national law could give rise to different legal conclusions based on identical facts, depending solely on the locus of the investment. Is that a problem? Can such a system actually increase predictability for investors?

---

5. Chapter 11's "Environmental Measures" Provision

Despite the large number of environment-related claims brought under Chapter 11, none have addressed in any detail the scope of Article 1114. Is it an exception? Does it include an obligation?

NAFTA Article 1114: Environmental Measures

1. Nothing in this Chapter shall be construed to prevent a Party from adopting, maintaining or enforcing any measure otherwise consistent with this Chapter that it considers appropriate to ensure that investment activity in its territory is undertaken in a manner sensitive to environmental concerns.

2. The Parties recognize that it is inappropriate to encourage investment by relaxing domestic health, safety or environmental measures. Accordingly, a Party should not waive or otherwise derogate from, or offer to waive or otherwise derogate from, such measures as an encouragement for the establishment, ac-

quisition, expansion or retention in its territory of an investment of an investor. If a Party considers that another Party has offered such an encouragement, it may request consultations with the other Party and the two Parties shall consult with a view to avoiding any such encouragement.

Would an "environmental exception" similar to GATT Article XX be more helpful for environmental measures? After *Methanex* and *Glamis Gold*, is there any apparent need for such an exception? Consider the arguments in the following excerpts, written before *Methanex* and *Glamis Gold* awards.

―――――――――

Chris Tollefson, *Games without Frontiers: Investor Claims and Citizen Submissions under the NAFTA Regime*
27 Yale J. Int'l L. 141, 151–153 (2002)

The relationship between these new "private" rights and the traditionally accepted prerogative of governments to take action to protect public health and the environment is not specifically addressed in the NAFTA text and is the source of considerable controversy and uncertainty. Unlike the GATT, Chapter 11 of NAFTA does not contain a generally applicable provision that prescribes how these competing private and public interests are to be balanced. Under the GATT, this balancing function is performed by Article XX (General Exceptions). This provision allows a state to defend a trade restrictive measure on the basis that it is "necessary to protect human, animal or plant life or health." * * *

Does the absence of an Article XX-like provision in Chapter 11 of NAFTA mean that a government cannot defend against an investor claim on the basis that its actions were motivated by bona fide health or environmental concerns? If this were true, those who have characterized the implications of Chapter 11 as "revolutionary" would be vindicated, as such an interpretation would represent a truly remarkable and unparalleled restriction on Westphalian sovereignty. Many would argue, however, that such an interpretation is implausible. For one, it is inconsistent with language in the preamble of NAFTA and the NAAEC [North American Agreement on Environmental Cooperation] affirming that environmental protection and economic development can and should be mutually supportive. It also appears to conflict with Article 1114 (Environmental Measures) of Chapter 11, a provision that is often cited in support of the argument that NAFTA is one of the greenest trade agreements ever negotiated. This provision states: "Nothing in this Chapter shall be construed to prevent a Party from adopting, maintaining or enforcing any measure otherwise consistent with this Chapter that it considers appropriate to ensure that investment activity in its territory is undertaken in a manner sensitive to environmental concerns."

Several trade experts have argued that the permissive nature of the language of Article 1114—in particular the caveat that such environmental measures must be "otherwise consistent with this Chapter"—suggests that it should be regarded as merely aspirational and of no legal consequence. In his separate opinion in S.D. Myers, however, Dr. Schwartz observes that such an interpretation is implausible in that it implies Article 1114 is "empty rhetoric."

―――――――――

John Wickham, *Toward a Green Multilateral Investment Framework: NAFTA and the Search for Models*

12 GEO. INT'L ENVTL. L. REV. 617, 622–625 (2000),
reprinted with permission of the publisher, Georgetown
International Environmental Law Review © 2000

NAFTA Article 1114(2) is the first provision of its kind seeking to prevent states from lowering environmental standards to attract international investment. In this regard, NAFTA truly breaks new ground and sets the bar higher for environmental language in all future trade and investment agreements. Nevertheless, measures aimed at achieving a minimum level of environmental regulation, or those encouraging international harmonization of environmental standards, are not unprecedented in trade agreements. As Charnovitz points out, there have been numerous trade agreements, some as early as 1924 and 1935, that included explicit and mandatory environmental standards in conjunction with trade liberalization. Indeed, Charnovitz believes that many earlier agreements were more environmentally stringent than NAFTA, and that NAFTA Article 1114(2) is flawed in at least three ways. [Steve Charnovitz, *The North American Free Trade Agreement: Green Law or Green Spin?*, 26 LAW & POL'Y INT'L BUS. 1 (1994).]

First, Charnovitz notes that Article 1114(2) is precatory, requiring only that "a Party should not waive or otherwise derogate from" environmental measures. Second, he points out that Article 1114(2) is ambiguous in key respects. For instance, he notes that the meaning of "relaxing" in "relaxing domestic health, safety or environmental measures" is unclear. Does "relax" mean enacting new legislation that lowers standards, he asks, or does it mean simply administrative action that interprets existing statutes in a more permissive way? More importantly, Charnovitz believes that there is "little doubt that parties are free to relax their laws for purposes other than attracting or retaining investment. For example, [he says,] they can relax laws to increase export competitiveness." Third, Charnovitz notes that, because Article 1114(2) recommends that parties pursue "consultations" in the event of competitive deregulation, this provision is considerably weaker than it would have been with language requiring dispute settlement.

Each of these critiques appears sound. Article 1114(2) certainly is weaker than it would have been with binding commitments and less ambiguous language. That said, Daniel Esty, an architect of NAFTA's environmental language, argues persuasively for one element of the voluntary commitments in Article 1114(2). Esty explains that:

> the drafters of this "pollution haven" language sought to establish a provision sufficiently rigorous to deter parties from using environmental degradation as a point of comparative advantage and yet not so easily invoked as a means of inflicting costs on competitors that it undermines the basic free trade thrust of NAFTA. They concluded that none of the NAFTA Parties could withstand the public pressure likely to be generated by awareness of any environmental performance lapse revealed in consultations, particularly in light of the active environmental communities in each country. Whether mechanisms will be established to ensure that the glare of publicity will be sufficiently bright to shame the NAFTA Parties into re-

forming any practice that is called into question under this provision remains an open issue—and one that bears ongoing scrutiny as NAFTA implementation goes forward.

* * * An important conclusion to draw from the literature on pollution havens and industrial migration is that, since so few industries migrate, a provision like NAFTA's Article 1114(2) … will only be of limited value in the face of other dynamics at play in trade expansion and industrial pollution. Although Esty and Geradin argue that the very perception or fear that industries will relocate can drive policy makers to freeze environmental standards (a phenomenon known as "regulatory chill" or "political drag"), this explains only why environmental standards do not rise, not why they fall, which is the concern of NAFTA Article 1114(2)….

In short, while governments might lower environmental standards to improve the competitiveness of existing domestic firms, there is little likelihood of their doing so to attract new firms to locate within their territory. This, coupled with the fact that very few industries have been shown to migrate on the basis of environmental considerations alone, makes NAFTA's Article 1114(2) …"Not Lowering Measures" seem too narrowly focused. To have a truly prophylactic effect, "not lowering measures" should not be applied only to "attracting investment," but instead should stand on its own, prohibiting retreat from environmental standards for any purely commercial reason.

An additional critique Charnovitz makes of NAFTA's Article 1114 and, more generally, of the NAFTA itself is more far-reaching. According to Charnovitz, "it is important to consider these [NAFTA] provisions in a broader context.… What international agreements generally do is to commit parties to adopt common standards or carry out common programs. A commitment to enforce one's own domestic standard may be the weakest form of international agreement." … Certainly it is better to encourage upholding domestic standards than it is to encourage nothing at all. Yet it raises the question: if the aim is collective action to protect and, ideally, to improve the environment, what is achieved by non-binding (or limited) promises to obey one's own laws? With NAFTA Article 1114(2)…, the answer would have to be "not much."

Questions and Discussion

1. Tollefson mentions the separate opinion of Dr. Schwartz in *S.D. Myers*. A fuller quotation from Dr. Schwartz is: "I do not think that Article 1114 must be viewed as empty rhetoric … I view Article 1114 as acknowledging and reminding interpreters of Chapter 11 (Investment) that the parties take both the environment and open trade very seriously and that means should be found to reconcile these two objectives and, if possible, to make them mutually supportive." S.D. Myers v. Canada (Separate Opinion of Dr. Schwartz), 118 (Nov. 12, 2000). Is that rhetoric just the same?

2. *Pope & Talbot, S.D. Myers*, and other tribunals have, to some degree, addressed Tollefson's question about the balance between private rights and public interests by suggesting that, in the context of Article 1102, environmental measures will receive no special consideration to the extent they exceed the "legitimate" exercise of police powers; that is, the ability of governments to enact and enforce laws and regulations for the general welfare of its citizens, including health and safety. In other words, government power on en-

vironmental measures under Article 1102 is co-extensive with traditional police powers, notwithstanding Article 1114 and language in NAFTA's preamble and the NAAEC underscoring the importance of environmental protection and sustainable development. Later U.S. free trade agreements, as discussed below, make explicit reference to police powers and even clarify that environmental measures will only "rarely" establish grounds for indirect expropriation claims.

IV. Post-NAFTA Investment Treaties

The controversy surrounding NAFTA's Chapter 11 has not gone unnoticed by the NAFTA Parties. As we have seen, the three governments have reacted both to public pressures and to their actual or anticipated losses in NAFTA litigation, by seeking to narrow the scope of their potential liability. In nearly two decades since the NAFTA, the United States has entered into numerous other free trade agreements, including United States-Chile Free Trade Agreement (U.S.-Chile FTA), the United States-Singapore Free Trade Agreement (U.S.-Singapore FTA), and the agreement with Costa Rica, El Salvador, Guatemala, Honduras, Nicaragua, and the Dominican Republic, known as DR-CAFTA. Each of these agreements includes investment provisions modeled on NAFTA but also learning from the lessons of NAFTA.

A. Minimum Standard of Treatment

With mixed success in getting tribunals to abide by the intent of the Free Trade Commission's Note on Interpretation (see Section III.E.3, above), the United States came up with the following language (almost identical language is included in the US-Singapore FTA, the DR-CAFTA, and other agreements):

U.S.-Chile Free Trade Agreement, June 6, 2003
available at http://www.ustr.gov/new/fta/chile.htm

Article 10.4 Minimum Standard of Treatment

1. Each Party shall accord to covered investments treatment in accordance with customary international law, including fair and equitable treatment and full protection and security.

2. For greater certainty, paragraph 1 prescribes the customary international law minimum standard of treatment of aliens as the minimum standard of treatment to be afforded to covered investments. The concepts of "fair and equitable treatment" and "full protection and security" do not require treatment in addition to or beyond that which is required by that standard, and do not create additional substantive rights. The obligation in paragraph 1 to provide:

(a) "fair and equitable treatment" includes the obligation not to deny justice in criminal, civil, or administrative adjudicatory proceedings in accordance with the principle of due process embodied in the principal legal systems of the world; and

(b) "full protection and security" requires each Party to provide the level of police protection required under customary international law.

3. A determination that there has been a breach of another provision of this Agreement, or of a separate international agreement, does not establish that there has been a breach of this Article.

In addition, in a footnote, the Parties are directed to Annex 10-A for "greater certainty" as to the meaning of minimum standard of treatment:

> The Parties confirm their shared understanding that "customary international law" … results from a general and consistent practice of States that they follow from a sense of legal obligation. With regard to Article 10.4, the customary international law minimum standard of treatment of aliens refers to all customary international law principles that protect the economic rights and interests of aliens.

Id. Does this understanding clarify how tribunals are to interpret minimum standard of treatment?

David A. Gantz, *Contrasting Key Investment Provisions of the NAFTA with the United States-Chile FTA*

NAFTA INVESTMENT LAW AND ARBITRATION, at 414–15

In paragraph 1, the United States and Chile have assured that there will be no confusion under this agreement as to the applicability of "customary international law" rather than simply "international law." Paragraph 2 attempts to deal with the inherent vagueness of the concepts of "fair and equitable treatment" and "full protection and security" by making it crystal clear that those concepts are not additive to the requirement of compliance with customary international law. Rather, they are part of that concept. Thus, "fair and equitable treatment" is defined as including (but not limited to) avoiding a denial of justice, and the concept of "due process embodied in the principal legal systems of the world" is offered as a rough definition.

The latter serves a second purpose … of seeking to equate fair and equitable treatment under customary international law with the U.S. standards of due process— so that the former is not broader than the latter. Presumably, the reference to due process in the principal legal systems of the world, rather than just in the United States, is an effort to avoid reducing "fair and equitable treatment" to no more than national treatment—i.e., non-discriminatory treatment where national treatment does not meet minimum standards of customary international law.…

At the same time, the language "principal legal systems of the world" seems at least partly inconsistent with what the United States has argued in *Methanex* … that "fair and equitable treatment" does not incorporate broad concepts of "equity, fairness, due process and appropriate protection." If the concepts define "fair and equitable treatment" and are found in principal legal systems of the world, it would seem far more difficult to argue that they are not violations of customary international law.

Paragraph 3 essentially adopts paragraph 3 of the [NAFTA] Interpretation, effectively eliminating the *S.D. Myers'* practice of using an Article 1102 violation as the principal basis for finding an Article 1105 "fair and equitable treatment" violation. (It also could have helped to avoid the bootstrapping undertaken by the *Metalclad* tribunal, where a violation of Article 1105 was used to support a finding of indirect expropriation under Article 1110.) The new language also avoids a possible argument by a claimant that the violation by a government of one of the provisions of a separate international agreement—one of the WTO agreements, as was argued in *Methanex*, or of a possible future agreement on anti-competitive practices or government procurement, for example—is, in and of itself, a denial of fair and equitable treatment.

A more or less classical definition of customary international law is provided in Annex 10-A. This definition, in analogous circumstances, would perhaps have shortened the debate over the meaning of customary international law in such cases as *Mondev*, *ADF* and *UPS*, but it necessarily fails to deal directly with the more critical question of the current scope of customary international law when seeking to define the reach of "fair and equitable treatment." Given that the United States has conceded that customary international law in this area has evolved since 1926, and continues to evolve, it would have been unwise for the United States to go beyond incorporating more explicit language on due process/denial of justice and customary international law as they affect the concept of "fair and equitable treatment."

B. Expropriation

While only *Metalclad* has found a governmental measure in an investor dispute to constitute an expropriation, the claims persist and, as a result, the United States seeks to limit the meaning of expropriation in more recent agreements. Again, although the language quoted below is from the U.S-Chile FTA, almost identical language is found in U.S.-Singapore FTA and DR-CAFTA.

U.S.-Chile Free Trade Agreement, June 6, 2003
available at http://www.ustr.gov/new/fta/chile.htm

Article 10.9 Expropriation and Compensation

1. Neither Party may expropriate or nationalize a covered investment either directly or indirectly through measures equivalent to expropriation or nationalization ("expropriation"), except:

(a) for a public purpose;

(b) in a non-discriminatory manner;

(c) on payment of prompt, adequate, and effective compensation accordance with paragraphs 2 through 4; and

(d) in accordance with due process of law and Article 10.4(1) through (3) [the equivalent of NAFTA Article 1105 on page 731].

Annex 10-D

The Parties confirm their shared understanding that:

1. Article 10.9(1) is intended to reflect customary international law concerning the obligation of States with respect to expropriation.

2. An action or a series of actions by a Party cannot constitute an expropriation unless it interferes with a tangible or intangible property right or property interest in an investment.

3. Article 10.9(1) addresses two situations. The first is direct expropriation, where an investment is nationalized or otherwise directly expropriated through formal transfer of title or outright seizure.

4. The second situation addressed by Article 10.9(1) is indirect expropriation, where an action or series of actions by a Party has an effect equivalent to direct expropriation without formal transfer of title or outright seizure.

(a) The determination of whether an action or series of actions by a Party, in a specific factual situation, constitutes an indirect expropriation, requires a case-by-case, fact-based inquiry that considers, among other factors:

(i) the economic impact of the government action, although the fact that an action or series of actions by a Party has an adverse effect on the economic value of an investment, standing alone, does not establish that an indirect expropriation has occurred;

(ii) the extent to which the government action interferes with distinct, reasonable investment-backed expectations; and

(iii) the character of the government action.

(b) Except in rare circumstances, nondiscriminatory regulatory actions by a Party that are designed and applied to protect legitimate public welfare objectives, such as public health, safety and the environment, do not constitute indirect expropriation.

David A. Gantz, *Contrasting Key Investment Provisions of the NAFTA with the United States-Chile FTA*

NAFTA INVESTMENT LAW AND ARBITRATION, at 421–22

Arguably, the only possibly significant (probably non-substantive) change from the NAFTA [in Article 10.9] is the substitution of the phrase "equivalent to expropriation or nationalization" for "tantamount to nationalization or expropriation." At least one NAFTA tribunal—*S.D. Myers*—had suggested that the terms "tantamount" and "equivalent" were functionally the same, and the NAFTA Article 1110 Spanish phraseology is "equivalente a la expropiacion," so the significance of this change should not be over-emphasized. * * *

[Annex 10-D] is a truly remarkable effort to provide detailed guidance—and constraints for future tribunals seeking to distinguish compensable expropriations from valid government regulations, particularly in light of the self-restraint under Article 1110 shown by most NAFTA tribunals to date. It unquestionably makes it more difficult for a foreign investor to successfully claim that any sort of government regulatory action is an expropriation. First, it confirms the intent of the parties that USCFTA Article 10.9 not go beyond customary international law in its protection of investment. Secondly, it seeks to limit expropriation claims to interference with tangible or intangible property rights (but certainly not to exclude partial takings). This would appear designed to exclude from coverage some trade-based claims, perhaps including those which were the subject of NAFTA claims in *Pope & Talbot* and *S.D. Myers,* or situations in which the relationship between the alleged taking and the effect on the claimant is very indirect, as in *Methanex* (a ban on MTBE impacts on a producer of the input product, methanol). Whether this will happen, given the breadth of definitions of such terms as "investment" in USCFTA Article 10.27, remains to be seen.

Third, indirect expropriation claims are circumscribed. Paragraph (a) stresses the need for "equivalency" of indirect takings to direct takings, absent only the formal transfer of title or outright seizure, perhaps again reflecting *Methanex,* among others. A case-by-case approach is acknowledged as necessary, but the adverse effect of government actions on an investment is not in itself to be considered an indirect expropriation. "Reasonable, investment based expectations" and the "character" of government action are also to be considered.

Most significantly, non-discriminatory regulatory actions protecting "legitimate public welfare objectives, such as public health, safety, and the environment" are not actionable as expropriations except in "rare" circumstances; this provision has *Methanex* written all over it, and also reflects the Trade Promotion Act objectives. As the U.S. Trade Representative summary notes, "Pursuant to the directives of the TPA of 2002, this article is supplanted by an annex that elaborates on relevant principles of United States takings law and clarifies the relationship of indirect expropriations and domestic regulation." This language undoubtedly reflects as well current United States government views as to the proper scope not only of Article 10.9 of the Chile FTA, but also of [NAFTA] Article 1110(1) as well, although it does not and could not, of course, modify the latter.

Questions and Discussion

1. Do the new expropriation provisions take into account the concerns expressed by governments and environmental groups regarding the distinction between expropriation and valid use of police powers to protect the environment?

2. The U.S.-Singapore Free Trade Agreement includes nearly identical language to that of the U.S.-Chile Free Trade Agreement concerning minimum standard of treatment and expropriation. However, the U.S-Singapore FTA memorializes the understanding of the meaning of expropriation, included in the Annex to the U.S.-Chile FTA, in an exchange of letters. *See* http://www.ustr.gov/new/fta/Singapore/final.htm. What legal significance do those letters have? Moreover, both agreements confirm the understanding *between the Parties* as to the meaning of expropriation. Is the investor bound by that understanding, even if it is included in an Annex? If the interpretations are so important, why wouldn't the Parties include it in the text of the treaty itself?

3. The United States free trade agreements with Chile and the Dominican Republic–Central America also contemplate the development at a later date of an appeals process for the investor-state mechanism, though no such process has yet been created. Several commentators have suggested an appellate body could help bring a more consistent and even approach to this evolving area of law. Would an appeals process be useful? In light of the many free trade agreements involving the United States, ranging from Oman and Bahrain to Israel, and Australia to several countries throughout Latin America, where would you locate such an appellate body and how would it operate?

V. Possible Paths Forward

A. The Constitutionalization of International Law

Providing private investors with a binding dispute resolution mechanism for claims against States is already eroding, and may ultimately breach, the seawall separating many aspects of domestic law and international law. In State-to-State models such as the WTO, Parties carefully weigh the costs and benefits of making claims that challenge another country's laws, regulations or practices. States often refrain from aggressively pursuing valid claims on any number of grounds, including diplomatic relations and concerns about its own nonconforming practices in similar areas. These considerations greatly reduce the number of international disputes, and also limit the intrusion of international legal principles and norms into domestic lawmaking. Private investors, in contrast, have but one key consideration in mind before pursuing a Chapter 11 claim: profitability. Companies may well consider the public and government relations implications of such decisions as well as numerous additional factors; nevertheless, the calculation is considerably narrower than the one facing national governments.

The profusion of BITs and the inclusion of investment provisions in trade accords is accelerating the evolution of international investment and trade law (*e.g.*, minimum standard of treatment), at the same time that it brings international legal norms and local law into closer orbit. In part, this helps explain a phenomenon that might aptly be described as the "constitutionalization" of international trade and investment law. The U.S. constitutional principles embodying due process (including takings and regulatory takings) and the dormant commerce clause find their approximate counterparts with the investment protections for minimum standards, direct and indirect expropriation, and national treatment, respectively. Indeed, at the urging of the U.S. Congress in the Bipartisian Trade Promotion Authority Act, the post-NAFTA trade agreements negotiated by USTR are converging further on U.S. Constitutional precepts by, for example, incorporating the latest constitutional test for indirect takings in *Penn Central Transportation Co. v. City of New York*, 438 U.S. 104 (1978). *See* Annex 10-D, at para. 4(a) of the U.S.-Chile FTA at page 767. The implications of this are striking. Consider that, soon, an arbitration panelist, who may not have any U.S. legal background, may be called upon to apply the *Penn Central* test developed by the U.S. Supreme Court in the murky waters of regulatory takings to a foreign investment located in the United States, Chile, or Singapore. Champions of internationalizing the U.S. Constitution may cheer this result even as the guardians of national sovereignty decry it. On the other hand, U.S. Supreme Court jurisprudence on takings is not a model of clarity or consistency. The Supreme Court itself has said:

> [O]ur decision in *Mahon* offered little insight into when, and under what circumstances, a given regulation would be see as going "too far" for purposes of the Fifth Amendment [and thus constituting a taking]. In 70-odd years of succeeding "regulatory takings" jurisprudence, we have generally eschewed any "'set formula'" for determining how far is too far, preferring to "engage in ... essentially ad hoc, factual inquiries[.]"

Lucas v. South Carolina, 505 U.S. 1003, 112 S.Ct. 2886, 120 L.Ed. 2d 798 (1992) (citations omitted). Can arbitration panelists from other parts of the world do better?

Mexico, Canada, and the United States have slowly awakened to the fact that public support for the investment provisions erodes rapidly if foreign investors are perceived to enjoy greater rights than local citizens. Yet, it will be exceedingly difficult for international jurists to apply mushy, multi-part tests to complex fact patterns and achieve results identical to national courts. For example, in the United States, the Commerce Clause jurisprudence weighs the burden that a state or local regulation may place on interstate commerce against the benefits of a legitimate public policy. This balancing process has proven elastic, and is fairly tolerant of trade-restrictive laws passed to preserve natural resources or to protect nature. Will foreign tribunal members from different legal and political cultures "balance" the same way nationals would? In Canada and Mexico, the constitutional sensitivities are no less deep-seated. Perhaps in view of this, the post-NAFTA generation of agreements has pulled some chips off the table by reaffirming the legitimacy of environmental and health and safety laws, and by restoring transparency to investor-state dispute resolution.

B. A Global Agreement on Investment?

Efforts to create a multilateral agreement on investment have so far failed. The negotiators of the Uruguay Round achieved some success in creating the Agreement on Trade Related Investment Measures (TRIMs). But TRIMS has limited scope; it governs only investment measures relating to trade in goods, such as domestic-content requirements. The TRIMs Agreement applies GATT's national treatment obligation and prohibition against quantitative restrictions to trade-related investments. It also creates an "illustrative list" of investment measures that are inconsistent with national treatment.

The members of the Organisation for Economic Cooperation and Development (OECD) strived for a more far-reaching agreement on investment—the Multilateral Agreement on Investment (MAI). The MAI text looked very much like NAFTA's investment chapter. As with the NAFTA, it very broadly defined investment to mean "[e]very kind of asset owned or controlled, directly or indirectly, by an investor." It also included national treatment and most favored nation treatment and minimum standard of treatment obligations, as well as prohibitions against expropriations and a range of performance requirements. Also like the NAFTA, the MAI would have granted investors the right to challenge governmental measures as inconsistent with the MAI without imposing any obligations on investors.

The negotiations of the MAI occurred largely without public attention. In 1998, when environmentalists unearthed a draft MAI, the negotiations quickly unraveled. The MAI negotiating process "was abandoned entirely after France withdrew, mainly because it could not shield its cultural industries from the MAI rules. The newly installed German government also decided to press for 'social and ecological compatibility,' which could not been accommodated in the technical draft under consideration." KONRAD VON MOLTKE, AN INTERNATIONAL INVESTMENT REGIME? ISSUES OF SUSTAINABILITY, at 28–29. In the United States, the influential work of Professor Robert Stumberg helped inform state governments, NGOs, and others about the potential state and local impacts of the MAI, and they soon mobilized to oppose the accord. Robert Stumberg, *Sovereignty by Subtraction: The Multilateral Agreement on Investment*, 31 CORNELL INT'L L.J. 491 (1998). For some environmentalists, the end of the MAI negotiations represented a victory that energized their campaign against the WTO Ministerial meeting in Seattle where the possibility of future investment negotiations was contemplated.

However, the larger question remains: what should an international investment agreement comprise? Clearly, investment rules are needed to provide security for investors to bring capital to places that may have deficient infrastructure and poor production facilities.

NAFTA created, and the MAI sought to create, an investment regime modeled in some respects on the GATT. Several of the core obligations, such as national treatment and most favored nation treatment, derived from the trade regime. Institutions similar to the GATT and WTO were chosen for dispute resolution—nonparticipatory, arbitral tribunals—except that corporate nonstate actors could bring claims, while other nonstate actors were shut out of the process. Konrad Von Moltke writes, "The tendency to construct an international investment regime modeled after the trade regime is understandable, even if it represents a serious error." KONRAD VON MOLTKE, AN INTERNATIONAL INVESTMENT REGIME? ISSUES OF SUSTAINABILITY, at 47. Among other reasons, Von Moltke contends that investments are fundamentally of a different character than goods or services. If this is true, then the demise of the MAI must be welcomed. Still, what should an international investment regime comprise? How would it differ from the NAFTA or WTO models?

Moltke provides some suggestions while leaving most of the specifics for another day. For example, based on the premise that different investment sectors may require different rules, he proposes a framework convention that would establish the basic institutions and organizational structure and defines a process for achieving specific goals. *Id.* at 69. Such an agreement would mirror international environmental agreements, such as the Framework Convention on Climate Change and the Vienna Convention for the Protection of the Ozone Layer which gave rise to more specific rules and binding commitments as scientific evidence grew and politically acceptable solutions were found.

As Moltke explains, such a strategy would allow specific rules to develop for specific, underfunded investment sectors or into existing agreements:

> Among the goods not sufficiently served by current flows of foreign direct investment are certain environmental values—such as the prevention of global climate change or the promotion of more sustainable exploitation of natural resources—as well as development in the poorer countries. It makes sense to tie the availability of certain internationally guaranteed investor rights to the provision of such international goods. In other words, it may be desirable to introduce investor rights into agreements such as the UN Framework Convention on Climate Change or an international forestry agreement, should one ever be agreed. This could be done before the creation of a global investment agreement that conveys rights to investors. In this manner it would become possible to achieve the kind of balancing between private rights and public goods that lies at the heart of any broader investment agreement. * * *

> It could be argued that segmenting the international investment regime is undesirable. After all, investment is a universal activity, and in principle more investment is a broadly desirable goal of public policy. But the problems associated with an international investment regime, outlined above, suggest that it is necessary to find organizations that can provide the necessary balance between rights and obligations. by inserting new investor rights into regimes that pursue some other legitimate policy goal—preventing global climate change or promoting sustainable forest practices for example—it becomes possible to create this balance in a more limited context.

Id. at 70–71.

In addition to creating investor obligations as well as rights, an investment regime should more comprehensively allow participation of non-State actors. NAFTA advances international law in some respects by allowing non-State investors to participate directly in international law by bringing investment challenges and obtaining binding judgments against States party to the international agreement. Such rights for non-State actors are extremely rare in international law. Just as with the WTO, however, public interest environmental and consumer groups have been denied corresponding rights, though some moves to accommodate their interests have been made. Non-State actors should be granted more formal and general rights to prepare *amicus* briefs in investment disputes and observe the hearings. If future agreements impose obligations on investors, then the right of non-State actors such as environmental and consumer groups to enforce those rights should be granted, just as citizens have the right to challenge violations of law by governmental and corporate entities under most domestic legal systems.

The International Institute for Sustainable Development (IISD) has advanced a proposal for reforming international investment agreements that seeks both to promote investment stability, fairness, and sustainable development and to balance private rights with public interests. The key to its proposal is establishing sustainable development as the goal of investment treaties. According to IISD, once a new goal is set, then new concepts and structures can be contemplated for rethinking investment treaties. IISD proposes a combination of rights and obligations for all parties, including minimum investor standards in environmental management, corporate accountability, compliance with basic human rights and core labor and environmental standards. The investment agreement would not develop these minimum standards. Instead, the investment agreement could incorporate existing international agreements. AARON COSBEY ET AL., INVESTMENT AND SUSTAINABLE DEVELOPMENT, at 29–34.

Chapter 11

Environment in Regional Trade Agreements — NAFTA and the European Union*

I. Introduction

Regional trade agreements (RTAs), which were discussed briefly in the introduction to Chapter 2, are now a major element of the legal framework for international trade. Although world trade data relating to RTAs is hard to come by, certainly the ever-expanding network of bilateral and regional preferential trading arrangements covers an ever-growing proportion of the world's cross-border exchanges of goods and services. For the two regions that are the focus of this chapter, the basic trade data show the significance of RTAs. For the United States, the value of its trade in goods and services with Canada and Mexico under the North American Free Trade Agreement (NAFTA) in 2008 was US$1.1 trillion, or approximately one-quarter of the U.S. total world trade of US$4.3 trillion. Canada and Mexico were the first and second largest trading partners, respectively, for the United States, with Mexico trade about twice the trade with China, the third-ranking trading partner. Europe is even more tightly bound to regional trade among the 27 member states of the European Union (EU). The volume of cross-border trade within the EU roughly equals the total of the EU's imports from and exports to non-EU trading partners. For more on RTAs in general, see David Gantz, Regional Trade Agreements: Law, Policy and Practice (2009).

Whatever the merits and demerits of RTAs vis-à-vis the multilateralism of the WTO from a trade and economic perspective, RTAs do offer an organizing framework for common approaches to environmental protection among smaller groups of countries that often share common airsheds, watersheds, and ecosystems. The purpose of this chapter is to look at two prime examples of such environmental collaboration in the context of trade integration. The NAFTA and EU represent quite different approaches to environmental issues in the context of free trade. The EU has become much more than a trade-focused customs union; it is by now committed by its governing treaties to a deep process of economic, legal, and political integration built on core principles of the free movement of goods and people. In perfecting its "internal market," the EU has embraced environmental protection and sustainable development as central policy goals, and it has

---

* The texts of the North American Free Trade Agreement and the European Union treaties are readily accessible in many locations. The government source for the NAFTA text in English is http://www.nafta-sec-alena.org/en/view.aspx. The new European Union treaties are available from the EU website; the English text is at http://europa.eu/lisbon_treaty/full_text/index_en.htm.

gradually fashioned fully-developed supra-national institutions and detailed legal frameworks to strive toward that goal. From the outset of their negotiations, the NAFTA parties, while cognizant of the deep-integration European approach, deliberately opted for a much less ambitious "shallow" integration model to meet their shared trade and development goals. The NAFTA has virtually no shared governance structure and quite notoriously does *not* include the free movement of people as part of economic liberalization and integration. Even with those differences, Europe and North America face many similar environmental and developmental challenges, including how to work across differing national regulatory regimes and enforcement practices and how to accommodate widely divergent environmental, technical, and institutional capacities. For example, the EU's joining of highly developed northern economies with less-developed economies such as Greece, Portugal and, more recently, the Eastern European States, presents parallels to the economic disparities in North America between the United States and Canada on the one hand and Mexico on the other.

As you read this chapter, consider the advantages and shortcomings of the NAFTA and EU approaches to key environment and trade issues. In particular, consider the extent to which the regional convergence of economic and competition policies calls for parallel efforts to harmonize environmental laws and policies, and if so, for which sectors or media. How well has each region addressed the principal environmental concerns about trade liberalization (scale, composition, competitive, and regulatory effects) outlined in Chapter 1. Have these regional arrangements struck a better balance between the values of free trade and environmental protection than we see in the WTO? Finally, you may wish to speculate about whether the forces of globalization will, over time, impel regions—and eventually the world—towards more sweeping efforts to harmonize environmental standards, much in the way European integration is moving forward.

II. NAFTA Negotiation and Environmental Concerns

The NAFTA links the combined US$16.5 trillion economies of Canada, Mexico, and the United States by eliminating most tariffs within North America and establishing rules for trade and investment for the goods and services produced and consumed by more than 450 million citizens of North America. The NAFTA goes beyond the GATT by introducing the most favored nation and national treatment obligations to new sectors, such as technical standards, services, intellectual property, and investment. Although a once-envisioned Free Trade Area of the Americas (FTAA) has fallen out of favor, the NAFTA template has been used by all three NAFTA parties in negotiating subsequent bilateral or regional free trade agreements in the Western Hemisphere, such as the Dominican Republic-Central America FTA of the United States, the Canada-Chile FTA, and a network of FTAs between Mexico and many of its Central American neighbors.

Thanks to the "fast-track" trade agreements procedure in the United States (see Chapter 2.V.A., pages 124–28), environmental issues became part of the NAFTA negotiations process from the outset. During 1991 debates on the legislation granting the President negotiating authority for the NAFTA, environmental organizations persuaded the Democratic-controlled Congress to press for specific mandates to address environmental questions in the trade agreement. In the end a more flexible approach was accepted; President George H.W. Bush submitted to Congress a detailed package of written "commitments" as part of the authorization process, which included a full section on the environment committing the administration to prepare a full review of potential environmental issues, include environmental officials in relevant parts of the negotiations, and appoint outside environmental advisors to the U.S. Trade Representative and to the President. All of this was accomplished during the ensuing 16 months leading up to the final agreement of the negotiators in August 1992.

Notwithstanding these first steps to include the environment as an element of trade policy, the labor and environmental communities in the United States were united in opposition to the NAFTA because both saw it as a threat to vital interests. While labor activists feared the southward migration of jobs to Mexico, environmentalists envisioned reduced health and safety regulations (the "race-to-the-bottom"), so-called "pollution havens," and increased pollution generally, the same reasons that they worried about free trade more generally as outlined in Chapter 1 of this book.

Environmental concerns over NAFTA were politically heightened for two additional reasons. First, the NAFTA debate followed closely on the controversial *Tuna/Dolphin* decisions under GATT, which demonstrated for the first time to many environmentalists that certain domestic environmental laws with widespread popular support could be held to violate trade agreements—and this at the behest of Mexico! Second, and more importantly, the NAFTA parties included both developed and developing countries. The United States and Canada are two of the world's most industrialized nations, each with a 1991 per capita GDP of more than $21,000. Although Mexico's economy was growing rapidly, its per capita GDP in 1991 was only $2,900. (Comparable figures for 2009, based on purchasing power parity calculations, are approximately $46,000 for the United States, $38,000 for Canada, and $14,000 for Mexico.) Such economic and other disparities between Mexico on the one hand and Canada and the United States on the other fueled a variety of concerns. One was the apparent gap between a well-developed body of environmental laws and regulations in Canada and the United States, with government agencies to carry them out, compared to new environmental legislation, immature regulatory programs, and poorly funded and inadequately staffed environmental agencies in Mexico. Mexico took steps during the NAFTA negotiations to strengthen its environmental enforcement capability, but substantial doubts remained. U.S. environmental groups pointed in particular to the rapid industrialization and equally rapid deterioration of air and water quality along the U.S.-Mexico border, brought about in large part through the Mexican "maquiladora" program, an economic development program promoting assembly plants and a wide range of other enterprises to serve the U.S. market by offering duty-free import of the raw and intermediate materials going into products destined for export. It was feared that further growth of "maquila"-style industrial activity would become the norm under NAFTA. *See* DANIEL C. ESTY, GREENING THE GATT: TRADE, ENVIRONMENT, AND THE FUTURE 2–3 (1997); PIERRE MARC JOHNSON & ANDRE BEAULIEU, THE ENVIRONMENT AND NAFTA 8 (1996).

U.S. environmental organizations, in collaboration with colleagues in Mexico and Canada, undertook a relentless advocacy campaign, preparing reports and position papers, encouraging media coverage of environmental problems in the border area, and personally lobbying state and federal government officials, members of Congress, and anyone else who might be able to influence the negotiations. Johnson and Beaulieu summarize their main demands as follows:

(1) Guarantees for upward harmonization of environmental standards in the NAFTA area; (2) more transparency and NGO participation in the administra-

tion and dispute settlement mechanism of NAFTA; (3) better enforcement of environmental regulations as well as some built-in procedure to make violations of this principle actionable under NAFTA ... ; (4) elaborated protection of environmental laws and regulations against preempted and NAFTA trade discipline challenges; and (5) a major and well-financed effort to clean up the Mexico-U.S. border area.

Johnson & Beaulieu, The Environment and NAFTA, at 28–29.

In response to this environmental advocacy, the United States pressed for, and the other parties accepted, some new language and some new provisions in the text of the NAFTA itself to assure some measure of protection for environmental laws and regulations. Although the negotiators could then say, with considerable truth, that the NAFTA text initialed in August 1992 was the "greenest trade agreement ever," these few environmental provisions were widely perceived by environmental groups as inadequate. Meanwhile, industrialist H. Ross Perot launched a populist political party, "We the People," with opposition to the NAFTA as its primary platform and then mounted a campaign for the Presidency, keeping NAFTA in the public spotlight.

Throughout the 1992 presidential campaign, environmental and labor groups called on the candidates to revise the NAFTA to include greater protection for labor and the environment and called on Congress to vote down the treaty (and the still unfinished WTO texts) unless such revisions were made. Environmentalists and labor unions are traditional key constituencies of the Democratic Party in the United States, so in October 1992, when then-candidate William Clinton announced his support for the NAFTA that had just been negotiated by his opponent, President Bush, he specifically conditioned his support on the need for additional arrangements to deal with neglected labor and environmental issues. When the Clinton Administration took office in January 1993, negotiating the labor and environmental side agreements to NAFTA became priority objectives for the new trade team. Giving environmental groups unprecedented access to, and significant influence on, the U.S. trade and environmental negotiators, the U.S. Trade Representative concluded the environmental and labor side agreements in August, followed by a bilateral agreement with Mexico on border environmental issues, the U.S.-Mexico Border Environment Cooperation Agreement (BECA). These agreements, as well as a summary assessment of the expected environmental effects of the all the agreements, became parts of the package submitted to Congress in advance of the vote on approval of the NAFTA. The side agreements and some other legislative commitments were enough to induce five major U.S. environmental organizations to support NAFTA, and Congress approved the agreement in November, allowing it to enter into force on January 1, 1994.

Questions and Discussion

1. Regional agreements such as the NAFTA are arguably faring somewhat better than the WTO at bridging the North-South divide over trade and environment policy. What trade-offs do you think a developing country like Mexico makes by engaging in one-on-one negotiations with the United States, rather than insulating itself by building a negotiating strategy within large coalitions of developing countries in the WTO, such as the Group of 77? For a Mexican environmental perspective on the NAFTA negotiations, *see* Gustavo Alanis-Ortega & Ana Karina Gonzalez-Lutzenkirchen, *No Room for the Environment: The NAFTA Negotiations and the Mexican Perspective on Trade and Environment,*

in GREENING THE AMERICAS: NAFTA'S LESSONS FOR HEMISPHERIC TRADE 41–60 (Carolyn L. Deere & Daniel. C. Esty eds., 2002); *see also*, BARBARA HOGENBOOM, MEXICO AND THE NAFTA ENVIRONMENT DEBATE: THE TRANSNATIONAL POLITICS OF ECONOMIC INTEGRATION (1998).

2. One of the key arguments of the Clinton Administration was that the environment would be better off with NAFTA and its side agreements than without them, because Mexico would become engaged as a partner on environmental law reform and environmental improvement measures. The U.S. environmental groups that supported NAFTA made similar arguments. As you continue reading about implementation of the side agreements since 1994, consider whether this argument has been vindicated or not.

III. NAFTA's Environmental Provisions

As noted above, at the insistence of U.S. negotiators, a few provisions were introduced into the text of the NAFTA itself to address some of the environmental concerns. This section gives a short summary of the NAFTA environmental provisions. With the exception of the environmental clauses in the investment chapter (see Chapter 10), it is fair to say that these provisions have not had any visible or substantive effect, but that is perhaps to be expected since they are primarily meant to defend national environmental measures from trade-based challenges.

Preambles to international agreements set the tone, and the NAFTA Preamble contains several references to the environment. The Parties commit themselves to the promotion of sustainable development and the strengthening of environmental laws and regulations. The Preamble specifically identifies the goal of ensuring a predictable commercial framework "in a manner consistent with environmental protection and conservation."

Article 104 of the NAFTA clarifies the relationship between its free trade provisions and the trade-restrictive measures contained in selected multilateral environmental agreements (MEAs). It does so by providing that the specific trade obligations of any of the enumerated MEAs take precedence over the provisions of NAFTA, so long as the Party invoking the MEA employs the alternative that is "the least inconsistent" with the other provisions of the NAFTA. The original list of MEAs includes: the Convention on International Trade in Endangered Species of Wild Fauna and Flora; the Montreal Protocol on Substances that Deplete the Ozone Layer; the Basel Convention on the Control of Transboundary Movements of Hazardous Wastes and Their Disposal; the Agreement Between the Government of Canada and the Government of the United States of America Concerning the Transboundary Movement of Hazardous Waste; and the Agreement between the United States of America and the United Mexican States on Cooperation for the Protection and Improvement of the Environment in the Border Area. By letter agreement, the Parties later added to the list the Convention on the Protection of Migratory Birds between Canada and the United States, and the Convention for the Protection of Migratory Birds and Game Mammals between the United States and Mexico.

The NAFTA chapters on sanitary and phytosanitary standards (SPS) and technical barriers to trade (TBT) contain important evidentiary burden shifting language and other provisions that differ from their WTO counterparts in ways meant to strengthen a Party's ability to set its own standards for protection of human health and the environment. *See* Chapter 7, Section III at pages 444–45 for a comparison of the NAFTA and WTO SPS provisions.

Finally, NAFTA Chapter 11 establishes rules pertaining to investments and investors, including a dispute resolution mechanism allowing private investors to challenge NAFTA governments directly for breach of its provisions. *See* Chapter 10 of this book. Article 1114 in particular contains novel, though nonbinding, language providing consultations in the event a Party suspects its trade partner is encouraging investment by relaxing domestic health, safety, or environmental measures. Without question, both the procedural and substantive provisions of Chapter 11 have proven to be the most controversial provisions of the NAFTA to date, eliciting a raft of unanticipated investor claims centered on national or local environmental decisions.

Most environmental organizations active in the trade and environment arena acknowledge that, taken together, the NAFTA's environmental language represents an improvement over prior regional agreements and similar provisions in the WTO, though it still falls well short of more comprehensive proposals for reconciling trade liberalization measures with environmental protection. Carolyn L. Deere & Daniel C. Esty, *Trade and the Environment in the Americas: Overview of Key Issues*, *in* Greening the Americas: NAFTA's Lessons for Hemispheric Trade 1, 14 (Carolyn L. Deere & Daniel C. Esty eds., 2002). Later in this chapter, we will see whether environmentalists have made much headway since the NAFTA by taking a brief look at the environmental content of bilateral and multilateral agreements negotiated after the NAFTA.

IV. The North American Agreement on Environmental Cooperation

A. Objectives and Commitments

A year after the NAFTA negotiations concluded but before the NAFTA came into force, Canada, Mexico, and the United States negotiated a self-standing agreement, the North American Agreement on Environmental Cooperation, Sept. 8, 1993, U.S.-Can.-Mex., 32 I.L.M. 1480 [hereinafter NAAEC]; the text is also available at http://www.cec.org. The NAAEC is a hybrid agreement, pairing U.S. concerns about economic competitiveness with the broader goal of fostering collaborative efforts for the improvement of the environment in North America. As a framework agreement, the NAAEC identifies numerous areas of potential cooperation, bound loosely by a broad conception of environment and, more practically, by the ability of the three countries to reach consensus on priorities and lines of action in its annual program of work.

Broadly, the NAAEC has three major elements. It establishes the North American Commission for Environmental Cooperation (CEC) and gives it a specific and unique institutional structure. It also defines the scope of the environmental issues within the authority of the CEC on which the three countries will cooperate. Finally, it contains innovative mechanisms for investigating the effectiveness of environmental enforcement.

The NAAEC is anchored by each country's commitment in Article 3 to ensure that its laws and regulations provide for "high levels" of environmental protection and in Article 5 to "effectively enforce its environmental laws and regulations through appropriate governmental action." Two mechanisms underscore the NAAEC's emphasis on enforcement. First, the citizen submission process, discussed in detail in Section D below, provides an avenue for groups or individuals to initiate an inquiry into a claim that a Party is failing to effectively enforce its environmental laws. Second, a Party-to-Party procedure allows a complaining Party to seek the imposition of a monetary assessment if a Party is found by a tribunal to have engaged in a "persistent pattern" of failure to enforce environmental law with potential competitive effects in the NAFTA region. These provisions constitute the enforcement "teeth" in what otherwise is primarily a framework for regional environmental cooperation.

On broader issues of the ambition of the Parties and their commitment to cooperate, the NAAEC includes an odd mix of mandatory language ("shalls") followed by words that often soften the obligation. For example, Article 3 requires that each Party "shall ensure that its laws and regulations provide for high levels of environmental protection and shall strive to continue to improve those laws and regulations." Yet, Article 3 also grants each Party the right to establish its own levels of domestic environmental protection and nowhere do the Parties define or establish threshold limits for "high levels." Other commitments are qualified by such words or phrases as "appropriate" (for example, Article 2(1)(e) says that each Party shall "assess, as appropriate, environmental impacts") or "to the extent possible" (for example, the Article 4(2) commitment to provide public notice and opportunity to comment on proposed environmental regulations) are framed in aspirational language such as "strive for," "promote," or "seek to."

Notwithstanding its blemishes, the NAAEC still manages to articulate a holistic and wide-ranging integration of environmental concerns within the new economic relationship. It is remarkable for its sweeping breadth. Article 10(2), for example, sets forth a nonexhaustive list of 19 areas for the Parties to consider and develop recommendations about, including: comparability of techniques and methodologies for data gathering and analysis; pollution prevention techniques and strategies; approaches and common indicators for reporting on the state of the environment; transboundary and border environmental issues; exotic species that may be harmful; the protection of threatened and endangered species; environmental matters as they relate to economic development; ecologically sensitive national accounts; ecolabeling; and "other matters as it may decide."

The NAAEC covers public participation and procedural questions as well. It contains commitments by each Party to ensure that its citizens have private access to remedies for violations of its environmental laws and regulations and that persons with a "legally recognized interest" have access to courts and administrative bodies for the enforcement of a Party's environmental laws and regulations (Article 6). Article 7 of the NAAEC enunciates a variety of procedural guarantees to ensure that such proceedings are "fair, open, and equitable."

For lawyers and law students, the most interesting experience under the NAAEC has been the operation of the citizen submission process. Section D below is devoted to that. Before getting to those issues, however, we will look at the unusual institutional structure of the CEC and at the programs of cooperative work it has carried out for the past 15 years.

B. Structure and Governance of the CEC

The NAAEC creates the Commission for Environmental Cooperation (CEC), an international organization headquartered in Montreal, Quebec. The CEC has a three-part structure that is unique among international organizations, comprising a Council, a Secretariat, and a Joint Public Advisory Committee (JPAC).

The Council is the governing body of the CEC. Its members are the cabinet-level environmental officials of each country. With a few important exceptions, Council decisions are taken by consensus. With an equal voice in governing the affairs of the CEC, each NAFTA Party contributes an equal share to its budget. The budget, US\$9 million per year, has held steady in nominal terms but has steadily declined in its purchasing power, forcing staff reductions and curtailed activities in recent years. The direct CEC expenditures are occasionally supplemented with contributions to specific activities, in money or in services, from other sources.

The Council meets at least once a year in regular sessions lasting two or three days, which must include at least one public meeting. NAAEC, art. 9(3). In practice, Council meetings routinely draw hundreds of stakeholders from all parts of the continent and provide, among other things, an important opportunity for NGOs to establish and fortify regional networks on issues of common concern. As a matter of practice, Council members have appointed a senior official in their agency to serve as "alternative representatives," who meet or teleconference throughout the year and oversee the day-to-day issues on behalf of the Council. The governments also establish working groups or committees to address a wide array of specific issues ranging from budgeting and implementation plans to government voting on factual records.

The CEC Secretariat acts as the technical, administrative, and operational arm of the Council. It also possesses some autonomous investigatory and reporting authority granted to it directly by the NAAEC, which is discussed in Section C below. The executive officer of the Secretariat is the Executive Director, who is appointed by and serves at the pleasure of the Council. Though the Parties held considerably different views regarding the optimal size of the Secretariat, the staff held fairly steady for the first ten years with approximately 20 program staff professionals recruited in roughly equal numbers from the three countries, but is now reduced to about 15. Professional staff manage programs in such areas as Environment and Trade, Conservation of Biodiversity, Environmental Law, Air Quality and Pollution, and Chemicals Management. The Director of Submissions on Enforcement Matters leads a small group of attorneys from the three countries who process citizen submissions and develop "factual records." There is a sizeable administrative staff as well, including people responsible for publication of the CEC's work in the three official languages. Regardless of their previous work, all CEC staff are international civil servants, subject to direction only by the Executive Director of the Secretariat.

The third element of the CEC is the most unusual. The Joint Public Advisory Committee—commonly known by its acronym, JPAC (pronounced jay-pack)—consists of fifteen private individuals (five from each country) appointed by their respective heads of State. Their broad mandate is to advise the Parties on any matter within the scope of the NAAEC. One of JPAC's distinguished former members highlights this innovative experiment in regional governance:

> Of the three branches of the North American Commission for Environmental Cooperation (CEC), the Joint Public Advisory Committee (JPAC) is arguably the most innovative. The fifteen citizens on JPAC—five from each country—are appointed by their governments to give advice to the CEC Council, to comment on the Secretariat's work plan, and to consult with the public in open meetings on aspects of the CEC's program.... Not surprisingly, there has been friction at times between nongovernmental JPAC members and the deputy ministers and

other federal officials who staff the Council, particularly over the rules and procedures for addressing citizen complaints over nonenforcement of environmental laws. In fact, a certain creative tension is built right into the JPAC's role. In the nearly eight years since it was constituted in 1994, JPAC has become an effective, visible and respected branch of the CEC. It continues to evolve as the CEC itself evolves as an institution.

John D. Wirth, *Perspectives on the Joint Public Advisory Committee, in* GREENING NAFTA: THE NORTH AMERICAN COMMISSION FOR ENVIRONMENTAL COOPERATION 199 (David L. Markell & John H. Knox eds., 2003) [hereinafter GREENING NAFTA]. Professor Wirth attributes the success of the JPAC, in part, to its early decision to eschew national identities, instead choosing "to interact as North Americans rather than [as] defenders of national positions or as representatives of any particular private voluntary organization or interest group." *Id.* at 201.

The interplay of the constituent bodies of the CEC—the Council, JPAC, and Secretariat—presents an interesting model for international institutions in areas touching on governance, accountability, and transparency. In its brief existence, the CEC has been no stranger to controversy; it has struggled to meet the expectations of its stakeholders while trying to balance the roles of regional facilitator, convener, statistician, and watchdog. The Council, after some early years actively promoting its new authority, has receded more recently into a posture more defensive of national agency interests. The JPAC has continued to serve as a high-level "representative" of the public interest in the large sense, actively soliciting the views of citizens in all three countries through public meetings and expressing its views, publicly and sometimes quite forcefully, to the Council. The Secretariat has worked hard, but not always with success, to maintain a degree of autonomy from the Council and serve as disinterested experts willing to engage with all sectors of the North American environmental community. As you read this section, think about whether you see the CEC as a mere "fig leaf" providing cover for trade interests, as a new breed of more muscular and participatory international environmental organizations, or something in-between.

Questions and Discussion

1. Article 43 of the NAAEC states:

Each Party shall contribute an equal share of the annual budget of the Commission, subject to the availability of appropriated funds in accordance with the Party's legal procedures. No Party shall be obligated to pay more than any other Party in respect of an annual budget.

On occasion, the Parties have discussed whether one or more Parties could contribute more than their agreed upon share to the operating budget of the CEC. While differing opinions were offered on whether such contributions would be permissible, the Parties never agreed on a common interpretation and have put aside the issue. Do you read Article 43 as permitting a Party to contribute more than its share of the annual budget? Why might a Party oppose such a practice?

2. Hungry for additional resources, the CEC Secretariat has actively sought government and nongovernmental partners, some of whom contribute funds directly to CEC programs. Does Council's acceptance of this practice render further discussion of the intent of Article 43 unnecessary?

3. The NAAEC includes commitments that could support more open and participatory decision-making and the strengthening of environmental law in courts and before administrative bodies. For example, Article 4 requires that each Party publish proposed laws and regulations in advance and allow citizens "a reasonable opportunity to comment." Article 6 requires Parties to ensure that citizens with legally recognizable interests under the law have access to administrative, quasi-judicial, and judicial proceedings and that Parties must provide remedies for violations of environmental law. What remedies are available for a breach of one or more of these provisions?

4. Given the origins of the NAFTA environmental side agreement, you might be surprised that the NAAEC deals less with trade and trade policy than with issues related to governance and the environment. While many of the subject areas dealt with in the NAAEC have the potential to intersect with trade policy, only Article 10(6) actually establishes an institutional linkage to the NAFTA through its Free Trade Commission. Subsequent free trade agreements such as the U.S.-Jordan and U.S.-Chile free trade agreements incorporate NAAEC-type environmental provisions directly into the text of the trade agreement. Which approach is preferable, and why? Does it matter which agency or department has oversight responsibility for the environmental provisions of the agreement (in the United States, EPA for the NAAEC; USTR for trade agreements)?

C. Cooperative Programs and Actions

1. NAAEC Article 13: Secretariat Reports

The NAAEC bestows some specific authorities on the CEC Secretariat separate from its function as the operational arm of the Council. One of these authorities is in Article 13: the autonomy for the Secretariat, on its own initiative, to bring important issues to the attention of the Council and the public through the preparation of reports. The Secretariat may prepare a report for the Council "on any matter within the scope of the annual program." NAAEC, art. 13(1). Also, the Secretariat may prepare a report "on any other environmental matter related to the cooperative functions" of the NAAEC unless the Council objects by a two-thirds vote. These environmental matters cannot, however, include issues related to Article 14 submissions. Article 13(2) gives the Secretariat wide latitude in drawing on public information, public consultations, and independent experts.

The Secretariat has employed Article 13 judiciously, alternating between specific circumstances where an independent assessment might assist in resolving an environmental problem, and broader emerging issues at the continental scale. As of June 2010, the Secretariat has completed six Article 13 reports, with one in progress.

The very first report involved the unexplained death of approximately 40,000 migratory birds in the State of Guanajuato, Mexico in 1994. Local and state authorities were unable to explain the causes for the die-off; the CEC Secretariat stepped in to empanel a group of internationally-recognized experts to examine the causes and develop recommendations for avoiding future incidents. The panel determined that the deaths had been caused by an outbreak of avian botulism, most likely triggered by the unsanitary conditions in the Silva Reservoir, as well as untreated municipal and industrial discharges into the Rio Lerma. CEC SECRETARIAT REPORT ON THE DEATH OF MIGRATORY BIRDS AT THE SILVA RESERVOIR (1995). The State of Guanajuato, and its then Governor Vincente Fox (who later became President of Mexico), embraced the report and capitalized on the international attention it generated to gain support for programs to reduce pollution discharges to the Rio Lerma.

Turning to an issue of more general concern, the CEC Secretariat convened a high-level team of North American experts to assess the long-range transport of atmospheric pollutants. CONTINENTAL POLLUTANT PATHWAYS: AN AGENDA FOR COOPERATION TO ADDRESS LONG-RANGE TRANSPORT OF AIR POLLUTION IN NORTH AMERICA (1997). While the report and recommendations were not widely disseminated, the process demonstrated to governments the high level of scientific consensus about the importance of this issue and probably helped facilitate negotiations for the Stockholm Convention on Persistent Organic Pollutants a few years later.

In response to concerns raised by a number of environmental organizations, the Secretariat used Article 13 to launch the Upper San Pedro Initiative to assess threats to critical migratory bird habitat along the shared bi-national upper San Pedro River basin in northern Mexico and southeastern Arizona. RIBBON OF LIFE: AN AGENDA FOR PRESERVING TRANSBOUNDARY MIGRATORY BIRD HABITAT ON THE UPPER SAN PEDRO RIVER (1999). Heavy withdrawals of groundwater near the San Pedro River in Arizona by farmers, fast-growing retirement communities, and expanded U.S. Army operations at Fort Huachuca threatened to interrupt the perennial flow of the river and impair its associated riparian habitats. Despite the outspoken opposition of Arizona Governor Symington, who characterized the initiative as a "drive-by eco study," the CEC pressed ahead with an experts' report to be considered by a tri-national advisory board. Over 650 people participated in CEC-sponsored "kaffee klatsches," workshops, and consultations on the groundwater management issues. In the end, the process successfully re-framed the issue, helping the Arizona communities to acknowledge the problem and to concentrate on finding solutions. Unfortunately, groundwater withdrawals have not been sufficiently reduced, so the threat to the San Pedro watershed and its riparian habitat persists. For further discussion, see Robert J. Glennon, WATER FOLLIES: GROUNDWATER PUMPING AND THE FATE OF AMERICA'S FRESH WATERS (2002).

The next Article 13 report again focused on a general matter of common concern and future interest. In ENVIRONMENTAL CHALLENGES AND OPPORTUNITIES OF THE EVOLVING NORTH AMERICAN ELECTRICITY MARKET (June 2002), the Secretariat conducted independent research to demonstrate the acute uncertainty environmental regulators face in trying to project future regional emissions scenarios for key air pollutants associated with electric power generation, including mercury and ozone precursors, as well as water management issues. Identifying poor coordination and incompatible requirements in federal, state, or provincial environmental laws, standards, or policies in the electricity sector, the report detailed how this regulatory fragmentation could frustrate domestic environmental and health strategies and lead to environment-related trade disputes.

Another Article 13 report on a salient and controversial environmental issue examined the impacts of genetically modified imported maize on native maize strains in Mexico. Again the Secretariat appointed a highly qualified group of scientists from the three countries who directed research efforts and prepared recommendations on how to avoid contaminating the gene pool in the world's most important repository of corn varieties. In March 2004, the background paper developed for the expert group was discussed at a public meeting with over 600 in attendance held in Oaxaca, Mexico—testimony to the interest sparked by an issue so closely linked to the cultural and historical identity of Mexico. See MAIZE AND BIODIVERSITY: THE EFFECTS OF TRANSGENIC MAIZE IN MEXICO (2004).

More recent reports have looked at complex questions about green building requirements and certification programs, and one in progress will examine sustainability issues in North American freight transport—one of the more direct environmental impacts of trade. All in all, Article 13 reports have had a considerable impact on policy, demonstrating the value of the CEC as an independent fact-finder on environmental issues of cross-border significance.

––––––––––

2. CEC Cooperative Programs

Each year, the CEC spends half its budget on an array of "cooperative programs," spread over several program areas and multiple projects, some of which continue for a period of years. The program areas and the specific projects change over time according to the long-term budgets and prioritization of activities recommended by the Secretariat and decided by the Council. In general, the program areas have included matters still in the current (as of mid-2010) list of program areas: Pollutants and Health; Biodiversity Conservation; Environment, Trade and Sustainability; and Environmental Information. Past and current projects show the typical range of projects and the way in which they are carried out.

In the first ten years or so, through a still-continuing project called Sound Management of Chemicals, the CEC brokered discussions and agreements involving governments, industry, and nongovernmental groups leading to the phase-out of the use of chlordane and DDT in Mexico and other reductions in the use of persistent organic pollutants in North America. Another continuing CEC initiative has been the development and publication of a North American Pollutant Release and Transfer Registry (PRTR), a comparative look at emissions releases to water, air, and land in the region. That work served to highlight specific industries, and sometimes specific facilities, as major pollution sources. As part of the project, Mexico gradually established and has now implemented its own national PRTR system. *See* the "Taking Stock" reports, available at http://www.cec.org/takingstock. While a number of CEC projects have sputtered or been taken over by slow-footed government working groups, others have accelerated cooperative activities in the region and deepened awareness of ecological, economic, and social linkages.

One long-term CEC project directly relevant to trade and the environment has been its assessment of the environmental effects of the NAFTA, a project in a larger program area now called Environment, Trade, and Sustainability. Two prominent American environmental advocates offered the following perspective on this project some years ago. The work continues; many more analyses of specific sectoral or country impacts have been prepared in the years since, and additional North American symposia on the subject were held in 2005 and 2008. The various analytical studies and the CEC's "framework for analysis" are all on the CEC website, at http://www.cec.org/Page.asp?PageID=1225&SiteNodeID=227&BL_ExpandID=.

Mary E. Kelly & Cyrus Reed, *The CEC's Trade and Environment Program: Cutting-Edge Analysis but Untapped Potential*
in Greening NAFTA, 101, 108–10 (2003)

A central element of the work of the Commission for Environmental Cooperation (CEC) is its Environment, Economy and Trade program. Included within this program are projects designed to assess the environmental effects of the

North American Free Trade Agreement (NAFTA), in accordance with Article 10(6)(d) of the North American Agreement on Environmental Cooperation (NAAEC). More recently, the CEC has undertaken projects to examine the environmental effects of an integrated North American electricity market, including expanded cross-border trade in electricity, and the effects of agricultural market integration on biodiversity, forestry, and freshwater resources.

Despite a slow and controversial start, the CEC's trade and environment work has succeeded in producing a cutting-edge analysis methodology. It has applied that methodology to explore and illuminate North American trade and environment linkages in the important areas of agriculture (corn, in particular), transportation, energy, forestry, hazardous wastes, industrial pollution, and electricity production. The CEC's work has shown that careful sector- or case-specific studies conducted in an open and transparent manner can provide a better understanding of the links between trade and environment than most of the limited-scope macroeconomic models in which effects are masked by modeling assumptions, data aggregation, and data unavailability. And in some instances the CEC's trade effects work has led to increased North American cooperation on environmental issues.

The NAFTA effects assessment work at CEC has, on the whole, helped illuminate many aspects of trade and environment linkages. There is also much to be learned from CEC's assessment methodology, especially as compared to many of the other previous and current attempts to apply macroscale economic modeling to environmental reviews of current or proposed trade agreements.

The CEC's own evaluation of its NAFTA effects work identifies several important lessons, including:

a. Specific environment-trade linkages do exist and should be examined, though other "nontrade driving forces," such as domestic political and economic conditions, global demand and others, should also be factored into the analysis.

b. Macroscale analyses, with their highly aggregated data and broad sweep, can mask or miss significant effects and are only useful if supplemented by smaller-scale analyses of local, regional, or sector-specific effects.

c. "Scale effects" associated with increased cross-border trade and investment flows may outstrip the available physical infrastructure and/or the ability of governments to monitor and regulate or prevent adverse environmental effects. In addition, the CEC concludes that to date there is "little evidence supporting the notion that, in the near term, greater revenues associated with increased trade correlate with increased resources for environmental authorities to address scale effects." Given the nonrenewable nature of many critical environmental resources, the lack of additional resources necessary to mitigate adverse effects at the time those effects are occurring should not be ignored.

d. The absence of available, high-quality environmental data, especially at the local, regional, and sectoral levels, hampers potentially useful smaller-scale analyses of trade/environment linkages.

e. Open, transparent, and inclusive approaches to analyzing trade and environment linkages are very important to the credibility, usefulness, and acceptability of the analyses.

The jury is still out on one aspect of the CEC's NAFTA effects work, however: how can or will the Commission's analyses have policy relevance? That is, can and will the studies be used to influence not only domestic environmental policies but also regional and even global trade policy and, maybe more important, regional development policy?

The available evidence on this question is still slim. It does not appear that the North American hazardous waste study sponsored under the CEC's NAFTA effects program, combined with domestic developments, policy advocacy, and media attention, has resulted in a proposal for stronger hazardous waste disposal regulations in Ontario. The CEC's NAFTA effects work is also contributing to trade and environment discussions at the World Trade Organization and the Organization for Economic Cooperation and Development. Notably, however, the CEC's assessment methodology was not even mentioned in the U.S. Trade Representative's proposal for an environmental review of the FTAA.

But the CEC's NAFTA effects work has implications that go well beyond just tinkering with trade or environment policy. It provides many indications that governments should be thinking in terms of "development policy," not just trade policy. If the goal of economic integration is indeed, as its backers claim, improving the economies, quality of life, and social conditions in participating countries, then the CEC's work indicates clearly that there are development policy conditions that must be in place if liberalized trade and investment are to make positive contributions to this goal on the environmental front.

The most important of these conditions may be the ability to identify and adequately fund the necessary environmental monitoring, regulatory, and enforcement functions and environmental infrastructure improvements in the developing country trading partners. This requires more than just putting in place reactive "flanking" policies to mitigate identified adverse environmental effects of increased trade and investment. Instead it implies a more comprehensive, and maybe even a more phased, approach to trade and investment liberalization, and it involves identifying clear and sufficient funding mechanisms for these development needs.

The NAFTA environmental effects work is only one part of the Trade, Environment, and Sustainability work program. Another element focuses on "Green Goods and Services," including a project for certification of shade-grown and organic coffee and another offering guidance and criteria for eco-tourism. Still other parts of this work area have a more industrial focus, including the automobile industry and North American transportation corridors.

D. Citizen Submissions on Enforcement Matters

In an innovation unique to an international agreement, Articles 14 and 15 of the NAAEC allow citizens of North America, whether individuals or civic organizations, to make a submission directly to the CEC Secretariat if they believe that a Party to the NAAEC is failing to effectively enforce its environmental law in a particular case or circumstance. Upon receiving such a citizen submission, the Secretariat first determines whether the submission meets the basic qualifying criteria established in Article 14(1). If so, the Secretariat then considers whether the submission merits requesting a response from the concerned Party in accordance with Article 14(2), which includes considerations such as environmental harm, the pursuit of private remedies, and the overall goals of the NAAEC. In light of any response by the Party, the Secretariat may recommend to the Council that a "factual record" be prepared to look further into the allegation. If at least two-thirds of the Council members agree, the Council will instruct the Secretariat to prepare a factual record on the matters raised in the submission. In preparing a factual record, the Secretariat shall consider any information furnished by a Party and it may consider other information that is publicly available, submitted to it, or developed by the Secretariat and independent experts. The final factual record is made publicly available upon a vote of the Council.

Scorned by some as "toothless" or an "odd procedural dead-end," the citizen submission process has been welcomed by others as an innovative "sunlight" mechanism that gives civil society a new voice in raising concerns about environmental enforcement in an increasingly globalized economy. For those who monitor the activities of the CEC, the process has generated considerable controversy and has captured the attention of the Council, scholars, and public policy advocates alike. In fact, many link the overall fate of the NAAEC to the functioning of the citizen submission process free from government meddling and interference. In the end, the mechanism is likely to be judged on the extent to which shedding light on enforcement practices stimulates on-the-ground results of improved government enforcement practices in the region.

The citizen submission process includes some peculiar provisions and definitions that limit the scope of the process and establish government defenses. As discussed below, these provisions have recently become hotly disputed in the context of specific submissions.

North American Agreement on Environmental Cooperation
Article 14: Submissions on Enforcement Matters

1. The Secretariat may consider a submission from any non-governmental organization or person asserting that a Party is failing to effectively enforce its environmental law, if the Secretariat finds that the submission:

   (a) is in writing in a language designated by that Party in a notification to the Secretariat;

   (b) clearly identifies the person or organization making the submission;

   (c) provides sufficient information to allow the Secretariat to review the submission, including any documentary evidence on which the submission may be based;

   (d) appears to be aimed at promoting enforcement rather than at harassing industry;

   (e) indicates that the matter has been communicated in writing to the relevant authorities of the Party and indicates the Party's response, if any; and

   (f) is filed by a person or organization residing or established in the territory of a Party.

2. Where the Secretariat determines that a submission meets the criteria set out in paragraph 1, the Secretariat shall determine whether the submission merits requesting a response from the Party. In deciding whether to request a response, the Secretariat shall be guided by whether:

    (a) the submission alleges harm to the person or organization making the submission;

    (b) the submission, alone or in combination with other submissions, raises matters whose further study in this process would advance the goals of this Agreement;

    (c) private remedies available under the Party's law have been pursued; and

    (d) the submission is drawn exclusively from mass media reports.

Where the Secretariat makes such a request, it shall forward to the Party a copy of the submission and any supporting information provided with the submission.

3. The Party shall advise the Secretariat within 30 days or, in exceptional circumstances and on notification to the Secretariat, within 60 days of delivery of the request:

    (a) whether the matter is the subject of a pending judicial or administrative proceeding, in which case the Secretariat shall proceed no further; and

    (b) of any other information that the Party wishes to submit, such as

        (i) whether the matter was previously the subject of a judicial or administrative proceeding, and

        (ii) whether private remedies in connection with the matter are available to the person or organization making the submission and whether they have been pursued.

Article 15: Factual Record

1. If the Secretariat considers that the submission, in the light of any response provided by the Party, warrants developing a factual record, the Secretariat shall so inform the Council and provide its reasons.

2. The Secretariat shall prepare a factual record if the Council, by a two-thirds vote, instructs it to do so.

3. The preparation of a factual record by the Secretariat pursuant to this Article shall be without prejudice to any further steps that may be taken with respect to any submission.

4. In preparing a factual record, the Secretariat shall consider any information furnished by a Party and may consider any relevant technical, scientific or other information:

    (a) that is publicly available;

    (b) submitted by interested non-governmental organizations or persons;

    (c) submitted by the Joint Public Advisory Committee; or

    (d) developed by the Secretariat or by independent experts.

5. The Secretariat shall submit a draft factual record to the Council. Any Party may provide comments on the accuracy of the draft within 45 days thereafter.

6. The Secretariat shall incorporate, as appropriate, any such comments in the final factual record and submit it to the Council.

7. The Council may, by a two-thirds vote, make the final factual record publicly available, normally within 60 days following its submission. * * *

Article 45: Definitions

1. For purposes of this Agreement:

A Party has not failed to **"effectively enforce its environmental law"** or to comply with Article 5(1) in a particular case where the action or inaction in question by agencies or officials of that Party:

(a) reflects a reasonable exercise of their discretion in respect of investigatory, prosecutorial, regulatory or compliance matters; or

(b) results from bona fide decisions to allocate resources to enforcement in respect of other environmental matters determined to have higher priorities; * * *

2. For purposes of Article 14(1) and Part Five:

(a) **"environmental law"** means any statute or regulation of a Party, or provision thereof, the primary purpose of which is the protection of the environment, or the prevention of a danger to human life or health, through

(i) the prevention, abatement or control of the release, discharge, or emission of pollutants or environmental contaminants,

(ii) the control of environmentally hazardous or toxic chemicals, substances, materials and wastes, and the dissemination of information related thereto, or

(iii) the protection of wild flora or fauna, including endangered species, their habitat, and specially protected natural areas

in the Party's territory, but does not include any statute or regulation, or provision thereof, directly related to worker safety or health.

(b) For greater certainty, the term **"environmental law"** does not include any statute or regulation, or provision thereof, the primary purpose of which is managing the commercial harvest or exploitation, or subsistence or aboriginal harvesting, of natural resources.

(c) The primary purpose of a particular statutory or regulatory provision for purposes of subparagraphs (a) and (b) shall be determined by reference to its primary purpose, rather than to the primary purpose of the statute or regulation of which it is part.

---

1. Implementation of Citizen Submission Process

As of May 2010, a total of 75 submissions have been filed with the CEC and 16 factual records have been prepared and made public—seven concerning Mexico, eight concerning Canada, and one concerning the United States. Another 15 submissions were under active consideration, including work in progress on three additional factual records and four pending recommendations for factual records made to the Council. The 44 other submissions were addressed as follows: 24 submissions were dismissed on grounds that they did not warrant further consideration based on Articles 14(1) and 14(2) (threshold criteria); three submissions were terminated under Article 14(3)(a) (pending judicial or administrative proceeding); 11 submissions were terminated pursuant to Article 15(1) (Secretariat decides not to proceed in light of Party response); four submissions were withdrawn by the submitters; and Council ended work on two submissions under Article 15(2) by rejecting the Secretariat's advice that the preparation of a factual record was warranted.

Virtually every independent review of the CEC conducted by the JPAC, National Advisory Committees, academics, and others has concluded that the Secretariat has performed its "quasi-autonomous" role in the process in a principled, professional, and even-handed manner. *See, e.g.,* John H. Knox, *A New Approach to Compliance with International Environmental Law: The Submissions Procedure of the NAFTA Environmental Commission,* 28 ECOLOGY L.Q. 1, 97, 121 (2001). Yet numerous issues have arisen with respect to the implementation of the citizen submission process. Some of these, such as the eligibility requirements related to "harm" and the applicability of the process to Congressional "riders," were addressed early in the life of the process and have not been revisited or seriously questioned by the Council or submitters. On other issues, however, the Secretariat—supported by the JPAC, National Advisory Committees, NGOs, and most scholars—appears to be locked in a struggle with the Council to maintain its independence and unfettered ability to investigate and report on government conduct relating to enforcement matters raised in submissions. In one sign of these problems, as of mid-2010, four recommendations by the Secretariat to the Council for preparation of factual records have yet to be voted on by the Council, even though some date back to 2007 and 2008. These issues have stimulated an impressive collection of academic scholarship and analysis. The discussion materials that follow provide a sampling of these issues and a sense of the gathering storm threatening the legitimacy of the process. Consider whether the tensions are the product of a flaw in the design of the mechanism or simply a series of adjustments and accommodations typically encountered early in the life of a process of this nature.

a. Legislative Measures and "Failures to Enforce Environmental Law"

A preliminary threshold issue is that the submitters must assert that a Party is failing to effectively enforce its environmental law. In two early submissions involving U.S. law, environmental groups challenged legislative actions of the U.S. Congress exempting particular activities from otherwise applicable environmental law and suspending implementation of key provisions of the Endangered Species Act. Secretariat's Determination under Article 14(2) (Spotted Owl), A14/SEM/95-001/04/14(2), (Sept. 21, 1995); Secretariat's Determination under Articles 14(1) (Logging Rider), A14/SEM/95-002/03/14(1), (Dec. 8, 1995). The environmental group submitters argued that the failure to apply existing law to specific projects or to prohibit an agency from conducting its work as required by law constituted a failure to effectively enforce environmental law. The Secretariat, however, disagreed. It determined that the "enactment of legislation which specifically alters the operation of pre-existing environmental law in essence becomes part of the greater body of environmental laws and statutes on the books." The Secretariat viewed these congressional actions as constituting a new legal regime, even though the laws were fully enforceable for other projects and fully enforceable after the expiration of the specific time restrictions included in the legislative actions.

The Secretariat concluded that it could not "characterize the application of a new legal regime as a failure to enforce an old one." Spotted Owl Article 14(2) Determination, at 6. The Secretariat also declined to recommend to the Council that the CEC become "a secondary forum for legislative debate." *Id.*

In an often overlooked passage at the conclusion of the decision terminating review of the Endangered Species Act submission, the Secretariat hinted at the potentially graver, but irremediable, implications of the legislative riders: "While the Submitters may contend that such legislative action amounts to a breach of the [NAAEC Article 3] obligation to maintain high levels of protection, Articles 14 and 15 do not repose in the Secretariat the power to explore aspects of the Agreement not arising from a failure to enforce environmental law." *Id.* In other words, the United States may have breached the substantive provisions of the NAAEC itself, but citizens have no rights under Articles 14 and 15 to redress such breaches. Nor are any such citizens' rights to be found elsewhere in the Agreement. Article 38 of the NAAEC provides that "[n]o Party may provide for a right of action under its law against any other Party on the ground that another Party has acted in a manner inconsistent with this Agreement."

---

b. Eligibility Requirements

In addition to asserting the failure of a Party to effectively enforce environmental law, the submitters must meet other eligibility requirements. These requirements of Article 14(1) had not caused any problems for submitters until recently, when the Council called on submitters to provide additional information on the grounds that it believed the submission lacked "sufficient information." Because of the context in which the issue has been raised, this matter is discussed in Subsection (f) below at pages 805–14.

With respect to Article 14(2), the Secretariat made several important findings. In one such decision, Mexico argued that submitters did not adequately allege harm to the members of their organizations. The Secretariat ruled that the burden to show harm under Article 14(2) was substantially less than for civil actions in many countries. The Secretariat ruled the plaintiffs had met their Article 14(2) burden, stating:

> In considering harm, the Secretariat notes the importance and character of the resource in question — a portion of the magnificent Paradise corral reef located in the Caribbean waters of Quintana Roo. While the Secretariat recognizes that the submitters may not have alleged the particularized, individual harm required to acquire legal standing to bring suit in some civil proceedings in North America, the especially public nature of marine resources bring the submitters within the spirit and intent of Article 14 of the NAAEC.

Secretariat Notification to Council under Article 15(1) (Cozumel), A14/SEM/96-001/07/ADV, at 5 (June 7, 1996).

---

c. Government Defenses

Once the Secretariat finds that submitters have met the eligibility requirements of Article 14(1) and 14(2), it forwards the submission to the relevant Party for a response. At this stage, a Party has two principal means for derailing a submission: it can claim that its nonenforcement is excused under Article 45 or it can claim that the matter is the subject of a pending judicial or administrative proceeding, in which case the Secretariat must terminate the submission.

From the outset, advocates for the citizen submission process feared that, unless constrained, governments could effectively derail most any submission by invoking either or both of these justifications. After all, many actions or inactions of an agency are attributable, at some level, to the exercise of discretion and resource allocation considerations. For its part, the CEC Secretariat was not provided with, nor sought, any guidance on the extent to which the Secretariat should defer to a Party's assertion of these justifications, which can be analogized to affirmative defenses in domestic legal proceedings. Early on, the governments employed these justifications judiciously, and the issue was largely skirted until the United States aggressively asserted the Article 45(1) justifications in the *Migratory Birds* submission. Party's Response (Migratory Birds), A14/SEM/99-002/04/RSP (Feb. 29, 2000).

The *Migratory Birds* submission was filed against the United States by nine American, Canadian, and Mexican environmental groups. The groups alleged that the United States was failing to enforce section 703 of the Migratory Bird Treaty Act (MBTA) against loggers. Section 703 prohibits any person from killing or "taking" migratory birds, including the destruction of nests, the crushing of eggs, and the killing of nestlings and fledglings, "by any means or in any manner," unless the U.S. Fish & Wildlife Service (FWS) issues a valid permit. 16 U.S.C. §703. The submitters argued that the United States, as a matter of internal policy, exempted logging operations from the MBTA's prohibitions without any legislation or regulation authorizing such an exception. The United States had never prosecuted a logger or logging company for a violation of the MBTA, even though it acknowledged that the MBTA had consistently been violated by persons logging on federal and non-federal land. The Director of the FWS stated that the FWS, "has had a long-standing, unwritten policy relative to the MBTA that no enforcement or investigative action should be taken in incidents involving logging operations, that result in the taking of non-endangered, non-threatened, migratory birds and/or their nests." The submitters argued that this policy did not reflect a reasonable exercise of the agency's discretion with respect to investigatory, prosecutorial, regulatory, or compliance matters. Submission (Migratory Birds), A14/SEM/99-002/01/SUB (Nov. 17, 1999).

The United States responded that it was exercising its enforcement discretion reasonably and using its scarce funding for other purposes. It noted that it enforced the Endangered Species Act vigorously and had implemented several other projects relating to the protection of waterfowl and other birds. The Secretariat found the contentions of the United States insufficiently substantiated and, in doing so, signaled that governments would not get a free pass on invoking Article 45(1) justifications.

Article 15(1) Notification to Council that Development of Factual Record Is Warranted (Migratory Birds)

A14/SEM/99-002/11/ADV, at 8–10, 25–27 (Dec. 15, 2000)

Preliminary Framework for Analysis of Article 45(1) Issues

This is the first Party response in which a Party has made a detailed assertion that Article 45 makes continued review of the submission inappropriate. The nature of the Secretariat's review of the submission in light of the response with respect to these issues will likely be determined on a case-by-case basis. The Secretariat anticipates, however, that the following analysis will generally be relevant.

In a particular submission, if a Party has asserted that its enforcement reflects a reasonable exercise of its discretion, the Secretariat should review at least two questions in assessing the extent to which the Party provides support for this assertion. First, to what extent has the Party explained how it has exercised its discretion? Second, to what extent has the Party explained why its exercise of discretion is reasonable under the circumstances? If the Party has provided a persuasive explanation of how it has exercised its discretion, and why its exercise of discretion is reasonable, then under Article 45(1)(a), the Party would not have failed to effectively enforce its environmental law. In such a situation there would seem to be little reason to continue with further study of the matters raised in the submission. If, on the other hand, the Party has not explained how it exercised its discretion or why its exercise of discretion is reasonable, dismissal would not be warranted under Article 45(1)(a). The Secretariat might nevertheless determine that dismissal is warranted for other reasons.

With respect to the assertion that a Party's enforcement practices result "from *bona fide* decisions to allocate resources to enforcement in respect of other environmental matters determined to have higher priorities," the Secretariat should review the extent to which the Party has explained at least three points: 1) its allocation of resources; 2) its priorities; and 3) the reasons why the Party's allocation of resources constitutes a *bona fide* allocation given the Party's priorities. If a Party has explained its allocation of resources and its priorities, and has provided a persuasive explanation of why its allocation of resources is *bona fide* in light of those priorities, then, again, under Article 45(1)(b), there is not a failure to effectively enforce. As a result, there is little reason to continue with further study of the submission.

How has the Party exercised its discretion?

In the Secretariat's view, the Party has provided substantial information concerning *how* it has exercised its discretion for purposes of Article 45(1)(a). The Party has done so by offering three basic points. First, the Party identifies its significant "enforcement" related initiatives. These include creation and implementation of a permitting scheme, issuance of regulations for the hunting of game birds that are designed to keep harvest levels in balance with a sustainable population, and related monitoring of game bird populations. The Party also identifies law enforcement investigations and prosecutions as enforcement-related approaches.

Next, the Party explains that its resources are limited. With respect to permitting, for example, the United States asserts that the FWS' Office of Migratory Bird Management lacks sufficient personnel to write permits for every incoming request. The response asserts that on average, approximately three million people each year engage in 22 million days of migratory bird hunting. The FWS has been able to commit 18 staff positions and a total nationwide budget of just over $1 million in an effort to manage approximately 40,000 active permits and process approximately 13,000 applications for intentional take permits annually. According to the United States, these resources are insufficient to the task and the agency faces "significant resource limitations." Thus, the Party asserts that simply addressing the large number of hunters and prospective hunters keeps its permitting resources more than fully occupied.

With respect to the impact of resource limitations on enforcement, the Party's response explains that the FWS' Division of Law Enforcement has "tremendous responsibilities" that include enforcement of a wide variety of statutes other than the MBTA that are designed to protect fish, wildlife, and plants. The combination of this broad range of responsibilities and existing personnel shortages makes

resource allocation decisions and the application of discretion in enforcement matters "unavoidable."

Third, the Party identifies the different types of activities that potentially violate
the Act and it explains how it has exercised its discretion in using the applicable
enforcement approaches to address these different types of activities. The Party
indicates that in light of its limited resources and the significant workload created by managing "intentional" killers of migratory birds through the permitting
process, it has exercised its discretion to focus its permitting program exclusively
on such intentional actors and not to allocate permitting resources to address
unintentional or incidental killings. Logging operations fit into this "unintentional" or "incidental" killings category, as do several other activities discussed
in more detail below, such as electric wires, oil pits, and other "attractive nuisance"-
type enterprises that the Party indicates attract birds, causing some to die. In
addition, the Party asserts that, due to its limited resources, it has "legitimately
concentrated its regulatory, enforcement, and scientific efforts to reducing unintentional takes of migratory birds caused by those activities where industry
has created hazardous conditions which often attract migratory birds to their
death." According to the Party, the FWS therefore "focuses less on preventing
takes ensuing from otherwise legal activities that modify the local environment
(logging, road construction)" than from intentional kills (such as from hunting) and from "activities where industry has created hazardous conditions which …
attract migratory birds to their death." * * *

*Is the Party's Exercise of Its Discretion Reasonable and/or its Allocation of Resources
Bona Fide Under the Circumstances?*

* * * The NAAEC is silent on the type of showing a Party should make in claiming under Article 45(1) that it is not failing to effectively enforce its environmental law. The NAAEC similarly is silent on how the Secretariat should review
such a claim in deciding whether to dismiss a submission or advise the Council
that development of a factual record is warranted. Neither the Council nor the
Secretariat have addressed these issues in detail previously.

It would appear that, to support dismissal on the basis of an Article 45(1) claim,
a Party must support the reasonableness, or *bona fide* nature, of its decisions, as
well as address the issues outlined above. To do so, a Party should provide a careful identification of the reasons why it chose to follow one course rather than
another. Here, such a showing includes providing a careful identification of the
reasons why the Party chose not to include logging operations in its permitting
scheme.

It is precisely that kind of explanation, justifying the reasonableness of the Party's
exercise of enforcement discretion in declining to establish a permitting scheme
under § 704 of the MBTA for activities, like logging operations, which result in
incidental killings, that is lacking in the response in this case. The United States
does not provide information, for example, on the relative number of birds killed
through intentional and incidental activities. Nor does the United States provide any other examples of where it has exercised its enforcement discretion
under any of its environmental laws so as to categorically exclude a portion of
the regulated community from permitting or prosecution. The U.S. has not provided this information, or any other facts, that explain why, as a policy matter,
a regulation and permitting scheme focused solely on intentional killings is a

reasonable exercise of discretion and bona fide allocation of resources to achieve the MBTA's goal of preventing the destruction of migratory birds.

The one assertion that the Party offers to support limiting the permit program to activities, such as hunting, whose purpose is to take migratory birds is that it is easier to monitor hunting than logging. The Party presumably is thereby asserting that the ease of monitoring hunters enhances the likelihood that permits issued will be complied with, thereby enhancing the value of the permitting scheme. Presumably, the Party is suggesting that the difficulty in monitoring compliance by loggers with any permits that are issued undermines the utility of a permitting scheme focused on them. Again, however, the Party does not provide factual documentation or other support for this assertion. Nor does the Party refute the Submitters' contention that the FWS has the flexibility to impose and enforce nesting and breeding season logging restrictions. It simply asserts that it is easier to monitor compliance by hunters than it would be to monitor compliance by loggers. This may well be the case, but in the Secretariat's view the Party needs to provide some support for its assertion that it is. * * *

[The Secretariat found that the United States had not provided persuasive explanations that it had exercised its enforcement discretion reasonably in making these other activities a higher priority, nor shown that its allocation of enforcement resources to these purported higher categories constituted a *bona fide* allocation of resources. For example, the Secretariat stated that it would "be helpful to develop additional information about how difficult it is to accumulate the information necessary to pursue enforcement of § 703 of the MBTA against logging operations, as compared to enforcement against other kinds of activities that the Party has decided to pursue," such as under the Endangered Species Act.]

For the reasons stated above, the Secretariat considers that the submission, in light of the Party's response, warrants development of a factual record. The Submitters assert that logging operations have violated and are continuing to violate the MBTA on a nationwide basis and in particular identified situations. The Submitters further assert that the Party has not brought a single prosecution under the MBTA for such alleged violations. In its response the Party does not challenge the first assertion. The Party acknowledges that no prosecution under the MBTA has been brought against a logging operation. In the Secretariat's view the Party has not adequately supported its claim that its failure to bring a single prosecution against logging operations is the result of a reasonable exercise of its discretion or a bona fide allocation of its resources. The Secretariat is not expressing a view as to the ultimate resolution of these issues. Instead, it has determined that the purposes of the NAAEC would be well served by developing in a factual record additional information of the types referred to above concerning them. In accordance with Article 15(1) of the NAAEC, the Secretariat so informs the Council and in this document provides its reasons.

Questions and Discussion

1. The Secretariat provided a detailed roadmap for the NAAEC Parties to follow when making claims that they are exercising reasonable discretion or making *bona fide* decisions to allocate resources to enforcement of other environmental matters. What must

the challenged Party show? Consider whether the invocation of these defenses should terminate a submission, as the NAAEC provides, or would it be better to have it considered by the public in a factual record along with other facts related to the alleged nonenforcement of environmental law.

2. The United States claimed that certain nonenforcement activities, such as bird population surveys, constituted a reasonable allocation of resources that excused it from enforcement of the MBTA. To what extent should nonenforcement activities satisfy a Party's commitment to effectively enforce environmental law?

3. See Subsection (f) below for further developments in *Migratory Birds*.

---

d. Matters Subject of a Pending Judicial or Administrative Proceeding

Where the matter raised in a submission is the subject of a pending judicial or administrative proceeding, Article 14(3)(a) requires the Secretariat to automatically terminate the submission. Despite the clarity of this provision, the Secretariat has pressed governments to fully substantiate their contentions that the matter is in fact the subject of a pending judicial or administrative proceeding. In *Oldman River I*, the Secretariat rebuffed Canada's attempt to invoke the automatic termination clause, even as it exercised its discretion to dismiss the submission on similar grounds. In this case, the Submitter alleged that Canada was failing to apply, comply with, and enforce the habitat protection provisions of the Fisheries Act and the Canadian Environmental Assessment Act to the detriment of fisheries habitat and riparian ecosystems.

Secretariat Determination under Article 15(1) (Oldman River I)
A14/SEM/96-003/12/15(1), at 3–5 (Oct. 8, 1996)

The Secretariat first considers whether Article 14(3)(a) compels the Secretariat to terminate review of the submission because the matter is currently pending before a Canadian court of law. Article 14(3) applies when the Secretariat has requested a response from a government following the initial review of a Submission. The Article provides that the Party "shall advise" the Secretariat within a prescribed time period "whether the matter is the subject of a pending judicial or administrative proceeding, in which case the Secretariat shall proceed no further."

Article 45(3) defines a "judicial or administrative proceeding" for the purposes of Article 14(3) to mean:

> a domestic judicial, quasi-judicial or administrative action pursued by the Party in a timely fashion and in accordance with its law. Such actions comprise: mediation; arbitration; the process of issuing a license, permit or authorization; seeking an assurance of voluntary compliance or a compliance agreement; seeking sanctions or remedies in an administrative or judicial forum; and the process of issuing an administrative order;

The pending Federal Court case called to the attention of the Secretariat by Canada is not an action *pursued by the Party* within the meaning of Article 45(3)(a). The term "Party" is employed consistently throughout the North American Agreement on Environmental Cooperation to refer to a government signatory to the Agreement. *See, e.g.,* Arts. 1(a), 2–8, 10–12, 48(1) and 50. Articles 14 and 15 clearly ascribe this meaning to "Party" as well. *See, e.g.,* Arts. 14(1), 14(2)(c), 14(3) and 15(1).

By limiting the ambit of "judicial or administrative proceedings" to those actions pursued by governments, the provision appears to contemplate the preemptory nature of directed efforts undertaken by a government in a timely manner to secure compliance with environmental law. In other words, where a government is actively engaged in pursuing enforcement-related measures against one or more actors implicated in an Article 14 submission, the Secretariat is obliged to terminate its examination of the allegations of non-enforcement. The examples listed in Article 45(3)(a) support this approach, since the kinds of actions enumerated are taken almost exclusively by the official government bodies charged with enforcing or implementing the law.

Since the current matter before the Canadian court was initiated and is being pursued by a private entity, and not a "Party" as that term appears to be employed in Article 45(3)(a), the Secretariat may consider other factors in its review of the Submission at this stage.

Notwithstanding the determination that Article 14(3) does not compel the Secretariat to terminate the submission process, the Secretariat nonetheless regards the pending judicial action as pertinent to our decision whether to recommend to development of a factual record. For the reasons discussed below, the Secretariat considers as relevant to its determination both the similarity of the issues which are the subject of the Submission and the pending judicial action, and the impact that the remedy sought in a court of law may have on the enforcement-related matters under consideration in this Submission. We regard these considerations as implicit in the guidance criteria set forth in Article 14(2) and in the information a Party can call to the attention of the Secretariat and Parties in Article 14(3). * * *

Although it is possible that the Federal Court may not rule on the arguments advanced under these paragraphs, the similarity of issues presented in both the submission and the lawsuit at this stage creates a risk that the preparation of a factual record may duplicate important aspects of the judicial action.

In addition to the possibility of duplication, the preparation of a factual record at this time presents a substantial risk of interfering with the pending litigation. * * *

In this instance, similar legal issues are before both the Federal Court and the Secretariat. The central issues addressed in the Submission could be rendered moot should the Federal Court rule in favor of the Applicant regarding the contentions they raise in paragraphs 7 and 8 of the Originating Notice of Motion. Both of these considerations weigh in favor of allowing the domestic proceeding to advance without risking duplication or interference by considering parallel issues under the Agreement.

Accordingly, the Secretariat considers that the submission does not warrant developing a factual record. *The Guidelines for Submissions on Enforcement Matters* do not empower the Secretariat to suspend submissions pending the resolution of judicial proceedings. However, the Submitter may wish in the future to file a new submission following a decision, dismissal or other resolution of paragraphs 7 and 8 of the Originating Notice of Motion currently before the Federal Court of Canada.

Questions and Discussion

1. The Secretariat continued to closely scrutinize government invocation of Article 14(3)(a) in later submissions. Review the Article 45(3)(a) definition of "judicial or administrative proceeding" quoted in *Oldman River I* above. Given the breadth of this definition and the very different processes and actions listed as examples of "proceedings," how would the Secretariat go about determining whether the Party pursued these proceedings in "a timely fashion"?

2. Once Canadian courts were no longer considering issues relevant to *Oldman River I*, the submitters filed a new submission, as the Secretariat had essentially invited them to do. In *Oldman River II*, A14/SEM/97-006, the Secretariat recommended the development of a factual record. In approving the preparation of a factual record, however, the Council considerably narrowed the scope of the inquiry by limiting it to a single example cited by the submitters.

3. Should the Secretariat terminate a submission if a government initiates a judicial or administrative proceeding after a submission has been filed?

---

e. Factual Records

After receiving the response of the government, the Secretariat may prepare a factual record, provided that at least two of the three Council members approve the Secretariat's recommendation to do so. Article 15(4) of the NAAEC describes the sources of information upon which the Secretariat can draw to prepare a "factual record," including information submitted by the Parties, public, and JPAC, and information "developed by the Secretariat or experts." Yet nowhere in the NAAEC is a "factual record" defined, and discussions entertained by the Parties during the drafting of the Guidelines for Submissions on Enforcement Matters Under Article 14 and 15 of the NAAEC ("Citizen Submission Guidelines") failed to reach common ground on specifying further what the countries meant by "factual."

As you review the following materials from factual records, consider how the content of factual records has evolved, as well as whether the facts do indeed "speak for themselves" or whether the process would benefit from the inclusion of conclusions and, perhaps, recommendations.

i. Cozumel

The first factual record completed by the Secretariat involved allegations by three Mexican NGOs that Mexican environmental authorities had failed to effectively enforce environmental law by not requiring the development and approval of an environmental impact assessment ("EIA") on the totality of the works proposed in relation to the construction of a port terminal and pier in Cozumel, Quintana Roo. Final Factual Record of the Cruise Ship Pier Project in Cozumel, Quintana Roo (Cozumel), A14/SEM/96-001/13/FFR, at 21–23 (Oct. 24, 1997). The submitters, represented by the Mexican Center for Environmental Law, argued that, by only assessing the pier and not the entire "Puerto Maya" tourist project, the project developers would fragment the approval process and defeat the purpose of EIA to consider all of the anticipated environmental impacts of a proposed project. The Government of Mexico contended that the project—and therefore the EIA—was limited to the construction of the pier and related facilities. Environmental authorities went so far as to state that "there is no real estate development as suggested by the Submitters, and that the onshore works referred to by the Submitters constitute only complementary elements of the pier described in the 1993 Concession." *Id.* at 21.

The Secretariat methodically collected and presented an authoritative body of documentation from a variety of sources conclusively establishing that the pier was only the first step of a massive 43 hectare real estate development project not identified in the Environmental Impact Assessment. In fact, the "Puerto Maya" project envisioned luxury hotels, restaurants, commercial centers, villas, a golf course, and other tourist establishments. *Id.* at 21–23.

Though dense, devoid of conclusions, and hardly suitable bedtime reading material, the *Cozumel* factual record established an important precedent through its meticulous compilation and exposition of facts. Mexico's initial complaint that an international organization should not squander scarce resources examining the construction of a single pier was answered by the wider policy implications of "segmenting" environmental impact assessment throughout Mexico. Later, the submitters attested to the usefulness of the *Cozumel* factual record and how the process and information it generated catalyzed change in the region. Kevin P. Gallagher, *The CEC and Environmental Quality, in* GREENING NAFTA, at 117, 128.

---

ii. BC Hydro

A very different fact pattern and factual record resulted from the next submission. In *BC Hydro,* SEM/97-001, several Canadian and U.S. environmental groups alleged that British Columbia Hydro, a provincially-owned company, operated its hydroelectric facilities in a manner that harmed fish and fish habitat in contravention of federal Canadian law. The submission and appendices detailed allegations of harmful practices at six BC Hydro-operated facilities and 39 specific incidents of alleged harm to fish habitat at some 33 facilities spread across the province. It noted the "particularly challenging" context in which, to obtain information and prepare the factual record, the CEC retained a distinguished B.C. resident, Professor Stephen Owen, to assist in "developing a process for obtaining information." Citing the "complex and highly technical" issues raised in the submission and response, the Secretariat went further and appointed an "Expert Group" comprising three experts, including individuals with expertise in hydroelectric operations, regulatory and compliance matters, and fish habitat-related issues.

In total, the *BC Hydro* Factual Record comprises 299 pages of text and appendices. The passages that follow provide a sampling of how the Secretariat employed the Expert Group to develop facts and to go beyond the *Cozumel* factual record by articulating the implications of factual findings, even considering future indicators of effective enforcement under Canada's new watershed protection strategy.

Final Factual Record for BC Aboriginal Fisheries Commission et al. (BC Hydro)
A14/SEM/97-001, at 126, 131–33, 140, 144–45 (May 30, 2000)

186. The Expert Group states that, "[i]n the end, there is little information relating to the effectiveness of prosecution as an enforcement tool given the lack

of use of this tool to date and the lack of information provided regarding the tool." (Appendix 8, para. 68). The July 1999 draft enforcement and compliance Policy contains a strategy for use of prosecutions, but little information was provided on actual implementation of this draft strategy. * * *

202. The Expert Group reviewed the information provided on each of the six BC Hydro facilities selected for relatively in-depth review. The Expert Group reviewed the allegations of the Submitters as well as the information concerning these allegations provided by Canada and BC Hydro. A series of specific questions was developed to supplement the information originally provided. (See 3 February 1999 Questions in Appendix 4, and 21 April 1999 Questions in Appendix 5). The Expert Group reviewed the follow-up information submitted. The Expert Group then developed its own information concerning the issues involved.

203. Section 5 of the Expert Group Report contains the Expert Group's compilation of information it developed or that was provided concerning each of these facilities. For each covered allegation, Section 5 begins by summarizing the allegation itself. It then summarizes Canada's response, in some cases including supplementary information provided by BC Hydro. The Expert Group then identifies the questions asked in order to develop additional information. Finally, the Expert Group provides the information it developed concerning each allegation.

204. The reader is referred to the Expert Group Report for the extensive information developed and summarized by the Expert Group concerning each of the six facilities. (See Appendix 8, paras. 102–218). In its "Overall Summary About the Six Facilities," the Expert Group makes five points concerning Canada's efforts to resolve the harm to fish habitat caused by BC Hydro operations (all paragraph references below are to the Expert Group Report in Appendix 8):

- In many situations, BC Hydro operations have caused and/or are continuing to cause harm to fish habitat. (para. 215)

- Canada has undertaken a number of actions to resolve the habitat issues at the BC Hydro operations. These actions vary widely in nature. They "rang[e] from technical discussion and negotiation to flow orders and occasional legal action." (para. 216).

- Based on the information provided, the amount of attention Canada has given to resolving various habitat issues has varied significantly depending on the facility involved....

The Expert Group notes:

The habitat problems created by construction and operation of hydroelectric facilities are complex and multifaceted and there is no scientific consensus about how best to deal with most of these problems. (para. 218). * * *

220. The Expert Group Report ... reviews Canada's enforcement activities, and their impacts, in considerable detail in the context of the six BC Hydro facilities selected for special consideration as part of the Factual Record process. Some salient information concerning Canada's activities to resolve harm to fish habitat and the impacts of these activities is summarized below.

- The Expert Group indicates that the level of effort Canada has invested in addressing habitat concerns seems to vary widely by facility. Some facilities have seen extensive efforts to resolve harm to fish habitat, while others have received relatively little attention, at least based on the information provided. (See, for example, Appendix 8, para. 216).

- Where actions have been taken to reduce harm to fish habitat caused by BC Hydro operations, in many instances these actions have paid dividends and have led to marked improvements in fish habitat. Canada, the Province of British Columbia, and BC Hydro provide considerable information concerning these actions. They also provide information concerning the results of some of these efforts. The Expert Group indicates that the fact that some activities produced benefits is clear but that information generally is limited concerning the degree and adequacy of benefit produced. The Expert Group also notes that in some situations it will be years before information on the effectiveness of these actions is available. (See, for example, Appendix 8, paras. 68, 76, 81–84, 101).

- The Expert Group highlights the importance of applying a comprehensive, system-wide approach in resolving harm to fish habitat. (See, for example, Appendix 8, para. 93). * * *

232. The Expert Group identifies a series of issues to monitor concerning whether the WUP process will prove to be effective. * * *

Along the same lines, the Expert Group states:

> If arresting the ongoing decline in fish habitat quality at most facilities is a "sufficient" outcome from WUP, as suggested by the documentation provided by Canada, then this will compromise the long term productivity of many important fish stocks. (para. 235).

Questions and Discussion

1. The preparation of the *Cozumel* factual record touched off a firestorm in Mexico, where the federal government attacked the process as "supranational" and accused the Secretariat of overstepping its authority to prepare factual records. A high profile campaign was waged in the media, and Mexico attempted to preempt the process by releasing a "factual record" of its own just weeks before the CEC completed its investigation. Is the citizen submission process supranational? How does it compare with the trade rules and dispute resolution procedures discussed elsewhere in this text?

2. Some Canadian officials were unhappy with the Secretariat's use of the *BC Hydro* Expert Group, viewing it as a surrogate means of reaching conclusions and making recommendations in a factual record. Canada reiterated its concerns in its comments on a draft factual record, published a few years later in *BC Mining*:

> Canada recognizes the Secretariat's authority to retain an independent expert in the preparation of a Factual Record, as needed. However, Canada considers the mandate given to the expert [to consider the effectiveness of the current Provincial remediation program in achieving compliance with the applicable law] to go well beyond the scope and purpose of a Factual Record. It is Canada's view that independent experts should not be drawing conclusions, or passing judgment on the actions taken by a Party.... Therefore, we request that the Secretariat review the information that has been attributed to the ARD expert, and remove any and all judgements, conclusions and/or opinions since they go beyond a compilation of facts.

Factual Record of BC Mining, SEM-98-004, Attachment 2: Comments of Canada, at 217, 218 (June 27, 2003).

3. Just what is a "fact"? Did the Secretariat present more than facts in *BC Hydro*? If an enforcement official's report concluded that an unauthorized release of water from a dam had resulted in the death of 100 salmon, would that be a fact? What if the number were disputed by experts or other officials? Could it be a fact that someone wrote, said, or held a belief, even if the belief itself was erroneous? Is it a "fact" that individuals or experts hold certain beliefs or opinions? Is the domestic law of each Party relevant in answering this question, such as rules governing the admissibility of evidence in trials or administrative proceedings?

Not all factual records present such complicated factual and legal questions. In *Rio Magdalena*, SEM-97-002, a Mexican nongovernmental organization asserted that Mexico was allowing three municipalities in the state of Sonora to discharge untreated wastewater into the Magdalena River in contravention of Mexican environmental law. The factual record left little doubt that discharges exceeding regulatory limits had taken place and were continuing. On the matter of enforcement, the Secretariat stated:

> The information the Secretariat presents in this factual record reveals that since the entry into force of the NAAEC on 1 January 1994, the [Mexican Water Authority] has not taken any enforcement action regarding the water pollution prevention and control environmental law provisions referred to in this factual record with respect to [the three named Municipalities].

Final Factual Record of the Río Magdalena Submission (Rio Magdalena), SEM-97-002, at 6 (Oct. 24, 2003). Mexico acknowledged and explained its enforcement record as follows:

> It should be mentioned that the treatment of wastewater from the country's population centers is a goal that the Mexican government has been unable to fully achieve and that progress in this area is subject to the availability of budgetary resources. This being the case, it must be stated that despite the existence of a general obligation in both federal and state law to treat wastewater from population centers, the economic limitations facing the country make it as yet impossible to fully enforce this provision; nevertheless, a clear strategy for a gradual solution to the wastewater treatment problem at the national level can be discerned in the corresponding government plans.

Id. at 12.

4. In later cases, the Secretariat began including an "Executive Summary" to aid readers in digesting what have become lengthy, detailed, and often complex factual records. (The quoted passages from the *Rio Magdalena* are taken from the Executive Summary.) Is a tighter summary of the findings a reader-friendly means of making factual records more accessible, or might the Secretariat be selecting salient facts as a backdoor way of suggesting sharper conclusions? Could it be both?

5. As discussed earlier, the Mexican government chafed at the *Cozumel* factual record, attacking the process at every turn. The Mexican government evinced a remarkably different attitude in *Rio Magdalena*, including a healthy dose of *mea culpa*. What changed? Do you find the Mexican government's implicit argument invoking the Article 45(1) justification on grounds of allocation of scarce enforcement resources more persuasive than the U.S. government's contentions in *Migratory Birds*? Is it worth the effort and expense to develop a factual record where a Party admits to a failure to enforce environmental law?

6. Article 7 of the NAAEC requires each NAAEC Party to ensure that its administrative and judicial proceedings are fair, open and equitable, and comply with due process of law and are open to the public, among other things. How would a Party enforce the breach of Article 7? Could a citizen raise any of these procedural and substantive guarantees as a basis for alleging that a Party is failing to effectively enforce its environmental law? How, if at all, does "effective enforcement" relate to any of these provisions? Are they related to trade?

---

f. Widespread Patterns and the Scope of Factual Records

In recent years, the Secretariat, Council, and JPAC have been locked in a dispute that has festered into the gravest threat to date to the legitimacy of the citizen submission process. The dispute initially involved the propriety of submitters alleging widespread patterns of nonenforcement and the extent to which a submitter must substantiate and particularize each instance of nonenforcement alleged in a submission. The Secretariat, exercising its independent screening and processing functions, recommended the development of factual records on several submissions alleging a widespread pattern of nonenforcement. The Council responded by approving the preparation of these factual records but significantly narrowing the scope of the inquiry to consider only those examples provided by the submitters with a much higher level of particularized, individual facts.

The Secretariat finally put its interpretation of the issue on record in the recommendation to the Council on the *Migratory Birds* submission discussed earlier in this chapter.

Secretariat Notification to Council under
Article 15(1) (Migratory Birds)
A14/SEM/99-002/11/ADV, at 8–10, 25–27 (Dec. 15, 2000)

Application of Articles 14 and 15 to Assertions of a Wide-ranging Failure to Enforce Environmental Law Effectively

The focus of the submission is on an asserted failure to effectively enforce that is nationwide in scope. While the Submitters identify some specific logging operations that allegedly violated the MBTA, the reference to particular operations is clearly intended to be illustrative. The Submitters' primary concern is with an asserted nationwide failure on the part of the Party to investigate or prosecute logging operations that violate the MBTA by killing birds or destroying bird nests.

Given the Submitters' broad focus on an asserted nationwide failure to effectively enforce, the Secretariat now considers whether the citizen submission process is intended for assertions of this sort. One possible view is that the citizen submission process is reserved for assertions of particularized failures to effectively enforce. Under this view a factual record would be warranted, only when a submitter asserts that a Party is failing to effectively enforce with respect to one or more particular facilities or projects. This view of the Article 14 process, in short, reads the opening sentence of Article 14(1) to confine the citizen submission process to asserted failures to effectively enforce with respect to particular facilities or projects. Under this view, assertions of a wide-ranging failure to effectively enforce that do not focus on individual facilities or projects would not be subject to review under the citizen submission process.

The text of Article 14 does not appear to support limiting the scope of the citizen submission process in this way. The opening sentence of Article 14 establishes three specific parameters for the citizen submission process. It thereby limits assertions of failures to effectively enforce to those meeting these three elements. First, the assertions must involve an "environmental law." Next, they must involve an asserted failure to "effectively enforce" that law (the assertion may not focus on purported deficiencies in the law itself). Third, assertions must meet the temporal requirement of claiming that there *is* a failure to effectively enforce.

The Parties' inclusion of these three limitations on the scope of the Article 14 process reflects that they knew how to confine the scope of the process and that they decided to do so in specific ways. The Parties could have limited the species of actionable failures to effectively enforce to either particularized incidents of such, or to asserted failures that are of a broad scope, in the same way that they included the limits referenced above. They did not do so. * * *

Moreover, in deciding whether to request a response from a Party, Article 14(2) of the NAAEC directs the Secretariat to be guided by whether a submission "raises matters whose further study in this process would advance the goals" of the Agreement. The goals of the NAAEC are ambitious and broad in scope. These goals include, for example, "foster[ing] the protection and improvement of the environment in the territories of the Parties for the well-being of present and future generations," as well as "enhanc[ing] compliance with, and enforcement of, environmental laws and regulations."

Assertions that there is a failure to enforce with respect to a single incident or project may raise matters whose further study would advance these goals. Indeed, the Secretariat has concluded that such assertions merit developing a factual record in several instances and the Council has concurred. But also, assertions that the failure to enforce extends beyond a single facility or project portend, at least potentially, a more extensive or broad-based issue concerning the effectiveness of a Party's efforts to enforce its environmental laws and regulations. In other words, the larger the scale of the asserted failure, the more likely it may be to warrant developing a factual record, other things being equal. If the citizen submission process were construed to bar consideration of alleged widespread enforcement failures, the failures that potentially pose the greatest threats to accomplishment of the Agreement's objectives, and the most serious and far-reaching threats of harm to the environment, would be beyond the scope of that process. This limitation in scope would seem to be counter to the objects and purposes of the NAAEC. The Secretariat declines to adopt a reading of the Agreement that would yield such a result.

On November 16, 2001, the Council issued five resolutions instructing the Secretariat to prepare factual records for five submissions, including the *Migratory Birds* submission discussed above. Four of the five Council resolutions dramatically altered the content of the factual record by sharply limiting or redefining the scope of the Secretariat inquiry. Instead of examining broad, programmatic failures to enforce specific environmental laws as the submitters had requested and the Secretariat had recommended, the Council directed the Secretariat to limit its investigation to the isolated examples cited by the submitters. The Secretariat says as much in a February 2002 memorandum to the chair of the Joint Public Advisory Committee:

> [T]he Council included instructions to prepare factual records regarding specific cases raised in the submissions, but did not include instructions regarding allegations in each of those submissions of widespread failures to effectively enforce environmental laws. For each of those four submissions, the Secretariat had recommended preparing factual records in regard to the widespread allegations of failures to effectively enforce.

Reprinted in David L. Markell, *The CEC Citizen Submission Process, in* GREENING NAFTA, at 274, 277.

In the Executive Summary of the *Migratory Birds* Factual Record, the Secretariat made sure that the procedural history of the submission became a matter of public record:

> Council Resolution 01-10 governs the scope of this factual record. The Resolution authorizes a factual record narrower in scope than the factual record that the Submitters sought and that the Secretariat considered to warrant development in its notification to Council under NAAEC Article 15(1). The focus of the factual record is on the two cases mentioned in the Resolution. Information regarding general policies and practices of the United States government for enforcing section 703 of the MBTA are included in the factual record to the extent that they provide context and background relevant to those two cases. Certain information that the Submitters suggested be included or that was discussed in the Secretariat Art. 15(1) notification is beyond the scope of Council Resolution.

Final Factual Record for Migratory Birds, SEM-99-002, at 7–8 (Apr. 22, 2003).

The Council's limitation on the scope of the factual record certainly shaped the nature of that factual record. Being restricted to two specific instances of nonenforcement, the *Migratory Birds* Factual Record shows that the State of California had prosecuted individuals in both cases, and reported that the federal authorities indicated that when state enforcement action had already been taken, the federal government would not also enforce except in unusual circumstances. But that was not the issue the submitters were trying to raise. Chris Wold, the lead attorney for the submitters, later acknowledged that the submitters had employed the process with the hope of generating information on the number of migratory birds "taken" as a result of logging in the United States and the nationwide effect of limiting the MBTA permit program to activities involving the intentional killing of migratory birds.

To make its own point to the Council and the public about the effect of the Council's limitations, the Secretariat provided in the *Migratory Birds* Factual Record a long list of examples of the kind of information that would *not* be included in the report. Similar recitals in later factual records drew protest from the Parties, who complained that the Secretariat's recounting of the narrowing of the scope of the factual record was itself outside the scope of a properly constituted factual record. *See, e.g.,* Factual Record for BC Mining, Canada's Comments on the Draft Factual Record, SEM-98-004, at 219 (June 27, 2003). In response to such complaints, Professor David Markell, former CEC Director of Submissions, has concluded that the Council's limiting of factual records upsets the careful balance established in the NAAEC and "raise[s] serious questions about the legitimacy of the Council's four November resolutions." David L. Markell, *The CEC Citizen Submission Process, in* GREENING NAFTA, at 285.

A later Council resolution in *Ontario Logging* opened a new line of attack on allegations of widespread patterns of nonenforcement, as the Council declined the Secretariat's recommendation to develop a factual record by questioning the "sufficiency" of the information presented by the submitter, despite the Secretariat's view that the submitters had met this burden. Council Resolution 04-03 (Ontario Logging), C/C.01/03-02/RES/05/final, (Apr. 22, 2003). For its part, the JPAC expressed strong concerns about the effect of these resolutions, but was urged by the Council not to conduct public consultations on their impact until after the factual records were completed. The JPAC did just that, and on their own authority conducted public consultations on limiting the scope of factual records. The excerpt below from the International Environmental Law Project (IELP) at Lewis & Clark Law School, one of the groups representing the submitters in Migratory Birds, illustrates the strong views held by advocates for a robust citizen submission process. In its comments, IELP also responds to the Council's decision to suspend a submission, despite the Secretariat's finding that all eligibility requirements had been met, until submitters provided "sufficient information."

International Environmental Law Project (IELP), Issues Relating to Articles 14 & 15 of the North American Commission on Environmental Cooperation

(Oct. 2, 2003)

Council Continues to Undermine the Integrity of the Citizen Submission Process by Impermissibly Narrowing the Scope of Factual Records

The Council's actions to narrow the scope of factual records and interpret provisions of the NAAEC clearly within the purview of the Secretariat are not only troubling, but are also *ultra vires,* beyond its authority in the NAAEC. Council's actions have eroded support for the NAAEC, as well as for the use of provisions similar to the Article 14/15 process in other free trade agreements. Council's refusal to respect the boundaries delineated in the NAAEC has led to repeated calls from the JPAC, NAC [National Advisory Committee] and independent review committees for Council to step back and allow the process to operate independently, as intended. Recently, for example, the U.S. Governmental Advisory Committee declared that the Council's decisions to narrow the scope of factual records had "eviserate[d]" the autonomy of the Secretariat to define the scope of the factual record.[13] JPAC has raised similar concerns, even charging that Council was narrowing factual records and taking other action on a case-by-case basis—through its Article 14/15 votes—as a means of circumventing the JPAC-led public consultation procedure for considering revisions to the Article 14 and 15 Submission Guidelines.[14]

The NAAEC carefully establishes a system of "checks and balances" by granting the Council and Secretariat distinct roles and clear boundaries. In this case, the

---

13. Letter of Advice to the EPA Administrator Christine Whitman from the Chair of the Governmental Advisory Committee to the U.S. Representative to the CEC, 1–2 (Oct. 19, 2001).

14. *See, e.g.,* JPAC Advice to Council No. 01-07 (Oct. 23, 2001) ("[JPAC] is compelled to express its frustration at being forced once again to advice on issues related to Articles 14 and 15, because past-agreed upon procedures are being ignored or circumvented."); JPAC Advice to Council No. 02-03 (Mar. 8, 2002) (stating Council's narrowing actions are "effectively eliminating an opportunity for public input into this very important issue; and … is considered by JPAC as a *de facto* change to the *Guidelines for Submissions on Enforcement Matters under Articles 14 and 15 of the NAAEC.*"

Secretariat has the duty to decide what the scope of the factual record should be. By its own terms, Article 15 of the NAAEC confers on Council the power to approve or reject the Secretariat's recommendation to prepare a factual record. Through substituting its own judgment of what constitutes "sufficient information" and the appropriate scope of a factual record, the Council is denying the Secretariat its proper role set out in the NAAEC. In so doing, Council is further undermining public confidence that the process will be allowed to operate as designed, even if that occasionally shines an embarrassing spotlight on government conduct.

Narrowing the scope of factual records beyond the Secretariat's specific recommendations has already radically altered the balance between Secretariat and Council functions. In the Migratory Birds submission, it is highly doubtful the Submitters ever would have employed the process had they known that Council would, in an arbitrary and unexplained fashion, limit the record to two specific instances cited only as examples of widespread government conduct. Moreover, it is highly doubtful whether the Secretariat would have recommended the development of a factual record to Council if the Secretariat had known that the scope of the submission would be narrowed in this manner. The absurdity of the result is patent: Council directed the Secretariat to develop a factual record that resembled neither the issues presented by the Submitter nor those recommended for study by the Secretariat. Indeed, it is the factual record that nobody wanted.

With respect to both points, the *ad hoc* nature of the Council's decision-making creates great uncertainty for both the Secretariat and Submitters. Without clear rules, neither the Secretariat nor Submitters know whether Council decisions constitute a type of "precedent" or whether the Council will establish a different rule in future cases. Even if we accept that the Council can override decisions of the Secretariat, a system must have clear rules that establish boundaries and definitions, and thus expectations, for all participants. The NAAEC Articles 14 and 15 establish such clear rules: Council votes "yes" or "no" on whether to instruct the Secretariat to prepare a factual record on the issues recommended for further study by the Secretariat.

Council Has Appropriated The Secretariat Function Of Assessing "*Sufficient Information*" And Has Defined It In A Manner Inconsistent With The Clear Language Of Article 14 Of The NAAEC

Council recently opened a new line of attack on the pattern issue by deciding in Ontario Logging (SEM-02-001) that the Submission did not contain sufficient information to warrant the development of a factual record.[16]

Article 14 explicitly states that the Secretariat alone has authority to determine whether a submission provides "sufficient information." It unambiguously commands that "[t]he Secretariat may consider a submission … if *the Secretariat* finds that the submission … provides sufficient information to allow *the Secretariat* to review the submission…." (emphasis added).

---

16. Council Resolution 03-05 (Apr. 22, 2003). Council questioned the sufficiency with the use of a statistical model which Submitters contend provides the best available information precisely because the government of Canada has abdicated its enforcement responsibilities by, among other things, failing to collect the kind of information required to assess the impact of commercial logging on bird populations protected by the Migratory Bird Treaty Act.

Instead of simply terminating the Ontario Logging submission with a thumbs up or down vote, Council impermissibly remanded the submission, allowing the Submitters to resubmit by supplementing the information upon which the submission was based. While innocent in form, this approach actually usurps the Secretariat function of reviewing the sufficiency of submissions by laying out markers the Secretariat must presumably follow in its reconsideration of the matter.[17] In other words, Council appears to be signaling to the Secretariat that it expects the "sufficiency" element to be applied in a much more restrictive and limiting way. Faced with a Secretariat that refuses to adopt a cramped definition of "sufficiency," Council may attempt to simply revise the *Guidelines*, defining "sufficiency" in a way that shuts down efforts to examine patterns of government conduct. Following this path will lead to the virtual extinction of the Citizen Submission Process, since it will have terminated its most useful applications.

Impacts of Council's Actions

The manner in which the Council has narrowed the scope of factual records—by rejecting investigations of general policy failures—allows Parties to disrupt the factual inquiry process, dictates where future claims will be brought and sidesteps the Council's commitment to ensure that JPAC and the public are involved in any process to amend the Article 14/15 *Guidelines*.

Derailment of the Factual Inquiry Process

Allowing Council to narrow factual records to isolated examples will enable governments to more easily derail factual inquiries by asserting that specific cases are the subject of ongoing proceedings or reflect a reasonable exercise of investigatory, prosecutorial, regulatory or compliance discretion. * * *

In response to public comments, the JPAC issued the following advice.

Joint Public Advisory Committee
Advice to Council No: 03-05, December 17, 2003

Re: Limiting the scope of factual records and review of the operation of CEC Council Resolution 00-09 related to Articles 14 and 15 of the North American Agreement on Environmental Cooperation

The Joint Public Advisory Committee (JPAC) of the Commission for Environmental Cooperation (CEC) of North America:

IN ACCORDANCE with Article 16(4) of the North American Agreement on Environmental Cooperation (NAAEC), which states that JPAC "may provide advice to Council on any matter within the scope of this agreement [...] and on the implementation and further elaboration of this agreement, and may perform such other functions as the Council may direct";

RECOGNIZING that the citizen submissions process under Articles 14 and 15 of the NAAEC plays a unique and indispensable role in fostering vigorous environmental enforcement;

---

17. The Secretariat promptly found that the new Submission, which continues to employ the statistical model objected to by Canada, met the sufficiency threshold and the Secretariat requested a response from Canada.

RECALLING JPAC's Lessons Learned Report to Council recommending that this process must be more timely, open, equitable, accountable and effective;

CONCERNED that the citizen submissions process is continuing to lose relevance, placing the CEC's credibility at risk; * * *

THEREFORE, on the matter of limiting the scope of factual records, JPAC strongly recommends that Council refrain in the future from limiting the scope of factual records presented for decision by the Secretariat.

JPAC supports this recommendation with the following reasons:

- By intervening in the fact-finding process, the Council is undermining the independence of the Secretariat and the credibility of the process.

- Interference by Council with the scope of a submission creates a situation where factual records no longer address the matters raised by the submitters, rendering the process less relevant.

- Such action jeopardizes the ability of those records to fully expose the controversy at issue.

- The factual records were not able to address evidence of widespread enforcement failures, cumulative effects that stem from such widespread patterns, or the broader concerns of submitters about implementation of enforcement policies.

- Restricting factual records to exploration of specific instances may also make it easier for the Parties to invoke other exceptions within the Agreement, such as Article 14(3) (excluding from the factual record matters subject to pending judicial or administrative proceedings), which are more readily invoked with respect to specific instances of nonenforcement than to allegations of widespread, systemic patterns of ineffective enforcement.

- Defining the scope of factual records to require citizens' groups to detail every specific violation to be included in the Secretariat's investigations potentially increases the financial and human resources burdens placed on these groups.

Related to this matter is the issue of what constitutes 'sufficient' information to support an allegation of failure to enforce. Council Resolution 03-05 relating to the Ontario Logging submission stated that this case "does not contain the sufficient information required to proceed with the development of a factual record at this time." With the benefit of input from the public and having been informed by the ELI report, JPAC concluded that:

- Such a decision adds to the existing "pleading" requirements of the NAAEC, a new and higher evidentiary threshold for the sufficiency of information necessary to support allegations of nonenforcement;

- While some evidentiary threshold is necessary to avoid frivolous or speculative allegations from submitters, according to the Article 14(1)(c) the Secretariat has the mandate, authority, and expertise to determine where this bar should be set; and

- In setting the bar for "sufficient information" too high, the Council may render it prohibitively difficult for citizens to participate in the process. * * *

Concerning Council Resolution 00-09, it is JPAC's considered opinion that Council's resolutions limiting the scope of factual records and rulings on the sufficiency of information provided in submissions, in conjunction with the Council's decision to delay public review of its decision to define the scope of factual records and subsequent delays in conducting a review of this resolution appear to:

- Jeopardize the commitment, expressed in Council Resolution 00-09, to increase transparency and public participation in the citizen submissions process; and

- Violate the object and purpose, or "spirit," of Council Resolution 00-09, which as we all recall was a hard-fought compromise designed to allow the process to move forward and re-establish public confidence. * * *

Questions and Discussion

1. Return to the language of Articles 14 and 15 on pages 789–91. Is IELP correct that the Council only has the authority to vote "yes" or "no" on a recommendation to prepare a factual record? Does the authority to vote "no" also imply the authority to limit the scope of a factual record? Could the Council likewise expand the scope of a factual record?

2. Whose role is it to determine whether a submission contains "sufficient information to allow the Secretariat to review the submission," as required by Article 14(1)(c)? Does the Council have the authority to overturn the Secretariat's determination that a submission includes "sufficient information" to proceed with the preparation of a factual record? Under Article 10(1)(b), the Council has the duty to "oversee the implementation and develop recommendations on the further elaboration of this Agreement." Does that give the Council the authority to define terms and provisions of the NAAEC through its power to approve and reject recommendations for the preparation of factual records?

3. Once trade tribunals are seized of a dispute, governments play virtually no role in shaping the outcome of the dispute except as litigants. Should the Council have such a role in a nonadjudicative process like the citizen submission process? IELP urges the governments to "recall their role as a steward of the NAAEC, and not solely as a defendant in a fact-gathering process." Is this possible? What would be the advantages and drawbacks of empowering an independent unit in the Secretariat to fully process, screen, and, where warranted, develop factual records without the intervention of the Council? Compare the dispute resolution remedies available to investors under Chapter 11 of NAFTA and similar provisions in other free trade agreements. Should citizens also have the right to redress intentional enforcement failures that adversely impact human health or the environment? What about for trade measures that can be demonstrated to cause harmful health or environmental effects?

4. Viewing the citizen submission process as too adversarial, the U.S. National Advisory Committee, which provides advice to the Environmental Protection Agency on issues relating to the NAAEC, recently proposed a cooperative mechanism for the resolution of environmental problems identified by citizens. This "problem-solving" process would allow citizens to approach an independent Secretariat with issues unrelated to enforcement failures and would not seek to assign blame for the specified environmental concern. Instead, the process would help resolve environmental problems:

[T]he Secretariat would work with the requestors and the Party or Parties concerned to resolve the issue. The Secretariat's functions would vary depending on the nature of the issue. It would seek to identify technology, information, financing, or other resources and catalyze resolution of the problem. (Those resources could be available through governments, businesses, academic institutions, non-profit institutions, international organizations, etc.) In some cases, it might simply pass on such information to the requestors; in others, it might facilitate direct contacts between the requestors and other interested parties; in still others, it might prepare a short report outlining an approach that all interested parties might consider taking. Finally, in some cases it might determine after further consideration that it cannot assist with resolution of the problem.

Advice 2007-1, (May 24, 2007), *in* Letter from M. Dolores Wesson, Chair, National Advisory Committee, to Stephen Johnson, Administrator, U.S. EPA, at 13 (May 24, 2007), *available at* http://www.epa.gov/ocem/nac/pdf/2007_may24_nac_letter.pdf. At its core, this proposal attempts to address the central issues that matter to citizens: that their voices are heard and that officials respond to their concerns in a meaningful way. It also seeks to ensure that specific environmental concerns are resolved. Do you think this is a better approach than the citizen submission process? Under what NAAEC provisions could such a process be implemented?

5. CEC observers continue to hold divergent views on the overall value of the citizen submission process. *Compare* Gustavo Alanís Ortega, *Public Participation within NAFTA's Environmental Agreement: The Mexican Experience, in* Linking Trade, Environment and Social Cohesion: NAFTA Experiences, Global Challenges 183 (John J. Kirton & Virginia Maclaren eds. 2002) (crediting the submission process with the creation of a protection area in Mexico and beneficial changes to Mexican environmental law); Chris Wold et al, *The Inadequacy of the Citizen Submission Process of Articles 14 & 15 of the North American Agreement on Environmental Cooperation,* 26 Loy. L.A. Int'l & Comp. L. Rev. 415 (2004) (noting that U.S. environmentalists have stopped using the process due to governmental intrusion in the process and the process's inherent limitations); John H. Knox, *Separated at Birth: The North American Agreements on Labor and the Environment,* 26 Loy. L.A. Int'l & Comp. L. Rev. 359 (2004) (arguing that despite the process's flaws, "environmental advocates are missing opportunities to extend the far more useful post-Westphalian procedures pioneered by the CEC").

6. *The Governmental Sanctions Process.* Part Five of the NAAEC establishes a "sanctions" process for a "persistent pattern" of nonenforcement of environmental laws that could ultimately lead to a withdrawal of NAFTA trade benefits for the country not enforcing its own environmental laws. This was an absolute must for U.S. negotiators so that the administration could assure Congress and the public that there was a way to guard against any competitive advantage deriving from nonenforcement of environmental law (Mexico being the implicit target of such concerns). The process leading to possible sanctions has several steps. First, NAAEC Article 22 provides that a government may request consultation for a "persistent pattern of failure [by a Party] to effectively enforce its environmental law," "persistent pattern" being defined as "a sustained or recurring course of action or inaction beginning after the date of entry into force of this agreement" (Article 45). As part of this consultation process, the CEC Council may, upon a two-thirds vote, convene an arbitral panel to prepare a report with recommendations for better enforcement. The trade linkage is explicit here; arbitral panels may only be convened for alleged persistent patterns of nonenforcement that relate to trade between the NAFTA Parties, including situations involving workplaces, firms, compa-

nies, and sectors (Article 24). If the panel finds a persistent failure to enforce environmental law by a Party, the disputing Parties "may" agree on a "mutually satisfactory action plan, which normally shall conform to the determinations and recommendations of the panel" (Article 33).

Now the "teeth" of this process come into play. If the Parties cannot agree on a plan or there is disagreement over implementation of a plan, any disputing Party may petition to reconvene the panel, which can impose a plan on the Parties. If the panel concludes that a Party is not fully implementing the plan, it may impose a monetary penalty not to exceed .007 percent of total trade between the Parties (Article 34 & Annex 34). (.007 of total trade is about $1.2 million today.) If a Party fails to pay, the other Party in the dispute can suspend NAFTA benefits in an amount not to exceed the monetary assessment (Article 36). As an inducement to pay the penalty instead of suffering a loss of trade benefits, the penalty money will go to the CEC, where it must then be spent "to improve or enhance the environment or environmental law enforcement in the Party complained against." This focuses any penalty on remediation of the problem rather than mere punishment.

To date, no NAAEC Party has availed itself of this process or even threatened to do so. The Parties have not even developed the Model Rules of Procedure to govern the process called for by Article 28 of the NAAEC. Is that surprising? Despite their dormancy, the sanctions provisions cast a long shadow over the cooperative nature of the NAAEC and arguably have made the Parties hypersensitive to the citizen submission procedure for fear that an issue raised by a citizen could later become the subject of the more consequential governmental sanctions process.

E. The NAFTA at Ten: Has the CEC Fulfilled Its Mission?

In January 2004, the NAFTA celebrated its ten-year anniversary. A blizzard of press releases extolled and excoriated the Agreement, and scores of conferences, retrospectives, and symposia examined the so-called "lessons learned" from NAFTA. Many analysts have tried to make objective assessments, but data for such assessments are hard to come by and subject to interpretation. For a useful compilation of some analyses, see GREENING THE AMERICAS: NAFTA's LESSONS FOR HEMISPHERIC TRADE (Carolyn L. Deere and Daniel C. Esty, eds., 2002) Yet, few have been swayed from their original positions on the issues.

Our focus here is the specific role of the CEC as one part of the NAFTA arrangement. As a former staff member of the CEC Secretariat, Greg Block offers one perspective.

Greg M. Block, *Trade and Environment in the Western Hemisphere: Expanding the North American Agreement on Environmental Cooperation into the Americas*
33 ENVTL. L. 501, 513–15, 520–21 (2003)

NAFTA's Impacts on Environment Revisited

If the first decade of NAFTA has failed to produce the kind of Chicken Little environmental impacts some opponents had forecast, it also failed to bolster many free traders' contention that higher incomes in Mexico inexorably would fuel an appetite for greater environmental protection. Despite some evidence of rising per capita income in Mexico, SEMARNAT (the Mexican Ministry of Environment) remains grossly underfunded, and major environmental indicators show little, if any, improvement.

The truth about how liberalizing trade in North America has affected the environment lies somewhere between the extremes, but just where remains hard to pinpoint. Not only is it difficult to assess the environmental effects of free trade, but it is also an arduous task to determine the counterfactual proposition—estimating how much worse (or better) things would be in the absence of free trade or NAFTA's environmental side accord. In the case of the NAAEC, assessments are even murkier respecting the many CEC initiatives that have little or nothing to do with trade.

Hard as it may be, policymakers must nevertheless attempt to evaluate the strengths and weaknesses of the NAAEC as one of the few models potentially applicable to the greater hemisphere in the FTAA. * * *

Opinions on the impact of the NAAEC are plentiful and varied. At the edges, hard-held views remain consistent with the positions advanced during the debate on NAFTA and the environment prior to its coming into force. Even if few people have changed their minds about the approach taken on environmental matters in the NAFTA, it is worthwhile to distinguish between the actual impact of the NAAEC on environment and trade policies in the region and the *potential* utility of the approach or model employed in the NAAEC. The distinction is important in determining whether the NAFTA approach itself is flawed, or if its full implementation merely lacks political support and adequate funding.

NAAEC Regional Impact

Early concerns that the side agreement and its sunlight mechanisms constituted an intrusive hindrance to trade in the region appear entirely unfounded. If anything, the CEC and its initiatives remain invisible to most business interests and the public at large. Indeed, few CEC actions directly impact specific trade interests. For precisely that reason, a number of commentators have expressed disappointment in the implementation of the environmental side agreement, especially those who had hoped the accord would help avoid or mitigate adverse impacts, or channel trade flows into more sustainable pathways.

Despite its inconspicuous public profile, over the past decade the successes and shortcomings of the CEC have drawn considerable attention from scholars, advisory committees, and others. Most commentators conclude that the impact of the CEC on major issues of regional concern has been modest, at best. Some welcome the emergence of the new institution as a much needed voice in regional environmental affairs. A less charitable opinion of the CEC is expressed by those who measure its accomplishments against the growing list of serious environmental issues calling for regional solutions. Those who expected the NAFTA and CEC to tackle these major areas of concern early on are understandably underwhelmed by the results so far. * * *

The CEC has also made some headway in providing many citizens with a fuller appreciation of "North American" or regional issues. As nonstate actors assume a growing role in public policy matters, the CEC provides a unique venue for nongovernmental bodies to forge alliances and develop regional campaigns. The heightened awareness of social, ecological and economic connectedness and an increasing openness and trust between governmental and non-governmental actors should, in the long run, help establish the foundations for finding enduring solutions to the seemingly intractable problems the region faces.

Impact on Trade and Trade Policy

Perhaps most disappointing to a number of environmental groups who supported the NAAEC has been its inability to impact everyday trade or trade policy in any noticeable way. The provisions enabling the CEC to provide expertise in environment-related trade disputes, as well as to proactively take measures to help avoid such disputes, have fallen into disuse after little more than quivering into life with a few procedural gatherings, and a series of aborted attempts to organize a trade and environment ministerial summit. Similarly, the CEC has been sidelined in the tri-national discussions over how to address growing concerns about the application of the investor-state provisions contained in NAFTA Chapter 11.

In the eyes of many of those who supported the side accord, the NAAEC must either improve environmental laws, policies, infrastructure and capacities as a bulwark against unsustainable trade patterns, or intervene directly by promoting environmental measures that may affect trade. At minimum, the CEC must provide independent information monitoring the environmental impacts of free trade in a timely and complete fashion. Yet, the CEC lacks rulemaking or adjudicative powers and, with its budget forever stuck at nine million dollars, has little monetary clout. Faced with these limitations, the organization has attempted to influence public policy by becoming an authoritative voice on a few key subjects. Against considerable odds, the CEC has managed to develop and apply a useful framework for assessing the impacts of free trade. Even if the CEC's analytical efforts have yet to yield many real world policy outcomes, the lessons-learned from developing and applying the framework stand as one of the less heralded achievements of the CEC. In the long-term, these lessons hold the potential to refine and reshape the nature of environmental concerns with trade agreements.

As the NAAEC turned 10, the CEC commissioned its own review of its effectiveness. The Ten-year Review and Assessment Committee (TRAC) agreed with IELP and others that the Council's actions, such as narrowing of factual records, had upset the balance set out in the NAAEC and undermined the Secretariat's role in the NAAEC's Article 14 process. Regarding the CEC's impact on the environment and understanding trade-environment linkages, the TRAC agreed with Mary Kelly and Cyrus Reed that the CEC had developed important methodologies for assessing the environmental impacts of trade that have supported and influenced similar efforts. It also agreed that macro studies must be supplemented with more geographically limited or media-specific studies but that the absence of data at the local and sectoral level makes such studies difficult. It further agreed that scale and composition effects warrant at least as much attention as competitiveness effects. Like Block, the TRAC noted that the CEC has done little to impact trade-environment linkages and that CEC actions have had few impacts on trade and trade policy.

In the excerpt that follows, the TRAC explains why the CEC has had trouble fulfilling its mandate and potential but also showing that its work has led to promise.

Ten-Year Review and Assessment Committee, Ten Years of North American Environmental Cooperation: Report of the Ten Year Review and Assessment Committee to the Council of the Commission for Environmental Cooperation

7–11, 13–15, 23–25 (June 15, 2004)

Has the CEC helped further a North American environmental agenda? * * *

The NAAEC is an agreement among three sovereign parties, each contributing equally to the CEC budget, and each represented equally on the CEC's decision-making structures. While the three Parties are ostensibly equal, they are in fact characterized by numerous asymmetries (*viz.*, in their economic size, political culture, natural resource endowment, in the environmental pressures they face, in their institutional capacities and in the level of national attention focused on the environment; ... Geography makes the United States the dominant partner in this relationship: straddling the middle of North American and being the only country sharing borders with both its partners, the United States has a greater stake in, and a greater influence over, the CEC's success than its neighbors.

The asymmetries above mean that the Parties often bring different priorities to the table. As one of the richest countries in the world in terms of biodiversity, Mexico, for example, has manifested a greater interest in "green" issues at the CEC than its neighbors. The United States, on the other hand, has shown a greater interest in the CEC's "accountability" agenda because it believes that greater public involvement, greater transparency and greater enforcement will lead all Parties to improve their environmental performance. These differing priorities flow in part from the different mandates of the environmental agencies represented on the CEC Council (while having a much bigger budget, the US EPA has a narrower mandate, focused on environmental protection, than either Environment Canada or Mexico's environment department, Semarnat, whose mandates include issues such as wildlife management. * * *

All these factors—the asymmetries among the three countries, their different interests and capacities, their domestic politics and the pressure to work on the basis of consensus—are basic constraints on any international organization but become highlighted when there are few members. They have made it difficult for the three Parties to develop and implement a common agenda, let alone address contentious issues.

The inherently-bilateral nature of some environmental issues also helps to explain why certain elements of the NAAEC cooperation agenda show so little progress ten years after the Agreement was signed. The Parties, for example, have developed recommendations on transboundary environmental impact assessment (Article 10(7)) but have been unable to conclude an agreement; they have made no meaningful progress on granting reciprocal access to their courts on environmental issues (Article 10(9)) or on establishing procedures allowing each other to seek to reduce transboundary pollution (Article 10(8)). The issues of reciprocal access are not only largely bilateral in nature but also involve primarily provincial and state law. For both Articles 10(8) and (9), a trilateral approach to what are essentially bilateral problems has not proven conducive to finding solutions.

It is all the more remarkable, therefore, that notwithstanding their differences and obstacles to trilateral action, the Parties have succeeded through the CEC in developing common programs on a number of issues such as biodiversity, children's environmental health and sound management of chemicals. * * *

The CEC Secretariat developed its first work program with little direction from the Parties. In the absence of stated Council priorities, the Secretariat spent the first several years deliberately testing various policy areas of activity listed in the NAAEC. This testing resulted in a broad work program with projects clustered under four general themes. Today, the CEC's four programs are: [Law and Policy; Environment, Economy, and Trade; Pollutants and Health; and Conservation of Biodiversity].

This is indeed a broad work program.... [M]ost observers, including JPAC, the NACs, government officials and some Secretariat staff, believe that the CEC program needs to be more focused and more results-oriented. Many observers have noted that the CEC's effectiveness has suffered from a short-term orientation to its work, unclear objectives for some projects and insufficient attention to strategic planning.... Given its limited resources, the CEC cannot afford to take on new projects unless it makes the difficult choice to shed some existing ones, nor can it continue to play its broad catalytic role unless it regularly turns over its programming. * * *

In its ten years, the CEC has helped Mexico build capacity most notably in the areas of (i) pollution prevention (with the CEC's assistance, Mexico has developed a pilot funding mechanism for small and medium-sized enterprises (SMEs) which is now being replicated, set up a chemicals department in Semarnat, expanded its technical capacities and established a round table of stakeholders); (ii) the management of toxic chemicals (Mexico's successful approach at phasing out DDT is now being adopted in Central America and has attracted India's interest); (iii) the development of a mandatory pollutant release and transfer registry (PRTR); and (iv) the conservation of wildlife habitat.

The CEC does not have a capacity building program *per se*. Instead, program managers have used a range of activities to create learning opportunities [including seminars on enforcement dealing with transboundary environmental issues; developed tools, emission inventories and methodologies for technology identification; and developed information systems and networks as part of its biodiversity work; among others].

The CEC's ability to fund the attendance of government and nongovernment individuals at its conferences and workshops has been critical to its capacity building efforts[.] * * *

In addition, all three countries have benefited from the CEC's coordination of trilateral activities in biodiversity conservation. This coordination is increasing the effectiveness of North American conservation efforts by (i) developing common priorities for the protection of certain species; (ii) developing North American Conservation Action Plans for three shared marine species; (iii) providing tools such as a map of terrestrial ecoregions which management agencies are using in their programs; and (iv) setting out common mechanisms for planning and monitoring bird conservation programs.

These efforts have to be placed in context: the CEC is a small organization and its own capacity development activities have only scratched the surface. As is the case in other capacity development projects, staff turnover in the recipient organizations has at times nullified the value of the training imparted. The absence of a stable supporting technical infrastructure in Mexico has sometimes meant that trained individuals were unable to use fully the skills they had acquired. In other instances, the policy approaches being transferred did not always reflect Mexican priorities or were not entirely appropriate to its conditions. More importantly, CEC staff and working groups have pursued these activities largely on their own, without common definition of, or strategy for, capacity building, and no systematic monitoring or evaluation of results achieved. As it continues its efforts in this area, one of the CEC's challenges will be to focus its efforts increasingly on institutional rather than individual capacity development. * * *

Has the CEC helped achieve the environmental goals and objectives of NAFTA? * * *

Article 10(6) of the NAAEC states that the Council shall cooperate with the NAFTA Free Trade Commission (composed of the three countries' trade ministers) to achieve the environmental goals and objectives of NAFTA by, *inter alia*:

"... (c) contributing to the resolution of environment-related trade disputes[;] ...

(d) considering on an ongoing basis the environmental effects of the NAFTA; and

(e) otherwise assisting the Free Trade Commission in environment-related matters."

In retrospect, the NAAEC may have raised unrealistic expectations about how much cooperation was possible between the CEC and the FTC. Where Parties have chosen to integrate environmental considerations in the negotiating positions they bring to the NAFTA working groups and committees, for example, they have done so internally through their usual interagency consultation process.... [T]he CEC, as a trilateral institution, has no role in the development of such national policies. NAFTA working groups and committees addressing environmentally-related trade issues (e.g., harmonization of automotive emissions standards; labelling practices for pesticides) have not sought the CEC's technical expertise because the Parties already had solicited the environmental advice they wanted from their own experts. An exception to this pattern has been the NAFTA working group on investment, which did consult JPAC on NAFTA's Chapter 11. * * *

The NAAEC represented a political acknowledgment that sustainable development requires the integration of environmental and trade considerations. A decade after negotiating the NAAEC, however, the Parties still pursue their trade and environmental policies largely separately rather than through the CEC. One of the results is that they are not always in a position to anticipate—and thus to prevent—environmental problems associated with increased trade and economic development. For some, this is one of the NAAEC's biggest disappointments. For others, the main value-added of the CEC is in the area of North American environmental cooperation, with the efforts to elaborate a trade component more of a distraction than a priority.

Questions and Discussion

1. Consider the strengths and weaknesses of the CEC as described by Mary Kelly & Cyrus Reed, Greg Block, and the TRAC. Do consistent themes or characteristics emerge

that explain why the CEC has succeeded in some areas and failed in others? As you look ahead to the next ten years, what mandate would you give the CEC? For example, should the CEC continue to play a role in building knowledge of trade and environment linkages? If yes, how should it pursue that goal? The TRAC recognized that the CEC has been an important provider of information, particularly with regard to pollutant releases. Should the CEC abandon an action-oriented workplan and instead focus on compiling information on various trade and environment issues for the NAAEC Parties?

2. The TRAC acknowledges various "asymmetries"—different interests and capacities, and different domestic politics—among the three NAAEC Parties that have hindered the CEC's success. It also noted that these factors become highlighted when there are few members. Do you agree? Would a CEC-like institution be more or less successful as the region grows? If not, what kind of institution should replace it?

3. One creative and promising CEC initiative that withered under budget constraints was the North American Fund for Environmental Cooperation. During its 8-year lifetime, this grant-making fund disbursed a total of nearly US$9.4 million to a variety of mostly local or regional cross-border collaborative efforts at environmental improvement developed by environmental NGOs or other citizen groups from two NAFTA countries, or occasionally from all three.

V. U.S.-Mexico NAFTA-Related Bodies

Environmental threats along the U.S.-Mexico border were one of the principal arguments against the NAFTA. Although the outcome of trade could only be predicted at the time the Parties signed the NAFTA, the Parties were aware that existing border conditions were deplorable. "Driven by the commencement of the Maquiladora Program, a program of U.S. trade incentives…, and the liberalization of Mexican trade rules in 1987, industrial development in the Border Region has turned the area into a 'virtual cesspool and a breeding ground for infectious disease.'" Robert F. Housman & Paul M. Orbuch, *Integrating Labor and Environmental Concerns Into the North American Free Trade Agreement: A Look Back and a Look Ahead*, 8 Am. U. J. Int'l L. & Pol'y 719, 777 (1993) (quoting American Medical Association report) (citations omitted).

Environmental and resource issues along the border were hardly new to those in the region. After years of conflict, the two countries agreed in 1942 on equitable sharing of boundary water resources, creating a bilateral International Boundary and Water Commission to oversee construction and management of water infrastructure and the allocation of water. In 1983, they concluded a broader Agreement on Cooperation for the Protection and Improvement of the Environment in the Border Area, commonly known as the La Paz Agreement. Aug. 14, 1983, U.S.-Mex., T.I.A.S. No 10,827. Under the La Paz Agreement, there have been specific measures taken on air pollution and waste management, among other issues. The environmental officials of the two countries have met annually since then to discuss environmental matters of common concern. The La Paz Agreement also provides the common legal definition of the "border area" as the area extending 100 kilometers in each direction from the land border (and its extensions in the Pacific and the Gulf of Mexico). But the NAFTA negotiations brought a more intense focus on the border environment. This part takes a brief look at some of the new environmental programs and institutions that the United States and Mexico negotiated in the NAFTA context.

A. The U.S.-Mexico Border Plan

The U.S.-Mexico border extends more than 3,100 kilometers (2,000 miles) from the Gulf of Mexico to the Pacific Ocean. The border region is biologically diverse, including many rare and endemic species, and a number of national parks and protected areas. It is also an ecologically fragile area of desert, mountains, and scarce water resources, but valuable estuaries and wetlands as well. At the same time, it is a very poor region on both sides of the border (excepting the city of San Diego), with local communities lacking the infrastructure and financial resources to handle the rapid industrialization and very rapid population growth of recent decades. The border area thus presents the classic challenge of sustainable development: how to improve economic welfare and social conditions while protecting a fragile environment. As EPA describes:

> The U.S.-Mexico border region is home to 12 million people ...
>
> Ninety percent of the border population resides in 14 paired, inter-dependent sister cities. These "sister-cities" are metropolitan areas in both countries. Rapid population growth in urban areas has lead to unplanned development, greater demand for land and energy, increased traffic congestion and waste generation, overburdened or unavailable waste treatment and disposal facilities, and more frequent chemical emergencies. Residents in rural areas suffer from exposure to airborne dust, pesticide exposure, inadequate water supply and waste treatment facilities. Projected population growth rates in the border region exceed anticipated U.S. average growth rates (in some cases by more than 40 percent) for each country. By 2020 the population is expected to reach 19.4 million.
>
> Border residents suffer disproportionately from many environmental health problems, including water-borne diseases and respiratory problems.

U.S. EPA, What is Border 2012, Introduction, www.epa.gov/usmexicoborder/framework/index.html (last modified June 24, 2009).

The 1983 La Paz Agreement is the legal basis for most of the ongoing cooperative environmental efforts in the border region. The La Paz Agreement empowers Mexican and U.S. environmental authorities to undertake cooperative initiatives implemented through multi-year binational programs. U.S. EPA and Mexico's environmental agency, SEMARNAT, serve as National Coordinators for these programs, which include the Integrated Environmental Plan for the Mexican-U.S. Border Area ("Border Plan") and its successors, Border XXI and Border 2012.

An early NAFTA-related effort to address conditions along the border came in February 1992 when the environmental minister of Mexico and the head of the U.S. EPA unveiled the Integrated Border Environmental Plan for the U.S.-Mexico Border Area. The border plan, its 1996 successor, the U.S.-Mexico Border XXI Program, and the current version, Border 2012, all set U.S. and Mexican priorities for improving environmental conditions, including those associated with Mexican border industrialization under the *maquiladora* program. The initiatives focus on cooperation, including efforts to: 1) strengthen the enforcement of environmental laws relating to polluting activities, 2) increase the understanding of pollution problems confronting citizens in the border region, and 3) provide environmental education and training.

The 1992 Border Plan called attention to pressing issues in the region and increased dialogue and communications between state, federal and local officials as well as the region's growing number of NGOs. Unfortunately, it failed to make sufficient funding available to conduct the cooperative efforts envisioned. Nor did the Plan prioritize activities sufficiently, and it soon devolved into an unintelligible jumble of poorly funded mini-projects spread across the breadth of the border. One commentator remarked at the time that the "plan's shortcomings stand as a vivid example of why environmental protection must occur contemporaneously with economic development." Robert Housman, *The North American Free Trade Agreement's Lessons for Reconciling Trade and the Environment*, 30 Stan. J. Int'l L. 379, 412 (1994).

Border 2012, the current framework for U.S.-Mexico cooperation among the environmental and natural resource agencies of the two governments, along with their state counterparts, expressly adopts a "bottom-up" approach to empower local communities to set priorities and implement projects to address the region's manifold environmental issues. Its mission — "to protect the environment and public health in the U.S.-Mexico border region, consistent with the principles of sustainable development" — is clear, though many questions persist about whether the initiative will bear more fruit than its predecessors. Border 2012 does set clear goals and timetables, enabling policymakers to measure the progress that has remained so elusive in the past in this troubled region. For more information on the Border 2012 program, *see* http://www.epa.gov/usmexicoborder.

B. The U.S.-Mexico Border Environment Cooperation Agreement

A particular finding in the environmental assessments done during the negotiation of NAFTA was the very poor capacity, in U.S. as well as Mexican border communities, for managing the major urban environmental problems such as sewage, solid waste, and air pollution. With impetus from influential political leaders from the U.S. border states, the United States and Mexico negotiated one more agreement, this one focused on border environmental infrastructure, to go with the NAFTA — the U.S.-Mexico Border Environment Cooperation Agreement. *See* Agreement Between the Government of the United States of America and the Government of the United Mexican States Concerning the Establishment of a Border Environment Cooperation Commission and a North American Development Bank, Nov. 16, 1993, U.S.-Mex., 32 I.L.M. 1545 [hereinafter the Agreement]. The Agreement establishes two new institutions, the Border Environment Cooperation Commission (BECC) and North American Development Bank (NADBank), to "help preserve, protect and enhance the environment of the border region in order to advance the well-being of the people of the United States and Mexico." Agreement, ch. I, art. I(1).

The main mission of the BECC is to provide technical assistance to border communities seeking to develop environmental infrastructure projects in the border region. The BECC is the agency responsible for certifying those projects for financing, under sustainability criteria it has developed. The NADBank was designed on the international development bank model to be a primary source of loan-based financing for these environmental infrastructure projects. The NADBank and the BECC are institutionally separate entities located in different cities (BECC in Ciudad Juárez, Mexico and the NAD-Bank in San Antonio, Texas).

Initially, the two institutions focused on water, wastewater, and municipal solid waste projects. In 2000, BECC and NADBank expanded the scope of projects eligible for financing to include air quality improvement, public transportation, clean and efficient energy, and municipal planning, development, and water management. By a "Protocol of Amendment" agreed in 2002, the designated "border area" for BECC and NADBank now extends 300 km into Mexico. According to the NADBank's 2009 annual report, by the end of 2008, the Bank had contracted for $870 million in financial support for 118 BECC-certified projects for which the total costs were $2.6 billion, and $748 million of that total had been disbursed. More than half of the contracted and disbursed amounts have been grant funds channeled to the NADBank by EPA under its Border Environment Infrastructure Fund program. EPA established this grant-funding mechanism in recognition that many deserving projects, especially in Mexico, would never have a sufficient user-fee rate base to generate the revenues needed to pay back loans.

The original governance structure of the BECC promoted the importance of local and nongovernmental participation by including members of the public and local and state officials on its governing board, augmented by a locally-based citizen advisory committee. Under that structure, the majority of the ten-member BECC Board of Directors (five from each country) were nonfederal officials, and board decisions required a majority of the members from each Party, thus giving local voices a controlling interest. For a detailed discussion of these elements, *see* Sanford E. Gaines, *Bridges to a Better Environment: Building Cross-Border Institutions for Environmental Improvement in the U.S.-Mexico Border Area*, 12 ARIZ. J. INT'L & COMP. L. 429 (1995). After some management problems at the BECC, by a "Protocol of Amendment" to the Agreement negotiated in 2002 and effective as of August 6, 2004, the Parties reorganized the governing structure to establish control by federal officials. The BECC and NADBank, while remaining separate operational entities, are now under a single Board of Directors with 10 appointed directors, including three federal officials from each Party, representing their departments of treasury, environment, and foreign affairs. One other director from each country is to represent a border state, and one from each country is to be a private citizen resident in a border state.

Nevertheless, the BECC has set a new standard for effective public participation in the affairs of a regional institution. The Agreement calls on the BECC to make all relevant information available to the public, establishes a means of considering complaints that procedures or policies have not been observed, and requires community participation in the development of projects considered for certification. *See* http://www.cocef.org. In the early years, BECC's wild and wooly public meetings might have caused some officials to have second thoughts about the wisdom of allowing citizens to vent their frustrations and desires in such an unrestrained and voluble manner. Tension between the more publicly-driven BECC processes and the comparatively bank-like behavior of the NADBank grew palpable as the NADBank denied funding to several BECC-certified projects on grounds that they failed to meet its financial feasibility and technical criteria. In time, the two institutions — and the different governmental departments that have managerial and oversight responsibility over their operations — have developed a more harmonious working relationship. Today, BECC meetings illustrate how well a remarkably diverse assortment of border interests — environmental and health NGOs, universities, local officials, businesses — have come together to collaborate on improving the quality of life in the border zone. While much remains to be done, the growing network of private and public actors in the region holds new promise for collaborative enterprises, just as the more open, accountable and transparent operation of the new generation of border institutions may hold promise for better regional governance structures in the future.

Questions and Discussion

1. The pre-NAFTA estimates for investments to mitigate border environmental problems approached US$20 billion. At current levels of funding, the BECC and NAD-Bank, though making a contribution, are clearly inadequate to address environmental problems at that scale. Moreover, these border institutions have little to do with trade and environment in a traditional sense, even though they were developed as part of the NAFTA package of agreements. Do they reflect mere opportunism by border region constituencies who have not received much political attention (or public resources) in the past? Do they instead (or also) represent a deeper, more holistic and encompassing approach to the relationship between trade, environment, and sustainable development?

2. Under the radar, so to speak, other federal, state, and local initiatives, many informal in character, have also contributed to the network of relationships mentioned in the concluding paragraph above. For example, U.S. EPA established a border liaison office in El Paso, Texas, which has become a point of almost daily face-to-face contact between U.S. and Mexican environmental officials and citizen groups at all levels. The EPA regional offices covering the border states (Regions VI and IX) have staff assigned to border issues. A U.S. EPA Good Neighbor Environmental Board fosters projects on the border on a wide range of environmental issues. These initiatives, along with working groups under Border 2012, draw in many state government environmental officials, provide funding for academic research by institutions in both countries, and have catalyzed cross-border citizen collaboration. The long-standing International Boundary and Water Commission, mentioned earlier, is engaged in a dialogue process including nongovernmental organizations in both countries to develop a management plan for the ecologically significant and highly stressed Colorado River delta region. Under a separate U.S. statute, experts on both sides are engaged in mapping transboundary groundwater resources, vitally important in this arid region. At the state level, the governors of the six Mexican border states and the four U.S. border states established the Border Governors' Conference, which holds an annual meeting and has an infrastructure of working committees, including ones on environmental issues, water resources, and science and technology.

Finally, there is considerable cross-border environmental work being done by local governments, business groups, environmental groups, university researchers, and others. A singular example is the citizen-driven binational collaboration addressing air quality in the El Paso/Ciudad Juárez airshed, now called the Joint Advisory Committee for the Improvement of Air Quality–Paso del Norte. *See* http://www.jac-ccc.org. This local initiative has gained formal recognition by both national governments and the affected state governments. For a somewhat dated but valuable look at such local initiatives, see ENVIRONMENTAL MANAGEMENT ON NORTH AMERICA'S BORDERS (Richard Kiy & John Wirth, eds. 1998).

VI. Beyond NAFTA: Free Trade in the Western Hemisphere

At about the same time the NAFTA entered into force, Heads of State from across the Western Hemisphere met in the Summit of the Americas in Miami, pledging to unite 800 million people and the economies of 34 countries in the region into the world's largest free trade area by 2005. *See* http://www.summit-americas.org. For many and complex reasons, the idea of a Free Trade Area of the Americas (FTAA) was stillborn, but the summit process continues, with attention to environmental issues along with other areas of common concern. *See, e.g.,* the Declaration of Commitment of Port of Spain, Securing Our Citizens' Future by Promoting Human Prosperity, Energy Security and Environmental Sustainability, adopted at the Fifth Summit of the Americas in 2009. (Link on the home page cited above.)

When the FTAA process stalled, the U.S. Trade Representative channeled its resources into bilateral or regional free trade agreements with many countries in Central and South America. Those countries in turn have expanded their own regional trade agreements among themselves. For the U.S. free trade agreements, NAFTA has been the template, but the environmental provisions of these agreements have evolved over time, and no two agreements are exactly alike.

As of 2010, the United States has free trade agreements with Chile, five Central American nations and the Dominican Republic (known as the Dominican Republic-Central American Free Trade Agreement ("DR-CAFTA")), Panama, and Peru. A negotiated agreement with Colombia has uncertain prospects in the U.S. Congress, as does another with South Korea. All of these agreements were negotiated under the authority of the Bipartisan Trade Promotion Authority Act of 2002, 19 U.S.C.A. §§ 3801–3813 (2002) [hereinafter TPA], described in more detail in Chapter 2 at pages 124–28.

The TPA represents a good barometer of the extent to which Congress has accepted the rationale—or at least the political necessity—of including environmental considerations in free trade agreements. Certain features of the NAFTA and its side agreement appear to have garnered substantial support from both political parties, and the TPA includes several environmental provisions in its overall goals and in its more specific trade negotiating objectives. Both the U.S.-Chile and DR-CAFTA agreements contain, in the main text, commitments to maintain high levels of environmental protection as well as including the State-to-State sanctions provisions for engaging in a recurring pattern of nonenforcement of environmental laws, based on the template of Part V of the NAAEC as discussed on page 813. Only DR-CAFTA contains a citizens' submission process similar to NAAEC Articles 14 and 15, and neither agreement establishes an independent Secretariat to implement programs or conduct monitoring and reporting. (DR-CAFTA does, however, establish a Secretariat directly controlled by the Parties for handling citizen submissions.) Environmental critics note that neither agreement assesses the environmental effects of free trade, nor do they establish a means of alleging that trade or trade measures are adversely impacting human health or the environment. The cooperative provisions are left without stable funding commitments or timetables, and each agreement studiously avoids mention of harmonization of any environmental laws, standards, or regulations.

Despite the imperfections of these agreements, the environment-trade "linkage" no longer appears in dispute. Each negotiation of a free trade agreement (FTA) brings some new ideas into play, and if some of the lessons of the NAAEC have not been "learned", other lessons have inspired some promising innovations, as Chris Wold explains.

Chris Wold, *Evaluating NAFTA and the Commission for Environmental Cooperation: Lessons for Integrating Trade and Environment in Free Trade Agreements*

28 St. Louis Univ. Public L. Rev. 201, 244–51(2008)

Before the United States and other countries negotiate new FTAs, they need to step back and learn the lessons of the NAFTA and NAAEC for the design of environmental linkages in FTAs. Because they are not doing that, they are failing to develop more effective ideas and institutions for improving trade-environment linkages. Building on the lessons of the NAFTA and NAAEC, FTAs should concentrate on scale effects from trade-based growth, identify the institutional needs of trading partners both for addressing scale effects and in the larger environmental context, and commit to effective public participation and public oversight of trade-environment linkages.

A. Focus on Scale Effects

While future FTAs should continue to include provisions that prevent competitiveness effects, such as requirements to enforce environmental law effectively, they should make efforts to identify, prevent, and mitigate scale effects.... [T]he work of the CEC and others has shown that scale effects are far more serious than competitiveness effects. In particular, much more work is needed before an FTA enters into force to assess the impact of trade liberalization caused by specific economic sectors and, to the extent possible, in particular regions. Moreover, once the FTA enters into force, processes must be in place to monitor impacts and strategies (or obligations) agreed upon to mitigate them.

A focus on scale will require a corresponding commitment to capacity building and obtaining relevant environmental data prior to entry into force of the FTA. Depending on the circumstances, capacity building may include information, technical training, technology, or substitute products. Again, the CEC's work shows that FTAs must invest far more in capacity building within regulatory agencies likely to be impacted by trade agreements to ensure that those agencies are able to monitor, assess, inspect, enforce and remediate environmental problems from increased trade. * * *

In addition, a greater emphasis must be placed on obtaining relevant environmental data before the FTA comes into force. This is one area where the United States has clearly learned from the CEC, which has concluded that the "lack of high-quality environmental data hampers analysis of trade-environment linkages." While some FTAs, including those in Latin America, are addressing the need for comparative environmental data in their ECAs [environmental cooperation agreements] or cooperative work programs, that information is coming *after* the impacts of FTAs come into force, thus eliminating the ability to gather baseline data for identifying the effects of trade. Without the relevant information prior to adoption of an FTA, it will be impossible to accurately assess the impacts of trade on the environment. Future FTAs should ascertain the need for common units of measurement for environmental factors, such as reporting on releases of toxic chemicals.

B. Identify Institutional and Other Needs

If FTAs focus on anticipating scale effects *prior to* liberalizing trade, then they will be better able to anticipate and "either improve environmental laws, policies, infrastructure, and capacities, as a bulwark against unsustainable trade patterns, or intervene directly by promoting environmental measures that may affect trade." While not necessarily adopting a focus on scale effects, the U.S.–Peru FTA does attempt to identify some of the legal, institutional, and capacity building needs of Peru. As such, it represents what is hopefully a new approach to trade and environment.

The U.S.–Peru FTA is in many respects very similar to other FTAs. It adopts the basic NAAEC approach which focuses on competitiveness effects and potential enforcement problems. However, it diverges significantly from the NAAEC approach by requiring substantial changes in Peru's forestry sector. It does so principally because of the high levels of illegal logging and trade, particularly in mahogany, in Peru.

As a result, environmental organizations successfully urged U.S. negotiators to include provisions in the U.S.–Peru FTA concerning forest management and trade in timber species. In an "Annex on Forest Sector Governance," Peru is required to "increase the number and effectiveness of personnel" devoted to enforcing laws relating to timber harvesting and timber trade, including within national parks legislation and indigenous lands. Peru must also develop and implement an anti-corruption plan for officials charged with the administration of forest resources and increase criminal and civil penalties to levels that deter illegal activity. Moreover, Peru must improve implementation of the Convention on International Trade in Endangered Species of Wild Fauna and Flora (CITES) by conducting comprehensive surveys of species protected by CITES, such as mahogany, establish export quotas for mahogany, and more generally, improve the administration and management of forest concessions by, among other things, physically inspecting areas designated for harvest of any CITES-listed tree species (i.e., mahogany), and develop systems to verify the legal chain of origin of CITES-listed tree species.

The demands on Peru do not stop here. For shipments of mahogany destined for the United States, the United States may ask Peru to investigate whether a particular Peruvian producer or exporter is in compliance with applicable laws; Peru is required to provide a written summary of its findings to the United States. With the consent of Peru, U.S. officials may participate in a site visit to determine a particular producer's or exporter's compliance with applicable law.

Beyond the provisions specific to the forestry sector, the U.S.–Peru FTA also establishes a Trade Capacity Building Committee to help the Parties, particularly Peru, make appropriate reforms to "foster trade-driven economic growth, poverty reduction, and adjustment to liberalized trade." This committee will, among other things, prioritize trade capacity building projects and monitor and assess progress in implementing trade capacity building projects. While this committee has no authority to make adjustments to the FTA where it identifies problems deriving from a lack of capacity, a permanent committee designed to assess capacity building needs is surely an important aspect of this FTA.

These provisions are quite extraordinary and "groundbreaking"—at least in the context of previous FTAs. In breaking the mold of FTAs, they point the way forward for future trade agreements by focusing the environmental provisions of trade agreements on problems likely to emerge or be exacerbated by liberalized trade. To the extent that these requirements fall short, it is that they must be adopted within 18 months *after*, not some time *prior to*, the date of entry into force of the FTA. Moreover, the FTA itself does not include any funding to help Peru implement these provisions. While the United States initially committed to funding implementation of the Annex on Forest Sector Governance, it now appears to be backing away from that pledge. In addition, it is not clear where the fund for the Trade Capacity Building Committee will come from. Without committed funding, these provisions may become nothing more than potential and promises unfilled, not unlike the NAAEC. * * *

2. Citizen Submission Process

The citizen submission process must be rethought. As many have proposed, the easiest way to transform the citizen submission process would be to eliminate the governments' role in determining whether a factual record is warranted. That simple change would help to ensure that process provides a valuable avenue for citizens of some countries to voice concerns about failures to enforce environmental law effectively. However, it is clear that governments view the process as adversarial and litigation-based and are "more inclined to weaken the procedure rather than strengthen it." As a consequence, they have made every effort to thwart its effectiveness; the process has clearly not lived up to expectations. Given the history of repression in Central America, it is entirely predictable that no Central American person or organization has used the citizen submission process of CAFTA–DR. The entire model is wrong.

Instead, future FTAs should design an approach that facilitates cooperation rather than encourages an adversarial process. The members of the U.S. National Advisory Committee, which provides advice to the Environmental Protection Agency on issues relating to the NAAEC, recently proposed a non-adversarial, cooperative mechanism for the resolution of environmental problems identified by citizens. This "problem-solving" process would allow citizens to approach an independent Secretariat with issues unrelated to enforcement failures and would not seek to assign blame for the specified environmental concern. Instead, the process would help resolve environmental problems. * * *

Another possible approach would focus the submission process on scale effects. Under this approach, citizens could seek review of the effects of trade liberalization on the environment. As with Article 13 reports under the NAAEC, the Secretariat could assemble experts to ascertain whether the environmental impacts were in fact caused by trade. If they were, then the Secretariat could propose measures, including recommendations for capacity building and technology, to mitigate those impacts. As with the previous proposal, this proposal seeks to eliminate the hostility that pervades the current submissions process by changing the focus of the process. This proposal does not cast blame on any particular agency, official, or company for environmental wrong doing. Rather, it asks whether a particular policy or measure is adversely affecting the environment.

Whether either of these processes can transform a valuable avenue for citizen participation in environmental decisionmaking is unknown. An opportunity for citizens to focus on scale effects in a way that suggests trade may not be beneficial could in fact be more controversial than the current mechanism. In any event, because the current process is clearly not working as intended, and with governments unwilling to let it work as intended, a new model should be tested.

_____

Questions and Discussion

1. Many commentators are urging policymakers to make a more determined effort to address the developmental components that exacerbate environmental market failures in free trade agreements. *See, e.g.,* JOHN AUDLEY, ISSUE BRIEF: OPPORTUNITIES AND CHALLENGES TO ADVANCE ENVIRONMENTAL PROTECTION IN THE U.S.-CENTRAL AMERICAN FREE TRADE NEGOTIATIONS 1–2, 5–8 (Carnegie Endowment for International Peace Feb. 2003), *available at* http://www.ceip.org/files/pdf/TED-CAFTA-and-environment.pdf. How can this be done? Is it practical to link trade liberalization measures to sustainability indicators in selected sectors like forestry or fisheries? What about regional sustainability committees with authority to recommend or authorize trade measures to brake environmental degradation?

2. Other commentators find weaker linkages than one might suspect between trade agreements, investments, and environmental conditions. For example, contributors to an edited volume on trade and sustainable development in Latin America concluded that there was no "independent" linkage between foreign direct investment flows in the region and the many trade and investment agreements those countries have entered into. Moreover, the region's generally weaker environmental regulations also had no independent effect on FDI flows. Finally, the contributors found that the environmental performance of multinational corporations in the region was mixed, better than local firms in some respects (e.g., environmental management systems), but not adequate in others (e.g, not consistently applying "best practices"). In general, the multinationals were also *not* better at compliance with environmental law than domestic firms. One lesson appears to be that *national* economic, social, and environmental policies are more important to sustainable development than international trade or environmental agreements. RETHINKING FOREIGN INVESTMENT FOR SUSTAINABLE DEVELOPMENT: LESSONS FROM LATIN AMERICA (Kevin Gallagher and Daniel Chudnovsky, eds., 2009). A separate analysis from the World Bank drawing similar conclusions is DANIEL L. LEDERMAN ET AL., LESSONS FROM NAFTA FOR LATIN AMERICA AND THE CARIBBEAN (2005).

3. Ironically, just as the U.S. Congress appears to have embraced the idea of sanctions for persistent failures to enforce environmental laws, some of the most vocal advocates are re-thinking that policy. Instead, they are calling for more developmental assistance for environmental infrastructure. What have we learned from the NAFTA experience?

4. In *Our Common Future*, the Brundtland Commission stated: "the ability to anticipate and prevent environmental damage requires that ecological dimensions of policy be considered at the same time as the economic, trade, energy, agricultural and other dimensions." U.N. GAOR, *Report of the World Commission on Environment and Development: Our Common Future*, 42d Sess., Agenda Item 83(e), U.N. Doc. A/43/427, at para. 28 (1987). Why is this so difficult to accomplish?

_____

VII. Environment and the European Union

A. Introduction

With its 27 Member States and more than 500 million citizens, the European Union (EU) represents the culmination of decades of effort to bring stability and prosperity to the continent by deepening political and economic integration. Starting as a small group of states liberalizing trade in steel and coal, the EU now embraces virtually the entire continent (among significant countries, only Switzerland and Norway are not members) and every economic sector in a "single market," with growing authority in other areas of policy such as finance and defense. As described in Chapter 2 (pages 128–32), under the Lisbon Treaty, which came into force in December 2009, the term European Union now applies to all aspects of the union; earlier terms like the "European Economic Community" are no longer in official use.

EU environmental law comprises scores of Europe-wide regulations, directives, court decisions, and policy statements. European law shapes, and sometimes controls, national and subnational environmental legislation. Environmental issues are increasingly integrated into other sectoral policies, including agriculture, transportation, and energy. EU law touches on virtually every area of environmental policy, from emissions standards and regulation of chemicals to environmental assessment and protection of habitats. Hundreds of matters have been the subject of cases in the EU judicial system, including several dealing with core trade and environment issues. Some of these decisions are covered in Chapter 4 (pages 255–65). This part provides an overview of the EU environmental law framework and the EU's approach to reconciling trade and environment tensions.

B. EU Institutions and Governance

The EU governance structure has four central institutions—the Council, the Commission, the European Parliament, and the Court of Justice—and several other important bodies and "agencies" with specific technical or scientific tasks, such as the European Environmental Agency.

The EU Council is a high-level decision making body, composed of one minister from each Member State who acts on behalf of his or her government. The composition of the Council depends on the issue before it; environmental ministers attend meetings convened by the Council in its "environment" configuration, and trade ministers attend Council meetings primarily dealing with trade issues. The Council passes EU laws (often jointly with Parliament), coordinates the broad policies of Member States, concludes international agreements with countries or international organizations, and approves the EU budget (with the Parliament).

The European Commission is the executive heart of the EU. It prepares policy analyses, consults with industry and nongovernmental organizations, and proposes legislation to the Parliament and the Council. The Commission also oversees the implementation of EU law by the Member States and serves as an enforcement agency by bringing cases against noncomplying Member States to the Court of Justice. The Commission also represents the EU internationally, for example in negotiation of agreements between the EU and other countries. There is a true "commission" of high-level members (often former ministers from Member States) that sets policy goals and is accountable to the European Parliament, but in practical terms the "Commission" means the approximately 24,000 civil servants who do the work, most of whom operate out of Brussels, Belgium.

The European Parliament is elected directly by the peoples of the Member States. The Parliament enjoys the power to legislate, exercise democratic supervision, and approve the EU budget. The most common procedure for approving EU legislation involves "co-decisions," requiring approval by both the Parliament and the Council. Parliament's approval is also required for many important political or institutional decisions. The Parliament may also provide the impetus for new legislative proposals by examining the Commission's annual program of work and by requesting the Commission to develop new proposals. The role of the Parliament in environmental policy has grown over the years; for example, it played an instrumental role in promoting environmental assessment, access to information, and eco-labeling. Parliament has also proved itself an insistent voice, calling attention to enforcement failures and urging EU members and institutions to redouble efforts to fully implement EU law.

The Court of Justice, first established in the 1952 Treaty of Paris by the original members of the Coal and Steel Community, enforces EU law and ensures that EU law is interpreted and applied in a consistent manner throughout the EU. The Court can settle disputes between Member States, between EU institutions and the Member States, and even disputes involving businesses and individuals where the subject matter concerns EU law. In some instances, environmental cases are the result of "infringement procedures" initiated by the Commission against Member States who fail to properly enact, implement, or enforce EU law. The Commission refers unresolved infringement claims to the Court, which makes binding judgments and may impose penalties.

A host of other players also participate in EU governance. The European Ombudsman addresses citizens' complaints about maladministration by any EU institution or body, and may bring to light a wide variety of issues related to EU environmental policies. The European Environment Agency (EEA), a scientific and technical expert agency, collects and analyzes data, prepares reports, and provides decision makers with the information needed for developing and improving environmental protection and sustainable development policies. The EEA manages the European environment information and observation network (EIONET), uniting over 300 environmental bodies, agencies, and public and private research centers across Europe.

The legal and political instruments applied to environmental policy consist mainly of directives, regulations, decisions, recommendations, and action programs. In EU parlance, *directives* are Council-approved documents that establish policy objectives and, in more or less detailed terms, direct the Member States to adopt laws and regulations in accordance with the directive. Some directives are "framework" directives setting broad objectives; others, like the directive on the emissions trading system, are very detailed. Member States must transpose directives into national laws and can be sanctioned for failing to implement directives. More than 300 directives addressing environmental matters are currently in force. *Regulations* are typically more specific and narrowly drawn than directives. Regulations are EU law, directly applicable and binding all Member States. *Decisions* cover a wide range of actions, including establishing committees, granting financial assistance for environmental projects, and establishing criteria for eco-labeling. *Recommendations* have no binding force, but are issued from time to time on environmental issues, such as coastal zone management and recycling. *Action programs* outline priority objectives for Community action, identify measures to achieve the objectives, and provide a timetable for conducting such actions. Most important for our purposes are the Environment Action Programs, currently in their sixth incarnation. *See* Ludwig Krämer, EC Environmental Law 54–61 (6th ed. 2007).

Questions and Discussion

1. By seeking outright harmonization and providing substantial developmental assistance to poorer regions, Europe has undertaken the most aggressive and far-reaching attempt to create a "level playing field" for its economic competitors within the region. EU expansion to incorporate former Eastern Bloc countries such as Poland, Latvia, Slovenia, and Bulgaria represents a challenge at least as great as the incorporation of Spain, Greece, and Portugal presented to the pre-2004 EU. In fact, the divergence in levels of development of most of the ten new EU members with Germany, France, and the United Kingdom is comparable to the economic disparity between Canada and the United States on the one hand and Mexico on the other.

The EU provided pre-accession structural funds for environmental infrastructure to candidate countries of more than 500 million Euros each year from 2000 to 2006. Notwithstanding this infusion of capital, the EU Commission estimated at the time that these countries would need to spend around 2–3 percent of GDP on environmental improvements over each of the next 15–20 years. How long should the EU subsidize environmental infrastructure and implementation in less developed regions? How might the addition of several less developed countries into the EU influence its environmental laws and policies? Since 2006, the EU has maintained a commitment of 500 million Euros for adjustment, but now focusing on employment issues under the Globalisation Adjustment Fund.

2. Although there is some modest harmonization work on technical standards under NAFTA, harmonization of environmental regulations is an explicit objective in the EU. In order to assist less prosperous regions of Europe to implement and comply with EU law as well as enhance economic integration, substantial resources are made available for environmental infrastructure, capacity building, conservation, and protection under so-called "Structural" and "Cohesion" funds. In general, these funds help promote more balanced socioeconomic development in furtherance of sustainable development in poorer regions of the EU. For the seven year period 2007–2013, the funding level is 277 billion Euros for the Structural Funds and 70 billion Euros for the Cohesion Fund, with three overall objectives: convergence (of poorer regions), regional competitiveness, and territorial (i.e. cross-border and regional) cooperation. Environmental protection and improvement is an explicit factor included in pursuit of each of these three objectives. Along with Europe's Common Agricultural Policy, these funds account for the great bulk of EU expenditures and EU funds going to governments.

3. Since the late 1990s, the EU has been much more assertive in advocating for a stronger application of environmental principles relating to trade law, especially with respect to the precautionary principle as it applies to genetically modified organisms, hormone-treated beef, chemicals, ecolabeling, and climate change. This position has brought the EU into conflict with the United States and Canada, among others, who have circled wagons around their strong domestic trade interests. Where is this leading?

C. Trade and the Environment in the EU

In announcing the establishment of an internal market, Article 3(3) of the Treaty on European Union says that the Union shall "work for the sustainable development of Europe based on balanced economic growth ... a high level of protection and improvement of the quality of the environment." The specific objectives related to the environment are found in Article 191 of the Treaty on the Functioning of the European Union (TFEU), which reads in pertinent part:

1. Union policy on the environment shall contribute to pursuit of the following objectives:

    – preserving, protecting and improving the quality of the environment,

    – protecting human health,

    – prudent and rational utilisation of natural resources,

    – promoting measures at the international level to deal with regional or worldwide environmental problems, and in particular combating climate change.

2. Union policy on the environment shall aim at a high level of protection taking into account the diversity of situations in the various regions of the Union. It shall be based on the precautionary principle and on the principles that preventive action should be taken, that environmental damage should as a priority be rectified at source and that the polluter should pay. * * *

3. In preparing its policy on the environment, the Union shall take account of:

    – available scientific and technical data,

    – environmental conditions in the various regions of the Union,

    – the potential benefits and costs of action or of lack of action,

    – the economic and social development of the Union as a whole and the balanced development of its regions.

———

Notwithstanding the explicit objectives of Article 191 of the TFEU, Article 3 of the Treaty on European Union reminds us of the close policy link between environmental protection and the development of the internal market. In particular, EU members must still abide by the free trade provisions of the Union even as they develop national environmental policies. At this point, read (or review) the discussion of the internal trade and environment law of the EU in Chapter 4, Section VI.B at pages 255–65).

———

Questions and Discussion

1. Recall from Chapter 4, Section VI.B the similarity of the free trade provisions of the TFEU and those of the GATT/WTO. Recall also the discussion there about the exceptions to those provisions, especially the excerpts from Jan Jans and Hans Vedder. Are the environmental and health justifications in Article 36 of the TFEU broader or more restrictive than their counterparts in GATT Article XX? Would the conservation of "exhaustible natural resources" constitute a legitimate justification in the EU?

2. The expansive area for potential EU environmental legislation established in Title XX of the TFEU (Articles 191–193) is further broadened by permissive mandates in areas such as agriculture, transport and energy—all areas into which environmental measures have crept.

———————

D. Subsidiarity and Harmonization

Article 5(3) of the Treaty on European Union, with minor changes from earlier language, confirms the principle of "subsidiarity," fundamental to EU law and jurisdiction.

> In areas which do not fall within its exclusive competence, the Union shall take action, in accordance with the principle of subsidiarity, only if and in so far as the objectives of the proposed action cannot be sufficiently achieved by the Member States, either at central or at regional and local level, but can rather, by reason of the scale or effects of the proposed action, be better achieved at Union level.

In practice, meeting the requirements of the subsidiarity principle has not presented a significant obstacle to the promulgation of EU-wide environmental directives and regulations. For one thing, several matters of environmental importance include transnational aspects which cannot be satisfactorily regulated without collective action. Reducing transnational or global pollution, protecting migratory birds and their habitats, and reducing ozone-depleting substances and greenhouse gas emissions are examples. Minimum EU standards for emissions, environmental packaging, product standards, and other areas also can level the economic playing field by avoiding a "race to the bottom" and reducing national restrictions and barriers to trade. Increasingly, the EU has developed minimum standards for processes and production methods, an area that remains contentious in the WTO. *See* Chapter 4.

Pursuing the twin goals of attaining EU environmental standards and establishing a common market has led the EU to embark on the world's most ambitious regional program of environmental regulatory harmonization. The harmonization program is pursued under Article 114(1) of the TFEU, which directs the Parliament and Council to "adopt the measures for the approximation of the provisions laid down by law, regulation or administrative action in Member States which have as their object the establishment and functioning of the internal market." For a more thorough discussion of EU harmonization, *see* Chapter 6, Section IV.D.2, at pages 426–30. Yet, as Professors Jans and Vedder describe below, harmonization itself comes in different flavors.

Jan H. Jans & Hans H.B. Vedder,
European Environmental Law
94–95, 98 (3rd ed. 2008)

Harmonisation is said to be *full* or *total* when a directive is intended to provide for a more or less uniform European standard in a particular field, from which it is no longer possible to derogate. In principle this kind of directive excludes both more stringent and less stringent national rules. * * *

Total harmonisation is found above all in those fields of environmental policy where there is a definite relationship with the free movement of goods. In particular, the Council makes use of total harmonisation in legislation to harmonise product standards, as it is the only way to ensure the free movement of the goods in question. This means the total harmonisation is encountered particularly frequently in environmental measures based on Article [114 TFEU].

Total harmonization precludes any derogation other than that allowed by the directive itself. * * *

As far as European environmental law is concerned, minimum harmonization can be defined as a form of European legislation which leaves Member States competent to adopt more stringent environmental standards than the European ones. It is often used in fields in which differences in national standards affect the functioning of the internal market less than do differences in product standards. This applies, for example, to measures to protect the quality of water and air, flora, fauna, and to measures in respect of waste, protection against radiation, etc. In this sense, European emission standards and quality standards can all be regarded as minimum standards.

Article 191 of the TFEU establishes the mandate for the EU to pursue policies for "preserving, protecting, and improving the quality of the environment ... aimed at a high level of protection." Article 192 then charges the Parliament and the Council with acting to meet those objectives. Article 193 of the TFEU then enshrines the practice of minimum harmonization as a means of attaining environmental goals into the Treaty:

The protective measures adopted pursuant to Article 192 shall not prevent any Member State from maintaining or introducing more stringent protective measures. Such measures must be compatible with this Treaty. They shall be notified to the Commission.

In light of the recognized legitimacy of harmonization in the EU, most of the disputes involve the intended sphere of application of a directive or regulation in order to determine whether any room remains for inconsistent national measures. Recent EU environmental legislation tends to delineate more clearly the scope of the legislation's application, providing greater certainty to affected parties. The same legislation, however, intensifies the push toward harmonization on a wide range of environmental requirements, such as product packaging and labeling, to take one example.

Questions and Discussion

1. Given the transboundary nature of many environmental problems, particularly in Europe, the principle of subsidiarity continues to play a significant role in the allocation of legal authority over environmental questions. Although not involving the subsidiarity principle as such, a 2009 ruling by the lower court in the European system (now known as the General Court) found that the Commission had exceeded its legal authority in rejecting the "national action plans" of Poland and Estonia under the EU's climate directives and requiring more emission reductions from the covered sectors in those countries. The court chastised the Commission for substituting its determinations for those committed to the Member States. Poland v Commission, Case T-183/07 and Estonia v Commission, Case T-263/07 (judgments of Sept. 23, 2009). As of mid-2010, the Commission's appeal of this ruling to the Court of Justice of the European Union is pending.

2. While the NAAEC commits the Parties to maintaining "high levels" of environmental protection, it does not seek to harmonize environmental policy or regulations in North America. The EU approach is usually distinguished on grounds that it represents a much deeper level of economic and social integration. Compare the EU approach with Article 10:3 of the NAAEC below:

> The Council shall strengthen cooperation on the development and continuing improvement of environmental laws and regulations, including ... (b) without reducing levels of environmental protection, establishing a process for developing recommendations on greater compatibility of environmental technical regulations, standards and conformity assessment procedures in a manner consistent with the NAFTA.

Imagine you are the environmental director for a state or province directly downwind from large sources of air pollution in the territory of a NAFTA partner that are in compliance with domestic standards in that country. Does the NAAEC provide a remedy? Can downwind jurisdictions implement state or provincial actions to boycott goods produced from the upwind sources? (For students of U.S. environmental law, compare your answer to a similar situation between upwind and downwind states under the Clean Air Act. Is the result different?) In general, is the "shallow" integration approach of the NAFTA a valid justification for not pursuing harmonization of some environmental policies and regulations in North America?

E. Implementation and Enforcement of Environmental Law

The ambitious pace of the development of EU environmental law and policy has not been matched by a similar zeal in implementation and enforcement. Several EU Members, nongovernmental organizations, and others have been increasingly exasperated over uneven implementation and compliance with EU environmental law throughout the region. In response, a series of measures is being taken to stimulate compliance, including a "name, shame, and fame" strategy to embarrass laggards. Environmental complaints giving rise to infringement proceedings are on the rise and European courts are rendering more decisions on environmental compliance. The full implementation of existing directives is a strategic priority within the EU's Sixth Environment Action Program, which runs through 2012. In 2007, the Commission opened 461 new environmental cases, including 113 of which were initiated by citizen complaints and 125 new infringement actions initiated against Member States. The Commission also responded to 146 petitions on environmental matters submitted by citizens to the European Parliament (more than one-third of all such petitions). The infringement actions span the full spectrum of environmental law. Approximately 20 to 25 percent involve nature conservation; waste management; environmental impact assessment; air, water, integrated industry pollution control. A variety of other subjects make up the remainder. Issues with respect to emission reductions and other mandates under the EU's climate policy are a major new area of enforcement action for the Commission. 25TH ANNUAL REPORT FROM THE COMMISSION ON MONITORING THE APPLICATION OF COMMUNITY LAW (2007) COM (2008) 777 final, and the accompanying staff report on The Situation in Different Sectors, SEC(2008) 2854.

1. The Duty to Implement EU Environmental law
Ludwig Krämer, *EC Environmental Law*
423–25, 429 (6th ed. 2007)

1. Obligations of Member States to Apply Community Law * * *

(b) Secondary Legislation * * *

12-07 ... Member States are under an obligation to ensure the practical application of Community environmental law. The transposition itself is only a formal legal act, whereas the protection of the environment begins when emissions are reduced, substances no longer put on the market or (the equivalent) into the environment, habitats protected, and so on. The practical application of environmental provisions is the most serious problem that national, Community and international environmental law faces. Even a piece of national legislation that copies a directive word for word will remain a mere piece of paper unless it is applied.

Some unique features which seriously affect the full application of Community environmental law in practice, must be remembered. Since environmental provisions try to protect the general interest of the Community, they differ markedly from agricultural, transport or industry legislation, which primarily affects specific vested interests. Where vested interests are in question, law making and law enforcement take place, in Western Europe, in constant public—and sometimes not so public—discussions with the representatives of those vested interests; this discussion also continues within the various administrations, parliaments and decision-making bodies. Vested interest groups are also used to ensure the transmission of knowledge on the specific legislation and in this way contribute either to ensuring compliance with the legal rule or bringing about concerted action against that rule, often even preventing its generation. This lobbying function of vested interest groups has become an integrated factor of decisionmaking at Community level and at the level of Member States.

The general interest "environment" has no vested interest defender. Environmental organisations in Western Europe are structurally and financially too weak to defend environmental interests effectively over a long period of time. While there is consensus that the environment needs adequate protection and that economic development should be "sustainable," the implementation of concrete, legally binding measures proves difficult wherever other, diverging interests appear. The environment, without a voice and without strong lobby groups, loses out in almost every specific conflict of interests. Since, furthermore, local, regional and national administrations in the 27 Member States are not all convinced to the same extent that Community environmental standards are to be enforced, complied with and applied in practice, practical application of environmental provisions varies within the Community.

12–08 General features also contribute to this situation. In a number of Member States, particularly in the south and in the new Member States, environmental problems are perceived to be the problems of affluent society; hence there is an attitude among economic operators, and also among administrations, that economic progress is of primary necessity and that environmental concerns should be tackled once the economic level of richer Member States has been reached. To this has to be added the different enforcement culture which exists in the Community, traditional weaknesses of central government in some Member States, the lack of national environmental infrastructures such as adequate administrations at local, regional and national level, and a lack of environmental information and education, of general awareness and attentive media, of environmental research bodies, laboratories and test or monitoring or enforcement bodies.

2. Monitoring Transposition and Application

(a) Implementation reports

12-09 Almost all Community environmental directives have contained, since the mid-1970s, a provision asking Member States to report on the implementation of the Directive. Typically, such reports had to be made every three years. The Commission was charged with producing, on the basis of these national reports, a Community report on the implementation of the directive in question; the normal period for these reports was, similarly, every three years.

This system did not lead to the desired result, since neither the Member States' implementation reports nor the Commission's comprehensive reports were drawn up regularly. * * *

In order to improve the reporting system, the Council adopted, in 1991, a Directive that restructured the reporting requirements. This Directive introduced the requirement for Member States to report, every three years, on the implementation of the different directives in a given sector (for instance, water, air or waste). The reports were to be based on questionnaires which were set up by committee procedure at Community level, in order to allow the national reports to address the same issues. The reporting period was three years.

The Directive has not significantly improved the situation. * * *

12-10 … Commission implementation reports were, overall, very disappointing, apart from the reports on the quality of bathing waters, which continue to be published annually.… * * *

(b) Monitoring by other bodies

12-14 The Community Ombudsman, set up under [Art. 228 of TFEU] has the task of controlling complaints of maladministration in the activities of the Community institutions or bodies. This might include maladministration in the treatment of citizen complaints in environmental matters or general omissions in the monitoring of application of environmental legislation. At the start of 2003, his office had a staff of 33 persons. His control activities occasionally deal with environmental issues, but try to avoid becoming a complaint instance against decisions taken by the Commission.

The Commission announced, in the fifth environmental action programme, that it would set up an implementation network which would aim "primarily at exchange of information and experience and at the development of common approaches at practical level, under the supervision of the Commission." However, at that time Member States had already started to set up an informal implementation network. As they vigorously opposed any mechanism at Community level that would give the Commission more options to monitor application of environmental provisions, they accepted the Commission as a member of that network, but kept its informal nature, and, since 1993, have called it the "European

Union Network for the Implementation and Enforcement of Environmental Law" (IMPEL).

---

2. Commission Enforcement Actions

In recent years, the EU has made good on its pledge to improve enforcement of Community environmental law. Spain became the second country fined by the Court of Justice for failure to comply with an environmental directive.

Case C-278/01, *Commission v. Spain*, 2003

http://curia.eu.int

[The European Commission sought penalties against Spain of EUR 45,600 per each day of delay in adopting the necessary measures to conform to the water quality limit values for inshore bathing water in accordance with Council Directive 76/160/EEC of 8 December 1975 concerning the quality of bathing water (OJ 1976 L 31, p.1) ("Directive") and the judgment of the Court of Justice in Case C-92/96 *Commission v Spain* [1998] ECR I-505.

The Directive was enacted to protect the environment and public health by reducing the pollution of bathing water and protecting such waters against further deterioration. The Directive requires Member States to set values applicable to bathing water for specified physical, chemical and microbiological parameters, which establish minimum standards. Member States had ten years—until January 1986—to conform to the water quality standards. EU countries are also required to report on their implementation each year.]

The pre-litigation procedure

8. By letter of 17 March 1998, the Commission drew the Spanish authorities' attention to the need to comply with the obligations ensuing from the judgment in *Commission v Spain*.

9. In response, by letters of 5, 11 and 19 June 1998, 5 January and 12 March 1999, the Spanish authorities notified the Commission of the measures adopted or in the course of being adopted to comply with that judgment. These included implementation of certain urban waste water purification projects undertaken in the context of the 1995 national purification plan, the supervision, monitoring and imposition of penalties for discharge and the prohibition on bathing in areas identified as not in conformity with the requirements, the adoption of certain specific measures and the launch in 1999 of a study of bathing areas, the discharge affecting the various areas, the qualitative characteristics of bathing water and the effect of discharge in each area and the solutions provided for and proposed depending on the conclusions reached.

10. On 24 January 2000 the Commission sent to the Kingdom of Spain a letter of formal notice under Article 228 EC, taking the view that it had not taken the necessary measures to comply with the judgment in *Commission v Spain*.

11. By letter of 26 May 2000 the Spanish authorities informed the Commission that the Ministry of the Environment had ordered a study to be carried out on the state of inshore waters designated for bathing in accordance with the Directive, a study which, according to those authorities, was to be completed

in the course of the year 2000. The Spanish authorities also set out the objectives and scope of the study and a timetable of action to be taken to ensure compliance with the Directive which, according to estimates, was to be completed in 2005.

12. On 27 July 2000, taking the view that those measures did not demonstrate that the infringement had been brought to an end, the Commission sent the Kingdom of Spain a reasoned opinion under Article 228 EC. In that opinion it concluded that, having failed to fulfil its obligations under Article 4 of the Directive by not adopting the measures necessary to ensure that the quality of inshore bathing water in Spain conformed to the limit values set in accordance with Article 3 of the Directive, the Kingdom of Spain had failed to comply with the judgment in *Commission v Spain* and had accordingly failed to fulfil its obligations under Article 228 EC. The Commission drew Spain's attention to the fact that if the case were brought before the Court of Justice, it would suggest that a penalty payment be imposed. It set a time-limit of two months for the Kingdom of Spain to adopt the measures necessary to comply with the reasoned opinion.

13. In response to that opinion, the Spanish Government sent two letters dated 26 and 27 September 2000 informing the Commission that there was a plan of action, notifying it of the extent of compliance of the quality of bathing water during the 1998 and 1999 bathing seasons and of the implementation of a national plan for the cleansing and purifying of urban waste water.

14. A meeting was held on 11 January 2001 between the Spanish Ministry of the Environment and the Commission's Directorate-General for the Environment in order to allow the Spanish Government to supplement the information relating to those measures.

15. On 16 January 2001 the Spanish Minister for the Environment sent to the Member of the Commission responsible for the environment a letter under cover of which he transmitted a new plan of action and undertook to complete the necessary steps in 2003.

16. On 26 March 2001 the Spanish authorities sent to the Commission a report drawn up by the Ministry of the Environment on progress on the action taken to comply with the judgment in *Commission v Spain*, together with a letter from the Secretary of State responsible for waters and coasts.

17. Taking the view that the Kingdom of Spain had not complied with that judgment, the Commission decided to bring this action. * * *

Findings of the Court

25. In its judgment in Commission v Spain the Court found that, by failing to take all necessary measures to ensure that the quality of inshore bathing water in Spain conforms to the limit values set in accordance with Article 3 of the directive, the Kingdom of Spain had failed to fulfil its obligations under Article 4 thereof.

26. Under Article 228(1) EC the Kingdom of Spain was required to take the necessary measures to comply with that judgment.

27. Article 228 EC does not specify the period within which the judgment must be complied with. However, in accordance with settled case-law, the importance of immediate and uniform application of Community law means that the process of compliance must be initiated at once and completed as soon as possible (Case

C-387/97 *Commission v Greece*[2000] ECR I-5047, paragraph 82, and case-law cited).

28. According to Article 228(2) EC, if the Member State concerned has not taken the necessary measures to comply with the Court's judgment within the time-limit laid down by the Commission in its reasoned opinion, the latter may bring the case before the Court of Justice, specifying the amount of the lump sum or penalty payment to be paid by the Member State concerned which it considers appropriate in the circumstances. * * *

35. In the light of all the foregoing considerations, it must be held that, by not taking the measures necessary to ensure that the quality of inshore bathing water in Spanish territory conforms to the limit values set in accordance with Article 3 of the Directive, notwithstanding its obligations under Article 4 of that directive, the Kingdom of Spain has not taken all the measures necessary to comply with the Court's judgment in Commission v Spain and has accordingly failed to fulfil its obligations under Article 228 EC.* * *

On those grounds, THE COURT (Full Court), hereby:

1. Declares that, by not taking the measures necessary to ensure that the quality of inshore bathing water in Spanish territory conforms to the limit values set in accordance with Article 3 of Council Directive 76/160/EEC of 8 December 1975 concerning the quality of bathing water, notwithstanding its obligations under Article 4 of that directive, the Kingdom of Spain has not taken all the measures necessary to comply with the Court's judgment of 12 February 1998 in Case C-92/96 Commission v Spain and has accordingly failed to fulfil its obligations under Article 228 EC;

2. Orders the Kingdom of Spain to pay to the Commission of the European Communities, into the account 'European Community own resources,' a penalty payment of EUR 624 150 per year and per 1% of bathing areas in Spanish inshore waters which have been found not to conform to the limit values laid down under Directive 76/160 for the year in question, as from the time when the quality of bathing water achieved in the first bathing season following delivery of this judgment is ascertained until the year in which the judgment in Commission v Spain is fully complied with;

3. Orders the Kingdom of Spain to pay the costs.

Questions and Discussion

1. The *Spanish Bathing Water* case provides a good illustration of the lengths that the EU will go to resolve disputes before bringing down the hammer. Nonetheless, the Court seems to have lost patience with Spain's approach, which included at least one study and two plans of action. Several enforcement actions have been launched since *Spanish Bathing Water*. The expansion of the EU to 27 Member States since this case may again change the enforcement dynamic on the continent as less developed regions of the EU struggle to implement EU law.

2. Compare the government sanctions process of the NAAEC with the EU process of enforcing EU law. How do the processes differ? Should the NAFTA Parties pursue a process like the EU's?

---

3. Citizen Complaints

EU citizens may complain to the Community Ombudsman for "maladministration" of the activities of the Community, such as the handling of environmental complaints or failure to monitor the implementation of Community environmental law. The Ombudsman investigates and attempts to resolve the complaints, more than 3,000 each year, many of which it finds arise from lack of information due to insufficient transparency in EU institutions. For further details, see the Ombudsman's most recent (2009) annual report at http://www.ombudsman.europa.eu/activities/home.faces.

Citizens may also complain directly to the Commission, as explained below.

Ludwig Krämer, *EC Environmental Law*
429–32 (6th ed. 2007)

12-15 As the Commission does not have any inspectors, controllers or decentralised administrations which would inform it on the application of Community environmental law within the whole of the Community, its main source of information on possible omissions in the application of Community environmental provision is the information that comes from outside the administrations, in particular from citizens.

The Commission instituted, in the late 1960s, a complaint system for citizens, in order to obtain information on non-technical barriers to the free circulation of goods. The Commission offered to intervene with Member States' administration in order to eliminate border controls and other barriers. Since the mid-1980s, the system has developed considerably as regards environmental complaints. The fact that individuals were able to register a complaint with the Commission stimulated Community-wide awareness of the environment, demonstrated to the citizen that the Commission was also accessible to the man in the street and made it clear to the individual that he had some responsibility for his environment, that he could become active in contributing to the preservation and protection of the environment and that environmental impairment should not be taken as an Act of God, against which nothing can be done. This was particularly important for southern European Member States.

Environmental complaints to the Commission came — and come — from individuals, environmental or professional organisations, national, regional or European deputies, local administrations, political parties, ambassadors and occasionally even from environment ministers of Member States.

12–16 The Commission considers as a complaint any written statement that invokes the breach of Community (environmental) law and asks the Commission to intervene to repair this breach. The formal requirements for such a complaint are very low … Procedurally, such an official inquiry is treated in exactly the same way as a complaint. To facilitate the introduction of complaints, the Commission has even drawn up and published a form.

12-17 The complaint is registered in a central Commission register. The Commission stated in 2002 that "all complaints received are registered, without any selection." This registration has as a consequence that the complainant is kept informed as to the evolution of the complaint and that only the Commission as an institution—not an individual official—may decide on the final outcome of it.

The Commission tries to obtain as much factual information from the complainant as possible, which often overburdens the person who has introduced the complaint. For the rest of the facts, the Commission seeks to obtain factual and legal information from the (central) administration of the Member State against which the complaint is directed. In rare cases, expert advice is taken. Hearings or witnesses' testimony are never taken in environmental cases. Also, inspections in Member States do not take place; in very rare cases visits to the affected sites in the form of fact-finding missions have been organised, but not more frequently than once per year.

In the 1980s, the Commission committed itself—both on the complaint form and in different declarations towards the public—to instruct each complaint; in 1999, it indicated that its administrations would decide according to the internal rules and priorities whether they would examine a complaint or not. And in 2002, the Commission further reduced its commitment to examine each complaint. This has led, during the last years, to a refusal to register complaints where Commission officials felt that no breach of Community law was likely, or to similar abuses, a clear contradiction to the Commission's own commitment to register *all* complaints. Anyway, no sanction exists against an omission to instruct properly, except for disciplinary measures and, eventually, the intervention of the European Ombudsman. The complainant has no direct rights as regards the omission to examine a complaint.

12–18 At the end of the instruction period, which shall not, according to the Commission's internal instructions, extend beyond one year, the Commission decides either to file the complaint or to open formal proceedings, under [Art. 258 TFEU] against a Member State. Upon intervention of the European Ombudsman, the Commission changed its rules in 1997; before it decides to file a complaint, the complainant is heard and has the right to present observations. These procedural guarantees, however, do not give any right to a complainant as regards the final decision which the Commission takes; neither can he oppose the filing of the complaint nor can he oblige the Commission to start legal proceedings under Art. [258 TFEU] against a Member State. The complainant also does not have a right to ensure the Commission makes adequate use of its discretion or, in other words, to see that the Commission's decision is not grossly arbitrary, for instance with regard to previous Commission decisions. The Court of Justice has rejected all attempts to oblige the Commission to start proceedings under [Art. 258 TFEU]. * * *

Practice has shown that an environmental complaint has a greater chance of leading to a positive result when the conflict between the environmental interests and the diverging economic interests is discussed in public. The mobilisation of public opinion constitutes an important element of ensuring the taking into consideration of environmental interests and demonstrates at the same time the—at least partly—political character of the complaint procedure; this political character also appears through the lack of control of the Commission's decisions, which facilitates policy interventions in the decision-making procedure.

Complaints procedures in environmental matters normally take a considerable time. Their lack of transparency and the-overall-limited results, in particular as regards large infrastructural projects, have not led to a situation where the Commission is perceived as a true complaint institution.

———————

The EU complaint process does not empower citizens or their organizations to bring direct actions to enforce EU law; the Commission must intervene on their behalf. When citizens bring claims in domestic courts, most EU Member States require individual, particularized harm to acquire legal standing, and some countries do not provide private rights of action to enforce environmental law. *See* Krämer, EC Environmental Law, at 440–41; Jan H. Jans, *EU Environmental Policy and the Civil Society, in* The European Convention and the Future of European Environmental Law 64–65 (Jan H. Jans, ed., 2003). This is changing, thanks to the Aarhus Convention on access to information, public participation in decisionmaking and access to justice in environmental matters. *See* Chapter 12, Part IV at pages 876–80 for some details on the Aarhus Convention and steps to implement it in the EU.

In limited circumstances, individual citizens may bring an action in the EU Court of Justice against a Member State under the doctrine of "direct effects." Generally, this doctrine allows such actions where a Member State has failed to transpose an EU directive into its national law, or has done so in an incomplete or flawed manner. A number of conditions must be fulfilled before an EU directive will be deemed directly applicable, including that the period for transposing a directive into national law has expired, that the provision of a directive is unconditional, that the provision is precise and "unequivocal," and that the provision explicitly or implicitly confers rights to an individual as against a Member State. Krämer, EC Environmental Law, at 432–33, *citing* Case C-236/92, Comitato di Difesa della Cava, 1994 E.C.R. I-483. To date, few individuals have availed themselves of this limited right, principally due to the burden of fulfilling each of the conditions required to invoke the doctrine.

———————

Questions and Discussion

1. The ombudsman process appears to be a much more powerful mechanism for citizen intervention in regional environmental issues than the NAAEC's citizen submission process. Yet, Krämer concludes that the process is not perceived as a true complaint institution. What are the limitations of the process? What are its strengths? Is the role of the citizen in the ombudsman process much different from the role of the citizen in the NAAEC's Article 14 process?

2. In 2002, the EU adopted its Sixth Environment Action Program (EAP) for the period 2002–2012, establishing priority actions, practical objectives, and a means to achieve them by 2012. Council Decision No. 1600/2002/EC. The action programs are now binding and must be adequately considered by EU decisionmaking bodies in developing and implementing EU policies. The Sixth EAP identifies four areas for urgent action: climate change; protecting nature and biodiversity; health and quality of life; and natural resources and waste. Under these four headings it identifies seven key areas for work: soil protection; marine environment; pesticides; air pollution; urban environment; sustainable use of resources; and waste prevention and recycling. The Sixth EAP also specifically identifies the objective of improved integration of environmental concerns into other policy areas. The 2007 Mid-term Review from the Commission announces no concrete progress on this objective, however, only promising further work on it. COM(2007)225 final.

3. In 1992, the EU established the "LIFE" program, devoted entirely to developing and funding EU environmental policy through financial support for private, public, or joint projects, including technology demonstration, best practices for implementation of directives, innovative projects, programs to build public awareness, and environmental monitoring initiatives. After going through several phases, it is currently operating as LIFE+ under Regulation (EC) 614/2007. Through 2006, LIFE had disbursed more than 2.2 billion Euros to support over 3,000 projects. LIFE+ is budgeted at another 2.1 billion Euros for the period 2007–2013. Many of the supported projects are related to habitat and biodiversity conservation. *See generally* http://ec.europa.eu/environment/life/index.htm. By comparison, recall the NAAEC priorities and its operating budget of US$9 million per year. Can North America hope to do more than improve coordination of a handful of regional actions at this level of funding?

4. Krämer is not alone in expressing frustration over the implementation and enforcement of EU environmental law and policy among its less environment-minded Members. In response, citizen groups and pro-environment Members are increasingly calling for more rigorous enforcement of the regulation conditioning the use of EU funds on full compliance with EU environmental law. KRÄMER, EC ENVIRONMENTAL LAW, at 149. Since EU funds may account for up to 80 percent of project costs, this gives the EU substantial leverage to ensure compliance. But as with similar provisions in some U.S. environmental legislation, authorities are reluctant to apply this sanction. In another approach, EU sectoral policies increasingly integrate environmental conditions into subsidy programs such as Europe's Common Agricultural Policy, including incentives for "ecological farming" and environmentally sound rural development. Are there comparable mechanisms in North America?

Chapter 12

Public Participation and Trade Law

I. Introduction

One of the hallmarks of the development of environmental law, first in the United States and then in many other countries, is increased access to government-held information, the government decision-making process, and the court system. This feature of environmental law is reflected in and given prominent international vindication in Principle 10 of the Rio Declaration on Environment and Development, which begins with the simple statement: "Environmental issues are best handled with the participation of all concerned citizens, at the relevant level." Principle 10 then discusses access to information, participation in decision-making, and access to administrative and judicial proceedings. These elements were later elaborated in treaty form in the Aarhus Convention, formally known as the Convention on Access to Information, Public Participation in Decision-making and Access to Justice in Environmental Matters, *done* June 25, 1998, http://www.unece.org/env/pp/documents/cep43e.pdf. The implementation of the Aarhus Convention is discussed in Part IV of this chapter.

Until fairly recently, the practice in the world of international trade policy making, negotiations, and dispute settlement was, by contrast, confidential, inscrutable, and outside the realm of public inquiry and participation by ordinary citizens. Growing concerns over certain aspects of globalization—including the power of trade bodies and the supranational character of trade rules they enforce—has dragged trade policy and its instruments and actors out of the shadows and into the sunlight. The governance of international institutions such as trade bodies is now under much greater scrutiny by civic organizations and is the subject of considerable political debate and scholarship. We have already covered some aspects of the previously closed world of government-to-government diplomacy and recent initiatives to make it more transparent and accessible in Chapters 2, 10, and 11 and in scattered sections elsewhere. This chapter consolidates some of the earlier sections and goes into more depth on public participation in trade law.

There are many facets to public participation and trade law, many of which are inextricably linked to each other, such as access to information as a precondition to meaningful participation in trade-related processes. This chapter samples some of these issues, including access to information, participation in trade committees and working groups, environmental assessment of trade agreements, and the right to observe or participate in trade disputes. As you read these materials, consider whether there is anything unique about trade processes and negotiations that should insulate them from the modalities of "open government" (notice and comment rulemaking, access to information) that apply to environmental law in particular and domestic legal processes in general (public legis-

latures and courtrooms). As you contrast these features with the wide spectrum of practice in other parts of the world—both in developed and developing countries—you will
begin to appreciate why establishing common "norms" of public participation has been
slow in coming.

II. Access to Trade Decisions and Documents

A. Dispute Settlement in the GATT and the WTO

As we have seen throughout this book, the outcome of trade disputes may significantly
impact environmental, health, and other public policies advocated or defended by national governments across the globe. Thus, it is not surprising that citizen watchdog
groups and others seek access to trade panel decisions, and to briefs and submissions
made by governments defending or prosecuting trade cases, as early in the process as possible. Gaining access to this information proved difficult, and, as we will see, litigious. In
the United States, litigation has pitted the pillars of "open government"—such as the
Freedom of Information Act (FOIA), the Federal Advisory Committee Act (FACA), and
the National Environmental Policy Act (NEPA)—against the traditionally insular operational modalities of trade organizations and the departments and agencies responsible
for interacting with them.

The citizen action group Public Citizen achieved an early milestone in its lawsuit against
the U.S. Trade Representative (USTR), invoking FOIA to gain prompt access to GATT
panel submissions and decisions. Public Citizen v. Office of the U.S. Trade Representative, 804 F. Supp. 385 (D.D.C. 1992). FOIA requires federal agencies to disclose agency
records to the public unless those records are subject to an exemption. Under FOIA, agencies must disclose final opinions made in the adjudication of cases, statements of policy
and interpretations that have been adopted by the agency and are not published in the Federal Register, administrative staff manuals and instructions to staff that affect a member
of the public, and all other records, regardless of form or format. Administrative Procedure Act, 5 U.S.C. §552(a)(2000). Exemptions from disclosure in FOIA are limited to
nine categories of documents, including inter-agency or intra-agency memorandums or
letters that would not be available by law to a party except in litigation with the agency
(especially draft documents), trade secrets and commercial information, information in
the interest of foreign policy, and certain information compiled for law enforcement purposes. 5 U.S.C. §552(b). When an agency seeks to withhold documents sought in a FOIA
request, the agency bears the burden to invoke a specific exemption.

Prior to Public Citizen's case, adopted GATT panel reports were made public, but there
was no formal mechanism for obtaining briefs (technically called submissions) or unadopted panel reports from governments or the GATT Secretariat. Recall that *Tuna/Dolphin
I* was such an unadopted panel report. Public Citizen invoked FOIA to compel the USTR
to disclose panel reports to the public before their consideration by the GATT Council,
and to disclose U.S. submissions to the panels, although portions of the submissions or
reports could be withheld if information contained in them was subject to an exemption.
With respect to U.S. submissions to GATT panels, Public Citizen underscored the important public policy dimensions at issue by arguing, in the language of FOIA, that U.S.
submissions embodied "statements of policy and interpretations which have been adopted

by the agency and are not published in the Federal Register." 5 U.S.C. §552(a)(2)(B) (2000). The court agreed:

> Plaintiffs have made an adequate showing, by providing examples of submissions that clearly contain interpretive statements, that these submissions contain statements of policy and interpretations adopted by USTR. The submissions constitute the agency's interpretation of the United States' international legal obligations, even if not personally approved by the Trade Representative herself. As such, they will have been subject to review by agency personnel in accordance with government policies.

Pub. Citizen v. U.S. Trade Representative, 804 F. Supp. at 387.

In compelling disclosure of these documents, the court rejected USTR's contention that it could withhold documents pursuant to FOIA's exemption for matters "in the interest of foreign ... policy." That exemption allows nondisclosure for documents relating to national defense and foreign policy "under criteria established by an Executive Order" but only if those documents are properly classified pursuant to such Executive Order. The United States feared that the release of negotiating positions, arguments made to dispute resolution panels, and pre-adoption panel decisions would harm foreign relations. However, the court could find no Executive Order or other U.S. law that would justify nondisclosure and it rejected USTR's assertion that GATT rules forbid disclosure. It concluded that GATT rules favored but did not require confidentiality. *Id.* at 388.

With the entry into force of the WTO agreements, changes in U.S. legislation, and pressure for greater transparency from a number of other governments, the handling of panel (and now Appellate Body) reports, country submissions, and amicus briefs has changed substantially from the practices that provoked the Public Citizen lawsuit. The implementing legislation for the Uruguay Round (which was drafted by the executive agencies) mandates that USTR make U.S. submissions available to the public promptly after they are submitted to a WTO panel. Uruguay Round Agreements Act, 19 U.S.C. §3537(c) (2000). USTR must also create a public file for each dispute settlement proceeding in which the United States is a party. In practice, USTR now posts its submissions in WTO disputes on its website, www.ustr.gov. It may, however, withhold information contained in the U.S. submission that another country treats as confidential; indeed, international practice obliges the United States to respect other nations' confidentiality claims. The WTO has followed suit, creating a comprehensive website of dispute settlement proceedings with complete documentation, including procedural rulings and all panel and Appellate Body reports, as soon as they are issued to the parties to the dispute. *See* http://www.wto.org/english/tratop_e/dispu_e/dispu_e.htm. Canada makes most of its trade dispute documents available through the Foreign Affairs and International Trade Canada website. *See* http://www.international.gc.ca/trade-agreements-accords-commerciaux/disp-diff/index.aspx?lang=en.

B. NAFTA and Other Investment Tribunals

The United States and Canada have generally pushed for greater openness and transparency in WTO trade settlement processes, but surprisingly (and perhaps inadvertently), both countries stumbled badly over public access to investor-State arbitration proceedings under Chapter 11 of the NAFTA. As discussed in Chapter 10, NAFTA (and several later agreements between the United States or Canada and other countries) permit private investors to bring claims directly against Parties to the NAFTA for breaching one or more enumerated investor rights. Not long after Canada's quiet settlement of one of the earliest of these claims brought by Ethyl Corporation (*see* Chapter 10 at pages 731–32), other companies filed investor claims against each of the NAFTA Parties, many of which called into question aspects of environmental regulation. Environmental advocacy groups in all three countries protested vehemently when they discovered that these proceedings were governed by procedural rules developed largely for private international arbitrations and so lacked public dockets, open hearings, or transcripts. Moreover, submissions by the parties to the arbitration were treated as confidential unless confidentiality was waived by all parties to the arbitration.

Further embarrassing the governments, an enterprising law professor, Todd Weiler, from the University of Windsor, Ontario, managed to secure many of the document sets for several such proceedings, which he promptly posted in full text on his website. He has maintained this practice over the years. *See* http://www.naftaclaims.com. Given the undeniable public importance of the issues at stake and the incongruity with practice and policy at the WTO, where decisions and other dispute settlement documents are placed on the WTO's website, the NAFTA partners partially rectified this anomaly by issuing a binding "note of interpretation" in 2001. The note clarified that "[n]othing in the NAFTA imposes a general duty of confidentiality on the disputing parties to a Chapter Eleven arbitration" and that the Parties were not precluded from providing public access to documents submitted to, or issued by, a Chapter 11 tribunal. NAFTA Free Trade Commission, Notes of Interpretation of Certain Chapter 11 Provisions (July 31, 2001), *available at* http://www.dfait-maeci.gc.ca/tna-nac/NAFTA-Interpr-en.asp. Accordingly, the Parties agreed to make available to the public in a timely matter all documents submitted to, or issued by, Chapter 11 tribunals, subject to standard confidentiality treatment of specified materials such as trade secrets. Nevertheless, UNCITRAL and ICSID rules governing these arbitrations do not automatically permit citizens the right to observe their proceedings. This issue is now being treated on an *ad hoc* basis; some Chapter 11 panels have allowed the public to attend hearings or to view the proceedings live on closed-circuit television, but others have not.

The U.S. Congress weighed in forcefully on public access issues in the Bipartisan Trade Promotion Authority Act of 2002 (TPA), which granted authority to the Administration to negotiate trade agreements. In the section declaring the U.S. principal trade negotiating objectives on foreign investment, Congress sought to ensure "the fullest measure of transparency" in the dispute settlement mechanism by ensuring that all requests for dispute settlement, proceedings, submissions, findings, and decisions were "promptly made public." Bipartisan Trade Promotion Authority Act of 2002 (TPA), 19 U.S.C. § 3802(b)(3) (2004). Congress also called for all hearings to be open to the public and for the establishment of a mechanism for acceptance of *amicus curiae* submissions from businesses, unions, and nongovernmental organizations. *Id.*

Many of these features have been incorporated into the bilateral and multilateral agreements the United States has negotiated under the TPA. For example, the U.S.-Dominican Republic-Central American Free Trade Agreement (DR-CAFTA) vests tribunals with authority to "accept and consider" *amicus curiae* submissions from persons or entities. DR-CAFTA, art. 10.20(3). Article 10.21 of DR-CAFTA entitled "Transparency of Arbitral Proceedings" provides for public access to all notices, pleadings, memorials, briefs, orders, awards, and decisions, as well as minutes or transcripts "where available." The article also requires tribunals to conduct hearings open to the public. DR-CAFTA, art. 10.21(2).

Questions and Discussion

1. With respect to submissions to WTO panels, the excision of the opposing member's arguments can make participation by the public difficult. A WTO member need only supply to the public a summary of its submission. An interested citizen group that wants to participate by filing an *amicus curiae* brief or by other means may therefore have only part of the argument if members excise parts of their arguments from the public version of their submission. Is there any value to such a rule? Similarly, interim decisions of a WTO panel are not made public. Why not? Do these limitations on disclosure differ from the handling of alternative dispute resolution or settlement negotiations between parties (including government parties) in domestic litigation?

2. Decisions rendered by trade tribunals can have far-reaching public policy implications. Countries may be called on to modify or abandon practices found to be inconsistent with trade rules or face punitive sanctions. As we have seen, some of these practices may implicate environmental policies that enjoy popular support at home, such as recycling or waste minimization strategies, wildlife protection measures, or bans on genetically engineered food products. Similarly, in investor-State actions, claimants may impugn popular governmental practices at the federal, state, or even local level. At the very least, citizens may be interested in scrutinizing the arguments advanced by both sides and holding government officials accountable for the vigor with which they defend the challenged practices. More engaged members of the public may wish to participate more directly in a dispute by submitting legal, scientific, or factual information to a panel as a "friend of the court" or "*amicus curiae.*" Chapter 2 reviews the evolving WTO policy regarding *amicus* filings, and Chapter 10 discusses the current practice on *amicus* briefs in investment arbitrations. *Amicus* filings are explicitly permitted in the U.S.-Singapore and U.S.-Chile free trade agreements, as well as DR-CAFTA.

C. Trade Agreement Negotiations and Trade Policy Making

1. Negotiating Documents

Environmental and other civic groups have also sought access to draft negotiating texts and related materials generated during trade agreement negotiations. In *Center for International Environmental Law v. Office of the U.S. Trade Representative*, 237 F. Supp. 2d 17 (D.D.C. 2002), the plaintiffs sought disclosure under FOIA of 269 documents concerning the negotiation of the U.S.-Chile Free Trade Agreement that fell into three general categories: 1) documents exchanged between the United States and Chile; 2) internal U.S. documents that described meetings with Chilean negotiators or proposals received from Chilean officials; and 3) classified documents created by or for the Trade Policy Review Group, an inter-agency group of senior officials that considers and determines U.S. trade policy.

To justify withholding the documents in the first two categories, the USTR relied on Exemption 5 of FOIA, which protects from disclosure documents that reveal an agency's deliberative process. 5 U.S.C. § 552(b)(5). The purpose of the deliberative process privilege is to encourage the frank discussion of policy issues among government officials and to protect the government's decisionmaking processes. For the exemption to apply, however, the documents must be "inter-agency" or "intra-agency" documents. The court did not accept USTR's argument that Chile was in a nonadversarial relationship with the United States and thus equivalent to an outside consultant with whom the USTR is exchanging "inter-agency" documents. The court ruled that Chile was an independent party promoting its own interests whose communications with the USTR necessarily fall beyond the scope of Exemption 5 for government deliberative documents. The court was mindful of the foreign policy concerns at stake:

> The Court is not oblivious to defendants' concern that disclosure of these documents may complicate international negotiations on free trade and other issues, and it recognizes the importance of confidentiality in treaty negotiations, particularly where, as here, the United States has promised confidentiality to its partner from the outset. Indeed, concern about confidentiality in communications between the government and the Tribes was at issue in *Klamath Water Users*. *See* 532 U.S. at 11. Ultimately, however, the Supreme Court concluded that such policy concerns cannot trump the plain language of the Freedom of Information Act or the underlying policy of the FOIA favoring public disclosure.

Center for Int'l Envtl. Law v. Office of the U.S. Trade Representative, 237 F. Supp. 2d at 29–30. The court also concluded that the five documents by or for the Trade Policy Review Group could be withheld pursuant to Exemption 1 for documents in the interest of foreign policy.

These and other legal actions have steadily eroded "business-as-usual" practices regarding the formulation and negotiation of trade agreements. The United States now routinely publishes draft texts of pending free trade agreements. Congress has also taken a more active role in shaping the content of free trade agreements by setting out general and specific negotiating objectives in trade legislation. Congressional committees may schedule progress report briefings or otherwise intercede more vigorously in the process, which in turn may enhance the public's ability to monitor negotiations or weigh in on selected matters.

Questions and Discussion

1. Should citizens be able to obtain documents relating to negotiations of a trade agreement? CIEL brought its case *after* the United States and Chile had signed their trade agreement. What if CIEL brought its case *before* the agreement was finalized? Should that kind of information, which may be subject to sensitive, ongoing diplomatic negotiations and negotiating tactics, be made public?

2. Even where negotiating documents have been exchanged with all the other negotiating countries and trade advisory committees, the USTR has made the same arguments for nondisclosure of such documents as it did in *Center for International Environmental Law v. Office of the U.S. Trade Representative*. If the documents have already been exchanged, who is left that does not have access to the documents? Why would the USTR refuse to disclose them under these circumstances? Would disclosure constitute a breach of trust with negotiating partners and impede international negotiations?

3. After its victory to obtain negotiating documents relating to the U.S.-Chile Free Trade Agreement, the Center for International Environmental Law sought documents re-

lating to the negotiations for a Free Trade Area of the Americas (FTAA). USTR, however, blocked disclosure of those documents under Exemption 5 as well as Exemption 1 (national security, including foreign relations). Exemption 1 allows an agency to withhold from disclosure documents that are "(A) specifically authorized under criteria established by an Executive order to be kept secret in the interest of national defense or foreign policy and (B) are in fact properly classified pursuant to such Executive order." 5 U.S.C. § 552(b)(1). USTR asserted that the documents were classified pursuant to Executive Order 12958, which provides in relevant part that information may be originally classified when "the information falls within one or more of the categories of information listed in Section 1.5 of the Order" and "the original classification authority determines that the unauthorized disclosure of the information reasonably could be expected to result in damage to the national security and … is able to identify or describe the damage." EO 12958, § 1.1(a)(3) & (4). In particular, USTR claimed that the documents contain information that falls within the Section 1.5(d) category relating to "foreign relations or foreign activities of the United States, including confidential sources." *Id.* § 1.5(d). When the Center for International Environmental Law sued, the USTR released all but one of the documents. See Center for Int'l Envtl. Law v. Office of the U.S. Trade Representative, Civil Action No. 01 CV 00498 (RWR/JMF) (Dec. 17, 2007); Personal Comm. With Martin Wagner, Earthjustice, Counsel for Plaintiffs (Oct. 25, 2010).

---

2. Trade Advisory Committees and Trade Committee Work

Most of the nuts-and-bolts drafting of the provisions of trade agreements takes place in working groups and committees formed by government negotiating teams. These teams are informed, in part, by a network of advisory committees established in response to a Congressional mandate. There are 28 advisory committees as of 2010. A few of these committees have broad mandates, but the vast majority (22) represent specific agricultural and industry sectors, such as "grain, feed and oilseeds" or "automotive equipment and capital goods." The more general committees include the highest-level committee, the Advisory Committee for Trade Policy and Negotiations (ACTPN), which is appointed by and advises the President, and committees providing input on labor, environment, the interests of state and local governments, and African issues. Trade representatives consult closely with affected economic interests, who lobby energetically to protect or expand their markets. Environment and labor hold much less sway. As of mid-2010, there is not a single non-industry member of such committees as the Agricultural Policy Advisory Committee or industry sector committees such as "energy and energy services" or "forest products"; several industry representatives, however, have seats on the Trade and Environment Policy Advisory Committee.

Patti Goldman describes the state of affairs more than a decade ago, and her description still captures the essence of the advisory committee process.

Patti Goldman, *The Democratization of the Development of United States Trade Policy*

27 Cornell Int'l L.J. 631, 672–77 (1994)

The Trade Acts establish an extensive advisory committee system that gives advisory committee members access to inside information about trade negotiations and related matters and offers opportunities to participate in the development of those trade policies....

These committees must be consulted and kept informed "on a continuing and timely basis" about "significant issues and developments and overall negotiating objectives and positions of the United States and other parties." In addition, the ACTPN and other committees whose subject matters are affected by a trade agreement must prepare a report on the trade agreement shortly after the conclusion of negotiations. This guarantees members of the advisory committees immediate access to the final trade agreement long before the agreement is generally available to the public. In addition, the advice given by these committees must be taken into account in determining the U.S. negotiating positions, and the committees must be informed of any "significant departures from such advice or recommendations."

Members of these committees have access to inside government information about the overall negotiating objectives and bargaining positions of the United States, even where such information is classified, contains trade secrets, or is otherwise confidential. A 1989 Commerce Department publication touting the benefits of serving on trade advisory committees during the negotiations leading to the 1979 Tokyo Round of GATT agreements reported that members had access to a vast store of classified documents concerning negotiations and a database that transmitted their views directly to government negotiators. With regard to the advisory committees' influence, the publication claimed:

> The advisory committee members spent long hours in Washington consulting directly with negotiators on key issues and reviewing the actual texts of proposed agreements. For the most part, government negotiators followed the advice of the advisory committees.... Whenever advice was not followed, the government informed the committees of the reasons it was not possible to utilize their recommendations.

More than 800 industry representatives serve on the advisory committees. Until recently, none had any representation of environmental or consumer interests. Rather, they had been comprised almost entirely of representatives of industry with a few representatives of labor organizations. Not only are these committees dominated overwhelmingly by industry, but a significant number of the industry members have poor environmental records and have worked to defeat strong environmental regulations.

In response to public and congressional objections at this skewed representation, expressed during the 1991 debates over extending fast-track authority, the USTR appointed representatives of environmental organizations to ACTPN and four other trade advisory committees in 1992. The remaining committees, even those dealing with important environmental and public health issues, such as those concerning chemicals, tobacco, fruits and vegetables, energy, wood products, and paper products, still lack any environmental or consumer representation. In response to requests for additional appointments of environmental and consumer representatives to the trade advisory committees, the USTR has taken the position that no such representation is legally required, and for years it had refused to make any additional appointments. Recently, however, a consumer representative and an environmental representative were appointed to the ACTPN. In addition, President Clinton issued an Executive Order establishing a trade and environment advisory committee as part of the trade advisory committee network. Only some of the members of this committee, however, represent environmental and consumer interests.

Virtually all of the meetings of the trade advisory committees are held in closed session, and the USTR routinely withholds their records from the public. Indeed, the U.S. Trade Representative recently directed that all meetings to be held by twenty-one of the trade advisory committees will be closed from March 1, 1994 to March 1, 1996. He did this by making a determination that all such meetings will be concerned with matters that would, if disclosed, seriously compromise the government's negotiating objectives and bargaining positions. This blanket determination runs counter to longstanding open meeting principles requiring that agency officials make closure determinations with respect to particular meetings based on the agenda for the meeting, that only those portions of meetings requiring secrecy may be closed, and that the public should receive notice of closure determinations in order to have some way to challenge those determinations administratively or in court.

In addition, secrecy rules prevent trade advisory committee members, including the few environmental representatives, from sharing any of the information that they gain through their service on the committees, even with their own staffs. Therefore, the trade advisory committees enable more than 800 industry representatives and only a few specially chosen environmental representatives to obtain more information about trade negotiations and have far greater opportunities to provide input into those negotiations than the general public.

This system was devised before trade agreements injected themselves into a whole array of domestic health and environmental matters, and thus it is poorly suited to the types of problems now arising in the negotiations. The trade advisory committees grant preferred access to a large number of insiders at the expense of the interested public at large. Congress and the USTR should rethink the entire trade advisory committee system and consider replacing it with other mechanisms for expert and public input.

If the trade advisory committee system is retained, however, several reforms are in order to make it more balanced and open. First, all of the advisory committees must have balanced representation of interests including environmental and consumer interests affected by the trade matters under consideration. The [George H.W.] Bush Administration belatedly and partially recognized the problem of unbalanced representation by appointing a few environmental representatives to some of the trade advisory committees. However, it left dozens of advisory committees without any environmental and consumer representation, including committees dealings with such matters as the chemical industry, tobacco, energy, and wood products. This type of one-sided advisory body is contrary to the Federal Advisory Committee Act (FACA) and rules of fair play. All trade advisory committees must be balanced in terms of the views represented.

The environmental and consumer representatives on the trade advisory committees should also present a balanced range of viewpoints. If, for example, all the environmental representatives supported NAFTA, an issue on which the environmental community was sharply divided, the committees would likely violate FACA's balanced viewpoint requirement and would, as a practical matter, lack the credibility and legitimacy that would enable them effectively to carry out their duties. The trade and environment advisory committee should also not be viewed as an excuse to maintain skewed memberships on other existing trade advisory committees; those committees should still be required to include consumer and environmental representation.

To achieve these goals, Congress should make it clear that all trade advisory committees are fully subject to the balanced membership requirements of the Federal Advisory Committee Act. In order to provide more explicit guidance to those appointing members to such committees, Congress should go further and spell out the precise interests that must be represented. The Trade Acts currently specify some interests that must be represented, and the USTR has justified excluding consumer and environmental representation where the statute does not explicitly require such representation. Therefore, it is critical that Congress specify that environmental and consumer representation is required on any advisory committee dealing with matters affecting the environment, health, or safety.

Under the Trade Acts, the ACTPN, the most powerful of the trade advisory committees, "shall include representatives of non-Federal governments, labor, industry, agriculture, small business, service industries, retailers, and consumer interests." The Trade Acts further require that the ACTPN "shall be broadly representative of the key sectors and groups of the economy, particularly with respect to those sectors and groups which are affected by trade." These mandates should apply not only to the ACTPN, but to all trade advisory committees.

The Trade Acts authorize the establishment of two other types of advisory committees but do not mandate that certain interests be represented. Lists of interests to be included on the committees are provided, but the Acts require their inclusion only "insofar as practicable" and do not specifically identify consumer or environmental interests. The USTR and the Department of Commerce have construed this omission to permit skewed trade advisory committees that exclude any environmental and consumer representation. To ensure representation of these interests, Congress should specifically identify them in the statute as ones that must (not "insofar as practicable") be represented on any trade advisory committee affecting environmental, health, safety, or consumer matters.

Second, the Trade Acts currently except the trade advisory committees from certain openness requirements of the FACA. In particular, their meetings are exempt from FACA's advance notice, openness, public participation, and open records provisions "whenever and to the extent it is determined by the President or his designee that such meetings will be concerned with matters the disclosure of which would seriously compromise the development by the United States Government of trade policy, priorities, negotiating objectives or bargaining positions…." By invoking this language, the USTR can close virtually all trade advisory committee meetings and refuse to make transcripts of those meetings available to the public, even when they pertain to a trade agreement that has been concluded.

This authority should be repealed. The FACA itself incorporates the exemptions to the open meeting requirements of the Government-in-the-Sunshine Act, and the national security exemption protects foreign government information and other information that would, if released, harm foreign relations. Likewise, the Freedom of Information Act exempts national security information from its mandate that the records of agencies and, through the FACA, of advisory committees be made available to the public. These exemptions provide ample authority to close those portions of trade advisory committee meetings and to withhold those records that must be kept secret to protect sensitive negotiating positions. They do not, however, enable the government to cloak trade negotiations in excessive secrecy that keep the public in the dark about non-sensitive matters. The largely discretionary and unconstrained authority given to trade advisory committees to operate in secret should be repealed.

In sum, Congress and the USTR should conduct a public assessment of the trade advisory committee system. The system gives a large number of insiders preferred access and lessens the incentive to develop mechanisms for obtaining input from the public at large. At a minimum, the trade advisory committee system should be made more balanced and open. Ultimately, however, it may be appropriate to replace the entire system with other mechanisms for expert and public input.

———————

At about the time this article was written, Patti Goldman and her colleagues mounted a series of challenges to the secrecy shrouding trade policy and negotiations. First, Public Citizen and others successfully sued USTR to rescind the blanket closure to the public of all trade advisory committee meetings. Pub. Citizen v. Kantor, No. 94-2236 (D.D.C. Oct. 17, 1994). In addition, Earthjustice, Public Citizen, and others challenged the failure of the USTR to create balanced membership of industry, environmental, and public health representatives on key trade advisory committees dominated by industry groups, as Goldman recommended above. Plaintiffs successfully argued that trade advisory committees, such as the 17 sectoral advisory committees established under the Trade Act of 1974, fell within the purview of the Federal Advisory Committee Act (FACA), enacted by Congress in 1972. Federal Advisory Committee Act, 5 U.S.C. app. 2 §§ 1–34 (2000). FACA governs the establishment, operation, and administration of advisory committees that provide advice to the president or to agencies. Section 5 of FACA requires that the membership of an advisory committee be "fairly balanced in terms of point of view represented and the functions to be performed by the advisory committee." In *Northwest Ecosystem Alliance v. Office of the U.S. Trade Representative*, No. C99-1165R (W.D. Wash. Nov. 9, 1999) (order granting summary judgment), the plaintiffs successfully sued to broaden the membership of the forest and paper product trade committee. In April 2000, Public Citizen and others filed suit against the USTR, seeking the inclusion of environmental representatives in the Industry Sector Advisory Committee on Chemicals and Allied Products for Trade Policy Matters (ISAC-3). In March 2001, the court approved a settlement agreement in which the USTR agreed to "make a good faith effort to expedite the appointment of one or more qualified environmental representatives to ISAC-3." Wash. Toxics Coalition v. Office of the U.S. Trade Representative, No. COO-73OR, at 3 (W.D. Wash. Jan. 16, 2003). That was hardly the end of the matter, however, as the plaintiffs soon returned to court, complaining that the USTR had appointed a representative who was consistently sympathetic to industry concerns. The judge agreed that the appointee failed to provide a voice for the environmental community, noting that there was nothing to indicate that he had "ever been affiliated with any environmental organizations or ever advocated on behalf of protecting the environment." *Id.* at 6.

Public interest groups sued again to obtain better representation on the Industry Trade Advisory Committees (ITACs, previously known as Industry Sector Advisory Committees (ISACs)), but with a much different result that throws their earlier victories into question. They noted that six ITACs did not include any members representing the public health community and that, as a result, the points of view represented on the ITACs were not fairly balanced. Earthjustice, on behalf of coalition of public health organizations, filed a lawsuit in December 2005 demanding that corporate interests be balanced with public interest representation on the ITACs. The U.S. District Court for the Northern District of California dismissed the complaint. D.C. No. CV-05-05177-MJJ (Martin J. Jenkins, District Judge, Presiding). In affirming the District Court, the Ninth Circuit concluded:

> The statutes at issue in this case—FACA and the Trade Act—are devoid of standards suggesting what Congress intended when it required all advisory committees to be "fairly balanced." As a result, determination whether a given ITAC is in compliance with the Trade Act's requirements is "hopelessly manipulable" and poses, as Judge Silberman noted, "a major political question of our time." [*Public Citizen v. National Advisory Committee on Microbiological Criteria for Foods*, 281 U.S. App. D.C. 1, 886 F.2d 419, 427, 429 (D.C. Cir. 1989)]. Given that context, analysis of whether the ITACs satisfy the "fairly balanced" requirement—both in terms of function and points of view represented—is a task "not properly undertaken by life-tenured, unelected federal judges." *Id.* at 427–28. Instead, we believe that this determination is a process best left to the executive and legislative branches of government.

Ctr. for Policy Analysis on Trade and Health v. Office of the United States Trade Rep., 540 F.3d 940 (9th Cir. 2008).

One U.S. trade advisory committee, the Trade and Environment Policy Advisory Committee (TEPAC), does include broad representation of key sectors and groups with an interest in trade and environment. TEPAC members are appointed by the USTR to provide policy advice on a large number of issues relating to trade and environment. Like the other advisory committees, TEPAC provides a report to the President, Congress, and the USTR at the conclusion of negotiations for each trade agreement, including an advisory opinion on whether and to what extent the agreement promotes the interests of the United States.

In March 2004, TEPAC delivered its report and advice on the draft text of the U.S.-CAFTA, which was concluded before the Dominican Republic joined the agreement. TEPAC, The U.S.-Central American Free Trade Agreement: Report of the TEPAC (Mar. 19, 2004). The report includes majority and minority opinions and raises interesting issues likely to have escaped mention, if not notice, prior to the creation of the body. A majority of TEPAC members believed that the DR-CAFTA met Congress's negotiating objectives as they relate to environmental matters and that the environmental provisions represented an improvement over the NAFTA and later bilateral agreements such as the U.S.-Chile Free Trade Agreement. Similarly, a majority of members felt that clarifications to the investment provisions eased concerns about their impact on environmental regulations, and most members applauded the enhanced mechanisms for public participation and access to information in the draft agreement. A minority view sharply disagreed, however, noting several inadequacies and deficiencies, including lack of funding for environmental provisions, the expansion of investor rights without commensurate responsibilities placed on investors or additional rights of protection for citizens, and several textual ambiguities. It remains to be seen how influential advisory bodies such as TEPAC will be, both in terms of influencing the scope and content of trade agreements and in engaging a broader group of citizens in the process. However effective TEPAC may be, it is no substitute for participating in the specific and focused work undertaken by the industry and agriculture sector committees.

Questions and Discussion

1. Once trade agreements enter into force, their implementation becomes a matter of domestic law, subject to most of the substantive and procedural guarantees attending to domestic legislation. Committees and working groups formed to implement trade agreements often address significant environmental issues, from automotive emissions to pesticide residues. As we have seen in this chapter, even those committees dealing with issues that indisputably have important implications for environmental policy or the environment seldom have adequate environmental representation within the spirit of FACA's "fairly balanced" requirement. Yet most environmental organizations lack the resources and expertise to staff such an extensive array of trade-related bodies, covering everything from customs practices and technical product standards to emergency planning for highway spills. (Consider that ISAC and TEPAC members are not provided funds for attending meetings). Is this a problem? If yes, how can it be overcome? If environmental and other organizations lack funds to attend meetings of advisory committees, should they focus their attention and resources on TEPAC? Why might they believe that TEPAC representation is not a substitute for representation on, for example, the forest and paper product advisory committee?

2. In 1997, the Secretariat of the CEC commissioned a report on the extent to which the more than 39 NAFTA committees, subcommittees, and working groups were paying heed to NAFTA's preambular commitment to sustainable development with respect to their environment-related responsibilities. CEC, *NAFTA's Institutions: The Environmental Potential and Performance of the NAFTA Free Trade Commission and Related Bodies*, ENVIRONMENT AND TRADE SERIES No. 5 (1997). These bodies often have a direct impact on important environmental questions, including risk assessment, pesticides, automotive emissions, agriculture, and transport practices. The results were decidedly mixed. In no case had NAFTA's economic bodies acted on their permissive environmental mandates and only a few recognized the environmental relevance of their work. The report authors cited "institutional rivalries" and "claims from particular societal interests" as reasons, as well as the absence of representatives from environmental groups as participants in these bodies. *Id.* at 16, 18. Institutional cooperation between the CEC and the NAFTA Free Trade Commission has not materialized, in part because the Free Trade Commission has no institutional structure or staff.

3. Patti Goldman is not alone in her criticisms of the advisory committee system as it is currently configured and with the people appointed to the committees. The General Accounting Office reached many similar conclusions in a 2002 report. GAO, INTERNATIONAL TRADE: ADVISORY COMMITTEE SYSTEM SHOULD BE UPDATED TO BETTER SERVE U.S. POLICY NEEDS (GAO-02-876). In a rare public moment, Teamsters President James Hoffa resigned from the ACTPN over his bitter resistance to the DR-CAFTA. In his letter of resignation to the President, he wrote: "Finally, your administration has failed to make the ACTPN broadly representative of the labor, environmental, and consumer communities." Letter of James P. Hoffa, General President, Teamsters Union, to President George W. Bush, June 24, 2004. In 2009, Professor Charnovitz chimed in: "Of the 32 members [of ACTPN], 27 come from business, two from universities or think tanks, one from a labor union, one from the federal government, and one from a state government. Clearly that is imbalanced." Cross-post from Steve Charnovitz to the International Economic Law and Policy blog, posted July 24, 2009, *available at* http://worldtradelaw.typepad.com/. Charnovitz goes on to recommend two new advisory committees—one on trade and public health and one on trade law.

———————

III. Environmental Impact Assessment and Trade Agreements

A. The U.S. National Environmental Policy Act

Environmental groups have long sought the preparation of an assessment of the environmental impacts of trade agreements at a point early enough in the process to have a meaningful influence on negotiations. A fuller appreciation and discussion of the potential environmental impacts of specific trade and investment liberalization measures, they believe, would lead to more informed policy debates and could help mitigate or avoid potential adverse impacts and maximize positive ones. The process of assessing trade agreements would also broaden the group of stakeholders participating in such policies and raise awareness and interest in trade policy among societal interests traditionally detached from this public policy arena.

In the United States, environmental groups initially sought to compel environmental assessments through the National Environmental Policy Act of 1969 (NEPA), 42 U.S.C. §§ 4321–4370e (2000). NEPA establishes a broad national commitment to protecting and promoting environmental quality by, among other things, requiring federal agencies to prepare an environmental impact statement (EIS)—a statement on the expected environmental impact of any agency action "significantly affecting the quality of the human environment." 42 U.S.C. § 4332(2)(C). NEPA and its implementing regulations, 40 C.F.R. §§ 1500–1517, require an agency to assess the direct, indirect, and cumulative impacts of the proposed legislation or project and propose measures to mitigate those impacts. It also requires the relevant agency to evaluate reasonable alternatives to the proposed project, as well as each alternative's potential direct, indirect, and cumulative impacts and possible mitigation measures.

NEPA allows citizens to participate in the preparation of the EIS by commenting at public hearings and on a draft EIS. The responsible agency must respond meaningfully and in writing to the comments of citizens, a duty which makes participation particularly significant. Moreover, NEPA directs agencies to initiate the EIS process "at the earliest possible time" to ensure that planning and decisions reflect environmental values. 40 C.F.R. § 1501.2. Nevertheless, the EIS process need not begin before there is a recommendation or report on a proposal for federal action.

NEPA thus seemed to offer an important means through which environmental advocates could participate in the development of trade policy and also require an assessment of the environmental impacts of a free trade agreement before it entered into force. If NAFTA would lead to pollution havens in Mexico or transboundary effects on the environment in the United States, then presumably that effect would be identified in an EIS and mitigation measures or alternatives could be proposed to avoid pollution havens.

NEPA, however, proved to be a tough fit for trade agreements. In *Public Citizen v. Office of the United States Trade Representative*, 970 F.2d 916 (D.C. Cir. 1992), the plaintiffs contended that, in negotiating the NAFTA and the Uruguay Round [WTO] agreements, USTR was required to prepare an EIS for each. NEPA lawsuits are brought under the Administrative Procedure Act (APA), which provides for court review only of "final agency action." *Id.* § 704. At the time of the lawsuit, no final agreement for either trade accord had been produced and delivered to the President for submittal to Congress, so the appeals court affirmed the lower court's dismissal of Public Citizen's claim on grounds that no final agency action had been taken.

Upon completion of the NAFTA negotiations (the NAFTA negotiations were finished before the Uruguay Round negotiations), Public Citizen again sued the USTR, alleging that NEPA required the preparation of an EIS on the completed agreements. In *Public Citizen v. Office of the United States Trade Representative*, 822 F. Supp. 21, 25 (D.D.C. 1993), the District Court agreed, holding that "the significant actions taken by the Defendant [USTR] in negotiating and drafting the NAFTA are sufficient to trigger the EIS under the NEPA." USTR had argued that the President, not the USTR, submits trade agreements to Congress, and thus USTR's actions could not constitute final agency action. The district court disagreed, ruling that the mere fact that the President submits the NAFTA to Congress did not bar review under the APA in this case, because "[t]he NAFTA that was negotiated and signed by the Trade Representative is the same document that shall be submitted to Congress and which is the subject of this suit." *Id.* at 26. The court further ruled that the fact that the President was under no obligation to submit the NAFTA to the Congress was not a bar to APA jurisdiction, because NEPA required an EIS for legislative proposals; NAFTA constituted a legislative proposal, which the USTR negotiated and drafted. *Id.*

The USTR appealed and that decision was reversed in *Public Citizen v. Office of the United States Trade Representative*, 5 F.3d 549 (D.C. Cir. 1993), *cert. denied*, 510 U.S. 1041 (1994). Clearly troubled by separation of powers issues and the ongoing political process involving Congress and the Executive Branch, the appeals court reverted back to the lack of final agency action:

> Even though [USTR] has completed negotiations on NAFTA, the agreement will have no effect on Public Citizen's members unless and until the President submits it to Congress.... [T]he Trade Acts involve the President at the final stage of the process by providing for him to submit to Congress the final legal text of the agreement, a draft of the implementing legislation, and supporting information. 19 U.S.C. § 2903(a)(1)(B). The President is not obligated to submit any agreement to Congress, and until he does there is no final action. If and when the agreement is submitted to Congress, it will be the result of action by the President, action clearly not reviewable under the APA. * * *

> The ultimate destiny of NAFTA has yet to be determined. Recently negotiated side agreements may well change the dimensions of the conflict that Public Citizen sought to have resolved by the courts. More importantly, the political debate over NAFTA in Congress has yet to play out. Whatever the ultimate result, however, NAFTA's fate now rests in the hands of the political branches. The judiciary has no role to play.

Id. at 551–53.

Questions and Discussion

1. Consider the different types of effects that environmental advocates worry about concerning trade agreements: scale and composition effects, regulatory effects, and competitiveness effects. *See* Chapter 1, Section I at pages 6–9. Which effects should be evaluated in an environmental impact assessment? Consider the breadth of scale and composition effects: impacts of increased production, depletion of various raw materials (timber, minerals, fish), transportation (shipping, automobile, airplane), and trade (in thousands of products). An assessment of regulatory effects could focus on, among other things, whether harmonization lowers or increases environmental standards and what

the effects of that might be. It could also analyze the effects of recognizing the technical regulations and sanitary and phytosanitary measures of other countries as equivalent. An assessment of competitiveness effects would review the potential for pollution havens. Now remember that NEPA and the EIA laws of almost all countries require an assessment of alternatives and mitigation measures. How should such an assessment be accomplished?

2. Environmental assessment of treaty negotiations creates a dilemma. An assessment before the negotiations begin, which would allow the environmental assessment to guide action, would necessarily be rather abstract. But an assessment after the negotiations are completed, when there are specific issues to be evaluated, can only influence the final decision whether or not to proceed with the agreement. In either case, the agreement as such has no environmental effect. Rather, it is the response of private businesses and governments to the new economic arrangements that will determine the environmental consequences. As described in Chapter 11 and also in Section III.B.4 of this chapter, the work of the Commission for Environmental Cooperation on the environmental effects of trade has attempted to create a methodology that copes with these difficulties. The USTR voluntarily prepared an "environmental review" of NAFTA near the beginning of the negotiations, and a "report" on environmental issues with relation to the final agreement and the side agreements at the time the NAFTA was submitted to Congress.

3. NEPA remains highly relevant to trade issues despite the difficulty plaintiffs face getting into court to enforce the statute under the APA. Another Public Citizen NEPA case concerned access to the United States by Mexican trucks under NAFTA. NAFTA called for a delayed liberalization of trucking services, but for many years the United States delayed opening the United States to Mexican trucks beyond the border area because of political opposition from various quarters, including labor, some state governments, and some environmental groups. Finally, Mexico initiated a trade complaint, and a NAFTA panel ruled that the U.S. failure to allow Mexican trucks entry into the United States beyond the border area violated several provisions of the NAFTA. In re Cross-Border Trucking Serv. (Mex. v. U.S.), NAFTA Arb. Panel, USA-MEX-98-2008-01 (Feb. 6, 2001). The President and Congress then reached a compromise, authorizing the U.S. President to lift the trucking ban if at the same time the U.S. Department of Transportation (DOT) issued safety rules for Mexican trucks. DOT then promulgated the regulations, and Public Citizen challenged that action under NEPA and the U.S. Clean Air Act. For its rulemaking, DOT prepared a very limited EIS that evaluated only the environmental effects of *processing* Mexican trucks that sought access to the United States, not the actual impacts caused by *driving* Mexican trucks. DOT justified this narrow EIS on the grounds that the U.S. President—in a decision not reviewable under NEPA—had already decided to open the border to Mexican trucks. Public Citizen argued that DOT had failed to assess the wider environmental impacts of air pollution in the region that may result from DOT's actions. The Ninth Circuit decided in favor of Public Citizen, concluding that DOT's approach constituted a "novel parsing of the regulations' effects" and that the environmental effects of government action had to be considered to "the fullest extent possible." Public Citizen v. Dep't of Transp., 316 F.3d 1002, 1022 (9th Cir. 2003). The United States sought review by the U.S. Supreme Court, which agreed to hear the case. The Supreme Court ruled in favor of DOT but largely avoided the thorny separation of powers issues by construing NEPA narrowly as not requiring a full assessment for an agency action when the agency has little or no authority to modify its action to account for any environmental impacts. In other words, since DOT lacked discretion to prevent cross-border operations of Mexican carriers, neither NEPA nor the Clean Air Act required

assessment of the environmental effects of such operations. Dep't of Transp. v. Public Citizen, 541 U.S. 752 (2004).

4. Is it possible for citizens to challenge other components of trade agreements that require implementation by an agency? Should it matter that EPA currently does not require Canadian or Mexican trucks to meet U.S. emission standards for domestic trucks? Is this the "deal" that other nations struck when they negotiated free trade agreements with the United States? How could this case be distinguished from U.S. practices requiring imported meats, produce, and other products to undergo inspections and meet demanding health, safety, and environmental standards?

B. Environmental Assessments and Sustainability Impact Assessments of Trade Agreements

1. "Environmental Reviews" in the United States

Bruised but not defeated, groups calling for NEPA-type assessment of the environmental impacts of trade agreements accomplished many of their goals by persuading the Clinton Administration to issue an Executive Order requiring such studies. As you look over the following materials on current trade assessment practice, consider whether similar assessments would look much different had they been conducted pursuant to NEPA, especially concerning the legal avenues open to citizens to challenge the accuracy, thoroughness, and scope of assessments prepared by government agencies.

Environmental Review of Trade Agreements, Exec. Order No. 13,141
64 Fed. Reg. 63169 (Nov. 18, 1999)

By the authority vested in me as President by the Constitution and the laws of the United States of America, and in order to further the environmental and trade policy goals of the United States, it is hereby ordered as follows:

§ 1. **Policy.** The United States is committed to a policy of careful assessment and consideration of the environmental impacts of trade agreements. The United States will factor environmental considerations into the development of its trade negotiating objectives. Responsible agencies will accomplish these goals through a process of ongoing assessment and evaluation, and, in certain instances, written environmental reviews.

§ 2. **Purpose and Need.** Trade agreements should contribute to the broader goal of sustainable development. Environmental reviews are an important tool to help identify potential environmental effects of trade agreements, both positive and negative, and to help facilitate consideration of appropriate responses to those effects whether in the course of negotiations, through other means, or both.

§ 3. (a) **Implementation.** The United States Trade Representative (Trade Representative) and the Chair of the Council on Environmental Quality shall oversee the implementation of this order, including the development of procedures pursuant to this order, in consultation with appropriate foreign policy, environmental, and economic agencies.

(b) Conduct of Environmental Reviews. The Trade Representative, through the interagency Trade Policy Staff Committee (TPSC), shall conduct the environmental reviews of the agreements under section 4 of this order.

§ 4. **Trade Agreements.**

(a) Certain agreements that the United States may negotiate shall require an environmental review. These include:

(i)   comprehensive multilateral trade rounds;

(ii)   bilateral or plurilateral free trade agreements; and

(iii) major new trade liberalization agreements in natural resource sectors.

(b) Agreements reached in connection with enforcement and dispute resolution actions are not covered by this order.

(c) For trade agreements not covered under subsections 4(a) and (b), environmental reviews will generally not be required. Most sectoral liberalization agreements will not require an environmental review. The Trade Representative, through the TPSC, shall determine whether an environmental review of an agreement or category of agreements is warranted based on such factors as the significance of reasonably foreseeable environmental impacts.

§ 5. **Environmental Reviews.**

(a) Environmental reviews shall be:

     (i)   written;

     (ii)   initiated through a Federal Register notice, outlining the proposed agreement and soliciting public comment and information on the scope of the environmental review of the agreement;

     (iii) undertaken sufficiently early in the process to inform the development of negotiating positions, but shall not be a condition for the timely tabling of particular negotiating proposals;

     (iv) made available in draft form for public comment, where practicable; and

     (v)   made available to the public in final form.

(b) As a general matter, the focus of environmental reviews will be impacts in the United States. As appropriate and prudent, reviews may also examine global and transboundary impacts.

§ 6. **Resources.** Upon request by the Trade Representative, with the concurrence of the Deputy Director for Management of the Office of Management and Budget, Federal agencies shall, to the extent permitted by law and subject to the availability of appropriations, provide analytical and financial resources and support, including the detail of appropriate personnel, to the Office of the United States Trade Representative to carry out the provisions of this order.

§ 7. **General Provisions.** This order is intended only to improve the internal management of the executive branch and does not create any right, benefit, trust, or responsibility, substantive or procedural, enforceable at law or equity by a party against the United States, its agencies, its officers, or any person.

WILLIAM J. CLINTON

THE WHITE HOUSE,

November 16, 1999.

Questions and Discussion

1. One reason for the preparation of an EIS is to trigger the public participation provisions of NEPA. NEPA allows citizens to comment on a draft EIS and to participate in public hearings before a draft is created. When should public participation occur in the development of a free trade agreement? When should federal, state, and local agencies participate? Does the Executive Order describe when citizens and agencies can participate? Are the public participation provisions of the Executive Order adequate?

2. Under NEPA, the EIS must include a discussion of direct and indirect impacts, as well as the cumulative impacts of past and reasonably foreseeable actions. What impacts must be assessed under the Executive Order? Moreover, the regulations that implement NEPA state that an assessment of reasonable alternatives to the proposed action is at the "heart" of the EIS. Environmental Impact Statement, 40 C.F.R. § 1502.14 (2004). The discussion of alternatives provides decisionmakers with the information necessary to evaluate the costs and benefits of a project. NEPA also requires the EIS to include mitigation measures. What does the Executive Order require?

3. The first Environmental Review prepared by the USTR pursuant to Executive Order 13,141 involved the bilateral free trade agreement with Jordan, which was signed on October 24, 2000. That agreement is atypical in a number of respects. First, total U.S.-Jordan trade was valued at only US$276 million in 1999, a tiny fraction of total U.S. trade valued at US$1.7 trillion in 1999. Jordan's global trade was valued at US$5.1 billion. Final Environmental Review of the Agreement on the Establishment of a Free Trade Area between the Government of the United States and the Government of the Hashemite Kingdom of Jordan (undated). The analysis of the environmental and regulatory effects of the agreement takes less than two pages of the environmental review. The review concludes that the environmental effects will be *de minimis*. Is that reasonable in light of the level of trade with Jordan?

By Spring 2010, USTR had completed 11 final environmental reviews and three interim reviews for agreements that have not yet been submitted to Congress for approval. The DR-CAFTA Environmental Review typifies the practice under Executive Order 13,141. Part of the review is a presentation of current trade data and expected trends under the agreement. The core of the environmental review is 13 pages, with only a brief and very general discussion of "economically-driven environmental effects" and "regulatory effects." Most of the focus is on transboundary and global effects, given the geographic proximity of Central America, its high biodiversity, and its important habitat for neotropical migratory birds. Here is a summary of the conclusions of this environmental review:

> 1. In this Final Environmental Review, the Administration has concluded that changes in the pattern and magnitude of trade flows attributable to the FTA will not have any significant environmental impacts in the United States. Based on existing patterns of trade and changes likely to result from provisions of the CAFTA-DR, the impact of the CAFTA-DR on total U.S. production through changes in U.S. exports appears likely to be small. As a result, the CAFTA-DR is not expected to have significant direct effects on the U.S. environment. While it is conceivable that there may be instances in which the economic and associated

environmental impacts are concentrated regionally or sectorally in the United States, we could not identify any such instances.

2. In considering whether provisions of the CAFTA-DR could affect, positively or negatively, the ability of U.S. federal, state, local or tribal governments to enact, enforce or maintain environmental laws and regulations, the Administration focused in particular on the provisions of the CAFTA-DR's Environment Chapter and related dispute settlement provisions. We concluded that the CAFTA-DR will not adversely affect the ability of U.S. federal, state, local or tribal governments to regulate to protect the U.S. environment, and that these and related CAFTA-DR provisions should have positive implications for the enforcement of environmental laws and the furtherance of environmental protection in both the United States and the FTA partner countries.

3. This review also carefully examined the provisions of the Investment Chapter and their environmental implications. We were unable to identify any concrete instances of U.S. environmental measures that would be inconsistent with the Agreement's substantive investment obligations. Given that U.S. environmental measures can already be challenged in U.S. courts, we do not expect the CAFTA-DR's investor-state mechanism to significantly increase the potential for a successful challenge to U.S. environmental measures. The CAFTA-DR's innovations in the substantive obligations and investor-state mechanism should provide coherence to the interpretation of the FTA's investment provisions.

4. As compared to the expected effects in the United States, the CAFTA-DR may have relatively greater effects on the economies of Central America and the Dominican Republic. In the near term, however, net changes in production and trade are expected to be relatively small because exports to the United States from these countries already face low or zero tariffs. Longer term effects, through investment and economic development, are expected to be greater but cannot currently be predicted in terms of timing, type and environmental implications.

5. Through increased economic activity in Central America and the Dominican Republic, the CAFTA-DR may have indirect effects on the U.S. environment through transboundary transmission of pollutants (air and water), and through effects on habitat for wildlife, including migratory species. This review examined a range of these possible impacts, but did not identify any specific, significant consequences for the U.S. environment. Nevertheless, the possibility of such effects requires ongoing monitoring. Monitoring of conditions in the U.S environment will continue as an element of existing domestic environment programs. Monitoring of environmental conditions in Central America and the Dominican Republic will be enhanced as a component of an Environmental Cooperation Agreement among the Parties.

6. The CAFTA-DR can have positive environmental consequences in Central America and the Dominican Republic by reinforcing efforts to effectively enforce environmental laws, accelerating economic growth and development through trade and investment and disseminating environmentally beneficial technologies. The public submissions process established by the Environment Chapter has significant potential to improve environmental decision-making and transparency in Central America and the Dominican Republic and to inform capacity-building activities in the region.

7. The CAFTA-DR provides a context for enhancing cooperation activities to address both trade-related and other environmental issues. As a complement to the CAFTA-DR, the United States and the FTA partner countries signed an Environmental Cooperation Agreement (ECA) that will enhance the positive environmental consequences of the Agreement. The ECA establishes a comprehensive framework for developing cooperative activities. An Environmental Cooperation Commission, consisting of high-level officials with environmental responsibilities from each Party, will oversee implementation of the ECA. The Agreement makes specific provision for benchmarking and monitoring of the progress of cooperative activities. The Parties are currently developing a Plan of Work that will identify specific areas of cooperation and provide more detail on how the benchmarking and monitoring provisions will be implemented.

Final Environmental Review of the Dominican Republic-Central America-United States Free Trade Agreement 1–3 (Feb. 2005). Office of the U.S. Trade Representative, Final Environmental Review, U.S.-Central America Free Trade Agreement (Feb. 2005), at 1–3, *available at* http://www.ustr.gov/trade-topics/environment/environmental-reviews.

4. Revisit the typology of potential environmental effects of trade set forth in Chapter 1, Section I at pages 6–9 (scale and compositional effects, regulatory effects, and competitiveness effects). Do USTR's preliminary conclusions regarding CAFTA speak to the main types of environmental effects identified by environmental economists?

5. The CAFTA Environmental Review lists the "most pressing" environmental issues in Central America as loss of biodiversity, air and water pollution, waste disposal, sustainable energy production, and degradation of land through erosion, nutrient depletion, and mismanagement. *Id.* at 9. If asked to "green" the CAFTA by seeking to improve the region's ability to contend with these challenges, what measures would you promote? Which of your measures would link directly to trade or to trade mechanisms?

6. The Bipartisan Trade Promotion Authority Act of 2002 included as a principal trade negotiating objective "reduc[ing] or eliminat[ing] government practices or policies that unduly threaten sustainable development." 19 U.S.C. §2102(b)(11)(E). The CAFTA Interim Environmental Review made no mention of subsidized and quota-protected U.S. sugar exports to CAFTA, but the omission did not escape the attention of the U.S. TEPAC, which commented:

> A majority of the Committee is extremely concerned about the Agreement's limited reductions in the above-quota sugar tariff rates over an extended period.... This is of particular concern with regard to sugar, where the overproduction of sugar caused by domestic subsidies places significant stress on delicate and endangered ecosystems like Florida's Everglades.

TEPAC CAFTA Report, at 5. In an attachment to the report, TEPAC members from Consumer Alert and Hudson Institute's Center for Global Food Issues amplified their critique, detailing how, in their view, U.S. sugar policy hurts the U.S. economy and environment. Imagine that U.S. domestic sugar supports ended along with the elimination of tariffs and quotas. Should USTR evaluate Central America's ability to irrigate sugar fields and control nutrient and pesticide run-off, along with other potential impacts of increased sugar cultivation in the region? In other words, how should we evaluate the spreading of environmental risks and benefits of such activities across the hemisphere?

2. Canada's Environmental Assessments

Canada also conducts environmental assessments of trade agreements pursuant to its 1999 *Cabinet Directive on the Environmental Assessment of Policy, Plan and Program Proposals* and the *Framework for Environmental Assessment of Trade Negotiations* ("the Framework"), released in 2001, Dept. of Foreign Affairs and International Trade website, http://www.international.gc.ca/enviro/assessment-evaluation/trade-commercial.aspx?lang=eng. The Framework outlines the process developed to ensure that environmental considerations are integrated into policy development stages and, ultimately, support negotiations. The process consists of three main phases: the Initial Environmental Assessment, the Draft Environmental Assessment, and the Final Environmental Assessment. The Initial Environmental Assessment is carried out for all negotiations and identifies the main environmental issues expected to arise as a result of negotiations. The Draft Environmental Assessment builds on the earlier report by including a more thorough examination and assessment of environmental impacts. The Final Environmental Assessment details the outcome of the negotiations as they relate to the issues in the Draft Environmental Assessment, including mitigation and enhancement. If the Initial Environmental Assessment does not identify "likely" or "significant" impacts, no further reports are prepared unless new information warrants reconsideration of the issue. *Id.*

Department of Foreign Affairs and International Trade, Framework for Environmental Assessment of Trade Negotiations
10–17 (Feb. 2001)

Analytical Framework to Conduct an Environmental Assessment of Trade Negotiations

This section outlines the analytical methodology to undertake an EA. The analysis will rely largely on existing information, augmented as necessary by additional research. Analysis will include quantitative and qualitative techniques and apply local and traditional knowledge when appropriate. As noted earlier, an EA of a trade negotiation has the potential to be a dynamic exercise, as it may have to focus on a "moving target." As such, the analytical stages described here may have to be undertaken at various points during the EA process. Regardless of when the analysis is undertaken during the course of an EA, the same analytical stages would be applied.

There are four stages in the analytical framework:

Stage 1. Identification of the economic effect of the negotiation

Stage 2. Identification of the likely environmental impacts of such changes

Stage 3. Assessment of the significance of the identified likely environmental impacts

Stage 4. Identification of enhancement/mitigation options to inform the negotiations

Stage 1: Identification of the Economic Effect of the Agreement to be Negotiated

The purpose of this stage is to identify the trade liberalization activity of the trade agreement to be negotiated. This stage will first identify what the potential agreement would entail and the overall **economic relevance** of the agreement to Canada. This will help to determine the scope of analysis required for the environmental assessment and to prioritize the issues to be assessed. * * *

Analysis during this stage would also endeavour to determine, when appropriate, if and how the trade liberalization activity could affect issues such as, for example:

- trade flows (product or technology);
- economic activity (scale and structural); and/or
- unique effects on the provinces or territories (other than the ability to regulate).

The **ability to regulate or legislate** refers to the likely legal and/or policy effects of agreements. Positive effects may result when appropriate environmental regulations, standards or other measures are in place to address macro- and micro-economic changes. Negative effects may result when appropriate environmental policies or regulations are not present, or if the agreement impedes the development or implementation of such policies or regulations.

The effects of trade flows cover both products and technology, including services. Product effects pertain to changes in trade flows of products. Positive effects may result when an agreement leads to increased trade in beneficial products, such as energy-efficient goods. Negative effects may result if the agreement leads to an increase in the production and trade of products that have direct or indirect negative impacts on the environment. Technology effects relate to changes in the flow of technologies, for example, technologies that reduce the resource requirements (energy, inputs) or reduce or eliminate pollution that may otherwise result from production.

The effects on **economic activity** include both scale and structure. *Scale effects* refer to changes in the overall *level* of economic activity or macro-economic effects of trade agreements. Positive effects may result from economic growth and financial gains when appropriate environmental policies or regulations are in place. In the absence of such policies or regulations, or when they are impeded or not enforced, negative environmental effects may result, such as unsustainable resource use or pollution resulting from trade-related increases in transportation. *Structural effects* refer to the changes in the *patterns* of economic activity or micro-economic effects of trade agreements. Positive effects may result when the agreement promotes the efficient allocation of resources and efficient patterns of production and consumption. Negative effects may result when the patterns of consumption are inefficient or unsustainable and/or when appropriate policies and regulations are not present. Baseline scenarios may be established as appropriate at this stage to help measure the changes resulting from the trade negotiations.

Stage 2: Identification of the Likely Environmental Impact of Such Changes

Once the economic effects of the trade agreement have been estimated, the likely environmental impacts of such changes are approximated. The EA will also identify those positive environmental benefits that might arise from the negotiations in the form of environmentally 'friendly' technologies and capacity-building initiatives.

For the purpose of this framework, "environment" refers to the components of the Earth, including land, water, air, including all layers of the atmosphere, all organic and inorganic matter and living organisms (including humans) and the interacting natural systems that include components of the foregoing.

Examples of questions to assist with the determination of likely environmental impacts—positive, negative, unknown, or neutral—may include:

- Will the trade negotiations be consistent with Canada's existing commitments under multilateral environmental agreements (MEAs), such as the Montreal Protocol, the Bio-diversity Convention, the Kyoto Protocol, etc.?

- Will the trade agreement affect the federal/provincial/territorial governments' ability to regulate environmental protection or to enhance environmental benefits?

- Will the trade negotiations affect the achievement of an environmental quality goal (e.g., reduction of greenhouse gas emissions or protection of endangered species)? * * *

If it is determined that no likely significant environmental impacts will result from the trade agreement to be negotiated, this will be documented and no further assessment action should be required. However, environmental factors will continue to be considered on an on-going basis particularly as new information arises during the course of negotiations.

Stage 3: Assessment of the Significance of the Identified Likely Environmental Impacts

If likely environmental impacts are identified, they will be assessed as to their significance. Possible factors to determine significance include:

- What is frequency and duration of the impact?

- What is the geographical scope and magnitude of the impact?

- Is there an established high level of risk to the environment associated with the impact?

- What sectors will be affected and what is the environmental relevance of those sectors?

- Are the impacts irreversible?

- Are the impacts likely to lead to cumulative impacts?

- Are there possible synergies among the impacts?

Additional criteria to determine the degree of significance will be developed as appropriate. This is an area where the views of SAGITs and outside 'experts' will be particularly useful.

This stage will require an initial survey of related existing information from various sources to help identify information gaps and areas where further work may be required. Every effort would be made to use or update relevant existing information and analysis. Once gaps in the information base have been identified and once resource requirements have been identified and allocated, further consultations with environmental assessment experts, provinces and territories, aboriginal groups, business groups and the public may be required to determine how and to what extent analysis will be undertaken to ascertain the magnitude of the likely environmental impact. This will include an analysis of those sectors that are clearly identifiable as being the subject of the agreement being negotiated and to which environmental impacts are attributable. An overriding consideration is that the level of effort in conducting any analysis will be commensurate with the level of anticipated environmental impact.

Stage 4: Identification of Enhancement/Mitigation Options to Inform the Negotiations

Previous stages of analysis identify the likely and significant environmental impacts of negotiations. Stage four identifies the policy options or actions to address negative impacts and to enhance positive impacts. * * *

Once cumulative impacts have been considered, enhancement and mitigation options would be identified. The mitigation and enhancement options would assist the negotiators to identify, as appropriate, what steps can be taken outside or within the negotiations to either address or enhance environmental outcomes. Examples of possible options include the establishment of new, or modifications to existing programs to address the likely negative environmental impacts identified and/or enhance the likely positive impacts. Additionally, there may be a need to establish mechanisms for follow-up to monitor the outcomes of an agreement in the course of its implementation. Another example could be to work with like-minded countries or organizations on issues identified during the course of the assessment.

In the absence of regulatory measures and institutions to address likely and significant negative environmental impacts, alternative policy responses to mitigate these impacts and to enhance the positive environmental impacts, would be examined. Again, because not all impacts can be examined, efforts will be focused on significant impacts as identified in stage 3.

In addition to identifying these options, other decisions that negotiators may make on the basis of the results of environmental assessments include the following:

- abandoning a negotiating position and developing a new approach;

- retaining the negotiating position; or

- retaining the negotiating position and taking other steps to mitigate the effects.

As noted, any new analysis undertaken during the course of negotiations due to new and unanticipated issues would be documented and included in the Final EA Report.

Public Participation

Environmental protection is a core Canadian value and priority. Canadians have a say in the development of Canada's environmental policy and trade agenda. Public input will continue to be sought by the Government when undertaking environmental assessments of trade negotiations. This framework identifies the form and at what point public input will be sought during an environmental assessment of a trade negotiation. While the timing and scope of public participation will vary depending on the nature of the agreement to be assessed, numerous opportunities for public participation are proposed as outlined throughout Section 2.1.

Given the confidentiality of the negotiating process, re-evaluations during the negotiations would not be shared with the public, but would be documented in the Final EA Report issued at the conclusion of negotiations. However, as noted in Section 2.1 (c), the EA Committees will seek the advice of Sectoral Advisory Groups on International Trade (SAGITs), comprising individuals from environmental non-governmental organizations, the private sector and academic institutions throughout the environmental assessment process. This would include any major new analysis required, or re-evaluations of the draft environmental assessment during negotiations.

———————

The focus of both U.S. and Canadian assessments is on forecasting environmental impacts in its own territory, not environmental impacts in the trading partner countries. The U.S. Executive Order 13,141 expands the scope of assessments to include global and transboundary impacts "as appropriate and prudent." Canada's Framework similarly limits the scope of most assessments to impacts on the Canadian environment due to "limited data, sovereignty issues, limited resources and practicality." *Id.* at § 2. The Framework does consider developing assessments for transboundary, regional, and global environmental impacts to the extent they have a "direct impact" on the Canadian environment. In the United States, limiting the scope of assessments of trade agreements in this manner has been widely criticized in view of the rather obvious fact that most developing countries' exports to the United States usually represent a small fraction of total U.S. trade in that good or service, whereas exports to, or imports from, the United States often represent a very significant percentage of traded goods or services in the sector at issue for a developing country. In other words, taken individually, impacts on the comparatively large economies of the United States are likely to be *de minimis*, even with trade agreements involving entire regions, such as the DR-CAFTA. Impacts on the environment in developing countries are more likely to be significant and may degrade natural resources well worth being concerned about, even if they do not present immediate "global" or "transboundary" concerns.

In practice, the USTR appears to have similarly concluded that little will be gained by the formulaic repetition of a finding that, say, U.S. tariff-reduced exports of baseball bats to El Salvador are unlikely to harm U.S. birch forests. In fact, most of the DR-CAFTA assessment evaluates the state of Central America's natural resources, with helpful statistics on forest depletion, air and water quality, and other environmental media.

———————

3. The European Union

The European Union employs a characteristically broader and more systematic approach than either the United States or Canada. It conducts what are called Trade "Sustainability Impact Assessments" (SIAs). SIAs have been prepared since 1999 for all the EU's major trade negotiations, including with Mercosur and, still active in 2010, a series of "economic partnership agreements" with diverse developing countries in Africa, the Caribbean, and the Pacific. In the SIA scheme, the assessments are carried out by private contractors who bid for each project. Contractors have included Manchester University in the United Kingdom and the consulting firm PriceWaterhouseCoopers. The work is carried out under the supervision of the Directorate General for Trade of the European Commission.

Several features differentiate EU's SIA process from the U.S. and Canadian assessment practices. To begin with, the explicit focus of SIA is on sustainability, meaning social factors as well as environmental effects and economic development are an integral part of the analysis. Second, the SIAs are explicitly directed to assess impacts on the non-EU trading partners as well as on EU members, and in that respect the other country or countries should be engaged in the assessment process. Third, the SIA is to be based on external consultation with all interested stakeholders, including civil society and, as appropriate, members of the European Parliament or member state officials and experts. Fourth, the process is to be fully transparent at every stage, with all documents made public. In short, trade SIAs seek to mainstream sustainable development into trade policy by using the assessment to guide negotiations in an effort to ensure that Europe's trade agreements are sustainable, enhance positive environmental and social effects of trade agreements and mitigate negative ones, and promote the consistency of international trade rules with sustainability objectives (including precaution, labeling, and consistency between WTO rules and MEAs).

SIA methodology employs a core group of sustainability indicators containing representative economic, environmental, and social data. A screening exercise first determines which trade or other measures in the scope of the proposed trade agreement require SIA because they are likely to have significant impacts. This is followed by a "scoping" process to determine which economic, social, or environmental components should be evaluated and the methodologies to be employed in the assessment. The third step is the assessment of the potential impacts on sustainable development, for each measure and for the agreement as a whole. Finally, there must be a mitigation and enhancement analysis to search out ways to reduce any negative impacts from trade liberalization and to enhance positive contributions to sustainable development. (A useful summary description of the SIA process is available in a "Handbook for Trade Sustainability Impact Assessment" (2006), *available at* http://trade.ec.europa.eu/doclib/html/127974.htm The Commission's homepage for trade SIA, with more details and links to all trade SIAs is: http://ec.europa.eu/ trade/analysis/sustainability-impact-assessments).

---

4. Rethinking Environmental Assessments of Free Trade Agreements

Researchers have made considerable progress in overcoming several of the methodological constraints hampering trade-economy-environment analysis. Nonetheless, environmental assessments of trade agreements have yet to yield many of the real world policy impacts that its proponents hoped for. (*See* NAFTA-related discussion in Chapter 11, Section IV.E at pages 814–20). The CEC Secretariat's own take on the state of trade and environment assessment, *The Picture Grows Clearer* (CEC 2002), offers some sober reflections on the practical limitations and constraints of trade impact assessment in addition to challenging some of the standard assumptions about trade and environment relationships.

The CEC report identifies six key considerations emerging from the assessment of the environmental effects of NAFTA. These include: designing trade/environment assessments to yield policy relevant outcomes without ignoring nontrade related forces; supplementing macro or large-scale studies with region-specific, media-specific, and sector-specific analyses; considering the impacts of environmental infrastructure and policy implementation resulting from increased trade flows; overcoming the lack of quality environmental data at the regional or local level; integrating sectoral policies more effectively; and underscoring the importance of evaluating economy-environment linkages in an "open, inclusive and transparent" manner.

CEC work has demonstrated just how important it is to supplement so-called "aggregated" or "macro" studies with more geographically limited or media-specific studies. Aggregate data may mask important conditions at the local level. For example, while overall

North American forest cover may be stable or increasing, this tells us little about the health of an ecologically significant stand of hardwood forest that may feel the pull of demand for lumber exports. Yet, researchers continue to lament the unavailability of precisely the kind of local data necessary to undertake such studies in a more systematic manner. At the same time, chronic shortages of resources for environmental monitoring dim the prospects for overcoming the data deficit anytime soon.

While useful, the so-called *ex ante* studies now being prepared in North America and Europe fail to compile or analyze local data and at times do little more than to state the obvious by pointing out that most developing countries lack the environmental infrastructure—technical, administrative, and legal—to protect vulnerable ecological assets during the critical transition to more open trade. Nor do they fully expose the deeper structural questions uncovered in trade and investment liberalization agreements. For example, these studies have not explored the land use impacts on communal or small-scale farming in Latin America (or elsewhere) of replicating U.S. and European agricultural models, which may include "factory farm"-type confined agricultural feedlot operations or may require more intensive application of fertilizers and pesticides. Nevertheless, environmental assessment establishes a framework for evaluating these issues in a more systematic, transparent, and inclusive manner, opening new vistas on the possibility of reform.

Questions and Discussion

1. Article 11 of the Treaty on the Functioning of the European Union states:

> Environmental protection requirements must be integrated into the definition and implementation of the Union's policies and activities, in particular with a view to promoting sustainable development.

Similarly, the Preamble to NAFTA pledges to promote "sustainable development" as well as to undertake its economic activities "in a manner consistent with sustainable development." Does either provision suggest the manner in which assessments of trade agreement should be conducted?

In both instances, critics have complained that economic considerations remain paramount in decisionmaking, with environmental factors playing a decidedly subordinate role. Gerd Winter, *Environmental Principles in Community Law, in* THE EUROPEAN CONVENTION AND THE FUTURE OF EUROPEAN ENVIRONMENTAL LAW 21–24 (Jan H. Jans, ed., 2003); JOCHEM WIERS, TRADE AND ENVIRONMENT IN THE EC AND THE WTO: A LEGAL ANALYSIS 18–21 (2002).

2. Scott Vaughan, former CEC head of Environment, Trade and Economy, conducted a study for the Carnegie Endowment for International Peace examining the impacts of NAFTA in Mexico with respect to: a) the rise in the overapplication of nitrogen, phosphorus, and other agrochemical inputs; b) the depletion of groundwater due to increased crop irrigation; and c) the vicious cycle of poverty and income divergence, subsistence farming, and high rates of deforestation and changes in land use. Scott Vaughan, *The Greenest Trade Agreement Ever? Measuring the Environmental Impacts of Agricultural Liberalization, in* NAFTA's PROMISE AND REALITY: LESSONS FROM MEXICO FOR THE HEMISPHERE 61 (John Audley et al. eds., 2003). Vaughan concludes that there is little evidence to suggest that the environmental safeguards in the NAFTA or its environmental side agreement have directly improved environmental quality in the farm sector. *Id.* at 63–64. NAFTA accelerated the structural shift toward large-scale, commercially viable, export-

oriented farms, which, on balance, are more water-intensive and increase concentrations of nitrogen and phosphorus, water-polluting agrochemicals used as inputs in larger-scale farms. Finally, Vaughan concludes that commercially oriented large-scale farms have not delivered environmental benefits associated with intensive farming, especially land-saving effects associated with an increase in production efficiency. Vaughan's article examining NAFTA and agriculture runs about the same length as the USTR's entire CAFTA Environmental Review (without annexes). Did the USTR give short shrift to these issues? Roughly one-quarter of Mexico's population lives in rural areas likely to be impacted in some way by the rapid modernization of Mexico's agricultural sector, mainly by replicating U.S. agribusiness models. In light of this fact, is the EU on track by including social issues within the ambit of its sustainability reviews?

Vaughan's study has the benefit of analyzing the effects of NAFTA ten years after it entered into force. Is it possible to make reasonable assumptions about the effects of a trade agreement before entering into it? Do any of the methodologies reviewed in this section provide the answer? If not, what else can be done? Some EIA laws, such as Chile's, require monitoring of a project to identify its actual environmental impacts. Would such a requirement in NEPA overcome its other defects as it relates to free trade agreements? Should free trade agreements include a specific provision that requires environmental and/or social impact analysis at periodic intervals? If an analysis of the WTO's SPS Agreement or of Article III of the GATT reveals significant environmental harm, what should happen?

3. Is it fair to lay the lack of capacity and resources to protect the environment in some developing countries at the doorstep of trade ministries? After all, don't many current small-scale local unsustainable practices merely become larger-scale ones as access and demand increases? Some would argue that whether it is fair or not is beside the point; since progress on environmental policy is slow and poorly funded, trade is the only game in town. Others note that trade agreements provide a framework for cooperation, and that our entanglement with these countries gives the developing world a greater stake in protecting valued resources and increases our levers over multinational corporations more likely to be sensitive to consumer demands for environmental stewardship. The debate will surely continue.

4. In 2000, the USTR sought public comment on procedures for obtaining trade policy advice from nongovernmental organizations. Request for Public Views, 65 Fed. Reg. 19,423-01 (Apr. 11, 2000). Several U.S. environmental NGOs jointly submitted a thoughtful and far-reaching proposal, outlining in detail many of the steps that should be taken to structure a "more balanced, open and democratic trade policy development process in the United States." The NGOs prefaced their comments by framing the larger picture:

> The recent World Trade Organization (WTO) Ministerial meeting in Seattle demonstrated that public confidence in international trade rules and institutions is eroding. Increasingly, average citizens do not feel that trade rules and institutions incorporate the full breadth and diversity of their values. The process by which trade policy is hindered by its lack of inclusiveness, balance and input from a broad range of civil society. As trade liberalization has grown beyond a traditional focus on tariff reduction, trade negotiations have increasingly addressed a widening range of issues, many of which deeply affect environmental and social values. Regrettably, the trade policy development process in the United States has not kept pace with this expansion and remains narrowly structured towards serving primarily commercial interests, with little regard for environmental or social issues.

The groups welcomed Executive Order 13,141 on Environmental Reviews but had reservations about its scope and implementation:

> Robust implementation of 13,141 should be an immediate objective of United States trade policy reform.... In his public remarks at the announcement of the E.O., Vice President Gore promised that the Order will "revolutionize the way the environment is dealt with in all future trade talks." The President's statement on the same day noted that E.O. 13,141 is meant to "to fully integrate environmental considerations into the development of U.S. positions in trade negotiations." * * *

> The critical question surrounding implementation of E.O. 13,141—and surrounding efforts to reform the mechanisms for making trade policy generally—is whether the result will be the proactive integration of significant environmental considerations into trade policies, or merely the gilding of conventional trade policies with de minimis environmental palliatives.

AMERICAN LANDS, ET AL., COMMENTS TO USTR (July 10, 2000).

5. In 2002, a team of economists and policy experts at Tuft University's Global Development and Environment Institute critiqued environmental assessment of trade in North America. After identifying several weaknesses in current assessment methodologies, the group proposed four recommendations for improving environmental reviews, including broadening the scope of environmental reviews to include areas such as the compositional and scale impacts of foreign direct investment, expanding the set of methodologies used to estimate economic impacts, increasing the number of environmental variables assessed, and enhancing existing levels of inter-governmental and public participation. Kevin Gallagher, Frank Ackerman & Luke Ney, *Economic Analysis in Environmental Reviews of Trade Agreements: Assessing the North American Experience*, GLOBAL DEV. & ENVTL INST. (Working Paper No. 02-01, Apr. 2002).

From what you have seen so far, are Executive Order 13,141 and similar efforts in other countries "revolutionizing" trade policy formulation, or do they appear to be the palliative some NGOs feared?

IV. New Frontiers in Public Participation: The Aarhus Convention

As we have seen, public participation and trade are cross-cutting issues that sometimes intersect in unforeseen ways in unconventional venues. Trade and environment issues may creep into state, provincial, or local fora as local governments consider measures dealing with waste, wildlife, land use, labeling, or investments. Trade issues also can surface in public participation mechanisms concerning a wide range of national issues such as organic farming standards, animal welfare regulations, and state renewable energy portfolios. Indeed, given the reach of our multilateral trade and investment rules and the increasing interdependencies of our economies, it is virtually impossible to predict the ways in which the public may suddenly find itself considering an important trade or investment related question. For that reason, the procedures and processes available to ensure transparency and openness in government decisionmaking and by international organizations are exceedingly important.

Much of this chapter has focused on the legal tools available to U.S. citizens to gain access to information and participate in policy making and dispute resolution in the trade arena. Key features of NEPA, FOIA, FACA, and the APA—the alphabet soup of U.S. legal devices employed to pry open government—are now rolled into one in a groundbreaking international agreement, the United Nations Economic Commission for Europe (UN/ECE) Convention on Access to Information, Public Participation in Decision-making and Access to Justice in Environmental Matters, more commonly called the Aarhus Convention. Hailed by UN Secretary-General Kofi Annan as "the most ambitious venture in environmental democracy undertaken under the auspices of the United Nations," the Aarhus Convention seeks to guarantee environmental procedural rights by ensuring public access to information, participation, and justice in environmental matters. Vera Rodenhoff, *The Aarhus Convention and its Implications for the 'Institutions' of the European Union,* 11 RECIEL 343 (2002). The Aarhus Convention was adopted at Aarhus, Denmark on June 25, 1998, and entered into force Oct 30, 2001. http://www.unece.org/env/pp/documents/cep43e.pdf. As of January 2010, 44 European and Central Asian countries, from Norway and Portugal to Tajikistan and Kyrgyzstan, are parties to the Convention.

The Aarhus Convention requires public authorities to gather and make public broad categories of environmental information, including proposed and existing activities that affect the environment. They must also regularly prepare state of the environment reports. Moreover, in 2003 the parties to the Aarhus Convention agreed on the Kiev Protocol on Pollutant Release and Transfer Registries, obligating a systematic approach to the collection and publication of data on sources of a wide variety of pollutants, including carbon dioxide. This protocol entered into force on October 9, 2009, and has 23 Parties as of early 2010. The Convention also commits its signatories to involve the public in decisionmaking for areas of environmental importance, and to take public input into account in decisionmaking. Finally, several provisions of the Aarhus Convention broaden and assure access to justice for citizens and nongovernmental organizations for environmental matters, as one of the Convention's most studious observers, Svitlana Kravchenko, notes below.

Svitlana Kravchenko, *Promoting Public Participation in Europe and Central Asia*

The New Public: the Globalization of Public Participation
95, 99, 101–102 (Carl Bruch ed., 2002)

The Aarhus Convention has the potential to bring about major changes in the way democracy is practiced in Europe and Central Asia. The Convention requires public participation in governmental decision-making far beyond previous practices and legislation in the region, particularly regarding specific development projects. * * *

The Aarhus Convention provides for access to justice in three circumstances: (1) for violations of national environmental laws, (2) if a request for information under Article 4 is improperly denied, and (3) to review any act or omission relating to public participation under Article 6, or other Articles if a party decides to do so.

A. Redressing Environmental Violations

Article 9.3 of the Aarhus Convention requires parties to the Convention to provide "administrative or judicial review" procedures for "members of the public" who meet the criteria, if any, in national law, to challenge "acts and omissions by private persons and public authorities which contravene provisions of national law relating to the environment." This article provides for enforcement by the public against private entities, such as polluting companies or developers, and also for remedies against governmental bodies that violate the law.

Members of the public may seek access to justice under the Convention against private persons, including corporations, which are "legal persons" under the law.

The public may also seek access to justice against public authorities. This provision potentially includes both public enforcement authorities, such as a Ministry of Justice or local prosecutors who fail to enforce the environmental laws, and also other public authorities, whether or not environmental, such as a forestry department, Ministry of Transportation, or local housing authority, that act contrary to the national environmental law or fail to fulfill required duties.

Members of the public may be provided with direct or indirect enforcement. Article 9.3 states that a party to the Convention may provide judicial review (in which members of the public can file lawsuits themselves in the court system) or administrative review (in which members of the public can formally invoke administrative procedures to stimulate public enforcement authorities to take action against the private persons or public authorities). * * *

B. Ensuring Access to Information

Article 9.1 of the Aarhus Convention allows access to a court of law or another independent and impartial body established by law if a request for information under Article 4 has been ignored, wrongfully refused, or inadequately answered. Final decisions by the court or independent body "shall be binding on the public authority holding the information." Since "any person" has this right of access injustice under Article 9.1, no test of the legitimacy of a person's interest can be imposed. In fact, even citizens or residents of another country can seek information-access to justice to enforce their right to information-under Article 3.9 of the Convention. * * *

C. Guaranteeing Public Participation

Article 9.2 provides access to justice to "members of the public concerned" to challenge the substantive and procedural legality of any decision, act, or omission subject to the provisions of Article 6 (public participation in decision-making regarding specific activities). Decisions, acts, or omissions subject to Article 7 (plans, programs, and policies) or Article 8 (executive regulations) can also be challenged if "so provided for under national law."* * *

Furthermore, "NGO standing" is explicitly provided in Article 9.2. Article 9.2 provides that "the interest of any non-governmental organization" that meets the requirements of Article 2.5 of the Convention (those "promoting environmental protection") "shall be deemed sufficient." Such NGOs are also deemed to have "rights capable of being impaired" in a legal system that requires an impairment of a right to seek judicial redress.

D. Conditions to Enable Access to Justice

Article 9.4 imposes general requirements applicable to all categories of access injustice, A review procedure should be "fair, equitable, timely, and not prohibitively expensive." A fair review procedure means a process that is impartial and free of prejudice. Article 3.9 separately requires that access to justice be made available "without discrimination as to citizenship, nationality or domicile." * * *

Access must also be effective. Article 9.4 states that remedies must be "adequate and effective," and include "injunctive relief as appropriate." This is significant, as injunctive remedies have traditionally not been as available in Europe as in some other parts of the world.

In addition, the Aarhus Convention provides that "Each party shall ensure that persons exercising their rights in conformity with the provisions of this Convention shall not be penalized, persecuted, or harassed in any way for their involvement." This is a significant protection for freedom of speech and advocacy.

Public participation is becoming part of the political landscape in the UN/ECE region. The Aarhus Convention has given people a voice.... Its adoption is a remarkable step forward in the development of international law as it relates to participatory democracy and citizens' environmental rights.

Like the U.S. laws discussed in this chapter, the Aarhus Convention provides a foothold for groups and citizens to gain access and participate in many kinds of trade-related matters. Annex I of the Aarhus Convention establishes procedures for public participation in 20 categories of activities with obvious links to trade, such as mining, the chemical industry, the energy sector, production and processing of metals, waste management, and industrial plants. Article 5.8 of the Convention calls on Parties to ensure that consumer information on products is provided to allow consumers to make "informed environmental choices" and Article 5.6 requires Parties to "encourage operators whose activities have a significant impact on the environment to inform the public regularly of the environmental impact of their activities and products, where appropriate within the framework of voluntary eco-labeling or eco-auditing schemes or by other means." As we have seen, many of the areas within the ambit of the Aarhus Convention are also the source of contentious trade and environment disputes in other fora.

The EU, which became a party to the Aarhus Convention in its own right through Council Decision 2005/370/EC, has adopted legislation to implement the Convention as a matter of EU law. Directive 2003/35/EC applies the Convention to Member States, and amends earlier directives on environmental impact assessment and on integrated pollution prevention and control to introduce the transparency and procedural elements of the Aarhus Convention into the administration of those programs by the Member States. Furthermore, Regulation 1367/2006 applies the Aarhus Convention requirements directly to the work of all EU institutions. The only ambiguous element is the handling of the sensitive issue of access to justice, in particular the question of who has standing to be a litigant in national courts. While explicitly asserting that NGOs must be given the same access to justice rights as individuals, Directive 2003/35/EC leaves it to each Member State to determine its own general principles and rules on the standing requirements for access to national courts.

Questions and Discussion

1. Review Article 11 of the Treaty on the Functioning of the European Union, quoted in Questions and Discussion on page 874. Consider how the implementation of the Con-

vention throughout the EU might help "operationalize" the pursuit of sustainable development in Article 11. If all NAFTA countries also signed and ratified the Aarhus Convention, would NAFTA's preambular commitment to sustainable development take on new meaning?

2. Another international agreement, known commonly as the "Espoo Convention," further amplifies environmental procedural rights by promoting access to information and public participation concerning the preparation of environmental impact assessments in a transboundary context. UN/ECE Convention on Environmental Impact Assessment in a Transboundary Context, Feb. 5, 1991, 30 I.L.M. 800. The Espoo Convention is open to UN/ECE member states and the EU, including Canada and the United States. The United States has signed but not ratified the Espoo Convention. Canada has signed and ratified this Convention, but entered a reservation limiting coverage to environmental impact assessment under federal jurisdiction. Under the North American Agreement on Environmental Cooperation, Mexico, the United States, and Canada pursued negotiation of an accord on transboundary environmental impact assessment, even publishing a draft agreement in 1997. Since then, however, negotiations have floundered, largely on grounds of reciprocity asserted by Mexico, which objected to the narrow scope of the proposed accord. (As in the Espoo Convention, the United States limited covered activities to those subject to NEPA or other federal laws requiring the functional equivalent, leaving out all nonfederal projects in the border regions.) *See* John H. Knox, *The Myth and Reality of Transboundary Environmental Impact Assessment*, 96 Am. J. Int'l L. 291 (2002). In the absence of a formal agreement, transboundary environmental impact assessment is practiced on an *ad hoc* basis in North America, with more routine application of the practice between Canada and the United States.

Selected Bibliography

We are indebted to the many authors and publishers for writing interesting and provocative articles that contribute to this book. We are especially grateful to those authors and publishers for permission to reprint materials used in this book.

The 2002 Environmental Sustainability Index 1, 14–17, *available at* http://www.ciesin. columbia.edu/indicators/ESI.

25TH ANNUAL REPORT FROM THE COMMISSION ON MONITORING THE APPLICATION OF COMMUNITY LAW (2007) COM (2008) 777 final.

Ackerman, Bruce & David Golove, *Is NAFTA Constitutional?* 108 HARVARD L. REV. 799 (1995).

Adelman, David E & John H. Barton, *Environmental Regulation for Agriculture: Towards a Framework to Promote Sustainable Intensive Agriculture,* 21 STAN. ENVTL. L.J. 3 (2002). Reprinted with permission of Stanford Environmental Law Journal.

Alanis-Ortega, Gustavo & Ana Karina Gonzalez-Lutzenkirchen, *No Room for the Environment: The NAFTA Negotiations and the Mexican Perspective on Trade and Environment, in* GREENING THE AMERICAS: NAFTA's LESSONS FOR HEMISPHERIC TRADE (Carolyn L. Deere & Daniel. C. Esty eds., 2002).

ALONSO, ALFONSO ET AL., BIODIVERSITY: CONNECTING WITH THE TAPESTRY OF LIFE (Alfonso Alonso et al., eds. 2001), *available at* http://www.nrcs.usda.gov/technical/ECS/ wildlife/primermedres.pdf.

AMBROSI, PHILLIPE & KARAN CAPOOR, STATE AND TRENDS OF THE CARBON MARKET 2009 (2009).

AMERICAN LANDS ET AL., COMMENTS TO USTR (July 10, 2000), *available at* http://www. consumerscouncil.org/trade/ustr71000.htm.

Anderson, Kym et al., *Distortions to World Trade: Impacts on Agricultural Markets and Farm Incomes,* 28 REVIEW OF AGRICULTURAL ECONOMICS (2006).

Anhang, Jeff & Robert Goodland, *Livestock and Climate Change,* WORLD WATCH (Nov./Dec. 2009).

ANSI EXECUTIVE STANDARDS COUNCIL, ANSI PROCEDURES FOR U.S. PARTICIPATION IN THE INTERNATIONAL STANDARDS ACTIVITIES OF ISO (Jan. 2004), *available at* http://publicaa. ansi.org/sites/apdl/isodocs/ANSI_Procedures_for_US_Participation_in_ the_International_Standards_Activities_of_ISO_2004_edition.doc.

Appleton, Arthur E., *Environmental Labelling Schemes Revisited: WTO Law and Developing Country Implications, in* TRADE, ENVIRONMENT, AND THE MILLENNIUM (Gary P. Sampson & W. Brandee Chambers eds., 2d ed. 2002). Reprinted with permission of United Nations University, United Nations University Press.

Article 15(1) Notification to Council that Development of Factual Record Is Warranted (Migratory Birds), A14/SEM/99-002/11/ADV, at 8–10, 25–27 (Dec. 15, 2000).

AUDLEY, JOHN J., GREEN POLITICS AND GLOBAL TRADE: NAFTA AND THE FUTURE OF ENVIRONMENTAL POLITICS 69 (Barry Rabe & John Tierney eds., 1997).

AUDLEY, JOHN, ISSUE BRIEF: OPPORTUNITIES AND CHALLENGES TO ADVANCE ENVIRONMENTAL PROTECTION IN THE U.S.-CENTRAL AMERICAN FREE TRADE NEGOTIATIONS (Carnegie Endowment for International Peace Feb. 2003), *available at* http://www.ceip.org/files/ pdf/TED-CAFTA-and-environment.pdf.

Australia, CoP12 Prop.39, Proposal to the Twelfth Conference of the Parties to Convention on International Trade in Endangered Species of Wild Fauna and Flora (CITES).

Australia's Quarantine and Inspection Service, Import Case Details—Public Listing, Condition C8592 (June 4, 2010).

Avery, Natalie, *Diet for a Corporate Planet: Industry Sets World Food Standards, available at* http://multinationalmonitor.org/hyper/issues/1993/08/mm0893_07.html (citing NATALIE AVERY ET AL., CRACKING THE CODEX: AN ANALYSIS OF WHO SETS WORLD STANDARDS (1993)).

Bacchus, James, *Open Up the WTO*, WASH. POST, Feb. 20, 2004, at A25.

Bamako Convention, Jan. 30, 1991, 30 I.L.M. 775 (1991) (entered into force Apr. 22, 1998).

Barbier, E.B., *The Environmental Effects of Trade in the Forestry Sector, in* OECD, THE ENVIRONMENTAL EFFECTS OF TRADE (1994).

Barg, Stephan et al., *A Sustainable Development Framework for Assessing the Benefits of Subsidy Reform, in* OECD, SUBSIDY REFORM AND SUSTAINABLE DEVELOPMENT: POLITICAL ECONOMY ASPECTS (2007).

Barker T. et al., *Technical Summary, in* CLIMATE CHANGE 2007: MITIGATION: CONTRIBUTION OF WORKING GROUP III TO THE FOURTH ASSESSMENT REPORT OF THE INTERGOVERNMENTAL PANEL ON CLIMATE CHANGE (B. Metz et al. eds., 2007).

Basel Convention, Mar. 22, 1989, 31 I.L.M. 657 (1989) (entered into force May 5, 1992).

Basse, Ellen Margrethe & Sanford E. Gaines, *How Thinking About Trade Can Improve Environmental Performance: Trade Issues in Environmental Labelling Systems*, 8 ENVTL. LIABILITY 71 (2000).

Beardsley, Eleanor, *In Europe, A Cow over Hormone-Treated U.S. Beef* (National Public Radio broadcast Sept. 29, 2009).

Beattie, Alan, *From a Trickle to a Flood: How Lawsuits Are Coming to Dictate the Terms of Trade*, FINANCIAL TIMES, Mar. 20, 2007.

BEAULIEU, ANDRE & PIERRE MARC JOHNSON, THE ENVIRONMENT AND NAFTA (1996).

BECC-NADB JOINT STATUS REPORT, Dec. 31, 2003, *at* http://www.cocef.org.

Becker, Elizabeth, *U.S. Subsidizes Companies to Buy Subsidized Cotton*, N.Y. TIMES, Nov. 4, 2003.

Bellman, Christophe et al., *Recent Trends in World Trade and International Negotiations*, REVUE INTERNATIONALE DE POLITIQUE DE DÉVELOPPEMENT (2010).

Benitah, Marc, *Ongoing WTO Negotiations on Fisheries Subsidies*, ASIL INSIGHTS (June 2004), *available at* http://www.asil.org/insights/insigh136.htm. Reproduced with permission from, ASIL Insights (2004) © The American Society of International Law.

BERRY, WENDELL,*Two Economies, in* HOME ECONOMICS (1987).

Bhaduri, Amit, *Nationalism and Economic Policy in the Era of Globalization, in* GOVERNING GLOBALIZATION: ISSUES AND INSTITUTIONS (Deepak Nayyar ed., 2002).

Bhagwati, Jagdish, *The Case for Free Trade,* 269 SCIENTIFIC AMERICAN 42 (Nov. 1993). Copyright © 1993 by Scientific American, Inc. All rights reserved.

Bhagwati, Jagdish, *Trade Liberalisation and "Fair Trade" Demands: Addressing the Environmental and Labour Standards Issues,* 18 THE WORLD ECONOMY 745 (1995). Reprinted with permission of the original publishers: Blackwell Publishing Ltd.

Bhagwati, Jagdish, *Trade and Environment: The False Conflict?, in* TRADE AND THE ENVIRONMENT: LAW ECONOMICS, AND POLICY (Durwood Zaelke et al. eds., 1993). From Trade and the Environment by Durwood Zaelke, et al., eds. Copyright © 1993 by Island Press. Reproduced by permission of Island Press, Washington, D.C.

BHALA, RAJ, INTERNATIONAL TRADE LAW: INTERDISCIPLINARY THEORY AND PRACTICE (3d ed. 2008).

Bhala, Raj, *The Myth about Stare Decisis and International Trade Law (Part One of a Trilogy),* 14AM. U. INT'L L. REV. 845 (1999).

Bhala, Raj, *The Precedent Setters: De Facto Stare Decisis in WTO Adjudication (Part Two of a Trilogy)* 9 J. TRANSNAT'L L. & POL'Y 1 (1999).

Bhala, Raj, *The Power of the Past: Towards De Jure Stare Decisis in WTO Adjudication (Part Three of a Trilogy),* 33 GEO. WASH. L. REV. 873 (2001).

BHALA, RAJ & KEVIN KENNEDY, WORLD TRADE LAW (1998). Reprinted from World Trade Law with permission. Copyright 1998 Matthew Bender & Company, Inc. a member of the LexisNexis Group. All rights reserved.

Bhutani, Shalini & Ashish Kothari, *Rio's Decade: Reassessing the 1992 Earth Summit: Reassessing the 1992 Biodiversity Convention: The Biodiversity Rights of Developing Nations: A Perspective from India,* 32 GOLDEN GATE U. L. REV. 587 (2002).

BIRNIE, PATRICIA W. & ALAN E. BOYLE, INTERNATIONAL LAW AND THE ENVIRONMENT (2002).

BIRNIE, PATRICIA, ALAN BOYLE, & CATHERINE REDGWELL, INTERNATIONAL LAW AND THE ENVIRONMENT (3d ed. 2009).

Block, Greg M., *Trade and Environment in the Western Hemisphere: Expanding the North American Agreement on Environmental Cooperation into the Americas,* 33 ENVTL. L. 501 (2003) (excerpt reprinted with permission of Environmental Law, Lewis & Clark Law School).

Borgen, Christopher J., *Resolving Treaty Conflicts,* 37 GEORGE WASH. INT'L L. REV. 573 (2005).

Bourgeois, Jacques H.J., *External Relations Powers of the European Community,* 22 FORDHAM INT'L L.J. 149 (1999).

BRACK, DUNCAN & KEVIN GRAY, INT'L INST. FOR SUSTAINABLE DEVELOPMENT REPORT, MULTILATERAL ENVIRONMENTAL AGREEMENTS AND THE WTO (Sept. 2003).

Brazil, China, India, Communication from Brazil, China, India, and Mexico, Fisheries Subsidies: Special and Different Treatment, TN/RL/GEN/163 (Feb. 11, 2010).

BROWNLIE, IAN, PRINCIPLES OF PUBLIC INTERNATIONAL LAW (5th ed. 1998).

Calbreath, Dean, SAN DIEGO UNION-TRIBUNE (Aug. 30, 2009).

Canada-Committee on Technical Barriers to Trade, G/TBT/W/21, WT/CTE/W/21 (Feb. 21, 1996).

CATCHING MORE BAIT: A BOTTOM-UP RE-ESTIMATION OF GLOBAL FISHERIES SUBSIDIES, 14 Fisheries Centre Research Reports No. 6 (Ussif Rashid Sumaila & Daniel Pauly eds. 2007).

CEC, CONTINENTAL POLLUTANT PATHWAYS: AN AGENDA FOR COOPERATION TO ADDRESS LONG-RANGE TRANSPORT OF AIR POLLUTION IN NORTH AMERICA (1997).

CEC, ENVIRONMENTAL CHALLENGES AND OPPORTUNITIES OF THE EVOLVING NORTH AMERICAN ELECTRICITY MARKET (June 2002).

CEC, MAIZE AND BIODIVERSITY: THE EFFECTS OF TRANSGENIC MAIZE IN MEXICO (2004).

CEC, *NAFTA's Institutions: The Environmental Potential and Performance of the NAFTA Free Trade Commission and Related Bodies*, ENVIRONMENT AND TRADE SERIES No. 5 (1997).

CEC, RIBBON OF LIFE: AN AGENDA FOR PRESERVING TRANSBOUNDARY MIGRATORY BIRD HABITAT ON THE UPPER SAN PEDRO RIVER (1999).

CEC, *Sustaining and Enhancing Riparian Migratory Bird Habitat on the Upper San Pedro River: Final Draft from the San Pedro Expert Study Team, in* RIBBON OF LIFE, Attachment 1 (1999).

CEC SECRETARIAT, REPORT ON THE DEATH OF MIGRATORY BIRDS AT THE SILVA RESERVOIR (1995).

Charnovitz, Steve, *An Analysis of Pascal Lamy's Proposal on Collective Preferences*, 8 J. INT'L ECON. L. 449 (2005).

Charnovitz, Steve, *Environment and Health under WTO Dispute Settlement*, 32 INT'L LAW. 901 (1998).

Charnovitz, Steve, *Environmental Harmonization and Trade Policy, in* TRADE AND THE ENVIRONMENT: LAW, ECONOMICS, AND POLICY (Durwood Zaelke et al., eds. 1993).

Charnovitz, Steve, *Environmental Trade Sanctions and the GATT: An Analysis of the Pelly Amendment on Foreign Environmental Practices*, 9 AM. U. J. INT'L L. & POL'Y 751 (1994).

Charnovitz, Steve, *Exploring the Environmental Exceptions in GATT Article XX*, 25 J. WORLD TRADE (1991).

Charnovitz, Steve, *Free Trade, Fair Trade, Green Trade: Defogging the Debate*, 27 CORNELL I. L. J. 459 (1994). Reprinted with permission of Cornell International Law Journal.

Charnovitz, Steve, *Improving the Agreement on Sanitary and Phytosanitary Standards, in* TRADE, ENVIRONMENT, AND THE MILLENNIUM (Gary P. Sampson & W. Bradnee Chambers eds., 2d ed. 2002). Ch. 7

Charnovitz, Steve, *The Law of Environmental "PPMs" in the WTO: Debunking the Myth of Illegality*, 27 YALE J. INT'L L. 59 (2002).

Chen, Jim, *Diversity and Deadlock: Transcending Conventional Wisdom on the Relationship Between Biological Diversity and Intellectual Property*, 31 ENVTL. L. REP. 10625 (2001).

CHENG, B., GENERAL PRINCIPLES OF LAW AS APPLIED BY INTERNATIONAL COURTS AND TRIBUNALS (1953).

CHOI, WON-MOG, LIKE PRODUCTS IN INTERNATIONAL TRADE LAW: TOWARDS A CONSISTENT GATT/WTO JURISPRUDENCE (2003).

Cline, William R., *Global Agricultural Free Trade Would Benefit, Not Harm, LDCs*, FINANCIAL TIMES, Aug. 9, 2004.

Cobb, Clifford et al.,WHY BIGGER ISN'T BETTER, THE GENUINE PROGRESS INDICATOR, (Redefining Progress, Nov. 1999).

Codex Alimentarius Commission, *Codex Principles and Guidelines on Food Derived From Biotechnology* (2003) (Codex *GMO Principles*).

Codex Alimentarius Commission, *Guidelines for the Production, Processing, Labelling and Marketing of Organically Produced Food*, GL 32-1999, Rev. 1-2001 (last amended in 2009).

CODEX ALIMENTARIUS COMMISSION, REPORT OF THE THIRTIETH SESSION OF THE CODEX COMMITTEE ON FOOD LABELLING, May 6–10, 2002, ALINORM 03/22.

CODEX ALIMENTARIUS COMMISSION, REPORT OF THE THIRTY-EIGHTH SESSION OF THE CODEX COMMITTEE ON FOOD LABELLING, ALINORM 10/03/22 (May 3–7, 2010).

Codex Alimentarius Commission, *Understanding the Codex Alimentarius: The Codex System: FAO, WHO and the Codex Alimentarius Commission*—The Commission's Operations (2004), *available at* http://www.fao.org/docrep/w9114e/W9114e04.htm #TopOfPage.

COLBORN, THEO ET AL., OUR STOLEN FUTURE (1996).

Colombia, *Environmental Labels and Market Access: Case Study on the Colombian Flower-Growing Industry*, WT/CTE/W/76, G/TBT/W/60 (Mar. 9, 1998).

Committee on Sanitary and Phytosanitary Measures, *Clarification of Paragraph 7 of the Decision on Equivalence*, G/SPS/W/128/Rev.2 (June 10, 2003).

Committee on Sanitary and Phytosanitary Measures, *Decision on the Implementation of Article 4 of the Agreement on the Application of Sanitary and Phytosanitary Measures*, G/SPS/19 (Sept. 26, 2001).

Committee on Technical Barriers to Trade, *First Triennial Review of the Operation and Implementation of the Agreement on Technical Barriers to Trade*, G/TBT/5 (Nov. 5, 1997).

Committee on Trade and Environment, *Compliance and Dispute Settlement Provisions in the WTO and in Multilateral Environmental Agreements*, Note by the WTO and UNEP Secretariats, WT/CTE/W/191 (June 6, 2001).

Convention on Biological Diversity, signed June 5, 1992, entered into force Dec. 29, 1993, *reprinted in* 31 I.L.M. 818 (1992).

COOK, GARY ET AL., APPLYING TRADE RULES TO TIMBER ECOLABELING: A REVIEW OF TIMBER ECOLABELING INITIATIVES AND THE WTO AGREEMENT ON TECHNICAL BARRIERS TO TRADE (CIEL Discussion Draft, Feb. 1997) (excerpts reprinted with permission of the Center for International Environmental Law).

Copeland, Brian R. & M. Scott Taylor, *Trade, Growth, and the Environment*, 42 J. ECON. LIT. 7 (2004).

CORDEN, W. M., TRADE POLICY AND ECONOMIC WELFARE (2d ed. 1997).

Cosbey, Aaron et al., Investment and Sustainable Development: A Guide to the Use and Potential of International Investment Agreements 3 (International Institute for Sustainable Development 2004) (excerpts reprinted with permission of the (International Institute for Sustainable Development).

Costanza, Robert et al., An Introduction to Ecological Economics (1997) (reprinted with permission. Copyright CRC Press, Boca Raton, Florida).

Council Directive (EC) No. 2009/142, Relating to Appliances Burning Gaseous Fuels, 2009 O.J. (L330/10).

Daly, Herman E., *Problems with Free Trade: Neoclassical and Steady-State Perspectives, in* Trade and the Environment: Law, Economics, and Policy (Durwood Zaelke et al. eds., 1993).

Daly, Herman, *Sustainable Growth: An Impossibility Theorem, in* Valuing the Earth: Economics, Ecology, Ethics (Herman E. Daly & Kenneth N. Townsend eds., 1993).

Daly, Matthew, *Northwest Timber Firm Backs Idea of Tariff Cuts*, Oregonian, June 12, 2004.

Davies, R.W.D. et al., *Defining and Estimating Global Marine Fisheries Bycatch*, 33 Marine Policy 661 (2009).

Dawkins, Kristin, *Biotech—From Seattle to Montreal and Beyond, The Battle Royale of the 21st Century*, Seedling, Mar. 2000, *at* http://www.biotechinfo.net/montreal_ beyond.html.

Deere, Carolyn L. & Daniel C. Esty, *Trade and the Environment in the Americas: Overview of Key Issues, in* Greening the Americas: NAFTA's Lessons for Hemispheric Trade (Carolyn L. Deere & Daniel C. Esty eds., 2002).

Demaret, Paul & Raoul Stewardson, *Border Tax Adjustments under GATT and EC Law and General Implications for Environmental Taxes*, 28 J. World Trade 5 (1994).

Demeter Association, Inc., Biodynamic Farm Standard (Mar. 18, 2010), http://demeter-usa.org/files/DemeterFarmStandardsm2.pdf.

Department of Foreign Affairs and International Trade, Cabinet Directive on the Environmental Assessment of Policy, Plan and Program Proposals and the Framework for Environmental Assessment of Trade Negotiations (Feb. 2001) ("the Framework"), *available at* .

Dernbach, John C., *Sustainable Development: Now More Than Ever*, 32 Envtl. L. Rep. 10003 (2002).

Developing Countries Block Extension of Green Subsidies Rules, Inside U.S. Trade, Dec. 24, 1999.

DiMascio, Nicholas & Joost Pauwelyn, *Nondiscrimination in Trade and Investment Treaties: Worlds Apart or Two Sides of the Same Coin?*, 102 Am. J. Int'l L. 48 (2008).

Downes, David, *The New Diplomacy for the Biodiversity Trade: Biodiversity, Biotechnology, and Intellectual Property in the Convention on Biological Diversity*, 4 Touro J. Transnt'l L. 1 (1993).

Downes, David R. & Brennan Van Dyke, Fisheries Conservation and Trade Rules (1998).

Draft Consolidated Chair Texts of the AD and SCM Agreements, TN/RL/W/213 (Nov. 30, 2007).

Driesen, David, *What is Free Trade?: The Real Issue Lurking Behind the Trade and Environment Debate*, 41 Va. J. Int'l L. 279 (2001).

Dunne, Matthew S., III, *Redefining Power Orientation: A Reassessment of Jackson's Paradigm in Light of Asymmetries of Power, Negotiation, and Compliance in the GATT/WTO Dispute Settlement System*, 34 Law & Pol'y Int'l Bus. 277 (2002).

Dunoff, Jeffrey L., *Border Patrol at the World Trade Organization*, 9 Y.B. Int'l Envtl. L. 21 (1998).

Dunoff, Jeffrey L., *Institutional Misfits: The GATT, the ICJ & Trade-Environment Disputes*, 15 Mich. J. Int'l L. 1043 (1994).

Dunoff, Jeffrey L., *Rethinking International Trade*, 19 U. Pa. J. Int'l Econ. L. 347 (1998).

Durning, Alan, How Much Is Enough? (1992).

Earth Island Institute, *ETP Bycatch Issue Misused By Opponents of Dolphin-Safe Fishing*, *available at* http://www.earthisland.org/immp/archive_dolphin7.htm.

Ehlermann, Claus-Dieter, *Six Years on the Bench of the "World Trade Court": Some Personal Experiences as Member of the Appellate Body of the World Trade Organization*, 36 J. World Trade 605 (2002). Reprinted with permission from Kluwer Law International © 2002, www.kluwerlaw.com.

Ekins, Paul, *The Sustainable Consumer Society: A Contradiction in Terms?*, 3 Int'l Envtl. Affairs 242 (1991).

Energy Subsidies: Getting the Prices Right, International Energy Agency (June 7, 2010), *available at* www.iea.org/files/energy_subsidies.pdf.

Epps, Tracey, International Trade and Health Protection: A Critical Assessment of the WTO's SPS Agreement (2008).

Erling, Uwe M., *Approaches to Integrated Pollution Control in the United States and the European Union*, 15 Tul. Envtl. L.J. 1 (2001).

Esty, Daniel C., Greening the GATT: Trade, environment, and the Future (1994). Copyright 1994 by Inst. for Int'l Economics. Reproduced with Permission of Inst. for Int'l Economics in the format Textbook via Copyright Clearance Center.

Esty, Daniel C., *A Term's Limits*, Foreign Policy No. 126 (Sept.–Oct. 2001).

Esty, Daniel C. & Damien Geradin, *Market Access, Competitiveness, and Harmonization: Environmental Protection in Regional Trade Agreements*, 21 Harv. Envtl. L. Rev. 265 (1997) © 1997 by The President and Fellows of Harvard College and The Harvard Environmental Law Review.

Esty, Daniel C. & Maria H. Ivanova, Global Environmental Governance: Options and Opportunities (2002).

European Commission, Communication from the Commission to the Council and the European Parliament: Enhancing the Implementation of the New Approach Directives (May 7, 2003).

European Commission, Guide to the Implementation of Directives Based on the New Approach and the Global Approach (2000), *available at* http://europa.eu.int/comm/enterprise/newapproach/legislation/guide/document/1999_1282_en.pdf.

European Commission, *The IPPC Directive*, *available at* http://europa.eu.int/comm/environment/ippc/index.htm.

European Commission, Report to the Trade Barriers Regulation Committee: TBR Proceedings concerning Chilean Practices Affecting Transit of Swordfish in Chilean Ports (Mar. 1999).

European Commission, Seal Hunting, *available at* http://ec.europa.eu/environment/biodiversity/animal_welfare/seals/seal_hunting.htm. (2009).

European Integrated Pollution Prevention and Control Bureau, *at* http://eippcb.jrc.es.

Faeth, Paul, *Growing Green: Enhancing the Economic and Environmental Performance of U.S. Agriculture* (1995).

FAO, Guidelines for the Production, Processing, Labelling and Marketing of Organically Produced Food, GL 32-1999, Rev. 1-2001, *available at* www.fao.org/organicag/doc/glorganicfinal.doc.

FAO, The State of World Fisheries and Aquaculture 2008 (2009).

FAO, World Review of World Fisheries and Aquaculture (2008).

FAO Fisheries Department, *Discards in the World,* FAO Fisheries Technical Paper 470 (2005), *available at* ftp://ftp.fao.org/docrep/fao/008/y5936e/y5936e00.pdf.

FAO Fisheries Department, *Marine Fisheries and the Law of the Sea: A Decade of Change. Special chapter (revised) of The State of Food and Agriculture 1992,* FAO Fisheries Circular No. 853 (1993).

Farber, Daniel A. & Robert E. Hudec, *Free Trade and the Regulatory State: A GATT's-Eye View of the Dormant Commerce Clause,* 47 Vand. L. Rev. 1401 (1994).

Farber, Daniel A. & Robert E. Hudec, *GATT Legal Restraints on Domestic Environmental Regulations, in* 2 Fair Trade and Harmonization (eds. Jagdish Bhagwati & Robert E. Hudec, 1996).

Federal, State Environment Officials Discussing Ways to Amend Packaging Law, 20 Int'l. Envt. Rep. 1009 (Oct. 29, 1997).

Ferris, Jeffrey & Juha Siikamäki, Conservation Reserve Program and Wetland Reserve Program: Primary Land Retirement Programs for Promoting Farmland Conservation (Aug. 2009) (citing B.A. Babcock et al., *The Economic, Environmental, and Fiscal Impacts of a Targeted Renewal of Conservation Reserve Program Contracts* (Working paper 95-WP 129, 1995).

Final Pacific Coast (USA) Regional Forest Stewardship Standard Version 7.9. Approved by FSC-US Board, Aug. 12, 2002, Accredited by FSC International, July 26, 2003.

Forest Stewardship Council, Principles and Criteria for Forest Management.

Forest Stewardship Council–United States, Standards and Policies, http://www.fscus.org/standards_criteria.

Free Trade's Green Hurdles, The Economist (June 15, 1991).

French, Hilary F., *Assessing Private Capital Flows to Developing Countries, in* State of the World (Worldwatch Institute 1998). © 1998, www.worldwatch.org.

French, Hilary F., Costly Tradeoffs: Reconciling Trade and the Environment (1993).

Gabcikovo-Nagymoros Project (Hung. v. Slovk.), 1997 I.C.J. 3 (Sept 25, 1997).

Gaines, Sanford E., *Considering WTO Law in the Design of Climate Change Regimes beyond Kyoto,* 8 IOP Conf. Series: Earth and Environmental Science 012002 (2009).

Gaines, Sanford E., *Processes and Production Methods: How to Produce Sound Policy for Environmental PPM-based Trade Measures,* 27 Colum. J. Envtl. L. 383 (2002). Reprinted with permission of the Columbia Journal of Environmental Law.

Gaines, Sanford E., *Protecting Investors, Protecting the Environment: The Unexpected Story of NAFTA Chapter 11, in* Greening NAFTA: The North American Commission for Environmental Cooperation (David L. Markell & John H. Knox eds., 2003).

Gaines, Sanford E., *Rethinking Environmental Protection, Competitiveness, and International Trade,* 1997 U. Chi. Legal F. 231 (1997).

Gaines, Sanford E., *The WTO's Reading of the GATT Article XX Chapeau: A Disguised Restriction on Environmental Measures,* 22 U. Pa. J. Int'l Econ. L. 739 (2001) (reprinted with permission of the Pennsylvania Journal of International Economic Law).

Gallagher, Kevin P., *The CEC and Environmental Quality, in* Greening NAFTA: The North American Commission for Environmental Cooperation (David L. Markell & John H. Knox eds., 2003).

Gallagher, Kevin, Frank Ackerman, & Luke Ney, *Economic Analysis in Environmental Reviews of Trade Agreements: Assessing the North American Experience,* Global Dev. & Envtl Inst. (Working Paper No. 02-01, Apr. 2002).

Gantz, David, *Contrasting Key Investment Provisions of the NAFTA with the United States-Chile FTA, in* NAFTA Investment Law and Arbitration: Past Issues, Current Practice, Future Prospects (Todd Weiler ed., 2004). © 2004 by TRANSNATIONAL PUBS INC (NY). Reproduced with permission of TRANSNATIONAL PUBS INC (NY) in the format Textbook via Copyright Clearance Center.

Gantz, David A., *Government-to-Government Dispute Resolution Under NAFTA's Chapter 20: A Commentary on the Process,* 11 Am. Rev. Int'l Arb. 481 (2000).

Gantz, David, Regional Trade Agreements: Law, Policy and Practice (2009).

Gardner, Gary. *Roundwood Production Up, in* Worldwatch Institute Vital Signs 2007–2008 (2007), *available at* http://www.worldwatch.org/vs2007.

GATT Contracting Parties, Decision of November 28, 1979 on Differential and More Favourable Treatment, Reciprocity and Fuller Participation of Developing Countries, B.I.S.D, 26th Supp. 203 (1980).

GATT Secretariat, *The Results of the Uruguay Round of Multilateral Trade Negotiations* (Nov. 1994).

GATT Secretariat, Trade and the Environment, GATT Doc. GATT/1529 (Feb. 3, 1991).

General Council, *Procedures for the Appointment of Directors-General,* WT/L/509 (Jan. 20, 2003).

Gilpin, Robert, Global Political Economy: Understanding the International Economic Order (2001).

Global Ecolabelling Network, http://www.gen.gr.jp.

Goldberg, Donald L. et al., UNEP, *Effectiveness of Trade & Positive Measures in Multilateral Agreements: Lessons from the Montreal Protocol* (1997), *available at* www.ciel.org/Publications/EffectivenessofTradeandPosMeasures.pdf. Reprinted with permission of the Center for International Environmental Law.

Goldman, Patti, *The Democratization of the Development of United States Trade Policy,* 27 Cornell Int'l L.J. 631 (1994) (excerpt reprinted with permission of the Cornell International Law Journal).

Goodland, Robert & Herman Daly, *Environmental Sustainability: Universal and Non-Negotiable,* 6 Ecological Applications 1002 (1996).

GOODSTEIN, EBAN, THE TRADE-OFF MYTH (1999).

Gray, Kevin, *Brazil-Measures Affecting Imports of Retreaded Tyres*, 102 S.J.I.L. 610 (2008).

Greenery and Poverty, THE ECONOMIST (Sept. 18, 1993).

Griswold, Daniel T., *Trade, Labor, and the Environment: How Blue and Green Sanctions Threaten Higher Standards*, Cato Institute Trade Policy Analysis No. 15, Aug. 2, 2001.

GROSSMAN, GENE & ALAN KRUEGER, ENVIRONMENTAL IMPACTS OF A NORTH AMERICAN FREE TRADE AGREEMENT (1991).

Grynberg, Roman & Martin Tsamenyi, *Fisheries Subsidies, the WTO and the Pacific Island Tuna Fisheries*, 32 J. WORLD TRADE 127 (1998).

Haavelmo, Trygue & Stein Hansen, *On the Strategy of Trying to Reduce Economic Inequality by Expanding the Scale of Human Activity, in* ENVIRONMENTALLY SUSTAINABLE ECONOMIC DEVELOPMENT: BUILDING ON BRUNDTLAND (Robert Goodland et al. eds., World Bank 1991).

Harmonized Tariff Schedule of the United States (2010) (Rev. 1), HTS 6203.43.40; 6203.49.20, available at http://www.usitc.gov/tata/hts/bychapter/index.htm.

Harrop, Stuart R., *The Agreements on International Humane Trapping Standards: Background, Critique and the Texts*, 3 J. INT'L WILDLIFE L. & POL'Y 387 (1998).

Heilprin, John, *Wasted Bycatch Detailed in Study*, SEATTLE PI, Dec. 1, 2005, *available at* http://www.seattlepi.com/national/250412_fish01.html.

HERNÁNDEZ-TRUYOL, BERTA ESPERANZA & STEPHEN J. POWELL, JUST TRADE: A NEW COVENANT LINKING TRADE AND HUMAN RIGHTS (2009).

HODA, ANWARUL, TARIFF NEGOTIATIONS AND RENEGOTIATIONS UNDER THE GATT AND THE WTO: PROCEDURES AND PRACTICES (2001).

HOGENBOOM, BARBARA, MEXICO AND THE NAFTA ENVIRONMENT DEBATE: THE TRANSNATIONAL POLITICS OF ECONOMIC INTEGRATION (1998).

Horn, Henrik & Robert L. Howse, *European Communities-Measures Affecting the Approval and Marketing of Biotech Products*, 8 WORLD TRADE REV. No. 1 (2009).

HOUSER, TREVOR ET AL., LEVELING THE CARBON PLAYING FIELD (2008).

Housman, Robert F., *Democratizing International Trade Decision-making*, 27 CORNELL INT'L L.J. 699 (1994) (excerpt reprinted with permission).

Housman, Robert F., *The North American Free Trade Agreement's Lessons for Reconciling Trade and the Environment*, 30 STAN. J. INT'L L. 379 (1994).

Housman, Robert & Durwood Zaelke, *Mechanisms for Integration, in* THE USE OF TRADE MEASURES IN SELECT MULTILATERAL ENVIRONMENTAL AGREEMENTS (Robert Housman et al. eds., 1995).

Housman, Robert F. & Paul M. Orbuch, *Integrating Labor and Environmental Concerns Into the North American Free Trade Agreement: A Look Back and a Look Ahead*, 8 AM. U. J. INT'L L. & POL'Y 719 (1993).

Howse, Robert, *The Appellate Body Rulings in the* Shrimp/Turtle *Case: A New Legal Baseline for the Trade and Environment Debate*, 27 COLUM. J. ENVTL. L. 491 (2002).

Howse, Robert & Donald Regan, *The Product/Process Distinction—An Illusory Basis for Disciplining "Unilateralism" in Trade Policy*, 11 EUR. J. INT'L L. 249 (2000).

HUDEC, ROBERT, ENFORCING INTERNATIONAL TRADE LAW (1993) (excerpt reprinted with permission of the European Journal of International Law).

Hudec, Robert E., *Differences in National Environmental Standards: The Level-Playing-Field Dimension*, 5 MINN. J. GLOBAL TRADE 1 (1996).

Hudec, Robert E., *Science and "Post-Discriminatory" WTO Law*, 26 B.C. INT'L & COMP. L. REV. 185 (2003).

Hudec, Robert E., *GATT/WTO Constraints on National Regulation: Requiem for an "Aim and Effects" Test*, 32 INT'L LAW. 619 (1999). Copyright 1992 American Bar Association. All rights reserved. Reprinted with Permission.

HUDSON, STEWART, *Trade, Environment and the Pursuit of Sustainable Development, in* INTERNATIONAL TRADE AND THE ENVIRONMENT (Patrick Low ed., 1992). © 1992 by WORLD BANK. Reproduced with permission of WORLD BANK in the format textbook via Copyright Clearance Center.

HUNTER, DAVID, JAMES SALZMAN, & DURWOOD ZAELKE, INTERNATIONAL ENVIRONMENTAL LAW AND POLICY (2d. ed. 2002) (excerpts reprinted with permission of Foundation Press).

HUNTER, DAVID, JAMES SALZMAN, & DURWOOD ZAELKE, INTERNATIONAL ENVIRONMENTAL LAW AND POLICY (3d. ed. 2007).

ICCAT, Recommendation 07-10 on an ICCAT Bluefin Tuna Catch Documentation Program (2007).

ICSID News Release, Methanex v. United States of America (NAFTA/UNCITRAL Arbitration Rules Proceeding), (Jan. 30, 2004).

International Dolphin Conservation Program Act (IDCPA), Pub. L. No. 105-42, 111 Stat. 1122 (1997).

INTERNATIONAL ENERGY AGENCY, ENERGY SUBSIDY REFORM AND SUSTAINABLE DEVELOPMENT: CHALLENGES FOR POLICY MAKERS (2001).

International Environmental Law Project (IELP), Comment, Issues Relating to Articles 14 & 15 of the North American Commission on Environmental Cooperation (Oct. 2, 2003).

International Forum on Globalization, *at* www.ifg.org/wto.html.

INTERNATIONAL INSTITUTE FOR SUSTAINABLE DEVELOPMENT, AN ENVIRONMENTAL IMPACT ASSESSMENT OF CHINA'S WTO ACCESSION: AN ANALYSIS OF SIX SECTORS (2004).

International Law Commission, Fragmentation of International Law: Difficulties Arising from the Diversification and Expansion of International Law, U.N. Doc A/CN.4/L.682 (Apr. 13, 2006) (finalized by Martti Koskenniemi).

International Pollution Control and International Trade, GATT Studies in International Trade No. 1 (1971).

IPCC, WORKING GROUP II, IMPACTS, ADAPTATIONS & MITIGATION OF CLIMATE CHANGE (Third Assessment Report, 2001)

IPCC, WORKING GROUP III, ECONOMIC AND SOCIAL DIMENSIONS OF CLIMATE CHANGE (Third Assessment Report, 2001).

IPCC, WORKING GROUP III, CLIMATE CHANGE 2007 SYNTHESIS REPORT (Fourth Assessment Report, 2007).

IUCN, *Trade Measures in Multilateral Agreements: A Report on the Effectiveness of Trade Measures Contained in CITES* (1999).

JACKSON, JOHN, THE WORLD TRADING SYSTEM (MIT Press: 2d ed. 1997) (excerpts reprinted with permission of MIT Press).

JACKSON, JOHN H., THE WORLD TRADE ORGANIZATION: CONSTITUTION AND JURISPRUDENCE (1998).

Jackson, John H., *World Trade Rules and Environmental Policies: Congruence or Conflict?*, 49 WASH. & LEE L. REV. 1227 (1992).

JACKSON, JOHN H., WILLIAM J. DAVEY, & ALAN O. SYKES, JR., LEGAL PROBLEMS OF INTERNATIONAL ECONOMIC RELATIONS (4th ed. 2002).

Jans, Jan H., *EU Environmental Policy and the Civil Society, in* THE EUROPEAN CONVENTION AND THE FUTURE OF EUROPEAN ENVIRONMENTAL LAW (Prof. Jan H. Jans ed., 2003) (excerpt reprinted with permission of Europa Law Publishing & Jan Jans).

JANS, JAN H. & HANS H.B. VEDDER, EUROPEAN ENVIRONMENTAL LAW (3d ed. 2008).

Jenks, C. Wilfred, *The Conflict of Law-Making Treaties*, 30 BRIT. Y.B. INT'L L. 401 (1953).

Johnson, Pierre Marc, *Beyond Trade: The Case for a Broadened International Governance Agenda*, 1 POLICY MATTERS No. 3 (June 2000).

Joint Public Advisory Committee, ADVICE TO COUNSEL NO: 03-05, December 17, 2003.

Kalderimis, Daniel, *Problems of WTO Harmonization and the Virtues of Shields and Swords*, 13 MINN. J. GLOBAL TRADE 305 (2004).

KATILA, MARKO & MARKKU SIMULA, SUSTAINABILITY IMPACT ASSESSMENT OF PROPOSED WTO NEGOTIATIONS: FINAL REPORT FOR THE FOREST SECTOR STUDY (June 19, 2005).

Kelly, Mary E. & Cyrus Reed, *The CEC's Trade and Environment Program: Cutting-Edge Analysis but Untapped Potential, in* GREENING NAFTA: THE NORTH AMERICAN COMMISSION FOR ENVIRONMENTAL COOPERATION (David L. Markell & John H. Knox eds., 2003). Copyright © 2003. All rights reserved. Used with the permission of Stanford University Press, www.sup.org.

KELLY, TRISH, THE IMPACT OF THE WTO: THE ENVIRONMENT, PUBLIC HEALTH AND SOVEREIGNTY (2007).

Kennedy, Kevin C., *The Illegality of Unilateral Trade Measures to Resolve Trade-Environment Disputes*, 22 WM. & MARY ENVTL. L. & POL'Y 375 (1998).

Khanna, Neha & Florenz Plassmann, *Household Income and Pollution: Implications for the Debate about the Environmental Kuznets Curve Hypothesis*, 15 J. ENVT. & DEV'T 3, 38 (2006).

Knox, John, *The Judicial Resolution of Conflicts Between Trade and the Environment*, 28 HARV. ENVTL. L. REV. 1 (2004). © 2001 by The President and Fellows of Harvard College and The Harvard Environmental Law Review.

Knox, John H., *The Myth and Reality of Transboundary Environmental Impact Assessment*, 96 AM. J. INT'L L. 291 (2002).

Knox, John H., *A New Approach to Compliance with International Environmental Law: The Submissions Procedure of the NAFTA Environmental Commission*, 28 ECOLOGY L.Q. 1 (2001).

Kopczynski, Mary, "The Haves Coming Out Behind: Galanter's Theory Tested in the WTO Dispute Settlement System," (2008) *available at*: http://works.bepress.com/mary_kopczynski/1.

Krämer, Ludwig, EC Environmental Law (5th ed. 2003).

Kravchenko, Svitlana, *Promoting Public Participation in Europe and Central Asia, in* The New Public: the Globalization of Public Participation (Carl Bruch ed., 2002) (excerpt reprinted with permission of the Environmental Law Institute).

Krugman, Paul, Pop Internationalism (1996).

Krugman, Paul R., Rethinking International Trade (1990).

Laborde, David et al., Implications of the 2008 Doha Draft Agricultural and Non-agricultural Market Access Modalities for Developing Countries (Jan. 22, 2010).

Laird, Ian, *Betrayal, Shock and Outrage, in* NAFTA Investment Law and Arbitration: Past Issues, Current Practice, Future Prospects (Todd Weiler ed., 2004).

LaNasa, Joseph A., *Rules of Origin and the Uruguay Round's Effectiveness in Harmonizing and Regulating Them,* 90 Am. J. Int'l L. 625 (1996).

Lankowski, Jussi, *Environmental Effects of Agricultural Trade Liberalization and Domestic Agricultural Policy Reforms,* UNCTAD/OSG/DP/126 (April 1997). Reprinted with permission of the author.

Lauterpacht, Hersch, The Development of International Law by the International Court (1958).

Leebron, David W., *Lying Down with Procrustes: An Analysis of Harmonization Claims, in* 1 Fair Trade and Harmonization: Prerequisites for Free Trade (Jagdish Bhagwati & Robert E. Hudec eds., 1996).

Letter from M. Dolores Wesson, Chair, National Advisory Committee, to Stephen Johnson, Administrator, U.S. EPA, at 13 (May 24, 2007), *available at* http://www.epa.gov/ocem/nac/pdf/2007_may24_nac_letter.pdf.

Macmillan, Fiona, WTO and the Environment (2001).

Maliti, Tom, *Developing Countries Could Earn Three Times the Aid They Receive if Subsidies Are Removed, WTO Says,* Associated Press (Feb. 11, 2002).

Manda, Olga, *Controversy Rages over "GM" Food Aid,* 16 Africa Recovery (Feb. 2003), *available at* http://www.un.org/ecosocdev/geninfo/afrec/vol16no4/164food2.htm.

Mann, Howard, Private Rights, Public Problems: A Guide to NAFTA's Controversial Chapter on Investor Rights (International Institute for Sustainable Development 2001). Reprinted with permission of the Institute for Sustainable Development.

Mann, Howard & Steve Porter, The State of Trade and Environment Law 2003: Implications for Doha and Beyond (International Institute for Sustainable Development and the Center for International Environmental Law, 2003). Reprinted with permission.

Marceau, Gabrielle, *A Call for Coherence in International Law: Praises for the Prohibition Against "Clinical Isolation" in WTO Dispute Settlement,* 33 J. World Trade 87 (1999). Reprinted with permission from Kluwer Law International © 2001. www.kluwerlaw.com.

Marceau, Gabrielle, *Conflicts of Norms and Conflicts of Jurisdictions: The Relationship between the WTO Agreements and MEAs and other Treaties,* 35 J. World Trade 1081 (2001).

Marceau, Gabrielle & Joel P. Trachtman, *The Technical Barriers to Trade Agreement, the Sanitary and Phytosanitary Measures Agreement, and the General Agreement on Tariffs and Trade: A Map of the World Trade Organization Law of Domestic Regulation of Goods*, 36 J. WORLD TRADE 811 (2002).

Markell, David L., *The CEC Citizen Submission Process, in* GREENING NAFTA: THE NORTH AMERICAN COMMISSION FOR ENVIRONMENTAL COOPERATION (David L. Markell & John H. Knox eds., 2003).

Martin, Gene S. Jr, and James W. Brennan, *Enforcing the International Convention for the Regulation of Whaling: The Pelly and Packwood-Magnuson Amendments*, 17 DEN. J. INT'L L. & POL'Y 293 (1989).

Mathews, Jessica Tuchman, *A Retreat on Trade?*, WASH. POST, Jan. 17, 1992.

MATSUSHITA, MITSUO, THOMAS J. SCHOENBAUM & PETROS MAVROIDIS, THE WORLD TRADE ORGANIZATION: LAW, PRACTICE, AND POLICY (2d ed. 2006).

Mattoo, Aaditya & Petros C. Mavroidis, *Trade, Environment and the WTO: The Dispute Settlement Practice Relating to Article XX of GATT, in* 11 INTERNATIONAL TRADE LAW AND THE GATT/WTO DISPUTE SETTLEMENT SYSTEM 327 (Ernst-Ulrich Petersmann ed., 1997) (excerpt reprinted with permission of Kluwer Law International). Reprinted with permission from Kluwer Law International © 2001. www.kluwerlaw.com.

McConnell, Irene, *The Asbestos Case at the World Trade Organization: The Treatment of Public Health Regulations under the General Agreement on Tariffs and Trade 1994 and the Agreement on Technical Barriers to Trade*, 10 TULSA J. COMP. & INT'L L. 153 (2002) (excerpt reprinted with permission of the Tulsa Journal of Comparative and International Law).

McDonald, Jan, *Domestic Regulation, Harmonization, and Technical Barriers to Trade* 19 (2004), *available at* http://www.iibel.adelaide.edu.au/docs/Jan%20McDonald.pdf.

McDorman, Ted L., *Dissecting the Free Trade Agreement Lobster Panel Decision*, 18 CANADIAN BUSINESS L.J. 445 (1991).

McDorman, Ted L., *The GATT Consistency of U.S. Fish Import Embargoes to Stop Driftnet Fishing and Save Whales, Dolphins and Turtles*, 24 GEORGE WASH. J. INT'L. L. & ECON. 477 (1991).

McDOUGAL, MYRES S., THE INTERPRETATION OF INTERNATIONAL AGREEMENTS (1994).

Meidinger, Errol, *Multi-Interest Self-Governance through Global Product Certification Programs*, (Buffalo Legal Studies Research Paper Series, Buffalo, N.Y., July 2006).

Memorandum of Understanding on Trade in Softwood Lumber, Dec. 30, 1986, United-States-Canada (as amended Oct. 31, 1990).

Menzie, David, et al., Some Implications of Changing Patterns of Mineral Consumption (USGS, Oct. 2003), *available at* http://pubs.usgs.gov/of/2003/of03-382/of03-382.html.

Milazzo, Mateo, SUBSIDIES IN WORLD FISHERIES: A REEXAMINATION, World Bank Technical Paper No. 406, at 16 (Apr. 1998).

Miller, Melissa Ann, *Note: Will the Circle Be Unbroken? Chile's Accession to the NAFTA and the Fast-Track Debate*, 31 VAL. U. L. REV. 153 (1996).

Mortensen, Jens L., *The Institutional Challenges and Paradoxes of EU Governance in External Trade: Coping with the Post-hegemonic Trading System and the Global Economy, in* THE UNION AND THE WORLD (A. Cafruny & P. Peters eds., 1998). Reprinted with permission.

Motall, Doaa Abdel, *Multilateral Environmental Agreements (MEAs) and WTO Rules: Why the "Burden of Accommodation" Should Shift to MEAs*, 35 J. WORLD TRADE 1215 (2001).

Murphy, Sean, *Biotechnology and International Law*, 42 HARV. INT'L L.J. 47 (2001).

Murphy, Sophia, *The World Trade Organization Agreement on Agriculture Basics* (Institute for Agricultural and Trade Policy, 2003). Reprinted with permission of the Institute for Agricultural and Trade Policy.

NAFTA FREE TRADE COMMISSION, NOTES OF INTERPRETATION OF CERTAIN CHAPTER 11 PROVISIONS (July 31, 2001), *available at* http://www.dfait-maeci.gc.ca/tna-nac/NAFTA-Interpr-en.asp.

National Organic Program, 65 Fed. Reg. 80,548 (Dec. 21, 2000) (implemented at 7 C.F.R. pt. 205).

Nayyar, Deepak, *Towards Global Governance*, *in* GOVERNING GLOBALIZATION: ISSUES AND INSTITUTIONS (Deepak Nayyar ed 2002).

Nell, Philippe G., *WTO Negotiations on the Harmonization of Rules of Origin: A First Critical Appraisal*, 33 J. WORLD TRADE 45 (1999).

Nordström, Håkan & Scott Vaughan, *Trade and Environment* 37 (1999), *available at* http://www.wto.org/english/news_e/pres99_e/environment.pdf.

OECD, AGRICULTURAL POLICIES IN OECD COUNTRIES: MONITORING AND EVALUATION (2009).

OECD, ENVIRONMENTALLY HARMFUL SUBSIDIES: CHALLENGES FOR REFORM (2005).

OECD, NATIONAL TREATMENT FOR FOREIGN-CONTROLLED ENTERPRISES (1993).

OECD, OECD GUIDELINES FOR MULTINATIONAL ENTERPRISES (2008), *available at* http://www.oecd.org/daf/investment/guidelines.

OECD, REPORT ON TRADE AND ENVIRONMENT TO THE OECD COUNCIL AT MINISTERIAL LEVEL, OCDE/GD(95)63 (May 24, 1995).

Okubo, Atsuko, *Environmental Labeling Programs and the GATT/WTO Regime*, 11 GEO. INT'L ENVTL. L. REV. 599 (1999).

Orellana, Marcos, *The EU and Chile Suspend the Swordfish Case Proceedings at the WTO and the International Tribunal of the Law of the Sea*, ASIL INSIGHTS (Feb. 2001), *available at* http://www.asil.org/insights/insigh60.htm.

Orellana Cruz, Marcos, *The Swordfish in Peril: The EU Challenges Chilean Port Access Restrictions at the WTO*, 6 BRIDGES 11 (July–Aug. 2000).

Organisation for Economic Cooperation and Development, Recommendation of the Council on Guiding Principles Concerning International Economic Aspects of Environmental Policies, C(72)128, Annex (May 26, 1972).

ORGANIZATION FOR ECONOMIC COOPERATION AND DEVELOPMENT, THE ENVIRONMENTAL EFFECTS OF TRADE (1994).

ORGANIZATION FOR ECONOMIC COOPERATION AND DEVELOPMENT, PROCESSES AND PRODUCTION METHODS (PPMs): CONCEPTUAL FRAMEWORK AND CONSIDERATIONS ON USE OF PPM-BASED TRADE MEASURES, OCDE/GD(97)137 (1997).

Ostruff, Joshua, *Transgenic Maize Goes under the Microscope*, *Trio* (Winter 2004), *at* http://www.cec.org/trio.

Oxfam International, *Dumping on the World: How EU Sugar Policies Hurt Poor Countries* (Oxfam Briefing Paper No. 61: March 2004).

Palmer, Alice & Richard Tarasofsky, *The WTO in Crisis: Lessons Learned from the Doha Negotiations on the Environment*, 82 INT'L AFFAIRS 899 (2006).

PALMETER, DAVID & PETROS C. MAVROIDIS, DISPUTE SETTLEMENT IN THE WORLD TRADE ORGANIZATION: PRACTICE AND PROCEDURE (1999).

Palmeter, David & Petros C. Mavroidis, *The WTO Legal System: Sources of Law*, 92 AM. J. INT'L L. 398 (1998). Reproduced with permission of American Journal of International Law. © The American Society of International Law ©.

Panagariya, Arvind, *The Tide of Free Trade Will Not Float All Boats*, FINANCIAL TIMES, Aug. 3, 2004.

PANAYOTOU, THEODORE, GLOBALIZATION AND ENVIRONMENT (CID Working Paper No. 53, 2000).

Pauwelyn, Joost, *The Limits of Litigation: "Americanization" and Negotiation in the Settlement of WTO Disputes*, 19 OHIO ST. J. ON DISP. RESOL. 121 (2003).

Pauwelyn, Joost, *Public International Law in the WTO System: How Far Can We Go?*, 95 AM. J. INT'L L. 535 (2001). Reproduced with permission of American Journal of International Law. © The American Society of International Law ©.

Pearce, David, *Environmentally Harmful Subsidies: Barriers to Sustainable Development*, *in* OECD, ENVIRONMENTALLY HARMFUL SUBSIDIES: POLICY ISSUES AND CHALLENGES (2003).

PEARCE, DAVID ET AL., BLUEPRINT FOR A GREEN ECONOMY (1989).

Pearson, Charles, *Environmental Control Costs and Border Adjustments*, 27 NAT'L TAX J. 599, 604 (1974).

Pearson, Charles S., *Testing the System: GATT + PPP=?*, 27 CORN. INT'L. L.J. 553, 560–561 (1994). Reprinted with permission of Cornell International Law Journal.

Pearson, Charles S. & Robert Repetto, *Reconciling Trade and Environment: The Next Steps*, *in* TRADE AND ENVIRONMENT COMMITTEE OF THE NATIONAL ADVISORY COUNCIL FOR ENVIRONMENTAL POLICY AND TECHNOLOGY, THE GREENING OF WORLD TRADE (1993).

Peel, Jacqueline, *Risk Regulation under the WTO SPS Agreement: Science As an International Normative Yardstick?* (Jean Monnet Working Paper 02/04, 2004).

Peterson, Luke, *Emerging Bilateral Investment Treaty Arbitration and Sustainable Development* (International Institute for Sustainable Development 2003), *available at* www.iisd.org/trade/investment_regime.htm.

Petition to Certify Japan Pursuant to 22 U.S.C. § 1978.

Petsonk, Annie, *The Kyoto Protocol and the WTO: Integrating Greenhouse Gas Emission Allowance Trading into the Global Marketplace*, 10 DUKE ENVTL. L. & POL'Y F. 185 (1999).

Plofchan, Thomas K., *Recognizing and Countervailing Environmental Subsidies*, 26 INT'L LAW. 763 (1992). Copyright 1992 American Bar Association. All rights reserved. Reprinted with permission of the Author and the America Bar Association.

Porrata-Doria, Rafael A. Jr., *Mercosur: The Common Market of the Twenty-First Century?*, 32 GA. J. INT'L & COMP. L. 1 (2004).

PORTER, GARETH, ESTIMATING OVERCAPACITY IN THE GLOBAL FISHING FLEET (WWF, 1998).

PORTER, GARETH, *The Euro-African Fishing Agreements: Subsidizing Overfishing in African Waters* (Background Paper for UNEP/WWF Workshop 1997).

PORTER, GARETH, FISHING SUBSIDIES, OVERFISHING AND TRADE (1997).

Postrel, Virginia, *Economic Scene: A Case in Free Trade: American Incomes Converge, but not at the Bottom*, N.Y. TIMES, Feb. 26, 2004, at C2. Copyright © 2004 by The New York Times Co. Reprinted with permission.

Press Release, European Commission, Environmental Democracy: Commission Promotes Citizens' Involvement in Environmental Matters (Oct. 28, 2003).

Press Release, European Environmental Bureau, Environmental NGOs Protest to Prodi Over Spanish Water Plan, *available at* http://www.eeb.org.

Press Release, Federal Trade Commission, FTC Charges Companies with 'Bamboo-zling' Consumers with False Product Claims (Aug. 11, 2009).

Press Release, IUCN, Extinction Crisis Continues Apace (2009), http://iucn.org/?4143/Extinction-crisis-continues-apace.

Press Release, U.S. Trade Rep., U.S., Brazil Agree on Framework Regarding WTO Cotton Dispute (June 17, 2010).

Press Release, UNEP, Turning the Tide on Falling Fish Stocks—UNEP-Led Green Economy Charts Sustainable Investment Path (May 17, 2010).

Proposal by ASEAN, WT/CTE/W/39 (July 24, 1996).

Public Citizen, *Global Trade Watch*, *at* www.citizen.org/trade/wto.

Ragosta, John A., *Natural Resource Subsidies and the Free Trade Agreement: Economic Justice and the Need for Subsidy Discipline*, 24 GEO. WASH. J. INT'L L. & ECON. 255 (1990).

Redefining Progress, The Genuine Progress Indicator, *at* http://www.cyberus.ca/choose.sustain/Question/GPI.html (1997).

Reid, Walter et al., *A New Lease on Life, in* BIODIVERSITY PROSPECTING: USING GENETIC RESOURCES FOR SUSTAINABLE DEVELOPMENT (Walter Reid et. al. eds, 1993).

The Relationship between the TRIPS Agreement and the Convention on Biological Diversity (CBD) and the Protection of Traditional Knowledge: Technical Observations on Issues Raised in a Communication by the United States, IP/C/W/443 (Mar. 18, 2005).

Repetto, Robert, *Complementarities Between Trade and Environment Policies, in* TRADE AND THE ENVIRONMENT: LAW, ECONOMICS, AND POLICY (Durwood Zaelke et al. eds., 1993).

REPETTO, ROBERT, THE FOREST FOR THE TREES? GOVERNMENT POLICIES AND THE MISUSE OF FOREST RESOURCES (World Res. Inst. 1988). Reprinted with permission of the World Resources Institute.

REPETTO, ROBERT C. ET AL., PUBLIC POLICIES AND THE MISUSE OF FOREST RESOURCES (Robert Repetto & Malcom Gillis eds., 1998).

REPETTO, ROBERT & WILLIAM B. MAGRATH, WASTING ASSETS: NATURAL RESOURCES IN THE NATIONAL INCOME ACCOUNTS (1989).

Report by the Chairman of the Group on Environmental Measures and International Trade, GATT Doc. L/7402, BISD, 40th Supp. 75 (1994).

Report (1996) of the Committee on Trade and Environment, WT/CTE/W/40 (Nov. 12, 1996).

Report (2009) of the Committee on Trade and Environment, WT/CTE/16 (Oct. 30, 2009).

Report of the Working Party on Border Tax Adjustments, adopted by the Contracting Parties in 1970, BISD, 18th Supp. 97. Ch. 4,

Report of the World Commission on Environment and Development: Our Common Future, U.N. GAOR, 42d Sess., Agenda Item 83(e), at para. 28, U.N. Doc. A/43/427 (1987). By permission of Oxford University Press.

RETHINKING FOREIGN INVESTMENT FOR SUSTAINABLE DEVELOPMENT: LESSONS FROM LATIN AMERICA (Kevin Gallagher and Daniel Chudnovsky, eds., 2009).

REUTER, PAUL, AN INTRODUCTION TO THE LAW OF TREATIES (1st ed. 1989).

Revesz, Richard L., *Rehabilitating Interstate Competition: Rethinking the "Race to the Bottom" Rationale for Federal Environmental Regulation*, 68 N.Y.U. L. REV. 1210 (1992).

Rio Declaration on Environment and Development, June 14, 1992, U.N. Doc. A/CONF.151/5/Rev. 1, *reprinted in* 31 I.L.M. 874 (1992).

Rodenhoff, Vera, *The Aarhus Convention and its Implications for the 'Institutions' of the European Union*, 11 RECIEL 343 (2002).

Rodrik, Dani, "Feasible Globalizations," NBER Working Paper 9129, Sept. 2002.

Roessler, Frieder, *Diverging Domestic Policies and Multilateral Trade Integration, in* 2 FAIR TRADE AND HARMONIZATION (Jagdish Bhagwati & Robert E. Hudec eds., 1997).

Romalis, John, *Factor Proportions and the Structure of Commodity Trade*, 94 AM. ECON. REV. 67 (2004).

Rose, Andrew K., *Do We Really Know that the WTO Increases Trade?*, 94 AM. ECON. REV. 98 (2004).

Rotterdam Convention, Sept. 10, 1998, U.N. Doc. UNEP/FAO/PIC/CONF/2, 38 I.L.M. 1 (1999) (entered into force Feb. 24, 2004).

Rugaber, Christopher S., *WTO Framework Makes "Historic" Changes to Farm Trade Talks, Johnson Says*, 21 INT'L TRADE REP. 1340 (Aug. 12, 2004).

Runge, C. Ford, *A Conceptual Framework for the Agricultural Trade and the Environment*, 33 J. WORLD TRADE 47 (1999).

Runge, C. Ford, *A Global Environment Organization (GEO) and the World Trading System: Prospects and Problems*, 35 J. WORLD TRADE 399 (2001).

Salzman, James, *Sustainable Consumption and the Law*, 27 ENVTL. L. 101 (1998).

SANDS, PHILLIPE, PRINCIPLES OF INTERNATIONAL ENVIRONMENTAL LAW (2d ed. 2003).

Schoenbaum, Thomas J., *International Trade and Protection of the Environment: The Continuing Search for Reconciliation*, 91 AM. J. INT'L L. 268 (1997).

Schorr, David K., *Fishery Subsidies and the WTO, in* TRADE, ENVIRONMENT, AND THE MILLENNIUM (eds. GARY P. SAMPSON & W. BRADNEE CHAMBERS, 2d. ed. 2002). Reprinted with permission of United Nations University, United Nations University Press.

Schwabach, Aaron, *How Free Trade Can Save the Everglades*, 14 GEO. INT'L ENVTL. L. REV. 301 (2001). Reprinted with permission of the publisher, Georgetown International Environmental Law Review © 2001.

Scott, Joanne, *On Kith and Kine (and Crustaceans): Trade and the Environment in the EU and WTO, in* THE EU, THE WTO AND THE NAFTA — TOWARDS A COMMON LAW OF INTERNATIONAL TRADE? (J.H.H. Weiler ed., 2000).

Sen, Amartya, *How to Judge Globalism*, THE AMERICAN PROSPECT, vol. 13, no. 1, January 1, 2002–January 14, 2002, *available at* http://www.cis.ksu.edu/~ab/Miscellany/globalism.html.

Shaffer, Gregory, *Reconciling Trade and Regulatory Goals: The Prospects and Limits of New Approaches to Transatlantic Governance Through Mutual Recognition and Safe Harbor Agreements*, 9 COLUM. J. EUR. L. 29 (2002).

Shaffer, Gregory C., *The World Trade Organization under Challenge: Democracy and the Law and Politics of the WTO's Treatment of Trade and Environment Matters*, 25 HARV. ENVTL. L. REV. 1 (2001). © 2001 by The President and Fellows of Harvard College and The Harvard Environmental Law Review.

Shapiro, Hal & Lael Brainard, *Trade Promotion Authority Formerly Known as Fast Track: Building Common Ground on Trade Demands More than a Name Change*, 35 GEO. WASH. INT'L L. REV. 1 (2003).

Shukla, S.P., *From the GATT to the WTO and Beyond*, *in* GOVERNING GLOBALIZATION: ISSUES AND INSTITUTIONS (Deepak Nayyar ed., 2002).

Silverglade, Bruce A., *The Impact of International Trade Agreements on U.S. Food Safety and Labeling Standards*, 53 FOOD & DRUG L.J. 537 (1998).

SINCLAIR, IAN M., THE VIENNA CONVENTION ON THE LAW OF TREATIES (2d ed. 1984).

Sizer, Nigel, David Downes & David Kaimowitz, *Tree Trade: Liberalization of International Commerce in Forest Products: Risks and Opportunities*, FOREST NOTES (World Res. Inst., Wash. D.C.), Nov. 1999, *available at* http://www.globalforestwatch.org. Reprinted with permission of the World Resources Institute.

Smithsonian Migratory Bird Center, Norms for Production, Processing and Marketing of "Bird Friendly®" Coffee (Apr. 4, 2002), http://nationalzoo.si.edu/SCBI/MigratoryBirds/Coffee/Certification/Norms-English_1.pdf.

Snape, William J. III & Naomi Lefkovitz, *Searching for GATT's Environmental Miranda: Are "Process Standards" Getting "Due Process?"* 27 CORNELL INT'L L.J. 777 (1994) (excerpt reprinted with permission of the Cornell Journal of International Law).

SOUTHWEST FISHERIES SCIENCE CENTER, REPORT OF THE SCIENTIFIC RESEARCH PROGRAM UNDER THE INTERNATIONAL DOLPHIN CONSERVATION PROGRAM ACT (Aug. 23, 2002).

Statement of the Free Trade Commission on Non-disputing Party Participation (Oct. 7, 2003).

Steinberg, Richard H., *Judicial Lawmaking at the WTO: Discursive, Constitutional, and Political Constraints*, 98 AM. J. INT'L L. 247 (2004).

STEINFELD, HENNING, LIVESTOCK'S LONG SHADOW: ENVIRONMENTAL ISSUES AND OPTIONS (Food and Agriculture Organization, 2006).

Stewart, Richard B., *Environmental Regulation and International Competitiveness*, 102 YALE L.J. 2039 (1993) (excerpt reprinted by permission of Yale Journal Company and William S. Hein Company from The Yale Law Journal, Vol. 102, pages 2039–2142.

Stewart, Terence P. & David S. Johanson, *A Nexus of Trade and the Environment: The Relationship between the Cartagena Protocol on Biosafety and the SPS Agreement of the World Trade Organization*, 14 COLO. J. INT'L ENVTL. L. & POL'Y 1 (2003) (excerpt reprinted with permission of Colorado Journal of International Environmental Law and Policy, Terence P. Stewart, & David S. Johanson).

Stiglitz, Joseph E., *A New Agenda for Global Warming*, 3 ECONOMISTS' VOICE (July 2006).

Stilwell, Matthew & Richard Tarasofsky, *Towards Coherent Environmental and Economic Governance: Legal and Practical Approaches to MEA-WTO Linkages* (WWF-CIEL Discussion Paper), Oct. 2001.

Stockholm Convention, May 22, 2001, U.N. Doc. UNEP/POPS/CONF/2,40 I.L.M. 532 (2001) (entered into force May 17, 2004).

Stockholm Declaration, June 16, 1972, UN Doc. A/CONF.48/14, *reprinted in* 11 I.L.M. 1416 (1972).

Stumberg, Robert, *Sovereignty by Subtraction: The Multilateral Agreement on Investment*, 31 CORNELL INT'L L.J. 491 (1998).

Sucharipa-Behrmann, Lilly, *Eco-Labels for Tropical Timber: The Austrian Experience, in* OECD, LIFE-CYCLE MANAGEMENT AND TRADE (1994).

Sweetland, John W., Professor of International Economics and Public Policy, University of Michigan, *at* http://www-personal.umich.edu/~alandear/glossary/.

Sykes, Alan O., *Countervailing Duty Law: An Economic Perspective*, 89 COLUM. L. REV. 199 (1989). Reprinted with permission of the author.

Taking and Importing of Marine Mammals, 68 Fed. Reg. 2010-11 (Jan. 15, 2003).

TALBERTH, DR. JOHN ET AL., THE GENUINE PROGRESS INDICATOR 2006: A TOOL FOR SUSTAINABLE DEVELOPMENT (Redefining Progress, 2006).

Tarasofsky, Richard G., *Ensuring Compatibility between Multilateral Environmental Agreements and the GATT/WTO*, Y.B. INT'L ENVTL. L. 52 (1996).

TBT Committee, G/TBT/9, Annex 4; TBT Committee, *Decision On Principles For The Development Of International Standards, Guides and Recommendations with Relation To Articles 2, 5 and Annex 3 Of The Agreement*, G/TBT/5 (Nov. 19, 1997).

Ten-year Review and Assessment Committee, Ten Years of North American Environmental Cooperation: Report of the Ten Year Review and Assessment Committee to the Council of the Commission for Environmental Cooperation (June 15, 2004). Reprinted with permission of the publisher, Commission for Environmental Cooperation.

TEPAC, THE U.S.-CENTRAL AMERICAN FREE TRADE AGREEMENT: REPORT OF THE TEPAC (Mar. 19, 2004).

TerraChoice Environmental Services, *Environmental and Other Labeling of Coffee: The Role of Mutual Recognition Supporting Cooperative Action* (Feb. 22, 2000), *available at* http://www.cec.org/files/pdf/ECONOMY/Terra-e_EN.pdf.

Tollefson, Chris, *Games Without Frontiers: Investor Claims and Citizen Submissions Under the NAFTA Regime*, 27 YALE J. INT'L L. 141 (2002).

Tolman, Jonathan, *Federal Agricultural Policy: A Harvest of Environmental Abuse* (Aug. 1995). Reprinted with permission of Competitive Enterprise Institute.

Trachtman, Joel P., *Trade and ... Problems, Cost-Benefit Analysis and Subsidiarity*, 9 EUR. J. INT'L L. 32 (1998).

Treaty on the Functioning of the European Union, May 9, 2008, 2008/C 115/59.

TRIBE, LAURENCE H., AMERICAN CONSTITUTIONAL LAW(3rd ed. 2000).

Turek, Bogdan, *Preparation of Packaging Recycling Law under Way to Meet EU Norms, Official Says,* 22 INT'L. ENVT. REP. 721 (Sept. 1, 1999).

U.N. Conference on Environment and Development, Agenda 21, ¶ 30.3, U.N. Doc. A/CONF.151/26 (1992).

U.N. Conference on Trade and Development, Environmental Policies, Trade and Competitiveness: Conceptual and Empirical Issues, TD/B/WG.6/6 (Mar. 29, 1995).

U.N. Department of Economic and Social Affairs, Division for Sustainable Development, *Johannesburg Plan of Implementation,* (Aug. 11, 2005), http://www.un.org/esa/sustdev/documents/WSSD_POI_PD/English/WSSD_PlanImpl.pdf.

U.N. Development Programme, Human Development Report, 1998 (1998).

U.N. Development Programme, Human Development Report, 2007 (2007).

U.N. Development Programme, Human Development Report, 2003, U.N. Sales No. 03.III.B.1 (2003).

UN/ECE Convention on Environmental Impact Assessment in a Transboundary Context, Feb. 5, 1991, 30 I.L.M. 800.

U.N. Economic & Social Council, Implementing Agenda 21: Report of the Secretary-General, U.N. Doc. E/CN.17/2002/PC.2/7 (2002).

U.N. GAOR, *Report of the World Commission on Environment and Development: Our Common Future,* 42d Sess., Agenda Item 83(e), U.N. Doc. A/43/427 (1987).

U.S. Dept. of Commerce, Fisheries Economics in the United States 2007 (Jan. 2010).

U.S. Environmental Protection Agency, Analysis of the Lieberman-Warner Climate Security Act of 2008 (2008).

U.S. Environmental Protection Agency, U.S.-Mexico Border 2012 Framework, www.epa.gov/usmexicoborder/.

U.S. Government Accountability Office, Livestock Grazing: Federal Expenditures and Receipts Vary, Depending on the Agency and the Purpose of the Fee Charged, GAO-05-869 (September 2005).

U.S. Secures Agreement Not to Use GATT to Allow Energy Tax Rebate, Inside U.S. Trade 19 (Jan. 28, 1994).

UNCTAD, *Environmental Policies, Trade and Competitiveness: Conceptual and Empirical Issues,* TD/B/WG.6/6 (Mar. 29, 1995).

UNCTAD, Global Investment Trends Monitor, No. 2 (Jan. 19, 2010) *available at* http://www.unctad.org/en/docs/webdiaeia20101_en.pdf.

UNCTAD, World Investment Report 2009 (2009), *available at* http://www.unctad.org/en/docs/wir2009overview_en.pdf.

UNEP Meeting on Developing Synergies and Enhancing Mutual Supportiveness of Multilateral Environmental Agreements and the World Trade Organization, Session 2: A Practical Approach Towards Developing Synergies in the Implementation of MEAs and the WTO (Oct. 2000).

UNEP, Report of the Ad Hoc Working Group on the Work of Its Third Session, U.N. Doc. UNEP/WG.172/2 (1992).

UNEP, The Trade and Environmental Effects of Ecolabels: Assessment and Response (2005).

United Nations, The Criteria for Identification of the LDCs, *available at* http://www.un.org/special-rep/ohrlls/ldc/ldc%20criteria.htm.

UNITED NATIONS ECONOMIC COMMISSION FOR EUROPE/FOOD AND AGRICULTURE ORGA-
NIZATION, FOREST PRODUCTS ANNUAL MARKET REVIEW 2005–2006 (2006).

United States, Communication from the United States, Fisheries Subsidies: Articles I.2,
II, IV, and V, TN/RL/GEN/165 (Apr. 22, 2010).

United States, *Environmental and Trade Benefits of Removing Subsidies in the Fisheries Sector*, WT/CTE/W/51 (May 19, 1997).

USLEAP, More Information on the Flower Industry, http://www.usleap.org/usleap-cam-
paigns/flower-workers-and-economic-justice/more-information-flower-industry.

Vasquez, Juan & Marceil Yeater, *Demystifying the Relationship Between CITES and the
WTO*, 10 RECEIL 271 (2000).

Vaughan, Scott, *The Greenest Trade Agreement Ever? Measuring the Environmental Impacts of Agricultural Liberalization, in* NAFTA's PROMISE AND REALITY: LESSONS FROM
MEXICO FOR THE HEMISPHERE (John Audley et al. eds., 2003).

Victor, David G., *The Operation and Effectiveness of the Montreal Protocol's Non-Compliance Procedure, in* THE IMPLEMENTATION AND EFFECTIVENESS OF INTERNATIONAL
ENVIRONMENTAL COMMITMENTS 137 (David G. Victor et al. eds., 1998).

Victor, David G., *The Sanitary and Phytosanitary Agreement of the World Trade Organization: An Assessment after Five Years*, 32 INT'L L. & POL. 865 (2000).

Vierdag, E.W., *The Time of the 'Conclusion' of a Multilateral Treaty: Article 30 of the Vienna Convention on the Law of Treaties and Related Provisions*, 59 BRIT. Y.B. INT'L. L.
100 (1988).

VINCENT, CAROL HARDY, GRAZING FEES: AN OVERVIEW AND CURRENT ISSUES (Congressional Research Service, updated March 10, 2008), *available at* http://www.publicland
sranching.org/htmlres/fs_buy_the_numbers.htm.

Vitousek, Peter, Paul Ehrlich, and Anne Ehrlich, *Human Appropriation of the Products of
Photosynthesis*, 36 BIOSCIENCE No. 6 (1986).

VON MOLTKE, KONRAD, AN INTERNATIONAL INVESTMENT REGIME? ISSUES OF SUSTAIN-
ABILITY (2000).

Vossenaar, Rene, *Eco-Labelling and International Trade: The Main Issues, in* ECO-LA-
BELLING AND INTERNATIONAL TRADE (Simonetta Zarrilli et al. eds., 1997).

Wagner, J. Martin, *International Investment, Expropriation and Environmental Protection*,
29 GOLDEN GATE U. L. REV. 465 (1999). Reprinted with Permission.

Wagner, Martin, *The WTO's Interpretation of the SPS Agreement Has Undermined the
Right of Governments to Establish Appropriate Levels of Protection Against Risk*, 31 LAW
& POL'Y INT'L BUS. 855 (2000).

Walker, Vern R., *Keeping the WTO from Becoming the "World Trans-science Organization":
Scientific Uncertainty, Science Policy, and Factfinding in the Growth Hormones Dispute*, 31 CORNELL INT'L L.J. 251 (1998) (excerpt reprinted with permission of Cornell International Law Journal).

WALLACH, LORI & PATRICK WOODALL, WHOSE TRADE ORGANIZATION? THE COMPRE-
HENSIVE GUIDE TO THE WTO (2004).

Ware, Patricia, *Biosafety Protocol Provides for Labeling of Modified Foods, House Member
Says*, 24 CHEMICAL REPORTER 280 (Feb. 21, 2000).

Weiler, Todd, *Interpreting Substantive Obligations in Relation to Health and Safety Measures, in* INVESTMENT LAW AND ARBITRATION (2004).

Weiler, Todd, *Prohibitions Against Discrimination in NAFTA Chapter 11, in* NAFTA INVESTMENT LAW AND ARBITRATION: PAST ISSUES, CURRENT PRACTICE, FUTURE PROSPECTS (Todd Weiler ed., 2004).

Weinberg, Aly, *Science and Trans-science,* 10 MINERVA 209 (1972).

Werksman, Jacob, *Greenhouse Gas Emissions Trading and the WTO,* 8 RECIEL 251 (1999).

Why Greens Should Love Trade, THE ECONOMIST (Oct. 9, 1999).

Wickham, John, *Toward a Green Multilateral Investment Framework: NAFTA and the Search for Models,* 12 GEO. INT'L ENVTL. L. REV. 617 (2000). Reprinted with permission of the publisher, Georgetown International Environmental Law Review © 2000.

Wiener, Jonathan Baert, *Global Environmental Regulation: Instrument Choice in Legal Context,* 108 YALE L. J. 677 (1999).

WIERS, JOCHEM, TRADE AND ENVIRONMENT IN THE EC AND THE WTO: A LEGAL ANALYSIS (2002) (excerpt reprinted with permission of Europa Law Publishing & Jochem Wiers).

Wilson, S. Bruce, *Can the WTO Dispute Settlement Body Be a Judicial Tribunal Rather than A iplomatic Club?,* 31 LAW & POL'Y INT'L BUS. 779 (2000).

Winter, Gerd, *Environmental Principles in Community Law, in* THE EUROPEAN CONVENTION AND THE FUTURE OF EUROPEAN ENVIRONMENTAL LAW (Jan H. Jans, ed., 2003).

Wirth, David A., *The Role of Science in the Uruguay Round and NAFTA Trade Disciplines,* 27 CORNELL INT'L L.J. 817 (1994) (excerpt reprinted with permission of the Cornell International Law Journal).

Wirth, John D., *Perspectives on the Joint Public Advisory Committee, in* GREENING NAFTA: THE NORTH AMERICAN COMMISSION FOR ENVIRONMENTAL COOPERATION (David L. Markell & John H. Knox eds., 2003).

Wise, Timothy A., *The Paradox of Agricultural Subsidies: Measurement Issues, Agricultural Dumping and Policy Reform* (Feb. 2004), http://ase.tufts.edu/gdae/Pubs/wp/04-02AgSubsidies.pdf.

Wiser, Glenn, *The Clean Development Mechanism Versus The World Trade Organization: Can Free-Market Greenhouse Gas Emissions Abatement Survive Free Trade?,* 11 GEO. INT'L ENVTL. L. REV. 531 (1999).

Wiser, Glenn M., *Frontiers in Trade: The Clean Development Mechanism and the General Agreement on Trade in Services,* 2 INT'L J. GLOBAL ENVT'L ISSUES No. 3/4 (2002) (reprinted with permission of Inderscience Publishers).

Wold, Chris, *An Analysis of the Relationship between CITES and the WTO* (May 31, 1997) (prepared for the 10th Meeting of the Conference of the Parties to CITES).

Wold, Chris, *Evaluating NAFTA and the Commission for Environmental Cooperation: Lessons for Integrating Trade and Environment in Free Trade Agreements,* 28 ST. LOUIS UNIV. PUBLIC L. REV. 201 (2008).

Wold, Chris, *Multilateral Environmental Agreements and Trade Rules: Conflict and Resolution,* 26 ENVTL. L. 841 (1996) (excerpt reprinted with permission of Environmental Law, Lewis & Clark Law School).

Wold, Chris, *The Status of Sea Turtles under International Environmental Law and International Environmental Agreements*, 5 J. Int'l Wildlife L. & Pol'y 11 (2002).

World Bank, Globalization, Growth, and Poverty: Building an Inclusive World Economy (2002).

World Bank, Global Economic Prospects 2004 (2004).

World Bank, Key Development Data & Statistics (2009).

World Bank, World Development Report, 1992 (1992).

World Bank, World Development Report 2008: Agriculture for Development (2007).

World Commission on Environment and Development, Our Common Future ["The Brundtland Report"] (1988).

World Health Organization & International Standards Organization, World Health Organization & World Trade Organization, *WTO Agreements & Public Health* (2002).

World Resources Institute's EarthTrends Database, *available at* http://earthtrends.wri.org/.

World Resources Institute et al., World Resources: A guide to the Global Environment — The Urban Environment (1996).

World Trade Organization Website, *10 Benefits of the WTO Trading System* (Apr. 2003), *available at* http://www.wto.org/english/thewto_e/whatis_e/10ben_e/10b00_e.htm.

World Trade Organization, *Goods Schedules, Members' Commitments*, *available at* http://www. wto.org/english/tratop_e/schedules_e/goods_schedules_e.htm.

World Trade Organization, Doha Work Programme Ministerial Declaration of 18 December 2005, Annex D, para 9, WT/MIN(05)/DEC (2005).

World Trade Organization, Ministerial Declaration, WTO Ministerial Conference, Fourth Session, Doha, Nov. 9–14 2001, WT/MIN(01)/DEC/W/1 (Nov. 14, 2001).

World Trade Organization, Ministerial Declaration of 20 November 2001, WT/MIN(01)/DEC/1, (Nov. 20, 2001).

World Trade Organization, TBT Information Management System, http://tbtims.wto.org.

WTO et al., World Tariff Profiles 16 (2009).

WTO Secretariat, *An Introduction to the GATS* (Oct. 1999), *available at* http://www.wto.org/english/tratop_e/serv_e/gsintr_e.doc. 9.

WTO Secretariat, *Negotiating History of the Coverage of the Agreement on Technical Barriers to Trade with Regard to Labelling Requirements, Voluntary Standards, and Processes and Production Methods Unrelated to Product Characteristics*, WT/CTE/W/10, G/TBT/W/11 (Aug. 29, 1995).

WTO Secretariat Note, *A Review of the Information Available in the WTO on the Export of Domestically Prohibited Goods*, WT/CTE/W/43 (Apr. 22, 1997).

WTO Secretariat Note, *Matrix on Trade Measures Pursuant to Selected Multilateral Environmental Agreements*, WT/CTE/W/160/Rev.4 (Mar. 14, 2007).

WWF, One Step Forward, Three Steps Back: Comment on TN/RL/GEN/163 (Apr. 28, 2010).

Wynne, Roger D., *The Emperor's New Eco-Logos?: A Critical Review of the Scientific Certification Systems Environmental Report Card and the Green Seal Certification Mark Programs*, 14 Va. Envtl. L.J. 51 (1994) (excerpt reprinted with permission of Virginia Environmental Law Journal).

Yale Center for Environmental Law & Policy and Center for International Earth Science Information Network, 2008 Environmental Performance Index (2008), http://sedac.ciesin.columbia.edu/es/epi/papers/2008EPI_mainreport_ july08.pdf.

Yoder, Christian G., The Canadian Forest Products Industry and U.S. Trade Laws, Resources: Newsletter, Can. Inst. Resources L. No. 17 (Winter 1987).

Zhu, Shushuai, Joseph Buongiorno & David J. Brooks, *Global Effects of Accelerated Tariff Liberalization in the Forest Products Sector to 2010* (U.S. Dep't of Agriculture, Forest Service Res. Pap. PNW-RP-534, Mar. 2002), *available at* www.fs.fed.us/pnw/pubs/rp534.

Index

U